23rd International Workshop on Rare Earth and Future Permanent Magnets and Their Applications (REPM2014)

Annapolis, Maryland, USA
17 - 21 August 2014

ISBN: 978-1-5108-4338-7

Printed from e-media with permission by:

Curran Associates, Inc.
57 Morehouse Lane
Red Hook, NY 12571

CURRAN ASSOCIATES INC.
proceedings
.com

Some format issues inherent in the e-media version may also appear in this print version.

Printed by Curran Associates, Inc. (2017)

REPM 2014
104 The Green, 217 Sharp Lab
University of Delaware
Newark, DE 19716
USA

Phone: (302) 831-8116

Additional copies of this publication are available from:

Curran Associates, Inc.
57 Morehouse Lane
Red Hook, NY 12571 USA
Phone: 845-758-0400
Fax: 845-758-2633
Email: curran@proceedings.com
Web: www.proceedings.com

The 23rd International Workshop

on

Rare Earth and Future Permanent Magnets and Their Applications

(REPM2014)

PROCEEDINGS

AUGUST 17-21, 2014

ANNAPOLIS, MARYLAND

WESTIN ANNAPOLIS

100 Westgate Circle, Annapolis, MD 21401

Organized by:

REPM2014 Organizing Committee

George C. Hadjipanayis, Chair

Christina H. Chen, Co-Chair

J. Ping Liu, Co-Chair

Dear Colleagues,

It is with great pleasure to welcome you to the 23rd International Workshop on Rare Earth and Future Permanent Magnets (REPM2014), which is held at the Westin in Annapolis, Maryland. This is the eighth time that this Workshop has been held in the U.S. (Dayton, OH 1974; Dayton, OH 1976; La Jolla, CA 1978; Roanoke, VA 1981; Dayton, OH 1985; Pittsburg, PA 1990; Newark, DE 2002).

Annapolis, the state capital of Maryland, is a beautiful historical seaport situated along the Chesapeake Bay. Annapolis is an easy day trip from Washington, DC. It is located in Anne Arundel County, approximately 16.4 miles from Baltimore/Washington International Airport (BWI), 31 miles from DC Roland Reagan National Airport (DCA) and 51.8 miles from DC Dulles International Airport (IAD). The city boasts more 18th century buildings than anywhere else in the United States, including the homes of all four Maryland signers of the Declaration of Independence. Annapolis, Maryland is a fun place to explore, with lots of great museums, shopping and restaurants.

The aim of this workshop is to bring together engineers and scientists from all over the world who work on permanent magnets and their applications to present their recent results and exchange ideas on wide range of relevant topics including resources, raw materials, recycling, processing, properties and applications of permanent magnets. The late Karl J. Strnat started this series of Workshops about 38 years ago and since then they have been very important and successful meetings.

We have been very successful in attracting speakers from many U.S. universities and respected institutions from around the world. The Workshop will serve as a proving ground for tomorrow's magneticians, bringing them together with many pioneers of rare earth magnets in this unique opportunity to exchange new ideas and experiences.

We received over 200 abstracts for this Workshop. Most of the submitted abstracts focused on Nd-Fe-B magnets. However, a large number of these abstracts are on non-rare earth magnets reflecting the increased research in this area worldwide because of the recent rare-earth crisis. Due to time constraints, the papers were not rigorously reviewed for their scientific and technical accuracy, but it will be the responsibility of the authors to defend their results throughout the meeting.

We would like to take this opportunity to thank all of those people who helped in organizing this meeting including the National and International Committees and the Program Committee. We also thank the Program Committee's assistance, especially Alexander Gabay, in organizing the submitted abstracts and editing the manuscripts.

The prevailing economic climate has meant that we were not able to offer as much financial support to the invited speakers and others as we would have liked. We express our gratitude to those organizations who sponsored the Workshop including the University of Delaware, DOE, Electron Energy Corporation, Molycorp, GE Global Research, YSM and NIMS-JSPS.

George C. Hadjipanayis Christina H. Chen J. Ping Liu

Program Committee

CHRISTINA H. CHEN (University of Dayton)
CHINS CHINNASAMY (EEC)
BAOZHI CUI (EEC)
ALEX GABAY (University of Delaware)
GEORGE C. HADJIPANAYIS (University of Delaware)
J. PING LIU (UT-Arlington)
MELANIA MARINESCU (EEC)
NARAYAN POUDAYL (UT-Arlington)

National Committee

JERRY BROWN (Kollmorgen)
STEVE CONSTANTINIDES (Arnold)
JUN CUI (PNNL)
GARETH P. HATCH (Technology Metals Research)
SAM JIANG (Argonne)
FRANK JOHNSON (GE)
MATT KRAMER (Ames)
JOHN LEBO (QM Power)
LAURA HENDERSON LEWIS (Northeastern Univ.)
JINFANG LIU (EEC)
FRED PINKERTON (GM)
JOHN PRATER (ARO)
CHUANBING RONG (Ford)
S.G. SANKAR (Advanced Materials Corporation)
DAVID SELLMYER (Univ. Nebraska)
RALPH SKOMSKI (Univ. Nebraska)
TAKAO SUZUKI (Univ. Alabama)
MATT WILLARD (Case Western)

REPM2014 International Advisory Committee

V. Bovda (Kharkiv Physics and Technics Institute)
W. C. Chang (National Chung Cheng University)
C. H. Chen (University of Dayton) Christina Chen
J.M.D. Coey (Trinity College Dublin)
Stephen Collocott (CSIRO)
Nora Dempsey (Institute Néel, CNRS/UJF)
J. Fidler (Technische Universität Wien)
H. Fukunaga (Nagasaki University)
Oliver Gutfleisch (TU Darmstadt)
George Hadjipanayis (University of Delaware)
I.R. Harris (University of Birmingham)
S. Hirosawa (ESICMM, NIMS)
Kazuhiro Hono (NIMS)
M. Katter (Vacuumschmelze GmbH & Co. KG)
C. O. Kim (Chungnam National University)
S. Kobe (Jožef Stefan Institute)
H. Kronmüller (Max-Planck-Institut)
M. K. Leonowicz (Warsaw University of Technology)
W. Li (CISRI – Central Iron & Steel Research Institute)
J. P. Liu (University of Texas at Arlington)
Shashi Prakash Narayan (AMPRI)
Dimitrios Niarchos (NCSR Demokritos)
A. G. Popov (Institute of Metal Physics)
G. Rieger (Siemens, GE)
M. Sagawa (Intermetallics CO., LTD.)
S. G. Sankar (Advanced Materials Corporation)
David Sellmyer (University of Nebraska)
L. Schultz (IFW Dresden)
R. M. W. Strnat (Magnet-Physics Inc.)
S. Sugimoto (Tohoku University)
Michael H. Walmer (Electron Energy Corporation)
A. Yan (Ningbo Institute of Material Technology and Engineering)
C. J. Yang (RIST, Korea)
J. B. Yang (Peking University)
J. P. Yonnet (Grenoble Institute of Technology)
M. Yue (Beijing University of Technology)

REPM2014 ORAL PRESENTATIONS

SUNDAY 8/17/2014	MONDAY 8/18/2014	TUESDAY 8/19/2014	WEDNESDAY 8/20/2014	THURSDAY 8/21/2014
	8:00-8:15 AM - **Opening Remarks**	8:00-10:30 AM **SYMPOSIUM** **Nanocomposite Magnets [Chair: Hono]** Skomski Fukunaga Jiang Neu/Sawatzki WB Cui Y. Hou Yan	8:00-10:30 AM **Non-Rare Earth Magnets I [Chair: Sankar]** J. Yang Lewis Kramer Ren Ener Mix Hozumi Carpenter	8:00-10:30 AM **Worldwide Consortia on PM [Chair: Kramer]** Hirosawa J. Cui F. Johnson Niarchos Kobe Suzuki Bollero
	8:15-9:00 AM **Keynote Address: Gutfleisch** *"Re-thinking Rare Earths: Demand, Sustainability and the Reality of Alternatives"*			
	9:00 - 10:30 AM **Resources/Markets I [Chair: Constantinides]** Zhang Collocott Eggert Rodrigues Gopalan			
	COFFEE BREAK - 15 minutes			
	10:45 - 12:30 PM **Resources/Markets II [Chair: Collocott]** King Hatch Richardson Walton Chinnasamy	10:45 - 12:30 PM **Grain Boundary Engineering in NdFeB Magnets [Chair: Jasinski]** Takagi K. Löwe Hioki Nakagawa C. Chang Jung-Goo Lee Wan W. Tang	10:45 - 12:30 PM **Non-Rare Earth Magnets II (Chair: Takeuchi)** Sankar Takahasi JP Wang Dirba Backen Menushenkov	10:45-12:30 PM **Nanocrystalline Magnets [Chair: Barandiaran]** KA Gschneidner Sepehri-Amin Zou D.S. Neznakhin V. Pop Viau S. Prakash Narayan S. Saito F. Pinkerton
LUNCH - 90 minutes				

SUNDAY 8/17/2014	MONDAY 8/18/2014	TUESDAY 8/19/2014	WEDNESDAY 8/20/2014	THURSDAY 8/21/2014
2:00 PM REGISTRATION	2:00-4:00 PM **Recent Developments in High Performance Magnets [Chair: Gutfleisch]** Sugimoto (Nd-Fe-B) JF Liu (SmCo) Herchenroeder/Brown ZH Guo U.M.R. Seelam M. Nakamura	2:00-4:00 PM **Status of PM Around the World [Co-Chairs: Sugimoto/Fidler]** Constantinides (USA) WeiLi/S. Dong (China) Iriyama (Japan) Katter (Europe) Dormidontov (Russia)	2:00-4:00 PM **SYMPOSIUM** **Coercivity-Grain Boundary Phases [Chair: Hirosawa]** Hono Nakamura Tsuchiura Hrkac A. Sakuma Woodcock	2:00-4:00 PM **Hard Magnetic Particles [Chair: Aru Yan]** Balasubramanian Liu (Poudyal) Gabay/Hadjipanayis Yue YC Yang OM Bovda
	COFFEE BREAK - 15 minutes			
4:30-5:30 PM **Needs, Opportunities and Funding in Magnets** Dr. S. Boyd Dr. H. Scott Coombe Dr. B. Gabriel Dr. JC Zhao	4:15-5:35 PM **Applications I [Chair: Katter]** Rieger Ding Morcos Chen/Horwath	4:15-5:50 PM **Novel Synthesis and Processing Techniques [Chair: Dempsey]** Marinescu Kocjan Berkowitz Hugonnet Popov Lopes/Wendhausen Feng M. Zakotnik	4:15-5:35 PM **Theory: Fundamental [Chair: Skomski]** Manchanda Mryasov L. Ke M. Werwinski R. Choudhary	4:15-6:30 PM **SYMPOSIUM** **Search for New Hard Magnetic Materials [Chair: Sellmyer]** CZ Wang Felser D. Johnson B. Sanyal D. Goll Takeuchi
5:30 - 7:30 PM **Reception**	5:35 - 6:45 PM **Thin Film PM [Chair: Suzuki]** Sellmyer Dempsey M. Nakano O. Akdogan	5:50-7:20 PM **Theory: Micromagnetics [Chair: Fukunaga]** Kronmueller Fidler Givord Fischbacher Wysocki/Antropov	5:35-7:05 PM **Applications II [Chair: Rieger]** Y. Asano Constantinides H. Choi/JF Liu S.P. Narayan	6:30-6:45 PM **Closing Remarks**
	7:00-9:00 PM **POSTERS**	**7:30 PM - BANQUET**	**7:00-9:00 PM** **POSTERS**	
		7:30 - 8:00 - Drinks **8:00 - 8:12** - ***Shuk Rashidi - "Karl Strnat Narrative"*** **8:12 - 9:00** - Dinner **9:00 - 9:30** - ***M.J.D. Coey "How Magnetism Has Changed the World - Three Times"*** **9:30 - 10:00** - Dessert		

The 23rd International Workshop on
Rare Earth and Future Permanent Magnets and Their Applications
(REPM2014)
Annapolis, Maryland USA - August 17-21, 2014

SCHEDULE
MONDAY, AUGUST 18, 2014

8:00 – 8:15 AM – **Opening Remarks**

8:15 – 9:00 AM – **Keynote Address – Dr. Oliver Gutfleisch**
"Re-thinking Rare Earths: Demand, Sustainability and the Reality of Alternatives"

9:00 – 10:30 AM Resources/Markets I [Chair: Constantinides]

COFFEE BREAK – 15 MINUTES

10:45 – 12:30 PM Resources/Markets II [Chair: Collocott]

COFFEE BREAK – 15 MINUTES

7:00 – 9:00 PM – POSTER SESSION

<u>**Posters A – Non-Rare Earth**</u>

Posters A – Thin Films

Posters A – Nd-Fe-B Sintered Magnets/Recycling

SCHEDULE
TUESDAY, AUGUST 19, 2014

8:00 – 10:30 AM SYMPOSIUM: Nanocomposite Magnets

COFFEE BREAK – 15 MINUTES

10:45 – 12:30 PM – Grain Boundary Engineering in NdFeB Magnets

7:30 BANQUET

7:30 – 8:00 PM Drinks
8:00 - 8:12 - Shuk Rashidi - "Karl Srnat Narrative"
8:12 - 9:00 – Dinner
9:00 - 9:30 - M.J.D. Coey "*How Magnetism Has Changed the World - Three Times*"
9:30 - 10:00 - Dessert

The 23rd International Workshop on Rare Earth and Future Permanent Magnets and Their Applications (REPM2014)
Annapolis, Maryland USA - August 17-21, 2014

SCHEDULE
WEDNESDAY, AUGUST 20, 2014

8:00 – 10:20 AM Non-Rare Earth Magnets I

2:22 – 2:44 PM - T. Nakamura[1], A. Yasui[1], Y. Kotani[1], T. Fukagawa[2], T. Nishiuchi[2], H. Iwai[3], T. Akiya[3], T. Ohkubo[3], K. Hono[3], S. Hirosawa[3], and Y. Gohda[4]
"Magnetism of Grain-boundary Phase in Nd-Fe-B Sintered Magnets Studied with Soft X-ray Magnetic Circular Dichroism Technique"
[1] Japan Synchrotron Radiation Research Institute, 1-1-1, Kouto, Sayo-cho, Sayo-gun, Hyogo 679-5198 Japan
[2] Magnetic Materials Research Laboratory, NEOMAX Div., Hitachi Metals, Ltd., 2-15-17 Egawa, Shimamoto, 618-0013, Japan
[3] National Institute for Materials Science, Tsukuba 305-0047, Japan
[4] Department of Physics, The University of Tokyo, 7-3-1 Hongo, Bunkyo-ku, Tokyo 113-0033, Japan

[1] Department of Applied Physics, Tohoku University, Sendai, Japan
[2] Institute of Physics of ASCR, Prague, Czech Republic

[1] College of Engineering, Mathematics and Physical Sciences, Univ. of Exeter, UK
[2] IFW Dresden, Institute for Metallic Materials, 01171 Dresden, Germany
[3] Centre for Sustainable Chemical Technologies, University of Bath, Bath, UK
[4] St. Pölten University of Applied Sciences, Matthias Corvinus Str. 15, Austria
[5] TU Darmstadt, Institute for Materials Science, Petersenstr. 23, Darmstadt, Germany

3:28 – 3:40 PM – **A. Sakuma[1,2]**
"Theoretical Study on the Magnetic Properties of Nd-Rich Grain-Boundary Phase of Nd-Fe-B Magnets"
[1] Department of Applied Physics, Tohoku University, Aoba 6-6-05, Aoba-ku, Sendai 980-8579, Japan
[2] CREST, Japan Science and Technology Agency, Aoba 6-6-05, Aoba-ku, Sendai 980-8579, Japan

[1]IFW Dresden, PO Box 270116, 01171 Dresden, Germany
[2]SuperSTEM Laboratory, STFC Daresbury Campus, Daresbury, WA4 4AD, UK
[3]Advanced Material Engineering Div., Toyota Motor Corporation, Susono 410-1193 Japan
[4]Materialwissenschaft, TU Darmstadt, Alarich-Weiß-Str. 16, 64287 Darmstadt, Germany

COFFEE BREAK – 15 MINUTES

4:15 – 5:35 PM Theory: Fundamental

[1]Physics and Astronomy and NCMN, University of Nebraska, Lincoln, NE, USA,
[2]School of Basic Sciences, Indian Institute of Information Technology, Mandi, Himachal Pradesh, India

4:37 – 4:59 PM - **O. Mryasov**[1,2], S. Okatov[2], J. Barker[2], S. Faleev[2], Yu. Gornostyrev[2]
"Understanding magnetization, magnetic anisotropy and their temperature dependence: manganese and iron based ferromagnets with large anisotropy"
[1]Department of Physics, University of Alabama, Tuscaloosa, USA
[2]MINT Center, University of Alabama, Tuscaloosa, USA

Posters B – Theory – Micromagnetics

BP21 - Alexander Edström, Erna Delczeg-Czirjak, Miroslaw Werwinski, Jan Rusz, and Olle Eriksson
"Stable tetragonal distortions and significantly increased magnetocrystalline anisotropies in FeCo alloys with C or B doping"
Department of Physics and Astronomy, Uppsala University, Uppsala, Sweden

BP22 - Marcos Flavio de Campos[1] , Daniel Rodrigues[1], Jose Adilson de Castro[1]
"On the suitability of micromagnetics for phases with high magnetocrystalline anisotropy"
UFF – Universidade Federal Fluminense – Volta Redonda RJ BRAZIL

BP23 - Jamileh Beik Mohhammadi[1,2], Andrew Tuggle[1,2], Claudia K.A. Mewes[1,2], Tim Mewes[1,2], Takao Suzuki[1,3]
"Micromagnetic Simulations to Optimize the Energy Product of Hard/Soft Nanocomposites"
[1] Center for Materials for Information Technology, University of Alabama, Tuscaloosa
[2] Department of Physics and Astronomy, University of Alabama, Tuscaloosa
[3] Electrical & Computer Engineering, Metallurgical and Materials Engineering, University of Alabama, Tuscaloosa

BP24 - P. Kharel,[1] R. Skomski,[2] P. Manchanda,[2] Y. Huh,[1] A. Nelson,[1] V. R. Shah,[2] G. C. Hadjipanayis,[3] and D. J. Sellmyer[2]
"Anisotropy and Micromagnetism of Heusler Alloys"
[1]Department of Physics, South Dakota State University, Brookings, SD USA
[2]Department of Physics & Astronomy and NCMN, University of Nebraska, Lincoln, NE USA
[3]Department of Physics and Astronomy, University of Delaware, Newark, DE USA

BP25 - Marcos Flavio de Campos[1], Fernanda A. Sampaio da Silva[1], Daniel Rodrigues[1], Jose Adilson de Castro[1], Sergio A. Romero[2] , Suzilene Real Janasi[3]
"Applicability of the SW-CLC Model"
[1] UFF – Universidade Federal Fluminense – Volta Redonda RJ BRAZIL
[2]IFUSP – Universidade de São Paulo – São Paulo SP BRAZIL
[3]BRATS - Cajamar SP BRAZIL

Posters B – Novel Synthesis and Processing

BP26 - M.Farr, A.Campbell, I.R.Harris, A.Bradshaw, R.S. Sheridan, V.S. Mann and **A.Walton**[a]
"The effect of Ni impurities on HDDR processing of scrap sintered NdFeB magnets" 352
School of Metallurgy and Materials, University of Birmingham, Edgbaston, Birmingham, UK

BP27 - R.S. Sheridan, V.S.J. Mann, A. Bradshaw, I.R. Harris, and **A. Walton**
"The development of microstructure during HDDR treatment of sintered NdFeB-type magnets" 355
School of Metallurgy and Materials, University of Birmingham, Edgbaston, Birmingham, UK

BP28 - Jose Adilson de Castro[1], **Daniel Rodrigues**[1], Marcos Flavio de Campos[1]
"From Neodymium oxide to NdFeB Alloy: An overview on the reduction methods" 358
[1)] PUVR– Federal Fluminense University, Volta Redonda, Rio de Janeiro, Brazil
[2)] BRATS - Sintered Filters and Metallic Powders, Cajamar, São Paulo, Brazil

BP29 - Rikio Soda*, Misaho Akada**, Kenta Takagi*, Kimihiro Ozaki*
"Development of particle-Based Simulation for magnetic-aligned compaction process" *361*
*) National Institute of Advanced Industrial Science and Technology (AIST)
**) Technology Research Association of Magnetic Materials for High-Efficiency Motors (MagHEM)

The 23rd International Workshop on Rare Earth and Future Permanent Magnets and Their Applications (REPM2014)
Annapolis, Maryland USA - August 17-21, 2014

SCHEDULE
THURSDAY, AUGUST 21, 2014

COFFEE BREAK – 15 MINUTES

10:45 – 12:30 PM – Nanocrystalline Magnets

12:30 – 2:00 PM – LUNCHEON

2:00 – 4:00 PM Hard Magnetic Particles

COFFEE BREAK – 15 MINUTES

4:15 – 6:30 PM SYMPOSIUM – SEARCH FOR NEW HARD MAGNETIC MATERIALS

6:30 – 6:45 PM – CLOSING REMARKS

Re-thinking Rare Earths: Demand, Sustainability and the Reality of Alternatives

O. GUTFLEISCH[1,2], M.D. KUZ'MIN[1], J. GASSMANN[2], R. GAUß[2]
[1]Technische Universität Darmstadt, Materialwissenschaft, Alarich-Weiß-Str. 16, 64287 Darmstadt, Germany
[2] Fraunhofer Project Group Materials Recycling and Resource Strategies IWKS, Fraunhofer Institute for Silicate Research ISC, Rodenbacher Chaussee 4, 63457 Hanau, Germany

Abstract: *This paper reviews briefly demand, sustainability and the reality of alternatives of rare earth elements REEs in high performance permanent magnets. It gives a short account of the rare earth oxide production leading up to the so-called Rare Earth Crisis and describes some of its consequences, both in economic and scientific point of views. The Rare Earth Crisis triggered around the world a number of renewed and sometimes significant, compare Japan, research activities into the development of resource efficient new high performance permanent magnets. It is interesting to compare the efforts put into this quest in terms of financing, timing and focus between the US, Europe and Japan. This paper looks also into the fundamentals of what is at all possible with 3d ferromagnets and ends with a criticality assessment of Co in order to understand whether cobalt-based magnets could be an alternative to Nd-Fe-B-type magnets.*

Keywords: *rare earth crisis, Nd-Fe-B, substitution, wind power, Co-based magnets*

Address: Prof. Oliver Gutfleisch, Technische Universität Darmstadt, Alarich-Weiß-Str. 16, 64287 Darmstadt, Germany, Tel: +49(0)6151-16-75559, E-Mail: gutfleisch@fm.tu-darmstadt.de

1. Demand and Sustainability of Rare Earths

Three years after the peak of the Rare Earth Crisis fundamental problems in the rare earth global supply and demand system remain. Prices have fallen, but rare earths are still classified as critical in terms of supply, particularly Nd, Dy and Tb [1]. Rare earths are critical for a variety of reasons. First of all, almost the entire value chain from mine to magnet is currently strongly concentrated in one country, that is, China. As a result of this monopole situation, there is a significant political dimension to the determination of respective prices. Figure 1 shows how an increased country concentration in combination with an increased overall demand in REE production correlates with prices that initially increased steadily and later on exploded. As a result of the 2010 and 2011 Rare Earth Crisis, demand seems to have decreased, although reliable figures are hard to find. As an example, whilst USGS argues that 110,000 t REO were produced in 2013, BGR lists an even much lower mass of 90,500 t [2], that is, almost twenty percent less. On the other hand, there is a lack of information on the consumer side: it is not straightforward to assess, where and in what quantities rare earth permanent magnets are installed. This lack of information causes a kind of market insecurity. It turns economic feasibility evaluations of new mining projects as well as projects that invest in recycling and remanufacturing routes into a challenging task; currently, REPM are not recycled on an industrial scale.

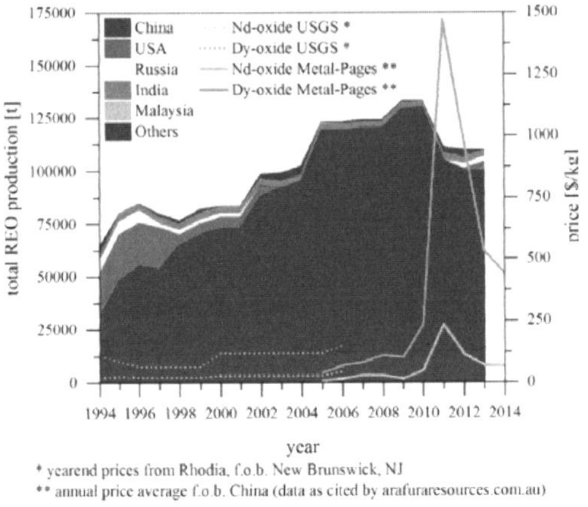

Fig. 1. Total REO production versus price development of Nd- and Dy-oxide. Production data are cited from USGS; the color code shows the relative distribution of the producing country [3,4].

Actually recycling of REEs is still in its infancy, basic hydrometallurgical, pyrometallurgical, chemical, physical and other processes need to be developed and assessed. Prior to that collection logistics ought to be implemented which involve also the development of effective dissembling methods. Environmental indicators of a product or device would certainly drastically improved if recycled REPMs were used.

Rare earths are critical, because in many applications they cannot be appropriately substituted: there are a number of existing and future technologies that fundamentally depend on high performance permanent magnets, thus rare earth metals (see below). Finally, the co-occurrence and co-extraction of the different kinds of REE has repeatedly led to the problem that – depending on the market situation driven by different kinds of emerging technologies – some particular REE drive the exploitation whilst others are produced in excess. This is the so-called 'Balance Problem': ideally, there would be a balance between the demand and supply of all REE, since production costs would then be shared by the selling of all REE; but this has never been the case. Currently, the LREE market is driven by the demand for Nd, those of the heavy rare earths by Dy [8,9].

Today, the greatest part, i.e. 30 to 40 %, of Nd-Fe-B magnets produced worldwide is used for the manufacture of motors and generators. This is followed by the use in hard disc, CD and DVD drives (10 to 15%) and a number of other applications, including e.g. audio equipment and home appliances [10,11]. As already mentioned, it is hard to find exact figures for each application field. However, it becomes clear, and it is important to note, that the demand by the frequently cited wind power and e-mobility devices have not yet had a decisive impact on the REPM market: using a bottom-up approach, Zepf estimates that about 800 t of Nd were used in magnets for wind generators and about 250 t for e-mobility devices in 2010, respectively [12]. This corresponds to about 4% and 1% of the entire Nd produced in this year [1]. We argue that these and other future CO_2-saving technologies will generate an enormous demand for high-performance permanent magnets. The *Energiewende* ("energy transition/ turnover – the exit from nuclear and fossil"), i.e. a systematic and sustainable investment into a renewable energies can be used as a case to underline this argument. The wind power capacity installed worldwide is expected to double from about 300 GW to 600 GW (Fig. 2) [4]. It is hard to say, which turbine technology will succeed in the long-term on a global scale. Regarding Germany, which currently accounts for about 10 % of the globally installed wind power capacity, we know that direct drive wind generators containing permanent magnets are increasingly popular, particularly for the use in offshore contexts. Permanent magnet driven turbines are more robust, have a greater energy yield and require less maintenance [13,14]. Assuming that 600 kg of (Nd,Dy)-Fe-B per MW is typically required in a modern wind turbine [11,14], one can estimate that approximately 7570 t of (Nd,Dy)-Fe-B are required for the installation of direct drive wind power generators in the period between 2012 and 2020. Assuming that a typical alloy would contain 28 wt.% Nd and 4 wt.% Dy, this corresponds to about 2120 t Nd and 300 t Dy, i.e. an average of 236 t and 34 t per year, respectively. Looking at the global production volume of these two elements, i.e. 21,000 t of Nd and 1,350 t of Dy (see [1] p167), these annual demands for wind power in Germany relate to about 1 % and 2.5 %, respectively.

The diagrams and figures estimated above may form the basis to estimate current and future demands of permanent magnets in wind turbines on a global scale. If we assume that – like in the case of Germany – in 2013 about 11 % of wind turbines installed every year contain (Nd,Dy)-Fe-B magnets [6] this would result in a global demand of about 650 t Nd and 92 t Dy, corresponding to 3% and 7% of the global production, respectively. If we assume that – as forecasted for the German case – in 2018 40 % of the newly installed turbines contain permanent magnets [7] and follow the same assumptions and calculations as above, the annual demands of Nd and Dy would amount to 4,370 t and 620 t respectively (see figures 2 and 3). These values would be equivalent to about 12 % and 40 %

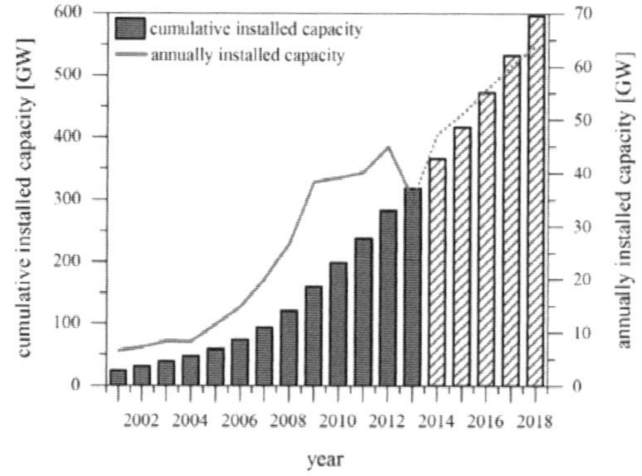

* forecast for the worldwide development of installed wind energy on the basis of data from GWEC (2014)

Fig. 2. Wind power installed worldwide, including projected data until 2018 [5].

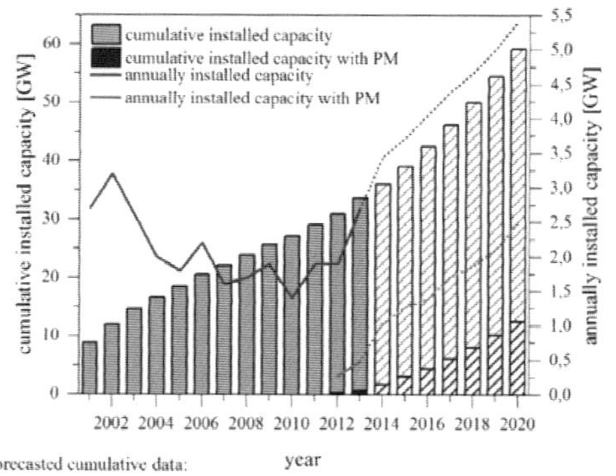

* forecasted cumulative data:
- assuming that Germany continues to have a 10% share of global wind power capac
* forcasted PM containing drives:
- assuming that by 2020 approx. 50% of the annually growth capacity is PM driven
- offshore capacity is expected to amount to 6500 MW by then

Fig. 3. Wind power capacity installed in Germany, including projected data until 2020 [5-7]; PM – permanent magnet.

of the Nd and Dy masses produced in 2018, respectively (see [1] p167 and p177 global Nd and Dy production of 37,000 t and 1,600 t in 2018, respectively). This scenario indicates the dynamics behind the rising demand of high-performance permanent magnets. Similar trends can be forecasted for other emerging technologies, such as those associated with e-mobility or magnetic refrigeration.

Currently, there is no equivalent alternative to Nd-Fe-B in terms of energy density and material cost. Significant progress is being made currently using grain boundary diffusion processes in sintered Nd-Fe-B magnets. This micro- and nanoengineering of the internal interfaces in REPMs enable significant savings in HREEs by efficiently using them where they are actually needed. However, research into substitution of critical metals must not end by looking at a material level. Instead, it must include research into finding substitutes on elemental, material, process, product and system levels. Regarding wind turbines, this certainly must include research into new machine designs. Regarding their magnetic properties, alloys containing the 3d elements Mn, Fe, Co, Ni are most interesting, which is discussed in the next section.

2. Alternatives: What is at All Possible with 3d Ferromagnets

2.1. Magnetization

The magnetization of 3d magnets is largely of spin nature; the orbital moment is quenched. Potentially, very high values of magnetization are possible. The maximum is reached in the hypothetical case of full spin polarization, where the 3d states are half filled, as shown in Fig. 4a. If the localized approach is adopted, the spin should obey the first Hund's rule,

$$S = \tfrac{1}{2} \max (N_{3d}, 10 - N_{3d}). \qquad (1)$$

The maximum value, $S_{max} = 5/2$, is obviously reached at the half-filling, $N_{3d} = 5$ (see Fig. 5). The

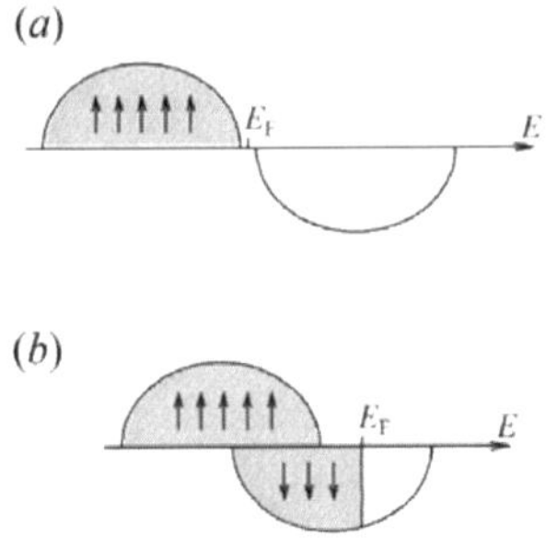

Fig. 4. Density of 3d states (schematic) in a hypothetical fully polarized ferromagnet (a) and a more realistic 3d metal with partial polarization (b).

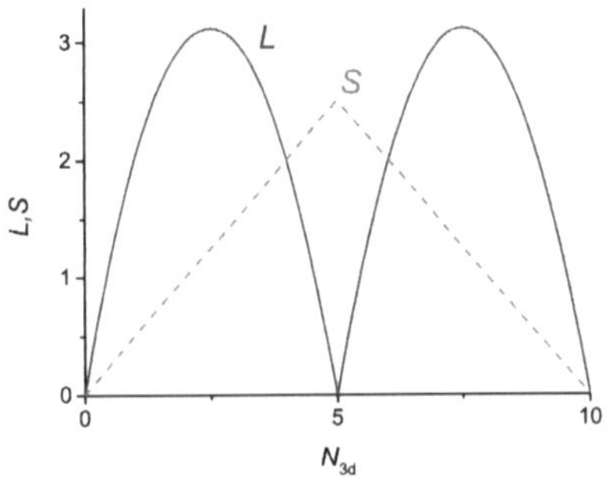

Fig. 5. Spin and orbital moments of a 3d system containing N_{3d} electrons per atom and obeying Hund's rules, Eqs. (1,2).

corresponding magnetic moment is 5 μ_B per 3d atom. For a solid containing ~8.5×10^{22} 3d atoms per cm^3 this results in a saturation polarization of about 5 T. This should be regarded as the highest possible value.

The value achieved in reality is only half as high, 2.5 T, as observed in permendur, $Fe_{0.65}Co_{0.35}$ [15]. (In practice, the permanent-magnet industry is happy to have anything between 1 T and 1.5 T.) That is to say, in real 3d ferromagnets the situation is rather more like the one shown in Fig. 4b. Of primary interest to us here are only materials with high magnetization, which are all either strong ferromagnets (the majority 3d subband is fully occupied) or at least close to being ones.

It should be remarked that the fully polarized case shown in Fig. 4a is not at all impossible – it just has not yet been observed in a concentrated 3d magnet. In compounds containing non-transition elements along with 3d ones, the latter can well be polarized to 5 μ_B/atom; however, the net magnetization is not particularly high due to dilution. Whether concentrated or not, a fully polarized 3d system is not suitable for making permanent magnets. The reason becomes clear from the second Hund's rule,

$$L = 2S\,(S_{max} - S), \qquad (2)$$

whereby the orbital moment is strictly zero if $S = S_{max}$ (see Fig. 5). Thus, the anisotropy vanishes where the magnetization is at its highest.

2.2. Anisotropy

Theoretically, very high values of anisotropy energy are possible in 3d compounds. The anisotropy constant of an itinerant ferromagnet is given by a simple expression [16]:

$$K_1 \approx \pm \tfrac{1}{4}\,\zeta\,\Delta L. \qquad (3)$$

Here ζ is the single-electron spin-orbit coupling constant and ΔL is the anisotropy of the orbital moment,

$$\Delta L = \langle L \rangle_{M\|Z} - \langle L \rangle_{M\perp Z} \quad (4)$$

where **Z** denotes a high-symmetry crystal direction. Equation (3) should be taken with a plus sign if the 3d shell is more than half full, as relevant to Fe, Co, and Ni. Both K_1 and ΔL should be normalized in a similar fashion, e.g., per atom or per unit cell. In principle, ΔL of a $3d$ atom could be as high as ~1, while density-functional calculations yield $\zeta_{Fe} \approx 0.055$ eV and $\zeta_{Co} \approx 0.07$ eV [17]. This would lead to a truly gigantic K_1, to the tune of several hundred megajoules per cubic meter. In reality, the anisotropy constants of 3d ferromagnets are at least 1.5 orders of magnitude smaller. Thus, the most strongly anisotropic compound, $LaCo_5$, has $K_1 \approx 10$ MJ/m^3, but the more common values are of the order of 1 MJ/m^3 or less.

The reason of the smallness of K_1 is that the expectation values of the orbital moment are typically ~0.1 rather than ~1, the differences (2) being yet smaller, ~10^{-2}. One says that the orbital moment is 'quenched'. Thus, the problem of anisotropy in a 3d-based magnet consists essentially in overcoming the quenching. Physically, two competing effects are responsible for the quenching of the orbital moment in 3d solids: crystal field and covalence. The former prevails in ionic insulators, the latter in metals. We are mainly interested in metallic materials. In that case the expectation values of the orbital moment can be estimated as

$$\langle L \rangle \sim \zeta_{3d}/W_{3d} \sim 0.1, \quad (5)$$

where W_{3d} is the corresponding bandwidth [16]. (Typically, $W_{3d} \sim 1$ eV.) However, this rough estimate does not suffice for the calculation of the anisotropy of the orbital moment ΔL (4) or the anisotropy constant (3). Accurate relativistic electronic structure calculations are needed instead.

It follows from Eq. (2) that L is a maximum at $S = S_{max}/2$, e.g., at $N_{3d} = 7.5$. One might think it to be an optimal filling of the 3d band – the majority subband is completely occupied, the minority one is half full. Yet, taking a closer look at the anisotropy, one finds that, on the contrary, $N_{3d} = 7.5$ is a value to avoid. Let us once again make use of the localized approximation and limit ourselves to $T = 0$. The leading anisotropy constant is then given by [18]:

$$K_1 = -\tfrac{3}{4}\, L\,(2L-1)\,\langle L\|\alpha\|L \rangle\, A_{20}, \quad (6)$$

where $\langle L\|\alpha\|L \rangle$ is a numerical coefficient playing the role of the Stevens factor in the L representation [19]:

$$\langle L\|\alpha\|L \rangle = \mp\tfrac{4}{21}\,(S_{max} - 2S)\,/\,(2L-1). \quad (7)$$

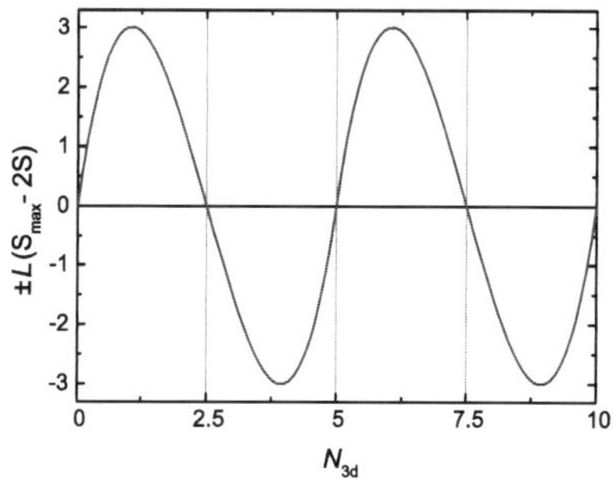

Fig. 6: The product $\pm L(S_{max}-2S)$ as a function of the filling number N_{3d}.

Hence,

$$K_1 = \pm\tfrac{1}{7}\, L\,(S_{max} - 2S)\, A_{20}. \quad (8)$$

The upper (lower) sign in Eqs. (7,8) should be taken for a 3d shell less (more) than half full. The quantity A_{20} in Eqs. (6,8) is the second-order crystal field parameter; all higher-order parameters have been neglected for simplicity. In the crudest approximation A_{20} does not depend on the filling number N_{3d}; K_1 vs N_{3d} then follows the product $\pm L(S_{max} - 2S)$, see Fig. 6. It is easy to see that the parenthesis in Eq. (8) vanishes at $N_{3d} = 7.5$, as well as at $N_{3d} = 2.5$ for early 3d elements. (In both cases $S = S_{max}/2$.) This is associated with a change of sign of the coefficient $\langle L\|\alpha\|L \rangle$ at those points. The product $\pm L(S_{max} - 2S)$ also has a node at $N_{3d} = 5$, where $L = 0$.

Given that the function plotted in Fig. 6 ignores the existence of energy bands in solids, it cannot be reasonably expected to provide an accurate description of the dependence of K_1 on N_{3d} for real ferromagnets. The most important effect neglected so far is the dependence on N_{3d} of the crystal field parameter A_{20}. This dependence will have a complex, oscillating character reflecting the band structure of a particular compound. One can infer from Eq. (8) that the resulting dependence $K_1(N_{3d})$ will acquire a more rugged shape, with more peaks and valleys. The nodes of the product $\pm L(S_{max}-2S)$ will be preserved, but extra nodes are likely to appear. In the absence of any information on a specific compound, one should at least try to avoid the nodes known a priori. It is known from experience that Co-based magnets tend to be strongly anisotropic. This is to be expected, since Co has $N_{3d} = 8.3$ [20].

3. Are Cobalt-based Magnets an Alternative?

Cobalt has a long history in magnetism. Its supply calamity and price volatility in the 1970s and early 80s was one of the key factors – and an example of a criticality of an element - that reinforced the search for alternative permanent magnet materials and finally led to the discovery of Nd-Fe-B for the use in this context. Since then, global production of cobalt has almost tripled, from 40,900 t Co in 1984 to 103,000 t in 2012 [21]. Thus, Co production is five times larger than that of Nd and ten times larger than that of Dy. With 56% of world production, the Democratic Republic of Congo is still the main producer, but there are a number of other countries that produce cobalt, most importantly China, Russia, and Zambia each with 6% of world production capacity; other production places are found in Canada, Australia, Cuba, Brazil and Morocco, each of which comprise 3 % to 4 % of world production capacity. Thus, production is not as highly concentrated as it is currently the case for the rare earths. Primary Co resources are estimated to comprise 15 million tonnes (see [1] p34-35). On the other hand, besides the political instability of its main producing country, there are a number of issues that might turn the supply of cobalt into a critical state. First of all, Co is a by-product of copper and nickel production, compare the metrics of metal ecology, thus would always depend on the prosperity of the Cu and Ni value chains. In addition, there are a number of critical competing technologies that also require Co, most importantly batteries (e.g. portable devices, e-mobility), super-alloys and catalysts. Co is also used in dissipative fields of applications, such as pigments and adhesives (see [1] p39). During the last 40 years, the price development of Co has been severely volatile. The 2014 EU report on critical raw materials classifies Co as critical, whilst an equivalent DOE report does not, most importantly because a greater number of Co production sites outside Africa will be coming online within the next decade [22,23].

In order to evaluate the potential of a Co-based magnet to replace Nd-Fe-B on a larger scale, we developed a stress test (Fig. 7) that calculates the market value of permanent magnets installed in wind turbines in 2013 in Germany, according to various magnet compositions and raw material prices. A Co-based magnet would at least contain more than 50% Co (1:5). The stress test enables us to conclude that a Co-based magnet could contain up to 81 wt.% Co to compete with a standard (Nd,Dy)-Fe-B alloy containing up to 4 wt.% Dy (estimates based on current prices and assuming that the Co-based magnet has the same energy density as (Nd,Dy)-Fe-B). Thus, apart from finding the high-energy density Co-based material itself, the key to bring such a material to a mass-market production is to secure global supply and to stabilize the Co price. In any case, to have at hand an alternative material with similar qualities to (Nd,Dy)-Fe-B when rare earth prices go off again would be a relaxing factor from the overall criticality perspective.

References

[1] European Commission, Report on critical raw materials for the EU – Report of the Ad hoc Working Group on defining critical raw materials (2014).

[2] http://www.bgr.bund.de/DE/Gemeinsames/Oeffentlichkeitsarbeit/Pressemitteilung/ BGR/

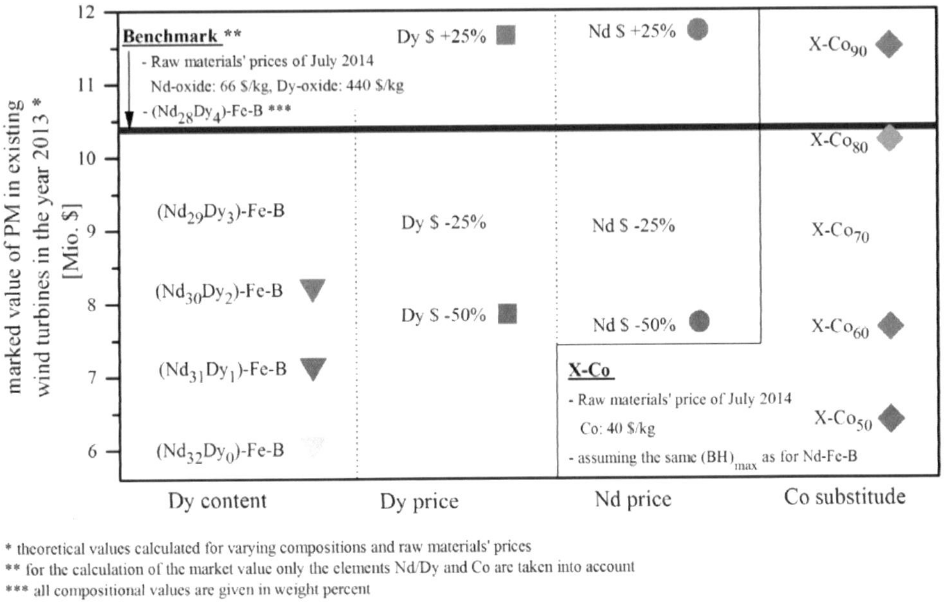

Fig. 7. Stress-test scenarios: raw materials' costs of Nd-Fe-B versus those of equivalent Co-based magnets. The data relate to the market volume in Germany in 2013.

bgr140312_Seltene%20Erden.html.
[3] USGS, *Minerals yearbook – Rare earths* (1994 – 2006).
[4] www.arafuraresources.com.au (2014).
[5] Global Wind Energy Council, *Global wind energy report - Annual market update 2013* (2014).
[6] Deutsche WindGuard GmbH, www.windguard.de (2014).
[7] R.L. Moss et al., *Critical metals in the path towards the decarbonisation of the EU energy sector* (2013).
[8] K. Binnemans et al., JOM **65** No. 7 (2013).
[9] P. Falconnet et al. J. Less-Common Met. Vol. **111** No. 9 (1985).
[10] D.N. Brown et al., *J. Phys. Condens. Matter.* **26**, 064202 (2014).
[11] www.helimagnet.com/applications.html.
[12] V. Zepf, *Rare Earth Elements – A new approach to the nexus of supply, demand and use; exemplified along the use of Neodymium in permanent magnets*, PhD thesis (2012).
[13] H. Polinder et al., 10 MW wind turbine direct-drive generator design with pitch or active speed stall control (2007).
[14] O. Gutfleisch et al., *Adv. Mater.* **23**, 821 (2011).
[15] G. Couderchon et al., J. Magn. Magn. Mater. Vol. **26**, 196 (1982).
[16] P. Bruno et al., Phys. Rev. B, Vol. **39**, 865 (1989).
[17] M. Richter, Density functional theory applied to 4f and 5f elements and metallic compounds. In: Handbook of Magnetic Materials, ed. K.H.J. Buschow (North-Holland, Amsterdam), Vol. **13**, Ch. 2 (2001).
[18] M.D. Kuz'min et al., Phys. Rev. B Vol. **46**, 8219 (1992).
[19] B. Bleaney et al., Rep. Prog. Phys. Vol. **16**, 108 (1953).
[20] J.C. Slater et al., J. Appl. Phys. Vol. **8**, 385 (1937).
[21] USGS – Cobalt statistics (2012).
[22] European Commission, Report on critical raw materials for the EU – Critical raw materials profiles (2014).
[23] U.S. Department of Energy, Critical materials strategy (2011).

General Situation of Rare Earth Resources and the Applications in China

A. ZHANG
Chinese Society of Rare Earth, Beijing, China

Abstract: *This paper gives the detailed information related to rare earth, including 1) the sustainable use of the resources; 2) the formation and development potential of a diversified pattern of rare earth supply; 3) the trend and forecast consumption structure of rare earth; 4) the rare earth industry's significant role in boosting strategic emerging industries; and 5) important applications of rare earth permanent magnets in related industries.*

Keywords: *rare earth elements; rare earth industries; rare earth magnets; rare earth applications*

Address: Anwen Zhang, zawcsre@126.com

I. The sustainable use of rare earth resources

1.1. Abundances of rare earth elements (RRE)

As shown in table 1, REE's abundances are not low. For example, cerium has about the same level as copper has. The abundance of terbium is equivalent to molybdenum. And the abundances of all the rare earth metals are much higher compared to those of gold, silver, platinum, and other precious metals.

- The total rare earth's highest abundance is 242.1, and the lowest is 159.9, and the average is 199.53. As a comparison, tin and cobalt are 40;
- The main REE average abundances are: Ce: 60.5, La: 29.2, Nd: 31.5, Pr: 7.72, Eu: 1.26, Tb: 1.23, Dy: 4.4, Y: 29.4, Sc: 17.5;

Table 1. REE crustal abundance (estimated) REE (listed in ascending order by atomic number). (units: ppm)

Rare earth element	Mason and Moore (1982)	Jackson and Christiansen (1993)	Sabot and Maestro (1995)	Wedepohl (1995)	Lide (1997)	McGill (1997)
Lanthanum	30	29	18	30	39	5~18
Cerium	60	70	46	60	66.5	20~46
Prasedynium	8.2	9	5.5	6.7	9.2	3.5~5.5
Neodymium	28	37	24	27	41.5	12~24
Samarium	6	8	6.5	5.3	7.05	4.5~7
Europium	1.2	1.3	0.5	1.3	2	0.14~1.1
Gadolinium	5.4	8	6.4	4	6.2	4.5~6.4
Terbium	0.9	2.5	0.9	0.65	1.2	0.7~1
Dysprosium	3	5	5	3.8	5.2	4.5~7.5
Holmium	1.2	1.7	1.2	0.8	1.3	0.7~1.2
Erbium	2.8	3.3	4	2.1	3.5	2.5~6.5
Thulium	0.5	0.27	0.4	0.3	0.52	0.2~1
Ytterbium	3.4	0.33	2.7	2	3.2	2.7~8
Lutetium	0.5	0.8	0.8	0.35	0.8	0.8~1.7
Yttrium	33	29	28	24	33	28~70
Scanium	22		10	16	22	5~10
Total	206.1	205.2	159.9	184.3	242.17	

- Ratio R of Tb+Dy / Pr+Nd is ~0.143, and the high coercivity NdFeB magnets generally have R = 5/31 or 0.161. Taking it from a statistical view of applications, can the REE supply be balanced? In fact the heavy REE (HRE) dispersed with high production costs, and the HRE metals are still in short supply.

1.2. The world has rich rare earth resources, and these data are shown in Table 2.

Table 2. The world's leading rare earth mineral resources (Excluding alluvial heavy mineral & rock phosphate deposits)

Country	Mine Name	Tonnage (Tons)	(%, TREO)	Reserve (TREO, 吨)
Australia	Brockman	50,000,000	0.23	11,000
Australia	Cummings	4,170,000	1.72	72,000
Australia	Du Bo	73,200,000	0.89	651,500
Australia	Weld Mountain	15,020,000	8.60	1,292,000
Australia	Nalabuma	55,000,000	0.03	16,500
Australia	Nolan	30,300,000	2.80	849,000
Australia	John Garde	382,000	7.96	30,400
Australia	Olympic Dam	>2,000,000,000	0.50	10,000,000
Australia	Yankee class	3,500,000	1.70	59,500
Canada	Huo Yi Das Lake	2,847,000	2.00	57,000
Canada	Strange Lake	137,639,000	0.97	1,335,000
Canada	Thor Lake (Lake Area)	175,900,000	1.43	2,516, 000
Canada	Thor Lake (N. Province)	1,136,000	0.71	8,000
Canada	Oka	210,000,000	0.127	267,000
Canada	Ortisei	2,270,000	0.11	2,500
USA	Mountain Pass	13,588,000	8.24	1,120,000
Greenland	Kirwan Neifeierde	457,000,000	1.07	4,890,000
Malawi	坎甘昆德	2,500,000	4.24	107,000
Brazil	Allah Berkshire	450,000,000	1.80	8,100,000
Brazil	Cattaro	10,000,000	0.90	90,000
Brazil	Pi Tingjia	164,000,000	0.15	246,000
Brazil	Pod Carlos			115,000
Brazil	Sheng Sila Lagos	2,900,000,000	1.50	43,500,000
Brazil	Tapia	5,200,000	10.5	546,000
Burundi	Casa Garvey	67,000	1.50	1,000
Kenya	Mo lima Mountain	6,000,000	16.2	972,000
Kirghizstan	阿克图吾兹	15,000,000	1.00	150,000
Kirghizstan	卡拉吉尔佳	957,000	0.70	6,700
Kirghizstan	Kunte Se	20,228,000	0.22-0.3	<60,000
Kyrgyzstan	Sale Isser	7,000,000	0.20	14,000
South Africa	Fort Pilaneisi	13,500,000	0.70	94,50
South Africa	Stephanie Campos Lal	249,500	11.80	29,500
South Africa	Like Dirk de Swift	31,500,000	3.60	1,130,000
Turkey	Lean Chigi Mallorca	4,695,000	2.78	130,500
Vietnam	Are Baio	500,000,000	1.40	7,000,000
Vietnam	Mau Xe North	557,000,000	1.40	7,000,000

1.3. The diversity of rare earth ore partition and HRE outside of China are shown in Tables 3, 4, and 5.

Table 3. Main feature of rare earth mine

Formula	Baotou China	China Ion-adsorbed REE Mine			China Sichuan mine	American Bastnaesite	Russia loparite	Australia monazite	Malaysia xenotime
		寻乌 Xunwu	信丰 Xinfeng	龙南 Nongnan					
La_2O_3	25.00	38.00	27.56	2.18	29.81	32.00	25.00	23.90	1.26
CeO_2	50.07	3.50	3.23	<1.09	51.11	49.00	50.00	46.30	3.17
Pr_6O_{11}	5.10	7.41	5.62	1.08	4.26	4.40	5.00	5.05	0.50
Nd_2O_3	16.60	30.18	17.55	3.47	12.78	13.50	15.00	17.38	1.61
Sm_2O_3	1.20	5.32	4.54	2.37	1.09	0.50	0.70	2.53	1.16
Eu_2O_3	0.18	0.51	0.93	<0.37	0.17	0.10	0.09	0.05	0.01
Gd_2O_3	0.70	4.21	5.96	5.69	0.45	0.30	0.60	1.49	3.52
Tb_4O_7	<0.1	0.46	0.68	1.13	0.05	0.01		0.04	0.92
Dy_2O_3	<0.1	1.77	3.71	7.48	0.06	0.03	0.60	0.69	8.44
Ho_2O_3	<0.1	0.27	0.74	1.60	<0.05	0.01	0.70	0.05	2.01
Er_2O_3	<0.1	0.88	2.48	4.26	0.034	0.01	0.80	0.21	6.52
Tm_2O_3	<0.1	0.13	0.27	0.60	-	0.02	0.10	0.01	1.14
Yb_2O_3	<0.1	0.62	1.13	3.34	0.018	0.01	0.20	0.12	6.87
Lu_2O_3	<0.1	0.13	0.21	0.47	-	0.01	0.15	0.04	1.00
Y_2O_3	0.43	10.07	24.26	64.9	0.91	0.10	1.30	2.41	61.87

Table 4. Main feature of rare earth ore relative value comparison (the lowest is set to 1)

	Baotou	寻乌 Xunwu	信丰 Xingfeng	龙南 Nongnan	四川 Shichuan	American Bastnaesite	Russia loparite	Australia monazite	Malaysia xenotime
La_2O_3	19.8	30.2	21.9	1.7	23.7	25.4	19.8	18.9	1
CeO_2	45.9	3.2	3.0	1	46.9	45.0	45.9	42.5	2.9
Pr_6O_{11}	10.2	14.8	11.2	2.2	8.5	8.8	10.0	10.0	1
Nd_2O_3	10.3	18.7	10.9	2.2	7.9	8.3	9.3	10.8	1
Sm_2O_3	2.4	10.6	9.1	4.7	2.2	1	1.4	5.1	2.3
Eu_2O_3	18	51	93	37	17	10	9	5.0	1
Gd_2O_3	2.3	14.0	19.9	19.0	1.5	1	2	5.0	11.7
Tb_4O_7		46.0	68.0	113.0	5.0	1		4.0	92.0
Dy_2O_3		59.0	123.7	249.3	2.0	1	20.0	23.0	281.3
Ho_2O_3		27.0	74.0	160.0		1	70.0	5.0	201.0
Er_2O_3		88.0	248.0	426.0	3.4	1	80.0	21.0	652.0
Tm_2O_3		13.0	27.0	60.0		2.0	10.0	1	113.0
Yb_2O_3		62.0	113.0	334.0		1	20.0	12.0	687.0
Lu_2O_3		13.0	21.0	47.0		1	15.0	4.0	100.0
Y_2O_3	4.3	100.1	242.0	649.0	91.0	1	13.0	24.1	618.7

With the highest Relative Partitions are:

- Ce: China Sichuan #1 - 46.9 , Baotou #2 - 45.9,
- Tb: China Longnan - 113 ,
- Dy: Malaysia xenotime - 281.3,
- Eu: China Xinfeng - 93, Y: Longnan - 649
- Tb+Dy: Longnan #1 -362.3, Xinfeng #2 -191.7
- Pr+Nd: Xunwu #1 - 33.5, Xinfeng #2 - 22.1, Baotou #3 – 20.5 (Baotou's total is world's highest based on the largest reserves)

Table 5. Relative Partitions

Composition	Weld Mountain in Australia	Cape, South Africa	Greenland TBBRZ
	REO	REO	By lanthanide meter
La_2O_3	24. 27	25. 36	22. 29
CeO_2	48. 83	44. 20	43. 37
Pr_6O_{11}	5. 22	4. 55	4. 38
Nd_2O_3	17. 33	15. 74	24. 72
Sm_2O_3	2. 37	2. 31	2. 86
Eu_2O_3	0. 47	0. 59	0. 28
Gd_2O_3	0. 83	1. 44	2. 62
Tb_4O_7	0. 05	0. 17	0. 50
Dy_2O_3	0. 18	0. 77	3. 32
Ho_2O_3	0. 02	0. 13	0. 72
Er_2O_3	0. 03	0. 32	2. 19
Tm_2O_3	0. 00	0. 04	0. 34
Yb_2O_3	0. 01	0. 23	2. 12
Lu_2O_3	0. 00	0. 03	0. 29
Y_2O_3	0. 38	4. 12	~20%
Total	100	100	100

Questions and Discussion:

- Compared to other rare metals resources, rare earths are widely distributed and abundant in the world. The problem is Not lack of global resources, but lack of rational exploitation and balanced use;
- Specific resource distributions are abundant for light RE, such as Ce, and tight-supply situation for HRE, such as Dy. However, the new technology in reducing the usage of HRE and RE luminescent materials will gradually improve the situation;
- Develop new applications and expand the application of RE in traditional industries will help to solve relatively surplus situation for the REE with high abundance.

II. The formation and development potential of a diversified pattern of rare earth supply

2.1. Current rare earths suppliers outside of China

Table 6. Current rare earth suppliers outside of China

No	Company	Country	Current Capacity	Capacity in 2015
1	Molycorp	USA	19000	40000
2	Lynas	Australia	10500	21000
3	Lovozersky	Russia	3000-4400	15000
4	Solikamsk Magnesium Works	俄罗斯		
5	Rare earth company	India	100	10000
6	丰田/双日/越南	Vietnam	20000	>20000
7	Neo	Thailand		
8	Lynas / Malaysia	Malaysia		
9	Brazilian Nuclear Energy Industry Corporation (INB)	Brazil	1500	>1500
	Total		55500	>107500

2.2. The planned rare earth projects

Table 7. Upcoming production of rare earths supplier

No.	Company	Country	2011-2013 Capacity (RE oxides -Ton)	2015 Expected Capacity (RE oxides – Ton)
1	Rareco/Great Western Minerals Group	South Africa / Canada	3000	5000
2	Sumitomo/Kazatomprom/ SARECO JV	Kazakhstan / Japan	3000	15000
3	Toyota/Sojitz/Govt. of Vietnam	Vietnam / Japan	300	5000
4	Toyota/Indian Rare Earths jv	India / Japan	5000	10000
5	Mitsubishi/Neo Materials Co.	Japan / USA / Canada / Brazil	500	1000
6	Alken Resources	Australia	2600	6000
	Total		14400	42000

2.3. REO production costs

Table 8. REO Production Cost

	Cost: USD/Kg-REO	Source
USA Mountain Pass	2.77?	Molycorp
China	5.58	Molycorp
Mount Weld	7.00	Molycorp
Nechalacho	3.70	Avalon Rare Metals
Strange Lake	0.51	Quest Rare Minerals

Questions and Discussions:

- The diversified pattern of world's RE supply has taken shape, and in the short-term Chinese dominance in the global RE supply chain continues;
- China's rare earth, especially light rare earth prices still have greater advantage;
- China needs to take control of the total mining and smelting separation production, strengthen self-discipline, improve the system of import / export trade rational design to stabilize the price of RE exports and prevent competing prices, which agree the long-term interests of both Chinese and foreign enterprises;
- Overseas Chinese RE supply and the China RE price have a positive correlation;
- In recent years, too much media stir in rare earth tension. We should ask: is it wise to depend on China as the sole supplier?

2.4. Analyses for RE supply and demand in the world

Table 9. World's rare earth supply and demand

Country	Operation	2011	2012	2013	2014	2015-2016
Australia	Dubbo	0	0	3,800	3,800	3,800
	Mount Weld	11,000	22,000	22,000	22,000	22,000
	Nolans Bore	0	20,000	20,000	20,000	20,000
Canada	Nechalacho	0	0	0	0	8,000
	Strange Lake	0	0	0	0	10,000
Greenland	Kvanefjeld	0	0	0	0	37,000
India	Chavara	2,700	2,700	2,700	2,700	2,700
Malaysia	Ipoh	450	450	450	450	450
Russia	Lovozero	3,000	3,000	3,000	3,000	3,000
South Africa	Steenkampskraal	0	0	5,000	5,000	5,000
United States	Bear Lodge	0	0	0	0	10,000
	Mountain Pass	3,000	19,050	40,000	40,000	40,000
Total:		20,150	67,200	96,950	96,950	161,950

USGS

2.5. Rare earth prices trend review

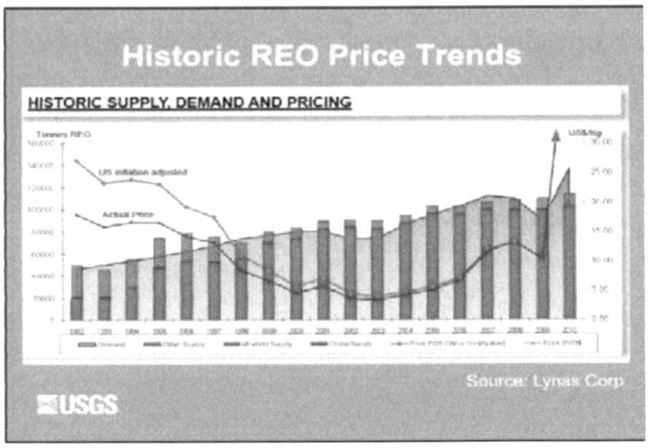

Fig. 1. Rare earth prices trend review

III. The trend and forecast consumption structure

3.1. Global applications of rare earth trends

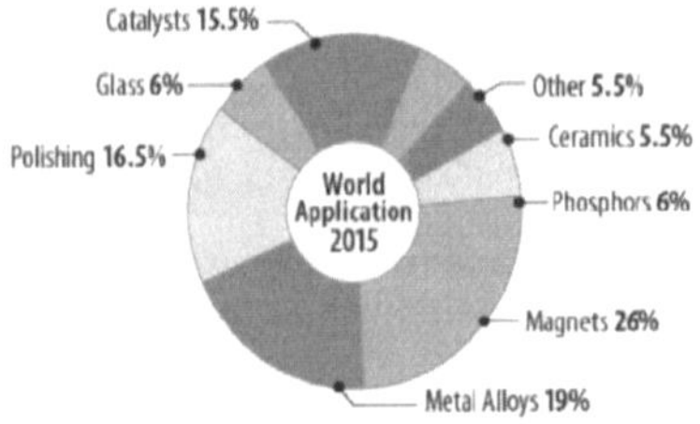

Fig. 2. The global application of rare earth trends [1]

3.2. CAGR (Compound Annual Growth Rate) forecast for the rare earth elements in 2012-2018

Table 10. Compound Annual Growth Rate (CAGR) forecast for the rare earth elements in 2012 ~ 2018

Application	2012~2018 CAGR	Rare earth metal
NiMH batteries	3.3	La、Nd
Magnets	10.1	Nd、Pr、Dy
Automobile exhaust purification	6.0	Ce
Oil catalytic cracking	8.0	La
Metallurgy	3.4	Ce、La
Light	-1.2	Eu、Tb、Y、Ce、La
Polishing	4.8	Ce、La
Optical lens	3.0	Ce
Optical glass	5.0	La、Gd
Others	3.0	Ce、La、Nd、Pr、Sm、Gd
Total	5.8	

Questions and Discussions:

- Three fastest growing areas of rare earth applications are: magnets, catalytic cracking of petroleum, automobile exhaust purification;
- Negative growth over the years for rare earth luminescent applications indicates a rapid LED development and reduction of the demand for HRE;
- Faced with the competition from lithium batteries and fuel cells, rare earth nickel-hydrogen batteries growth slows down;
- What is the progress of developed countries to reconstruct the rare earth industry chain with rare earth permanent magnet as the major part?

IV. Strategic emerging industries on the rare earth industry has a significant role in boosting

4.1. The correlation of rare earth and strategic emerging industries

Table 11. The correlation of rare earth and strategic emerging industries

Economy	Current Application	Future Application
Energy and environmental conservation	Various energy-saving motors tricolor fluorescent light LED hydrogen strorage (energy storage) devices exhausted gas purification Sensor instrument disposal of waste	Solar power energy-saving equipment environmental conservation
New generation information technology	Basic eletronic materials Basic component 3C product Optical fibre	New semiconductor devices Micro-electronics devices Quantum devices The internet of things、Cloud computing
Bioindustry	Armarium (MRI etc.) Agriculture Forestry Animal husbandry Aquaculture High grade cosmetic medicine、reagent	Breed of new medicinal bacteria and enzyme diagnostic reagent cancer、prevent AIDs
Equipment manufacturing industry	High cost performance structural materials Sensor Detector Control devices Micro and specialmotors Airplane, spacecraft, robot	marine & ocean engineering equipment Trains andRailroads Airspace infrastructure system

4.2. The rare earth (RE) consumption structure in China

Fig. 3 shows China's RE consumption structure in 1987–2012. The total RE usage was 4888 tons in 1987 and 83,110 tons in 2011: the annual growth rate was 12.5%. The RE new materials accounted for 66.20% of the total in 2011 and increased to 72.1% in 2012, but the total RE usage dropped to 64,797 tons.

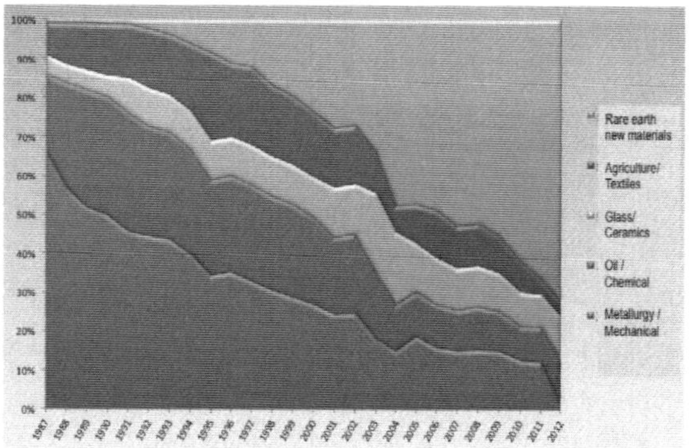

Fig. 3. China's consumption structure in 1987-2012 and consumption of rare earths

Table 12 shows the forecast for RE demand in China. The nationwide NdFeB output would be 150k tons in 2015. According to the calculation on the ratio of (Pr+Nd)/RE = 2/10, it requires 250k tons of rare earth oxides. In this case, the amount of Ce+La+Sm equals 190k tons (=76% x 250k). We should develop the light rare earth application market in addition to Pr and Nd.

Table 12. Rare earth demand in China

	Wind power	HEV	E-Bike	NMR	Inverter air conditioner
Unit Usage	0.67t/MW	1.5～3kg/unit	0.32kg/unit	0.5～3t/ unit	0.1kg/unit
Relative usage	PMG ~1/4	PM motor	PM motor	Most use	2010 ~50%
Total Usage	2020 200 million KW	2020 5 million units	2011: 26 million 2011～2015 6% increase/y	~1000/y	2010 24 million units

Questions and Discussion:

- In some materials, RE may be regarded as "vitamin" role; but in RE permanent magnets and other functional materials, RE is main component;
- As a by-product of RE production, thorium (Th) should be given attention in for its applications;
- Rare earth materials in the Internet, networking (sensors and actuators), bio-engineering, marine engineering equipment, robotics, rail transportation, space-based setting new applications look promising and worth the wait;
- RE materials in the military services (land, sea, air, aerospace, and electronics) will continue to emerge;
- Some proposed alternative technologies for RE metals might seriously affect the performance of some devices with higher energy consumption, lower efficiency or higher costs. From the aspects of technology, economy and energy preservation, we should ask if these alternatives are reasonable?

V. Important applications of rare earth permanent magnets (REPM) in related industries in China

5.1. NdFeB Application Profiles

The quantity demanded for the following applications will have steady growth: lifting machinery, mining pump motor, magnetic separators, electric tools, rail transportation, especially for industrial use various types of PM motors, micro motors, which require high performance with rare earth permanent magnets

- China is expected to reach 150k tons of REPM demands nationwide in the next five years,
- For RE functional materials, the emphasized point is to enhance the material properties to expand the high-end applications and increase the added values.
- Actively develop high performance REPM with energy product + coercivity >> 65 (MGOe +kOe)
- The RE Functional Materials Bases: Focus on the construction in Beijing, Inner Mongolia Baotou, Ganzhou, Jiangxi, Sichuan Liangshan, Longyan, Fujian, Zhejiang, Ningbo and other bases.
- In 2015 Chinese new material value of ¥2,000 bullion: three times of the "Eleventh Five-Year Plan"

Table 13. Table NdFeB Application Profiles

Industry	Type	Unit usage - Kg	Total usage	Advantage	Notes
Wind power	Permanent magnet direct drive motor	670/MW	Based on 20% rare earth magnets, 2013 ~ 2017 global 41,000 tons	Low voltage ride through capability, power savings	If the magnet price is too high, will be replaced by the traditional technology
Automobile: EV、HEV、PHEV	PM Synchronous motors (PMSM)	1-3/unit	2011 to 2015 by HEV800 million, you need 12,000 tons, based on 1.5Kg / car	High specific power, good performance	Difficult to replace or substitute the weight of a large increase fuel consumption
Automotive electronic power steering system	EPS	0.25/unit	In China in 2014 :11490000 units result in 2,873 tons usage	Small, energy-saving, reliable	Gradually replace the power steering device
Elevator	traction motors	10.5/unit	2012 Nationwide in China: Elevator estimated 530,000 units, 90% of rare earth permanent magnet motor, with 5,000 tons Magnets	High efficiency, low power consumption, small size, long life, no room	In the past decade China lift production increased> 20%
Industry	Type	Unit usage - Kg	Total usage	Advantage	Notes
Air conditioning	Inverter air conditioner	0.1/unit	In 2010 China produced 24 million units, if 50% use REPM motor, it counted for 1200 tons/y	Energy-saving, low noise, precision temperature control	Japan accounted for 97%. Inverter washing machine, Invert refrigerator to be developed
Electronic information	Mobile phone	0.0025/unit	In 2011 -1.8 billion units, with 4,500 tons Magnets	Small size, high efficiency	Not easy to replace
	Hard drive		In 2011 - 6300 tons of sintered magnets, 1,300 tons bonded magnets	High recording density, small size	Faced with solid-state memory competition
E-Bike (EB)	Drive motor	0.32	China in 2010 EB yield 29.54 million (magnetics 9500 tons) In 2012: EB 20.28 million (magnets 6489 tons)	High Power, energy-saving	In small cities and rural areas have great potential for development
Medical Equipment	NMR-MRI	0.5~3 tons	In the future if global demand 1,000 units/y , the magnet would be 500 to 3000 tons	High definition	Faces competition superconducting MRI

5.2. The application of rare earth in the wind power

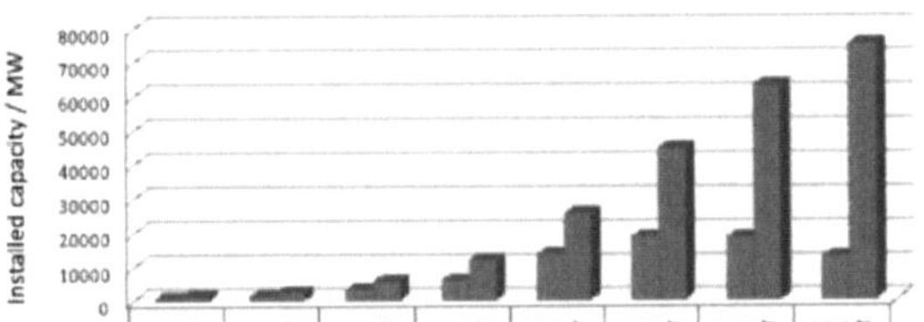

	2005年	2006年	2007年	2008年	2009年	2010年	2011年	2012年
Annual	507	1288	3311	6154	13803	18928	18491	12936
Total	1250	2538	5849	12003	25806	44734	63225	75380

Fig. 4. Total installed capacity of China wind power

Table 14. China 2015-2020 Wind power predicted [2]

	Conservative (MW)		Optimistic (MW)		Aggressive (MW)	
	Cumulative installed	Annual	Cumulative installed	Annual	Cumulative installed	Annual
2015	80000	9000	112000	15000	180000	18000
2020	150000	14000	202000	18000	230000	20000

※Source: China Wind Energy Association

China Wind Power Renewable Energy Society of Professional Committee (CWEA) Statistics:

- In 2012 China has 7872 installed new wind turbine units, added 12.93 GW, and the nationwide has total ownership of 53,764 units with 75.38 GW.
- In 2012 U.S. added 13.1 GW, and the total has cumulated to 60GW.
- In 2012 China's total wind power generating capacity vs. country's total generating capacity was 2%.
- In 2012 global offshore wind power installed capacity reached 5.41GW
- Global Wind Energy Council forecasts that wind power capacity will double from 2013 to 2017, reaching 536 GW in 2017; an annual growth rate of 13.7%.
- Asia will have new installation of 112GW, reaching 200GW in 2017;
- In 2013, China is restored the number one in the world in installed capacity of wind power;

Advantages of Wind power permanent magnet (PM) direct drive motors include a higher conversion efficiency and low rate of abandoned wind off-grid; the future PM direct drive offshore wind power installed capacity is expected to count for 70% offshore wind power.

5.3. The application of rare earth in the new energy vehicles in China

Table 15. China's major automobile groups: current production capacity of electric vehicles and the "Twelfth Five-Year Plan" (These models mainly use PM synchronous motors)

Company No	Current capacity (1000/y)	Major Product	Capacity investment (billion RMB)	Predicted capacity (10,000/y)
1	10	A0 pure electric cars, hybrid cars Pentium, H platform for hybrid cars	5.498	15
2	—	Pure electric vehicles, plug-in hybrid cars, hybrid cars	—	~1
3	3	Pure electric mini passenger cars	0.42	5
4	10	Hybrid vehicles, pure electric vehicles, key components	7.2	20
5	20	Q60FB、C30DB、M30RB BSG weak level of pure electric vehicles hybrid vehicles	2.5	15
6	2	Hybrid vehicles, pure electric buses	1.0	1
7	50	BSG、EVM1 The new platform、ISGA0、A grade platform、T31Plug—in platform	0.4	30
8	20	Plug-in hybrid vehicles	0.3	5
9	10	Pure electric and plug-in hybrid vehicles	0.5	10
10	80	F3DM、e6、K9	1.0	40
11	20	Electric light goods, cars, light passenger	0.86	10
合计	225		19.678	152

Questions and Discussion:

- Strong demand for wind power and new energy vehicles as the representative of emerging industries will push forward the research, production and sale of rare earth permanent magnetic materials;
- Rare earth permanent magnets take important role in the strategic emerging industries with the relevant product performance. Scope and applications of rare earth permanent magnets to some extent reflect the level of high-tech development of a country;
- How to establish rare earth price formation mechanism that avoids price roller coaster ups and downs? How to build an interactive win-win environment for the rare earth raw materials, magnet materials, and their applications in the whole industry chain system?

Concluding Remark

Rare earth industry is a sunrise industry, and rare earth materials industry has more room for development in the fast growing high-tech industry's strategy. Efforts have been made and to be made to solve environmental and ecological problems generated in the production of rare earth metallurgical to benefit all mankind.

References

1. http://thewatchers.adorraeli.com/2012/04/25/rare-earth-mine-in-bayan-obo-in-the-nei-mongol-autonomous-region/ IMCOA, 2011
2. China Wind Energy Association (2013) and various documents

Rare-Earths in Australia: A Perspective

S. J. COLLOCOTT
CSIRO Materials Science and Engineering, Lindfield NSW, Australia 2070

Abstract: *Australia has significant reserves of rare and precious metals. Of global economic reserves of rare-earth oxides (REO), Australia has 2.8% (3.19 million tonnes (Mt) of Economic Demonstrated Resource) cf. China 47.7%. Australia's rare-earth resources may be relatively small, but Australia has well developed mining operations, for example the Lynas Corporation Mount Weld project with its associated processing plant in Malaysia, that are at a level of maturity capable of supplying significant quantities of rare-earths to global markets. Australia also has significant paramarginal, submarginal and inferred resources of rare-earths. Exploration continues apace by a range of small mineral exploration companies to identify new deposits and to prove up known mineralisation. A number of promising deposits have been identified, but commercial production from these is some years in the future. More broadly, the future development of the rare-earth industry in Australia will depend on factors beyond the resource and its extraction. Important will be an economic environment that fosters the development of value-chains that go from the ore body to high-technology product. What happens in the broader Australia economy, which largely escaped the global financial crisis of 2008 unscathed, will drive commercial viability of rare-earth projects and enterprises. Australia is by world standards an open economy, having concluded eight Free Trade Agreements with key trading partners. Important to the future prosperity of all involved in the rare-earth industry, and in ensuring a stable and secure supply of rare-earths, is an open global and transparent trading regime, free of distortions that may result in barriers to commodities, products, services and investment, conducted in a best practice commercial environment.*

Keywords: *Australia; rare-earth resources; industry*

Address: Dr. S. J. Collocott, CMSE, PO Box 218, Lindfield NSW, Australia 2070,
E-mail: stephen.collocott@gmail.com

1. Introduction

Australia is a resource rich country, and in recent years it has prospered from an unprecedented boom in demand for its high quality bulk resources, mainly from rapidly expanding Asian economies. Minerals and fuels make-up close to 51% of Australia's exports, with the top three commodities iron ore and concentrates, coal and gold [1]. In addition to bulk commodities, Australia has significant reserves of rare and precious metals. Of global economic reserves of rare-earth oxides (REO) Australia has 2.8% (3.19 Mt of Economic Demonstrated Resources) [2], compared with China 47.7%, and the USA 11.3% [2]. In recent years China has dominated the global rare-earth industry, supplying over 90% of global demand, as well as being a major consumer. The global dependence of supply of rare-earths from China, and a concern that supply may be reduced, or cut, due to geopolitical reasons has led to countries putting in place strategies to ensure security of supply. Australia's rare-earth resources may be relatively modest, but Australia has well developed projects, for example the Lynas Corporation Mount Weld mine and associated processing plant in Malaysia, that are at a level of maturity capable of supplying significant quantities of rare-earths to global markets. Australia also has significant paramarginal, submarginal and inferred resources of rare-earths. The search for new deposits, and to prove up known mineralisation, is driven by a range of small mineral exploration companies. A number of promising deposits have been identified, but commercial production from these is some years in the future.

The future prosperity of the rare-earth industry in Australia will depend on factors beyond the resource and its extraction. The development of new mines will require considerable capital, and this capital may be difficult to raise, as lenders often view such enterprises as being high risk. Value adding and development of value-chains that go from the ore resource to high-technology product will require not only research and development, applied at all stages of the value-chain, but an economic environment that encourages the necessary financial investment throughout the value-chain. The future success of the Australian rare-earth industry is perhaps best assured by ensuring it has a strategic position in the global supply chain for rare-earths. This will be facilitated if countries avoid polices that could distort markets for rare-earths, and conduct trade on the basis of commercial considerations in-line with well-established multilateral trading rules.

2. The Resource

Though rare-earths are relatively abundant in the Earth's crust, minable concentrations are scarcer compared to commonly exploited metals. Australia has mined rare-earths for over 100 years, with yittrium-rich minerals (gadolinite) mined in 1913 near Marble Bar in Western Australia. Beach sands, widely mined for their ilmenite, rutile, leucoxene and zircon content, also contain the rare-earth bearing heavy minerals monazite and xenotime. In the 1950's small amounts of monazite were extracted from sand mining in Byron Bay, NSW, from which cerium oxide was produced for use in glass polishing. Beach sand mining expanded in the 1970's and 1980's, with activities in Western Australia, Queensland and New South Wales. In 1985 Australia produced 18,735 tonnes of monazite, making it the world's largest producer. In 1995 beach sand mining largely ceased (some small operations still continue at Cooljarloo, Western Australia, and North Stradbroke Island, Queensland), due to low prices for rare-earths and environmental concerns associated with some of the mining activities. During what may be termed the 'the beach sand' era of rare-earth mining from 1952 to 1995, Australia exported some 265,000 tonnes of monazite [3]. During the last decade interest has switched from sand minding to hard rock containing rare-earth deposits.

As of 31 December 2012, Geoscience Australia [2], estimated Australia's reserves of rare-earths (reported as rare-earth oxides REO) amounted to 3.19 Mt of Economic Demonstrated Resources (EDR) (2.8% of global economic reserves, compared with China 47.7% and the USA 11.3%), 0.42 Mt Paramarginal and 31.14 Mt in the Submarginal Resource categories. There is an additional 16.13 Mt REO in the Inferred Resources category. A significant proportion of the Submarginal and Inferred Resources are in the Olympic Dam iron oxide-copper-gold deposit in South Australia (predominantly 0.2% La and 0.3% Ce). The REO at Olympic Dam is currently not recovered and is stored in tailings dams at the mine site. The long closed Mary Kathleen uranium mine in Queensland has a remanent resource of 5.5 Mt of REO contained in tailings. An estimated 4.68 Mt of REO is contained in monazite deposits, but extraction of rare-earths from these deposits is currently considered not viable due to cost, and environmental issues associated with the disposal of thorium and uranium present. The best known hard rock deposit (a carbonatite laterite - carbonatites are igneous rocks composed of more than 50% carbonate minerals) is at Mount Weld, Western Australia. On current knowledge, it is the world's highest grade REO deposit. Generally, rare-earth deposits and prospects in Australia are associated with igneous, sedimentary and metamorphic, rock groups which may be found in a wide range of geological environments. Deposits that are commercially important tend to be associated with alkaline igneous rocks, and secondary placer deposits, such as heavy-mineral sand deposits. Exploration activities focusing on alkaline igneous rocks would seem to offer the best chance for discovery of new high-tonnage high-grade REO deposits. Figure 1 shows Australian rare-earth deposits and prospects. Globally, the main types of rare-earth deposits are rare-earth—iron ores with

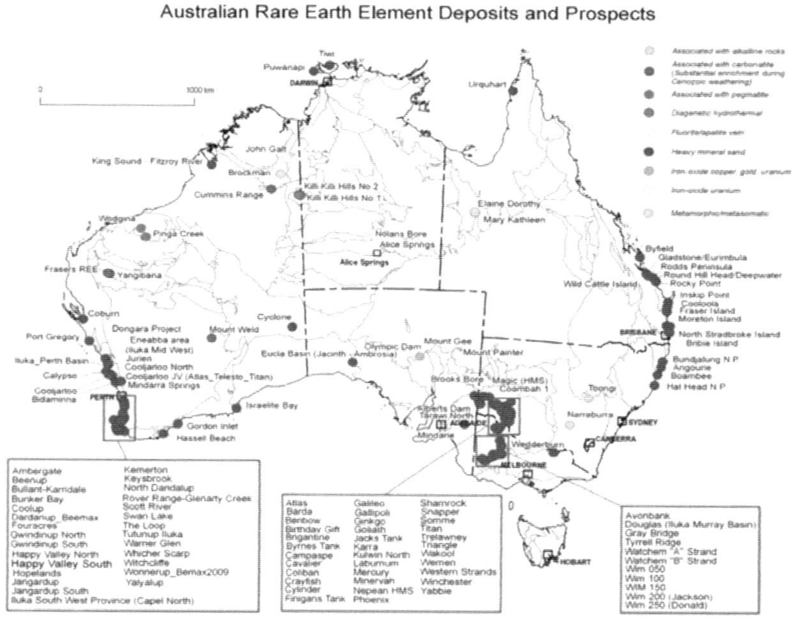

Fig. 1. Australian rare-earth element deposits and prospects (see [3]).

bastnasite and monazite as the main rare-earth containing ores e.g. the Bayan Obo deposit in China. At the Mountain Pass mine in California, USA, the resource is a carbonatite of 20 Mt at 8.2% REO, cf. Mt Weld, WA with 9.7 Mt at 11.7% REO [4].

3. Industry Activity

There is a plethora of exploration activity by many mainly small mining companies. These companies vary in size and the maturity of their activity covers the spectrum from exploration to establish the resource, scoping studies, beneficiation, extraction, separation, right through to the start-up phase and production of commercial quantities of REO. A summary of significant Australian rare-earth projects (the choice is somewhat arbitrary and does not pretend to be exhaustive) is given in Table 1. The projects viewed as being most advanced are those of Lynas and Alkane (shaded rows), with all others at stages closer to exploration, understanding the mineralogy and scoping.

The best known, and most significant project on a world scale, is that of Lynas, with ore mined and concentrated at the Mount Weld mine site, then shipped to the Lynas Advanced Materials Plant (LAMP) facility in Kuantan, Malaysia, for processing through to the REO stage. Lynas suffered some delays due to legal obstacles from local groups in Malaysia, but these have been overcome and the LAMP plant is now operational. At Mount Weld, Phase 2 of the Concentration plant is completed and operating at 80% capacity, with 18.4 kt of dry bagged concentrate, as of September 2013 (note Lynas has tailored the mine output to better meet demand and low REO prices), ready for shipping to Malaysia. The LAMP facility is expected to achieve a Phase 1 capacity of 11,000 t/yr (916.7 t per month) of REO by June 2014, with a planned Phase 2 expansion to 22,000 t/yr of REO. Estimated production of REO in April 2014 was 700 t. Lynas has some financial challenges, reporting a A$59.3 million loss for the first half of the 2013/14 financial year, and announcing a capital raising program in May 2014 for A$40 million, to cover a cash shortfall as it renegotiates a US$325 million loan. Lynas expects to be cash-flow neutral if it achieves monthly sales of 750 t of REO. There has been considerable volatility in the Lynas share price, A$0.145 (May 2014) compared to A$2.60 (April 2011).

The Alkane project at Dubbo, NSW, is primarily a zirconia project with significant quantities of rare-earths. The project is still in the feasibility stage, with the process flow sheet for extraction of REOs completed, and trials conducted with a pilot plant to confirm rare-earth recoveries. Plant construction is expected to begin in 2014. Alkane has a MoU with Shin-Etsu, Japan, for toll treatment and sale of REO. Alkane also has a gold project at nearby Tomingley, and its first gold pour of an 8 kg bar, containing ~230 oz of gold, occurred in February 2014. Still at a very early stage, but of potential importance, is the Hasting's project that has the potential to supply 10% of world demand for Dy, and the Northern Minerals project which has significant Dy content. TUC Resources is now Spectrum Rare Earths.

Table 1. Summary of significant Australian rare-earth projects. Note the format of Total Reserve and REO Content and Distribution tends to be company specific. Numbers given are only a guide. Details should be checked with individual companies. In some cases Measured (M) and Inferred (I) Reserves are given. Sources are company websites [5], Geoscience Australia [2], and industry reviews [4].

Company	Deposit	Total Reserve Estimate (Mt)	REO content	REO distribution
Lynas	Mt Weld, WA	9.7	11.7%	Ce 47.55%, La 23.88%, Nd 18.13%, Dy 0.25%
Lynas	Duncan, WA	8.992	4.8%	Ce 39.38%, La 24.87%, Nd 17.89%, Dy 1.27%
Alkane	Dubbo, NSW	35.7M (37.5I) (Total 73.2)	0.75%M (0.75%I)	Production @ 1Mtpa: Light REO 20% (4,665 t), Heavy REO 5% (1,309 t)
Arafura	Nolans Bore, NT	47	2.6%	Ce 48.72%, Nd 20.58%, La 19.13%, Dy 0.32%
Hastings	Halls Creek, WA	36.2	0.21%	Heavy REO 0.18% (140 t pa of Dy for +25 yrs)
Crossland	Charley Creek, NT	418	0.0289%	17% Heavy REO (167,235 t monazite)
Navigator	Cummins Range, WA	4.9	1.74%	Light REO 95.6%, Heavy REO 0.3%
Northern Minerals	Browns Range, NT	4.37M (2.12I) (Total 6.48)	0.72% (0.77I)	Y 58.21%, Dy 8.79%, Gd 5.71%, Er 5.33%
Spectrum Rare Earths	Skyfall, Fish River, NT	To be determined	0.48%-1.25%	Dy 7.4% TREO

4. Future Outlook

Australia largely escaped the global financial crisis of 2008 and has enjoyed a period of solid growth fuelled by an unprecedented demand for high quality bulk resources, mainly from rapidly expanding Asian economies. For the 2013-14 financial year, key economic indicators are 2.75%, 2.5% and 6% for annual growth rate, interest rate and unemployment, respectively. The Australian rare-earth industry has little vertical integration with minimal up-stream manufacturing of high-value added products. Indeed, manufacturing in Australia is seen as 'high-cost' and globally uncompetitive, with industries such as appliance and automotive (vehicle manufacture by Ford, GM Holden and Toyota will cease by 2017) in decline. This is attributed, perhaps simplistically, to a high A$ and small domestic market. The Liberal-National Party Government, led by PM Tony Abbott, elected September 2013, is averse to Government intervention to support 'failing' manufacturing industries. There is scope for the development of value chains from the ore resource to high-technology product, and Australia has excellent R&D capabilities to assist in this process. Australia is by world standards an open economy, having concluded eight Free Trade Agreements (nine if the recently announced, but not yet formalised, agreement with Japan is included) with key trading partners. It is important that all countries avoid polices that could distort markets for rare-earths, and trade must be conducted on commercial terms in-line with well-established multilateral trading rules. Australia with its portfolio of projects and prospects is well positioned to be a secure and reliable supplier of rare-earths.

References

[1] *Trade at a Glance 2012*, Department of Foreign Affairs and Trade, Australian Government.

[2] http://www.australianminesatlas.gov.au/aimr/commodity/rare_earths.html#Rare_earths

[3] D. M. Hoatson, S. Jaireth, and Y. Miezitis, *The major rare-earth-element deposits of Australia: geological setting, exploration, and resources.* Geoscience Australia, 2011, 204 pp.

[4] D. J. Kingsnorth, *Rare Earths: An Industry Undergoing Rejunvenation*, IMCOA-Curtin University, June 2013.

[5] http://www.lynascorp.com/Pages/rare-earths-project.aspx; http://www.alkane.com.au/; http://www.arafuraresources.com.au/; http://www.hastingsraremetals.com/; http://www.crosslandstrategic.com/; http://www.navigatorresources.com.au/Projects/Cummins-Range-%28REE%29; http://northernminerals.com.au/; http://www.tucresources.com.au/index.php/projects/rare-earth-project

(The author is retired and ceased being a CSIRO Fellow February 2014)

Vertical Integration and the Rare-Earth Supply Chain

R. G. EGGERT
Colorado School of Mines, Golden, Colorado 80401 USA

Keywords: *vertical integration, rare-earth elements*

Address: Roderick G. Eggert, Division of Economics and Business, Colorado School of Mines, Golden, CO 80401 USA, Tel: +1 303 273 3981, E-mail: reggert@mines.edu

The Chinese government is consolidating what previously were a large number of companies operating at different stages of the rare-earth supply chain into a small number of vertically integrated companies. The U.S.-based multinational company Molycorp mines rare-earth minerals and produces rare-earth oxides and chemicals, magnet materials, and magnets. Yet many if not most potential producers of rare-earth minerals have no plans to extend their activities downstream into production of intermediate and final products, and instead plan to sell mixed or separated oxides to others. Does it matter whether rare-earth producers are vertically integrated? Should rare-earth miners manufacture magnets? These and related questions are the focus of this paper.

A supply chain sometimes is referred to as a *vertical* chain of activities—from acquisition of raw materials to manufacturing and distribution of final products, and everything in between. Vertical integration occurs when multiple stages of production within a supply chain are organized within a single company. Complete vertical integration occurs when an entire supply chain is organized within a single firm. The degree of vertical integration varies from industry to industry, as well as within industries (that is, some firms in an industry are vertically integrated, others are not). When should firms partially or completely integrate their activities? When is it better to focus on only one section of a supply chain?

In an idealized market—in which each stage of a supply chain consists of many firms with similar costs of production producing identical products, and writing and enforcing contracts is simple and straightforward—firms would be indifferent to vertical integration. It would not matter, in terms of profits, product quality and efficiency, whether firms were vertically integrated.

Most real markets, however, do not satisfy all the requirements of this idealized market. Whether to vertically integrate, or not, matters to a company. Vertical integration in rare earths and other sectors is neither inherently good nor bad but rather depends on the circumstances of a particular company. Considering whether to vertically integrate requires evaluating the advantages (benefits) and disadvantages (costs) of integration. Among the potential benefits of vertical integration, three stand out. Compared to contracting with an outside firm, vertical integration makes it easier to (1) protect confidential information, (2) efficiently coordinate activities between and among different stages in the vertical chain, and (3) avoid being taken advantage of by a powerful supplier of an input or a powerful buyer of an output.

On the other hand, the potential disadvantages or costs of vertical integration include (1) not benefitting from the scale, scope or learning economies (or efficiencies) available from outside firms (in other words, not taking advantage of existing market experts), and (2) suffering inefficiencies when an internal unit is shielded from the disciplining effects of the market because it does not have sell its services or products to an outside firm.

The rest of this paper takes these general principles and applies them to the rare-earths supply chain. It finds that the strongest arguments for vertical integration involve (1) coordination benefits in a supply chain characterized by specialized products and, in many cases, very high purity and quality requirements and (2) avoiding being taken advantage of by powerful, existing firms in the sector to, for example, gain access to a downstream activities or distribution channels. Even when the case for vertical integration is strong, there are alternatives to integration such as strategic alliances and joint ventures.

Acknowledgment
Initial work on this topic was supported by the Japan Oil, Gas and Metals National Corporation. Current work is supported by the Critical Materials Institute, an Energy Innovation Hub funded by the U.S. Department of Energy, Office of Energy Efficiency and Renewable Energy, Advanced Manufacturing Office.

Perspectives for Rare-Earth Magnets in Brazil

D. RODRIGUES [1,2], J.A. DE CASTRO [2], M.F. DE CAMPOS [2]
[1]BRATS - Sintered Filters and Metallic Powders, Cajamar, São Paulo, Brazil
[2]EEIMVR – Federal Fluminense University, Volta Redonda, Rio de Janeiro, Brazil

Abstract: *Brazil has large reserves of rare-earth minerals. Relevant sites are Araxá, Serra Verde, Catalão and Pitinga. Many of the occurrences of rare-earth in Brazil consist in monazite, which present big amount of light rare-earths as Neodymium and Praseodymium. However, Pitinga mine presents larger amount of heavy rare-earth as Dysprosium. High efficiency electrical motors are a subject where the Brazilian industry has large tradition, generating internal demand for high energy product magnets. The present situation enables the establishment of a rare-earth magnet industry in Brazil, where several mines are starting rare-earth oxide production.*

Key words: *rare earth, Brazil, reserves, magnets*

Address: Daniel Rodrigues, BRATS, São Paulo, Brazil, E-mail: daniel@brats.com.br, marcosflavio@id.uff.br

1. Introduction

That the rare earths (REs) are not in fact rare is very well known. However, some rare earths are hard to find and have larger prices. The heavy rare earths are much more scarce than the light rare earths. Besides, the applications determine the price. As example, Samarium was expensive in the eighties, because the high demand for SmCo magnets, but now Samarium price has been reported as low as the price of cerium [1]. Greenland and Australia have large RE reserves, besides China. However, Catalão, State of Goiás (Brazil) is reported - unofficially - to have 120 million of tons of rare earth oxides [2]. Even it is basically monazite, it is a considerable RE amount. In the last November of 2013, CBMM, a Brazilian Company responsible for most of the niobium extracted in the world, officially announced reserves estimated in 26.69 millions of tons in Araxá, state of Minas Gerais [3]. All those data confirm Chen [4], which already in 2011 pointed out that Brazil is the country with the largest reserves of rare-earth in the world, exceeding China. The usual high amount of Thorium associated with monazite is a long time problem. However, Thorium nowadays is seriously considered as a source of nuclear energy, and this renewed the interest on monazite and similar ores. Several of the relevant occurrences of Niobium and Tantalum in Brazil are associated with monazite. An exception is Pitinga in Amazon, where there is a large cassiterite mine, with also production of Tantalum and a large amount of heavy are earths. Excluding Pitinga, most of the significant reported Brazilian occurrences of rare earth are monazite, with large amounts of light RE as Neodymium and Praseodymium, but scarce in Dysprosium. The recent prices (June/2014) [1] suggest that the heavy REs Europium, Terbium and Dysprosium, and that the light REs Praseodymium and Neodymium are now the most relevant. Yttrium and Samarium prices are not far from Cerium [1]. Nowadays, there is significant oversupply of Cerium, and its price is predicted to decrease in the next years. The price of rare-earths now in 2014 decreased to the level before of the 2011 peak, and thus many projects for rare-earth production need to be reconsidered. Although Niobium business was clearly profitable, rare-earth business was never seen as profitable in Brazil, in the last 20 years. Because this, nobody in Brazil was interested in rare-earths until 2011, when the prices spiked. Brazil was in the past a relevant producer of rare-earth minerals [5]. At the present time, Brazilian production is very small, but CBMM plans to produce 1000 tons/year of rare-earth oxide within a couple of years, with possible expansion in forthcoming years [3]. Lanthanum is a low price RE with large application in catalysis: an amount of 1000 tons/year of La_2O_3 is requested for Brazilian state oil company, needed for cracking of crude Oil [5]. Wind energy plants, rapidly growing in Brazil, maybe a possible market for neodymium iron boron magnets. High efficiency electrical motors are a subject where the Brazilian industry has large tradition, generating demand for high energy product magnets. Besides, the opportunities for new energy sources, as wind power and high demand from automotive industries enables the establishment of a rare-earth magnet industry in Brazil, especially if, besides CBMM, other mines start rare-earth oxide production. As the price of rare-earth is very small now, extraction of rare earth in Brazil only could be justified if the rare-earths were exported not as commodities, but inside high technology products, following the example of China.

2. Brazilian Rare-Earth Reserves

Some of the most relevant RE sites are displayed in Fig. 1. Brazilian giant Company Vale do Rio Doce has announced reserves in Salobo, state of Pará, but

Fig. 1. Sites in Brazil with relevant occurrences of rare-earths.

focus on iron ore and does not have plans at the moment for commercial production of rare-earth ore. In terms of relevance, Catalão-GO appears at the moment as the site with largest reported reserves [2]. Anglo American mining company has produced iron-niobium in Catalão. Araxá has large reserves reported by CBMM [3]. Near the CBMM site in Araxá, Vale do Rio do Doce and MbAC [6] companies also have large reserves of Niobium, Rare Earths, Thorium, and other minerals [7]. Minaçu, Serra Verde in Goiás is promising to produce 5000 ton/year of separate rare-earth oxides starting in 2019 [8]. Morro do Ferro, in Poços de Caldas [9], presents Thorium associated with rare earths. Guarapari is a very beautiful beach resort, famous by its black sands, a characteristic of monazite. All coasts from the north of state of Rio de Janeiro the south of Bahia (from Delta do Paraíba to Cumuruxatiba) are rich in monazitic sand. In the 1950s, from these reserves, Europium was extracted for the Nautilus submarine [5], but the amount of rare earth at the Brazilian coast is small, if compared with those of Goiás and Amazon. The reserves of Morro dos Seis Lagos and Serra do Repartimento have large potential, but they remain in evaluation. Besides, Serra do Repartimento is in indigenous area, and this may limit its commercial use. Other places with heavy rare earths as Pitinga may exist in Amazon, in less explored areas, as for example Maicuru, state of Pará [10].

3. Demands for Rare-Earth Magnets

Brazil already produced rare-earth metal in the past; CIF produced mischmetal (using fluorides) by fused-salt electrolysis [11], but focused only on the tantalum production since mid 1990s. The fused salt process remains in use today for neodymium [12]. Brazilian companies are at the present moment developing technology for rare-earth oxide separation and for metallic rare-earth production.

It is general belief that the investment of CBMM and other mining companies is only viable with existence of magnet manufacturing plants in Brazil. Unfortunately, Brazilian government is typically focused on commodities, rather than in industry. There is internal market for magnets in Brazil from both: high-efficiency electrical motors industry as well as automotive industry. Besides, wind energy plants could benefit substantially from the use of NdFeB magnets.

4. Conclusion

Although the reported numbers are not official, the Brazilian reserves of rare-earths may be larger than those of China. The recent interest in Thorium as nuclear fuel, together with the interest on rare-earths for magnets and catalysis, has increased the relevance of the Brazilian reserves of monazite and associated minerals. The Brazilian rare-earth market for catalysis (La_2O_3) and for magnets make viable the rare earth oxide production in Brazil. However, the only application able to sustain the economic viability of the rare-earth business (cost plus volume) is the magnet production. The production of rare-earth magnets may boost high-technology industries in Brazil, since the government and entrepreneurs gives a proper attention and support for this area.

Acknowledgment
The authors would like to thank the National Council for Scientific and Technological Development (CNPq).

References

[1] www.frontierrareearths.com/rare-earths/rare-earth-prices.
[2] www.cetem.gov.br/antigos/noticias/cetem%20midia/2011/11_07_28_china_terras_raras_brasil.html.
[3] www.cbmm.com/us/p/229/employees-develop-process-to-recover-rare-earths.aspx.
[4] C. Zhanheng. *J. Rare Earth*, 2011, Jan., 29, 1, 1.
[5] O. Serra., *J. Braz. Chem. Soc.*, 2011, 22, 5, 811.
[6] www.mbacfert.com/projects/araxa.aspx
[7] www.senado.gov.br/noticias/jornal/emdiscussao/Upload/201304%20-%20setembro/pdf/em%20discuss%C3%A3o!_setembro_2013_internet.pdf.
[8] www.miningweekly.com/article/msv-aims-to-lead-western-rare-earths-production-with-low-cost-project-2014-03-11.
[9] N. Waber. *J. Geochem. Explor.*, 1992, 45, 113–157.
[10] www.rbg.sbgeo.org.br/index.php/rbg/article/download/365/58.
[11] www.cif.ind.br/historia.html.
[12] D. Kennedy, *StrategischeRohstoffe-Risikovorsorge*, 2014, Springer Spektrum, Berlin, 201-217.

The Critical Materials Institute

A.H. KING
Critical Materials Institute, The Ames Laboratory, Ames, IA 50011-3020, U.S.A.

Abstract: *Within the span of a third of a century, the permanent magnet industry has been impacted twice by supply-chain issues. In 1978 concerns over cobalt supplies drove a search for alternatives to Sm-Co. In 2010 the rare earths, notably including Nd and Dy, became the archetype for critical materials when their prices spiked and access to them was used as a bargaining chip in geopolitical negotiations. In 2011, the U.S. Department of Energy published a Critical Materials Strategy for clean energy needs, which includes permanent magnets because of the anticipated growth in electrical generating capacity and the use of electric motors. DOE's strategy has three primary pillars: (1) diversifying primary sources of supply; (2) inventing substitute materials; and (3) encouraging more efficient use of available supplies, through advanced manufacturing, re-use and recycling. The Critical Materials Institute (CMI) was established as a means to carry out this strategy.*

Keywords: *Nd; Dy; critical materials; energy*

Address: Alexander H. King, Critical Materials Institute, The Ames Laboratory, 134 Wilhelm Hall, Iowa State University, Ames IA 50011-3020, U.S.A., Tel: (1-515) 296-4500; Fax: (1-515) 296-4515; E-mail: alexking@ameslab.gov

1. Introduction

Rare earths are sold as oxides, elemental metals, and in other forms, and although they are not traded through an open commodities market, public attention was drawn to rapid price increases for many of the rare earth elements, beginning in 2010. As prices rose to astronomical levels – eventually reaching more than 10 times their pre-2010 levels for some elements – concerns emerged concerning the needs for these elements, and the security and stability of their supply. Metals that had previously been the province of a few technical specialists began to be discussed in the popular media, and political attention soon followed.

Concerns about the rare earths were further heightened in September of 2010, when a dispute over fishing rights and the control territorial waters resulted in the arrest of a Chinese fishing boat captain by the Japanese coastguard. China retaliated by cutting off exports of rare earths to Japan, resulting in the emergence of the term "rare earth diplomacy." It was widely reported that the late Chinese leader, Deng Xiaoping, had commented that while the Middle East has oil, China dominates the rare earths [1].

Starting late in 2010, hearings were held on the rare earths by various committees in the U.S. Congress, and the term "critical material" came into widespread use. A number of reports emerged on the topic and it was recognized that the rare earths were indeed archetypal "critical materials" but were possibly not the only ones that needed to be considered [2-10]. In the spring of 2011 President Obama's budget request to Congress included funds for an Energy Innovation Hub for Critical Materials, and following an open competition, the funds for the hub were awarded to a team led by the Ames Laboratory, in January 2013.

2. Critical Materials

A critical material is a substance used in modern technology, which is subject to supply risk and for which there are no easy substitutes. The materials that fall within this definition are not fixed. Lists of critical materials vary with location, because industrial needs and materials sources tend to be localized: distinct differences can therefore be seen between the lists of critical materials produced by studies conducted for different governments, as seen in Refs. 2 - 10. Critical materials lists also vary with time, as supply and demand vary: sources of materials can cease to be available for a number of reasons, and new sources can emerge, while demand can be altered quite radically by the demise of old technologies or the emergence of new ones. Even within a particular region at a particular time, any list of critical materials will depend on who compiles it: an automotive manufacturer will have a different list than an electronics manufacturer, although there will be overlaps.

There have been critical materials for nearly as long as there have been man-made materials, and some historians now believe that criticality of copper may have contributed to the end of the bronze age and the ensuing collapse of the ancient Greek civilization. Other critical materials have emerged from time to time, and the 20th Century case of cobalt provides an instructive example. In the early 1970's the central African nation of Zaire was the dominant source. Cobalt was used in superalloys and had emerging uses in magnets following the development of Sm-Co as a permanent magnet material. In 1978, a revolt overtook the mining province of Katanga, cutting off supplies of cobalt and several other materials. The price history of cobalt before, during and after the revolution can be seen in Fig. 1: decades of price instability are common in the aftermath of materials criticality events.

3. Critical Materials for Clean Energy Technologies

The Critical Materials Institute was established to assure secure supplies of materials needed for clean energy technologies in the USA, over the next ten to fifteen years. Its initial program addresses seven elements identified as either "critical" or "near critical" over this timeframe, in the Critical Materials Strategy developed by the US Department of Energy [8]. These include five of the rare earths: yttrium, neodymium, europium, terbium and dysprosium, in addition to lithium and tellurium.

These elements are widely applied in modern technologies, as illustrated by the partial list of their uses in Table 1. They have uses beyond clean energy and may therefore be of concern to constituencies other than DOE. The rare earths, in particular, are subject to supply risk primarily because one country – China – dominates the world's supply. Until very recently, China provided as much as 97% of the world's industrial rare earth supplies. There are no easy substitutes for the rare earths in most of their applications because they impart highly specialized properties to magnets, phosphors and other specialized applications, largely enabled by the effects of the 4f electrons that define the lanthanide series.

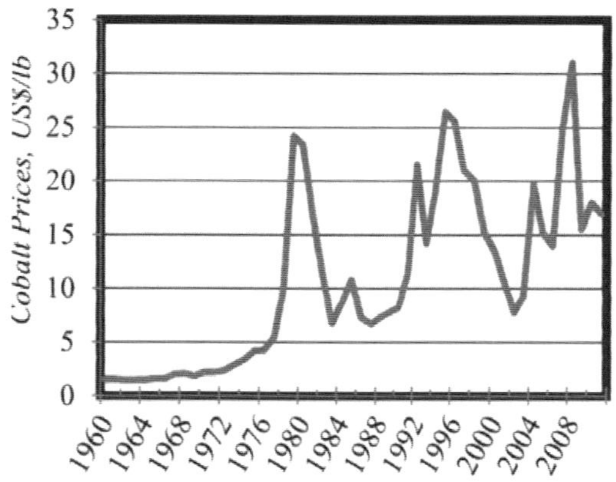

Fig. 1. Annual average prices of cobalt from 1960 to 2011. Note the price spike associated with the Katangan revolt of 1978, and severe price instability that continues today.

Table 1. Principal uses of the materials addressed by CMI, applicable to clean energy technologies.

	Photovoltaics	Magnets	Batteries	Lighting
Li			◆	
Te	◆			
Y				◆
Nd		◆	◆	
Eu				◆
Tb				◆
Dy		◆		

4. The CMI Approach

CMI is one of DOE's five Energy Innovation Hubs. These are integrated research centers that combine basic and applied research with engineering to accelerate scientific discovery in critical energy issue areas. Leadership is vested in scientists who are given the authority to assign funds where they are most effectively used and the funding level was initially set at $20M - $25M per year, for 5 years, renewable for an additional five.

CMI deploys a strategy with three fundamental pillars, or focus areas, tied together by a fourth crosscutting area that provides underlying research germane to two or more of the pillar focus areas. The three pillars of the CMI strategy are

- Diversifying supply
- Developing substitute materials
- Driving reuse, recycling, and more efficient use of materials in manufacturing

The Institute brings together world-class expertise across all of these areas in addition to basic physics and chemistry, along with advanced lifecycle and economic analysis. With such broad needs, our research team is dispersed over 18 partnering institutions, and maintaining the integrated team approach is one of CMI's major challenges.

A second challenge revolves around matching the CMI research program to the timescale of materials criticality events. As seen in Figure 1, and also reflected in the 2010 rare earth price spike, the initial emergence of criticality is reflected by a price excursion that typically lasts three or four years, although prices tend to remain unstable for decades to follow. In crafting responses to criticality events, we note that

- Diversifying sources is often taken to mean mine development, which takes at least 10 years, *when a known resource already exists*.
- Deploying a substitute material in an existing product takes an average of 4 years, *when there is an existing option* – which is not the case for any of the materials addressed by CMI.
- Development and deployment of *new* substitute materials takes an average of 18 years.

The timescales for conventional responses to materials criticality events are clearly not commensurable with the timescales over which criticality emerges, with the result that technologies that rely upon the affected materials may not survive in the marketplace.

A case in point is the choice of technologies for electricity generation using wind-turbines. The most efficient and reliable wind turbine technology for utility-scale units (750 kW and up) utilizes direct-drive generators, which are enabled by high-strength Nd-Fe-B permanent magnets, (which also contain significant amounts of Dy). Alternative technologies use less powerful magnets and increased generator rotation rates enabled by gearboxes, or use induction-type generators, which have no permanent magnets, but are much larger. Various hybrid technologies also exist. The high failure-rate of wind-turbine gearboxes increases their operating costs, but do not completely offset their cost advantage over comparable direct-drive turbines, whose price is dominated by the cost of the magnet materials. The result is that (according to data provided by the American Wind Energy Association) only 223 of the 33,000 utility-scale wind turbines installed so far in the U.S. are direct-drive units. Anecdotal information suggests that direct-drive units command a much larger market share in China.

CMI houses lifecycle and economic analysis functions that have the specific role of guiding the research emphasis in pursuit of reducing the criticality of any particular material, in the interest of providing manufacturers with viable options in a timely manner. For example, it is recognized that demand for europium and terbium is partly driven by the adoption of high-efficiency fluorescent lighting technologies including compact fluorescent bulbs and T5 long-tube lamps. These technologies are expected to give way to LEDs in ten to fifteen years, so the current bulge in demand will level off or decline at that point. As we seek solutions to the criticality of Eu and Tb, then, short-term solutions are preferred over longer-term ones, and we have a strong focus on recycling, and no direct effort to diversify supply, since the development of new conventional mines is a decade-long effort. In other cases, where we see continued long-term growth in demand, such as lithium and neodymium, our efforts focus more heavily on matters related to the diversification of supply. The Critical Materials Institute focuses on producing workable solutions on a schedule that is relevant to the projected demand for the materials in question.

5. The Research Program

The Critical Materials Institute has started work on 35 discrete projects, each of which has a specific target for deployment and a timescale determined by considerations like the ones described above. The timescales range from very short (3 years) to quite long (10 years) but in each case, the timescale relates to projections for needs that are addressed by the individual projects.

Work on source diversification focuses on developing technologies that can lower the cost of existing mineral processing and improve the economics of existing sources by finding new uses for by-products. We are also looking at methods for accessing unconventional sources in the form of existing mineral streams such as phosphate processing. Some of these projects have the fastest anticipated impact, among the CMI program.

In the area of materials substitution, CMI is working toward new magnet materials with reduced rare earth content, and also on enabling the spring magnet concept through novel manufacturing methods. We are developing new red and green phosphors, to replace europium and terbium, and we are developing new methodologies for materials design, linking computation and experimentation in a novel framework.

To drive more efficient use, reuse and recycling of materials, CMI is developing methods for recycling rare earths from available streams such as lamp phosphors and magnets, and tellurium from solar cells. It is also developing new separations technologies including supercritical fluids, membrane solvent extraction, electro-recycling, pyroprocessing and bioleaching.

Supporting all of the other scientific work, CMI has a crosscutting research function, to develop basic scientific knowledge and databases germane to all of the other projects, environmental assessments, and supply-chain, lifecycle and economic analysis. As noted above, the economic aspects of this work guide and direct of all of our projects.

Every project that we undertake has a comer-cialization plan and is monitored by technology transfer experts. If conditions change sufficiently to affect the viability of its commercialization plan, then a project will be redirected or possibly terminated, even if it is producing outstanding science.

In addition to the CMI's research projects and commercialization efforts, the hub provides outreach efforts that include education programs, coordination with other U.S. funded critical materials efforts, and an information service called the Critical Materials Information Center. An industrial affiliates program provides input into the CMI research directions, access to CMI results and licensing opportunities for CMI-developed technologies.

In its initial five-year funding period, CMI aims to deliver four major outcomes:

(1) Assured materials supply chains for clean energy manufacturing in the U.S.:
 - by solving current critical materials issues;
 - by identifying and averting future criticality issues;

(2) Assured supplies of technical talent and expertise;

(3) Provision of critical materials information to researchers, producers & OEMs;

(4) Coordination of Federal critical materials research efforts for maximum impact.

Acknowledgement
This work is supported by the Critical Materials Institute, an Energy Innovation Hub funded by the U.S. Department of Energy, Office of Energy Efficiency and Renewable Energy, Advanced Manufacturing Office.

References

[1] K. Bradsher, Amid Tension, China Blocks Vital Exports to Japan, *New York Times*, Sept. 22, 2010.

[2] *Minerals, Critical Minerals, and the U.S. Economy* U.S. National Research Council, (Washington, DC, National Academies Press, 2008).

[3] *Critical Elements for New Energy Technologies*, (Cambridge, MA, MIT Energy Initiative, 2010).

[4] *Critical Raw Materials for the EU*, (Brussels, European Commission, 2010).

[5] *Critical Materials Strategy*, (Washington DC, U.S. Department of Energy, 2010).

[6] *Energy Critical Elements: Securing Materials for Emerging Technologies*, (Washington, DC, American Physical Society & Materials Research Society, 2011).

[7] *Risk List 2011*, (London, British Geological Survey, 2011).

[8] *Critical Materials Strategy*, (Washington DC, U.S. Department of Energy, 2011).

[9] V.B. Grasso, *Rare Earth Elements in National Defense: Background, Oversight Issues, and Options for Congress*, Congressional Research Service, 2012.

[10] R. Silberglitt, J.T. Bartis, B.G. Chow, D.L. An and K. Brady, *Critical Materials: Present Danger to U.S. Manufacturing*, Rand Corporation, 2013.

[11] J.C. Waldbaum, *From Bronze to Iron: The Transition from the Bronze Age to the Iron Age in the Eastern Mediterranean*, Göteborg, Sweden, Paul Aströms Förlag, 1978.

[12] J.C. Waldbaum, in: *The Coming of the Age of Iron*, ed. T.A. Wertime and J.D. Mulhy, New Haven, Conn.: Yale University Press, 1980, pp. 69-98.

The Development of Future Sources of Rare-Earth Supply

G. P. HATCH[1,2]
[1] Technology Metals Research LLC, Carpentersville, Illinois, USA
[2] Innovation Metals Corp, Toronto, Ontario, Canada

Abstract: *Recent years have seen an explosion of interest in the future production of rare-earth elements (REEs) from new sources of supply outside of China. Initially driven by anticipated growth in demand for energy-efficient electrical devices, more recent focus has been on reducing the geopolitical risks associated with the dominance of China in the REE supply chain. This paper provides a review of the present status of new REE project development outside of China. A review of the most advanced of the REE projects currently under development is presented, highlighting the specific characteristics of individual projects that make them attractive for commercial development.*

Keywords: *rare earths; REEs; rare-earth production; mineral resources*

Address: Gareth P. Hatch, Technology Metals Research LLC, 180 S. Western Ave #150, Carpentersville, IL 60110, USA, Tel: +1-847-867-3091, Email: ghatch@techmetalsresearch.com

1. Introduction

Rare-earth elements (REEs) are a vital component of a wide variety of high-tech devices and assemblies. The last ten years has seen a significant interest in the development of new sources of REEs, in order to satisfy growing demand for their use in permanent magnets, phosphors, ceramics, energy-storage batteries, catalysts and other applications [1]. The market is dominated by China and in recent years, issues of a geopolitical nature have threatened the ability of non-China-based manufacturers to fully utilize the REE supply chain. This included unprecedented price spikes in 2010 and 2011, leading to a significant increase in interest to find alternative sources of supply [1].

2. Stages of Project Development

Any future mining project goes through a series of development stages, and REE projects are no exception. All projects start with initial exploration and characterization of prospective deposits of geological interest. Such work includes field surveys and testing of grab samples. Such work identifies prospective areas for further scrutiny, leading to drilling, trenching and other means of obtaining enough materials to characterize the deposit.

Once enough data has been obtained, estimates of the size and concentrate of the deposit can be made, in the form of mineral resource estimates. Such estimates typically conform to recognized guidelines for such estimates, such as Canada's NI 43-101, Australia's JORC Code or South Africa's SAMREC code. Technology Metals Research (TMR) tracks the various REE projects currently underway outside of Chin, with resource estimates that conform to these guidelines (per their respective operators) [2]. As of June 2014, the TMR Index included 51 advanced REE projects being operated by 48 companies, located in 34 regions within 16 countries outside China [2].

Mineral resource estimates have different levels, corresponding to increasing degrees of confidence in the geological data that has been analyzed. Inferred resources represent a minimum level of confidence, based on limited information derived from widely-spaced drilling, with little demonstrated continuity between sample points [3]. Further drilling to increase the density of data points leads to estimates of Indicated resources, while even more drilling leads to Measured resources, representing the highest level of confidence in the geological model that results.

The so-called junior mining companies operating such projects are constantly trying to raise money to go to the next stage of development. The most common method for doing this is to utilize the mineral resource estimates in order to produce technical reports that describe the projects. Economic and other considerations are applied to the estimates, in order to produce preliminary economic assessments (PEA) or scoping studies, pre-feasibility studies (PFS) or definitive feasibility studies (FS). The work required to produce a PFS or FS is substantially more than for a PEA; such work may include the conversion of some portion of the Indicated and / or Measured resources in to mineral reserves – those portions of a mineral resource that have been shown to be economically viable. Such reserves include Probable reserves, typically based on Indicated (and sometimes Measured) resources, and Proven reserves, based on Measured resources [3].

In order to finance the construction of the future mining project, a definitive FS is usually required, to allow equity and debt financing providers to properly assess the risk and potential rewards of providing capital to such projects. Off-take agreements with specific customers are also usually a pre-condition of financing.

3. REE Minerals Processing

Alongside the work required to determine the geology and mineralogy of a REE deposit, processes must be developed for the conversion of REE-bearing minerals in the ground, into useful end products. The mineralogy of each REE deposit in development is unique, and although some REE-bearing minerals are common to numerous deposits, in general specific processes have to be developed and optimized for each individual deposit.

Beneficiation is the process of taking mined ore and processing it through comminution and physical separation, in order to concentrate the minerals of interest, and to removing the gangue or waste minerals. Physical separation techniques used for REE ore processing are similar to those used for other ores, and might include magnetic separation, gravity separation, flotation and other means.

Once a REE mineral concentrate has been produced, it may then be subject to a variety of hydro- and pyrometallurgical processes, to 'crack' the mineral and to extract the REEs contained within them, putting them into solution. A wide variety of techniques are used for these processes, which are tailored to the specific minerals of interest. Impurities that come along with the REEs into solution have to be dealt with. The end goal is a high-purity mixed REE concentrate that can be subject to further processing.

The final step for the production of useful REE products is the separation of the individual REEs from each other. Today this is almost entirely achieved through the process of solvent extraction (SX), through which the REEs are put back into solution and are then progressively separated into groups or REEs, until finally they are produced as into individual products. This is a laborious and time-consuming process, because REEs are chemically very similar to each other.

The processes developed for particular REE deposits are documented and presented in the various PEA, PFS and FS technical reports. Such processes will also be piloted, before being tested in larger-scale demonstration plants, in order to fine-tune the processes.

4. Projects with Proven and Probable Reserves

Of the 57 REE mineral resource estimates associated with the 51 projects on the TMR Index, 10 have been converted to proven and / or probable mineral reserves, as of June 2014.

a) Bear Lodge (Wyoming, USA)

The Bear Lodge deposit has a total mineral reserve of 7.2 Mt with an average TREO grade of 3.12%, resulting in 224 kt of contained REOs [4]. Operated by Rare Element Resources (RES), the project is predominantly LREO in character, with Nd_2O_3 + Pr_6O_{11} constituting 22.60% of TREO content, and Dy_2O_3 0.28% of TREO. Located relatively close to infrastructure in the northeastern part of Wyoming, the deposit is a carbonatite, with the primary REE-bearing minerals including bastnaesite, monazite and ancylite. RES has completed a PFS on the project and has completed extensive beneficiation and extraction pilot-plant work, with the goal of producing a mixed REO concentrate for sale.

b) Browns Range (Western Australia, Australia)

Browns Range, operated by Northern Minerals (NTU) consists of a number of prospects, which have a combined total mineral reserve of 3.4 Mt with an average TREO grade of 0.69%, resulting in 23.6 kt of contained REOs [5]. The project has one of the highest distributions of HREOs of any project currently under development (78.6% of TREO). While only 4.6% of TREO consists of Nd_2O_3 + Pr_6O_{11}, Dy_2O_3 makes up 8.4% of TREO, the second highest Dy_2O_3 content of any project on the TMR Index. The primary mineral of interest is xenotime, with the main deposits hosted in breccia hydrothermal systems. NTU has recently completed a PFS on the project as well as a variety of pilot-plant programs for beneficiation and extraction, with the current goal of producing a mixed REO concentrate for sale.

c) Dubbo Zirconia Project (New South Wales, Australia)

As the name implies, the primary mineral of interest at the Dubbo project in Australia is zirconia, but the deposit contains significant quantities of REEs. The total mineral reserve is 35.9 Mt with an average TREO grade of 0.88%, resulting in 317 kt of contained REOs [6]. Dubbo is located close to major centers of population in New South Wales. Operated by Alkane Resources (ALK), the project is relatively rich in HREOs, with Dy_2O_3 making up 2.02% of TREO, alongside a Nd_2O_3 + Pr_6O_{11} content of 16.29% of TREO. The primary REE-bearing minerals in this polymetallic deposit are eudialyte, armstrongite and basnaesite. ALK has completed a comprehensive FS on the project and has operated a demonstrate plant for a number of years. It is in the process of project financing to get the project into operation. The company is looking to partner with Shin Etsu Chemical in order to toll process REO concentrates, so that they can be separated into individual REOs and other REE compounds.

d) Kipawa (Quebec, Canada)

Kipawa is located in the southern part of Quebec, with good access to infrastructure and logistics. Matamec Explorations (MAT) is developing the deposit in conjunction with Toyota Tsusho (TT), which has a significant ownership stake in the deposit. Kipawa has a mineral reserve of 19.8 Mt with a TREO grade of 0.41%, resulting in 81 kt of contained REOs [7]. The principal REE-bearing minerals of interest are eudialyte, mosandrite and britholite, contained is a peralkaline granite / syenite system. The deposit skews to the HREOs, with Dy_2O_3 constituting 3.56% of TREO. Nd_2O_3 + Pr_6O_{11} make up 16.94% of TREO. MAT completed a FS on Kipawa in 2013, and after completing a range of pilot-plant testing, is further optimizing the metallurgy for future processing. The company currently plans to produce a L/MREO-rich and a M/HREO concentrate, with the latter subject to potential future offtake by TT.

e) Mount Weld Central Lanthanide Deposit (Western Australia, Australia)

The Mount Weld Central Lanthanide Deposit (CLD) is currently in production, with the initial mining campaign completed a few years ago, resulting in enough feedstock for processing for a number of years. Operated by Lynas (LYC), the mined material is beneficiated close to the mine site, before being sent to the Lynas Advanced Materials Plant (LAMP) in Malaysia. Initial operations at the LAMP were delayed but the facility is in the process of ramping up to a target production rate of 11 kt / year TREO. The CLD has a total mineral reserve of 9.7 Mt with a grade of 11.73%, the richest of any deposit with a mineral reserve [8]. This results in a contained TREO content of 1.1 Mt. Skewing to the LREOs, the CLD TREO contains 23.29% Nd_2O_3 + Pr_6O_{11} alongside 0.25% Dy_2O_3. The deposit is a carbonatite, with supergene monazite the primary REE-bearing mineral of interest. LYC is current producing separated LREOs and carbonates, as well as M / HREO concentrates.

f) Mountain Pass (California, USA)

Mountain Pass has a storied history, first being put into operation in the 1950s and ramping up in the 1960s. For many years the Mountain Pass mine was the largest producer of REEs in the world, before price pressure from China in the 1980s and 1990s, and environmental issues forced its closure. The mine is once again in operation, being operated by Molycorp (MCP) and in the process of ramping up to over 19,000 t / year of TREO production. The deposit is a carbonatite, with bastnaesite the primary REE-mineral of interest. It has a mineral reserve of 16.7 Mt with a grade of 7.98%, one of the highest grades of any deposit worldwide [9]. This results in 1.3 Mt of contained TREOs, primarily LREOs. 16.30% of the TREO is made up of Nd_2O_3 + Pr_6O_{11} with only trace amounts of Dy_2O_3. MCP produces separated LREOs and carbonates, as well as other concentrates. Much of the Nd_2O_3 + Pr_6O_{11} produced is converted into metals for use in MCP's Magnequench magnetic powders division.

g) Nechalacho Basal (Northwest Territories, Canada)

Avalon Rare Metals (AVL) operates the Nechalacho project, located close to the Great Slave Lake in the Northwest Territories of Canada, a relatively remote region of the country. The Basal Zone at Nechalacho has a total mineral reserve of 4.6 Mt with an average TREO grade of 1.70%, resulting in 248 kt of contained REOs [10]. The project has significant quantities of HREOs, with Dy_2O_3 constituting 3.32% of TREO. Nd_2O_3 + Pr_6O_{11} comprise 20.88% of TREO. The deposit is a peralkaline granite / syenite, and contains numerous REE-bearing minerals including fergusonite, zircon, allanite, monazite, bastnaesite and synchysite, making for a relatively complex hydrometallurgical process. AVL has completed multiple pilot-plant programs for the beneficiation and extraction of REEs, as well as initial work on the separation of individual REEs into oxides and other compounds. The company has completed a FS for the Nechalacho project, and recently announced plans to toll-process REO concentrates at the Solvay Rhodia facility in France, as a means of producing separated REOs for future sale.

h) Ngualla (Mbeya, Tanzania)

The Ngualla project is a relative newcomer to the TMR Index, with its owner Peak Resources (PEK) accelerating development work to produce a mineral reserve estimate of 20.7 Mt with an average TREO grade of 4.54%. This results in 940 kt of contained REOs [11]. Skewing mostly to the LREOs, Nd_2O_3 + Pr_6O_{11} comprise 21.33% of TREO alongside 0.32% Dy_2O_3. The REE-bearing mineral of interest in bastnaesite, with the deposit itself a carbonatite. PEK has produced a PFS for Ngualla, with some initial pilot-plant work completed. The company plans to produce separated LREOs and a single mixed M/HREO product for sale into the marketplace.

i) Nolans (Northern Territory, Australia)

Arafura Resources (ARU) has been developing the Nolans project in central Australia for a number of years. The deposit has a mineral reserve of 24 Mt, with a grade of 2.80% TREO. This results in 672 kt of contained REOs [12]. Nolans has one of the highest Nd_2O_3 + Pr_6O_{11} contents of any deposit on the TMR index, at 26.52% of TREO. There are only trace amounts of Dy_2O_3 present. Nolans is a hydrothermal stockwork vein-type deposit, with the primary REE-bearing minerals of interest including apatite, allanite and monazite. ARU has completed the equivalent of a PFS with a FS underway. The company has also completed demonstration plant work on beneficiation, extraction and separation of REOs. ARU plans to produce and to sell separated LREOs, and mixed MREO and HREO products.

j) Steenkampskraal (Western Cape, South Africa)

Steenkampskraal was once a thorium mine, located in western South Africa, until the market for this material collapsed. It has subsequently been reborn as a REE project, operated by Great Western Minerals (GWG) with a mineral reserve of 800 kt, and a grade of 8.68% TREO, one of the highest of any project on the TMR Index. This results in contained TREO content of 69 kt [13]. The company recently completed a comprehensive FS on the deposit, and continues to pilot beneficiation and extraction processes. GWG has recently indicated an interest in toll processing its future materials in order to produce separated REOs. The company does not plan to produce separated La and Ce compounds, electing to stockpile these instead. Some of the materials produced will be utilized in GWG's subsidiary Less Common Metals, for the production of metals and alloys for using in the permanent-magnet industry. The deposit is hydrothermal in mature, with monazite being the primary REE-bearing mineral of interest.

5. Other Projects of Interest

In addition to REE projects with defined mineral reserves, there are numerous others that have completed mineral-resource estimates. Some of these have also completed PEA, PFS and FS reports, without having yet completed mineral reserve estimated (unusual in the case of a PFS & very unusual for an FS). Table 1 shows the projects on the TMR Index that have completed these technical reports. In addition to these projects, there are numerous others that have completed an initial mineral resource estimate [2].

6. Final Thoughts

It can be seen that there is a wide variety of REE projects under development outside of China, and in numerous countries and jurisdictions. The degree of difficulty in developing such projects depends on the complexity of the minerals to be exploited, the location of the deposits in relation to existing infrastructure and most important of all, the ability of operating companies to raise the sometimes signify-cant amounts of capital to bring such projects into operation.

Nevertheless, given the number of projects currently underway, the development of a REE supply chain originating outside of China has what it needs in terms of mineral resources and reserves, to get underway.

References

[1] G. P. Hatch, in: *Proc. 22nd Int. Workshop on Rare-earth Permanent Magnets and their Applications*, Nagasaki, 2012, 4-9.

[2] G. P. Hatch, *TMR Advanced Rare-earth Projects Index*, TMR, Carpentersville, USA, www.rareearths.org (accessed July 8, 2014).

[3] R. G. Eggert, *Rare-Earths Resources, Reserves, and Mining Economics*, presented at the TMR Rare-Earths Bootcamp, Toronto, 2011.

[4] Roche Engineering, *Rare Element Resources Inc, Bear Lodge Project - Technical Report on the Mineral Reserves on Development of the Bull Hill Mine*, April 2012, available at www.sedar.com (accessed July 8, 2014).

[5] Northern Minerals, *Maiden Ore Reserve for the Browns Range Project*, June 2014, available at www.asx.com.au (accessed July 8, 2014).

[6] Alkane Resources, *Definitive Feasibility Study Confirms Robust Dubbo Zirconia Project*, April 2013, available at www.asx.com.au (accessed July 8, 2014).

[7] Roche Engineering, *Matamec Explorations – Feasibility Study for the Kipawa Project, Temiscamingue Area, Quebec, Canada*, October 2013, available at www.sedar.com (accessed July 8, 2014).

[8] Lynas, *Significant Increase in Ore Reserves at Mount Weld*, September 2012, available at www.asx.com.au (accessed July 8, 2014).

[9] Molycorp, *Molycorp's Rare Earth reserves at Mountain Pass Increase by 36%*, April 2012, available at www.edgar.com (accessed July 8, 2014).

[10] Avalon Rare Metals, *Avalon Announces Results of Positive Feasibility Study for the Nechalacho Rare Earth Elements Project*, April 2013, available at www.sedar.com (accessed July 8, 2014).

[11] Peak Resources, *Ngualla Rare Earth Project – Maiden Ore Reserve*, March 2014, available at www.asx.com.au (accessed July 8, 2014).

[12] Arafura Resources, *Nolans Rare Earths Project: Maiden JORC Ore Reserve*, December 2012, available at www.asx.com.au (accessed July 8, 2014).

[13] *Great Western Minerals Reports Feasibility Study Results for Steenkampskraal Rare Earth Element Project*, May 2014, available at www.sedar.com (accessed July 8, 2014).

Table 1. Current status, ownership and distribution of rare earths in the most advanced production- and development-stage projects (as of June 2014) that publish technical reports conforming (according to the operators) to internationally recognized guidelines such as NI 43-101, JORC, SAMREC etc. PRV = Proven mineral reserve, PRB = Probable mineral reserve, MEA = Measured mineral resource, IND = Indicated mineral resource, INF = Inferred mineral resource; LREO = light rare-earth oxides (oxides of La, Ce, Pr & Nd), MREO = middle rare-earth oxides (oxides of Sm, Eu & Gd) & HREO = heavy rare-earth oxides (oxides of Tb, Dy, Ho, Er, Tm, Yb, Lu & Y). Percentages may not add up to 100% due to rounding. Data derived from company reports.

Mineral Deposit	Location	Data Estimates	Operator	LREO	MREO	HREO
In Production						
Mount Weld CLD	AUS	PRV+PRB	Lynas	94.7%	4.1%	1.2%
Mountain Pass	USA	PRV+PRB	Molycorp	98.6%	1.1%	0.3%
Completed Feasibility Study						
Dubbo Zirconia Project	AUS	PRV+PRB	Alkane Resources	74.6%	4.4%	21.0%
Kipawa	CAN	PRV+PRB	Matamec Explorations & Toyota Tsusho	60.4%	6.3%	33.4%
Nechalacho Basal	CAN	PRV+PRB	Avalon Rare Metals	69.4%	7.9%	22.7%
Steenkampskraal	ZAF	PRV+PRB	Great Western Minerals	89.2%	4.9%	5.9%
TANBREEZ	GRL	INF	Rimbal	66.5%	5.2%	28.4%
Completed Pre-Feasibility Study						
Bear Lodge	USA	PRV+PRB	Rare Element Resources	94.1%	4.6%	1.3%
Browns Range	AUS	PRB	Northern Minerals	13.1%	8.3%	78.6%
Kvanefjeld	GRL	IND+INF	Greenland Minerals & Energy	86.6%	2.8%	10.6%
Ngualla	TZA	PRV+PRB	Peak Resources	97.1%	2.5%	0.4%
Nolans	AUS	PRB	Arafura Resources	94.4%	3.7%	2.0%
Strange Lake Enriched	CAN	IND	Quest Rare Minerals	47.8%	5.3%	46.8%
Completed Preliminary Economic Assessment / Scoping Study						
Aksu Diamas	TUR	INF	AMR Mineral Metal	88.7%	3.9%	7.4%
Araxá	BRA	MEA+IND+INF	MBAC Fertilizer	95.8%	2.5%	1.7%
Ashram Main	CAN	MEA+IND+INF	Commerce Resources	94.1%	3.6%	2.3%
Ashram MHREO	CAN	MEA+IND+INF	Commerce Resources	88.8%	5.6%	5.6%
Bokan	USA	IND+INF	Ucore Rare Metals	56.3%	7.7%	36.0%
Buckton	CAN	IND+INF	DNI Metals	71.6%	6.4%	22.0%
Charley Creek	AUS	IND+INF	Crossland Strategic Metals & Pancontinental Uranium	75.9%	5.8%	18.3%
Eco Ridge	CAN	IND+INF	Pele Mountain Resources	88.3%	4.3%	7.4%
Foxtrot	CAN	IND+INF	Search Minerals	76.7%	5.2%	18.1%
Glenover	ZAF	IND+INF	Galileo Resources & Fer-Min-Ore	89.6%	6.4%	4.0%
Hastings	AUS	IND+INF	Hastings Rare Metals	12.0%	5.8%	82.1%
Milo	AUS	INF	GBM Resources			
Mount Weld Duncan	AUS	MEA+IND+INF	Lynas	86.9%	5.6%	7.5%
Norra Kärr	SWE	IND+INF	Tasman Metals	46.7%	6.5%	46.8%
Round Top	USA	MEA+IND+INF	Texas Rare Earth Resources	25.7%	3.8%	70.6%
Sarfartoq	GRL	IND+INF	Hudson Resources	96.1%	3.3%	0.7%
Strange Lake Granite	CAN	IND+INF	Quest Rare Minerals	60.6%	5.3%	46.8%
Zandkopsdrift	ZFA	IND+INF	Frontier Rare Earths & Korea Resources	89.9%	4.3%	5.8%

Metal and Magnet Value Chain

ED RICHARDSON
President – USMMA, Vice President – Thomas & Skinner, Inc.

Given the recent volatility in the global market for rare earths, the US is facing an important question: "Are we dependent on countries such as China for key magnetic components, like sintered Nd-Fe-B magnets?" The answer is yes. An analysis of the US value chain for sintered Nd-Fe-B magnets reveals that there are gaps in the domestic manufacturing capabilities and other areas of weakness.

- While mining has restarted at Molycorp's Mountain Pass mine, the collapse of rare earth prices since 2011 has created financial challenges for the company. Other proposed rare earth mining projects are now in doubt due to a lack of funding - especially those with low percentages of rare earth elements in their deposits. Also, rare earth deposits in the US are typically low in heavy rare earth content, providing scant amounts of dysprosium for magnet production.
- Once ore is mined, the rare earth elements must be separated and refined into pure metal, prior to becoming a magnet alloy. Currently, the US does not have commercial capacity for processing rare earth oxides into metals. Without this capability, rare earth oxides must be shipped overseas for conversion into metals. The US has the ability to melt rare earth metals into Nd-Fe-B alloys and create powder for pressing into magnets. Also, the US now has the capability to press, sinter and finish sintered Nd-Fe-B magnets at the recently opened Hitachi plant in North Carolina.
- There is concern regarding the ability of the US industrial base to build the equipment necessary for neo magnet production. Other metal industries use similar pieces of equipment, such as vacuum jet mills and sintering furnaces. However, the presses used for sintered Nd-Fe-B magnets require the incorporation of a strong magnetic field. This type of press is unique to the magnet industry, and presses of this design have likely not been built in the US for well over 10 years. While it is possible that presses could be built in the US to meet the requirements of a neo magnet manufacturer, it would require a considerable amount of engineering and design work to re-create this capability.

In sum, the US does not have the commercial ability to convert rare earth oxides into metals, and there are weaknesses both in the mining of heavy rare earths and in the ability to manufacture equipment for a sintered Nd-Fe-B plant.

Recycling of sintered Nd-Fe-B magnets has been suggested as an alternative source for US manufacturers. Unfortunately, few sintered Nd-Fe-B magnets are recycled today. Removing magnets from devices is extremely labor intensive. Separation of the rare earths from the other metals, like the separation required after mining, is capital intensive and technologically challenging. Economically, recycling has not been shown as a viable alternative to production of virgin materials.

The US value chain for sintered Nd-Fe-B magnets has improved dramatically in recent years, but problems still remain. Fortunately, steps can be taken to alleviate the most obvious deficiencies. Stockpiling rare earth metals, with special emphasis on the heavy rare earths like dysprosium, is a low cost way of preventing shortages during supply interruptions. Supporting industry through focused research and development projects might also encourage the emergence of a new generation of sintered Nd-Fe-B manufacturing experts - just as the previous generation of US magnet experts nears retirement age.

In light of these gaps and weaknesses in the sintered Nd-Fe-B manufacturing supply chain, the U.S. Government may wish to evaluate the following actions to ensure a stable supply of sintered Nd-Fe-B magnets:

- Initiate a stockpile or vendor-managed inventory of neodymium, praseodymium, didymium, and / or dysprosium metals. This would provide metals for alloying into Nd-Fe-B if supplies of these magnets were restricted or disrupted.
- Continually monitor the economic health of Molycorp and, in particular, its US assets: Mountain Pass and Molycorp Metals and Alloys. This should include monitoring the level of foreign ownership, given that a foreign company, Molymet, already owns 27% of Molycorp.
- Notify Hitachi Metals that the China Grove facility is a strategic lynchpin of the defense industrial base, and discuss how the Defense Production Act (Title I) might apply to that facility. This is critical, since Hitachi has stated a corporate reluctance to supplying sintered Nd-Fe-B magnets for military use - especially those used for weapons of mass destruction.
- Defense Production Act (DPA) project to establish a domestically owned and operated magnet manufacturing capability. This would mitigate risks from Hitachi's control of the current US sintered Nd-Fe-B magnet production capabilities.
- ManTech program to assist current producers of other magnet materials to upgrade capabilities to be a reserve, second source of magnet material. This would mitigate US risks from Hitachi's position as the sole US producer of sintered Nd-Fe-B magnets. Hitachi has previously closed their US sintered

Nd-Fe-B magnet plant, and left the US without a source of sintered Nd-Fe-B magnets.

- DPA project to build rare earth oxide to rare earth metal processing capacity. This would provide the US with an ability to produce rare earth metals without shipping US rare earth oxides overseas for processing.
- ManTech project to commercialize new rare earth metal making technology. An example of this is the technology at Infinium, which could be a significant new advance.

Recycling of Rare Earth Magnets

A. WALTON, A. CAMPBELL, R.S. SHERIDAN, V.S.J. MANN, J.D. SPEIGHT, I.R. HARRIS, B.GUERRERO*, C. BAGAN*, A. CONESA* V. SCHALLER**

Magnetic Materials Group, University of Birmingham, Edgbaston, Birmingham, UK B15 2TT.
*Leitat Technology Centre - C/ de la Innovació, 2 · 08225 Terrassa, Barcelona, Spain.
**Stiftelsen Chalmers Industriteknik, Chalmers Science Park, Gothenburg, Sweden

Abstract: *In recent years there has been significant price volatility for rare earth metals, due in part to supply restrictions from China, the predominant supplier. In particular, this has had a very significant impact on the market for neodymium iron boron (Nd-Fe-B) magnets. To increase the availability of these magnets, one of the possible solutions would be to recycle the existing stock contained in electrical equipment. However there are major challenges for recycling and the barriers differ significantly across a wide range of applications. This paper highlights some of the challenges, which are faced for a range of these applications, in order to recycle these magnets. The individual steps required for recycling are discussed including: identification, detection, separation, purification and re-processing. The options for re-processing are addressed, including re-sintering, HDDR processing, re-melting or by separating the rare earth fraction from the magnets.*

Keywords: *recycling, hydrogen; Nd-Fe-B; urban mining; magnet*

1. Introduction

Due to pressure on supplies of the rare earth elements, in recent years there has been a drive towards recycling of these materials. The waste streams available for recycling can take several forms including: (i) manufacturing scrap, (ii) end of life goods (urban mining) or (iii) landfill mining of historical industrial waste residues. In this paper, only products from the urban mine source will be considered.

For La, Eu, Y, Ce and Tb recycling already takes place to some degree from batteries, lamp phosphors and polishing materials [1]. However, this is often only economically viable when the rare earth prices are high. Therefore to counter possible price variability, it is essential that any recycling process for NdFeB magnets is extremely efficient and cost effective.

2. Scrap Processing / Scrap Availability

Despite current efforts, there is only very limited recycling of rare earth magnets from the urban mine [1]. This is due in part to a combination of insufficient collection rates of electrical products containing rare earth magnets, historically low prices for rare earths and the technical challenges associated with extraction and re-processing. The barriers for recycling often differ significantly from one application to another and a couple of examples are shown in this paper. The first step for recycling to occur on a large scale is the identification of products, which contain significant and sufficient quantities of rare earth magnets. One of the major challenges for the recycling of rare earth magnets is that the magnets are often distributed over a large number of different applications, particularly in the electronics sector where they are used both in resin bonded and sintered forms in devices such as ear phones, DVD players, phones, cameras etc. Many of these products are processed together in a mixed WEEE stream. Therefore if the Nd-Fe-B magnets are to be recycled, detection in the mixed waste stream would be required and it is likely that the detection technique would have to be remote. Normally, shredding would be used to expose the surface of the material to be detected. However it has been shown previously, that when these electronic goods are shredded then the magnets break apart and then stick magnetically to the ferromagnetic components [2]. Therefore in these shredded electronic goods, Nd-Fe-B would be detected throughout the waste. External detection could for example take the form of a magnetic technique. One other major issue is that, depending on the particular device, many common applications can use either Nd-Fe-B or strontium ferrite magnets. For example, many lower performance hand held drills will use ferrite magnets whereas the high-end drills will employ Nd-Fe-B magnets. Therefore if an external magnetic detection technique is used then it is likely that, initially, different magnet types will be separated together.

Du et al [3] attempted to quantify the availability of scrap Nd-Fe-B into different categories such as loud speakers, hard disk drives (HDDs) etc. However, a more detailed breakdown is required in order to identify key products which contain significant quantities of Nd-Fe-B in applications which can be collected and separated readily. There are several products which have already been identified by several workers including air conditioning compressors, automotive applications and HDDs [1-3]. It should be noted that, in the coming years, the available scrap from these markets will change dramatically. Whilst the HDD market is likely to decline gradually due to the partial replacement with solid state devices and the fact that HDDs are becoming smaller as more people move to laptops, the automotive sector will expand due to more hybrid cars and electric vehicles (EVs) reaching their end of life.

HDDs are one of the most abundant and readily available forms of scrap from the electronics sector which contain Nd-Fe-B magnets. HDDs are already collected in large numbers as companies and individuals want to protect confidential information stored on HDDs. Consequently the HDDs are often disposed of by shredding the hard drives often whilst under the surveillance of cameras to guarantee safe destruction. This material not only becomes widely distributed as a coarse powder but it will also pick up significant quantities of oxygen which could limit the possible reprocessing routes which could be used to transform this material into a new magnet. Therefore it is likely that any technology, which can be used to separate the magnets from the waste, will have to be applied prior to the shredding operation. It should be noted that many HDDs are repaired or sold on in their current form which can make it difficult to get accurate figures on the quantity of available scrap from this market. An example of a HDD (with the case removed) is shown in Fig. 1. There are two main Nd-Fe-B magnets in the HDD. A resin bonded magnet in the central spindle motor and one or two, fully dense, sintered magnets in the voice coil motor (VCM) assembly which controls the position of the read head over the disk. It is unlikely that the resin bonded magnets will be recycled as this represents only a relatively small amount of material and the magnet is very difficult to remove from the compression fitted sleeve in which it is housed. There are also inherent difficulties in recycling of the sintered magnets from HDDs which are often common across the electronics sector. Firstly, the device itself has a rather complicated architecture which requires the removal of 8 - 12 security screws to reach the point where the VCM can be removed. The magnets are also coated with Ni, glued into position and are fully magnetised so that they are attracted to the ferritic plates positioned either side of the magnets.

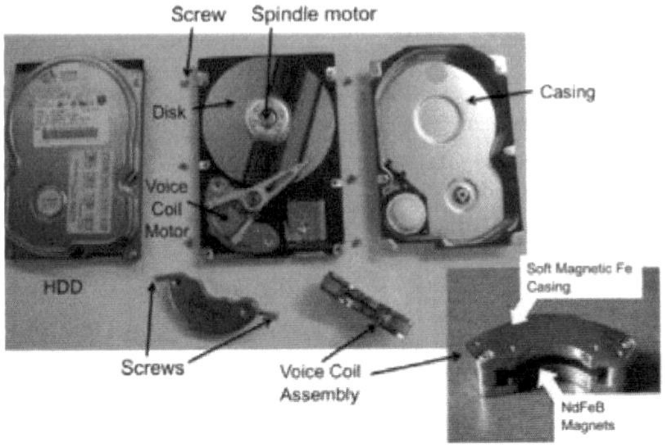

Fig. 1. Hard disk drive with the case removed.

If the Nd-Fe-B can be separated and purified as an alloy, then one of the major issues with regard to the choice of the particular re-processing technology, is the compositional range of the magnets that have been used in that particular application. Through the passage of time, the composition of the magnets in all applications is likely to have changed as improvements have been made to such properties as the corrosion resistance, coercivity and Curie temp of the magnets. The composition of the magnets will also determine the scrap value of the magnets. Of particular note is the Dy content of the magnets. The Dy price is currently around 460$/kg [4] which is over 5 times the current price of Nd. As part of the EU Remanence project, 80 HDDs were dismantled (provided by Stena Metall) and the sintered magnets removed manually from the VCM assemblies. ICP analysis was then performed at the Leitat Technology Centre to assess the composition of the sintered magnets.

The Nd and Dy weight percentages are shown in Figures 2 to 4 by year and by individual manufacturer (indicated by symbols only to maintain confidentiality). The average composition of the magnets taking into account all 80 samples was 27.94 wt.% Nd, 3.94wt.% Pr and 1.68 wt.% Dy. As a scrap source this will be relatively low in value compared to those of many of the other scrap sources which will come on line in the coming years. For example, the magnets used in drive motors in the automotive sector could have > 6wt.% Dy. The greatest number of samples summarised in Fig. 2 contained less than 1wt.% Dy but it is evident from Fig. 4 that the Dy content of the magnets various dramatically with the year of the device and with the producer of the HDD. There is a general downward trend in terms of the Dy content of the samples per manufacturer, with a noticeable drop in 2010 when the dramatic price rises were observed for Dy in particular.

In the future, one of the likely sources for rare earth magnets will be from the automotive sector. Modern vehicles use significant quantities of magnets in many components around the vehicle from seats motors to loud speakers. However, as with the electronics

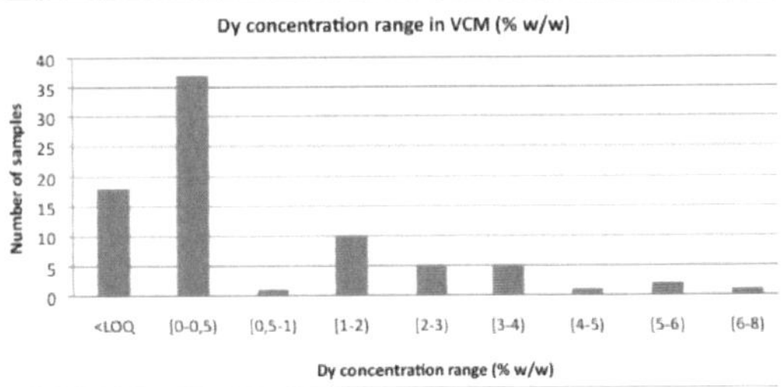

Fig. 2. Number of Nd-Fe-B samples vs. the Dy content for magnets extracted from HDDs.

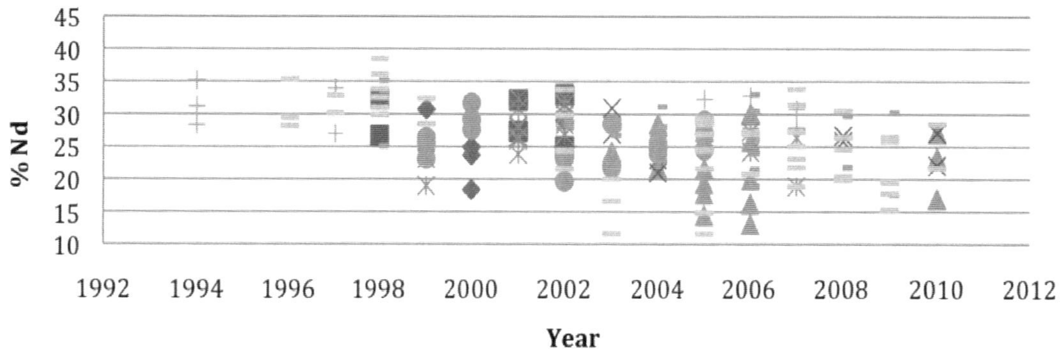

Fig. 3. Compositional variation of Nd content (wt.%) in the sintered Nd-Fe-B magnets of HDDs (voice coil) as a function of year and manufacturer (each symbol type represents one manufacturer).

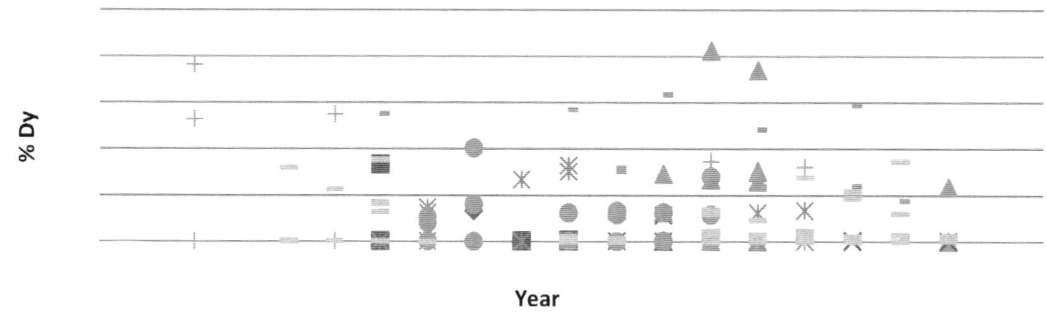

Fig. 4. Compositional variation of Dy content (wt.%) in the sintered Nd-Fe-B magnets of HDDs (voice coil) as a function of year and manufacturer (each symbol type represents one manufacturer).

sector, there will be key applications which contain significant quantities of Nd-Fe-B magnets which should be in a form which is easier to recycle. For example, hybrid and electric vehicles will often have a rare earth containing permanent magnet drive motor and a generator which are likely to contain together, between 1 - 2 kg of Nd-Fe-B. In modern vehicles there has also been the development of electric power steering and stop start technology, both of which can employ significant quantities of sintered Nd-Fe-B magnets. The key to developing an economical recycling process will be to develop methods for separating these key components in an efficient manner before the vehicle is shredded. The architecture of the device will again play a significant role in how readily the magnet containing component can be remove from the vehicle, as will the position of the component within the vehicle. Design for recycling will have a significant role to play in determining the efficiencies of these processes. Once the magnet containing components are separated from the car, then the magnets themselves have to be separated from their surrounding support structures. Unlike the HDD market described earlier, for each component there are likely to be many designs. This is likely to result in different challenges for separation, depending upon how the magnets are held in the device. Figure 5 illustrates a couple of designs for rotors from drive motors on vehicles. In some devices the magnets are surface mounted by gluing small magnets onto the surface of a rotor. This is typically sheathed in carbon fibre or Inconel. In other devices the magnets are embedded in the rotor itself, as in the Toyota Prius. It is possible to heat the rotor to demagnetise the magnets, however it is unclear what level of contamination could arise from the carbon fibre composite material or the epoxy resins which are used typically to hold the magnets in place. In addition, if the rotor is heated in air then, to some degree, the surface of the magnets will become oxidised. All of these impurities may limit the subsequent reprocessing options available to convert the separated material into new forms of magnet.

Fig. 5. Rotors from electric vehicles.

Although it is known that, in order to improve the thermal stability, the magnets in drive motors in vehicles will contain a significant quantity of Dy, it is unclear, at this juncture, what the spread of compositions is by year and manufacturer and therefore a detailed study is required, similar to the study reported here for the HDDs. The particular value of the magnet waste can then be determined more accurately. However, if for arguments sake the Dy content is around 6 wt.%, then it would be substantially more than the value of the raw material compared to that of the magnet contained in HDDs.

3. Separation of Magnets from the Waste

One of the major challenges for nearly all types of urban mine waste is how to separate the Nd-Fe-B fraction from the general waste in a cost effective manner. Hitachi has disclosed that they use a mechanical technique to remove the magnet containing components from HDDs and air conditioning motors but, in the open literature, there are few technical details. At REPM 2012, Walton et al disclosed a hydrogen-based route to separate Nd-Fe-B magnets from HDDs [2]. In this technique the hydrogen decrepitaiton (HD) process is used to break down the Nd-Fe-B magnets into a friable demagnetised powder. During this process the Ni coating on the surface of the magnet peels away. By tumbling the products in a porous drum after the HD process it is possible to liberate the powdered hydrogenated material together with the Ni flakes. Then, by mechanical sieving with ball bearings, it is possible to preferentially mill the hydrogenated Nd-Fe-B in preference to the other components thus producing a powder with a Ni content of between 300-400pmm which is very close to the Ni-content in the initial material. Since REPM 2012, this hydrogen-based process has been scaled up at the University of Birmingham to a larger pilot scale within a 300 litre hydrogen reactor. The trials using this equipment have shown that around 4 – 5 kg of Nd-Fe-B can be separated from 250 HDDs (equating to 16 - 20 g of Nd-Fe-B / HDD), although this does depend on the size of the HDDs being processed. The extracted materials were then sieved using a course 1mm sieve followed by burr-milling of the friable powdered material. This increased significantly the milling rate compared to that of the standard mechanical sieving process. The powder was passed subsequently through a sieve stage at 90 or 45 microns and ICP analysis of the material showed that it contained $\leq$ 400 ppm of Ni.

4. Re-Processing Routes

There are many ways in which to re-process the extracted Nd-Fe-B from electrical equipment either directly from the alloy or by chemical extraction of the rare earth elements [1]. The choice of route will be determined initially, by the compositional range of the material and the impurity levels contained in the Nd-Fe-B fraction. If the impurity level is too high then a direct alloy route is less likely. The schematic diagram shown in Fig. 6 demonstrates where the extracted Nd-Fe-B material could potentially be put back into the primary production route for a magnet. The further one moves down this flow diagram, then the higher the quality of magnet which can be produced. However, if short loop recycling can be employed (towards the top of the diagram) then the cost and energy of processing will be lower but this is likely to be associated with a drop in magnetic performance. It is possible to re-process the magnet in alloy form in several ways including re-sintering [5], HDDR processing [6,7], melt-spinning [8] and re-melting to form a master alloy.

Each of these routes will be affected by the composition of the input scrap. For example, Sheridan et al showed that an increase in the Dy and Co content of sintered magnets by around 1 at.% and 5 at.% respectively, resulted in the disproportionation pressure for HDDR increasing by around 800 mbar [6]. If, for example, a mixed VCM waste stream was collected with a range of compositions as in Figures 2, 3 and 4 and processed using the HDDR route then it might be difficult to tailor the conditions to avoid either over or under processing of the material possibly leading to an overall drop in the magnetic properties.

Any impurities in the Nd-Fe-B magnet will also have an impact upon the quality of the re-processed magnet. For example it has previously been reported that due to the higher oxygen content of sintered magnets (2000 – 5000 ppm) it is much harder to re-sinter the HD powder directly back into new magnets due to a lack of Nd for the liquid phase sintering process [5]. One way round the oxygen problem would be to re-melt the extracted Nd-Fe-B magnets to produce a master alloy. The oxidised material will form in the slag which can then be separated from the

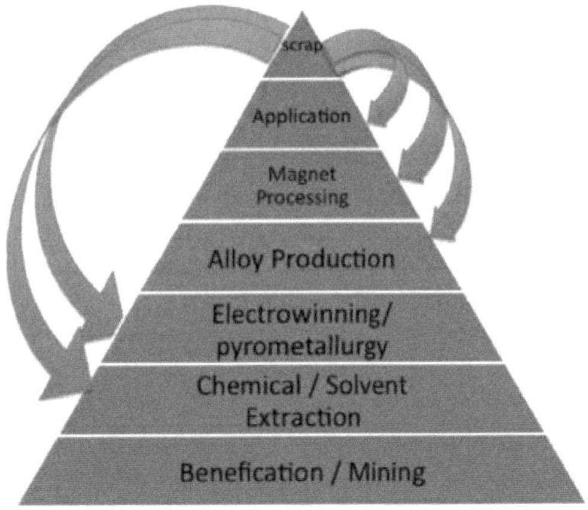

Fig. 6. Diagram of possible recycling routes for Nd-Fe-B

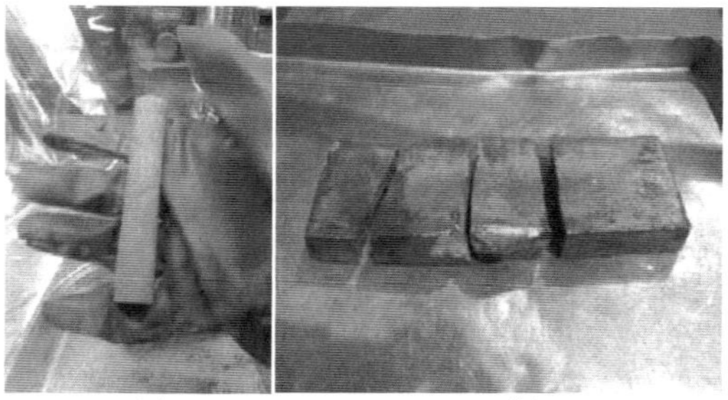

Fig. 7. (a) pelletized degassed Nd-Fe-B. (b) cast master alloy.

remainder of the cast material. However this would be associated with a yield loss due the concentration of Nd_2O_3 in the slag layer. In collaboration with Less Common Metals (LCM) this route has now been demonstrated successfully for the hydrogen extracted material from hard disk drives. About 5 kg of hydrogenated Nd-Fe-B was degassed at 900 °C in powder form at the University of Birmingham. The degassed material was then isostatically pressed into green compacts of around 100 – 150 g (Fig. 7a). 2.15 kg of pellets were loaded into an vacuum induction furnace alongside 4.85 kg of primary cast alloy which acted as a heal. A cast master alloy was produced which had an average oxygen content of around 300 – 700 ppm (see Fig. 7b). Further work is ongoing to optimise this route to market.

5. Conclusions

This paper has outlined many of the challenges which have to be addressed before widespread recycling of NdFeB magnets can be implemented. If a viable recycling route can be achieved then a recycled source of material could offer many advantages over primary sources including; a lower environmental footprint, lower energy production and potentially a cheaper source of raw material, particularly if a short loop process can be implemented directly from the alloy.

Acknowledgements
Less Common Metals are thanked for their technical support. WRAP (UK) and the EU Remanence and EREAN projects are thanked for supporting this work.

References

[1] K.Binemanns et al, *J. Clean. Tech.* **51**, 2013, 1.
[2] A. Walton et al, in: *Proc. REPM 2012*, 10–13.
[3] Du et al, *J. Ind. Ecol.* **15**, 2011, 836.
[4] www.metal-pages.com
[5] M.Zakotnik et al, *J. Alloys. Compd.* **469**, 2009, 314.
[6] R.S. Sheridan et al, *J. Magn. Magn. Mater.* **350**, 2014, 114.
[7] O. Gutfleisch et al, *Adv. Energy Mater.* **3**, 2013, 151.
[8] M. Itoh et al, *J. Alloys. Compd.* **374**, 2004, 393.

Large Scale Recycling of Industrial Scrap Sm(Co, Fe, Cu, Zr)$_z$ Magnets into Valuable Permanent Magnets

C. CHINNASAMY, M. MARINESCU, J. LIU
Electron Energy Corporation, Landisville, PA 17601, USA

Abstract: *Rare earth element recovery from the "urban mine" is on the verge of being the next big thing in electronics recycling. We have developed a cost-effective rare earth element (REE) recycling process for converting industrial scrap Sm(Co, Fe, Cu, Zr)$_z$ magnets into valuable permanent magnets. The surface-cleaned Sm(Co, Fe, Cu, Zr)$_z$ scrap magnets were induction melted, crushed and either ball milled or jet milled to a 3-4 μm particle size range. Based on elemental analysis, the alloy powder was compensated with different percentages of Sm-rich additive powders produced from the virgin elements to make the optimum Sm_2Co_{17} alloy composition, and isopressed to make sintered magnets. The magnetic properties were: remanent magnetization (B_r) = 10.52-10.61 kG, intrinsic coercivity (H_{ci}) = >28.52 kOe, H_k = 15.79-17.59 kOe and the energy product $(BH)_{max}$ = 26.25-26.54 MGOe, with good mechanical and thermal properties. These recycled 2:17 magnets show almost equivalent properties compared to commercial magnets of the same grade. This process will produce specialty and master alloys of sufficient quality to be blended with other magnet alloys or to be used as virgin alloys for the production of rare earth permanent magnets.*

Keywords: *rare earth magnets recycling, urban mine, Sm-Co recycling, recycled sintered Sm(Co, Fe, Cu, Zr)$_z$ magnets, 2:17 magnets.*

Address: Chins Chinnasamy, Electron Energy Corporation- Technology Center, 924 Links Avenue, Landisville, PA 17601, USA, Tel. (1-717) 898-2294, E-mail: cnchinnasamy@electronenergy.com

1. Introduction

Rare earth element (REE) based Nd-Fe-B and Sm-Co magnets have been widely used because of their excellent magnetic properties. The applications of Nd-Fe-B and Sm-Co rare earth permanent magnets include hybrid electric vehicles (HEVs), power generators for wind turbines, high performance industrial motors, hard disk drives for computers, travelling wave tubes for satellite communications, headphones and speakers, washing machines, and other consumer electronic devices. Electric cars use about seven pounds of rare-earth magnets, while each clean-energy wind turbine uses more than 600 pounds of neodymium. Dy is used as an additive to Nd-Fe-B magnets to increase the coercivity (because it increases the magnetocrystalline anisotropy) in motor applications. However, the limited supply of Nd, and especially Dy, and other heavy rare earth elements, is a major concern and therefore these elements have been internationally classified as strategic materials [1-3]. Other rare earth elements, such as Sm, Pr, etc, have a lower supply risk but experience less-controllable market fluctuations. According to IMCOA/Roskill data [4], magnets represented about 21% of the market for rare earth elements in 2008 and were estimated to reach 24% in 2013. Moreover, in a typical neodymium-iron-boron (Nd-Fe-B) magnet manufacturing facility, about 20–30% of the magnet material is wasted as scrap and swarf, mostly from machining blocks into particular geometries, which is estimated to be about 1500–2500 tons/year. In the case of Sm-Co magnets, about 20-30% of the raw materials are wasted as scraps at typical Sm-Co manufacturing sites. This material can end up in landfills with negative implications for the environment. The magnet scrap generated within manufacturing sites is fully traceable, which provides a clearer opportunity than the uncategorized post-consumer magnets from discarded electronic devices. The financial justification for recycling pre-consumer rare earth magnets waste is that the value of the scrap is estimated to be between US$100-200 million per year. However, to date, only very small quantities of rare earth elements (estimated at less than 5%) have been recycled from pre-consumer scrap. Hence, rare earth element recovery from the "urban mine" is on the verge of being the next big thing in electronics recycling [5]. In this paper, we present a cost effective approach to recycle Sm(Co, Fe, Cu, Zr)$_z$ magnet scraps, targeting the stream from magnet manufacturing sites (Fig. 1), into sintered Sm(Co, Fe, Cu, Zr)$_z$ magnets with good magnetic, mechanical and thermal properties.

2. Experimental

About 50 lbs of SmCo-2:17 type Sm(Co,Fe,Cu,Zr)$_z$ industrial scrap magnets in the form of unmachined blocks and magnet pieces were collected, surface cleaned and melted using an industrial induction melting furnace. Before melting, the sintering skin of the unmachined blocks was removed to decrease the

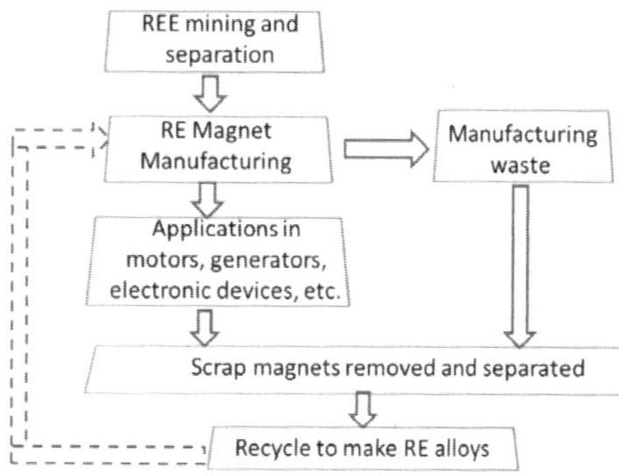

Fig. 1. The life cycle of rare earth element (REE) in permanent magnets with EEC's (Electron Energy Corporation) low cost recycling approach.

percentage of virgin elements needed to be added for compositional compensation. An elemental analysis was carried out using induction coupled plasma spectroscopy (ICP-AES) to ensure the correct composition and the absence of any other impurity elements. The induction melted $Sm(Co,Fe,Cu,Zr)_z$ alloy ingot was crushed and either ball milled or jet milled to produce the alloy powders with a particle size in the range of 3-4 μm. After milling, the powders were dried in an inert atmosphere. In order to compensate it further, the powder produced by ball milling was blended and isopressed with different percentages of Sm-rich additives. The additives were prepared either from the $Sm(Co,Fe,Cu,Zr)_z$ scrap magnets or by using virgin elements. After evaluating the magnetic properties of the test parts, standard large block size magnets were made for each additive percentage, and were processed with the standard sintering, solution and aging techniques to produce sintered magnets. The sintered $Sm(Co,Fe,Cu,Zr)_z$ magnets were machined to remove the skin and the magnetic properties were studied. Magnetic measurements were performed with a KJS instrument on test parts pulse-magnetized at 70 kOe. The oxygen content was measured with an oxygen analyzer (LECO Model RO-300). Densities of the magnets were determined by a water immersion technique. Mechanical properties were measured by three point break test method. The zero reversible temperature coefficients of these recycled $Sm(Co, Fe, Cu, Zr)_z$ magnets were also measured and compared with the production grade 2-17 magnets.

3. Results and Discussion

Figure 1 shows the demagnetization curves of test parts made at different locations in a sintered sample block with an optimized additive percentage. The best magnetic properties of the recycled sintered $Sm(Co, Fe, Cu, Zr)_z$ magnets are: remanent magnetization (B_r) = 10.52-10.61 kG, intrinsic coercivity (H_{ci}) = >28.52 kOe, H_k = 15.79-17.59 kOe and energy product $(BH)_{max}$ = 26.25-26.54 MGOe, with good

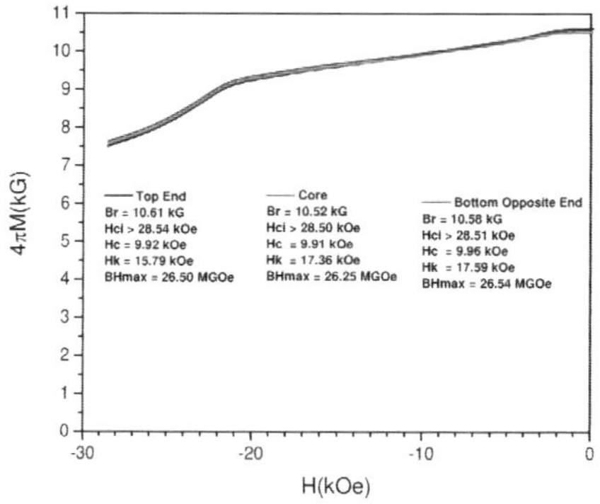

Fig. 2. Demagnetization curves of test parts made from the recycled sintered Sm_2Co_{17} magnet blocks with optimized additive showing uniform magnetic properties throughout a large magnet block.

curve shape. These recycled magnets show almost equivalent properties compared to commercial magnets of the EEC 2:17 - 27 grade.

The magnetic properties of the recycled sintered $Sm(Co, Fe, Cu, Zr)_z$ magnets are shown in Fig. 2. Twelve 1.66" x .246" x .090" parts were cut and machined from a magnet block with the same optimized additive level that produced the aforementioned magnetic properties. 3-point break tests were performed on this rectangles and the average results obtained were within 98% of break tests of EEC Sm_2Co_{17}-27 material of the same size. Hence, the recycled 2-17 magnets also show good mechanical properties required for device applications.

Sintered 2-17 magnets usually have excellent thermal characteristics and can withstand much higher operating temperatures and are more corrosion resistant then the sintered Nd-Fe-B magnets. In order to confirm that the recycled sintered $Sm(Co, Fe, Cu, Zr)_z$ magnets have good thermal stability, a reversible temperature coefficient study was performed between -60 and 100°C. The measured reversible temperature coefficient (RTC) of Br is defined as $\alpha = (\Delta B_r/B_r) \times (1/\Delta T) \times 100\%$. The measured RTC of Br for the recycled sintered $Sm(Co,Fe,Cu,Zr)_z$ magnets is -0.042%/°C which is close to the α value of EEC 2:17-27 grade magnets.

Using the currently most successful recycling method, industrial scrap $Sm(Co,Fe,Cu,Zr)_z$ magnets were recycled with good magnetic and mechanical properties and are eligible for commercial use.

Acknowledgements
This work was supported by the National Science Foundation Environmental Protection Agency (EPA) under SBIR phase II contract No. EP-D-13-047.

References

[1] U. S. Department of Energy, *"Critical Materials Strategy"*, 2011, Dec.
[2] P. C. Dent, "Rare earth future", Magnetics Technology International, 2011, 56-59.
[3] X. Du, T. E. Graedel, "Global rare earth in-use stocks in NdFeB permanent magnets", *J. Industrial Ecology*, 2011, 15, 6, 836-843.
[4] http:// www.roskill.com.
[5] Chins Chinnasamy, Melania Marinescu, Jinfang Liu, Peter Dent, "Rare earth magnet recycling", *International Cooperation Symposium Toshikohzon "Urban Mine"- Its Potential Resources*, 2012, Oct., Kyoto, Japan, 8-15.

Recent Progress in High-Performance Magnets

S. SUGIMOTO[1], M. NAKAMURA[1], K. ISOGAI[1], M. MATSUURA[1], Y. UNE[2], H. KUBO[2], M. SAGAWA[2]
[1] Department of Materials Science, Graduate School of Engineering, Tohoku University
[2] Intermetallics Co., Ltd.

Abstract: *This paper describes recent progress in techniques for reducing Dy content in Nd-Fe-B magnets and the development of new types of magnets. An effective method for increasing coercivity in Nd-Fe-B sintered magnets is the refinement of the $Nd_2Fe_{14}B$ grains. We have decreased the powder size of the grains to less than 1 μm by combining hydrogenation–disproportionation–desorption–recombination, hydrogen decrepitation, and helium (He) jet-milling. The coercivity of the ultrafine powders increased dramatically after annealing above 600 °C because of the formation of a liquid Nd-rich phase. We also found that Mn-Sn-Co-N alloys showed a high coercivity of $\mu_0 H_{cJ}$ = 1.59 T after homogenization at 1050 °C for 20 h in Ar, annealing at 950 °C for 5 h in N_2 (first nitriding), and subsequent annealing at 500 °C for 5 h in N_2 (second nitriding). The microstructural analyses showed that the alloys had a fine two-phase microstructure consisting of β-Mn and perovskite phases.*

Keywords: *dysprosium saving, coercivity, hydrogenation-disproportionation-desorption-recombination, hydrogen-decrepitation, helium jet mill, annealing*

Address: Satoshi Sugimoto, Department of Materials Science, Graduate School of Engineering, Tohoku University, 6-6-02 Aramaki Aza Aoba, Aoba-ku, Sendai, 980-8579, Japan, Tel & Fax: +81-22-795-3785, E-mail: sugimots@material.tohoku.ac.jp

1. Introduction

Nd-Fe-B sintered magnets are widely used in many applications. One of the most promising applications for these magnets is in motors for hybrid electric vehicles. However, if the operating temperature of the magnets exceeds 150 °C, a room temperature coercivity around $\mu_0 H_{cJ}$ = 3 T is required. Although the heat resistance and coercivity of Nd-Fe-B sintered magnets can be improved by adding Dy, the magnetic moment of Dy is coupled anti-parallel to that of Fe, which decreases the magnetization and maximum energy product of the magnet. In addition, the natural abundance of Dy is low and the number of countries that produce it is limited. Therefore, the development of Dy-free or Dy-lean Nd-Fe-B sintered magnets with high coercivity is desirable. It has been 39 years since the development of Nd-Fe-B sintered magnets by Sagawa et al. Therefore, there is intense interest in the development of new types of magnet. In this paper, we discuss recent progress in Dy-saving techniques for Nd-Fe-B magnets [1] and the research we are doing on new types of magnets [2,3].

2. Dy-Saving Techniques

2.1. New preparation method for ultrafine powders for Nd-Fe-B sintered magnets

Decreasing the grain size of the $Nd_2Fe_{14}B$ phase is an established method for increasing coercivity of Nd-Fe-B sintered magnets. Therefore, the grain refinement of the $Nd_2Fe_{14}B$ phase by decreasing the grain size of strip-cast (SC) alloys, the jet-milled powder size, and the grain size of sintered magnets has been reported [4-7]. However, conventional N_2 jet milling can only produce particles around 3 μm in diameter. Une and Sagawa [8-10] decreased the size of jet-milled powder to around 1 μm by He jet milling SC Nd-Fe-B alloys. The resulting Dy-free Nd-Fe-B sintered magnets exhibited a coercivity of about 2.0 T and a maximum energy product $(BH)_{max}$ of 400 kJ m^{-3} (Fig. 1).

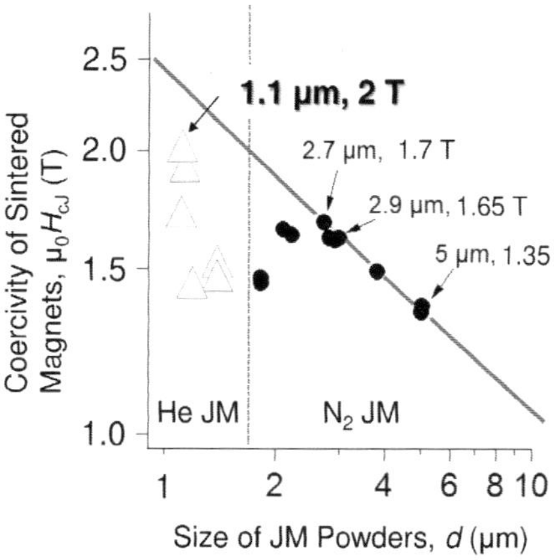

Fig. 1. Relation between jet-milled (JM) powder size (d) and coercivity ($\mu_0 H_{cJ}$) of Nd-Fe-B sintered magnets. Triangle and closed circle represent $\mu_0 H_{cJ}$ of the samples prepared using He JM and N_2 JM, respectively [4].

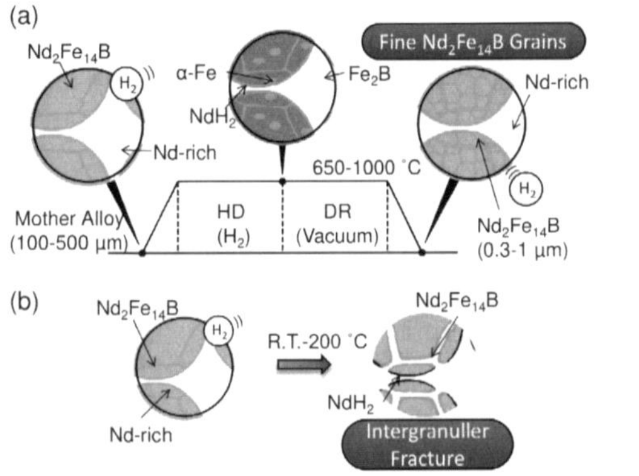

Fig. 2. Schematic of (a) HDDR and (b) HD processes.

These results show that the grain size must be decreased further to increase the coercivity. Recently, we have decreased the size of jet-milled powders to 0.3 μm by combining hydrogenation–disproportionation–desorption–recombination (HDDR), hydrogen decrepitation (HD) and helium jet milling [1]. Figure 2 shows a schematic illustration of the HDDR and HD processes.

HDDR is a well-known method for refining the grain size of the $Nd_2Fe_{14}B$ phase in Nd-Fe-B alloys. The $Nd_2Fe_{14}B$ phase decomposes into NdH_2, Fe, and Fe_2B by heat treatment at temperatures of 650–1000 °C under a hydrogen atmosphere. During subsequent heat treatment in a vacuum, the hydrogen is desorbed from the NdH_2, and NdH_2, Fe, and Fe_2B recombine into fine $Nd_2Fe_{14}B$ grains. Fine $Nd_2Fe_{14}B$ grains with a size of approximately 0.3 μm can be obtained through the HDDR process [11]. The HDDR-treated Nd-Fe-B alloy exhibits a homogeneous microstructure consisting of $Nd_2Fe_{14}B$ and Nd-rich grain boundary phases [12]. Hydrogen decrepitation (HD) [13] is also used in the conventional production of Nd-Fe-B sintered magnets. During HD, the Nd-rich phase in Nd-Fe-B alloys absorbs hydrogen at room temperature and undergoes volume expansion, which results in grain boundary fracture.

HD can be used to obtain coarse powders directly from ingots, and to induce grain boundary fracture in HDDR-treated alloys. Ultrafine jet-milled powder can be obtained by He jet milling hydrogen decrepitated HDDR alloys. Accordingly, we expected that we could prepare ultrafine jet-milled powders for Nd-Fe-B sintered magnets by using a combination of HDDR, HD, and He jet milling. A schematic of this process is shown in Fig. 3.

2.2. Experimental procedure

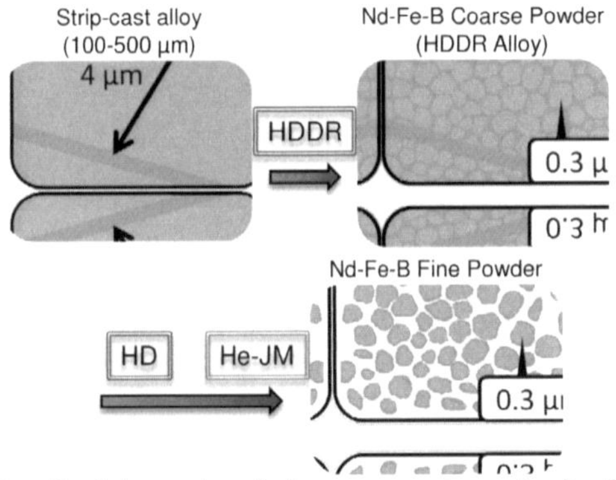

Fig. 3. Schematic of the preparation of ultrafine powders.

The starting material was a SC $Nd_{11.9}Pr_{2.2}Fe_{bal.}B_{5.7}Al_{0.5}Cu_{0.1}Co_{1.1}$ (at. %) alloy. The alloy was crushed into a coarse powder HD at room temperature. The coarse powders were treated by HDDR at 900 °C for 60 min under a H_2 atmosphere, at 800 °C for 10 min under an Ar atmosphere, and then at 800 °C for 60 min in vacuum. The HDDR treated powders underwent HD treatment at 200 °C for 5 h in H_2, and were then crushed into ultrafine powders by He jet milling. The magnetic properties were measured with a vibrating sample magnetometer (VSM). The microstructure was investigated by X-ray diffraction (XRD) and field-emission scanning electron microscopy (SEM).

2.3. Results and discussion

Figure 4 shows an SEM image of the microstructure of the jet-milled powder prepared by conventional He jet milling and the backscattered electron (BSE) images of the SC alloy and the HD-treated alloy. In the BSE images of the SC and HD treated alloys, the dark and bright regions correspond to the $Nd_2Fe_{14}B$ and Nd-rich phases, respectively. The BSE image of the SC alloy (Fig. 4(a)) shows a lamellar microstructure consisting of $Nd_2Fe_{14}B$ and Nd-rich phases with a lamellar spacing of 3.2 μm, which is similar to the previously reported spacing.

The BSE image of the alloy after HD treatment (Fig. 4(b)) shows the grain boundary fracture along the Nd-rich phase and the intergranular fracture into $Nd_2Fe_{14}B$ grains. The SEM image of the He jet milled powders (Fig. 4(c)), which were prepared using the HD treated alloy, shows that the average powder size was 1.07 μm. However, the coercivity of the jet-milled powders measured by VSM was low at around 0.09 T.

Figure 5 shows SEM images of the HDDR-treated alloy, the HD-treated alloy, and the He jet-milled

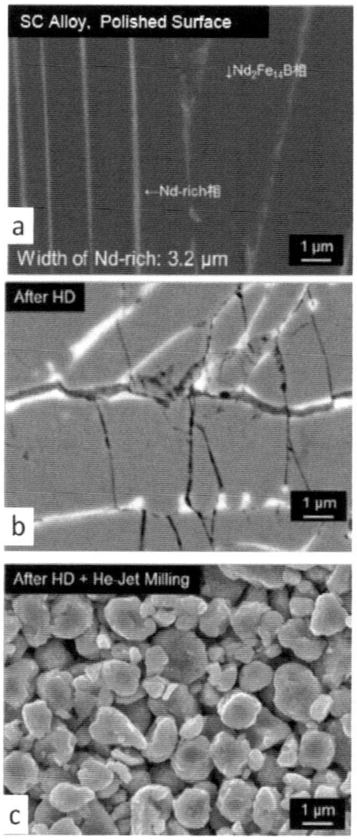

Fig. 4. BSE image of the (a) SC alloy and (b) HD-treated alloy, and (c) SEM image of the He jet-milled powder from the HD-treated alloy.

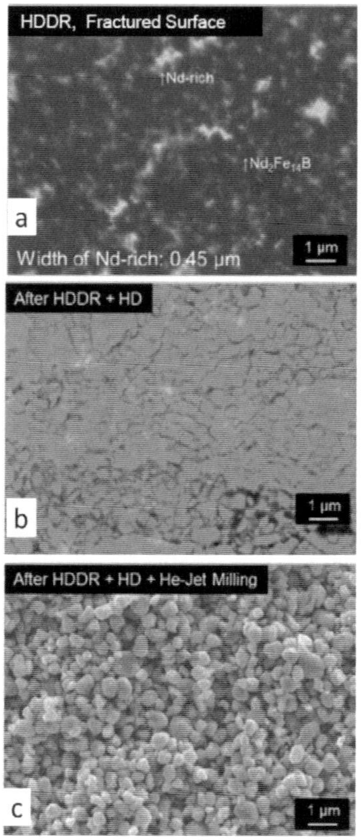

Fig. 5. BSE image of the (a) HDDR-treated alloy and (b) HDDR- and HD-treated alloy, and (c) SEM image of the He jet-milled powder from the HDDR- and HD-treated alloy.

powder of the HDDR- and then HD-treated alloy. In the HDDR-treated alloy (Fig. 5(a)), the Nd-rich phase along the grain boundary of the $Nd_2Fe_{14}B$ phase is observed and the average $Nd_2Fe_{14}B$ grain size is 0.33 μm. After the HD treatment (Fig. 5(b)), the grain boundary fracture of the HDDR alloy is visible. Comparing the SEM images of the powders in Fig. 5(c) and 4(c) shows that the powder size of the He jet-milled powder of the HDDR- and HD-treated alloy is less than that of the HD-treated alloy. The powder size of the HDDR- and HD-treated alloy is 0.33 μm, which is comparable to the grain size of the $Nd_2Fe_{14}B$ phase after HDDR treatment shown in Fig. 5(a).

In addition, the coercivity of He jet-milled powders from the HDDR- and HD-treated alloy was 0.20 T, which was higher than the coercivity of the jet-milled powders of SC alloys (0.09 T). The coercivity also increased after annealing at temperatures around 600 °C because of the presence of a liquid Nd-rich phase.

In conclusion, the combination of HDDR, HD and He jet milling is effective for preparing ultrafine powders for Nd-Fe-B sintered magnets.

3. New Types of Magnets

3.1. Mn-Sn-Co-N alloy

No material has yet been reported that shows better magnetic properties than Nd-Fe-B magnets. However, compounds such as $Fe_{16}N_2$ [14], L10-FeNi [15], nanocomposite magnets [16], and Sm-Fe-N magnets [17] have been widely studied. Recently, we reported that Mn-Sn-Co alloys show a high coercivity ($\mu_0 H_{cJ}$ = 1.59 T) comparable to that of rare earth magnets, after heat treatment in a nitrogen atmosphere [3][4]. In the present paper, the relationship between heat treatment and magnetic properties is discussed.

3.2. Experimental procedure

The $Mn_{82.5}Sn_{10}Co_{7.5}$ (at %) alloy was prepared by arc melting. The alloy was homogenized at 1050 °C for 20 h in Ar, and crushed into particles with a size of 500–850 μm. The alloy particles were annealed at 950 °C for 1–20 h in N_2 and then quenched to room temperature (first nitriding). Subsequently, the alloy

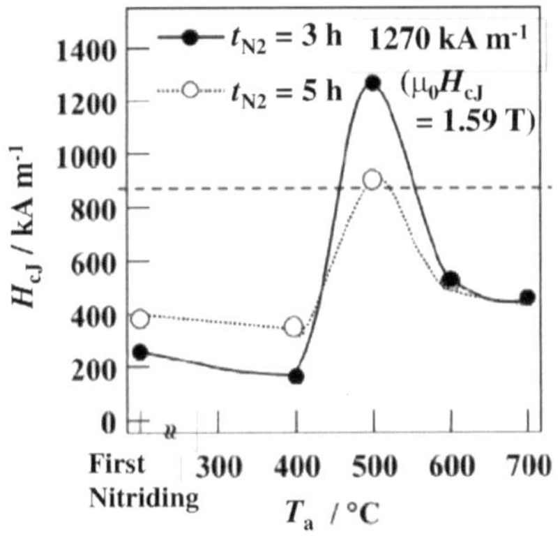

Fig. 6. Dependence of the coercivity on the second nitriding temperature (t_{N2}) for the $Mn_{82.5}Sn_{10}Co_{7.5}$ alloy.

was annealed at 400–700 °C for 5 h in N_2 and then quenched to room temperature (second nitriding). The magnetic properties were measured with a VSM and the phases were identified by XRD. The microstructure was observed by SEM.

3.3. Result and discussion

Figure 6 shows the dependence of the coercivity on the second nitriding temperature for the $Mn_{82.5}Sn_{10}Co_{7.5}$ alloy annealed during the first nitriding for 3 or 5 h. The coercivity strongly depended on the second nitriding temperature. The sample that showed the highest coercivity of 1.59 T (1270 kA m^{-1}) underwent the second nitriding at 500 °C.

Figure 7 shows the XRD patterns of the $Mn_{82.5}Sn_{10}Co_{7.5}$ alloys after homogenization, first nitriding for 3 h, and second nitriding at 400–700 °C for 5 h. The homogenized alloy consisted of a β-Mn phase. In the XRD pattern after the first nitriding, the main peaks of the ζ (or ζ') phase in the Mn-N system, and small peaks corresponding to β-Mn were observed. However, the peaks of the ζ (or ζ') phase

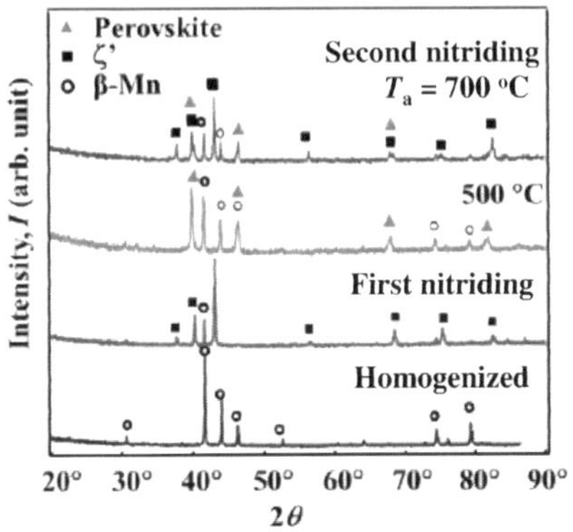

Fig. 7. XRD patterns of $Mn_{82.5}Sn_{10}Co_{7.5}$ alloys after homogenization. First nitriding for 3 h and second nitriding at 400–700 °C for 5 h.

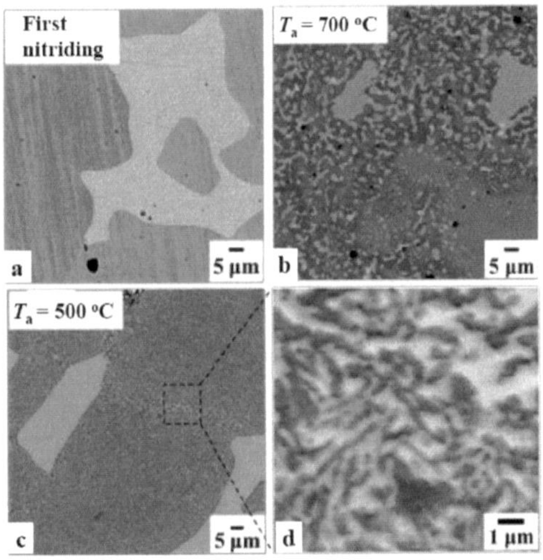

Fig. 8. BSE images of $Mn_{82.5}Sn_{10}Co_{7.5}$ alloys after (a) first nitriding at 900 °C for 3 h in N_2, and after second nitriding for 5 h in N_2 at (b) 700 and (c) 500 °C. (d) Magnified section of (c).

disappeared and peaks of perovskite (Mn_4N-like) and β-Mn phases were present in the sample that underwent the second nitriding at 500 °C. This indicates that the phase transformation of ζ' into the perovskite and β-Mn phases occurred during the second nitriding at 500 °C.

Microstructural changes during the second nitriding were also observed by SEM. Figure 8 shows the BSE images of $Mn_{82.5}Sn_{10}Co_{7.5}$ alloys at the following stages after the first nitriding at 900 °C for 3 h in N_2 and the subsequent second nitriding at 500 or 700 °C for 5 h. The sample subjected to the second nitriding at 500 °C (Fig. 8(c)) or 700 °C (Fig. 8(b)), show a two-phase structure with white and gray contrast. Based on the XRD analysis results in Fig. 7, these two phases were a perovskite phase and a β-Mn phase. The two-phase structure of the sample after the second nitriding at 500 °C was finer that that at 700 °C. Figure 8(d) shows a magnification of a section of Fig. 8(c). Considering that the highest coercivity was obtained after the second nitriding at 500 °C, the formation of the fine two-phase microstructure may be closely related to the increased coercivity of the Mn-Sn-Co-N alloy.

Acknowledgement

This study was supported by the "Future Pioneering Projects/Development of magnetic material technology for high-efficiency motors" from the Ministry of Economy, Trade and Industry, by Japan CREST project (Core Research for Evolutionary Science and Technology) in JST (Japan Science and Technology Agency), and by a JSPS KAKENHI, Grant-in-Aid for JSPS Fellows, 255050.

References

[1] M. Nakamura, M. Matsuura, N. Tezuka, S. Sugimoto, Y. Une, H. Kubo, M. Sagawa, *Appl. Phys. Lett.*, 2013, 103, 022404-1.

[2] K. Isogai, K.Shinaji, T. Mase, M. Matsuura, N. Tezuka, S. Sugimoto, *Mater. Trans.*, 2013, 54, 1236.

[3] K. Sinaji, T. Mase, K. Isogai, M. Matsuura, N. Tezuka, S. Sugimoto, *Mater. Trans.*, 2013, 54, 2007.

[4] M. Sagawa, Y. Une, *Proc. 20th Int. Workshop on Rare Earth Permanent Magnet & their Applications*, 2008, 103.

[5] T. Hattori, H. Ishihara, S. Sugimoto, R. Goto, N. Tezuka, Y. Une, M. Sagawa, *Mater. Trans.*, 2009, 50, 2347.

[6] R. Goto, S. Nishio, M. Matsuura, N. Tezuka, S. Sugimoto, *IEEE Trans. Magn.*, 2008, 44, 4232.

[7] T. Hattori, N. Fukamachi, R. Goto, N. Tezuka, S. Sugimoto, *Mater. Trans.*, 2009, 50, 479.

[8] Y. Une, M. Sagawa, *J. Jpn. Inst. Met.*, 2012, 76, 12 (in Japanese).

[9] S. Sugimoto, *Proc. of the 20th International Workshop on Rare Earth Permanent Magnets and Their Applications*, 2008, 106.

[10] T. Fukada, M. Matsuura, R. Goto, N. Tezuka, S. Sugimoto, Y. Une, M. Sagawa, *Mater. Trans.*, 2012, 53, 1967.

[11] T. Takeshita, R. Nakamura, *Proc. of the 10th International Workshop on Rare Earth Magnets and Their Applications*, 1989, 1, 551.

[12] K. Hono, H. Sepehri-Amin, *Scr. Mater., 2012,* 67, 530.

[13] I. R. Harris, P. J. McGuiness, *J. Less-Common Met.*, 1991, 172–174, 1273.

[14] T. K. Kim, M. Takahashi, *Appl. Phys. Lett.*, 1972, 20, 492.

[15] T. Shima, M. Okamura, S. Mitani, K. Takanashi, *J. Magn. Magn. Mater.*, 2007, 310, 2213-2214.

[16] E. F. Kneller, R. Hawig, *IEEE Trans. Magn.,* 1991, 27, 3588.

[17] J. M. D. Coey, H. Sun, *J. Magn. Magn. Mater.*, 1990, 87, L251.

Recent Developments in $Sm(Co,Cu,Fe,Zr)_z$ Magnets

J.F. LIU, M. MARINESCU
Electron Energy Corporation, 924 Links Ave, Landisville, PA 17538, USA

Abstract: *For applications requiring both high density of magnetic energy and thermal stability, the permanent magnets of choice are $Sm(Co,Cu,Fe,Zr)_z$ magnets. Other advantages include better corrosion resistance and relative abundance of Sm as compared to Dy, which is required for most of the Nd-Fe-B magnets. To satisfy various applications, different $Sm(Co,Cu,Fe,Zr)_z$ magnet grades have been developed over the years, including high $(BH)_{max}$ grade with 31- 33 MGOe, high temperature grades with operating temperature up to 550 °C, and temperature compensated grades with a reversible temperature coefficient of B_r, α = -0.001 %/°C. Many current applications of these magnets would be well-served by advancements in the properties of the $Sm(Co,Cu,Fe,Zr)_z$ materials. These possible advancements, which also make the points of discussion for this paper, are: (1) an increase of B_r and $(BH)_{max}$ in high energy product magnet grade; (2) an increase of $(BH)_{max}$ in temperature compensated grades; (3) thermal and structural stability in vacuum; (3) an increase of electrical resistivity to reduce eddy current losses; (4) an improvement of mechanical properties.*

Keywords: permanent magnets, $Sm(Co,Fe,Cu,Zr)_z$, 0TC, thermal stability, thermal stability in vacuum, electrical resistivity, mechanical properties.

Address: Jinfang Liu, Electron Energy Corporation, 924 Links Ave, Landisville, PA 17538, USA; tel: 717 898 2294; fax: 717 898 0660; liu@electronenergy.com

$Sm(Co,Fe,Cu,Zr)_z$ magnets with high maximum energy product

Sm-Co magnets with higher residual induction, B_r, and maximum energy product, $(BH)_{max}$, would be of great benefit for many applications such as motors, generators, actuators, isolators, circulators, accelerometers and other magnetic devices. Because of supply chain risk of Nd and Dy and high temperature stability issues related to Nd-Fe-B magnets, $Sm(Co,Fe,Cu,Zr)_z$, magnets can be a very good viable alternative for many applications with operating temperatures above 150 °C. Currently, the performance of Nd-Dy-Fe-B at temperatures up to 150 °C is superior, and, as long as the market still permits, and with the development of new grain boundary engineering technology that minimizes the needed amount of Dy for high temperature operation, these magnets will dominate their respective applications area. However, for applications at temperatures as high as 200 °C , the addition of large amounts of Dy is required for Nd-Fe-B magnets, which significantly reduces the magnetic properties and makes them fairly expensive. $Sm(Co,Fe,Cu,Zr)_z$ magnets then become the best option. Table 1 shows a direct comparison between the magnetic hysteresis parameters of Nd-Dy-Fe-B and $Sm(Co,Fe,Cu,Zr)_z$ magnet grades with operating temperatures above 200 °C.

The highest $Sm(Co,Fe,Cu,Zr)_z$ magnet grade commercially available has a $(BH)_{max}$ = 31- 33 MGOe, B_r = 11.5- 11.7 kG and H_{ci} > 25 kOe (at room temperature) and can operate up to 250 °C. These magnets can actually still operate above this temperature, but a knee appears in the second quadrant of the hysteresis loop. The hysteresis parameters of these magnets at 250 °C are: $(BH)_{max}$ = 25.4 MGOe, B_r = 10.5 kG and H_{ci} = 10.3 kOe.

Table 1. *Comparison of the magnetic properties of sintered Nd-Fe-B and Sm-Co magnets at 25 °C and elevated temperatures.*

	B_r (kG)			H_{ci} (kOe)			$(BH)_{max}$ (MGOe)		
Temperature(°C)	25	200	240 - 250	25	200	240 - 250	25	200	240 - 250
Nd-Fe-B*	10.8	9.0	8.0	>30	7.0	4.0	28	< 20	< 16
Sm-Co**	11.5	10.7	10.5	>25	13.1	10.3	31.3	26.7	25.4

* The properties at 200 °C are of NEOMAX-28EH (NEOMAX Co., Ltd., Japan), T_{op} = 200 °C. The properties at 240 °C are of VACODYM 688AP (VACUUMSCHMELZE GmbH, Germany)
** The properties at 25, 200, and 250 °C are of EEC 2:17-31 (Electron Energy Corporation, U.S.A)

High magnetization and high $(BH)_{max}$ values in $Sm(Co,Fe,Cu,Zr)_z$ magnets, can be achieved via compositional optimization and development of a defect-free cellular micro structure by thermal treatments [1]. In this case, the most important element is Fe, located in the interior of the cells with the rhombohedral 2:17 structure. The saturation magnetization $4\pi M_s$ of the rhombohedral Sm_2Co_{17} phase is about 12 kG. With the addition of Fe, the saturation magnetization increases to about 13.5 kG for $Sm_2(Co_{0.8}Fe_{0.2})_{17}$ and reaches a maximum of $4\pi M_s$ = 16.3 kG for the $Sm_2(Co_{0.3}Fe_{0.7})_{17}$ compound [2]. On the other hand, when Fe doping in $Sm(Co,Fe,Cu,Zr)_z$ magnets is more than 25wt%, the cell size increases too much, beyond 150- 180 nm and the cellular structure becomes inhomogeneous, which in turn results in a decreased coercivity and poor squareness of the demagnetization curve.

Recent reports [3] suggest that morphology related issues in magnets with increased Fe content can be addressed by an added thermal treatment segment in the already complicated sintering-solution treatment – aging protocol. This 'pre-aging' extra treatment at a temperature below the regular aging temperature is shown to help with the formation of a finer cell microstructure, which in turn is beneficial for achieving a better squareness of the demagnetization curve. Thus, magnets with a composition of $Sm(Co_{bal}.Fe_{0.35}Cu_{0.06}Zr_{0.02})_{7.8}$ containing about 25.04 wt% of Fe, reached the following magnetic properties: $4\pi M_r$ = 12.4 kG, H_{ci} = 18.7 kOe and $(BH)_{max}$ = 33.4 MGOe. For comparison, the non 'pre-aged' magnets, although they had the same remanent magnetization, reached only $(BH)_{max}$ = 31.5 MGOe.

The criticality of the thermal treatment segments, as well as the compositional homogeneity of the precursor material was proven by our work, too. Figure 1 shows the demagnetization curve of a $Sm(Co,Fe,Cu,Zr)_z$ magnet block with an Fe content of about 20 wt% and a $(BH)_{max}$ of 33 MGOe. The complexity of the microstructure and its critical dependence on the process parameters make this grade of magnets somewhat difficult to fabricate. Figure 1 shows the effect of re-solution and re-aging on the intrinsic coercivity, H_{ci}, and squareness of the demagnetization curve. The H_{ci} is increased from 16.3 kOe to over 25 kOe, while H_k (the field at which the magnetization drops by 10%) is increased from 7.9 kOe to over 14.8 kOe. Higher remanence levels (e.g. $4\pi M_r$ = 12.0 kG) are accompanied by a low H_k and implicitly lower $(BH)_{max}$, as shown in Figure 1.

Pushing the limit of $(BH)_{max}$ above 33 MGOe, although seems within the reach, may take more effort to

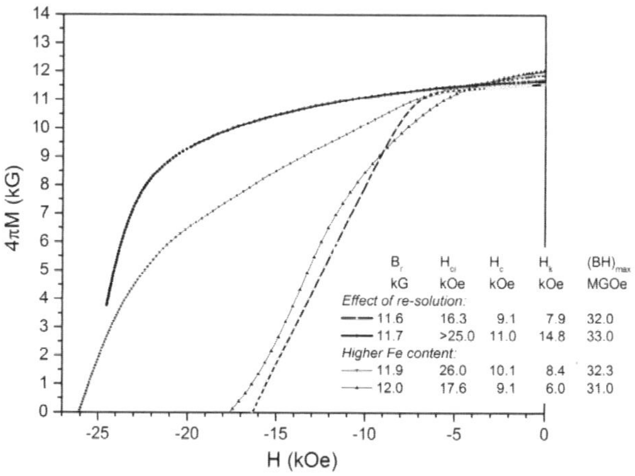

Fig. 1. Effect of Fe content enrichment and re-solution plus re-aging treatment on the demagnetization curves of $Sm(Co,Fe,Cu,Zr)_z$ magnet grades with high B_r and $(BH)_{max}$.

accomplish consistently in large scale production. From very early research [4], only 6% of the samples intended to perform above 30 MGOe reached the 33- 34 MGOe level.

The record of $(BH)_{max}$ = 36 MGOe is still held by the report in [5] for $(Sm_{0.59}Pr_{0.41})(Co_{0.68}Fe_{0.20}Cu_{0.11}Zr_{0.02})_{6.68}$ magnets, in which the substitution of Pr for Sm allowed, with an optimum thermal treatment, for an intrinsic coercivity H_{ci} = 11.2 kOe, while the reported saturation magnetization was $4\pi M_s$ = 12.4 kG.

High temperature operation of $Sm(Co,Fe,Cu,Zr)_z$ magnets in vacuum

Space applications such as high power Xe^+ ion propulsion engines (> 10 kW) utilize high temperature permanent magnets to create an axial magnetic field that extends the electron paths and increases the probability of an ionizing collision. In such applications, the temperatures could be well above 400°C in a vacuum of about 10^{-5} Torr. Moreover, a consistent magnetic field provided by these magnets is essential for the ion engines performance. The best choices for these applications are the 2:17 Sm-Co magnets with relatively high maximum energy product $(BH)_{max}$, low reversible temperature coefficient of residual induction B_r and of coercivity H_c, and linear demagnetization curves up to 550°C.

The saturation vapor pressure of Sm is of the order of 10^{-10}, 10^{-7}, 10^{-5} and 10^{-4} Torr at 300, 400, 500 and 600°C, respectively. It might be therefore expected that in a vacuum of 10^{-4} Torr and a temperature of around

600°C, the magnets might become Sm-depleted at surface over a long period of time. However, the scanning electron microscopy studies have shown that the surface of the subject magnets kept in vacuum at up to 700 °C is morphologically similar to the surface of the magnets exposed at the same temperatures in air. Figure 2 shows the existence of two layers on the surface of a $Sm(Co,Fe,Cu,Zr)_z$ magnet with listed maximum operation temperature of 400 °C (and noted as T400), kept at 550°C for 240 h in a vacuum of 10^{-5} Torr. The top layer, with a thickness of 1 μm or less, is Sm depleted and consists of Co and Fe oxides and Cu-rich precipitates (see the corresponding elemental maps in Fig. 3). The second layer with a thickness of 10- 20 μm is complex and it develops toward the magnet body through the migration of the atoms and formation of

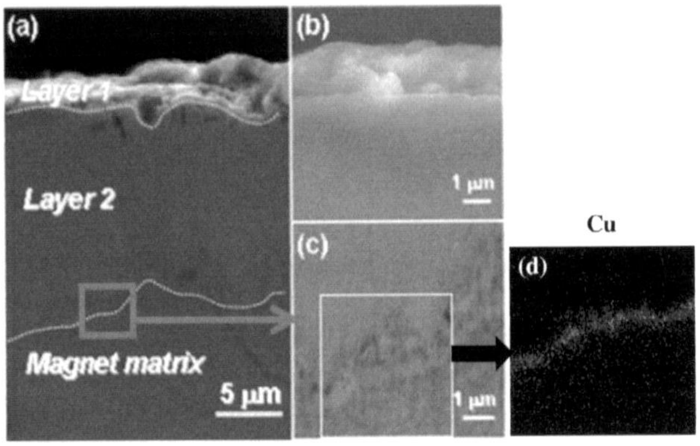

Fig. 2. (a) SEM image of a cross section in a T400 magnet exposed to 550 °C for 240 h in a vacuum of 10^{-4} Torr. (b) Top outermost layer, layer 1, of the same magnet. (c) Interface between layer 2 as shown in (a) and the magnet matrix. (d) EDX elemental mapping of Cu atomic distribution.

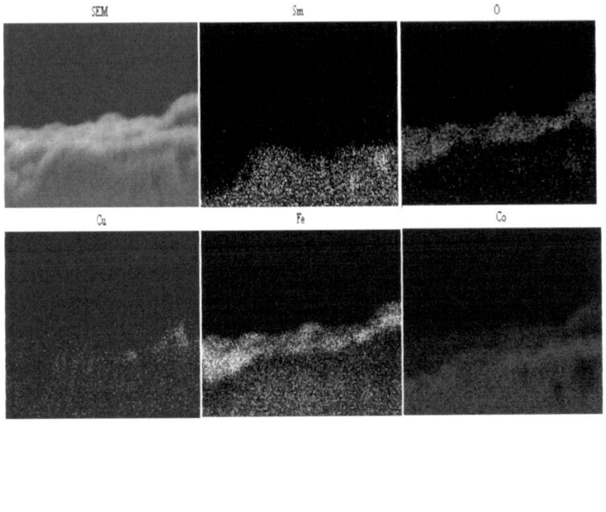

Fig. 3. EDX elemental map of layer 1 (the top outermost layer) in a T400 magnet after exposure to 550 °C for 240 h in a vacuum of 10^{-4} Torr.

(Fe, Co)-rich and Cu-rich fine regions simultaneously with oxygen penetration. Although not detected, it is natural to expect that the oxygen in this layer forms an increased amount of very fine Sm oxide. The elemental map at the interface between the second layer and the central part of the magnet is shown in Figure 2d. It should be noted that at the very edge of the interface, there is a distinct Cu-rich layer formed through the diffusion of Cu from layer 2. We could not confirm that the Cu-rich segregations are located near microcracks.

The surface alteration was similar for the magnets exposed in vacuum at 700 °C, except that the thickness of the layer 2 was larger, of about 30 μm. For lower temperatures, the second layer may not develop or may be very thin for an exposure time of 240 h. For comparison, the thickness of surface alteration due to the exposure in air at 550 °C of the same types of magnets can be as high as 550 μm. The morphology of the surface layers was found similar for all $Sm(Co,Fe,Cu,Zr)_z$ magnet specimens regardless the particular stoichiometry (or maximum operating

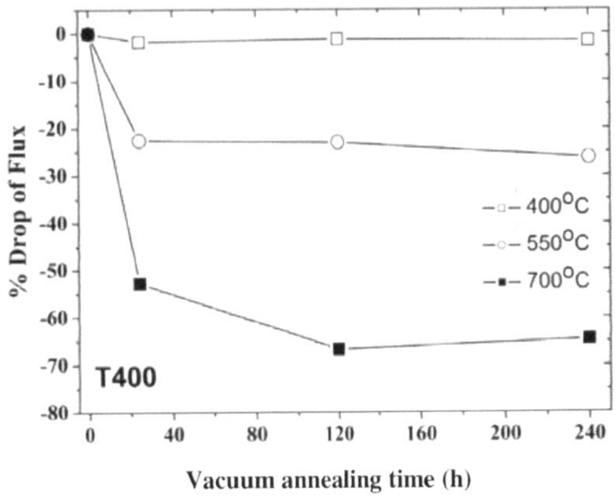

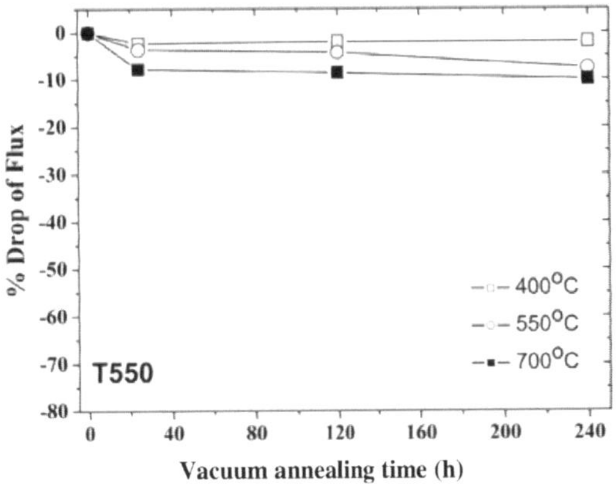

Fig. 4. Magnetic flux change versus time after exposure to various temperatures under vacuum (10^{-5} Torr) for T400, and T550 Sm-Co magnets.

temperature), when treated in vacuum under the same conditions of temperature and time.

The magnetic flux change with time at various temperatures under a vacuum of 10^{-5} Torr is shown in Figure 4 for two grades of uncoated magnets with a defined maximum operating temperature, T_M, as 400, and 550 °C, noted as T400, and T550, respectively. The magnetic flux change is very small if the magnets are only exposed to a temperature below their maximum operating temperature. In general, the maximum energy product decreases by less than 10% even at temperatures 100 °C above their specified T_M. The residual induction of T550 magnets decreases by 8.5% after the exposure to 700 °C for 240 h under vacuum. The maximum energy product at room temperature for the T550 magnet sample was $(BH)_{max}$ = 16.95 MGOe.

$Sm(Co,Fe,Cu,Zr)_z$ magnets with almost zero reversible temperature coefficient of residual induction

While the irreversible change with temperature of the magnetic flux of a permanent magnet can be avoided by thermal stabilization, the reversible part may become critical in applications that require a constant magnetic flux while the service temperature varies. The rate of the reversible change of residual induction, B_r, with temperature ΔT, is given by the relation:

$$\alpha = \frac{\Delta B_r}{B_r} \cdot \frac{1}{\Delta T} \cdot 100\% \qquad (1)$$

The typical values of the reversible temperature coefficient of B_r for the major classes of permanent magnets are α = -0.2 %/°C for ferrites, α = -0.03 to -0.02 %/°C for Alnico, α = -0.11%/°C for $Nd_2Fe_{14}B$, α = -0.04 %/°C for $SmCo_5$ and α = -0.035 %/°C for conventional Sm_2Co_{17}-type magnets. Permanent magnets with very low α over a temperature span between -50 °C and 250 °C are needed in applications such as traveling wave tubes, accelerometers, gyroscopes, especially for military and aerospace operations.

In RE-TM (TM = transition metal) compounds, when the RE is a light rare earth element (such as Sm, Nd, Pr, Ce), the magnetization decreases with increasing the temperature, whereas when the RE is a heavy rare earth element (such as Gd, Tb, Dy, Ho, Er, Tm), the magnetization has a non-monotonous trend: over specific temperature range it can increase with the temperature rise until ultimately decreasing to zero. The explanation for this behavior is that the magnetic moments of the light RE sublattice couples parallel to

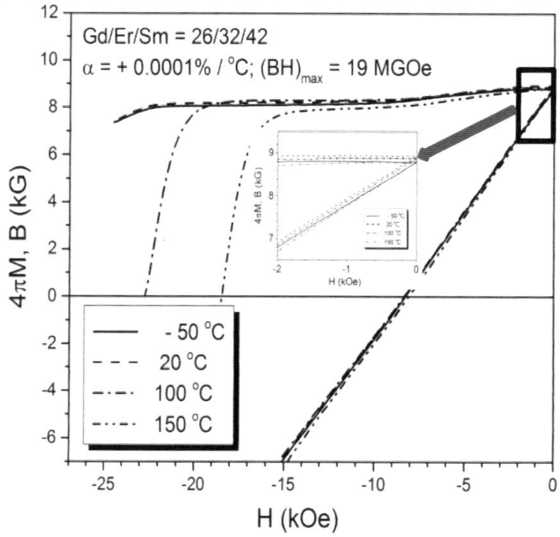

Fig. 5. Demagnetization curves at different temperatures for temperature compensated $(Sm,Gd,Er)(Co,Fe,Cu,Zr)_z$ magnets with $(BH)_{max}$ = 19 MGOe.

those of the TM sublattice, while for the heavy RE atoms, the coupling is antiparallel. Therefore, by combining the two effects, it is possible, within a certain temperature range, to achieve a near-zero reversible temperature coefficient of residual induction.

Most of the pioneering work in this area was done a few decades ago and the research activities seemed to cease about ten years ago. Singular partial substitutions of Sm by Gd , Er , (Ho, Tm, Dy, Tb) were reported to provide α values on the order of tens of ppm/°C for particular temperature ranges, with reasonable to good values of maximum energy products [6]. However, most of the optimally compensated magnets with a high $(BH)_{max}$ had a low H_k, which constrains their practical use.

Fully temperature-compensated magnets are doped with Gd and have α ~ -0.001%/°C in the temperature range of -50 °C to 150 °C and $(BH)_{max}$ = 16 MGOe at room temperature. An increase of $(BH)_{max}$ up to 18 MGOe can be achieved by shifting the Sm/Gd ratio towards more Sm content, which has in turn an adverse effect on α that increases up to -0.02 %/°C.

We report here that a low, positive α and a very good magnetic performance, $(BH)_{max}$ = 19 MGOe, can be obtained with a certain mixed Er and Gd substitution for Sm and an optimum heat treatment protocol. The reversible temperature coefficient of B_r in the temperature range of -50 °C to 150 °C, calculated from close circuit magnetic measurements of B_r, was α = 0.0001 %/°C (Fig. 5).

Sequentially laminated Sm(Co,Fe,Cu,Zr)$_z$ magnets with increased electrical resistivity

Finite element analysis [7] showed that for a single-phase permanent magnet brushless DC motor, the eddy current loss in the permanent magnets can be reduced from 75 W to 23 W by segmenting the rotor ring magnet into 8 segments.

We have developed a method to produce sequentially laminated Sm(Co,Fe,Cu,Zr)$_z$ / dielectric magnets with the direction of magnetization parallel to the dielectric layer plane. The magnetic, electric and mechanical properties of these laminated magnets critically depend on the dielectric material and dielectric layer thickness. The optimum dielectric thickness was found to be less than 100 µm to prevent layer discontinuity.

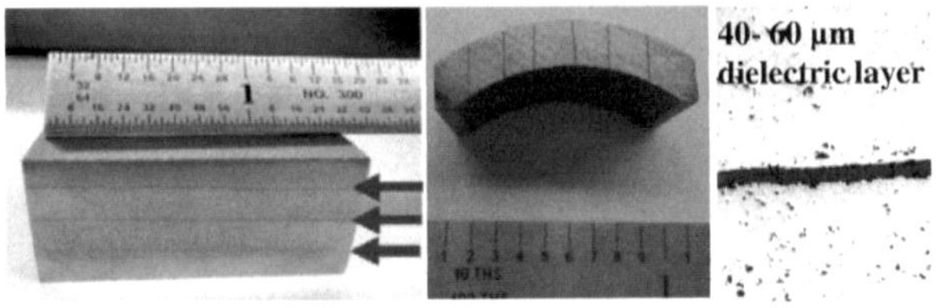

Fig. 6. Sequentially laminated Sm(Co,Fe,Cu,Zr)$_z$/dielectric sintered magnets and the typical thickness of the dielectric layer.

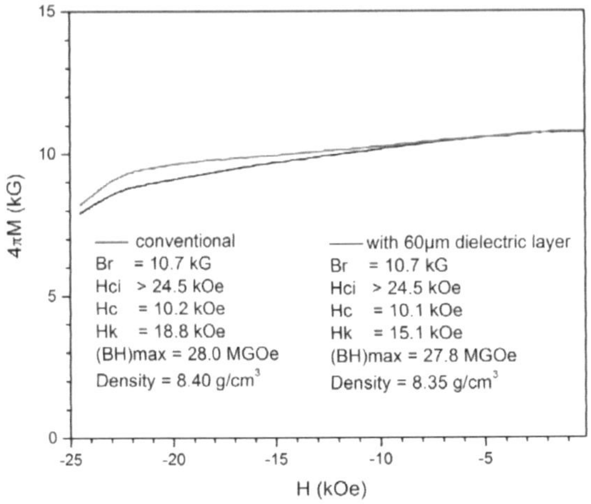

Fig. 7. Demagnetization curves and magnetic properties of Sm(Co,Fe,Cu,Zr)$_z$/dielectric sintered magnets compared to the conventional counterparts.

The fabrication method involves spraying a colloidal dielectric solution onto layers of pressed Sm(Co,Fe,Cu,Zr)$_z$ magnet powder. Fig. 6 shows sequentially laminated Sm(Co,Fe,Cu,Zr)$_z$ / dielectric magnets in form of blocks or arcs having a dielectric layer thickness of 40- 60 µm. The magnetic hysteresis parameters of Sm(Co,Fe,Cu,Zr)$_z$ /dieletric magnets do

Table 2 Electrical resistivity and room-temperature mechanical properties of Sm(Co,Fe,Cu,Zr)$_z$/dielectric sintered magnets.

	Break force	Resistivity
Conventional Sm(Co,Fe,Cu,Zr)$_z$	44.5 lb	50- 70 µΩ·cm
Seq. laminated Sm(Co,Fe,Cu,Zr)$_z$/dielectric (40- 60 µm)	38.2 lb	No overall electrical conductivity

not deteriorate compared to conventional Sm(Co,Fe,Cu,Zr)$_z$ counterparts (Fig. 7) and their overall electrical resistance can be in the range of hundreds of ohms to infinite, basically showing complete electrical insulation (Table 2).

When subjected to the 3-point break test, the Sm(Co,Fe,Cu,Zr)$_z$ /dieletric magnets with a dielectric layer thickness less than 100 µm, shown acceptable mechanical strength, with a break force at an 85% level compared to the monolithic sintered magnets with the same composition (Table 2)

Mechanical properties of Sm(Co,Fe,Cu,Zr)$_z$ magnets

It is well know that Sm(Co,Fe,Cu,Zr)$_z$ sintered permanent magnets have a high-risk of mechanical failure when subjected to mechanical stress such as vibration and mechanical shock. These magnets can only be shaped by grinding, lapping, and electric discharge machining (EDM), which often result in chipping, cracking and fracture, with material losses ranging from 5% to 20%. Fig. 8 shows a low fracture toughness for anisotropic sintered RE magnets that exhibit the best $(BH)_{max}$. Permanent magnets in the

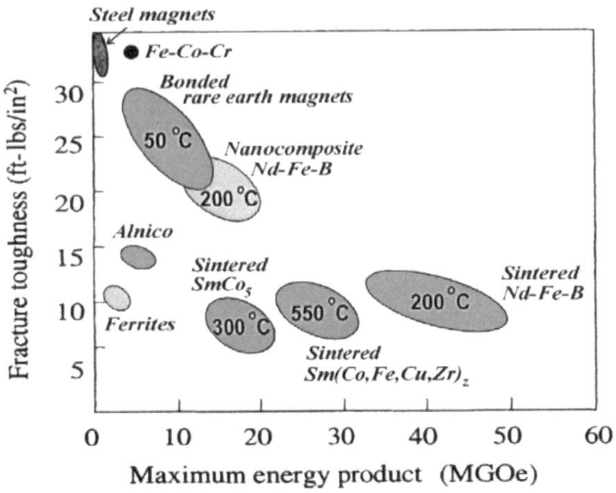

Fig. 8. $(BH)_{max}$ and fracture toughness of the most common types of permanent magnets. For magnets with $(BH)_{max}$ greater than 10 MGOe, the maximum operating temperatures are also shown.

Table 3 Room-temperature Vicker's hardness for $Sm(Co,Fe,Cu,Zr)_z$ magnets. For comparison a Rockwell hardness of 60 C is a equivalent to a Vicker's hardness of 700.

$Sm(Co,Fe,Cu,Zr)_z$ magnet grade	Average (HV)	Stdev (HV)
High $(BH)_{max}$	771.13	38
$T_{max} = 400^oC$	806.3	53
$T_{max} = 550^oC$	786.3	55
Fully compensated 0TC	722.7	37

magnetized state have lower toughness in the transverse direction. Suppliers of $Sm(Co,Fe,Cu,Zr)_z$ magnets provide the room temperature mechanical properties, but, due to the experimental difficulties, not much data exists yet for mechanical properties at higher temperatures, at which the magnets actually operate. For sintered $Sm(Co,Fe,Cu,Zr)_{7.4}$ magnets, it was reported [8] that the fracture toughness, K_{IC}, values increase from 2 - 3 MPa $m^{1/2}$ at the room temperature to 3 - 5 MPa $m^{1/2}$ at 500 ^oC.

Table 3 shows the room-temperature Vicker's hardness for $Sm(Co,Fe,Cu,Zr)_z$ magnets, which are higher than the catalog values reported by others. The typical trend of hardness which should increase with decreasing grainsize was not confirmed by our results, suggesting that the mechanical hardness behavior is more complex in this type of materials.

References

[1] O. Gutfleisch, High temperature samarium cobalt permanent magnets, Nanoscale Magnetic Materials and Applications, ed. J.P. Liu et al., Springer Science+Business Media, LLC 2009, p. 337.

[2] A. E. Ray and K. J. Strnat, Research and development of rare earth – transition metal alloys as permanent magnet materials, *Technical Report AFML-TR-72-202*, 1972

[3] Y. Horiuchi et al., *Materials Transactions*, **55**, 3, 2014, 482

[4] S. Liu and A. E. Ray, *IEEE Trans. Magn.*, **25**, 5, 1989, 3785

[5] G. V. Ivanova, et al., *Phys. Met., Metall.*, **59**, 6, 1985, 64

[6] C. H. Chen et al., J. Appl. Phys., **91**, 10, 2002, 8483

[7] Y. Chen, Z. Q. Zhu, Y. Chen, D. Howe, J.H. Gliemann, Industry Applications Conference, 42nd IAS Annual Meeting, *IEEE*, **23-27** , 2007, 537.

[8] L. Ren, G.C. Hadjipanayis, A. Parvizi-Majidi, *J. Magn. Magn. Mater.*, **257**, 2003, 58.

Recent Developments with Melt-Spun NdFeB for Permanent Magnet Applications

DAVID N. BROWN[1], LIM YONG KEAT[1], ZHAO WEI[1], HE FENG[2], JAMES W. HERCHENROEDER[3]
[1]Magnequench Technology Centre, 01-19 The Galen, 61 Science Park Road, Singapore 117525
[2]Magnequench (Tianjin) Co. Ltd., 19 Quanzhou Rd, Wuqing Development Area, Tianjin, China, 301700
[3]Magnequench International, Inc., 237 S. Pendleton Ave, Pendleton, IN 46064, USA

Abstract: *Melt-spun Nd-Fe-B powders can be net-shape formed into a variety of shapes for a range of permanent magnet applications. The melt-spinning process produces flake powder with a fine, uniform array of nano-scale $Nd_2Fe_{14}B$ grains. These powders are then either formed into isotropic polymer-bonded magnets or hot formed into fully dense magnets. This paper discusses the critical factors affecting the success of melt spun Nd-Fe-B material in applications. Requirements such as high remanence, thermal stability and low cost are being addressed by the development of anisotropic powder, special compositions for higher density bonded magnets, nano-scale protective powder coatings and lower cost alloy compositions.*

Keywords: *Nd-Fe-B; bonded magnets; nanocrystalline; melt-spinning*

Address: James W. Herchenroeder, Magnequench International, Inc., 237 S. Pendleton Ave., Pendleton, IN 46064, USA, Tel.: 859 734 9345, E-Mail: jim.herchenroeder@molycorp.com

1. Introduction

The majority of commercial Nd-Fe-B permanent magnets are produced by sintering [1] and melt-spinning techniques [2], with sintered Nd-Fe-B representing about 90% of the total rare-earth permanent magnet market. Sintered and hot deformed melt-spun Nd-Fe-B magnets exhibit the highest magnetic performance due to their strong crystallographic alignment. Meanwhile most bonded Nd-Fe-B are isotropic and offer advantages in ease of manufacture and ability to be formed into complex magnet shapes.

The Nd-Fe-B magnet market has enjoyed significant growth over recent years and is expected to continue to grow with increasing demand from the burgeoning clean technology sector, with new applications in electric vehicles and wind turbines. The entire Nd-Fe-B magnet market is currently about 60,000 ton/year and bonded melt-spun magnets represent about 6,000-8,000 ton/year of this total. Figure 1 illustrates melt-spun Nd-Fe-B bonded magnet applications and their respective market segments.

There are many factors that govern the suitability of a permanent magnet for a particular application.

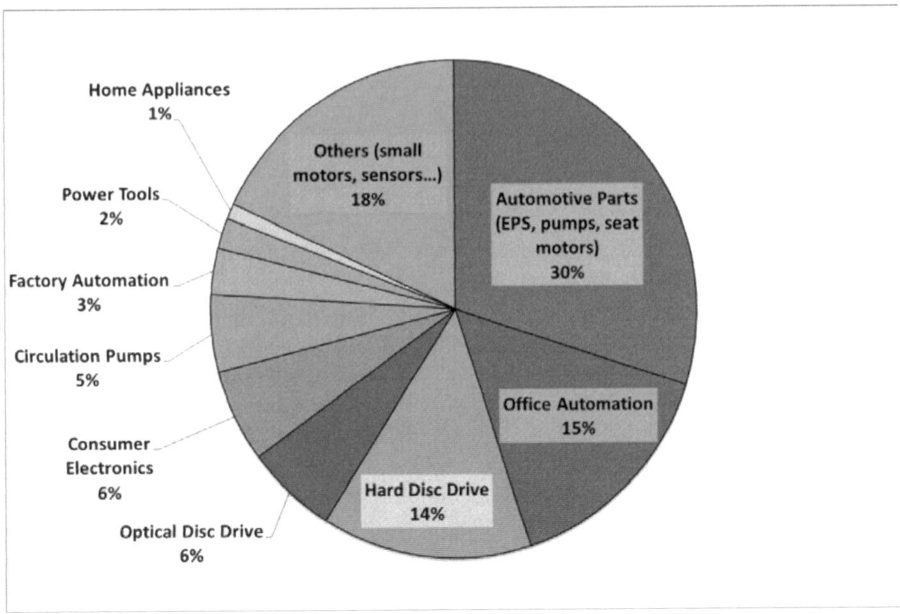

Fig. 1. Applications of bonded melt-spun Nd-Fe-B permanent magnets.

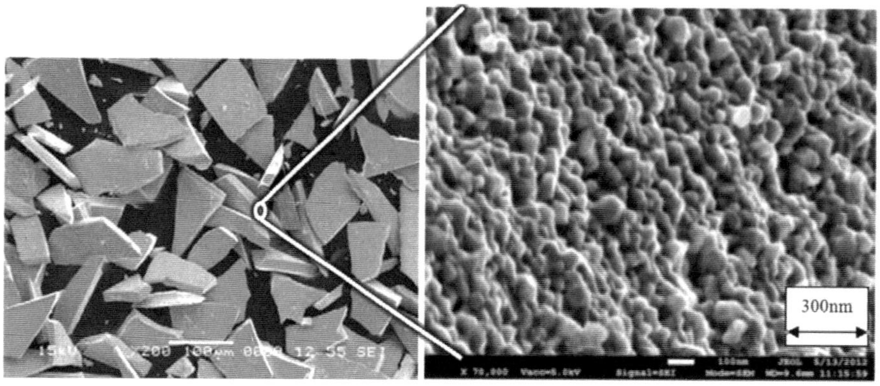

Fig. 2. Melt-spun Nd-Fe-B flakes and internal grain structure revealed on fracture surface of a flake.

Traditionally, high remanence (B_r) and maximum energy product [$(BH)_{max}$] have been priorities. However, enhanced intrinsic coercivity (H_{ci}), good thermal stability and low alloy cost have become increasingly important. This article will discuss how a melt-spun Nd-Fe-B powder supplier is addressing these concerns.

2. Melt Spun Nd-Fe-B Powder and Magnets

Melt spinning is the process of pouring a stream of molten alloy on to a high-speed rotating quench wheel. The alloy solidifies at 10^6 °C/second and forms an amorphous or nanocrystalline microstructure. The rapidly quenched alloy forms ~30 μm thick flakes, which are mechanically brittle, chemically stable and crystallographically isotropic. Figure 2 shows SEM images of melt-spun flakes and the $Nd_2Fe_{14}B$ grain structure revealed on the fractured surface of an individual flake. These $Nd_2Fe_{14}B$ grains are randomly oriented and approximately 50 nm in diameter.

3. Isotropic Polymer Bonded Magnets

Most applications of melt-spun Nd-Fe-B powder are in the form of isotropic polymer-bonded magnets with $(BH)_{max}$ values between 5 and 10 MGOe. These are typically cured compacts of between 60 and 80 vol. % Nd-Fe-B powder in an epoxy- or nylon-based resin. These magnets can be net-shape formed into intricate parts, like thin-walled rings for spindle motors in drive systems. Bonded Nd-Fe-B magnets are significantly stronger than sintered ferrite magnets [$(BH)_{max} \leq 4$ MGOe] but weaker than sintered Nd-Fe-B magnets [$(BH)_{max} > 35$ MGOe]. Therefore, if this material is to compete with the high flux density of sintered Nd-Fe-B magnets, it needs to be fully densified by hot pressing and crystallographically oriented by hot deformation processes.

4. Development Areas with Bonded Nd-Fe-B Magnets

Current developments within the bonded Nd-Fe-B business tend to eveolve around teh themes of lower cost, higher perfromance and improved thermal stability.

4.1. Lower cost polymer bonded magnets

The problems of rare earth supply and cost seen in 2011/12 have been addressed in a number of ways.

4.1.1. Alternative supply of rare earth elements

With the reopenning of the Molycorp mine in Mountain Pass and Molycorp's acquistion of Magnequench, the bonded Nd-Fe-B industry has moved toward a position of greater reliability and diversity of supply, increased security of supply chains and better price predictability.

4.1.2. Use of lower cost chemistries

Rare earth elements like Ce and La are relatively abundant compared to Nd and Pr. Therefore, these elements tend to be lower cost and less vulnerable to price fluctuations. On the downside, substituting Ce and La for the rare earth component in Nd-Fe-B tends to reduce the magnetic performance. However, a new range of melt-spun powders are available for magnetic applications where low cost is critical.

Figure 3 and Table 1 illustrate the range in magnetic performance for (Nd,La,Ce)-Fe-B melt-spun powders with various Ce and La substitutions.

Figure 4 illustrates the decline in magnet remanence with increasing amounts of cerium substituted for Nd in the melt-spun powder.

4.2. Higher performance Nd-Fe-B bonded magnets

4.2.1 Anisotropic polymer bonded magnets

In an effort to address the need for higher flux density in bonded magnets Magnequench has developed a range of anisotropic powders with energy products between 36 and 38 MGOe. Anisotropic powder is produced from melt spun material by hot pressing and

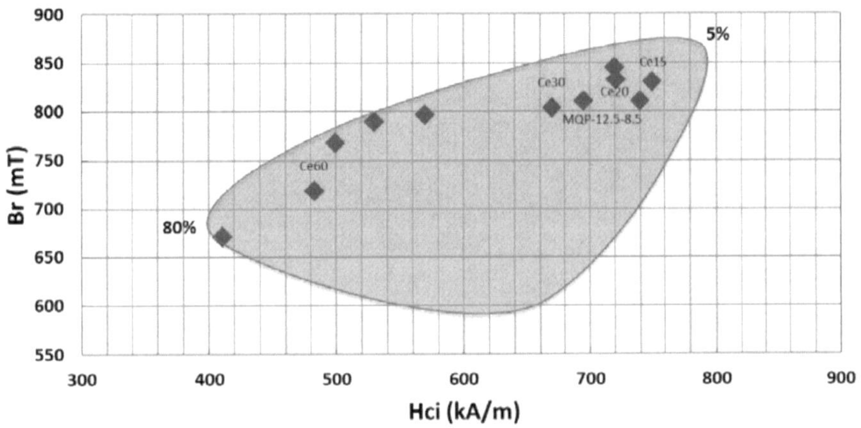

Fig. 3. Range in magnetic performance of lower cost (Nd,Ce,La)-Fe-B powders.

Table 1. Magnetic properties of melt-spun powder and bonded magnets with different levels of Ce and La substitution.

Amount of Ce/La	Powder			Magnet (PC = 2)		
	B_r (mT)	H_{ci} (kA/m)	$(BH)_{max}$ (kJ/m^3)	B_r (kG)	H_{ci} (kOe)	$(BH)_{max}$ (MGOe)
0%	873	869	123	6.92	10.29	9.13
5%	857	838	117	6.8	9.91	8.80
10%	843	851	114	6.69	10.00	8.50
15%	829	777	107	6.58	9.13	8.10
20%	815	710	101	6.51	8.51	7.82
30%	800	661	97	6.39	7.91	7.45
40%	769	580	85	6.22	6.88	6.83
50%	751	549	81	6.08	6.51	6.50
60%	718	483	71	5.84	5.71	5.80
80%	671	411	63	5.43	5.03	5.42
80%	599	663	54	4.74	7.84	4.11

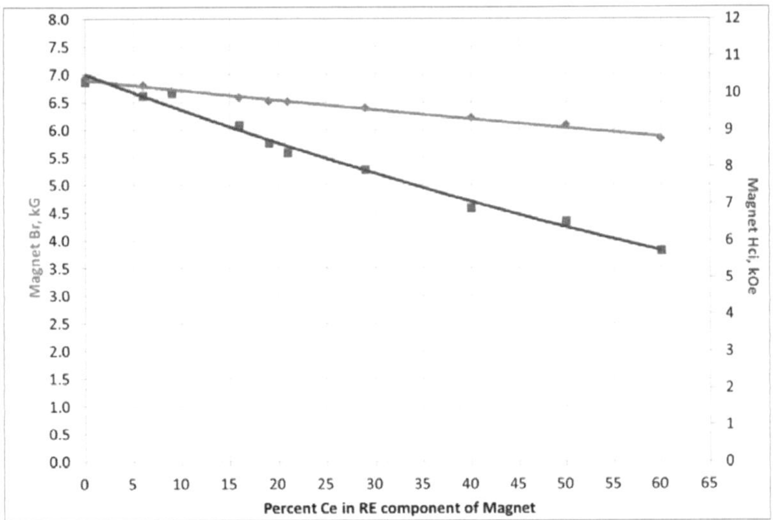

Fig. 4. Effect of using progressive amounts of cerium on the remanence of bonded (Nd,Ce)-Fe-B magnets.

die-upsetting compacts of the flake. The rare earth content needs to be between 28 and 32 wt.% to facilitate the liquid grain boundary deformation mechanism [3]. The grain structure within the material becomes textured during the hot deformation, as illustrated in Figure 5. At low magnification, on the left side, the original melt-spun flake structure can be seen in a flattened, elongated form, flowing perpendi-

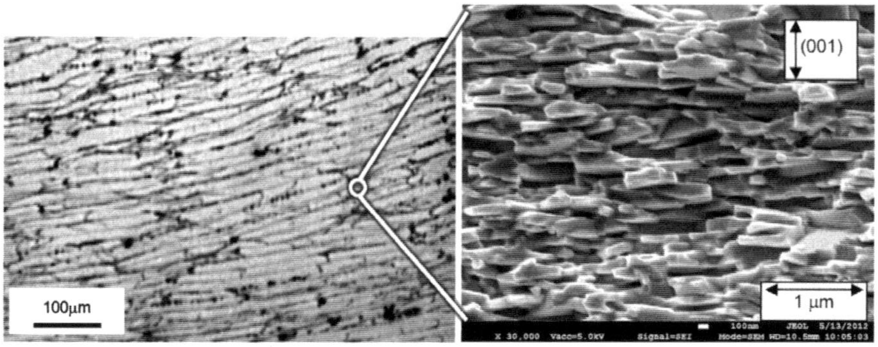

Fig. 5. Hot deformed magnet microstructure, showing elongated flake structure on left and an intergranular fracture surface on right side.

cular to the force direction. Fracture surfaces can reveal the individual $Nd_2Fe_{14}B$ grains at higher magnification (right side). These $Nd_2Fe_{14}B$ grains appear as 50 x 500 x 500 nm platelets having grown in their (010) and (100) orientations, resulting in the magnetically preferred orientation (001) being aligned perpendicular to the grain-growth direction.

The deformed compacts are crushed to a desired particle size (< 400 μm), mixed with a polymer and pressed into anisotropic bonded magnets. Maintaining particle alignment requires an external magnetic field while pressing anisotropic bonded magnets, which make the process more complicated than pressing conventional isotropic magnets. However, these magnets have the potential to offer higher energy product and remanence than isotropic materials. The performance of four grades of anisotropic powder is detailed in Table 2 and Figure 6. Demagnetization curves of the anisotropic bonded magnets are illustrated in Figure 7. There are challenges to achieving full powder alignment in high density

Table 2. Anisotropic powder properties.

		MQA-37-11	MQA-38-14	MQA-37-16	MQA-36-18
B_r	mT	1300	1310	1290	1240
	kG	13	13.1	12.9	12.4
$(BH)_{max}$	kJ/m^3	290	300	295	285
	MGOe	36.5	38	37	36
H_c	kA/m	955	1120	1270	1430
	kOe	12	14	16	18

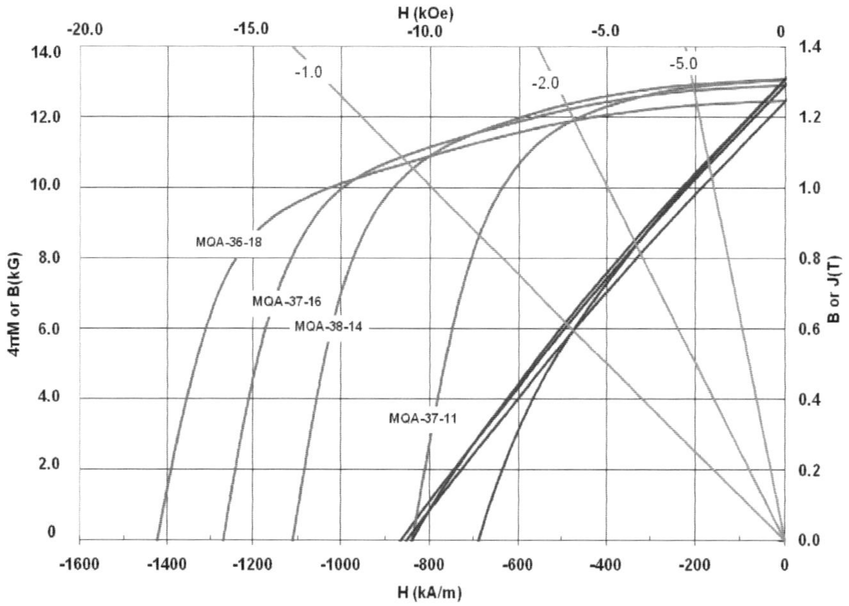

Fig. 6. Illustration of the demagnetization curves of anisotropic powders.

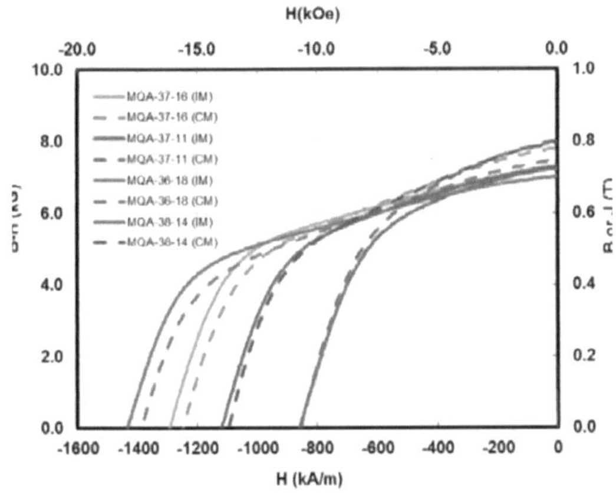

Fig. 7. Illustration of the demagnetization curves of magnets made from anisotropic powders.

compression molded magnets (CM), however injection molded magnets (IM) can readily achieve full alignment of the anisotropic Nd-Fe-B powder.

4.2.2. Melt-spun HD powder for higher density polymer bonded magnets

Melt-spun HD powder can be pressed into higher density bonded magnets than traditional melt-spun powders, and therefore can exhibit superior performance in the magnet form. These HD powders also offer lower spring-back and require lower ejection forces in the magnet making operation. The magnetic properties of these types of powder and their magnets are detailed in Table 3. The magnet remanence will increase proportionally with magnet density. Spring-back is a term that discribes the increase in compact dimensions between being compressed and being released from the mould. Larger spring-back percentages in the compact dimensions are generally a detrimental factor. Figure 8 plots the radial spring-back percentage observed when compression moulding MQP-B+ and MQP-15-9HD at pressures between 500 and 1000 MPa. For each compaction pressure less spring-back occured with the MQP-15-9HD. These MQP-15-9HD compact were also more dense.

4.3. Improving thermal stability of polymer bonded magnets

To limit the oxidation of melt spun NdFeB powder at elevated temperatures a nano-scale protective coating has been developed. Once the melt-spun powder has been crushed to a desired size (say <100 μm) it can then be surface treated with an anti-ageing technology

Table 3. Magnetic properties of HD powders and their typical bonded magnets.

Powder Name	Powder			Magnet (PC = 2)				B_r(magnet) / B_r(powder)
	B_r (kG)	H_{ci} (kOe)	$(BH)_{max}$ (MGOe)	B_r (kG)	H_{ci} (kOe)	$(BH)_{max}$ (MGOe)	Density (g/cc)	
MQP-16-9HD-20177	8.78	9.4	15.5	7.13	9.1	10.4	5.97	81%
MQP-15-9HD-20178	8.72	9.3	15.3	7.04	9.3	10.2	6.01	81%
MQP-B+-20056	8.97	9.8	15.7	7.00	9.3	9.9	5.93	78%

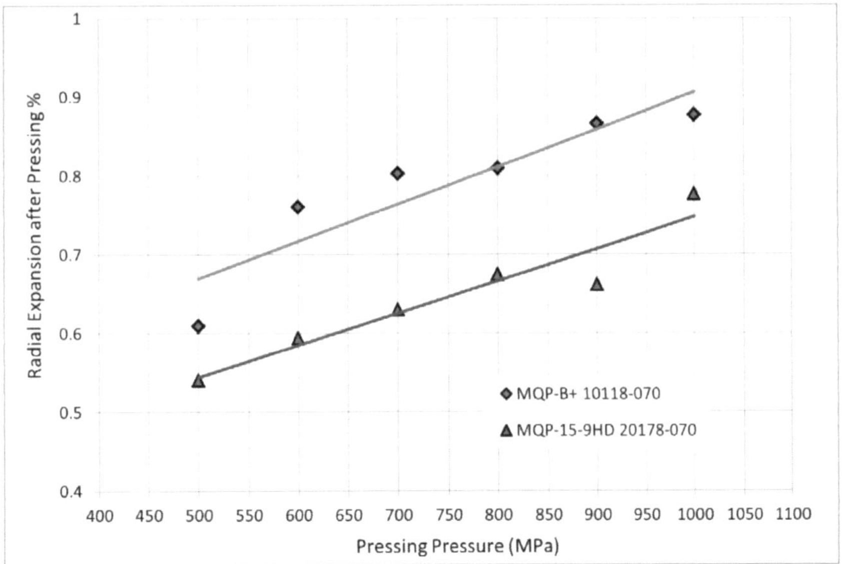

Fig. 8. Radial spring-back observed when compression moulding MQP-B+ and MQP-15-9HD at compaction pressures between 500 and 1000 MPa.

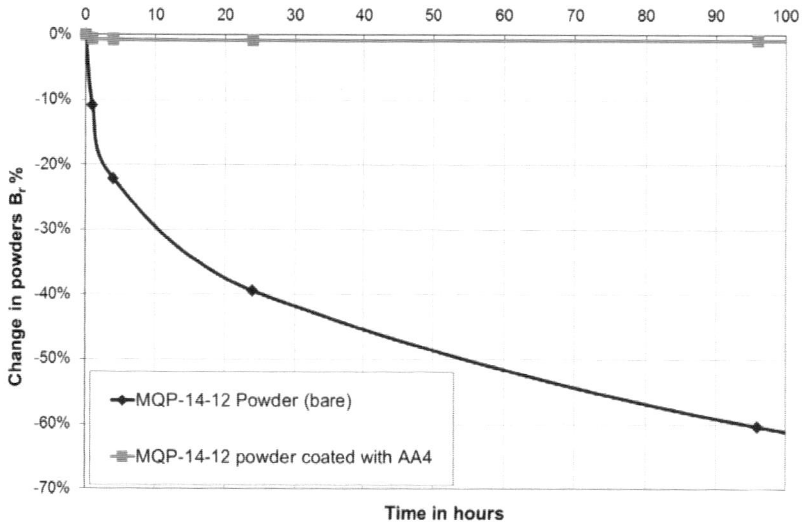

Fig. 9. Difference in thermal flux ageing between an untreated and an AA4-coated MQP-14-12 powder that were held at 275 °C for 100 hours.

known as AA4. Freshly exposed Nd-Fe-B fracture surfaces are particularly vulnerable to oxidation, and the AA4 treatment puts a barrier layer between the exposed Nd-Fe-B and external atmosphere. An example of the effectiveness of this barrier is shown in Figure 9. AA4-coated MQP-14-12 and standard uncoated MQP-14-12 were both crushed to <106 μm and placed in an air oven at 275 °C for 100 hours. After this time the untreated powder sample had lost over 60% in room temperature remanence, presumably due to oxidation of the magnetic phase. Meanwhile the AA4 coated sample was barely affected by the test.

5. Conclusions

The topical interests of higher performance, greater thermal stability and lower cost have been the focus of developmental work on melt-spun Nd-Fe-B material. Anisotropic powder and HD powder aim to offer higher performance magnets. The AA4 coating technology improves the thermal stability of bonded magnets. Substituting Nd with some portion of the more abundant Ce or La will offer lower cost magnet solutions.

References

[1] M. Sagawa, S. Fujimura, N. Togawa, H. Yamamoto and Y. Matsuura, *J. Appl. Phys.* **55,** 1984, 2083.

[2] J. J. Croat, J. F. Herbst, R. W. Lee and F. E. Pinkerton *J. Appl. Phys.* **55**, 1984, 2078.

[3] W. Grünberger, D. Hinz, A. Kirchner, K.-H. Müller and L. Schultz *J. Alloys Compd.* **257,** 1997, 293.

High Performance Anisotropic Nanocrystalline Rare-Earth Magnets

Z.H. GUO, X. DU, H.J. WANG, B. LAI, W. PAN, M.G. ZHU, W. LI
Division of Functional Materials, Central Iron & Steel Research Institute, Beijing 100081, China

Abstract: *The effects of composition, preparation process on the microstructure, magnetic properties, and crystal alignment of hot pressing/hot deformation nanocrystalline Nd-Fe-B magnets have been investigated. Magnets with the best magnetic properties contain 28.9 wt.% Nd. The replacement of Nd with a small amount of Pr can improve the crystal alignment, then enhance remanence and maximum magnetic products. The mechanism of the texture formation of nanocrystalline magnets during hot deformation process was analyzed. The optimal magnetic properties of* B_r*=14.70 kGs,* H_{cb}*=9.21 kOe,* H_{cJ}*=9.55 kOe, and* $(BH)_{max}$*=53.67 MGOe were obtained.*

Keywords: *rare earth permanent magnet;* $Nd_2Fe_{14}B$*; hot pressing; hot deformation; die-upset; nanocrystalline; anisotropy*

Address: Zhaohui Guo, Division of Functional materials, Central Iron & Steel Research Institute, Beijing 100081, China, Tel: 086-10-62185125, Email: zhguo@vip.sina.com

1. Introduction

Hot pressing/hot deformation (die-upset) has become one of the basic production routes to prepare high performance nanocrystalline Nd-Fe-B permanent magnets with full density and high anisotropy [1,2]. These magnets offer some advantages over the widely used sintered magnets, such as better anticorrosion properties, and the ability to be formed into complex near-net shapes with isotropic or highly anisotropic magnetic properties. One particular application is the backward extruded ring magnets [3,4]. These radially oriented Nd-Fe-B ring magnets find application in various electric motors, such as EPS (Electric Power Steering) motors, brushless motors, and alternating current servo motors, where high power, low cogging, quiet and smooth rotation are required.

For the hot deformed Nd-Fe-B magnets, the magnetic properties are extremely sensitive to the size, shape, crystal structure, and the orientation of crystallites of the magnetic phase as well as the distribution of the second phase. These microstructural parameters, however, depend on the composition and the processing conditions. In this work, the effects of the composition, hot pressing, and hot deformation process on the microstructure, magnetic properties, and crystal alignment of magnets have been investigated. Based on extensive studies, the high performance anisotropic Nd-Fe-B magnets have been prepared by hot pressing/hot deformation method.

2. Experimental

Bulk nanocrystalline rare earth magnets with compositions of (Nd,Pr)-Fe-Co-Ga-B were prepared by the process of melt spinning, hot pressing, and hot deformation. The optimally quenched melt-spun ribbons have equiaxed and randomly oriented $Nd_2Fe_{14}B$ grains with grain size of about 10 nm. After melt spinning, the ribbons were crushed into powder particles of < 500μm and then hot pressed at 500 °C – 700 °C under 200 MPa – 350 MPa in vacuum. Hot pressing of ribbon powder achieves complete densification while maintaining essentially an isotropic magnetic structure. Excessive grain growth could be avoided due to very short hot pressing process, typically only 2 minutes. The hot-pressed magnet specimens were further hot deformed at 600 °C – 900 °C with a height reduction of 0% - 90% in argon atmosphere. The hot deformation process modifies the equiaxed grains to platelet-like grains, which have high magnetic anisotropy with c-axis parallel to the pressing direction, and dramatically improves the magnetic properties. The magnetic properties were tested in closed-circuit with a hysteresisgraph meter (NIM-2000HF) after pre-magnetization in a pulsed magnetic field of 70 kOe. The microstructure was studied on fracture surfaces of the magnets by a scanning electron microscope (SEM, JMS-6400). Thermal analysis was conducted by differential scanning calorimetry (DSC, NETZSCH STA 449 F3) at a heating rate of 20 K/min.

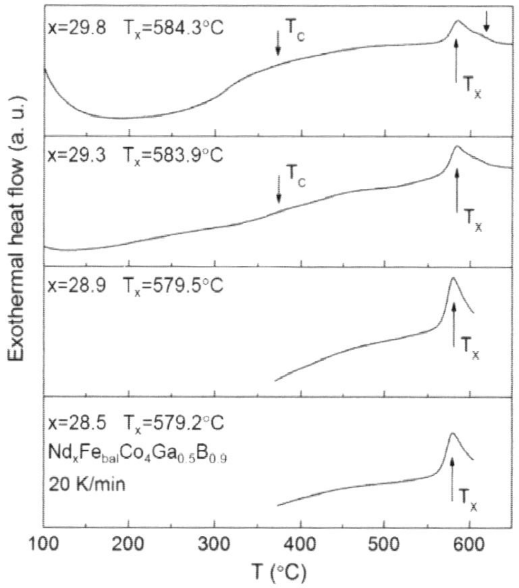

Fig. 1 DSC curves of melt-spun $Nd_xFe_{bal}Co_4Ga_{0.5}B_{0.9}$ powders with different Nd content.

3. Results And Discussion

Bulk nanocrystalline magnets with a nominal composition of $Nd_xFe_{bal}Co_4Ga_{0.5}B_{0.9}$ (wt.%) (x=28.5, 28.9, 29.3, and 29.8) were prepared by the process of melt spinning, hot pressing, and hot deformation. Fig. 1 displays the DSC curves of melt-spun ribbons with different Nd content at quenching velocity of 30m/s. With decreasing the content of Nd, the intensity of the crystallization exothermic peaks of $Nd_2Fe_{14}B$ phase increase gradually, indicating that the degree of amorphous increases. The crystallization temperatures, which are maintained at about 580°C, slightly decrease for lower Nd content. A weak exothermic peak can be observed at 620°C for Nd content x=29.8 and 29.3, which may possibly correspond to the crystallization temperature of 2:17 phase. The magnetic properties of the optimized as-deformed magnets with different Nd content are plotted in Fig. 2. Nd content has a great impact on the intrinsic coercivity H_{cJ}, which decreases monotonically from 12.88kOe for Nd content x=29.8 to 6.88kOe for x=28.5. The remanence B_r increases slightly with decreasing Nd content, mainly due to higher proportion of $Nd_2Fe_{14}B$ main phase in the magnet with lower Nd content. The maximum energy product $(BH)_{max}$ first increases then decreases with decreasing Nd content, and the maximum has been obtained when x=28.9. Magnets with the best magnetic properties contain 28.9 wt.% Nd.

The replacement of Nd with a small amount of Pr can improve the crystal alignment, then enhance remanence and maximum magnetic products. Table 1 gives the magnetic properties of hot deformation magnets with the nominal compositions of Nd-Fe-Co-Ga-B and Nd-3%Pr-Fe-Co-Ga-B under the same preparation condition. The substitution of 3wt.% Pr for Nd increases the remanence and decreases the intrinsic coercivity a little, meanwhile the substitution obviously improves the maximum energy product mainly due to the improvement of the squareness of demagnetization curve. Fig. 3 shows the SEM images of melt spun ribbons and hot deformation magnets without and with the substitution of 3wt.% Pr for Nd in Nd-Fe-Co-Ga-B magnets. A small amount of Pr substitution refines the grains of the melt spun ribbons obviously as shown in Fig. 3a and 3b. For as-deformed magnets, Pr substitution improves the microstructure from two aspects, firstly refining the grain size, and secondly improving the degree of orientation of Nd-Fe-B grains as shown in Fig. 3c and 3d.

Table 1 Magnetic properties of hot deformation magnets with the compositions of Nd-Fe-Co-Ga-B and Nd-3%Pr-Fe-Co-Ga-B

Compositions	B_r kGs	H_{cb} kOe	H_{cJ} kOe	$(BH)_{max}$ MGOe
Nd-Fe-B	14.42	12.84	14.02	50.19
Nd-3%Pr-Fe-B	14.69	12.83	13.77	52.32

For the hot deformed Nd-Fe-B magnets, isotropic nanocrystalline magnets with full density can be obtained after the hot pressing. Further hot deformation of the isotropic magnets can create crystallographic texture and obtain anisotropic nanocrystalline magnets. The magnetic properties, especially the remanence and the maximum energy product, are determined largely by the degree of crystallographic alignment of the $Nd_2Fe_{14}B$ phase. The mechanism of the c-axis alignment of the $Nd_2Fe_{14}B$ phase under stress during hot deformation process is very important for improving the magnetic properties of these nanocrystalline magnets. Fig. 4 shows the changes of the microstructure during hot deformation process. Fig. 5 shows the corresponding remanence. Obviously, there is a close correlation between the remanence and the microstructure, especially the crystal texture, in hot deformation magnets. The remanence increases rapidly in the beginning of the hot deformation. Then the rate of increase slows down when the deformation ratio larger than 51%, and the remanence approaches saturation after 65%. Based on the evolution of microstructure, the hot deformation process can be divided into three stages: (1) the initial stage, $Nd_2Fe_{14}B$ grains grow anisotropically, i.e. the growth perpendicular to the c-axis faster than that parallel to the c-axis, as shown in Fig. 4a to 4c; (2) intermediate stage, the c-axes of $Nd_2Fe_{14}B$ grains rotate to the direction of the pressure gradually under stress, as shown in Fig. 4b to 4d; (3) final stage, $Nd_2Fe_{14}B$ grains grow mainly along the direction perpendicular to the c-axis and do not grow basically in the direction parallel to the c-axis as shown in Fig. 4d to 4f. The final magnets are composed of elongated and aligned platelet-like grains with grain size of 50-100nm thick and 500-1000nm long. The texture formation during hot formation process involves the preferred growth of $Nd_2Fe_{14}B$ nanograins along the easy growth direction a-axis, grain rotation, grain boundary sliding, and so on.

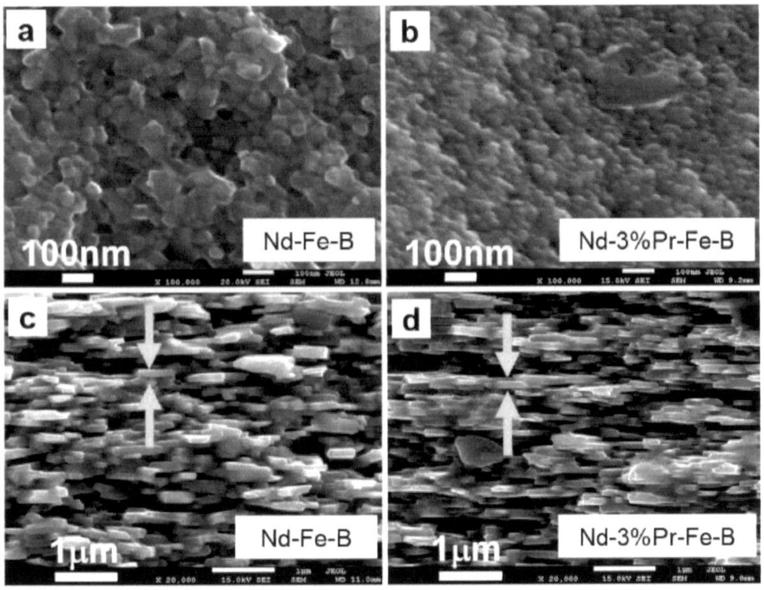

Fig. 3 SEM images of melt spun ribbons (a, b) and hot deformation magnets (c, d) without and with the substitution of 3wt.% Pr for Nd in Nd-Fe-Co-Ga-B

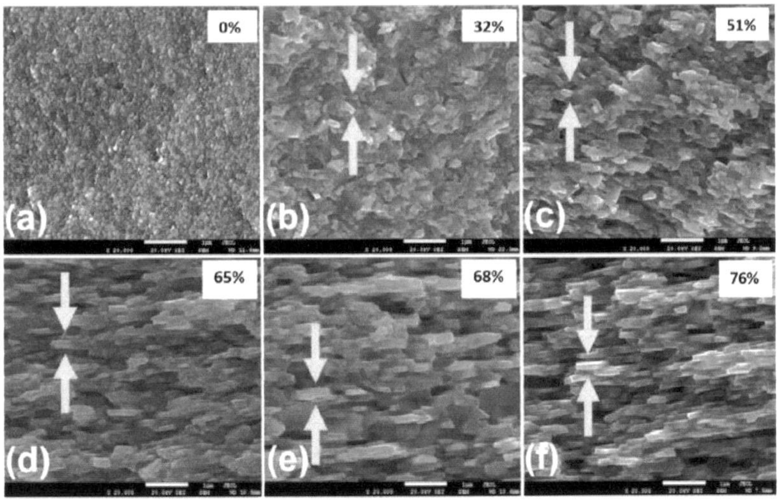

Fig. 4 SEM images of hot deformation magnets with different deformation ratio (a - 0%,b - 32%, c - 51%, d - 65%, e - 68%, and f - 76%) (The directions of the arrows in SEM images are parallel to the directions of pressure during hot deformation process.)

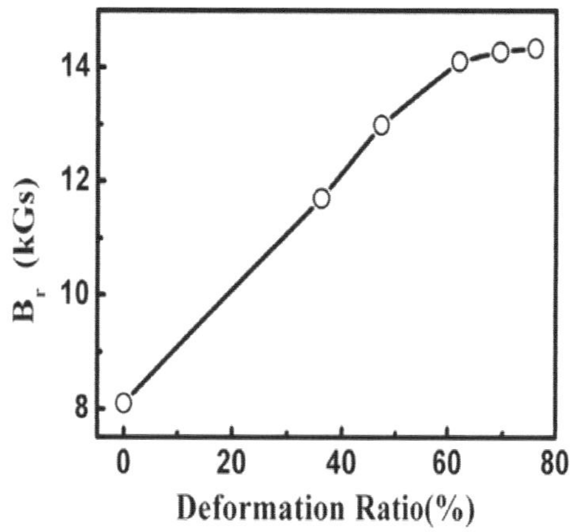

Fig. 5 *and the corresponding remanence B_r as a function of deformation ratio*

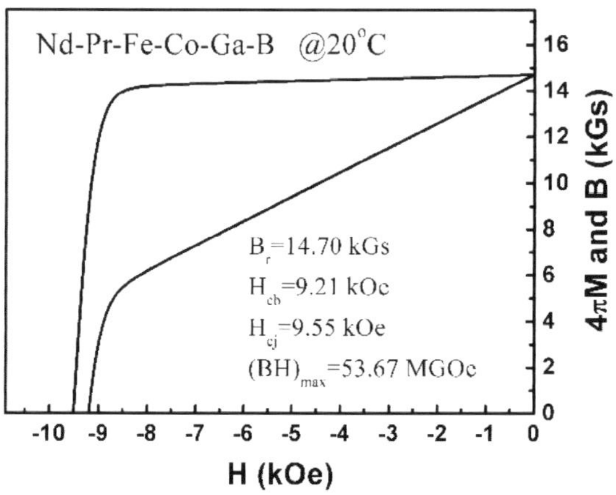

Fig. 6 Demagnetization curves and magnetic properties of the high performance anisotropic nanocrystalline Nd-Fe-B magnets

Magnets with optimal magnetic properties have been prepared with the compositions of (Nd, Pr)-Fe-Co-Ga-B under the process of rapid quenching velocity of 25m/s, hot-pressing temperature of 550°C - 600°C, deformation temperature of 800°C - 850°C, and deformation ratio of 80%. The best magnetic properties of B_r =14.70kGs, H_{cb}=9.21kOe, H_{cJ} =9.55kOe, and $(BH)_{max}$= 53.67MGOe were obtained as shown in Fig. 6.

4. Conclusions

Rare earth content has a great impact on the magnetic properties of high performance anisotropic nanocrystalline magnets. The texture formation during hot formation process involves the preferred growth of $Nd_2Fe_{14}B$ nanograins along the easy growth direction a-axis, grain rotation, and grain boundary sliding. The optimal magnetic properties of B_r=14.70kGs, H_{cb}=9.21 kOe, H_{cJ}=9.55kOe, and $(BH)_{max}$=53.67MGOe were obtained.

Acknowledgements

This work was supported by the National Basic Research Program of China (2010CB934601) and the National Natural Science Foundation of China (51331003).

References

[1] R. W. Lee, Appl. Phys. Lett. **1985**, 46, 790
[2] D. Lee, S. Bauser, A. Higgins, C. Chen, S. Liu, M. Q. Huang, Y. G. Peng, and D. E. Laughlin, J. Appl. Phys. **2006**, 99, 08B516
[3] A. H. Li, W. Li, B. Lai, H. J. Wang, M. G. Zhu, and W. Pan, J. Appl. Phys. **2010**, 107, 09A725
[4] I. Dirba, S. Sawatzki, O. Gutfleisch, J. Alloys Comp. **2014**, 589, 301

Microstructure and Coercivity of Tb_4O_7 Grain Boundary Diffusion Processed Sintered Nd-Fe-B Magnets

U.M.R. SEELAM[1], T. OHKUBO[1], H. NAKAMURA[2], K. HONO[1]
[1]Elements Strategy Initiative Center for Magnetic Materials (ESICMM), National Institute for Materials Science, 1-2-1 Sengen, Tsukuba 305-0047, Japan
[2]Magnetic Materials Research Center, Shin-Etsu Chemical Co. Ltd., Fukui 915-8515, Japan

In the grain boundary diffusion (GBD) process of Nd-Fe-B magnets, heavy rare earth elements (HREs) such as Dy and Tb are incorporated preferentially along the grain boundaries rather than alloying into the entire grains. This results in a dramatic improvement in coercivity without losing remanence, leading to substantial savings in HREs [1-3]. However, it is well known that the alloying of Dy to the matrix is required to attain the coercivity higher than 2 T. In this study, microstructural characterization was carried out on terbium oxide (Tb_4O_7) GBD processed (Nd,Dy)-Fe-B sintered magnets with four different Dy contents in order to understand the combined effect of Dy alloying and Tb GBD process. The nominal Dy compositions of the four base-alloys (prepared by two-alloy method) are 0, 2, 5, and 11 wt.% (dimensions: 15 x 15 x 2.2 mm^3). Before the GBD process, the magnets were post-sinter annealed at about 550 °C under Ar atmosphere for about 1-3 hours. They were then coated with terbium oxide (Tb_4O_7) as a diffusing agent and kept in an elevated temperature about 900 °C for 10 hours to allow penetration of Tb into the magnet. Back-scattered electron (BSE) imaging in scanning electron microscopy (SEM) and energy dispersive spectroscopy (EDS) mapping in scanning transmission electron microscopy (STEM) mode were used for the analysis.

Figure 1 shows the coercivity as a function of Dy content of the magnets before and after the GBD process. Coercivity values of the four magnets before and after GBD process are, 1.2 and 1.9 T, 1.5 and 2.4 T, 2.1 and 3.2 T, and 3.6 and 4.3 T, respectively. The GBD process could enhance the coercivity by about 0.7 - 0.9 T. In this report, a case study is presented on the microstructure of the magnet without any Dy content in it. Figure 2 shows in-lens and BSE images of the magnet with 0 wt.% Dy. Tb-enriched shells were observed along the grain boundaries after the GBD process. Figure 3(a) shows STEM-EDS mapping of a core/shell region near the surface of the magnet. The thickness of the shells near the surface is about few hundreds of nanometers, while the average concentration of Tb in the shells is evaluated to be 1.93 at.%. Figure 3b shows STEM-EDS mapping of a region from the center of the bulk of the magnet. Near the center, the thickness of these shells is typically less than 100 nm, with an average Tb concentration of ~ 0.66 at.% from the region shown in Figure 3c. Finally, the overall average concentration of Tb in the shells from the surface and center regions is ~ 1.3 at.% or 3.1 wt.%. Using the magnetocrystalline anisotropy fields (H_A) of $Tb_2Fe_{14}B$ (22 T) and $Dy_2Fe_{14}B$ is (15 T), Tb concentration in the shells is converted to an equivalent Dy concentration, which is evaluated to be 1.9 at.% Dy or 4.6 wt.% Dy. The coercivity of the conventional sintered magnet with 4.6 wt.% Dy is 1.9 T. The observed coercivity of this GBD magnet is also 1.9 T, which matches well with the above estimated coercivity from the shell

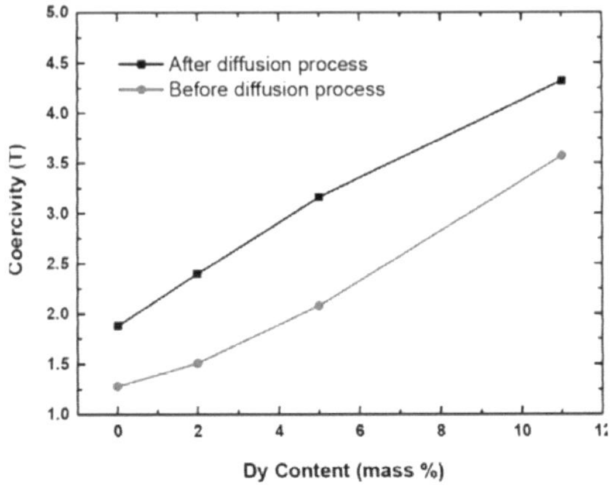

Fig. 1. Coercivity of the (Nd,Dy)-Fe-B sintered magnets at various Dy levels before and after Tb_4O_7 GBD process.

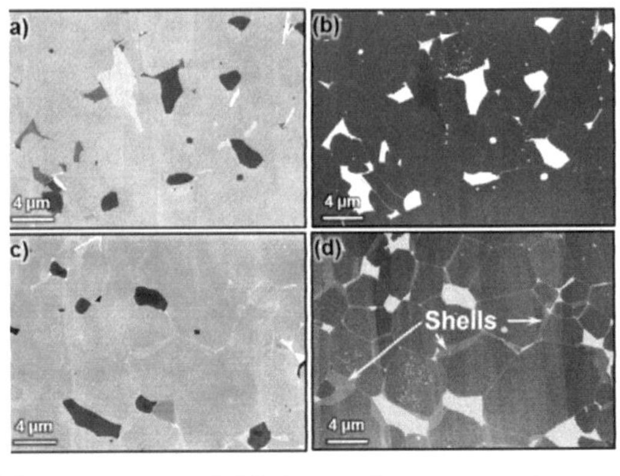

Fig. 2. In-lens and BSE images from near surface of the magnet without Dy addition; before (a,b) and after (c,d) the GBD process. C-axis is out-of-plane.

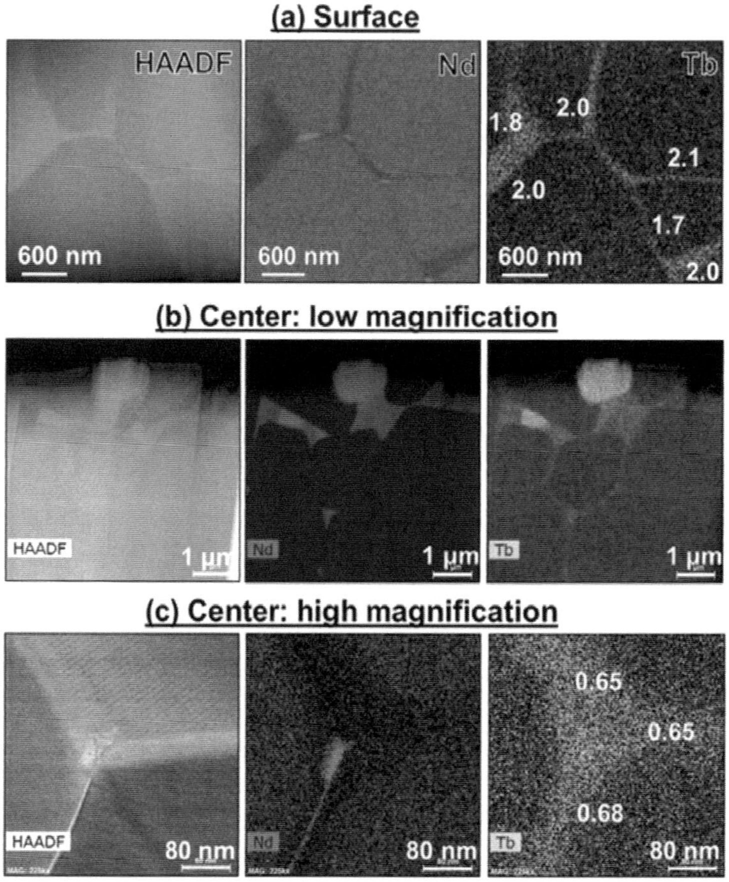

Fig. 3. (a) STEM/EDS mapping from the surface of the magnet; (b) from the center of the bulk magnet at low magnification and (c) at high magnification: Tb concentration (at.%) is shown.

concentration of Tb of 1.3 at.%. Thus it is concluded that the coercivity of the GBD processed magnet is a function of the average concentration of heavy rare earth element in the shells.

References

[1] H. Nakamura, K. Hirota, M. Shimao, T. Minowa, M. Honshima, *IEEE Trans. Magn.* **41**, 2005, 3844.

[2] Z. Samardzija, P. McGuiness, M. Soderznik, S. Kobe, M. Sagawa, *Mater. Charact.* **67**, 2012, 27.

[3] H. Sepehri-Amin, T. Ohkubo and K. Hono, *Acta Mater.* **61**, 2013, 1982.

Effect of Annealing on Magnetic Properties and Microstructure of Ultrafine Nd-Fe-B Powders

MICHIHIDE NAKAMURA[1*], MASASHI MATSUURA[1], NOBUKI TEZUKA[1], SATOSHI SUGIMOTO[1], YASUHIRO UNE[2], HIROKAZU KUBO[2], MASATO SAGAWA[2]
[1]Department of Materials Science, Graduate School of Engineering, Tohoku University, Sendai 980-8579
[2]Intermetallics Co., Ltd., Nagoya 463-0003

Abstract: *In this paper, the effects of annealing on the magnetic properties and microstructure of ultrafine Nd-Fe-B powders were investigated. The ultrafine Nd-Fe-B powders, which had an average particle size (D_{50}) of 0.67 μm, were prepared from hydrogenation–disproportionation–desorption–recombination-treated Nd-Fe-B alloys by hydrogen decrepitation and helium jet milling. Spherical ultrafine particles were obtained, and the relative span was 0.85. Annealing below 500 °C increased the coercivity (μ_0H_c) of the ultrafine powders slightly. Annealing above 600 °C increased the coercivity drastically. Annealing at 950 °C resulted in a large coercivity drop, which was attributed to abnormal grain growth.*

Keywords: *ultrafine neodymium-iron-boron powders; annealing temperature, magnetic properties; hydrogenation-disproportionation-desorption-recombination; helium jet milling*

Address: Michihide Nakamura, Department of Materials Science, Graduate School of Engineering, Tohoku University, Aoba-yama 02, Aoba-ku, Sendai 980-8579, JAPAN, Tel: (+81)-22-795-7333, E-mail: b2td5305@s.tohoku.ac.jp

1. Introduction

Nd-Fe-B sintered magnets are the most widely used type of rare earth magnet and are essential for many products, including hard disk drives, electric motors, and generators. However, they have a large temperature coefficient of coercivity; thus, they require a high coercivity of about 3 T at room temperature to function at temperatures around 200 °C. The coercivity of Nd-Fe-B sintered magnets can be increased by adding Dy, although this is expensive and decreases the saturation magnetization. Grain refinement of the $Nd_2Fe_{14}B$ phase can also increase coercivity [1-4]. He jet milling has been used to prepare fine Nd-Fe-B powders about 1.1 μm in size from strip-cast (SC) Nd-Fe-B alloys [5-7]. Grain-refined Nd-Fe-B sintered magnets with a high coercivity of 2.0 T have been prepared from these powders without Dy. Ultrafine Nd-Fe-B powders less than 1 μm in size are now required to improve the coercivity of Nd-Fe-B sintered magnets further.

Ultrafine Nd-Fe-B powders must contain $Nd_2Fe_{14}B$ and Nd-rich phases. During sintering and heat treatment, the Nd-rich phase melts and diffuses along the grain boundaries, and reduces the number of nucleation sites [8]. High coercivity is achieved by the homogeneous coating of the $Nd_2Fe_{14}B$ phase with the Nd-rich phase. Thus, it is crucial to develop a Nd-Fe-B alloy consisting of homogeneous $Nd_2Fe_{14}B$ grains smaller than 1 μm covered with a Nd-rich phase for preparing ultrafine Nd-Fe-B jet-milled powders (< 1 μm) for Nd-Fe-B magnets.

Hydrogenation-disproportionation-desorption-recombination (HDDR) is used to produce ultrafine $Nd_2Fe_{14}B$ grains with an average size of approximately 0.3 μm in Nd-Fe-B alloys [9,10]. Hydrogenation–disproportionation (HD) involves heating at 650–1000 °C under a hydrogen atmosphere to decompose the $Nd_2Fe_{14}B$ phase into NdH_2, Fe, and Fe_2B. Desorption–recombination (DR) removes hydrogen from NdH_2 by heating in a vacuum, and fine $Nd_2Fe_{14}B$ grains are formed from NdH_2, Fe, and Fe_2B recombining, producing a homogeneous micro-structure consisting of $Nd_2Fe_{14}B$ and Nd-rich grain boundary phases [11-13].

We identified a combination of HDDR and hydrogen decrepitation as a promising method for obtaining ultrafine Nd-Fe-B powders. We have used hydrogen decrepitation and He jet milling to fabricate ultrafine Nd-Fe-B powders with an average particle size of 0.33 μm from HDDR-treated Nd-Fe-B alloy [14]. However, the effects of annealing on ultrafine Nd-Fe-B powders have not been reported. It is important to understand how annealing affects the magnetic properties and microstructure of ultrafine Nd-Fe-B powders intended for Nd-Fe-B sintered magnets. In this work, we examined the effects of annealing on the magnetic properties and microstructure of ultrafine Nd-Fe-B powders.

2. Experimental procedure

An SC Nd-Fe-B alloy with a composition of $Nd_{27.5}Pr_{4.15}Fe_{bal.}B_{1.0}Al_{0.23}Cu_{0.1}Co_{0.96}$ (mass %) was used as the starting material. The HDDR treatment conditions were as follows. First, HD treatment was performed under a hydrogen atmosphere (0.1 MPa) at 950 °C for 60 min. The alloy was annealed at 800 °C for 10 min under Ar atmosphere, and then it was also annealed under vacuum (<10 Pa) for 60 min. Finally, the alloy was cooled to room temperature, and DR treatment was performed. The HDDR-treated alloy underwent hydrogen decrepitation for 5 h at 200 °C under hydrogen, and was then pulverized by He jet milling. The original SC alloy was also pulverized by hydrogen decrepitation and He jet milling. We refer to the jet-milled powders from the HDDR alloy and SC alloy as 'jet-milled HDDR alloy powder' and 'jet-milled SC alloy powder', respectively. The jet-milled HDDR and SC alloy powders were annealed from 100 to 1000 °C for 30 min under high vacuum (10^{-4} Pa), and were quenched to room temperature. A vibrating sample magnetometer (VSM) was used to measure the magnetic properties of the powders. VSM samples were prepared by the following steps: aligning the powders in an external magnetic field of 2.0 T, fixing them in paraffin wax, and magnetizing them in a pulsed magnetic field of 8.0 T. Field-emission scanning electron microscopy (FE-SEM) was used to observe the microstructure. The average grain and particle sizes were defined as the median diameters (d_{50} and D_{50}, respectively) and the dimensionless value of grain and particle size distribution (Q) was defined as the relative span (RS_{grain} and $RS_{particle}$, respectively):

$$RS_{grain} = \frac{(d_{90}-d_{10})}{d_{50}}, \quad (1)$$

$$RS_{particle} = \frac{(D_{90}-D_{10})}{D_{50}}. \quad (2)$$

The values of d_{50}, D_{50}, RS_{grain}, and $RS_{particle}$ were calculated from the electron microscopy images.

3. Results and discussion

Figure 1 shows the secondary electron (SE) image of a fracture surface of the HDDR alloy. The grain size of the $Nd_2Fe_{14}B$ phase was less than 1 μm, indicating that the HDDR process resulted in grain refinement. Figure 2 shows the grain size distribution of the $Nd_2Fe_{14}B$ grains in the HDDR alloy calculated from the SE image. The grain sizes for cumulative distributions of 10% and 90% are defined as d_{10} and d_{90}, respectively. The average grain size is the size at which the cumulative distribution reaches 50% (d_{50}). We evaluated d_{50} as 0.60 μm in the HDDR-treated alloys. As the grain size distribution narrows, the relative span approaches zero. Using the d_{10}, d_{50}, and d_{90} values shown in Fig. 2, we calculated the value of RS_{grain} for HDDR alloys as 0.88.

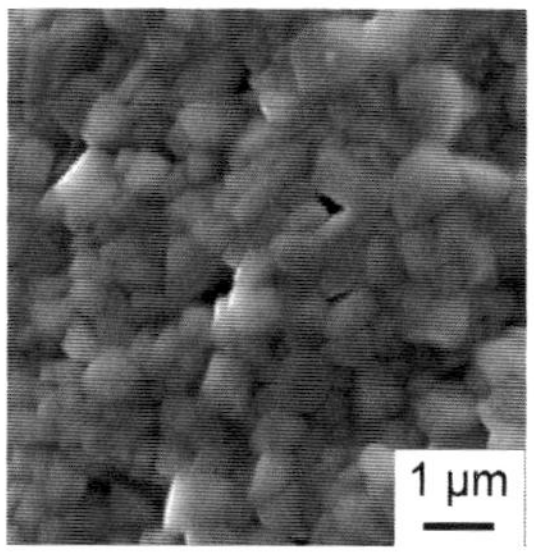

Fig. 1. SE image of the HDDR-treated alloy.

The HDDR alloy was hydrogen decrepitated under heating at 200 °C for 5 h in H_2, and the alloy was pulverized by He jet milling. For comparison, the SC alloy was also hydrogen decrepitated and subsequently He jet-milled. In Fig. 3, the SE images show that the particles of jet-milled HDDR alloy powder were spherical and smaller than the particles of jet-milled SC alloy powder. The particle size distribution of the jet-milled HDDR and SC alloy powders is shown in Fig. 4. As the particle size of the jet-milled HDDR alloy powder increased from 0.43 to 1.00 μm the cumulative distribution increased from 10% to 90%. From Fig. 4, D_{50} was calculated as 0.67 μm and $RS_{particle}$ was calculated as 0.85 for the jet-milled HDDR alloy powder. The increase in the cumulative curve of the jet-milled SC alloy powder was gradual. The values of D_{50} and $RS_{particle}$ for the jet-milled SC alloy powder were 1.12 μm and 1.53, respectively. Thus, the average particle size of the jet-milled HDDR alloy powder was half that of the jet-milled SC alloy powder. In addition, the jet-milled HDDR alloy powder exhibits a narrower particle size distribution ($RS_{particle}$ = 0.85) than the jet-milled SC alloy powder ($RS_{particle}$ = 1.53). Comparing the grain and particle size distribution of the jet-milled powder of HDDR alloy with the grain size distribution of the HDDR alloy before jet milling from the results of Figs. 2 and 4(a), we see that the RS_{grain} and $RS_{particle}$ values are

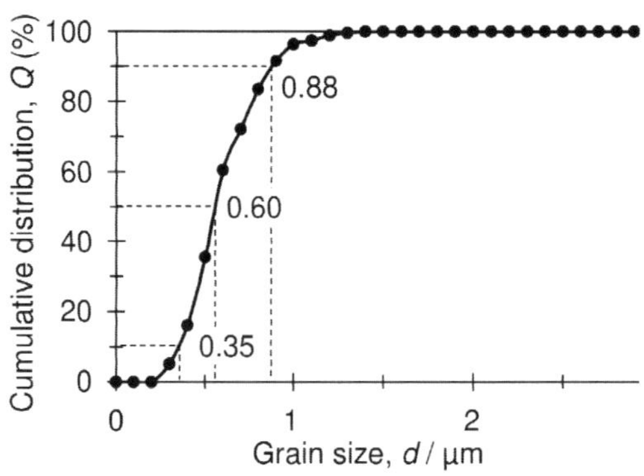

Fig. 2. Grain size distribution of $Nd_2Fe_{14}B$ in HDDR-treated alloy.

Fig. 3. SE images of the jet-milled (a) HDDR and (b) SC alloy powders.

approximate. This result indicates that Nd-Fe-B jet-milled powders are comparable with the $Nd_2Fe_{14}B$ grain-boundary-fractured hydrogen-decrepitated HDDR-treated alloy.

The jet-milled HDDR and SC alloy powders were annealed at 100 - 1000 °C for 30 min under high vacuum (10^{-4} Pa). The value of magnetization measured under an applied field of 2 T, and is referred as $\mu_0 M_{2T}$. Without annealing, the value of $\mu_0 M_{2T}$ was 1.32 T for both the jet-milled HDDR and SC alloy powders.

Annealing at a low temperature decreased the value of $\mu_0 M_{2T}$ for the jet-milled HDDR and SC alloy powders slightly, whereas annealing around 600 °C decreased it sharply.

For the jet-milled HDDR alloy powders, the value of $\mu_0 H_c$ before annealing was 0.14 T, which was higher than the value of 0.06 T for the jet-milled SC alloy powders. The value of $\mu_0 H_c$ was increased slightly by annealing at 300 °C for both powders: For the jet-milled HDDR alloy powder $\mu_0 H_c$ increased from 0.28 to 0.61 T, and for the jet-milled SC alloy powder it increased from 0.10 to 0.23 T. The jet-milled HDDR alloy had a larger $\mu_0 H_c$ than the jet-milled SC alloy powder after annealing below 500 °C. The value of $\mu_0 H_c$ for both the jet-milled powders was increased considerably by annealing above 600 °C, from 0.64 to 1.52 T for the jet-milled HDDR alloy powder and from 0.27 to 1.60 T for the jet-milled SC alloy powder. Annealing above 950 °C resulted in a drastic drop in $\mu_0 H_c$ for only the jet-milled HDDR alloy powder. Some coarse $Nd_2Fe_{14}B$ grains of several tens of micrometers in size were observed in the jet-milled HDDR alloy powders. In contrast, such abnormal grain growth was not observed in the jet-milled SC alloy powder. Consequently, the large drop in $\mu_0 H_c$ was attributed to the abnormal grain growth.

4. Conclusion

We examined the effect of annealing on the magnetic

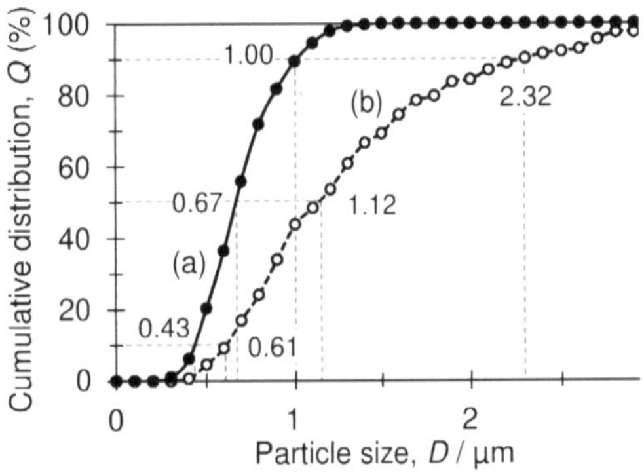

Fig. 4. Particle size distribution of the jet-milled (a) HDDR and (b) SC alloy powders.

properties and microstructure of ultrafine Nd-Fe-B powder. The jet-milled HDDR and SC alloy powders had average particle sizes (D_{50}) of 0.67 and 1.12 µm, respectively. The jet-milled HDDR and SC alloy powders were annealed at 100 to 1000 °C for 30 min under high vacuum (10^{-4} Pa). Without annealing, the value of $\mu_0 M_{2T}$ for both the jet-milled HDDR and SC alloy powders was 1.32 T. The value of $\mu_0 M_{2T}$ for both the jet-milled HDDR and SC alloy powders was slightly decreased by annealing at a low temperature, and was sharply decreased by annealing around 600 °C. The coercivity of both the jet-milled powders was slightly increased by annealing at 300 °C, and was drastically increased by annealing above 600 °C.

Acknowledgments
This work was supported by the "Future Pioneering Projects/Development of magnetic material technology for high-efficiency motors" from the Ministry of Economy, Trade and Industry, and by JSPS KAKENHI (Grant-in-Aid for JSPS Fellows, 255050).

References
[1] R. Ramesh and K. Srikrishna, *J. Appl. Phys.* **64**, 1988, 6406.
[2] R. Ramesh, G. Thomas, and B. M. Ma, *J. Appl. Phys.* **64**, 1988, 6416.
[3] M. Sagawa and Y. Une, in: *Proceedings of the 20th International Workshop on Rare Earth Permanent Magnets and Their Applications*, Crete, Greece, edited by D. Niarchos, (Admore, Greece, 2008) 103.
[4] T. Fukada, M. Matsuura, R. Goto, N. Tezuka, S. Sugimoto, Y. Une, and M. Sagawa, *Mater. Trans.* **53**, 2012, 1967.
[5] T. Hattori, H. Ishihara, S. Sugimoto, R. Goto, N. Tezuka, Y. Une, and M. Sagawa, *Mater. Trans.* **50**, 2009, 2347.
[6] S. Sugimoto, in: *Proceedings of the 20th International Workshop on Rare Earth Permanent*

Magnets and Their Applications, Crete, Greece, 2008, edited by D. Niarchos, (Admore, Greece) 106.
[7] Y. Une and M. Sagawa, *J. Jpn. Inst. Met.* **76**, 2012, 12 (in Japanese).
[8] R. Goto, S. Nishio, M. Matsuura, N. Tezuka, and S. Sugimoto, *IEEE Trans. Magn.* **44**, 2008, 4232.
[9] T. Takeshita and R. Nakamura, in: *Proceedings of the 10th International Workshop on Rare Earth Magnets and Their Applications*, **1** (Kyoto, 1989) 551.
[11] K. Hono and H. Sepehri-Amin, *Scr. Mater.* **67**, 2012, 530.
[12] W. F. Li, T. Ohkubo, K. Hono, T. Nishiuchi, and S. Hirosawa, *Appl. Phys. Lett.* **93**, 2008, 052505.
[13] H. Sepehri-Amin, W. F. Li, T. Ohkubo, T. Nishiuchi, S. Hirosawa, and K. Hono, *Acta Mater.* **58**, 2010, 1309.
[14] M. Nakamura, M. Matsuura, N. Tezuka, S. Sugimoto, Y. Une, H. Kubo, and M. Sagawa, *Appl. Phys. Lett.* **103**, 2013, 022404.

The use of Permanent Magnets in Industrial and Energy Applications at Siemens

G. RIEGER
Siemens AG, Corporate Technology, Muenchen, Germany

Abstract: *Electrical machines based on Permanent Magnets (PM) with high energy density are well suited as drives and generators in a wide range of industrial applications and power generation. Permanent magnetic synchronous motors (PMSM) up to the MW class have been introduced by Siemens in the 1990ies, only a few years after the discovery of Nd-Fe-B magnets and their availability from mass-production. Nowadays also generators of the MW range based on PM have found their way into high volume applications, especially in large direct drive wind power turbines. For all of those applications, high performance permanent magnets with maximum energy density and long-term stability are required. Moreover, temperature behavior, electrical conductivity and production tolerances are key properties for increased overall efficiency and integration into electrical machines. Besides reduction of size and weight further improvement in shapability and machinability of magnetic materials for automated handling and mounting will lead to increased competitiveness of medium and large size PM based electrical machines.*

Keywords: *permanent magnets; motors; generators; energy density; magnet material requirements*

Address: Gotthard Rieger, Siemens AG, Corporate Technology, Research & Technology Center, CT RTC MAT MSR-DE, Otto-Hahn-Ring 6, 81739 Muenchen, Germany, Tel: +49 89 636-48728, Fax: +49 89 636-42256, E-mail: gotthard.rieger@siemens.com

1. Introduction

Permanent magnets (PM) have been successfully used in electrical machines from the early days of the invention of electric motors in the middle of the 19th century. Triggered by the development of hard ferrites, and later by the invention of RE based magnets, PMs have formed the success story of permanent magnetic excitation in synchronous electrical machines. This was only possible by continuous improvements in material properties especially with regard to temperature stability (mainly by increased coercivity), and due to overall reliability (like corrosion resistance). The most important advantage of permanent magnetic excited machines of the medium to high power class is their high degree of efficiency. Due to the permanent magnetic excitation there are no ohmic losses in the rotor. Therefore, depending on the application the overall losses of PM machines are estimated to be 20 % to 45 % less than conventional asynchronous machines or electrically excited synchronous machines as outlined in ref. [1]. Additionally, PM based machines outperform other designs in terms of power density (torque/volume), weight, noise level and robustness.

Today Siemens offers a comprehensive range of electric motors and generators for all industries, application fields and performance levels. The spectrum ranges from energy efficient low voltage motors, high dynamic servo and torque motors, high-performance high-voltage motors to a broad range of generators and their applications.

2. Permanent Magnet Based Motors for Process Industry and Motion Control Applications

For many years synchronous motors based on PM have been well received by the market. Siemens has introduced high torque direct motors of the SIMOTIC HT-direct series (Fig. 1), especially for applications which demand high torques at low speeds. Within a wide speed range (0 to 800 rpm) these systems do not require any intermediate gearboxes. Therefore, the motors allow reliable and low-maintenance drive systems of excellent overall efficiency. The direct drive concept permits compact configurations and low noise operation making it interesting for a wide range of applications. Examples are in mining industry for mill drives, in steel industry e.g. for shears and roller gates, in plastics industry to drive high torque extruder worms, in crane industry for the widest range of applications, in sugar industry for sugar centrifuges and in paper industry as roller and press drive.

Motors for motion control applications cover both linear as well as high torque motors. They are typically based on permanent magnet motor designs. Applications are drives in machine tools, production machines handling, assembling systems and robotics. Built-in torque motors from the series SIMOTICS-1FW6 are optimized for use in high precision machine tools. The system is available as liquid-cooled or

a)  b) 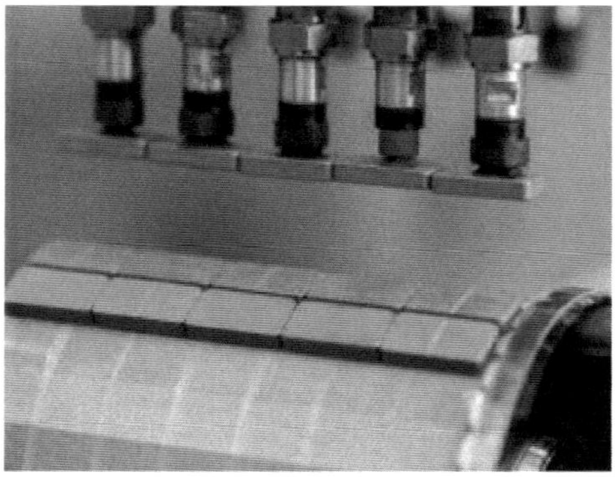

Fig. 1. a) High torque motor of direct series. b) The brushless rotor is equipped with surface mounted permanent magnets.

a)  b) 

Fig. 2. a) Different built-in torque motors. b) Typical components, e.g. hollow-shaft rotor.

convection cooled and built-up as a multi-pole permanent magnet AC synchronous motor with hollow-shaft rotor as shown in Fig. 2. The motors are supplied as built-in components while for a complete drive unit, an additional bearing and shaft encoder are required. Each frame size is available in different axis lengths. Most stators and rotors are equipped with flanges at each end with centering surfaces for installation in the machine.

Linear motors are available for all applications with long traveling paths and high demands on dynamic performance and precision. Typically the magnets are integrated on the secondary sections track. In 2008 a new concept in synchronous technology (1FN6 - linear motor, see Fig. 3) has been introduced. This innovative motor concept has all the advantages of direct drives such as high power density, high dynamic response, good control features and outstanding precision. The advantage is that the secondary section track is no longer equipped with permanent magnets. Those are just present inside the primary section. The target applications are linear axes with traverse paths of approximately 4 m or more which are found in the field of production machines and machine tools, e.g. as highly dynamic and precise feed axes in x-y-tables of water and laser cutting machines.

In recent years, Siemens has observed a growing demand for large diameter direct drives, particularly in precision industry applications. It was found that this could be satisfied by standardized linear motor modules arranged in rotational symmetry. By applying this modular concept a broad torque and power range could be covered [2].

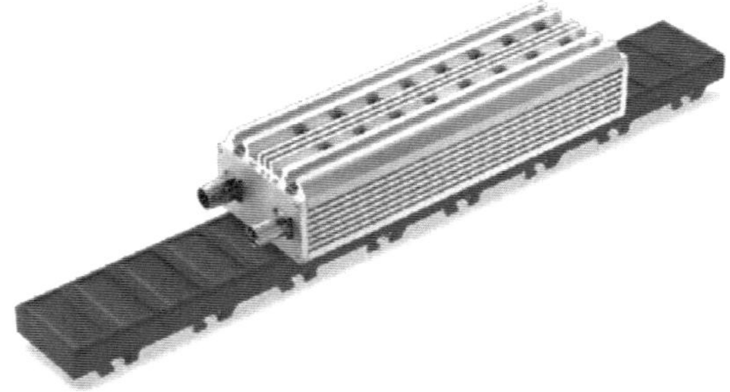

Fig. 3. Linear motor with concept of permanent magnets inside the primary section (top). The secondary section is formed by a segmented (PM-free) iron track.

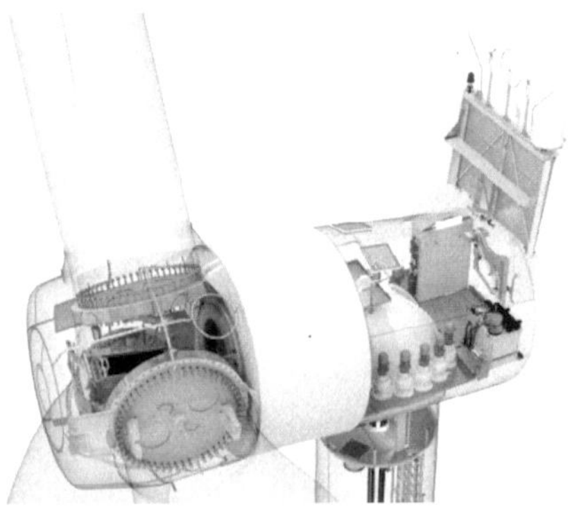
a)

b)

Fig. 4. a) Siemens wind turbine using direct drive generator with permanent magnets on outer rotor. b) Generator test of the D3 platform.

3. Permanent Magnet Based Generators

In conventionally designed wind energy systems, a massive gear set converts the relatively slow rotation of the blades into fast rotation, which then generates electric power in a high-speed generator either using PMSM or asynchronous designs. Gearless direct drive generators (Fig. 4) mostly employ permanent magnets to generate power directly from slow rotation. In Siemens Wind Power systems the rotor is built up as cylinder with PM mounted on the inner side, and this rotor spins around a column-like stator. The advantages of this concept are numerous, strongly relying on the performance of PM materials. The first prototype of a 3 MW turbine (D3 platform) has been installed in 2009 and since then many of these direct drive systems have been delivered and are fully operating in wind farms all over the world. The 6 MW generator has been launched in 2012 and in spring 2014 a new onshore 3.2 MW wind turbine (rated up from 3 MW) has been presented. Improvements are reached in the turbine control system and increased efficiency through the use of stronger magnets.

4. The Future Belongs to Green Propulsion

Drive technology of Siemens has also been used for decades in many mobility solutions, including railway systems, hybrid buses and marine applications.

For diesel-electric ship propulsion Siemens developed motors and generators which are excited by means of PM. The poles and coils are designed for minimal power loss. The motor achieves higher torque at low speed compared to conventional drive solutions and is therefore able to drive larger propellers with much greater efficiency. The diameter and the weight of the PM motor are significantly lower compared to electrically excited synchronous machines, especially in terms of the torque delivered. The motor itself is about 2% more efficient.

Those PM motors are used in Siemens Solutions for Podded Propulsion (eSiPOD) which are fully rotational single- and twin-propeller outboard systems with electrical power transmission of up to 12 MW per unit (Fig. 5a). The performance of this system is the result of a combination of dual-propeller

a)

b)

Fig. 5. a) Twin-propeller outboard ship propulsion system b) Volvo C 30 Electric permanent magnet synchronous motor.

technology with a hydrodynamically optimized drive module and a permanently excited motor. During the development phase, eSiPOD was tested on various types of ships. The tests have confirmed excellent efficiency gains and significant reduction in noise.

The broad range of applications and ongoing substitution of conventional systems show that both motors and generators using PM are essential parts for future power generation, automation, logistics and mobility. Substitution of conventional combustion engines has already started with the introduction of hybrid and full electric cars. A permanent magnet synchronous motor from Siemens has found its first application in the Volvo C 30 Electric (Fig. 5b). The motor has a continuous power of 62 kW and provides up to 108 kW peak power. The rated torque is 119 Nm and the peak torque is 220 Nm.

5. Future Demand and Requirements for High Energy Permanent Magnets

Current market predictions and estimations for future demand of high energy density (rare earth) permanent magnets show strong and steady increase. This is mainly assigned to the ongoing trend of electrification driven by e-mobility and decentralized medium size power generation (e.g. by wind energy). A preliminary long-range prediction of Neodymium is shown in Fig. 6 including the supply from primary and secondary sources. Demand on Dysprosium as needed for temperature stability respectively coercivity is also projected by some studies. These studies forecast a growth by a factor of 10 to 30 in 2050 in comparison to 2011 [3]. While material recovery for some scare materials like Copper from motor/generator windings already reaches double-digit values, rare earth element or magnet recovery is still marginal (below 1%) in many countries.

In terms of technical requirements the stability of electrical machines and their components to high temperatures tends to become even more important. This is due to the broad range of environmental conditions together with a trend for some applications towards higher speed level. This issue in combination with the goal of reduced content of heavy rare earth elements (like Dy or Tb) has led to numerous activities for the improvement of coercivity in sintered Nd-Fe-B magnets. Typical approaches are based on grain-size reduction and grain-boundary engineering (Dysprosium diffusion technology, see e.g. ref. [4]).

At high motor speed and therefore high frequencies in the kHz range eddy currents (unavoidable in the metallic sintered PM) lead to additional losses, self-heating and the risk of demagnetization. Therefore the rather high conductivity of sintered rare earth magnets has to be treated and strategies and solutions for improving temperature stability have to be found. This could be tackled by changes in magnetic circuit design as well as by suitable cooling concepts and isolated segmented/laminated magnet structures. On the other hand new material developments are needed to suppress eddy currents in the bulk by lowering the magnet electrical conductivity. This might be achieved by novel magnetic powder processing routes leading to composite magnets with low electrical conductivity by isolated particles but with still high magnetic remanence achieved by improved filling factors and orientation degree. New machine topologies e.g. for ultra-light motor applications are also becoming more important for future applications. They are potentially more sensitive to magnetization issues and specific flux distribution in the hard magnetic material.

From a manufacturing perspective the assembly of motors and generators are increasingly automated even for smaller volume applications [5]. Therefore tolerances in both magnet shape and performance

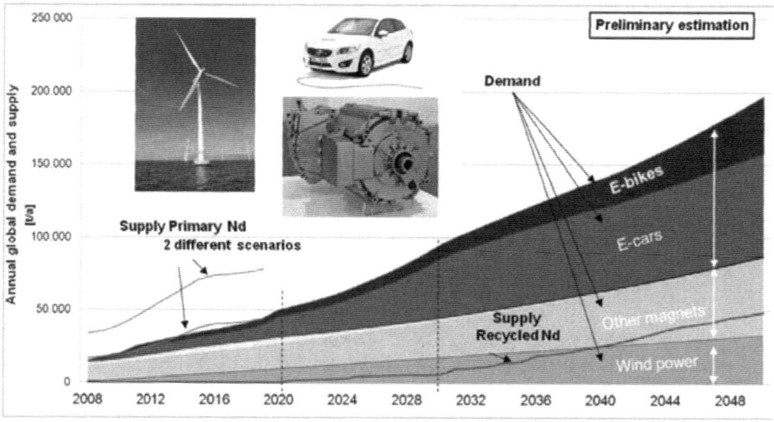

Fig. 6. Scenario till 2050 for annual global Neodymium demand and supply from recovery (source: Fraunhofer Institute ISI).

must be further minimized. Each of these measures will lead to increased competitiveness of PM based electrical machines in a long-term growth market.

References

[1] M. Kaufhold, A. Joeckel, *etz.*, *Elektrotechnik + Automation* **123**, 2002, 8.

[2] Z. Jajtic, F. Ulmar, C. Volmert, S. Fretzschner, H. Pommer, M. Dorfner, in: *1st Int. Electric Drives Production Conf.*, 2011, pp. 36-39.

[3] S. Hoenderdaal, L. T. Espinoza, F. Marscheider-Weidemann, W. Graus, *Energy* **49**, 2013, 344.

[4] C. Brombacher, K. Löwe, O. Gutfleisch, M. Rührig, M. Katter, in: *Proc. 22th Workshop on Rare-Earth Permanent Magnets and their Applications,* 2012, p2-034.

[5] E. Joseph, J. Tremel, B. Hofmann, A. Meyer, J. Franke, S. Eschrich, in: *3rd Int. Electric Drives Production Conf.*, 2013, pp. 82-87.

Axial Magnetic Field and Its Uniformity in Wide-Aperture Permanent Magnet Solenoids

C.H. CHEN [1,4], J.C. HORWATH[2], B.W. HOFF [3]
[1] University of Dayton Magnetics Lab., 300 College Park, Dayton, OH 45469, USA
[2] Air Force Research Laboratory, Propulsion Directorate, Wright-Patterson Air Force Base, OH 45433, USA
[3] Air Force Research Laboratory, Directed Energy Directorate, Kirtland Air Force Base, NM 87117, USA
[4] Magnet Energy Corp., San Jose, CA 95125, USA

Abstract: *Wide-aperture rare earth permanent magnet (PM) solenoids with various configurations were simulated using finite element computer modeling, in which the effect of configuration on the axial field B_z and its uniformity ΔB_z was analyzed. The magnetic orientation of individual segments and the aspect-ratio of the solenoid have significant effect on B_Z and ΔB_z. Two-layered configurations assembled with trapezoidal or arc segments result in a more uniformed B_z compared to the configuration assembled with five-faced polyhedrons. The two-layered configuration that avoids sharp angles also has the advantage of easier fabrication.*

Keywords: *permanent magnet solenoid, wide aperture, magnet configuration, axial field uniformity*

1. Introduction

A concentrated magnetic flux density can be generated by arranging permanent magnets in the form of hollow cylindrical or spherical shells, such as those described as a magic ring or a magic sphere [1,2]. The principle behind such design is the superposition theorem, based on which Halbach array was developed for various particle beam devices [3-5]. By arranging the magnetization vectors of each magnet, a concentrated magnetic field can be achieved [1,2,6-8]. A magnetic circuit design primer was extensively described by Leupold & Potenziani [6] for various PM solenoids, one of which is a PM solenoid made of five-faced polyhedrons as shown in Fig. 1a. The objective of this research is not to achieve the highest magnetic field, but a targeted axial field B_z, a minimum variation ΔB_z, and a minimum radial field B_y in the work zone.

2. Computer Modeling Procedure and PM Solenoid Configurations

Ansoft's Maxwell 3D was used for the finite element modeling with errors setting < 0.1%. Fig. 1a shows the configuration with polyhedral magnets, proposed by Leupold & Potenziani [6]. The two-layered configurations assembled with trapezoidal segments (Fig. 1b) and arc segments (Fig. 1c) are developed in this research. The inner-diameter (ID) of the solenoids was fixed, while the outer-diameter (OD) and the length (L) could be varied. Both Nd-Fe-B and Sm-Co magnets with linear B-H curves in the second quadrant were used for the simulation. The Nd-Fe-B of 47MGOe has a coercivity H_c = 13.4 kOe (1066 kA/m) and recoil permeability $\mu = 1.045$. The Sm-Co of 28MGOe has H_c = 10.31 kOe (820 kA/m) and μ = 1.038. The results shown below are obtained from the configuration of Fig. 1c.

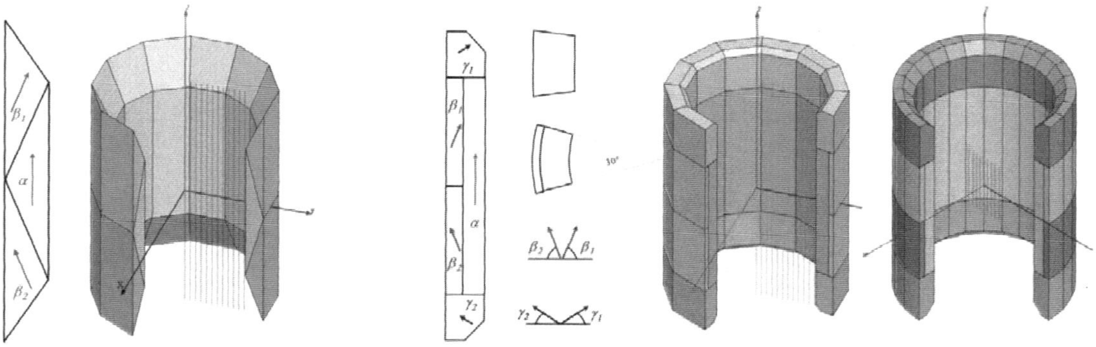

(a) Polyhedron assembly proposed by [6]. *(b) Trapezoid and (c) arc 2-layered assemblies developed in this study.*

Fig. 1. Magnetic configurations viewed in 2D and 3D cut-view with $\alpha = 90°$, $\beta = 0° - 90°$, and $\gamma = 0° - 60°$.

3. Results and Discussion

3.1. Magnet orientation influence

The magnets used for this set of simulations had magnetic orientations $\alpha = 90°$ and $\beta = 0°, 27°, 45°, 74°$, and $90°$. The solenoids have OD = 330 mm, ID= 254 mm, and L = 410 mm. The working zone has y (radius) of 50mm and z (length) of 120mm (z = ± 60). Fig. 2a ($\beta = 27°$) and Fig. 2b ($\beta = 74°$) show the B_Z vectors plotted along eight lines parallel to z-axis with y (radius) = 0, 30, 50, 70, 80, 90, 100, and 110 mm. The 27° has B_z (max) = 0.295T, which is 42% higher than that of 74°. However, the ΔB_z in the work zone is 34.1% for the 27° and 11.5% for the 74°. β of 27° also results in an unwanted larger B_y, and the B_y(max) in the work zone is 2.96 times of that of the 74°. The relationship of the magnetic field vectors vs. β is plotted in Fig. 3, showing a nonlinear relationship between B_z and the β. The linear relationships of ΔB_z and B_y versus β can be expressed as the following equations.

$$\Delta B_z = -0.496\,\beta + 48.121 \quad (1)$$
$$B_y = -0.0006\,\beta + 0.0575 \quad (2)$$

These plots show that the magnet orientation makes a significant difference on the axial field strength and its uniformity in the working zone. An angle β with a set of suitable data can be determined and selected according to the plots and the equations.

3.2. Aspect ratio influence

Sm-Co magnets were used for this set of simulations with $\beta = 74°$. The ID and OD were the same as above, and the aspect ratio or L/ID ranges from 1.0 to 2.1. As plotted in Fig. 4, a smaller L/ID results in a higher B_z(max) but larger ΔB_z & B_y in the work zone. All the values of B_z, B_y and ΔB_z have a nonlinear relationship versus L/ID. The radial field B_y and variation ΔB_z have a 3rd order polynomial relationship with the aspect-ratio L/ID, which can be expressed as equations (3) and (4). A better uniformity can be achieved in the work zone if a larger L/ID is selected, but it is compromised by a lower B_z(max).

$$\Delta B_z = -0.2545\beta^3 + 1.5702\beta^2 - 3.3602\beta + 2.5199 \quad (3)$$
$$B_y = 0.0067\beta^3 - 0.0136\beta^2 - 0.0363\beta + 0.0769 \quad (4)$$

3.3. Two-layered configuration

The configuration consisting of polyhedrons (Fig. 1a) having sharp angles was initially used in this study, which did not result in a satisfactory uniformity. The two-layered configurations were then developed. Fig. 5 shows uniform axial field B_z in the work zone with ΔB_z < 1.1% and B_y < 0.0005T for an optimized solenoid with arc segments (Fig. 1c), the two-layered structures without all the sharp angles also have the advantage of easier manufacturing.

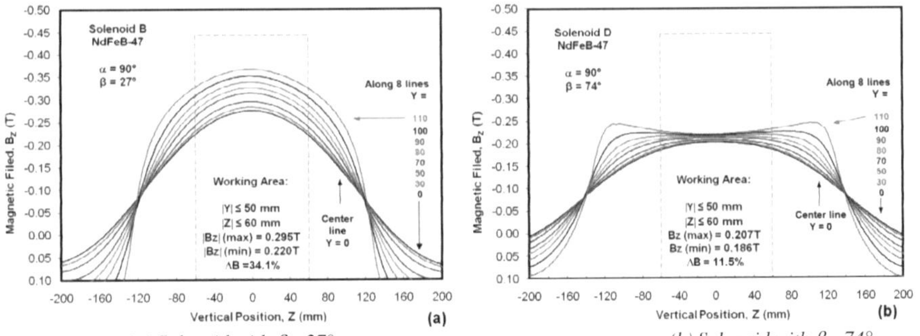

(a) Solenoid with β =27°. *(b) Solenoid with β =74°.*

Fig. 2. Magnetic field B_Z vectors along the lines parallel to z axis in the solenoid.

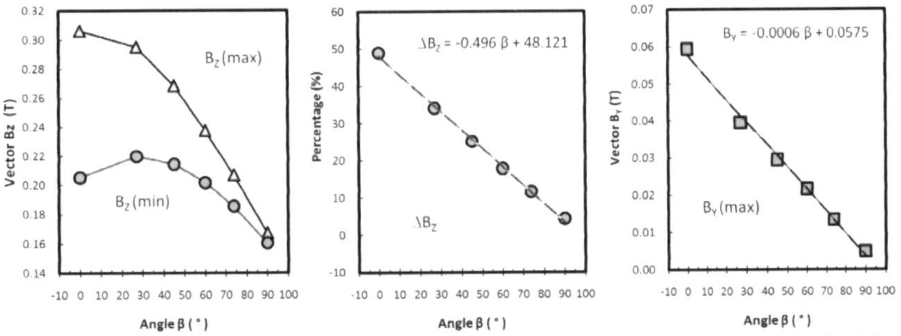

(a) max & min B_Z. *(b) ΔB_Z.* *(c) B_y (smaller is better).*

Fig. 3. The magnetic vectors in work zone versus the angle β (from 0° to 90°).

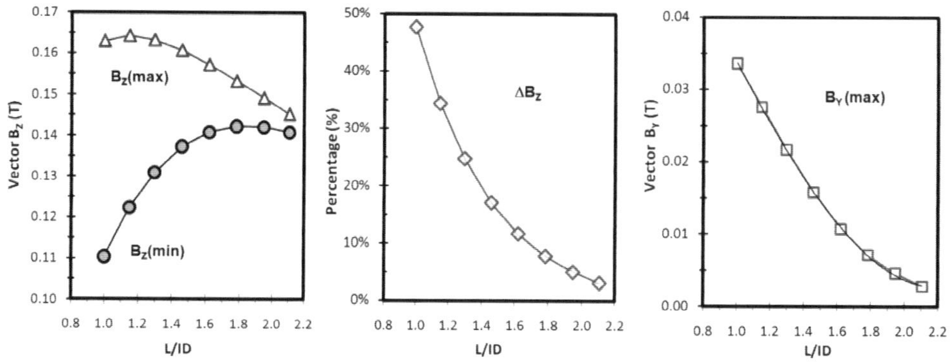

Fig. 4. The magnetic vectors in work zone versus the aspect-ratio for a set of Sm-Co solenoids.

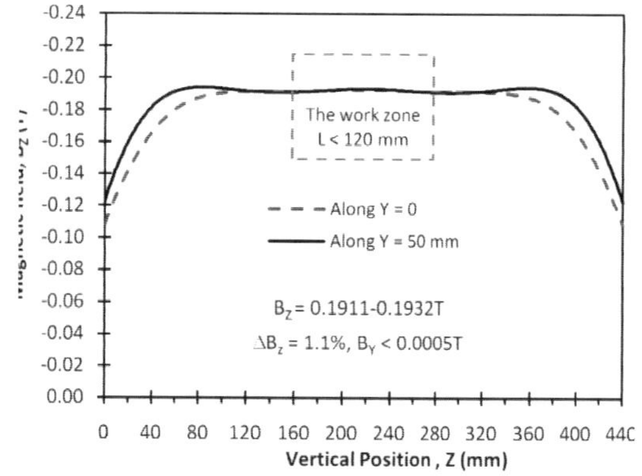

Fig. 5. Magnetic vectors B_z and B_y for the 2-layer configuration assembled with Nd-Fe-B arc segments.

4. Summary

The magnetic orientation has the most significant effect on the axial field and its uniformity. A smaller angle β results in a higher axial field B_z but a larger radial field B_y and deviation ΔB_z. The aspect ratio of the solenoid also has a large effect on the axial field and its uniformity. A smaller aspect ratio of L/ID results in a higher B_z but a larger ΔB_z and a higher B_y in the work zone for L/ID in the range of 1.0 to 2.1.

The two-layered configuration assembled with arc segments was developed [9], resulting in a uniform axial field B_z in the work zone with ΔB_z < 1.1% and B_y < 0.0005T. A Nd-Fe-B solenoid prototype, based on the two-layered arc segment configuration, was built and tested, which was designed to have a length to inner diameter ratio of approximately 5:3 and an axial field B_z of 1.8 kG. Experimental measurements agree with simulation predictions to within < 5% [10].

Acknowledgment

This work was funded by the Air Force Research Laboratory.

References

[1] H.A. Leupold and E. Potenziani II, *IEEE Trans. Magn.* **23**, 3628 (1987).

[2] H.A. Leupold, *IEEE Trans. Magn.* 29, 2341 (1993).

[3] K. Halbach, *Nucl. Instr. and Methods* **169**, 1 (1980).

[4] K. Halbach, *Proc. 5th Int. Workshop on RE-cobalt permanent magnets and their applications*, Virginia, USA, 73 (1981).

[5] K. Halbach, *Proc. 8th Int. Workshop on RE-cobalt permanent magnets and their applications*, Dayton, USA, 123, (1985).

[6] H. A. Leupold and E. Potenziani II, Army Research Laboratory Technical Report ARL-TR-946 (July 1996).

[7] O. Cugat and F. Bloch, *Proc. 15th Int. Workshop on RE magnets and their Applications*, Dresden, Germany, 807 (1998).

[8] M. Kumada, Y. Iwashita, M. Aoki, E. Sugiyama, *Proc. 2003 Particle Accelerator Conf.*, 1993 (2003).

[9] B.W. Hoff, C. H. Chen, J. C. Horwath, M. D. Haworth, P. J. Mardahl, and S. L. Heidger, *J. App. Phys.* **111**, 07A711 (2012).

[10] B. W. Hoff, P. J. Mardahl, C. H. Chen, J. C. Horwath, M. D. Haworth, US 8,358,190B1 (2013).

Nanostructuring and Properties of Strong Permanent-Magnet Films

D.J. SELLMYER,[1] Y. LIU,[1] W.Y. ZHANG,[1] P. KHAREL[1,2]
[1] Nebraska Center for Materials and Nanoscience and Department of Physics and Astronomy, University of Nebraska, Lincoln, NE 68588
[2] Department of Physics, South Dakota State University, Brookings, SD 57007

Abstract: *In this paper we present recent results on FePt-based and MnBi-based films in which special attention has been paid to the achievement of excellent easy-axis alignment to promote high perpendicular anisotropy and magnetization. In addition, we focus on nanostructuring and/or alloying to achieve enhanced properties such as saturation magnetization (M_s) and coercivity (H_c). The FePt:X films are based on the $L1_0$ structure and are nanostructured to contain $Fe_{1-x}Co_xPt$, $FePt_{1-x}Ni_x$ single phases or $L1_0$ (Fe,Co)Pt:fcc(Fe,Co)Pt hard-soft phases. The films are [001] oriented with perpendicular magnetic anisotropy (PMA) by growth at 830°C on MgO (001). In the case of $L1_0$ FePt:fcc Fe-Pt, the properties are clear examples of exchange-coupled hard-soft magnets with increasing M_s and decreasing H_c as the soft-phase fraction increases. Maximum values of M_s, H_c and nominal $(BH)_{max}$ are 1416 emu/cm^3, 51 kOe, and 64 MGOe, respectively. Exchange-coupling between the $L1_0$ grains is critical in controlling H_c. MnBi:X films have the hexagonal NiAs structure and are oriented with c normal to the film plane. Strong PMA is observed with $J_s = 4\pi M_s = 8.3$ kG, $H_c = 20$ kOe, and $(BH)_{max} = 16.3$ MGOe in the pure film at room temperature. H_c rises to 31.6 kOe at 540 K. Alloying with various elements including X = Au, Pt, Fe and rare earths generally leads to a decrease in M_s. This is explained by antiferromagnetic spin correlations in agreement with DFT calculations for X = Fe.*

Keywords: *permanent-magnet films; exchange-coupled grains*

Address: David J. Sellmyer, Nebraska Center for Materials and Nanoscience, University of Nebraska, Lincoln, NE 68588-0113, USA, Tel.: 402-472-2407, Fax: 402-472-6148, E-mail: dsellmyer@unl.edu

1. Introduction

High-anisotropy permanent-magnet films have attracted much attention because of their potential for emerging applications [1-5]. Examples include extremely high-density media for heat-assisted magnetic recording, thermally stable magneto-electronics devices with perpendicular anisotropy, actuators in micro-electro-mechanical systems, and nanoscale biomagnetic and other sensors [6-14]. In considering the fabrication and properties of permanent-magnet films, it is useful to consider the intrinsic properties of known high-anisotropy materials such as those listed in Table I. Naturally, the well-known magnetic materials such as $Nd_2Fe_{14}B$, $SmCo_5$ and related materials have excellent properties including saturation magnetic polarization J_s and first anisotropy constant K_1. However, these materials have the deficiencies that they are chemically reactive which is particularly troublesome for film magnets, and they contain critical and/or expensive rare-earth materials. For this reason much of our recent work on film magnets has been focused on the Fe-, Co-, or Mn-based materials with the ordered tetragonal $L1_0$ or hexagonal NiAs structures. Considerable effort has been placed on special techniques to grow highly c-axis oriented films with strong perpendicular magnetic anisotropy (PMA). In addition, methods to modify and improve the properties of the basic "pure" phases have been studied through substitutional alloying and/or nanostructuring to include a second, soft phase to increase the average magnetization. The specific systems investigated include FePt:Fe and FePt:$Fe_{65}Co_{35}$ nanocomposite films, $Fe_{50}Pt_{50-x}Ni_x$, and MnBi and MnBi-X alloys, where X = Fe, Pt, Pr and other metals.

Table I. High-Anisotropy bulk compounds.

Compound	Crystal Structure	J_s (kG)	K_1 (Mergs/cm^3)
$Nd_2F_{14}B$	Tetragonal	16.1	50
$SmCo_5$	Hexagonal ($CaCu_5$)	10.7	172
YCo_5	Hexagonal ($CaCu_5$)	10.6	55
$LaCo_5$	Hexagonal ($CaCu_5$)	9.0	50
FePt	Tetragonal ($L1_0$)	14.3	66
CoPt	Tetragonal ($L1_0$)	10.0	49
MnBi	Hexagonal (NiAs)	7.8	12
MnAl	$L1_0$	6.5	17
MnGa	$L1_0$	7.8	26
$HfCo_7$	Orthorhombic	10.8	16
Zr_2Co_{11}	Rhombohedral	8.0	11

2. Film-Growth Methods and Structures

An AJA International sputtering system was used to prepare FePt-based films. Films with various compositions were deposited on (001) oriented single-crystal MgO and on Si substrates by co-sputtering Fe, Co, Pt or Ni targets with *in-situ* heating at 830 °C. The sputtering rates of Fe, Co, Pt and Ni were adjusted to obtain films with specified Fe, Co, Pt and Ni

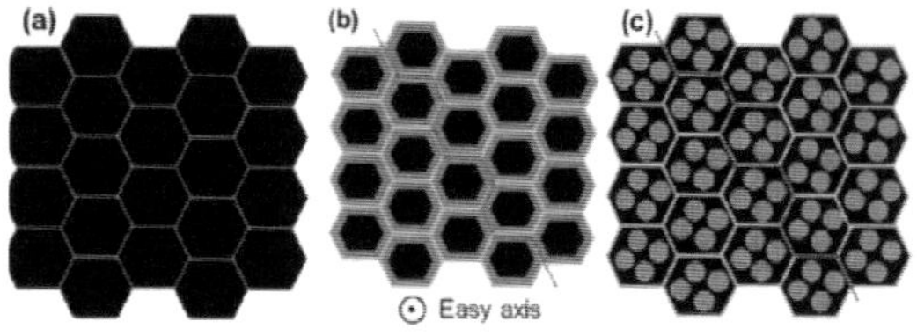

Fig. 1. Schematic aligned nanostructures.

concentrations. Before each deposition, a vacuum of better than 4 x 10^{-8} Torr was achieved in the deposition chamber, and the Ar pressure for deposition was 5 mTorr. An AJA e-beam evaporation system was used to deposit the Mn/Bi trilayers. Bi(l)/Mn(m)/Bi(n) layers were alternatively deposited on glass substrates at 125 ^{0}C. The deposition rate for Bi and Mn was 8 and 5 Å/s. The trilayers were *in situ* annealed at 290 ^{0}C for 1h and subsequently at 400 ^{0}C for 1 h. These growth methods have been shown to produce highly oriented structures with the *c* axes oriented perpendicular to the film plane.

Various types of single- or two-phase nano-structures can be envisioned from the growth methods employed. Some of these are shown schematically in Fig. 1. The hard-phase grains are shown as black hexagons and are assumed to have their easy axes out of the figure. Figure 1(a) shows a polycrystalline single-phase film with aligned easy axes. Figure 1(b) could represent a hard-soft (black-gray) core-shell arrangement or a collection of hard grains that are separated and exchange decoupled by a gray non-magnetic phase (or vacuum). Finally, Fig. 1(c) shows schematically a hard-soft nano-composite with the soft (cross-hatched) sub-grains embedded randomly in the hard (black) grains. The hard grains are more or less exchange decoupled through a thin intergranular phase that could promote pinning of domain walls as shown by the dashed line. Approximations to these structures will be discussed below.

3. FePt:Fe-Pt Composite System

Aspects of the nanostructures shown in Figure 1 have been realized in the FePt:Fe-Pt films [15]. Figure 2 is a TEM image of a FePt:Fe-Pt film on MgO substrate. This image is similar to the models shown in Fig. 1(b) and (c) but with less packing density. The soft phase appearing white is visible but the contrast is blurred due to the MgO substrate. The separation of the magnetic grains ensures low exchange coupling and high coercivity in this film. The soft phase enhances the magnetization. The volume fraction, the size of the soft phase, and the separation between the composite grains must be optimized to achieve the highest energy product. The FePt films are [001] oriented with perpendicular magnetic anisotropy

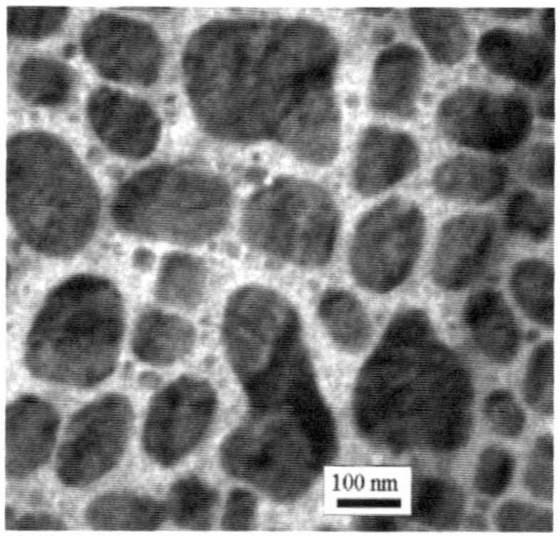

Fig. 2. TEM image of a FePt:Fe film.

(PMA) by growth at 830 °C on MgO (001). The magnetic properties as a function of the volume fraction of the soft phase are plotted in Figure 3. Significant magnetic properties achieved for a volume percent of 5.4 are: coercivity H_c = 40 kOe, saturation magnetization M_s = 1287 emu/cc, and nominal energy product $(BH)_{max}$ ≈ 54 MGOe. The volume fraction of the soft phase is deduced by using the hysteresis loops of both perpendicular and parallel measurement. This measurement is confirmed by phase-diagram calculations as well.

4. $(Fe_{0.65}Co_{0.35})Pt$:$Fe_{0.65}Co_{0.35}$ Composite System

The magnetic properties of the films were improved by choosing a high-magnetization soft phase, $Fe_{0.65}Co_{0.35}$. The hard phase FePt was replaced by $(Fe_{0.65}Co_{0.35})Pt$ through considera-tion of phase equilibrium. The Fe:Co ratio is sustained at 65:35 [16]. Figure 4 displays the plots of magnetic properties variation with volume fraction of the soft phase in $(Fe_{0.65}Co_{0.35})Pt$:$Fe_{0.65}Co_{0.35}$ films. The increase of the Fe-Co concentration from 57.3 to 68.3 at% enhances the saturation magnetization M_s from 1245 emu/cm^3

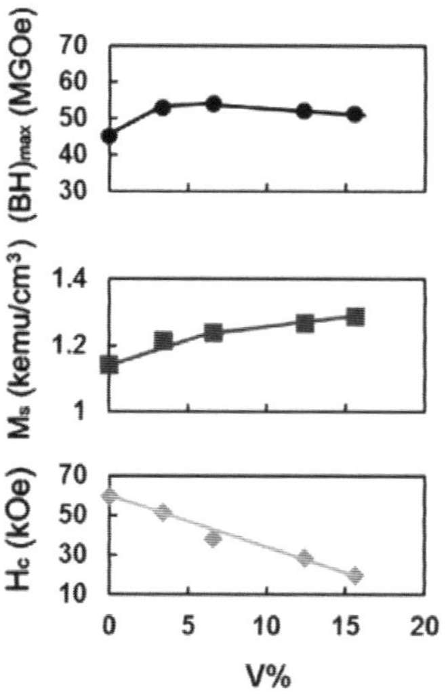

Fig. 3. Magnetic properties variation of FePt films with volume fraction of soft phase.

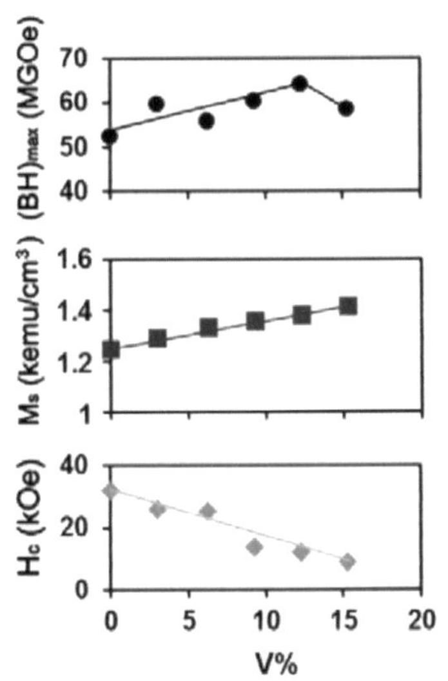

Fig. 4. Magnetic properties variation of (Fe,Co)Pt films with volume fraction of soft phase.

to 1416 emu/cm^3, and the coercivity decreases from 32 kOe to 8.9 kOe. The highest nominal maximum energy product per grain is 64 MGOe.

5. $Fe_{50}Pt_{50-x}Ni_x$ Films

We have investigated the effect of replacing some Pt by a third element on magnetic properties of FePt. The requirement for the third element is that it can substitute for Pt and sustain the stability of the $L1_0$ FePt structure. It is also desirable that the third element can improve the magnetic properties of FePt. After screening of usable elements by the method described in [17], we determined that Ni is a suitable element. $Fe_{50}Pt_{50-x}Ni_x$ (x = 0, 6, 12, 18, 25) films were deposited on (001) oriented single-crystal MgO and on Si substrates by co-sputtering Fe, Pt and Ni targets. Figure 5 shows the magnetic properties variation with Ni content. With increase of the Ni concentration from 0 to 25 at.%, the saturation magnetization M_s increases from 1060 emu/cm^3 to 1320 emu/cm^3, the coercivity decreases from 26.8 kOe to 0.7 kOe. A nominal maximum energy product of 52.9 MGOe was obtained in the film $Fe_{50}Pt_{44}Ni_6$.

6. MnBi:X Films

Mn-Bi-based films have been studied because of their strong magnetocrystalline anisotropy energy and good high-temperature properties [18-21]. Figure 6 shows XRD patterns of the Mn_xBi_{100-x} films (Fig. 1a, 1b). The films consist of the NiAs-type low-temperature-phase (LTP) MnBi. The intensity from the (002) peaks is the strongest, implying the c-axis of the LTP grain is perpendicular to the film plane. Its lattice parameters were determined to be a = 4.29 and c = 6.12 Å, close to those reported in the bulk LTP [22].

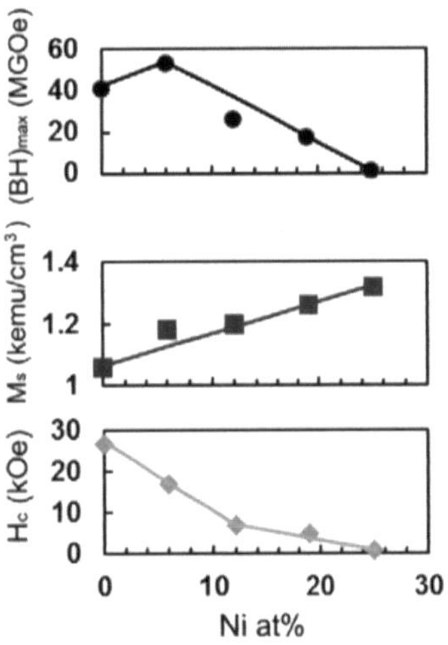

Fig. 5. Magnetic properties variation of $Fe_{50}Pt_{50-x}Ni_x$ films with Ni concentration.

Compared to the x = 57 and 48 films, the x = 52 film has the fewest diffraction peaks from misoriented grains and the weakest relative intensity of diffraction `indicates that the x = 52 film has the best c-axis alignment perpendicular to the film plane and highest content of the hard magnetic LTP. The thermomagnetic curve of the x = 52 film was measured in a field of 3 kOe. The transition temperature is estimated from the peak value in the dM/dT curve. Only one transition was seen in the heating $M(T)$ curve. The transition temperatures from LTP to high-temperature-phase (HTP) and from HTP to LTP are 627 K and 591 K, which are close to the reported values in the $Mn_{55}Bi_{55}$ film [23]. Figure 7a shows $J(H)$ curves of the Mn_xBi_{100-x} films. The x = 52 film has the largest concentration and best c-axis grain alignment of the hard magnetic LTP. Thus, its saturation magnetization and coercivity are higher than those of the other two films (x = 48 and 57). The squareness of its hysteresis loops is also better than the others. The huge difference of the remanence ratio

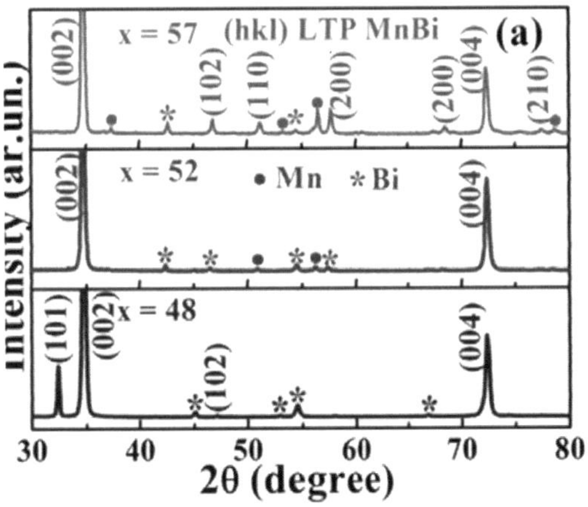

Fig. 6. X-ray diffraction of MnBi films.

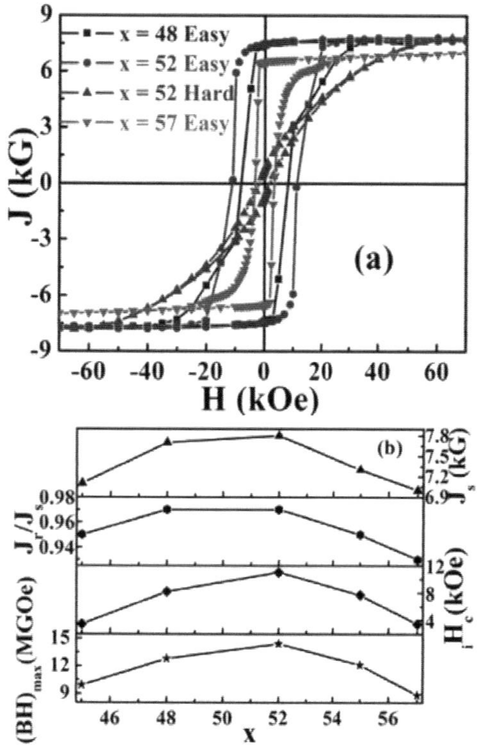

Fig. 7. (a) Hysteresis loops of MnBi films. (b) Magnetic properties variation with Mn concentration.

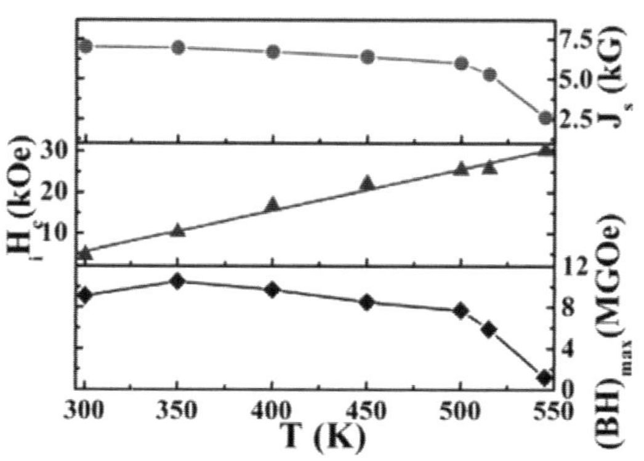

Fig. 8. Magnetic properties variation of $Mn_{57}Bi_{43}$ with temperature.

and coercivity between the easy- and hard-axis $J(H)$ curves means good grain orientation in the $x = 52$ film in agreement with the XRD results. The crossing point between the easy- and hard-axis $J(H)$ curves at 61 kOe corresponds to the magnetocrystalline anisotropy field of the LTP. The magneto-crystalline anisotropy constant was estimated to be 14.0 Mergs/cc using the Sucksmith-Thompson method. Figure 7b gives the deduced magnetic properties of the Mn_xBi_{100-x} films. The J_s and H_c increased with x increasing, so the $(BH)_{max}$ was improved. The best magnetic properties: $J_s = 7.8$ kG, $H_c = 11.0$ kOe, and $(BH)_{max} = 14.4$ MGOe has been achieved for the $x = 52$ film.

Figure 8 shows the temperature dependence of magnetic properties for the $x = 57$ film. The direction of the applied field is perpendicular to the film plane. The H_c increases from 4.6 kOe at 300K to 30.2 kOe at 545K possibly due to the enhancement of the magnetocrystalline aniso-tropy field [24]. The squareness of hysteresis loops was improved, but J_s slightly decreases with the increase of T ($T \leq 500$K). Therefore, the energy product slightly decreases. In order to improve the high energy product at high temperature, a certain amount of high-magnetization soft magnetic layer may be added to increase remanence. We also have performed experiments on alloying MnBi with various elements including X = Au, Pt, Fe and rare earths; this generally leads to a *decrease* in M_s [25,26]. This is explained by antiferromagnetic spin correlations involving Mn atoms in interstitial sites in the NiAs structure, which are in agreement with DFT calculations for X = Fe [26].

7. Conclusions

Using in-situ heating during the sputtering, we have fabricated exchange-coupled nano-structures of FePt-based films with a high degree of alignment. The energy product of exchange coupled FePt:Fe films exceeds the pure hard phase FePt. The energy product is further improved to 64 MGOe by using a high-magnetization soft phase ($F_{65}Co_{35}$) and hard phase. Ni was shown to be a suitable element for partially substituting for Pt. The magnetization is enhanced with some H_c reduction in $FePt_{1-x}Ni_x$ films. In MnBi:X films, Strong PMA is observed with $J_s = 4\pi M_s = 8.3$ kG, $H_c = 20$ kOe, and $(BH)_{max} = 16.3$ MGOe in the pure film at room temperature. H_c rises to 31.6 kOe at 540 K [4]. Attempts to improve the magnetization of MnBi by alloying with Fe, Pr and other metals were foiled by structure- specific antiferro-magnetic correlations involving interstitial Mn atoms.

Acknowledgements
Research supported by US DOE (DE-FG02-04ER46152), NSF (DMR-082052 and DMR-0960110, electron microscopy), and NCMN-NRI (Central Facilities).

References

[1] S.D. Bader, *Rev. Mod. Phys.* **78**, 2006, 1.
[2] D.J. Sellmyer, R. Skomski (Eds.): *Advanced Magnetic Nanostruc.*, Springer, Berlin, 2006, 1-508.
[3] Y. Liu, D.J. Sellmyer, D. Shindo (Eds.): *Handbook of Advanced Magnetic Materials*, Springer, Berlin, 2006, Vol. 1, pp. 1-373, Vol. 2, pp. 1-601, Vol. 3, pp. 1-352, Vol. 4, pp. 1-448.

[4] H. Kronmüller, S.S.P. Parkin (Eds.): *Handbook of Magnetism and Adv. Magn. Matls.*, Wiley, West Sussex, UK, 2007, 1-5.
[5] J.P. Liu, E. Fullerton, O. Gutfleisch, D.J. Sellmyer (Eds.): *Nanoscale Magnetic Mater. and Applic.*, Springer, Berlin, 2009, pp. 1-710.
[6] D. Weller, T. McDaniel, in: D.J. Sellmyer, R. Skomski (Eds.): *Advanced Magnetic Nanostruc.*, Springer, Berlin, 2006, pp. 295-324.
[7] S. Rivoirard, D. Givord, in: D.J. Sellmyer, R. Skomski (Eds.): *Advanced Magnetic Nanostruc.*, Springer, Berlin, 2006, pp. 325-357.
[8] N.M. Dempsey, in: J.P. Liu, E. Fullerton, O. Gutfleisch, D.J. Sellmyer (Eds.): *Nanoscale Magnetic Mater. and Applic.*, Springer, Berlin, 2009, pp. 661-684.
[9] S.M. Lindsay, *Introduction to Nanoscience*, Oxford, UK, 2010, pp. 1-445.
[10] J. Gao, H. Gu, B. Xu, *Acc. Chem. Res.* **42**, 2009, 1097.
[11] J.T. Zhang, Y. Tang, L. Weng, M. Ouyang, *Nano Letters* **9**, 2009, 4061.
[12] C.L. Zha, Johan Åkerman, *IEEE Trans. Magn.* **45**, 2009, 3491.
[13] D.P. Arnold, W.G. Wang, *J. Microelect. Syst.* **18**, 2009, 1255.
[14] C.J. Xu, Z. Yuan, N. Kohler, J. Kim, M.A. Chung, S. Sun, *J. Am. Chem. Soc.* **131**, 2009, 15346.
[15] Y. Liu, T.A. George, R. Skomski, D.J. Sellmyer, *Appl. Phys. Lett.* **99**, 2011, 172504.
[16] Y. Liu, T.A. George, R. Skomski, D.J. Sellmyer, *J. Appl. Phys.* **111**, 2012, 07B537; *IEEE Trans. Magn.* **49**, 2013, 3292.
[17] Y. Liu, T. Takasugi, O. Izumi, *Metall. Trans.* **17A**, 1986, 1433.
[18] P. Ravindran, A. Delin, P. James, B. Johansson, J.M. Wills, R. Ahuja, O. Eriksson, *Phys. Rev. B* **59**, 1999, 15680.
[19] P. Kharel, P. Thapa, P. Lukashev, R.F. Sabirianov, E.Y. Tsymbal, D.J. Sellmyer, B. Nadgorny, *Phys. Rev. B* **83**, 2011, 024415.
[20] P. Kharel, R. Skomski, D.J. Sellmyer, *J. Appl. Phys.* **109**, 2011, 07B709.
[21] D. Chen, R.L. Aagard, *J. Appl. Phys.* **41**, 1970, 2530.
[22] A.F. Andresen, W. Halg, P. Fischer, E. Stoll, *Acta Chem. Scand.* **21**, 1967, 1543.
[23] P. Kharel, S. Valloppilly, X.Z. Li, W.Y. Zhang, R. Skomski, J.E. Shield, D.J. Sellmyer, *J. Phys. D: Appl. Phys.* **46**, 2013, 095003.
[24] H. Kronmüller, J.B. Yang, D. Goll, *J. Phys.: Cond. Matt.* **26**, 2014, 064210.
[25] P. Kharel, R. Skomski, P. Lukashev, R. Sabirianov, D.J. Sellmyer, *Physical Review B* **84**, 2011, 014431.
[26] P. Kharel, X. Z. Li, V. R. Shah, N. Al-Aqtash, K. Tarawneh, R. F. Sabirianov, R. Skomski, D. J. Sellmyer, *J. Appl. Phys.* **111**, 2012, 07E326.

Nanocomposite Thick-film Magnets with Nd-Fe-B + α-Fe Phases Prepared under High Laser Energy Density

M. NAKANO, K. MOTOMURA, K. FUJIYAMA, T. YANAI, H. FUKUNAGA
Graduate School of Engineering, Bunkyo-machi 1-14, Nagasaki 852-8521, Japan

Abstract: *The small spot size of laser beam with the high energy density above 10 J/cm^2 enabled us to prepare an isotropic nano-composite thick-film magnet with a high remanence value. In the as-deposited films, the structure of amorphous phase including α-Fe grains by taking advantage of the emitting process of Fe and Nd atoms from an Nd-Fe-B target. Through a rapid annealing process, nano-composite thick-films with Nd-Fe-B and α-Fe phases could be obtained. Resultantly, we succeeded in preparing a 16 μm -thick-film magnet with remanence, coercivity and $(BH)_{max}$ values of approximately 1.0 T, 400 kA/m and 100 kJ/m^3, respectively, indicating a promising material usable for a miniaturized cylindrical motor.*

1. Introduction

Many researches on anisotropic Nd-Fe-B thick-film magnets have been demonstrated to develop microelectro–mechanical systems (MEMS) technology [1][2]. Recently, we reported that the preparation of a multi-polarly magnetized rotor comprising the rapidly-quenched thick-film magnets with isotropic properties is effective to develop a miniaturized cylindrical motor [3], and the required values of coercivity, remanence and $(BH)_{max}$ for the films are higher than 0.9 T, 400 kA/m, and 90 kJ/m^3, respectively. We also have prepared isotropic Nd-Fe-B+α-Fe nano-composite thick-film magnets by using a PLD (Pulsed Laser Deposition) method with the laser energy density lower than 1 J/cm^2 [4]. The characteristics of the method are a high deposition rate above 40 μm/h and a reliability of magnetic properties because of the good transfer of composition from a target to a film [4-6]. Furthermore, we demonstrated that the additives such as Zr and Nb are effective to enhance coercivity in nano-composite Nd-Fe-B thick-films, however the microstructure was inhomogeneous due to the partial existence in coarse grains larger than 100 nm, and resultantly the remanence didn't exceed 0.8 T [4]. The results indicated that the usage of low energy density together with the additives is insufficient to suppress the grain growth in PLD-made nano-composite Nd-Fe-B films. Other deposition and annealing processes are, therefore, required to achieve better magnetic properties.

In this study, we focused on the use of high laser energy density above 10 J/cm^2 in order to adopt a different deposition process by taking advantage of the explosively emitting process of atoms from a target. As a result, the fabrication of Nd-Fe-B+α-Fe nanocomposite thick-film magnets usable for the above cylindrical motor has been demonstrated.

2. Experimental Procedures

The rotated targets with various compositions of $Nd_XFe_{14}B$ (x=1.8-2.8) were ablated by an Nd-YAG pulse laser (wave length = 355 nm). The films deposited on each Ta substrate ere fabricated in the vacuum atmosphere of 10^{-5}Pa. The laser energy density (LED) is changed by the spot size of the laser which could be controlled by moving the distance between a focal lens and a target intentionally. The two ranges of laser energy density were adopted as below 1 J/cm^2 and above 10 J/cm^2 at fixing the laser power of 4 W. The laser power was measured with a power meter in front of the entrance lens of a chamber. The deposition rate became from 20 to 40 μm/h by using the distance of 10 mm between a target and a substrate. All the as-deposited films thicker than 10 μm were crystallized by a pulse annealing (PA) method in the vacuum atmosphere of 2-5×10^{-5}Pa. The pulse-annealing time varied from 1.7 to 2.2 s with an infrared furnace at output power of 8 kW, and then they were cooled down to room temperature[7]. The magnetic properties of the sample were measured with a vibrating sample magnetometer (VSM) under maximum applied magnetic field of 2.5 T after magnetization under a pulsed field.

3. Results and Discussion

Figure 1 shows the remanence values of Nd-Fe-B thick-film magnets prepared by using two regions of LED as a function of Nd contents in each film. Here, an $Nd_{2.4}Fe_{14}B$ target was used. In the case of LED ≦ 1 J/cm^2, each film indicated almost the same compositions compared with that of the target. At LED larger than 10 J/cm^2, the reduction in Nd contents of the films by approximately 5 at. %. The evaluation of composition on the ablated surface area in the target indicated that no selectivity of the emitted Fe and Nd atoms. It is, therefore, considered that Fe atoms tend to move directly to a substrate and Nd atoms tend to be widely emitted under the explosive deposition process using the high laser energy density.

We further investigated the relationship between coercivity and remanence of each sample thicker than

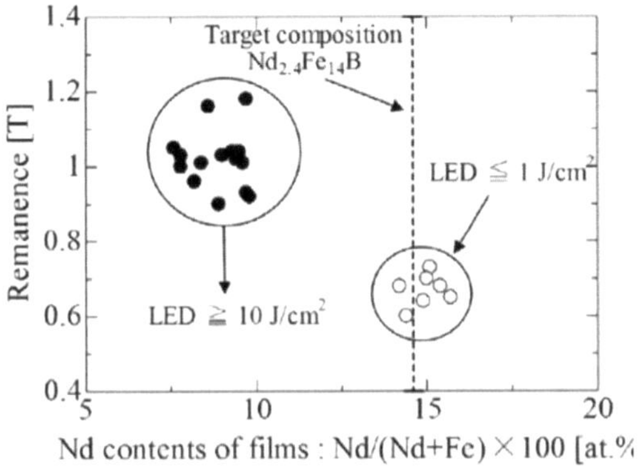

Fig.1. Remanence of thick-film magnets prepared by using an $Nd_{2.4}Fe_{14}B$ target together with two ranges of LED as a function of Nd contents.

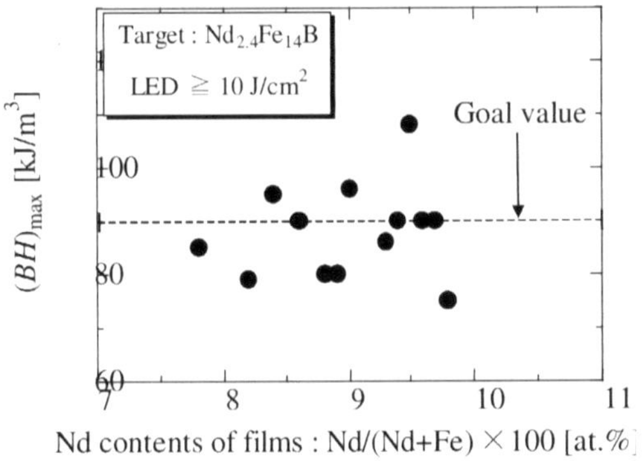

Fig. 3. $(BH)_{max}$ values as a function of Nd contents in each thick-film prepared by using LED above 10 J/cm² together with an $Nd_{2.4}Fe_{14}B$ target.

10 μm prepared by six Nd-Fe-B targets with various compositions under LED ≧ 10 J/cm² as displayed in Fig. 2. In all the targets, the deposition rate was higher than 20 μm/h and the reduction in the Nd contents of each film by several atomic percentages was observed compared with that of the corresponding target. The samples prepared by using an $Nd_{2.4}Fe_{14}B$ target had relatively large values of coercivity and remanence. In addition, the $(BH)_{max}$ values of the films fabricated from the $Nd_{2.4}Fe_{14}B$ target showed around 90 kJ/m³ as seen in Fig. 3. Figure 4 shows the *M-H* loop of a 16 micron-thick-film magnet with remanence, coercivity and $(BH)_{max}$ values of 1.04 T, 426 kA/m and 108 kJ/m³, respectively. From these results, although the dispersion of magnetic properties was observed, the use of an $Nd_{2.4}Fe_{14}B$ target with the LED ≧ 10 J/cm² was an effective method of attaining the required properties usable to the cylindrical motor.

In order to investigate the mechanism for obtaining superior magnetic properties by using the high LED together with an $Nd_{2.4}Fe_{14}B$ target, the crystal structure of as-deposited and annealed films was examined. Figure 5 shows the X-ray diffraction patterns of three as-deposited films prepared by different deposition conditions. The lowest pattern was corresponded to a sample prepared from an $Nd_{2.4}Fe_{14}B$ target by using LED ≧ 10 J/cm². The residual two samples were fabricated by using LED

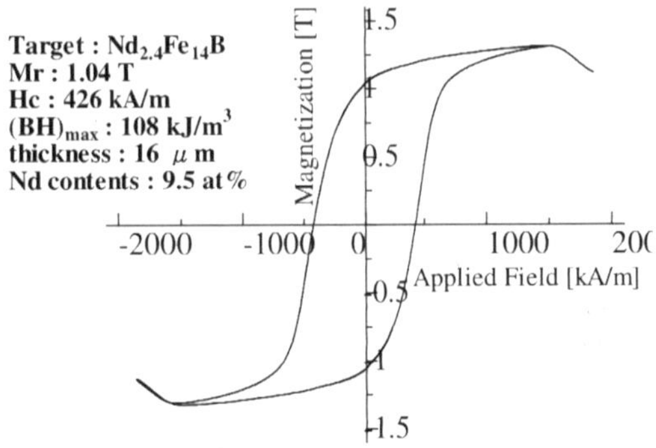

Fig. 4. M-H loop of a 16 μm-thick Nd-Fe-B film magnet prepared by using LED above 10 J/cm² together with an $Nd_{2.4}Fe_{14}B$ target.

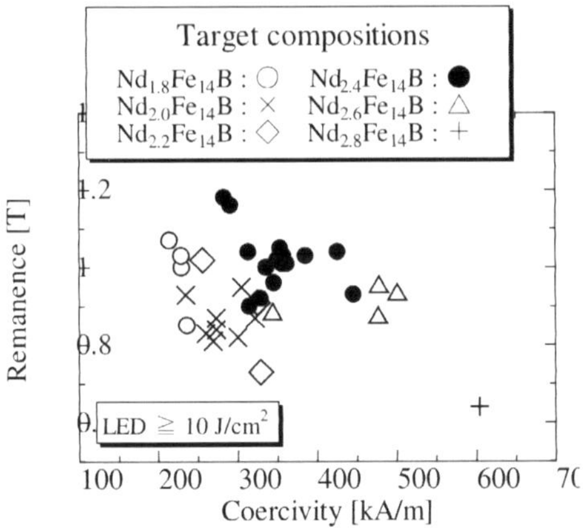

Fig.2. Relationship between remanence and coercivity values of films thicker than 10 μm by using six targets with various compositions.

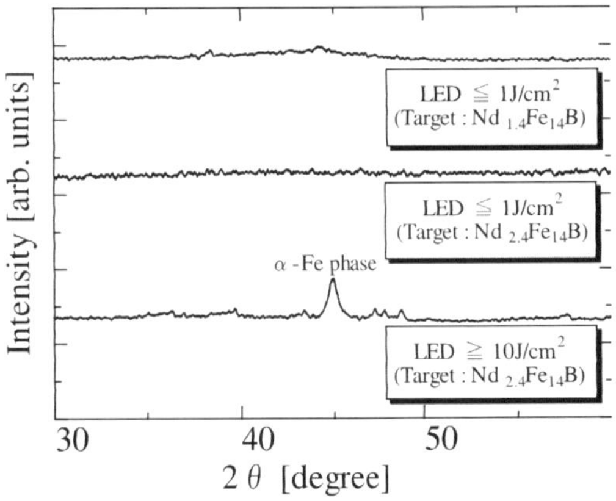

Fig. 5. X-ray diffraction patterns of as-deposited films prepared by different conditions.

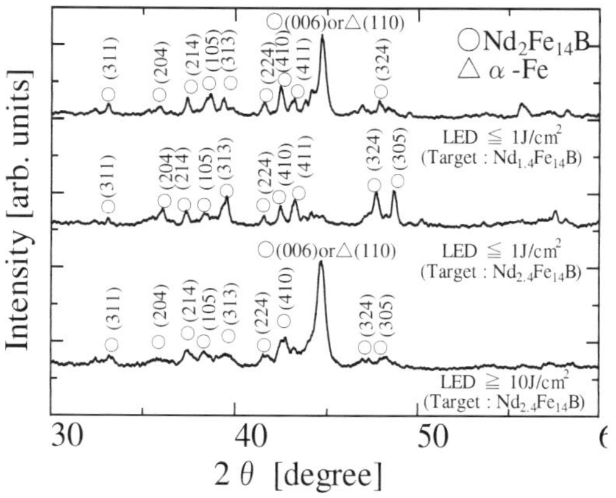

Fig. 6. X-ray diffraction patterns of annealed films shown in Fig. 5. Usage of LED ≧ 10 J/cm² together with an $Nd_{2.4}Fe_{14}B$ target enabled us to obtain isotropic Nd-Fe-B/α-Fe nano-composite film magnets.

≦ 1 J/cm². Furthermore, each sample corresponding to the highest and middle diffraction patterns were fabricated by using $Nd_{1.4}Fe_{14}B$ and $Nd_{2.4}Fe_{14}B$ targets, respectively. The Nd contents range for two films corresponding to the lowest and highest diffraction patterns were almost the same. The as-deposited samples prepared under the LED ≦ 1 J/cm² had amorphous structure, on the other hand a crystallization peak corresponding to α-Fe phase could be observed in the high LED-made sample. Figure 6 shows the diffraction patterns of annealed samples displayed in Fig. 5. Except the sample corresponding to the middle diffraction pattern, the residual two samples were composed of Nd-Fe-B and α-Fe phases. The estimation on the average grain sizes in each sample showed approximately 15 nm (LED ≧ 10 J/cm²) and 20 nm (LED ≦ 1 J/cm²), respectively.

It was clarified that the usage of LED ≧ 10 J/cm² in an $Nd_{2.4}Fe_{14}B$ target enabled us to obtain an as-deposited film with amorphous structure including α-Fe phase. Furthermore, the grain growth of α-Fe phase of the above-mentioned films was suppressed by approximately 3 nm through the annealing. These results are probably attributed to the explosively emitting deposition process which is much different phenomenon from the previous one [4], however further investigations of the mechanism are required.

4. Conclusion

Isotropic Nd-Fe-B/α-Fe nano-composite thick-film magnets with the remanence above 0.9 T were prepared by taking advantage of the high laser energy density over 10 J/m². The as-deposited films had amorphous phase including α-Fe grains, and a nano-composite structure could be obtained after the pulse annealing. We succeeded in obtaining Nd-Fe-B thick-film magnets with the required properties usable to the cylindrical motor.

References

[1] M. Uehara, N. Gannai, M. Fujiwara, and T. Tanaka," *IEEE Trans. Magn.* **41**, 2005, 3838.

[2] N. M. Dempsey, A. Walther, F. May, D. Givord, K. Khlopkov, and O. Gutfleisch, *Appl. Phys. Lett.* **90**, 2007, 092509.

[3] F. Yamashita, S. Nishimura, O. Kobayashi, M. Itoh, M. Nakano, H. Fukunaga and K. Ishiyama, *J. Appl. Phys.* **109**, 2011, 07A712.

[4] M. Nakano, M. Itakura, T. Yanai, F. Yamashita, and H. Fukunaga, *IEEJ. Trans. on Fundamentals and Materials.* **132**, 2012, 844.

[5] M. Nakano, S. Sato, F. Yamashita, T. Honda, J. Yamasaki, K. Ishiyama, M. Itakura, J. Fidler, T. Yanai, and H. Fukunaga, *IEEE Trans. Magn.* **43**, 2007, 2672.

[6] H. Fukunaga, T. Kamikawatoko, M. Nakano, T. Yanai, and F. Yamashita, *J. Appl. Phys.* 109, 2011, 07A758.

[7] H. Fukunaga, K. Tokunaga, and J. M. Song, *IEEE Trans. Magn.* **38**, 2002, 2970.

Effect of Grain Size on Spinodal Decomposition and Magnetic Properties of Melt-Spun Alnico

KONRAD LÖWE[1], FARZIN TABARY[1], BIANCA FRINCU[1], RAJASEKHAR MADUGUNDO[3], OLIVER GUTFLEISCH[1, 2] GEORGE C. HADJIPANAYIS[3]
[1]TU Darmstadt, Petersenstr. 23, 64287 Darmstadt, Germany
[2]Fraunhofer ISC, IWKS Group Materials Recycling and Resource Strategy, Hanau, Germany
[3]Department of Physics and Astronomy, University of Delaware, Newark, DE, USA

Abstract: *The aim of this work is to investigate the effect of very fine grain sizes on the spinodal decomposition in the Alnico system. Commercial Alnico 8 was melted and melt-spun with varying copper wheel speeds, which led to a grain size of around 2µm. This value was further reduced to sub-micrometer size by a small addition of Boron (1at%). The spinodal decomposition was induced through a two-step annealing treatment in the range of 600-900°C under a magnetic field. It was found that the nanometer-sized spinodal structures become bigger with increasing wheel speeds and smaller with the addition of Boron. Contrary to expectations, the coercivity of the sample containing Boron is slightly reduced compared to the one without it, which is attributed to the formation of unwanted secondary phases.*

1. Introduction

Permanent magnets are used in many commercial applications with the most important ones in motors and generators. The recent rare earth crisis calls for the development of rare earth-lean/free permanent magnets [1]. Alnico magnets are the first modern permanent magnets discovered by Mishima [2] which do not contain rare earths and have a relatively high energy product. The magnetic hardness of these magnets originates from the shape anisotropy of Fe-Co-rich magnetic rods which are embedded in a non-magnetic Ni-Al rich matrix. This microstructure is obtained through spinodal decomposition after a special heat-treatment. However, the low coercivity (~2 kOe) of Alnico magnets, limits their use for high temperature applications. The theoretical value of the coercivity based on rod shape anisotropy is expected to be much higher (>7 kOe). Recent electron microscopy observations revealed that the morphology of the rods is inhomogenous and the matrix is weakly magnetic, both of which can lead to the low coercivity [3]. The aim of this work is to investigate the effect of grain size on the spinodal decomposition in Alnico melt-spun alloys and hopefully be able to tailor the spinodal structures by varying the grain size and processing routes to include magnetic annealing that may lead to higher coercivity.

2. Experimental

An Alnico 8 magnet was used in this study. Samples with different grain sizes were prepared by varying the copper wheel speed of the melt-spinner from 5-60 m/s. Another set of samples was also prepared with the addition of a small amount of B (1 at.%) in order to obtain a smaller grain size. Spinodal decomposition was induced by subjecting the as-spun samples to an annealing heat treatment at temperatures in the range of 600 - 900 °C. The ribbons were heat-treated under vacuum at temperatures 900 °C (for 30 minutes) and then were cooled to 600 °C at ~100 °C/min cooling rate. The heat-treatment was continued at this temperature for 120 min. The ribbons were under magnetic field of 1T during the whole heat-treatment. Magnetic properties of the ribbons were measured with Quantum Design VersaLab vibrating sample magnetometer. Microstructure characterization of the ribbons was carried out by scanning electron microscopy using a SEM JEOL JSM 7600F.

3. Results and Discussion

The grain size as expected was found to decrease with the wheel speed. Figure 1 shows the microstructure of as-spun sample prepared at high wheel speeds. As one can see the grain size in both cases is similar with an average size below one micron. The average grain size is doubled after the heat treatment to induce the spinodal decomposition.

High resolution SEM studies show the microstructure that develops in the samples after the heat treatment. The spinodal structures are observed in the micron size grains with a spinodal size in the range 45-80 nm with the larger size corresponding to the higher wheel speed samples (Fig. 2).

Samples containing B have a smaller grain size and a finer spinodal structure (Fig. 3). Contrary to expectations the coercivity was found to be smaller in the B-containing samples, despite their somewhat finer spinodal structures. After annealing the alnico ribbons showed a coercivity of 348 G which decreased to 273 G after B addition (Fig. 4). This effect might be attributed to the forming of The microstructure of these samples is currently being studied by transmission electron microscopy to

Fig. 1. Microstructure of melt-spun alnico spun at 40 m/s (top) and 60 m/s (bottom).

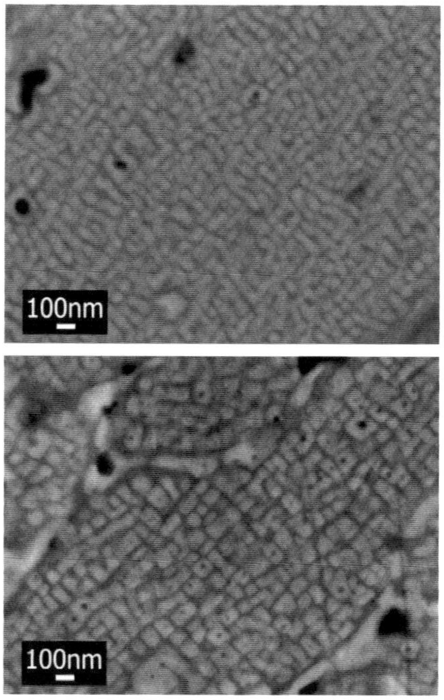

Fig. 2. Spinodal structures observed in the samples spun at 5 m/s (top, $d_{mean} \approx 45 - 50$ nm) and 60 m/s (bottom, $d_{mean} \approx 55 - 80$ nm)

determine further the fine details of the spinodal structure that would allow us to understand the development of coercivity in the melt-spun ribbons.

Acknowledgment
This work was supported by DOE BES DE-FG02-04ER4612.

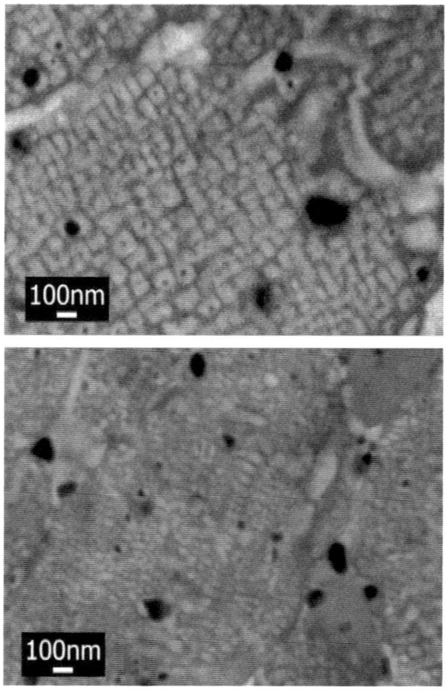

Fig. 3. Spinodal structures in a sample without B (top) and with B addition (bottom), produced at approximately same wheel speeds. A finer spinodal structure is observed in the samples containing 1 at.% B.

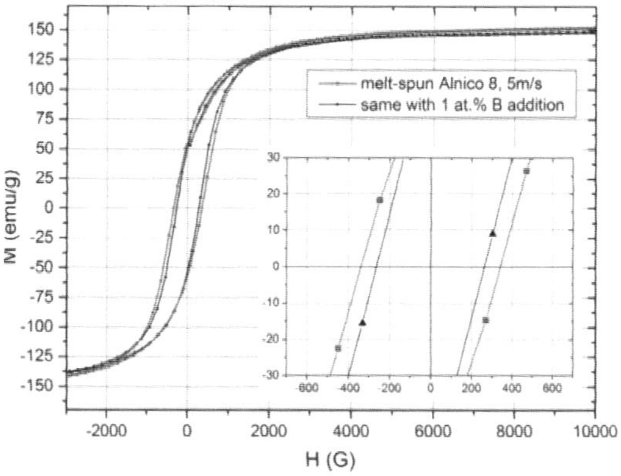

Fig. 4. Hysteresis loops of Alnico without and with B addition.

References

[1] M. J. Kramer, R. W. McCallum, I. A. Anderson, and S. Constantinides, *JOM* **64**, 2012, 752.

[2] T. Mishima, *Stahl u. Eisen* **53**, 1931, 79

[3] Lin Zhou , M. K. Miller, Ping Lu, Liqin Ke, R. Skomski, M. McCartney, D. Smith, H. Dillon, Q. Xing, A. Palasyuk, S. Constantinides, R.W. McCallum, I. E. Anderson, V. Antropov, and M. J. Kramer, Architecture and Magnetism of Alnico, *Acta Mater.* **74**, 2014, 224.

Magnetic Relaxation in La-Co Substituted Strontium M-Type Hexaferrites

P. HERNÁNDEZ-GÓMEZ[1], XIANSONG LIU[2], J. M. MUÑOZ[1], C. TORRES[1], O. ALEJOS[1]
[1]Univ. Valladolid, Dpto. Electricidad y Electrónica, 47071 Valladolid, Spain
[2]Univ. Anhui, School of Physics and Materials Science, Hefei 230039, PR China

Abstract: *Magnetic relaxation has been measured in La-Co M-type polycrystalline Sr hexaferrites with two different initial compositions, one of them with equal substitution of La and Co and other with different amount of substituting cations. The samples have been prepared by means of standard ceramic techniques, sintered 4h in air at 1350° C, and then rapidly quenched. XRD measurements reveal the formation of single phase magnetoplumbite. In the temperature range between 80 and 420 K the isochronal disaccommodation spectra show the presence of different relaxation processes. When the amount of substituting cations is the same, processes centred at 180 K and 300 K are noticeable. Increase in doping content lowers the amplitude of relaxation processes and supresses the 300 K process. On the other hand, when the amount of Co is lower than La, the 300 K process is not present and the diminution of amplitude of 180 K peak is more abrupt with increasing doping. The results are interpreted in terms of the effect of cation occupation in electronic and ionic relaxation processes.*

Keywords: *strontium ferrites; rare earth hexaferrites; magnetic disaccommodation; magnetic relaxation*

Address: Pablo Hernández-Gómez, Dpto. Electricidad y Electrónica, Facultad de Ciencias, Universidad de Valladolid, 47011 Valladolid, Spain, Tel: +34983423895, Fax: +34983423225, E-mail: pabloher@ee.uva.es

1. Introduction

Hexagonal ferrites have been widely used as permanent magnets owing to their appropriate magnetic properties as big saturation magnetization, large uniaxial magnetic anisotropy, and high Curie temperature, as well as their low manufacturing cost. In addition, they show promising properties in microwave devices and magneto-optic or perpendicular recording media [1]. There are different stable phases derived from the M-type $AFe_{12}O_{19}$ (A: Ba, Sr, Pb). The physical properties needed for the different applications mentioned are fulfilled choosing the most appropriate phase, carrying out adequate cation substitutions and improving the microstructure, by using different synthesis methods. Among the different cation substitutions, it has been discovered that the addition of rare earth La^{3+} and transition Co^{2+} can improve the performance of the permanent magnetic hexagonal ferrites [3].

Regarding magnetic properties, the magnetic after-effect processes have to be taken into account in order to minimize the losses. In addition, the study of this kind of processes provides information about the underlying mechanisms governing the dynamic behaviour of Bloch walls [4]. Among the different techniques available, the magnetic disaccommodation measurements are a powerful tool in the detection of this kind of phenomena. It consists in the time variation of the mobility of domain walls after a magnetic shock, and is shown by a temporal evolution of the magnetic permeability after a demagnetization stage, and the relaxation time, which characterizes each relaxation process, is strongly temperature-dependent. This relaxation phenomenon has been observed firstly in spinel ferrites [4], but is also present in hexaferrites [5,6], garnets [7] and ferrimagnetic perovskites [8]. In this paper we analyse the magnetic disaccommodation observed in SrM hexaferrites with different La-Co substitution.

2. Experimental setup

For this study, we have prepared two series of polycrystalline samples of La-Co substituted M-type hexaferrites. The initial materials $SrCO_3$ (98%, industry purity), La_2O_3 (98%), Fe_2O_3(99%), Co_2O_3(98.5%) were mixed together in the two different initial compositions which were investigated: one of them with equal substitution of La and Co, i.e. $Sr_{1-x}La_xFe_{12-x}Co_xO_{19}$ (x=0.09 to 0.18), and other with different amount of substituting cations: $Sr_{1-x}La_xFe_{12-y}Co_yO_{19}$ (x=0.09, y=0.08; x=0.13, y=0.11; x=0.16, y=0.13) which exhibit increased magnetic properties [9]; additional substitution rate degrade the main magnetic parameters. The mixtures of these raw materials were milled in water for 2 h with an angular velocity of 200 r.p.m. and a ball to power weight ratio of 8 : 1. The milling processes were performed in a centrifugal planetary ball mill using three sizes of hardened steel balls with diameters of 8, 10 and 12 mm. The mixed powder was dried, crushed and sifted. These samples were shaped into balls of about Ø8 mm, pre-sintered in a furnace at temperatures up to 1250–1300°C in air, and then were cooled in the furnace down to room temperature. The pre-calcined samples were dry-milled using a vibration mill, then wet-milled with additives ($CaCO_3$, SiO_2, Al_2O_3 or Cr_2O_3) using an attritor. The finely milled slurry with a diameter of about 0.8 μm was pressed into rods in the magnetic field of 800 kA/m parallel to the pressing direction. The pressed compacts were sintered at 1350 °C in air atmosphere, keeping the top temperature for 4 hours and then they were quenched.

The powder X-ray diffraction (XRD) patterns were collected on a Mac Science (MXP18AHF) Powder X-ray diffractometer using Cu-Ka radiation 0,15418 nm. Magnetic disaccommodation measurements were carried out with a computer aided system based on a LCR bridge [8], in the 80 K < T < 420 K temperature range. The results have been represented as isochronal curves, i. e, the relative variation of the initial permeability after sample demagnetization between an initial time t_1= 2 s and different window times t_2 = 4, 8, 16, 32, 64 and 128 s in the form

$$\frac{\mu(t_1,T)-\mu(t_2,T)}{\mu(t_1,T)}(\%) \qquad (1)$$

When the time window (t_2-t_1) is of the same order of magnitude that the relaxation time at a specified temperature, this curve exhibits a maximum. In this way, isochronal spectra disclose the different after-effect processes in the temperature range tested, and the characteristic parameters of the relaxation process, as activation energy, can be obtained.

3. Results and Discussion

X-ray diffraction patterns for samples with compositions $Sr_{1-x}La_xFe_{12-x}Co_xO_{19}$ are shown in Fig. 1. It is clear that the samples are composed of single phase of magnetoplumbite crystal structure, i.e. hexagonal M-phase ferrite. Similar results are obtained for the samples corresponding to composition $Sr_{1-x}La_xFe_{12-y}Co_yO_{19}$

In Fig. 2 the magnetic disaccommodation of pure M-type Sr ferrite sintered in air at a similar temperature is represented. We can see that with increasing sintering temperature several relaxation processes emerge at temperatures 380 K (A peak), 300 K (B), 165 K (D) and 90 K (F). Processes C and E at intermediate temperatures that appear in other hexaferrite systems are absent here [6]., and A_0 process at temperatures around 500 K is also noteworthy; the diffusive nature of this process comes from the high temperature range where this process is observed, according to the high activation energy involved. Magnetic disaccommodation processes are strongly coupled to the presence of both anisotropic cations, usually ferrous cations in octahedral sites, and lattice vacancies. Unless the sintering temperature is below the characteristic temperature for iron reduction in air (1380 °C), some amount of Fe^{2+} is present when sintering at 1340-1350 °C. This type of magnetic relaxation processes is due to anisotropic reorientations of vacancy and interstitial-type point defects in the crystal lattice (orientational processes), as well as diffusion of anisotropic cations via lattice vacancies (diffusional processes) [5] The reorientation of point defects within the Bloch walls from the initial state after demagnetization towards another one that minimize the free energy, creates a local induced anisotropy that stabilize the domain walls, leading to a time dependent decrease of initial permeability after demagnetization, and the relaxation time which characterizes each relaxation process is strongly temperature-dependent.

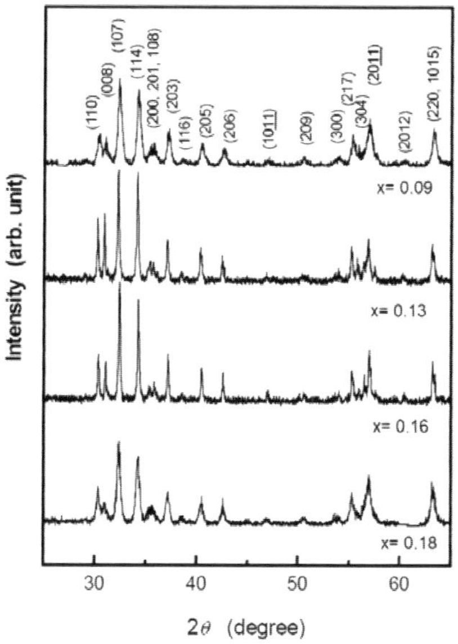

Fig. 1 XRD patterns of $Sr_{1-x}La_xFe_{12-x}Co_xO_{19}$ samples (x=0.09 to 0.18)

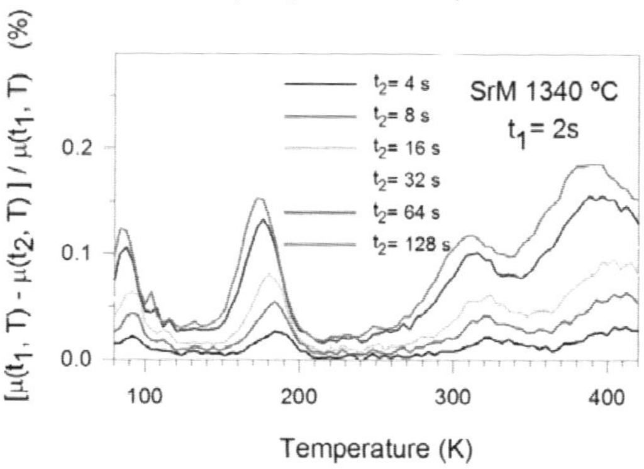

Fig. 2 Disaccommodation spectra of pure M phase $SrFe_{12}O_{19}$ sintered in air at 1340 ºC. Isochronal curves according to Eq.(1) with the increasing times t_2 referred in the text correspond to the plots from bottom to top in each graph

A close inspection reveals strong similarities, regarding the metallic sites, among cubic and hexagonal close packed structures. In addition, the magnetoplumbite structure can be described in terms of the stacking of two simple blocks, one of them with spinel structure ($S=Fe_6O_8$) and the other with hexagonal close-packed structure, that contains the Sr (resp. Ba and substituting La) cation ($R=SrFe_6O_{11}$), in the form RSR*S*. For this reason it is feasible the assumption that the relaxation processes detected in hexagonal ferrites are caused from similar underlying mechanisms responsible for the magnetic after-effects in spinel ferrites, and the presence of additional relaxation processes can be due to the existence of additional interstitial sites in the crystallographic structure. In the case of M-type phase we can find three octahedral sites (12k, $4f_2$, 2a), one tetrahedral ($4f_1$) and one bipiramidal trigonal (2b) site. In this way B process, with activation energies of 0.84 eV, close to the well-known III peak observed in magnetite [4] is caused by reorientation of the local symmetry axis of a vacancy located in an octahedral site due to the jump of a ferrous cation from a neighbour octahedral site towards the vacancy. In the case of hexaferrites this relaxation process involves the octahedral sites 2a located in spinel S blocks within the hexagonal lattice. The A peak has a similar origin with increased activation energies (1 eV) due to the presence of the Sr ion. On the other hand, the D peak is attributed to anisotropic rearrangement of ferrous cations in the octahedral $4f_2$ sites located in R blocks. These are face-sharing sites so that the energy involved in this process, 0.5 eV, is lower than the corresponding to the B peak. Finally, the F process (95K, 0.25eV) is connected to electronic hopping processes among ferrous and ferric cations, as it happens in magnetite below Verwey temperature.

In Fig. 3, the magnetic disaccommodation spectrum of the analyzed LaCo M-type hexaferrites is presented. For $Sr_{1-x}La_xFe_{12-x}Co_xO_{19}$ samples we can observe the B and D peaks, whereas A peak has very low amplitude, and A_0 process can be inferred from inspection of some spectra. The increase in doping rate causes a progressive diminution of relaxation processes, especially in B peak, and a shift of D process peak temperature to higher values (from 165 K to 180 K in the samples investigated). At the higher substitution rate analyzed the disaccommodation processes are small, and further doping will suppress them, in a similar way than observed in cobalt doped magnetite [10]. Electronic F process is completely suppressed, as observed also in several doped magnetite systems, caused by the destruction of the crystalline periodic potential. Mössbauer investigations of La^{3+}-Co^{2+} substitution M-type ferrite samples revealed that most of the Co^{2+} cations enter into the structure by substituting in the octahedral 2a sites [11], and then causing the observed diminution of B peak amplitude, and making energetically unfavorable the A process. In addition, local neutrality favors the presence of the divalent ferrous cation in the vicinity of La^{3+} thus enhancing the D relaxation process which takes place in face-sharing octahedral $4f_2$ in R blocks. On the other hand, substitution of part of Sr^{2+} (ionic radius 1.27 Å) with La^{3+} (ionic radius 1.16 Å), and Co^{2+} instead Fe^{3+} (ionic radii 0.65 Å and 0.55 Å resp) has to be taken into account, as it distorts the hexaferrite structure. With this in mind, increased doping rate almost suppresses B peak, due to the small amount of Fe^{2+} in 2a sites occupied by cobalt, and also modifies the D peak in two ways: increasing its characteristic activation energy due to lattice distortion and lowering its amplitude, because the unit cell is smaller and then the presence of localized ferrous cations in $4f_2$ sites is less probable in favour of interstitial diffusion of anisotropic cations via lattice vacancies, thus increasing the high temperature A_0 process.

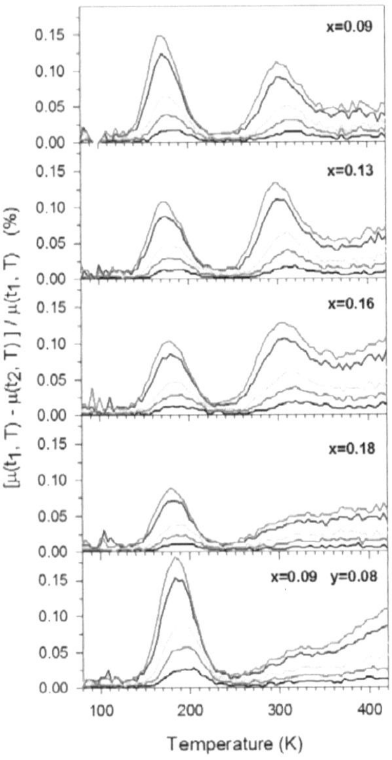

Fig. 3 Disaccommodation spectra of samples of composition $Sr_{1-x}La_xFe_{12-x}Co_xO_{19}$ (x=0.09 to 0.18) and representative $Sr_{1-x}La_xFe_{12-y}Co_yO_{19}$ sample with (x=0.09, y= 0.08)

Concerning $Sr_{1-x}La_xFe_{12-y}Co_yO_{19}$ samples, the effect observed with doping rate is similar, i.e. diminution of relaxation amplitudes with increasing substitution. In this case we can see that D peak is prominent, and B peak is strongly diminished, even for the lower substitution rate analyzed. In this case, the amount of Co^{2+} is lower than La^{3+} substitution, thus favouring a higher amount of Fe^{3+} changing its valence to Fe^{2+} to maintain electrical neutrality. As commented before, the preference of Co^{2+} for octahedral 2a sites promotes the preferential occupation of ferrous cations in octahedral sites in R blocks near La^{3+}, thus enhancing the D process and almost suppressing the B process regarding $Sr_{1-x}La_xFe_{12-x}Co_xO_{19}$ samples. The increased amount of ferrous cations cannot enter completely in the $4f_2$ sites due to higher ionic radium of Fe^{2+} (0.61 Å) regarding Fe^{3+} (0.55 Å) hence increasing the diffusion of interstitial ferrous cations at high temperatures, i.e, the A_0 relaxation.

Acknowledgements

Financial support of Junta de Castilla y León (project ref VA202U14) and Universidad de Valladolid (travel funds) is acknowledged.

References

[1] M. P. Sharrock, IEEE Trans Magn. 25(6) (1989) 4374
[2] H. Kojima in: Ferromagnetic Materials vol. 3, ed. E.P. Wohlfarth (North-Holland, Amsterdam, 1982) 305-391
[3] R. Skomski, J.M.D. Coey, Phys. Rev. B 48 (1993) 15812
[4] F. Walz, V.A.M. Brabers, S. Chikazumi, H. Kronmüller and M. O. Rigo, Phys. Stat. Sol. B, 110 (1982) 471
[5] P. Hernández-Gómez, J. Muñoz, C. Torres, C. de Francisco, O. Alejos, J. Phys. D: Appl. Phys. 36 (9) (2003) 1062
[6] P. Hernández-Gómez, C. Torres, C. de Francisco, J. M. Muñoz, O. Alejos, J. I. Iñ iguez, V. Raposo, J. Magn. Magn. Mat. 272–276 (2004) e1843.
[7] P. Hernández-Gómez, C. Torres, C. de Francisco, J.I. Iñiguez, J.M. Perdigao, Mat. Sci. Forum, 514-516 (2006) 319.
[8] C. de Francisco, J.M. Muñoz, M. Zazo, A.G. Flores, J. Iñiguez, L. Torres, J. Appl. Phys. 89 (2001) 7642
[9] X. Liu, C. H. Cheng, Z. Ruan, F. Hu, D. R. Zhu, K L. Jiang, C. Wang, Adv. Mater. Res. 284-286 (2011) 2311.
[10] S. Iida, J. Phys. Soc. Jpn. 17 (1962) 123
[11] L. Lechevallier, J. M. Le Breton, J. Magn. Magn. Mater. 290-291 (2005) 1237

Magnetic and Structural Properties of MnAl Thin Films

SIQIAN ZHAO[1], TOSHIYA HOZUMI[1,2], PATRICK LECLAIR[1], GARY MANKEY[1], TAKAO SUZUKI[1]
[1]Center for Materials for Information Technology (MINT), University of Alabama, Tuscaloosa, U.S.A.
[2]Advanced Technology Development Center, TDK Corporation, Narita, Japan

Abstract: *A systematic study has been carried out to elucidate the correlation between magnetic anisotropy K and saturation magnetization M_s in the τ-phase MnAl thin films. In the present study, it is found that the relation between K and M_s obeys a 1.3^{th} power law over a temperature range of 5 to 400 K. This result is at variance with the prediction based on the single ion mechanism.*

Key words: *τ-phase MnAl; thin films; magnetic anisotropy; saturation magnetization*

Address: Siqian Zhao, Center for Materials for Information Technology (MINT), The University of Alabama, Tuscaloosa, AL 35487, Tel: (1-205)239-8755, E-mail: szhao6@crimson.ua.edu

1. Introduction

Manganese alloy systems with nearly equiatomic composition with Al, Bi and Ga are known to exhibit high magnetic anisotropy. Among them, τ-phase MnAl has been commercially used as a permanent magnet since it exhibits a high magnetic anisotropy of 10^7 erg/cc at room temperature [1,2]. While there has been voluminous work regarding MnAl compounds, little research on the magnetic anisotropy has been carried out [3,4]. This work has been motivated to elucidate the origin of magnetic anisotropy in the τ-MnAl thin films.

2. Experimental

Multilayer thin films of [Mn (x nm)/Al (y nm) x N] with x, y = 0.5 ~ 7, N = 10 ~ 40 were fabricated by using a DC magnetron sputtering system with a base pressure of approximately 10^{-9} Torr. A 5 to 8 nm Ru buffer layer was deposited onto SiO_2 substrates. The samples were deposited at room temperature and post-annealed without breaking vacuum at temperatures T_a from 430 to 580 °C for annealing times t_a from 10 to 600 min. Capping layers of Ru were deposited after the samples cooled to room temperature.

Measurements of magnetic properties were carried out with a vibrating sample magnetometer in fields up to 9 T over a temperature range from 4 to 400 K. Structural characterizations were performed by X-ray diffraction (XRD) with Co Kα radiation and also by high-resolution transmission electron microscopy.

3. Results and discussion

Figure 1 shows X-ray diffraction patterns for the samples with x = 1, y = 1.25, N = 30 and T_a = 580 °C for various t_a from 10 to 600 min, together with the one for an as-deposited sample. The as-deposited sample shows only the diffraction peaks for f.c.c. Al and h.c.p. Ru under- and overcoat layers. No diffraction peaks for the τ-phase are present. In the sample with t_a = 10 min, there is a rather sharp peak for β-Mn. Upon annealing for longer time, the τ-phase peaks of (101) and (110) were observed, though the (110) peaks are rather weak. In addition, the peaks for the non-magnetic ε-MnAl phase were observed. The values of d_{101} of the τ-phase for the samples with t_a = 190 and 600 min are 2.143 Å and 2.137 Å, respectively, smaller by 2.1%, and 2.4%, as compared to the bulk value (= 2.19 Å). There is very little change in d_{101} with t_a except for t_a =10 min.

Figure 2 shows magnetization M at 1.8 T and both in-plane coercivity ($H_{c//}$) and out-of-plane coercivity ($H_{c\perp}$) for different annealing time t_a ranges from 10 to 600 min. The magnetization M remains nearly the same for samples annealed for 10, 70 and 130 min. After that, M decreases from t_a = 190 to 600 min. In the case of coercivity, $H_{c\perp}$ gradually increases from t_a = 10 to 300 min, then decreases at t_a = 600 min. On

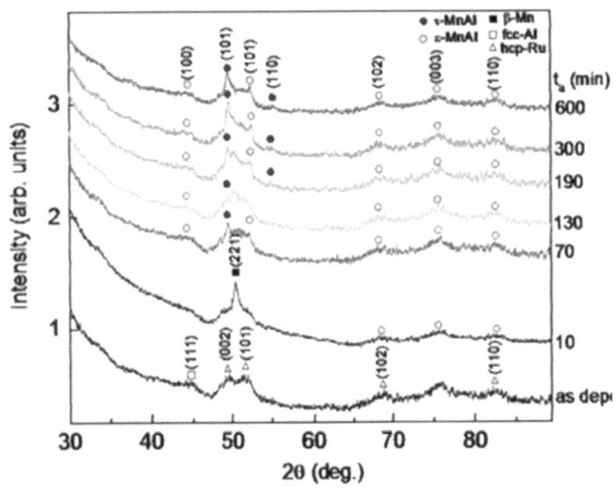

Fig. 1. Demagnetization curves of annealed ribbon powder with different conditions.

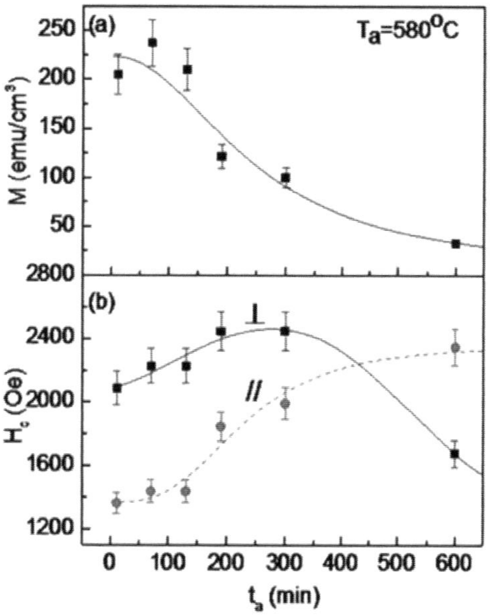

Fig. 2. The annealing time dependence of (a) magnetization at 1.8 T and (b) coercivity H_c for samples x = 1, y = 1.25, N = 30 and annealed at T_a = 580 °C for various t_a = 10 to 600 min.

the other hand, $H_{c//}$ doesn't change much for t_a less than 130 min. For samples annealed for times greater than 190 min, it increases with t_a. The sample with t_a = 10 min shows a rather high magnetization despite the fact that there is no τ-phase peak detected in the XRD patterns.

Figure 3 shows the temperature dependence of magnetic anisotropy constant K and saturation magnetization M_s of the sample with x = 1, y = 1.25, N = 30 and annealed at T_a = 580 °C for t_a = 190 min. The magnetic anisotropy constant K was estimated at different temperatures in two ways: (i) K_{MH} = (1/2) M_sH_s, where H_s is a saturation field defined as the field where magnetization becomes saturated and M_s is defined as the magnetization at maximum applied field 4 T; (ii) K_T is estimated from the extrapolation of the torque amplitude for the two fold symmetry to $H = \infty$ at a given temperature.

The M_s values are shown in Fig. 3 together with the K_{MH} and K_T values. It was found that both the K_{MH} and K_T decrease monotonically with increasing temperature from 4 to 400 K.

Based on the temperature dependence of K_{MH}, K_T and M_s, the relation between K and M_s is plotted in the log scale, as shown in Fig. 4. To be more accurate, some estimated data points of M_s obtained from a fitted polynomial curve of M_s vs. T, were added in between the data points in the K_T vs. M_s curve. According to previous theoretical expectations [5-8], K is proportional to M_s^n. The data was fitted to a power law to acquire n for both K_{MH} and K_T. In the present study, it is found that the value of n is approximately 1.3 for the power law fits describing both K_{MH} and K_T. Much theoretical work has been carried out concerning the relationship between $K(T)$ and $M(T)$ [5-8]. Among them, an effective spin Hamiltonian model predicts values of n = 3 and 2 for the single and two ion models, respectively [8].

Since Mn is believed to be a dominating contribution to magnetic anisotropy of the τ-phase MnAl [3], a single ion model is most likely the case, which leads to the 3rd power dependence. The present result of the 1.3th power is in disagreement. The reason for this discrepancy may be due to that i) a two ion mechanism could be responsible rather than single ion mechanism, resulting in a much higher spin-orbit coupling constant of the τ-phase MnAl than that for single Mn or Al atom [9-10], and ii) the present result is based on the data for a wide range of temperature from 4 to 400 K, whereas the theoretical work found

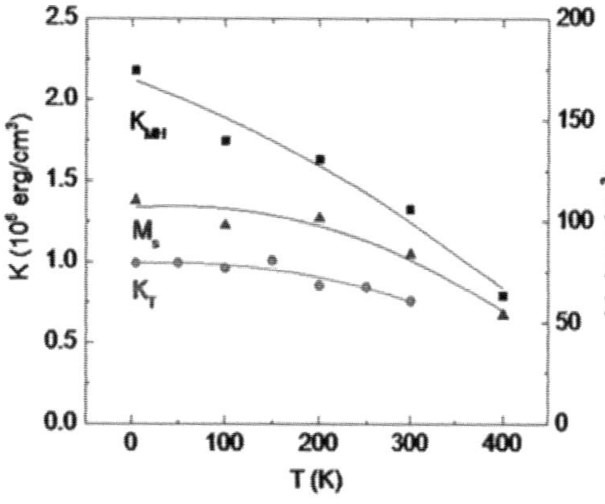

Fig. 3. Temperature dependence of K_{MH}, K_T and M_s for sample with x = 1, y = 1.25, N = 30 and annealed at T_a = 580 °C for t_a = 190 min.

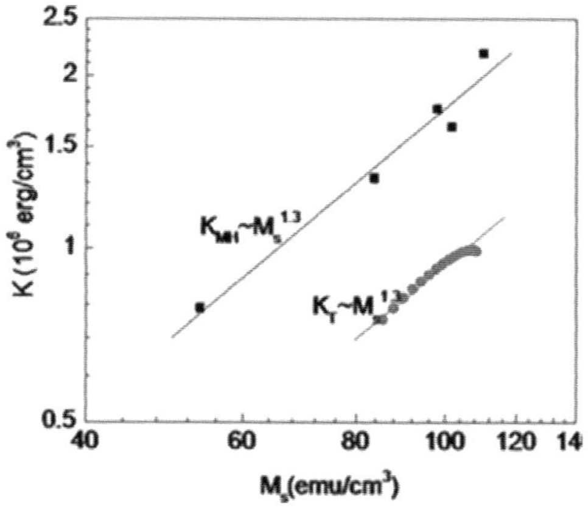

Fig. 4. K vs. M_s power law fits for K_{MH} and K_T at different measuring temperatures.

the exponent for temperatures much lower than the Curie point.

In summary, the present study reports for the first time the correlation between the magnetic anisotropy and the magnetization. The result is at variance with the prediction based on the single ion mechanism.

Acknowledgement
The work was supported in part by the G8 project (NSF-CMMI 1229049) and also by TDK Corporation. The authors express their gratitude to Dr. Hono's group at NIMS for fruitful discussions and their detailed TEM characterizations.

References
[1] H. Kono, *J. Phys. Soc. Jpn.* **13**, 1958, 1444.
[2] A. J. J. Koch, P. Hokkeling, M. G. v. d. Steeg, and K. J. de Vos, *J. Appl. Phys.* **31**, 1960, S75.
[3] A. Sakuma, *J. Phys. Soc. Jpn.* **63**, 1994, 1422.
[4] S. H. Nie et al., *Appl. Phys. Lett.* **102**, 2013, 152405.
[5] N. Akulov, *Z. Phys.* **100**, 1936, 197.
[6] C. Zener, *Phys. Rev.* **96**, 1954, 1335.
[7] H. B. Callen and E. Callen, *J. Phys. Chem. Solids* **27**, 1966, 1271.
[8] O. N. Mryasov et al., *Europhys. Lett.* **69**, 2005, 805.
[9] A. Sakuma, *J. Phys.Soc. Jpn.* **82**, 2013, 073704.
[10] A. Sakuma, *J. Phys. Soc. Jpn.* **83**, 2014, 034715.

Towards Exchange-Biased Permanent Magnets: Structure-Property Correlations in FeMn Alloys

I.J. McDONALD, L.G. MARSHALL, L.H. LEWIS
College of Engineering, Northeastern University, Boston, Massachusetts, 02115, USA

Abstract: *Efforts to realize novel types of permanent magnet materials have been motivated by the need for greater control over technical magnetic properties in inexpensive and readily-accessible materials. Towards this goal, FeMn-based alloys exhibit a range of tailorable magnetic anisotropies and thus may be promising candidates for permanent magnetic materials. Depending upon the precise composition, alloys in the Fe-Mn system can exhibit ferromagnetism or antiferromagnetism, facilitating the development of enhanced coercivity donated by exchange anisotropy in multiphase FeMn systems. In this study, alloys of composition* $Fe_{1-x}Mn_x$ *(x=0.1, 0.3) have been rapidly solidified by melt-spinning to produce FeMn nanocomposites for fundamental study:* $Fe_{0.9}Mn_{0.1}$ *is primarily ferromagnetic while* $Fe_{0.7}Mn_{0.3}$ *is primarily antiferromagnetic. Moderate annealing produces nanoscaled minority phases in these alloys with the capability to support the development of exchange bias. Correlation of the multiphase microstructural evolution with intrinsic and extrinsic magnetic attributes will inform the future development of this system.*

Keywords: *exchange bias, FeMn, permanent magnet, rare-earth-free*

Address: Laura H. Lewis, Dept. of Chemical Engineering, Northeastern University, Boston, MA 02115, USA.
E-mail: *lhlewis@neu.edu*

1. Introduction

In recent years there has been initiative to develop inexpensive, sustainable rare-earth-element-free permanent magnets motivated by instabilities in supply and pricing in the markets for these elements [1,2]. With availability, sustainability, and cost all major considerations in the search for alternative materials systems, investigation of bulk FeMn-based alloys is very attractive [1, 3]. The FeMn system is exceptional in its ability to exhibit a range of tailorable magnetic anisotropies including, but not limited to, magnetocrystalline, shape and exchange anisotropies. The primary focus of this work is the realization of controllable exchange bias in the FeMn system that can lend enhanced coercivity to provide an appreciable magnetic energy product. Exchange bias refers to exchange coupling occurring at the interface of a ferromagnetic and an antiferromagnetic material which acts to pin interfacial magnetic spins; this results in a horizontal shift of the magnetic hysteresis, thereby increasing coercivity [4]. It is desired to establish exchange anisotropy in a FeMn alloy system through control of composition and processing to produce a multiphase nanostructured ferromagnetic-antiferromagnetic system [1,5,6]. Previous work has been limited to investigation of exchange bias in film systems consisting of single-phase FeMn coupled with another magnetic alloy such as FeNi [7-11]. While a large body of work is available on the phase behavior in the FeMn binary system, there is considerably less literature regarding the associated magnetic character [12-15]. This current work examines multiphase FeMn-based systems with potential for application as permanent magnet materials.

2. Experimental Techniques

$Fe_{(1-x)}Mn_x$ (x = 0.1 and x = 0.3) were arc-melted from elemental sources (99.98%) and then rapidly solidified via melt-spinning to produce uniform ribbons. These compositions were chosen in order to produce alloys consisting of majority phases α-Fe(Mn) (ferromagnetic) and γ-Fe(Mn) (antiferromagnetic) [5]. Compositions were verified using EDAX Energy Dispersive Spectroscopy (Hitachi S4800 Scanning Electron Microscope). Hysteretic and thermomagnetic characterization was carried out using a Quantum Design VersaLab Vibrating Sample Magnetometer in the field range ±3 T and in temperature range 300 K - 1000 K; heating and cooling were performed under an applied field of 200 Oe at a rate of 10 K/min. In parallel, these heat-treatment sequences were repeated in a tube furnace, to prepare samples for structural examination. Structural information was obtained by X-ray diffraction using a Phillips PANalytical X'Pert Pro X-ray laboratory diffractometer (Cu-K_α radiation, λ=1.54184 Å) and using synchrotron radiation at beamline X16C at the National Synchrotron Light Source at Brookhaven National Laboratory (λ=0.700271 Å). Lattice parameters were determined using a least-squares fit to the data, and the constituent crystallite sizes were assessed using the Scherrer formula [16].

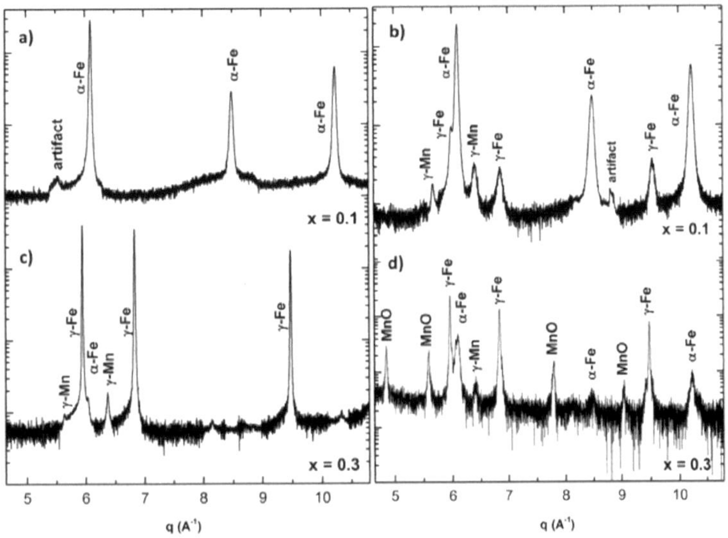

Fig. 1. X-ray diffraction patterns for $Fe_{1-x}Mn_x$ (x = 0.1, 0.3) in the a,c) as-made state and b,d) after 3 heating cycles.

3. Structural Analysis of Melt-spun and Heat-treated Ribbons

In the as-made state, $Fe_{0.9}Mn_{0.1}$ was determined to consist solely of bcc α-Fe with a slightly expanded lattice parameter relative to reported values for this composition [12,17]. The average α-Fe crystallite size was found to be on the nanoscale. After 3 successive heating cycles, X-ray diffraction revealed the presence of the fcc γ-Fe and γ-Mn phases with an average size of tens of nanometers, Fig. 1 (a-b).

The $Fe_{0.7}Mn_{0.3}$ as-made sample primarily consists of fcc γ-Fe phase with a small minority bcc α-Fe phase; crystallite sizes were also nanoscale in this sample. The γ-Fe phase was similarly determined to have a larger lattice parameter than reported in the literature [12,15]. The amount of α-Fe phase was found to increase after heat-treatment, as shown in Fig. 1 (c-d). Additional γ-Mn and MnO phases were also detected after heat-treatment.

4. Magnetic Characterization of Melt-Spun and Heat Treated Ribbons

The magnetic character of the samples was recorded in the as-made state as well as after each successive heating cycle to understand the magnetic evolution of the samples. As-made $Fe_{0.9}Mn_{0.1}$ had a small coercivity of 15 Oe and a saturation magnetization M_S=111 emu/g, which is about half of that expected from pure α-Fe. After each heating cycle M_S decreased while the coercivity increased to roughly 60 Oe, as shown in Fig. 2.

In the as-made state, $Fe_{0.7}Mn_{0.3}$ showed only a very small magnetization that rapidly increased upon heat-treatment, Fig. 2, to roughly 0.5 emu/g. The coercivity remained relatively unchanged.

Thermomagnetic cycling showed a reproducible hysteretic behavior where the overall magnetic moment remained constant until 850 K and 950 K, for $Fe_{0.9}Mn_{0.1}$ and $Fe_{0.7}Mn_{0.3}$ respectively, at which point it dropped to nearly zero. Upon cooling there was no significant increase in magnetic moment until roughly 500 K and 650 K, for $Fe_{0.9}Mn_{0.1}$ and $Fe_{0.7}Mn_{0.3}$, respectively, as shown in Fig. 3.

5. Analysis

In this study, samples of $Fe_{0.9}Mn_{0.1}$ and $Fe_{0.7}Mn_{0.3}$ were rapidly solidified to attain a nanocomposite bulk system that is anticipated to exhibit exchange bias. Characterization revealed that melt-spun $Fe_{0.9}Mn_{0.1}$ consists of the ferromagnetic bcc α-Fe(Mn) phase;

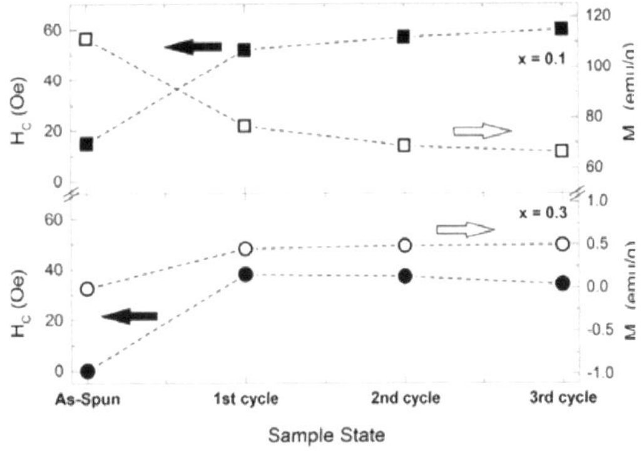

Fig. 2. Evolution of magnetic character in $Fe_{1-x}Mn_x$ (x = 0.1, 0.3) alloys after each heating cycle.

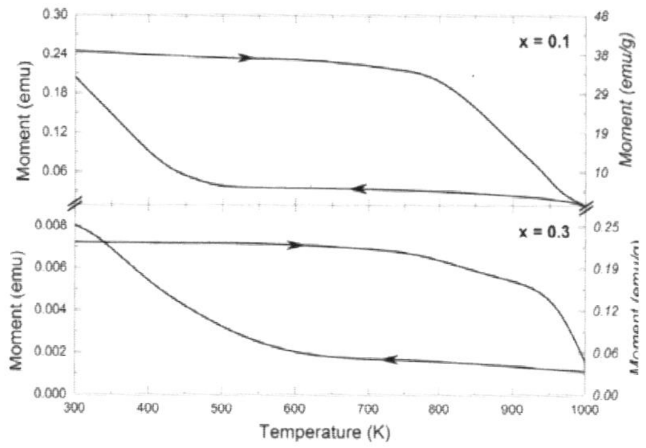

Fig. 3. Thermomagnetic behavior of $Fe_{(1-x)}Mn_x$ (x = 0.1, 0.3).

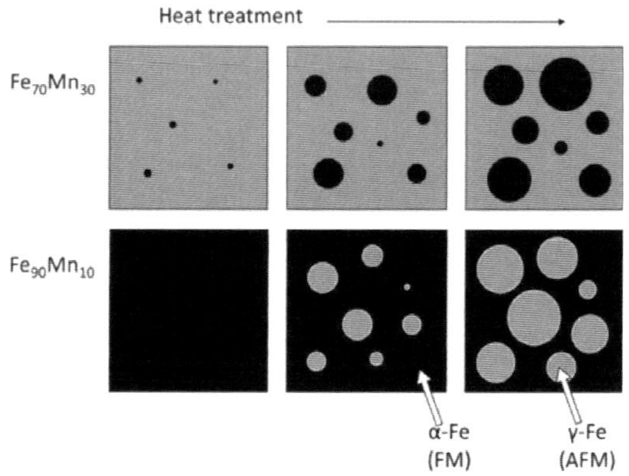

Fig. 4. Proposed model of microstructural evolution in FeMn systems with heating cycles.

upon heat-treatment, the antiferromagnetic fcc γ-Fe(Mn) phase was detected. Conversely, the $Fe_{0.7}Mn_{0.3}$ sample in the as-spun state consists of antiferromagnetic γ-Fe(Mn) with minority γ-Mn and α-Fe phases. Heat-treatment of this alloy causes an increase in the amount of ferromagnetic α-Fe phase as evidenced by both structural and magnetic measurements.

Magnetic transitions observed upon heating and cooling are hypothesized to be associated with the structural transformation between α-Fe and γ-Fe. [12]. These results support a conceptual model, illustrated in Fig. 4, of a nanoscale multiphase system that is amenable to the development of exchange bias. In the $Fe_{0.9}Mn_{0.1}$ sample the majority phase is ferromagnetic while the minority phase is antiferromagnetic; the $Fe_{0.7}Mn_{0.3}$ sample consists of the inverse configuration. In this way, these FeMn-based systems may be studied to better understand the development and optimization of exchange bias in multiphase binary alloys for permanent magnet application.

Acknowledgments
This work is supported by the U.S. Office of Naval Research; Grant #N00014-10-1-0553.

References

[1] L. H. Lewis, F. Jiménez-Villacorta, *Met. Mater. Trans. A* **44**, 2012, S2.
[2] M. J. Kramer, R.W. McCallum et al., *JOM* **64**, 2012, 752.
[3] A. Palasyuk, E. Blomberg, R. Prozorov et al., *JOM*, **65**, 2013, 862.
[4] W. H. Meiklejohn, C. P. Bean, *Phys. Rev.* **102**, 1956, 1413.
[5] H. Baker et al. *ASM Handbook*, Vol. 3 – Alloy Phase Diagrams. ASM Intl., 1992.
[6] F. Jiménez-Villacorta, J.L. Marion, T. Sepehrifar et al., *Appl. Phys, Lett,* **100**, 2012, 112408.
[7] C. Schlenker, S.S.P. Parkin, J.C. Scott, K. Howard, *J. Magn. Magn. Mater.* **54-57**, 1986, 801.
[8] S. Zhong, D. Jun, Z. Shi-Ming, *Chinese Phys. B* **23**, 2014, 027503.
[9] A. V. Svalov, P.A. Savin, V.N. Lepalovskij et al., *AIP Adv.* 3, 2013, 092104.
[10] J. K. Howard, T.C. Huang, *J. Appl. Phys.* **64**, 1988, 6118.
[11] A. Tan, J. Li, C.A. Jenkins et al., *Phys. Rev. B* **88**, 2013, 104404.
[12] A. R. Troiano, F.T. McGuire, *Trans. Am. Soc. Met.* **31**, 1943, 340.
[13] P. Marinelli, A. Baruj, J. Pons, M. Sade et al., *Matls Sci and Eng*, **2002**, A335, 137.
[14] A. T. W. Kempen, F. Sommer, E.J. Mittemeijer, *Acta Mater.* **50**, 2002, 3545.
[15] C-M. Li, F. Sommer, E.J. Mittemeijer, *Mater. Sci. Eng. A* **325**, 2002, 307.
[16] A.L. Patterson, *Phys. Rev.* **56**, 1939, 978.
[17] L. Zwell, J.T. Michalak, H.A. Wriedt, *J. Appl. Cryst.* **3**, 1970, 357.

High Coercivity in Mn_xGa Alloys with the $D0_{22}$ structure

A.A. El-GENDY[1,2], G.C. HADJIPANAYIS[1]
[1]Department of Physics and Astronomy, University of Delaware, Newark, DE 19711, USA
[2]Nanotechnology and Nanometrology Lab., National Institute for Standards, Giza 12211, Egypt

Abtract: *Synthesis of Mn-Ga nanoscale particles is a challenging problem due to the large number of phases which can be formed at different alloy compositions. These phases exhibit different magnetic properties which can be exploited in many applications such as permanent magnets.* $D0_{19}$ Mn_xGa *is a stable antiferromagnetic phase at high temperature. This phase has poor magnetic properties but with heat treatment it can be transformed to the ferrimagnetic* $D0_{22}$ *phase which in comparison shows high anisotropy and magnetization. However,* $D0_{22}$ *is a metastable phase which is difficult to be formed at normal conditions. In this study, we synthesize* $D0_{22}$ *MnxGa nanocube shape particles via a heat treatment of ball milled powders. The samples have been prepared by arc-melting and planetary ball milling for 2 hours at 250 rpm. The XRD results show the presence of* $D0_{19}$ *structure in the as-made samples which then transforms to* $D0_{22}$ *after annealing at 723 K for long time. This transformation results in a high* H_C *of 8.3 kOe and a magnetization of 14 emu/g at room temperature. SEM images in the as-milled particles, show the presence of rod- shape particles with the size in the range of 10 to 15 µm. This homogeneous structure, after annealing for long time, transforms to* $D0_{22}$ *cubical shape nanoparticles with a size in the range of 30 to 50 nm. The results of this study show that* $D0_{22}$ Mn_xGa *alloys can acquire good hard magnetic properties at the nanoscale.*

Keywords: *rare earth free magnets; high coercivity;* $D0_{22}$

Address: Ahmed El-Gendy, Department of Physics and Astronomy, University of Delaware, Newark, DE 19711, USA. Email: aelgendy@udel.edu

1. Introduction

The demand for rare earth-free permanent magnets with high-temperature performance is high for many applications such as wind turbines and hybrid vehicles. In the last decades the rare earth elements have gained the commercial market in permanent magnet industry because of their excellent performance. However, the recent rare earth crisis which was followed by substantial increase in the price of rare earths lead to a significant problem for the industry [1- 5]. Because of this much of the research today, is focused on the development of novel rare earth free magnets with good magnetic properties and much lower materials costs than the rare earths [4]. One of these materials is the binary Mn-Ga alloy which has a rich phase diagram including the presence of many magnetic phases according to the composition such as ferromagnetic $L1_0$ or ferrimagnetic $D0_{22}$ phases [6]. The $D0_{22}$ structure has lower magnetisation but higher coercivity than the $L1_0$ structures [6]. Detailed studies on these alloys have not been published to date and in addition, the high raw materials costs of Ga are likely to prevent the commercial application of Mn-Ga magnets. For that reason the current work focuses on a Mn-rich composition to produce the $D0_{22}$ phase. According to the phase diagram of Mn-Ga alloys, the synthesis of this metastable phase is difficult to be obtained at normal conditions. In this study, we prepared the crystalline $D0_{22}$ phase by heat treating the amorphous Mn_xGa alloys which are formed in as-made ball milled powders..

2. Experimental

$Mn_{2-3}Ga$ samples were prepared by arc-melting the corresponding amounts of the constituent elements under a 10 mbar argon atmosphere. The resulting polycrystalline ingots were ball milled for 2 hours at 250 rpm. The resulting powders were subsequently annealed at 723 K in an evacuated quartz tube for 12 days. The annealing temperature was chosen to be safely below the structural transformation temperature in this alloy which is reported to be at around 800 K [8] and is high enough to ensure sufficient diffusion. After annealing, the samples were cooled in air. This procedure resulted in samples exhibiting the $D0_{22}$ structure as confirmed by powder x-ray diffraction using the Cu-Kα radiation. The magnetic properties were measured using a Quantum Design Versa Lab vibrating sample magnetometer (VSM), with magnetic fields up to 3 T. The morphology and elemental analysis of the samples have been obtained using a Jeol scanning electron microscope (SEM) equipped with energy dispersive x-ray (EDS) detector.

3. Results and Discussion

Figure 1 shows the XRD pattern of the as-made and annealed ball milled powders. The broadening of the XRD peaks of the as- milled powders is attributed to the amorphous phase which is present together with the D019 phase.

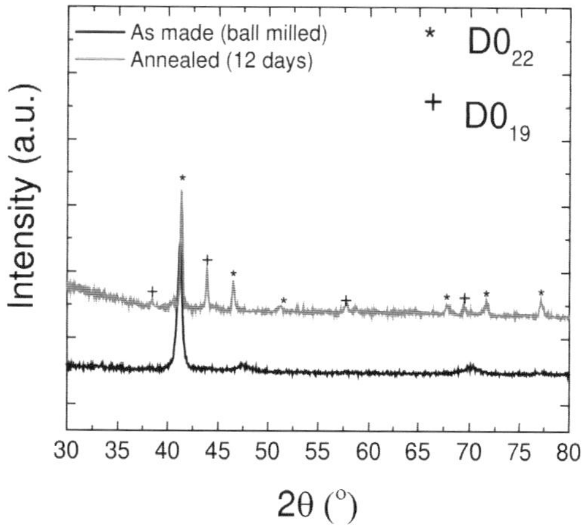

Fig. 1. XRD diffraction patterns for as-made ball milled and annealed powders at 723 K for 12 days.

Afer heat-treating the as-made powders at 723 K for 12 days, the peaks become sharp indicating the formation of crystalline $D0_{22}$ tetragonal phase with a percentage of 75%. This value was determined from the XRD pattern of the annealed ball milled powders shown in Fig. 1.

The morphology of the samples was investigated by SEM (Fig. 2) which shows the formation of nanocube-like structure in the annealed ball milled powders. The size of the nanocubes is in the range of 30 to 50 nm. The EDS analysis reveals the exact composition of the particles which is $Mn_{72}Ga_{28}$.

Fig. 2. SEM image of the cube-like nanostructure in annealed ball milled Mn_xGa powders.

Figure 3 shows the hysteresis loops of the as-prepared and annealed ball milled powders. The as-made powders show weak magnetic properties with a small magnetization at 3T (M(3T)) and coercivity (H_C) of 3.5 emu/g and 600 Oe, respectively.

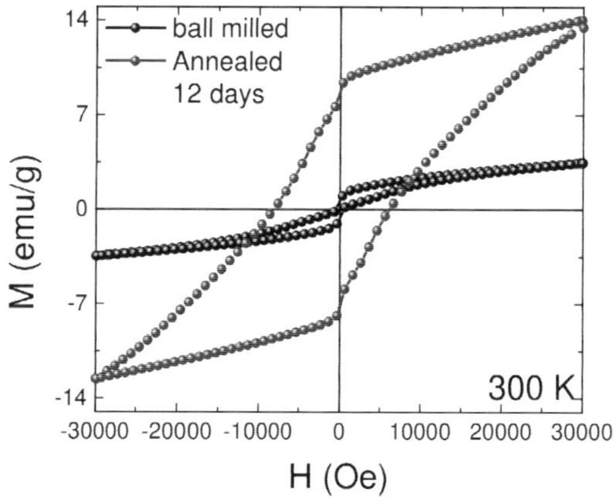

Fig. 3. Hysteresis loops at room temperature for as-made and annealed ball milled powders.

However, after annealing at 723 for 12 days, the magnetic properties are improved to 14 emu/g and 8.3 kOe for M(3T) and H_C, respectively. The hysteresis loop shown is a minor loop with a shape characteristic of isotropic samples with a very high anisotropy. The $D0_{22}$ ferrimagnetic phase is most predominant in the annealed ball milled powders leading to higher magnetization and coercivity in comparison to the as-made ball milled in which the amorphous $D0_{22}$ and D019 phases arepresent. In comparison to recent published results [8], the H_C of our annealed ball milled powders is two times larger, while the M(3T) is almost the same.

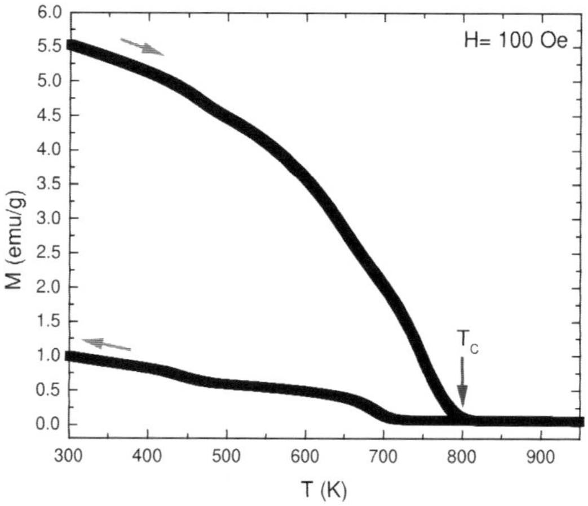

Fig. 4. Temperature dependent on magnetization at 100 Oe for Mn_xGa nanocubes

Figure 4 shows the temperature dependence of magnetization up to 950 K in a field of 100 Oe. The data suggest a Curie temperature for the ferrimagnetic D022 phase approximately 800 K which is in good agreement with values reported in the literature [8].

4. Conclusion

$Mn_{72}Ga_{28}$ ($Mn_{2\text{-}3}Ga$) alloys with the $D0_{22}$ phase were synthesized using planetary ball milling. Annealing at 723 K for 12 days led to enhanced magnetic properties because of an increased amount of the $D0_{22}$ tetragonal phase as compared to as-made $D0_{19}$ hexagonal phase. Our work showed that it is very difficult to obtain a pure $D0_{22}$ phase due to the metastability of this phase. However, our data yielded an enhancement in the magnetic properties of the Mn_xGa compared to the recent published results [8-10]. Further work is needed to optimize a single phase $D0_{22}$ tetragonal phase in order to get better magnetic properties to be used for the development of rare earth free permanent magnets.

Acknowledgement
The authors would like to thank the support by NSF-G8.

References

[1] A. A. El-Gendy, T. Almugaiteeb, and E. E. Carpenter, *J. Magn. Magn. Mater.* 348 (2013) 136.
[2] A. A. El-Gendy, M. Qian, Z. J. Huba, S. N. Khanna, and E. E. Carpenter, *Appl. Phys. Lett.* 104 (2014) 023111.
[3] O. Gutfleisch, M.A. Willard, E. Brück, C.H. Chen, S.G. Sankar, J.P. Liu, *Adv. Mater.* 23 (2011) 821.
[4] J.M.D. Coey, *Scr. Mater.* 67 (2012) 524.
[5] M.J. Kramer, R.W. McCallum, I.A. Anderson, S. Constantinides, *JOM.* 64 (2012) 752.
[6] H. Niida, T. Hori, H. Onodera, Y. Yamaguchi, and Y. Nakagawa, *J. Appl. Phys.* 79 (1996) 5946.
[7] F. Wu, S. Mizukami, D. Watanabe, H. Naganuma, M. Oogane, Y. Ando, and T. Miyazaki, *Appl. Phys. Lett.* 94 (2009) 122503.
[8] J. Winterlik, B. Balke, G. H. Fecher, and C. Felser, *Phys. Rev. B* 77 (2008) 054406.
[9] T. J. Nummy, S. P. Bennett, T. Cardinal, and D. Heiman, *Appl. Phys. Lett.* 99 (2011) 252506.
[10] B. Z. Cui, M. Marinescu, and J. F. Liu, *IEEE Trans. Mag.* 49 (2013) 7.

Analytical Calculation of Permanent Magnet and Coil Interaction

H. ALLAG [1,3] **, J. P. YONNET** [1,2]
[1] Université Grenoble Alpes, G2E Lab, F-38400 St Martin d'Hères, France
[2] Centre National de la Recherche Scientifique, G2E Lab, F-38000 Grenoble, France
[3] Jijel University, Jijel, Algeria

Abstract: *Permanent magnets are used with coils to create force and movements. For simple shape configurations, the analytical calculation is possible, giving a very easy and fast optimization. 3D analytical calculation has been developed for magneto-mechanical applications, working with forces exerted between permanent magnets: passive magnetic bearings, magnetic couplings, etc. The forces component and the interaction energy are obtained after four successive integrations of arctangent and logarithm functions. The results between two permanent magnets can be easily used to calculate the interaction between a magnet and a thin sheet of current. Unfortunately, the thickness of real coils cannot be neglected. The coil thickness gives an additional parameter in the calculation, which leads to a more complicated problem, with five successive integrations. Recently, the interaction calculation between a magnet and a thick coil has been fully analytically solved, giving a real 3D solution. To illustrate the use of the 3D analytical expressions, the calculation of an actuator is presented.*

Key words: *analytical calculation; force; VCM*

Address: Jean-Paul Yonnet, G2E Lab, Université Grenoble Alpes – CNRS Grenoble, ENSE3, Bât Ampère, BP 46, 38402 St Martin d'Hères cedex, E-mail: Jean-Paul.Yonnet@g2elab.grenoble-inp.fr

1. Introduction

The 3D analytical calculation of the interactions between two magnets has been developed since the 1980s. The first publications were made on long shaped magnets in interaction for magnetic bearings. These long magnets can be treated as a 2D problem. In 1984, the first calculation in 3D was published for cuboidal magnets with parallel magnetizations [1]. The analytical calculation has been extended for perpendicular magnetizations, allowing analytical calculations with any magnetization direction. In the 2010s, the torque components have been analytically calculated [2].

Important results in analytical calculations have also been obtained by Janssen [3] for magnet suspensions and Ravaud [4] for cylindrical shape magnets and arc-shaped magnets. Recently, new 3D analytical results have been obtained for the calculation of interaction between rectangular coils and magnets (Fig. 1). Rover [5] has obtained interesting results.

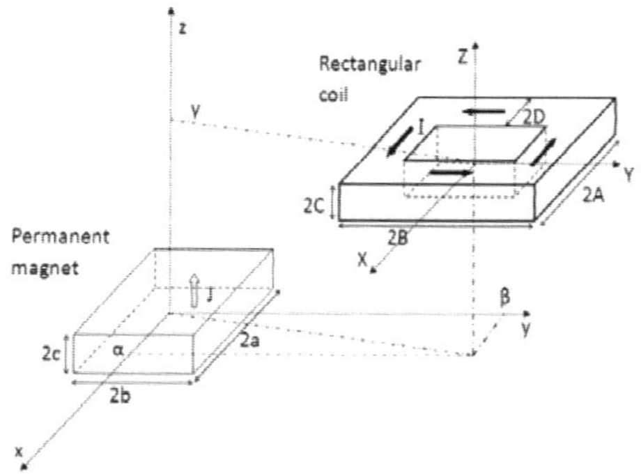

Fig. 1. Interaction between a thick coil and a permanent magnet.

A new approach using amperian model of the magnetization has been developed. It allows calculating of all the force components between a thick coil and a magnet after five integrations. The analytical expressions are used to calculate the force in an actuator.

2. Basic Mathematical Model

The interactions between two parallelepiped magnets will be considered in a first step. Magnets are supposed to be perfect, with their polarizations J and J' rigid and uniform, and a relative permeability of 1.

The magnet edges are respectively parallel (see Fig. 2) in the basic model. The dimensions of the first magnet are 2a x 2b x 2c, and its polarization is J parallel to 2c. Its centre is O, and the origin of the axes is Oxyz. For the second magnet, the dimensions are 2A x 2B x 2C, its polarization is J' parallel to 2C, and the coordinates of its centre O' are (α, β, γ). The side 2a is parallel to the side 2A, and so on.

For the units, in the international system SI, polarization J and charge density σ are in Tesla [T], and all the lengths are in meters [m]. Energy, force and torque are respectively in Joule [J], Newton [N],

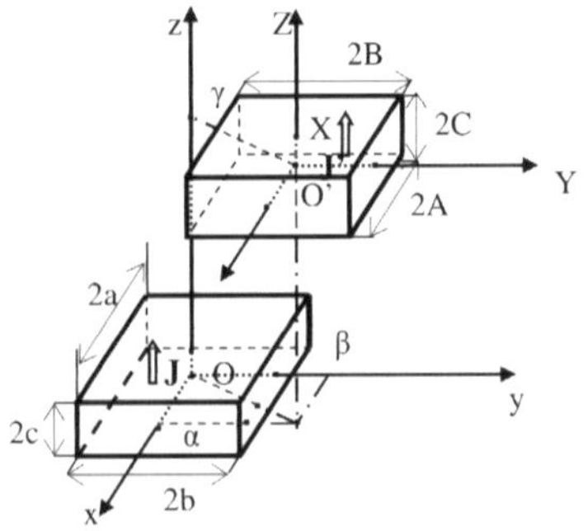

Fig. 2. Magnet configuration. The geometrical parameters are given in Table I.

and Newton.meter [N.m].

3. Interaction between a Magnet and a Coil

In addition to the calculation of the interaction between two magnets, the analytical calculation is also possible between coils, or between magnets and coils. Between rectangular coils, it is possible to calculate the interaction energy, the force and the torque, and also the mutual inductance. Between a magnet and a coil, the interaction force can be calculated, allowing the design of electromagnetic actuators.

At the beginning, the coulombian model of the magnetization has been used. The magnetization is replaced by magnetic charge distributions on the magnet poles. The magnetization can also be represented by sheets of currents around the magnet. This is the amperian model, which is equivalent to the previous coulombian model. For example, the calculation of the interaction forces or energy between two magnets can be made with sheet of currents around the magnets (Fig. 3). It allows obtaining interaction energy, force components, torque components like the coulombian model. In addition, the mutual inductance between the "magnet – equivalent" coils can be calculated. For thin sheets, the amperian model works immediately. But real coils are not only thin sheets of currents. They have a thickness, labelled as 2D on Figure 1.

With thin rectangular coils, the result is obtained after four integrations like magnetic charge representation. With thick coils, an additional integration is necessary

Table 1. Magnet Dimensions and Position.

Axis	Ox	Oy	Oz
First magnet dimension(J)	2a	2b	2c
First magnet parameter [0,1]	i	k	p
Second magnet dimension (J')	2A	2B	2C
Second magnet parameter	j	l	q
Second magnet position centre O'	α	β	γ

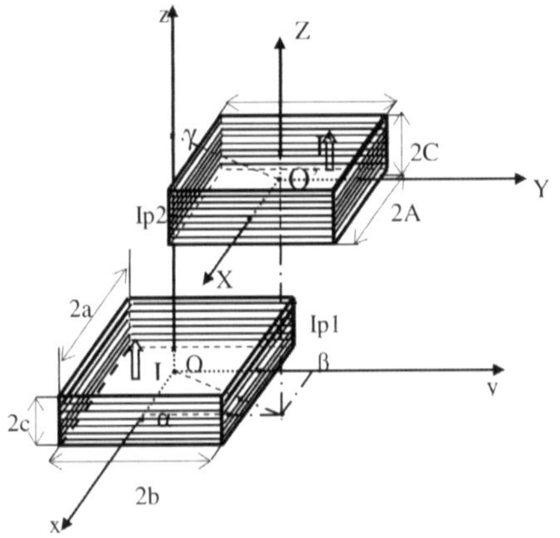

Fig. 3. Sheets of current around the magnet.

to take into account the coil thickness. Five successive integrations are now necessary. The calculation principle has been developed in a recent article [6]. For the case of a coil and a magnet, the calculation will be made by the mutual inductance between thin coils.

For the force calculation:

F = -grad E

$$E = I_{p1} \cdot I_{p2} \cdot M_T = \left(\frac{J \cdot 2c}{\mu_0} \right) \cdot (I_{cond}) \cdot M_T$$

with

$$M_T = \sum_{n=0}^{1} (-1)^n \left[Mx + My \right]$$

The force calculation is linked to the mutual inductance expression Mx and My between the amperian currents.

For the F_x component:

$$F_x = -\frac{\partial}{\partial x}\left[\left(\frac{J \cdot 2c}{\mu_0} \right) \cdot (I_{cond}) \cdot M_T \right] = -\left(\frac{J \cdot 2c}{\mu_0} \right) \cdot (I_{cond}) \cdot \frac{\partial M_T}{\partial x}$$

$$= -\left(\frac{J \cdot 2c}{\mu_0} \right) \cdot (I_{cond}) \cdot \frac{\partial \left(\sum_{n=0}^{1} (-1)^n \left[Mx + My \right] \right)}{\partial x}$$

It gives two components to the force, the first component coming from M_x is called F_{x1}, and the second one from M_y called F_{x2}.

$$F_x = F_{x1} + F_{x2}$$

$$F_{x1} = \frac{J}{4\pi} \frac{(I_{cond})}{S_{CX}} \sum_{n=0}^{1} \sum_{i=0}^{1} \sum_{j=0}^{1} \sum_{k=0}^{1} \sum_{l=0}^{1} \sum_{p=0}^{1} \sum_{q=0}^{1} (-1)^{i+j+k+l+p+q+n} \psi_{x1}(U_{ij}, V_{kl}, W_{pq}, r)$$

The expressions of the functions ψ is given by:

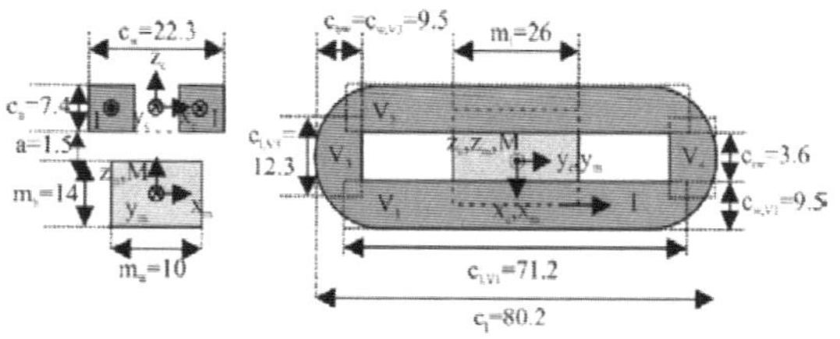

Fig. 4. The studied actuator: a cuboidal permanent magnet and a rectangular coil; the dimensions are in millimeters [5].

$$\psi_{x1}(U,V,W,r) = -\frac{V(V^2-3W^2)}{6}\ln(U+r) - \frac{U(U^2-3W^2)}{6}\ln(V+r) - UVW\cdot\ln(-W+r)$$
$$-\frac{W}{6}\left(3V^2\mathrm{tg}^{-1}\left(\frac{UW}{V\cdot r}\right)+3U^2\mathrm{tg}^{-1}\left(\frac{WV}{U\cdot r}\right)+W^2\mathrm{tg}^{-1}\left(\frac{VU}{W\cdot r}\right)\right)-\frac{V\cdot U\cdot r}{3}$$

with

$$U_{ij} = \alpha + (-1)^j(Lx-D) - (-1)^i a$$
$$V_{kl} = \beta + (-1)^n(Ly-D) + (-1)^l D - (-1)^k b$$
$$W_{pq} = \gamma + (-1)^q C - (-1)^p c$$

Similar results are obtained for F_{x2}, giving the full analytical expression of F_x. The components F_y and F_z, can be obtained by the same way.

4. Application to the Calculation of an Actuator

The analytical calculation between a magnet and a coil can be used for an actuator calculation [5]. These actuators work with the forces created between coils and magnets. The calculated device has been built by the Technical University of Eindhoven for a magnetic suspension. The dimensions are shown on Figure 4, and the measurements are compared with the calculated force components on Figure 5. The calculations have been made by analytical integration.

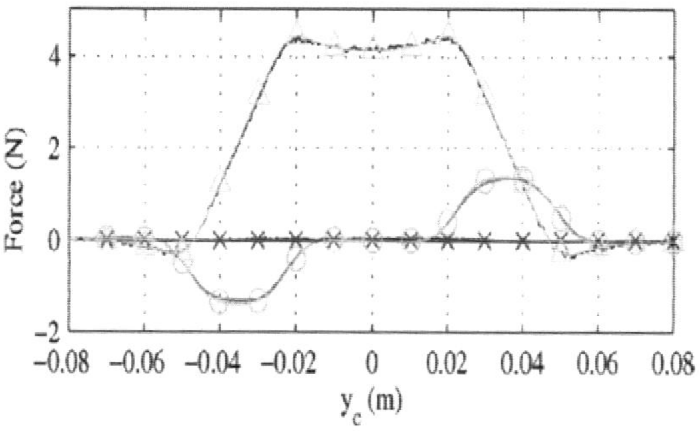

Fig. 5:
Fx obtained from measurements (blue solid line),
Fx obtained from analytic integration (blue X),
Fy obtained from measurements (red dashed line),
Fy obtained from analytic integration (green circle),
Fz obtained from measurements (light blue line),
Fz obtained from analytic integration (cyan triangle) [5].

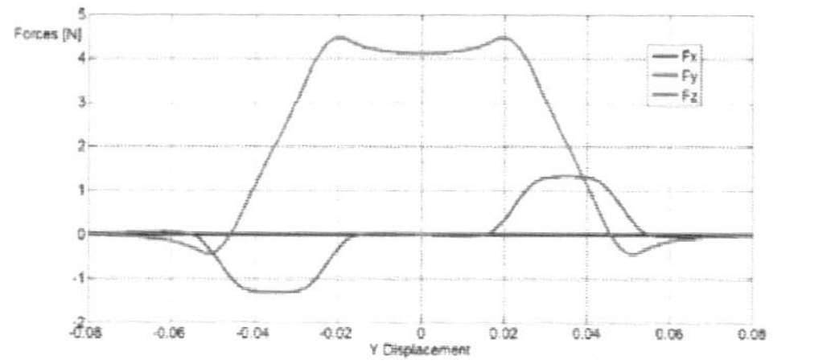

Fig. 6: Analytical calculation of the force components of the TUE actuator.

The same actuator has been calculated with our analytic formulas. The results are given on Figure 6. The obtained force components are in perfect agreement.

5. Conclusion

Analytical calculation is a very powerful method to calculate permanent magnet systems. The representation of the magnetization by sheets of currents allows the analytical calculation of the interaction between magnets, and the interaction between coils and magnets. For thick coils, the problem needs five successive integrations. The analytical results are illustrated by the calculation of the force created by an actuator.

References

[1] G. Akoun, J-P. Yonnet, *IEEE Trans. Magn.*, 1984, 20, 5, 1962-1964.

[2] J.-P. Yonne, H. Allag, *IEEE Trans. Magn.*, 2011, 47, 8, 2050-2055.

[3] J. L. G. Janssen, J. J. H. Paulides, E. A. Lomonova, *IEEE Trans. Magn.*, 2011, 47 , 10, 4286- 4289.

[4] R. Ravaud, G. Lemarquand, V. Lemarquand, C. Depollier, *IEEE Trans. Magn.*, 2008, 44, 8, 1982-1989

[5] J. M. M. Rovers, J. W. Jansen, Elena A. Lomonova, *IEEE Trans. Magn.*, 2010, 46, 6, 1656-1659.

[6] M. Aissaoui, H. Allag, J-P. Yonnet, "Mutual Inductance and Interaction Calculation between Conductor or Coil of Rectangular Cross Section and Parallelepiped Permanent Magnet", to be published in *IEEE Trans. Magn.*, 2014, 50.

Magnetic Properties of Hydrogenation-Disproportionation-Desorption-Recombination (HDDR)-Processed Dy-Free Nd-Fe-B Bulk Magnets Prepared from Magnetically Aligned Compacts of a Mixture of Fine Nd-Fe-B-Based Alloy Powder and Nd-Al Powder

N. NOZAWA, T. MURATA, T. NISHIUCHI
Magnetic Materials Research Laboratory, Magnetic Materials Company, Hitachi Metals, Ltd.

Abstract: *To improve the coercivity of Nd-Fe-B-based bulk porous magnets with submicron-sized grains obtained by hydrogenation-disproportionation-desorption-recombination (HDDR) processing of compacts of aligned anisotropic fine Nd-Fe-B powder, we applied a mixture of Nd-Fe-B-based alloy powder and Nd-Al powder as a starting material in this study. The coercivity and the density of samples after HDDR treatment were increased in proportion to the added ratio of Nd-Al alloy powder. After hot-pressing into shape, the obtained full dense magnets maintained high coercivity.*

Key words: *hydrogenation-disproportionation-desorption-recombination; Nd-Fe-B magnet; porous; Nd-Al powder; hot-pressing*

Address: Noriyuki Nozawa, Magnetic Materials Research Laboratory, Magnetic Materials Company, Hitachi Metals, Ltd. 2-15-17, Egawa, Shimamoto, Osaka 618-0013 Japan., Tel: +81-75-961-3173, Fax: +81-75-962-9690, E-mail: noriyuki.nozawa.ug@hitachi-metals.com

1. Introduction

A hydrogenation-disproportionation-desorption-recombination (HDDR) process is able to produce anisotropic Nd-Fe-B magnetic powder [1,2]. During HDDR processing, the $Nd_2Fe_{14}B$ phase hydrogenates and disproportionates into $NdH_{2\pm x}$, α-Fe and Fe_2B under heat treatment (about 700 to 900 °C) in a hydrogen atmosphere ("hydrogenation-dispropotionation (HD) reaction"). After the HD reaction, hydrogen is removed from $NdH_{2\pm x}$ by decreasing the hydrogen partial pressure. The phases resulted from the HD reaction recombine into an $Nd_2Fe_{14}B$ phase ("desorption-recombination (DR) reaction"). Magnetic powder from HDDR processing ("HDDR powder") has submicron-sized grains, which is one order of magnitude smaller than those in a conventional sintered magnet, and shows anisotropic hard magnetic property. Thus, this process is expected to be useful towards obtaining high coercive magnets without Dy and Tb [3,4].

Recently, the use of Nd-M alloy (M=Cu, Al, etc.) diffusion processing to make Dy-free Nd-Fe-B magnets of high coercivity from HDDR powder was reported by many researchers [5-7]. Coercivity enhancement in HDDR powder has also been reported without diffusion processing, by adding Al and increasing Nd content in a starting alloy of the HDDR process [8]. On the other hand, we proposed a unique process for producing porous bulk magnets with submicron-sized grains by applying HDDR processing to compacts of magnetically-aligned fine Nd-Fe-B powder [9]. The squareness of both these magnets and full dense magnets by hot-pressing to them was better than that of conventional HDDR powder. But, coercivity was low (about 1 MA/m) against the expectations of obtaining a high coercive magnet. In order to increase coercivity in such a bulk magnet, we applied HDDR processing to compacts of fine Nd-Fe-B-based alloy powder incorporated with Nd-Al alloy powder as a coercivity enhancer, in this study.

2. Experimental Procedure

A flowchart of sample preparation used in this study

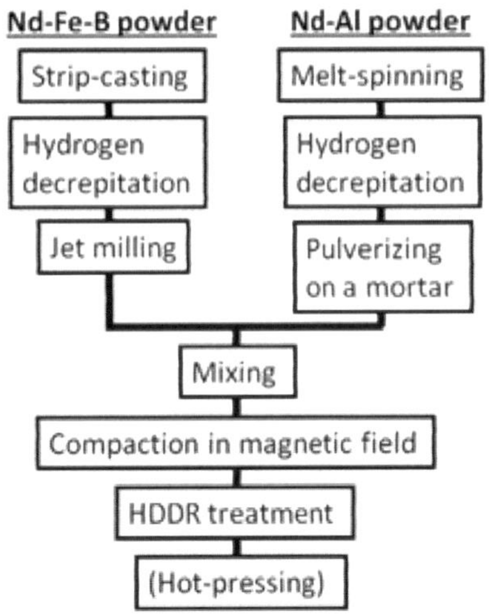

Fig.1. Flowchart of sample preparation.

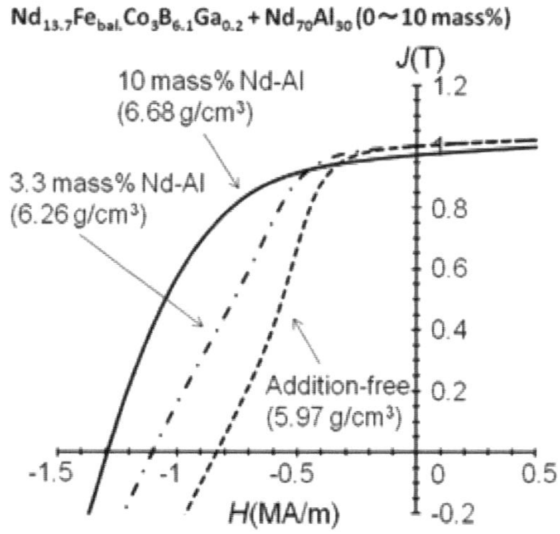

Fig. 2. Demagnetization curves of samples prepared from $Nd_{13.2}Fe_{bal.}Co_3B_{6.1}Ga_{0.2}$ and $Nd_{70}Al_{30}$ powders with different mixing ratio.

is shown in Fig. 1. $Nd_xFe_{bal.}Co_3B_{6.1}Ga_{0.2}$ (mol%, x = 12.7, 13.2, 13.7 and 14.2) alloys were made by strip-casting. After hydrogen decrepitation, each alloy was jet-milled into a fine powder of an average particle size of around 5 μm. On the other hand, $Nd_{70}Al_{30}$ and $Nd_{40}Al_{60}$ alloys were made by melt-spinning. After hydrogen decrepitation, each alloy was pulverized and sieved to make a powder of a particle size of 53 μm or less. The Nd-Al powder was added to the Nd-Fe-B-based alloy powder in a ratio of 1 to 10 mass %. Then, the mixed powder was magnetically aligned in an applied field of 1.5 T and compacted to a density of 4.2 g/cm^3. After that, the compacts were subjected to HDDR treatment as follows. Each compact was heated from 20 °C to 600 °C for 42 min in a hydrogen atmosphere at a pressure of 0.1 MPa, and from 600 °C to 840 °C or 860 °C for 18 min in an argon atmosphere of 0.1 MPa, and then kept at 840 °C or 860 °C for 15 min in an Ar atmosphere of 0.1 MPa, and for 120 min in a hydrogen atmosphere of 0.1 MPa to promote the HD reaction. After that, the sample was annealed at the same temperature as the HD reaction for 60 min in an argon atmosphere of low pressure to promote the DR reaction, and subsequently cooled to room temperature in an argon atmosphere. Several samples after HDDR treatment were further compressed by hot-pressing in a vacuum at 800 °C and 50 MPa for 20 min. Magnetic properties of the samples after HDDR treatment and after hot-pressing were evaluated by B-H tracer, and their microstructures were observed by field emission scanning electron microscopy (FE-SEM) and electron probe micro analysis (EPMA).

3. Results and Discussions

3.1. Coercivity and microstructure of samples

Figure 2 shows demagnetization curves after HDDR treatment at 860 °C for three samples of $Nd_{13.7}Fe_{bal.}Co_3B_{6.1}Ga_{0.2}$ powders with additions of $Nd_{70}Al_{30}$ powder in different ratios. Coercivity (H_{cJ}) and density of the samples after HDDR treatment increased in proportion to the added ratio of Nd-Al alloy powder. The coercivity in the sample with a 10 mass% Nd-Al powder addition showed 1.30 MA/m, which is much higher than that in the non-additive sample (0.83 MA/m).

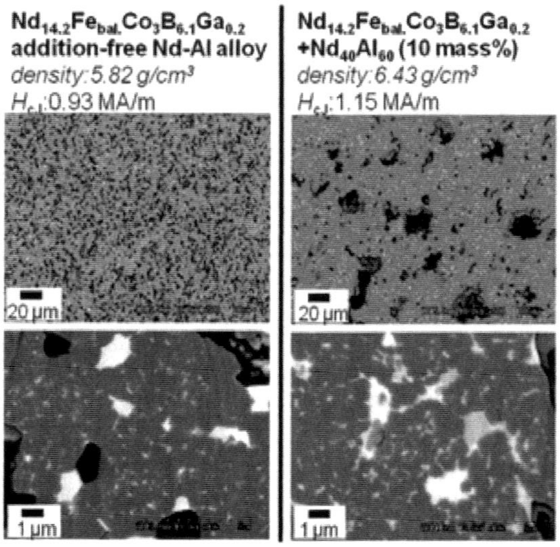

Fig. 3. FE-SEM images of polished surfaces of samples of $Nd_{14.2}Fe_{bal.}Co_3B_{6.1}Ga_{0.2}$ powders with and without addition of $Nd_{40}Al_{60}$ powder (Added ratio: 10 mass%).

Figure 3 shows FE-SEM images of polished surfaces of the samples obtained from $Nd_{14.2}Fe_{bal.}Co_3B_{6.1}Ga_{0.2}$ powders with $Nd_{40}Al_{60}$ powder added (10 mass%) and not-added after HDDR treatment at 840 °C. Coercivity and density of the samples also increased with the addition of Nd-Al alloy, as in the case of the $Nd_{70}Al_{30}$ powder. FE-SEM observations show that the addition-free sample has numerous pores of a size of around 1-3 μm, which is the same result as our previous study [8]. On the other hand, the microstructure of the sample with Nd-Al powder addition showed different features from the non-addition sample, including large pores of a size greater than 10 μm. These pores likely resulted from the original Nd-Al powder. In addition, the Nd-rich phase in the sample with Nd-Al powder addition increased compared with addition-free sample. According to the Nd-Al binary phase diagram, $Nd_{40}Al_{60}$ composition should not generate a liquid phase at 800 °C. Therefore, these results suggest that a portion part of the Nd and Al in the Nd-Al powder diffused into the Nd-Fe-B-based alloy powder during HDDR treatment, and helped to form Nd-rich phases in the samples, which likely caused the increase in the density of the samples during HDDR treatment and the enhancement of coercivity.

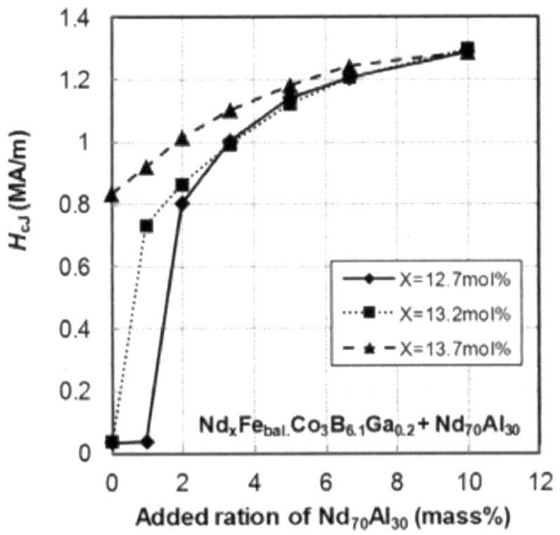

Fig. 4. Relationship between added ratio of $Nd_{70}Al_{30}$ and coercivity of samples of three kinds of $Nd_xFe_{bal.}Co_3B_{6.1}Ga_{0.2}$ (mol%, x = 12.7, 13.2 and 13.7) powders and $Nd_{70}Al_{30}$ powder.

3.2. Effect of Nd content in Nd-Fe-B-based alloy powder

Figure 4 shows the relationship between the added ratio of $Nd_{70}Al_{30}$ and coercivity after HDDR treatment at 860 °C for a sample of a mixture of $Nd_xFe_{bal.}Co_3B_{6.1}Ga_{0.2}$ (x = 12.7, 13.2 and 13.7) powder and $Nd_{70}Al_{30}$ powder. The coercivity of the addition-free samples obtained from compacted powders with compositions of $Nd_{12.7}Fe_{bal.}Co_3B_{6.1}Ga_{0.2}$ and $Nd_{13.2}Fe_{bal}Co_3B_{6.1}Ga_{0.2}$ was extremely low. On the contrary, the coercivity drastically increased when Nd-Al powder was added to the Nd-Fe-B-based alloy powders of these compositions. It is assumed that there was not enough Nd-rich phase to develop coercivity at the grain boundaries in the addition-free samples because a portion of the Nd had reacted with O, C and N in the sample during HDDR treatment as shown in our previous study [8], and added Nd-Al powder helped to form an Nd-rich phase at the grain boundaries of the samples, which is the same effect shown in Fig. 3.

When the added ratio of Nd-Al powder was less than 3.3 mass%, the coercivity of the samples increased in proportion to the Nd content (x) in the Nd-Fe-B-based alloy powder. On the other hand, the coercivity of the samples with a 10 mass% of Nd-Al powder addition was almost same level for different amounts of x (12.7, 13.2 and 13.7) in the Nd-Fe-B-based alloy powder. These results suggest that a portion of the excess Nd in the stoichiometric composition of $Nd_2Fe_{14}B$ did not help to enhance coercivity in the HDDR-processed samples in this study.

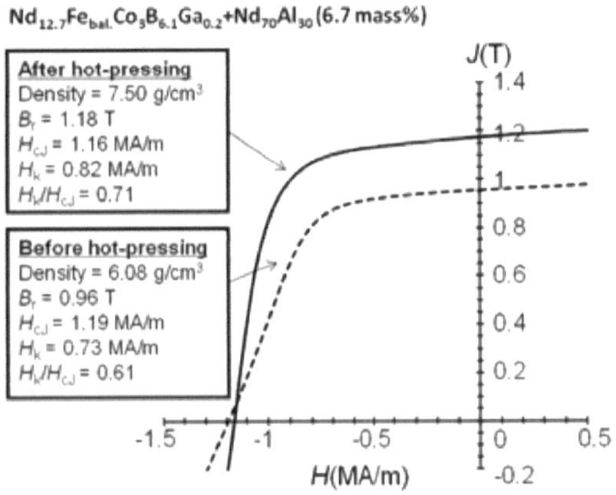

Fig. 5. Demagnetization curves of magnets before and after hot-pressing.

3.3. Densification of samples by hot-pressing

A porous magnet obtained by HDDR treatment was compressed by hot-pressing to improve remanence (B_r). When total Nd content of the mixture of Nd-Fe-B-based alloy powder and Nd-Al powder exceeded 15 mol%, the sample after hot-pressing could not be pushed out of the die because of the liquid phase extruded from the sample during hot-pressing. Figure 5 shows demagnetization curves, densities and magnetic properties before and after hot-pressing for the samples with $Nd_{12.7}Fe_{bal.}Co_3B_{6.1}Ga_{0.2}$ powder with $Nd_{70}Al_{30}$ powder addition (added ratio = 6.7 mass% , total Nd content of the sample = 14.9 mol%). The density (6.08 g/cm^3) of the porous magnet increased to almost full density (about 7.50 g/cm^3) under hot-pressing, which resulted in an increase in remanence. The coercivity of the sample after hot-pressing was equivalent to that before hot-pressing.

4. Summary

We applied hydrogenation-disproportionation-desorption-recombination (HDDR) processing to compacts of aligned anisotropic fine Nd-Fe-B powder mixed with Nd-Al powder. The coercivity and the density of the samples after HDDR treatment increased in proportion to the added ratio of the Nd-Al alloy powder. The samples added Nd-Al powder had differing porous microstructures that included some large pores of a size of more than 10 µm. And more of an Nd-rich phase was observed in the samples added Nd-Al powder compared with the addition-free samples. When the added ratio of Nd-Al powder was less than 3.3 mass%, the coercivity of the samples with $Nd_{70}Al_{30}$ addition increased in proportion to the Nd content (x) in the $Nd_xFe_{bal.}Co_3B_{6.1}Ga_{0.2}$ (mol%, x=12.7, 13.2 and 13.7) powder. On the other hand, the coercivity of the samples with 10 mass% of $Nd_{70}Al_{30}$ powder added were almost the same level for different amounts of x (12.7, 13.2 and 13.7) in the Nd-Fe-B-based alloy powder, which suggests that a portion of the excess

Nd in the stoichiometric composition of $Nd_2Fe_{14}B$ did not contribute to enhancing coercivity in the HDDR-processed sample in this study. In the case that the total Nd content of the Nd-Fe-B powder mixed with Nd-Al powder was less than 15 mol%, (e.g. $Nd_{12.7}Fe_{bal.}Co_3B_{6.1}Ga_{0.2}$ powders with $Nd_{70}Al_{30}$ powder added [added ratio = 6.7 mass% , total Nd content of the sample = 14.9 mol%) a fully densified magnet was successfully obtained by hot-pressing after HDDR treatment, and it maintained high coercivity.

References

[1] T. Takeshita, R. Nakayama, *Proc. 12st Int. Workshop on Rare-Earth Magnets and Their Applications, Canberra, Australia*, 1992, 670-681.

[2] R. Nakayama, T. Takeshita, *J. Alloy. Compd.*, 1993, 193, 259.

[3] T. Nishiuchi, S. Hirosawa, M. Nakamura, M. Kakimoto, T. Kawabayashi, H. Araki, Y. Shirai, *IEEJ Trans. Electr. Electr. Eng.* 2008, 3, 390.

[4] W. F. Li, T. Ohkubo, K. Hono, *Proc. 20st Int. Workshop on Rare-earth Permanent Magnets and Their Applications, Crete, Greece,* 2008, 114-117.

[5] H. Sepehri-Amin, T. Ohkubo, T. Nishiuchi, S. Hirosawa, K. Hono, *Scripta Mater.*, 2010, 63, 1124.

[6] C. Mishima, K. Noguchi, M. Yamazaki, H. Mitarai, Y. Honkura, *Proc. 21st Int. Workshop on Rare-earth Permanent Magnets and Their Applications, Bled, Slovenia,* 2010, 253-256.

[7] T. Nishicuhi, N. Nozawa, T. Murata, T. Kawata, S. Hirosawa, *Hitachi Metals Tech. Rev.,* 2013, 29, 38 (in Japanese).

[8] K. Morimoto, N. Katayama, H. Akamine, M. Itakura, *J. Magn. Magn. Mater.*, 2012, 324, 3723.

[9] N. Nozawa, T. Nishiuchi, S. Hirosawa, *Proc. 21st Int. Workshop on Rare-earth Permanent Magnets and Their Applications, Bled, Slovenia,* 2010, 257-260.

Annealing Effect on $L1_0$ FePt Nanoparticles Prepared by Ball Milling of Layered Crystal $Fe(H_2O)_6PtCl_6$

X.C. HU[1,2], G.C. HADJIPANAYIS[2], D.J. SELLMYER[3]
[1]Department of Materials Science and Engineering, University of Delaware, DE 19716, USA
[2]Department of Physics and Astronomy, University of Delaware, DE 19716, USA
[3]Department of Physics and Astronomy, University of Nebraska, Lincoln, NE 68588, USA

Abstract: *In this work, a new green chemical approach was used to synthesize magnetically hard $L1_0$ FePt nanoparticles. The precursor, a polycrystalline molecular complex ($Fe(H_2O)_6PtCl_6$) with Fe and Pt atoms arranged on alternating planes, was milled with NaCl by planetary ball milling. Annealing in the temperature range from 300 °C to 500 °C was applied on both the precursor and ball milled mixture of precursor and NaCl. Both bulk FePt and FePt NPs with the $L1_0$ structure were obtained. Due to the special layered structure of the precursor, the transformation temperature was decreased to 350 °C for bulk FePt and 400 °C for FePt NPs as compared to the commonly reported value of 650 °C for equiatomic FePt. The highest coercivity obtained in FePt NPs is 10.9 kOe.*

Key words: *green chemical synthesis; $L1_0$ FePt nanoparticles; high coercivity; annealing effect*

Address: Xiaocao Hu, Department of Physics and Astronomy, University of Delaware, DE, USA, Tel: +1 302-831-3515, Fax: +1 302-831-1637, E-mail: xiaocaoh@udel.edu

1. Introduction

FePt nanoparticles (NPs) attracted much interest in recent years because of their promising applications in ultra-high density biomedical technologies [1], recording [2] and permanent magnet composites [3,4]. FePt NPs in $L1_0$ phase are considered to be a promising material for ultra-high density recording media due to the high anisotropy of $L1_0$ (7×10^7 erg/cc) which makes the nanoparticles thermally stable at room temperature (RT) even with a particle size as small as 2.8 nm [5-7].

The most popular chemical fabrication method of FePt NPs was first reported by Sun et al. [8]; however, the as-made FePt NPs are usually in the magnetically soft fcc phase. To transform the NPs to magnetically hard fct phase, post annealing above 600 °C is needed which usually leads to undesirable agglomeration and sintering [9-11]. To solve this problem, a green chemical synthesis method to fabricate $L1_0$ FePt NPs is reported in this paper. Crystalline saline complex hexaaquairon(II) hexachloroplatinate ($[Fe(H_2O)_6]PtCl_6$) is used as the precursor, mixed with NaCl and then ball milled by planetary milling. The effect of annealing is investigated on the structure and properties of the precursor and FePt NPs obtained after washing away the NaCl from the annealed mixture.

Experimental

A 0.5M water solution with equal atomic concentration of $FeCl_2{\cdot}H_2O$ and $H_2PtCl_6{\cdot}6H_2O$ (from Aldrich) was evaporated to fabricate the $[Fe(H_2O)_6]PtCl_6$ crystal. Then, 50 mg precursor was mixed with 20 g NaCl and is planetary ball milled at 250 rpm for 5 h. After the milling, the light-yellow powder mixture was annealed under an atmosphere of forming gas (95% Ar and 5% H_2) at temperatures varying from 350 °C to 500 °C for 2 h. The following reduction reaction takes place:

$$[Fe(H_2O)_6]PtCl_6 + 3H_2 \rightarrow FePt(L1_0) + 6H_2O + 6HCl.$$

Finally, the annealed mixture was washed by deionized water to obtain the FePt NPs. To demonstrate the influence of ball milling, the precursor was annealed directly at different temperatures (from 300 °C to 500 °C for 2 h) without ball milling with NaCl.

The morphology of the annealed precursor was observed by scanning electron microscopy (SEM) (Auriga 60 by Zeiss). The morphology and size of FePt NPs were decided by transmission electron microscopy (TEM) (JEOL 2010). The crystal structure can be obtained from X-ray diffraction (XRD) patterns (Rigaku Ultima IV with Cu Kα radiation) using a θ-2θ plane reflection geometry. Hysteresis loops were measured by a Versa Lab vibrating sample magnetometer (Quantum Design).

Results and Discussion

Fig. 1 demonstrates the morphology of FePt NPs and annealed precursor. From the SEM and TEM images,

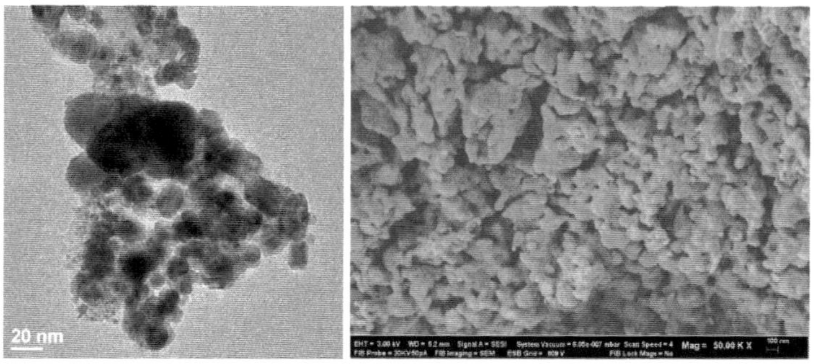

Fig. 1. Typical TEM images for FePt NPs and SEM images for annealed precursor.

one can see that direct annealing of precursor produces bulk FePt with the L10 structure as shown in XRD patterns in Fig. 2. Ball milling breaks the larger FePt pieces into NPs.

To investigate the phase transformation temperature from fcc to fct in the particles made by our method, different annealing temperatures were used in the range of 350 °C to 500 °C. For comparison, the precursor was also annealed at the same temperatures. Fig. 3 shows the XRD patterns FePt NPs. The XRD patterns in Fig. 3 show the characteristic (001), (110) peaks of fct phase and the splitting of (200) peaks in the samples annealed at 450 °C and 500 °C. For the 400 °C sample, the (111) and (200) peaks are broadened and shifted towards the angle of fct phase; however, the (001) and (110) peaks are so weak and broad that can't be seen clearly. This indicates an early stage of phase transformation from the fcc phase to the fct phase. The XRD patterns in Fig. 2 showed that direct annealing of the precursor led to the formation of FePt but with larger size (as indicated by the narrower peaks).

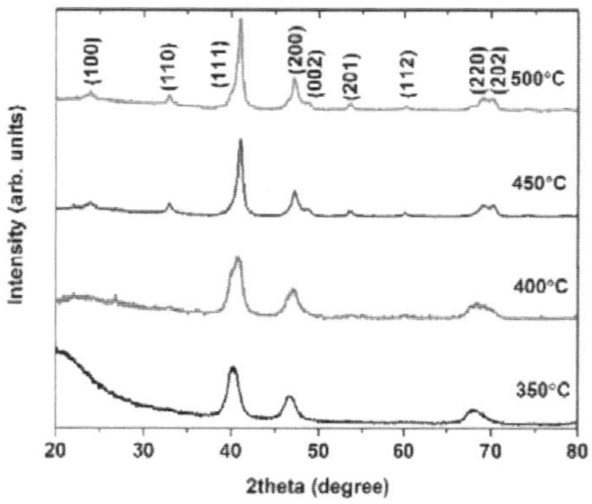

Fig. 2. XRD patterns of FePt NPs annealed at (a) 350 °C (b) 400 °C (c) 450 °C (d) 500 °C.

The hysteresis loops are shown in Fig. 4. The room temperature (RT) coercivity of 4.9 kOe shown in Table 1 indicates that the phase transformation at around 400 °C occurred. Compared with the coercivity at a higher annealing temperature (up to 10.9 kOe at RT), the lower coercivity values at 400 °C indicate an incomplete phase transformation. Also, Fig. 4 shows a magnetization increase as the annealing temperature is increased which can also be explained by the degree of phase transformation which increases with higher annealing temperature.

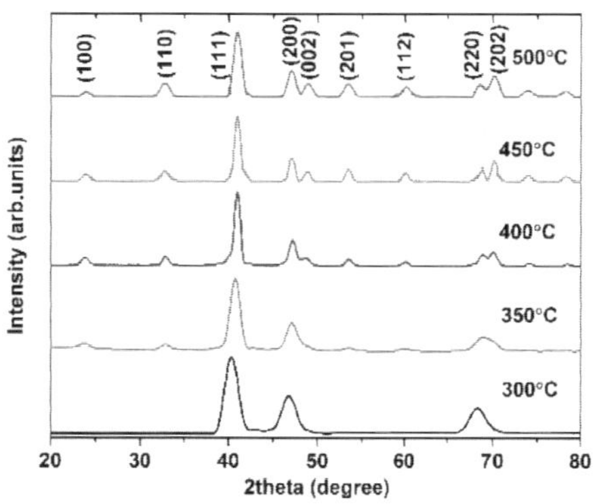

Fig. 3. XRD patterns of annealed precursor at (a) 300 °C, (b) 350 °C, (c) 400 °C, (d) 450 °C, (e) 500 °C.

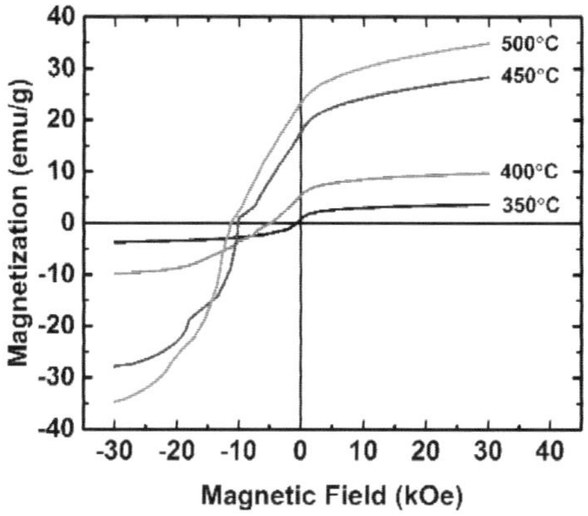

Fig. 4. RT hysteresis loops of FePt NPs annealed at different temperatures.

Table 1. Coercivity and magnetization values at 30 kOe of FePt NPs annealed at different temperatures.

Annealing temperature (°C)	350	400	450	500
H_c (kOe)	0.5	4.9	9.2	10.9
M_s (emu/g)	3.7	9.7	28.4	34.9

For the bulk FePt, the phase trans-formation temperature was further decreased to 350 °C, with a coercivity around 5.4 kOe (shown in Fig 5 and Table 2). The highest coercivity was 13.4 kOe which was obtained at 500 °C.

The phase transformation temperature observed in particles prepared by our method is much lower than the values reported in the literature which are at 600 °C or above. This is due to the layered structure of Fe and Pt atoms in the precursor which was reported in our previous paper [12,13]. A lower energy is needed to rearrange and order the atoms leading to a decrease of the phase transformation temperature. Similar results were obtained in film systems through annealing the sputtered Fe and Pt multilayer [14].

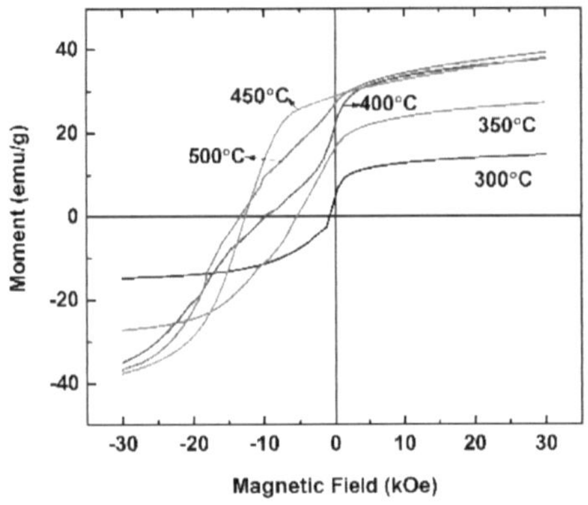

Fig. 5. RT hysteresis loops of annealed precursor annealed at different temperatures.

Table 2. Coercivity and magnetization values at 30 kOe of bulk FePt annealed at different temperatures.

Annealing temperature (°C)	300	350	400	450	500
H_c (kOe)	0.8	5.4	9.8	12.3	13.4
M_s (emu/g)	14.7	27.2	37.7	38.1	39.3

Conclusions

In this paper, a green method is described to fabricate $L1_0$ FePt NPs with high coercivity using environment-friendly chemicals NaCl and deionized water. FePt NPs were obtained by planetary ball milling of a mixture of precursor $[Fe(H_2O)_6]PtCl_6$ and NaCl. The influence of annealing on both the FePt NPs and annealed precursor was investigated. In the particles prepared by this method, the phase transformation takes place at around 400 °C, which is much lower than the commonly reported temperature of around 650 °C. For bulk FePt, the phase transformation was further decreased to 350 °C.

Acknowlegment
This work was supported by DOE.

References

[1] L. X. Tiefenauer, A. Tschirky, G. Kuhne, and R. Y. Andres, *Magn. Reson. Imaging* **14,** 1996, 391.
[2] H. W. Zhang, Y. Liu, and S. H. Sun, *Front. Phys. China* **5,** 2010, 347.
[3] B.Balamurugan, D.J. Sellmyer, G.C. Hadjipanayis, and R. Skomski, *Scr. Mater.* **67,** 2012, 542.
[4] A. Mari, E. Agostinelli, D. Fiorani, A. Flamini, S. Laureti, D. Peddis, A. M. Testa, G. Varvaro, M. V. Mansilla, A. Mezzi, and S. Kaciulis, *Superlattices Microstruct.* **46,** 2009, 95.
[5] K. Inomata, T. Sawa, and S. Hashimoto, Journal of Applied Physics **64,** 2537 (1988).
[6] J. P. Wang, *Proc. IEEE* **96,** 2008, 1847.
[7] T. Miyazaki, O. Kitakami, S. Okamoto, Y. Shimada, Z. Akase, Y. Murakami, D. Shindo, Y. K. Takahashi, and K. Hono, *Phys. Rev. B* **72,** 2005.
[8] S. H. Sun, C. B. Murray, D. Weller, L. Folks, and A. Moser, *Science* **287,** 2000, 1989.
[9] S. H. Sun, *Adv. Mater.* **18,** 2006, 393.
[10] P. Gibot, E. Tronc, C. Chaneac, J. P. Jolivet, D. Fiorani, and A. M. Testa, *J. Magn. Magn. Mater.* **290,** 2005, 555.
[11] Q. Dong, G. J. Li, C. L. Ho, M. Faisal, C. W. Leung, P. W. T. Pong, K. Liu, B. Z. Tang, I. Manners, and W. Y. Wong, *Adv. Mater.* **24,** 2012, 1034.
[12] A. Capobianchi, M. Colapietro, D. Fiorani, S. Foglia, P. Imperatori, S. Laureti, and E. Palange, *Chem. Mater.* **21,** 2009, 2007.
[13] E. A. X. C. Hu, C. Ni, G. C. Hadjipanayis, A. Capobianchi, *Green Chem.* **16**, 2014, 2292.
[14] Y. Endo, N. Kikuchi, O. Kitakami, and Y. Shimada, *J. Appl. Phys.* **89,** 2001, 7065.

Effect of Non-Magnetic Layer Diffusion for Nd-Fe-B Thin Films with Particulate Structure

T. FURUUCHI, H. IWAMA, M. DOI, T. SHIMA
Tohoku Gakuin University, Tagajo 985-8537, Japan

Abstract: *The microstructural and magnetic properties for particulate Nd-Fe-B thin films with several cap layer materials have been investigated. The Nd-Fe-B thin films with different film thickness were prepared on MgO (100) single crystal substrate and subsequently, the Nd-Fe alloy cap layers with different composition were deposited. High coercivity* H_c *of 20 kOe was obtained for the Nd-Fe-B thin films with t = 5 nm. With increasing Nd content x in the* Nd_xFe_{100-x} *films, a saturation magnetization was decreased and hold maximum at x = 20. Further increase of Nd content reduces the magnetization. After the deposition of Nd-Fe alloy cap layers on the Nd-Fe-B thin films, a shape of the initial magnetization curve was changed, indicating that magnetization process was affected by the thin additive layer.*

Key words: *Nd-Fe-B thin film; particulate structure; sputtering; Nd-Fe alloy; magnetization process*

Address: Takahiro Furuuchi, Graduate school of Engineering, Tohoku Gakuin University, Tagajo 985-8537, Japan, Tel: (81) 22-368-1128, Fax: (81) 22-368-1272, E-mail: s1494305@mail.tohoku-gakuin.ac.jp

1. Introduction

Since the discovery of $Nd_2Fe_{14}B$ compound [1], Nd-Fe-B permanent magnets have been widely used for the applications such as sensors, actuators and motors, since they possess large magnetocrystalline anisotropy (K_{u1} = 4.5x10^6 J/m^3 at room temperature) and relatively high magnetization (M_s = 1.6 T) among all permanent magnets [2]. Recently, the consumption of Nd-Fe-B sintered magnets has increased due to the expansion in the markets for hybrid vehicles (HVs), electric vehicles (EVs) and wind power generators resulting from an environmental and energy issues. One critical issue is how to reduce an indispensable addition of heavy rare earth elements such as Tb and Dy to the Nd-Fe-B sintered magnet for the enhancement of coercivity at high temperature utilization [3]. This issue is caused by the scarce natural resources of these elements. The actual value of the coercivity for commercial Nd-Fe-B sintered magnets is much lower than the theoretically predicted one [4], and the reason for the gap between them has not been clarified yet. Therefore, the elucidation of the coercivity mechanism is essential for reducing the amount of heavy rare earth elements from the Nd-Fe-B magnets and for improving the hard magnetic properties.

The present study demonstrates the effect of the thickness for particulate Nd-Fe-B thin films and also the effect of the composition of Nd-Fe cap layers, which constitute the grain boundary phase, for the Nd-Fe-B thin films on the structure and magnetic properties.

2. Experimental Procedure

All the samples were prepared by co-sputtering of Nd (3N), $Fe_{80}B_{20}$ (at%) and Fe (4N) targets using an ultra-high vacuum (UHV) compatible dc magnetron sputtering system. The base pressure was below 5×10^{-8} Pa. The MgO (100) single crystal substrate was used and it was heated up to 700 °C before deposition for surface treatment. First of all, a Mo buffer layer of 20 nm was deposited at room temperature (R.T.). Then, the substrates were heated to 550 °C during the deposition of the Nd-Fe-B layer. The thickness of the Nd-Fe-B layer was varied in the range of 3 - 20 nm. Finally, a Mo layer of 10 nm was deposited at R.T. as an oxidation protective layer. Composition of the Nd-Fe-B layer was determined to be $Nd_{19.7}Fe_{68.6}B_{11.7}$ (at.%) by an electron probe micro analyzer. Structural analysis was performed by X-ray diffraction (XRD) with Cu-Kα radiation. The magnetic properties were measured by a superconducting quantum interference device (SQUID) magnetometer in the field up to 70 kOe.

3. Results and Discussion

The magnetization curves for Nd-Fe-B thin films at various film thicknesses are shown in Fig. 1. All the measurements were performed at R. T.. The magnetic field was applied in the direction perpendicular to the film plane. The magnetic easy axis is perpendicular to the film plane for all the samples, since the c-axis of $Nd_2Fe_{14}B$ is perpendicular to the film plane as characterized by XRD. The initial magnetization curves were changed with increasing the films thickness. A steep increase in the initial magnetization curves begins to observe at a low magnetic field for the

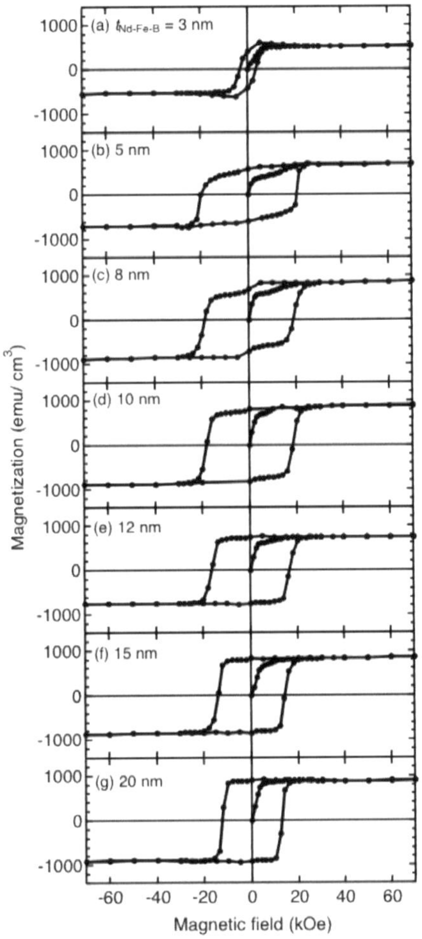

Fig. 1. The magnetization curves for Nd-Fe-B thin films at various film thicknesses. (a) $t_{Nd-Fe-B}$ = 3 nm, (b) 5 nm, (c) 8 nm, (d) 10 nm, (e) 12 nm, (f) 15 nm and (g) 20 nm.

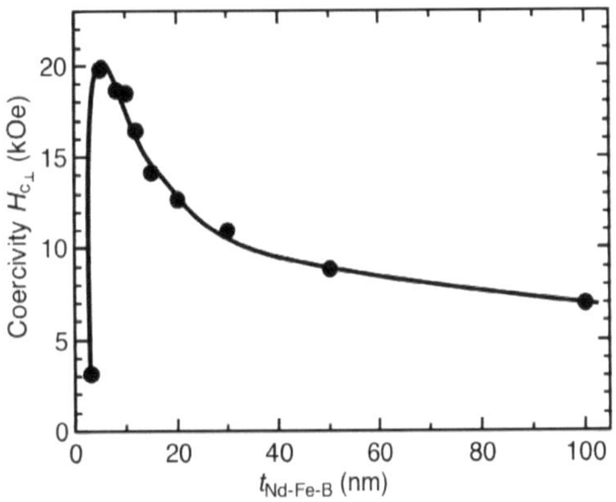

Fig. 2. Effect of the thickness of Nd-Fe-B layer ($t_{Nd-Fe-B}$) on the coercivity for Nd-Fe-B thin films.

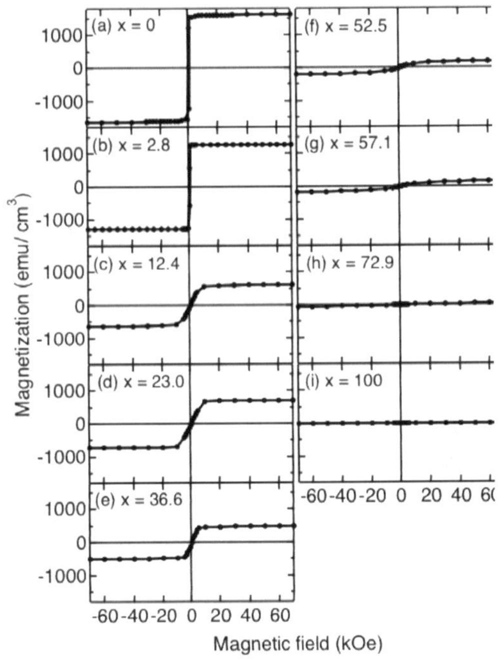

Fig. 3. The magnetization curves for Nd_xFe_{100-x} alloy films at various Nd content x (at.%). (a) x = 0 (Fe), (b) 2.8, (c) 12.4, (d) 23.0, (e) 36.6, (f) 52.5, (g) 57.1, (h) x = 72.9 and (i) 100 (Nd).

films with $t_{Nd-Fe-B} \geq 8$ nm. The squareness of the magnetization curve was improved for the film with $t_{Nd-Fe-B}$ = 10 nm, and also relatively high coercivity H_c of 18.6 kOe was obtained. With further increasing of $t_{Nd-Fe-B}$, H_c decreased. H_c as a function of $t_{Nd-Fe-B}$ are shown in Fig. 2. Highest H_c of 20 kOe was obtained for the film with $t_{Nd-Fe-B}$ = 8 nm and then it was gradually decreased with increasing $t_{Nd-Fe-B}$, this is thought to arise from the change of the magnetization process from the rotation of the magnetization to the domain wall displacement.

The magnetization curves for Nd_xFe_{100-x} alloy films at various Nd content x are shown in Fig. 3. x is (a) 0 (Fe), (b) 2.8, (c) 12.4, (d) 23.0, (e) 36.6, (f) 52.5, (g) 57.1, (h) 72.9 and (i) 100 (Nd) at.% and the film thickness was fixed at 300 nm. The magnetic field was applied in the in-plane directions. No large Hc was observed for all the films and the value of the remanent magnetization was decreased for the film with x ≥ 12.4. From these magnetization curves, saturation magnetization as a function of Nd content are summarized in Fig. 4. With increasing Nd content x in the Nd-Fe films, a saturation magnetization was decreased and hold maximum at x = 20. Further increase of Nd content reduces the magnetization. This is well consistent with the theoretical calculation of the fcc Nd-Fe alloys done by Prof. Sakuma [9].

The magnetization curves for the Nd-Fe-B with Nd_xFe_{100-x} alloy cap layer are shown in Fig. 5. The thicknesses of the Nd-Fe-B and Nd-Fe layers are 10 nm and 2 nm, respectively. x is (a) 0 (Fe), (b) 23.0, (c) 52.5, (d) 72.9 and (e) 100 (Nd) at.%. No post annealing

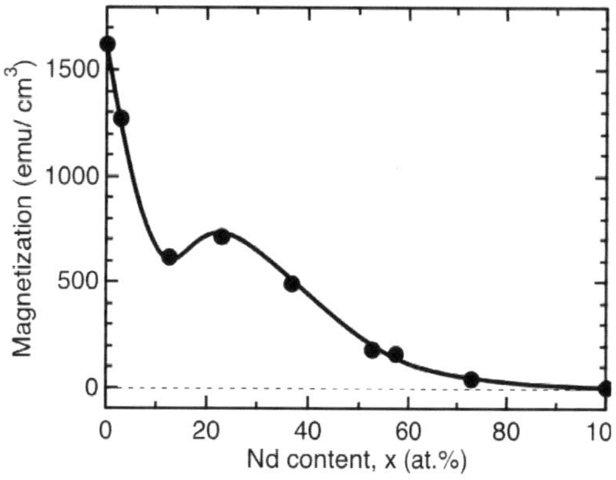

Fig. 4 The saturation magnetization as a function of Nd content for Nd_xFe_{100-x} alloy films.

was performed for all the samples. The saturation magnetization was increased for the film without Nd addition (a), however, the reduction of the remanent magnetization was observed. The squareness of the magnetization curve was improved for the films with x = 23.0 at.% and further increasing of x, high H_c of 20.5 kOe was obtained for Nd-Fe-B film with x = 52.5 at.%. The saturation magnetization was monotonically decreased with increasing the Nd content in the Nd-Fe layer. It is noteworthy that the different behavior at the shape of the initial magnetization curve was observed for the films with x = 23.0 and 72.9 at.%. This result indicates that thin Nd-Fe alloy cap layer affect the magnetization process in the Nd-Fe-B thin films, although no heat treatment was performed.

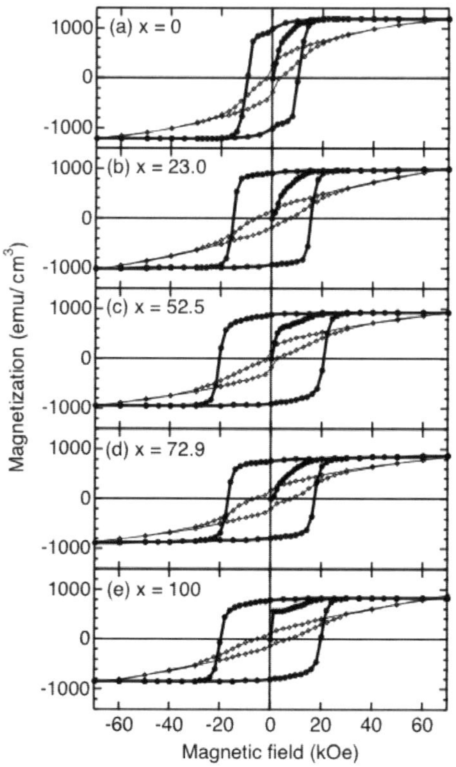

Fig. 5 The magnetization curves for the Nd-Fe-B films with Nd_xFe_{100-x} alloy cap layer. (a) x = 0 (Fe), (b) 23.0, (c) 52.5, (d) 72.9 and (e) 100 (Nd).

4. Conclusion

High coercivity *Hc* of 20 kOe was obtained for the Nd-Fe-B thin films with t = 5 nm. With increasing the Nd content in the Nd_xFe_{100-x} films, a saturation magnetization was decreased and hold maximum at x = 20 at.%. Further increase of Nd content reduces the magnetization. After the deposition of Nd-Fe alloy cap layers on the Nd-Fe-B thin films, a shape of the initial magnetization curve was changed, indicating the influence of magnetization process.

Acknowledgment

This work was supported in part by the Ministry of Education, Culture, Sports, Science and Technology (MEXT) project for the ''Hi-Tech Research Center Preparation Program'' and performed at the Hi-tech Research Center of Tohoku Gakuin University.

References

[1] M. Sagawa, S. Fujimura, N. Togawa, H. Yamamoto, Y. Matsuura, *J. Appl. Phys.*, **55**, (1984) 2083.
[2] D. Harimoto and H. Matsuura, Hitachi Giho, **23** (2007) 69.
[3] M. Sagawa, S. Hirosawa, K. Tokuhara, H. Yamamoto, S. Fujimura, Y. Tsubokawa and R. Shimizu, *J. Appl. Phys.*, **61**, (1987) 3559.
[4] K. Hono, H. Sepehri-Amin, *Scripta Mater.* **67** (2012) 530.
[5] S. L. Chen, W. Liu, C. L. Chen, and Z. D. Zhang, *J. Appl. Phys.*, **98**, (2005) 113905.
[6] W. B. Cui, Y. K. Takahashi, K. Hono, *Acta Mater.*, **59** (2011) 7768.
[7] C. Y. You, Y. K. Takahashi, and K. Hono, *J. Appl. Phys.*, **108**, (2010) 043901.
[8] H. Sepehri-Amin, T. Ohkubo, T. Nishiuchi, S. Hirosawa and K. Hono, *Scripta Mater.* **63** (2010) 1124.
[9] Private communication.

Development of High-Anisotropy MnBi Thick Films

W.Y. ZHANG[1,2], P. KHAREL[1,3] D.J. SELLMYER[1,2]
[1]Nebraska Center for Materials and Nanoscience, University of Nebraska, Lincoln, NE 68588 USA
[2]Department of Physics and Astronomy, University of Nebraska, Lincoln, NE 68588 USA
[3]Department of Physics, South Dakota State University, Brookings, South Dakota 57007, USA

Abstract: *Hexagonal MnBi films with different thicknesses have been fabricated by multilayer deposition and annealing, using an e-beam evaporation system. The effect of the thickness of the film on structure and magnetic properties has been investigated. The films contain mainly NiAs-type MnBi with small amount of Bi. The thinner films show c-axis texture but become more isotropic as the thickness increases. However, the c-axis texture can be developed in relatively thick films by magnetic field annealing. As a result of magnetic field annealing, there is a significant improvement in both the squareness of the hysteresis loops and the remanence ratio of thick films. The remanence ratio of 2 μm film increased from 0.48 to 0.95 after magnetic field annealing. This improvement in squareness led to large increase in energy product* $(BH)_{max}$*. For example, the* $(BH)_{max}$ *of the 1 μm film increased from 6.4 MGOe to 13.5 MGOe at 300 K due to magnetic field annealing. The above results suggest that thick MnBi films could be promising candidates for magnetic MEMS application.*

Keywords: *high-anisotropy; thick film; magnetic properties; magnetic field annealing*

Address: Wenyong Zhang, Nebraska Center for Materials and Nanoscience & Physics and Astronomy, University of Nebraska, Lincoln, NE-68588, U.S.A., E-mail: wenyong.zhang@unl.edu

1. Introduction

Hard magnetic thick films (>1μm) exhibiting high coercivity and energy product are useful for magnetic microelectromechanical system (MEMS) applications, including microactuators, micromotors, sensors, and radiofrequency (RF) microswitches [1-3]. Because of their superior magnetic properties, the thick films of the rare-earth-element-based materials are preferred for MEMS applications. However, there are some technical and materials issues such as high preparation temperature (>773K), low corrosion resistance, and unchangeable texture direction, which limit the broad application of these materials in MEMS [4-6]. This situation has attracted much research attention to the search for alternative high-anisotropy compounds which are free of rare-earth elements. Our interest is in a ferromagnetic Mn-based compound NiAs-type MnBi, which shows a strong perpendicular magnetic anisotropy in thin films.

The hexagonal MnBi (Low Temperature Phase-LTP) has been a subject of extensive research due to its unique magnetic and magneto-optical properties [7, 8]. The LTP-MnBi is ferromagnetic at room temperature, has high coercivity that increases with increasing temperature and shows an almost rectangular M(H) hysteresis loop when the magnetic field is applied along its crystallographic *c*-axis. As the temperature increases above room temperature, the hexagonal MnBi undergoes a magnetostructural phase transition at 630 K and transforms into a paramagnetic orthorhombic $Mn_{1.08}Bi$ phase called the high-temperature phase (HTP) [9]. The reported values of the room-temperature magnetocrystalline anisotropy constant and saturation polarization for the LTP-MnBi are 12 Mergs/cm^3 and 8.1 kG, respectively [10]. Highly c-axis oriented MnBi thin films, with their c-axis perpendicular to the film plane, can be easily grown even in a glass substrate by optimizing the film synthesis conditions [11, 12]. We have found that the c-axis texture is thickness dependent and the films start losing their c-axis texture when thickness increases above 500 nm; they become completely isotropic at a thickness of about 2 μm. Here, we discuss how magnetic field annealing can be used to grow highly textured MnBi thick films with thickness more than 500 nm. We also discuss the effect of magnetic field annealing on the structural and magnetic properties of these thick films.

2. Experimental methods

Hexagonal MnBi films of thickness about 0.5, 1.0, and 2.0 μm were prepared by multilayer deposition and annealing using an e-beam evaporation system. The Bi(347 nm)/Mn(123 nm)/Bi(30 nm) multilayer, $[Bi(241\ nm)/Mn(82.7\ nm)]_3/Bi(30\ nm)$ multilayer, and $[Bi(241\ nm)/Mn(82.7\ nm)]_6/Bi(60nm)$ multilayer were deposited on a glass substrate maintained at 398 K. Figure 1 shows the schematic of Bi/Mn multilayer growth. The thickness ratio of Bi and Mn layers was 3.05. The deposition rate for Bi and Mn was 8 Å/s and 5 Å/s, respectively. The Bi/Mn multilayers were annealed *in situ* first at 563 K for 1h and subsequently at 673 K for another one hour. The annealed samples were coated with a 20 nm thick Ti layer to prevent oxidation. We call these samples the as-prepared MnBi thick films. The total thicknesses of the as-prepared thick films were determined using Bruker Dektak-XT stylus surface profiling system. In order to

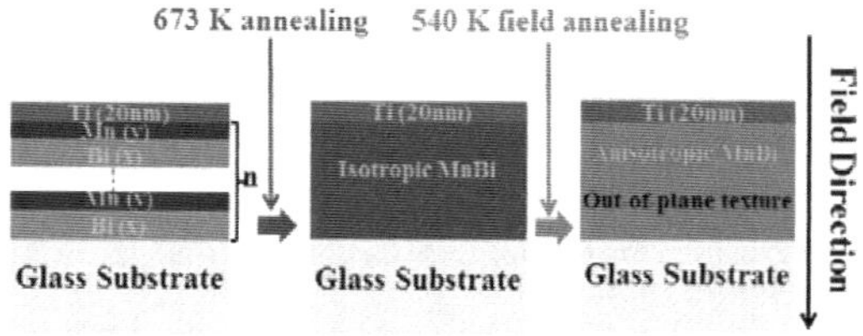

Fig.1. Schematic of Bi/Mn multilayer and film growth.

develop a texture in the thick films, the as-prepared films were annealed at 540 K for 30 minutes in an external magnetic field of 70 kOe. The magnetic field was applied perpendicular to the film surface, which facilitated the MnBi crystallites to align with their *c*-axis along the field direction. The phase compositions and degree of texture of the grains were determined by X-ray diffraction (XRD). The magnetic properties of the films were investigated using the Quantum Design Magnetic Property Measurement System (MPMS) and Physical Property Measurement System (PPMS).

3. Results and Discussion

Figure 2 shows XRD patterns of the MnBi films with various thicknesses. Almost all peaks in the diffraction patterns can be indexed with the standard pattern for the hexagonal LTP-MnBi. The XRD patterns of the 0.5 μm- and 1 μm-thick films contain strong diffraction peaks from the (00*l*) planes, indicating that the films still have *c*-axis texture perpendicular to the film plane. We note that there are many diffraction peaks from the misoriented grains in the diffraction pattern of 1 μm-thick film, although the pattern of 0.5 μm thick films mainly contains peaks from (00*l*) reflections. This indicates that self-alignment of grains in the 0.5μm-thick film is much better than that in the 1μm-thick film. Further, the presence of multiple peaks from different crystal planes and the intensity ratios of the (101), (110), (102) diffraction peaks in the 2 μm-thick film indicate that the films are polycrystalline and isotropic. The lattice parameters a = 4.288 Å and c = 6.122 Å determined from the analysis of the XRD patterns using TOPAS software are consistent with the previously reported values for bulk MnBi in the hexagonal NiAs structure [13]. This analysis also indicates that there is a small fraction of Bi in the samples, where the volume fractions of the LTP-MnBi and Bi are 92.5% and 7.5%, respectively.

Grain alignment in hard magnetic materials is necessary to improve the remanence, which increase the energy product, a parameter that determines the efficiency of a permanent magnet. Our recent investigation on the arc-melted Bi-rich MnBi ribbons shows that magnetic field annealing is highly effective to develop c-axis texture by aligning MnBi grains along the direction of external magnetic field [14]. We have used the same approach to develop c-axis texture in our MnBi thick films. As mentioned above, the as-prepared 2μm-thick films are polycrystalline and isotropic. However, the magnetic field annealing has produced a big change in the degree of c-axis texture in these films. XRD pattern of the magnetic field annealed thick MnBi film is shown in Fig. 3, where the main reflections are from the (00*l*) plane. For comparison, the XRD pattern of the as-prepared film is also shown in the upper panel of Fig. 3. This clearly shows that the magnetic field annealing has developed a *c*-axis texture perpendicular to the film plane in the MnBi thick films. The peaks indexed as Al_2O_3 in the magnetic-field-annealed samples are from the Zircar cement, which was used to cover the sample while mounting on the heater stick.

Figure 4a shows the *J*(H) hysteresis loops of the as-prepared MnBi films of different thicknesses. The *M*(H) loop of the 0.5μm-thick film is almost rectangular but those of other two thick films are not

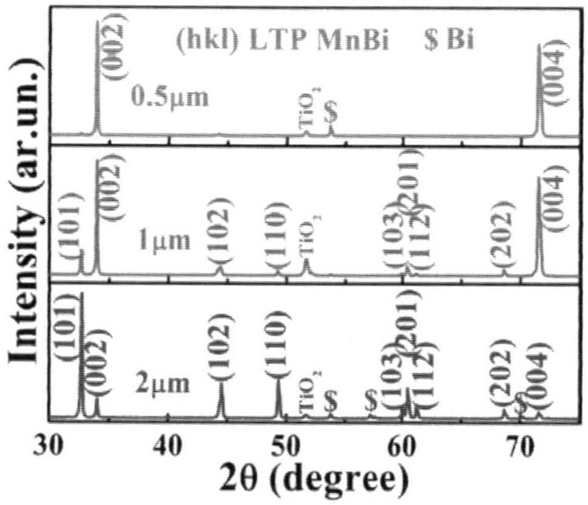

Fig.2. XRD curves of MnBi films with various thickness.

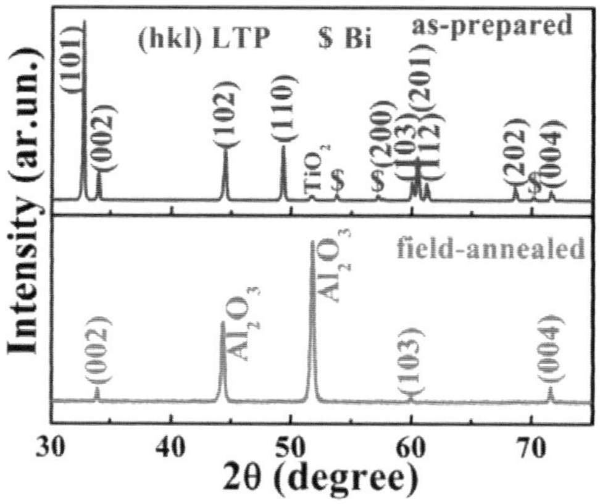

Fig.3. XRD curves of as-prepared and field-annealed 2 μm MnBi films.

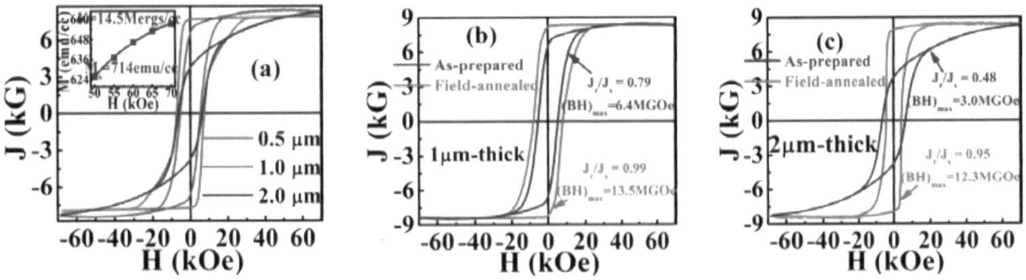

Fig.4. Hysteresis loops of as-prepared MnBi film with various thickness (a), 1μm (b) and 2 μm (c) as-prepared and field-annealed MnBi film.

saturated even at a magnetic field of 70 kOe. The remanence ratio for the 0.5μm-thick film is 0.97, indicating that the sample has a very good c-axis texture, consistent with the XRD results. As thickness increases, the remanence ratio and the squareness of the hysteresis loops worsen reducing the energy product. The remanence ratio for the 2μm-thick film is about 0.5, implying that the sample is isotropic. Figure 4b and 4c show the *J*(H) hysteresis loops of the as-prepared and field annealed films. Magnetic field annealing has produced significant improvement in the ramanence ratio and squareness of the *J*(H) and *M*(H) loops of the MnBi thick films. This large increase in the remanence ratios is caused by the alignment of the MnBi grains with their c-axis along the direction of external magnetic field and is consistent with our XRD data as discussed above. The increase in the squareness of the *M*(H) loops has led to a large increase in the $(BH)_{max}$. The $(BH)_{max}$ increases from 3.0 MGOe for the as-prepared 2 μm film to 12.3 MGOe for the field-annealed 2 μm film. The magnetocrystalline anisotropy constant of the LTP determined using the approach to saturation method is 14.5 Mergs/cm^3. For this calculation, the high field region in the *J*(H) loop of the as-prepared sample was fitted to the expression: $M = M_s[1-A/H^2]+\chi H$, $A = 4K^2/15M_s^2$ [14]. We note that the saturation magnetization of the as-prepared film is almost the same as that of the field-annealed films, indicating that there is no change in the phase compositions due to magnetic field annealing.

4. Summary

The MnBi films with different thicknesses have been prepared on glass substrate by $[Bi/Mn]_n$ multilayer deposition and *in situ* annealing using an e-beam evaporation system. The relatively thin films show strong structure anisotropy. The thick film is crystallographically isotropic, but the samples develop strong crystalline and magnetic anisotropy after magnetic field annealing due to the alignment of the MnBi grains with their c-axis along the direction of external magnetic field. Magnetic field annealing has significantly increased the remanence ratio, the squareness of the hysteresis loops, and energy product. An energy product as high as 13.5 MGOe has been achieved for the field-annealed MnBi films. These highly c-axis textured MnBi thick films, which can be synthesized at a relatively low annealing temperature even on a glass substrate, show interesting magnetic properties such as high energy product and high Curie temperature above room temperature. They are potential candidates for the magnetic MEMS applications.

Acknowledgement
This work is supported by ARO (WF911NF-10-2-0099).

References

[1] O. Cugat, J. Delamare, and G. Reyne, IEEE Trans. Mag., **2004**, 39, 3607.
[2] H.H. Gatzen, ECS Trans., **2009**, 16, 235.
[3] E.R. Brown, IEEE Trans. Microwave Theory and Techniques, **1998**, 46, 1868.
[4] A. Walther, D. Givord, N.M. Dempsey, K. Khlopkov, and O. Gutfleisch, J. Appl. Phys., **2008**, 103, 043911.
[5] K. Tokuhara and S. Hirosawa, J. Appl. Phys., **1991**, 69, 552.
[6] N.M. Dempsey, A. Walther, F. May, D. Givord, K. Khlopkov, and O. Gutfleisch, Appl. Phys. Lett., **2007**, 90, 092509.
[7] P. Ravindran, A. Delin, P. James, B. Johansson, J.M. Wills, R. Ahuja, O. Eriksson, Phys. Rev. B, **1999**, 59,15680.
[8] D. Chen, R.L. AAGard, and T.S. Liu, J. Appl. Phys., **1970**, 41, 1395.
[9] T. Chen, J. Appl. Phys., **1974**, 65, 2358.
[10] H. Kronmüller, J.B. Yang, and D. Goll, J. Phys.: Cond. Matt., **2014**, 26, 064210.
[11] J.X. Shen, R.D. Kirby, and D.J. Sellmyer, J. Appl. Phys., **1991**, 69, 5984.
[12] P. Kharel, R. Skomski, and D.J. Sellmyer, J. Appl. Phys., **2011**, 109, 07B709.
[13] A.F. Andresen, W. Halg, P. Fischer, E. Stoll, Acta Chem. Scand. **1967**, 21, 1543.
[14] W.Y. Zhang, P. Kharel, T. George, X.Z. Li, P. Mukherjee, S. Vallopilly, and David J. Sellmyer (to be submitted)
[15] G.C. Hadjipanayis, D.J. Sellmyer, and B. Brant, Phys. Rev. B, **1981**, 23, 3349.

Magnetization Reversal Behavior of FePt/ MgO/ FePt Circular Dot Arrays

H. IWAMA, H. MAKUTA, S. TAKEYAMA, K. YUSA, M. DOI, T. SHIMA
Tohoku Gakuin University, Tagajo 985-8537, Japan

Abstract: *FePt/ MgO/ FePt multilayer films and their circular dot arrays deposited on various buffer layers have been investigated. The bottom FePt layer was epitaxially grown on buffer layer of Au, $Au_{55.3}Pt_{44.7}$ and Pt. The different chemical ordering of the FePt layers was achieved by the different growth conditions. A remarkable step in the magnetization curves was clearly observed. The four states of the magnetic domain structure corresponding to the step in the magnetization curves have been successfully observed for the Au/ FePt (10 nm)/ MgO (5 nm)/ FePt (5 nm) circular dot arrays.*

Key words: *$L1_0$ ordered FePt, circular dot arrays, magnetic domain, magnetic force microscope*

Address: Hiroki Iwama, Tohoku Gakuin University, 1-13-1, Chuo, Tagajo 985-8537, Japan, Tel: +81-22-368-1128, Fax: +81-22-368-1272, E-mail: s1394351@tjcc.tohoku-gakuin.ac.jp

1. Introduction

$L1_0$ ordered FePt alloy with high uniaxial magnetocrystalline anisotropy (K_u = 7.0×10^7 erg/cc) [1] has attracted much attention, since it is good candidate for future magnetic devices such as next-generation ultrahigh-density magnetic storage media and biasing nanomagnets [2]. It is also thought to overcome the problem of thermal fluctuation in nano-meters scale. A lot of studies have been studied for thin films [3, 4] and self-assembled nano particles [5, 6]. In our previous study [7], FePt multilayer films can be successfully grown epitaxially on MgO layer. A remarkable step in the third quadrant of the magnetization curve, which arise from the different magnetic properties of top and bottom FePt layers, are clearly observed for FePt/ MgO/ FePt multilayer films. However, magnetic domain observation of FePt bilayer films with different buffer layer materials has not yet done. In this study, in order to see the effect of lattice mismatch between buffer layer and bottom FePt layer on the magnetization reversal behavior, FePt/ MgO/ FePt multilayer films and their circular dot arrays have been fabricated on various buffer layers and their structure, magnetic properties and magnetic domain structure have been investigated.

2. Experimental Procedure

All the samples were prepared using an ultrahigh vacuum magnetron sputtering system with separate targets of Fe, Pt, Au and MgO. The base pressure was under 5.0×10^{-8} Pa. A Fe seed layer of 1 nm and various buffer layers of Au, $Au_{55.5}Pt_{44.7}$ and Pt of 40 nm were deposited on a MgO (100) single crystalline substrate at room temperature (R.T.), and then they were annealed at 300 °C for 1 hour. The FePt layer of 10 nm was co-deposited with Fe and Pt at 300 °C. Then the MgO intermediate layer of 5 nm was deposited at R.T. Top FePt layer of 5 nm was deposited at 300 °C. Finally, the samples were annealed at T_a of 500 °C to promote the $L1_0$ ordering of FePt layer. FePt circular dot arrays were microfabricated through the use of electron beam (EB) lithography and Ar ion etching. A negative-type EB resist (TGMR 3.6 cp) was spin-coated on the films and the circular dot arrays were patterned. Then, the FePt layer was milled by Ar ions through the EB resist mask. Since the Ar ion etching was stopped at the buffer layer. Finally, dot arrays of the FePt layer were obtained. The diameter of circular dots (D) was 1 μm and the distance between two adjacent dots was 1 μm. The magnetic properties were measured by a superconducting quantum interference device (SQUID) magnetometer and magneto-optical Kerr effect (MOKE). The structure analysis was performed by X-ray diffraction (XRD) with Cu $K\alpha$ radiation. The

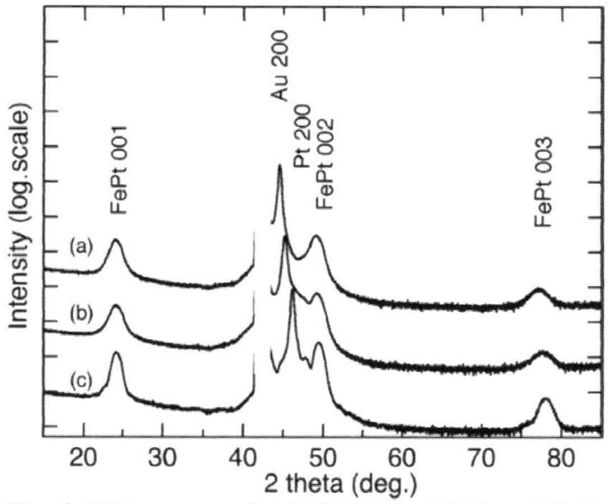

Fig. 1. XRD patterns for buffer layer X (40 nm)/ FePt (10 nm)/ MgO (5 nm)/ FePt (5 nm) films with various buffer layers. X = (a) Au, (b) $Au_{55.3}Pt_{44.7}$ and (c) Pt.

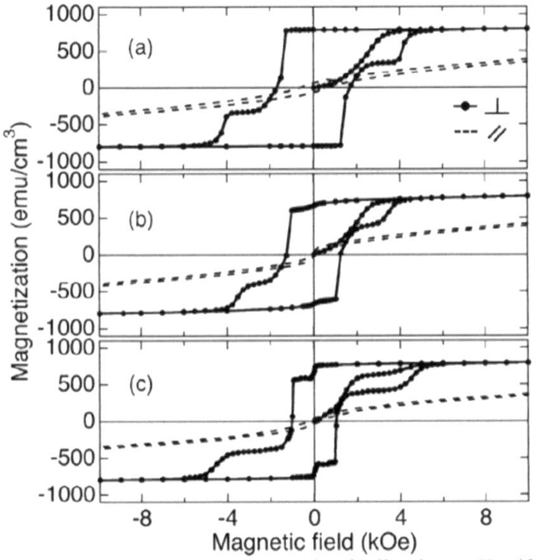

Fig. 2. Magnetization curves for buffer layer X (40 nm)/ FePt (10 nm)/ MgO (5 nm)/ FePt (5 nm) films with various buffer layers. X = (a) Au, (b) $Au_{55.3}Pt_{44.7}$ and (c) Pt.

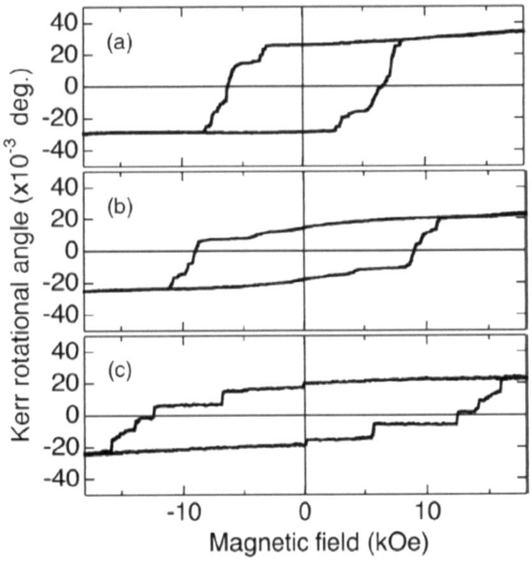

Fig. 3. MOKE loops for buffer layer X (40 nm)/ FePt (10 nm)/ MgO (5 nm)/ FePt (5 nm) films with various buffer layers. X = (a) Au, (b) $Au_{55.3}Pt_{44.7}$ and (c) Pt.

composition was determined to be $Fe_{48.8}Pt_{51.2}$ (at.%) measured by electron probe X-ray micro analysis (EPMA). The size, the shape of the dots and the distance between the dots were confirmed using atomic force microscope (AFM) with dynamic force mode (DFM). The magnetic domain structure was observed by a magnetic force microscope (MFM) in applied fields up to ±6 kOe at the direction perpendicular to the film plane.

3. Results and Discussion

XRD patterns for buffer layer X (40 nm)/ FePt (10 nm)/ MgO (5 nm)/ FePt (5 nm) films are shown in Fig. 1. Buffer layer was selected as (a) Au, (b) $Au_{55.3}Pt_{44.7}$ and (c) Pt. In addition to a fundamental (002) peak, (001) and (003) superlattice peaks from the face centered tetragonal phase have been clearly observed for all the films, indicating the formation of $L1_0$ ordered structure. The peak from the other plane of the $L1_0$ structure was not observed. With increasing Pt content in the buffer layer, the peaks from the FePt $L1_0$ phase were shifted to a higher angle.

Magnetization curves for FePt/ MgO/ FePt films with various buffer layers are shown in Fig. 2. All the measurements were performed at R.T. The magnetic field was applied in the directions perpendicular to the film plane (solid line) and in-plane (broken line). The magnetic easy axis was perpendicular to the film plane for all the samples, since the [001] axis of the tetragonal $L1_0$ ordered structure was perpendicular to the film plane as demonstrated in Fig. 1. With increasing Pt content in the buffer layer, H_c was decreased from (a) 1.7 kOe to (b) 1.2 kOe and (c) 1.0 kOe, this is thought to due to the reduction of the lattice mismatch between the buffer and the bottom FePt layers. The remarkable steps of magnetization curves were observed in the first and third quadrant for all samples, owing to the different thicknesses and chemical ordering of top and bottom FePt layers. Since the nucleation filed (H_N), at which the magnetization begins to drop with decreasing the field after saturation of each layer, is changed and magnetization reversal occurred individually. This remarkable step in the magnetization curve for FePt/MgO/FePt thin films is thought to be due to the formation of the MgO intermediate layer without interdiffusion.

MOKE loops of FePt/ MgO/ FePt circular dot arrays with a diameter of D = 1 μm are shown in Fig. 3. The magnetic field was applied in the directions perpendicular to the film plane. With increasing Pt content in the buffer layer, H_c was increased from (a) 6.1 kOe to (b) 8.9 kOe and (c) 12.4 kOe. In addition, the steps of magnetization curves were also observed. However, the position was changed to the second quadrant for the films with (a) Au and (c) Pt. Enhancement of H_c is thought to arise from the restriction of the domain wall replacement, while the change of the position is due to the damage at the edge of the circular dots during Ar ion etching.
A minor loop of the magnetization curve for the Au/ FePt/ MgO/ FePt circular dot arrays is shown in Fig. 4. The magnetic field was applied in the in range of ±6 kOe, this is corresponding to the maximum applied filed of electromagnet of MFM apparatus. The closed circles ((b) ~ (i)) denote the field at which magnetic domain observation was performed.

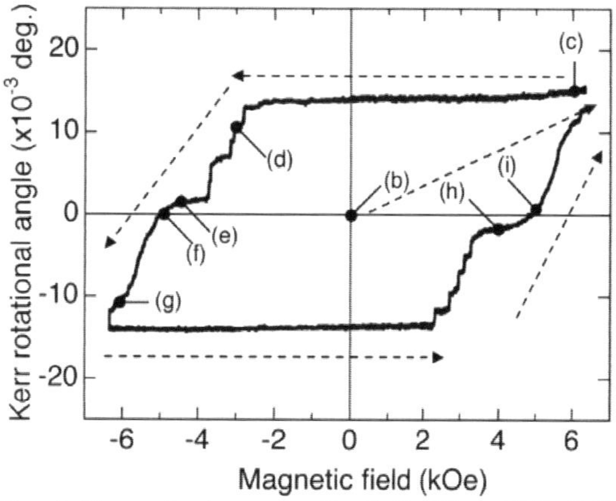

Fig. 4. Magnetization curve for FePt (10 nm)/ MgO (5 nm)/ FePt (5 nm) circular dot arrays with Au buffer layers in the range between +6 kOe and -6 kOe.

Figure 5 shows the surface morphology and the magnetic domain patterns for the Au/ FePt/ MgO/ FePt circular dot arrays observed by DFM and MFM. A maze-like domain pattern with dark and bright contrasts was observed at a virgin state (b). However, as the magnetic field was increased, the dark regions in the magnetic domain pattern almost disappeared at +6 kOe (c). Once the applied field was reduced and the reverse field was applied, a drastic change in the domain pattern was observed between -3 kOe (d) and -4.5 kOe (e), which corresponds to the first drop in the minor loop as demonstrated in Fig. 4. An abrupt transition of the domain patterns was clearly observed at -5 kOe (f) and -6 kOe (g). This is well consistent with the result of the magnetization drop in Fig. 4. From the magnetic domain observation, four remarkable distinct states of the magnetization were successfully confirmed for the circular dots with FePt double layers. The first state was an upward direction of the magnetization (+6 kOe (c)) for both FePt layers. The second one was a downward (-6 kOe (g)) direction of the magnetization for both FePt layers. The third and fourth ones were an anti-parallel state (opposite direction) (-4.5 kOe (e) and +5 kOe (i)) for the vertical FePt layers.

4. Summary

The structure and magnetic properties of FePt films and circular dot arrays with a multilayered structure were investigated. The different chemical ordering of the FePt layers was achieved by different growth conditions: the bottom FePt layer was epitaxially grown on an buffer layer of Au, $Au_{55.3}Pt_{44.7}$ and Pt, while the top FePt layer was epitaxially grown on an MgO layer. A remarkable step in the magnetization curves was clearly observed. The origin of the coercivity difference between two FePt layers is thought to arise from the strain that was induced into the FePt layers. The lattice mismatch of the top FePt layer grown on an MgO layer was higher than the one grown on an Au layer. From an in-field magnetic

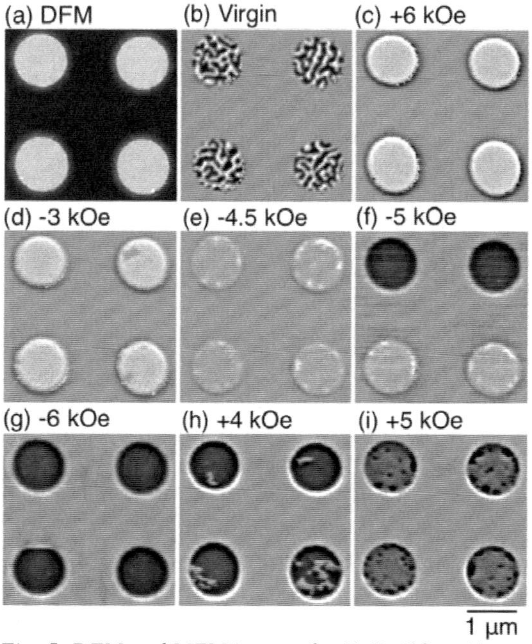

Fig. 5. DFM and MFM images for FePt (10 nm)/ MgO (5 nm)/ FePt (5 nm) circular dot arrays with Au buffer layer. DFM image (a) and MFM images: (b) virgin, (c) +6 kOe, (d) -3 kOe, (e) -4.5 kOe, (f) -5 kOe, (g) -6 kOe, (h) +4 kOe and (i) +5 kOe.

domain observation, independent magnetization reversal of the bottom and top FePt layers was clearly observed by in-field MFM measurement. The four states of the magnetic domain structure corresponding to the step in the magnetization curves have been successfully observed for the Au/ FePt (10 nm)/ MgO (5 nm)/ FePt (5 nm) circular dot arrays. These results are expected to provide fruitful information for multi-level (three dimensional) magnetic recording of future ultra high density magnetic storage systems.

References

[1] O. A. Ovanov, L. V. Solina, V. A. Demshina, *Phys. Met. Metallogr.*, 1973, 35, 81.

[2] T. Shima, K. Takahashi, Y. K. Takahashi, K. Hono, G. Q. Li, S. Ishio, *Appl. Phys. Lett.*, 2006, 99, 033516.

[3] C. Moutafis, S. Komineas, C. A. F. Vaz, J. A. C. Bland, T. Shima, T. Seki, K. Takanashi, *Phys. Rev. B*, 2007, 76, 104426.

[4] T. Seki, H. Iwama, T. Shima, K. Takanashi, *J. Phys. D. Appl. Phys.*, 2011, 44, 335001.

[5] T. Shima, K. Takahashi, Y. K. Takahashi, K. Hono, *Appl. Phys. Lett.*, 2002, 81, 1050.

[6] S. Matsumoto, T. Shima, *J. Phys.: Conf. Ser.*, 2011, 266, 012038.

[7] S. Matsumoto, H. Iwama, T. Shima, *J. Magn. Soc. Jpn.*, 2012, 36, 86.

Structural Characterization of Rare Earth-Transition Metal Alloy Thin Film with Ordered Structure by Diffraction

MITSURU OHTAKE, MASAAKI FUTAMOTO

Faculty of Science and Engineering, Chuo University, Tokyo 112-8551, Japan

Abstract: *A rare-earth-transition (R-T) metal alloy film may involve multiple hexagonal ordered phases such as R_2T_{17}, R_2T_7, and RT_3 in addition to RT_5 phase. The crystallographic phase and the order degree are investigated by employing a combination of reflection high-energy electron diffraction (RHEED) and X-ray diffraction (XRD). Identification of RT_5 phase is carried out by analyzing a reciprocal lattice map measured by RHEED. A simplified method for estimating the order degree, where only intensity ratio of (0001) superlattice to (0002) fundamental XRD reflection is considered, is proposed for some of the typical RT_5 film materials of $SmCo_5$, $PrCo_5$, YCo_5, etc.*

Key words: *RT_5 ordered alloy, epitaxial thin film, reciprocal lattice, order degree*

Address: Mitsuru Ohtake, Faculty of Science and Engineering, Chuo University, Tokyo 112-8551, Japan, Tel: +81-3-3817-1862, Fax: +81-3-3817-1847, E-mail: ohtake@futamoto.elect.chuo-u.ac.jp

1. Introduction

Magnetic films with high magnetic anisotropy energies have attracted much attention to magnetic applications such as recording media, microsensors, and micromotors. Ordered alloys consisting of rare earth (*R*) and 3*d* ferromagnetic transition (*T*) metals with hexagonal $D2_d$ structure such as $SmCo_5$, $PrCo_5$, etc. show uniaxial magnetocrystalline anisotropy energies (K_u) of 10^7–10^8 erg/cm^3 along the *c*-axis. An epitaxial film is useful for the orientation control of easy magnetization axis, since the crystallographic orientation can be controlled by the substrate orientation. RT_5 epitaxial films have been prepared by employing bcc-W, bcc-Cr, fcc-Cu, and hcp-Ru underlayers [1]–[5]. However, multiple hexagonal crystallographic phases such as R_2T_{17}, R_2T_7, and RT_3 may be involved in a film in addition to RT_5 phase [2]. Conventional out-of-plane and in-plane X-ray diffractions (XRD) are not easy to distinguish these phases, since the lattice spacings of these compounds are very similar each other. Reciprocal lattice map measurement like reflection high-energy electron diffraction (RHEED) is effective for the phase identification. In the present study, $SmCo_5$ epitaxial films with the easy magnetization axes parallel and perpendicular to the surface are prepared. The structure is carefully investigated by using a combination of RHEED and XRD ($\lambda_{Cu\text{-}K\alpha}$ = 0.15418 nm).

2. Experimental procedure

A molecular beam epitaxy system equipped with an RHEED facility was used for film preparation. The base pressures were lower than 7×10^{-9} Pa. $Sm_{17}Co_{83}$ (at. %) films were deposited on Cr(100), Cr(211), Co(1-100), and Cu(111) underlayers hetero-epitaxially grown on single-crystal substrates at 500 °C. The details of deposition condition are shown in our previous papers [3], [4].

3. Results and discussion

The epitaxial orientation relationships of $SmCo_5$ films with respect to Cr(211), Cr(100), and Cu(111) underlayers are determined in previous studies [2]–[4] as $SmCo_5$(1-100)[11-20] || Cr(211)[1-1-1], $SmCo_5$(11-20)[0001], [1-100] || Cr(100)[011], and $SmCo_5$(0001)[11-20], [1-100] || Cu(111)[1-10], respectively. The *c*-axes of (1-100) and (11-20) films are lying in the film plane, whereas that of (0001) film is perpendicular to the surface. Figs. 1(a)–(c) show the schematic diagrams of RHEED patterns simulated for (1-100), (11-20), and (0001) films with hexagonal R_2T_{17}, RT_5, R_2T_7, and RT_3 structures epitaxially grown in the orientation relationships shown above. Figs. 1(d) and (e) show the RHEED patterns observed for $Sm_{17}Co_{83}$ films deposited on Cr(211) and Cr(100) underlayers. The diffraction patterns are showing that RT_5(1-100) and RT_5(11-20) crystals are formed with the *c*-axis lying in the film plane. The streaks along the perpendicular direction in the pattern of Fig. 1(d) indicate that the film deposited on Cr(211) underlayer possesses an atomically flat surface (or terraces). Fig. 1(f) shows the RHEED pattern observed for an $Sm_{17}Co_{83}$ film deposited on Co(1-100) underlayer. The observed pattern also corresponds to the pattern calculated for RT_5(1-100) film [Fig. 1(a-2)], similar to the case of film deposited on Cr(211) underlayer. However, streaks along the [0001] are involved in the pattern of Fig. 1(f), which indicates that the film includes a small volume of other hexagonal phases. The reason is possibly due to that Co atoms diffuse from the underlayer to the $Sm_{17}Co_{83}$ film and the film composition shifts from $SmCo_5$ stoichiometry to a Co-rich composition. Fig. 1(g) shows the RHEED pattern observed for an $Sm_{17}Co_{83}$ film deposited on Cu(111) underlayer. The RHEDD pattern corresponds to the pattern calculated for RT_5(0001) film with the *c*-axis normal to the surface. The streaks along the perpendicular direction indicate formation of flat surface and/or involvement of other phases. Fig. 1(h) shows the cross-sectional transmission electron microscope (TEM) image of the sample. A layer-by-layer structure consisting of RT_5(0001) and RT_5(0002) is clearly recognized. Therefore, the streaks are considered to show realization of flat surface, similar to the case of film deposited on Cr(211) underlayer.

The order degree of RT_5 film can be calculated by comparing the XRD intensities of (0001) superlattice and (0002) fundamental reflections, I_s and I_f. I is proportional to structure factor (F) and the complex conjugate (F^*), Lorentz-polarization factor (L), and absorption factor (A) [6]. F_s and F_f are respectively $S(f_R-f_T)$ and f_R+5f_T, where f is atomic scattering factor. L and A are respectively expressed as $(1+\cos^2 2\theta)/(\sin^2\theta\cos\theta)$ and $[1-e^{-\mu(2\Lambda/\sin\theta)}]/2\mu$, where μ is the linear absorption coefficient of RT_5 alloy and $2\Lambda/\sin\theta$ is the X-ray path length. Here, Λ corresponds to ∞ or film thickness (t) for either in-plane or out-of-plane XRD. Therefore, $S = [(f_R+5f_T)_f/(f_R-f_T)_s] \times [(LA)_f/(LA)_s]^{1/2} \times (I_s/I_f)^{1/2}$. The parameters of f, L, and A vary depending on the diffraction angle and the material properties. The approximate diffraction angles of superlattice and fundamental reflections can be evaluated from the lattice constant, *c*, of bulk material. When a parameter of C is introduced as $[(f_R+5f_T)_f/(f_R-f_T)_s] \times [(LA)_f/(LA)_s]^{1/2}$, the equation can be simply expressed as $S = C(I_s/I_f)^{1/2}$. The C values of typical RT_5 magnetic film materials are calculated as shown in Table 1. The S value of $Sm_{17}Co_{83}$ film deposited on Cr(211) underlayer is calculated by using the $C_{(IP)}$ value to be 0.77.

4. Summary

The structural properties of rare earth-transition metal films are investigated by RHEED and XRD. The reciprocal lattice map measurement by RHEED identifies the kind of ordered phase (R_2T_{17}, RT_5, R_2T_7, RT_3). The order degree of RT_5 film is investigated by XRD. A simplified method for estimating the order degree, where only intensity ratio of (0001) superlattice to (0002) fundamental XRD reflection is considered, is explained for some of the typical RT_5 film materials ($SmCo_5$, $PrCo_5$, YCo_5, etc.)

References

[1] E. E. Fullerton et al., *Appl. Phys. Lett.*, 69, 1996, 2438.

[2] M. Benaissa, K. M. Krishnan, E. E. Fullerton, J. S. Jiang, *IEEE Trans. Magn.*, 34, 1998, 1204.

[3] T. Yanagawa *et al.*, *J. Appl. Phys.*, 115, 2014, 17A759.

[4] M. Ohtake, Y. Nukaga, F. Kirino, M. Futamoto, *J. Cryst. Growth*, 311, 2009, 2251.

[5] M. Seifert, V. Neu, L. Schultz, *Appl. Phys. Lett.*, 94, 2009, 022501.

[6] B. D. Cullity: *Elements of X-Ray Diffraction, Addison-Wesley*, Massachusetts, 1956.

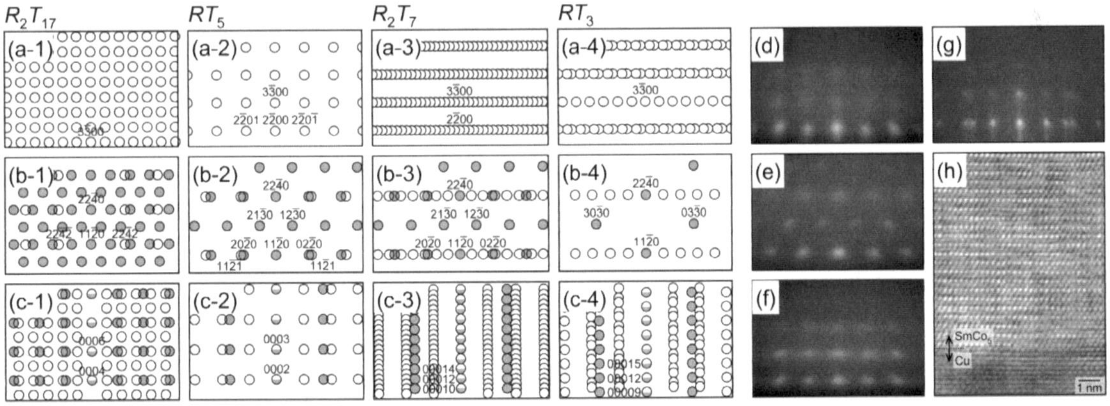

Fig.1 *(a)–(c) Schematic diagrams of RHEED patterns simulated for (a) (1-100), (b) (11-20), and (c) (0001) surfaces with (a-1)–(c-1)* R_2T_{17}, *(a-2)–(c-2)* RT_5, *(a-3)–(c-3)* R_2T_7, *and (a-4)–(c-4)* RT_3 *structures. The incident electron beam is parallel to (a) [11-20], (b) [0001]+[1-100], or (c) [11-20]+[1-100]. (d)–(g) RHEED patterns observed for* $Sm_{17}Co_{83}$ *films deposited on (d) Cr(211), (e) Cr(100), (f) Co(1-100), and (g) Cu(111) underlayers. (h) Cross-section TEM image observed for an* $Sm_{17}Co_{83}$ *film deposited on Cu(111) underlayer.*

Table 1 Summary of crystallographic properties of typical RT_5 *magnetic film materials.*

Material	YCo_5	$LaCo_5$	$CeCo_5$	$PrCo_5$	$NdCo_5$	$SmCo_5$	$GdCo_5$	$TbCo_5$	$DyCo_5$	$HoCo_5$	$ErCo_5$	$SmNi_5$	$SmFe_5$	$SmCu_5$
c (nm) [Bulk]	0.3969	0.3976	0.4016	0.3988	0.3977	0.3971	0.3967	0.3982	0.3988	0.3996	0.3981	0.3974	0.4140	0.4099
$C_{(OP\_10\ nm)}$	3.99	1.72	1.68	1.61	1.56	1.48	1.41	1.37	1.34	1.32	1.29	1.58	1.40	1.75
$C_{(OP\_20\ nm)}$	4.00	1.73	1.68	1.61	1.57	1.48	1.42	1.38	1.35	1.32	1.29	1.58	1.41	1.75
$C_{(OP\_50\ nm)}$	4.03	1.75	1.70	1.63	1.58	1.50	1.43	1.39	1.36	1.34	1.30	1.59	1.42	1.76
$C_{(OP\_100\ nm)}$	4.08	1.77	1.73	1.66	1.61	1.53	1.46	1.42	1.39	1.35	1.32	1.61	1.45	1.78
$C_{(OP\_1000\ nm)}$	4.84	2.16	2.13	2.04	1.98	1.89	1.81	1.75	1.70	1.63	1.59	1.86	1.79	2.03
$C_{(IP)}$	5.63	2.43	2.36	2.27	2.20	2.08	1.99	1.94	1.89	1.86	1.81	2.23	1.98	2.46

Preparation of $SmCo_5$ Alloy Single-Crystal Thin Films on bcc(211) and hcp(1-100) Underlayers

ATARU SUZUKI[1], TAKATO YANAGAWA[1], YUSUKE HOTTA[1], MAKOTO YAMADA[1], MITSURU OHTAKE[1], FUMIYOSHI KIRINO[2], MASAAKI FUTAMOTO[1]
[1]Faculty of Science and Engineering, Chuo University, Tokyo 112-8551, Japan
[2]Graduate School of Fine Arts, Tokyo University of the Arts, Tokyo 110-8714, Japan

Abstract: *$Sm_{17}Co_{83}$ (at. %) films are deposited on Cr(211), Fe(211), $Fe_{65}Co_{35}$(211), and Co(1-100) underlayers hetero-epitaxially grown on MgO(110) substrates by using a molecular beam epitaxy system. The film growth behavior and the detailed film structure are investigated. Sm-Co films grow epitaxially on the underlayers. The Sm-Co films consist of RT_5(1-100) crystal with the c-axis lying in the film plane. The degrees of RT_5 ordering for the films deposited on Cr, Fe, $Fe_{65}Co_{35}$, and Co underlayers are determined to be 0.77, 0.67, 0.67, and 0.71, respectively. Small volumes of other hexagonal R-T crystals other than RT_5 are included in the films deposited on Fe, $Fe_{65}Co_{35}$, and Co underlayers. The reason is interpreted to be due to that Co and/or Fe atoms of underlayers have diffused into a Sm-Co film and the film composition has shifted from $SmCo_5$ stoichiometry.*

Key words: *$SmCo_5$ ordered alloy; thin film, epitaxial growth; single-crystal substrate; underlayer*

Address: Ataru Suzuki, Faculty of Science and Engineering, Chuo University, Tokyo 112-8551, Japan, Tel:+81-3-3817-1862, Fax: +81-3-3817-1847, E-mail: a-suzuki@futamoto.elect.chuo-u.ac.jp

1. Introduction

Nanocomposite materials with exchange-coupled hard and soft magnetic phases have the potential to achieve high energy products. Fe or Fe-Co alloy with bcc structure has been used as a soft phase, whereas $SmCo_5$ ordered alloy with hexagonal RT_5 structure has been frequently employed as a hard phase. In order to align the easy magnetization axis parallel to the surface, a well-defined epitaxial film is useful, since the crystallographic orientation can be controlled by the substrate orientation. $SmCo_5$ epitaxial films with the *c*-axis lying in the film plane have been prepared on MgO(100) and MgO(110) substrates by employing W [1], Cr [2], and Fe [3] underlayers. However, multiple hexagonal crystallographic phases like R_2T_{17}, RT_5, R_2T_7, and RT_3 may be included in an Sm-Co film [2]. It is not easy to determine the phase by employing conventional out-of-plane and in-plane X-ray diffractions (XRDs), since the lattice spacings of hexagonal phases are very similar. Reciprocal lattice map measurement like electron diffraction is useful for such identification. In our previous studies [4], [5], $SmCo_5$ epitaxial films of (0001) and (11-20) orientations were prepared by using a ultra-high vacuum molecular beam epitaxy system equipped with a reflection high-energy electron diffraction (RHEED) facility.

The purpose of the present study is to prepare $SmCo_5$(1-100) single-crystal films with the *c*-axis parallel to the surface and to investigate the film growth behavior and the detailed structure.

2. Experimental Procedure

$Sm_{17}Co_{83}$ (at. %) films of 20 nm thickness were deposited on $Cr(211)_{bcc}$, $Fe(211)_{bcc}$, $Fe_{65}Co_{35}(211)_{bcc}$, and $Co(1\text{-}100)_{hcp}$ underlayers hetero-epitaxially grown on MgO(110) substrates. The substrate temperature during deposition was fixed at 500 °C. The details of deposition condition were similar to our previous studies [4], [5]. The surface structure during film formation was studied by *in-situ* RHEED. The resulting film structure was investigated by out-of-plane and in-plane XRDs with Cu-Kα radiation (λ = 0.15418 nm).

3. Results and Discussion

Fig. 1(a) shows the RHEED patterns observed during formation of an Sm-Co film on a Cr(211) underlayer. A clear diffraction pattern starts to be recognized from the early stage of film growth and it remains unchanged till the end of deposition. A Sm-Co film epitaxially grows on the Cr underlayer. Fig. 1(e) shows the schematic diagrams of RHEED pattern simulated for the (1-100) surface of R_2T_{17}, RT_5, R_2T_7, and RT_3 structures. The observed RHEED patterns correspond to the diffraction pattern calculated for RT_5(1-100) surface. The film consists of RT_5(1-100) crystal with the *c*-axis lying in the film plane. Figs. 1(b)-(d) show the RHEED patterns observed for Sm-Co films deposited on Fe(211), $Fe_{65}Co_{35}$(211), and Co(1-100) underlayers. The RHEED patterns are also showing that RT_5(1-100) epitaxial crystals are formed. However, streaks along $SmCo_5$[0001] are

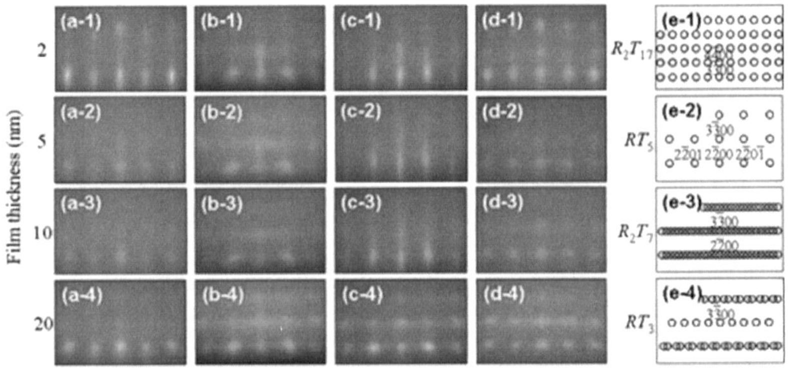

Fig. 1. (a)-(d) RHEED patterns observed during formation of $Sm_{17}Co_{83}$ films on (a) Cr, (b) Fe, (c) $Fe_{65}Co_{35}$, and (d) Co underlayers. (e) Schematic diagrams of RHEED pattern simulated for (1-100) surface of (e-1) R_2T_{17}, (e-2) RT_5, (e-3) R_2T_7, and (e-4) RT_3 structures.

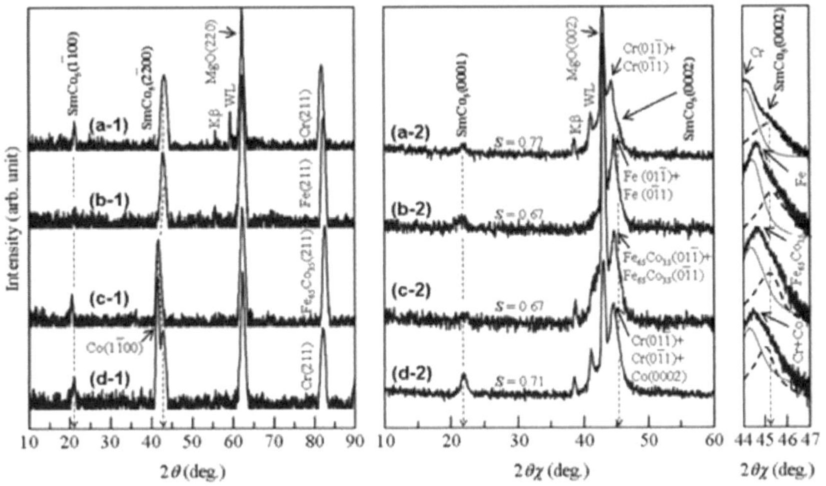

Fig. 2. (a-1)–(d-1) Out-of-plane and (a-2)–(d-2) in-plane XRD patterns of $Sm_{17}Co_{83}$ films deposited on (a) Cr, (b) Fe, (c) $Fe_{65}Co_{35}$, and (d) Co underlayers.

recognized in these RHEED patterns. The result indicates that hexagonal crystallographic phases other than RT_5 are included. This is possibly because Co and/or Fe atoms of underlayers have diffused into the Sm-Co films causing compositional shifts from the $SmCo_5$ stoichiometry. Fig. 2 shows the out-of-plane and in-plane XRD patterns. (0001) in-plane superlattice reflections are observed in addition to the (1-100) out-of-plane, (2-200) out-of-plane, and (0002) in-plane fundamental reflections. The long-range order degree (S) was calculated by comparing the intensities of (0001) and (0002) reflections. The S values of Sm-Co films deposited on Cr, Fe, $Fe_{65}Co_{35}$, and Co underlayers are determined to be 0.77, 0.67, 0.67, and 0.71, respectively.

4. Summary

$Sm_{17}Co_{83}$ alloy films are deposited on Cr(211), Fe(211), $Fe_{65}Co_{35}$(211), and Co(1-100) at 500 °C. The film growth behavior and the detailed film structure are investigated by RHEED and XRD. Sm-Co films with RT_5 structure epitaxially grow on the underlayers. The order degrees of films deposited on Cr, Fe, $Fe_{65}Co_{35}$, and Co underlayers are 0.77, 0.67, 0.67, and 0.71, respectively. Small volumes of hexagonal R-T phases other than RT_5 are included in the films deposited on Fe, $Fe_{65}Co_{35}$, and Co films, possibly due to that Fe and/or Co atoms have diffused from the underlayers into the Sm-Co films and the film composition has shifted from the $SmCo_5$ stoichiometry.

References

[1] E. E. Fullerton *et al.*, *Appl. Phys. Lett.* **69**, 1996, 2438.
[2] M. Benaissa *et al.*, *IEEE Trans. Magn.* **34**, 1998, 1204.
[3] M. J. Pechan, *et al.*, *J. Appl. Phys.* **87**, 2000, 6686.
[4] M. Ohtake *et al.*, *J. Cryst. Growth.* **107**, 2009, 2251.
[5] T. Yanagawa *et al.*, *J. Appl. Phys.* **115**, 2014, 19.

Waste Nd-Fe-B sintered magnets recycling by doping with DyH_3 nanoparticles

W. Q. LIU[1], C. LI[1], M. ZAKOTNIK[1], M. YUE[1], D. T. ZHANG[1], T. Y. ZUO[2]
[1]College of Materials Science, Beijing University of Technology, Beijing, 100124, China;
[2]Institute of Recycling economy, Beijing University of Technology, Beijing, 100124, China.

Abstract: *Waste sintered Nd-Fe-B permanent magnets were recycled via doping DyH_3 nanoparticles. The effect of the DyH_3 nanoparticles on the microstructure and magnetic properties of the recycled magnets has been studied. DyH_3nanoparticles additives between 0.0 wt. % and 1.0 wt. % have little effect on the remanence (B_r) of the recycled magnet. When the additive content is more than 1.0 wt. %, the remanence (B_r) begins to decrease. The coercivity of recycled magnet increases gradually as the DyH_3 nanoparticles additive increases. The magnetic properties of the resulting magnet were: $(BH)_{max}$ = 36.54 MGOe and B_r = 12.96 kGs, representing decreases of 13% and 4%, respectively, and recovered coercivity resulting of 17 kOe of the initial magnet.*

Keywords: *recycling; Nd-Fe-B; DyH_3; nanoparticles; magnetic properties*

Address: W. Q. Liu, College of Materials Science and Engineering, Beijing University of Technology, Beijing, 100124, China, Tel:(86-10)6739-1760, Fax: (86-10)6739-1760, Email: liuwq@bjut.edu.cn

1. Introduction

Since their invention in 1984 [1-2], the sintered Nd-Fe-B magnets have played an important role in many fields, such as voice-coil motor (VCM) devices, hybrid electric vehicles (HEV), turbine motor, magnetic resonance imaging (MRI), etc. Recycling of waste Nd-Fe-B magnets is inevitable for the reduction of industrial waste. However, few commercially scalable methods for recycling or regeneration of the waste magnets in mass production are readily available. In the past years, numerous researchers [3-9] reported compelling results on the production of recycled anisotropic Nd-Fe-B powders. In this study, we report recycling of waste Nd-Fe-B magnets with rare earth hydride nanoparticles. The magnetic properties and microstructure of the recycled magnets were investigated and compared to the starting material.

2. Experiments

First, the hydrogen decrepitation (HD) process was conducted by placing the uncoated waste magnet pieces in a vacuumed furnace and admitting hydrogen at a pressure of 1 bar. The waste Nd-Fe-B magnet ($Nd_{22.57}Dy_{0.79}Pr_{7.1}Al_{0.17}Fe_{67.15}Tb_{0.41}Co_{0.74}Cu_{0.09}B_{0.98}$) absorbed hydrogen at 423 K for 4 hours, followed by insitu degassing at 873 K for 10 hours, until the vacuum had recovered and was greater than 10^{-3} Pa. The DyH_3 nanoparticles were prepared by the inert gas condensing method. The DyH_3 nanoparticles and the degassed Nd-Fe-B powders were homogeneously mixed by low energy ball milling in hexane for 1.5 hours. The DyH_3 additions to waste powders were set between 0 and 2.0 wt. %. The ball-to-powder weight ratio was 10:1. Powders were aligned under 3 T and pressed to form the green compacts. The green compacts were sintered at 1403 K under vacuum for 1 hour, followed by heat treatment. The magnetic properties of the recycled magnets were measured by permeameter. The densities of the sintered samples were measured using Archimedes method. The microstructure of recycled magnets was observed using the Scanning Electron Microscope (SEM). The proportion of Nd-rich phase and the grain size were examined using the image analyzer software (ImageJ).

3. Results and Discussions

The magnetic properties of the recycled magnets as a function of DyH_3 nanoparticles content are plotted in Figure 1 and compared with the starting material. The best recycled magnet yields B_r of 13.52 kGs, H_{cj} of 16.75 kOe, and $BH_{(max)}$ of 41.25 MGOe. The recycled magnets with DyH nanoparticle content between 0.0 wt. % and 1.0 wt. % have maintained the remanence (B_r), but, with higher additions, the B_r begins to decrease rapidly due to the antiparallel coupling of Dy with Fe in the ϕ-phase ($Nd_2Fe_{14}B$) [10]. The coercivity (H_{cj}) exhibits a linear increase for all the recycled magnets doped with DyH_3 nanoparticles peaking at 20 kOe, which exceeded the initial coercive force of 17 kOe for the starting material. This increase is expected and is ascribed to the formation of the $Dy_2Fe_{14}B$ phase, which has lower magnetization saturation and a higher anisotropy field than that of the $Nd_2Fe_{14}B$ phase. The additional decrease in the B_r can be contributed further to the incomplete densification.

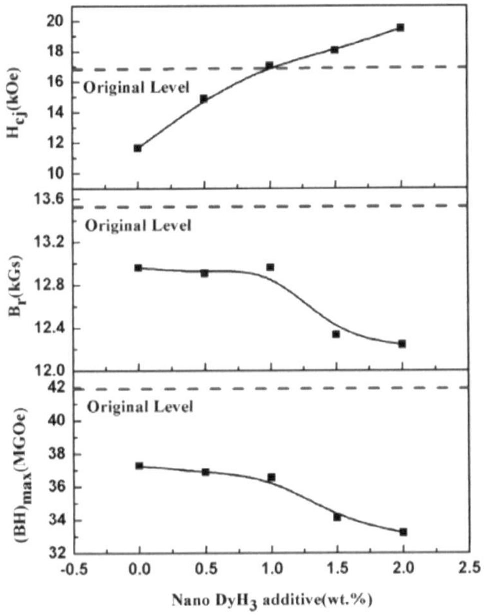

Fig. 1. The magnetic properties of the recycled magnets as a function of DyH_3 nanoparticles content.

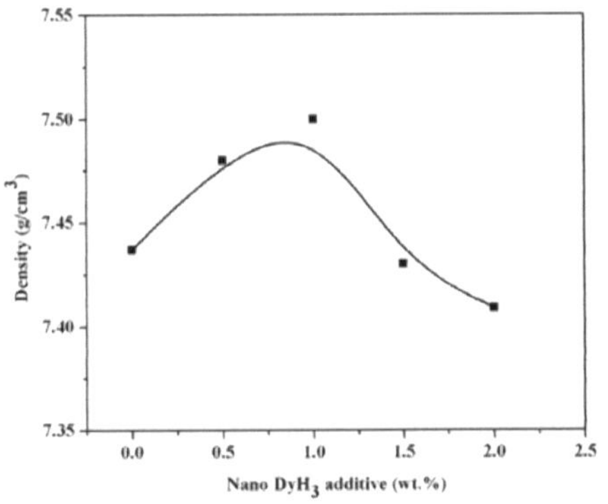

Fig. 2. The densities of the recycled sintered magnets with different DyH_3 nanoparticles additives.

When these recycled materials were processed to produce high coercive recycled magnets, we found that the best density was obtained for the recycled product with 0.5 wt.% and 1.0 wt.% DyH_3 (see Fig. 2). Using less or more DyH_3 additions resulted in materials with lower densities. For the five series of recycled product, which varied in DyH_3 content from 0 to 2.0 wt.%, significant changes were observed in the sintered microstructure, e.g., a greater percentage of Dy in the recycled magnets resulted in the increased porosity (see Fig. 3). A quantitative assessment using the image analysis technique revealed that the amount of porosity is increasing with increased content of DyH_3 nanoparticles. Large holes appear in the recycled magnet with 2.0 wt.% additive, which could be explained by residual hydrogen that was not completely desorbed from DyH_3 nanoparticles. This hydrogen is then released during the sintering process, and contributes to the formation of large cracks present in the recycled sintered magnet product.

Fig. 4 shows the proportion of the Nd-rich phase and the average grain size of recycled magnets as a function of DyH_3 nanoparticle additive when compared to the starting material. Significant changes were observed in the volume fraction of ~50 wt.% Nd-rich phase loss for the recycled sample without additive. The amount of the initial DyH_3 additions to the recycled magnets was observed to have an influence on the rate of grain size, and yields nearly three times the average grain size when compared to the starting magnet. It seems that the better coercivities obtained with the DyH_3 additions are not the result of microstructural advantage, but rather the result of the increased anisotropy field and formation of the $Dy_2Fe_{14}B$ phase.

4. Conclusion

Waste sintered Nd-Fe-B magnets were recycled by means of adding DyH_3 nanoparticles to Nd-Fe-B powders. The best recycled magnet produced contained 1.0 wt.% of DyH_3 nanoparticles when compared to the properties of the starting waste sintering magnet. The H_{cj}, B_r and $(BH)_{max}$ values of 101.7%, 95.4%, and 88.58%, respectively, were

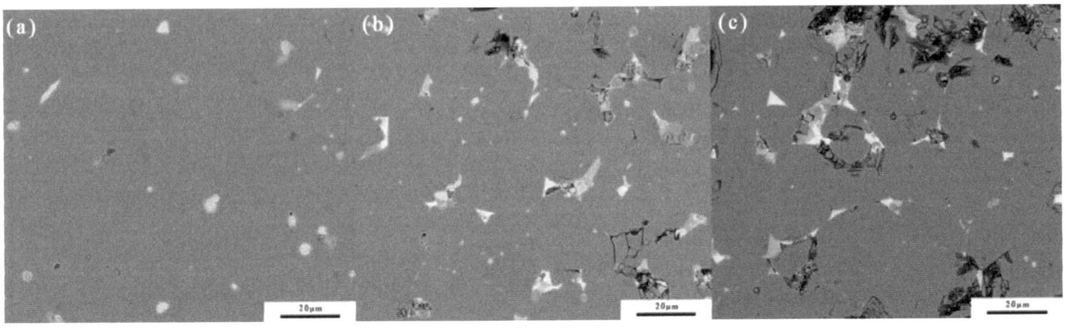

Fig. 3. SEM BSE images of the recycled sintered magnets (a). without DyH_3 nanoparticles additive, (b). with 1.0 wt.% DyH_3 nanoparticles additive, and (c). with 2.0 wt.% DyH_3 nanoparticles additive.

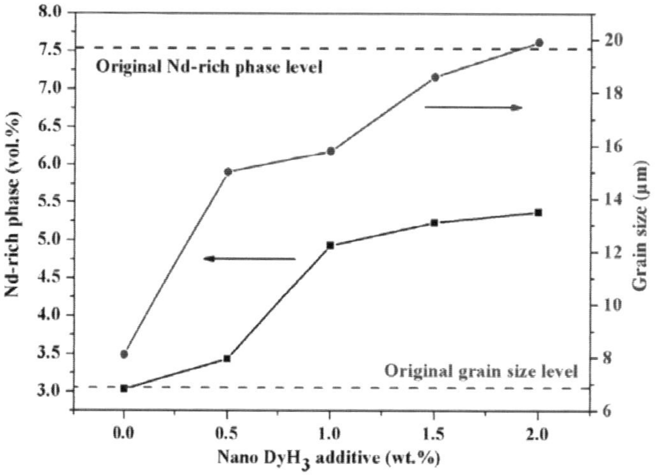

Fig. 4. Nd-rich phase contents and grain size of the recycled sintered Nd-Fe-B magnets with different DyH_3 nanoparticles additive percentages.

recovered. The average grain size of the recycled magnets is about three times larger than that of the original waste magnet, and the grain size increases further as the DyH_3 nanoparticles content in magnet increases. We will be investigating nano additions more closely using other nano elemental additions in order to better understand the recovery of magnetic and microstructural performance of recycled magnets.

Acknowledgment

This work was supported by the National High Technology Research and Development Program of China (2012AA063201), National Natural Science Foundation of China (51001002 and 51371002), Jinghua Talents of Beijing University of Technology, Rixin Talents of Beijing University of Technology, The Importation and Development of High-Caliber Talents Project of Beijing Municipal Institutions, Technology Foundation for Selected Overseas Chinese Scholar of Beijing.

References

[1] M. Sagawa, S. Fujimura, M. Togawa, H. Yamamoto, Y. Matsura, *J. Appl. Phys.* **55**, 1984, 2083.

[2] J. J. Croat, J. F. Herbst, R. W. Lee, F. E. Pinkerton, *J. Appl. Phys.* **55**, 1984, 2078.

[3] K. Miura, M. Itoh, K. Machida, *J. Alloys Compd.*, 466, 2008, 228.

[4] E. A. Périgo, S. C. da Silva, R. V. Martin, H. Taklishi, F. J. G. Landgraf, *J. Appl. Phys.* **111**, 2012, 07A725.

[5] R. S. Sheridan, R. Sillitoe, M. Zakotnik, I. R. Harris, A. J. Williams, *J. Magn. Magn. Mater.* **324**, 2012, 63.

[6] M. Zakotnik, I. R. Harris, A. J. Williams, *J. Alloys Compd.* **450**, 2008, 525.

[7] M. Zakotnik, I. R. Harris, A. J. Williams, J. Alloys Compd. **469**, 2009, 314.

[8] M. Itoh, M. Masuda, S. Suzuki, K. Machida, *J. Alloys Compd.* **374**, 2004, 393.

[9] O. Gutfleisch, K. Güth, T. G. Woodcock, *Adv. Energy Mater.* **3**, 2013, 151.

[10] J. F. Herbst, $R_2Fe_{14}B$ materials: Intrinsic properties and technological aspects, *Rev. Mod. Phys,* **63**, 1991, 819.

Corrosion Behaviors and Mechanism of Sintered Rare-Earth Magnets

A.H. LI, W. LI, J.J. LI, S.L. HUANG, Y.C. SUN, H.B. FENG, M.G. ZHU
Division of Functional Materials, Central Iron & Steel Research Institute, Beijing 100081, China

Abstract: *Sintered rare-earth magnets possessing outstanding magnetic properties are widely applied in many fields. However, the corrosion resistance of the magnets is poor because the rare earth-rich phases in them are easily oxidized. In this article, the corrosion resistance of sintered Nd-Fe-B and Sm-Co magnets was investigated in steady-state damp heat (HH), neutral salt spray (NSS) and pressure cooker (PCT) climates. The effects of alloy composition and different corrosive environments on magnetic flux loss were studied. The weight losses of the magnet specimens in the NSS test are higher than that in the HH and PCT tests, because erosive chlorine ions translated through the voids of the corrosion film, destroyed its stable status, deepened and accelerated the corrosion process. The corrosion resistance of sintered Nd-Fe-B magnets can be improved by Dy partially substitution for Nd and minor Co addition. The sintered Sm-Co magnets show very good corrosion resistance in the above three kinds of climates. Potentiodynamic polarization experiments were carried out at room temperature in different electrolytes. It shows that: a typical active dissolution occurred in 0.1mol/L HCl electrolyte; anode passivation happened in 3.0%NaOH electrolyte; in 3.5%NaCl electrolyte, the active dissolution was very remarkable in the anode reaction due to the existence of erosive chlorine ions.*

Address: A. H. Li, E-mail: li_ah@sina.com

1. Introduction

Sintered rare-earth magnets possessing outstanding magnetic properties are widely applied in many high-tech fields such as hybrid electric vehicles (HEV), wind generators, permanent magnetic motors, medical apparatus, consumer electronics, computers, etc. However, corrosion resistance has been a problem with the magnets owing to the high chemical activity of the phases rich in rare earth elements [1]. The electro-chemical corrosion occurs for Nd-Fe-B magnets in a damp- heat atmosphere because of the difference of corrosion potential between the matrix $Nd_2Fe_{14}B$ phase and the boundary Nd-rich phase [2-4]. Methods of alloying-element addition, surface passivation and coating are often applied to protect the metal materials from environmental erosion. It is important work to investigate the corrosion behavior and mechanism of sintered rare-earth magnets in different environmental conditions and in different types of electrolytes, since it will be helpful to find methods of improving the corrosion resistance of the magnets by composition designating and surface passivation-treating. In this article, corrosion resistance of sintered Nd-Fe-B and Sm-Co magnets was investigated in steady-state damp heat, neutral salt spray, and pressure cooker climates. The effects of alloy composition and different corrosive environments on magnetic flux loss were also studied. Polarization curves were measured, and electrochemical impedance spectroscopy tests were carried out to investigate the corrosion kinetics for sintered rare-earth magnets in different electrolytes.

2. Experimental Procedures

The magnets used in this study, with nominal compositions of A: $Nd_{27.9}Dy_{0.2}Fe_{bal}Co_{0.5}M_{0.4}B_{1.0}$ (wt. %), B: $Nd_{22.3}Dy_{8.8}Fe_{bal}Co_{2.1}M_{0.8}B_{1.0}$ (wt. %) (M=Al, Cu, and Ga), and C: $Sm(Co_{bal}Fe_{0.2}Cu_{0.1}Zr_{0.02})_{7.4}$, were fabricated by the conventional powder metallurgy process. The magnet specimens were magnetically saturated by a pulsed magnetic field. The magnet specimens were divided into three equivalent groups. The three groups of specimens were tested in a constant humid heat chamber at 85°C, 1atm, 85%RH (heretofore referred to as the "HH" test), in an autoclave at 120°C, 2atm, 100%RH (heretofore referred to as the "PCT" test), in a neutral salt spray tester at 35°C, 5%NaCl (heretofore referred to as the "NSS" test), respectively. After corrosion testing, the weight losses of the specimens were measured with a balance after brushing off the corrosion products from the specimens. The magnetic fluxes of the specimens before and after testing were measured by using a fluxmeter. The corrosion behavior and the magnetic flux loss were studied. Potentiodynamic polarization experiments were carried out with a PARM273A potentiostat.

All the experiments were performed in a standard three-electrode system consisting of Nd–Fe–B working electrode (see Fig. 1), saturated calomel reference electrode, and Pt counter electrode. Electrochemical impedance spectroscopy measurements were also performed. The electrochemical tests were carried out at room temperature in 3.0%NaOH, 3.5%NaCl, and 0.1mol/L HCl electrolytes. A scanning electron microscope (SEM) with energy dispersive X-ray spectroscopy

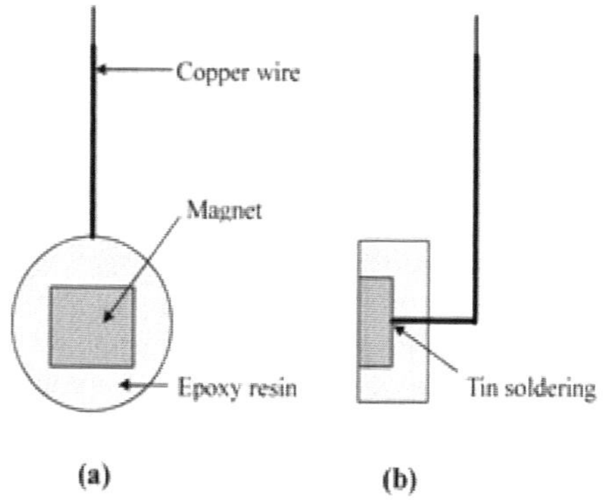

Fig. 1. A sketch, (a) in front view, and (b) side view, of NdFeB working electrode.

(EDX) was used to study the corrosion microstructure of the tested specimens.

3. Results and Discussion

The weight losses and the magnetic flux losses of the magnet specimens after the different corrosion tests (HH, PCT, and NSS) for 70 hours are listed in Table 1. The weight losses and the magnetic flux losses of Specimen A in different corrosion tests are all higher than that of Specimen B. It suggests that the corrosion resistance of sintered Nd-Fe-B magnets can be improved by Dy partially substitution for Nd and minor Co addition. The sintered Sm-Co magnets showed very good corrosion resistance in the above three kinds of climates. The corrosion rates of sintered Nd-Fe-B magnets in HH and NSS test exhibit an obvious parabolic trend. The weight loss of the magnet specimens was very small in the PCT test due to an oxygen-deficient atmosphere. The flux loss in the above three kinds of climates have an approximate linear trend. The variations of the weight losses and the magnetic flux losses of the magnet specimens with test times in the NSS test are shown in Fig. 2, and Fig. 3, respectively.

The potentiodynamic polarization curves of sintered Nd-Fe-B magnets in different electrolytes are shown

Table 1. Weight losses and magnetic flux losses of the magnet specimens after the corrosion tests for 70 hours.

Test type / Specimen No.	HH	PCT	NSS
	Weight loss /Flux loss	Weight loss /Flux loss	**Weight loss /Flux loss**
A	27.30 /13.0%	0.15 /9.4%	**12.50 /3.3%**
B	21.44 /7.9%	0.10 /3.8%	**4.42 /2.9%**
C	**~0 /~0**	**~0 /~0**	**~0 /~0**

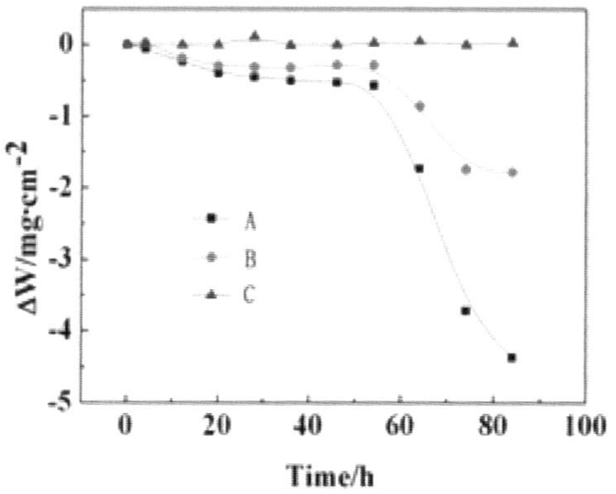

Fig. 2. The weight losses of the magnet specimens for different test times in the NSS test.

in Fig. 4. In 0.1mol/L HCl electrolyte (see Fig. 4a), a typical active dissolution proceeded once the magnet electrode was immersed in the acid solution, and many of bubbles formed on the surface on the magnets. The passivity phenomenon was not found in the measured regions. However, the anode reaction went through three stages of activation, passivation, and transpassivation in 3.0%NaOH electrolyte. The anode passivation happened in the potential of from -420mv to 500mv, which is probably because the corrosion products $Nd(OH)_3$ and $Fe(OH)_2$ absorbed on the surface of the magnet electrode hindered the corrosion reaction. When the electrode potential was higher than 500mv, the dissolution rate of the passivation film was higher than its generation rate, so transpassivation happened (see Fig. 4b). In 3.5%NaCl electrolyte, for the anode polarization curve, the corrosion current density rapidly increased with increasing electrode potential (see Fig. 4c), suggesting that the active dissolution is very remarkable. It is because the erosive chlorine ions can translate through the voids of corrosion film and reach the matrix. Thereby, chlorine ions substituted for oxygen on the surface of the metal, destroyed its passivitaion status, further formed soluble compounds and so accelerated the corrosion process of the magnet [5]. The cathode polarization curve was very steep in 3.5%NaCl electrolyte, revealing that the electrode

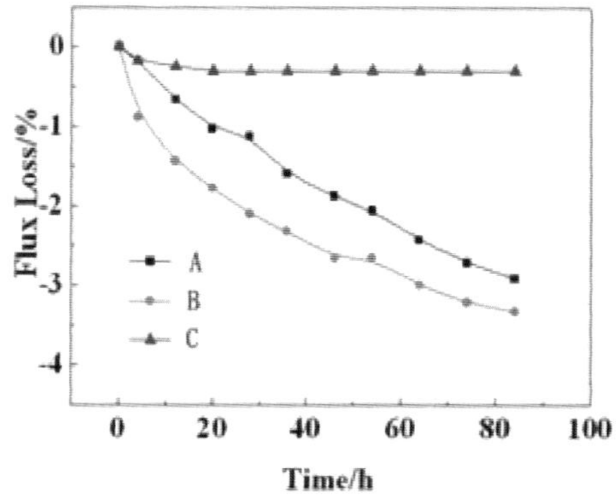

Fig. 3. Magnetic flux losses of the magnet specimens for different test times in the NSS test.

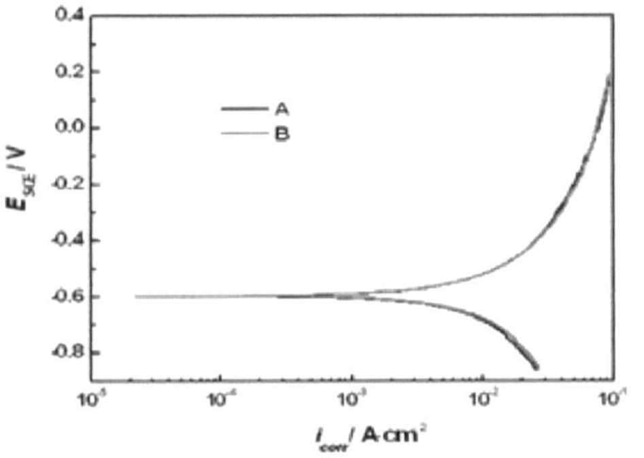

(a) 0.1mol/L HCl: Active dissolution in both anode and cathode

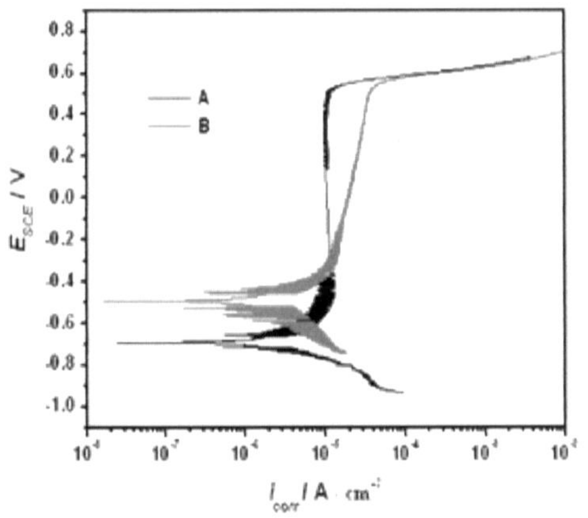

(b) 3.0%NaOH: Evident passivation occuring

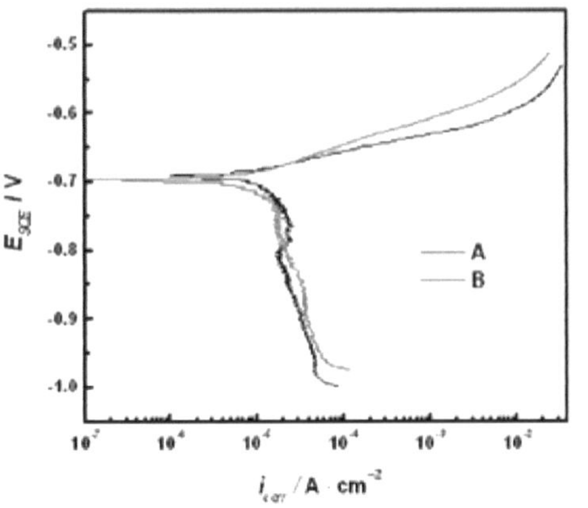

(c) 3.5%NaCl : Active dissolution in anode

Fig. 4. Polarization curves of sintered Nd-Fe-B magnets in different electrolytes.

reaction was controlled by the process of concentration polarization.

The corrosion macromorphologies and micro-morphologies of sintered rare-earth magnets were studied. The typical SEM micromorphologies of sintered Nd-Fe-B magnets after 70 h of the NSS test are shown in Fig. 5. It can be seen that: there are many of pits in the surface of the corroded specimens (see Fig. 5a). "Turtle cracks" were found in high-magnification SEM images (see Fig. 5b), due to the erosive chlorine ions which translated through the voids of corrosion film, destroyed its stable status, and deepened and accelerated the corrosion process. The weight losses of the magnets specimens in the NSS test were higher than that in the HH and PCT tests (the flux losses were lower in the NSS test because it was performed at room temperature).

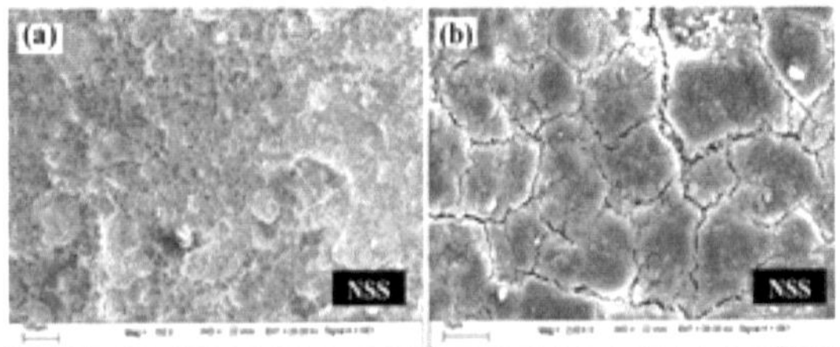

Fig. 5. SEM corrosion micromorphologies of sintered Nd-Fe-B magnets for the NSS test in (a) low magnification and (b) high magnification.

In this article, the corrosion resistance of sintered Nd-Fe-B and Sm-Co magnets was investigated in steady-state damp heat (HH), neutral salt spray (NSS) and pressure cooker (PCT) climates. The weight losses of the magnets specimens in the NSS test were higher than that in the HH and PCT tests, which was because erosive chlorine ions translated through the voids of corrosion film, destroyed its stable status, accelerated the corrosion process. The corrosion resistance of sintered Nd-Fe-B magnets can be improved by Dy partially substitution for Nd and minor Co addition. The sintered Sm-Co magnets showed very good corrosion resistance in the above three kinds of climates. Potentiodynamic polarization experiments were carried out at room temperature in three different electrolytes. It showed that a typical active dissolution proceeded in 0.1mol/L HCl electrolyte; anode passivation happened in 3.0%NaOH electrolyte; and in 3.5%NaCl electrolyte, the active dissolution was very remarkable in the anode reaction due to the existence of erosive chlorine ions.

Acknowledgement
We thank the national science and technology support program of China (2012BAE02B01), and the National Basic Research Program of China (2014CB643701) for financial support for the study.

References

[1] D. F. Cygan, M. J. McNallan, *J. Magn. Magn. Mater.*, 1995, 139, 131.
[2] A. S. Kim, F. E. Camp, T. Lizzi, *J. Appl. Phys.*, 1996, 79, 4840.
[3] M. Katter, L. Zapf, R. Blank, W. Fernengel, W. Rodewald, *IEEE Trans. Magn.*, 2001, 37, 2474.
[4] G. L. Yan, P. J. McGuiness, J. G., *J. Alloys Compd.*, 2009, 478, 188.
[5] A. A. El-Moneim, A. Gebert, *J. Appl. Electrochem.*, 2003, 33, 795.

On the Texture Evaluation of Nd-Fe-B Magnets with Different Alignment Degrees

L.U. LOPES[1], E.C. SANTOS[1], T. HARTWIG[2], P.A.P WENDHAUSEN[1]
[1] MAGMA-Labmat, Department of Mechanical and Materials Engineering, UFSC - Brazil
[2] Fraunhofer IFAM, Bremen - Germany

Abstract: *In this work, Nd-Fe-B magnets fabricated by Powder Injection Molding technique, and aligned under low and high fields; for reference purposes, isotropic magnets were also prepared. The texture of the magnets was evaluated by several techniques, such as magnetic characterization, XRD, pole figures and EBSD orientation mapping. The obtained results were discussed and it was found that all techniques could detect minor differences in the degree of alignment. Moreover, some of the techniques used, such as EBSD orientation mapping, provide additional information on the alignment homogeneity throughout the magnet. Combined, these techniques serve as a good evaluation of magnet's texture and provide extremely useful data for improvements in the alignment processes.*

1. Introduction

The presence of crystallographic texture in Nd-Fe-B based magnets is a key factor that make possible obtaining high remanence, and combined with the intrinsic high anisotropy field for the 2:14:1 phase, remarkable values for maximum energy product. In this regard, texture evaluation is critical to bring improvements to the aligning process and can be performed by several techniques. XRD characterization is one of the most common ways to determine texture in Nd-Fe-B magnets [1] and can detect minor improvements in texture, but on the other hand requires time and specialized instrumentation. In addition to XRD, the utilization of a goniometer provide more information, allowing the draw of pole figures [2] and an easier evaluation of the present texture.

Magnetic characterization in easy and hard magnetization axis and quantification of the average angle of misorientation [3] is a fast method to determine the degree of alignment in the whole magnet. For a more localized investigation of the texture, the utilization of the Electron Backscatter Diffraction (EBSD) is being widely applied [4]–[7] and make possible the visualization of the crystallographic orientation for each grain in the microstructure, allowing the evaluation of the alignment homogeneity throughout the magnet.

In Powder Injection Molding process applied to fabricate Nd-Fe-B magnets, the alignment process is influenced by many factors beyond the conventional PM process [8], raising the necessity of a detailed texture quantification.

This work will cover the utilization of several tools for texture quantification in Powder Injection Molded Nd-Fe-B magnets, which show different degrees of alignment due to process modification. The main objective is to determine the strengths of each technique, in order obtain information about the texture development associated with a specific process condition.

2. Experimental

Powder Injection Molding process was applied to manufacture Nd-Fe-B magnets according to conditions described in a previous publication [8]. In this study, high (1 T) and low (0.6 T) fields were applied during injection molding to generate crystallographic texture. Isotropic magnets were also fabricated to serve as a reference. Magnetic characterization was performed in a hysteresisgraph in easy and hard directions.

3. Results and Discussion

Magnetic characterization results for magnets aligned in high and low fields, and for an isotropic magnet is shown in Fig. 1. The characterizations were carried out in easy and hard directions for anisotropic magnets. It can be noticed that remanence increases in

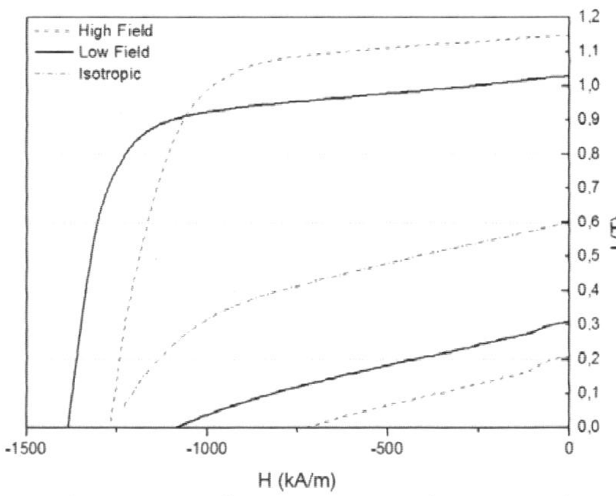

Fig. 1. Magnetic characterization of magnets aligned with high and low fields and of an isotropic magnet.

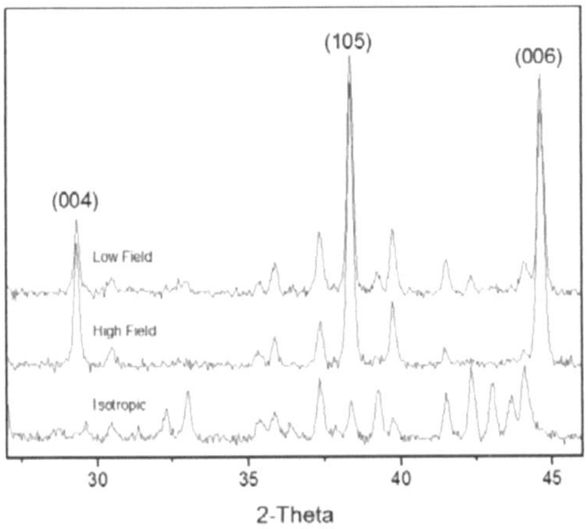

Fig. 2. X-ray diffraction patterns of bulk magnets aligned in high and low fields and isotropic.

easy direction and decreases in hard direction for the magnet aligned in high field, compared to the low field alignment. To quantify the alignment, different methods were used. A quick approach can apply an isotropic magnet as a reference, by calculating the percentage of the remanence in the easy axis in relation to the square value of the isotropic magnet's remanence. By this method, it is found a degree of alignment of 85,6 % for the low field alignment, and 95,4 % for the high field alignment.

The second method that can be applied to quantify the degree of alignment is the calculation of the average misalignment angle [3]. The calculation is based in the remanence in easy and hard directions for the same magnet. It was found an average misalignment angle of 20° in the magnets aligned with high field, while the low field aligned magnets exhibit an angle of 31.1°. With the average misalignment angle, it is possible to infer the degree of alignment, achieving the value of 94,4 % for high field alignment and 85,6 % for low field alignment. The results for both methods were in fair agreement, indicating the

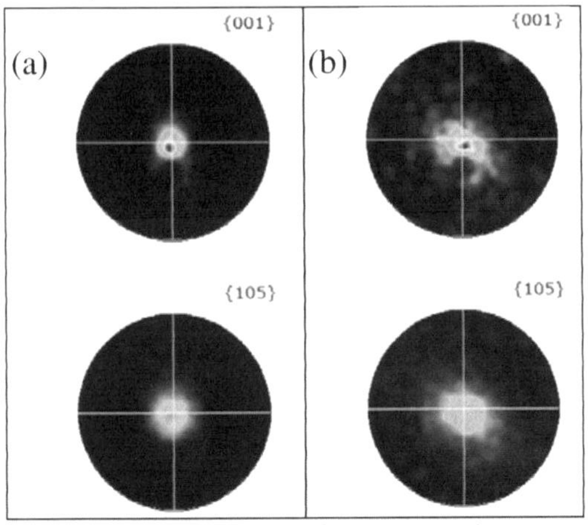

Fig. 3. XRD pole figures for anisotropic magnets aligned with (a) high and (b) low fields.

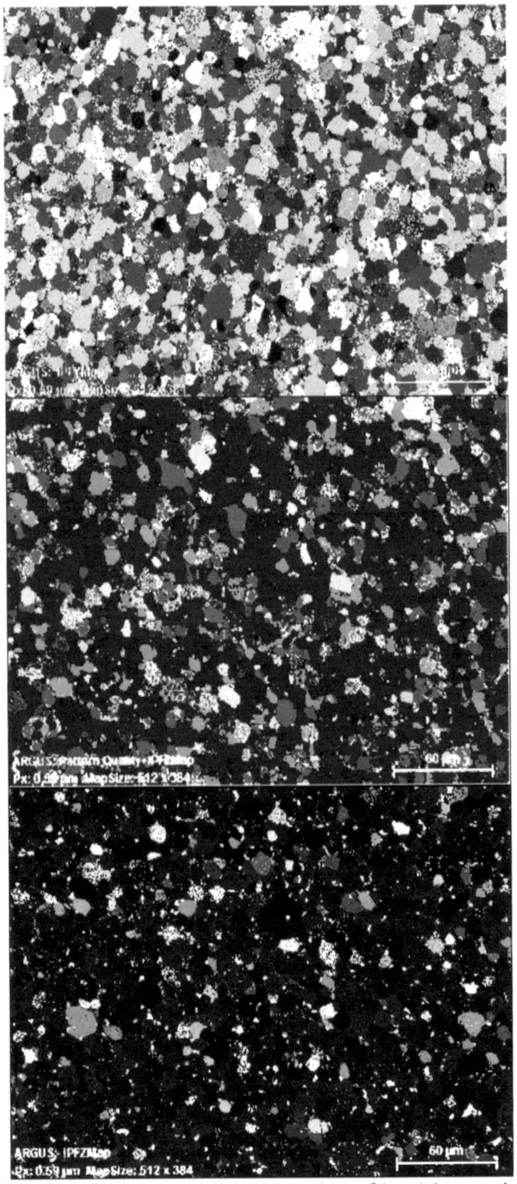

Fig. 4 – EBSD orientation mapping of (top) isotropic, (middle) low-field aligned and (bottom) high-field aligned magnets

possibility to apply both methods in the case of availability to measure the magnet in two directions or fabricate an isotropic magnet with the same powder and process conditions.

X-ray diffraction for bulk specimens results are shown in Fig. 2. The presence of texture is clearly detectable by the reflection intensities of preferred oriented planes, principally (004), (006) and (105). It can be seen that the intensity of such reflections is directly proportional to the degree of alignment present in the magnets.

As an aid to evaluate the quality of the present texture, XRD pole figures for reflections of planes

(001) and (105) are shown in Fig. 3. It can be seen significant differences from the magnet aligned with high and low fields, with less dispersion of intensity around the origin, which indicates a higher degree of alignment. Stronger texture is present in pole figure of {*00l*} reflections due to privileged orientation in *c*-axis of $Nd_2Fe_{14}B_1$ cell induced by the aligning field.

In Fig. 4, EBSD orientation maps are shown for isotropic, high and low-field aligned magnets. Better viewed in color, here the maps are presented in grayscale, with a darker color grains indicating a *c*-axis crystal orientation perpendicular to the plane of paper. From the random grain orientation found in isotropic magnet, a texture improvement can be seen in low-field aligned magnet. In high field aligning, the higher texture can be noticed with just a few misaligned grains. White areas are mostly Nd-rich phase or reminiscent porosity and are not influenced by the aligning field. EBSD maps cannot express the texture of the whole magnet but are very useful for localized evaluation, e.g. inhomogeneous texture throughout the magnet due to aligning field variations or, in the case of PIM process, lack of texture in the surface due to quick cooling of injection feedstock.

4. Summary

Several techniques were applied to evaluate the texture of magnets fabricated by the Powder Injection Molding process. A very straight-forward method to quantitatively evaluate the degree of alignment is by means of magnetic characterization, with an isotropic sample as a reference or by the measurement in easy and hard directions. XRD and pole-figure are useful for a deeper texture investigation, in specific planes, and can infer the alignment quality, but are time consuming, and requires specialized equipment. EBSD orientation mapping was also investigated and could discriminate different degrees of alignment, giving useful and visual information, but only in a small area, which can be handy to evaluate texture homogeneity.

Acknowledgement

The authors would like to thank Dr. Gert Nolze from BAM Institute for the support in EBSD characterization.

References

[1] D. Givord, A. Liénard, R. Perrier, *et al.*, *J. Phys.-Paris,* 1985, 9, 46, 313–317.
[2] W. C. Chang, T. B. Wu, K. S. Liu, *J. Appl. Phys.*, 1988, 63, 8, 3531.
[3] W. Fernengel, A. Lehnert, M. Katter, *J. Magn. Magn. Mater.*, 1996, 158, 19–20.
[4] K. Khlopkov, O. Gutfleisch, D. Eckert, *et al.*, J. *Alloys Compd.*, 2004, 365, 1–2, 259–265.
[5] K. Khlopkov, O. Gutfleisch, D. Hinz, *et al.*, *J. Appl. Phys.*, 2007, 102, 2, 023912.
[6] T.G. Woodcock, K. Khlopkov, A. Walther, *et al*, *Scr. Mater.*, 2009, 60, 9, 826–829.
[7] T.G. Woodcock, O. Gutfleisch, *Acta Mater.*, 2011, 59, 3, 1026–1036.
[8] L.U. Lopes, T. Hartwig, P.A.P. Wendhausen, *IEEE Trans. Magn.*, 2013, 49, 8, 4618–4621.

Temperature Effect on Microstructure and Magnetic Properties of NdFeB Sintered Magnets Mixed with Small DyCo Alloy Powder

M.W. LEE[1], D.R. DHAKAL[1], T.S. JANG[1], T.H. KIM[2], S.R. LEE[2], H.J. KIM[3]
[1]Department of Hybrid Engineering, Sunmoon University, Asan 336-708, Republic of Korea
[2]Department of Materials Science and Engineering, Korea University, Seoul 136-713, Republic of Korea
[3]R&D Center of Jahwa Electronics Co. Ltd, Cheongwon 363-922, Republic of Korea

Abstract: *Microstructural change and corresponding effect on coercivity of aNd-Fe-B sintered magnet mixed with small Dy-Co powder addition was investigated. Thin Dy-rich shell was found to enclose magnetic grains uniformly at low sintering temperature (1040 °C) while the shell thickness increased with increasing sintering temperature. Segregation of cobalt in Nd-rich triple-junction phase followed by the formation of Co-rich phase was beneficial for the coercivity enhancement, resulting in the stabilization of the metastable c-Nd_2O_3 phase. After the optimization of sintering and annealing temperature, enhancement of the coercivity was found to be more than 1 kOe without deterioration of the remanence.*

Address: T. S. Jang, Department of Hybrid Engineering, Sunmoon University, Asan 336-708, Republic of Korea, E-mail : tsjang@sunmoon.ac.kr

1. Introduction

Having excellent magnetic properties, Nd-Fe-B sintered magnets are used in the driving motors of hybrid vehicles although they are unable to sustain at high-enough temperature operation because of low Curie temperature and high temperature coefficient of the coercivity. This disadvantage can be overcome when their coercivity is enhanced by adding heavy rare earth elements like Tb or Dy, creating high anisotropy [1,2]. However, the remanence reduction always accompanies the usage of these heavy rare earth elements. The antiferromagnetic coupling between heavy rare earth elements and Fe leads to reduced saturation magnetization and the energy product $(BH)_{max}$. Nevertheless, the reduction of the remanence and energy product can be minimized by forming the Dy-rich core-shell type structures [3,4]. The mixing of metallic Dy or Dy compound powder to Nd-Fe-B magnet powder in magnet making process can lead to the formation of such core-shell type structure.

Cobalt in Nd-Fe-B sintered magnet is beneficial for the improvement of remanence and Curie temperature but the creation of planar anisotropy in main phase decreases the coercivity [5,6]. However, in real cases, Co concentration is found to be higher in Nd-rich phase of Nd-Fe-B sintered magnets, which results in considerable microstructural change of Nd-rich phase. The low melting element like Cu increases the wettability and continuity of Nd-rich phase thereby increasing the coercivity [7]. Furthermore, metastable c-Nd_2O_3 phase ($Ia\bar{3}$, a= 1.108 nm) becomes stable due to Cu segregation in Nd-rich triple-junction phase (TJP) and grain boundary phase (GBP) [8]. Co also lowers the melting point of Nd-rich phase as Cu does; therefore, it is possible to improve the characteristics of Nd-rich phases.

When Co is added to Nd-Fe-B sintered magnet the optimum sintering temperatureand temperature of the 1st post-sintering annealing (PSA) are lowered, meanwhile the simultaneous addition of Co and Dy can easily reduce the thickness of Dy-rich shell. In this study, therefore, we intended to increase the coercivity of Nd-Fe-B sintered magnets by adding Dy-Co alloy powder to improve the microstructure of Nd-rich TJP and GBP. In particular, we tried to optimize the sintering and 1st PSA temperature by investigating the magnetic properties in terms of microstructural change.

2. Experimental Procedure

Starting alloy with the composition (at.%) $Nd_{14.7}Fe_{76.5}B_{6.0}M_{2.8}$ (M = Cu, Co, Al, Nb) was prepared by strip casting. The strips were HD-treated and jet-milled to produce magnetic powder. The average particle size of the powder was about 5 μm. The jet-milled powder was wet-mixed with 1.1 wt.% of Dy-Co alloy powder. The solvent was removed by creating vacuum atmosphere. The mean particle size of Dy-Co alloy powder was about 4 μm. The mixed powder was aligned under the magnetic field of 2.2 T and pressed to form green compacts. The green compacts were sintered at 1040, 1050, 1060 and 1070 °C for 4 h and subjected to the 1st PSA at 600, 630, 660 and 690 °C for 2 h, respectively. The 2nd PSA and 3rd PSA were done at 530 °C for 2 h and at 500 °C for 2 h, respectively. Microstructural studies were carried out using Scanning Electron Microscopy (SEM, Hitachi S-3000N). Phase analysis was carried out using an Electron Probe Micro Analyzer (EPMA,

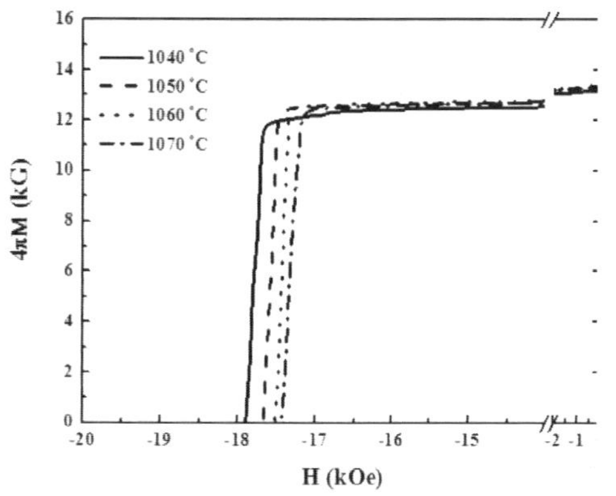

Fig. 1. Demagnetization curves of Nd-Fe-B magnets mixed with small Dy-Co alloy powder and sintered at various temperatures.

SHIMADZU EPMA-1720), and High Resolution Transmission Electron Microscopy (HRTEM, JEOL JEM 2100F). Magnetic properties were measured using a *B-H* loop tracer (Magnet-Physik Permagraph C300).

3. Results and Discussion

Fig. 1 shows the demagnetization curves of Nd-Fe-B magnets mixed with small Dy-Co alloy powder and sintered at various temperatures. As the sintering temperature decreased, the coercivity increased from 17.4 kOe to 17.9 kOe. The magnet was sintered to full density regardless of sintering temperature (ρ ≥ 99 %). Moreover, the average grain size decreased as the sintering temperature decreased (from 5.98 μm at 1070 °C to 5.72 μm at 1040 °C). Fig. 2 shows the EPMA maps of Co and Dy in the magnets for all sintering temperatures. Formation of Dy-rich shell around the main magnetic grains was found in all Dy-Co alloy powder-added magnets, whereas Co was segregated mainly in Nd-rich TJP. The variation of shell thickness according to the sintering temperatures is given in Table 1. As can be seen in the table, the shell thickness also decreased as the sintering temperature decreased.

Fig. 3 shows the demagnetization curves of Dy-Co alloy powder-added Nd-Fe-B sintered magnet annealed at various temperatures. In order to compare the effect of the annealing steps on magnetic properties and microstructure, annealing of the sintered magnets was carried out in two ways. The first annealing procedure consisted of three annealing steps (1st PSA, 2nd PSA, and 3rd PSA) and the second - of two annealing steps (1st PSA and 2nd PSA). Magnetic properties of such annealed magnets are summarized in Table 2. The coercivity was high when 1st PSA temperature was 690 °C and decreased with decreasing 1st PSA temperature. Furthermore, the two-step-annealed magnets always show higher

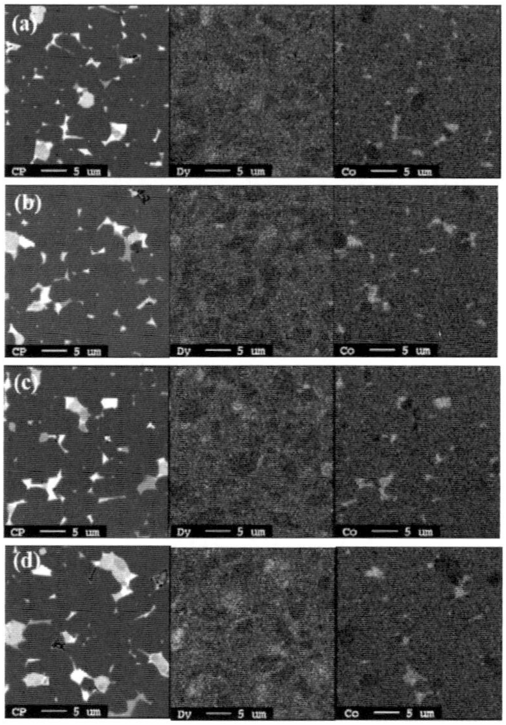

Fig. 2. EPMA maps ofDy-Co-alloy-added magnets sintered at (a) 1040 °C, (b) 1050 °C, (c) 1060 °C and (d) 1070 °C.

coercivity than the three-step annealed magnets. In order to find out the reason of this difference, TEM investigation and EDX analysis were performed for both the three-step-annealed magnets (690, 530 and 500 °C) and the two-step-annealed magnets (690 and 530 °C).

Fig. 4 (a) shows the TEM bright field image of the two-step annealed one, and (b) and (c) shows the EDX images of Cu and Co distribution in (Co,Cu)-rich TJP, respectively. In general, Nd-rich TJP is composed of Nd-Co-Cu-O. The EDX map shown in Fig. 4 revealed that Cu and Co are not mixed perfectly throughout the TJP but separated to form Cu- and Co-rich region with approximate at.% compositions of $Nd_{32.5}Co_{2.6}Cu_{30.2}O_{34.8}$ and $Nd_{32.9}Co_{39.4}Cu_{12.7}O_{13.7}$, respectively. On the other hand, the Cu- and Co-poor region (dark contrast in TJP) has the composition of $Nd_{44.3}Co_{0.25}Cu_{0.43}O_{51.2}$. In case of Co and Nd, the eutectic decomposition reaction can occur at ≈ 630 °C. Therefore, L↔ Nd + Nd_3Co eutectic reaction can occur during the 2nd

Table 1. Variation of Dy shell thickness with sintering temperature.

Sintering temperature (°C)	1040	1050	1060	1070
Shell thickness (μm)	0.96	1.14	1.48	1.57

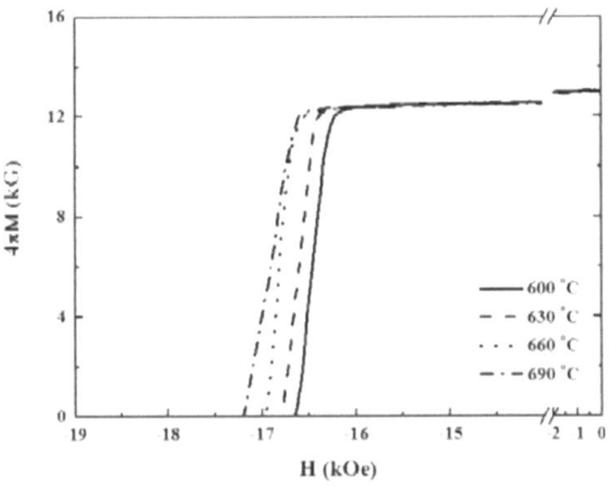

Fig. 3. Demagnetization curves of Dy-Co-alloy-added Nd-Fe-B magnets sintered at 1040 °C and annealed at different 1st PSA temperatures. The 2nd and 3rd PSA were done at 530 and 500 °C, respectively.

PSA. Because of this eutectic decomposition, the TJP has Co-rich region as well as Co-poor region. In case of Cu and Nd, however, the eutectic decomposition occurs at ≈ 500 °C; thus, there is no chance to form Cu-rich phase from eutectic reaction during the 2nd PSA. Also, Cu has no solubility to the main magnetic phase at the 2nd PSA temperature and Cu can move towards the Co-poor region resulting in the formation of Cu-rich phase [8].

The HRTEM images and selected area diffraction pattern (SADP) of Cu-rich TJP and Co-rich TJP regions are shown in Fig. 5(a) and (c), respectively. As shown in Fig 5(a), the Nd-oxide phase in Cu-rich TJP was found to be c-Nd_2O_3. This phase was stabilized when Cu segregation was more than 30 at. %, hence increasing the coercivity by reducing the interfacial lattice mismatch [8]. Fig. 5(b) shows the GBP area near Cu-segregated (Co,Cu)-rich TJP. The phase in this area was also found to be stable

Table 2. Magnetic properties of Dy-Co-alloy-added Nd-Fe-B sintered magnets processed in various annealing steps.

1st PSA (°C)	Number of PSA steps	B_r (kG)	$_iH_c$ (kOe)	$(BH)_{max}$ (MGOe)
600	3	13.0	16.7	41.0
	2	13.0	17.3	41.0
630	3	13.1	16.8	41.3
	2	13.1	17.5	41.3
660	3	13.1	17.0	41.3
	2	13.1	17.9	41.3
690	3	13.1	17.7	41.3
	2	13.1	18.5	41.3

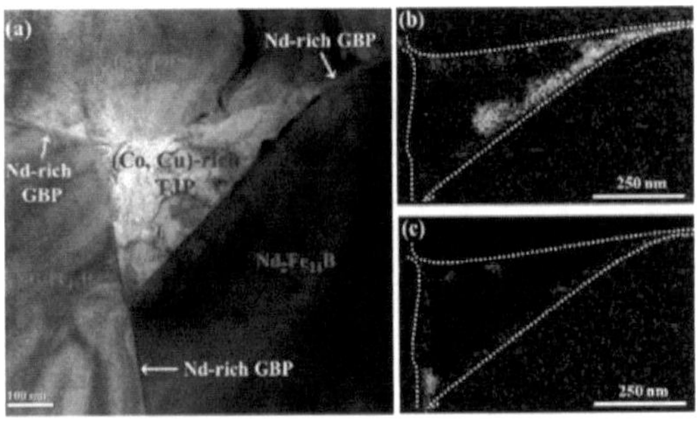

Fig. 4. (a) TEM bright field micrograph, (b) EDX Cu map at Nd-rich TJP and (c) EDX Co map at Nd-rich TJP of two-steps-annealed Nd-Fe-B sintered magnet mixed with Dy-Co alloy powder.

c-Nd_2O_3. The Co-segregated TJP and GBP were also found to be stable c-Nd_2O_3 phase as can be seen Fig. 5(c) and (d), respectively. The formation of stable c-Nd_2O_3 phase in TJP, although Co and Cu segregated separately in the TJP, seemed to be the main reason of the coercivity enhancement in two-step annealed magnets.

Fig. 6 shows TEM bright field and SADP images of Nd-rich TJP in the magnet annealed in three steps. The Co-rich region (marked A) and Cu-rich region (marked B) can be seen in this figure. The composition of Co-rich and Cu-rich regions was found to be approximately $Nd_{28.0}Co_{23.1}Cu_{8.0}O_{40.9}$ and $Nd_{17.1}Co_{0.5}Cu_{19.7}O_{62.7}$, respectively. Microstructure of three-step annealed magnets was found to be similar to the one in two-step annealed magnets. Separation of Co-rich and Cu-rich regions in TJP was also found in the three-step-annealed samples.

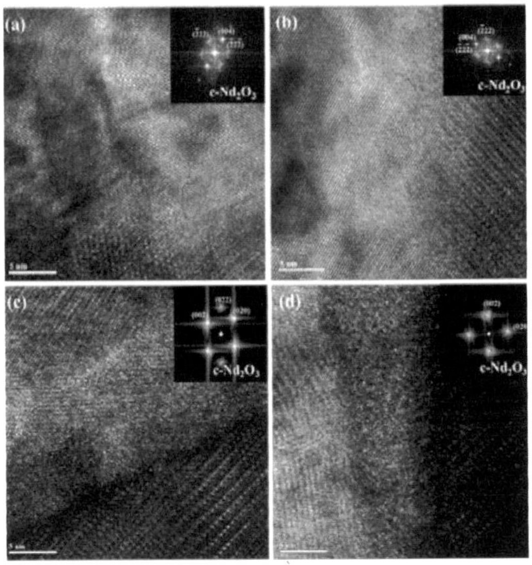

Fig. 5. HRTEM micrograph and corresponding SADP images of (a) Cu-rich TJP, (b) Cu-rich GBP, (c) Co-rich TJP, and (d) Co-rich GBP at Nd-rich TJP of a two-step-annealed Nd-Fe-B sintered magnet mixed with Dy-Co alloy powder.

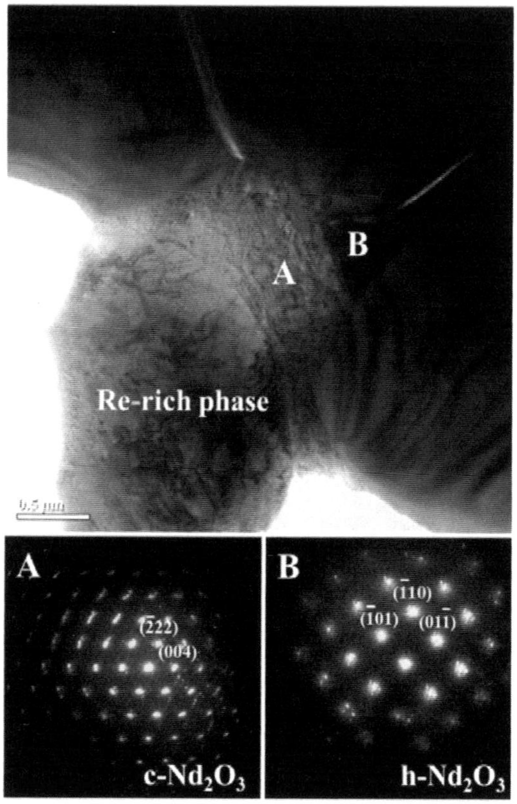

Fig. 6. TEM bright-field micrograph showing different contrast at Co-rich phase (region A) and Cu-rich phase (region B) at Nd-rich TJP of three-step-annealed Nd-Fe-B sintered magnet mixed with Dy-Co alloy.

However, the crystal structure analysis revealed that the Co-rich TJP was *c*-Nd_2O_3, but the Cu-rich TJP was *h*-Nd_2O_3 phase. The quantity of Co was found to be sufficient enough to stabilize the *c*-Nd_2O_3 phase in both annealing cases, although it was somewhat lower in region 'A' in three-step-annealed magnet (39.4 at.% in two-step-annealed one vs. 23.1 at. % in three-step- annealed one). The quantity of Cu segregation was also found to be lower in region 'B' in three-step- annealed magnet (30.2 at.% in two-step-annealed one vs. 19.7 at. % in three-step-annealed one). However, unlike Co, this was insufficient for the stabilization of the *c*-Nd_2O_3 phase, yielding the *h*-Nd_2O_3 phase. As mentioned above, separation of the Cu- and Co-rich phases occurred at Nd-rich TJP during the 2nd annealing. However, during the 3rd annealing at 500 °C, the eutectic reaction between Nd and Cu occurred again that led to further separation of Cu-rich and Cu-poor regions, which eventually took place Cu-poor regions in Nd-rich TJP. This phenomenon eventually deteriorated the microstructure in such way that was not beneficial for the coercivity enhancement.

4. Conclusion

The coercivity of Nd-Fe-B sintered magnet mixed with small Dy-Co alloy powder was increased from 17.4 kOe to 18.5 kOe after the optimization of sintering and annealing temperature as well as annealing steps without deterioration in remanence. The magnet sintered at 1040 °C and annealed in two steps at 690 °C and 530 °C exhibited higher coercivity due to the formation of uniform Dy-rich shell around magnetic grains and the stabilization of *c*-Nd_2O_3 phase in Cu-rich and Co-rich TJP. When the magnet was annealed further at 500 °C, the microstructure was deteriorated due to further separation of Cu, resulting in Cu-poor region in Nd-rich TJP thereby the formation of *h*-Nd_2O_3 phase in the TJP.

Acknowledgment
This work is supported by the Strategic Core Material Technology Development Program (No. 10043780) funded by the ministry of Trade, Industry and Energy (Korea) and the New and Renewable Energy of the Korea Institute of Energy Technology Evaluation and Planning (KETEP) funded by the Ministry of Knowledge Economy, Republic of Korea (No. 2011T100200304).

References

[1] K. Hirota, H. Nakumara, T. Minowa M. Honshima, *IEEE Trans. Magn.* **42**, 2006, 2909.
[2] M. Komuro, Y. Satsu, H. Suzuki, *IEEE Tans. Magn.* **46**, 2010, 3831.
[3] Y.C. Yang, W.J. James. X.D. Lo, H.Y. Chen, L.G. Xu, *IEEE Trans. Magn.* **22**, 1986, 757.
[4] K.H.J. Buschow, *J. Mater. Sci. Res.* **1**, 1986, 1.
[5] B. E. Davies, R. S. Mottram, I. R. Harris, *J. Mater. Chem. Phys.* **64**, 2001, 272.
[6] A. Kowalczyk, A. Wrzeciono, *J. Magn. Magn. Mater.* **74**, 1988, 260.
[7] W.F. Li, T. Ohkubo, T. Akiya, H. Kato, K. Hono, *J. Mater. Res.* **24**, 2009, 413.
[8] T.H. Kim, S.R. Lee, M.W. Lee, T.S. Jang, J.W. Kim. Y.D. Kim, H.J. Kim, *Acta Mater.* **66**, 2014, 12.

Temperature Dependence of Coercive Force Decrease Ratio in Nd-Fe-B Sintered Magnets

YUTAKA MATSUURA, NOBUYUKI KITAI, MITSUTOSHI NATSUMEDA, RINTARO ISHII, JUN HOSHIJIMA, FUTOSHI KUNIYOSHI
Hitachi Metals Ltd., 2-15-17 Egawa, Shimamoto-cho, Mishima-gun, Osaka, Japan 618-0013

Abstract: *We investigated the temperature dependence of coercive force decrease ratio of Nd-Fe-B sintered magnets from room temperature to 473K. The coercive force decrease ratios for aligned magnets gradually decreased as temperature increased and became close to the calculation results which were obtained from the alignment distribution of grains and by the postulation that every grain independently obeys the 1/ cos θ law.*

The temperature dependence of coercive force of a magnet of α = 0.95 alignment and without Dy quickly decreased compared with a magnet of α= 0.8. The coercive force decrease ratios of magnets with Dy required a higher temperature to reach the calculation results than those of magnets without Dy. These results mean that the pinning force depends on the alignment and the Dy content. It was also found that the temperature dependence of the coercive force decrease ratio co-relates with the temperature properties of the angular dependence of coercive force. Our experiments strongly suggest that the coercive force is determined by the domain wall motion accompanied by domain wall leaps through several grains with weak pinning sites.

Keywords: *magnet; permanent magnets; NdFeB sintered magnets; coercive force; coercive force mechanism*

1. Introduction

Motor applications such as traction motors for the hybrid electric vehicles and compressor motors for air conditioners must achieve high efficiency to reduce energy consumption and gas emissions, which are considered one of factors of climate change. Permanent magnets, especially Nd-Fe-B sintered magnets of very high performance, are considered key materials for achieving high efficiency in motor applications.

In these applications, magnets are subjected to a very high demagnetization field from the stator coil, and demagnetization might occur when the magnet is used in high temperatures. High coercive force materials are required to prevent demagnetization in these applications and many studies to improve coercive force are still continuing [1], [2]. In these studies, it is considered that the elucidation of the coercive force mechanism is also very important towards indicating how to improve the coercive force.

In our previous paper [3], we reported that the coercive force of Nd-Fe-B sintered magnets related to the alignment (α) of $Nd_2Fe_{14}B$ grains. As alignment improves, coercive force gradually decreases, and it is found that the coercive force steeply decreases in the high alignment area (α > 0.95). We also defined coercive force decrease ratio (β) as follows.

$$\beta = (H_{cJ} - H_{cJisotropy}) / H_{cJisotropy} \qquad (1)$$

H_{cJ} is the coercive force with various alignments, and $H_{cJisotropy}$ is the coercive force of an isotropically aligned magnet.

From the alignment distribution of magnetization and the angular dependence of coercive force, it is expected that the magnetic domain wall motion model qualitatively explains our empirical data on the relation between alignment and coercive force decrease ratio [3].

But, the calculation results, using the alignment distributions obtained by electron back scattered diffraction (EBSD) and the postulation that every grain independently obeys the 1/cos θ law [4], differ considerably from the empirical data of coercive force decrease ratio shown in Fig. 1 [5].

It is considered that this difference comes from our speculation, and it could be solved if we postulate that the magnetic domain wall is pinned at a strong

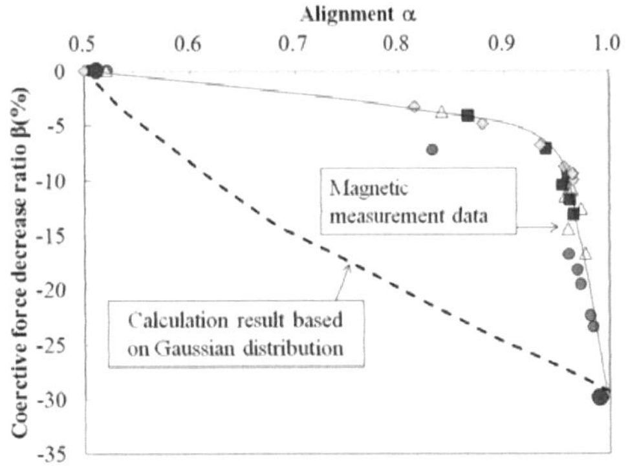

Fig. 1. Relation between alignment and coercive force decrease ratio. [3] Dotted line is the calulation results based on the Gaussian distribution and 1/cos θ law [5].

pinning site existing in grains tilted from easy magnetization direction. Using this speculation, it is expected that the coercive force is determined, when the magnetic domain wall jumps through several grains with weak pinning sites after the magnetic domain wall de-pinned from a strong pinning site.

These speculations could be proven by checking the temperature dependence of coercive force decrease ratio.

2. Experiment

Magnets of several different compositions were made by powder metallurgical method. Alloys were made by strip casting and crushed to 3 - 5 μm. The powder was pressed into different magnetic fields to make magnets of different alignment, then sintered at 1350 K. The sintered magnets were heat-treated at 773 K for coercive force enhancement.

The alignment of these magnets was evaluated from the alignment distribution obtained by electron back scattered diffraction (EBSD).

Compositions of $Nd_{13.48}B_{5.76}Co_{0.55}Fe_{bal.}$ for magnets without Dy and $Nd_{12.75}Dy_{0.84}B_{5.81}Co_{0.55}Fe_{bal.}$ for magnets with Dy were used to determine the temperature dependence of the coercive force decrease ratio.

Coercive force was measured by permeameter at room temperature. For elevated temperatures, a permeameter with a magnetic circuit was installed in an oven. Demagnetization was measured at room temperature, 313 K, 333 K, 353 K, 373 K, 393 K, 413 K, 433 K, 453 K and 473K for magnets without Dy and at room temperature, 333 K, 373 K, 413 K and 453 K for magnets with Dy. We also measured the temperature properties of the angular dependence of coercive force of $Nd_{14.33}B_{6.20}Co_{1.00}Fe_{bal.}$ to compare with the coercive force decrease ratio. Samples are embedded in glass as shown in Fig. 2, and are measured at 296 K, 333 K, 373 K and 413 K using a permeameter.

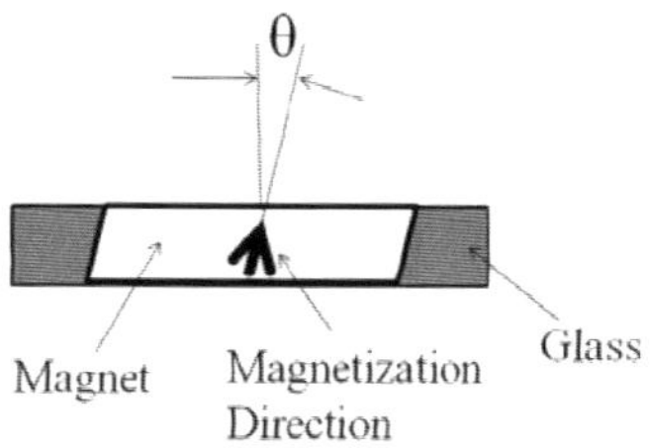

Fig. 2. Magnet samples used for the angular dependence of coercive force. Magnets were cut from a block magnet at different angles,

3. Results and Discussion

Figure 3 shows the temperature dependence of coercive force for magnets without Dy and of different alignments; an isotropically aligned magnet (α = 0.5) and aligned magnets (α = 0.8, α = 0.95). As temperature rises, the coercive forces of these magnets monotonically decrease, and the difference of coercive force between the istotropically aligned magnet and the aligned magnets also decreases.

It is well known that the temperature dependence of coercive force relates to the temperature properties of the anisotropy field (H_A) and the saturation magnetization (J_s) of $Nd_2Fe_{14}B$ compound [6,7]. From equation (1), it was expected that the temperature dependence of coercive force decrease ratio would be small because the magnets used in this experiment have the same composition, and the temperature dependence of H_A and J_s cancelled out. Figure 4 shows the temperature dependence of coercive force decrease ratio. As temperature increases, the coercive force decrease ratio steeply decreases from room temperature and gradually decreases in high temperatures. And, it was found that the coercive force decrease ratio of the magnet with high alignment (α = 0.95) decreased quickly compared with the magnet of low alignment (α = 0.8).

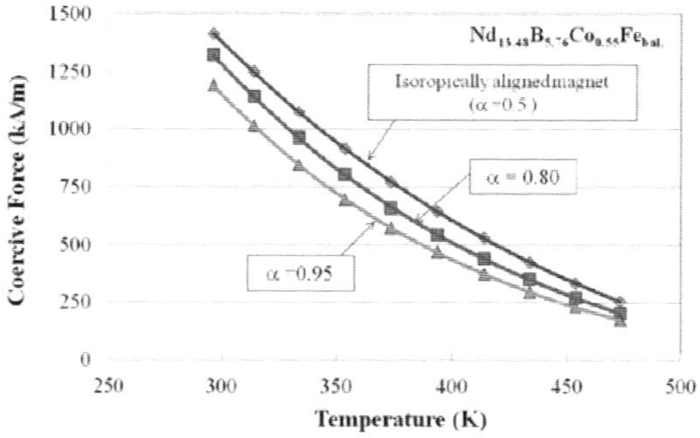

Fig. 3. Temperature dependence of coercive force of isotropically oriented magnets of 0.8 and 0.95 alignment.

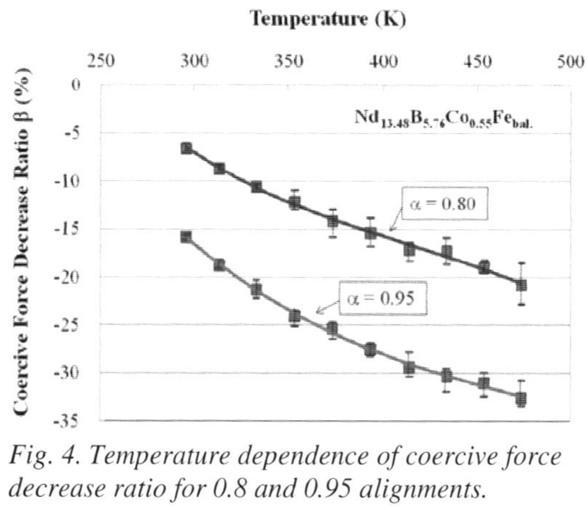

Fig. 4. Temperature dependence of coercive force decrease ratio for 0.8 and 0.95 alignments.

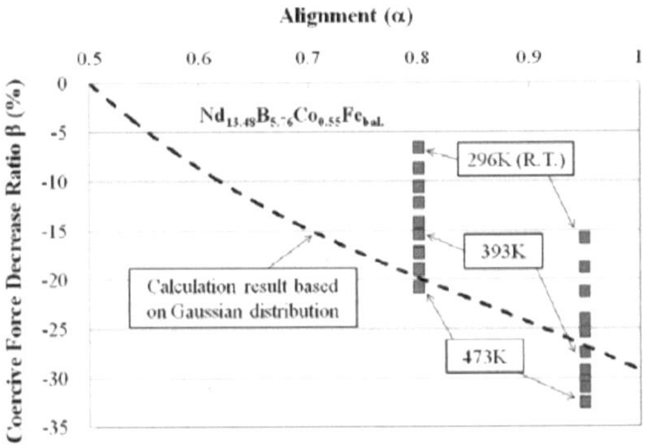

Fig. 5. Relation between alignment and coercive force decrease ratio of $Nd_{13.48}B_{5.76}Co_{0.55}Fe_{bal.}$ at various temperatures.

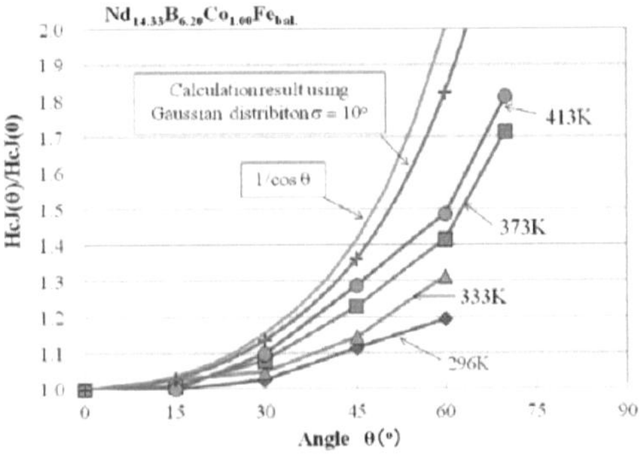

Fig. 7. Temperature properties of the angular dependence of coercive force.

Figure 5 shows the alignment dependence of coercive force decrease ratio of the magnet without Dy at various temperatures. From this figure, it was found that the coercive force decrease ratios of various alignments decreased and became close to the calculation results as temperature increased. The coercive force decrease ratio of the magnet with α = 0.95 reached the calculation results around 393 K. But, the magnet with α = 0.8 reached the calculation around 473 K.

Figure 6 shows the temperature dependence of coercive force decrease ratio for the magnet with Dy. The coercive force decrease ratio of this magnet has a similar temperature dependence to the magnet without Dy except for the temperature which it reached the calculation results.

If we presume that there exists a pinning force which depends on the alignment and Dy content, and the pinning force decreases as temperature rise, the discrepancy in coercive force decrease ratio between the calculation and the magnetic measurement at room temperature could be reasonably explained.

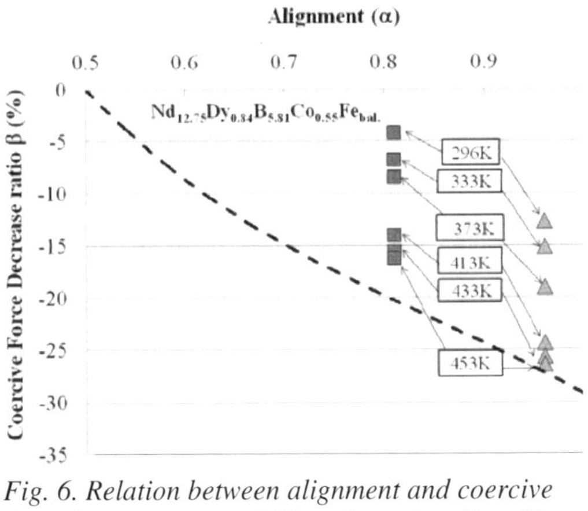

Fig. 6. Relation between alignment and coercive force decrease ratio of $Nd_{12.75}Dy_{0.84}B_{5.81}Co_{0.55}Fe_{bal.}$ at various temperatures.

This data on the magnet without Dy and the magnet with Dy strongly suggests that the coercive force of Nd-Fe-B sintered magnets was determined by the magnetic domain wall motion accompanied with the domain wall leap through grains with weak pinning force. And, the leap of the magnetic domain wall at elevated temperatures is shorter than that of room temperature. In other words, the number of reverse grains by the magnetic domain wall leap becomes smaller and smaller as temperature increases.

Fig. 7. shows the temperature properties of the angular dependence of coercive force of $Nd_{14.33}B_{6.20}Co_{1.00}Fe_{bal.}$. The angular dependence is temperature dependent and it is close to 1/cos θ as temperature increases, which is similar to the temperature dependence of the coercive force decrease ratio. It seems that the temperature dependence of coercive force decrease ratio co-relates with the temperature properties of the angular dependence of coercive force decrease ratio.

References

[1] H. Nakamura, K. Hirota, M. Shimao, T. Minowa, M. Honshima, *IEEE Trans. Magn.* **41**, 2005, 3844.
[2] T. Yamazaki, R. Muraoka, K, Nakajima, H. Hasegawa, in: *Proc. Autumn Conf. Jpn. Soc. Powder Powder Metallurgy*, 2013, 79.
[3] Y. Matsuura, J. Hoshijima, R. Ishii, *J. Magn. Magn. Mater.* **336**, 2013, 88.
[4] E. Kondorskii, *Comptes Rendus (Doklady) de l'Academie des Scieces de l'URSS* **15**, 1937, 457.
[5] Y. Matsuura, N. Kitai, R. Ishii, M. Natsumeda, J. Hoshijima, *J. Magn. Magn. Mater.* **346**, 2013, 113.
[6] D. Givord, P. Tenaud and T. Viadieu, *IEEE Trans. Magn.* **24**, 1988, 1921.
[7] H. Kronmueller, K. D. Dust, M. Sagawa, *J. Magn. Magn. Mater.* **74**, 1988, 291.

Optimum Hard-Soft Geometries: Science, Wishful Thinking, and Technology

R. SKOMSKI
University of Nebraska, Lincoln, NE 68508.

Abstract: *The geometrical optimization of aligned hard-soft nanocomposites is investigated by model calculations and analyzed in the context of industrial permanent magnetism. Physically transparent analytical solutions in terms of Bessel functions $J_{d/2-1}$ are obtained for hyperspherical soft inclusions. This includes layers (d = 1), cylinders (d = 2), and spheres (d = 3), as well as extruded hyperspheres, such as cuboids, and geometries with free soft surfaces. Embedded soft cubes exhibit a volume-fraction enhancement of 91% compared to embedded soft spheres, with a coercivity reduction of only 25%. Considering nucleation field and the volume fraction of the soft phase, we find that soft-magnetic cubes and long rods with square cross section are most promising from the viewpoint of energy product. Practical limitations arise from the need to actually produce the optimized structures — the corresponding challenges are well-understood but difficult to overcome in practice.*

Keywords: *nucleation field; hard-soft composites; coercivity; energy product*

Address: Ralph Skomski, Department of Physics and Astronomy and Nebraska Center for Materials and Nanoscience, University of Nebraska, Lincoln, NE 68588, E-mail: rskomski@neb.rr.com

1. Introduction

Geometrical optimization is an important aspect of the ongoing research on *c*-axis aligned hard-soft nanostructures for permanent magnets. The aim is to enhance magnetization and energy product by adding nanoscale soft regions without destroying the coercivity [1,3,5]. This requires the sacrifice of excess anisotropy to enhance magnetization and energy product beyond that of the hard phase [1-5], up to an upper limit of about 1000 kJ/m^3, or twice the value achievable in $Nd_2Fe_{14}B$. There are various experimental proofs of principle [6,7], but progress towards an industrial magnets has been demanding, and the search for optimum geometries is one aspect of this challenge.

In 1991, Kneller and Hawig [1] used layered structures to outline the positive effect of aligned hard-soft nanostructuring and to establish that the soft-phase regions cannot be much larger than twice the Bloch-wall width of the hard phase, $\delta_h = \pi (A/K_h)^{1/2}$ [1-3], The underlying micromagnetics of layered two-phase structures was well understood at that time, due to earlier papers by Goto *et al.* [8], Kronmüller [9], and Nieber and Kronmüller [10]. While δ_h has been confirmed as the dimensionality-independent length scale for effective hard-soft interactions [3], this does not mean that geometry effects are unimportant, and nucleation-field variations by factors of up to 16 have been calculated for several simple geometries [11].

The corresponding geometrical optimization or "rational design" of three-dimensional hard-soft nanostructures was initiated by Skomski in 1992 [2] and by Skomski and Coey in 1993 [3]. The calculations on spherical soft inclusions [2] were soon followed by several articles on a variety of geometries and limits, such as embedded soft cylinders [11-13], embedded soft cubes [14], disordered nanostructures [3,12,13], and interacting soft regions [12,13]. This predominantly analytic research complements analytical and numerical calculations by other groups, for example on granular nanocomposites [15] and core-shell-structures [16]. The geometrical optimization has recently attracted renewed attention due to the recent rare-earth supply bottlenecks [11,17].

2. Shape and Size of Soft Regions

The simplest nontrivial approach to the geometry of hard-soft composites is to embed the soft regions in a very hard matrix [2,3]. Figure 1 shows some basic geometries.

As derived elsewhere [3,14,18], the coercivity can be estimated by solving the differential equation for the nucleation field H_N

$$- A \nabla^2\phi + K_1(\mathbf{r})\,\phi + \tfrac{1}{2}\,\mu_0 M_0\, H_N\,\phi = 0, \qquad (1)$$

subject to the appropriate boundary conditions. In this equation, A is the exchange stiffness, $K_1(\mathbf{r})$ is the local anisotropy constant ($K_1 = 0$ in the soft phase), M_0 the local saturation magnetization and $\phi(\mathbf{r}) \sim m(\mathbf{r})$ is the nucleation mode, that is, the angle ϕ between magnetization and *c*-axis, or alternatively the magnetization deviation $\mathbf{m} = \mathbf{M} - M_0\,\mathbf{e}_z$. In the hard-

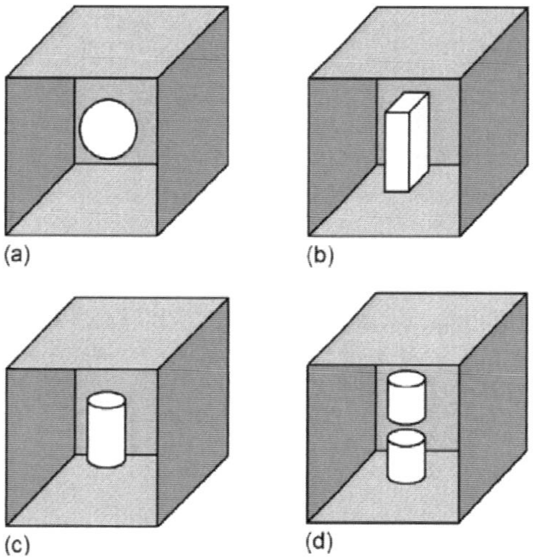

Fig. 1. Some soft-in-hard geometries: (a) embedded sphere, (b) embedded cuboid, (c) embedded cylinder, and (d) interacting soft regions. Dark and bright gray denote hard and soft regions, respectively, and the aspect ratios of the cuboids (a:b:c) and cylinders (L:R) can assume arbitrary values.

magnetic limit considered in this section, the solutions of Eq. (1) are the Bessel functions $J_p(x)$, so that

$$\phi(r) = r^{1-d/2}\, J_{d/2-1}(\kappa r) \qquad (2)$$

For half-integer order p, that is, for odd dimensionalities, the Bessel functions are analytical: $\phi(r) \sim \cos(\kappa r)$ for layers (d =1) and $\phi(r) \sim \sin(\kappa r)/r$ for spheres (d = 3). By separation of variables, it is also possible to treat extruded geometries, such as cylinders of finite aspect ratios $\xi = L/2R$:

$$H_N = \frac{2A}{\mu_o M_s R^2}\,(c_2^{\,2} + \pi^2/4\xi^2) \qquad (3)$$

where c_2 = 2.4048 is the first zero of the "two-dimensional" Bessel function $J_o(\kappa r)$. For rectangular cuboids of volume $a \times b \times c$,

$$H_N = \frac{2A}{\mu_o M_s}\,(1/a^2 + 1/b^2 + 1/c^2) \qquad (4)$$

This includes the limits of thin films ($a = b = \infty$, $c = t$) and cubes ($a = b = c$).

Relative to embedded spheres, this method yields nucleation-field reductions by factors of 3/4 (embedded cubes), 1/2 (embedded wires with square cross section), and 1/4 (embedded layers). Free soft-magnetic surfaces, as in Fig. 2(b), are particularly harmful to the nucleation field, as explained in the caption of Fig. 2.

3. Volume Fraction of the Soft Phase

To optimize the permanent-magnet performance, it is important to maximize the volume fraction of the soft phase without having soft regions too far away from the hard phase. The volume fraction of the soft phase is limited by nucleation-mode delocalization [13]. Figure 2 compares different surface and delocalization effects. The delocalization mechanism, where the nucleation mode tunnels through the hard phase like an electron through a potential barrier, is unrelated to the geometrical connectivity and to the percolation behavior of the soft phase. For example, when two

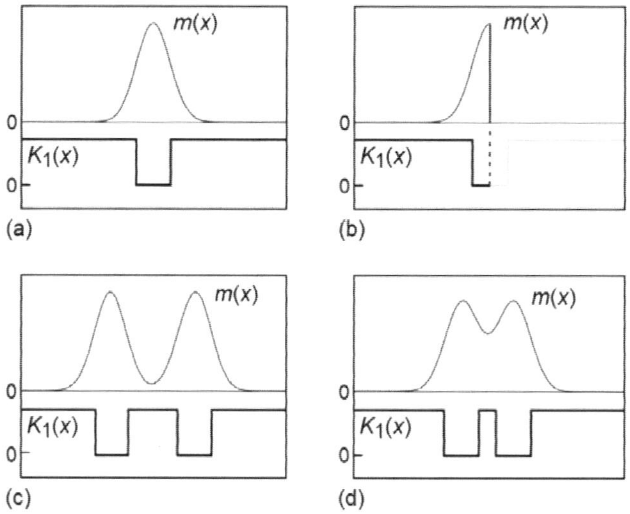

Fig. 2. Surface and interaction effects: (a) soft-in-hard inclusion, (b) surface, (c) weakly interacting soft regions, and (d) strongly interacting soft regions with emerging nucleation-mode delocalization. The modes of (a) and (b) are micromagnetically equivalent, because $\nabla m(r) = 0$ in both cases. This meaning that the nucleation field $H_N \sim 1/t^2$ of an embedded layer of thickness t is four times as big as that of a layer having the same thickness but a free surface [11].

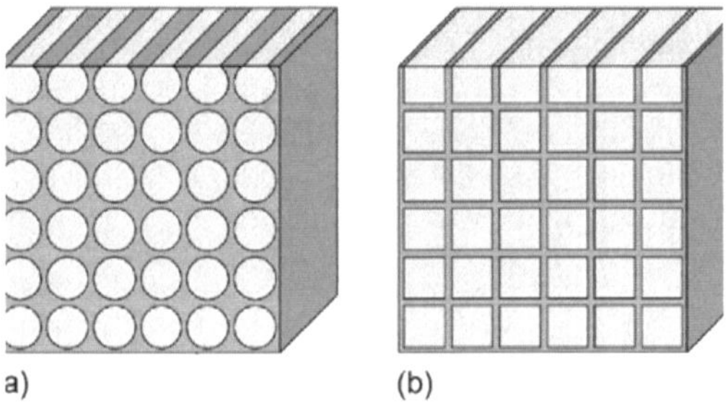

Fig. 3. Schematic hard-soft geometries: (a) embedded spheres and (b) embedded cubes.

cylinders of aspect ratio 1.3 are moved together, as schematically shown in Fig. 1(d), the relative nucleation field continuously decreases from a value 1 (infinite distance) to 0.878 when the two cylinder touch (zero distance).

Embedded soft cubes are more promising than embedded soft spheres, because they waste less "dead" hard-magnetic volume distant from the soft phase. Straight-forward comparison of the volumes of cubes and spheres yield a volume-fraction factor $6/\pi$ = 1.91 in favor of the embedded cubes. On the downside, the coercivity of cubic inclusions is somewhat reduced compared to spherical inclusions, by 25% according to the analysis of Sect. 2.

A similar analysis comparing embedded long rods with square and circular cross sections, Fig. 3, shows that f increases by a factor $4/\pi = 1.273$, whereas H_N decreases by a factor $\pi^2/2c_2^2 = 0.852$. Note that isolated long wires (f < 15%) of any cross-section geometry show a substantial coercivity enhancement due to shape anisotropy [17], but this enhancement diminishes as f increases [11,19].

4. Magnetostatic Effects

Equation (1) is exact in the limit of very fine-grained hard magnets ($K_1 \gg \mu_0 M_s^2/4$) but cannot incorporate magnetostatic effects beyond the introduction of effective "shape" anisotropies K_{eff} and effective interaction fields H_{eff} [14]. The magnetostatic self-interaction energy is an integral involving $\mathbf{M}(\mathbf{r})\,\mathbf{M}(\mathbf{r}')\,dV\,dV'$. If the magnet is very inhomogeneous, then the regions around $\mathbf{r}$ and $\mathbf{r}'$ switch at different points on the hysteresis loop, making it possible to define an interaction field by integration over dV'. If $\mathbf{M}(\mathbf{r}) \approx \mathbf{M}(\mathbf{r}')$, then the integration is effectively over $\mathbf{M}(\mathbf{r})^2$, thereby establishing a $K_{eff}(\mathbf{r})$.

In reality, K_{eff} and H_{eff} are not sufficient to describe the magnetostatic interaction. Figure 4 uses a simple two-spin model to explain the reason. The model [18,20,21] has only two magnetic degrees of freedom, namely two rotation angles about a common axis. Magnetostatically, it favors an antiparallel (↑↓) spin configuration (d), in close analogy to compass needles located side by side. On the other hand, exchange tries to keep the spins parallel, as in (a) and (c).

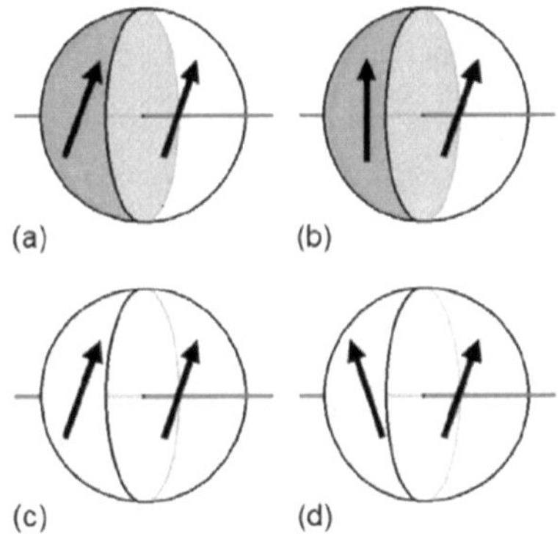

Fig. 4. Nanoscale magnetization reversal: (a) coherent rotation in a two-phase particle, (b) localized nucleation in a two-phase particle, (c) coherent rotation in a single-phase particle, and (d) rudimentary "curling" in a single-phase particle.

As the feature size increases, there is a transition from a cooperative or "military" regime (a) with effective anisotropy to a noncooperative or "civilian" regime (b) where each region behaves differently and experiences a local interaction field. However, curling or "vortex" states [22-24], realized as (d) in the model, cannot be described by effective parameters H_{eff} and K_{eff}.

5. Wishful Thinking and Technology

The practical realization of aligned hard-soft nano-structures is demanding, because structures such as those shown in Figs. 1 and 3 are extremely difficult to produce. In fact, creating a powerful nanocomposite permanent magnet by simply mixing hard and soft powders is not possible. Imperfections of all kinds, including big soft regions, act as nucleation centers and reduce nucleation field, coercivity, and energy product. This real-structure dependence of the coercivity, also known as "Brown's paradox" [22,23], is not a failure of theory but an indicator of our limited knowledge about real-structure defects in real materials [23]. Furthermore, even advanced numerical simulation methods [15] are not able to treat magnets having sizes larger than a few μm.

As the volume fraction of the soft phase increases, the coercivity tends to break down rapidly. The main reasons are nucleation-mode delocalization (Fig. 2) and the difficult-to-control size of the soft regions. The term "incomplete exchange coupling", occasionally applied to two-phase hysteresis loops caused by big soft regions, is somewhat unfortunate. In fact, the hard-soft interface exchange is usually assumed to be perfect, and even moderately reduced exchange has little or no effect on the hysteresis loops [14]. Two-phase loops only arise if the interface exchange is zero or negative (AFM), as it is sometimes the case for Fe-rich atomic environments [18,25].

Concerning the *choice of materials*, the effective range of the hard-soft exchange scales as $(A/K_h)^{1/2}$, so that "semihard" materials with reduced K_h, such as MnBi and MnAl, can be nanostructured on a somewhat larger length scale. At fixed length scale, this mechanism improves the Kronmüller factor α by a factor scaling as $1/K_h^{1/2}$, but this gain is normally outweighed by the reduction in the anisotropy field K_h. However, nanostructuring is a complicated technology, and gains in length scale may be beneficial in some cases, for example at high temperatures, where K_h is relatively small.

Note that this paper focuses on magnets where the *c*-axes of the hard phases are *aligned*, as contrasted to isotropic magnets. While the latter promise less high energy products, because the hard phase does not fully contribute to the magnetization, isotropic two-phase nanostructures such as $Nd_2Fe_{14}B$:Fe [26-28] are much easier to produce. Two-phase magnets with *c*-axis alignment are usually only partially *c*-axis aligned or "textured", but such magnets are physically closer to fully aligned magnets [14,29]. For example, in the limit of very small grain sizes, the average anisotropy $\langle K \rangle$ of isotropic magnets becomes zero [30], whereas those of partially aligned magnets remain comparable to K_1 [29].

6. Conclusions

In summary, we have investigated how the performance of aligned hard-soft nanocomposites depends on nanogeometry. Approximate but physically transparent model results have been obtained for a variety of soft-phase geometries. High volume fractions of the soft phase, as required for substantially enhanced energy products, yield a coercivity reduction due to micromagnetic delocalization, as contrasted to percolation. The best geometries are embedded soft cubes and wires with square cross section, but such structures are particularly difficult to produce.

Acknowledgment
This work has benefitted from discussions with B. Balamurugan, J. Cui, G. C. Hadjipanayis, S. J. Jiang, L. H. Lewis, J. P. Liu, P. Manchanda, T. Rana, D. J. Sellmyer, J. E. Shield, and I. Takeuchi. This research is supported by PNNL ARPA-E, Argonne ARPA-E, and BREM.

References

[1] E. F. Kneller and R. Hawig, *IEEE Trans. Magn.* **27**,1991, 3588.
[2] R. Skomski, *Phys. Status Solidi (b)* **174**, 1992, K77.
[3] R. Skomski and J. M. D. Coey, *Phys. Rev. B* **48**, 1993, 15812.
[4] E. E. Fullerton, S. J. Jiang, and S. D. Bader, *J. Magn. Magn. Mater.* **200**, 1999, 392.
[5] N. Jones, *Nature* **472**, 2011, 22.
[6] P. Liu, C. P. Luo, Y. Liu, and D. J. Sellmyer, *Appl. Phys. Lett.* **72**, 1998, 483.
[7] D. Roy and P. S. Anil Kumar, *J. Appl. Phys.* **106**, 2009, 073902.
[8] E. Goto, N. Hayashi, T. Miyashita, and K. Nakagawa, *J. Appl. Phys.* **36**, 1965, 2951.
[9] H. Kronmüller, *Phys. Status Solidi (b)* **144**, 1987, 385.
[10] S. Nieber and H. Kronmüller, *Phys. Status Solidi (b)* ***153***, 1989, 367.
[11] R. Skomski, P. Manchanda, P. Kumar, B. Balamurugan, A. Kashyap, and D. J. Sellmyer, *IEEE Trans. Magn.* **49**, 2013, 3215.
[12] R. Skomski and J. M. D. Coey, *IEEE Trans. Magn.* **30**, 1994, 607.
[13] R. Skomski, *J. Appl. Phys.* **83**, 1998, 6503.
[14] R. Skomski, *J. Phys.: Condens. Matter* 15, 2003, R841.
[15] T. Schrefl and J. Fidler, *J. Appl. Phys.* **83**, 1998, 6262.
[16] A. Szlaferek, *Phys. Status Solidi (b)* **241**, 2004, 1312.
[17] J. S. Jiang and S. D. Bader, *J. Phys.: Condens. Matter* **26**, 2014, 064214.
[18] R. Skomski and J. M. D. Coey, *Permanent Magnetism*, Institute of Physics, Bristol, 1999.
[19] R. Skomski, Y. Liu, J. E. Shield, G. C. Hadjipanayis, and D. J. Sellmyer, *J. Appl. Phys.* **107**, 2010, 09A739.
[20] J.P. Liu, R. Skomski, Y. Liu, and D.J. Sellmyer, *J. Appl. Phys.* **87**, 2000, 6740.
[21] J. Lyubina, K.-H. Müller, M. Wolf, and U. Hannemann, *J. Magn. Magn. Mater.* **322**, 2010, 2948.
[22] W.F. Brown, *Micromagnetics*, Wiley, New York 1963.
[23] A. Aharoni, *Rev. Mod. Phys.* **34**, 1962, 227.
[24] R. Skomski, J.-P. Liu, and D. J. Sellmyer, *Phys. Rev. B* **60**, 1999, 7359.
[25] Y. Toga, H. Moriya, H. Tsuchiura, and A. Sakuma, *J. Phys.: Conf. Ser.* ***266***, 2011, 012046.
[26] R. Coehoorn, D. B. de Mooij, J. P. W. B. Duchateau, and K. H. J. Buschow, *J. Phys.* **49**, 1988, C-8 669.
[27] J. Schneider, D. Eckert, K.-H. Müller, A. Handstein, H. Mühlbach, H. Sassik, and H. R. Kirchmayr, *Mater. Lett.* **9**, 1990, 201.
[28] A. Manaf, R. A. Buckley, H. A. Davies, *J. Magn. Magn. Mater.* **128**, 1993, 302.
[29] R. Skomski, *J. Magn. Magn. Mater.* **157-158**, 1996, 713.
[30] G. Herzer, *J. Magn. Magn. Mater.* **112**, 1992, 258.

Micromagnetic Approaches to Future Magnets - $SmCo_5$ /α-Fe Nanocomposite Magnets

H. FUKUNAGA, R. HORIKAWA, T. YANAI, M. NAKANO
Graduate School of Engineering, Nagasaki University, Bunkyo-machi 1-14, Nagasaki 852-8521, Japan

Abstract: *Magnetic properties of $SmCo_5$ /α-Fe nanocomposite magnets with core-shell structure and layered structures were computer-simulated at 300 K and 470 K. The achievable (BH)max values of anisotropic $SmCo_5$/α-Fe magnets were approximately 800 kJ/m^3 at 300 K and 700 kJ/m^3 at 473 K, while extremely fine nanostructures were needed for obtaining the above values. The achievable $(BH)_{max}$ value at 473 K was much higher than that for $Nd_2Fe_{14}B$/α-Fe magnets. The consideration for the magnetic hardness and thermal agitation limited the achievable $(BH)_{max}$ to 670 kJ/m^3 at 300 K and 570 kJ/m^3 at 473 K, and revealed that a nanostructure with the size of approximately 10 nm is a suitable size for good magnetic properties. In spite of these limitations, $SmCo_5$/α-Fe magnets are still expected to have clear advantage over Nd-Fe-B-based magnets at 473K. For isotropic magnets with a layered structure, the calculated $(BH)_{max}$ values were approximately 300 and 250 kJ/m^3 at 300 and 473 K, respectively.*

Keywords: *$SmCo_5$, nanocomposite; core-shell; layered structure; micromagnetics; $(BH)_{max}$, high temperature*

Address: Hirotoshi Fukunaga, Graduate School of Engineering, Nagasaki University, Nagasaki 852-8512, Japan, TEL/FAX: +81-95-819-2552, E-mail: fukunaga@nagasaki-u.ac.jp

1. Introduction

High performance permanent magnets usable at a high temperature have increased in importance. As the coercivity of Nd-Fe-B magnets decreases drastically at a high temperature, an increase in coercivity of Nd-Fe-B has been investigated intensively, and several methods such as the segregation $Nd_2Fe_{14}B$ grains [1], the Dy diffusion in grains boundary phases [2, 3], and the refinement of grain size [4] have been reported.

On the other hand, Sm-Co-based magnets are also expected as high performance magnets usable at a high temperature [5] because of their high Curie temperatures [6]. Thus, a Sm-Co/α-Fe nano-composite magnet is a good candidate for a high performance magnet for use at a high temperature. The high magneto-crystalline anisotropy of Sm-Co alloys enables the presence of a large amount of α-Fe in the magnet while necessitating a small grain size [7, 8]. Therefore, the microstructural design is an important issue in developing Sm-Co/α-Fe magnets. First-principle calculations have been reported on effects of microstructure on magnetic properties of Sm-Co/α-Fe powders and layered structures [9-12]. The temperature dependence of H_c for the $SmCo_5$/ Sm_2Co_{17} magnets also has been calculated [13].

The synthesis of isotropic and anisotropic Sm-Co/α-Fe nanocomposite magnets has been reported [14-20]. For anisotropic $SmCo_5$/α-Fe multi-layered films, $(BH)_{max}$ values exceeding the theoretical limit of $SmCo_5$ have been achieved [15,19]. A small temperature coefficient of H_c, approximately −0.3%/K, has been also reported for a Sm-Co/α-Fe multi-layered thick film-magnet [14]. These results suggest the importance of Sm-Co/α-Fe nanocomposite magnets, and the clarification of potential of these magnets is needed for further investigations.

The present contribution focused on $SmCo_5$/α-Fe nanocomposites with core-shell and layered structures. The former structure is a suitable for preparation of bulk magnets and the latter one is for control of a nanostructure. In this contribution, their potentials at 300 and 470 K were computer-simulated based on the miciromagnetics, and the results were discussed in terms of the magnetic hardness and the comparison of the magnetic anisotropy energy with thermal agitation energy.

2. Calculation Model and Method

We assumed the cubic particle with a core-shell structure and the layered structure illustrated in Fig.1. The model core-shell structure of size L (Fig.1 (a)) was composed of anisotropic $SmCo_5$ and isotropic α-Fe parts. The layered structure (Fig.1 (b)) is composed of $SmCo_5$ and α-Fe layers stacked periodically. In the calculation, the total thickness L of $SmCo_5$ and α-Fe layers (the stacking period) was kept constant and the ratio of $SmCo_5$ thickness to

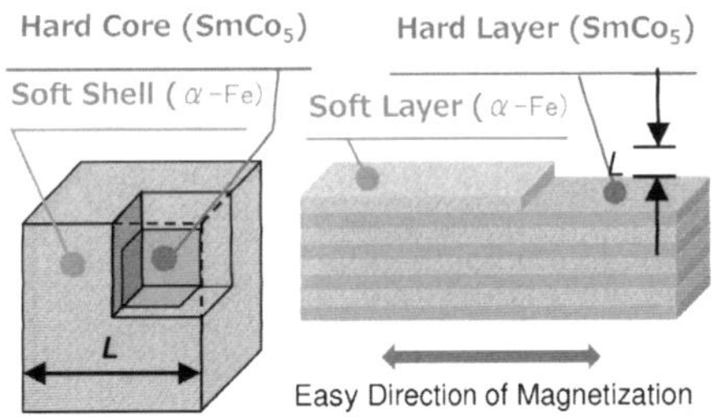

(a) Core-Shell Structure (b) Layered Structure
Fig.1 Simulation Models.

TABLE I SIMULATION PARAMETERS.

	$SmCo_5$		α-Fe	
Temperature T [K]	300	473	300	473
Anisotropy constant K_u [MJ/m^3]	10.0	6.80	0.00	0.00
Saturation Polarization M_s [T]	1.00	0.95	2.15	2.09
Exchange stiffness constant A [×10^{-11} J/m]	1.20	1.09	2.50	2.36
Exchange constant J_{sh} at 300 K [J/m^2]	1.0×10^{-3}			

α-Fe one was varied. In anisotropic magnets, the in-plane uniaxial magnetic anisotropy was assumed for the $SmCo_5$ layer, and an external field was applied in the easy direction of magnetization. The calculation region ($L\times L\times L$) was divided into 32768 cubic elements, and periodic boundary conditions were adopted in three directions so that infinitely large magnets were assumed.

Table I shows the assumed simulation parameters at 300 K and 473 K. The parameters at 300 K were taken from Ref. 6. The saturation polarization M_s and the magnetic anisotropy constant K_u for $SmCo_5$ at 473 K and M_s for α-Fe at 473 K estimated from the declination of the curves indicated in references [21], [22], and [23], respectively. The exchange constant A at 300 K was also taken from Ref.6, and the constants at 473 K were estimated by using the following equation [24]

$$A = cM_s(T)^2 . \tag{1}$$

The exchange constant J_{sh} at the interface between $SmCo_5$ and α-Fe is not known, so a value of 1.0x10^{-3} J/m^2 was assumed, which is approximately two thirds of the value for the Fe–Fe interface [25].

The total magnetic energy W stored in the model magnet when an external field $\boldsymbol{H}$ is applied is given as

$$W = K_u^{(H)}V\sum_{i=1}^{N^3}\left\{\frac{K_{ui}}{K_u^{(H)}}(\mathbf{u}_i\cdot\mathbf{m}_i)^2 - \sum_{j=1}^{6}\left[\frac{J_{eij}S}{6K_u^{(H)}V}(\mathbf{m}_i\cdot\mathbf{m}_j)\right] - \frac{M_{si}}{K_u^{(H)}}(\mathbf{m}_i\cdot\mathbf{H})\right\} + W_m, \tag{2}$$

where the subscriptions i and j denote the numbers of the corresponding elements. W_m represents the magnetostatic energy due to a local demagnetizing field. N is the total number of elements, while S and V are the surface area and volume of each element, respectively. Furthermore, $\boldsymbol{u}_i$ and $\boldsymbol{m}_i$ are unit-vectors in the directions of the easy axis of magnetization and polarization, respectively, in the ith element.

The intra-phase exchange interaction constant J_{ss} or J_{hh} was calculated from the exchange stiffness constant A for α-Fe or $SmCo_5$ under the assumption that the element size δD is sufficiently small, as

$$J_{eii} = A_{ii} / \delta D . \tag{3}$$

The stable directions of magnetization under a given applied field were determined by rotating magnetization in each element so as to diminish magnetic torque acting upon the magnetization. Hysteresis loops were traced by changing an applied field in magnitude. Details of the calculation method were reported elsewhere [8].

3. Calculation Results for Anisotropic Magnets

3.1. Magnetic Properties at 300 K

Demagnetization curves of particles with a core-shell structure are shown in Fig.2. Those for the particles with the α-Fe core and $SmCo_5$ shell structure are also shown as a reference. The fraction of α-Fe was kept at approximately 50%. The magnetic properties of both models significantly depended on L. When L was larger than 10 nm, magnetization reversal occurred incoherently. The incoherent magnetization reversals for the α-Fe core structure tended to be more remarkable than those for the $SmCo_5$ core structure. This phenomenon is explained by the fact that the magnetization reversal tended to occur more easily in the α-Fe core, because α-Fe phase was thicker than in the $SmCo_5$ core structure. On the other hand, as L became smaller than 10 nm, coherent magnetization reversals occurred in both models. These results suggest that a hard $SmCo_5$ core and a soft α-Fe shell is the better structure for obtaining superior squareness of the demagnetization curves. Therefore, we indicate the results for the magnets with the hard $SmCo_5$ core and soft α-Fe shell structure.

Figure 3 shows the coercivity H_c as a function of the α-Fe fraction. A decrease in L improved H_c, whereas H_c decreased with increasing α-Fe fraction for all L values. The coercivity H_c for magnets with a layered structure behaved similarly, and the nearly same H_c values were calculated as shown in Fig.4 for α-Fe fractions exceeding 70 %.

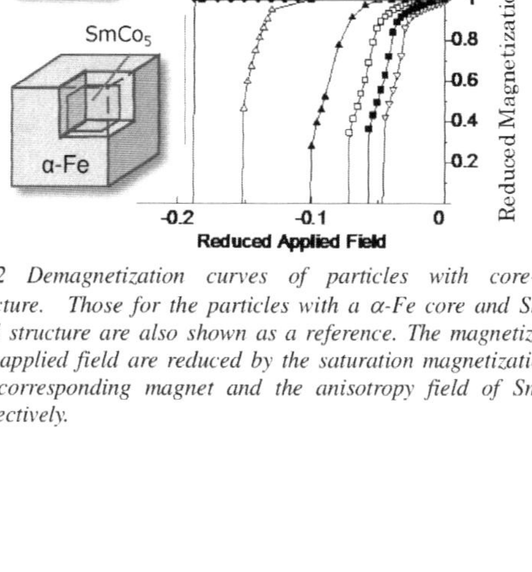

Fig.2 Demagnetization curves of particles with core-shell structure. Those for the particles with a α-Fe core and $SmCo_5$ shell structure are also shown as a reference. The magnetization and applied field are reduced by the saturation magnetization of the corresponding magnet and the anisotropy field of $SmCo_5$, respectively.

An increase in the α-Fe fraction increased the remanence while decreasing H_c. Resultantly, the calculated $(BH)_{max}$ vs α-Fe fraction curves had a peak for each particle size L as shown in Fig.5. The peak position shifted to the right with decreasing L, and a $(BH)_{max}$ value of approximately 800 kJ/m^3 was calculated with L=6.4 nm and an α-Fe fraction of 87.5%.

The $(BH)_{max}$ value for the layered structure are shown in Fig.6, together with the results for the core-shell structure and those for $Nd_2Fe_{14}B$/α-Fe nano- composite magnets. As seen in the figure, the achievable $(BH)_{max}$ value for the layered structure is roughly same as that for the core-shell structure, 800 kJ/m^3. The $(BH)_{max}$ value of $Nd_2Fe_{14}B$/α-Fe nanocomposite magnets peaked at the α-Fe fraction of approximately 75 % and reached 800 kJ/m^3. Therefore, the achievable $(BH)_{max}$ value for $SmCo_5$/α-Fe nanocomposite magnets is comparable to that for $Nd_2Fe_{14}B$/α-Fe ones. The large $(BH)_{max}$ value for $SmCo_5$/α-Fe can be attributed to the large magnetic anisotropy of $SmCo_5$, which enables the inclusion of a large amount of α-Fe.

The size of the $SmCo_5$ core for the α-Fe fraction of 87.5 % and L=6.4 nm, which give the largest $(BH)_{max}$ value, is 3.2 nm. For the layered structure with L=8 nm, the thickness of a $SmCo_5$ layer is calculated to be 1 nm. Considering the lattice constants of $SmCo_5$ (a=0.50 nm, c=0.40 nm), we need extremely fine microstructure for obtaining the largest $(BH)_{max}$ value.

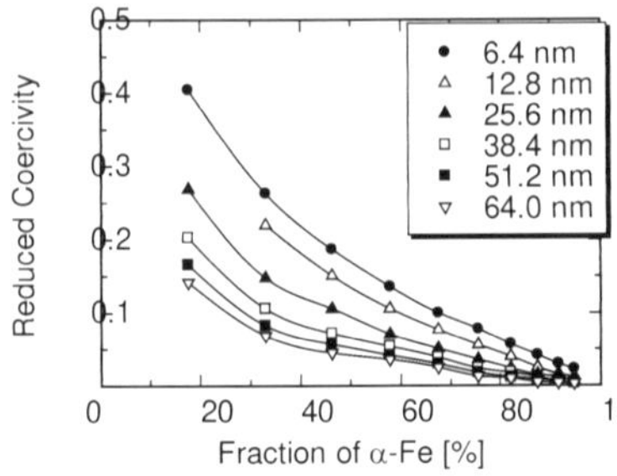

Fig.3 Coercivity of $SmCo_5$/α-Fe nanocomposite magnets with core-shell structure at 300 K as a function of α-Fe fraction. The coercivity is reduced by the anisotropy field of $SmCo_5$.

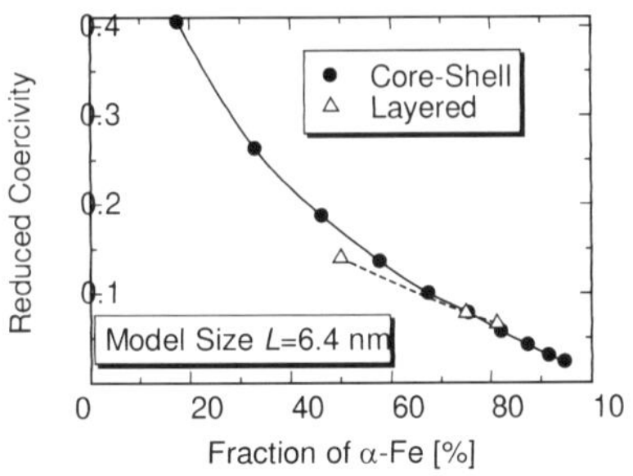

Fig.4 Coercivity of $SmCo_5$/α-Fe nanocomposite magnets with core-shell and layered structures at 300 K as a function of α-Fe fraction. The coercivity is reduced by the anisotropy field of $SmCo_5$.

Therefore, it might not be clear if the physical parameters assumed in Table 1 would be valid.

Coey has discussed the potential of variety of magnets from the viewpoint of the magnetic hardness κ [26]. κ relates to the ratio of the magnetic anisotropy energy to that due to demagnetizing field, and is defined as

$$\kappa = \sqrt{\mu_0 K_u / J_s^2}, \qquad (4)$$

where K_u, J_s, and μ_0 are the magnetic anisotropy constant, the saturation polarization, and the permeability of the vacuum, respectively. κ for composite magnets would be expressed as

$$\kappa = \sqrt{\mu_0 (1-f) K_{uh} / \{f J_{ss} + (1-f) J_{sh}\}^2}, \qquad (5)$$

where f is the volume fraction of magnetically soft phase, and the subscription s and h denote the magnetically soft and hard phases, respectively. We calculated κ for $SmCo_5$/α-Fe and $Nd_2Fe_{14}B$/ α-Fe magnets, and indicate the f values corresponding to κ =1 by the arrows in Fig.6. It is clearly seen that the achievable $(BH)_{max}$ values are limited to approximately to 670 kJ/m^3 for both magnets under condition of κ >1. From Fig.5, it was also revealed that this $(BH)_{max}$ value can be obtained for the particle with L=12.8 nm.

3.2. Magnetic Properties at 473 K

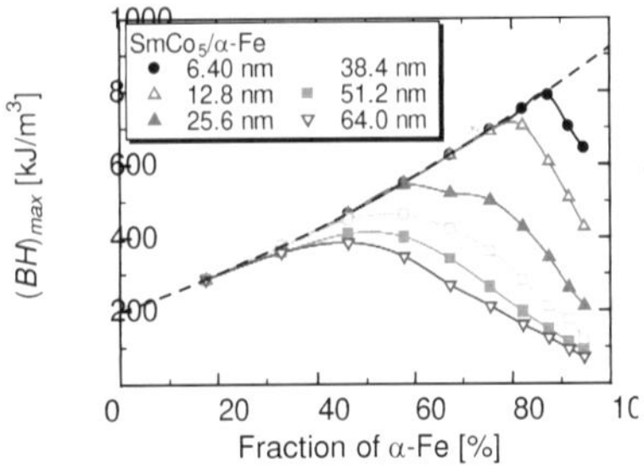

Fig.5 $(BH)_{max}$ values of $SmCo_5$/α-Fe nanocomposite magnets with core-shell structure at 300 K as a function of α-Fe fraction. The broken line indicates the theoretical limit calculated from the saturation polarization.

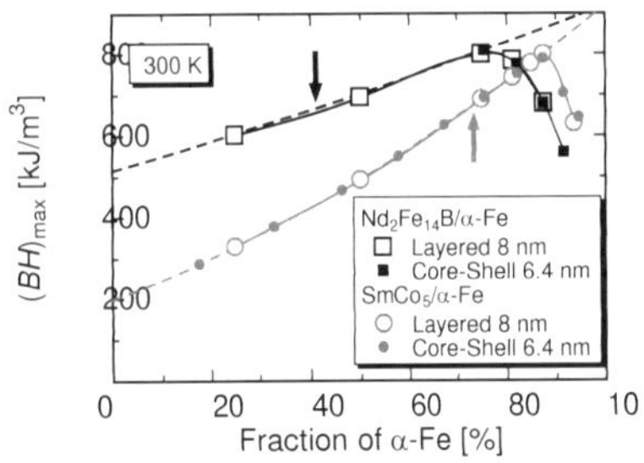

Fig.6 $(BH)_{max}$ values of $SmCo_5$/α-Fe and $Nd_2Fe_{14}B$/α-Fe nano-composite magnets with core-shell and layered structures at 300 K. The size of the particles with the core-shell structure and the stacking period of the layered structure were set at 6.4 and 8 nm, respectively. The broken line indicates the theoretical limit calculated from the saturation polarization. The arrows indicate the α-Fe fractions corresponding to κ =1. The definition of κ is explained in the text (See eqs. (4) and (5)).

Figure 7 shows H_c of $SmCo_5$/α-Fe and $Nd_2Fe_{14}B$/α-Fe magnets with a layered structure at 300 and 473 K as a function of the α-Fe fraction. The stacking period L was set at 8 nm. The calculated temperature coefficient, β, values were −0.26 ~ −0.19 %/K for $SmCo_5$/α-Fe magnets and −0.37 ~ −0.33 %/K for $Nd_2Fe_{14}B$/α-Fe ones. The small β values of the $SmCo_5$/α-Fe magnets can be attributed to the small temperature coefficient of anisotropy field H_A of $SmCo_5$, because the temperature coefficients of H_A of $SmCo_5$ and $Nd_2Fe_{14}B$ are −0.2 and −0.3 %/K, respectively.

The improved temperature stability of H_c resulted in large $(BH)_{max}$ values at 473 K. The calculated $(BH)_{max}$ values at 473 K are shown in Fig.8. The highest $(BH)_{max}$ was approximately 700 kJ/m^3 for $SmCo_5$/α-Fe magnets, whereas the highest one for

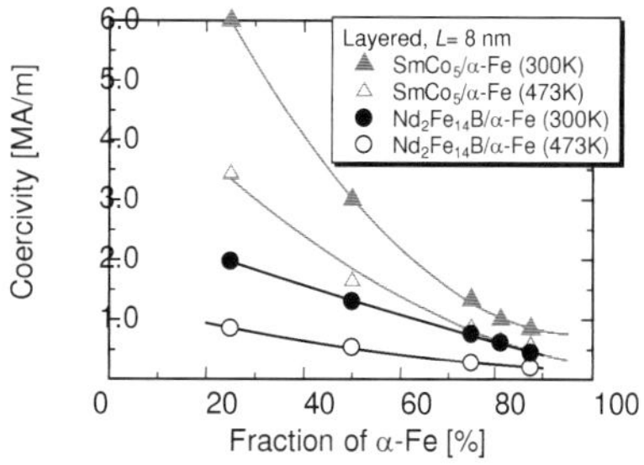

Fig.7 Coercivity of $SmCo_5$/α-Fe and $Nd_2Fe_{14}B$/α-Fe nano-composite magnets with layered structure at 300 and 473 K as a function of α-Fe fraction. The stacking period L is set at 8 nm.

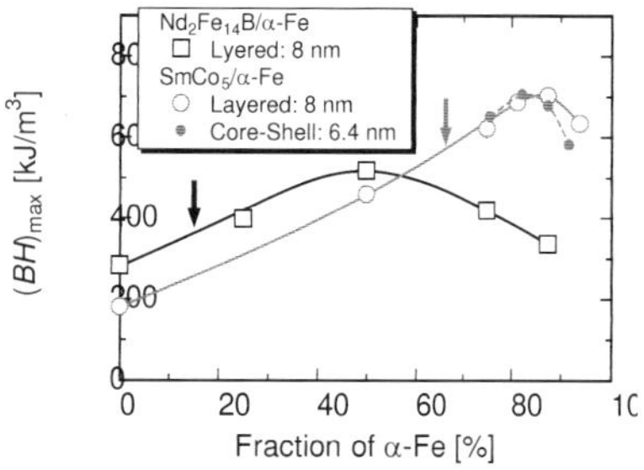

Fig.8 $(BH)_{max}$ values of $SmCo_5$/α-Fe and $Nd_2Fe_{14}B$/α-Fe nano-composite magnets with core-shell and layered structures at 473 K. The size of the particle with the core-shell structure and the stacking period of the layered structure were set at 6.4nm and 8 nm, respectively. The arrows indicate the α-Fe fractions corresponding to κ =1. The definition of κ is explained in the text (See eqs. (4) and (5)).

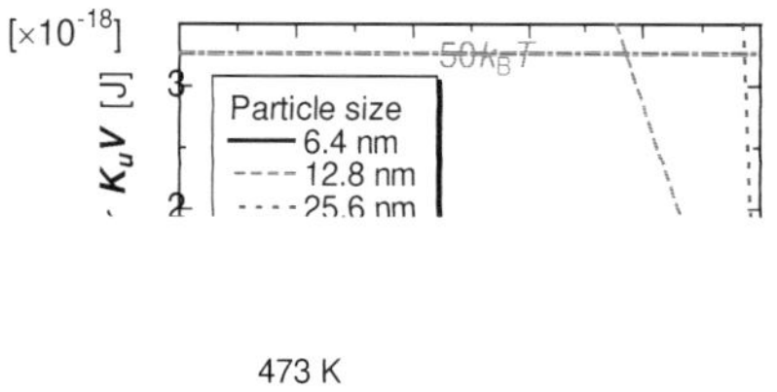

Fig.9 Energy barrier $K_{uh}V_h$ at 473 K for magnetization reversal of an isolated $SmCo_5$/α-Fe particle with core-shell structure as a function of α-Fe fraction.

$Nd_2Fe_{14}B$/α-Fe magnets was approximately 500 kJ/m^3.

The α-Fe fractions corresponding to κ =1 are also shown by the arrows in Fig.8. The inclusion of a large amount of α-Fe seems to be difficult in Nd-Fe-B based magnets used at a high temperature. The achievable $(BH)_{max}$ values are limited to 570 and 350 kJ/m^3 for $SmCo_5$/α-Fe and $Nd_2Fe_{14}B$/α-Fe magnets, respectively, under the condition of κ>1. In spite of these limitations, $SmCo_5$/α-Fe magnets have clear advantage at a high temperature.

Particles with a core-shell structure need to be consolidated to a bulk magnet. When each particle is isolated magnetically from others in a magnet, their magnetization would be affected by thermal agitation. The energy barrier against magnetization reversal for a nanocomposite magnet would be expressed as $K_{uh}V_h$, where K_{uh} and V_h are the magnetic anisotropy constant and the volume of a magnetically hard phase, respectively. The calculated $K_{uh}V_h$ values for $SmCo_5$/α-Fe magnets are shown in Fig.9 as a function of α-Fe fraction. The energies corresponding to $25k_BT$ and $50k_BT$, where k_B and T are the Boltzmann constant and temperature, respectively, are also shown in the figure. We need a particle size exceeding 12.8 nm under the condition of $K_{uh}V_h > 50 k_BT$. For the particle size of 12.8 nm, the magnet can includes only 77% α-Fe, and the achievable $(BH)_{max}$ value is limited to approximately 650 kJ/m^3. Since the condition of κ>1 limits the $(BH)_{max}$ to 570 kJ/m^3, $(BH)_{max}$ values of the particle with L=12.8 nm is limited by the magnetic hardness rather than thermal agitation. It should be noted that the particle size of 12.8 nm is enough to achieve the $(BH)_{max}$ value limited by κ, and that the obtainable $(BH)_{max}$ value is much higher than that expected for Nd-Fe-B-based magnets.

4. Calculation Results for Isotropic Magnets

We simulated magnetic properties of isotopic $SmCo_5$/α-Fe nanocomposite magnets with a layered structure. The fraction of α-Fe was set at 50%, and a $SmCo_5$ layer was assumed to be composed of cubic grains whose size is a half of the thickness of a $SmCo_5$ layer. The easy directions of magnetization of $SmCo_5$ grains were determined so that the average of cosθ becomes 0.5, where θ is the angle between the easy direction of magnetization and an applied field. The coercivity H_c at 300 and 473K is shown in Fig.10 as a function of the stacking period L. The averaged H_c values for five models and error bars are indicated. The H_c vs L curve had a broad peak at around L=20~30 nm and the increase in temperature shifted the peak toward right-hand side. The peak H_c values at 300 and 473K were 500 and 350 kA/m, respectively. The calculated β value was approximately −0.28 %/K, which roughly agrees with that for the Sm-Co/α-Fe multi-layered film synthesized by the pulsed laser deposition method [14].

The calculated rapid decrease in H_c in the small L region can be explained by the averaging effect of the magnetic anisotropy, because the reduction in the grain size increases the effective inter-grain exchange interaction and decreases the effective magnetic anisotropy [25, 27]

Figure 11 showed $(BH)_{max}$ of isotropic magnets at 300 K and 473K as a function of L. The $(BH)_{max}$ values for five models were indicated. The $(BH)_{max}$ vs L curves had a peak, and the peak value at 300 and 473K were approximately 300 and 250 kJ/m^3, respectively. The $(BH)_{max}$ value at 300 K agrees roughly with that calculated for a dispersed $Nd_2Fe_{14}B$/α-Fe nanocomposite magnet [8].

5. Conclusions

Magnetic properties at 300 K and 470 K of $SmCo_5$/α-Fe nanocomposite magnets with core- shell and layered structures were computer-simulated based on the miciromagnetics. The achievable $(BH)_{max}$ values of anisotropic $SmCo_5$/α-Fe nanocomposite magnets were approximately 800 kJ/m^3 at 300 K and 700 kJ/m^3 at 473 K. At 470 K, the achievable $(BH)_{max}$ value for $SmCo_5$/α-Fe magnets was much higher than that for $Nd_2Fe_{14}B$/α-Fe ones. It is also found that we need an extremely fine nanostructure for obtaining the above values.

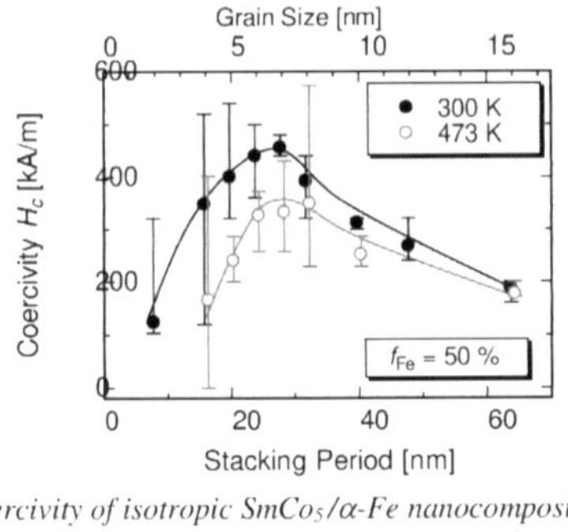

Fig.10 Coercivity of isotropic $SmCo_5$/α-Fe nanocomposite magnets with layred structure at 300K and 473K as a function of the stacking period, L. The averaged H_c values for five models and error bars were shown.

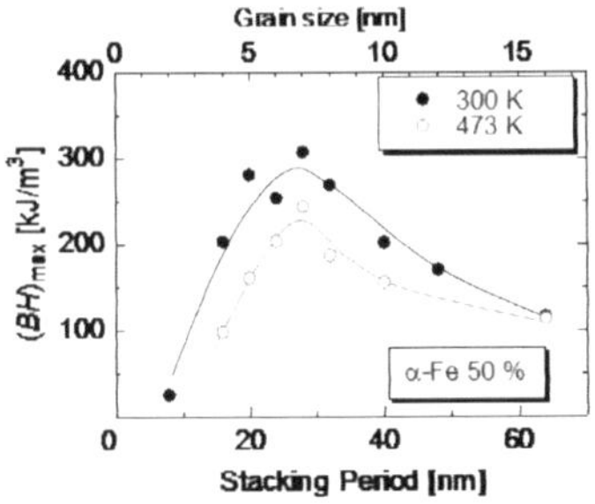

Fig.11 $(BH)_{max}$ of isotropic $SmCo_5$/α-Fe nanocomposite magnets with layered structure at 300K and 473K as a function of the stacking period, L. The averaged values for 5 model magnets are shown.

The consideration for the magnetic hardness and thermal agitation limited the achievable $(BH)_{max}$ to 670 kJ/m^3 at 300 K and 570 kJ/m^3 at 470 K, and revealed that a nanostructure of approximately 10 nm is a suitable size for good magnetic properties. In spite of these limitations, $SmCo_5$/α-Fe magnets are still expected to have clear advantage over Nd-Fe-B-based magnets at 473K.

For isotropic magnets with a layered structure, the $(BH)_{max}$ vs the stacking period curves had a peak. The peak $(BH)_{max}$ values were approximately 300 and 250 kJ/m^3 at 300 and 473 K, respectively.

References

[1] N.M. Dempsey, T.G. Woodcock, H. Sephri-Amin, Y. Zhang, H. Kennedy, D. Givord, K. Hono, O. Gutfleish, *Acta Mater.* **2013**, *61*, 4920-4927.

[2] K. Hirota, H. Nakamura, T. Minowa, and M. Honshima, *IEEE Trans. Magn.* **2006**, *42*, 2909-2911.

[3] D.S. Li, S. Suzuki, T. Kawasaki, and K. Machida, *Jpn. J. Appl. Phys.* **2008**, *47*, 7876-7878.

[4] Y. Une and M. Sagawa, *J. Japan Inst. Metals* **2012**, *76*, 12-16.

[5] W. Tang, Y. Zhang, and G. C. Hadjipanayis, *IEEE Trans. Magn.* **2000**, *36*, 3294-3296.

[6] K.H.J. Buschow, *Ferromagnetic Materials vol.1*, **1980**, *ch.1*, ed. E.P. Wolfarth, North-Holland, Amsterdam.

[7] E.F. Kneller, and R. Hawig, *IEEE Trans. Magn.* **1991**, *27*, 3588-3600.

[8] H. Fukunaga, J. Kuma, and Y. Kanai, *IEEE Trans Magn.* **1999**, *35*, 3235-3240.

[9] R. Lardé, J.-M. Le Breton, A. Maìtre, D. Ledue, O. Isnard, V. Pop, and I. Chicinas, *J. Phys. Chem.* **2013**, *C 117*, 7801-7810.

[10] V. M. Uzdin, A. Vega, A. Khrenov, W. Keune, V. E. Kuncser, J. S. Jiang, and S. D. Bader, *Phys. Rev.* **2012**, *B 85*, 024409.

[11] R. F. Sabiryanov and S. S. Jaswal, *Phys. Rev.* **1998**, *B58*, 12071.

[12] T. Schrefl, H. Forster, R. Dittrich, D. Suess, W. Scholz, and J. Fidler, *J. Appl. Phys.* **2003**, *93*, 6489-6491.

[13] C.-B. Rong, H.-W. Zhang, R.-J. Chen, and B.-G. Shen, *J. Appl. Phys.* **2006**, *100*, 123913.

[14] H. Fukunaga, A. Tou, M. Itakura, M. Nakano, and T. Yanai, *IEEE Trans. Magn.* **2014**, *50*, 2101504.

[15] Neu, S. Sawatzki, M. Kopete, Ch. Mickel, and L. Schultz, *IEEE Trans. Magn.* **2012**. *48*, 3599-3602.

[16] W.Q. Liu, J.H. Zuo, M. Yue, Z.Z. Cui, D.T. Zhang, J.X. Zhang, P.Y. Zhang, H.L. Ge, Z.H. Guo, W. Li, *J. Appl. Phys.* **2011**, *109*, 07A741.

[17] Y. Zhang, M.J. Kramer, C. Rong, and J.P. Liu, *Appl. Phys. Lett.* **2010**, *97*, 032506.

[18] N.V. R. Rao, R. Gopalan, M. M. Raja, V. Chandrasekaran, D. Chakravarty, R. Sundaresan, R. Ranganathan, and K. Hono, *J. Magn. Magn. Mater.* 2007, *312*, 252-257.

[19] J. Zhang, Y. K. Takahashi, R. Gopolan, and K. Hono, *Appl. Phys. Lett.* **2005**, *86*, 122509.

[20] J. Zhang, S. Zhang, H. Zhang, and B. Shen, *J. Appl. Phys.* **2001**, *89*, 5601-5605.

[21] K.-D. Durst, H. Kronmüller, and W. Ervens, *Phys. Stat. Sol. (a)* **1988**, *108*, 403-416.

[22] I. A. Al-Omari, R. Skomski, R. A. Thomas, D. Leslie-Pelecky, and D. J. Sellmyer, *IEEE Trans. Magn.* **2001**, *37*, 2534-2536.

[23] R. Becker, W. Döring, "*Ferromagnetisms*," Springer, Berlin, **1939**, 32.

[24] Chuan-Bing Rong, Hong-Wei Zhang, Ren-Jie Chen, and Bao-Gen Shen, *J. Appl. Phys.* **2006**, *100*, 123913.

[25] H. Fukunaga and K Inoue, *Jpn. J. Appl. Phys.* **1992**, *31*, 1347-1352.

[26] Coey, *IEEE Tans. Magn.* **2011**, *47*, 4671-4681.

[27] G. Herzer, *IEEE Trans. Magn.* **1989**, *25*, 3327-32

Rational Design of the Nanocomposite Structure for High-Performance Permanent Magnets

J.S. JIANG
Argonne National Laboratory, Argonne, IL 60439, U. S. A.

Abstract: *Permanent magnet materials based on the "exchange spring" mechanism, in which a soft magnetic phase is hardened via interfacial exchange coupling to a hard magnetic phase, promise superior maximum energy product [$(BH)_{max}$] and are a potential solution to the supply criticality in rare earth elements. The properties of exchange-spring magnets are intimately connected with not only the intrinsic material characteristics but also the geometry and spatial arrangement of the phases. A rational design of the structure that balances property enhancement and the feasibility of scalable fabrication can help select viable synthesis routes. The magnetization processes in model exchange-spring structures with close-packed 1-D multilayer, 2-D cylindrical and 3-D spherical motifs have been analyzed with both micromagnetic simulations and nucleation theory. The multilayer geometry and the soft-cylinders-in-hard-matrix geometry have the highest achievable $(BH)_{max}$, while the soft-spheres-in-hard-matrix geometry has the lowest upper limit for $(BH)_{max}$. The cylindrical geometry permits the soft phase to be large and does not require strict size control. Nanocomposite exchange-spring permanent magnets based on the cylindrical geometry may be amenable to scaled-up fabrication.*

Keywords: exchange-spring, nucleation, optimal structure, energy product.

Address: J. Samuel Jiang, Materials Science Division, Argonne National Laboratory, 9700 S. Cass Ave., Argonne, IL 60439, U.S.A., Tel: (630) 252-7738, Fax: (630) 252-5219, E-mail: jiang@anl.gov

1. Introduction

The exchange-spring principle [1] is a promising new pathway to achieving high-performance permanent magnet materials [2]. In an exchange-spring magnet, a nanometer-scale soft magnetic phase, which usually has high magnetization, is hardened by the exchange interaction at the interfaces with a hard phase. The average magnetization and the maximum energy product $(BH)_{max}$ of the exchange-spring magnet material become enhanced in comparison to those of the hard phase alone. Additionally, the exchange-spring magnet can reduce or even eliminate the expensive rare earth elements that are often necessary in the production of modern permanent magnet materials.

Exchange-spring magnets have been fabricated as random nanocomposites mainly by rapid-quenching and subsequent annealing, or by mechanical alloying [3]. Their $(BH)_{max}$, although improved over single phase isotropic hard magnets, is still significantly lower than that of oriented single-phase magnets due to the lack of control over the microstructure. $(BH)_{max}$ values as large as 400 kJ/m^3 (~ 48 MGOe) has been reported in fully epitaxial exchange coupled $SmCo_5$/Fe multilayers [4]. Nevertheless, the multilayer structure may not be practical for the scale-up production of permanent magnet materials, because it is rather difficult to extend the practice of sequential deposition of ultra-thin layers to fabricate a multilayer of macroscopic thickness. Bottom-up assembly using pre-synthesized nanoparticles [5,6,7] allows the dimension of the soft and hard phases to be controlled and has the potential to be scaled up. However, to develop a viable bulk synthesis strategy that fully exploits the microstructural control afforded by bottom-up assembly of nanoparticles, it is necessary to identify the optimal exchange-spring structure.

This paper presents a theoretical calculation of the nucleation field (H_N), at which the reversal of the soft phase magnetization first occurs, and the maximum energy product $(BH)_{max}$ of several exchange-spring magnet structures. Based on the comparison of the dependence of $(BH)_{max}$ on the geometric characteristics, and the consideration of practical constraints in material fabrication, an optimal microstructure for the exchange-spring permanent material is identified.

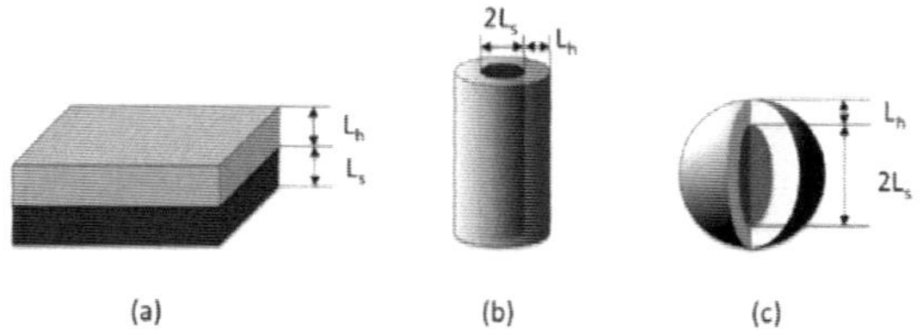

Fig. 1. Schematic illustration of the (a) bilayer, (b) cylindrical core/shell, and (c) spherical core/shell exchange-spring geometries.

2. The Exchange-Spring Geometries

There are three elemental exchange-spring geometries that differ in the dimensionality of composition variation: a 1D bilayer geometry, a 2D cylindrical core/shell geometry and a 3D spherical core/shell geometry. These geometries are illustrated in Fig. 1. The dimensions (radius or thickness) of the hard and soft phases are denoted as L_h and L_s, respectively. The easy axis of the hard phase is in-plane for the 1D bilayer, axial for the 2D cylindrical core/shell geometry, and arbitrary for the 3D spherical geometry.

A core/shell geometry can have either the soft core surrounded by a hard shell or a hard core surrounded by a soft shell. Only the soft core/hard shell geometries will be considered here, because it can be shown with micromagnetic modeling that when units of hard core/soft shell exchange-spring elemental structures are packed together, the soft shells come in contact with each other, the connectedness of the soft phase matrix has no means to impede a nucleated magnetization reversal from propagating. The cascading effect leads to a much earlier reversal of the total magnetization in the assembly than in an isolated hard core/soft shell element [8].

3. The Nucleation Fields

The nucleation of magnetic reversal can be theoretically treated with the linearized Brown's equation [9]:

$$\left[2A\nabla^2 - 2K - M\left(H - N_z M\right)\right]\mathbf{m}(\mathbf{r}) = M\vec{\nabla}U(\mathbf{r}), \quad (1)$$

where $\mathbf{m}(\mathbf{r})$ is the small transverse deviation from the saturated local magnetization, $\mathbf{M}$. The applied field $\mathbf{H}$ defines the z-axis, and N_z is the demagnetizing factor along the field direction in the saturated state before nucleation. A and K are the local exchange and anisotropy constants, respectively. The term $\vec{\nabla}U(\mathbf{r})$ comes from the demagnetizing field due to the starting deviation from saturation. Thus, $U(\mathbf{r})$ denotes the scalar potential created by the magnetization distribution $\mathbf{m}(\mathbf{r})$, and is given by the magnetostatic Poisson equation:

$$\nabla^2 U(r) = 4\pi M\vec{\nabla}\bullet\mathbf{m}(r). \quad (2)$$

In general, Eqns. (1) and (2) need to be solved self-consistently, along with the appropriate boundary conditions. Nucleation corresponds to the highest field ($H = -H_N$) at which Eqn. (1) has a solution. A textbook example is when the transverse demagnetizing field $-\vec{\nabla}U(\mathbf{r})$ can be written in a closed form as $-N'M\mathbf{m}(\mathbf{r})$, such as in the case of coherent rotation and curling in ellipsoids, then Eqn. (1) becomes the familiar Helmholtz equation and is readily solved. To simplify the calculations, it is assumed that the hard phase is perfectly rigid. The boundary condition is thus given by $\mathbf{m}(L_s)=0$.

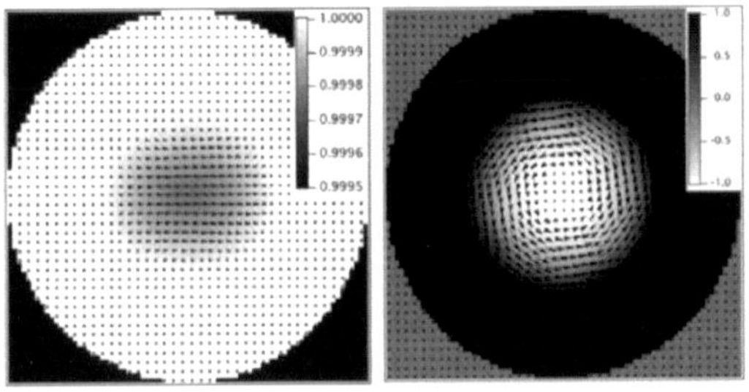

Fig. 2. The magnetization distribution of (a) the modified bulging and (b) the modified curling nucleation modes. The transverse components of the magnetization are shown as arrows and the longitudinal components are shown in gray scale.

For the bilayer geometry with an in-plane easy axis for the hard layer, the nucleation of the soft phase reversal proceeds via a quasi-Bloch wall. The magnetization distribution $\mathbf{m}(\mathbf{r})$ is sinusoidal and the demagnetizing field is zero. The solution of Eqn. (1) gives:

$$H_N = \frac{2K_S}{M_S} + \frac{\pi^2 A_S}{2M_s L_S^2}, \quad (3)$$

where A_S, K_S and M_S are the exchange constant, the anisotropy constant, and the saturation magnetization of the soft phase, respectively. The second term Eqn. (3) is exactly the same as that derived by Goto *et al.* [10] for an exchange-spring bilayer with perfectly hard and perfectly soft magnetic layers.

For the cylindrical soft core/hard shell geometry, the nucleation can proceed in either a modified bulging mode or a modified curling mode (Fig. 2) [8]. The modified bulging mode is favored at low L_s values, and is very similar to the bulging mode proposed by Skomski *et al.* [11]. The bulging mode, where $\mathbf{m}(\mathbf{r})$ is uniform but the amplitude varies radially, is not an exact nucleation mode because the magnetostatic self-interaction energy is not zero as argued in Ref. **Error! Bookmark not defined.**, nor can the demagnetizing field be written in a closed form. However, by treating the demagnetization field as a perturbation, the approximate solution for the nucleation field in the modified bulging mode can be written as [8]:

$$H_N = \frac{2K_s}{M_s} + 11.57\frac{A}{M_s L_s^2} + 1.43\pi M_s. \quad (4)$$

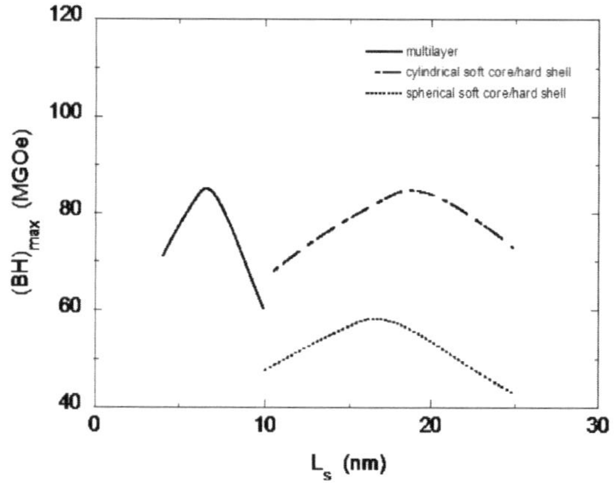

Fig. 3. The energy density $(BH)_{max}$ plotted as a function of the soft phase size L_s for several $SmCo_5$/ $Fe_{65}Co_{35}$ exchange-spring structures.

The modified curling mode, where **m**(**r**) is tangential and independent of the polar angle, is favored at larger L_s values, and has a vanishing demagnetizing field because of the flux closure. The nucleation field for the modified curling mode is given straightforwardly by:

$$H_N = \frac{2K_s}{M_s} + 29.36\frac{A}{M_s L_s^2}. \quad (5)$$

At a given L_s, the mode that has the lower H_N is the true nucleation mode. The crossover between the two modes occurs at $L_s^{coh} \approx 1.99\sqrt{A_s / M_s^2}$.

Similarly, the nucleation field for the modified bulging mode for the spherical soft core/hard shell geometry is given by

$$H_N = \frac{2K_s}{M_s} + 19.74\frac{A}{M_s L_s^2} + 0.39\pi M_s - \frac{4\pi}{3}(M_s - M_h). \quad (6)$$

The M_h contribution in the last term represents the magnetizing effect of the hard phase cavity. For the modified curling mode, the nucleation field is

$$H_N = \frac{2K_s}{M_s} + 40.382\frac{A}{M_s L_s^2} - \frac{4\pi}{3}(M_s - M_h). \quad (7)$$

There is no correction for transverse demagnetization because of the flux closure of magnetization curling. For a spherical soft α-Fe core and hard NdFeB shell exchange-spring structure, the nucleation fields calculated from Eqns. (6) and (7) are in excellent agreement with those [12] obtained from finite-element micromagnetic simulations [8].

4. The Maximum Energy Product

The maximum energy product of an exchange-spring magnet is determined by the average magnetization and by the nucleation field [13,14]:

$$(BH)_{max} = \begin{cases} (2\pi M_{sat})^2, & for \quad H_N \geq 2\pi M_{sat}, \\ H_N(4\pi M_{sat} - H_N), & for \quad H_N < 2\pi M_{sat}. \end{cases} \quad (8)$$

where M_s (M_h), and v_s (v_h) are the magnetization and volume fraction of the soft (hard) phase, respectively, and $M_{sat}=M_s v_s+M_h v_h$ is the saturation magnetization of the exchange-spring composite. v_s and v_h are determined by the geometry.

In Fig. 3, the calculated $(BH)_{max}$ is plotted as functions of L_s for close-packed bilayer, cylindrical core/shell, and spherical core/shell exchange-spring structures having $SmCo_5$ as the hard phase (with A_h=1.2 μerg/cm, $K_h=1.72\times10^8$ erg/cm^3, M_h=859 emu/cm^3), and $Fe_{65}Co_{35}$ as the soft phase (with A_s=2.2 μerg/cm, $K_s=2\times10^5$ erg/cm^3, M_s=1950 emu/cm^3). The hard phase size is kept constant at L_h=5 nm. For all the exchange-spring structures, $(BH)_{max}$ initially increases with increasing L_s as M_{sat} increases, peaks at an L_s when $H_N=2\pi M_{sat}$, and then decreases due to the rapid reduction in H_N with increasing L_s. The multilayer geometry has the largest peak $(BH)_{max}$ value of 85.2 MGOe at L_s=6.5 nm; and the peak $(BH)_{max}$ value for the geometry with cylindrical soft inclusions is only slightly lower, at 84.8 MGOe with L_s=18.7 nm. Although the cylindrical geometry has a lower M_{sat} than the layered geometry with the same value of L_s, it maintains a substantial H_N at large L_s, enabling $(BH)_{max}$ to catch up. The geometry with spherical soft inclusions has the lowest alue of $(BH)_{max}$ because, even though its H_N value is similar to that of the cylindrical geometry with the same L_s, it has the lowest packing efficiency and lowest soft-to-hard volume ratio, and, thus, the lowest value of M_{sat}.

Shown in Fig. 4 is the map of $(BH)_{max}$ of the close-packed cylindrical $Fe_{65}Co_{35}$ core/$SmCo_5$ shell exchange-change magnet, with the soft and hard phase dimensions as the coordinates. The gray scale represents $(BH)_{max}$ value in MGOe. The curves mark equi-$(BH)_{max}$ contours. As expected, $(BH)_{max}$ increases with decreasing L_h, and peaks at L_s ~20 nm.

5. Discussion

It is worth noting that the elongated Fe-Co core/ ferrite shell permanent magnet material has been reported decades ago by Falk and Hooper [15], and magnetic nanowires with large aspect ratios have been produced with various techniques [16,17]. Nearly the same $(BH)_{max}$ can be achieved with the cylindrical soft core/hard shell geometry, at a much larger soft-

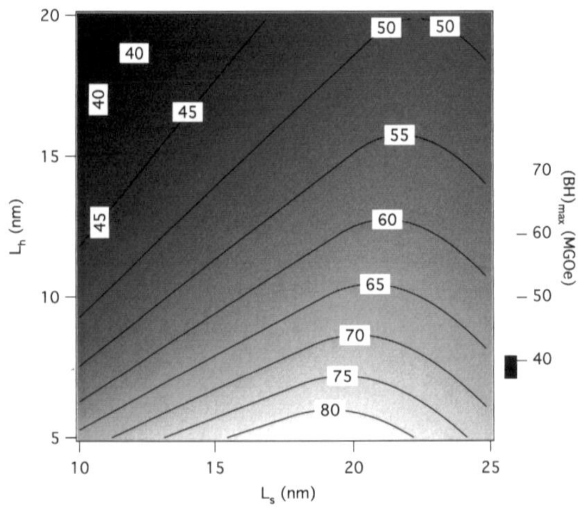

Fig. 4. The $(BH)_{max}$ map with the soft and hard phase dimensions as the coordinates, for the close-packed cylindrical $Fe_{65}Co_{35}$ core/$SmCo_5$ shell exchange-change magnet.

core diameter of a few tens of nm. At the soft-phase size where $(BH)_{max}$ peaks, nucleation is via the flux closed modified curling mode, thus the packing density has no effect on the nucleation field. The relatively weak dependence of $(BH)_{max}$ on the soft core diameter also relaxes the need for strict size control. Therefore, the geometry of cylindrical inclusions embedded in a hard matrix is an optimum exchange-spring structure, since it balances the requirements of exchange hardening and magnetization enhancement, with the feasibility of scalable fabrication for the production of high-performance permanent magnet materials.

6. Conclusion

The nucleation fields have been calculated and the potential for maximizing $(BH)_{max}$ is assessed for various exchange-spring geometries. The geometry with cylindrical soft inclusions in a hard matrix is optimal for the exchange-spring permanent magnet because it has an upper limit for $(BH)_{max}$ that is nearly the same as that of the multilayers, and because it permits the soft phase to be larger and does not require strict size control. Exchange-spring permanent magnets based on the cylindrical geometry may be amenable to scaled-up fabrication.

Acknowledgment
This work was supported by the U.S. Department of Energy, Office of Science, Basic Energy Sciences, Materials Sciences and Engineering Division.

References

[1] E. F. Kneller, R. Hawig, *IEEE Trans. Mag.*, 1991, 27, 3588.
[2] R. Skomski, J. M. D. Coey, *Phys. Rev.*, 1993, B48, 15812.
[3] See review, G. C. Hadjipanayis, *J. Magn. Magn. Mater.*, 1999, 200, 373, and references therein.
[4] V. Neu, S. Sawatzki, M. Kopte, Ch. Mickel, L. Schultz, *IEEE Trans. Magn.*, 2012, 48, 3599.
[5] H. Zeng, J. Li, J. P. Liu, Z. L. Wang, S. Sun, *Nature*, 2002, 420, 395.
[6] Y. Hou, S. Sun, C. Rong, J.P. Liu, *Appl. Phys. Lett.*, 2007, 91, 153117.
[7] M. Marinescu, J. F. Liu, M. J. Bonder, G. C. Hadjipanayis. *J. Appl. Phys.*, 2008, 103, 07E120.
[8] J. S. Jiang, S. D. Bader, *J. Phys.: Cond. Mater.*, 2014, 26, 064214.
[9] A. Aharoni, *Introduction to the Theory of Ferromagnetism*, 2000, Oxford University Press, Oxford.
[10] E. Goto, N. Hayashi, T. Miyashita, K, Nakagawa, J. Appl. Phys. 36, 1965, 2951.
[11] R. Skomski, J. P. Liu, D. J. Sellmyer, *Phys. Rev.*, 1999, B60, 7359.
[12] R. Fischer, T. Leineweber, H. Kronmüller, *Phys. Rev.*, 1998, B57, 10723.
[13] E. E. Fullerton, J. S. Jiang, M. Grimsditch, C. H. Sowers, S. D. Bader, *Phys. Rev.*, 1998, B58, 12193.
[14] J. S. Jiang, J. E. Pearson, Z. Y. Liu, B. Kabius, S. Trasobares, D. J. Miller, S. D. Bader, D. R. Lee, D. Haskel, G. Srajer, J. P. Liu, *Appl. Phys. Lett.*, 2004, 85, 5294.
[15] R. B. Falk, G. D. Hooper, *J. Appl. Phys.*, 1961, 32, 190S.
[16] T. M. Whitney, J. S. Jiang, P. C. Searson, and C. L. Chien, *Science*, 1993, 261, 1316.
[17] T. Maurer, F. Ott, G. Chaboussant, Y. Soumare, J.-Y. Piquemal, G. Viau, *Appl. Phys. Lett.*, 2007, 91, 172501.

Preparation, Microstructure and Coupling Mechanism of NdFeB-Based Nanocomposite Films with Ta Spacer Layer

W. B. CUI, Y. K. TAKAHASHI, H. SEPHERI-AMIN, K. HONO
National Institue for Materials Science (NIMS), Sengen 1-21-1, Tsukuba, Ibaraki, Japan

Address: Weibin Cui, National Institue for Materials Science (NIMS), Sengen 1-21-1, Tsukuba, Ibaraki, Japan, E-mail: cui.weibin@nims.go.jp

Hard/soft-magnetic nanocomposite have attracted much interests for their potential of achieving the maximum energy product $(BH)_{max}$ that exceeds the upper limit for a single-phase magnet. However, the experimental results are far behind such a theoretical prediction that ignores the reduction of the coercivity by the exchange coupling with soft magnetic phases. How to create anisotropic nanocomposite magnets while keeping the coercivity high is a major challenge. In this study, we demonstrate an anisotropic nano-composite thin film in $Nd_2Fe_{14}B$ / FeCo magnetic multilayer thin films with relatively high coercivity ($\mu_0H_c \approx 1.38$ T) by using a spacer layer. Meanwhile, due to the existence of spacer layer, the coupling mechanism between soft/hard-magnetic layers was also investigated by experiments along with micromagnetic calculations.

The thin films with structure of Ta(50 nm) / [HM / Ta(1 nm) / $Fe_{65}Co_{35}$(10 nm) / Ta(1 nm)$]_N$ / Nd-Fe-B / Ta(20 nm) were prepared by magneto-sputtering, where HM layer stands for $Nd_{15}Fe_{75}B_{10}$(30 nm) / Nd(3 nm), which is deposited at 600 °C. The other layers were deposited at room temperature. The whole thin films are finally annealed at 650 °C for 30 min. The microstructure was characterized by energy filtering transmission electron microscopy and magnetic properties were measured by SQUID VSM. The micromagnetic simulations were performed by FEMME software [1]

As demonstrated in the Ta(50 nm) / $Nd_{15}Fe_{75}B_{10}$(50 nm) Nd(5 nm) / Ta(x nm) Fe(5 nm) / Ta(20 nm) bi-layer system, when there is no Ta spacer (x = 0 nm), the coercivity is reduced to zero [2], as seen in Figure 1a. After sputtering a Ta (2 nm) spacer layer, the coercivity was recovered to 2.7 T, which was nearly compared with nearly 3 T of diffusion-processed Nd-Fe-B single-layer film [3]. Such result indicates the special role of interface in the Nd-Fe-B / Fe nanocomposite films. So, the multilayer films with structure of Ta(50 nm) / [HM / Ta(1 nm) /

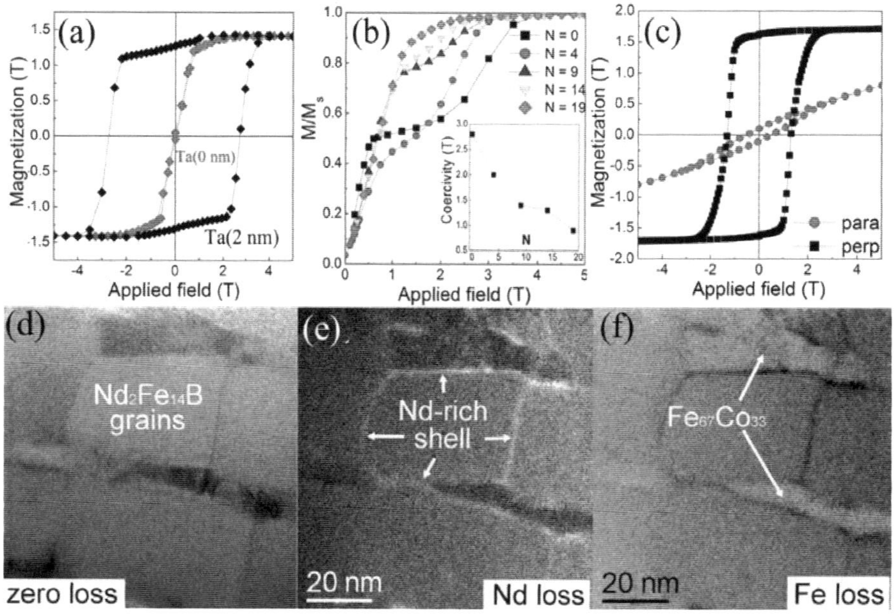

Fig. 1 (a) Hystersis loops of Ta(50 nm)/$Nd_{15}Fe_{75}B_{10}$(50 nm)Nd(5 nm)/Ta(x nm)Fe(5 nm)/Ta(20nm) bilayer films (x = 0 and 2 nm). (b) Initial magnetization curves of multilayer films Ta(50nm)/[HM/Ta(1 nm)/$Fe_{65}Co_{35}$(10 nm)/ Ta(1 nm)$]_N$/HM/Ta(20 nm). The inset figure shows the dependence of coercivity on the layer number N; (c) Hysteresis loop of multilayer film with N = 14. (d) high magnification cross-sectional bright-field TEM image of N = 14 multilayer thin films and the corresponding Nd loss image(e) and Fe loss image (f).

$Fe_{65}Co_{35}$(10 nm) / Ta(1 nm)$]_N$ / HM / Ta(30 nm) were prepared. When $N = 0$, which stands for the SL film, the coercivity is 2.8 T due to diffusion process. In the inset figure of Fig. 1b, with increasing number of N, $\mu_0 H_c$ decreases monotonously to 0.9 T at $N = 19$ due to more soft-magnetic phase. Fig. 1b compares the initial magnetization curves of films with various N. The step-behaviour gradually diminishes and a lower pinning field is observed. Finally, the step behavior disappears at $N = 19$. Fig. 1c shows the hysteresis loops of the composite film of $N = 14$. The magnetization curves in the perpendicular and parallel directions to the films indicate that the film has very strong perpendicular anisotropy. Coercivity is 1.38 T and the M_r is nearly 1.61 T, leading to the ultrahigh $(BH)_{max}$ of 486 kJ/m^3. No kinks on the demagnetization curve and nearly linear in-plane magnetization curve indicate the good coupling between soft and hard magnetic phases. From the low-magnification cross-sectional TEM images, the multilayer thin films show a lamella microstructure. The high-magnification TEM images and the corresponding Nd and Fe loss images are shown in Fig 1(d) to Fig. 1(f). The square $Nd_2Fe_{14}B$ grains can be seen, surrounded by a thin Nd-rich shell. Such core-shell structure is thought to be the reason for high coercivity. While, in the grain boundary regions, Fe_2Co phase is seen without alloying with Nd-rich phase, contributing to both high coercivity and high saturations.

As seen in Fig.1a, when the Ta spacer appears at the interface region, the coercivity is recovered. It is believed that the coupling between soft/hard-magnetic layer would be tuned dependent on the thickness of Ta spacer layer. To investigate such effect, a simplified system such as Ti(20 nm) / Nd-Fe-B(100 nm) Nd(10 nm) / Ta(x nm) / Fe(10 nm) / Ti(20 nm) (x = 0 – 400 nm) was prepared and the typical hysteresis loops are shown in Figure 2. In Ti(20 nm) / Nd-Fe-B(100 nm) Nd(10 nm) /Ti(20 nm) single-layer film (Fig. 2a), good squareness is achieved. By directly depositing Fe onto Nd-Fe-B layer, the coercivity was lowered. By inserting Ta(2 nm) spacer layer, the coercivity along perpendicular direction was enhanced to 0.8 T. when the Ta thickness is varied from 2 nm to 250 nm, the coercivity is not changed substantially. With further increasing Ta thickness to 400 nm, a kink is observed along out-of-plane direction, indicating the decoupling between soft/hard-magnetic layers. Meanwhile, the coercivity is also increased to be comparable with that of single-layer film. However, along in-plane direction, the kink gradually appears in the thin film with Ta(0 nm) and Ta(2 nm). And a sharp kink along in-plane direction is observed finally in the films with Ta thickness thicker than Ta(2 nm), compared with the kinks observed along out-of-plane direction in thin film of Ta(400 nm).

The micromagnetic simulations were applied in the Nd-Fe-B(100-nm) / Ta(x nm) / Fe(10 nm) model system with various thickness of Ta. By inserting Ta spacer, the exchange coupling is seriously weakened while magnetostatic coupling is not so weakened. The antiparallel configuration of Nd-Fe-B moments with Fe moments can be more easily accommodated compared with the case of spacer layer-free films. Also due to the existence of spacer layer, the coupling between soft/hard- magnetic layers is decreased slowly along out-of-plane direction, leading to the

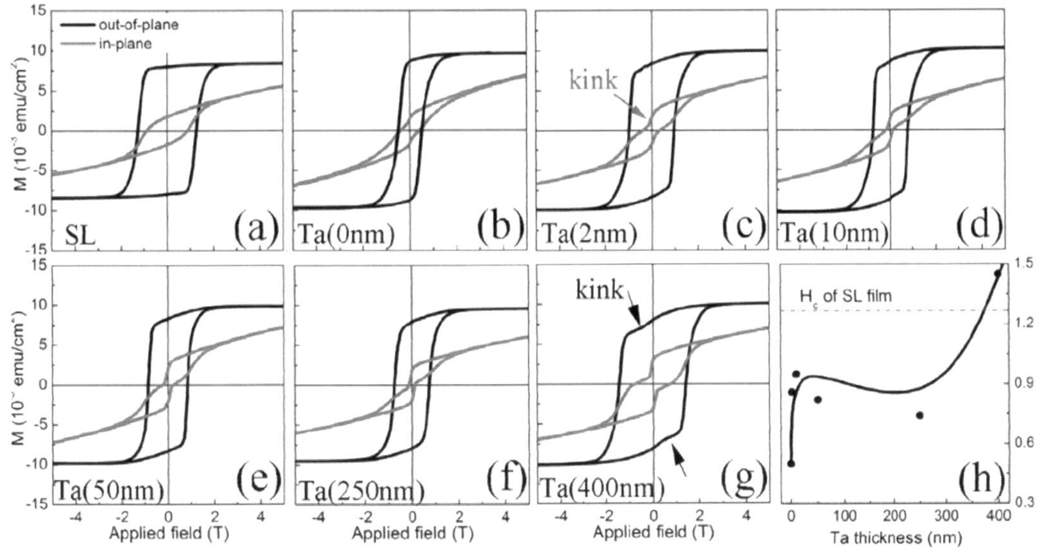

Fig. 2. Hysteresis loops of Ti(20 nm)/Nd-Fe-B(100 nm)Nd(10 nm)/Ti(20 nm) single-layered (SL) film (a) and Ti(20 nm)/Nd-Fe-B(100 nm) Nd(10 nm)/Ta(x nm)/Fe(10 nm)/Ti(20 nm) nanocomposite films [x = 0 nm (b), 2 nm(c), 10 nm (d), 50 nm (e), 250 nm(f) and 400 nm(g)]; Ta-thickness dependence of the coercivity (h).

kinks observed at Ta thickness of around 400 nm. [4]

In conclusion, in the thin film system, by diffusion process, the coercivity of Nd-Fe-B thin film can be enhanced to the level of 3 T. By using Ta spacer layer, the coercivity can be recovered. In a multilayer system, a coercivity of 1.38 T and $(BH)_{max}$ of 486 kJ/m^3 can be achieved. The unique Nd-rich shell / $Nd_2Fe_{14}B$ grain core structure is thought to be responsible for high performance. The reason of coercivity recovery by using Ta spacer layer is clarified by micromagnetic simulation. Magnetostatic coupling and seriously weakened exchange coupling lead to the easier accommodation of untiparallel configurations of Nd-Fe-B moments and Fe moments, which explains the enhanced coercivity by using spacer layer and the kinks observed in film with 400 nm thickness of Ta. From our experimental results, it can be seen that spacer layer is indispensible for making high-performance soft/hard-magnetic nano-composite magnets. By weakening the exchange coupling, the better magnetic properties can be achieved by using spacer layer.

References

[1] J. Fidler, T. Schrefl, *J. Phys. D: Appl. Phys.* **33**, 2000, R135.
[2] W.B. Cui, Y.K. Takahashi, K. Hono, *Adv. Mater.* **24**, 2012, 6530.
[3] W.B. Cui, Y.K. Takahashi and K. Hono, *Acta Mater.* **59**, 2011, 7768.
[4] W.B. Cui, H. Sepheri-Amin, Y.K. Takahashi and K. Hono, submitted.

Magnetic and Mechanical Properties of α-Fe Doping Hot-Pressed NdFeB Magnets

M. LIN[1], H. WANG[2], A. YAN[1]
[1] Ningbo Institute of Material Technology & Engineering Chinese Academy of Science, Ningbo 315201, People's Republic of China
[2] Ningbo Jinji Strong Magnetic Material Company, Ningbo 315041, People's Republic of China

Abstract: *The hot deformed magnets by blending melt-spun flakes and α-Fe particles were studied. The doping of coarse α-Fe particles on the magnetic properties and mechanical properties of hot deformed magnets were tested. It shows that the* B_r *and the* $(BH)_{max}$ *get improved when the doped α-Fe powders are less than 3 wt%. The* H_{cj} *always decreases with the increasing α-Fe powders. The bending test shows that the bending strength was enhanced by the elongated α-Fe phase embedded in the matrix 2:14:1 phase. The binding between the α-Fe phase and the matrix phase is strong compared with that of the matrix. The fracture surface morphology shows that the bending strength is improved by the crack deflection and the α-Fe extraction effects.*

Keywords: *hot deformed magnets; composite Nd-Fe-B magnets; bending strength*

1. Introduction

Hot pressed Nd-Fe-B magnets have been commercially available for a number of years [1]. Despite of the extraordinary magnetic properties of hot pressed Nd-Fe-B magnets, their mechanical properties such as bending strength and fracture toughness are poor, as compared with the sintered forms [2]. High die-upset levels tend to promote cracks, which reduce the magnetic density and remanence.

The anisotropic hot-pressed magnets made of the blending of the melt-spun Nd-Fe-B ribbons and coarse α-Fe/Fe-Co powders were reported [3], where the composite magnets exhibited a uniform demagnetization behavior and some showed the enhanced values of the B_r and the $(BH)_{max}$. The α-Fe was elongated during the hot deformation, where a special structure that the flake-like plastic α-Fe embedded in the $Nd_2Fe_{14}B$ matrix phase was formed.

Our previous work showed that plastic phase helped to improve the mechanical properties of sintered Nd-Fe-B magnets [4]. Unlike the traditional sintering, the convenient doping of α-Fe by the hot deformation process may potentially combine both the magnetic properties and mechanical properties of the hard phase and the soft phase together. This also provides a clue for the development of composite magnets with improved both magnetic properties and mechanical properties. The change of magnetic properties and the bending strength of hot deformed Nd-Fe-B/α-Fe composite magnets were analyzed in this paper.

2. Experiments

The magnetic alloys with composition $Nd_{13.5}Fe_{80}Ga_{0.5}B_6$ were prepared by induction melting. Melt spinning was then used to make ribbons with a wheel speed 40-50 m/s. The ribbons were crushed into about 500μm powders. The melt-spun powders with and without α-Fe doped were blended. In vacuum they were hot-pressed at 600-800°C under 100-200 MPa and then they were hot-deformed at 700-900°C under 80-150MPa. The specimens were reduced to the 40% of their original thickness.

The magnetic properties were measured with a hysteresis loop tracer. The microstructure was investigated with a SEM. The alignment in the press direction was detected with a XRD. Bending strength was measured by a 3-point bend test with a span of 14.5 mm. The specimens with a size of 5× 6 × 19 mm were tested with the easy axis parallel to the load direction.

3. Result and Discussion

The particle size of the α-Fe powders used in this study was analyzed. Most of them were 15-40μm.

The XRD patterns of the Fe-free and Fe-doped(1&3 wt.%) hot-deformed magnets are shown in fig.1. According to the rule that A better grain alignment is represented by enhanced (004),

(006), and (008) intensities and agreater than 1 intensity ratio of (006) over (105) [3], the 1 wt.% α-Fe particles doped do good to the c-axis alignment of the magnetic main phase in the press direction, while the c-axis alignment of the 3wt% α-Fe particles doped magnet is almost the same with the Fe-free magnet.

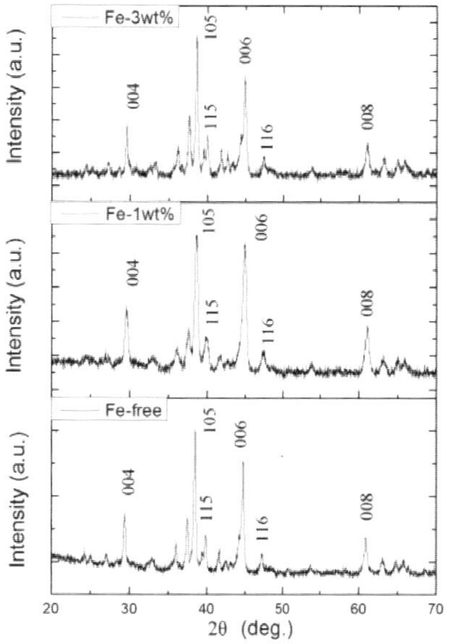

Fig.1. XRD patterns of the Fe-free and the α-Fe doped hot-deformed magnet

The change of magnetic properties before and after the α-Fe particle doping is shown in fig. 2. With the Fe fraction increasing, the Hcj always decrease but the B_r and $(BH)_{max}$ get improved before Fe fraction at 3%.

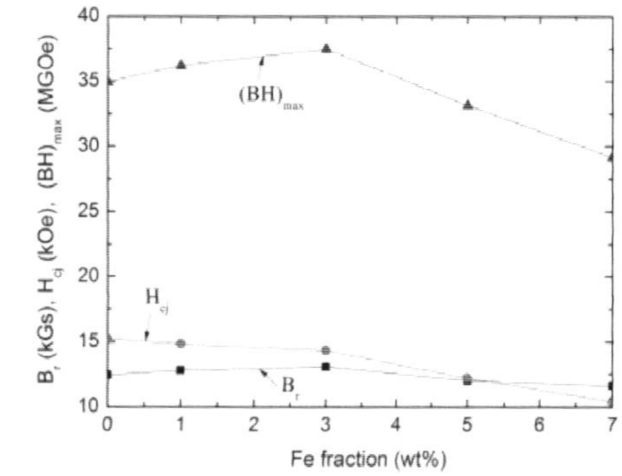

Fig.2. Effects of Fe fraction on magnetic properties of composite $Nd_{13.5}Fe_{80}Ga_{0.5}B_6$ /Fe magnets

Fig.3 is the backscattered electron image of the polished surface of hot-deformed magnets with α-Fe doping. The dark gray phase is the α-Fe, while the light gray is the 2:14:1 phase. The α-Fe has a length of up to over 50μm and a thickness of 10-40μm. Apparently, the α-Fe particles were elongated in the perpendicular to the press direction. The improved B_r and $(BH)_{max}$ may arise from the magnetic coupling between the hard matrix phase and the soft α-Fe flakes by the long-range magnetostatic interactions [5].

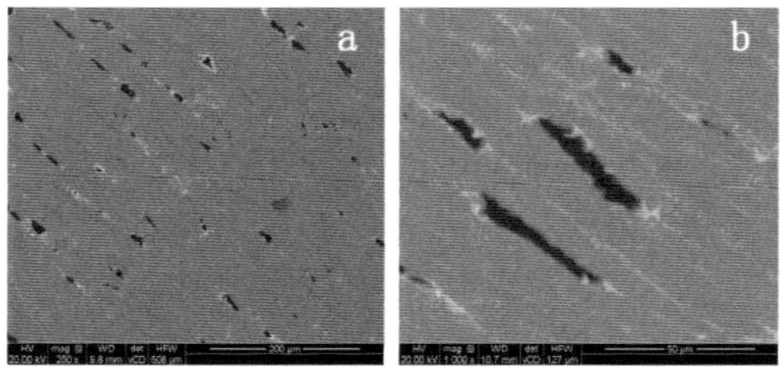

Fig. 3. SEM images of the α-Fe doped magnets

The mechanical tests were repeated for seven times in order to obtain average values. The deviation of maximum fracture strength was 5%. The mechanical test showed that the α-Fe doping help to improve the bending strength from 210 to 240MPa and the strain percentage increase after Fe doped in fig.4. For the α-Fe doped magnet, the protruding α-Fe phase can be clearly detected on the fracture surface. It can also be found that the α-Fe particles were coated by the matrix 2:14:1 phase, which indicate that the binding between the matrix phase and the α-Fe particles were stronger than that between the matrix particles.

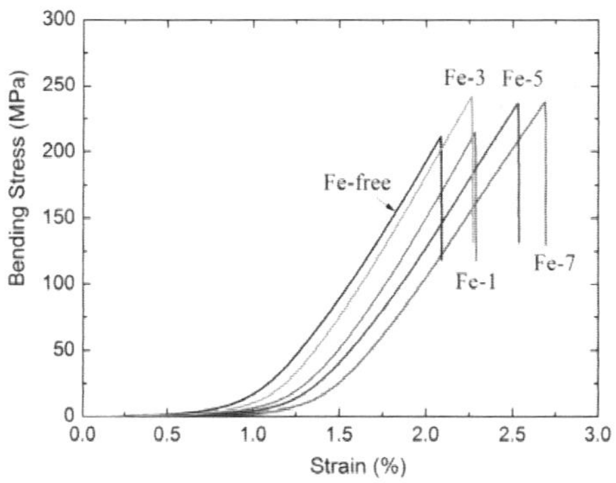

Fig. 4. Bending true stress–strain curves of the Fe-free and the Fe doped hot-deformed magnet

The normal stress of an arbitrary spot in transverse section is directly proportional to its distance from the impartial axis. Bending strength is the biggest tensile stress achieved when the tensile area fracture because the tensile stress is much lower that compressive stress in Nd-Fe-B sintered magnets. When fracture occurs, a crack tip is located in the tensile area all the time. The crack tip moves and propagates through the whole specimen. When the crack is propagating, it is deflected when touching the elongated α-Fe phase. Another effect is that the elongated α-Fe particles will be extracted from the matrix phase and consume the fracture energy. Both of these may account for the improvement of the bending strength.

As for the α-Fe doping magnets, the grain growth at the flake boundary was successfully suppressed. This may closely related to the altered deformation process due to the doping of α-Fe particles. When an increasing compressive stress is applied to a hot-pressed sample, plastic deformation occurs in the flakes. Previous study reported the addition of internal lubricant to produce the die-upset magnets [6]. The low-melting lubricants help to decrease the friction between the particles, improve the formability during the hot-working step and make the uniformly plastically deformed grains through the products. The plastic deformation α-Fe particles during die upset may help to decrease the friction between the flakes and have effects similar to the low melting additions.

However, the effect of grain growth suppression by α-Fe particle doping still need further research. The microstructural change on the flake boundary may be another reason for the improvement of bending strength after the α-Fe particle doping. The further optimization of the grain size of the soft phase would lead to an increase in both the magnetic properties and mechanical properties.

4. Conclusions

The less than 3wt% α-Fe powders doped have little influence on the c-axis alignment of the hot-deformed magnet. The B_r and the $(BH)_{max}$ get improved after the blending of the less than 3wt% α-Fe powders. The Hcj always decreases with the increasing α-Fe powders. The bending strength was enhanced by the elongated α-Fe phase embedded in the matrix 2:14:1 phase. The binding between the α-Fe phase and the matrix phase is strong, as compared with that of the matrix.

References

[1] D.Hinz, A. Kirchner, D.N.Brown, B.-M.Ma, O.Gutfeisch, *Journal Materials Processing Technology.* 135 (2003) 358.

[2] J. A. Horton, J. L. Wright and J. W. Herchenroeder, *IEEE Trans. Magn.* 32 (1996) 4374.

[3] D. Lee, S. Bauser, A.Higgins, C.Chen etc, *J. Appl. Phys.* 99 (2006) 08B520-1.

[4] H.J. Wang, A.H. Li, M.G. Zhu, W. Li, , *J. Magn. Magn. Mater* 307 (2006) 268.

[5] A.M.Gabay and G.C.Hadjipanayis, *J. Appl. Phys.* 101 (2007) 09K507.

[6] Iwasaki Katsunorl, Tanigawa Shigeho, Tokunaga Masuaki, Eur. Patent 89119269.2 (1990).

Microstructure and Magnetic Properties of Fine-Grained Nd-Fe-B Sintered Magnets Derived From HDDR-Processed Powder

K. TAKAGI[1], M. ISHII[2], R. SODA[1], K. OZAKI[1]
[1]National Institute of Advanced Industrial Science and Technology (AIST), Nagoya, 463-8560, Japan
[2]Research Association of Magnetic Materials for High-Efficiency Motors (MagHEM), Nagoya, 463-8560, Japan

Abstract: *HDDR-processed Nd-Fe-B powder was consolidated by a current sintering with uniaxial pressure in the range from 38 to 600 MPa. This sintering method was able to fabricate dense compacts regardless of the pressure; however the low-pressure sintering required high sintering temperatures close to the grain growth temperature of 850 °C. On the other hand, the coercivity of the obtained compacts was lower than the raw powder. In particular, the coercivity first dropped and thereafter recovered in the course of densification. Scanning electron microscope observation and X-ray diffractometry did not find obvious correlations between the coercivity decrease and the changes in Nd-rich phase and internal strain. The sintered compacts were then annealed, and the coercivity of all the compacts was recovered to the level of raw powder.*

Keywords: *Nd-Fe-B, sintered magnets; HDDR-processed powders; coercivity*

Address: Kenta Takagi, Green Innovative Magnetic Materials Center, National Institute of Advanced Industrial Science and Technology, Nagoya, 463-8560, Japan, Tel: +81-52-736-7561, E-mail: k-takagi@aist.go.jp

1. Introduction

Nd-Fe-B powders prepared via HDDR process are expected as a heavy-rare-earth-free magnet because they exhibit high coercivity and good thermal coefficients due to their fine-grained microstructure. These days, the HDDR powders were commercialized, and these powders have the coercivity, H_{cj} more than 14 kOe and the maximum energy product, $(BH)_{max}$ of 40 MGOe [1]. Further development for enhancement of magnetic properties is also under way. On the other hand, the HDDR powders are hard to sinter with maintenance of the original magnetic properties by traditional sintering technique. In particular, the coercivity is suddenly decreased by heating over the production temperature (around 850 °C) due to grain growth. Therefore, it is necessary to use low-thermal-load sintering method enabling reduction of sintering temperature and time. So far, some research groups have tried the consolidation of the HDDR powders with ingenious approaches [2,3]. We are currently developing sintered magnets of the HDDR powders by a current sintering which is one kind of rapid hot-press sintering methods. In this sintering process, the phenomena that have not appeared in the conventional Nd-Fe-B sintered magnets were found: constantly-observed decrease in coercivity independent of grain growth, and an anomalous drop in coercivity related to the sintered density.

In this study, we investigated the relationship between the microstructure and magnetic property for these sintered magnets, and discussed an appropriate sintering process for the HDDR powder.

2. Experimental procedure

Coarse HDDR Nd-Fe-B powder with a mean particle size of 117 μm (Aichi Steel Co.) was used in this study as a raw powder. This powder had B_r of 13.3 kG, H_{ci} of 14.4 kOe, and $(BH)_{max}$ of 40 MGOe. The powder was put in a cylindrical die set, and sintered in vacuum under uniaxial compression by our developed current sintering system. In this study, we used a graphite die as well as a WC-FeAl cemented carbide die which was capable of withstanding a high pressure under a high temperature. The sintering was performed at various temperatures in the range from 600 to 1000 °C, and the pressure was varied from 38 to 600 MPa depending on the material of die set.

The density of the obtained compacts was measured by the Archimedes method. The magnetic properties were measured using a pulsed magnetometer (Nihon Denjisokki PBH -1000) and PPMS/VSM (Quantum Design Dynacool). Microstructural observations of the sintered compacts were conducted using field emission scanning microscope (FE-SEM, JEOL JSM-7800F) and transmission / scanning transmission microscope equipped with energy dispersive X-ray spectrometer (TEM-STEM-EDX, JEOL JEM-2100F / JED2300). Internal strain was determined using X-ray diffraction (XRD) with Co-K_α radiation.

3. Result and discussion

In the case where the sintering was performed under the low-pressure of 38 MPa with the commonly-used graphite die set, dense bulks with the relative density more than 98% were obtained at the sintering temperatures above 840 °C. This temperature was fairly close to the critical temperature that the coercivity was decreased due to the grain growth. Meanwhile, sintering at the higher pressures of 200 ~ 600 MPa with the cemented carbide die was able to densify the powder below 760 °C.

Figure 1 shows the coercivity of the obtained compacts as a function of relative density. In the case of the low-pressure sintering, the coercivity first decreased and thereafter recovered in the course of densification. This phenomenon was observed in the previous study [2]. Meanwhile, the compacts sintered at the high pressure showed the decrease in coercivity by 7–25 % but not the anomalous coercivity decrease that took place in the low- pressure sintering.

The coercivity decrease had several possible causes: the change in Nd-rich/Nd-oxide boundary phases, the presence of internal micro-strain, and the morphological change in the boundary phase/grain interface [4-7]. FE-SEM observation was first performed for the compacts sintered at the low-pressure in order to understand this anomalous coercivity decrease. Fig. 2 compares the Nd-rich phase networks on the grain boundaries between the compact showing the anomalous coercivity decrease and the compact that the coercivity was recovered by densification. It was found that the compact with the anomalously low coercivity had clearer Nd-rich phase networks than the compact with the recovered coercivity. The STEM-EDX analysis revealed that the compositions of Nd-rich phases in both two compactions almost agreed. In particular, the atomic ratios of Nd and Fe in the Nd-rich phases were about 13.4 : 86.6 for both the compacts. This means that the Nd-rich phases might not be nonmagnetic. These results suggested that the anomalous decrease

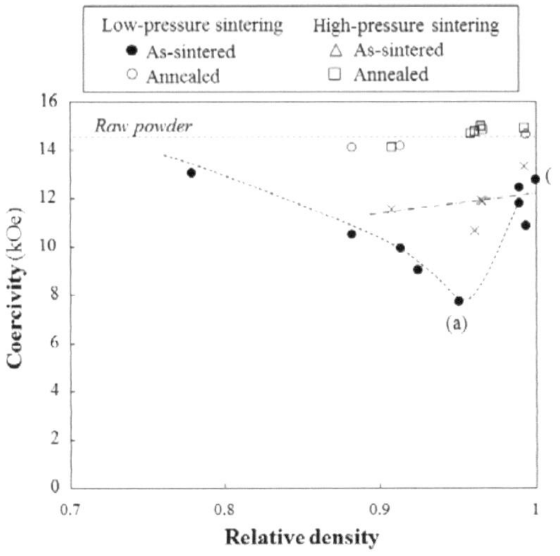

Fig. 1. Relationships the coercivity and relative density for the as-sintered compacts and post-annealed compacts

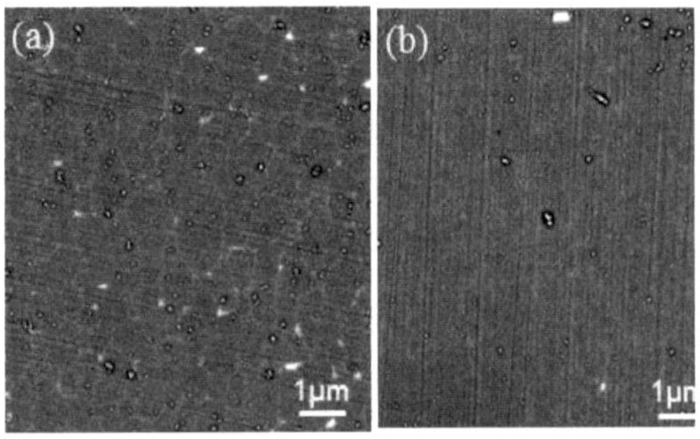

Fig. 2. Cross-sectional SEM-BSE images of the compact sintered at the low pressure. (a) the compact that showed the anomalous coercivity decrease, and (b) the compact with the recovered coercivity.

phenomenon of coercivity might not be caused by the difference in Nd-rich phase networks. The EDX analysis also revealed that the grain boundaries barely contained oxygen. Thus, the change of Nd-oxide boundary phase was not major reason for the coercivity decrease.

The TEM observation was also conducted. As a result, it was observed that the compact showing the anomalous coercivity decrease tended to have more local strains at the triple junction than the high-coercive compact. Therefore, some of the sintered samples were rapidly annealed at 750 °C. After annealing, the coercivity of the compacts showing the anomalous coercivity decrease was recovered to that of the raw powder, as shown in Fig. 1. Furthermore, even the coercivity of the dense compacts did not reach to that of the raw powder regardless of the sintering pressure. But, the annealing also increased their coercivity to the values over 14 kOe. However, X-ray diffractometry did not find obvious correlation between the coercivity and internal strain. Therefore, the most likely cause of the coercivity decrease by the sintering might be due to the change in the boundary phase/grain interface. The detailed investigation of the cause is now in progress. Consequently, a combination of the current sintering and adequate annealing was able to densely consolidate the HDDR powder while remaining the high coercivity. At this point, the anisotropic sintered samples have H_{cj} of 14.9 kOe, M_s of 11.1 kG, and $(BH)_{max}$ of 27.7 MGOe. The low remanence of the present magnets was caused by a low degree of orientation. Improvement of magnetic–alignment process is also under way.

4. Summary

A current sintering method was able to fabricate the dense sintered magnets from the HDDR- processed powder below the grain growth temperature. However, the sintered compacts showed the decreases in coercivity, and in particular the decrease depending on the density was anomalous. Detailed observations did not find the correlations between the changes of Nd-rich boundary phase and internal strain and the coercivity variation. The coercivity was fully recovered by annealing. Thus, the coercivity decrease might be caused by the morphological change in the boundary phase/grain interface.

Acknowledgement
This work has been supported by Future Pioneering Projects / Development of magnetic material technology for high-efficiency motors from Japanese Ministry of Economy, Trade and Industry.

References

[1] http://www.magfine.net/eng/index.html

[2] N. Nozawa, H. Sepehri-Amin, T. Okubo, K. Hono, T. Nishiuchi, S. Hirosawa, *J. Magn. Magn. Mater.* **323**, 2011, 115.

[3] K. Suresh, T. Ohkubo, Y. K. Takahashi, K. Ohishi, R. Goplan, K. Hono, T. Nishiuchi, N. Nozawa S. Hirosawa, *J. Magn. Magn. Mater.* **321**, 2009, 3681.

[4] F. Vial, F. Joly, E. Nevalainen, M. Sagawa, K. Hiraga, K. T. Park, *J. Magn. Magn. Mater.* **242-245**, 2002, 1329.

[5] T. Fukunaga, S. Hirosawa, *J. Appl. Phys.* **104**, 2008, 013911.

[6] M. Matsuura, R. Goto, N. Tezuka, S. Sugimoto, *Mater. Trans.* **51**, 2010, 1901.

[7] H. W. Kwon, J. G. Lee, J. H. Yu, *J. Appl. Phys.* **115**, 2008, 17A727.

Coercivity Enhancement of Hot-Deformed Nd–Fe–B Magnet by Grain Boundary Diffusion Process with the Sputtering Technique

K. HIOKI, A. HATTORI, T. IRIYAMA
Daido Steel Co., Ltd., 2-30 Daido-cho, Minami-ku, Nagoya 457-8545, Japan

Abstract: *Hot-deformed Nd–Fe–B magnets have a fine microstructure owing to their unique fabrication procedure. Their fine crystal grains (200–500 nm) allow higher coercivity compared with sintered magnets. However, the grain size alone does not markedly increase the coercivity. In this study, the coercivity was enhanced by a grain boundary diffusion process using raw powder coated with* $Tb_{0.85}Cu_{0.15}$ *(wt.%). The proposed diffusion process improved the magnetic properties of the base magnet from* $B_r = 14.1$ *kG,* ${}_iH_c = 14.8$ *kOe (1180 kA/m) to* $B_r = 13.7$ *kG,* ${}_iH_c = 20.4$ *kOe (1625 kA/m).*

Keywords: *coercivity; hot-deformed magnet; grain boundary diffusion process; sputtering*

Address: Keiko Hioki, Daido Corporate Research & Development Center, Daido Steel Co., Ltd., 2-30 Daido-cho, Minami-ku, Nagoya 457-8545, Japan, Tel: 81-52-611-9671, Fax: 81-52-611-2199, E-mail: k-hioki@ac.daido.co.jp

1. Introduction

Recently, considerable attention has been focused on the development of high coercivity Nd–Fe–B magnets without using heavy rare earth elements (HREE), such as Dy or Tb, which are scarce and subject to price fluctuations. Such magnets are demanded for clean energy applications such as hybrid electric vehicles, consumer electronics and wind turbines, which require high remanence and large coercivity. Hot-deformed Nd–Fe–B magnets possess a fine microstructure because of their nanocrystalline starting material and lower temperature production process. Consequently, hot-deformed Nd–Fe–B magnets exhibit better coercivity than sintered magnets and Dy and Tb contents are reduced [1]. Their crystal grain size is close to the critical diameter of the single domain of $Nd_2Fe_{14}B$ [2]. However, the grain size alone cannot confer a large coercivity advantage. Therefore, some attempts to increase coercivity have been made [3-8].

Generally, the grain boundary diffusion process for hot-deformed magnets is more difficult relative to sintered magnets, because both Dy and Tb easily diffuse into the bulk of the grains and the grains easily grow during the diffusion heat treatment. This study proposes coating the raw powder with a uniform and thin layer of Tb–Cu with the aim of diffusing Tb both in the grain boundary phase and on the surface of grains uniformly into the whole sample. Our novel grain boundary diffusion process using Tb–Cu alloy is expected to increase coercivity without sacrificing the remanence.

2. Experimental Procedures

The starting material was prepared by rapid quenching, followed by coating of the HREE free raw powder with a thin layer of $Tb_{0.85}Cu_{0.15}$ (wt.%). The coating (amount = 1.0 wt.%) was applied by the sputtering technique. The chemical compositions of the raw powders before and after sputtering were $Nd_{9.4}Pr_{3.3}Co_{3.8}B_{5.8}Ga_{0.46}O_{0.09}C_{0.16}Fe_{bal.}$ (at.%) and $Nd_{9.3}Pr_{3.3}Co_{3.8}B_{5.7}Ga_{0.46}Tb_{0.3}Cu_{0.14}O_{0.30}C_{0.17}Fe_{bal.}$ (at.%), respectively. Oxygen content was increased after sputtering. The sputtered powders were hot-pressed and hot-deformed at 800 °C then subjected to heat treatment at 730 °C for 10 h. The optimal heat treatment condition was decided from many trial-and-error experiments. Here, $Tb_{0.85}Cu_{0.15}$ (wt.%) was selected as the diffused material because we expected small quantities of it would largely increase coercivity. In addition, we presumed that the lower eutectic point of $Tb_{0.85}Cu_{0.15}$ (750 °C) compared with the Dy alloy was suitable for heat treatment of the hot-deformed magnet.

To measure the magnetic properties of the hot-deformed magnets, samples were cut by a wire electrical discharge machine into blocks measuring 5.6 mm (easy axis) × 7 mm × 7 mm. Magnetic properties at room temperature (RT) and 180 °C were measured with a DC recording fluxmeter. Microstructures were observed using a field emission-scanning electron microscope. The Tb diffusion conditions were characterized by field emission-electron probe microanalyzer (FE-EPMA) and electron energy loss spectroscopy (EELS).

3. Results and Discussion

Figures 1(a) and (b) show the demagnetization curves and temperature dependence of coercivity for the hot-deformed magnets fabricated from the noncoated powder and 1.0 wt.% Tb–Cu coated powder. Curves B and C show the results before and after heat treatment (at 730 °C for 10 h), respectively. Magnetic properties of base magnet were B_r=14.1 kG, ${}_iH_c$=14.8 kOe (1180 kA/m), while magnetic properties of diffusion processed magnet were B_r=13.7 kG, ${}_iH_c$=20.4 kOe (1625 kA/m). The temperature coefficient of coercivity β between RT and 180 °C was also improved from −0.511 to −0.465. From these results, the proposed process clearly improved the coercivity while preserving the square shape of the demagnetization curve. In other words, the coated powders suppressed the coercivity distribution in the depth direction of the magnet.

Figure 2 shows the magnetic properties of the hot-deformed Tb-diffused magnets and Tb bulk added magnets, which were also fabricated for comparative purposes. As seen from this figure, the Tb-diffused magnet displays superior magnetic properties to the Tb-added magnet. However, the property differences between the two magnets are less than expected. To clarify the reasons for this unexpected result, we conducted microstructural observations.

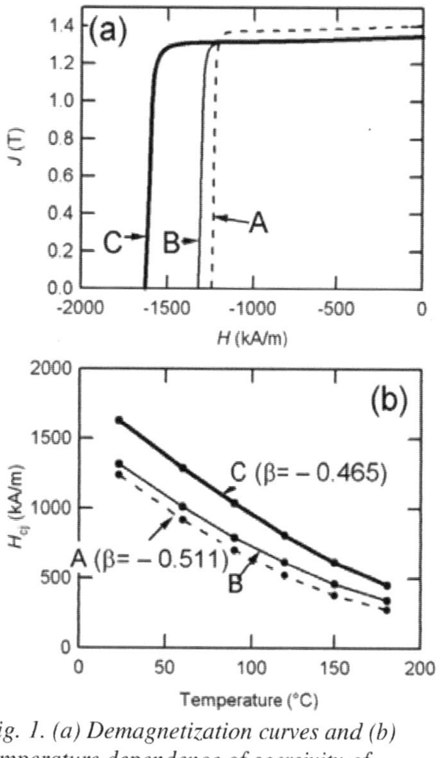

Fig. 1. (a) Demagnetization curves and (b) temperature dependence of coercivity of hot-deformed magnets fabricated from raw uncoated powder (A) and powder coated with 1.0 wt.% Tb–Cu (B, C). B and C correspond respectively to samples with and without heat treatment at 730 °C for 10 h. In Fig. 1(b), β is the temperature coefficient of the coercivity between RT and 180 °C.

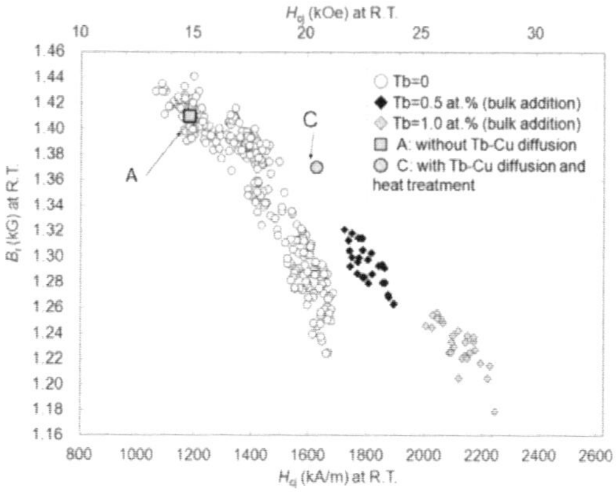

Fig. 2. Magnetic property map of Tb-free and Tb bulk added (Tb = 0.5, 1.0 at.%) hot-deformed magnets. Here, A and C respectively indicate hot-deformed magnets fabricated from raw uncoated powder and powder coated with 1.0 wt.% Tb–Cu, and then heat treated at 730 °C for 10 h.

Figures 3(a)–(d) show SEM images of the uniform fine grain areas, looking at the plane parallel to the c-axis. From Fig. 3(b), we can observe that while some grains grow at the powder boundaries (indicated by the white arrows), most of the grains are unchanged by heat treatment. Therefore, the unexpectedly small increments in the magnetic properties are not attributable to altered grain size.

Next, the Tb diffusion condition was examined the by FE-EPMA. The composition and Tb mapping images are shown in Figs. 4(a)–(d). Comparing these images,

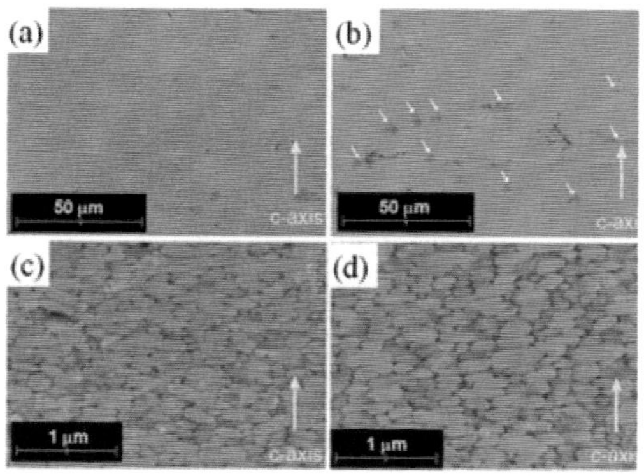

Fig. 3. FE-SEM images of the microstructure along a plane parallel to the c-axis (a), (c) before and (b), (d) after heat treatment at 730 °C for 10 h. The white arrows in (b) indicate the grain growth.

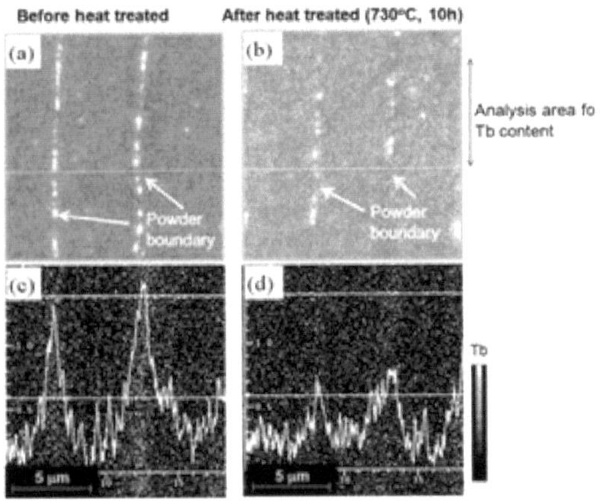

Fig. 4. (a), (b) Composition images and (c), (d) Tb mapping images of the plane parallel to the c-axis (a), (c) before and (b), (d) after heat treatment at 730 °C for 10 h.

Tb at the powder boundary clearly diffuses into the powder during heat treatment. However, most of the Tb is retained at the powder boundary. We infer that insufficient diffusion of Tb into the powder is responsible for the small increments in the magnetic properties. This presumption is supported by TEM-EELS images of the Tb diffusion conditions near the powder boundary. Figures 5(a)–(d) show TEM-EELS images of the diffusion-processed sample (sample C in Fig. 1). These images reveal that Tb is restricted to the grain boundary phase, where the Nd- and Pr-rich phases reside. No Tb is visible on the grain surfaces.

4. Conclusions

1) The coercivity and its temperature coefficient were improved by the grain boundary diffusion process using Tb–Cu coated powders; 1. Without the grain boundary diffusion process: B_r = 14.1 kG, ${}_iH_c$ = 14.8 kOe (1180 kA/m) and β= −0.511, 2. With the grain boundary diffusion process: B_r = 13.7 kG, ${}_iH_c$ = 20.4 kOe (1625 kA/m) and β= −0.465.

2) The magnetic properties of Tb-diffused hot-deformed magnets were superior to those of Tb bulk-added magnets, but the improvement was smaller than expected because of insufficient Tb diffusion.

3) The following measures may enable effective diffusion. 1. Choose an HREE alloy with lower melting point (e.g., three-alloy system). 2. Reduce the level of contaminants such as oxygen and carbon in the raw powders.

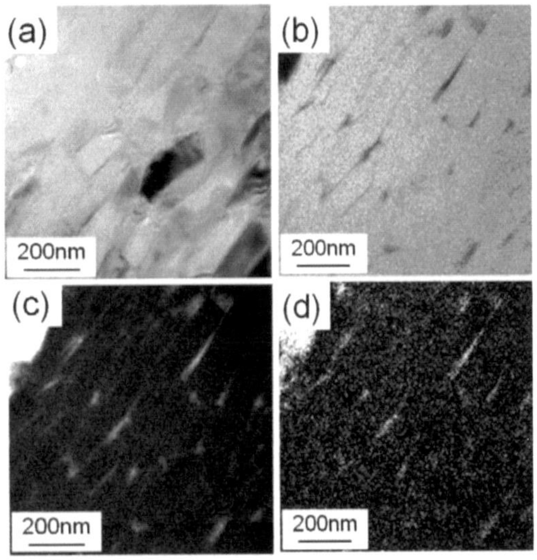

Fig. 5. TEM-EELS images of the microstructure parallel to the c-axis of a hot-deformed magnet after heat treatment. (a) TEM image and (b) Fe, (c) Nd, and (d) Tb composition.

Acknowledgment

The authors would like to thank K. Jinushi, Y. Iizumi, and A. Ito at Furuya Metal Co., Ltd. for the surface treatment of the powders.

References

[1] K. Hioki, A. Hattori, and, T. Iriyama, *J. Magn. Soc. Jpn.* **38**, 2014, 79.

[2] W. Szmaja, *J. Magn. Magn. Mater.* **301**, 2006, 546.

[3] H. Sepehri-Amin, T. Ohkubo, T. Nishiuchi, S. Hirosawa, and K. Hono, *Scr. Mater.* **63**, 2010, 1124.

[4] H. Sepehri-Amin, J. Liu, T. Ohkubo, K. Hioki, A. Hattori, and K. Hono, *Scr. Mater.* **69**, 2013, 647-650.

[5] T. Akiya J. Liu, H. Sepehri-Amin, T. Ohkubo, K. Hioki, A. Hattori, and, K. Hono, *J. Appl. Phys.* **115**, 2014, 17A766.

[6] T. Akiya, J. Liu, H. Sepehri-Amin, T. Ohkubo, K. Hioki, A. Hattori, and K. Hono, *Scr. Mater.* **81**, 2014, 48 - 51

[7] S. Sawatzki, I. Dirba, L. Schultz, and O. Gutfleisch, *J. Appl. Phys.* **114**, 2013, 133902.

[8] S. Sawatzki, I. Dirba, H. Wendrock, L. Schultz, and O. Gutfleisch, *J. Magn. Magn. Mater.* **358-359**, 2014, 163-169.

Effect of Dy/ Cu Cap Layers for Nd-Fe-B Thin Films After Heat Treatment

R. NAKAGAWA, M. DOI, T. SHIMA
Tohoku Gakuin University, Tagajo 985-8537, Japan

Abstract: *In order to understand the coercivity mechanism of Nd-Fe-B magnets, we have investigated the effect of Dy/ Cy cap layers for Nd-Fe-B thin films after heat treatment. Remarkable enhancement of the coercivity was obtained for the Nd-Fe-B thin films prepared at 520 °C followed by the post annealing at 625°C. Especially, the value of* H_C *was changed from 5.7 kOe to 25.0 kOe for Nd-Fe-B (100 nm)/ Dy (4 nm)/ Cu (2 nm) thin film. This result suggests that the volume fraction of Dy and Cu layers is close to a eutectic composition of binary Dy-Cu alloys, and Dy is thought to infiltrate into both* $Nd_2Fe_{14}B$ *phase and grain boundary phase.*

Keywords: *Nd-Fe-B thin film; grain boundary phase; diffusion; eutectic reaction*

Address: Ryosuke Nakagawa, Department of Electronics Engineering, Tohoku Gakuin University, Tagajo 985-8537, Japan, Tel: (81) 22-368-1128, Fax: (81) 22-368-1272,
E-mail: s1494302@tjcc.tohoku-gakuin.ac.jp

1. Introduction

Nd-Fe-B sintered magnets [1] exhibit a highest maximum energy products $(BH)_{max}$ among all permanent magnets, so they have been used for wide variety of applications. Particularly, their usage to traction motors for hybrid and electric vehicles (HEVs) have been increased recently and also will be increased in the future due to the consideration for the environmental issues. Since the Nd-Fe-B sintered magnets show a relatively low curie temperature of 315 °C, the substitution of heavy rare earth elements (HRE) such as Dy and Tb for Nd is essential for realizing a high thermal stability [2]. However, due to the scarce and localized natural resources of the HRE elements, Dy-free or less permanent magnet is strongly required. It is well known that the structure and the chemistry of the grain boundary phase between $Nd_2Fe_{14}B$ phases play an important role to understand coercivity mechanism. Recent studies revealed that the magnetic coupling between the $Nd_2Fe_{14}B$ main phases is thought to reduce by the grain boundary phase with Nd-rich and Cu-rich alloy phases after post-sinter annealing [3-4]. Hence, control of grain boundary phase is essential to increase the coercivity with much lower amount of Dy. Thus, it is important to investigate the microstructure including a grain boundary phase for Dy-containing Nd-Fe-B sintered magnets. In addition, in order to realize an ideal microstructure of the Nd-Fe-B magnet, thin film fabrication technique is known as one of useful and powerful routes [5]. In this study, in order to understand the coercivity mechanism, the samples have been prepared by the alternative deposition of the Dy and Cu cap layers onto Nd-Fe-B layer and the effect of the post annealing for the diffusion of cap layers into grain boundary phase have been investigated.

2. Experimental Procedure

The samples were prepared by using an ultrahigh vacuum compatible magnetron sputtering system. The base pressure is below 5×10^{-8} Pa. The compositions of the Nd-Fe-B layer was controlled by co-sputtering with Fe, $Fe_{80}B_{20}$ (at%), and Nd targets and it was determined to be $Nd_{14.2}Fe_{78.2}B_{7.6}$ by electron probe X-ray microanalysis (EPMA). A Mo buffer layer of 10 nm was deposited onto thermally oxidized silicon substrates (SiO_2) at 520 °C. The substrate temperature T_s was kept at 520 °C during the deposition of the Nd-Fe-B layer. The thickness of the Nd-Fe-B layer was fixed at 100 nm. The Nd-Fe-B layer was prepared at different conditions before the deposition of Dy and Cu cap layers: one is crystallized and the other is amorphous state. When T_s is around 520 °C, the structure of the Nd-Fe-B layer shows partially crystalline but mainly amorphous state. However, the structure turned into crystalline after annealed at 600 °C for 30 min. Subsequently, the substrates were cooled down to room temperature (R.T) and then both Dy and Cu layers were deposited. The nominal thickness of Dy layer (t_{Dy} nm) was varied in the range of 0 - 10 nm, the thickness of the Cu layer (t_{Cu} nm) was fixed at 2 nm. Then, a Mo layer of 10 nm was deposited at R.T. for the prevention of oxidation. Finally, the samples were annealed at 625 °C for 30 min for the diffusion of cap layers. The structural analysis was performed by X-ray diffraction (XRD) with Cu Kα radiation. The magnetization curves were measured using a superconducting quantum interference device (SQUID) magnetometer in the field up to ±70 kOe. All the measurements were performed at R.T.

3. Results and Discussion

In order to see the effect of volume fractions of Dy layer on the structure for crystallized Nd-Fe-B thin films, t_{Dy} was varied. X-ray diffraction patterns for the Nd-Fe-B (100 m)/ Dy (t_{Dy} nm)/ Cu (2 nm) films are shown in Fig. 1. The intensity of the peaks from c-plane of the $Nd_2Fe_{14}B$ phase in the Nd-Fe-B layer is clearly observed for all the samples. This indicates that Nd-Fe-B layer is thought to grow with columnar structures toward c-axis orientation. In addition, the peak identified as $Nd_2Fe_{14}B$ (220) was observed at $2\theta = 28.6$ ° for the film with t_{Dy} = 10 nm. However, no peak corresponding to the Dy and Cu layer was observed.

Magnetization curves for the Nd-Fe-B/ Dy/ Cu films are shown in Fig. 2. All the films were measured in the direction perpendicular to the film plane (solid line) and parallel to the film plane (broken line). The Nd-Fe-B thin films with Dy/ Cu cap layers show a slightly higher H_c than the one without cap layers. However, remarkable enhancement of H_c was not observed. This suggests that the Dy and Cu cap layers deposited on the crystallized Nd-Fe-B layer does not enough to infiltrate even after post-annealing at 625 °C.

In order to see the effect of volume fractions of Dy layer on the structure for amorphous Nd-Fe-B thin films, t_{Dy} was varied. X-ray diffraction patterns for the Nd-Fe-B (100 nm)/ Dy (t_{Dy} nm)/ Cu (2 nm) films are shown in Fig. 3. After the deposition of Nd-Fe-B layer of 520 °C, T_s was cooled down to R.T. and then Dy and Cy layers were deposited. The intensity of the peaks from c-plane of the Nd-Fe-B layer is clearly

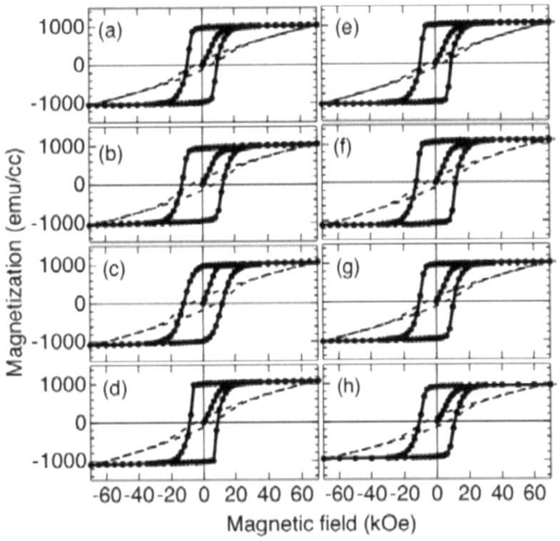

Fig. 2. Magnetization curves for Nd-Fe-B (100 nm)/ Dy (t_{Dy} nm)/ Cu (2 nm) thin films. After the deposition of Nd-Fe-B layer, the samples were post annealed at 600 °C for crystallization. (a): the Nd-Fe-B film without cap layer, (b) t_{Dy} = 0, (c) 1, (d) 2, (e) 3, (f) 4, (g) 5, and (h) 10 nm.

observed for all the samples and no significant change was observed, compared with Fig. 1.

Magnetization curves for the Nd-Fe-B (100 m)/ Dy (t_{Dy} nm)/ Cu (2 nm) films are shown in Fig. 4. With increasing t_{Dy}, H_c was increased and hold maximum of 25.0 kOe at t_{Dy} = 4 nm. This enhancement suggests that the composition of Dy and Cu layer is almost close to a binary Dy-Cu alloy eutectic composition. Since that, the Dy and Cu layers were probably infiltrated into the grain boundary and $Nd_2Fe_{14}B$ main phase. However, due to the antiferromagnetic coupling of the magnetic moments of Fe with Dy,

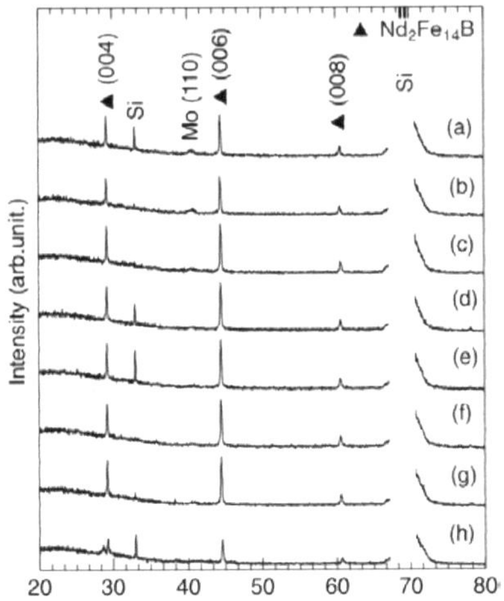

Fig. 1. X-ray diffraction patterns for Nd-Fe-B (100 nm)/ Dy (t_{Dy} nm)/ Cu (2 nm) thin films. After the deposition of Nd-Fe-B layer, the samples were post annealed at 600 °C for crystallization. (a): the Nd-Fe-B film without cap layer, (b) t_{Dy} = 0, (c) 1, (d) 2, (e) 3, (f) 4, (g) 5, and (h) 10 nm.

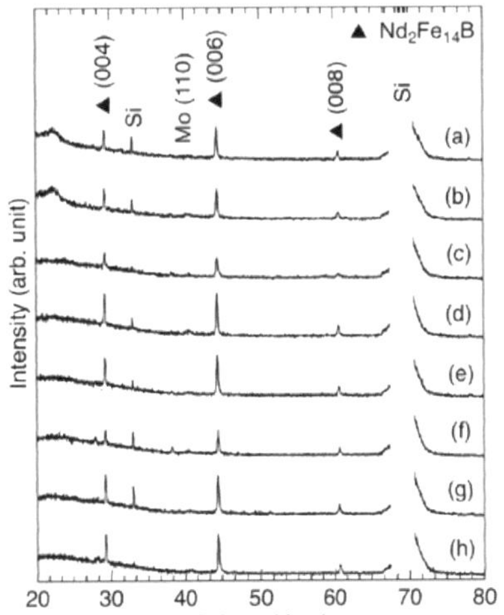

Fig. 3. X-ray diffraction patterns for Nd-Fe-B (100 nm)/ Dy (t_{Dy} nm)/ Cu (2 nm) thin films. After the deposition of Nd-Fe-B layer, T_s was cooled down to R.T. (a): the Nd-Fe-B film without cap layer, (b) t_{Dy} = 0, (c) 1, (d) 2, (e) 3, (f) 4, (g) 5, and (h) 10 nm.

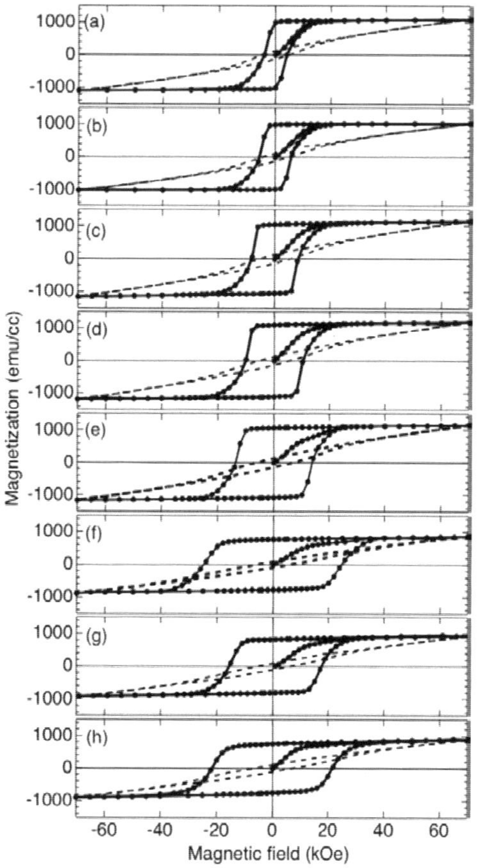

Fig. 4 Magnetization curves for Nd-Fe-B (100 nm)/ Dy (t_{Dy} nm)/ Cu (2 nm) thin films after annealing at 625 °C. After the deposition of Nd-Fe-B layer, T_s was cooled down to R.T. (a): the Nd-Fe-B film without cap layer, (b) t_{Dy} = 0, (c) 1, (d) 2, (e) 3, (f) 4, (g) 5, and (h) 10 nm.

remanence was reduced.

H_c as a function of the thickness of Dy layer for Nd-Fe-B (100 nm)/ Dy (t_{Dy} nm)/ Cu (2 nm) thin film was summarized in Fig. 5. No remarlable change was obtained for the film with post annealing after the deposition of Nd-Fe-B layer. While, with increasing t_{Dy}, H_c was increased for the film without post annealing. In particular, highest H_c of 25.0 kOe was obtained for the film with t_{Dy} = 4 nm. This is thought to due to the formation of $(Nd,Dy)_2Fe_{14}B$ shell around each grain [6-9] that impedes the nucleation of reversed domains and the domain wall displacement.

4. Summary

Effect of Dy/ Cu cap layers for two states of crystallized and amorphous Nd-Fe-B layer has been investigated. The Dy and Cu cap layers deposited on the crystallized Nd-Fe-B layer did not enough to infiltrate even after post annealing at 625 °C, while the films deposited on the amorphous Nd-Fe-B layer probably infiltrated into the grain boundary phase and

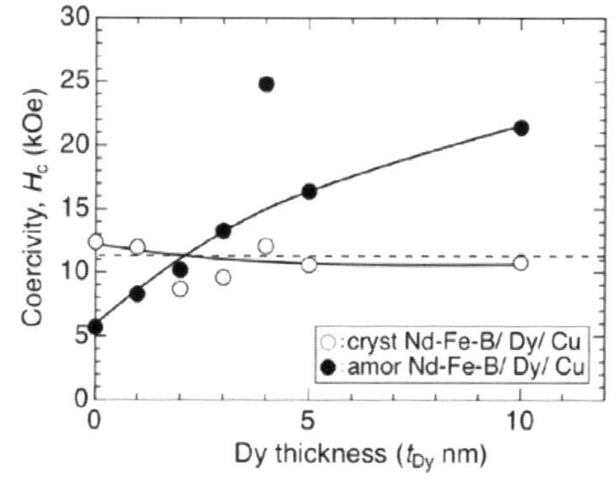

Fig. 5. Effect of Dy layer thickness on the coercivity for Nd-Fe-B (100 nm)/ Dy (t_{Dy} nm)/ Cu (2 nm) thin films. The open and closed circles denote the Nd-Fe-B thin films with the post annealing after the deposition of Nd-Fe-B layer and without the post annealing, respectively. The dashed line also denotes the results from the Nd-Fe-B (100 nm) single-layer films without cap layer.

$Nd_2Fe_{14}B$ main phase. As a result, due to the formation of $(Nd,Dy)_2Fe_{14}B$ shell around each grain that impedes the nucleation of reversed domains and the domain wall displacement, highest H_c of 25.0 kOe was obtained for the film with t_{Dy} = 4 nm without post annealing after the deposition of Nd-Fe-B layer.

Acknowledgment

This work was supported in part by the Ministry of Education, Culture, Sports, Science and Technology (MEXT) project for the "Hi-Tech Research Center Preparation Program" and performed at the Hi-tech Research Center of Tohoku Gakuin University.

References

[1] M. Sagawa, S. Fujimura, N. Togawa, H. Yamamoto, Y. Matsuura, *J. Appl. Phys.* **55**, 1984, 2083.
[2] M. Sagawa, S. Hirosawa, K.Tokuhara, H. Yamamoto, S. Fujimura, Y. Tsubokawa, and R. Shimazu, *J. Appl. Phys.* **61**, 1987, 3559.
[3] S. Suzuki, Y. Hatayama, H. Iwama, and T. Shima, *IEEE Trans. Magn.* **47**, 2011, 2796.
[4] T. Sato, N. Oka, T. Ohsuna, Y. Kaneko, S. Suzuki and T. Shima, *J.Appl. Phys.* **110**, 2011, 023903.
[5] T. Shima, K. Sato, Y. Mishina, Y. Ohtsuki, H. Iwama, *J. Jpn. Inst. Metal.* **76**, 2012, 52.
[6] H. Nakamura, K. Hirota, M. Shimao, T. Minowa, M. Honshima, *IEEE Trans. Magn.* **41,** 2005, 3844.
[7] H. Suzuki, Y. Satsu, M. Komuro, *J. Appl. Phys.* **105**, 2009, A734.
[8] K. Hirota, H. Nakamura, M. Shimao, T. Minowa, M. Honshima, *IEEE Trans. Magn.* **42,** 2006, 2909.
[9] H. Seperi-Amin, T. Ohkubo K. Hono, *J.Appl. Phys.* **107**, 2010, A745.

Coercivity Enhancement of Bulk Sintered Nd-Fe-B Magnets by DyH_3 Nanoparticles Grain Boundary Diffusion

C. CHANG[1], W. Q. LIU[1], D. WU[1], M. YUE[1], D. T. ZHANG[1], T. Y. ZUO[2]
[1]College of Materials Science, Beijing University of Technology, Beijing, 100124, China
[2]Institute of Recycling economy, Beijing University of Technology, Beijing, 100124, China

Abstract: *The coercivity enhancement of bulk sintered Nd-Fe-B permanent magnets by grain boundary diffusion technique with DyH_3 nanoparticles was studied. The magnetic properties and microstructure of these magnets were systematically studied. The coercivity and remanence of grain boundary diffusion magnets were improved by 16% and reduced by 2.9%, respectively, compared with those of the original magnets. The investigation shows that Dy is preferentially enriched as $(Nd,Dy)_2Fe_{14}B$ phase in the surface region of the $Nd_2Fe_{14}B$ matrix grains, as indicated by the remarkable enhancement of the magneto-crystalline anisotropy field of the magnets. As a result, magnets diffused with a small amount of DyH_3 nanoparticles possess enhanced coercivity without remarkably sacrificing its magnetization.*

Keywords: *bulk Nd-Fe-B magnets, grain boundary diffusion, DyH_3 nanoparticles; coercivity*

Address: W. Q. Liu, College of Materials Science and Engineering, Beijing University of Technology, Beijing, 100124, China, Tel: (86-10)6739-1760, Fax: (86-10)6739-1760, Email: liuwq@bjut.edu.cn

1. Introduction

Nd-Fe-B sintered magnets for elevated temperature applications have received considerable interest with the increased demanding in permanent magnetic motors [1]. It is well known that the addition of heavy rare earths (Dy or Tb) effectively enhances coercivity. Unfortunately, it leads to a considerable decrease of remanence and energy product of the magnets [2, 3]. Recently, grain boundary diffusion method has been widely used to prepare Dy-less Nd-Fe-B sintered magnets [4, 5]. Previous investigations focus on micro-scale Dy_2O_3, DyF_3 and TbF_3 powder diffusion and thin magnets with thicknesses less than 5 mm. However, little is known concerning the effects of nanoparticle diffusion on the magnetic properties of bulk Nd-Fe-B permanet magnets. In the present study, DyH_3 nanoparticles have been applied to prepare bulk Nd-Fe-B sintered magnets via grain boundary diffusion method. The microstructure and magnetic properties of these prepared magnets were investigated.

2. Experiments

Bulk Nd-Fe-B permanent magnets with the dimensions of 10×10×7 mm were etched in a nitric acid solution to clean the surfaces. DyH_3 nanoparticles were prepared by inert gas condensation method, and then were mixed with ethyl alcohol in different ratios from 1:4 to 2:1. The magnets were immersed in the mixture and ultra-sonicated for two minutes, and dried immediately by hot air. The magnets with the DyH_3 coating were then heat treated at 800-875 °C for 3 h and subsequently annealed at 500 °C for 5 h in vacuum. Magnetic properties were measured using a B-H loop line instrument with a magnetic field of 3 T. The microstructure of the magnets was analyzed using a scanning electron microscopy (SEM).

3. Results and discussion

Figure 1 shows the TEM image of DyH_3 nanoparticles. The size of the DyH_3 nanoparticles ranges from 50 to 200 nm.

The influence of the weight ratio between DyH_3 nanoparticles and alcohol on the magnetic properties of bulk sintered Nd-Fe-B permanent magnets is shown in Fig. 2. It shows that increasing the weight ratio results in the gradual augmentation of the coercivity of the magnets, while the remanence and maximum energy energy product of the magnets drop simultaneously. The magnet that exhibited optimal overall magnetic properties had coercivity (H_{ci}) of 1282 kA/m (raised by 15.7% compared to that of

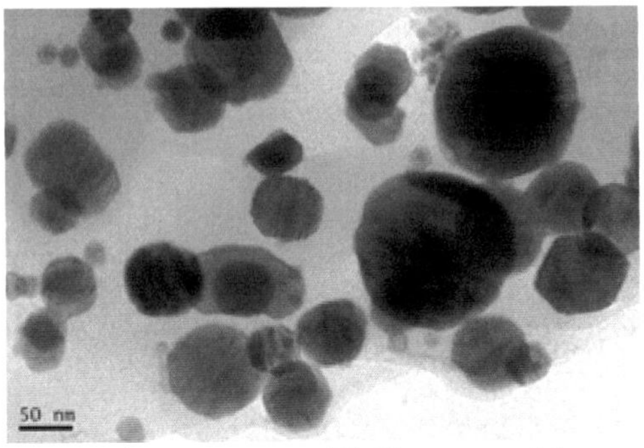

Fig. 1. TEM image of DyH_3 nanoparticles.

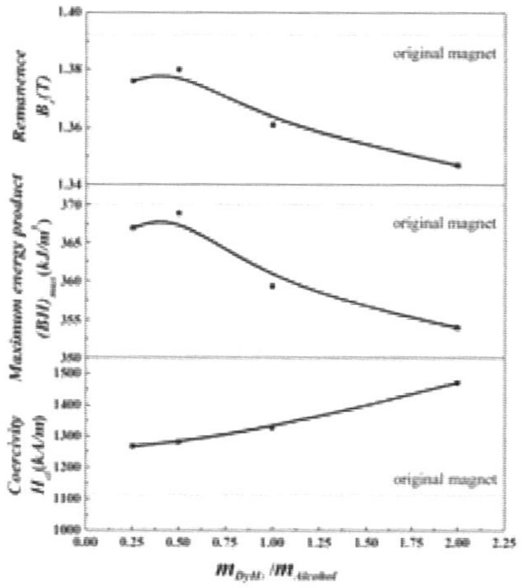

Fig.2. The influence of weight ratio between DyH_3 nanoparticles and alcohol on the magnetic properties of bulk sintered Nd-Fe-B permanent magnets.

original magnet) , remanence (B_r) of 1.38 T (reduced by 0.9%) , and maximum energy product [$(BH)_{max}$] of 369 kJ/m^3 (reduced by 0.3%), using the weight ratio of 1:2.

Figure 3 shows the magnetic properties of the magnets by grain boundary diffusion process as a function of heat treatment temperatures. With the increasing of the heat treatment temperature, the remanence and maximum energy product of magnets decrease gradually. However, the coercivity of the magnets remarkably increases first, peaks at 825 °C, then falls. The decrease of coercivity is due to the excessive grain growth at high temperatures. Considering the overall magnetic properties, the heat treatment temperature was optimized at 825 °C. The coercivity of the magnets increases by 180 kA/m (16%), while the remanence and the maximum energy product of the magnets reduces by 0.04 T (2.9%) and 15 kJ/m^3 (4%), respectively, compared to those of the original magnet.

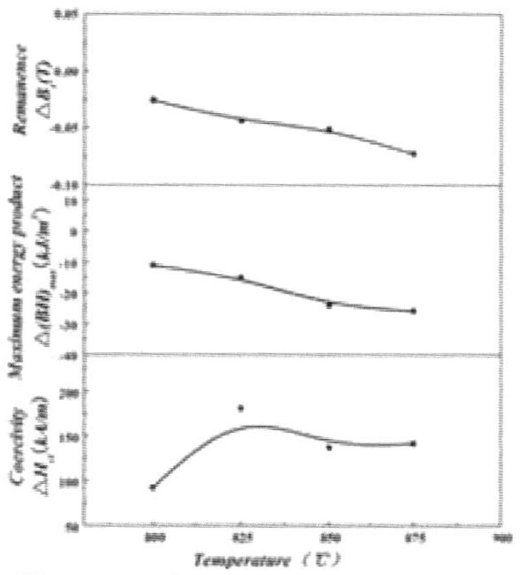

Fig.3. The magnetic properties of the magnets by grain boundary diffusion process as a function of heat treatment temperatures.

Fig. 4. Backscatter electron image of the magnet by grain boundary diffusion process

To clarify the distribution of the Dy element in the Nd-Fe-B magnet after the diffusion process, the microstructure as well as the concentration distribution of Fe, Nd, Pr and Dy both in the Nd-rich grain boundary phase and in the $Nd_2Fe_{14}B$ matrix phase grains were examined, and the results are shown in Fig. 4. It can be seen that the magnets are mainly composed of the $Nd_2Fe_{14}B$ main phase (the dark grey area), the Nd-rich grain boundary phase (the white area), and the grain surface region (the light grey area). Further quantitative investigations of Dy distribution in Nd-rich phase, grains surface region, and center of the $Nd_2Fe_{14}B$ grains, which were respectively indicated by number a, b, and c in Fig. 4, shows that Dy enriches mainly the surface region of $Nd_2Fe_{14}B$ grains, where the Dy concentration is higher than in both the Nd-rich phase and the center of $Nd_2Fe_{14}B$ grains (Table I). Furthermore, the enriched Dy element in the grains surface region of the $Nd_2Fe_{14}B$ grains is expected to exist as the $(Nd,Dy)_2Fe_{14}B$ phase, which has the larger H_A than that of the $Nd_2Fe_{14}B$ phase. As a result, the H_{ci} of the Nd-Fe-B magnets is remarkably enhanced due to the restraint of magnetic reversal of the magnet during the demagnetization process.

4. Conclusion

In summary, high coercivity bulk magnets without obvious degradation of the remanence were fabricated by applying grain boundary diffusion technology with

TABLE 1. Energy dispersive X-ray analysis in Nd-rich phase (a), grain surface region (b), and center of the $Nd_2Fe_{14}B$ grains (c) in the Nd-Fe-B magnets diffused with Dy nanoparticles (wt.%).

Position	Fe	Nd	Pr	Dy
a	3.24	65.04	18.14	13.58
b	62.79	16.76	4.52	15.93
c	67.99	23.19	5.95	2.86

DyH_3 nanoparticles. H_{ci} was improved by 16%, B_r reduced by 2.9% and $(BH)_{max}$ reduced by 4%. The diffusion Dy element was found to preferentially enrich the $(Nd, Dy)_2Fe_{14}B$ phase in the surface region of the $Nd_2Fe_{14}B$ matrix grains. The specially distributed $(Nd,Dy)_2Fe_{14}B$ phase was expected to improve the coercivity of the Nd-Fe-B magnets by enhancing the H_A and restraining of the magnetic reversal of the magnet during the demagnetization process.

Acknowledgement
This work was supported by the National Natural Science Foundation of China (51001002, 51371002), National High Technology Research and Development Program of China (2012AA063201), Rixin Talents of Beijing University of Technology, Jinghua Talents of Beijing University of Technology, The Importation and Development of High-Caliber Talents Project of Beijing Municipal Institutions, Technology Foundation for Selected Overseas Chinese Scholar of Beijing.

References

[1] M. H. Walmer, J. F. Liu, P. C. Dent, Proceedings of 20th International Workshop on Rare Earth Permanent Magnets and Their Applications, Crete, Greece, 2008, pp. 1-6.
[2] S. Hirosawa, Y. Matsuura, H. Yamamoto, S. Fujimura, M. Sagawa, H. Yamauchi, *J. Appl. Phys.*, 59, 1986, 873
[3] M. Sagawa, S. Fujimura, H. Yamamoto, K. Hiraga, *IEEE Trans. Magn.*, 20, 1984, 1584
[4] H. Nakamura, K. Hirota, M. Shimao, T. Minowa, M. Honshima, *IEEE Trans Magn.*, 41, 2005, 3844
[5] K. Hirota, H. Nakamura, T. Minowa, M. Honshima, *IEEE Trans. Magn.*, 42, 2006, 2909.

Thermal Stability of Nd-Fe-B HDDR Powder and Hot-Pressed Compact

JUNG-GOO LEE[1], HEE-RYOUNG CHA[1], SHU LIU[1], JI-HUN YU[1], HAE-WOONG KWON[2], TAE-HOON KIM[3], CHEOL-WOONG YANG[3]
[1]Powder & Ceramics Division, Korea Institute of Materials Science, Changwon, Korea
[2]Department of Materials Science and Engineering, Pukyong National University, Busan, Korea
[3]School of Advanced Materials Science Engineering, Sungkyunkwan University, Suwon, Korea.

Abstract: *Thermal stability of the $Nd_{12.5}Fe_{80.6}B_{6.4}Ga_{0.3}Nb_{0.2}$ hydrogenation, disproportionation, desorption and recombination (HDDR)-treated powder and its effect on magnetic properties of hot-pressed compact, were studied. Coercivity of the HDDR-treated powder was markedly reduced by heating above 600 °C. In addition, coercivity of the hot-pressed compact was also radically reduced when the compaction was performed at the temperature above 650 °C. The HDDR-treated powder contained a significant amount of hydrogen, and it influenced the thermal stability of the material. The residual hydrogen existed in the form of $Nd_2Fe_{14}BH_x$ hydride, and it was disproportionated into α-Fe, Fe_2B and NdH_2 phases at an elevated temperature. The radical coercivity reduction was attributed to the presence of the soft magnetic phases, α-Fe and Fe_2B formed via disproportionation of the $Nd_2Fe_{14}BH_x$.*

Keywords: *coercivity; disproportionation; HDDR; hot-pressing; residual hydrogen*

Address: Jung-Goo Lee, Powder & Ceramics Division, Korea Institute of Materials Science, Changwon, Korea, Tel/Fax: +82 55 280 3606/3392, E-mail: jglee36@kims.re.kr

1. Introduction

The coercivity of the commercial Nd-Fe-B magnets without heavy rare earth (HRE) elements is considerably lower than that expected from their anisotropic magnetic field. And it has been generally accepted that the low coercivity is attributed to insufficient microstructure control and one of the key requirements for achieving high coercivity in Nd-Fe-B magnet is having a fine grain structure. The hydrogenation, disproportionation, desorption and recombination (HDDR) process is an effective means of obtaining the fine grain structure [1-2]. The usual HDDR-treated material is, however, in powder form. Therefore, it would be very promising if the HDDR powder can be consolidated into high density bulk magnet keeping the ultrafine microstructure in the HDDR powder state. Previous reports revealed that hot-pressing technique was applied successfully to consolidate the HDDR powder into a high density compact [3-6]. It is believed that a significant amount of hydrogen is contained in the Nd-Fe-B HDDR powder and this residual hydrogen may be desorbed and react again with the powder during the hot-pressing under vacuum. The residual hydrogen may, therefore, influence the magnetic properties, in particular, the coercivity of the consolidated compact.

Based upon this premise, in this article, desorption of the residual hydrogen in the HDDR-treated powder during hot-pressing, and its effects on the coercivity of the consolidated compact were investigated.

2. Experimental Procedure

The starting material used in the present study is HDDR-treated powder of $Nd_{12.5}Fe_{80.6}B_{6.4}Ga_{0.3}Nb_{0.2}$ alloy. Details of HDDR treatment can be found elsewhere [7, 8]. The thermal stability of HDDR powder was studied over a temperature range from 500 to 800 °C in vacuum and Ar atmosphere. Hydrogen content in the HDDR-treated powder was determined by Hydrogen Determinator (LECO, RH-600). The desorption behavior of the HDDR-treated powder was examined by vacuum gauge and thermopiezic analyzer (TPA) up to 800 °C. The powder was compacted by hot-pressing with induction heating in vacuum at a temperature ranges from 400 to 850 °C. Magnetic characterization of the materials was undertaken by means of vibrating sample magnetometer (VSM). Morphology of the powder was observed by SEM.

3. Results and Discussion

Figure 1 shows the coercivity of HDDR-treated powder measured at room temperature after heat treatment in vacuum and Ar atmosphere over the temperature range from 500 to 800 °C. It appears that coercivity of the powder was reduced significantly above 600 °C, and interestingly, the coercivity reduction was much more profound for the material heated in Ar atmosphere than in vacuum. One of the possible reasons for the coercivity reduction would be an excessive grain growth caused by the heating at elevated temperature. However, this is not the case. Microstructure observation showed that no significant

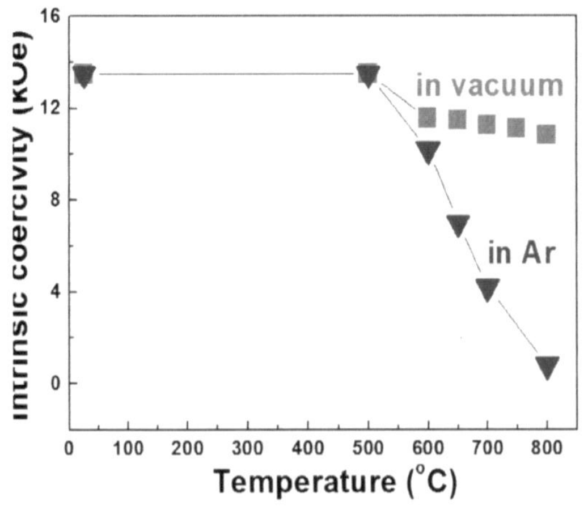

Fig. 1. Coercivity variation of HDDR-treated powder after heat treatment in vacuum and Ar atmosphere over the temperature range from 500 to 800 °C [12].

difference in the grain size was noticed before and after the heating both in Ar and in vacuum as shown in Fig. 2. The radical coercivity reduction in the sample heated in Ar may be closely related to the residual hydrogen in the HDDR-treated powder. The desorption of residual hydrogen in the HDDR-treated powder was studied by vacuum gauge, and the desorption trace was shown in Fig. 3. Also included in Fig. 3 is the hydrogen desorption trace for the fully hydrogenated bulk alloy with identical composition for comparison. For full hydrogenation, the bulk alloy was heated up to 500 °C in 1 bar hydrogen. It appears that the HDDR powder showed a similar hydrogen desorption pattern with that of the fully hydrogenated alloy except that the amount of desorbed hydrogen was much smaller. The residual hydrogen in the HDDR powder is desorbed through three steps at specific temperatures around 200 °C, 300 °C and 700 °C, respectively. The desorption at around 200 °C is corresponding to the hydrogendesorption due to the transition from $Nd_2Fe_{14}BH_x$ to $Nd_2Fe_{14}B$. The desorption events at 300 °C and 700 °C are corresponding to the hydrogen desorption due to the transition from $NdH_{2.7}$ to NdH_2, and NdH_2 to Nd, respectively [9,10]. These results clearly indicated that the HDDR powder contained a significant amount of hydrogen. The residual hydrogen is considered to be a common feature of Nd-Fe-B HDDR powder. Previous work also reported that the hydrogen content did not come down to zero after completion of optimum HDDR process [11]. The amount of Nd-rich phase in the present alloy is considered to be fairly small due to the slightly over stoichiometric composition. Therefore, it is more or less reasonable to assume that most of the hydrogen in the HDDR-treated material may exist in the $Nd_2Fe_{14}B$-type magnetic phase as form of $Nd_2Fe_{14}BH_x$.

On the other hand, the coercivity of the hot-pressed compact was lower than that of the initial HDDR powder, and it decreased with increasing the hot-pressing temperature. It is worth noting that coercivity of the compact was radically reduced when the compaction was performed at the temperature above 650 °C. It was also confirmed that there is no significant grain growth before and after the hot-pressing at higher temperature as shown in Fig. 2. More detailed microstructural observation of the compact hot-pressed at higher temperature was carried out by TEM. Interestingly, in some local area in the compact hot-pressed at 800 °C, the α-Fe and Fe_2B phases were found as shown in Fig. 4. It is

Fig. 2. SEM micrographs showing the grain structure of (a) initial powder, (b) powder heated up to 800 °C in Ar, (c) powder heated up to 800 °C, and (d) compact hot-pressed at 800 °C [12,13].

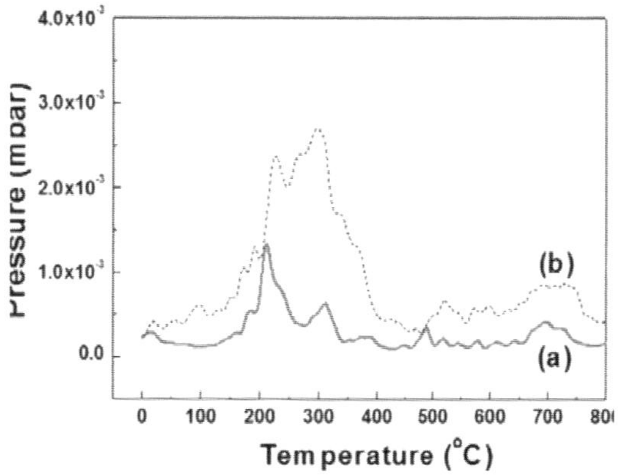

Fig. 3. TPA trace showing the hydrogen desorption and absorption of HDDR-treated powder in closed system [13].

believed that these α-Fe and Fe_2B phases may have been formed by the disproportionation of the $Nd_2Fe_{14}BH_x$.

4. Conclusions

HDDR-treated powder contained significant amount of residual hydrogen. Coercivity of the hot-pressed compact of the powder was radically reduced when the compaction was performed at the temperature above 650 °C. Some of the residual hydrogen was released during hot-pressing and it was confined in the closed-type die and rehydrogenated the powder again. Resulting hydrogenated phase was disproportionate during hot-pressing above 650 °C, leading to formation of α-Fe and Fe_2B phases. The radical coercivity reduction in the compact hot-pressed above 650 °C was attributed to the presence of the softmagnetic phases, α-Fe and Fe_2B formed via disproportionation of the $Nd_2Fe_{14}BH_x$.

Acknowledgment
This research was supported by a grant from the Fundamental R&D Program for Core Technology of Materials funded by the Ministry of Knowledge Economy, Republic of Korea.

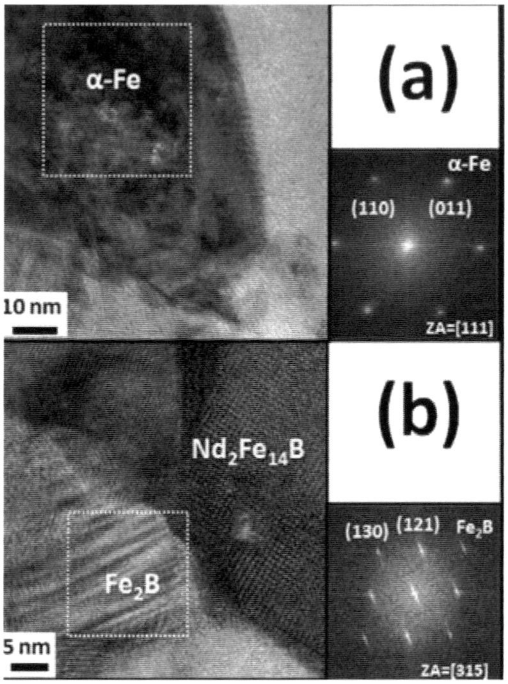

Fig. 4. TEM micrographs showing the presence of (a) α-Fe and (b) Fe_2B phases in the compact hot-pressed at 800 °C [13].

References

[1] T. Takeshita and R. Nakayama, in: *Proc. 10th Int. Workshop on RE Magnets and Their Applications*, 1989, 1, 551.
[2] P. J. McGuiness, X. J. Zhang, X. J. Yin, and I. R. Harris, *J. Less-Common Met.* **158**, 1990, 359.
[3] E. Estevez, J. Fidler, C. Short, and I. R. Harris, *J. Phys. D: Appl. Phys.* **29**, 1996, 951.
[4] O. Gutfleisch, A. Kirchner, W. Grunberger, D. Hinz, H. Nagel, P. Thompson, J. N. Chapman, K.-H. Müller, L. Schultz, and I. R. Harris, *J. Phys. D: Appl. Phys.* **31**, 1998, 807.
[5] N. Nozawa, H. Sepehri-Amin, T. Ohkubo, K. Hono, T. Nishiuchi, and S. Hirosawa, *J. Magn. Magn. Mater.* **323**, 2011, 115.
[6] K. Morimoto, E. Niizuma, K. Igarashi, K. Mori, M. Watanabe, and R. Nakayama, *J. Magn. Magn. Mater.*, 2003, *265*, 345–351.
[7] J. I. Lee, H. W. Kwon, and Y. S. Kang, *J. Magn.* **13**, 2008, 102.
[8] H. R. Cha, J. H. Yu, Y. K. Baek, H. W. Kwon, Y. D. Kim, and J. G. Lee, *J. Magn.* **19**, 2014, 49.
[9] D. Book and I. R. Harris, *J. Alloy Compd.* **221**, 1995, 187.
[10] M. Zakotnik, I. R. Harris, and A. J. Williams, *J. Alloy Compd.* **450**, 2008, 525.
[11] T. Nishiuchi and S. Hirosawa, *IEEE IEE J. Trans.* **3**, 2008, 390.
[12] Md. A. Matin, H. W. Kwon, J. G. Lee, and J. H. Yu, *IEEE Trans. Magn.* **50**, 2014, 2100504.
[13] Md. A. Matin, H. W. Kwon, J. G. Lee, J. H. Yu, T. H. Kim, and C. W. Yang, *IEEE Trans. Magn*, **49**, 2013, 3398.

Improvement of Coercivity and Thermal Stability of NdFeB-type Magnetic Powders by Alloy Diffusion

FANGMING WAN, JINGZHI HAN, YINGCHANG YANG, JINBO YANG
State Key Laboratory for Mesoscopic Physics, and School of Physics, Peking University, Beijing 100871, China

Abstract *Alloy diffusion can be used to improve the magnetic property of Nd-Fe-B. In this work, we have used Pr-Cu alloy diffusion effect to improve the magnetic properties of HDDR Nd-Fe-B and MQA powders. The diffusion of Pr-Cu alloy into the powders can prevent the grain from growing, and improve the coercivity of the powders. This enhancement in coercivity is mainly attributed to the modification of grain boundaries including the formation of a nonmagnetic boundary layer and the increase of boundary thickness. The modified boundaries can work as effective pinning layers for domain walls. The diffusion treatment also improves the thermal stability of the magnetic powders. By diffusion of Pr-Cu alloy into the powders, the room temperature coercivities of HDDR and MQA powders can increase to 18 and 24 kOe, respectively.*

Keywords: *Nd-Fe-B; permanent magnet; coercivity; alloys diffusion*

Address: School of Physics, Peking University, hanjingzhi@pku.edu.cn and jbyang@pku.edu.cn

1. Introduction

$Nd_2Fe_{14}B$-type permanent magnets are widely used because of their excellent magnetic performance at room temperature [1,2]. There are two typical methods to prepare anisotropic $Nd_2Fe_{14}B$-type powders. One is the hydrogenation disproportionation desorption recombination (HDDR) process [3], another is pulverizing die-upset or hot deformed magnets [4,5]. However, the processed powders usually exhibit a relatively low coercivity (about 10 - 13 kOe), which limits the applications at high temperature due to the unsatisfying thermal stability associated with their low Curie temperatures. At present, the diffusion of Dy element on the surface of the powders is an effective way to increase the coercivity, but the addition of Dy raises costs of raw materials since the Dy resource is scare. Therefore, developing the Dy-free anisotropic powders with high coercivity is desired for the technique applications.

Recently, it was found that the coercivity of HDDR $Nd_{12.5}Fe_{72.8}Co_{8.0}B_{6.5}Ga_{0.2}$ powders can be improved by diffusing Nd-Cu alloy into the boundary areas [6]. In this work, we have used $Pr_{68}Cu_{32}$ alloy as the diffusing agent. The eutectic point (472 °C) of $Pr_{68}Cu_{32}$ alloy is much lower than that of $Nd_{70}Cu_{30}$ (520 °C). Thus, compared to Nd-Cu-type alloy, the $Pr_{68}Cu_{32}$ powders may melt and diffuse more effectively into the grain boundaries of $Nd_2Fe_{14}B$-type powders under the same heat treatment condition. By diffusing $Pr_{68}Cu_{32}$ alloy into Nd-Fe-B powders, the coercivities of the HDDR and MQA powders were improved from 13 kOe to 18 and 24 kOe, respectively. The thermal stability of these powders was also improved.

2. Experimental Detail

HDDR $Nd_{13}Fe_{79.4}B_7Nb_{0.3}Ga_{0.3}$ powders were prepared according to the experimental procedure described in reference [7]. The commercial MQA (Magnequech Int.) Dy-free anisotropic powders with mean size of about 100 μm were also used as the starting materials [8]. The $Pr_{68}Cu_{32}$ ribbon was prepared by melt spinning method and was pulverized into fine powders in the argon atmosphere. The anisotropic HDDR and MQA powders were mixed with various ratios of $Pr_{68}Cu_{32}$ powders. The mixtures were grinded and annealed in vacuum (~10^{-3} Pa) at 600 °C for 1 h. The obtained powders were bonded by epoxy resin, and were oriented in a magnetic field of 1.5 T. Magnetic measurements were performed using VSM. The microstructure of the samples was investigated by scanning electron microscopy (SEM) and transmission electron microscopy (TEM).

3. Results and Discussion

Figure 1 shows the magnetic properties of the HDDR $Nd_{13}Fe_{79.4}B_7Nb_{0.3}Ga_{0.3}$ powders before and after heat treatments with Pr-Cu alloys. The HDDR powders show a remanence of 1.4 T, an intrinsic coercivity of 13 kOe, and a maximum energy product of 41 MGOe at room temperature. The ratio of residual magnetization to saturation magnetization is B_r / B_s = 0.915. After the heat treatment, the coercivity of HDDR powders increases from 13 to 18 kOe. A 40% increase of the coercivity was observed with an addition of 5 wt. % $Pr_{68}Cu_{32}$ powders and a heat treatment at 650 °C for 1 h. The enhancement of the coerecivity is much higher than that (20%) of using Nd-Cu alloy reported by Sepehri-Amin et al. [6]. This discrepancy may result from the different eutectic

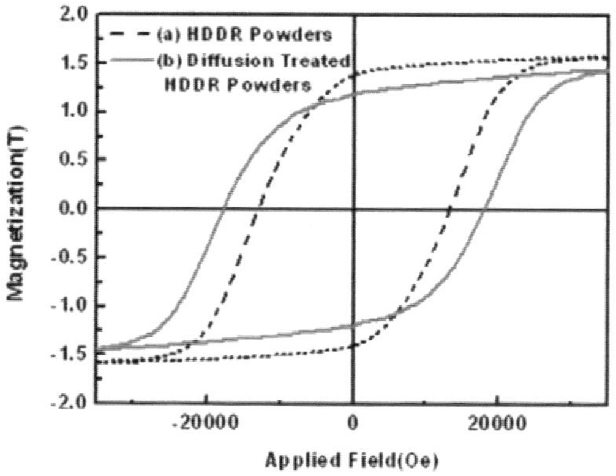

Fig. 1. Room temperature hysteresis loops of HDDR $Nd_{13}Fe_{79.4}B_7Nb_{0.3}Ga_{0.3}$ powders (a) before and (b) after diffusion treatment.

points of R-Cu (R = Nd and Pr) alloys. The $Pr_{68}Cu_{32}$ diffusion-treated powders are still anisotropic, as can be identified by the relative changes in X-ray diffraction intensity before and after magnetic alignment. It is thus inferred that diffusing $Pr_{68}Cu_{32}$ alloy can increase the coercivity and maintain the crystal texture of HDDR $Nd_{13}Fe_{79.4}B_7Nb_{0.3}Ga_{0.3}$ powders. A balance between the coercivity increment and remanence decrement, and possessing higher magnetic properties may possibly be achieved if the amount of $Pr_{68}Cu_{32}$ alloy and the condition of the heat treatment could be adjusted.

Figure 2 shows the TEM images of HDDR $Nd_{13}Fe_{79.4}B_7Nb_{0.3}Ga_{0.3}$ before and after the heat treatment. The average grain size remains comparable to the single domain size of $Nd_2Fe_{14}B$ phase, indicating there is no obvious grain growth under the heat treatment at 650 °C for 1 h. It is noted that more

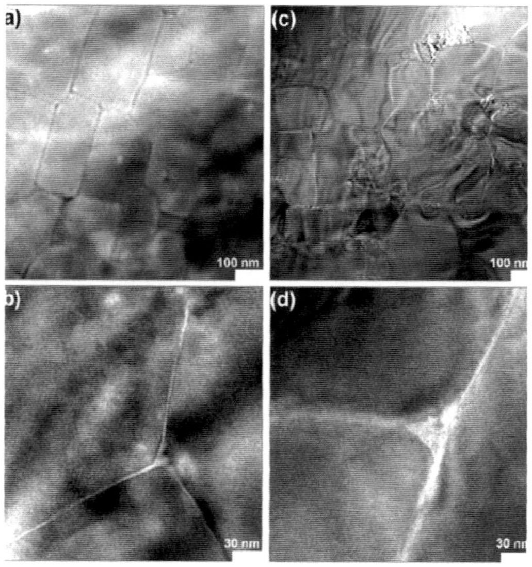

Fig. 2. TEM images of the $Nd_{13}Fe_{79.4}B_7Nb_{0.3}Ga_{0.3}$ HDDR powders before (a), (b) and after(c), (d) Pr-Cu diffusion.

$Nd_2Fe_{14}B$ grains are surrounded by continuous grain boundary layers and in averagely speaking the boundary layers become thicker. According to Energy Dispersive X-ray Spectroscopy analysis (EDX), Cu and Pr elements are mainly concentrated within grain boundary region. The diffusion of Pr and Cu elements into the Nd-Fe-B grain boundary region may be approached by the following way. The HDDR processed powders have numerous micro-cracks mainly in the boundary regions. When the $Pr_{68}Cu_{32}$ alloy is heated at 650 °C, it melts and the Pr-Cu liquid tends to seep through the cracks via the capillarity effect. Then Pr-Cu liquid gradually diffuses along the grain boundaries. As a result, the boundary area is enlarged by the diffusion [Fig. 2(d)].

Figure 3 shows the room temperature hysteresis loops of the anisotropic MQA powders before and after the diffusion treatment. It can be seen that the coercivity of MQA powders increases with increase of diffusion agent content, and reaches to a maximum value of 2.4 T with 30 wt.% diffusion agent. The decrease of the remanence is mainly due to the addition of nonmagnetic Pr-Cu alloy. As a comparison, the hysteresis loop of simply heat treated MQA powders under the same conditions without the Pr-Cu addition was also shown in Fig. 3. Without Pr-Cu addition, the magnetic properties of MQA powders after heat treatment were deteriorated as compared to those of the initial powders. This indicates that the enhancement in coercivity is mainly due to the diffusion of Pr-Cu alloys into the MQA powders but not the heat treatment itself.

The TEM images of the MQA powders before and after the diffusion process indicates the initial MQA powders without heat treatment consist of platelet-like grains with a length of about 200 nm and a thickness of about 50 nm. The thickness of the boundary layer is not uniform with some grains being almost in contact with each other. In the presence of Pr-Cu, the

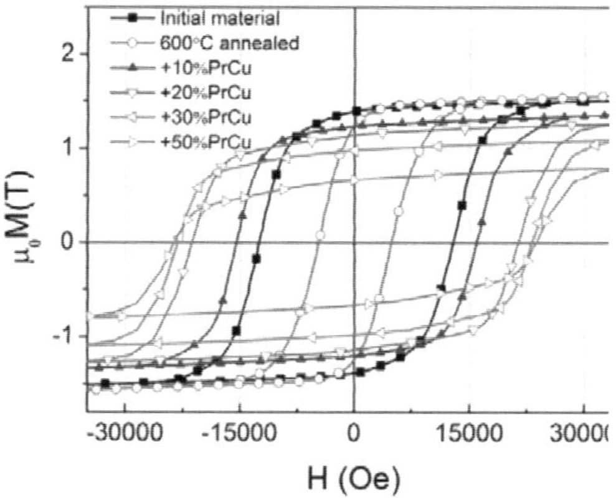

Fig. 3. Hysteresis loops of initial and diffusion-treated anisotropic MQA powders.

diffusion treatment did not change the shape and size of the platelet-like grains, but the average thickness of the grain boundary layer increases significantly (about 6 nm). These indicate that Pr-Cu alloy diffuses into the boundary layers of the MQA powders and prevents the neighboring Nd-Fe-B grains from welding. As a result, the thickness of the boundary layer increases, and the contents of Fe and Co in the boundary layers decrease. The modified boundary layers may cause an increase of the nucleation field and lead to an enhancement in the coercivity.

4. Summary

The temperature coefficient of coericivity for HDDR powders after diffusion treatment show a lower β(T). The coercivity remains nearly 10 kOe at 110 °C. Although the remanence at room temperature of diffusion-treated powders is lower than that of the untreated one, the thermal stability of the remanence for diffusion treated powers has been improved. The coercivity of the initial MQA powders is 3.6 kOe at 160 °C and 2.2 kOe at 200 °C. After the diffusion treatment, the powders show coercivities of 8 kOe at 160 °C and 4.2 kOe at 200 °C. The coercivity of the powders at 200 °C is improved, which will be very helpful for the application of the corresponding bonded magnets at elevated temperatures.

References

[1] M. Sagawa, S. Fujimura, N. Togawa, H. Yamamoto and Y. Matsuura, *J. Appl. Phys.* **55**, 1984, 2083.
[2] J. J. Croat, J. F. Herbst, R. W. Lee, and F. E. Pinkerton, *J. Appl. Phys.* **55**, 1984, 2079.
[3] T. Takeshita, R. Nakayama, in: *11th Workshop on Rare Earth Magnets and their Applications*, Pittsburg, USA, 1990, p. 49.
[4] Y. Nozawa, K. Iwasaki, S. Tanigawa, M. Tokunaga and H. Harada, *J. Appl. Phys.* **64**, 1988, 5285.
[5] L. Eshelman, K. Young, V. Panchanathan and J. Croat, *J. Appl. Phys.* **64**, 1988, 5293.
[6] H. Sepehri-Amin, T. Ohkubo, T. Nishiuchi, S. Hirosawa, and K. Hono, *Scr. Mater.* **63**, 2010, 1124.
[7] Z. Lin et al., *Appl. Phys. Lett.* **100,** 2012, 052409.
[8] F. Wan et al., *J. Appl. Phys.* **113**, 2013, 193902.
[9] Z. Lin et al., *J. Appl. Phys.* **112**, 2012, 073924.
[10] D. I. Paul, *J. Appl. Phys.* **53**, 1982, 1649.
[11] R. Friedberg and D. I. Paul, *Phys. Rev. Lett.* **34**, 1975, 1234.

Microstructure and Magnetic Properties of Zn-Coated (Nd,Dy,Y)-(Fe,Co)-B Ribbon Powder and Subsequent Hot Deformed Magnets

W. TANG, L. ZHOU, K.W. DENNIS, M.J. KRAMER, I.E. ANDERSON, R.W. McCALLUM
Ames Laboratory USDOE, Iowa State University, Ames, IA 50010

Abstract: *Milled melt-spun ribbon flake of MRE-Fe-B coated with Zn using a vapor transport technique were found to have significant increases in coercivity without degrading the magnetization when the Zn thickness and heat treatment were optimized. Magnetic measurements show that 0.5-1.0 wt.% Zn coating increases the coercivity about 1 kOe over the initial ribbon powder. After vacuum hot deformation (VHD), the VHD magnet with Zn coating of 0.5 wt.% results in a nearly 3 kOe higher coercivity than an un-coated alloy magnet. The microstructures of the ribbon powder and VHD magnets show that an elongated and aligned grain structure was mainly evolved from the nucleation and growth of previous platelet-like but randomly distributed grains in the initial ribbon powder. A deformed force combined with a transient liquid phase formed by Zn and excess Nd at grain boundaries induced the grains to rotate, align and finally produce the elongated grains with a high anisotropic texture.*

Keywords: *$RE_2Fe_{14}B$ magnets; nanocrystalline magnets; hot deformation; Zn coating*

Address: Wei Tang, Ames Lab of DOE, Ames, IA50011, USA, Tel: (515)294-8685, E-mail: weitang@ameslab.gov

1. Introduction

It has been demonstrated that enhanced high temperature performance of $RE_2Fe_{14}B$ magnets with decreased Dy can be obtained by refining the grain size in conventional sintered magnets for grain sizes less than 1μm [1], this approach brings difficulties both in the milling process and in protecting the extremely high surface area powders from oxidation. An alternative approach is the die-upsetting process. This technique uses $RE_2Fe_{14}B$ melt-spun ribbon powder (predominantly amorphous) as a feedstock to produce anisotropic magnets with lower Dy content and enhanced temperature stability of the magnetic properties. Extensive research has documented that the existence of a transient liquid phase during hot-deformation is essential in forming the required texture and nano-scaled microstructure [2,3]. Previously, anisotropic $MRE_2(Fe,Co)_{14}B$ (MRE = Nd + Dy + Y) magnets were successfully produced by a single stage vacuum hot deformation (SSVHD) approach, where Zn powder was blended or coated with glassy magnet alloy powder and crystallized under pressure to develop increased magnetic anisotropy texture and magnetic properties [4]. In this work, a vacuum-assisted vapor transport technique was used to coat uniformly the surface of the ribbon powder with Zn. The microstructure and magnetic properties of Zn-coated ribbon powder and subsequent VHD magnets with different Zn contents were studied. Zn distribution in the microstructure and its effect on magnetic properties were analyzed and discussed.

2. Experimental Methods

Ribbon flakes with initial compositions of $[Nd_{0.45}(Y_{0.75}Dy_{0.25})_{0.55}]_{2.5}Fe_{13}Co_1B$ were prepared by arc-melting and then melt spinning at a wheel speed of 25 m/s in an Ar atmosphere. The ribbon flakes were pulverized into powder with a size of less than 75 μm and Zn-coated by physical vapor deposition (PVD). Three samples without Zn and with an initial Zn mass of 0 and 0.5 wt.% were respectively prepared and annealed at 750 °C for 30 min. The resulting Zn-coated powders were die-upset by the SSVHD method. The detailed PVD and SSVHD processes were described in Ref. 4 and 5. Microstructure and composition profiles of the resulting Zn-coated powder and SSVHD magnets were examined using a scanning electron microscope (SEM) and a transmission electron microscope (TEM). Magnetic properties were measured using a Quantum Design SQUID magnetometer and a VersaLab VSM.

3. Results and Discussion

The magnetic properties of ribbon powders without Zn coating and with 0 and 0.5 wt% Zn coating, respectively, are shown in Fig. 1. It was seen that the coercivity of the 0% Zn-sample is the same with that of the starting material, indicating that the low temperature at which the coating was performed did not affect the material. However, the coercivity of the 0.5 wt.% Zn-coated sample increases to 15.3 kOe from 14 kOe compared to the Zn-free samples. No significant change in remanence was observed. This

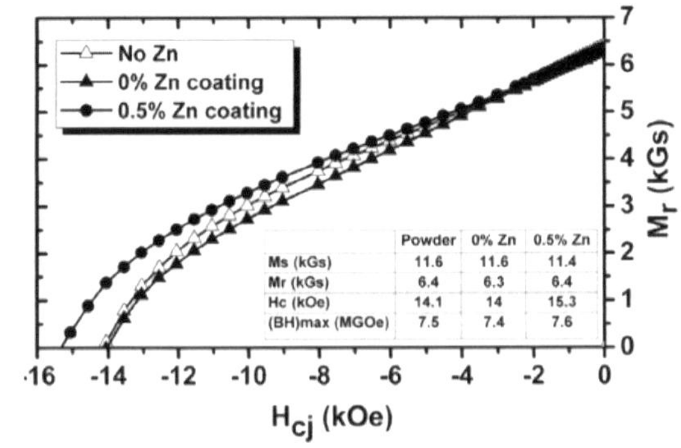

Fig. 1. Demagnetization curves of annealed ribbon powder with different conditions.

indicates that the addition of Zn can improve the coercivity of ribbon powder. A high-angle-annular-dark-field (HAADF) scanning transmission electron microscopy (STEM) image and its EDS composition analysis of the annealed ribbon powder with 0.5 wt.% Zn coating are shown in Fig. 2 and Table 1. Region 1 and 2 in Fig. 2 present a grain boundary and interior grain area, respectively. It is known from Table 1 that no Zn was detected in the interior grain area. A 3.9 wt.% Zn was detected only in the grain boundary area, indicating that Zn diffused along the grain boundaries where the Zn then reacts with the RE-rich grain boundary phase to form a new phase distribution. In addition, it is seen from Fig. 2 that most of grains exhibit a platelet-like (or rod-like in 3 dimensions) morphology with ~30 nm in thickness and ~100 nm in length, while a few of grains exhibit equiaxed morphology with average size of 50 nm. The equiaxed grains should be closed to the wheel surface areas of the initial ribbon, while the platelet-like grains should lie at middle or free surface area of the ribbon. These platelet-like grains are randomly oriented.

Zn-coated ribbon powders also were hot-deformed to fabricate VHD magnets as stated goal of the study. A

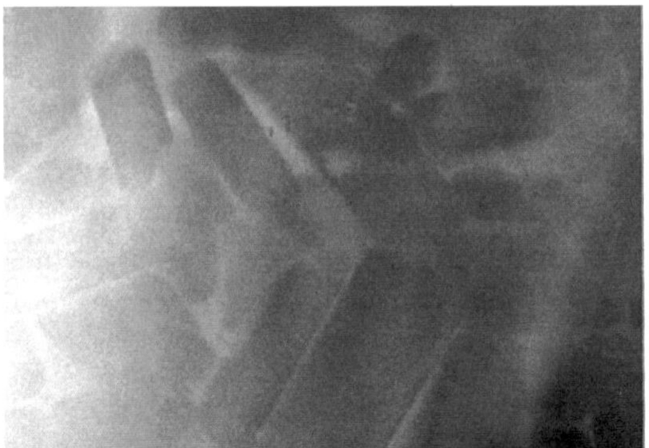

Fig. 2. HAADF STEM image *of annealed ribbon powder with 0.5 wt% Zn coating.*

Table 1. EDS composition profiles (wt.%) of annealed ribbon powder with 0.5 wt.% Zn.

	Region	Fe	Co	Zn	MRE
750 °C	R1	2.8	7.6	3.9	85.7
30 min	R2	78.6	5.9	0	15.5

typical bright field TEM image (Fig. 3) of a transverse section of the VHD sample with 0.5 wt.% Zn [arrows in the figure indicate the pressing direction, Fig. 3(a)], shows platelet-like 2-14-1 grains whose long-axes are perpendicular to the pressing direction. It is obvious that these elongated and aligned grains are mainly evolved from the nucleation and growth of previous platelet-like grains in the ribbon powder. As seen in Fig. 2, a platelet-like grain structure was developed after the initially ribbon powder was fully crystallized at 750 °C without applying any pressing force. However, the platelet-like grains were randomly distributed. When the ribbon powder was deformed (also simultaneously crystallized) at 735 °C, the platelet-like grains were rotated, aligned and grown under a deformed force. Compared Fig. 2 to Fig. 3(a), it was found that the thickness (~ 30 - 60 nm) of the platelet-like grains was not changed much but the length (> 300 nm) was significantly increased after hot deformation, indicating that the deformed force can inhibit the grain growth of direction parallel to the pressing direction but greatly induces preferential grain growth along with the direction perpendicular to the pressing direction, and finally leads to the elongated grain structure with a high degree of texture. Fig. 3(b) is a HAADF STEM image of the same sample. The compositions for the different regions labeled in Fig. 3(b) were analyzed by EDS and listed in Table 2. Almost no Zn was detected in the interior of these nano-grains, i.e., in Regions 3 and 4, but a small amount of Zn was detected in the triple junctions of grains and along grain boundary areas, i.e., in Region 1. Region 2, which is a RE-segregated spot with very high Y concentration, also contains a certain amount of Zn. These results demonstrate that Zn diffused into the intergranular boundaries from the interparticle regions in the VHD magnets.

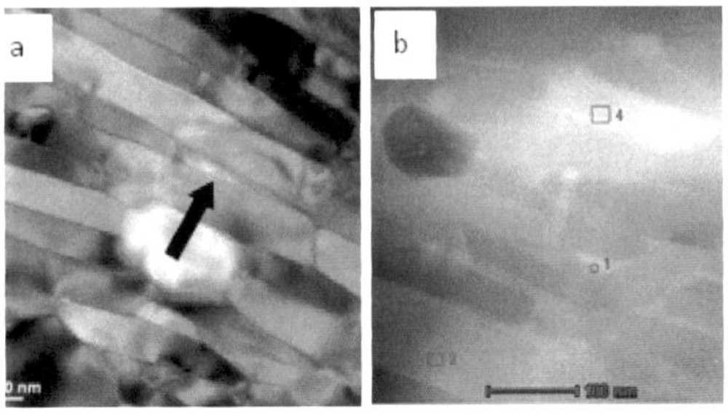

Fig. 3. Bright field TEM image (a) and HAADF STEM image (b) of VHD magnet with 0.5 wt.% Zn coating. The EDS data in Table 2 is from the red rectangle regions in (b).

Table 2. EDS composition profiles of VHD magnet with 0.5 wt.% Zn coating.

wt. %	R1	R2	R3	R4
Fe & Co	41.2	28.7	84.7	82.3
RE	72.1	69.7	15.3	17.3
Zn	2.2	1.5	0	0.3

The effect of different Zn coating on magnetic properties is shown in Fig. 4. With increasing Zn content from 0 to 1.5 wt.%, the H_c and $(BH)_{max}$ first increased from 8.8 kOe to 13.7 MGO, reached a peak value of 11.2 kOe and 23.0 MGOe, and then decreased to 7.2 kOe and 10.4 MGOe, respectively, while the M_r remained nearly constant. With further development, especially elevated temperature testing, this Zn coating technique, combined with the hot deformation approach may offer a route to higher coercivity magnets that require a reduced Dy content.

4. Conclusion

Zn coated on the surface of ribbon powder diffused into grain boundaries after the ribbon powder was annealed or hot-deformed. An appropriate amount of Zn can improve the coercivity of the ribbon powder and VHD magnets. While the annealed ribbon powder shows a platelet-like but randomly distributed grain structure, the VHD magnet exhibits elongated and aligned grains with a high anisotropic texture. The deformed force combined with a transient liquid phase formed by Zn and excess Nd at grain boundaries promote the formation of the aligned grain structure and thus improve coercivity of the VHD magnets. An optimized VHD magnet with 0.5 wt.% Zn-coating obtains a coercivity of 11.2 kOe and $(BH)_{max}$ of 23 MGOe, respectively.

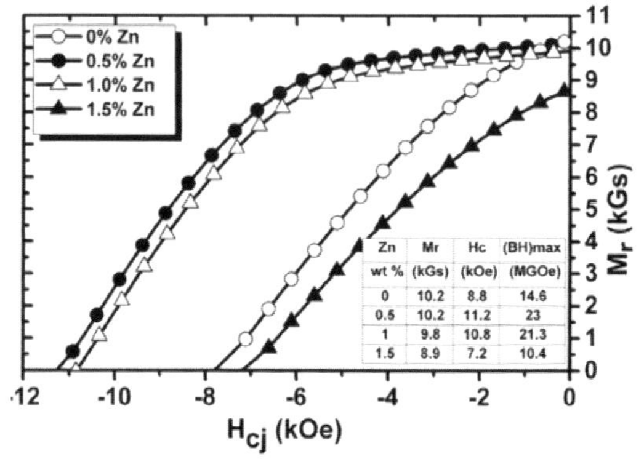

Fig. 4. Demagnetization curves of VHD magnets coated with different amount of Zn.

Acknowledgement

This work was supported by DOE-EERE-VT-PEEM and Propulsion Materials Programs at the Ames Laboratory. Ames Laboratory is operated for the U.S. DOE by Iowa State University under contract no. DE-AC02-07CH11358.

References

[1] P. Nothnagel, K. H. Müller, D. Eckert, and A. Handstein, *J. Mag Mag Mater.* **101**, 1991, 379.

[2] R. W. Lee, *Appl Phys. Lett.* **46**, 1985, 790.

[3] J. Liu, H. Sepehri-Amin, T. Ohkubo, K. Hioki, A. Hattori, T. Schrefl, and K. Hono, *Acta Mater.* **61**, 2013, 5387.

[4] W. Tang, Q. F. Xing, K.W. Dennis, M. J. Kramer, I. E. Anderson and R. W. McCallum, *IEEE Trans. Magn.* **48**, 2012, 3147.

[5] W. Tang, L. Zhou, K. W. Sun, K.W. Dennis, M. J. Kramer, I. E. Anderson and R. W. McCallum, *J. Appl. Phys.* **115**, 2014, 17A725.

Status of Permanent Magnets – Around the World

S. CONSTANTINIDES
Arnold Magnetic Technologies, Rochester, NY, USA

Abstract: *The last decade has been marked by dramatic changes in magnetic technologies, products, raw materials sourcing and price, intellectual property, and new or greatly modified applications. One driver for these changes has been an increase in the standard of living for hundreds of millions of persons with the expectation of additional advances. This has led to increases in consumption of energy and raw materials. Magnetic materials can help by providing improvements in efficiencies and facilitating new technologies.*

Key Words: *permanent magnets, sintered magnets, rare earth, ferrite, motors*

Address: Steve Constantinides, Arnold Magnetic Technologies, Rochester, NY, 14625, U.S.A., Tel: +1 (585) 385-9010, E-mail: sconstantinides@arnoldmagnetics.com

1. Introduction

Reducing a discussion of the permanent magnet industry to a few pages (and a few minutes) is a severe challenge. Various issues come into play, including, for magnet manufacturers, the much-discussed availability of raw materials, raw material prices and rapid changes thereto, export quotas and tariffs, intellectual property constraints, new magnet and processing developments, etc. The user community is involved in device design choices - to use one material versus another - or in the selection of devices that use no magnets at all. Markets for products continually change and adapt, but usually at a rate that is easily absorbed. Rapid change is often disruptive.

Adjusting to change is more easily accomplished when the market is "elastic", that is, when alternative materials or designs are available. Elasticity helps to stabilize raw material prices and balance supply and demand. However, some technologies have become so dependent upon rare earth magnets that the price spike and fear of unavailability that occurred in late 2010 through early 2012 caused significant shifts in product design strategies and roll-out schedules for new products.

Within this context, let us examine a major driving force behind changes in the permanent magnet industry and then offer details on magnet usage in three key market segments: automotive traction motors, wind power generators and data storage technologies. Finally, an assessment of the overall permanent magnet market will be offered.

2. "It's All about Energy"

Electricity literally drives our lives. A typical home contains dozens of devices dependent upon electricity – refrigerators, washing machines, computers, printers, power tools, electric shavers, garage door openers, TVs, phones, etc. Magnetic materials are important in the production, transmission and use of electrical energy. Magnetically "soft" alloys such as silicon-iron (Si-Fe) are used in electrical generators, distribution transformers, and in end-use devices such as motors. Permanent magnets contribute to the power generation market and permanent magnet (PM) motors are increasingly used to improve efficiency of end use applications, especially in variable speed requirements.

Lawrence Livermore National Laboratory (LLNL) has produced energy flow (Sankey) diagrams (https://flowcharts.llnl.gov/) showing sources of energy for electricity generation, through distribution to end use. Diagrams have been produced for numerous countries. Net delivered energy is usually lower than 50 per cent of the input energy. For example, in the USA in 2011, the net delivered energy was 41.7%.

Part of the energy debate is the role of carbon dioxide in weather change. Carbon dioxide is largely a product of burning fossil fuels to make electricity or to power transportation. Whether or not carbon dioxide is actually a cause of global warming, it is becoming increasingly obvious that additional sources of electrical energy will be necessary to ensure a high standard of living for all people, all-the-better if these additional sources minimize the generation of harmful byproducts (carbon dioxide, radioactive wastes).

Emphasis is placed on minimally polluting, renewable energy. For example, in China renewables are sought to reduce air pollution, and in Europe to reduce dependence on imported fossil fuels.

Figure 1 shows the current and forecast production of electricity, including that produced by renewables. It highlights that even with the expected significant

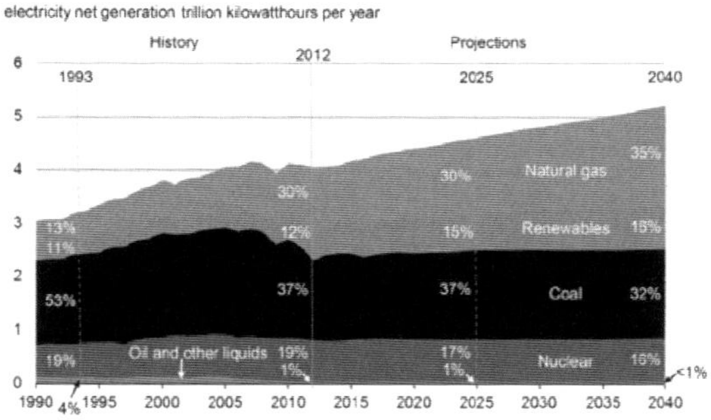

Fig. 1. Over time the electricity mix gradually shifts to lower-carbon options, led by growth in natural gas and renewable generation [1,11].

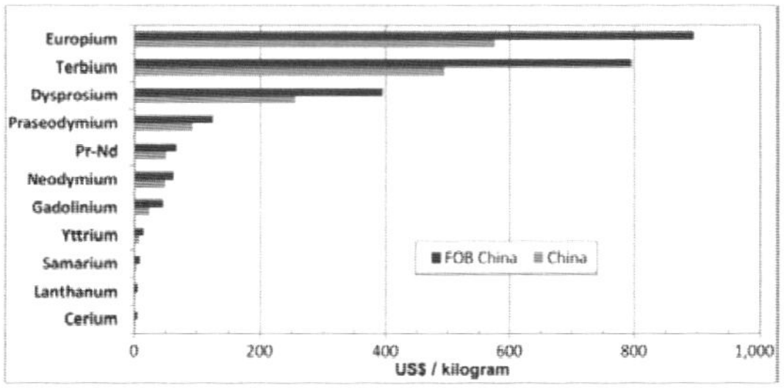

Fig. 2. Rare earth oxide prices as of June 5, 2014 as reported by Metal Pages (www.metal-pages.com).

growth in renewables, they will remain a minor portion of the total energy requirement. Perhaps the best take-away is that we will need 1) additional sources of input energy, 2) improvements in efficiency of production and distribution, 3) higher efficiency of end-use applications, 4) new technologies requiring lower electric consumption and 5) more flexibility in energy sourcing. Permanent magnets can play an important role in these efforts [12].

3. Raw Material Supply and Pricing

There has been a lot of "press" regarding rare earth raw material prices. A rapid run-up of pricing from late 2010 to mid-2011 was disruptive to producers and users of neodymium iron boron (Neo) magnets. However, every magnet raw material has experienced price volatility at one time or another resulting from an imbalance in supply and demand made worse by commodities trading. For example, iron tripled in price from 2009 to mid-2011, copper increased fivefold between 2003 and 2011, nickel increased from \$5 to \$55 between 2001 and 2007 then dropped to \$29 in 2011. Aluminum, one of the most common elements in the crust of the earth, has experienced fluctuations of 100% price change.

An exacerbating issue is that, while most materials can be sourced from many countries and regions, during the 2003 to 2012 period, over 97% of rare earth raw material (oxides, metals and alloys) was supplied both directly and indirectly from China. Furthermore, China instituted tariffs on exports of rare earths of between 10 and 25% - depending on element. Rare earths have been sold under private contract – there has not been transparency in pricing. Asian Metals obtained and reported information regarding "claimed" prices which were one to three weeks delayed from actual contracts and inflated over actual contract pricing. It has been generally accepted that the reported prices, while not exact, have offered directionally correct market information. Figure 2 shows reported rare earth oxide prices as of June 5, 2014, sorted from high (Europium) to low (Cerium).

Unlike Neo magnets, samarium cobalt (SmCo) magnet raw material supply has been adequate and prices rose far less than for Nd, Pr and Dy. Cobalt prices did experience a spike in early 2008 due to use of the element in batteries and to supply industry realignment. Cobalt use in magnetic materials represents about 7% of production and includes the following products: alnico, SmCo, Fe-Cr-Co, Vicalloy, and Fe-Co soft magnetic alloys. Earlier price shifts have been due to instability in one of the producing countries (Zaire, Belgian Congo). There has been adequate supply and materials have been available globally. Samarium comes primarily from light rare earth ores as a by-product from mining for neodymium – the more neodymium that is mined and processed, the more samarium will be available. As a result, there has been an excess of samarium available. By some estimates, SmCo production could be quadrupled without distorting the supply-demand ratio.

Ferrite magnets use widely available raw materials: 1) iron oxide from ore and from pickle liquor and 2) strontium carbonate. Ferrite magnet pricing has been far more stable and the global supply of magnets adequate. As a result, users of permanent magnets were forced to shift away from Neo magnets and use 1) ferrite magnet devices, 2) SmCo magnets or 3) non-PM motor designs.

4. Market Segments

The specific requirements of each application determines which magnet material will be used. Factors considered in selecting the optimal permanent magnet include:

- Flux density: Residual Induction, B_r
- Energy Product: $(BH)_{max}$
- Resistance to demagnetization (H_{cJ})
- Usable temperature range
- Change in magnetics with temperature
- Demagnetization curve shape (2nd quadrant)
- Recoil permeability (close to 1.0)
- Magnetizing field requirement
- Corrosion resistance (water, salts, gases)
- Physical strength and toughness

Table 1. Devices and applications that use permanent magnets.

Actuators	Mag lev transportation
Advertising (signage)	Motors: industrial, automotive accessories, consumer, etc.
Air conditioning compressors and fans	MRI
Electric bicycles	Pipe inspection systems
Energy storage systems	Relays and switches
Gauges	Reprographics (magnetic toner rolls)
Generators	Sensors
HDD, CD, DVD	Torque-coupled drives
Hysteresis clutch	Traction drive motors (transportation)
Magnetic braking	Transducers, loudspeakers
Magnetic refrigeration	Wave guides (TWT, undulators, wigglers)
Magnetic & eddy current separation	Wind power generators

- Electrical resistivity
- Available sizes, shapes, and manufacturability
- Value: performance at competitive price

Where are permanent magnets used? Table 1 provides a list of devices and applications which use permanent magnets. The uses can be categorized as providing:

- Field for sensing
- Field for induction (separators, brakes)
- Flux for holding, latching, clamping
- Energy product for motors/generators
- Energy product for torque coupling
- "Shaped" field for guidance of EM transmissions (radar and microwave)

The market for permanent magnets has been changing at an accelerated pace due to several factors including supplier technological innovation and user requirements. For example, automotive CAFÉ standards (USA) coupled with high fuel cost (global) has propelled innovation in fuel efficiency (turbo-diesel) and a switch from reliance on direct use of fossil fuels to electric motor traction drive systems. In the area of information data storage, solid state drives (SSDs) are replacing hard disk drives in smaller portable computers and expanding data storage in phones and tablet computers. However, servers continue to rely on the less expensive hard disk drive (HDD) technology. The biggest change appears to be in the optical drive arena (CD-ROMs and DVDs) where SSDs are the medium of choice for recording and playing music and displaying pictures. We'll examine three markets in more detail: transportation, wind power generation, and information storage.

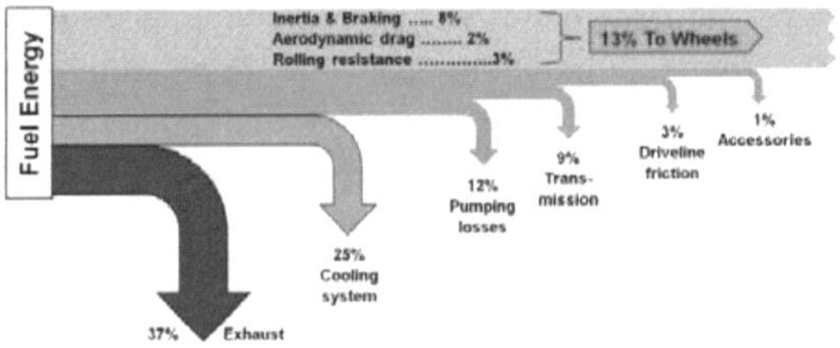

Fig. 3. The Internal Combustion Engine Energy Budget. Adapted from [4].

4.1. Transportation

There are numerous devices in automobiles and trucks that utilize permanent magnets. A typical car contains at least 100 magnets and some luxury vehicles are reputed to contain over 170 magnets. Devices using magnets include the engine cooling fan, windshield wipers, starter motor, alternator, electronic throttle control, antilock braking system, HVAC blower, power seat adjusters, power window motors, door lock actuators, fuel pump, etc. The most interesting issue may be the drive system where there is an emphasis on converting from fossil fuels to electric drives.

Production of fossil fuels includes natural gas, coal and oil. Oil is refined into diesel, home heating oil, gasoline, jet fuel, kerosene, and numerous industrial hydrocarbons (hexane, pentane, etc.). The energy content per unit volume of liquid fuels is very high and delivery via pipeline and truck is convenient and well-established and local storage is straightforward. However, the efficiency of the internal combustion drive system is low – about 13%, as shown in Figure 3.

Alternative propulsion systems have been developed that depend upon compressed gases: methane (natural gas), propane, or hydrogen. While one or more of these may become more widely used in the future, they require the installation of a distribution infrastructure and consumer acceptance.

Electrically propelled vehicles offer an alternative to the combustion engine and have been in use for over 150 years. There are now numerous versions as follows.

HEV, Hybrid Electric Vehicle: Uses both an electric motor and internal combustion engine (ICE) to propel the vehicle.

PHEV, Plug-in Hybrid Electric Vehicle: Plugs into the electric grid to charge the battery – is similar to a pure hybrid – and also utilizes an internal combustion engine.

EREV, Extended Range Electric Vehicle: Operates as a battery electric vehicle. An internal combustion engine is used to re-charge the battery, allowing extended range travel.

BEV, Battery Electric Vehicle: Powered exclusively by electricity from an on-board battery that is

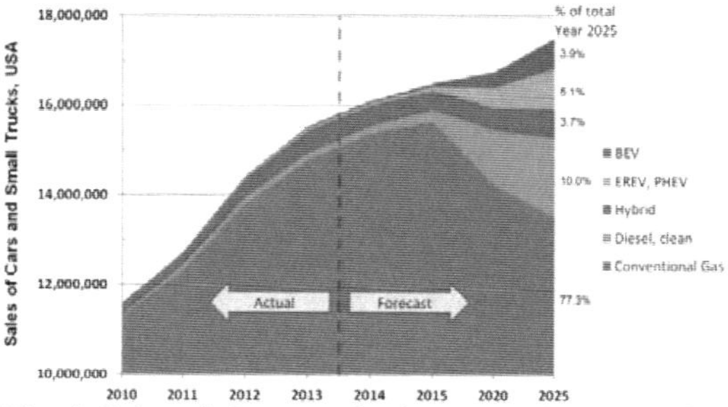

Fig. 4. Sales of electric vehicles, recent history and forecast [3,5,6].

periodically charged by connecting to the electric grid.

FCEV, Fuel Cell Electric Vehicle: Converts the chemical energy from a fuel, such as hydrogen and oxygen, into electricity to power the drive motor.

Forecasts for the introduction and sale of electric vehicles have been optimistic. J.D. Power and Associates in their 2011 US Green Automotive Study predicted alternative powertrain models to reach about 6.5% of US sales in 2013 [2]. The actual was 3.8%. The number of models at 59 has also lagged the forecast of 124. However, growth in both sales and number of models has been increasing. Figure 4 shows actual growth in sales of these vehicles and a forecast through year 2025.

The forecast is dependent upon retention of the CAFÉ standards, continued increases in gasoline prices and improvements in the value proposition – price of electric vehicle combined with its feature set. Note that this aggressive forecast shows a continuing reliance on fossil fuel engines (ICE) at about 77% of all new vehicles. It also seems likely that the CAFÉ standard for 2025 of 54.5 mpg may not be met [7,8].

Switching from gasoline to electric drives will cause a greater dependence on commercial electric power production and the grid distribution system [9]. Conventional electric power generation uses mostly fossil fuels, especially coal (US and China). A switch to plug in electric vehicles may not produce a reduction in greenhouse gases.

4.2. Wind Power

Generators using energy contained in wind have been producing electricity for several decades. Charles Brush built a wind "mill" in 1888 to produce electricity [10] .The early units were small, only a few kilowatts in output, and most often serving a remote cabin, a business or a remote data collection facility. Wind power is divided into three categories of Small Wind, generators up to 100 kW in output, Community or Mid Wind, 100 kW to 1 MW, and Utility or Large Wind, 1 MW and more. Some of the earlier Utility Wind installations used ~650 kW generators, the largest units available at the time, but the current division is at 1 MW.

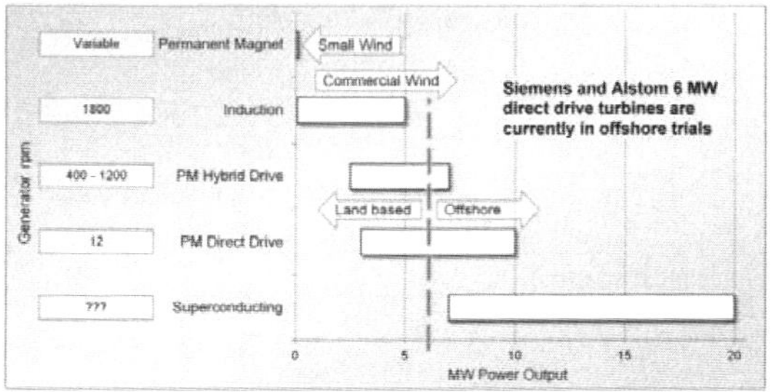

Fig. 5. Types of wind power generators and likely use locations [6,7].

Utility scale installations have flourished especially in regions where alternate energy is expensive or where government subsidies promote installation. There are numerous wind energy organizations. Some of the more prominent are:

- Global Wind Energy Council (GWEC, www.gwec.net)
- American Wind Energy Association (www.awea.org)
- European Wind Energy Association (www.ewea.org)
- World Wind Energy Association (www.wwindea.org)
- Centre for Wind Energy Technology (India, www.cwet.tn.nic.in/html/relatedlinks.html)
- List of a few dozen more organizations is at www.thewindpower.net/actors_wea_en.php.

According to the GWEC, at the end of 2013, China had installed 91 GW of utility scale electrical power generation, the USA 61 GW, Germany 34 GW, India 20 GW and the world total was 318 GW.[6] Approximately 10% additional capacity is being installed each year.

The largest installed generators are 6 MW direct drive (Siemens and Alstom) and are being evaluated for long term performance and reliability. Direct drive turbines use permanent magnets on a large diameter rotor with 100 +/- poles for high switching frequency during low rpm rotation (12-15 rpm). Maximum generator size has been limited by the strength of the blades. As improvements have been made allowing greater swept area, the limiting factor has become the weight and size of the gearbox and induction generator. It is generally accepted that 5 MW and larger turbines will depend upon permanent magnet or superconducting generators.

A consensus estimate is that direct drive generators require 600 kg of Neo magnets per MW output. Therefore a 6 MW turbine is expected to contain 3.6 tons of Neo magnets. Until the price bubble and fear of inadequate supply that occurred in 2010-2011,

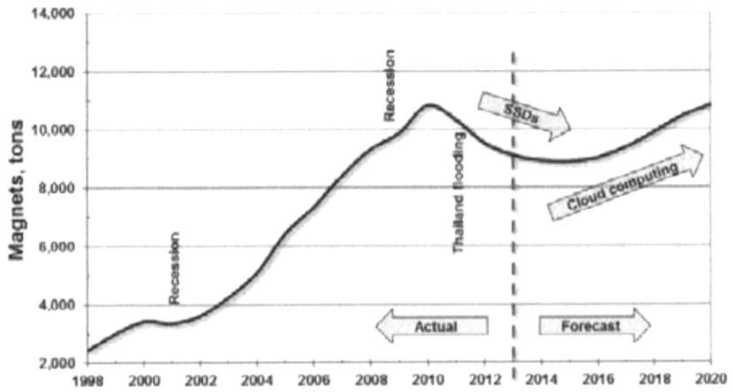

Fig. 6. Use of Neo magnets in hard disk drives (HDDs).

direct drive generators were planned by most, if not all, of the commercial, utility scale generator manufacturers. It may still be appropriate to install these larger generators in offshore wind farms where maintenance is more difficult and steady wind provides name plate output a high percentage of the time.

An intermediate type of generator, the hybrid, uses a one or two-stage gearbox – instead of three – to improve dependability and reduce the maintenance cycle while still benefitting from some size and weight reduction through the use of permanent magnets. It is estimated that the hybrid generators require between 165 and 250 kg of Neo per MW output.

4.3. Information Storage

Hard disk drives from the 1970s and early 1980s used large ferrite magnets to move the read/write head. The discovery of Neo coincided with the explosion of personal computers and permitted small form factor drives to be built and at a reasonable price. My first hard drive in 1985 was a 10 MB, 5 ¼ inch drive that cost $600 or $60 per MB. Fast forward to 2014 and drives of 1 terabyte cost $70 – a cost of $0.00007 per MB – about one millionth as much as in 1985.

A relatively new form of bulk memory storage is the flash ROM. Both size and dependability have improved. Common forms of this memory are "thumb drives" and solid state drives (SSDs). There are no moving parts and memory access is several times faster than for a hard disk drive. SSDs are proliferating, especially in tablet computers, smart phones, cameras, and in smaller portable computers where 124 to 256 GB storage is typical. HDDs remain more affordable than SSDs, so high volume data storage found in servers is expected to continue to use HDDs. High performance desktop systems are now being built with hybrid systems – the SSD runs the operating system and key functional software, while the HDD stores the bulk of the data. What we see is, therefore, a balance between the two storage types where use of HDDs will grow back to 2010 levels by 2020.

Table 2. Permanent magnet usage by application. Ferrite estimates for 2012-2013; Neo estimates for 2010. Price and availability issues have disrupted the Neo market.

Ferrite Magnet Applications	%
Motors - Automotive	18%
Motors - Appliances	13%
Motors - HVAC	13%
Motors - Industrial & Commercial	12%
Motors - All Other	5%
Loudspeakers	9%
Separation Equipment	5%
Advertising & Promotional Products	5%
Holding & Lifting	5%
MRI	3%
Relays & Switches	1%
All Other - Miscellaneous	11%

Rare Earth Magnet Applications	%
Motors, industrial, general auto, etc	24.7%
HDD, CD, DVD	15.8%
Electric Bicycles & Scooters	8.2%
Acoustic Transducers	8.2%
Unidentified	5.8%
MRI	5.6%
Air conditioning compressors and fans	3.6%
Magnetic Separation	4.7%
Wind Power Generators	1.9%
Torque-coupled drives	3.4%
Generators	3.0%
Sensors	2.9%
Energy Storage Systems	1.9%
Hysteresis Clutch	2.8%
Hybrid & Electric Traction Drive	0.7%
All other	6.8%

This has relevance for the magnet industry since each hard disk drive contains a bonded Neo spindle drive magnet and a sintered Neo voice coil motor (VCM) magnet with a total weight of ~13 grams per drive, market average [7]. Optical drives contain a variety of technologies for spindle rotation and read/write head movement. As mentioned, optical drives are often omitted from smaller portable computers. We see their use diminishing, albeit slowly. Approximately 11,000 tons of Neo magnets were used in HDDs, CDs and DVDs in 2010. This dropped to 9,000 tons in 2014 and is expected to rise back to 11,000 tons by 2020 [18,19,20].

5. Overall Permanent Magnet Market – Current and Forecast

Recent estimates for the use of permanent magnets in various applications are shown in Table 2. For both ferrite and rare earth, about 70% of the totals, by weight, are used in motors and generators including

Table 3. Global sales for common magnet materials.

	2010				2015			
	tons	%	$$$	%	tons	%	$$$	%
NdFeB	67,300	10.5%	5,700	65.1%	80,015	8.2%	9,305	62.6%
SmCo	2,310	0.4%	270	3.1%	3,510	0.4%	540	3.6%
Ferrite	567,000	88.2%	2,600	29.7%	881,120	90.7%	4,760	32.0%
Alnico	5,555	0.9%	125	1.4%	6,440	0.7%	185	1.2%
Other	540	0.1%	65	0.7%	580	0.1%	75	0.5%
Totals	**642,705**	100.0%	**8,760**	100.0%	**971,665**	100.0%	**14,865**	100.0%

Sales $$$ are in millions; 2015 is forecast

linear motors and acoustic generators (e.g. Hi-Fi speakers). The choice of rare earth over ferrite is almost always one of smaller size and lower weight. However, other factors influence the decision such as corrosion resistance, which is important in automotive starter motors.

The two main kinds of rare earth magnets are Neo and SmCo. A decision to use SmCo instead of Neo is usually a function of application temperature and/or temperature stability. SmCo is a naturally good high temperature magnet with standard grades useful to 350 °C, and with minor composition shift to less iron/more cobalt, SmCo can be used to over 500 °C. The transition in price and performance between Neo and SmCo occurs between 120 and 180 °C depending on material grades. The newer HRE diffused Neo is pushing the transition closer to 180 °C.

Table 3 provides global sales for the common magnet materials in weight and dollars. Figures for 2010 are best estimates based on the "transparent" market – where published data both for the magnet and the user industries allows estimates to be made. A significant, but unquantified portion of the market exists internal to China, India, Russia, and to a lesser extent in several other countries. I refer to this as the "opaque" market.

Estimates for Neo in 2015 are based on demand since we are still unsure exactly how much raw material will be available for Neo magnets, both the light rare earths (LREs) and the heavy rare earths (HREs, esp. Dy and Tb) are at issue. Ferrite surprises by contributing 88+% by weight of permanent magnets in 2010. Growth to 90+% in 2015 is due in part to the higher performing La-Co (series 12) grades manufactured by Hitachi and TDK for sale outside of China and by several Chinese manufacturers for sale outside of the PCT countries.

References

[1] A.S. Sieminski, *Annual Energy Outlook 2014, Early Release Reference Case, AEO2014 Early Release Rollout Presentation*, 2013, December 16, Paul J. Nitze School of Advanced International Studies, Johns Hopkins University, Washington, DC.

[2] J.D. Power and Associates, *US Green Automotive Study*, 2011, https://pictures.dealer.com/jdpower/f0391cbb0a0d02b7004dd014ba12057d.pdf.

[3] D. Kodjak, *Consumer Acceptance of Electric Vehicles in the US, International Council on Clean Transportation*, 2012, December.

[4] T.A. Keim, I. Celanovic, *Convergence*, 2008, Direct Conversion of Heat to Electricity.

[5] EDTA (Electric Drive Transportation Association, http://electricdrive.org

[6] www.hybridcars.com

[7] Internal company report, *Global Automotive Market Forecast for Permanent Magnets*, 2013, January 25.

[8] International Energy Agency, *Global EV Outlook: Understanding the Electric Vehicle Landscape to 2020*, 2013, April.

[9] DNV GL Energy Storage Group, *Managing the Challenges of Electricity Storage*, www.dnvkema.com/Images/DNV%20KEMA%20Energy%20Storage%20Group_06-07-13.pdf .

[10] Wikipedia, *Charles Francis Brush*, http://en.wikipedia.org/wiki/Charles_F._Brush.

[11] U.S. Energy Information Administration, *Annual Energy Outlook with Projections to 2040*, 2014, April, DOE/EIA-0383(2014).

[12] International Energy Agency (IEA), *Key World Energy Statistics*, 2013.

[13] International Energy Agency (IEA), *Technology Roadmap, Wind Energy*, 2013.

[14] Global Wind Energy Council, *Global Wind Statistics*, 2013.

[15] Global Wind Energy Council, *Global Wind Report – Annual Market Update*, 2013.

[16] *USGS Minerals Yearbooks*, 1995-2013, http://minerals.usgs.gov/minerals/pubs/commodity/rare_earths/

[17] *USGS Mineral Commodities Summaries*, http://minerals.usgs.gov/minerals/pubs/commodity/rare_earths/

[18] V. Filkes, J. Unsworth, J. Monroe, S. Zaffos, *Gartner, Inc.*, 2013, April 15, Solid State Drives will Complement, Not Replace, Hard-Disk Drives in Data Centers.

[19] Samsung, *The Benefits of SSDs on Computing Speed, Reliability and Performance*, www.samsung.com/us/system/b2b/resource/2013/09/09/White_Paper_SSD-Advantage_Final.pdf .

[20] T. Coughlin, *HDD Decline Expected to Slow and Reverse*, www.forbes.com/sites/tomcoughlin/2014/02/10/hdd-decline-expected-to-slow-and-reverse/ .

Development of Rare Earth Permanent Magnet in China

SHENGZHI DONG[1], YANG LUO[2], WEI LI[1]
[1]Central Iron & Steel Research Institute, Beijing 100081, China
[2]IEEE TC-15 Voting Member, Beijing, China

Abstract: *Owning the richest rare earth deposit, China has great advantage of developing rare earth magnets. With the rapid increase of output capability the competition becomes hot and fiercer. The status of permanent magnet industry in China will be presented. Analysis around the rare earth resource and possible market change in the future will be made in this study. Some typical R&D efforts, such as Dy saving technology, low cost magnet leverage of cheap rare earth elements like Ce et al. and radially oriented ring magnet will be introduced.*

Keywords: *rare earth magnet, production, market, R&D status, low cost magnet*

Address: Shengzhi Dong, No.76 Xueyuan Nanlu, Haidian District, Beijing, 100081, China, Tel:+86-10-6218-5006, Email:dong_shengzhi@163.com

1. Introduction

As a country possessing the largest rare earth deposits, China has made a lot of efforts to support and develop the rare earth related industry. As the most important application of rare earth, rare earth permanent magnets, consuming more than 40% of RE products produced in China annually, develop rapidly in the past 30 years. It has been noticed and should be alerted that with the over estimation of the demand, the output capability of Nd-Fe-B magnets increases much faster than requirement resulting a tough competition situation.

It is well known there is an abnormal price change for rare earth in 2011. Within about half a year the price of almost all rare earth elements increases sharply about 5-10 times. Although the price drops back not long after, it affects the permanent magnet industry heavily.

In this paper we will give a brief introduction of the status of permanent magnet industry and make a discussion in rare earth market. Some R&D efforts on REPM in China will be reviewed and discussed.

2. Status of Rare Earth Permanent Magnet Industry

With the continuous increase of the application of REPM, especially of Nd-Fe-B, in computer, mobile phone, wind generator, autos, air conditioner, elevator, and varieties of motors, the rare earth permanent magnet industry keeps growing rapidly for many years[1]. With the advantage of rich rare earth resource and low production cost, China dominated the sintered Nd-Fe-B magnet production from the beginning of 21 century. The average annual growth rate in China is more than 25% before 2005. Figure 1 presents the annual output of Nd-Fe-B from 2003 to 2013. It is evident the annual output drops two times in 2008 and in 2012 respectively, corresponding to the year of global financial crisis and the year after the "rare earth crisis" in 2011.

From the data shown in Table 1 one can notice easily that the growth rate of Nd-Fe-B magnet slows down gradually from the year of 2005. During the period of 2003 to 2013, the average growth rate is no more than 13%.

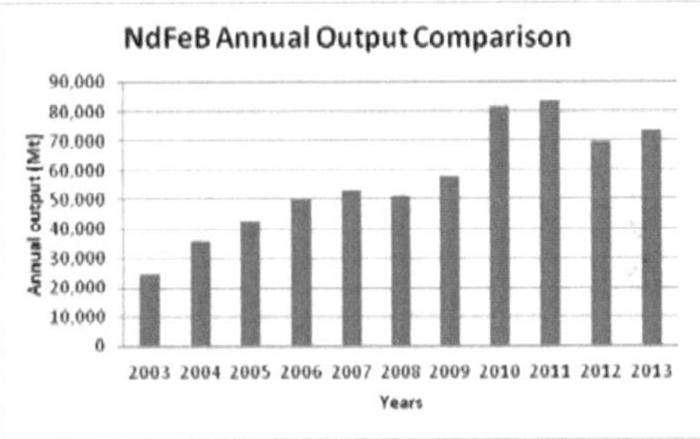

Fig. 1 The annual output of sintered Nd-Fe-B from 2003 to 2013

Table 1. Annual output of sintered NdFeB magnet and growth rate

Year	2003	2004	2005	2006	2007	2008	2009	2010	2011	2012	2013
Output(Mt)	24459	35660	42360	49781	53480	51200	57742	81825	83400	69658	**73720**
Growth		45.8%	18.8%	17.5%	7.4%	-4.3%	12.8%	41.7%	1.9%	-16.5%	5.8%

In 2010 the output increases sharply with a rate higher than 40%. This big jump should be considered as a rebound after the drop in 2008 instead of a signal of faster increasing demand. Based on the tremendous increasing of Nd-Fe-B magnet demand in 2010, a lot of magnet manufacturer and financial investor felt incredible promising and made most ambitious expansion plan. At least three companies claim in early 2011 they will invest and establish new factory with production capability of 10,000 tons of sintered Nd-Fe-B. These unusual expansion plans misleading the expectation of Rare Earth market, which becomes one of the key factors pushing the rare earth price higher and higher in 2011. In 2012, the magnet industry experienced the biggest market shrinkage in the history. Although the requirement recovers to a certain extent in 2013 the total output of Nd-Fe-B magnet is less than in 2010 and 2011.

In 2013 the total requirement for the sintered Nd-Fe-B magnets in the world is about 92500 tonnes, in which about 80% comes from China, 18% comes from Japan, the rest is mainly from Europe, as shown in Figure 2.

There are more than 200 sintered Nd-Fe-B manufacturers in China now. Less than 10% of these companies have production capacities larger than 3kMt.

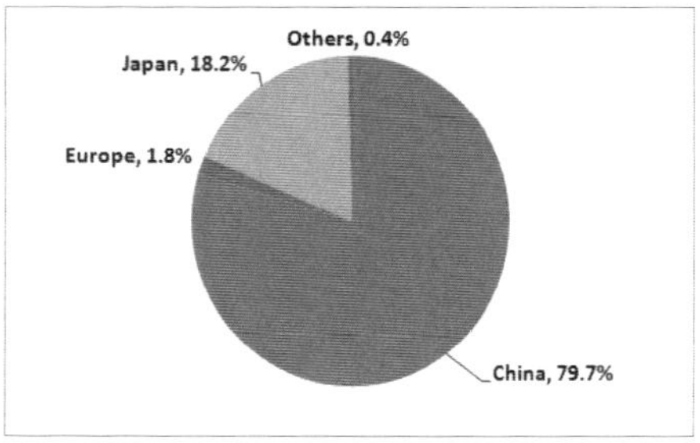

Fig. 2 Sintered Nd-Fe-B output distribution in the world in 2013

About 30% of these sintered magnet companies have capacities in between 1-3kMt. The total production capacity is over 200kMt. Compared with the actual output 73kMt in 2013, which is basically decided by market demand, the production capacity is far exceeding the requirement. The oversupply situation of Nd-Fe-B magnet leads to a fierce competition in the market. Most of the Nd-Fe-B companies can only leverage 30-60% of their production capabilities. Even for the public companies like Sanhuan and Yunsheng, their rate of operation is no more than 75%. As a result, the operation income and the profit drop significantly for most of the Nd-Fe-B magnet companies in 2013.

Table 2. Operation income and profit of some typical Chinese Nd-Fe-B companies (in million RMB)

		Income	Cost	Profit	Gross profit rate
Sanhuan	2012	4933	3302	925	33.1%
	2013	3638	2602	449	28.5%
	change	-26.3%	-21.2%	-51.4%	-4.6%
Yunsheng	2012	2919	1820	646	43.2%
	2013	2138	1478	362	36.5%
	change	-26.8	-18.8	-44.0%	-6.7
Zhenghai	2012	812.4	589.0	168.4	26.61
	2013	547.6	406.4	87.4	24.64%
	change	-32.6%	-31.0%	-48.1%	-1.97%

For a long period of time, there are only five companies (Sanhuan, Yunsheng, AT&M, Jingci, Thinova) in China authorized with sintered Nd-Fe-B production and sales license by Hitachi Metals. After several month's lawsuit action, three Chinese companies: Yantan Zhenghai, Ningbo Jinji and Earth Panda settled down a compromise agreement with Hitachi in May 14,2013 and became the new licenced sintered Nd-Fe-B magnet manufacturers. From then on, the hot competition happens not only for those companies without license but for 8 licensed companies as well. This might be part of the reason that the gross profit rate of Zhenghai dropped much less than Sanhuan and Yunsheng since Zhenghai just got the privilege as a licensed manufacturer.

There are more than 30 bonded Nd-Fe-B manufacturers in China. The typical outstanding companies include AT&M (Shenzhen, Highmag), Zhong Ke San Huan(Shanghai, Epson)、Chengdu Galaxy、Zhejiang Innuovo、 Dongguan Jiangmen and Ningbo Yunsheng. Due to the great advantage of precision dimension, net shape compaction, flexible for making complex shape, the bonded magnets have widely used in many high end application such as computer, auto, home appliance, office automation et al. The annual output of bonded Nd-Fe-B magnets in China and in the world is shown in Figure 3. From 2003 to 2013, the global requirement for bonded Nd-Fe-B magnet increase at an average rate of 5% per year while the output in China increases 11% annually. In 2003 only 37% bonded magnets were made in China. Now more than 67% is supplied by China. The other two important supply area/country are south east (17%) and Japan (10%).

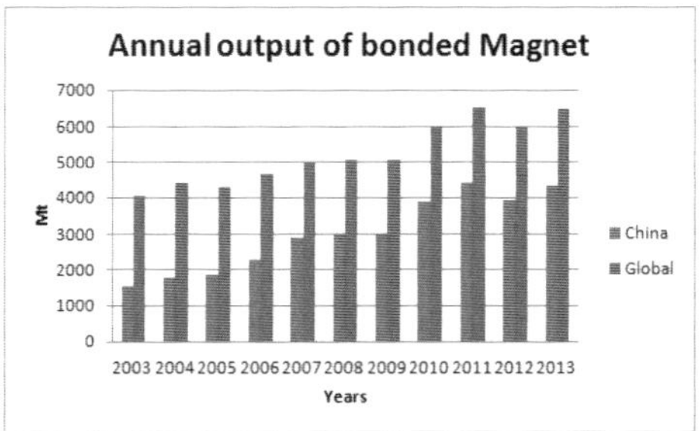

Fig. 3 Annual output of bonded Nd-Fe-B magnet in the world

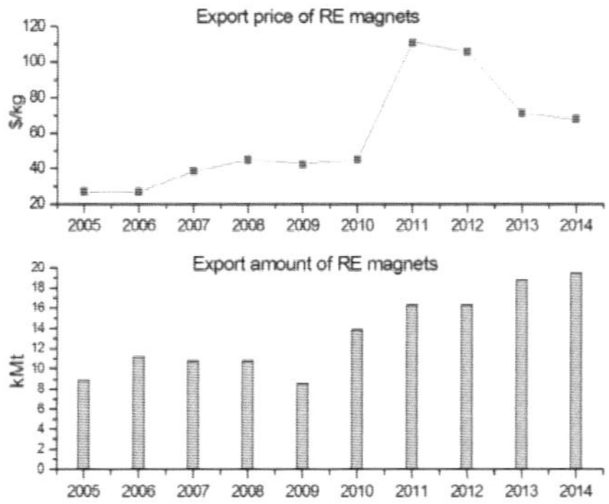

Fig.4 Comparison of export quantities and average price of rare earth magnet

Figure 4 shows the export quantities and average sale price of rare earth magnet from 2005 to 2014 based on Customs' published data, in which the data for 2014 is calculated upon the first 4 month's data. Compared with figure 1, one may notice the influence of rare earth price fluctuation around the year of 2011 on the export quantities of rare earth magnet is much less than Chinese domestic market. The requirement outside China keeps growing even in 2012 while the total output of Nd-Fe-B in 2012 dropped 16.5% which implies the demand outside China is much less sensitive to the price of rare earth.

Figure 5 shows the export quantities and average sale price of non rare earth magnet (mainly for ferrite hard magnet). The total output of hard ferrite in 2013 is about 750kMt in China which is about 2/3 of the global output. Different from Nd-Fe-B magnet, the peak price of ferrite magnet appears in 2012 rather than in 2011 when the rare earth price reaches its top. This is in corresponding to the fact that some original RE magnet demand turn to ferrite magnet due to the abnormal price change in 2011. The sudden demand increase of ferrite magnet in China in 2012 causes its price increase while the price of Nd-Fe-B decreases.

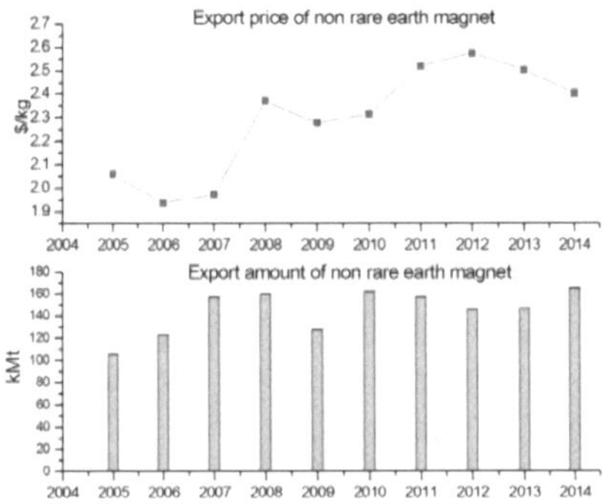

Fig.5 Comparison of export quantities and average price of non rare earth magnet

3. Discussion of Rare Earth Market

In 2011 the rare earth market experienced an abnormal "crisis". Figure 6 presents the price trend of Nd (export to Japan) as a typical representative of rare earth metal. It can be seen the Neodymium price reached to its bottom, about 15$/kg, in the beginning of year 2009. Then it gradually increased before 2011 and reaches its top at 460$/kg in July 2011 shortly. The rare earth "crisis" starts almost at the beginning of year 2011. For the purpose of environmental protection and make full use of Chinese precious rare earth resource, the government issues a series of policy and regulation to manage the rare earth production process. The total supply of rare earth was suppressed due to some rare earth manufacturers have to stop their production until they meets the strict requirements for environment protection. As mentioned, Nd-Fe-B output of 2010 increased by 40%. This positive data caused the over promising estimation to the future magnet market. Emerging Nd-Fe-B production capabilities were planed and established continually, which implies that the demand for rare earth would keep increasing dramatically. A clear market prediction that the demand is far more supply was widely accepted. A lot of speculators started to enter into this market. At this time, the rare earth price is not only decided by consumers and producers but by government and speculators as well. All these factors constructed a "rare earth crisis"----the price of all rare earth elements rocketed up with an incredible speed. Price of some rare earth metals such as Dysprosium increased by 10 times within 200 days.

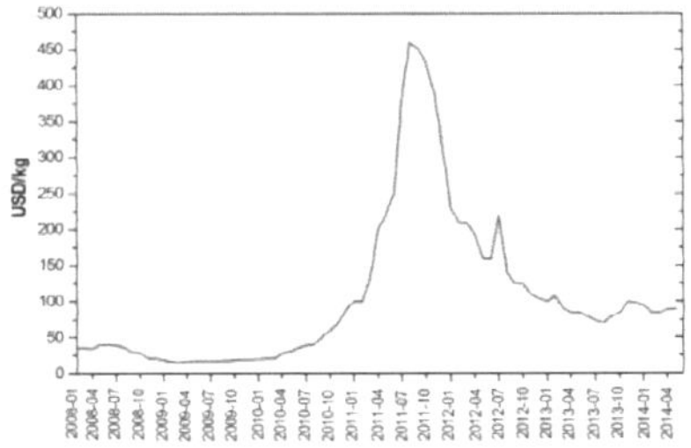

Fig.6 Export price trend of rare earth Nd metal

With the tremendous increase of rare earth price the Nd-Fe-B market is heavily damaged. Some users have to change their design to use hard ferrite instead of Nd-Fe-B magnet. Some users even stop using magnet. The abnormal increased price supported by speculators could not last for long time. It started to drop back at almost the same speed as it climbed up. Now the rare earth price is decided by the supply and demand market again. Although there're some concerns that the rare earth price may increase dramatically again as what happened in 2011, we don't think its probability is big enough to worry about. The main reasons for our judgment include three points: 1. The growth rate of Nd-Fe-B demand has been slowed down to less than 15%. 2. The RE supply comes not only from China but also from US, Australia, Vietnam et al and grows quickly. 3. More and more people realize that rare earth is actually not so "rare" as they considered before.

4. Research and Development of REPM in China

As the largest REPM production and application country, China makes a lot of efforts to support the research and development activities on REPM. Due to the fact that the oversupply situation will last for a relative long time more and more REPM manufacturers invest more in R&D activities to enhance their competition capabilities.

(1) Progress on production equipments

Strip casting alloying, HD+JM pulverizing, sealed pressing and multi-stage sintering process are widely used in production now. 600-1000kg SC furnace with two separated cooling chambers facilitating semi-continue alloying is developed for production. The rotary HD furnace is widely adopted. Automatic press and multi-chamber sinter furnace are helpful to get low oxygen uniform magnet and increase the manufacture efficiency.

(a) semi-continuous SC furnace (b) automatic magnetic aligning pressor

(c) Rotary HD furnace (d) Multi-chamber sinter furnace

Fig.7 Advanced manufacturing equipment used in Chinese Nd-Fe-B factory

(2) Excellent magnetic performance

With the development of advanced equipments and new technologies[2], great progress has been made in manufacturing high end sintered Nd-Fe-B magnets. Some factories, taking AT&M and Sanhuan for example, can make world class high grade magnets such as N55, 52M, 48SH, 42UH et al.

Central Iron & Steel Research Institute worked together with Sanhuan to develop the top high end magnets. They have successfully developed fantastically high coercivity magnet with excellent magnetic performance Hcj=40.3kOe, BHm=32.75MGOe as demonstrated in figure 8. The comprehensive hard magnet performance (CHMP): BHmax(in MGOe)+Hcj(in kOe)=73.05 which is one of the best performance in the world. This is a symbol indicating that in developing high CHMP magnet the researchers and manufacturers in China have made a lot of progress.

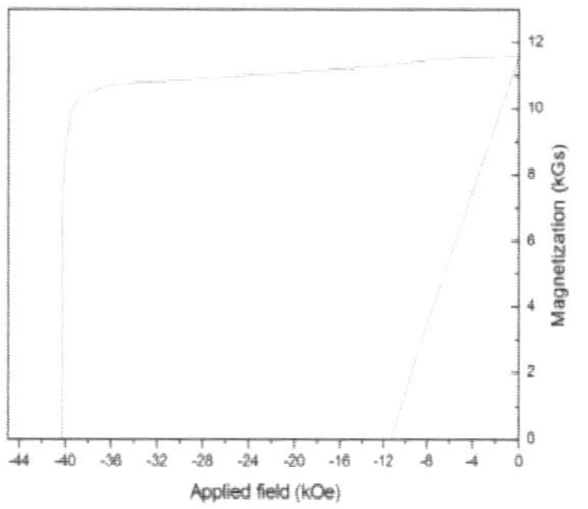

Fig.8 Demagnetization curve of new developed magnet with excellent performance

(3) Mechanical property modification [3,4]

Adopting the dual alloy process, via adjusting the composition of liquid phase, the grain boundary phase can be modified and the mechanical properties of sintered Nd-Fe-B can be effectively improved. The bending strength can be enhanced to 400MPa. The anti overloading impact capability is higher than 10^5g as shown in Fig.9

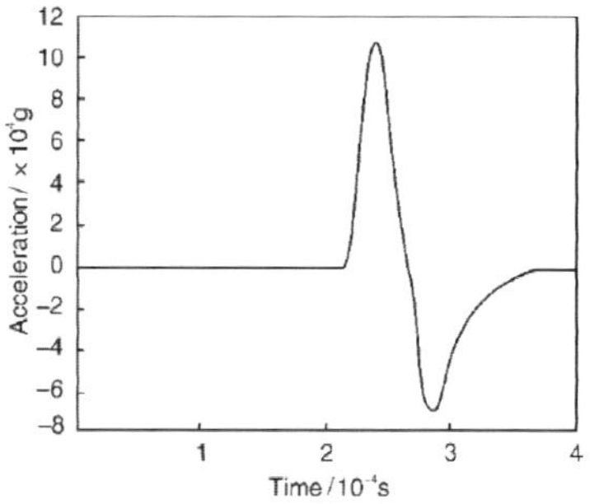

Fig.9 Anti overloading impact test curve of high strength and toughness magnet

(4) Dy saving technology

Grain boundary modification technique has been proved to be an effective way to enhance intrinsic coercivity with less Dy by different experiments[5-7]. Similar grain boundary diffusion process is studied in a number of Chinese research groups with different ways and some promising progress was achieved. It's obvious that with grain boundary diffusion process, the coercivity of the magnet can be effectively enhanced. Magnet with intrinsic coercivity of 20kOe can be obtained with much less Dy or even no Dy compared with traditional process. But for actual application of this technique, there's a long way to go to benefit from both performance and total cost.

(5) Hot Press Magnet (Extrude radial orientation ring)

Central Iron & Steel Research Institute cooperated with Ningbo Material Institute studying the hot pressing magnet at very early stage.

Starting from rapid-quenching material with microcrystalline grains, hot-press process is applied to obtain full density magnet alloy which is isotropic oriented. After further hot deformation the magnetic crystals align along the extrude direction through texturing. With this so called back extrusion technique the radially oriented anisotropic magnets can be successfully obtained. The advantage of hot deformation magnet include: 1. Excellent magnetic properties (53.7MGOe is obtained in CISRI). 2. Larger magnet density, better corrosion resistance. 3.Higher grade for small radial ring magnet (>43MGOe).

The hot press and deformation process on the microstructure and magnetic properties are demonstrated in figure 9.

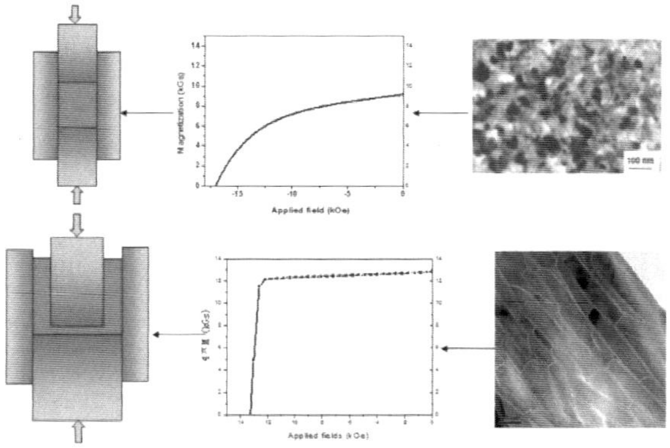

Fig.9 Microstructure and magnetic properties demonstration for hot press and deformation

(6) Dual main phase Cerium magnet

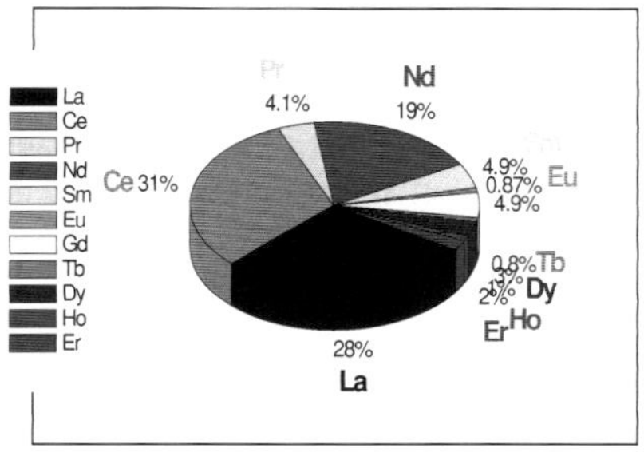

Fig.10 Composition percentage of different rare earth in the nature

As shown in figure 10, Ce takes the largest portion in the existing rare earth deposit. Making full use of Ce in permanent magnet is economically and socially meaningful. CISRI makes a lot of efforts to develop Ce rich magnet for comprehensive utilization of RE resource.

It is found when both Ce-Fe-B and Nd-Fe-B alloys were prepared separately and then mixed together in a designed ratio which is defined as dual hard main phase process, the final magnet presents a higher coercivity than the magnet with same composition but made by single alloy process. This coercivity enhancement phenomena happened in "dual hard main phase(DHMP) magnets" has been confirmed for different Ce magnet such as hot pressing magnet.

The mechanism of coercivity enhancement of DHMP magnet is still under discussion. Some explanation has been made though further verification experiments are required. Two of the typical preliminary explanations are "hard phase exchanging interaction" and "dispersion strengthening".

(7) Sm-Co magnet for extremely high temperature application

Based on Sm(Co,Fe,Cu,Zr)z alloy, the extremely high temperature operation magnet is studied and successfully prepared with adjusting Fe composition and applying strip casting technology. Its maximum energy product is larger than $84kJ/cm^3$ at 500C which is one of the best performance for an extremely high temperature application.

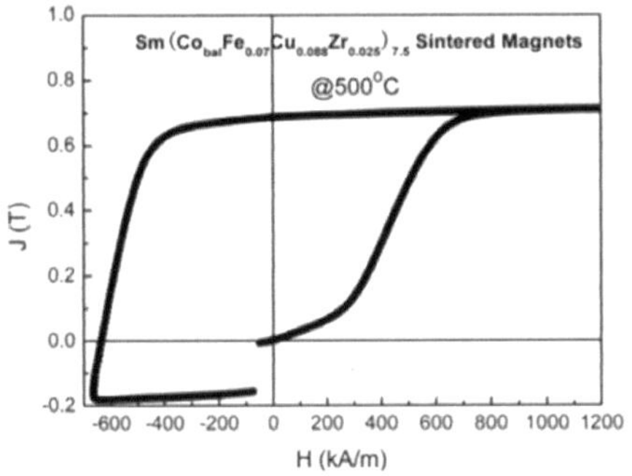

Fig.11 The hysteresis loop of SmCo magnet at high temperature

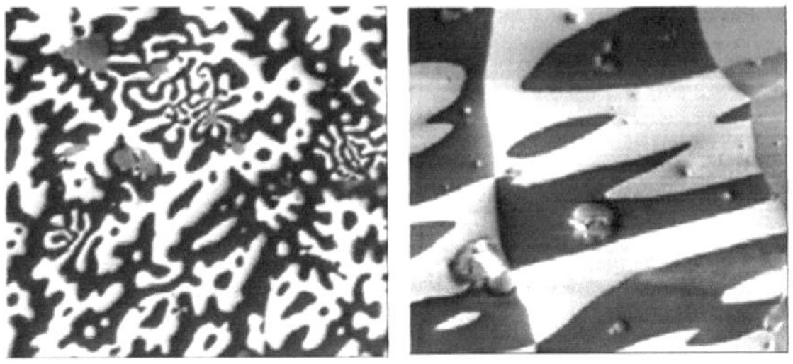

//C ⊥C

Fig.12 Domain structure of SmCo at high temperature observed with MFM

5. Discussion of Research and Development Trends in China

For future technology development, the focus will be how to improve the service properties and to reduce the cost. More research and development efforts will be deployed in the following areas:

(1) Balanced usage of rare earth in REPM

With the development of enabling technology such as dual hard main phase process, grain boundary diffusion, and fine-grained magnet, high abundance RE elements Y, La, Ce which is considered unsuitable for hard magnet application becomes promising and attractive to obtain low cost magnet with acceptable performance. Recycling technology to leverage the RE resource in scrapped magnets and machined fragments is important as well.

(2) Technology for low temperature coefficient of intrinsic coercivity to improve thermal stability

Same intrinsic coercivity but better thermal stability? This will be a noval direction to save Dy and meet the requirements of low irreversible loss for many high temperature application.

(4) Technology for making near net shape magnet

For sintered magnets about 20-40% of the material will be machined off to get the final products. Technology development for near net shape magnet will be driven strongly by the market competition situation.

(5) Technology enable better service life: low weight loss magnet, better anticorrosion surface treatment, better mechanical strength and toughness.

References

[1] Y.Luo, "25 years development of NdFeB magnet industry", in: *Proc. 20 Int. Workshop on Rare Earth Permanent Magnet & Their Applications*, Greece, 2008, p. 27.

[2] W. Li, W. Pan, Y.Q. Guo et al., *Phys. Status Solidi C* **4**, 2007, 4611.

[3] H.J. Wang, A.H. Li, Y.Q. Guo et al., *J. Appl. Phys.* **103**, 2008, 07E119.

[4] H.J.Wang, A.H. Li, W. Li, *Intermetallics* **15**, 2007, 985.

[5] D.S. Li, S. Suzuki, T. Horikawa, M. Itoh, and K.Machida, in: *The Papers of Tech. Meeting. Magn. IEE Hapan*, MAG-05-117(2005).

[6] N. Fujimori, in: *Proc. Techno-Frontier 2006*, Japan Management Association, 2006, B1-1-1.

[7] H. Nakamura, K. Hirota, M. Shimao, T. Minowa and M. Honshima, *IEEE Trans. Magn.* **41**, 2006, 3844.

Recent Trends and Perspectives on Development of Permanent Magnets in Japan

T. IRIYAMA
Daido Steel Co., Ltd./Intermetallics Co., Ltd., Nagoya 457-8545, Japan

Abstract: *The grain boundary diffusion (GBD) process has recently been developed as a very effective technique to enhance the magnetic properties of sintered Nd-Fe-B magnets with a lower amount of Dy addition than that in a conventional process. Fine-particle Nd-Fe-B magnets fabricated using the pressless process (PLP) or hot deformation process are promising candidates as next-generation Nd-Fe-B magnets that come closer to achieving the optimal magnetic properties. Sm-Fe-N materials have demonstrated excellent magnetic properties when used as bonded magnets. Extensive research to find new magnetic materials is being carried out under a Japanese national project. However, the development of new magnetic materials with high performance is expected to take a long time, and therefore, it is important to improve the conventional Nd-Fe-B or Sm-Fe-N materials for realizing their optimal properties. An overview of these new trends in the development of magnetic materials in Japan is presented in this article.*

Keywords: *Nd-Fe-B; Sm-Fe-N; grain boundary diffusion; pressless process; hot-deformed magnets*

Address: Takahiko Iriyama, Daido Corporate R&D Center, Daido Steel Co., Ltd., Nagoya 457-8545, Japan, Tel: (81-52) 611-9412, Fax: (81-52) 611-9494, E-mail: t-iriyama@ac.daido.co.jp

1. Introduction

The demand for permanent magnets for use in clean energy applications such as hybrid electric vehicles (HEVs), electric vehicles (EVs), auxiliary devices for automobiles, consumer electronics, and wind turbines has increased rapidly in recent years. Typically, these applications require that the magnets not only have high remanence (B_r) but also large coercivity (H_c). Fig. 1 shows the magnetic properties of various commercial permanent magnets available in Japan. The Nd-Fe-B magnet [1] is the most attractive of these because it has the highest $(BH)_{max}$ value of all the commercial magnetic materials. The addition of heavy rare-earth elements (HREEs) such as Dy or Tb is the most common method of increasing the coercivity of Nd-Fe-B magnets [2]. However, one of the problems of HREE addition is that it reduces B_r, as shown in Fig. 1. Another serious problem is the declining HREE supply owing to the restricted production of HREEs. Accordingly, efforts to reduce HREE use have been undertaken all over the world. In this paper, an overview of the recent trends on the development of permanent magnets in Japan is presented.

2. Recent Trends on Development of Permanent Magnets in Japan

Table 1 lists some major examples of the recent research and development efforts in the field of permanent magnets being carried out by Japanese magnet producers or as part of Japanese national projects [3-23]. These efforts can be classified into the following categories: 1) improvement in the magnetic properties of Nd-Fe-B materials, 2) development of rare-earth magnets other than the Nd-Fe-B ones, and 3) search of non-rare-earth magnetic materials. In addition to these efforts, studies to improve the magnetic properties of ferrite magnets are also being carried out [24-26]. These studies are also important for the permanent magnet industry, because ferrite magnets are the most produced magnets in the world owing to their low prices, and because they will be used for a very long time.

2.1. Improvement in magnetic properties of Nd-Fe-B materials

2.1.1. Grain boundary diffusion process

The grain boundary diffusion (GBD) process has recently been developed as a very effective technique for reducing HREE usage by more than 50% [3-8, 27]. Various methods for performing GBD, such as rare-earth-fluoride coating [3], rare-earth-powder mixing [4], rare-earth-alloy coating [5, 6], and sputtering [7], have been reported. Fig. 2 shows a typical example of the effects of the GBD technique.

Mizoguchi et al. showed that the reduction of oxygen and carbon inclusions is important in order to obtain better effects from the GBD process [6]. Fig. 3 shows the demagnetization curves for sintered Nd-Fe-B magnets fabricated by the pressless process (PLP)

before and after the GBD process (magnet A: ~0.11 wt% carbon, magnet B: ~0.07 wt% carbon). Here, Tb alloy powder was used as HREE for the GBD process. The coercivity of magnet A was increased by 743 kA/m, whereas that of magnet B increased by 1025 kA/m. The line profiles for Tb from the surface to a depth of 3 mm in the magnets, obtained using characteristic X-rays, are shown in Fig. 4. Tb atoms diffuse from the surface to a depth of 3 mm through the grain boundaries in magnet B, whereas they diffuse only to a maximum depth of 1 mm in magnet A. It is thought that carbon compounds at the triple points of grain boundaries block Tb diffusion and trap Tb atoms near the magnet surface. Consequently, coercivity increase in magnet A with a higher carbon content was less than that in magnet B. GBD-processed Nd-Fe-B sintered magnets have been already realized and their applications are expanding gradually.

2.1.2. Fine-particle Nd-Fe-B magnets

Fine-particle Nd-Fe-B magnets fabricated using the PLP process [5, 9] or hot deformation process [10, 11] are promising candidates as next-generation Nd-Fe-B magnets that come closer to achieving the optimal magnetic properties. Fig. 5 shows the ideal and actual microstructure of sintered Nd-Fe-B magnets. The actual sintered Nd-Fe-B magnets include various defects such as coarse grains, non-metallic inclusions, misoriented grains, and lack of intergranular phase region that deteriorate their hard magnetic properties. It seems that it is easier to obtain the ideal microstructure using the PLP or hot deformation process than using the conventional sintered process. The digests of PLP and hot-deformed magnets are described below.

The fabrication process for PLP magnets as proposed by Sagawa is shown in Fig. 6 [5]. One of the important features of PLP magnets is that they have larger coercivity than those fabricated using the conventional process, because the atmosphere in the PLP process is inert throughout the process and the resulting magnets contain a low level of oxygen inclusions. Fig. 7 shows the coercivities and SEM images of PLP magnets. By optimizing the fabrication process and microstructure, a large coercivity of 1600 kA/m (20 kOe) was obtained for a Dy-free PLP magnet with a particle size of about 1 □m, as shown in Fig. 7 [9]. Sagawa et al. have taken up the challenge to fabricate a high-performance nanostructured PLP magnet under the Japanese national project MagHEM [14].

Figure 8 shows the microstructures of a hot-deformed and a conventional sintered magnet. The hot-deformed magnet has a fine microstructure that is one order of magnitude finer than that of the sintered magnet (grains of the hot-deformed magnet are platelet-shaped). Thus, hot-deformed Nd-Fe-B is a promising material for realizing HREE-free Nd-Fe-B magnets with high performance. Fig. 9 shows the fabrication process for radially oriented (ring) hot-deformed magnets. A schematic model of the lateral profile of a radially oriented hot-deformed ring magnet is shown in Fig. 9. The major differences between the hot deformation and sintering processes are the former's requirement of a lower processing temperature and nanocrystalline starting materials to yield a much finer grain size, as shown in Fig. 8. Fig. 10 shows the magnetic property map of Dy-free and Dy-saving hot-deformed Nd-Fe-B magnets measured at room temperature (RT) and 180 °C, respectively. The coercivity of the Dy-free hot-deformed magnets reached more than 1600 kA/m. Additionally, a coercivity of 2300 kA/m for a Dy content of 2.1 at% was achieved. This Dy content was less than that found in conventional sintered magnets. Therefore, it can be said that this magnet exhibits high performance without the addition of HREEs.

<u>2.2. Development of rare-earth magnets other than Nd-Fe-B materials</u>

2.2.1. Sm-Fe-N, Sm-Fe, Sm-Co magnets

Sm-Fe-N materials have demonstrated excellent magnetic properties when used as bonded magnets [18, 28]. Tada et al. reported an injection-molded Sm-Fe-N magnet with a coercivity of 1.52 MA/m that was larger than that of a conventional magnet [15, 16]. Takagi and Ozaki succeeded in fabricating a highly dense Sm-Fe-N magnet by using the SPS process [19]. Sakurada et al. reported a newly developed Sm-Co sintered magnet with a high Fe content that showed high performance at high temperatures [21].

2.2.2. Nanocomposite magnets

Fe-$Nd_2Fe_{14}B$ and Fe-SmCo nanocomposites are being researched by several groups [12-14, 22]. However, large coercivities for these materials have not reported yet. It is thought that obtaining the ideal microstructures for nanocomposite magnets is very difficult.

<u>2.3. Search for non-rare-earth magnetic materials</u>

Extensive research to find new magnetic materials

such as $L1_0$-FeNi [12-14], $L2_0$-Fe-Co [13], and $Fe_{16}N_2$ [14] is being carried out as part of a Japanese national project. However, the development of new magnetic materials with high performance is expected to take a long time, and therefore, it is important to improve the conventional Nd-Fe-B or Sm-Fe-N materials to realize their optimal properties in the immediate future.

3. Perspectives

Fig. 11 shows the desirable magnetic properties of next-generation magnets, which the author personally hopes for. In order to achieve these properties, several big hurdles have to be crossed first. For instance, it is required to develop a fabrication process for obtaining the ideal microstructure that would result in large coercivity.

References

[1] M. Sagawa, S. Fujimura, N. Togawa, H. Yamamoto, Y. Matsuura, *J. Appl. Phys.*, **55**, 1984, 2083.
[2] J. F. Herbst, J. J. Croat, F. E. Pinkerton, W. B. Yelon, *Phys. Rev.*, **29**, 1984, 4176.
[3] H. Nakamura, *Materia Japan*, **50**, 2011, 374 (in Japanese).
[4] T. Hidaka, C. Ishizaka, M. Hosako, Proceedings of the 21st International Workshop on Rare-Earth Permanent Magnets and their Applications, 2010, pp. 100-102.
[5] M. Sagawa, Proceedings of the 21st International Workshop on Rare-Earth Permanent Magnets and their Applications, 2010, pp. 183-186.
[6] T. Mizoguchi, M. Sagawa, N. Iwata, H. Matsui, A. Kimura, Proceedings of 2014 International Conference on NdFeB Magnets: Supply Chain, Critical Properties & Applications, 2014, pp. 154-157.
[7] K. Hioki, A. Hattori, T. Iriyama, Abstracts of 58th Annual Conference on Magnetism and Magnetic Materials, 2013, p. 645.
[8] T. Akiya, J. Liu, H. Sepehri-Amin, T. Ohkubo, K. Hioki, A. Hattori, K. Hono, *Scripta Materialia*, **81**, 2014, 48.
[9] Y. Une, M. Sagawa, *J. Japan Inst. Metals*, **76**, 2012, 12 (in Japanese).
[10] K. Hioki, T. Morita, A. Hattori, Proceedings of the 22nd International Workshop on Rare-Earth Permanent Magnets and their Applications, 2012, pp. 89-92.
[11] K. Hioki, A. Hattori, T. Iriyama, *J. Magn. Soc. Jpn.*, **38**, 2014, 79.
[12] http://www.element.jst.go.jp/researchers/index.html
[13] http://www.jst.go.jp/kyousou/theme/h23theme01.htm l
[14] http://www.maghem.jp/project.html
[15] S. Tada, T. Tomomoto, M. Kume, Proceedings of the 22nd International Workshop on Rare-Earth Permanent Magnets and their Applications, 2012, pp. 48-53.
[16] S. Tada, H. Maehara, M. Yamamoto, M. Kume, Abstracts of Spring Meeting of Japan Society of Powder and Powder Metallurgy, 2014, p. 73 (in Japanese).
[17] S. Sakurada, T. Hirai, A. Tsutai, *J. Magn. Soc. Japan*, **21**, 1997, 181 (in Japanese).
[18] R. Omatsuzawa, K. Murashige, T. Iriyama, *Trans. Magn. Soc. Japan*, **4**, 2004, 113.
[19] K. Takagi, K. Ozaki, Proceedings of the 22nd International Workshop on Rare-Earth Permanent Magnets and their Applications, 2012, pp. 273-276.
[20] T. Saito, Abstracts of Annual Meeting 2014 IEE Japan, 2014, pp. 17-18 (in Japanese).
[21] S. Sakurada, Y. Horiuchi, M. Hagiwara, T. Kobayashi, T. Kobayashi, K. Okamoto, M. Endo, N. Sanada, Abstracts of Spring Meeting of Japan Society of Powder and Powder Metallurgy, 2014, p. 64 (in Japanese).
[22] H. Fukunaga, A. Tou, R. Horikawa, T. Yanai, M. Nakano, Abstracts of Spring Meeting of Japan Society of Powder and Powder Metallurgy, 2014, p. 63 (in Japanese).
[23] K. Shinaji, T. Mase, K. Isogai, M. Matsuura, N. Tezuka, S. Sugimoto, *Mater. Trans.*, **54**, 2013, 2007.
[24] Y. Minachi, H. Taguchi, KINZOKU Materials Science & Technology, **79**, 2009, 12 (in Japanese).
[25] Y. Kobayashi, Abstracts of Annual Meeting 2014 IEE Japan, 2014, pp. 19-22 (in Japanese).
[26] G. Obara, Abstracts of Annual Meeting 2014 IEE Japan, 2014, pp. 23-26 (in Japanese).
[27] K. T. Park, K. Hiraga, M. Sagawa, Proceedings of the 16th International Workshop on Rare-Earth Permanent Magnets and their Applications, 2000, pp. 257-264.
[28] T. Iriyama, Kidorui no zairyou gijutu handbook, NTS, Japan, 2008, pp. 157-165 (in Japanese).

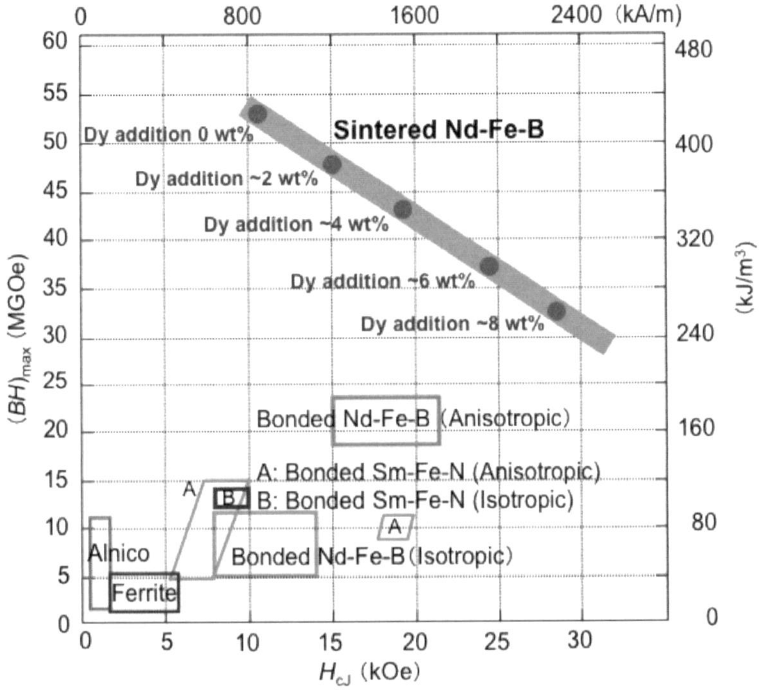

Fig. 1 Magnetic properties of various commercial permanent magnets in Japan.

Table 1 Major examples of the recent research and development efforts in the field of permanent magnets being carried out by Japanese magnet producers or as part of Japanese national projects.

Category	Research and development	Ref.
1) Improvement in the magnetic properties of Nd-Fe-B materials		
Grain boundary diffusion technique	Rare-earth-fluoride coating	[3]
	Rare-earth-powder mixing	[4]
	Rare-earth alloy coating	[5, 6]
	Rare-earth alloy sputtering	[7]
	Nd-Cu eutectic diffusion under expansion constraint	[8]
Fine-particle magnet	Pressless process (PLP) magnet	[5, 9]
	Hot-deformed magnet	[10, 11]
Fundamental study	Microstructure/Magnetic domain structure/Computer simulation	[12-14]
2) Development of rare-earth magnets other than the Nd-Fe-B materials		
Sm-Fe-N	Anisotropic bonded $Sm_2Fe_{17}N_3$ with large coercivity	[15, 16]
	Isotropic bonded $SmFe_9N$	[17, 18]
	Highly dense isotropic $SmFe_9N$	[19]
Sm-Fe	Sm_5Fe_{17} with large coercivity	[20]
Sm-Co	High performance $Sm(CoFeCuZr)_{7.8}$ sintered magnet	[21]
Nanocomposite	$Fe\text{-}Nd_2Fe_{14}B$ multi-layer	[12-14]
	Fe-SmCo PLD (pulsed laser deposition) multi-layer	[22]
3) Search of non-rare-earth magnetic materials		
	$L1_0$ FeNi	[12-14]
	$L2_0$ FeCo	[13]
	$Fe_{16}N_2$	[14]
	MnSnCoN	[23]

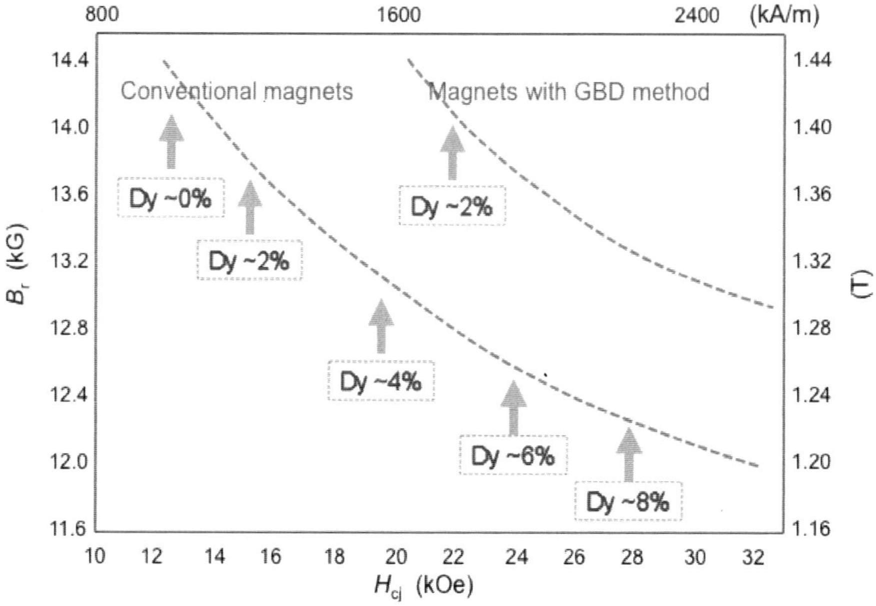

Fig. 2 Typical example of the effects of the GBD technique.

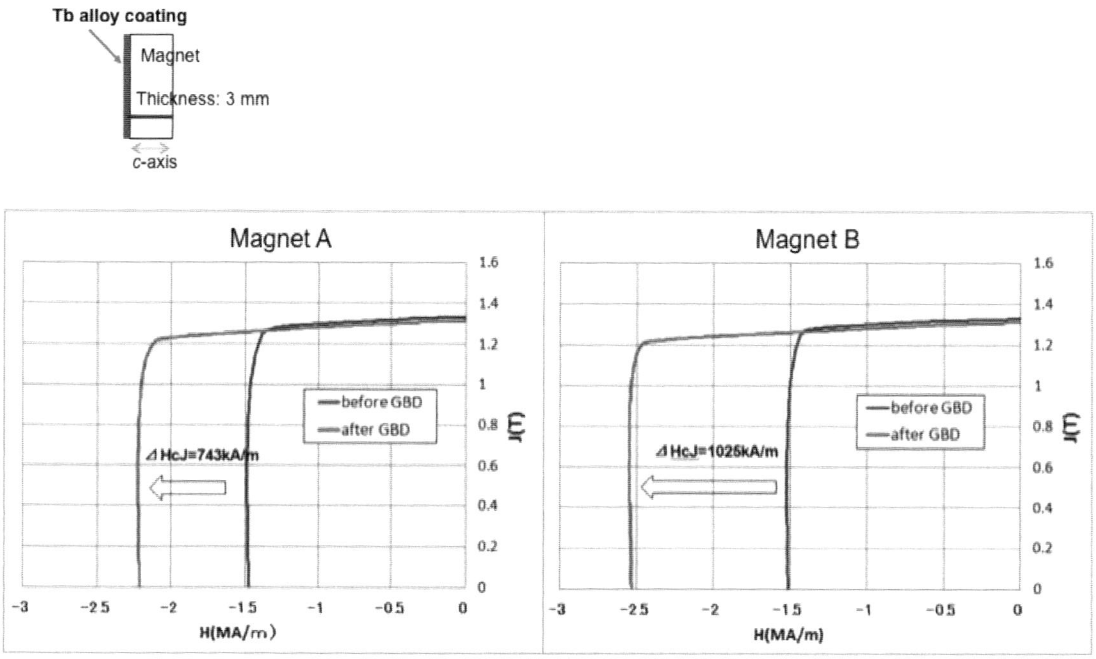

Fig. 3 Demagnetization curves for sintered Nd-Fe-B magnets fabricated by the pressless process (PLP) before and after the GBD process.
Magnet A: Oxygen inclusion ~0.08 wt%, Carbon inclusion ~0.11 wt%
Magnet B: Oxygen inclusion ~0.08 wt%, Carbon inclusion ~0.07 wt%

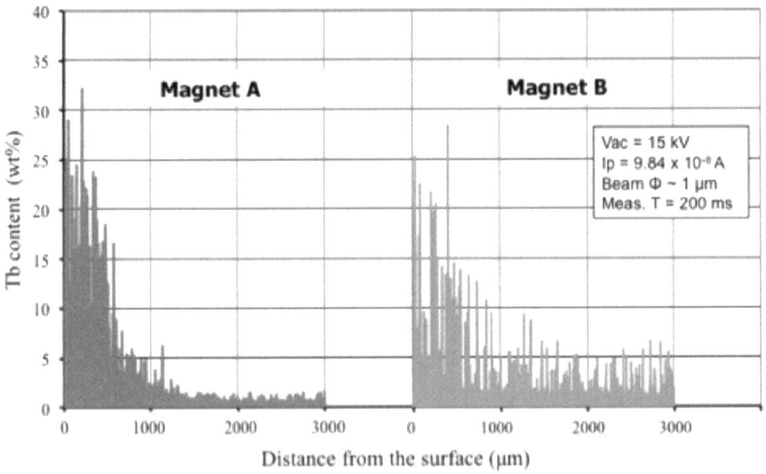

Fig. 4 Line profiles for Tb from the surface to a depth of 3 mm in the magnets obtained using characteristic X-rays.

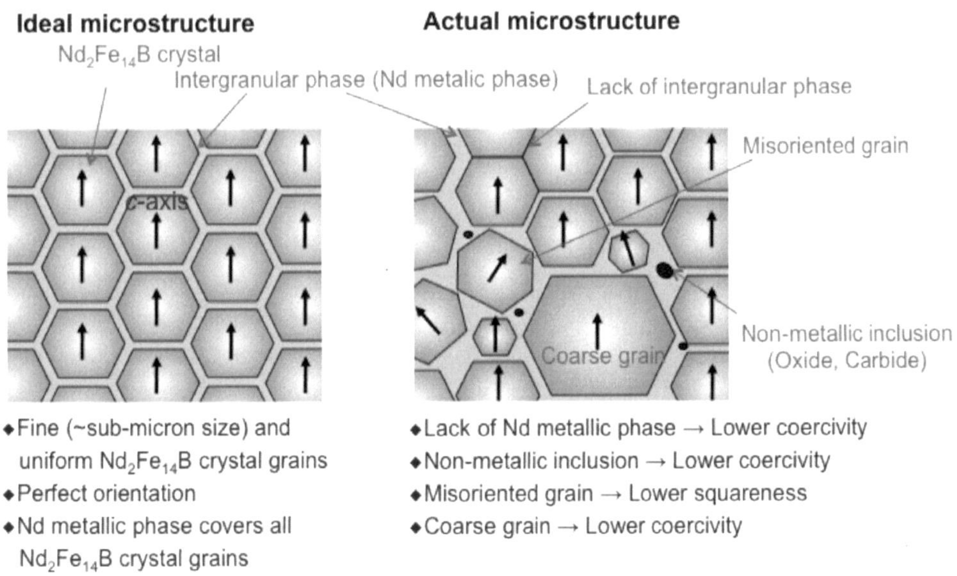

Fig. 5 Ideal and actual microstructure of sintered Nd-Fe-B magnets.

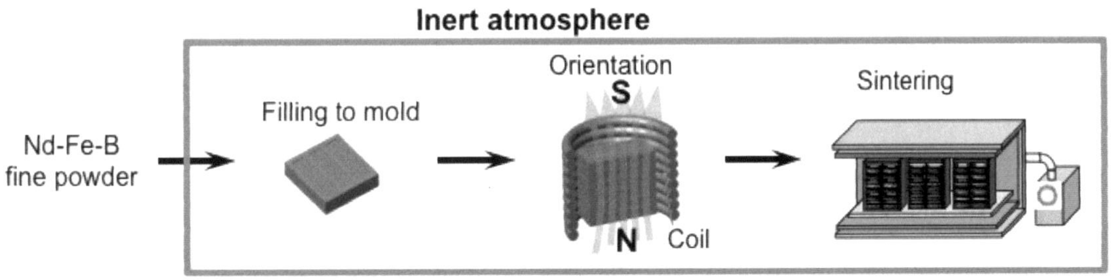

Fig. 6 Fabrication process for pressless process (PLP) magnets.

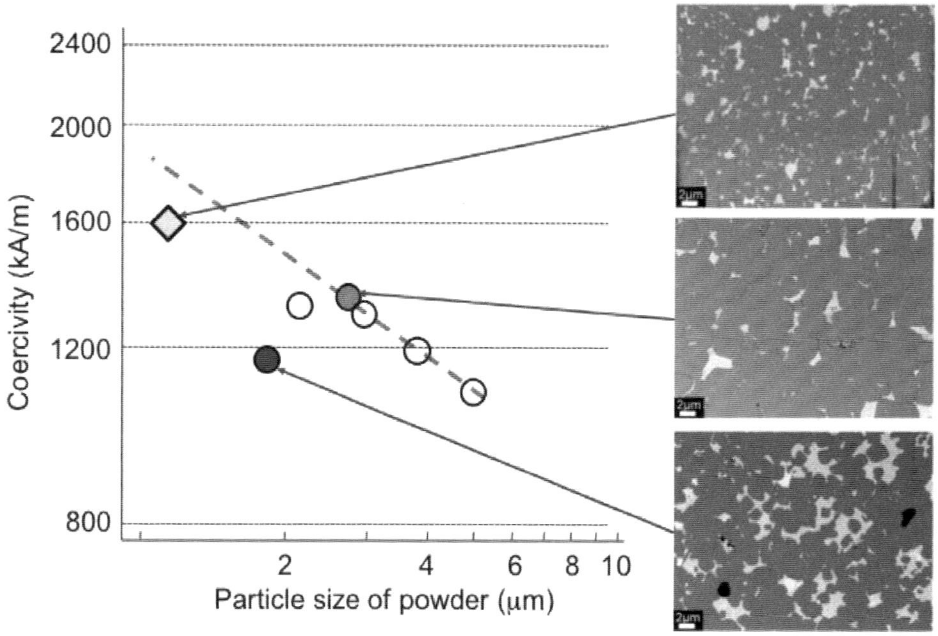

Fig. 7 Coercivities and SEM images of pressless process (PLP) magnets. (SEM observation was done by Prof. Hono of NIMS.)

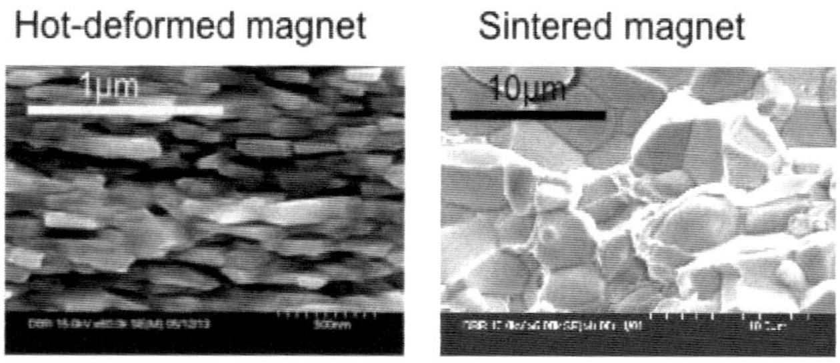

Fig. 8 Microstructures of a hot-deformed and a conventional sintered magnet.

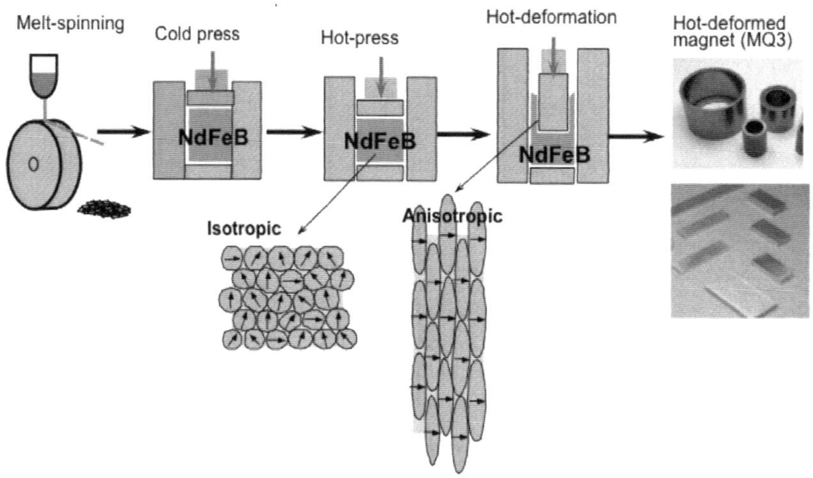

Fig. 9 Fabrication process for radially oriented hot-deformed magnet.

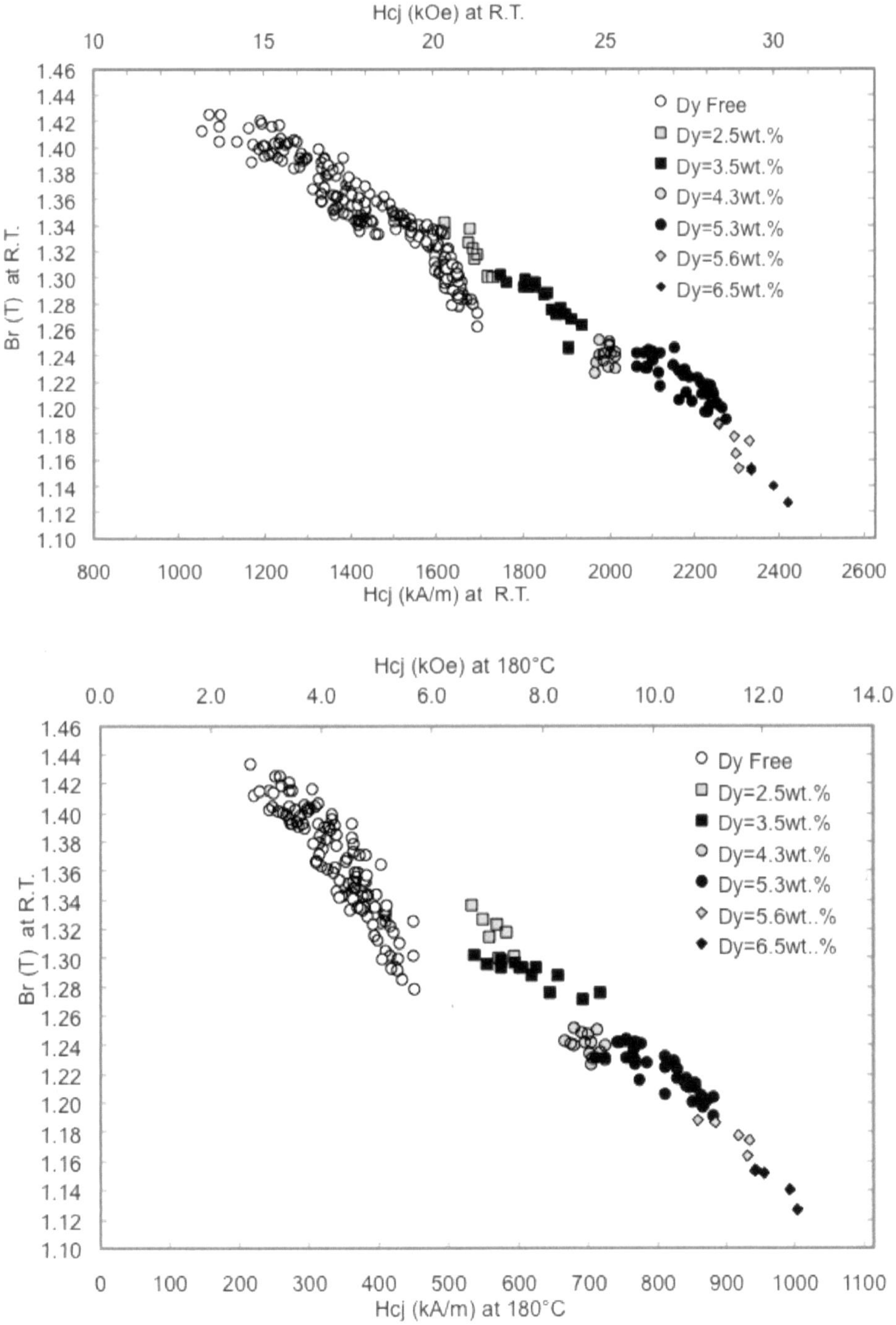

Fig. 10 Magnetic property map of Dy-free and Dy-saving hot-deformed Nd-Fe-B magnets measured at room temperature (RT) and 180 °C.

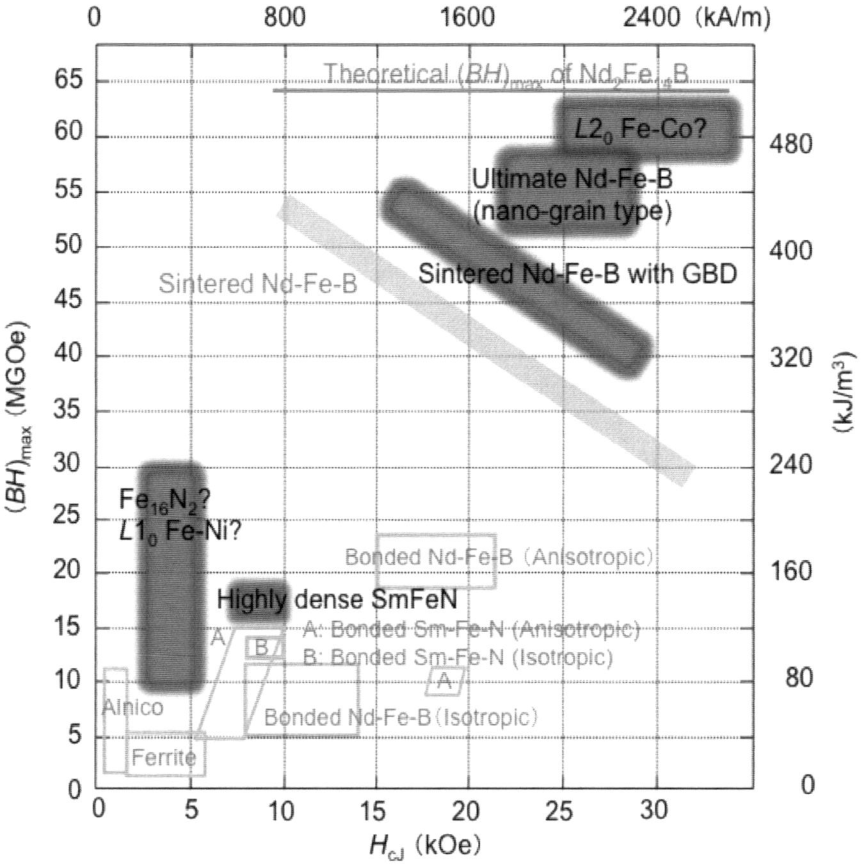

Fig. 11 Desirable magnetic properties of next-generation magnets, which the author personally hopes for.

The Status of Rare Earth Permanent Magnets in Europe

M. KATTER
Vacuumschmelze GmbH & Co. KG, Hanau, Germany

Abstract: *In Europe there is still a production capacity of about 1500 t/a for sintered rare earth permanent magnets (REPM). Based on a new license agreement with Hitachi Metals Ltd, Vacuumschmelze GmbH & Co. KG in Germany together with its affiliate Neorem Magnets Oy in Finland produces REPM for industrial motors, automotive applications like electric power steering and sensors as well as generators for offshore wind mills. Now Dy-free magnet grades with a coercivity,* H_{cJ}*, of 1350 kA/m and a remanence,* B_r*, of 1.37 T are available. By application of a grain boundary diffusion process REFeB magnets with a content of heavy RE of only 3.8 wt.% with* $B_r = 1.33$ *T and* $H_{cJ} = 2440$ *kA/m could be produced recently. Furthermore new magnet grades based on PrFeB have been developed for cryogenic applications. In addition there is a strong focus on near net shape single part die pressing technologies with an increased yield and optimized distribution of the alignment directions for sensor applications and scientific applications like undulators but also for motors, e.g. to reduce torque ripple. Vacuumschmelze has developed several lacquers which allow to produce cost-effectively segmented magnets with good electrical insulation and corrosion resistance to reduce heating caused by eddy currents. The paper will give an overview about the actual technological development trends in Europe. In addition there is also a lot of academic research on RE magnets which resulted in many national and European funded research projects which will be briefly described in the paper.*

Key words: *NdFeB; PrFeB; SmCo; sintered magnets*

Address: M. Katter, Vacuumschmelze GmbH & Co. KG, Grüner Weg 37, 63450 Hanau, Germany, Tel: +49 6181 382083, Fax: +49 6181 3882083, E-Mail: Matthias.Katter@vacuumschmelze.com

1. Introduction

Rare Earth Permanent Magnets (REPM) are known since 1966 when K.J. Strnat described the extremely large magnetocrystalline anisotropy of YCo_5 [1]. Industrial production of SmCo magnets started in the early 1970´s, mainly in the US, Europe and Japan. Due to the high price and the volatile availability of the main constituents the applications where initially restricted to high end applications. The situation changed when in 1984 the NdFeB permanent magnets were discovered which are based on cheaper and more abundant raw materials [2,3]. In the 1980´s many companies in Japan, US and Europe started the industrial production of sintered and also rapidly quenched NdFeB magnets. Until about 2004 the largest share of sintered NdFeB magnets were used in voice coil motors for hard disc drives, followed later by motors and generators [4]. In the 1990´s most of the REPM were produced in Japan in the form of sintered magnets, dominated by Sumitomo Special Magnets. The capacity in US and Europe stayed more or less constant whereas the production capacities in China increased considerably. Since 2000 most of the sintered NdFeB magnets are produced in China and in 2003 in US the production of NdFeB magnets was stopped at all [5]. Contrary to the development in the US in Europe Vacuumschmelze GmbH & Co. KG (VAC) in Germany and Neorem Magnets Oy (Neorem) in Finland continued their production of sintered REPM until today. The paper will report the actual status of REPM in Europe including the technology trends and a brief review of funded academic research projects.

2. General

Besides the large production capacities for rare earth (RE) permanent magnets in China and Japan there is still a considerable industrial production of NdFeB and SmCo magnets in Europe. VAC in Germany is together with its affiliate Neorem in Finland by far the largest producer of sintered RE magnets in Europe with a total capacity of about 1500 t/a. Based on a new license agreement, signed in 2013, both companies are fully licensed by Hitachi Metals Ltd and can deliver the magnets worldwide including Japan. Smaller amounts of sintered REPM are also produced by Magnetfabrik Schramberg in Germany, Arnold Magnetic Technologies in Switzerland and Magneti Ljubljana in Slovenia. Bonded REPM are produced among others by Max Baermann GmbH, Magnetfabrik Bonn, Kolektor Magnet Technology in Germany, Sura Magnets in Sweden and Sintex in Denmark. Most of the bonded REPM are based on isotropic, rapidly quenched NdFeB but there are also some anisotropic NdFeB- (HDDR type powder) and SmCo-based magnets produced. The powders for the bonded NdFeB magnets are all produced in Asia whereas some of the SmCo powders are also produced in Europe.

The main application for REPM in Europe is still industrial motors. However, recently automotive applications like electric power steering and generators for offshore wind mills gain on importance. Besides these applications which are related to electromechanical power conversion there are many magnets used in sensor applications, magnetic bearings and scientific applications like undulators. Especially these high end applications require very sophisticated magnets regarding the mechanical and magnetic tolerances which can be provided by the specialized European magnet producers.

3. Technology Trends in Europe for REPM

Dy has been used for many years as a standard substitute for Nd to increase the coercivity and thus the temperature stability of sintered NdFeB magnets. At least since the huge price peak for Dy in 2011 there is a strong demand to reduce the Dy content by increasing the coercivity of such magnets by other means. One of the most elegant methods to achieve this is the reduction of the grain size of the magnets [6]. However, up to now for Dy-free sintered NdFeB magnets it has not been reported that the coercivity could be increased above 1600 kA/m at room temperature using this technique alone. In addition, the handling of such extremely fine powders under industrial conditions is very difficult. Therefore additional methods are required to increase the coercivity using as low as possible amounts of heavy rare earths.

One way to increase the coercivity of Dy-free magnets is the substitution of Al in combination with small amounts of Co, Cu and Ga, s. Fig. 1. However, the remanence of such magnets decreases by 0.1 T per wt.% Al which is about four times faster than for the substitution with Dy or Tb. By choosing an optimizedamount of Co, Cu, Ga, Al and adding a small amount of 0.2 wt.% Tb, magnet grades with a coercivity, H_{cJ}, of 1350 kA/m and a remanence, B_r, of 1.37 T can be produced under industrial conditions. Such magnets are suitable for many applications up to 120°C and are almost independent on the supply of heavy rare earths. By applying an additional grain boundary diffusion (GBD) process [7] to such magnets a coercivity, H_{cJ}, of 1920 kA/m and a remanence, B_r, of 1.37 T at room temperature can be achieved under production conditions, as shown in Fig. 1. Such magnets can be used at temperatures up to 150°C.

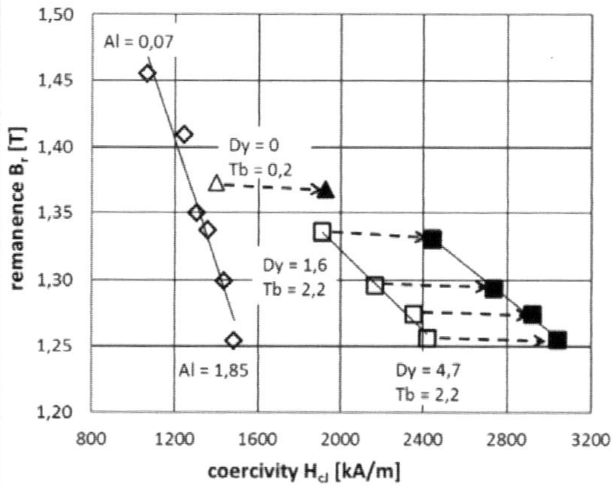

Fig. 1. Magnetic properties at room temperature of NdFeB based sintered magnets with various Al, Dy and Tb content. The compositions are given in wt.%. The diamonds represent isostatically pressed laboratory samples which do not contain any Dy and Tb, the triangles and squares stand for magnets which are pressed in a transverse magnetic field under production conditions and the solid symbols represent grain boundary diffused (GBD) magnets.

But the increase of the coercivity depends on the thickness of the magnets. Fig. 2 shows the dependence of the gain in coercivity on the distance from the magnet surface where the heavy rare earths were applied. For a magnet thickness of 5 mm a minimum increase of coercivity of 400 kA/m can be reached in the center of the magnet. This behavior is almost independent on the particular magnet grade. This means that any sintered NdFeB magnet grade can benefit from the increased coercivity due to the GBD process under the above mentioned dimensional restrictions.

For even higher application temperatures recently magnet grades with optimized amounts of Dy and Tb have been developed. Depending on the Dy-content such magnets reach remanences of 1.22 – 1,35 T and coercivities of 2550 – 1850 kA/m, respectively, s. Fig. 1. Since these magnet grades are not produced utilizing the GBD process, there are no restrictions regarding the thickness of such magnets. After application of the GBD process such magnets reach a B_r of 1.33 T and a H_{cJ} of 2440 kA/m at room temperature for a total heavy rare earth content of only 3.8 wt.%. Such magnet grades can be produced in large scale under industrial production conditions.

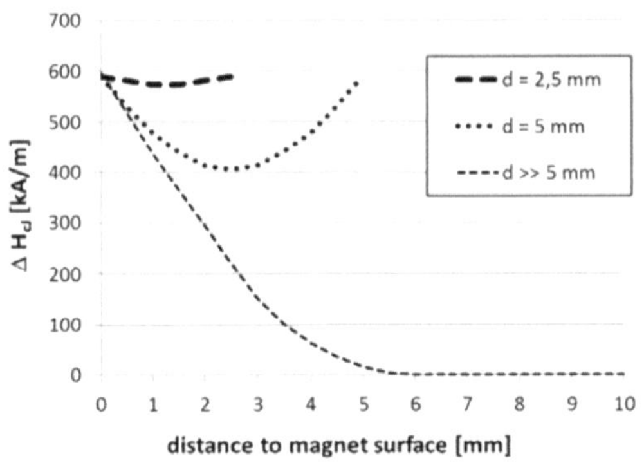

Fig. 2. Increase of the coercivity of NdFeB based sintered magnets after the application of a GBD process in dependence on the distance from the magnet surface. The 2.5 and 5 mm thick magnets were treated on all faces, the magnet with d >> 5 mm was treated only from one side

Furthermore new magnet grades based on PrFeB have been developed in Europe for cryogenic applications [8]. Such magnets do not suffer from the spin reorientation of the $Nd_2Fe_{14}B$ phase below 150 K and reach a remanence of 1.62 T at 77 K, s. Fig. 3. Although these magnet grades are designed for cryogenic applications for some applications it is required that they can be handled at moderately elevated temperatures without demagnetization. For this purpose VAC has developed the grade VACODYM® 131 DTP where the coercivity at room temperature is increased to more than 1650 kA/m by a GBD treatment, as shown in Fig. 3 [9].

Besides these alloy developments, in Europe there is a strong focus on near net shape single part die pressing technologies with an increased yield. In close cooperation with customers' production processes and magnet designs could be developed with reduced or even without any grinding or cutting of the magnets. Another advantage of the single part die pressing technology compared to magnets cut out of larger blocks is that each single magnet is identical regarding its distribution of the alignment directions. This feature is not only important for sensor applications and scientific applications like undulators but it can also be used beneficially in motors, e.g. to reduce torque ripple.

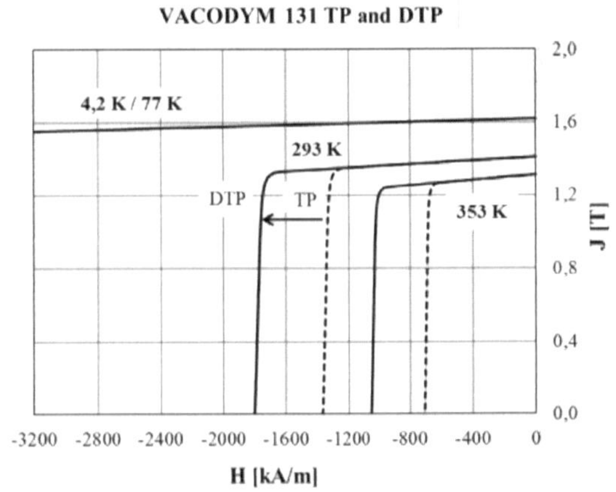

Fig. 3. Magnetic characteristics of PrFeB magnets before and after the application of a GBD process.

There is also a trend to use segmented magnets to reduce heating caused by eddy currents. VAC has developed several lacquers which allow to produce cost-effectively segmented magnets with good electrical insulation and corrosion resistance, as shown in Fig. 4.

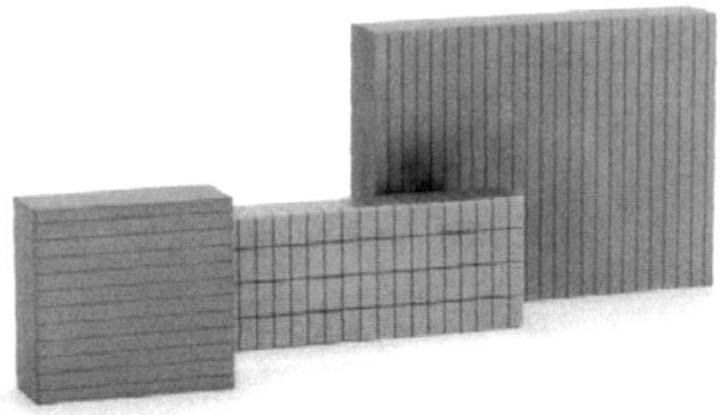

Fig. 4. Overview of segmented magnets to reduce eddy currents.

Table 1. Selection of public funded European and national research projects related to REPM

project	topic	consortium
EURARE	Exploitation scheme for Europe´s RE ore deposits	NTU Athens (GR), RWTH Aachen (GER), GME (Greenland), Less Common Metals (UK), NEOREM (FI)…
PerEMot	Grain boundary diffusion process	Siemens, Vacuumschmelze, TU Darmstadt (all GER)
MAG-DRIVE	REPM with reduced grain size	IJS (SLO), Valeo (FR), Uni. Birmingham (UK), Magneti Ljubljana (SLO), …
ROMEO	Magnets with reduced amount of heavy RE and RE-free magnets	JSI Ljubljana (SLO), TCD Dublin (IRL), CNRS Grenoble (FR), Vacuumschmelze (GER), IFW Dresden (GER), PUAS St. Pölten (AT),…
NANOPYME	RE-free exchange coupled magnets	IMDEA (ES), IFE (N), DTU (DK), INSTM (I), IMA (ES), INNOVENT (GER), …
REFREEPERMAG	RE-free magnets	NCSR Demokritos (GR), TU Vienna (AT), TU Darmstadt (GER), Magnetfabrik Bonn (GER),...
REMANENCE	recycling of REPM	C-Tech Innov. (UK), Uni. Birmingham (UK), Kolektor (GER), Magneti Ljubljana (SLO), …
MORE	recycling of REPM	Siemens, Umicore, Daimler, Frauenhofer ISI, Vacuumschmelze , Öko-Institut, Uni Erlangen, TU Clausthal (all GER)

4. Public Funded Research Projects

In Europe there is also a lot of academic research on REPM. There are currently about 50 national and European funded research projects where about 200 partners from academics and industry work together on the optimization of REPM [10]. Table 1 lists a selection of some major actual projects. The projects span a wide range from the exploitation of Europe´s RE ore deposits, over the optimization of the GBD process, reduction of RE consumption in REPM, completely RE-free permanent magnets down to the development of recycling methods for REPM. The total budget for the projects funded by the European Commision, mainly in the framework of FP7, is about 75 Mio. € [10]. This framework will be followed now by Horizon 2020 where the first projects are already in the application process.

5. Conclusions

Despite the large production capacities and competition for REPM in China and Japan there is still a vital industry in Europe producing sintered and bonded permanent magnets based on NdFeB and SmCo. The industry has specialized itself on magnets for the main applications like motors and generators with an increasing share on automotive applications. To serve the demands of the market several new NdFeB magnet grades with reduced amount of heavy RE as well as special variants of the GBD process have been developed. In contrast to China there is a strong focus on near net shape pressing techniques and automation of the production lines. The activities of the industry are supported by many research and university institutes which are collaborating among each other in the frame work of about 50 national and European funded research projects. On this innovative basis the European REPM industry is well prepared to be competitive also in future.

6. Acknowledgments

P. McGuiness is gratefully acknowledged for sharing the data regarding the funded research projects.

References

[1] K.J. Strnat, *Ferromagnetic Materials*, Volume 4, North-Holland, Amsterdam, 1988, pp. 131-209.

[2] M. Sagawa, S. Fujimura, M. Togawa, Y. Matsuura, *J. Appl. Phys.* **55** (1984) 2083.

[3] J.J. Croat, J.F. Herbst, R.W. Lee, F.E. Pinkerton,

J. Appl. Phys. **55** (1984) 2078.

[4] Y. Kaneko, in: *Proc. 18th Workshop on High Performance Magnets & their Applications*, edt. N.M. Dempsey and P. de Rango, Annecy (2004) 40.

[5] Y. Luo, in: *Proc. 18th Workshop on High Performance Magnets & their Applications*, edt. N.M. Dempsey and P. de Rango, Annecy (2004) 28.

[6] K. Uestuener, M. Katter, W. Rodewald, *IEEE Trans. Magn.* **42** *(*2006*)* 2897.

[7] K.T. Park, K. Hiraga, M. Sagawa, in: *Proc. 16th international Workshop on Rare-Earth Magnets and Their Applications*, JIM, Sendai (2000) 257.

[8] K. Uestuener et al., in: *Proc. 20th Int. Workshop on Rare Earth Permanent Magnet & Their Applications*, edt. D. Niarchos, Knossos (2008) 397.

[9] C. Brombacher, K. Uestuener, F.-J. Boergermann, M. Katter, in: *Proc. 23rd Int. Workshop on Rare Earth Permanent Magnet & Their Applications*, edt. G. Hadjipanayis, Annapolis (2014) submitted.

[10] P. McGuiness, "Permanent Magnet Activities supported by the EU", paper presented at Joint European Magnetic Symposia 2013, Rhodes (2013).

Status of Permanent Magnets in the World: Russia

A.G. DORMIDONTOV[1], A.S. LILEEV[2], N.V. KUDREVATYKH[3,4]
[1] JSC "SPETSMAGNIT", Moscow, Russia
[2]National Research University "MISIS", Moscow, Russia
[3]Ural Federal University,
[4]Ural Institute of Metrology, Yekaterinburg, Russia

Abstract: *History and the present status of Russia permanent magnet industry are reviewed. The sources of raw rare earths - including ore deposits, existing extraction practices and the future prospects - are discussed in detail. The latest developments in rare-earth-based permanent magnet materials and design of magnetic systems are illustrated by multiple examples.*

Keywords: *permanent magnets; Russia; rare-earth ore deposits; magnetic systems*

1. Introduction

The present day status of permanent magnets in Russia has evolved in two stages. The first one goes back to the collapse of the USSR in December 1991. The second began in January 2013 with publication of a program "Development of Rare and Rare-Earth Metals Industry" as a part of state program "Development of the Industry and Increase of Its Competitiveness". The program introduced simultaneously funding of all links of the production chain including the products with a high added value, such as permanent magnets and magnetic systems.

Before 1990, the USSR was among the major manufacturers of permanent magnets. In 1988, USSR produced 12900 tons of Alnico magnets, 23 t of Fe-Cr-Co magnets, 47 t of Sm-Co magnets and 2500 t of strontium and barium ferrite magnets. Manufacturers of magnets in the USSR were never experiencing difficulties with supply of the row materials; the domestic raw materials industry could satisfy needs - in both the quantity and quality - for all required components, from electrolytic Ca and Fe to Nb, Zr to rare earth metals (REMs). Today, when discussing the production of magnets, it is first necessary to address the current shortage in REMs. The unprecedented increase in manufacturing and consumption of the REM-based magnets has resulted in an enormous interest to raw RE materials.

2. Sources of Raw Rare Earths

There were three producers of raw REMs in the USSR (see Table 1). Presently Russia possesses the world second - after China - explored RE reserves (about 30%) and the world largest expected resources [1,2]. Seventeen ore deposits are on the state balance-sheet. Although, the majority of them contain rather poor ores, there are exceptions. In particular, the ore of *Alluaiv* deposit contains the rare mineral *evdialite* which can be found only in two other places on Earth - in significantly smaller quantities [1]. Its reserves available for surface mining are estimated to be 80 million tons; the overall expected reserves may be 1000 times larger.

The concentration of REMs in the ores of *Tomtorsky* deposit reaches 8 - 13%; its explored reserves are 150 million t, and expected reserves are 2 billion t. Apart from REMs, its ores contains about 5% Nb. A similar to the *Tomtorsky* deposit but more modest *Chuktukonsky* deposit is located in Krasnoyarsk Region.

At the present, Russia does not have regulations against incomplete processing of natural resources. This leads to considerable losses of mineral resources during selective enrichment of the raw materials. Consider the *apatite* ores being extracted on the Kola Peninsula for production of the phosphoric fertilizers and containing 1 - 2% of REMs. In the case of a complex processing, the present volumes of production and enrichment of these ores would allow for annual production of 40 000 t of REMs. However, in a pursuit of a quick profit these enormous resources are left behind. According to [1], during 1994 - 2008 more than 3 million t of REO and 4.5 million t of Sr oxide were written off the state balance-sheet. For many years, a considerable part of the *apatite* - 85% -

Table 1. Sources of raw rare earth materials in the USSR.

Deposit name and region	Ore type	Main elements	Output (10^3 t/year)
Lovozerskoe, Russia, Murmansk region, Kola Peninsula	Loparites	Ti, Ta, Nb, RE	6.5
KutessayII, Orlovka, Kirgizia	Ittrohinsizit	RE	1.5
Aktau, Mangushlak Peninsula, Kazakhstan	Uranium phosphorus	U, P, RE	0.5

Table 2. Key parameters of RE-metal deposits prime for operating up in Russia [3].

Deposit name and region	Ore and RE-content		Ore reserves and their status	
Alluayv. Lovozerskiy Mts., Murmansk Region	Loparites	TR – 1 %, incl. TR_{Ce} до 99 %, $Y+TR_Y \leq 1$ %	Explored	$80x10^6$ t
	Evdialite	TR – 2,7 %, incl. TR_{Ce} – 60-62 %, $Y+TR_Y$ – 38-40 %	Expected	$80x10^9$. t
Tomptor , Buranny Area, Sakha Republic, Yakutiya	Natural Pirochlor –monatcit-krandalite concentrate	TR – 8-13 %, Incl. TR_{Ce} – 60-62 %, $Y+TR_Y$ – 38-40 %	Explored	$43x10^6$ t
			Expected	$1.2x10^9$ t
			Explored REM	$3.2x10^6$ t
			Expected REM	$157x10^6$ t
			Explored Nb_2O_5	$1.3x10^6$ t
			Expected Nb_2O_5	$74x10^6$ t
			Explored Sc	$21x10^3$ t
			Expected Sc	$1.13x10^6$ t
Chuktukonsky, Boguchansky district. Krasnoyarsk Region	Natural Pirochlor –monatcit-krandalite concentrate	TR – 5,1-5,33 %, Incl. TR_{Ce} – 94 %, $Y+TR_Y$ – 6 %	State balance	$6.8x10^6$ t
Waste after sulfuric acid treatments of Hibin apatite	phospho-gypsum	TR – 0,5 %, incl. TR_{Ce} – 85-95 %, $Y+TR_Y$ – 5-15 %	Dumps at European parts of Russia	$200x10^6$ t
			Annually produced	$8x10^6$ t
Waste after nitric acid treatments of Hibin apatite	FRZK	TR – 1-2 %, incl. TR_{Ce} – 85-95 %, $Y+TR_Y$ – 5-15 %	Annually produced	$5.7x10^3$ t

is processed via a sulfate method when most of RE- and Sr-containing materials end up in the phospho-gypsum waste. Only on JSC *PhosAgro* enterprises, 8 million t of a fresh phospho-gypsum go to dumps annually, and their total amount reaches more than 200 million t with 1.6% of Sr and 0.5% RE in average [2]. Facilities for extraction of nitrate apatite concentrates are controlled by JSC *Acron*, JSC *UralChem* and JSC *Rossoshanskiye Udobreniya*. The produced nitrates are superior-quality raw materials for extraction of the REMs. The general capacity of these enterprises is more than 1 million t of *apatite* concentrate a year; with the available technologies this would allow extraction of more than 5000 tons of REOs [1,2]. The most promising Russia sources of the REMs are listed in Table 2.

The new RE-industry development program has already encouraged JSC *Acron* and *Skaygrad Group* to undertake efforts on REM extraction from fertilizers production leftovers, such as the *phospho-gypsum*. There is a hope that these efforts will eventually produce positive results.

3. Processing of Concentrates

In the USSR production of REM arose in the mid-1950s during the technology and defense race with the USA. The Middle Range Machinery Ministry which supervised the nuclear industry was put in charge of processing actinide-containing RE ores, whereas the Ministry of Nonferrous Metallurgy was responsible for processing ores without radioactive inclusions. An annual output of up to 8500 t of REO not only completely covered the domestic demands, but also allowed for export. The USSR REO production output was the world third, following those of USA and France. The REOs in the USSR were produced by nine plants located in what is now Russia, Kazakhstan, Kyrgyzstan, Estonia and Ukraine [4,5].

The scheme of REM freight traffics on the former USSR territory is presented in Fig. 1. The full cycle of pure REMs production was carried out only at the *Kyrgyz Mining and Metallurgical Plant* (presently owned by the Canadian Stans Energy Corp.). Part of its products was additionally refined at *Podolsk Chemical Iron and Steel Works* to be used in electronics manufacturing. Other concentrating ore works shipped concentrates to the next technological chain enterprises according to their affiliations with the specific Ministry.

These producers are presented by two production branches. In the first, a concentrate from *Aktau* (earlier known as Shevchenko) in Kazakhstan was separated from phosphorus and deactivated at the *Dnieper Chemical Plant (*DCP) in Dneprodzerzhinsk, Ukraine. It was then subjected to separation and recombination at the Moscow *Polymetals* plant. Thus, about 1500 t of REM from this plant together with 500 t from Kyrgyzstan satisfied the USSR industry demand for the yttrium group REMs [4,5]. The second production chain began with Murmansk region deposits. Loparite ore was enriched at the *Lovozersky* mining and processing works (MPW), then at the

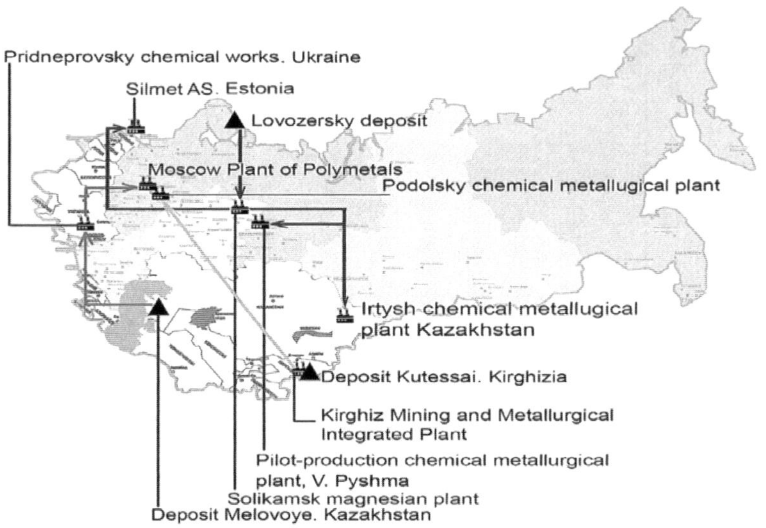

Fig. 1. Production of REM in the USSR.

Solikamsk Magnesian Plant (*SMP*), from which the concentrate in the form of chloride melts was moved for separation and recombination to the *Giredmet pilot plant POZ* (Verkhnyaya Pyshma, Sverdlovsk Region), *Irtysh Chemical Steel Works* (*ICSW*, Kazakhstan) and eventually to *Silmet Plant* (Sillamyae, Estonia). These enterprises produced annually about 6500 t of REMs [4,5].

The collapse of the USSR undermined the close cooperation between the enterprises, decreased – temporarily – the demand for REMs from the industry and the military, and also caused flight of skilled workers and highly qualified specialists from Kazakhstan and Kyrgyzstan to Russia, Ukraine and Belarus. Privatization of the production branches put those of the enterprises which were the main market players into hands of the local elite which often lacked understanding of a role and value of the production. Mining and processing works in Kyrgyzstan and Kazakhstan were closed. Lacking the raw materials supply, the *Pridneprovsky CMP,* the *Moscow Plant of Polymetals*, *Irtysh CMP*, *POZ Giredmet* also discontinued production of the REMs.

In 2000, *SMP* was acquired by JSC *Silvinit.* The new owner has restored the traditional chain of REM production and acquired additionally the *Lovozersky MPW* and *Silmet*. On *Lovozersky MPW*, serious investment events were thus held, which raised the efficiency of *MPW* machinery complexes, increased its productivity and reopened – after a reconstruction – the earlier closed facilities. *SMP* started from production of REM chloride melts to the production of REM carbonates. However, the investors had, apparently, overestimated the commercial opportunities and were forced to sell *Sylvinite* with *SMP* and *Lovozersky MPW* to *Uralkaliy*'s structures. At this sale, *Silmet company* through the mediation of Estonian speculators, passed under control to the *American Molicorp*. Since 2010, the largest Russia state corporations such as *Rosatom* and *Rostekh Group*, being in great demand for the REM products, began preparation of a state program for the REM industry development. By this time, the private industrial groups *Acron* and *Apatite*, controlling raw material resources, and the *IST* financial and industrial group which had been already Russia first and the world fourth manufacturer of silver (and partially owned five largest Russia gold mining companies) also became interested in the REM production. Prospects for the rare-earth industry development after 2010 in Russia are summarized in Fig. 2.

Following of the state program for development of the REM industry, *Rostekh* and *IST-groups* created JV *RT-Globalnye Resources*, which is planning to invest $1 billion in development of the *Buranny* site of the *Tomtor* deposit. The first stage of the JV's program calls for putting into operation the capacities which will provide by 2017 – 2018 the production of 4500 t of a ferroniobium and 10000 t of REM [6] at Krasnoyarsk chemical and metallurgical enterprise. JSC *Atomredmetzoloto* – a part of *Rosatom State Corporation* - has begun production of a collective concentrate of REM and scandium oxide from uranium solutions of JSC *Dalur* and JSC *Hiagda*. The latter two are operators of uranium deposits by the same names. Completion of all the facilities and reaching the maximum planned production of 1800 tons of uranium annually is scheduled for 2019. The private partner of *Rosatom* - JSC *Intermiks Mat* assumes the scandium extraction from *Dalur* and *Hiagda* deposits concentrates at the plant in *Lermontov* city at *Stavropol Region*. The REM separation is also planned at the *Chepetsk Mechanical Plant,* a part of *Rosatom* holding – *Tvel*. For internal market of the yttrium-group REMs, *Rostekh* assumes

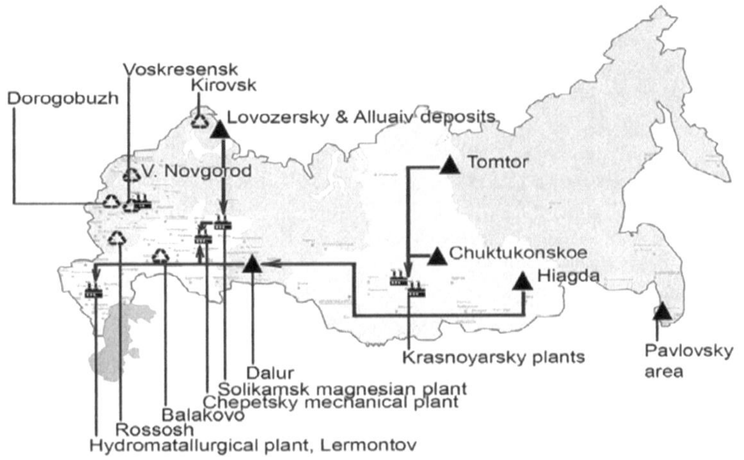

Fig. 2. Rare earth ore deposits and the processing enterprises involved to the first stage of the REM development Program in Russia.

the development of *Pavlovskaya Square* (Primorye) deposits containing ore bodies with new type yttrium-earth mineralization. Technologically, these ores don't concede, but their RE-contents often surpass the ion-sorption ores of the Southern China deposits which are now the main global source of yttrium-group REMs. The use of *Pavlovskaya Square* is tempting also due to the developed infrastructure –power lines, highway and railroad at the deposit borders [7]. It is expected that after the first stage of the REM industry development Program is completed in 2017-2018, Russia will be producing about 10% of the global REMs output, *i.e.*, 16000 – 18000 t in terms of the REOs.

4. Magnets

In the Soviet Union, manufacturing of permanent magnets (PMs) was both controlled and stimulated by the government. The infrastructure pyramid which supported the PMs industry is shown in Fig. 3. The development of the PMs technology was equal to that

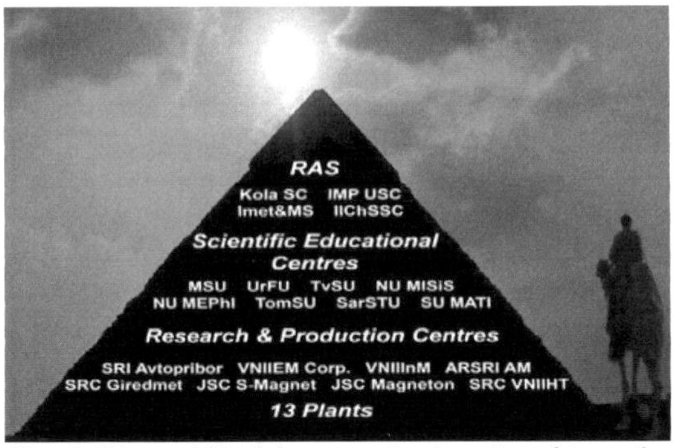

Fig. 3. "Pyramid" of the organizations in subject of RE magnets in Russia (see also Table 3).

of the world top manufacturers. Suffice to remind that *single-crystal* Alnico PMs were commercially manufactured by only two companies, *Philips* in the Netherlands and NPO *Magneton* in the USSR.

The present output of the PMs manufacturing Russia is nowhere close to that of China. By our estimates, the 2012 production of RE PMs in Russia was 130 – 140 t. The level of the PMs properties is, generally, equivalent to that by the other manufacturers; at least, the tests performed at the certified laboratories by those companies which trade China-made PMs in Russia indicated a full parity. The typical properties of the RE PMs produced by Russian manufacturers are listed in Table 4.

5. Magnetic Systems

Many of PMs manufacturers in Russia traditionally provide their customers with a full complex of products and services – calculation, optimization, design, production and delivery of magnetic elements and magnetic systems (MS) or assembles. In fact, they can assure precise 3D magnetic fields for any technical application. Not only hysteresis characteristics of the magnetic material and their temperature dependences, but also the mechanical strength, thermal and electric properties and chemical resistance in various environments are considered when designing the MSs. We are talking here not just about offering PMs from a catalog, but about designing PMs for the specific products; this includes customized magnet structure, shape, distribution of magnetization directions, etc.

Table 4 presents various classes of magnet applications in specific designs. A significant amount of the A class magnets is used in the nondestructive control systems, where there are no high requirements to thermal stability and heat resistance but a high maximum energy product is required [9]. Examples of such devices are shown in Figs. 4 and 5.

It should be noted that PM application in MS devices and the nondestructive control apparatuses is a fairly trivial task. However, it is necessary to consider that dimensions of the magnets, magnetic elements and whole systems often measure in meters. This calls for uncommon approaches to MS designing and for development of special technology/equipment for their assembling. Customized operational protocols and equipment have been developed for such devices to account for impossibility to switch off the most powerful sources of magnetic field and for the eddy currents and magnetic viscosity of the PM material.

Table 3. Institutions and companies involved in R&D and PM production in USSR and Russia [5,8].

No.	Short Name	Full Name	Role	Location
		Russian Academy of Sciences		
1	Kola SC	Kola Science Centre	1	Apatity, Murmansk region
2	IMP USC	Institute of Metal Physics of the Ural Science Centre	1	Ekaterinburg
3	Imet&MS	Institute of Metallurgy and Metal Science	1	Moscow
4	IICh SSC	Institute of Inorganic Chemistry of the Siberian Science Centre	1	Novosibirsk
		Scientific Educational Centres		
1	MSU	Moscow State University	1	Moscow
2	UrFU	Ural Federal University	1	Ekaterinburg
3	TvSU	Tver State University	1	Tver
4	NU MISiS	National University of Science and Technology MISiS	1	Moscow
5	NU MEPhI	National Research Nuclear University MEPhI	1	Moscow
6	TomSU	Tomsk State University	1	Tomsk
7	SarSTU	Saratov State Technical University	1	Saratov
8	SU MATI	State Technical University MATI	3	Moscow
		Branch Research & Production Centres		
1	SRI Avtopribor	Scientific Research and Experimental Institute Avtopribor	1	Moscow
2	VNIIEM Corp.	R & P Corp. Space Monitoring Systems, Information & Control and Electromechanical Complexes	1	Moscow
3	VNIIInM	All-Russia S & R Institute of Inorganic Materials VNIIInM	1	Moscow
4	ARSRI AM	All-Russia S & R Institute of Aviation materials	1	Moscow
5	SRC Giredmet	Federal State R & D Institute of Rare-Metal Industry "Giredmet"	1	Moscow
6	JSC S-Magnet	JSC S-magnet	1	Moscow
7	JSC Magneton	R & P JSC Magneton	1	Vladimir
8	SRC VNIIHT	Federal State R & P Institute of Inorganic Chemistry VNIIHT	1	Moscow
9	RPU Composit	R & P Union Composit Ltd.	3	Korolev, Moscow region
10	SRPI Chermet	Federal State R & P Institute of Ferrous Metallurgy Chermet	3	Moscow
11	RPU TulaCM	R & P Union Tulachermet	3	Tula
12	VNIIMET	All-Union S & R Institute of Electronics Materials VNIIMET	4	Kaluga
		Plants		
1	POZ-Progress	POZ - Progress, Ltd.	1	V. Pyshma, Svedlovsk region
2	PPP S-Magnet	Pilot-production plant JSC S-magnet	1	Moscow
3	PPP Magneton	Pilot-production plant R & P JSC Magneton	1	Vladimir
4	RPU Almaz	JSC R & P Union Almaz	1	Saratov
5	MSZ Elemash	JSC Mashinostroitelny Zavod MSZ Elemash	1	Electrostal, Moscow region
6	UrEMP	FSUE Ural Electromechanical Plant	1	Ekaterinburg
7	Neva-ferrit., Ltd.	Neva-ferrit., Ltd.	1	Kr. Selo, Leningrad region
8	Valtar	ValtaR Co., Ltd.	2	Korolev, Moscow region
9	SG-Magnet	Skygrad-Magnet Co., Ltd.	2	Korolev, Moscow region
10	ERGA	R & P Group Co. ERGA	2	Kaluga
11	ELIS	ELIS-firm, Ltd.	2	Ozersk, Chelyabinsk region
12	ELMA-T	R & P Co. ELMA-T	2	Saratov
13	MMS	R & P Co. Magnets and magnetic systems., Ltd.	2	Moscow
14	MAGNIT	JSC MAGNIT	3	Novocherkassk, Rostov region
15	MPPm	Moscow Plant of Polymetals	3	Moscow
16	Sib ChIW	JSC Sibir Chemical Integrated Works	3	Seversk, Tomsk region
17	KF ETS	Kusinsky Factory of Exact Technological Stones	3	Kusa, Chelyabinsk region
18	Pl Magneton	JSC Plant Magneton	3	St. Peterburg
19	Pod ChMW	JSC Podolsk Chemical Metal Works	3	Podolsk, Moscow region
20	PChP	Pridneprovsky Chemicals Plant	3	Dneprodzerzhinsk, Ukraina
21	NFRM	Novosibirsk Factore of Rare Metals	3	Novosibirsk
22	Silmet	Molycorp Silmet AS	3	Sillamae, Estonia
23	1MIMF	1st Moscow Instrument-making Factory	4	Moscow
24	PPP VNIIMET	Pilot-production plant VNIIMET	4	Kaluga
		1 - traditionally work on RE-magnets; 2 - new private companies; 3 - liquidated divisions RE-magnets; 4 - liquidated units		

Table 4. Grades of RE permanent magnets manufactured by Russian companies.

Russian name	Class	B_r (kGs)	$_jH_c$ (kOe)	$(BH)_{max}$ (MGOe)	α_b @ -60 – 100 °C (%/°C)	Max. T_{op}, (°C)
KS37 (1:5 Sm-Co)	A_{1-5}	8.8 – 10.0	14 - 30	18 - 24	< - 0.040	200
	B_{1-5}	8.0 – 9.0	25 - 30	16 - 20	< - 0.040	250
	C_{1-5}	7.2 – 8.0	16 - 20	12 - 16	< - 0.010	150
KS25DC (2:17 Sm-Co)	A_{2-17}	10.8 – 11.4	14 - 20	26 - 30	< - 0.035	250
	B_{2-17}	10.0 – 10.6	22 - ≥30	22 - 26	< - 0.030	350
	B^*_{2-17}	8.8 – 9.4	≥30	18 - 21	< - 0.035	580
	C_{2-17}	8.0 – 9.6	10 - 16	16 - 22	< - 0.010	150
Nd-Fe-B	A_{2-14-1}	13.0 – 14.4	12 - 15	40 - 52	< - 0.120	120
	B_{2-14-1}	10.0 – 12.0	30 - 40	25 - 35	< - 0.120	200
	C_{2-14-1}	11.0 – 11.2	30 - 40	30 - 32	< - 0.055	120
	C^*_{2-14-1}	0.85 – 0.95	20 - 23	16 - 20	< - 0.010	120

A – general industrial applications with limited operating temperature,
B – generalindustrial applications with increased operating temperature (heat-resistant),
C – specialized applications with the lowered value of reversible remanent induction temperature coefficient (thermostable).

The B class magnets find their applications in a wide range of electric motors, from DC microrotors for aviation equipment to multipolar rotors of powerful valve engines and generators. They are also used in chemical, oil and gas machinery engineering, in particular, for production of high-moment magnetic couplings for the toque transfer through isolating wall of various devices, and in production the down-loaded electric centrifugal and screw oil pumps working in oil wells 600 - 4000 m deep (Fig. 6 [9]).

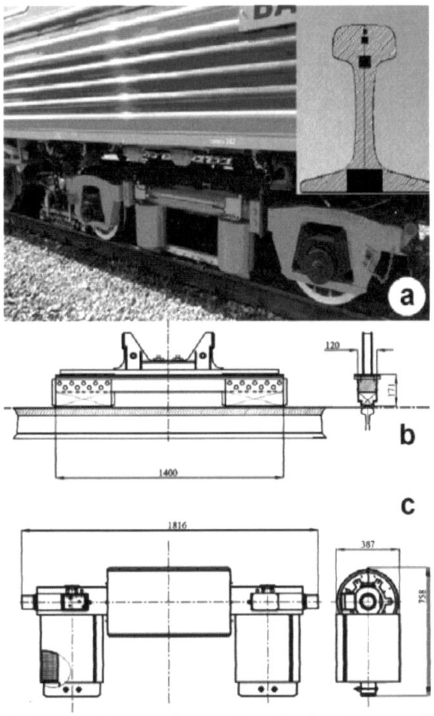

Fig. 4. Cart of the Railway Line Defect Scoper for detection of size and in-depth defects: (a) place of installation; (b) MS on RE-type PM base (size 1400 x 171 x 120; does not require power supply); (c) MS on an electromagnet (size 1816 x 758 x 387, input power 5 kW).

Another example of the A class magnets applications is their use as magnetic suspension for the bearings in energy storage machines. Magnetic suspension with a loading capacity of 1.55 x 10^4 N is intended for the maximum reduction of flywheel kinetic energy losses due to friction decrease in supporting bearings. The suspension is executed in the form of a vertical support with two built-in magnetic systems blocks with axial force of 0.775 x 10^4 N each. The magnetic block is an independent system which can be used in other similar devices as a unified element [10]. The design of the block provides the independence of carrying load on axial positioning (within possible movement) of rotating and motionless parts of magnetic system (see Table 5). The suspension load is 45 kg. The ratio of loading capacity to the mass of PMs is greater than 400. The tested frequency of rotation is up to 4500 rpm. The size of the unified PM element is Ø108 mm x 144 mm.

Analytical simulation of electric machines determining the eddy currents in continuous conductive medium for the specific shape and physical characteristics of the medium is rather complicated task; simplified models are have to be used in the engineering practice. A software package incorporating the results of multiple studies has been developed in Russia; it allows for precise calculation of electrodynamics system with PM-based *eddy-current brakes*. Using this software, both design of the system creating DC magnetic fields and configuration of the braking tire are optimized and dynamic characteristics of the braking process – the braking force $F(t)$, speed $V(t)$, braking distance $X(t)$ and arising overloads $P(t)$ - are calculated. Fig. 7 presents the parameters calculated for braking of a lifting machine weighing 4500 kg and equipped with Nd-Fe-B PMs which is in a free fall from the 40

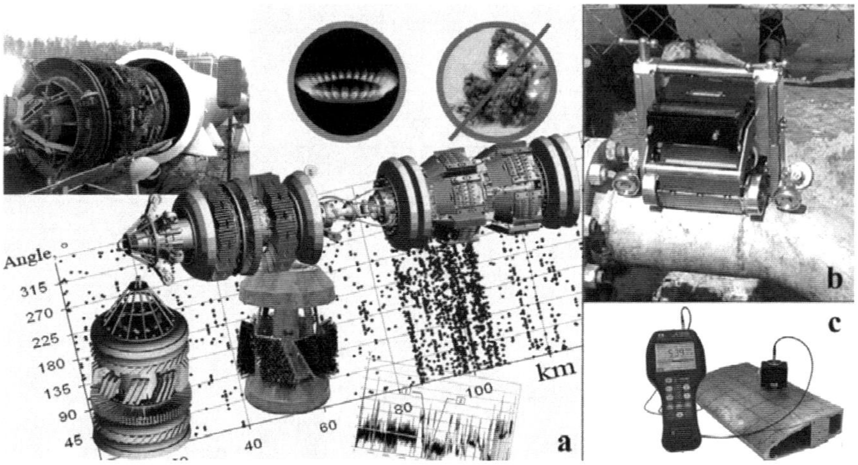

Fig. 5. Devices for cleaning and nondestructive testing of oil and gas pipelines with MS based on Nd-Fe-B magnets: (a) the scanner of a welded seam; (b,c) thickness detectors with EMA on PMs.

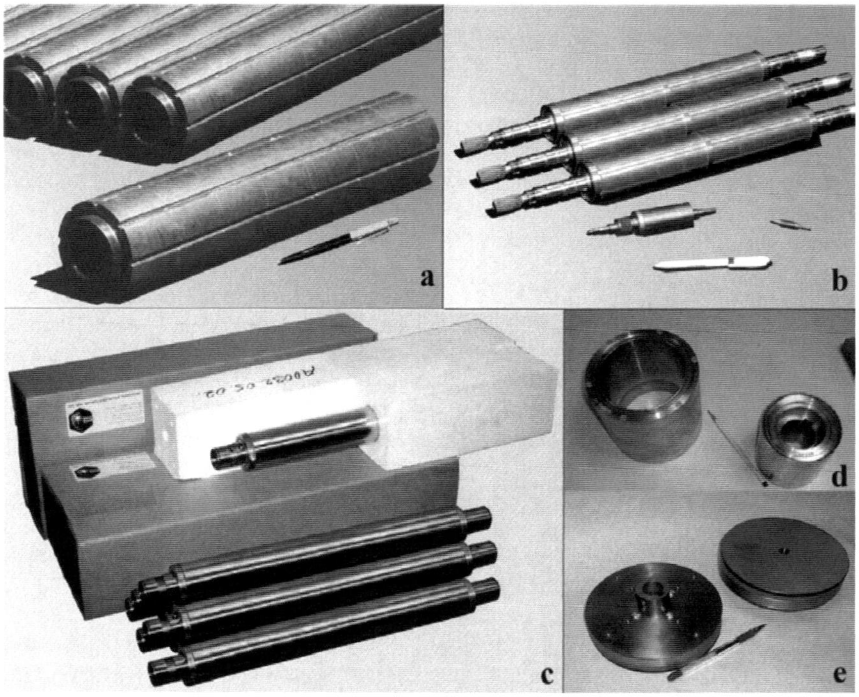

Fig. 6. Two- and multipolar rotors of electric motors:(a - c) synchronous coupling of the chemical reactor; (d) asynchronous coupling of the coil-winding machine with Nd-Fe-B PMs.

meters height by the beginning of the braking [11]. Results of the calculations have been confirmed by numerous practical tests. More than 60 electrodynamics systems with the eddy-currents brakes are now being used in various applications.

The other examples of the A class magnets use are magnetic systems for monochromatic microwave generators of millimeter and submillimeter electromagnetic waves developed in Russia on the base of the backward-wave tubes (BWT) [12] (Fig. 8) and dispersing magnetic system (DMS) for mass-spectrometer MTI-350G [13] (Fig. 9). The first device has no foreign analogs and it is unique in its ability for a ±30% change of the working frequency. Its BWT generation is reproducible up to 1500 GHz. A 20 kg MS for BWT produces a 1.4 T magnetic field in cylindrical working space 45 mm in diameter and 33.5 mm long. The maximum field inhomogeneity in a Ø12 mm x 26 mm zone for arrangement of the slowing-down BWT system is 1.5%.

DMS for arrangement of an ions passing tube is based on the high-energy-product Nd-Fe-B PMs; it produces the magnetic field of 0.72 T in the arc shaped working space with the length of 600 mm and gap of 17 mm

Table 5. Technical parameters of magnetic suspension (δ is the gap between the horizontal mobile and motionless planes of magnetic system, σ is the interval of working gaps, φ is the interval with guaranteed constant lifting force).

δ (mm)	0.05	0.10	0.20	0.30	0.40	0.50	0.60	0.70	0.80
$F\times10^{-4}$ (N)	1.52	1.55	1.55	1.55	1.55	1.55	1.55	1.55	1.55
σ (mm)									
φ (mm)									

with the maximum inhomogeneity not exceeding 1.0%. It is three times lighter than electromagnet (170 kg vs. 550 kg) and does not require a power supply, thus allowing for reduction of the both spectrometer price and maintenance cost (electricity, stabilization power supply, cooling of the coils, etc.).

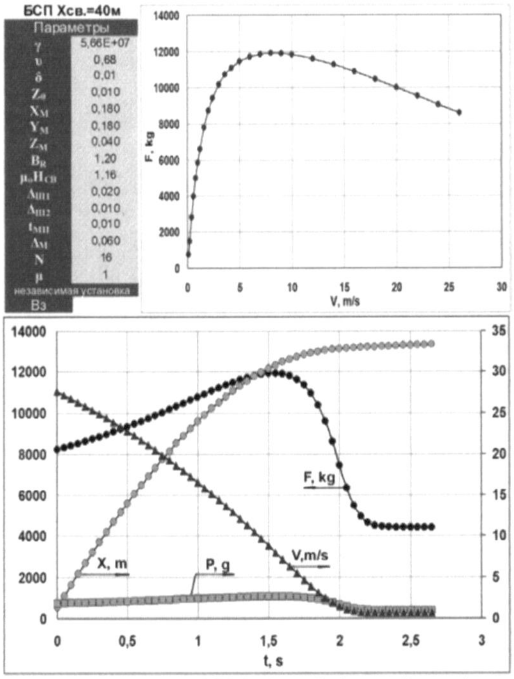

Fig. 7. Parameters of PMs-based electrodynamic eddy-currents braking system: F(t) is braking force, V(t) is speed, X(t) is braking distance and P(t) is arising overload.

Let's now consider an example of a C class magnet application in a serial MS. The system with a longitudinal magnetic induction component of 165 – 230 mT (depending on adjustment) ensures many years of operation of the pulse magnetrons with output power P = 2.5 MW, P_{av} = 5 kW, with a frequency of 2800 ±10 MHz and τ = 6 μsec as a part of medical accelerators [9]. RE PMs found the broadest application in the production of magnetic focusing systems (MFS) with regular and reversed magnetic fields (MRFS) for powerful broadband single-beam and multibeam (up to 49 beams) klystrons. Tens of MFS and MRFS are presently in a mass production.

Narrowing the reverse field domains and adjusting the homogeneity of longitudinal magnetic field component to 4% or better and transverse field component to 3 mT or lower (Fig. 10) makes it possible to realize the current conductivity at the level of 99 - 100%.

The C class Nd-Fe-B magnets with the reversible temperature coefficient of remanent induction α_b = -0.055 %/°C in the -60 °C to 100 °C range have been developed in Russia at the early 1990s specifically for electro-vacuum electric and electronic devices [14,15] For many microwave applications, the $|\alpha_b|$ value of 0.055%/°C is too high. In such cases, the Alnico magnets (known in Russia as YuNDK), or Sm-Co

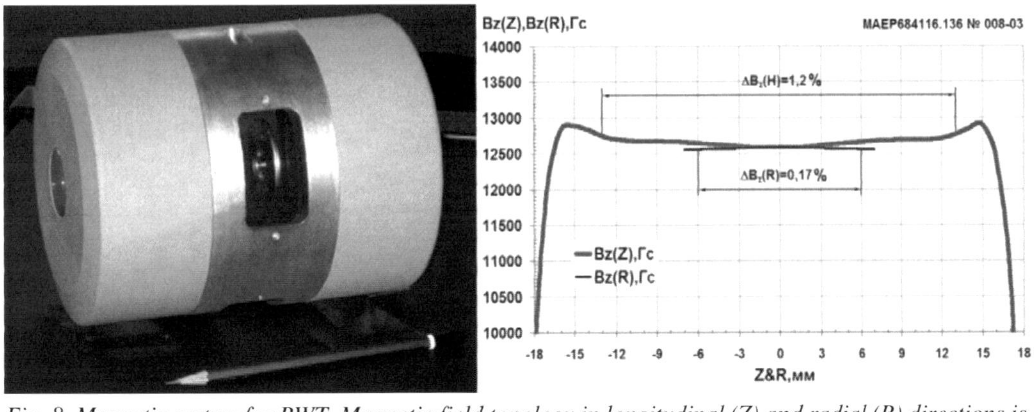

Fig. 8. Magnetic system for BWT. Magnetic field topology in longitudinal (Z) and radial (R) directions is plotted.

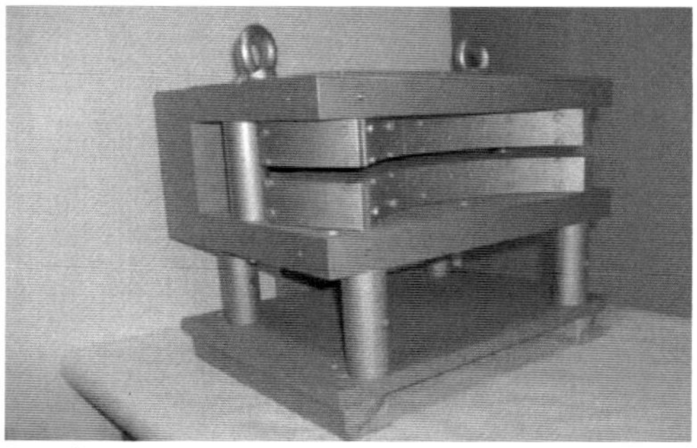

Fig. 9. Dispersing Magnetic Systems for MTI-350G Mass-Spectrometer for uranium products control.

magnets with a flux thermo compensation circuit [15] were used. Recently, several research groups developed for these or similar applications requiring a stable magnetic field in a wide temperature range new Nd-Fe-B-based PMs with the α_b close to zero (the $C^*_{2\text{-}14\text{-}1}$ class) [15-17]. The new magnets are being used in specialized microwave applications (Table 5).

Magnets of the B* class are usually used in the equipment of specific applications [18,19].

Thus, the work carried out in recent years shows the evident success of development of the REMs and their use in the traditional or new Russia industry sectors. This increases confidence in the eventual success of the government program on development of rare and rare-earth metals Industry.

References

[1] E. Kozlowski, *Metals of Eurasia* **3**, 2011, 56 (in Russian).

[2] A.E. Samonov, in: *Proc. 1st All-Russia Conf. on Prospects of Ore Mining, Production and REM Application in Russia*, 2011, pp. 114-117 (in Russian).

[3] A.E. Samonov, in: *Proc. 1st All-Russia Conf. on Prospects of Ore Mining, Production and REM Application in Russia*, 2011, pp. 122-123 (in Russian).

[4] V.D. Kosynkin, V.A. Glebov, in: *Proc. III Int. Conf. on Functional Nanomaterials and High-Purity Substances*, Suzdal, 2010 (in Russian).

[5] Yu.A. Vereschagin, N.V. Kudrevatykh, M.A. Malygin, T.N. Emelina, in: *Proc. 19th Workshop on REPM and Their Applications*, Beijing, China, 2006, pp. 23-32.

[6] A. Dzhumaylo, A. Balashova, *The Businessman*, Nov. 2013 (in Russian).

[7] D.S. Klyucharev, G.N. Trach, in: *Proc. 1st All-Russia Conf. Prospects of Ore Mining, Production and REM Applications in Russia*, 2011, pp. 71–75 (in Russian).

[8] A.G. Dormidontov, V.A. Sein, in: *Proc. XVIII Int. Conf. on Permanent Magnets*, Suzdal, Russia, 2011, pp. 188 – 189.

[9] A.G. Dormidontov, E.I. Kanevsky, A.A. Lukin, P. S. Perevoshchikov, S.V. Sergeyev, K.L. Sergeyev, in: *Proc. XVIII Int. Conf. on Permanent Magnets*, Suzdal, Russia, 2011, pp. 194 – 195.

[10] Ya.D. Rabinovich, A.G. Dormidontov, S.B. Mukho, N.N. Khludov, in: *Proc. XIV Int. Conf. on Permanent Magnets*, Suzdal, Russia, 2003, pp. 226–227.

[11] I.F. Tulupov, S.V. Sergeyev, A.G. Dormidontov, P.S. Perevoshchikov, in: *Proc. XIV Int. Conf. on Permanent Magnets*, Suzdal, Russia, 2003, pp. 154 –155.

[12] A.G. Dormidontov, S.V. Sergeyev, P.S. Perevoshchikov, K.L. Sergeyev, in: *Proc. XIV Int. Conf. on Permanent Magnets*, Suzdal, Russia, 2003, pp. 152–153.

[13] N.V. Kudrevatykh, B.G. Djavaev, A.N. Maslov, D.S. Neznakhin, A.S. Volegov, S.V. Andreev, A.I. Kozlov, in: *Proc. XIX Int. Conf. on Permanent Magnets*, Suzdal, Russia, 2013, pp. 88–89.

[14] A.G. Dormidontov, A.A. Lukin, K.L. Sergeyev, in: *Proc. XIX Int. Conf. on permanent magnets*, Suzdal, Russia, 2013, pp. 54–55.

[15] A.A. Lukin, A.G. Dormidontov, N.B. Kolchugina, E.S. Semenova, E.I. Kanevsky, A.L. Dyomin, P.S. Perevoshchikov, S.V. Sergeyev, K.L. Sergeyev, in: *Proc. XIX Int. Conf. on permanent magnets*, Suzdal, Russia, 2013, pp. 120–121.

[16] G.S. Burkhanov, A.A. Lukin, P.S. Perevoshchikov, S.V. Sergeyev, N.B. Kolchugina, A.G. Dormidontov, *Russian Federation Patent 2493628*, 2013.

[17] G.S. Burkhanov, A.A. Lukin, P.S. Perevoshchikov, S.V. Sergeyev, N.B. Kolchugina, N.E. Klyuev, A.G. Dormidontov, *Russian Federation Patent 2500049*, 2013.

[18] A.G. Popov, A.V. Queens, N.N. Shchegoleva, *Phys. Met. Metallogr.* **3**, 1990, 100 (in Russian).

[19] V.N. Beketov, V.N. Moskalev, A.V. Ogurtsov, D.V. Taranov, M.K. Shadrin, E.I. Kanevsky, in: *Proc. XIX Int. Conf. on Permanent Magnets*, Suzdal, Russia, 2013, pp. 132–133

Rare Earth Based Permanent Magnets Processed by Friction Consolidation and Extrusion

M. MARINESCU[1], J. CUI[2], G. GRANT[2], S. JANA[2], J. DARSELL[2], M. J. KRAMER[3], S. KODAT[1], J. LIU[1]
[1]Electron Energy Corporation (EEC), Landisville PA, USA
[2]Pacific Northwest National Laboratory (PNNL), Richland WA, USA
[3]Ames Laboratory, Ames IA, USA

Abstract. *Friction consolidation and extrusion (FC&E) technology has been used to fabricate bulk, close to full density, nanocrystalline rare earth based permanent magnets. The technology has been applied on both Nd-Fe-B based powder and composite Nd-Fe-B / Fe blended powders. The friction consolidation segment of the process generates a nanostructure with an out of plane texture, controllable to some degree. The extrusion segment of the process generates a texture depending on the material composition and it can be radial or axial. The best magnetic performance obtained so far for Nd-Fe-B nanocrystalline magnets fabricated by FC&E were:* $(BH)_{max}$ *= 23.5 MGOe,* B_r *= 11.2 kG,* H_{ci} *= 6.0 kOe. The nanocomposite Nd-Fe-B / Fe magnets fabricated by friction consolidation show a uniform distribution of the phases, but further process optimization is needed to reach the expected magnetic performance.*

Keywords: friction consolidation and extrusion, solid state processing, nanocrystalline magnets, nanocomposite magnets.

Address: M. Marinescu, Electron Energy Corporation, 924 Links Ave, Landisville, PA 17538, USA; tel: 717-898-2294; fax: 717-898-0660; melania@electronenergy.com

1. Introduction

The key to the more efficient use of rare earth (RE) resources while maintaining high performance-to-weight ratios in permanent magnets is to develop grain-aligned exchanged-coupled microstructure. While the architecture of exchange-coupled nanocomposites has been worked out theoretically, and confirmed to some degree in thin films [1, 2], the technical challenge over the last two decades has been to put the concept into practice at the macroscopic, industrial-scale level.

In a radical departure from the techniques that have previously been applied to permanent magnet processing, Friction Consolidation and Extrusion (FC&E) offers unique advantages that can help solve the problems in the fabrication of anisotropic exchange-coupled nanocomposite magnets. FC&E is based on the principles of friction stir processing (FSP). FC&E uses a non-consumable rotating tool to generate frictional heat and large plastic deformation resulting in a solid-state processing of materials. Continuous dynamic recrystallization occurs in the shearing solid, and if the load and temperature are suddenly reduced, a microstructure with the desired texture and nanoscale features could be attained. Microstructural refinement, densification, and homogeneity of the processed zone are the result of intense plastic deformation that are controllable by adjusting parameters such as tool rotation speed, load, feed rate, and chamber boundary conditions, such as temperature, cooling rate and, possibly, external magnetic fields.

FC&E process is a solid state method to densify powders and to produce compacts with customized microstructure induced by severe plastic deformation. The texture development from the friction consolidation step may be difficult to control within an extended depth of processed material. Therefore, the extrusion step of the process is aimed at a more precise control of the crystallographic texture in the final product.

2. Experimental Details

Although the FC&E can be a continuous process, in our experiments we have employed a non-continuous setting, where first, the powder was densified by friction consolidation, and then the formed disk was subjected to the extrusion process. The FC&E system at PNNL is a customized MTI friction machine. The unconsolidated powders are loaded in a can. A rotating tool is plunged into the can and a force is applied to the powder charge. As heat and pressure build below the tool face, the powder is consolidated by the effect of shear stress combined with a hydrostatic state of stress.

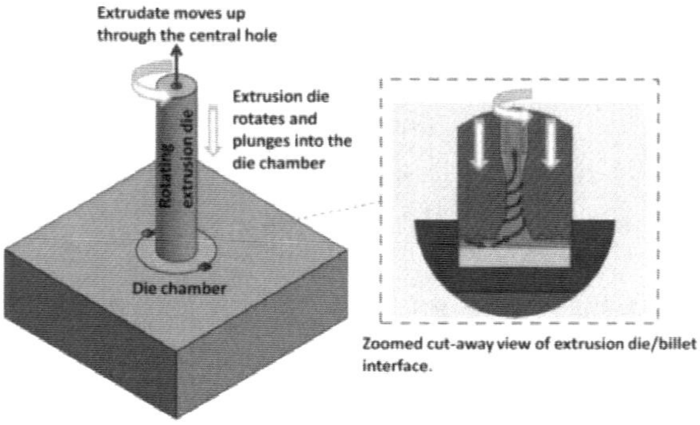

Fig. 1. Schematic showing the extrusion segment of FC&E process with rotational movement of the die.

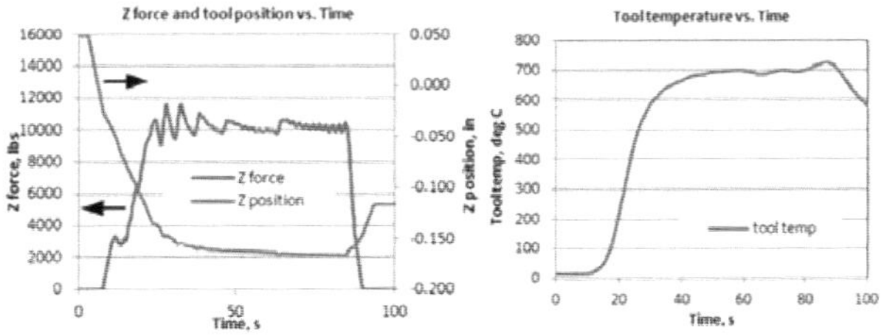

Fig. 2. Time dependent profile of (a) load and tool position and (b) tool temperature, during the friction consolidation of M1 powder.

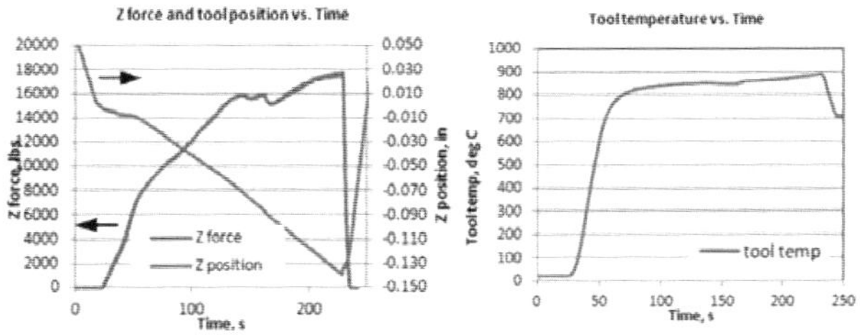

Fig. 3. Time dependent profile of (a) load and tool position and (b) tool temperature, during the extrusion segment of FC&E of M1 powder.

Figure 1 depicts the extrusion segment of the FC&E process with rotational movement of the die. A layer from the top of the puck shears and flows into the die cavity with both extrusion and rotational motion. A dynamic cooling system was built to control the temperature of the can as well as of the extrusion die.

Two types of feedstock material have been used, Nd-Fe-B powder and a mixture of Nd-Fe-B and Fe powders. The experiments have been done using two Nd-Fe-B based precursors in form of ground melt spun ribbons with the following stoichiometries in at%: $(Nd,Y,Dy)_{12.39}Fe_{bal}Co_{8.74}B_{5.83}$ (noted as M1) and $(Nd,Pr)_{13.90}Fe_{bal}Co_{4.46}Ga_{0.47}B_{5.47}$ (noted as M2). The crystallite size of the Nd-Fe-B precursor flake powder was less than 100 nm, and the powder particle dimensions along directions other than flake thickness were less than 250 μm. The experiments on mixed two phase powders used Fe powder produced by atomization with a particle size less than 10 μm. The powder was severely plastically deformed, while in the solid state, by friction consolidation using a hardened tool at very high speeds between 125 to 500 rpm and under forge loads of 10,000 to 25,000 lb. The extrusion ratio was 26:1, the typical die feed rate during extrusion was 0.05"/min. and the diameter of the extrusion tool was 0.2".

2. Results and Discussions

In order to establish an understanding of the behavior of Nd-Fe-B material subjected to FC&E, initial experiments were carried out without the addition of Fe powder. Both M1 and M2 compositions were overstoichiometric and M2 had a larger amount of the RE-rich phase.

The M1 powder was subjected to the friction consolidation process under a tool rotational speed of 125 rpm and a forge load of 10,000. Figure 2 shows the load and temperature profile of the friction consolidation event. In about 30 s, the powder was compacted close to the final density, while the tool temperature increased to about 600 °C. The dwell time under maximum load was 60 s.

The shearing action during the friction consolidation process resulted in a high density of defects leading ultimately to grain size reduction and possibly a quasi-amorphous state followed by a recrystalization process. The friction consolidated sample in form of a disk had a diameter of 1" and a thickness of ¼". The density achieved within the targeted thickness was 7.2 g/cm^3, which is about 95% of the bulk value.

Figure 3 shows the load and temperature profile of the extrusion segment of FC&E process applied to the M1 powder. The rotational speed of the tool reached 500 rpm, the forge load had a z-position control and it reached almost 18,000 lb while the tool temperature increased to 850 °C at the end of the 200 s process. The extruded sample was a rod with a length of 2.2" and diameter of 0.2".

Figure 4 shows the demagnetization curves of two samples machined from the unextruded friction consolidated disk and extruded rod fabricated by using M1 powder precursor. It can be noted that the test sample from the disk has a strong magnetic texture with the easy magnetization direction along the thickness of the disk (out of plane), while the test sample from the

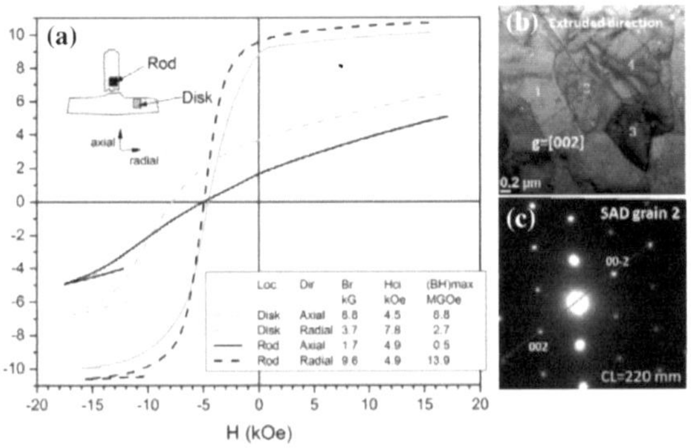

Fig. 4. (a) Demagnetization curves for the unextruded disk and extruded rod fabricated by FC&E using M1 powder; (b) TEM micrographs and (c) electron diffraction patterns of M1 extruded sample.

extruded rod shows a strong radial texture (perpendicular to the long axis of the rod). The sample from the disk has the following parameters of the magnetic hysteresis along the disk axis: $(BH)_{max}$ = 8.8 MGOe, B_r = 8.8 kG, H_{ci} = 4.5 kOe. The sample from the extruded rod has the following parameters of the magnetic hysteresis perpendicular to the rod axis: $(BH)_{max}$ = 13.9 MGOe, B_r = 9.6 kG, H_{ci} = 4.9 kOe.

TEM analysis performed on the M1 extrudate revealed a nanocrystalline structure with the grains elongated in the extrusion direction (Fig. 4 b-c). It was confirmed that the [001] direction was orthogonal to the extrusion direction, i.e., basal plane flow.

Compared with the M1 material, the M2 powders with higher RE content behaved differently during the FC&E process. The rotational speed of the tool during the extrusion segment of the FC&E process reached about 800 rpm, although the tool temperature increased to only 825 °C. The extruded sample was a rod with a length of 1" and diameter of 0.2".

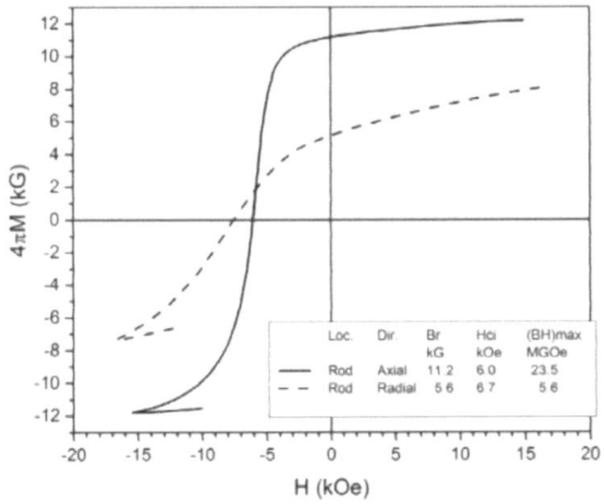

Fig. 5. Demagnetization curves and hysteresis parameters for the unextruded disk and extruded rod fabricated by FC&E using M2 powder.

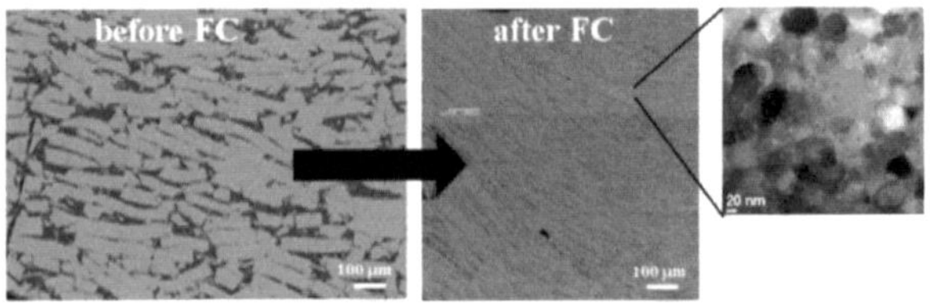

Fig. 6. SEM and TEM micrographs of nanocomposite M1 / 20 wt% Fe sample produced by friction consolidation.

Figure 5 shows the demagnetization curve of a sample machined from the extruded rod fabricated by using the M2 powder precursor. The sample has an axial texture, with the following parameters of the magnetic hysteresis along the rod axis: $(BH)_{max}$ = 23.5 MGOe, B_r = 11.2 kG, H_{ci} = 6.0 kOe.

The experiments on the FC&E of blends of Nd-Fe-B nanocrystaline powder (M1) and microcrystalline Fe powder are promising. The friction consolidation segment of the process is efficient in generating a uniform distribution of the two phases, decreasing the size of the Fe phase to submicron and nanoscale while the 2:14:1 phase is maintained (or rather recrystallized) at the nanoscale (Fig. 6). The excellent mixing effect is a consequence of the high shear strain at a limited temperature developed during the FC process. The FC processed nanocomposite samples have a density of 95-98% of bulk value. The best magnetic properties obtained so far in the nanocomposite M1 / 20 wt% Fe sample produced by friction consolidation are: $(BH)_{max}$ = 4.2 MGOe, B_r = 7.3 kG, H_{ci} = 4.7 kOe. Further optimization of the process condition, as well as the feedstock powder chemistry, shape and size, is needed to reach a good magnetic performance.

Acknowledgements
This work was supported by the U.S. Department of Energy, Advanced Research Projects Agency – Energy (ARPA-E), award DE-AR0000325.

References

[1] V. Neu, S. Sawatzki, M. Kopte, C. Mickel, L. Schultz, *IEEE Trans. Magn.*, 48, 11, 2012, 3599.
[2] W.B. Cui, Y. K. Takahashi, K. Hono, *Adv. Mater.*, 2012, DOI: 10.1002/adma.201202328.

MnBi Single Domain Particles Produced by Spark Erosion

AMI BERKOWITZ[1], PHI-KHANH NGUYEN[1], DAVID J. SMITH[2]
[1]University of California, San Diego, La Jolla, California
[2]Arizona State University, Tempe, Arizona

Abstract: *MnBi is a very promising rare-earth-free permanent magnet material with the unique property that its high magnetocrystalline anisotropy at room temperature increases with increasing temperature until ~275°C. It has been a problem to produce the desired low-temperature phase (LTP) of MnBi due to the complex nature of the Mn-Bi phase diagram with its peritectic regions. As a result, most of the MnBi powder samples that show interesting permanent magnet properties are produced by time-consuming grinding/annealing procedures. Alternatively, we have produced single domain MnBi particles more directly from bulk material with high yields by spark erosion. The best properties are obtained from bulk material with highest fraction of LTP MnBi. Accordingly, we have developed processing methods that yield superior bulk properties.*

Keywords: *permanent magnets; MnBi; spark errosion*

Address: Ami Berkowitz, University of California, San Diego, CMRR, M.S. 0401, 9500 Gilman Drive, La Jolla, CA 92093-0401, E-mail: aberk@ucsd.edu

1. Background

The low-temperature phase of MnBi (LTP) has an anisotropy, K, at room temperature of 1.6 x 10^6 ergs/cm^3, T_C = 360 °C, and M_s (R.T.) ≈ 79 emu/g. The LTP also has the unique property that *K increases with temperature* to 2.2 x 10^7 ergs/cm^3 at 277 °C [1]. Notwithstanding the rather low magnetization, these properties make MnBi LTP an attractive candidate for a rare-earth-free permanent magnet. However, several obstacles to achieving large-scale production of the LTP are present. The Mn-Bi phase diagram is rather complex, with peritectic regions that prevent simple cooling from the liquidus to the LTP; conversely, annealing within the LTP region, < T_C, is very slow due to the low diffusion rates. As a consequence, a variety of melt-spinning [2], chemical [3], mechanical [3], cryo-milling [4], and other methods have been used to prepare suitable powders of LTP MnBi. However, these methods often do not produce satisfactory MnBi properties, and they are generally not appropriate for economical, large-scale processing. We describe an alternative, high-rate, scalable processing method, spark erosion [5], in which single domain particles are produced more directly from suitable bulk material. The best spark-eroded powders are produced from bulk alloys having the highest fraction of LTP. Therefore, we have also developed a processing protocol for producing bulk alloys with high LTP MnBi fractions. We discuss the bulk alloy processing and the spark-eroded powders after a description of the spark erosion process.

2. Spark Erosion Apparatus

As sketched in Fig. 1, a 10 cm diameter spark erosion cell is mounted in a double-walled, vacuum-jacketed glass container that holds the dielectric liquid. Two electrodes of the alloy of interest are mounted in the cell. 'Charge' pieces of the same alloy, ~2 cm in diameter, fill the perforated Delrin support, making contact with the electrodes. The glass container is vibrated so that contacts among the electrodes and charge pieces are made and broken frequently. Thus, electrical contact between the electrodes is made randomly, as are the gaps among the charge pieces across which the sparks are generated. A charged capacitor is attached to the electrodes. When the electric field across the electrodes, due to a sufficiently small gap in the charge pieces, is larger than the dielectric breakdown field, the capacitor

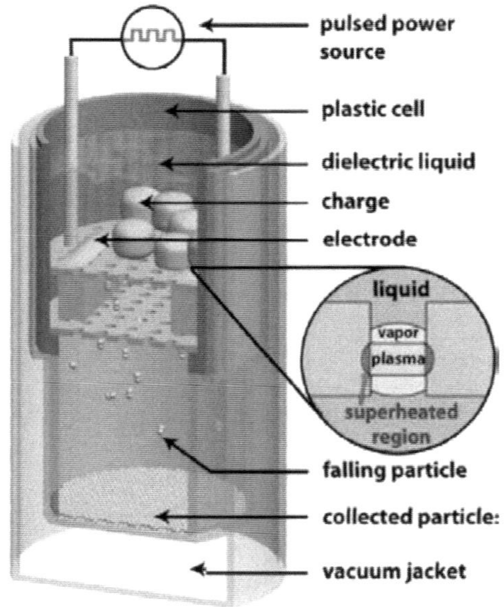

Fig. 1. Sketch of spark erosion apparatus. Operation described in text.

discharges producing a spark (micro-plasma) between the pieces involved. This micro-plasma, consisting of electrons and positive ions, is very hot, of order 10 000 K. The kinetic energies of the faster electrons and slower ions are deposited on localized regions on the charge pieces or the electrodes, where the spark was initiated, superheating them to boiling. When the spark collapses, vaporized alloy and molten droplets are violently ejected from the boiling regions and propelled through the plasma region into the dielectric liquid where they are very rapidly quenched and drift to the bottom of the glass container.

3. Spark-Eroded Particles

The first MnBi alloys for the electrodes and charge were made by chill casting [6]. We report on particles spark-eroded in liquid nitrogen from the best of these alloys. The use of liquid nitrogen as the dielectric, with subsequent processing of the particles in a glove box with < 5 ppm oxygen insures that oxidation is not an issue. The as-sparked powders were sieved <53 μm to remove any chips from the electrodes and charge. The as-sparked powder included 20 – 50 nm particles, as well as much larger spherical and irregular particles with diameters up to 25 μm. Closer inspection showed that these larger particles were, primarily, aggregates of 20 – 50 nm particles [6].

The magnetization of the as-sparked powder in 7 T was 17 emu/g with H_c = 0.7 T, as seen in Fig. 2. After a short anneal in the glove box (temperature ramped to 300 °C in ~ 15 minutes, then power turned off), the magnetization increased to 69 emu/g and H_c dropped to 0.4 T. The 4-fold increase in magnetization after such a short anneal at 300 °C seemed most likely to result from the crystallization of amorphous or poorly crystallized particles, which was also suggested by a

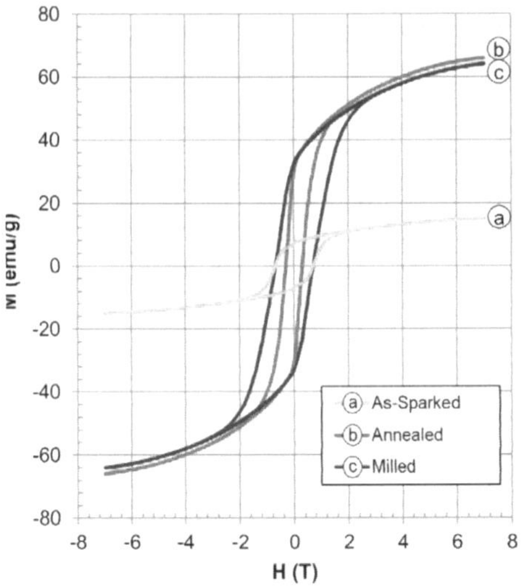

Fig. 2. Magnetization of powders, (a) as-sparked; (b) ramp-annealed to 300 °C; (c) low-energy milled after ramp-anneal.

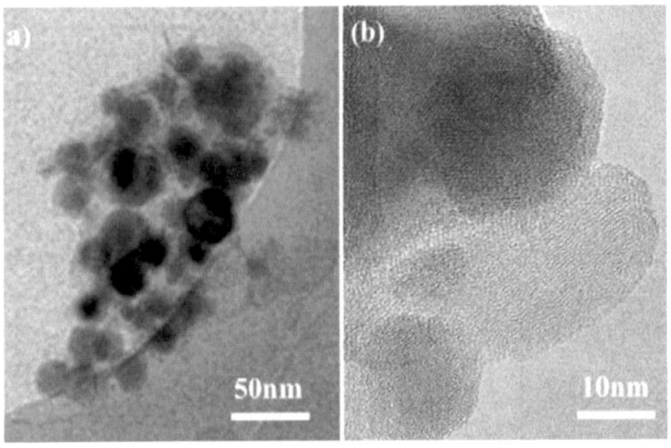

Fig. 3. Transmission electron micrographs of as-sparked particles. (a) Lower magnification. (b) Higher magnification, showing lattice fringes ending abruptly, changing orientation, etc., indicating poor crystallization.

weak background in the x-ray diffraction pattern of the as-sparked particles that was not present in the pattern of the annealed particles [6]. Figure 3 shows transmission electron micrographs of some of the as-sparked particles. Some poorly crystallized particles are shown in Fig. 3(b), in which lattice fringes end abruptly, change orientation, etc. Scherrer analysis of the XRD line widths indicated that the average MnBi crystallite size increased from 42 nm in the as-sparked powders to 62 nm after the anneal. The magnetization increase of 52 emu/g on annealing the as-sparked powders indicates that ~66% of the as-sparked powder is amorphous or poorly crystallized. This is a consequence of the rapid quenching associated with spark erosion. The lowered H_c after annealing seemed to be associated with the generally denser appearance, necking among particles, etc. Therefore, the annealed powders were milled at low energy to break up interparticle bonds and reduce the dipolar interactions arising from the increased density. The results, as seen in Fig. 2, were quite favorable. H_c increased to 1.0 T with very little reduction in magnetization to yield an energy product of 3.0 MGOe.

Another feature of the annealed powders is shown in Fig. 4. H_c rose with temperature until ~550 K for the ramp-annealed powders. After the low-energy milling of the ramp-annealed powders, H_c increased by > 6 kOe and followed the same temperature dependence as the annealed powder. This behavior testifies to the likelihood that the low-energy milling disperses the aggregated grains, thereby reducing the dipolar and exchange interactions, and increasing H_c.

4. Yield

The yield for spark-eroded single domain particles of MnBi offers an outstanding economic advantage over other preparation methods. All of the powders reported here were made in the 10 cm diameter laboratory cell illustrated in Fig.1. The yield for the powders discussed above (Figs. 2, 3, and 4) was > 100

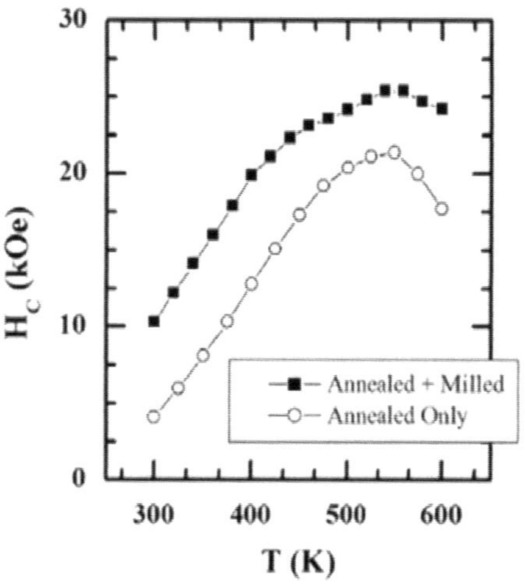

Fig. 4. Temperature dependence of H_c for spark-eroded MnBi powders after -anneal to 300 °C, and after low-energy milling of annealed powders.

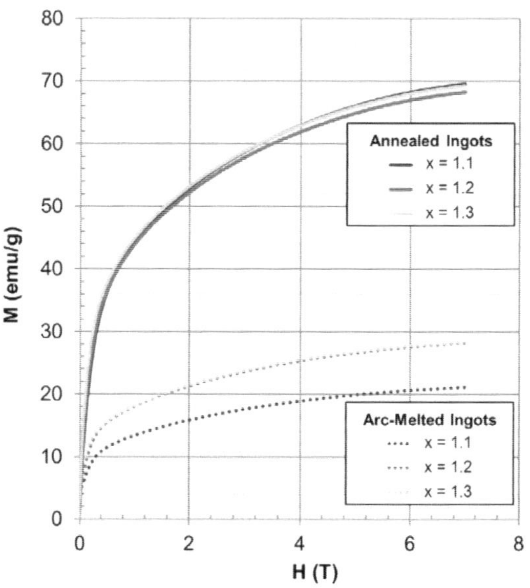

Fig. 5. Magnetization curves for arc-melted ingots with compositions $Mn_xBi_{1.0}$, with x = 1.1, 1.2, 1.3, before and after 64 h anneals at 330 °C in 10^{-6} Torr.

g/h. We have since spark-eroded MnBi powders under optimized conditions with a *yield of ~360 g/h* in the same 10 cm diameter cell. Considering that it has been shown that spark erosion is a readily scalable technique with high energy efficiency [7], with only modest processing required to obtain optimum properties, it seems likely that this production technique should be very competitive in the marketplace.

5. Optimized Starting Alloys

We have recently developed a better method than chill-casting for preparing the bulk material for the MnBi electrodes and charge. The starting ingots are arc-melted under argon. The magnetization of these ingots is reduced by the presence of unreacted Mn and Bi. To promote the reaction of Mn and Bi to form MnBi, and to draw out unreacted Bi (melting point = 271 °C), the arc-melted ingots were annealed at 330°C in a vacuum of 10^{-6} Torr for 64 h. Figure 5 shows the magnetization curves for three compositions of arc-melted ingots, as-prepared and after the vacuum anneal specified above. A dramatic increase in the magnetization after the anneal is noted for all the samples, with little dependence on composition. Spark-eroding these alloys is in process at this writing.

6. Summary

Spark erosion is a very competitive method for making single domain particles of MnBi with high H_c and magnetization ~87% of the theoretical value. The spark-eroded powders require only a short (~ 15 min) ramp-anneal and a nominal low-energy dispersion milling to achieve useful properties. Processing of the powders can be conveniently carried out in a glove box with no oxidation issues. The unique temperature dependence of the MnBi magnetocrystalline anisotropy is observed in the increase of H_c from 1.0 T to ~ 2.7 T as the temperature increased from 300 K to ~550 K. It is of impressive economic significance that yields as high as 360 g/h have been produced in the 10 cm diameter laboratory cell, especially since the process is eminently scalable. Finally, a protocol for producing starting alloys with very attractive properties has been developed.

References

[1] Tu Chen and W. E. Stutius, *IEEE Trans. Magn.* **10**, 1974, 581.
[2] T. Saito, R. Nishimura, and D. Nishio-Hamane, *J. Magn. Magn. Mater.* **349**, 2014, 9.
[3] N. V. Rama Rao, A. M. Gabay, X. Hu, and G. C. Hadjipanayis, *J. Alloys Compd.* **586**, 2014, 349.
[4] N. V. Rama Rao, A. M. Gabay, W. F. Li, and G. C. Hadjipanayis, J. *Phys. D: Appl. Phys.* **46**, 2013, 265001.
[5] A.E. Berkowitz and J.L. Walter. *J. Mater. Res.* **2**, 1987, 277.
[6] Phi-Khanh Nguyen, Sungho Jin, and Ami E. Berkowitz, *J. Appl. Phys.* **115**, 2014, 17A756.
[7] Unpublished experimental demonstration by AEB during development of spark erosion technique, and later work by P-KN at UCSD.

Sintering Analysis of NdFeB Materials

B. HUGONNET[1], G. LARGILLER[1], F. SERVANT[1], C. RADO[1], J. M. MISSIAEN[2,3]
[1]CEA, LITEN, 17 rue des Martyrs, F-38054 Grenoble, France
[2]Univ. Grenoble Alpes, SIMAP, F-38000 Grenoble, France
[3]CNRS, SIMAP, F-38000 Grenoble, France

Abstract: *Nd-Fe-B magnets present high magnetocrystalline anisotropy that leads to outstanding magnetic properties. This anisotropy is also present during the sintering and plays a role into the mechanisms driving the densification. Sintering was studied along and perpendicular to the easy magnetization axis for an optimized thermal cycle leading to high magnetic properties and full densification. The perpendicular strain rate is significantly lower than the parallel strain rate, especially at low temperature. The sintering kinetics at high temperature would be mainly controlled by solid state diffusion with a high apparent activation energy (450-474 kJ/mol).*

Keywords: *Nd-Fe-B; sintered magnets; sintering anisotropy; liquid-phase sintering; activation energy*

Address: Cyril RADO, CEA, LITEN, 17 rue des Martyrs, F-38054 Grenoble, France. Tel: (+33) 438781131, E-mail: cyril.rado@cea.fr

1. Introduction

Nd-Fe-B permanent magnets are known as high energy product $(BH)_{max}$ materials. Coercivity decrease with temperature is the weakness of this material. Indeed, theoretical anisotropy field value of $Nd_2Fe_{14}B$ (73 kOe [1]) is far from coercivity values currently obtained. Moreover studies concerning coercivity improvements by means of heavy rare earth addition usually leads to a drastic remanence loss and price increase. Another way to improve the coercivity without significant remanence decrease is to control the microstructure.

High-coercivity Nd-Fe-B magnets are currently obtained through a powder metallurgy route. Nd-Fe-B magnetic materials have a complex microstructure mainly constituted of two phases: $Nd_2Fe_{14}B$ and a Nd-rich phase which plays a key role on coercivity increase. Liquid phase sintering process allows to optimize the magnetic properties of the material by controlling the phase repartition and microstructure during the thermal cycle.

Previous investigations have been carried out by Popov et al. [2] and Davies et al. [3] on the sintering of Nd-Fe-B material. The first one deals with the optimization of powder manufacturing as well as processing parameters in order to have the best final magnetic properties. The second one gives a complete analysis of the sintering shrinkage along the easy magnetization axis.

In this study, sintering of Nd-Fe-B powder has been evaluated based on dilatometric experiments along the easy magnetization axis as well as along the perpendicular direction (called parallel direction and perpendicular direction, respectively). DSC measurements have been performed to identify phase transformations during sintering. Samples have been quenched to observe the microstructure at different temperatures. This allows us to establish a better understanding of the sintering path.

2. Experimental

Strip-cast ribbons of nominal composition $Dy_{0.2}(Nd,Pr)_{13.6}Fe_{78.6}B_6(Co,Cu,Al)_{1.6}$ were used. Ribbons were hydrogenated and desorbed (HD), then turned into powder with a jet mill under nitrogen gaz. Powder is characterized by D50 = 5.0 μm, D10 = 1.3 μm and D90 = 10.1μm and SBET = 0.6 m²/g. Powder was then filled in a cylindrical mold and oriented parallel to the axial direction of the cylinder using a pulsed magnetic field of 6 T. Finally samples were shaped at a pressure of 150 MPa into a cold isostatic press to obtain a green density close to 4 g/cm^3.

A thermal treatment consisting in a 2 °C/min temperature ramp until a 4 h plateau at 750 °C (to remove hydrogen induced by powder's synthesis) followed by 2 °C/min ramp until 1050 °C for a 4 h plateau was used.

Dilatometric experiments were done in a Setaram vertical differential high temperature dilatometer with a vacuum below $6 \cdot 10^{-5}$ mbar.

To identify phase transformations happening during sintering, DSC measurements were performed on HD ribbons with a Netzsch Pegasus. This material has the same composition as the powder used during dilatometric studies but has a lower specific surface and is less sensitive to oxidation. Samples of 50 mg underwent a thermal cycle similar to dilatometric experiments until 950 °C (maximum temperature of the device) using an alumina crucible with He as heat transfer gaz.

Interrupted heat treatments were performed in a dedicated high vacuum. Thermal ramp up were followed by a quenching at a speed of 60 °C/min at several temperatures. Microstructures were observed in SEM and magnetic properties were determined with a hysteresigraph.

3. Results & Discussion

Densification of 99.5% and high magnetic properties were obtained at 1050 °C for 4 h (B_r = 1.38 T, H_{cj} = 11.3kOe, $(BH)_{max}$ = 46.7 MGOe).

3.1. Sintering anisotropy

Fig. 1 represents the sintering parallel and perpendicular to easy magnetization axis. At the end of the sintering, at room temperature, the ratio between the two strains is about 2. Popov et al. [2] have found the value of 1.5. The difference can be explained by a different powder processing.

On Fig. 2, at low temperature (before dehydration plateau at 750 °C) sintering starts at 570 °C for the parallel direction and 20 °C later for the perpendicular direction. The two strain rate curves have the same shape as they reach a plateau but parallel strain rate increases again at 650 °C whereas perpendicular strain rate remains constant for a temperature increase of almost 100 °C. The large endothermic DSC signal which can be attributed to the dehydration of NdH_2 phase [4,5] occurs in the same temperature range. This temperature range also covers possible liquid formation through NdCu/Nd or $Nd_2Fe_{14}B$/Nd eutectics. Thus the onset of shrinkage can be attributed to liquid formation, to dehydration of NdH_2 or both.

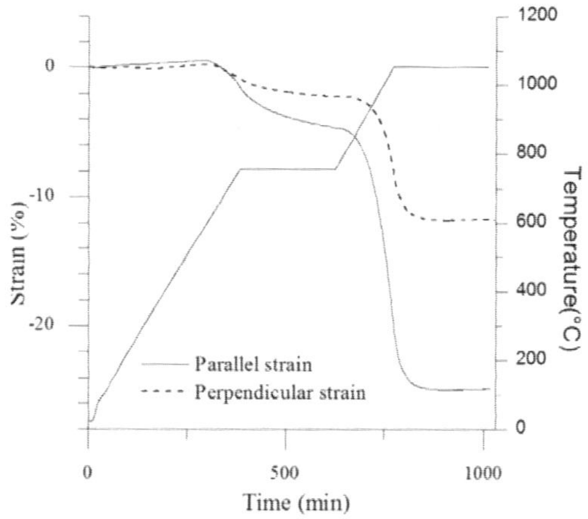

Fig. 1. Parallel versus perpendicular strains.

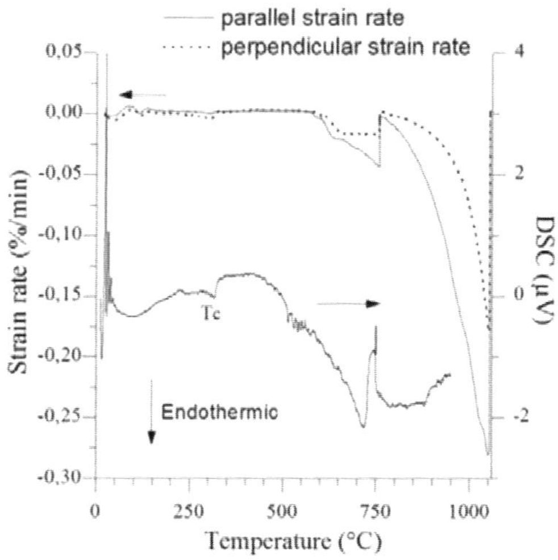

Fig. 2. Perpendicular, parallel strain rates and DSC analysis of the hydrated ribbons versus temperature.

The strain rate curves differences in the two directions reveal two different behaviors that could be attributed to an anisotropy of interface energy or to a heterogeneous distribution of Nd-rich phase in the green compact. Figs. 4(a) and 4(b) compare the powder and the compact quenched at 670 °C during sintering. Before sintering, Nd-rich phase (white on the picture) is spread on grain surfaces. After quenching at 670 °C, Nd-rich phase is drop-shaped on grain surfaces and forms localized necks (black arrows) between grains indicating a fusion before quenching temperature.

After the dehydration plateau, during the temperature increase until the final plateau at 1050 °C, the two strain rate curves have the same kind of shape. The

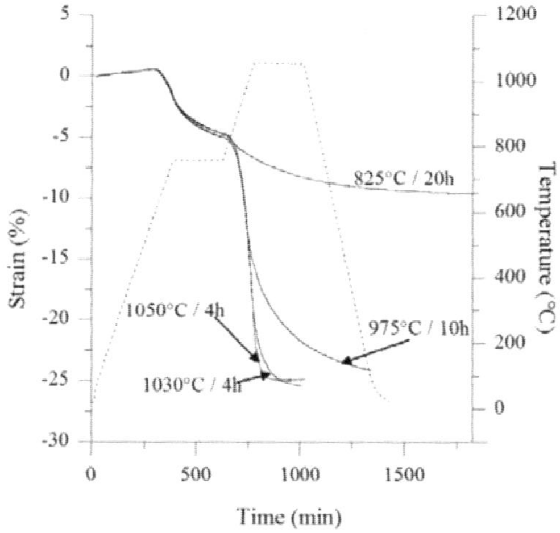

Fig. 3. Isothermal treatments strain parallel to easy magnetization axis (the dotted line represents the thermal cycle at 1050 °C).

Fig. 4. Backscattered SEM image of: (a) the powder, (b) the sample quenched at 670°C, (c) the sample quenched at 1054°C after a 1 h plateau.

strain rate is smaller in the perpendicular direction but it tends to increase relative to the parallel direction as temperature increases. The strain rate curve shapes could not be compared to those obtained by Popov et al. [2] and Davies et al. [3] as a dehydration plateau was used in our study.

3.2. Sintering kinetics at higher temperatures

Isothermal dilatometric experiments have been made in order to find the activation energy of sintering after the dehydration plateau. This study was done in the parallel direction (Fig. 3).

In order to calculate the activation energy, the following equation was used:

$$\dot{\varepsilon} = A(\varepsilon) \times \exp(-\frac{Q}{RT})$$

where $\dot{\varepsilon}$ is the strain rate, ε is the strain, Q is the apparent activation energy, R is the gas constant and T is the temperature. $A(\varepsilon)$ is a strain-dependent constant.

Fig. 5 shows the Arrhenius plots at fixed strains between -20.4% and -23.4%. The activation energy calculated for these strains is comprised between 450 kJ/mol and 474 kJ/mol which would indicate a control either by solid state diffusion or interfacial reaction rather than diffusion through the liquid. In Fig.4(c) the

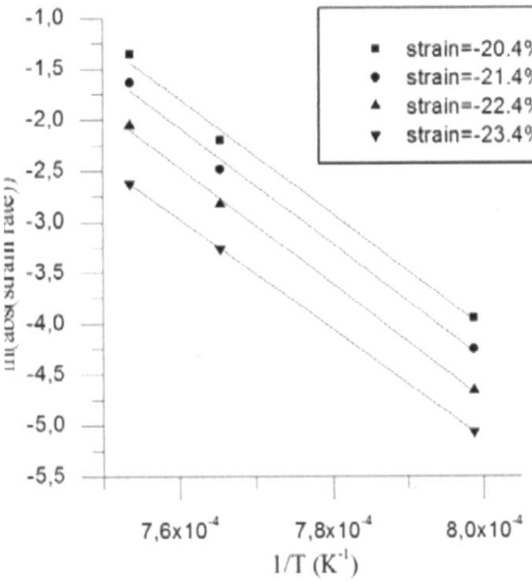

Fig. 5. Arrhenius plot of the strain rate for different fixed strains.

quenched sample exhibits flat contact surfaces between $Nd_2Fe_{14}B$ grains which seem to be free from liquid, whereas former liquid phase is localized at triple grain boundaries and in former pores that have been filled. If quenched microstructures are representative of the microstructure at the sintering temperature, this observation is in agreement with a kinetic control by lattice or grain boundary diffusion in the solid state.

4. Conclusion

High magnetic property dense Nd-Fe-B magnets have been made using liquid phase sintering process. The onset of sintering is related with the dehydration of the powder and probably to the early formation of a eutectic liquid. Anisotropic shrinkage behavior parallel and perpendicular to the easy magnetization axis is observed at the beginning of the sintering and tends to be reduced as sintering proceeds. Sintering kinetics at high temperatures would be controlled by diffusion in the solid state from activation energy measurements and microstructural observations. Still, more work is needed to precise the exact sintering mechanism and to explain the anisotropic shrinkage behavior.

References

[1] J. F. Herbst, *Rev. Mod. Phys.* **63**, 1991, 819.
[2] A. G. Popov, E. G. Gerasimov, D. Y. Vasilenko, V. A. Bykov, and K. Y. Shunyaev, in: *Proc. 22nd Int. Workshop on Rare-Earth Permanent Magnets and Their Applications*, 2012, 225-228.
[3] B. E. Davies, R. S. Mottram, and I. R. Harris, *Mater. Chem. Phys.* **67**, 2001, 272.
[4] J. M. Cadogan and J. M. D. Coey, *Appl. Phys. Lett.* **48**, 1986, 442.
[5] D. Book and I. R. Harris, *J. Alloys Compd.* **221**, 1995, 187.

Effect of Internal Lubricants on Microstructure and Magnetic Properties of Sintered Nd-Fe-B Magnets Produced by PLP

A.G. POPOV[1], V.S. GAVIKO[1], P.B. TERENTEV[1], T.I. GORBUNOVA[2], N.V. PECHISCHEVA[3], G.C. HADJIPANAYIS[4]
[1] Institute of Metal Physics, UB of the RAS, Ekaterinburg, 620990, Russia
[2] Institute of Organic Synthesis, UB of the RAS, Ekaterinburg, 620137, Russia
[3] Institute of Metallurgy, UB of the RAS, Ekaterinburg, 620016, Russia
[4] University of Delaware, Newark, DE 19716, USA

Abstract: *Magnetic properties and microstructure of sintered Nd-Fe-B magnets prepared by pressless process have been investigated. It is shown that an addition of the internal lubricants in toluene upon milling of the Nd-Fe-B alloy increases remanence of the sintered magnets by 5 - 7%.*

Key words: *Nd-Fe-B, sintered magnets, pressless process, internal lubricants*

Address: Aleksandr G. Popov, Institute of Metal Physics, UB of the RAS, 18 S. Kovalevskoy Str., Ekaterinburg, 620990, Russia, apopov@imp.uran.ru

Pressless process (PLP) of the powders, developed by Sagawa and Uno [1], for production of the sintered Nd-Fe-B magnets is one of modern approaches in Dy-free technology. A crucial issue of the PLP is the simultaneous development of high density and degree of texture in the sintered magnets. In previous investigations [1-3], it has been shown that in order to obtain sintered PLP-magnets with high density, it is necessary to have high filling density ρ_f of powders (ρ_f > 3 g/cm^3) placed into molds. However, the high ρ_f increases friction between the powder particles and obstructs their alignment in magnetic field. In order to increase the values of remanence B_r and maximum energy product $(BH)_{max}$ of sintered Nd-Fe-B magnets produced by PLP, one has to enhance the degree of texture. One way to achieve this goal is to increase strength of the applied pulse magnetic field; the other way is to reduce the frictional forces between the powder particles. This can be achieved by coating the particles with a thin layer of a lubricant. The present work is dedicated to the application of several lubricants used to enhance the alignment of the powders in pulse magnetic field of moderate strength.

After hydrogen decrepitation and coarse grinding the strip casting alloy, which consisted of 31.5 Nd, 1 B, bal. Fe (wt. %), was milled in a vibratory mill in toluene. Lubricant additives - zinc stearate powder or esters - were put into the mill vessel together with the alloy powder. The content of the added lubricants was calculated in wt. % of the alloy powder. Some properties of the lubricants are presented in Table 1.

After milling to the average particle size of 3 - 5 μm, wet powders were loaded into molybdenum molds with the filling density of 3.0 to 3.5 g/cm^3. Alignment of powders was accomplished in the pulsed magnetic field of 46 kOe; after PLP the magnets were sintered in vacuum at 1090 °C. The low evaporation temperatures of the lubricants allow one to remove them from the surface of powder particles by slow heating under vacuum at the temperature not higher than 500 °C. The X-ray diffraction investigations were performed using a DRON-6 diffractometer in Cr $K\alpha$ radiation. The oxygen content in the sintered samples was determined by the reduction method using an ELTRA-ONH 2000 gas analyzer.

Fig.1 shows how the properties of the PLP magnets depend on the content C of the added lubricants.

Table 1. Some properties of lubricants used for production of PLP magnets.

Lubricant	Chemical formula	Molecular mass	ρ (g/cm^3)	T^*_m (°C)	T^{**}_b (°C)	Oxygen concentration, (wt.%)
ethyl butyrate	$CH_3(CH_2)_2COOC_2H_5$	116.16	0.879	-98	120	27.55
ethyl caprylate	$CH_3(CH_2)_6COOC_2H_5$	172.27	0.867	-45	208	18.09
methyl caprylate	$CH_3(CH_2)_6COOCH_3$	159.24	0.878	-40	193	19.00
ethyl laurate	$CH_3(CH_2)_{10}COOC_2H_5$	228.40	0.866	-11	275	12.85
zinc stearate	$(C_{17}H_{35}COO)_2Zn$	632.30	1.100	130	277	10.12

T^*_m – melting point; T^{**}_b – boiling point

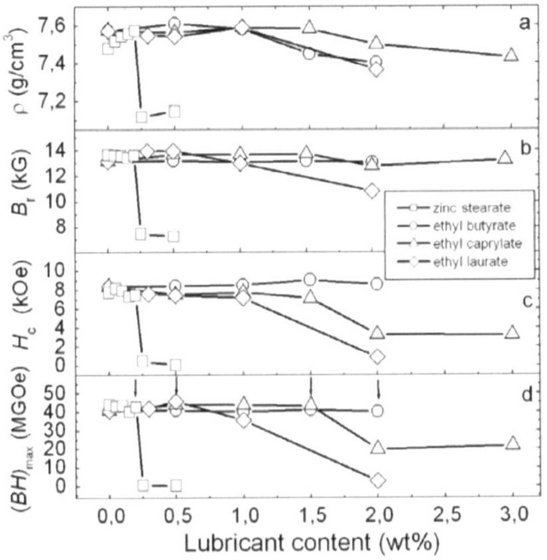

Fig.1. Effect of the added lubricants on the properties of PLP magnets.

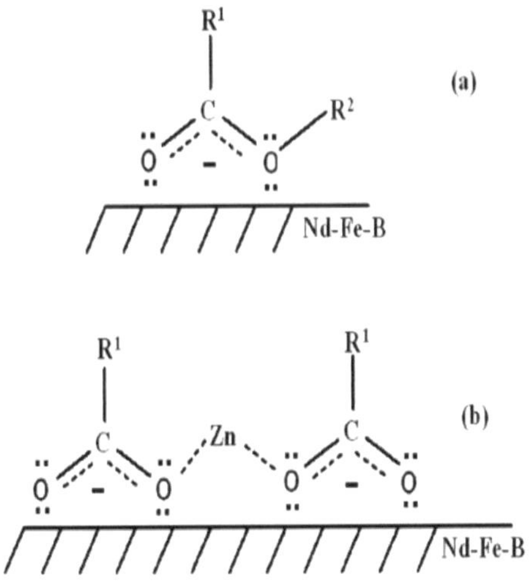

Fig.2. Scheme of interaction of the lubricant molecules with surface of the alloy particles: (a) esters, (b) zinc stearate.

Addition of ethyl butyrate in the range of 0-2 wt % almost does not influence properties of the magnets. This fact, especially the constant B_r values, shows that ethyl butyrate does not reduce the friction forces between the particles. Increasing concentrations of the other internal lubricants in toluene upon milling of the Nd-Fe-B alloy up to critical content C_{cr} increases the B_r and $(BH)_{max}$ of the sintered magnets by 5 - 7%. At $C > C_{cr}$, the properties of the magnets and, particularly coercive force, start to decrease. The critical contents (shown with arrows in Fig. 1d) are 1.5, 0.5 and 0.2 wt. % for ethyl caprylate, ethyl laurate and zinc stearate, respectively. It can be seen from Fig. 1 and Table 1 that the higher are the molecular mass and boiling temperature of the lubricants, the lower are the C_{cr} values; therefore, the process of lubricant removal from the surface of the particles is more difficult.

The esters employed as lubricants are described by the R^1-C(O)O-R^2 chemical formulas (where R^1 = CH_3-$(CH_2)_n$, n = 2, 6, 10 and R^2 = CH_3 or CH_3CH_2) and they belong to the class of the organic compounds with uneven distribution of electron density. The ester group C(O)O-R^2 contains two atoms of oxygen, both having two lone pairs of electrons. Because of the surplus of the electron density, this group is polarized and freely connects to the surface of Nd-Fe-B particles (Fig. 2a). The alkyl residue R^1 does not have surplus electrons and it is oriented at an angle of about 90° to the surface of the alloy particles. Densely packed molecules of the lubricant form a layer on the surface of Nd-Fe-B particles; its thickness is equal to the length of one or several molecules. These layers prevent direct contact between particles and, thus, reduce boundary friction.

The fact that ethyl butyrate does not affect the friction forces between particles is probably caused by the short molecular chain. Molecules of the lubricants with number of methylene groups $(CH_2)_n$ $n \geq 6$ effectively reduce boundary friction.

Fig. 3 shows the microstructure of the fracture of magnets produced without addition and with addition

Fig. 3. Microstructure of the fracture of PLP magnets prepared without lubricant addition (a) and with addition of ethyl caprylate (b) and ethyl laurate (c).

of 1% ethyl caprylate and 1% ethyl laurate. The size of grains of the $Nd_2Fe_{14}B$ phase monotonically decreases, and the amount of spherical Nd_2O_3 oxides increases as the molecular mass of the employed lubricant grows. Probably, the lubricants serve also as surfactants, and their addition enhances milling of the alloy powder. The finer is the powder particle, the larger is an area of their surface, and more of the unextracted lubricant molecules remain in the powder. The unextracted lubricants lead to excess oxidation of the Nd-rich phase in the course of the sintering of magnets and decrease their H_c.

Table 2. Content of oxygen and oxides in the sintered magnets produced with addition of lubricants with concentration higher than C_{cr}.

Sample	Lubricant	Lubricant content (wt. %)	NdO_x content (vol. %)	Oxygen content (wt. %)	Carbon content (wt. %)	H_c (kOe)
C0	no lubricant	0	2.0	0.355	-	8.17
C1	ethyl butyrate	2.0	3.1	0.430	0.098	8.13
C2	ethyl caprylate	2.0	3.3	0.433	0.131	3.11
C3	methyl caprylate	1.5	3.5	0.466	0.116	3.91
C4	ethyl laurate	1.0	3.7	0.443	-	3.86
C5	zinc stearate	0.5	5.0	0.975	-	0.11

Table 2 presents oxygen and oxides contents determined for the magnets prepared at $C > C_{cr}$. Despite the fact that in samples C1 - C5 the concentration of the added lubricants decreases, the contents of oxygen and NdO_x oxides increase more than by 1.5 times in comparison with the magnet produced without lubricant addition. Coercivity also sharply declines. This negative effect of oxidation is the strongest in the case of zinc stearate addition. Unlike the ester molecule which has a single polar group, the molecule of the zinc stearate contains two polar carboxylate groups (Fig. 2b); this strengthen its bond with the surface of the Nd-Fe-B particles and complicates the removal process.

Thus, it is shown that the addition of the internal lubricants in toluene upon milling of the Nd-Fe-B alloy increases the remanence of the sintered magnets by 5 - 7%. The maximum concentration of the zinc stearate and esters should not exceed 0.2% and 1.0% of the mass of Nd-Fe-B powder, respectively. The higher lubricant concentrations lead to the interaction of the lubricant with the Nd-rich phase in the course of the sintering of the magnets resulting in a decrease of the magnetic hysteresis properties. The PLP magnets prepared using lubricant additives with optimal content exhibit a density of 7.5 g/cm^3, $B_r \geq 14$ kG, $H_c \geq 8$ kOe and $(BH)_{max} \geq 46$ MGOe.

Acknowledgment

The work is supported by CRDF GLOBAL – UB RAS (project RUP2-7104-EK-13) and UB RAS (project No. 12-M-23-2066).

References

[1] M. Sagawa and Y. Une, in: *Proc. 20th Int. Workshop on Rare Earth Permanent Magnets and Their Applications*, Crete, 2008, pp. 103-105.

[2] A. G. Popov, A. V. Shitov, E. G. Gerasimov *et al.*, *Phys. Met. Metallogr.* **113**, 2012, 331.

[3] A.G. Popov, E.G. Gerasimov, P.B. Terent'ev *et al.*, *Phys. Met. Metallogr.* **114**, 2013. 285.

Investigation of the Carbon Role on the Magnetic Properties of Powder Injection Molded Nd-Fe-B Magnets

L.U. LOPES[1], E.C. SANTOS[2], N. UENAL[3], T. HARTWIG[3], P.A.P WENDHAUSEN[1]
[1] MAGMA-Labmat, Department of Mechanical and Materials Engineering, UFSC – Brazil
[2] Instituto SENAI de Inovação em Laser, FIESC-SENAI – Brazil
[3] Fraunhofer IFAM, Bremen – Germany

Abstract: *One of the issues that Powder Injection Molding (PIM) is facing to be stablished as a manufacturing process for complex-shaped Rare-Earth magnets is the remaining carbon residue found in the material after the binder extraction step. In this work, thermal binder extraction was performed at various rates and atmospheres in order to obtain magnets with different carbon content levels. Magnetic characterization in sintered magnets showed a strong correlation between coercivity and carbon content: an increase of the latter from 640 PPM to 1300 PPM reduced coercivity from 1400 kA/m to less than 500 kA/m. Investigation of both low and high carbon magnets by WDS mapping and high resolution FEG was focused on understanding the impact of the carbon content on coercivity, concerning carbon dispersion within the material's microstructure.*

1. Introduction

The fabrication of Nd-Fe-B full-dense magnets by Powder Injection Molding (PIM) has been investigated in previous works [1]–[4]. Such studies were motivated by PIM advantages in attaining complex-shaped magnets without diluting the remanence as in the case of injection molded bonded magnets In this technique, the polymeric binders that act as a temporary vehicle that provide rheology for injection molding, are extracted by thermo-chemical routes prior to the sintering stage. This process is controlled by the applied heating rate and furnace atmosphere, which influence the binder decomposition that, in turn, invariably leaves carbon rich residues.

It is known that carbon might have detrimental effects to the hard magnetic properties of Nd-Fe-B based magnets [5], [6]: in high amounts carbon reacts with $Nd_2Fe_{14}B$ and by forming more stable Nd carbides, releases α-Fe [7]. In smaller amounts, however, there is no observable α-Fe formation and the coercivity drop mechanism is not well understood, but carbon seems to be concentrated in Nd-rich phase along with oxygen impurities [5]. The aim of this work is to shed some light on this carbon issue by microstructural investigation, in order to evaluate the carbon dispersion and how magnetic properties are affected.

2. Experimental

$(Nd,Dy)_{14.35}Fe_{79.4}B_{6.14}$ alloy was jet-milled to an average particle size of 4,6 μm. The feedstock for injection molding was prepared by mixing the alloy powder under argon atmosphere at 120 °C with a binder system having a ratio of 60% by volume of powder. The selected binder comprises a mixture of polyethylene (PE), waxes and stearic acid. In such a multicomponent binder, PE acted as the backbone polymer, a stiff resin that provides structural stability to the green part. The injection molding of cubic samples (10 mm side) was carried out at 90 °C and 300 bar, by means of a Thermo Scientific Minijet. The injected parts underwent solvent debinding in hexane for 48 h at room temperature. During this process, the mass loss was monitored, assuring over 95% wax extraction. Samples were then subjected to a thermal debinding cycle under argon or hydrogen gas flux. Heating rates of 0.5, 1.0 and 1.5 °C/min were maintained up to 610 °C. After this step, the atmosphere was changed to high vacuum and a two-step sintering cycle was performed, consisting of a first step at 1080 °C for 2 h followed by a second step at 1120 °C for 30 min. Magnetic properties were determined with a hysteresisgraph, through sample magnetization with 4 T pulsed field. Carbon and oxygen levels were determined by hot gas extraction techniques.

3. Results and Discussion

Demagnetization curves for sintered magnets debound

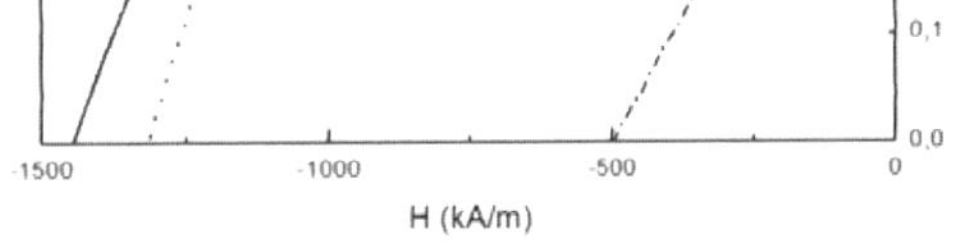

Fig. 1. Demagnetization curves of sintered magnets debound under hydrogen with different heating rates.

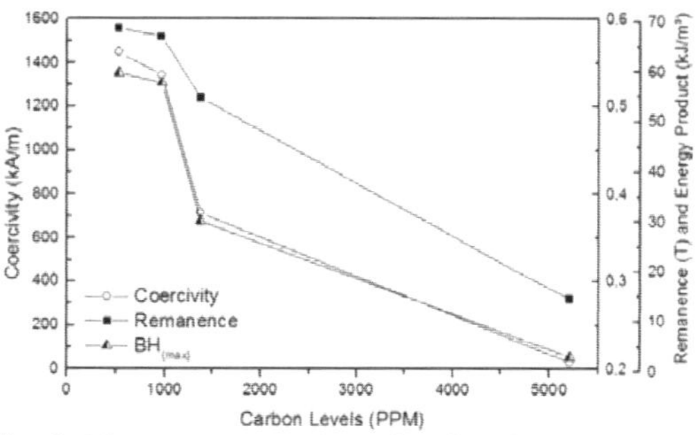

Fig. 2. Magnetic properties related to the carbon levels in sintered samples.

under hydrogen at the three studied rates are shown in Fig. 1. Debinding under argon resulted in very low coercivity and the data is not shown. A correlation of heating rate and the final magnetic properties during binder extraction can be clearly observed. It has been established that slower rate results in highest coercivity.

In Fig. 2, the main magnetic properties are shown in relation to the carbon content levels. The lower amounts of carbon are related to the slower heating rates during the thermal debinding, and the highest amount, over 5000 PPM, corresponds to debinding under argon. A slower heating rate allows for a complete polymer decomposition, aided by the reaction with the hydrogen gas. When a fast heating rate is applied, the polymer is not fully extracted and its remains undergo pyrolysis. In the absence of a reactive gas, polymer chains cannot be broken into small, volatile molecules, therefore thermal debinding loses its efficiency. During sintering stage the carbon from the pyrolysed polymer reacts with the Nd-rich liquid phase and, in case of high amounts, with 2:14:1 phase.

Fig. 3 shows a BSE-SEM microstructure image of the magnet that underwent binder extraction in argon atmosphere, resulting in a high carbon residue. The

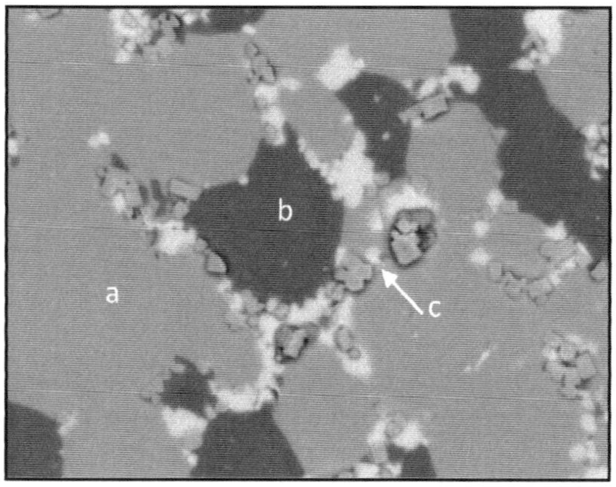

Fig. 3. BSE-SEM image of an argon debound magnet, with carbon level of 5300 PPM. (a) 2:14:1 phase; (b) Free iron; (c) Nd carbides.

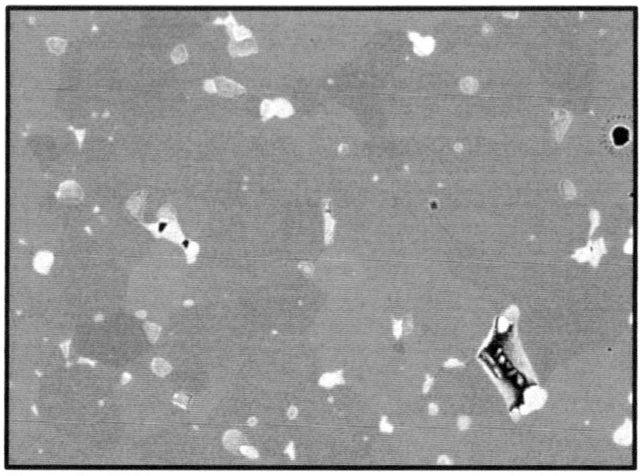

Fig. 4. BSE image of a magnet with 1400 PPM carbon, no visible α-Fe can be observed.

disproportionation of the 2:14:1 phase is clearly visible as α-Fe islands were formed, strongly reducing the coercivity. This result is in agreement with the study performed by Pan et al. [7], indicating that the formation of α-Fe is proportional to the amount of carbon present.

In Fig. 4, the microstructure of an alloy with 1400 PPM of carbon is shown. Despite the improvement in microstructure compared to the magnet with 5300 PPM of carbon, the coercivity is still low at 500 kA/m. Even with no visible α-Fe formation, the coercivity is still affected by the presence of carbon and this is thought to be related to a different mechanism.

In order to evaluate how carbon is being distributed within this microstructure, EPMA-WDS mapping was performed for carbon, iron and neodymium, as shown in Fig. 5. The element mapping indicates that carbon and neodymium-rich phase seems to coexist, while no α-Fe could be found. Similar results are reported by

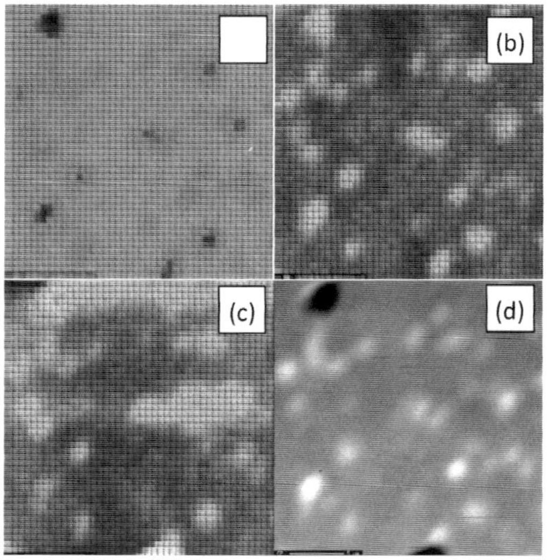

Fig. 5. EPMA-WDS element mapping for: (a) Fe, (b) Nd, (c) C and (d) SEM-BSE Imaging of the same area. White color stands for higher concentration.

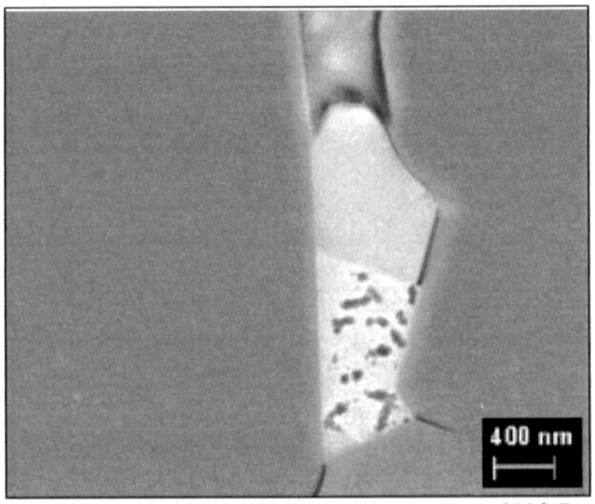

Fig. 6. High resolution BSE-FEG imaging of Nd-Rich phase with internal precipitates.

Minowa et al [5] detecting a higher concentration of carbon in Nd-rich phase. Carbon is expected to react with Nd during sintering while this phase is liquid.

In Fig. 6, a detailed image of the Nd-rich phase of the magnet with 1400 PPM carbon shows the presence of internal precipitates that may consist of neodymium carbides and oxide. Such precipitates could not be found in grain boundaries where they could act as a nucleation sites for reverse domains, decreasing coercivity. It is however expected that small precipitates are present inside the grain boundary phase, or even located elsewhere in the microstructure. Another possibility for the reduction in coercivity without α-Fe formation is the interference of carbon in the wettability of liquid phase during sintering [1]. In this case, no proper grain boundary film can be generated during sintering, which would lower the coercivity according to the most widely accepted theories on coercivity generation in Nd-Fe-B sintered magnets [8].

4. Conclusion

Nd-Fe-B magnets fabricated by PIM process may contain different levels of carbon contamination, which strongly affects the material's coercivity. The amount of carbon is related to the binder extraction step and when in high concentrations it reacts with the 2:14:1 phase, releasing a soft-magnetic α-Fe phase. In case of smaller concentrations, no visible α-Fe formation could be found, but coercivity was still affected. The results suggest that carbon reacts with the Nd-rich phase and affects the coercivity by interfering with the formation of a continuous intergranular film, or by carbide nano-precipitates within grain boundaries, where it acts as a nucleation site for reverse domains. Further investigations of such mechanisms by TEM are underway to support these assumptions.

Acknowledgment

The authors would like to thank Dr. Zanatta and Mr. Alexsandro Rabelo from Instituto SENAI de Inovação in Sistemas de Manufatura for the SEM analysis. The contribution of Prof. Persiano, Departamento de Fisica - ICEx – UFMG, with the WDS measurements was also of great importance.

References

[1] S.H. Lee, W. Lee, W.Y. Jeung, T.J. Moon, *Powder Metall.*, 1998, vol. 41, no. 3, 185–188.

[2] C. Drescher, N. Ünal, L. U. Lopes, T. Hartwig, F. Petzoldt, *Proc. 22nd REPM*, 2012, 27–30.

[3] M.A.Carvalho, L.U. Lopes, W.H.D. Luna, *et al.*, *Proc. of the 22nd REPM*, 2012, 31–34.

[4] L.U. Lopes, T. Hartwig, P.A.P. Wendhausen, *IEEE Trans. Magn.*, 2013, vol. 49, no. 8, 4618–4621.

[5] T. Minowa, M. Shimao, M. Honshima, J. *Magn. Magn. Mater.*, 1991, vol. 97, 107–111.

[6] L.U. Lopes, M.A. Carvalho, R.S. Chaves, *et al.*, *Mater. Sci. Forum*, 2012, Aug., vol. 727–728, 124–129.

[7] F. Pan, M. Zhang, R. Zhao, *et al.*, *J. Phys. D. Appl. Phys.*, 1998, vol. 31, no. 5, 488.

[8] J. Fidler, *Magn. IEEE Trans.*, 1987, vol. M, no. 5, 2106–2108.

Coercivity Enhancement of the Sintered Magnets with Blending Magnetic Grains

HAIBO FENG, ANHUA LI, SHULIN HUANG, YANFENG LI, MINGGANG ZHU, WEIXING XIA, WEI LI
Division of Functional Materials, Central Iron & Steel Research Institute, China Iron and Steel Research Institute Group, Beijing 100081, P. R. China

Abstract: *The blending-magnetic-grain (BMG) method we developed and the grains with different Ce content were obtained in the magnets. The demagnetization curve of BMG magnet is smooth which is similar with the single-grain magnets. Microstructure and domain-structure of the BMG magnets were investigated. A hard-hard coercivity reinforcement mechanism was proposed and discussed. This coercivity enhancement effect is applicable in magnets with ternary and multi-magnetic grains system magnets.*

Keywords: *rare-earth; sintered magnet; $Nd_2Fe_{14}B$; microstructure; magnetic properties*

Address: Haibo Feng, Division of Functional Materials, Central Iron & Steel Research Institute, China Iron and Steel Research Institute Group, Beijing 100081, P. R. China

1. Introduction

With the growing demand for sintered $Nd_2Fe_{14}B$-type rare-earth magnets in new energy economic areas, reducing consumption of magnetic rare-earths and their substitution in the magnets were investigated [1-3]. Substitutes for Nd, such as La and Ce, were used in sintered RE-Fe-B magnets. Since the $Ce_2Fe_{14}B$ has lower saturation magnetization and weaker anisotropy than $Nd_2Fe_{14}B$, the magnetic properties decrease when Ce added to the magnets. Recently, we developed a blending-magnetic-grain (BMG) method: two powders with nominal composition of $Nd_{30}Fe_{bal}B_1$ and $RE_xNd_{30-x}Fe_{bal}B_1$ were prepared and mixed, then, aligned and sintered. The resulting magnet consists of Ce-free/lean grains and Ce-rich grains. A higher coercivity was obtained in the magnets with the BMG grains. The coercivity enhancement mechanism of the BMG magnets was proposed and discussed.

2. Experimental

The strip cast flakes with nominal compositions $Nd_{30}Fe_{bal}B_1$ (wt. %) and $(Nd_{0.5}Ce_{0.5})_{30}Fe_{bal}B_1$ were prepared. The two alloys were hydrogen-decrepitated (HD) and jet milled. Mixed powders with nominal composition of $(Nd_{0.7}Ce_{0.3})_{30}Fe_{bal}B_1$ were obtained by blending the two powders. Then, the powders were aligned and isostatically cold pressed. The compacts were vacuum sintered at 1000 - 1030 °C for 2 h. Then the magnets were annealed at 900 °C for 2 h and at 520 °C for 2 h and water-quenched to room temperature. Magnetic properties of the magnets were measured by the NIM-2000 hysteresis loop instrument. Microstructure was investigated by scanning electron microscopy (SEM, JSM-7001F) and transmission electron microscopy (JEM-2000).

3. Results and Discussion

The $(Ce_{0.3}Nd_{0.7})_{30}Fe_{bal}B_1$ magnet has a high performance when sintered at 1030 °C for 2 h: B_r = 13.5 kG, H_{ci} =9.5 kOe and $(BH)_{max}$ =42.8 MGOe. Fig. 1 presents the BSE image of the sintered magnet. The magnet has a grain size of ~5 μm, and the boundary phase is distributed between the $Re_2Fe_{14}B$ grains homogenously. As it can be seen in Fig. 1, the boundary phase is continuous and envelops the magnetic $Re_2Fe_{14}B$ grains thus contributing to the coercivity improvement. Because, the melting point of boundary phase decreases with the Ce content, the magnet can be sintered at lower temperature. A density of 7.61 g/cm^3 can be obtained for the $(Ce_{0.3}Nd_{0.7})_{30}Fe_{bal}B_1$ magnet sintered at low temperature. The EDS analysis results are presented given in Table1. Two kinds of grains with different Ce content were observed in the magnets. In the Ce-lean grains, the Ce content is below 2.5 at.%; Ce-free grains were observed. At the same time, the Ce content is above 6.5 at.% in the other grains. This indicates that the microstructure with BMG was obtained in the magnets.

Magnetic properties of the magnets with BMG were compared with the magnet prepared by the conventional method. The results are presented in Table 2. The remanence and maximum energy product of the BMG magnets were similar to the conventional magnets, but the coercivity of BMG magnets is 30% higher than that of common magnets. Moreover, the demagnetization curve of BMG magnet is smooth which is similar to that of the single-grain magnets, as given in Fig. 2. Demagnetization curve is not a linear combination of couplings between the $Nd_2Fe_{14}B$, $(Ce,Nd)_2Fe_{14}B$ grains and Ce-Nd-Fe grains. This indicates that an enhanced effect exists in

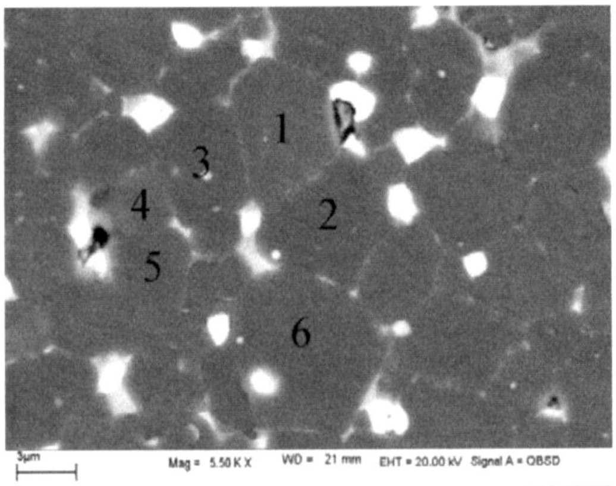

Fig. 1. BSE image of the sintered magnet.

Table 1. EDS results of the grains (at.%).

Grain	Ce	Nd	Fe
1	0.42	14.51	85.07
2	6.55	7.81	85.64
3	6.95	7.57	85.48
4	2.29	12.76	84.95
5	7.08	7.53	85.39
6	1.71	13.72	84.57

the magnets with BMG microstructure. Typical magnetic domain structure of the BMG magnets is given in Fig. 2. Most magnetic domains stretch over several grains. So, the coercivity of (Ce,Nd)-Fe-B grains can be enhanced by the adjacent Nd-Fe-B grains with higher coercivity by a hard-hard reinforcement mechanism. This coercivity enhancement effect is applicable in magnets with ternary and multi-magnetic grains system magnets. So, higher coercivity can be obtained in the magnets with BMG microstructure. This coercivity enhancement effect is applicable in all the magnets with ternary and multi-magnetic grains.

4. Conclusions

High performance Ce-Nd-Fe-B system magnets were obtained by BMG method. Two kinds of grains with different Ce content present in the magnets. The $Nd_2Fe_{14}B$ and $(RE,Nd)_2Fe_{14}B$ magnetic grains are distributed randomly in the magnets and they are surrounded by the RE-Nd-Fe boundary phase. The coercivity of (Ce,Nd)-Fe-B grains is enhanced by the higher-coercivity adjacent Nd-Fe-B grains by a hard-hard reinforcement mechanism. Higher coercivity of H_{ci} = 9.53 kOe was obtained; this is 30% higher than the magnets prepared by the conventional method.

Table 2. Magnetic properties of $Ce_9Nd_{21}Fe_{bal}B_1$ magnets.

Fabrication method	B_r (kG)	H_{cj} (kOe)	$(BH)_{max}$ (MGOe)
Conventional	13.43	7.22	42.5
BMG	13.53	9.53	42.8

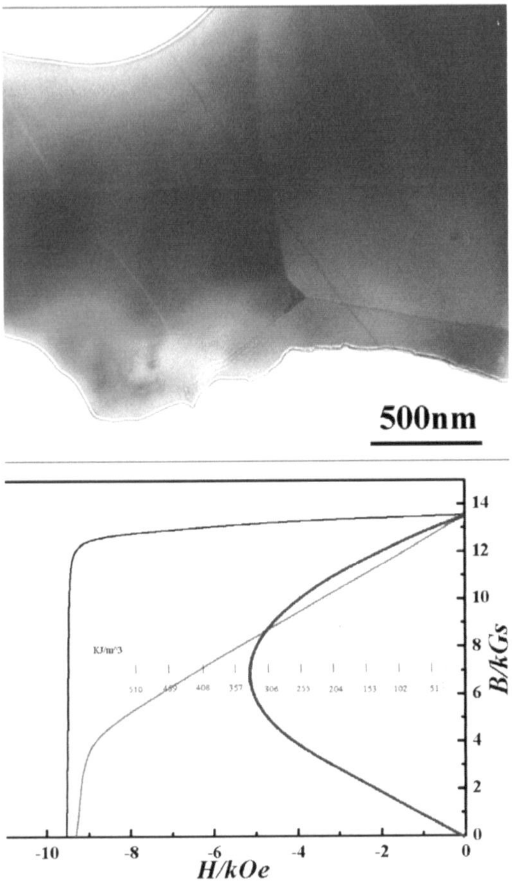

Fig. 2. Domain structure and demagnetization curve of the BMG magnet.

Acknowledgements
This work was supported by National Natural Science Foundation of China (Grant NO. 50931001 and 51171048) and National Key Technology R&D Program.

References

[1] J.F. Herbst, *Rev. Mod. Phys.* **63**, 1991, 819.
[2] M. Velicescu, P. Schrey, W. Rodewald, *IEEE Trans. Magn.* **31**, 1995, 3623.
[3] S.X. Zhou, Y.G. Wang, R. Høier, *J. Appl. Phys.* **75**, 1994, 6268.

Mass Production of Recycled NdFeB-type Sintered Magnets and a Novel Grain Boundary Modification Process

M. ZAKOTNIK, C.O. TUDOR
Urban Mining Technology Co., Perryville, Maryland 21903, USA

Abstract: *First attempts to recycle the NdFeB-type sintered magnets started at the beginning of the 21st century and have continued only on a laboratory scale ever since. We are reporting for the first time a large up scaling in rare earth based magnet recycling. The magnetic properties were compared to the starting material, i.e., NdFeB-type sintered magnets from waste material streams. Waste NdFeB-type sintered magnets were acquired and subjected to a recycling method that uses a significantly less energy intensive process when compared to the traditional magnet-manufacturing route. By carefully controlling the processing parameters and blending small amounts of elemental additives, we were able to produce various NdFeB-type sintered magnets suitable for a wide range of commercial applications. The new recycled magnet yielded a best energy product of 391 kJ/m^3, Br of 1.423 T, and iHc of 1041 kA/m. The overall rare earth content of the recycled magnet was 13.7 at.%, with 99.5 at.% of waste material used, and hence recovered, in the recycling process. Furthermore, aiming to improve the thermal stability, we succeeded in accomplishing an iHc of 1.9 MA/m, yielding a high-energy performance recycled NdFeB-type sintered magnet suitable for motor applications. In conclusion, we present a new recycled NdFeB-type sintered magnet readily available in mass production and suitable for a wide range of commercial applications. A novel grain boundary modification process is also presented, which is suitable for both recycled and virgin magnets to improve magnetic properties using minimal heavy rare earth additions.*

Keywords: *recycling, NdFeB-type sintered magnets, restoration/improvement of magnetic performance, high energy recycled permanent magnets, grain boundary modification, processing technology*

Address: Miha Zakotnik, Urban Mining Technology Co., Perryville, Maryland 21903, USA, Phone +1 (302) 345 2950, E-mail: miha.zakotnik@gmail.com

1. Introduction

The consumer market based on NdFeB sintered magnets, first developed in the 1980s [1], has shown rapid growth in recent years, thanks in part to the increase in consumer applications using high performance magnets. Indeed, publicly available data has estimated that the global output of sintered NdFeB-based magnets reached ~83,000 tonnes in 2011 [2] and ~100,000 tonnes in 2013. Meanwhile, the production capacity of magnet manufacturers in China alone reached 300,000 tons per year, suggesting a further increase in global output by the end of 2014. Today, the market for NdFeB-based magnets is 80% in consumer goods, with the remaining market share of 20% in business-to-business products.

The amount of NdFeB-based material in products that are approaching end of life in the world is vast. The potential advantages of recycling this material include: cost, resource availability, and reduced environmental impact. While NdFeB magnets used in wind turbines and MRI machines may undergo a different end-of-life recycling treatment, the magnets embedded in end-of-life consumer goods are not yet separated, because no such regulation is yet enforced in the USA. In fact, it is safe to assume that NdFeB magnets coming from this latter group are directly shredded together with the end product. The amount and quality of rare earths in the resulting material mixture are very low and, thus, their recovery may imply a long sequence of separation processes not likely to be economically feasible. To alleviate this problem, desirable recycling processes for NdFeB must be simple and able to recover the quality and quantity of the metals in order to ensure the standards for input back into the market.

Various recycling approaches for rare earths and the recovery of NdFeB-type sintered magnets have previously been reviewed [3]. However, most of the recycling solutions to this date have been presented on a laboratory scale in ideal conditions. Previous work has shown that recycling magnets on a laboratory scale can be accomplished using hydrogen decrepitation [4]. In this work, it was shown that, using a powder blending addition of 1 at.% of neodymium before sintering, the recycled magnet can maintain and, in some cases, improve the magnetic properties of the starting magnet. This technique has a substantial advantage, not only because of its simplicity, but also because of its low cost. Moreover, it allows for the development of a close loop recycling system for rare earth magnets, thus considerably

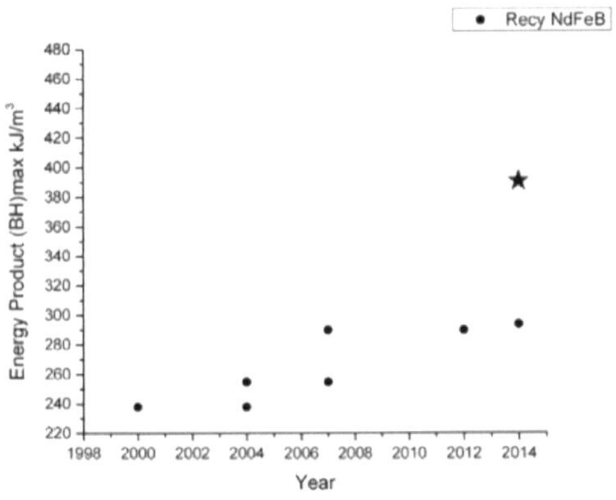

Fig. 1. Progress of developing recycled NdFeB-type sintered magnets in laboratory (black circles). The star shows the recycling in mass production of this work.

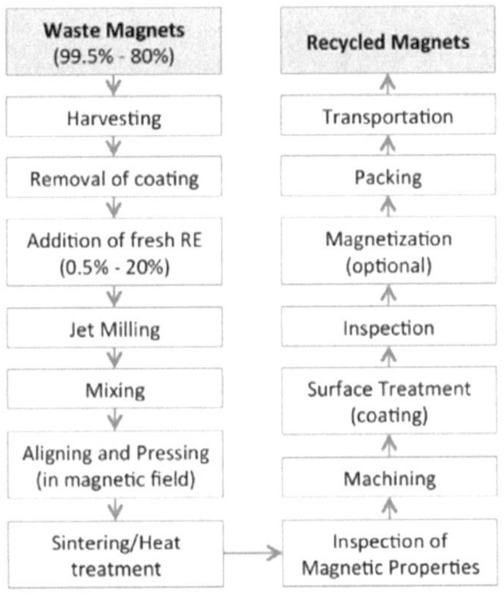

Fig. 2. Typical manufacturing process used to recycle NdFeB-based sintered magnets.

reducing the environmental impact generated by the extraction and processing of primary rare earths.

In this paper, we contrast the traditional way of manufacturing the NdFeB-based sintered magnet with a recycling technique that was applied and tested on a pilot plant scale. Fig. 1 also shows the energy product of the recycled NdFeB-type sintered magnet achieved in mass production using commercial equipment (star), when compared to the laboratory achievements (black circles) over the years. Our work extends and builds upon work proposed by Zakotnik et al. [4][5][6]. The magnetic properties have also shown an improvement by the use of a developed grain boundary modification technique, which has also been demonstrated on a pilot plant scale. This technique can be applied on both recycled and virgin NdFeB magnets to enhance magnetic performance.

The challenges of restoring or improving the magnetic properties of recycled NdFeB-type sintered magnets are as follow: (1) waste material preparation; (2) composition control; (3) restoration and modification of grain boundary phase; (4) densification through sintering; (5) control of grain size; and (6) alignment of $Nd_2Fe_{14}B_1$ grains.

2. Experimental Setup

Batches consisting of 300 kg of recycled NdFeB-type sintered magnets have been processed through a powder metallurgy process, as shown in Fig. 2. The starting material was harvested from a range of end-of-life applications (e.g., MRI machines, voice coil motors, loudspeakers). Chemical composition was analysed using inductive coupled plasma (ICP) before, during, and after the recycling process. The recovered magnets from the end-of-life applications were coated with a protective coating to reduce their susceptibility to corrosion. This coating was mechanically removed before further processing, ensuring a clean, uncoated NdFeB-based starting material. The recovered NdFeB-based sintered magnets were then coarse milled and homogenized, and fresh Nd, Pr, and Dy were added using a hydrogen-mixing reactor. This reactor was evacuated before admitting hydrogen at a pressure of 0.9 bar. The sintered magnets absorbed the hydrogen at room temperature and were then partially degassed at 600°C in situ until the vacuum was recovered. The material was further homogenised by jet milling to achieve an approximate powder size of 3.5 μm, which was then sieved to remove large oxidised particles. Powders were then compacted in a magnetic field to form a green compact. The green body was then transferred to a hydraulic chamber and subjected to an isostatic pressure of 60 MPa. Densities of the recycled NdFeB-based sintered magnets were determined using the Archimedes principle and a temperature controlled liquid. Cylindrical magnets (10 mm in diameter and 10 mm in height) were cut from a sintered block using a wire-cutting machine, and the magnetic properties were then measured using a close looped permeameter after pulse magnetising the magnet in a field of 4T. The microstructure of recycled magnets was also characterised by scanning electron microscope (SEM). The proportion of the Nd-rich material was determined by image analysis using the imageJ software.

3. Results and Discussion

The compositions of the starting 'scrap' magnets and recycled magnets were analysed using ICP, with results shown in Table 1. An increase in the Nd-content and Dy-content of the recycled magnet can be observed, whereas the content of the other metallic elements remains fairly constant. The expected build up in the oxygen and carbon content during the recycling process can also be observed. Removing

	Nd (at.%)	Pr (at.%)	Dy (at.%)	B (at.%)	Al (at.%)	Fe (at.%)	C (at.%)	O (at.%)
Starting Material	10.50	3.04	0.12	6.92	0.52	bal.	0.31	0.95
High Energy	11.39	3.01	0.37	6.85	0.52	bal.	0.31	1.00
	Nd (at.%)	Pr (at.%)	Dy (at.%)	B (at.%)	Al (at.%)	Fe (at.%)	C (at.%)	O (at.%)
Starting Material	9.97	3.18	0.17	5.81	0.75	bal.	0.37	0.22
High Coercivity	9.80	2.98	1.37	5.62	0.76	bal.	0.62	0.53

Table 1. Analysis of the typical composition of the magnet (+/- 0.009-0.08). Some of the minor additions are being omitted. "High Energy" and "High Coercivity" refer to the recycled material with 0.5 at.% and 3 at.% additions, respectively.

larger and not friable rare earth oxides throughout the recycling process reduces the oxygen build up. This would reduce the amount of both Nd-rich and Nd_2O_3 material, but will not reduce the overall Nd content to such a level that would dramatically lower the magnetic performance. The excess of freshly added Nd prior to the recycling process would lead to formation of Nd-rich pockets and of other Nd phases, depending on the oxygen levels present in the process [7][8][9][10]. Additionally, in order to achieve improved magnetic performance of the new composition of the recycled NdFeB-type sintered magnets, the restoration of both microstructure and grain boundary rich phase is extremely important.

Fig. 3 shows a comparison of the typical microstructure between the waste NdFeB-based magnets (starting material, Fig. 3A) and the recycled NdFeB-type sintered magnets (new material, Fig. 3B). The starting material has a similar microstructure to the recycled material, with white scattered rare-earth rich phase uniformly surrounding the $Nd_2Fe_{14}B_1$ phase. A quantitative analysis using imageJ reveals that the average grain size in the waste magnet is 11.5 μm, while, in the recycled NdFeB-type sintered magnet, the grain size is 4.5 μm. The bright regions are most probably both metallic Nd and their oxides, while the dark areas represent the porosity where the Nd-rich was pulled out during sample preparation.

The scaled-up 300 kg batches of recycled NdFeB-based sintered magnets were found to yield consistent restored remanence and improved coercivity over the starting material. Demagnetization loops are shown in Fig. 4. The highest value of Br was found within the batch blended with 0.5 at.% additions, with a value of 1.42 T, corresponding to almost 90% of the theoretical value for the $Nd_2Fe_{14}B$ compound. The iHc value was found to improve by 29%, peaking at 1042 kA/m. The volume fraction of $Nd_2Fe_{14}B$ phase was measured at ~95% (±). It is very apparent from Fig. 4 that the magnetic properties of the recycled magnets can be not just restored but also improved by carefully controlling the amount of additives, processing parameters, composition, and waste material preparation. The high coercive grade (Fig. 4B) exhibits a slight decrease in remanence values, which may be due to the antiparallel coupling of added heavy rare earth Dy migrating from grain boundary into the matrix phase and coupling with Fe within the $Nd_2Fe_{14}B$ phase [11]. It is also worth noting that the small addition of Dy resulted in ~80% increase in coercivity and ~6% decrease in remanence, which allows the recycled NdFeB-type sintered magnets to be used in high temperature applications.

Generally, the additions of metals (e.g., Nd, Dy, Pr, Tb, etc.) will cause the formation of a thin boundary layer, which results in a continuous and smooth interface, hence reducing the number of sites available for the formation of reverse domains. If the inter-granular material were either paramagnetic or anti-ferromagnetic, this would result in better magnetic isolation of the $Nd_2Fe_{14}B$ grains and improve the overall magnetic performance. These two factors help to explain the increased coercivity observed with additions of heavy rare earths such as Dy. Mostly, the square loop shape has been maintained or improved for all recycled magnets with Dy additions. There is either a restoration in the remanence or improvement of the intrinsic coercivity and maximum energy product for all recycled sintered magnets when compared to that of the starting material.

4. Highlights

Traditionally, the magnet production starts by melting pure raw materials (e.g., pure electrolytic iron 99.9%, ferroboron, rare earths (RE) and other transitional metals (T)) forming REFeTB alloys. The basic steps are: (1) the alloy is formed using the *strip casting* method consisting of molten elements being poured on a rotating water-cooled copper wheel forming 0.2-0.3 mm thick flakes resulting in a grain size ranging from 5 to ~80 μm [12][13]; (2) the alloy is exposed to *hydrogen decrepitation* (HD), causing the formation of a fine powder; (3) the powder is further milled using a *jet milling* apparatus to ~5 μm particle size; (4) the particles are single crystals, which have a preferred direction of magnetization, that can be *aligned* in a magnetic field and pressed to give a green compact, which is (5) *sintered* and (6) *annealed* under vacuum.

Recycling of the waste NdFeB-type sintered magnets and applying grain boundary modification was performed by blending the waste material with a combination of small amounts of virgin rare earths and transitional metals (see U.S. Patent Application No. 14/307,267). This recycling process is very different from the traditional process commonly employed by magnet manufacturers to produce magnets from virgin material. The recycling process

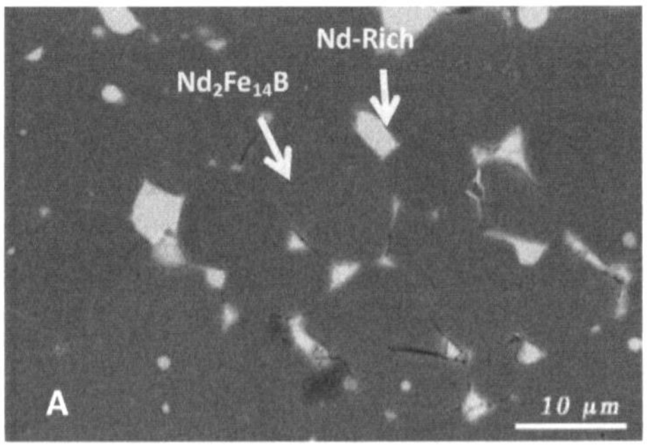

Fig. 3. Backscatter electron images showing the comparison (the appearance and the microstructure) of sintered and etched (A) NdFeB-type waste material and (B) recycled NdFeB-type magnet.

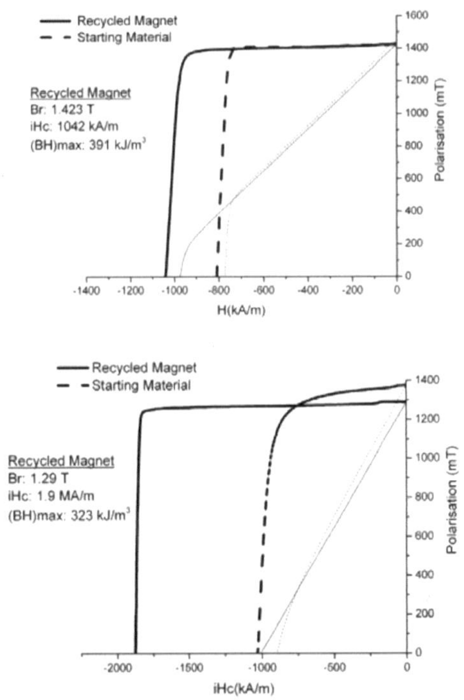

Fig. 4. Demagnetisation variations of recycled NdFeB-type sintered magnets (A) with 0.5 at.% additions resulting in high energy, and (B) with 3 at.% additions resulting in high coercivity suitable for high temperature applications. Density of the recycled magnets is 7.56 g/cm³.

is now commercially viable, producing new recycled magnets that can have dramatically improved magnetic and physical properties, when compared to their virgin magnet predecessors. These new recycled magnets have an acceptable and reproducible microstructure, and are designed with the magnetic performance required by a wide variety of applications.

4.1. High grades of recycled NdFeB magnets

In order to avoid the material cost of both virgin and recycled NdFeB-type sintered magnets, we have been investigating a process that improves the coercive force with the optimum amount of Dy content through the grain boundary modification process. In particular, the Dy or Tb is necessary for high temperature applications, such as electric motors. It is therefore imperative to control not only the composition and grain size throughout the processing, but also the grain boundary phase. One important solution in preparing the material, either virgin or recycled NdFeB-type sintered magnets, is to reduce impurities (e.g., coating removal) and oxygen content (e.g., rare earth-rich oxide).

This work has shown that NdFeB-based magnets can effectively be recycled with a controlled oxygen content (see Table 1). This work has also shown that the overall magnetic performance of recycled magnets can be recovered, if not improved, with minimum amount of dopants. This novel process resulted in 29% increase in coercivity and 0% decrease in remanence (see Fig. 4A), or 80% increase in coercivity and 6% decrease in remanence (see Fig. 4B).

Grain boundary modification has also been evaluated on a large pilot scale representing an alternative to other grain boundary diffusion processes [14][15][16], where the increase of iHc is about 40% with a small drop in Br of ~0.6%. It is worth noting here a distinction between the novel process developed and the conventional grain boundary diffusion – the former is not limited to a thickness of about 6 mm of the magnet sintered body.

Fig. 5 shows how the grain boundary modified (GBM) technique described herein can be applied to sintered magnets on a pilot scale to improve remanence and coercivity when compared to the starting material. The results show advantages of the GBM process, which include: no limitation on the magnet thickness, controlled amount of doped material, and precise tailoring of magnetic performance to meet customer requirements.

The performance of commercially available recycled NdFeB-type sintered magnets is shown in Fig. 6.

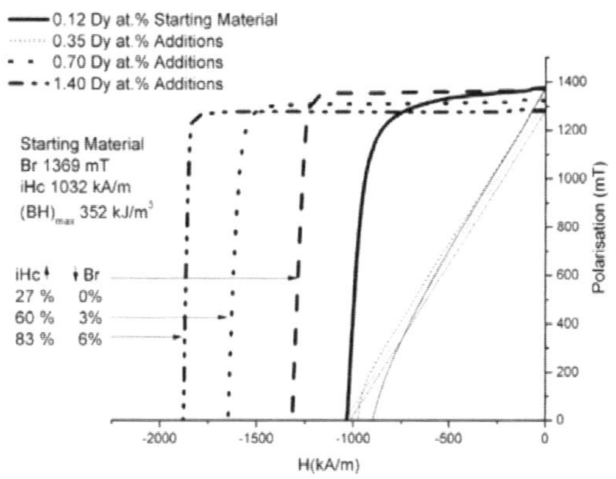

Fig. 5. Demagnetization curves of GBM-processed sintered magnets containing different Dy content.

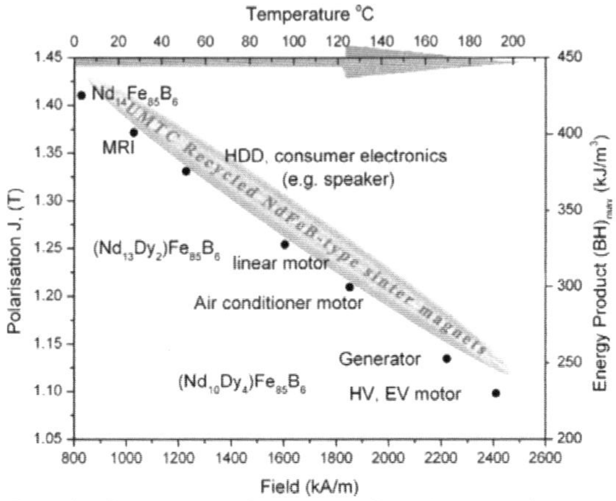

Fig. 6. Magnetic performance of virgin (•) and recycled (shaded area) NdFeB-type sintered magnets suitable for a wide range of applications.

4.2. Future challenges

The next stage in the development is to further upscale to a 250-tone plant capacity to produce recycled NdFeB-type sintered magnets. The novel processes presented in this work provide a good ground for optimism on mass recycling NdFeB-type sintered magnets, as well as diminishing the dependence on the heavy rare earth content. Furthermore, Urban Mining Technology Co. has also developed a series of patented tools for the harvesting of the NdFeB-type sintered magnet material from actual devices, such as disk drives. The results included here, as well as measurements of other magnetic properties (e.g., temperature and field dependence of the coercive field) show that the recycling method described herein is applicable and scalable. Further results will be published in the near future.

5. Conclusion

Two new methods have been presented and tested in mass production, including the recycling of waste NdFeB sintered magnet and grain boundary modification.

The recycled NdFeB-type sintered magnets have reached a commercial level with improved magnetic performance. This was achieved through increased energy-cost performance and novel processing, which controls composition, microstructure, and sintering behaviour. Waste sintered magnets can be processed with small rare earth additions and transitional metals, leading to full densification, resulting in both restored and increased magnetic properties.

The second method, grain boundary modification, which has also been evaluated in mass production, resulted in high coercivity and a controlled drop in remanence without limit to the magnet thickness. Although the remanence decreased by 86 mT after grain boundary modification, the increase in the coercivity was more than 800 kA/m.

The development of permanent magnets has shown that each incremental increase in high-energy magnet retains a niche market even when undermined by newer improved products. Hence, it is reasonable to expect that any new magnet having properties that are unique in one way or another will be able to take a portion of the market.

Acknowledgment
The authors are grateful to Urban Mining Technology Co. for the financial support and for believing in the process and product herein. The authors would also like to thank Sreco D. Skapin from the Institute Josef Stefan (IJS), as well as Wu Dan and Yue Ming from Beijing University of Technology (BJUT) for providing some characterizations.

References

[1] M. Sagawa, S. Fujimura, N. Togawa, H. Yamamoto, Y. Matsuura, *J. Appl. Phys.* 1984, 55, 2083.
[2] O. Gutfleisch, M.A. Willard, E. Brück, C.H. Chen, S.G. Sankar, J.P. Liu, *Adv. Mater.* 2011, 23, 821-842.
[3] K. Binnemans, P. T. Jones, B. Blanpain, T. Van Gerven, Y. Yang, A. Walton, M. Buchert, *Journal of Cleaner Production*, 2013, 51, 1-22.
[4] M. Zakotnik, I.R. Harris, A.J. Williams, *J of Alloys and Compounds*, 2008, 450 (1-2), 525-531.
[5] M. Zakotnik, I.R. Harris, A.J. Williams, *J. of Alloys and Compounds*, 2009, 469 (1-2), 314-321.
[6] M. Zakotnik, I.R. Harris, and A.J. Williams, *Proceedings of 19th International Workshop on*

Rare Earth Permanent Magnets & Their Applications 2006, 289-295.

[7] T.G. Woodcock, O. Gutfleisch, *Acta Mater,* 2011, 59, 1026.

[8] R.K. Mishra, J.K. Chen, G. Thomas, *J. Appl. Phys.,* 1986, 59, 2244.

[9] K. Makita, O. Yamashita, *Appl. Phys. Lett.,* 1999, 74, 2056.

[10] K. Hono, H. Sepehri-Amin, *Scripta Materialia,* 2012, 67, 530-535.

[11] N. Oono, M. Sagawa, R. Kasada, H. Matsui, A. Kimura, *Journal of Magnetism and Magnetic Materials,* 2011, 323, 297-300.

[12] O. Gutfleisch, *J. Phys. D: Appl. Phys,* 2000, 33, R157–R172.

[13] J. Bernardi, J. Fidler, M. Sagawa, Y. Hirose, *J. Appl. Phys.,* 1998, 83, 6396.

[14] M. Komuro, Y. Satsu, H. Suzuki, *IEEE Transactions on Magnetics*, 46, 11.

[15] K. Hirota, H. Nakamura, T. Minowa, M. Honshima, *IEEE Trans. Magn.,* 2006, 42, 2909.

[16] D. Li, S. Suzuki, T. Kawasaki, K. Machida, *Jpn. J. Appl. Phys.,* 2008, 47, 7876

.

Micromagnetic Analysis of Hardening Mechanisms in Supermagnets

H. KRONMÜLLER[1], D. GOLL[2], J.B. YANG[3], Y.B. YANG[3], Y. CHEN[1], E. GOERING[1]
[1]Max Planck Institute for Intelligent Systems, Heisenbergstr. 3, 70569 Stuttgart, Germany
[2]Material Research Institute, Aalen University, Beethovenstr. 1, 73430 Aalen, Germany
[3]Department of Physics, State Key Laboratory for Mesoscopic Physics, Peking University, Beijing 100871, P. R. of China

Abtract: *Numerous discussions took place since the discovery of rare-earth transition metal intermetallic compounds dealing with the relevant hardening mechanism in these permanent magnets (PMs). These discussions resulted from the fact that as outlined by Brown and Kronmüller the technically realized coercive fields always were a factor 4 – 10 smaller than the values predicted by the continuum theory of micro-magnetism. The ideal maximum coercivities for nucleation hardened PMs are* $H_c = 2K_1 / J_s$ *and for pinning hardened PMs* $H_c = K_1 / 2J_s$ *(*K_1 *= first anisotropy constant,* $J_s = \mu_0 M_s$ *= magnetic polarization,* M_s *= magneti-zation). At room temperature (RT) nucleation hardened* $SmCo_5$ *should lead to* $\mu_0 H_c$ *= 41 Tesla and for pinning hardened* Sm_2Co_{17} *based PMs* $\mu_0 H_c$ *= 2 – 3 Tesla. In the case of nucleation hardened PMs, including the* $RE_2Fe_{14}B$ *sintered magnets, the low coercive fields are known as Brown's paradox. It will be the topic of the paper to show that this paradox can be solved considering the effects of the microstructure.*

Keywords: *micromagnetism; coercivity; nucleation; pinning*

Address: Helmut Kronmüller, Max Planck Institute for Intelligent Systems, Heisenbergstraße 3, 70569 Stuttgart, Germany, Tel: (+49-711) 689-1910, Fax: (+49-711) 689-1912, E-mail: kronmueller@is.mpg.de

1. Introduction

The magnetic hardening mechanisms governing the large coercive fields of rare earth-transition metal based PMs has been the topic over decades of years. This holds for all PMs based on $SmCo_5$, Sm_2Co_{17}, $Nd_2Fe_{14}B$, $Sm_2Fe_{17}N_x$ as well as for non-rare earth PMs as MnBi, MnAl or Mn_2Ga. Whereas in the case of the conventional PMs as Alnico and Ba-Sr-ferrites it is generally accepted that in both cases the nucleation mechanism is governed by the form effect (Alnico) and by the magnetocrystalline anisotropy (Ba-Sr-ferrites), in the case of the rare earth metal based PMs, nucleation as well as domain wall pinning (DWP) models have been discussed [1-5]. These controversial discussions are due to the fact that the complex microstructures of sintered PMs lead to coercive fields smaller than a factor 4 – 10 as compared to the predictions of theory. In the case of isolated particles with uniaxial symmetry and prolate shape the maximum nucleation field leading to a spontaneous reversal of magnetization is given by

$$H_N = \frac{2K_1}{\mu_0 M_s} + \frac{1}{2} M_s \qquad (1)$$

(K_1 = first anisotropy constant, M_s = spontaneous magnetization, $\mu_0 M_s = J_s$, spontaneous polarization, μ_0 = vacuum permeability). As shown in Fig. 1, the experimental ratios H_c / H_N of the most important

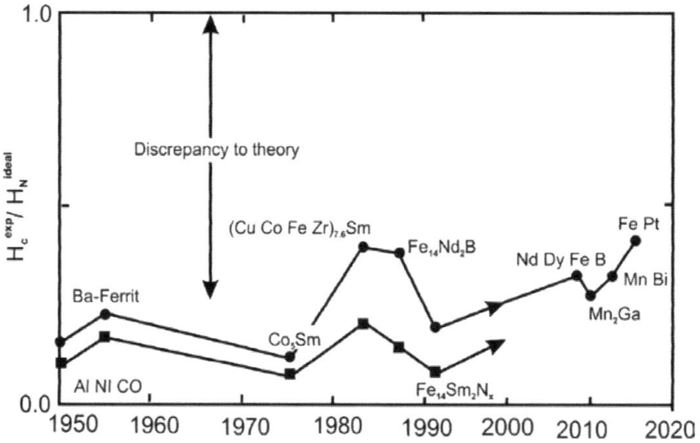

Fig. 1. The H_c/H_n *ratios of laboratory (●) and technical (■) PMs as developed during the last eight decades. Brown's paradox I.*

PMs developed during the last 8 decades are a factor 4 – 10 smaller as predicted by theory. Only in the case of laboratory PMs the ratio may be somewhat larger. This failure of achieving no better coercive fields is known as Brown's paradox [6,7] and is related to the deteriorating role of the microstructure.

There exists a further important aspect of Brown's paradox related to the role of single domain particles which are the origin of nucleation based reversal processes. In thermodynamic equilibrium the critical diameter, D_c, for the formation of single domain particles of $Nd_2Fe_{14}B$ are 120 nm for platelets and 250 nm for spherical shape. However, in sintered PMs of $Nd_2Fe_{14}B$ the grains' diameters are of the order of 5 – 10 μm and even larger. Therefore, as demonstrated in Fig. 2 after cooling down from above the Curie temperature, T_C, the grains become multi-domain grains. If these multidomain grains are magnetically saturated by applying the saturation field, H_s, ideal grains remain in the single domain state after reducing the field again to $H = 0$. The grains cannot develop the thermodynamic equilibrium state because the demagnetizing field is smaller than the nucleation field. In the case of non-ideal grains, i.e., grains with nucleation fields smaller than M_s, a multidomain state develops either at $H = 0$ or if the field is applied antiparallel to the original magnetization. This latter case more or less is realized in sintered magnets depending on the perfectness of the grains and the paramagnetic intergranular phase. Accordingly, there exists a large potential for improving the coercivities of supermagnets by optimizing the microstructure. In order to raise H_c to one half of the ideal $2K_1/J_s$ value the following improvements of the microstructure are required as will be discussed in the following.

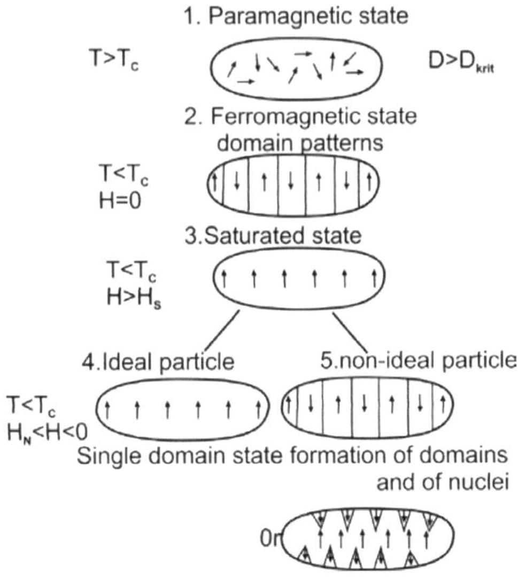

Fig. 1. Domain patterns in small grains after different pretreatments: Cooling from above T_c. Remanent states after saturation. Brown's paradox II.

2. Micromagnetic Background

2.1. Coercive field of nucleation hardened PMs

The nucleation field of single domain particles originally has been determined by Stoner and Wohlfarth [8]. Taking into account demagnetization fields and the second anisotropy constant, K_2, Kronmüller et al. [9] obtained for the extended Stoner-Wohlfarth theory for single domain particles misaligned by an angle ψ with respect to the inversely applied magnetic field

$$H_c(\psi) = \frac{2K_1 + (N_\perp - N_\parallel)\,\mu_0 M_S^2}{J_S} \times \frac{1}{\left[(\sin\psi)^{2/3} + (\cos\psi)^{2/3}\right]^{3/2}} \times \left[1 + \frac{2K_2}{K_1 + \frac{1}{2}(N_\perp - N_\parallel)\,\mu_B M_S^2} \times \frac{(\mathrm{tg}\,\psi)^{2/3}}{1 + (\mathrm{tg}\,\psi)^{2/3}}\right]. \quad (2)$$

$N_\parallel$ and $N_\perp$ correspond to the demagnetization factors parallel and perpendicular to the c-axis of an ellipsoidal particle eq. (2) holds for the nucleation field within the angular range $0 \le \psi \le \pi/2$, however, is valid for the coercive field only in the range $0 \le \psi \le \pi/4$. In the angular range $\pi/4 \le \psi \le \pi/2$ the coercive field is given by

$$H_c(\psi) = \frac{2K_1 + (N_\perp - N_\parallel)\,\mu_0 M_S^2}{J_S} \times \frac{1}{2}\sin 2\psi \times \left(1 + \frac{2K_2\cos^2\psi}{K_1 + \frac{1}{2}(N_\perp - N_\parallel)\,\mu_B M_S^2}\right). \quad (3)$$

Eqs. (2) and (3) may be written as

$$H_c(\psi) = \frac{2K_1}{J_S}\,\alpha_\psi - N_{\mathrm{eff}}\, M_S\, \alpha_\psi\ , \quad (4)$$

where α_ψ denotes the second term of eqs. (2) and (3) and $N_\perp - N_\parallel$ has been replaced by N_{eff}. Fig. 3 presents the ψ-dependence of H_c for different ratios K_2/K_1 revealing the shape of a ski-jump. Due to the effect of K_2, $H_c(\psi)$ becomes flattened for $\psi < \pi/4$ as compared to the classical Stoner-Wohlfarth behaviour and becomes steeper for $\psi > \pi/4$. For $\psi \le \pi/4$ the H_c value is determined by an irreversible nucleation process and within the range $\pi/4 \le \psi \le \pi/2$ by reversible rotations because in this case the nucleation field H_N is larger than H_c. Eqs. (2) and (3) hold for single domain particles which are fully isolated from each other by a paramagnetic inter-granular phase. Other systems with individual particles are nanopatterned thin films as recently published [10,11]. Fig. 4 presents a comparison of the angular dependences of H_c as measured for the non-rare earth systems of MnBi and FePt. In the case of MnBi H_c has been investigated for a melt-spun polymer bonded, oriented PM [12,13]. Excellent

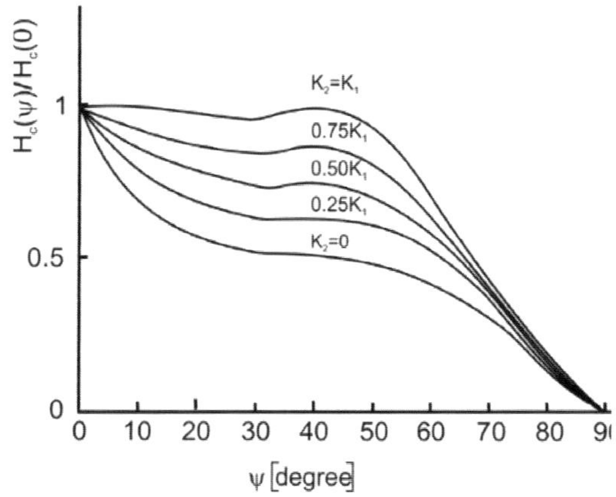

Fig. 3. Angular dependence of $H_c(\psi)/H_c(0)$ for different ratios K_2/K_1 [17].

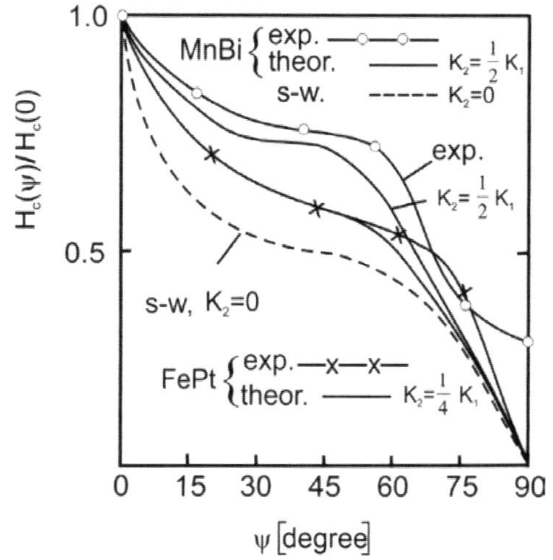

Fig. 4. Comparison of measured angular dependences of $H_c(\psi)/H_c(0)$ for MnBi PMs [13] and nanopatterns of FePt [11,17] with eqs. (2) and (3).

agreement between experiment and the predictions by eqs. (2) and (3) is obtained for $K_2 = (1/2)\,K_1$, which also agrees with measurement of Albert and Carr [14] who found $K_2/K_1 = (1/2.3)$.

At $\psi = \pi/2$ H_c/H_N of MnBi reveals a finite value of 0.25 which has to be attributed to the existence of misaligned grains. In the case of an isotropic distribution of grain's easy axes for $2K_2/K_1 = 1$ the average value $\langle\alpha_\psi\rangle = 0.6$ holds and for $K_2 = 0$ $\langle\alpha_\psi\rangle = 0.47$. Assuming a Gaussian distribution of misalignment angles $p(\theta) = 1/(\pi\theta^2)^{1/2}\exp(-\theta^2/\theta_0^2)$ where θ_0 denotes the mean standard deviation [15] the average value of α_ψ for $\psi = \pi/2$ is given by 0.25 for $\theta_0 = \pi/12$ in agreement with the experimental result. In the case of FePt nanopatterns, H_c/H_N vanishes at $\psi = \pi/2$ as predicted by eq. (2), because in this case due to the epitaxial growth dots are ideally (001) oriented.

Of course, the agreement of the angular dependence of H_c with the extended Stoner-Wohlfarth theory does not give an interpretation of the actual values of H_c. Besides the misaligned grains there are at least three further deteriorating effects which lead to the existence of Brown's paradox. These effects either act separately or in combination. Not outlining the detailed backgrounds of the micromagnetic equations [4,16] the results of its solutions are summarized in the following. In terms of microstructural parameters, α_K, and N_{eff} leading to a generalized equation for H_c

$$H_c = \frac{2K_1}{J_s}\,\alpha_\psi\,\alpha_K - N_{\text{eff}}\,M_S \quad . \qquad (5)$$

2.2. Reduced anisotropies at grain surfaces

In order to derive analytical results for α_K it has been assumed that K_1 varies at the grain surface as $K_1(z) = K_1 - \Delta_K/\text{ch}^2(z/r_0)$, where Δ_K denotes the reduction of K_1 at the grain's surface $z = 0$. The linearized micromagnetic equations have been solved rigorously for the above ansatz of $K_1(z)$. For $\Delta_K = K_1$ three regions of α_K values have been found (r_0 = width of deterioration):

1. $\alpha_K = 1 - \pi^2 r_0/\delta_B$ for $2\pi\,r_0 < \delta_B$
2. $\alpha_K = (1/\pi)\,\delta_B/r_0$ for $2\pi\,r_0 > \delta_B$
3. $\alpha_K > 0$ for $2\pi\,r_0 >> \delta_B$.

From the rigorous result obtained for α_K the following relation between α_K and r_0 may be derived:

$$r_0 = \delta_B\,\sqrt{1-\alpha_K}\,/\,\pi\,\alpha_K \ . \qquad (6)$$

As an example, Fig. 5 presents a plot of $\mu_0 H_c/J_s$ vs. $2K_2/M_sJ_s$ of MnBi [17] for the determination of $\alpha_K\alpha_\psi = 0.3$ and $N_{\text{eff}} = 0.75$. With $\langle\alpha_\psi\rangle = 0.6$ this gives $\alpha_K = 0.5$ and $r_0 = 3.3$ nm. In the case of sintered PMs like Nd-Fe-B or MnBi PMs, r_0 values of

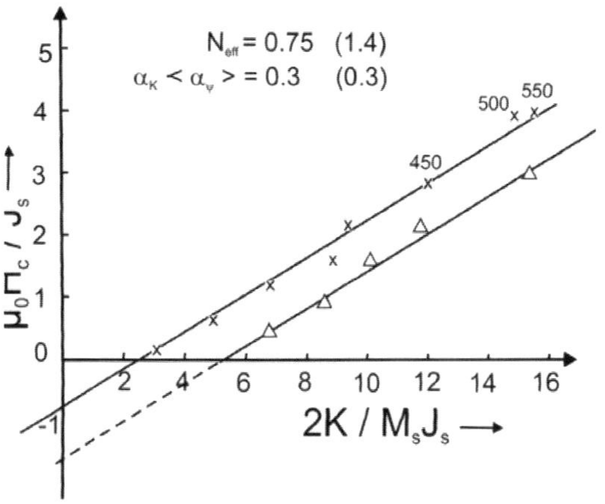

Fig. 5. Analysis of the temperature dependence of H_c for MnBi PMs (–×– [12,17]; –△– [17,25]).

1 – 3 nm are derived [2,16].

In order to reduce the ideal value for H_c only by a factor of two according to the above results r_0 should be smaller than (2/3) δ_B, i.e., in the case of Nd-Fe-B smaller than 3 nm.

2.3. Soft magnetic intergranular phases

As a model system a soft magnetic film of thickness, d_s, is embedded between two hard magnetic grains. The nucleation field and the α_K parameters of this composite system have been determined previously [18] as shown in Fig. 6. As a function of d_s/δ_B according to Fig. 6 α_K reveals three ranges:

i) $\alpha_K = 1$ holds for $d_s < \delta_B$ due to complete exchange coupling between the soft and the hard phases the ideal H_c value holds.

ii) α_K decreases rapidly in the range $\delta_B < d_s < 8\delta_B$. In this range α_K decreases to 0.1.

iii) α_K = prop. $(d_s)^{-1.8}$ for $d_s > 8\delta_B$.

According to these results soft magnetic precipitations within the intergranular phase should have thicknesses not exceeding δ_B.

2.4. Dipolar demagnetizing fields

Dipolar interaction in general reduce the coercive field as described by the term (–)$N_{eff} M_s$ in eq. (4). The magnetic field, H_i, acting on an individual grain of a sintered PM is composed of three contributions [7,19]:

$$\mu_0 H_i = N_m \cdot \langle J \rangle + N_g J_s - N_n \langle J_n \rangle . \qquad (7)$$

The first term of eq. (7) denotes the macroscopic demagnetization field of the PM, the second term describes the demagnetizing field of the isolated grain, and the third term corresponds to the demagnetizing field of the hole if the grain is removed. In eq. (6), $\langle J \rangle$ denotes the global polarization of the PM, J_s = spontaneous polarization and J_n corresponds to the average polarization of the neighboring grains. If $\langle J_n \rangle$ in a first approximation corresponds to $\langle J \rangle$ and $\langle J \rangle = \beta J_s$ holds ($\beta \sim 0.9 - 1$), the effective demagnetization factor is given by $N_{eff} = (N_m - N_n)\, \beta + N_g$.

An upper limit for N_{eff} is obtained for platelet-like shapes of the pm and of the grains, with $N_{eff} \sim 1$. A lower limit is obtained for spherical or cubic shapes of the pm and the grains, with $N_{eff} \sim 1/3$. According to these results $\mu_0 H_c$ may be reduced considerably by dipolar demagnetizing field in case of Nd-Fe-B, e.g., by 1.6 Tesla.

3. Theoretical Aspects of Pinning-Hardened PMs

Whereas conventional PMs before the discovery of Alnico were based on the pinning of DWs at defect structures it is generally accepted that also Sm_2Co_{17} based PMs below 600 K also are governed by DW pinning [3,20]. DW pinning in this case takes place at planar zigzag precipitates of $SmCo_5$ embedding the pyramidal Sm_2Co_{17} phase. In the case of planar defects as phase boundaries, or anti-phase boundaries the following ratios of material constants are introduced (I soft and II hard phase):

$$\varepsilon_J = J_s^{I} / J_s^{II}, \quad \varepsilon_K = K_1^{I} / K_1^{II}, \quad \varepsilon_A = A^{I} / A^{II}.$$

1. Sharp phase boundary [21]

$$H_c = (\, 2\, K_1^{II} \,/\, J_s^{II} \,)$$

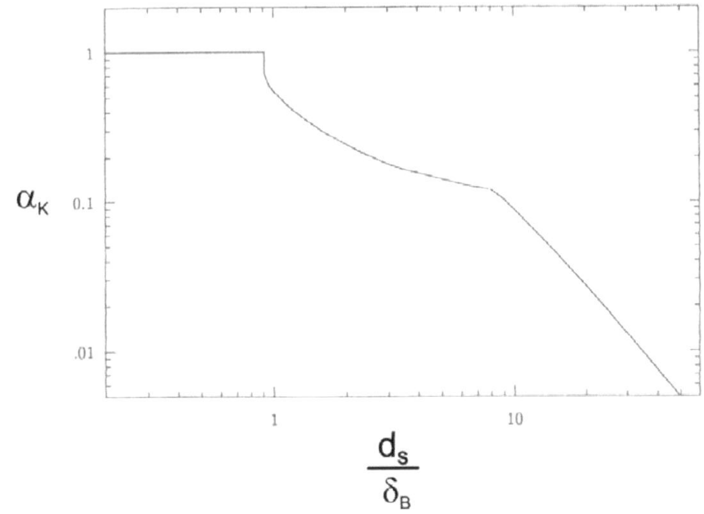

Fig. 6. Dependence of the microstructural parameter α_K on the thickness, d_s, of a soft film embedded between two magnetically hard films of Nd-Fe-B [18].

$$(1-\varepsilon_K\,\varepsilon_A)\,/\,\left(1+\sqrt{\varepsilon_A\,\varepsilon_J}\right)^2\,. \quad (8)$$

2. Narrow precipitation [22,23] (width $d < \delta_B{}^h$)

$$H_c = \frac{\pi}{3\cdot\sqrt{3}}\,\frac{2K_1^{\mathrm{II}}}{J_s^{\mathrm{II}}}\,\frac{1}{\cos\psi_0}\,\frac{d}{\delta_B^{\mathrm{II}}}\,\left|\sum_{i=1}^{N-1}\left(\varepsilon_A^i-\varepsilon_K^i\right)\right|\,, \quad (9)$$

where the index i denotes the i'th atomic plane of N planes within the planar precipitation and $\delta_B{}^{h}$ the dw width of the hard phase.

3. Extended phase boundary of width D

$$H_c = (K_1^{\mathrm{II}}/\,2J_s^{\mathrm{II}})\left(1\,/\,(1+D/\,\delta_B^{\mathrm{II}})\right). \quad (10)$$

Using the material parameters of Sm_2Co_{17} and $SmCo_5$ eq. (8) leads to H_c values of ~ 3 Tesla. Also eq. (10) leads to similar values if $D < \delta_B$ holds. Eq. (9) may be applied to antiphase boundaries, stacking faults and small angle boundaries leading to coercivities of 0.1 – 4 Tesla [24].

Acknowledgement
The authors gratefully acknowledge the support of the Deutsche Forschungsgemeinschaft for the project HPPMSNG.

References

[1] K. J. Strnat, *J. Magn. Magn. Mater.* 7, 1978, 351.
[2] H. Kronmüller, K. D. Durst, M. Sagawa, *J. Magn. Magn. Mater.* **74**, 1988, 291.
[3] M. Marinescu, A. Gabay, G. C. Hadjipanayis, in: *Handbook of Magnetism and Advanced Magnetic Materials*, Eds. H. Kronmüller, S. Parkin, John Wiley & Sons, Chichester 2007, pp. 2005-2034.
[4] H. Kronmüller, R. Fischer et al., *J. Phys. D* **29**, 1996, 2274.
[5] D. Givord, D. Tenaud, T. Viadien, *IEEE Trans. Magn.* **24**, 1988, 1921.
[6] W. F. Brown, *Rev. Mod. Phys.* **17**, 1945, 15.
[7] H. Kronmüller, *Phys. Status Solidi (b)* **144**, 1987, 385.
[8] E. C. Stoner and E. P. Wohlfarth, *Phil. Trans. Roy. Soc. A* **240**, 1948, 599.
[9] H. Kronmüller, K. D. Durst, G. Martinek, *J. Magn. Magn. Mater.* **69**, 1987, 149.
[10] T. Bublat and D. Goll, *Nanotechnlogy* **22**, 2011, 315301.
[11] D. Goll and T. Bublat, *Phys. Status Solidi (a)* **2010**, 2013, 1261.
[12] J. B. Yang et al., *Appl. Phys. Lett.* **99**, 2011, 082505.
[13] J. B. Yang et al., *J. Magn. Magn. Mater.* **330**, 2013, 106.
[14] P. A. Albert and W. J. Carr Jr., *J. Appl. Phys. Suppl.* **32**, 1961, 201S.
[15] G. Rieger et al., *Phys. Status Solidi (a)* **171**, 1999, 583.
[16] H. Kronmüller, in: *Supermagnets, Hard Magnetic Materials*, Eds. G. J. Long, F. Grandjean, Kluwer, Dordrecht, 1991, pp. 461-498.
[17] H. Kronmüller et al., *J. Phys.: Condens. Matter* **26**, 2014, 064210.
[18] T. Leineweber and H. Kronmüller, *J. Magn. Magn. Mater.* **176**, 1997, 145.
[19] V. M. Dobrynin, V. M. T. S. Barthmetal et al., *Phys. Rev. B* **81**, 2010, 172403.
[20] D. Goll, H. Kronmüller, H. H. Stadelmeier, *J. Appl. Phys.* **96**, 2004, 6534.
[21] H. Kronmüller and D. Goll, *Physica* **319**, 2002, 122.
[22] H. R. Hilzinger and H. Kronmüller, *Phys. Lett.* **51A**, 1975, 59.
[23] R. Friedberg and D. Paul, *Phys. Rev. Lett.* **34**, 1975, 1234.
[24] H. R. Hilzinger, *Appl. Phys.* **12**, 1977, 253.
[25] Y. Chen, A. Leineweber et al., submitted to *Adv. Mater.*, 2014.

Ab-Initio and Micromagnetic Calculations on Novel Permanent Magnets

J. FIDLER[1], P. TOSON[1], A. ASALI[1], G. ZICKLER[1], M. HAJDUGA[1] T. SCHREFL[2]
[1] Vienna University of Technology, Institute of Solid State Physics, Wiedner Hauptstr. 8-10, A-1040 Vienna, Austria.
[2] Center for Integrated Sensor Systems, Danube University Krems, Wiener Neustadt A-2700, Austria.

Abstract: *On the basis of density functional theory (DFT) and numerical finite element micromagnetic calculations we have analyzed the magnetocystalline anisotropy energy of distorted $(Pr,Dy)_2Fe_{14}B$ in order to understand the mechanisms for magnetization reversal in Dysprosium free rare earth permanent magnets. In the second part we have studied the limits of crystal anisotropy and shape anisotropy as candidates for rare earth free hard magnetic materials based on Fe and Co nanorods.*

Keywords: *anisotropy calculation; coercivity modeling; $RE_2Fe_{14}B$; Co and Fe nanorods*

Address: Josef Fidler, Vienna University of Technology, Institute of Solid State Physics, Wiedner Hauptstr. 8-10, A-1040 Vienna, Austria, E-mail: josef.fidler@tuwien.ac.at

1. Introduction

The search for candidates of suitable magnetic materials, structures and their expected behavior as reduction of the dysprosium content or the replacement for rare earth containing permanent magnets is of great economical and scientific interest [1]. We have performed first principle calculations using the Wien2k code which is based on the density functional theory in order to determine the magnetocrystalline anisotropy of the rare earth (RE) intermetallic compounds $RE_2Fe_{14}B$. The aim is to obtain anisotropy values in dependence on the crystal lattice distortion and the individual substitution of rare earth atoms within the unit cell in order to understand the effect of the variation of crystal anisotropy near grain boundaries in sintered rare earth permanent magnets. Finite element micromagnetic simulations based on the Landau-Lifshitz-Gilbert equation for magnetization reversal have been carried out in order to study the influence of the microstructure on the hysteresis properties. The results of the micromagnetic simulations are compared with high resolution and nanoanalytical TEM investigations of grain boundary regions of various Dy-free RE-Fe-B sintered magnets with different RE content and coercive field, respectively. In the second part we will concentrate on the evaluation of elongated Co and Fe based nanopillars for the usage as bulk permanent magnet material.

2. Dysprosium Free RE Permanent Magnets

The hysteresis properties of the magnets are governed by a combination of the intrinsic properties, such as saturation polarization J_s, magnetic exchange A and magnetocrystalline anisotropy K_1 of various phases and the influence of the microstructure on the magnetization reversal process. The intergranular structure and phases occurring between the grains play a significant role determining the magnetic properties, thus a detailed understanding of the microstructure and grain boundaries is necessary. Magnetic domain structures, which are a result of the occurrence of magnetic stray fields, are directly influenced by the microstructural features. The direct observation of microstructure and magnetic domain structure leads to a deeper insight of the origin of the coercive field of $RE_2Fe_{14}B$ based rare earth magnets, where the nucleation and expansion of reversed domains determines H_c. The nucleation field is given by the local anisotropy field H_A and the local demagnetizing field H_d [2]

$$H_c = H_n = \alpha\frac{2K_1}{J_s} - \frac{N_{eff}J_s}{\mu_0}, \quad \alpha = 0.4 - 0.6$$

Nucleation occurs, if the local demagnetizing field exceeds the local anisotropy and external field:

$$\text{local } H_d \geq \text{local } H_A - |H_{ext}|$$

The TEM micrograph of Fig. 1a shows the granular microstructure of a sintered $(Nd,Pr)_2Fe_{14}B$ magnet, with RE_2O_3 grain boundary junctions and different RE-rich grain boundaries (GB) perpendicular ("*x*") and parallel ("*y*") to the alignment direction [001]. The thickness of type "*x*" GB is in the order of 4 - 5 nm (Fig. 1c). Local strain contour contrast on the 2:14:1 crystal lattice is observed in Fig.1b surrounding the grain boundary junction. H_c is determined by the local decrease of K_1 and J_s at GB and the amount of decoupling of grains. The formation of reversed domains after nucleation near

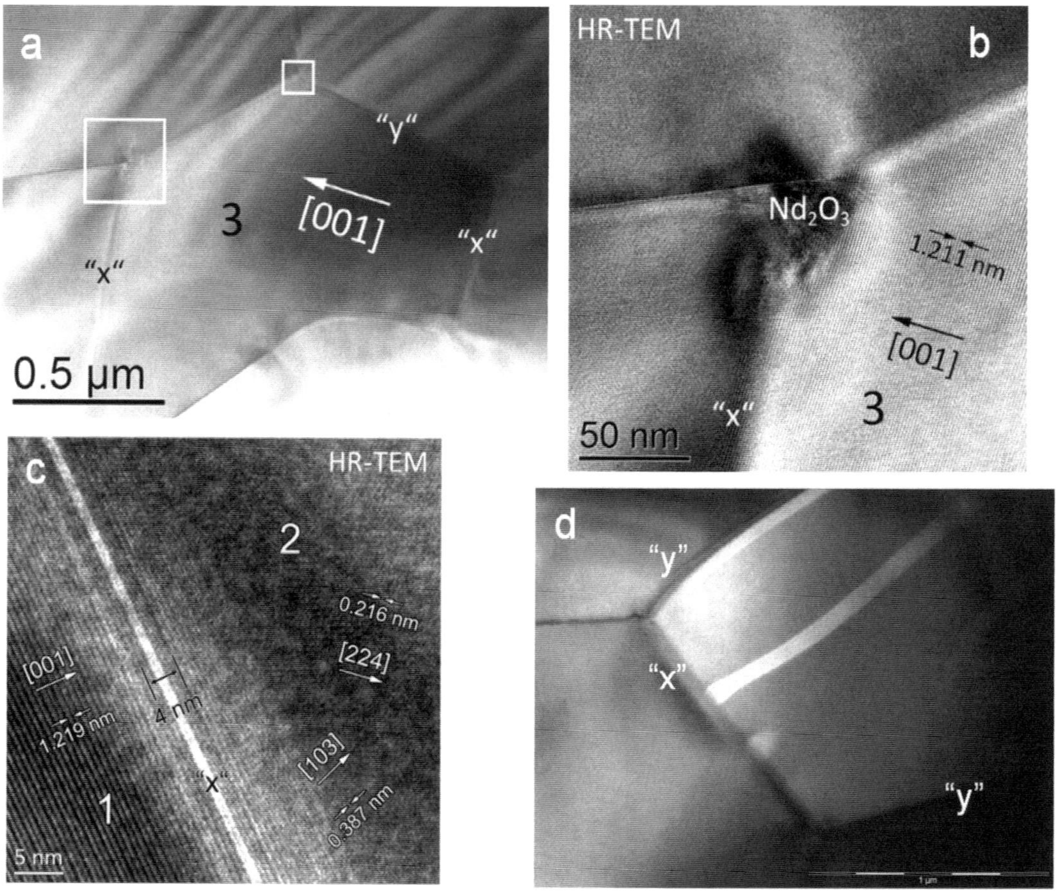

Fig.1. TEM micrographs of a $(Nd,Pr)_2Fe_{14}B$ magnet showing grain boundary (GB) junctions and GB perpendicular ("x") and parallel ("y") to [001]. The nucleation of domains is shown in the Lorentz TEM micrograph (d).

the "x" GB is shown in the Lorentz TEM Foucault image of Fig.1d. The electronic structure calculations were carried out with the WIEN2k code [3], a full potential, linearized augmented plane wave DFT method, where the core states are treated fully relativistically and taking into account the scalar relativistic effects for the valence states in the SCF calculation phase, which, though, omit the spin-orbit coupling (SOC). The SOC is afterwards introduced as a second variational treatment [4]. Hence, after the convergence of the scalar relativistic SCF, the SOC is calculated. The initial spin magnetic moments are calculated during the SCF procedure, but the orbital moments, as well as the correct spin moments (including the SO effect) only after the SOC, by calculating the density matrix. For the calculation of the magnetic anisotropy energy, the difference of the sum of the eigenvalues calculated for two different crystallographic directions (the hard and the easy axis) is obtained and divided by the structure volume [5].

The reason, that the difference in the sum of eigenvalues and not the values of total energy is used for the calculation of MAE, lies in the fact, that the values for total energy are of the order of 300 KRy, while the sum of eigenvalues, in the order of 1 KRy. In both cases, nevertheless, the difference of values in the easy and the hard directions are of the order of 10^{-3} to 10^{-5} Ry. It is obvious that a calculation of this difference through eigenvalues demands less computational precision and is more reliable. We have studied the dependency of the magnetization (moments), and the anisotropy energy on the change of the crystal lattice parameter close to the distorted grain boundary regions.

The calculations [6] show for $Pr_2Fe_{14}B$ a decreasing and a negative MAE (an in-plane easy direction of magnetization) for a c/a value $\geq$ 1% (Fig. 2b). For $Dy_2Fe_{14}B$ the calculated MAE values remain nearly constant in the range -1% $\leq c/a \leq$ +1%. In general, the total magnetization per formula unit increases with increasing c/a ratio for all cases. The coercive field of $(Pr,Dy)_2Fe_{14}B$ permanent magnets is determined by the local minimum value of $2K_1/\mu_0 M_s$ and the local demagnetizing field at grain boundaries, which is proportional to M_s.

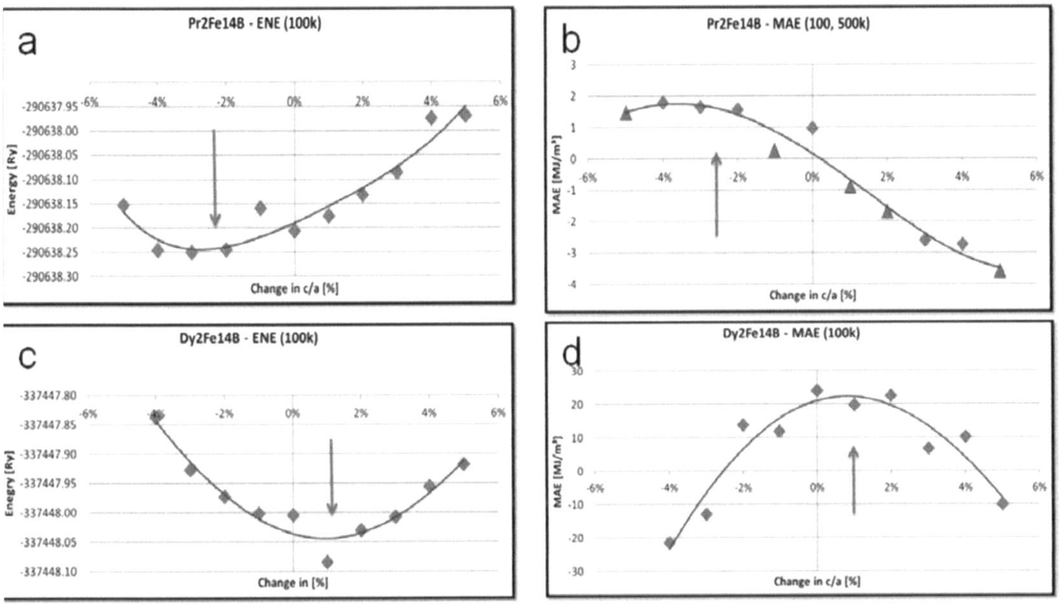

Fig.2. (a) and (c) Energy values for all materials in dependence of c/a for a mesh of 100 k-points. (b) and (d) MAE values for all materials in dependence of c/a for a mesh of 100 k-points. Lattice Parameters Pr: a = 0.8799 nm, c = 1.2242 nm; Dy: a = 0.874 nm, c = 1.183 nm.

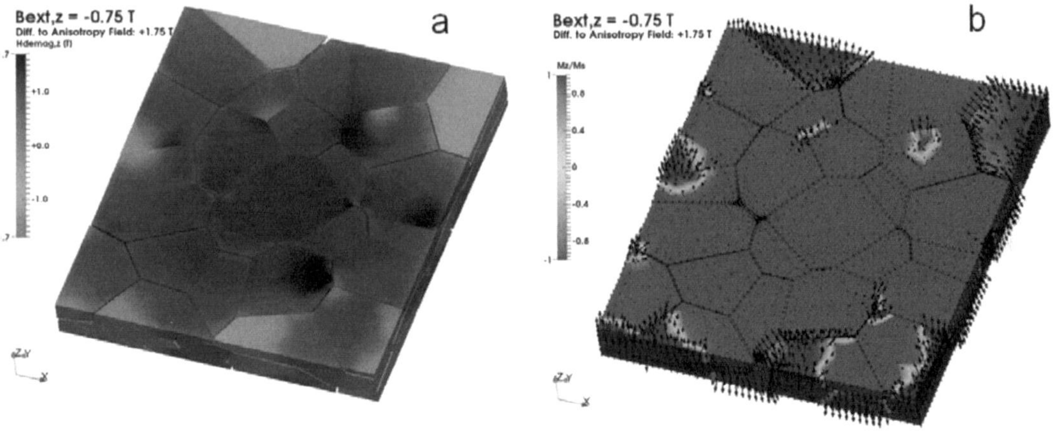

Fig. 3. Micromagnetic finite element simulation of the demagnetizing field (a) and magnetization (b) showing the reversal processes near grain boundaries and grain boundary junctions for $Pr_2Fe_{14}B$ assuming a reduced anisotropy of 1.65 MJ/m^3. The grain size is in the order of 100 - 200 nm.

Numerical micromagnetic simulations of the demagnetizing field (Fig. 3a) and the magnetization reversal (Fig. 3b) of a granular microstructure with a grain size of about 100 - 200 nm show that the regions with low anisotropy field and large demagnetization field near grain boundaries and grain boundary junctions are the centers for magnetization reversal. The material parameters are J_s = 1.65 T and K_1 = 1.64 MJ/m^3.

3. Magnets Based on Packed Co and Fe Nanorods

Besides the modeling of the coercivity of RE permanent magnet materials we also have performed numerical finite element micromagnetic simulations in order to study the possibility and determine the limits of shape anisotropy effects on packed Fe and Co nanorod structures as candidates for rare earth free permanent magnetic applications. Recent developments in nanoscience enabled the production of the nanostructured systems with dimensions approaching the order of few nanometers. We have studied nanorod structures on a regular grid and in an irregular packing. Both types of models describe structures which can be produced experimentally; regular grids of nanorods can be created by electro deposition in an alumina template [7] and irregularly packed structures can be obtained by compacting nanorods synthesized in a polyol process [8].

As result of our investigations on various nanorods with different diameter *D* and height *H* we observed an increasing contribution of inhomogeneous magnetization reversal processes for a diameter larger than 20 nm. Figure 4a shows the formation of end domains in Co and Fe nanopillars with D = 60 nm and H = 1000 nm. The following material parameters for hcp Co have been used: uniaxial anisotropy constant K_1 = 450 kJ/m³, saturation polarization J_s = 1.76 T and exchange constant A = 13 pJ/m. The easy axis of the magnetocrystalline anisotropy is parallel to the nanorod's long axis. For bcc iron we used cubic anisotropy constants K_1 = 45 kJ/m³ and K_2 = 1.5 kJ/m³, J_s = 2.15 T and A = 25 pJ/m. According to the inhomogeneous magnetization reversal the calculated coercive field is remarkable lower than the theoretical maximum values for Co ($\mu_0 H_A$ = 0.64 T) and Fe ($\mu_0 H_A$ = 0.05 T). Both, the magnetocrystalline anisotropy together with the shape anisotropy determine the theoretical coercive field lead for a perfect rotational ellipsoid [2]:

$$H_c = H_n = \frac{2K_1}{J_s} + (N_\perp - N_{//})\frac{J_s}{\mu_0} \quad \text{for } K_1 > 4K_2$$

$N_\perp$ and $N_{//}$ are the demagnetization factors for polarization perpendicular and parallel to the easy axis. The exact calculation of demagnetizing factors is no-trivial for non-ellipsoidal shapes. Fig. 4b shows the simulated hysteresis curves for a single Fe and Co nanorod with D = 20 nm and H = 100 nm. An aspect ratio of 1:5 is sufficient for increasing the coercive field due to the shape anisotropy contribution.

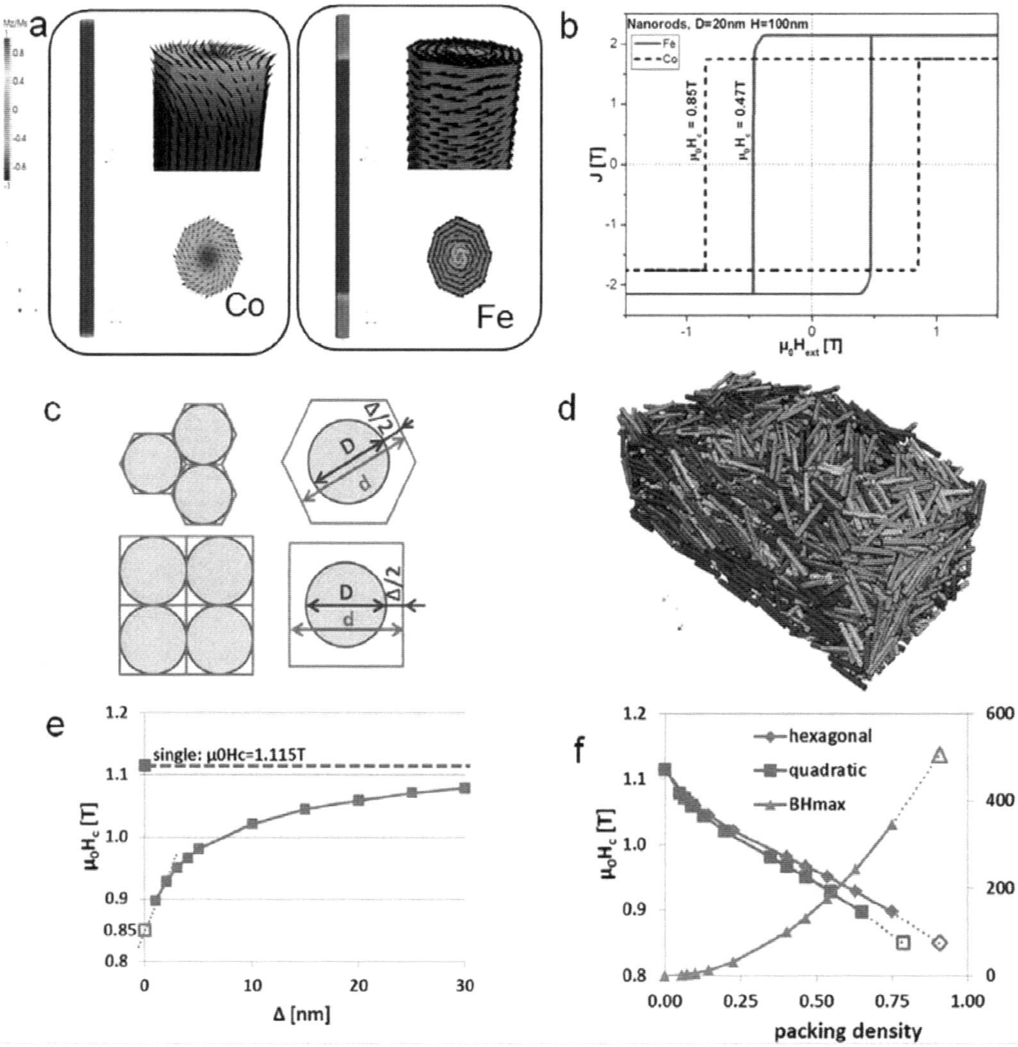

Fig. 4. Micromagetic modelling of magnetization reversal of hcp Co and bcc Fe nanorods with D = 60 nm and H = 1000 nm (a). D = 20nm, H = 100 nm (b). Assembly of periodic (c) and irregularly packed structures (d). Dependency of the coercivity on the surface-surface distance Δ (blue solid line) (e). Dependency of H_c and energy density product on packing density for periodic structures.

The packed structures have been generated by a packing algorithm based on gravity and collision forces and have a packing density of up to 58% (Fig. 4c). The algorithm places nanorods very sparsely in a box and compacts the nanorods using gravity and collision forces [9]. In addition, a torque which orients the nanorods parallel to the x axis is applied to each nanorod. This torque mimics the orientation of magnetic dipoles in a homogenous external field. For a periodic packing the nanorods are arranged either in a hexagonal or quadratic grid with size d (incycle diameter of the hexagon/square). This leaves a surface-to-surface distance $\Delta = d - D$ between the nanorods (Fig. 4d). The coercivity of multiple nanorods is dominated by the surface-surface distance Δ and not by the overall packing (Fig. 4e). Fig. 4f plots the coercivity values over the packing density of a regular grid of nanorods with the same surface-surface distance Δ. The simulations on the regular hexagonal or quadradic grid of nanorods show that energy density products $(BH)_{max}$ of up to 200 kJ/m³ can be reached with a packing density of about 55%, but the calculations on irregularly packed structures exhibit only energy density products of up to 85 kJ/m³. The discrepancy can be explained by the misalignment of nanorods which reduces both coercive field and remanence of the structure.

In addition to this, we also studied the increase of coercivity of capped Fe nanorods with an antiferromagnetic layer. The antiferromagnetic caps on Fe nanorods suppress the formation of nucleation centers at the tips and increase the coercivity of the nanorod by 11% in the case of asymmetric hysteresis loops with hard caps (K_1, cap = 4.6 MJ/m³) and 25% in the case of symmetric hysteresis with softer caps (K_1, cap = 460 kJ/m³).

Acknowledgments
The financial support from the European Community's Seventh Framework Programme (FP7-NMP) under grant agreement no. 280670 (REFREEPERMAG) and no: 309729 (ROMEO) is acknowledged.

References

[1] O. Gutfleisch, M.A. Willard, E. Brück, C.H. Chen, S.G. Sankar, J.P. Liu, *Adv. Mater.*, **23**, 2011, 821.
[2] H. Kronmüller and M. Fähnle, *Micromagnetism and the microstructure of ferromagnetic solids*, Cambridge University Press, 2003.
[3] K. Schwarz, *J. Solid State Chem.* **176**, 2003, 319.
[4] K. Schwarz, P. Blaha, *Comp. Mat. Sci.* **28**, 2003, 259.
[5] P. Larson, I.I. Mazin, D.A. Papaconstantopoulos, *Phys. Rev. B* **67**, 2003, 214405.
[6] A. Asali, P. Toson, P. Blaha, J. Fidler, *IEEE Trans. Magn.* 2014 (in press).
[7] L.G. Vivas, Yu.P. Ivanov, D.G. Trabada, M.P. Proenca, O. Chubykalo-Fesenko and M. Vázquez, *Nanotechnology* **24**, 2013, 105703.
[8] K.A. Atmane, F. Zighem, Y. Soumare, M. Ibrahim, R. Boubekri, T. Maurer, J. Margueritat, J.Y. Piquemal, F. Ott, G. Chaboussant, F. Schoenstein, N. Jouini and G. Viau, *J. Solid State Chem.* **197**, 2013, 297.
[9] E. Coumans, Bullet Physics Library (Online). http://www.bulletphysics.com/

Hard Magnet Coercivity

S. BANCE[1], G. CIUTA[2,3], T. SHOJI[4], T. GAO[3], G. HRKAC[5], M. YANO[4], A. MANABE[4], N.M. DEMPSEY[2,3], T. SCHREFL[1,6], D. GIVORD[2,3]

[1] Dep. of Technology, St Pölten University of Applied Sciences, Austria
[2] Univ. Grenoble Alpes, Inst NEEL, F-38042 Grenoble, France
[3] CNRS, Inst NEEL, F-38042 Grenoble, France
[4] Toyota Motor Corp., Toyota City, Japan
[5] CEMPS, University of Exeter, Exeter, UK
[6] Center for Integrated Sensor Systems, Danube University Krems, Austria

Abstract: *Based on a critical analysis of the experimental coercive properties, general considerations on the reversal mechanisms in RFeB magnets are recalled. By plotting together the experimental parameters obtained in various magnets, common features of the reversal processes are demonstrated. Modeling provides an almost quantitative description of coercivity in these materials and permits connecting the defect characteristic properties to reversal mechanisms.*

Keywords: *hard magnets, coercivity, global model, micromagnetic modeling*

Address: Dominique Givord, Institut Néel, CNRS/UJF, BP166 38042 Grenoble-cedex 9 France, +33476881090
E-mail: dominique.givord@neel.cnrs.fr

1. Introduction

The understanding of coercive phenomena is one of the most challenging aspects of the study of hard magnetic materials [1,2]. As well known, the reversal process of reference is coherent rotation, as described by the Stoner-Wohlfarth model and the associated coercive field, H_c, is equal to the anisotropy field, H_A [3]. The real coercive field is significantly smaller than the anisotropy field and this is ascribed to the influence of defects. The reversal process involves the formation of transitory heterogeneous magnetic states. Schematically, these can be listed as: nucleation of a region of non-saturated magnetization (with respect to the initial magnetic state), propagation/expansion and (possibly) pinning [2]. The study of reversal processes aims at identifying the one that is critical, i.e. governs full reversal within the individual objects (grains) from which the magnet is made. Reversal phenomena are not accessible to direct experimental observation and their analyses rely on indirect measurements. These are the temperature dependence of the coercive field, the angular dependence of the coercive field and the temperature dependence of the activation volume. In the first sections of this paper, the conclusions that can be drawn from such measurements are discussed. This part of the manuscript is not original but it is necessary to understand the significance of the second part, in which common experimental features of the reversal mechanisms are revealed and the results of numerical modeling are presented. Modeling provides an almost quantitative description of coercivity and permits connecting the defect characteristic properties to reversal mechanisms.

2. Physical Significance of the Temperature Dependence of the Coercive Field

In the analysis of coercivity, it is common to compare the temperature dependence of the coercive field to that of intrinsic physical parameters characterizing the hard magnetic phase. On purely phenomenological grounds, Kools introduced the expression [4] :

$$\mu_0 H_c = \alpha_m \mu_0 H_A - \mu_0 H_D, \qquad (1a)$$

where H_A is the hard phase anisotropy field and $H_D = -N_{eff} M_s$ is the demagnetizing field (M_s is the spontaneous magnetization), α_m and N_{eff} are adjustable parameters. The evaluation of the strength of the demagnetizing field (i.e. of the parameters N_{eff}) in such hard magnetic materials is a difficult task [1]. Due to the heterogeneous character of the magnetic configuration, the divergence of the magnetization is not zero. In addition to the usual surface charges, volume charges contribute to the demagnetizing field and their value depend on the reversal processes themselves. However, the demagnetizing field is not expected to modify qualitatively the nature of the reversal mechanisms. Since the focus of the present paper is on the discussion of such mechanisms, N_{eff} is considered here as a purely phenomenological parameter. Expression (1a) can be re-written as:

$$\mu_0 H_T = \alpha_m \mu_0 H_A, \qquad (1b)$$

where $\mu_0 H_T = \mu_0 H_c - \mu_0 H_D$ is the total field determining reversal, obtained by subtracting H_D to the experimental coercive field H_c ($|H_T| > |H_c|$).

Within the so-called micromagnetic model, developed by Kronmüller and co-workers [1,6], a planar defect is assumed. The possible reversal mechanisms are coherent rotation-like or domain-wall de-pinning. The nature of the dominant mechanism may be derived from the value of the parameter α_m in expressions (1). In the case of the NdFeB magnets, its value is about $1/3$. Within the present model, this is incompatible with pinning. This led to conclude that the reversal process is coherent rotation-like [1,5].

The other expression to which the temperature dependence of the field H_T may be compared is obtained within the so-called global model [6, 7]. This model considers that the various possible reversal mechanisms, except coherent rotation, involve the formation of a heterogeneous magnetic configuration. This must be somehow similar to a domain wall, the magnetic configuration of minimum energy that incorporates magnetization reversal. This gives:

$$\mu_0 H_T = \alpha_G \frac{\gamma}{v^{1/3} M_s} \qquad (2)$$

where γ is the domain wall energy within the hard phase and v, the activation volume, an experimental parameter. Expression (2) is expected to account for the changes in both the domain wall energy and the domain wall surface area that may occur during reversal, i.e. it may represent the various processes described in the introduction.

The present discussion suggests that the nature of the reversal mechanisms may be identified, at least partially, from the analysis of the temperature dependence of the coercive field, More precisely, the applicability of expression (2) and not that of expression (1) should exclude that reversal occurs by coherent rotation. However, it turns out that this argument does not apply. Both expressions (1) and (2) generally provide satisfactory account for the experimental temperature dependence of H_c [2, 8]. This is due to the fact that the experimental value of $v^{1/3}$ is approximately proportional to the domain wall width, δ (see next section) [2]. Most hard magnetic materials crystallize within a uniaxial structure for which the magnetocrystalline anisotropy is generally dominated by second-order terms. In this case, the domain wall thickness $\delta = \pi\sqrt{A/K}$ and $\gamma = 4\sqrt{AK}$, leading to $\gamma/v^{1/3} \sim \gamma/\delta \sim K$ (A is the exchange constant and K the second order magnetocrystalline anisotropy coefficient). Since relations (1) and (2) are formally equivalent, they cannot be used to distinguish between reversal mechanisms.

However, this argument does not apply to NdFeB magnets below typically 200 K. In this temperature range, higher order anisotropy terms become important in $Nd_2Fe_{14}B$, leading to the spin reorientation that takes place at 135 K. It is then found that the global model tends to provide better account for the temperature dependence of H_c than the micromagnetic model (see [2]).

At the end of this section, it should be stressed that the applicability of both expressions (1) and (2) implies that the coercive field H_c is proportional to some intrinsic parameters characterizing the hard magnetic phase. Assuming that reversal occurs by coherent rotation, then, $H_c << H_A$ implies that $H_{A'} << H_A$, whereby H_A' is the anisotropy field in the defect region. From one material to another, $H_A(T)$ may vary considerably, and it is puzzling that $H_{A'}$ should remain proportional to H_A. Amongst others, this experimental observation led us to conclude that reversal at H_c, is governed by the passage/expansion of a pre-formed nucleus [7].

3. Temperature Dependence of the Activation Volume

The concept of the activation volume is intrinsically linked to that of coercivity [6, 9-11]. Magnetization reversal occurs when the difference between the minimum energy configuration and the saddle point energy configuration can be provided by thermal activation. The characteristic time for magnetic measurements is of the order of 1s, leading to the classical thermal energy value of $25k_BT$. Experimentally, the activation volume is obtained by comparing the field dependence and the time dependence of the magnetization. At "low temperature" (up to room temperature for NdFeB magnets), v remains approximately proportional to δ^3 [2,11], i.e. the activation volume magnetic properties are relatively close to the main phase properties, in agreement with previous section. At higher temperature, the activation volume increases much faster with T than δ^3. This suggests that the anisotropy in the activation volume decreases faster with T than its main phase value. The anisotropy is approximately proportional to the magnetization at some power (anisotropy coefficients of order l should vary as $M_s^{l(l+1)/2}$ according to the Akulov law), suggesting that the magnetization in the activation volume decreases faster than bulk magnetization with increasing temperature. Numerical modeling (see below) reveals that defects that are less than 1 nm thick, already affect considerably the value of the coercive field. The high temperature dependence of v may thus be tentatively related to the temperature dependence of the magnetization being higher at the surface than in the bulk.

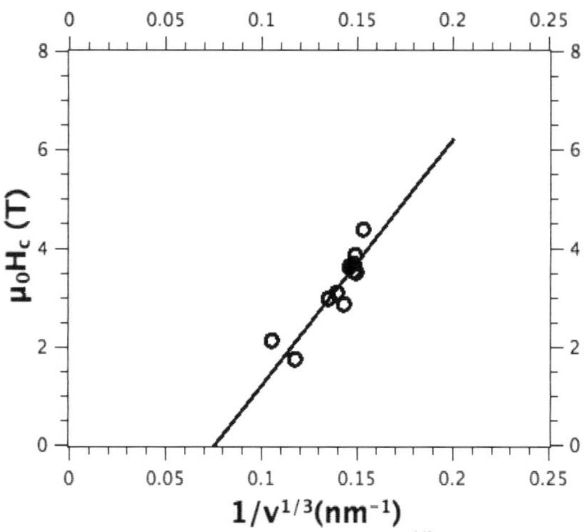

Fig. 1. Coercive field, μ_0H_c versus $1/v^{1/3}$ (v = activation volume) for a series of RFeB magnets.

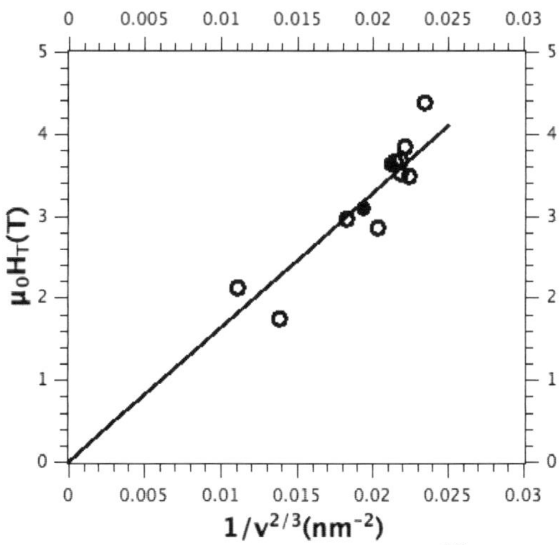

Fig. 2. Coercive field, μ_0H_c, versus $1/v^{2/3}$ (v is the activation volume) (same samples as Fig. 1). The line is a fit to the data, with slope 160 T/nm^2.

4. Angular Dependence of the Coercive Field

The angular dependence of the coercive field has been discussed in previous publications [12-14]. It is closer to Kondorsky's $1/\cos\theta$ law than to Stoner-Wohlfarth's law. This is another result suggesting that magnetization reversal does not occur by coherent rotation but involves the formation of a domain wall-like configuration, so that low coercive field can be reconciled with an anisotropy in the activation volume of the same order as main phase anisotropy.

5. Comparing the Room Temperature Coercivity in Various NdFeB Magnets

At this stage, the activation volume and the coefficient α_G are parameters that permit describing the temperature dependence of coercivity, but to which no special physical significance is attached. To go beyond this, the properties of different samples and the associated parameter values should be compared. Equation (2) suggests plotting H_T as a function of $1/v^{1/3}$. This is done in Fig 1 for various RFeB magnets. H_T increases as the size of the activation volume decreases, as expected. However, the approximate linear variation seen in Fig. 1, does not extrapolate to the origin of the coordinates, as it would do for constant α_G. The slope of the variation, higher than expected, tells us that the parameter α_G increases with the coercive field.

Coming back to expression (2), we will now assume that the magnetocrystalline anisotropy is determined by second order terms only. The domain wall energy and the domain wall width in v, are given by $\gamma' = 4\sqrt{A'K'}$ and $\delta' = \pi\sqrt{A'/K'}$ where A' is the exchange constant in the activation volume. Assuming the activation volume proportional to δ'^3 leads to [7]:

$$\mu_0 H_T = \alpha'_G \frac{4\pi A}{v^{2/3} M_s} \quad (3)$$

Expression (3) presents a fundamental difference with expression (2) above. No a priori assumption on the value of the anisotropy in the activation volume is made. The exchange constant, A', is assumed proportional to the exchange constant, A, within the hard phase. This is a much less stringent hypothesis than the usual assumption K' proportional to K, since anisotropy is by far more sensitive to small structural defects than exchange interactions are.

Expression (3) may account for $H_c(T)$ in ferrite and Pr-Fe-B magnets [7]. It cannot be used however to describe $H_c(T)$ in NdFeB magnets for which a spin-reorientation occurs at 135 K, i.e. anisotropy constants of higher orders are not negligible and even larger than the second order anisotropy constant in a certain temperature range. However, at room temperature, relation (3) should apply. The field $\mu_0 H_T$ is plotted as a function of $1/v^{2/3}$ in Fig. 2 for the same magnets as in Fig. 1. An approximate linear relationship is found and the corresponding line extrapolates to the origin of the coordinates. This shows that the coefficient α'_G has approximately the same value in all samples. The slope derived from figure 2 amounts to 160 T/nm^2. Using $A = 8\ 10^{-12}$ J/m and $\mu_0 M_s = 1.61$ T, gives $\alpha'_G = 2$.

The constancy of the parameter α'_G implies that the fundamental geometry of the reversal process remains essentially unchanged as the coercive field is varied within a factor of almost 3. Assuming $A'=A$, a simple expression for α_G, is obtained by comparing expressions (2) and (3) :

$$\alpha_G = \frac{\alpha'_G}{v^{1/3}}\delta = 2\frac{\delta}{v^{1/3}} \quad . \quad (4)$$

The increase of α_G with H_T (Fig. 1) is thus an illustration of the inverse dependence between H_T and v ([2,7]). The coefficient α_G given by expression (4) is

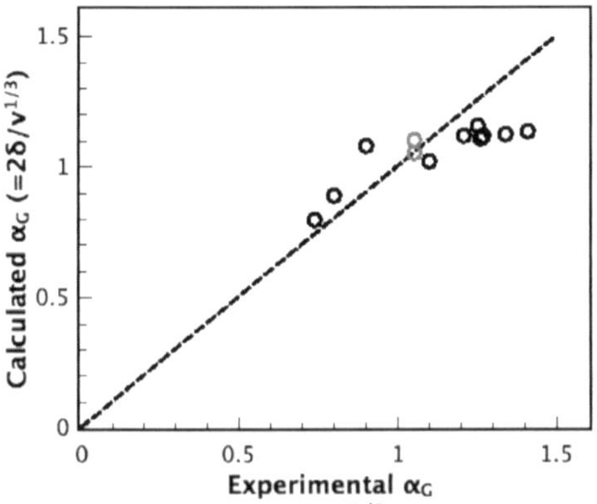

Fig. 3. Calculated α_G (= $2\delta/v^{1/3}$) compared to experimental α_G derived from the temperature dependence of the coercive field; δ is the $R_2Fe_{14}B$ domain wall width and v the activation volume.

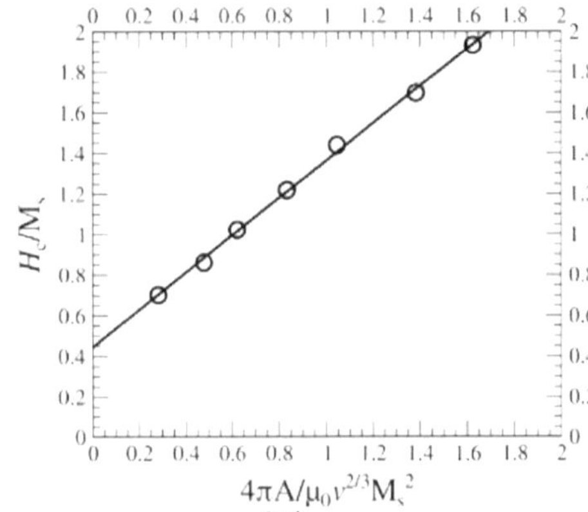

Fig. 4. H_c/M_s versus $\frac{4\pi A}{\mu_0 v^{2/3} M_S^2}$ derived from numerical modeling, including thermal activation, for $Nd_2Fe_{14}B$ with a defect thickness of 0.8 nm.

plotted in Figure 3 as a function of the experimental α_G, derived from the analysis of the temperature dependence of H_c. A striking correspondence is found between both coefficients, despite the fact that they were derived using two different methods and that the calculation of α_G, involves a unique adjustable parameter, α'_G of which value is the same for all samples. These results demonstrate the global consistency of the present analysis.

6. Numerical modeling

The analysis described in the above section provides a consistent description of coercivity, within a certain physical representation of the reversal process. In the present section, the reversal processes are examined in the framework of recent numerical modelling studies [15]. The polyhedral hard magnetic grains were approximated by simple cubes with a defect shell of zero anisotropy. The magnetization reversal process was computed numerically by solving the equation of motion for the magnetization, with temperature-dependent intrinsic material paramaters. As opposed to linearized micromagnetic models, both the linear and non-linear nature of the equations were taken into account. It was found that magnetization reversal begins at a corner of the cube, where increased demagnetizing field causes localized curling of the magnetization.

As expected, in the absence of any defect, the coercive field ($\mu_0 H_c \sim 5.8\ T$) approaches the value for coherent rotation ($H_c = H_A$), once the demagnetizing field contribution is considered ($\mu_0 H_D \sim \mu_0 M_s \sim 1.6T$). However, as noted above, even in this case, reversal does not occur by coherent rotation. Due to the heterogeneous character of the demagnetizing field, a magnetic configuration forms that appears to resemble a domain wall. It is generally accepted that the existence of defects is almost unavoidable, of which presence might actually be intrinsic to the material surface [17]. The existence of defects is simply taken into account by assuming the presence of a zero anisotropy layer at the grain surface. As the thickness of the defect layer, t, is increased up to 2 nm, the 300 K coercive field decreases from 5.8 T to 1.6 T. Most importantly, as soon as the defect thickness exceeds 0.5 nm, a stable non-uniform magnetic configuration forms under a finite negative applied magnetic field, H_n, which can be associated to the usual "nucleation field" of micromagnetics equation. The field strength needs to be further increased for full reversal to occur, at $H_c > H_n$. For t=1.2 nm, the 300 K coercive field reaches values close to experimental values.

To account for thermal activation, the minimum energy path during reversal is calculated using the nudged elastic band method [18] The magnetic configuration of minimum energy at $H=H_c$ is $25k_BT$ lower than the energy of the magnetic configuration at the saddle point. The activation volume can then be calculated from the difference in magnetization between the saddle point and the local minimum.

We calculated the thermally-activated coercivity and associated activation volumes for the same cube model with a defect thickness of t = 0.8 nm, and material properties for $Nd_2Fe_{14}B$ ranging from T = 200 K to T = 500 K. Thermal activation reduced the coercivity value by between 31 and 47 percent, increasing with higher temperature. The associated activation volume at 200 K amounts to around 140 nm^3, to be compared to about 2200 nm^3 at 500 K. From the calculated temperature dependence of the coercive field, the calculated ratio H_c/M_s is plotted in Figure 4 as a function of $4\pi A/\mu_0 v^{2/3} M_S^2$, with the results following a linear trend [19]. The derived slope is ≈1, to be compared to α'_G = 2 derived from Fig. 2. Despite the fact that the model appears to describe most experimental observations, this indicates that further model refining is needed.

References

[1] H. Kronmüller, *Phys. Status Solidi*, 1987, B144, 385-396.
[2] D.Givord, M.F. Rossignol, *Coercivity*, in: J.M.D. Coey (Ed.), *Rare-Earth Iron Permanent Magnets*, 1996, Clarendon Press, Oxford, 219.
[3] E.C. Stoner, E.P. Wohlfarth, *Philos. Trans. Roy. Soc. London*, 1948, 240A, 599-642.
[4] F. Kools, *J. Phys.*, 1985, C6, 46-48.
[5] H. Kronmüller, K.-D. Durst, M. Sagawa, J. *Magn. Magn. Mater.*, 1988, 74, 291-302.
[6] D. Givord, P. Tenaud, T. Viadieu, *IEEE Trans. Magn.*, 1988, 24, 1921- 1923.
[7] D. Givord, M.F. Rossignol, V.M.T.S. Barthem, *J. Magn. Magn. Mater.*, 2003, 258–259, 1-5.
[8] X.C. Kou, H. Kronmüller, D. Givord, M.F. Rossignol, *Phys. Rev. B*, 1994, 50, 3849-3860.
[9] E.P. Wohlfarth, *J. Phys.*, 1984, F14, L155.
[10] P. Gaunt, *J. Appl. Phys.*, 1986, 59, 4129-4132.
[11] D. Givord, A. Liénard, P. Tenaud, T. Viadieu, *J. Magn. Magn. Mater.*, 1987, 67, L281-L285.
[12] H. Kronmüller, K.D. Durst, G. Martinek, *J. Magn. Magn. Mater.*, 1987, 69, 149-157.
[13] D. Givord, P. Tenaud, T. Viadieu, *J. Magn. Magn. Mater.*, 1988, 72, 247-252.
[14] D. Elbaz, D. Givord, S. Hirosawa, F.P. Missell, M.F. Rossignol, V. Vilas-Boas, *J. Appl. Phys.*, 1991, 69, 5492-5494.
[15] S. Bance, H. Oezelt, T. Schrefl, G. Ciuta, N. M. Dempsey, D. Givord, M. Winklhofer, G. Hrkac, G. Zimanyi, O. Gutfleisch, T. G. Woodcock, T. Shoji, M. Yano, A. Kato, A. Manabe, *Appl.Phys. Lett.* 2014, 104, 182408.
[16] R. Dittrich, T. Schrefl, T., D. Suess, W. Scholz, H. Forster, H., & J. Fidler, *J. Magn. Magn. Mater.*, 2002, 250, 12-19.
[17] G. Hrkac, T. Woodcock, C. Freeman, A. Gontacharov, J. Dean, T. Schrefl, O. Gutfleisch, *Appl. Phys.Lett.*, 2010, 97, 232511.
[18] T. Schrefl, *et al.* in: *Kronmüller & Parkin Handbook of Magnetism and Advanced Materials*, ed, Wiley & Sons, 2007.
[19] S. Bance, *et al.*, unpublished.

Micromagnetics for the Coercivity of Nanocomposite Permanent Magnets

J. FISCHBACHER[1], S. BANCE[1], M. GUSENBAUER[1], A. KOVACS[1], H. OEZELT[1], F. REICHEL[1], T. SCHREFL[1,2]
[1]St. Poelten University of Applied Sciences, 3100 St. Poelten, Austria
[2]Center for Integrated Sensor Systems, Danube University Krems, Austria

Abstract: *Exchange spring permanent magnets may be a route towards high energy product permanent magnets with low rare-earth content. In composite magnets soft magnetic phases act as nucleation sites for magnetization reversal. We use micromagnetic simulations in order to understand the role of the size and shape of the soft inclusions on the magnetization reversal. We compare the switching field of magnetically soft spheroids, cuboids and cylinders embedded in a hard magnetic matrix. Whereas there is only little difference in the switching field for enclosed spherical or cubical soft shapes, prolate inclusions enhance the stability of the magnet.*

Keywords: *two phase nanocomposite magnets; micromagnetics simulations*

Address: Johann Fischbacher, Industrial Simulation, St. Poelten University of Applied Sciences, Matthias Corvinus-Strasse 15, 3100 St. Poelten, Austria, Tel: +43 2742 313 228 – 638, Fax: +43 2742 313 228 – 609, E-mail: johann.fischbacher@fhstp.ac.at

Introduction

Micromagnetics is a continuum theory that describes magnetization processes on a length scale ranging from about a nanometer to micrometers. Using the finite element method in order to discretize the micromagnetic equations we can compute the coercive field of a permanent magnet depending on its physical and chemical structure. Especially simple geometrical models are useful, in order to understand and quantify the different factors that determine the coercive field of a composite magnet. The theory of exchange spring permanent magnets was discussed by Kneller [1], Skomski [2], and Schrefl [3]. Skomski and co-workers [4] compared the nucleation field of different hard-soft geometries. Spheres were reported to show a higher nucleation field as compared to cylinders or layered structures. In this work we apply numerical micromagnetics, in order to evaluate hard-soft shapes and their influence on magnetization reversal. In particular we are interested in the effect of shape and size of a single soft inclusion in a hard magnetic matrix. The influence of magnetostatic interactions between several soft inclusions in a hard matrix is discussed in [5].

Method

We use a finite element micromagnetic software for the solution of the Landau-Lifshitz Gilbert equation [6]. First the external field H_e is kept zero for 10 ns, in order to obtain a remanent magnetic state. Then H_e is applied at a rate of -80 mT/ns up to -8 T. The field is applied at an angle of 0.5 degrees with respect to the easy axis of the hard magnetic material. The Gilbert damping constant is one. We use a soft phase (α-Fe) with a magnetic polarization $J_s = 2.15$ T and an exchange constant $A = 21$ pJ/m. As magnetically hard phase we use $Nd_2Fe_{14}B$ with uniaxial anisotropy constant $K_1 = 4.9$ MJ/m³, $J_s = 1.61$ T and $A = 8$ pJ/m. A single α-Fe spheroid, cuboid or cylinder is embedded into a $Nd_2Fe_{14}B$ spherical or ellipsoidal shell. The demagnetizing field of a uniformly magnetized sphere or ellipsoid is uniform. Therefore we avoid any reduction of the coercive field by strong demagnetizing fields near corners or edges of the macroscopic sample [7]. Still the macroscopic demagnetizing field of the shell creates an additional field that acts on the soft inclusions. Thus when comparing the switching field of different soft shapes we add the macroscopic demagnetizing field $-NM$ of the sample to correct the loop. N is the demagnetizing factor of the macroscopic shape and M the magnetization. We define the switching field, H_{sw}, as the critical field when the hard phase switches irreversibly. For fair comparison, the volume of the differently shaped inclusions is kept the same and placed inside the same shell. For samples varying in size the volume ratio between α-Fe and $Nd_2Fe_{14}B$ is kept constant.

Results

We start with investigating the influence of the particle shape on the magnetization of an isolated $Nd_2Fe_{14}B$ particle. Fig. 1 shows that the non-uniform demagnetizing fields reduce the coercive field of a cube with respect to the coercive field of a sphere. But embedded into a hard magnetic matrix, soft spheres and soft cubes with equal volume, V_s, yield almost the

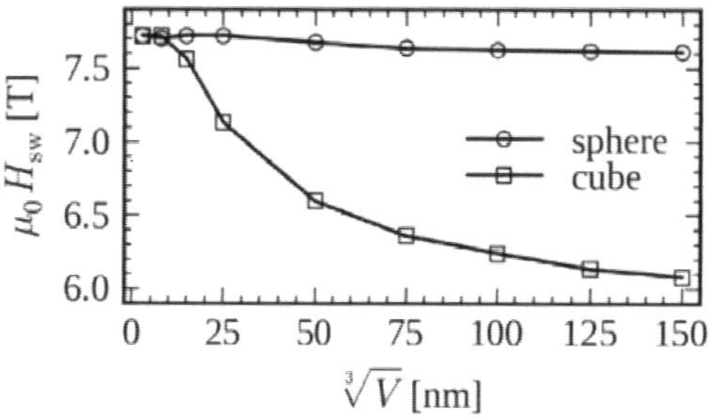

Fig. 1. Switching field of $Nd_2Fe_{14}B$ cubes and spheres with volume V.

same switching field. Increasing the share of magnetically hard material increases the switching field only for small inclusions with an edge length or diameter less than 10 nm to 12 nm, respectively (Fig. 2). Even for a small 4x4x4 nm³ inclusion, H_{sw} is reduced by 2 T compared to H_{sw} of a pure $Nd_2Fe_{14}B$ sphere.

In order to study the influence of reduced exchange coupling between the magnetically hard matrix and the soft magnetic inclusion, we introduce a 1 nm thick interlayer. The volume of the shell plus interlayer is seven times the volume of the soft body, V_s. The material constants of the interlayer are adjusted according to $A_i = fA_{hard}$, $J_{s,i} = J_{s,hard}(A_i/A_{hard})^{1/2}$, and $K_{1,i} = K_{1,hard}(J_{s,i}/J_{s,hard})^3$, whereby the subscript 'hard' refers to the $Nd_2Fe_{14}B$ constants. Fig. 3 shows the soft phase reversal field (open markers) and the hard phase switching field (filled markers). Here we define the soft phase reversal field as the critical field at which the magnetic polarization reaches $0.9J_s$.

With full coupling (square markers) we observe the transition from a one-step magnetization reversal for small inclusions (V_s < 10x10x10 nm³) to a two-step reversal for larger embeddings. The difference between the soft phase reversal field and the hard phase switching field is less than 0.6 T shrinking with the size of the soft body. With reduced exchange coupling the switching fields of the two phases are

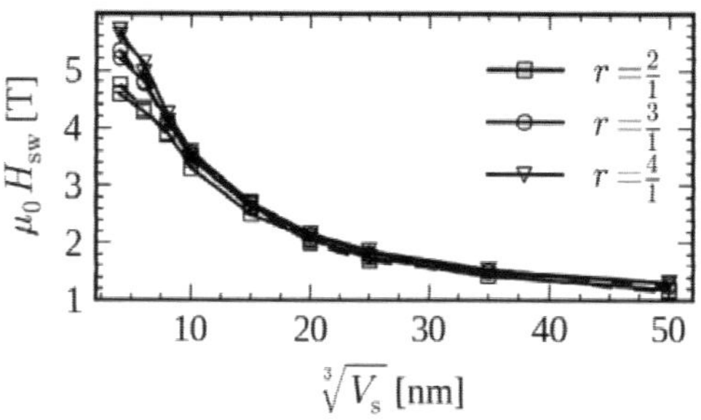

Fig. 2. Switching field of α-Fe cubes (solid line) and spheres (dashed line) with equal volume V_s in a $Nd_2Fe_{14}B$ spherical shell. r denotes the ratio of hard to soft magnetic volume.

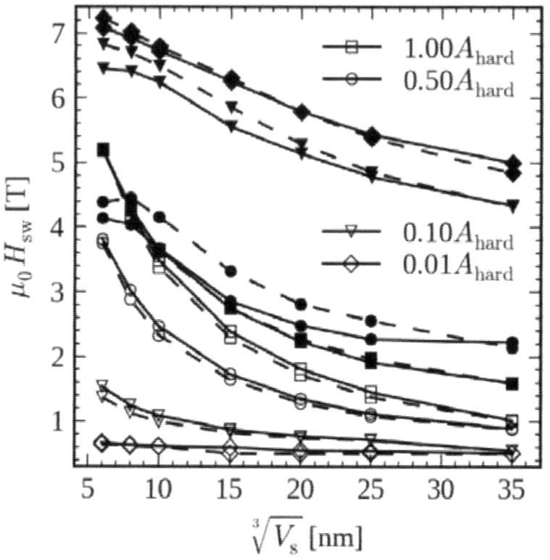

Fig. 3. α-Fe cubes (solid line) and spheres (dashed line) enclosed by a 1 nm interlayer in a $Nd_2Fe_{14}B$ spherical matrix. The interlayer exchange constant $A_i=fA_{hard}$ is reduced to decouple inclusion and shell. Open markers refer to the soft phase reversal field and filled markers to the hard phase switching field.

clearly distinct. The difference in H_{sw} increases to about 1.5 T when the coupling is reduced by $f = 0.5$. For f = 0.01 the soft phase reversal field approaches for the macroscopic demagnetizing field *NM* whereas the hard phase reverses at switching fields between 5 T and 7.2 T depending on the size of the inclusion. The shape of the inclusion has only little influence on the reversal of the soft phase. But samples with a spherical inclusion show a more stable hard phase when coupling is reduced.

In [8] it has been reported that the nucleation field can be enhanced significantly by transforming a soft magnetic sphere to an elongated shape such as a cylinder or a prolate spheroid but H_c plateaus for aspect ratios larger than 5. Fig. 4 shows the switching field for such prolate soft inclusions inside a $Nd_2Fe_{14}B$ prolate spheroid. The shell's minor axis is twice the inclusion diameter. The major axis is adjusted to fit the elongated inclusions keeping the ratio of magnetically hard to soft material at 4:1. We compare two orientations. In the upper figure of Fig. 4 we choose the long axis of the soft inclusion to be perpendicular to the easy axis of the hard material and the applied external field. We refer to this orientation with 'x'. The figure below deals with a configuration with the long axis parallel to the easy axis and external field ('z'). In general, an ellipsoidal shaped inclusion stabilizes the magnet better than a cylinder or cuboid. With raising diameter the differences diminish. Unlike the single phase results, elongating the soft magnetic inclusions still decreases the switching field but it plateaus again for higher aspect ratios. For small diameters, an inclusion aligned parallel to the easy axis results in a more stable

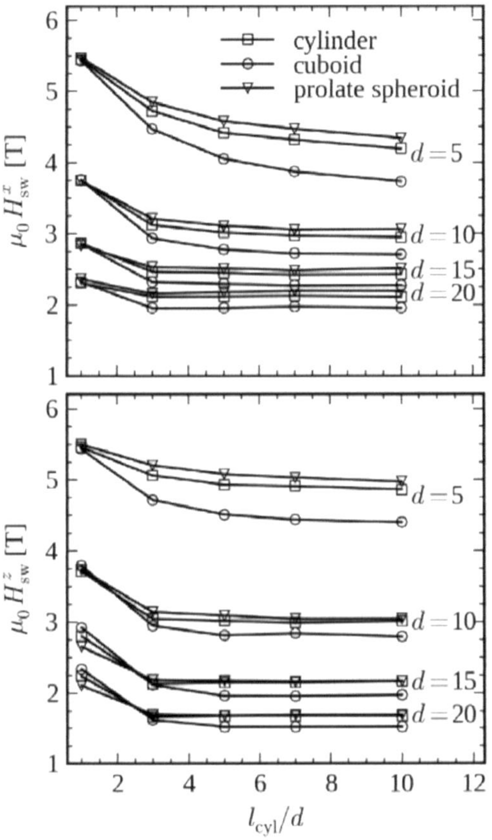

Fig. 4. Switching field of prolate α-Fe inclusions in an ellipsoidal hard magnetic shell. The volume of the soft phase is equal to the volume of a cylinder with diameter d and length l_{cyl}. The diameter d is common for all three embeddings but the length is adjusted to comply with the volume constraint. The volume ratio of shell to inclusion is 4:1. 'x' and 'z' in the axes labels refer to an orientation of the inclusions' long axis perpendicular or parallel to the the easy axis of the hard phase, respectively.

magnet than a configuration with an inclusion perpendicular to the easy axis. The difference in the switching field is 0.6 T shrinking with lower aspect ratios l_{cyl}/d. However, for diameters larger than 10 nm a soft phase in 'x'-orientation results in a 0.2-0.5 T higher switching field. If we compare H_{sw} of similar inclusion volumes in Figures 2 and 4 we notice significantly higher switching fields for prolate inclusions than for cubes or spheres. (Cylinder: d = 10 nm, l_{cyl} = 100 nm; cube 20x20x20 nm³).

Conclusions

For small soft magnetic inclusions within a hard magnetic matrix, the shape of the soft inclusions was found to contribute to the coercive field with prolate spheroids showing the highest switching field. If lateral extension of the soft inclusion was greater than 10 nm the shape effect was suppressed. For elongated soft inclusions such as cylinders or prolate spheroids it is preferable to align them parallel to the easy axis if the diameter is smaller than 10 nm. For wider soft inclusions an orientation perpendicular to the easy axis leads to better stability.

References

[1] E. Kneller, R. Hawig, IEEE Trans. Magn. 27, 1991, 3588.
[2] R. Skomski, J. M. D. Coey, Phys. Rev. B 48, 1993, 15812.
[3] T. Schrefl, H. Kronmüller, J. Fidler, J. Magn. Magn. Mater. 127, 1993, L273.
[4] R. Skomski, P. Manchanda, P. Kumar, B. Balamurugan, A. Kashyap, D. J. Sellmyer, IEEE Trans. Magn. 49, 2013, 3515.
[5] J. Fischbacher, S. Bance, L. Exl, M. Gusenbauer, H. Oezelt, F. Reichel, T. Schrefl, Eur. Phys. J. B 86, 2013, 100.
[6] T. Schrefl, G. Hrkac, S. Bance, D. Suess, O. Ertl, and J. Fidler. "Numerical Methods in Micromagnetics (Finite Element Method)." in Handbook of Magnetism and Advanced Magnetic Materials. Helmut Kronmüller, Stuart Parkin (Eds), John Wiley & Sons, Ltd., 2007.
[7] H. F. Schmidts, H. Kronmüller, J. Magn. Magn. Mater. 94, 1991, 220–234.
[8] S. Bance, J. Fischbacher, T. Schrefl, I. Zins, G. Rieger, C. Cassignol, J. Magn. Magn. Mater. 363, 2014, 121-124.

Nanocrystalline MnBi with High Degree of Texture and Coercivity

JINBO YANG[1,2], Y.B. YANG[1], H. ZHAO[1], Y.C. YANG[1]
[1]State Key Laboratory for Mesoscopic Physics, School of Physics, Peking University, Beijing, China
[2]Collaborative Innovation Center of Quantum Matter, Beijing, China

Abstract: *Magnetically hard and textured nanocrystalline MnBi has been prepared by melt spinning and subsequently low temperature annealing. The size of MnBi grains is about 20-30 nm, which is much smaller than the size of single domain (250 nm). Well-shaped hexagonal MnBi grains are observed in the samples. These grains are crystallographically textured with their c-axes tending to be parallel due to the diffusion growth process. This texture is critical for obtaining anisotropic magnetic powders. Coercivity* $_iH_c$ *of nanocrystalline MnBi can be greatly improved by further grinding. The coercivity of MnBi shows a positive temperature coefficient and it reaches a maximum of 2.5 T at 540 K before decreasing to 1.8 T at 610 K. The magnetization reversal mechanism for the 7-hours-ground sample is controlled by coherent rotation in the single domain grains. The temperature dependence of the coercivity is related to that of the magnetocrystalline anisotropy. The nanocrystalline powders of MnBi show anisotropic characteristics with* M_r/M_s *ratio of about 93.4%. The maximum energy product* $(BH)_{max}$ *of the powders is about 9.0 MGOe at room temperature.*

Keywords: *MnBi; nanocrystalline; texture; magnetocrystalline anisotropy; permanent magnet; coercivity*

Address: Jinbo Yang, School of Physics, Peking University, Beijing, 100871, P. R. China, Tel: (86-10) 62753459, Fax: (86-10) 62761615, E-mail: jbyang@pku.edu.cn

1. Introduction

The intermetallic compound MnBi has been studied extensively because of its unusual magnetic properties. The high temperature phase (HTP) shows excellent magneto-optical properties, while the low temperature phase (LTP) with NiAs-type hexagonal crystal structure exhibits unique magnetic and structural properties. It is remarkable that the coercivity $_iH_c$ of the LTP has a positive temperature coefficient from 150 to 550 K, which is favourable for the high temperature applications [1-6]. Although MnBi is a very interesting compound, it is very difficult to prepare the single phase compound using conventional methods such as arc-melting, mechanical milling [7] and sintering [8] which is mainly due to that Mn tends to segregate from the Mn-Bi liquid below the peritectic temperature 719 K. So far, many methods have been tried to avoid the segregation. Guo et al. [9-11] have prepared high purity LTP MnBi using melt-spinning method, but the $_iH_c$ was only 0.2 T at room temperature (RT). Saha et al. [12] have used grinding method to increase the $_iH_c$, but the saturation magnetization decreased severely after grind due to the impurity phase. In this paper, nanocrystalline LTP MnBi with high performance were prepared. The effects of alloy compositions, quenching speeds and heat treatment conditions on the purity of final products and magnetic properties were systematically investigated. Nanocrystalline MnBi with high texture and coercivity was obtained. The formation of the texture and the mechanism of the coercivity were presented.

2. Experimental methods

Mn_xBi_{100-x} ($50 \leq x \leq 70$) ingots were prepared by arc-melting with high purity manganese (99.99%) and bismuth (99.99%). The ribbons of Mn_xBi_{100-x} were obtained by melt-spinning with speed of the wheel altered from 10 to 70 m/s. The ribbons were then annealed at different temperatures from 473 to 773 K [13]. The structure of the ribbons was studied by x-ray diffraction (XRD) and neutron diffraction at different temperatures [14]. Microstructure of MnBi ribbons were observed by scanning electron microscope (SEM) and transmission electron microscope (TEM). The ribbons were grinded into powders, mixed with epoxy resin and then aligned in a magnetic field of 1.5 T. Magnetic properties were measured using Superconductivity Quantum Interference Device (MPMS-7T platform).

3. Results and discussions

Different quenching speeds (10 - 65 m/s) were tried to prepare amorphous phase MnBi. The amorphous ribbons were obtained with a speed of 65 m/s, which was confirmed by their XRD patterns. In order to transfer amorphous MnBi into LTP MnBi without other phases, ribbons were annealed at different temperatures. As shown in Fig. 1, XRD investigations indicated that LTP MnBi started to form at 533 K, and single phase MnBi could be obtained in the temperature range of 533 to 593 K. Purity of LTP MnBi reduced if the amorphous ribbons were annealed at a temperature higher than 593 K. The ribbons annealed at 613 K and 653 K contain more

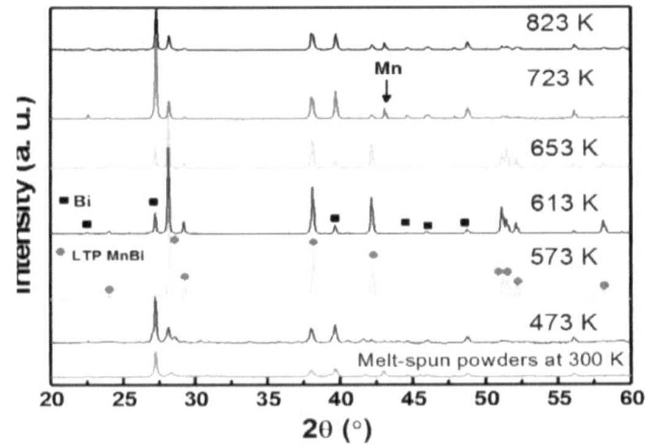

Fig. 1. XRD patterns of the $Mn_{55}Bi_{45}$ ribbons annealed at different temperatures.

nonmagnetic phases of Bi and Mn than those annealed at 573 K. This is due to the fact that Mn segregates from the Bi at a higher annealing temperature, which prevents the formation of LTP MnBi. The magnetization-versus-applied-magnetic-field curves of MnBi ribbons annealed at different temperatures were measured at RT. It was found that saturation magnetization (M_s) of ribbons also reduced at annealing temperature above 593 K, which was consistent with the purity of LTP MnBi.

Fig. 2 shows the XRD patterns of annealed Mn_xBi_{100-x} ($50 \leq x \leq 70$) melt-spun at 65 m/s. It can be seen from the patterns that high purity MnBi sample can be prepared for $x = 55$. A large amount of Bi phase appears when Mn content is reduced to $x \leq 53$, while Mn and a small amount of MnO_2 phases appear for the $x \geq 57$ sample. Thus, the excess Mn in the composition is very important to get the high-purity MnBi since a large amount of Mn may be volatilized during arc-melting and melt-spinning processes. Therefore, the amount of Mn should be carefully controlled to compensate the loss of Mn and avoid the excess of Mn existed in finally annealed ribbons.

The XRD pattern of $Mn_{55}Bi_{45}$ alloy was refined with Rietveld method [15] using the FULLPROF software.

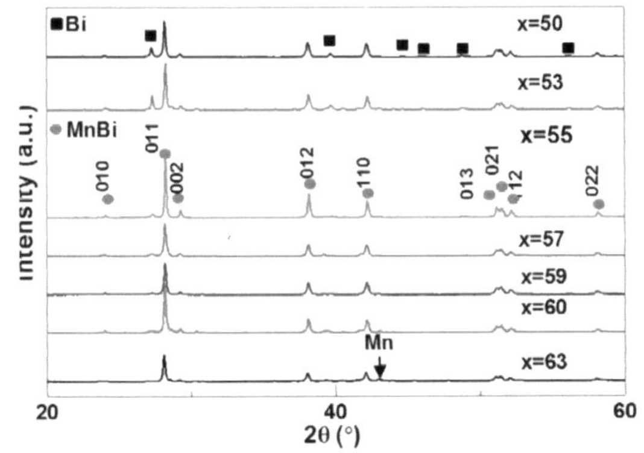

Fig. 2. XRD patterns of Mn_xBi_{100-x} annealed at 573 K after melt-spun at 65 m/s.

The LTP MnBi showed a hexagonal structure with lattice parameter $a = 4.2853(5)$ Å and $c = 6.1229(1)$ Å at RT, and Mn atoms were supposed to occupy 2a site. From the XRD pattern of the annealed MnBi ribbons, it could be seen that the intensity of the Bi peaks was quite weak, indicating that there was only a little amount of Bi. The content of MnBi was determined to be higher than 95%. The obtained MnBi shows a saturation magnetization of 75 emu/g at RT, which is very close to its theoretical value of 80 emu/g.

In order to improve the coercivity, the ribbons were grinded for different lengths of time. It is found that ${}_iH_c$ increases with the grinding time, and reaches a value of about 1.0 T after grinding for 7 hours (Fig. 3). The ratio of remanence (M_r) to M_s is about 0.935 after grind, indicating that most of the particles have their c-axes aligned. Since most nanocrystalline compounds prepared by melt-spinning are isotropic and normally an M_r/M_s ratio of less than 60%, such high squareness of the hysteresis loop of nanocrystalline MnBi is unique and indicates high texture of the c-axes. The maximum energy product $(BH)_{max}$ of the ribbons is 9.0 MGOe and 5.0 MGOe at room temperature and 400 K, respectively.

The TEM images of the annealed MnBi with various quenching speeds are shown in Fig. 4. Well-shaped hexagonal MnBi grains with an average size of 200 nm are observed in the samples with a speed of 20 m/s [Fig. 4(a)]. According to the electron diffraction patterns featuring the characteristic hexagonal spot pattern along the [001] direction [see Fig. (4b)], the MnBi grains are crystallographically oriented by their c-axes. This orientation is critical for obtaining anisotropic magnetic powders. The average grain size decreases to about 20–30 nm when a quenching speed of 65 m/s is applied [see high resolution lattice image in Fig. 4(c)]. The in-situ x-ray diffraction at different temperatures (data not shown) revealed that the Bi crystals start to form at very low temperature. Since Bi crystal has the same hexagonal geometry as the LTP MnBi, this helps to form MnBi crystal along the [001] axis by diffusion.

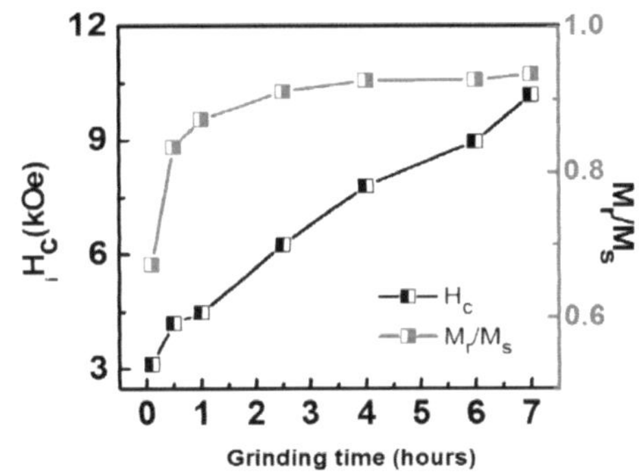

Fig. 3. Grinding time dependence of ${}_iH_c$ and M_r/M_s for the annealed MnBi ribbons.

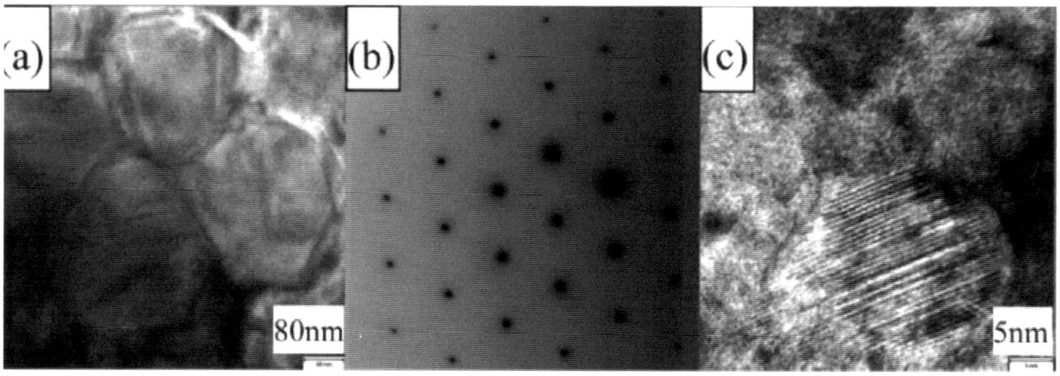

Fig. 4. TEM images of the annealed MnBi with quenching speed, 20 m/s (a), the electron diffraction pattern of MnBi grains (b), and the TEM images of annealed MnBi with quenching speed of 65 m/s (c).

Fig. 5 is the temperature dependence of coercivity for MnBi compound. The coercivity exhibits a positive temperature coefficient and reaches a maximum at 540 K, and then decreases slowly to 1.8 T at 610 K. The variation of the coercivity on temperature is supposed to be controlled by the change of magnetocrystalline anisotropy [16]. However, the coercivity of the sample ground for 7 hours increases between 450 K and 540 K faster than that of sample ground for 3 hours. The particle size after grinding for 7 hours is much smaller and it is close to the single domain size of MnBi (250 nm). Furthermore, the small grains in the particles are tending to have their *c*-axes (the easy axes) aligned. From the hysteresis loops, the M_r/M_s ratio is about 0.934 for the sample ground for 7 hours and 0.884 for the sample ground for 3 hours indicating that the *c*-axes of the grains are better aligned in the former sample.

The angular dependence of coercivity was obtained from the hysteresis loops measured at various angles. The measurements were performed as follows: after magnetic saturation by a pulsed field applied along the alignment direction, the sample was exposed to a reversing magnetic field applied at the angle φ with

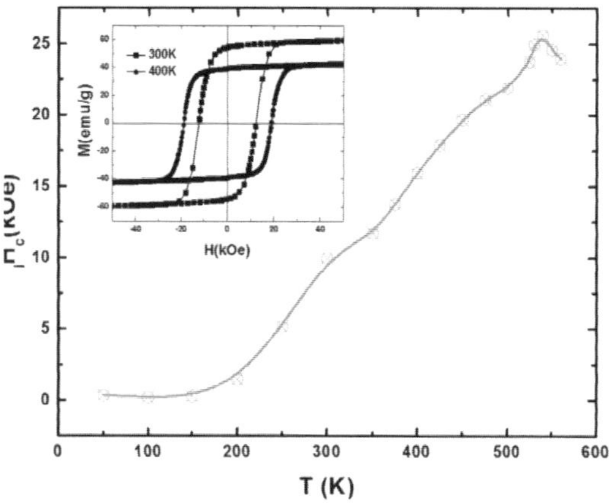

Fig. 5, Temperature dependence of coercivity for MnBi. The inset figure shows the hysteresis loops of anisotropic MnBi powders at 300 and 400 K.

respect to the alignment direction, as shown in Fig. 6 (a). The mechanism of coercivity was then analyzed by comparing the experimental results with three theoretical models: (1) The S-W model with $H_N^{ideal}(K_1\neq0,\ K_2=0,\ K_3=0)$ for $K_2 = 0$ and $K_d = 0$ originally proposed by Stoner and Wohlfarth [17]. The parameters K_1, K_2 are the anisotropy constants of MnBi and K_d is the anisotropy constant related to the demagnetization field. (2) The nucleation field model developed by Kronmüller et al. [18] considering the second anisotropy constant K_2 (K_2/K_1 = 0.318 for MnBi at room temperature [19]), as shown in the $H_N^{ideal}(K_1\neq0,\ K_2\neq0,\ K_d=0)$ curve. (3) For the third model [20], $_iH_c^{Pin}$ represents the angular dependence of pinning field which is proportional to $1/cos\theta$. The angular dependence of the theoretical nucleation and pinning fields for ideal grain alignment were plotted in Fig. 6(b). The value of the *y* axis were normalized to the value for $\varphi = 0$. The angular dependence for the critical field H_N and coercive field $_iH_c$ of MnBi measured at 300 K were also plotted in Fig. 6(b). Here, the critical field H_N is defined as the point of inflection of the hysteresis loops in the second or third quadrant[i], and the coercive field $_iH_c$ is defined as the magnetic field where the magnetization is zero. It is found that H_N^{exp} initially decreases with the increasing φ, and then increases for $45^o \leq \varphi \leq 90°$ which fits the $H_N^{ideal}(K_1\neq0,\ K_2=0,\ K_d=0)$ curve best. The disparity of the H_N between the experimental measurement and S-W model may be caused by the ignoring the second anisotropy constant K_2 which will increase the critical field. In addition, the coercive field $_iH_c^{exp}$ shows a different dependence on the φ. The variation trend of $_iH_c^{exp}$ is in accordance with that of H_N^{exp} for $0° \leq \varphi \leq 45°$. However, the $_iH_c^{exp}$ starts to deviate from H_N^{exp} in the range of $45° \leq \varphi \leq 90°$, which was predicted by the Stoner-Wohlfarth model. In conclusion, the magnetization reversal process of the MnBi powders is supposed to be mainly controlled by coherent rotation of the magnetization of single domain grains. Because the grain sizes in the LTP MnBi do not show apparent change from 300 to 540 K, the Stoner-Wohlfarth model is also supposed to be the appropriate coercivity mechanism for MnBi

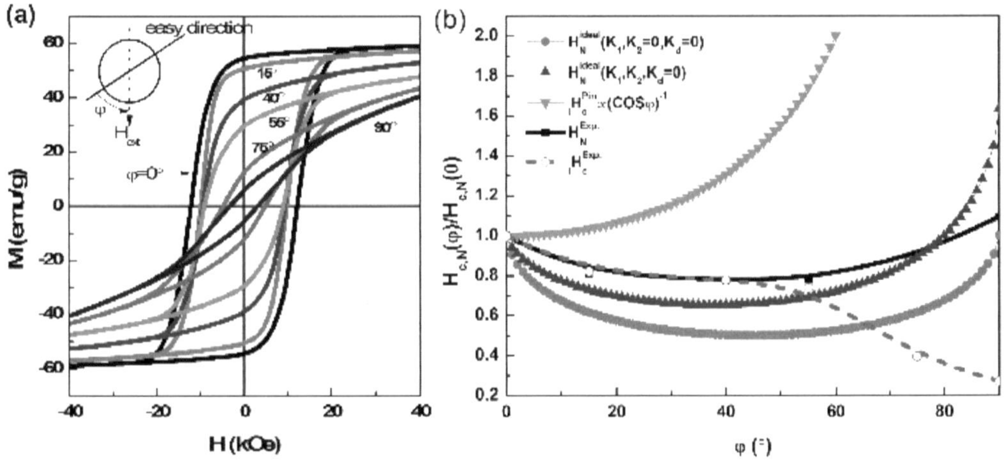

Fig. 5, Temperature dependence of coercivity for MnBi. The inset figure shows the hysteresis loops of anisotropic MnBi powders at 300 and 400 K.

at temperature between 300 and 540 K.

4. Summary

In summary, LTP MnBi was prepared by melt-spinning and subsequently annealing. The maximum energy product $(BH)_{max}$ of the ribbons is about 9.0 MGOe at room temperature. The coercivity of MnBi exhibits a positive temperature coefficient, and the magnetization reversal mechanism for the sample ground for 7 hours is controlled by coherent rotation in the single domain grains. The temperature dependence of coercivity is related to that of the magnetocrystalline anisotropy and to the sizes of the MnBi particles. The average size of the MnBi grains is 20 nm, much smaller than the single domain size of 250 nm. Importantly, the *c*-axes of the nanocrystalline MnBi grains tend to be parallel to each other

Acknowledgements
This work was supported by the National Natural Science Foundation of China (Grant Nos 51371009, 50971003 and 51171001), the National Basic Research Program of China (No 2010CB833104, MOST of China), the National High Technology Research and Development Program of China (No. 2011AA03A403).

References

[1] C. Guillaud, *J. Phys. Radium* **12**, 1951, 143.
[2] R. R. Heikes, *Phys. Rev.* **99**, 1955, 446.
[3] T. Chen, *J. Appl. Phys.* **45**, 1974, 2358.
[4] R. Coehoorn and R.A. Degroot, *J. Phys. F: Met. Phys.* **15**, 1985, 2135.
[5] X. Guo, X. Chen, Z. Altounian, and J.O. Stromolsen, *Phys. Rev. B* **46**, 1992, 14578.
[6] J.B. Yang, K. Kamaraju, W.B. Yelon, W.J. James, Q. Cai, and A. Bollero, *Appl. Phys. Lett.* **79**, 2001, 1846.
[7] A. Szlaferek and A. Wrzeciono, *Acta Phys. Pol. A* **92**, 1997, 315.
[8] F.X. Yin, N.J. Gu, T. Shigematsu, and N. Nakanishi, *J. Mater. Sci. Tech.* **12**, 1996, 335.
[9] X. Guo, A. Zaluska, Z. Altounian, and J.O. Stromolsen, *J. Mater. Res.* **5**, 1990, 2646.
[10] X. Guo, Z. Altounian, and J.O. Stromolsen, *J. Appl. Phys.* **69**, 1991, 6067.
[11] X. Guo, A. Zaluska, Z. Altounian, and J.O. Stromolsen, *Mat. Sci. Eng. A* **133**, 1991, 509.
[12] S. Saha, R.T. Obermyer, B.J. Zande, V.K. Chandhok, S. Simizu, S.G. Sankar, and J.A. Horton, *J. Appl. Phys.* **91**, 2002, 8525.
[13] J.B. Yang et al., *Appl. Phys. Lett.* **99**, 2011, 082505.
[14] Y.B. Yang et al., *J. Magn. Magn. Mater.* **330**, 2013, 106.
[15] L.B. McCusker, R.B. Von Dreele, D.E. Cox, D. Louer, and P. Scardi, *J. Appl. Crystal.* **32**, 1999, 36.
[16] X. Guo, X. Chen, Z. Altounian, and J.O. Stromolsen, *J. Appl. Phys.* **73**, 1993, 6275.
[17] E.C. Stoner, E.P. Wohlfarth, *Phil. Trans. Royal Soc. London A* **240**, 1948, 599.
[18] H. Kronmüller, K.D. Durst, G. Martinek, *J. Magn. Magn. Mater.* **69**, 1987, 149.
[19] P.A. Albert and W.J. Carr, *J. Appl. Phys.* **32**, 1961, S201.
[20] E. Kondorsky, *J. Phys.* **11**, 1940, 161.

Prospects of Chemically-Ordered FeNi (Tetrataenite) for Permanent Magnet Development

L.H. LEWIS
Department of Chemical Engineering, Northeastern University, Boston, Massachusetts, 02115, USA

Abstract: *Equiatomic FeNi with the tetragonal $L1_0$ structure, known as tetrataenite, possesses the a high Curie temperature, high magnetization and sufficient magnetocrystalline anisotropy to qualify it as a highly attractive candidate for high-performance permanent magnet applications. However, tetratenite is highly challenging to synthesize: it is only found naturally and in appreciable volumes as a component of stony, stony-iron and iron meteorites subjected to extraordinarily slow cooling rates, as low as 0.3 K per million years. This slow cooling rate fosters long-range polymorphic chemical ordering from the chemically-disordered cubic parent phase to the chemically-ordered tetragonal form at T = 320 °C. Considerations of the chemical ordering process as well as a review of results obtained from characterization and analysis of massive tetrataenite extracted from the meteorite NWA 6259 inform the potential of tetrataenite in advanced permanent magnet applications.*

Keywords: permanent magnet, rare-earth-free, ferrous, meteorite

Address: Laura H. Lewis, Dept. of Chemical Engineering, Northeastern University, Boston, MA 02115, USA.
E-mail: lhlewis@neu.edu

1. Introduction: Crystal Structure Design for Enhanced Magnetic Anisotropy

The goal of realizing rare-earth (RE)-free permanent magnetic materials with high-energy products $(BH)_{max}$ means that the principle source of the magnetic anisotropy, the magnetocrystalline anisotropy arising from the 4*f* electronic state, is no longer available for exploitation. This situation defines the subset of elements and materials that may be suitable as high-energy-product magnets. Magnetic anisotropy may be recovered in rare-earth-free compounds, to various degrees, in magnetic materials that adopt lower symmetry crystal structures, such as hexagonal or tetragonal crystal structures. These structures typically display magnetic moment alignment that is perpendicular to the basal plane, providing two energy minima to define the uniaxial magnetic anisotropy state. The majority of strongly-magnetic non-RE alloys assume a high-symmetry cubic crystal structure with low magnetocrystalline anisotropy; however, certain promising compounds form in the tetragonal $L1_0$ (space group P4/mmm or AuCu I structure type) structure, with an associated appreciable uniaxial magnetic character. The $L1_0$ structure forms in binary equiatomic compounds of general composition AB. Figure 1 illustrates the chemically-ordered $L1_0$ (AuCu I) crystal structure that is comprised of alternating layers of the two constituent A, B elements stacked parallel to the tetragonal *c*-axis, thereby creating a natural superlattice. The chemically-ordered $L1_0$ compound forms through a disorder-order phase transformation from a parent phase, which is often a chemically-disordered, face-centered- cubic (fcc) solid solution of the two elements (top image, Figure 1). This chemical ordering phase transformation is polymorphic, preserving the phase composition, and therefore ideally only involves extremely short-range physical interchange of the elemental components A and B. The decrease in symmetry concurrent with the formation of the $L1_0$ structure leads to a tetragonal distortion, which usually, results in a contraction along the unit cell *c*-axis, [001].

2. $L1_0$-Type FeNi – Tetrataenite

The $L1_0$ structure is well known and thoroughly

Fig. 1. (Top) The chemically-disordered fcc (A1) binary crystal structure and (bottom) the chemically-ordered $L1_0$ (AuCu I) crystal structure.

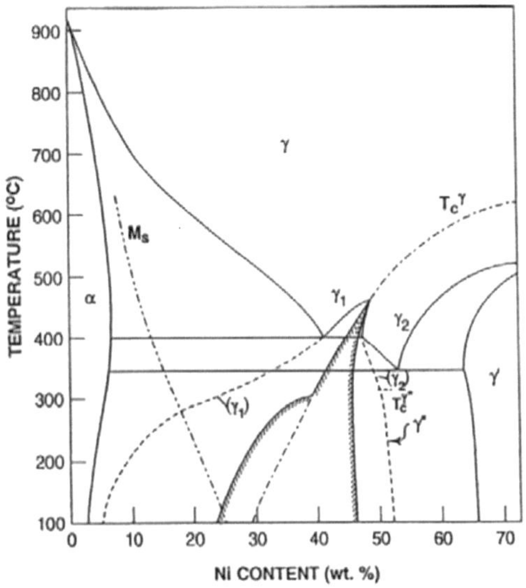

Fig. 2. Fe-Ni phase diagram showing γ" tetrataenite (the $L1_0$ chemically-ordered phase of FeNi). The α is a low Ni bcc phase, γ is a high Ni fcc phase, $γ_1$ is a low Ni paramagnetic fcc phase, $γ_2$ is a high Ni ferromagnetic fcc phase, γ' is ordered Ni_3Fe, M_S is the martensite starting temperature. $T_{Cγ}$ is the Curie temperature of the γ phase. $T_{Cγ''}$ is the ordering temperature of FeNi, γ".

studied in magnetic compounds such as FePt and FePd; these intermetallic alloys possess a high magnetization and significant magnetocrystal-line anisotropy, donating large coercivity, that would be very appropriate for advanced permanent magnet applications. However, due to the costliness of Pt and Pd, these intermetallic ferromagnetic compounds are under consideration only for thin-film-based devices, precluding their use as bulk permanent magnets.

An intriguing alternative is found in the isostructural ferromagnetic $L1_0$-type FeNi phase known as tetraenite. This compound is comprised of much less expensive and more readily available constituents. Figure 2 shows the modern binary iron-nickel phase diagram, derived from microprobe studies of phases and compositions found in meteoritic materials [1]. Tetrataenite is identified in Figure 2 as the γ" line compound phase; it is reported to possess an equilibrium order-disorder phase transformation temperature of 320 °C. This compound is only found naturally and in appreciable volumes as a component of stony, stony-iron and iron meteorites.

As discussed later in this manuscript, tetratenite has been confirmed to possesses relatively high and thermally-stable magnetocrystalline anisotropy combined with a magnetization equal to that of $Nd_2Fe_{14}B$. These attributes indicate that tetrataenite would be an excellent permanent magnet, especially for high-temperature applications. However, this

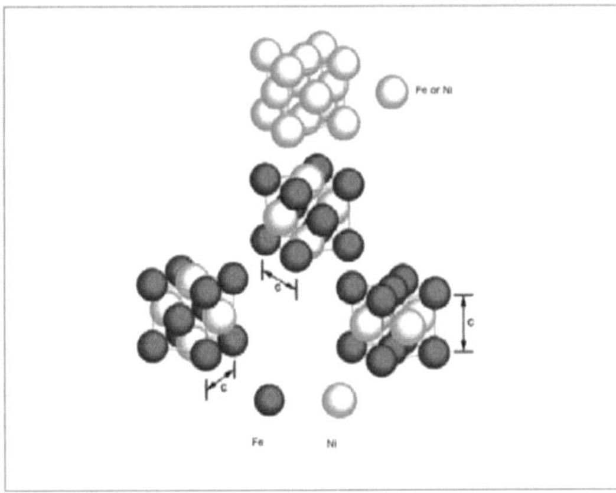

Fig. 3. The unit cells of the A1 (top) and $L1_0$ (bottom) phases. The figure shows the three variants of $L1_0$.

compound has a number of very significant materials synthesis and processing challenges that must be addressed before it can enter the technological marketplace. Particular issues are: i) chemically-ordered $L1_0$-type FeNi is only slightly more stable than polymorphic disordered structure; ii) the Fe-Ni interdiffusion rates for temperatures below this chemical order-disorder temperature are extraordinarily slow; iii) the $L1_0$ structure possess three crystallographically-equivalent, mutually-perpendicular structural variants, each with an associated easy axes of magnetization, that impede achievement of magnetic texture to foster high magnetic remenance. Despite these formidable challenges, investigation and directed engineering of the crystal structure, microstructure and magnetic structure of tetrataenite have only just begun, and it is anticipated that focused research will provide many clues to turn this extraterrestrial material into an engineering solution.

3. Tetrataenite Formation Considerations:

The only natural sources of tetrataenite exist in selected meteorites that cool over millions of years. with a calculated diffusivity of one atomic jump per 10,000 years at 300 °C [2]. There is a very low thermodynamic driving force to form the chemically-ordered $L1_0$ structure in the Fe-Ni binary system as it is only marginally more stable than the disordered structure that is entropically stabilized above the equilibrium chemical order-disorder temperature of 320 °C. The cooling rates necessary to foster tetrataenite formation are in the range 0.2 to 10,000 K/Myr, pointing to an extraordinarily low Fe-Ni interdiffusion rates such that the $L1_0$ structure does not form in the Fe-Ni system under normal laboratory conditions. This low interdiffusion rate is somewhat surprising, given that only local atomic rearrangement, not long-range diffusion, is required to form the ordered phase. It is known that the local atomic rearrangements necessary to achieve chemical ordering can be facilitated by the creation of point

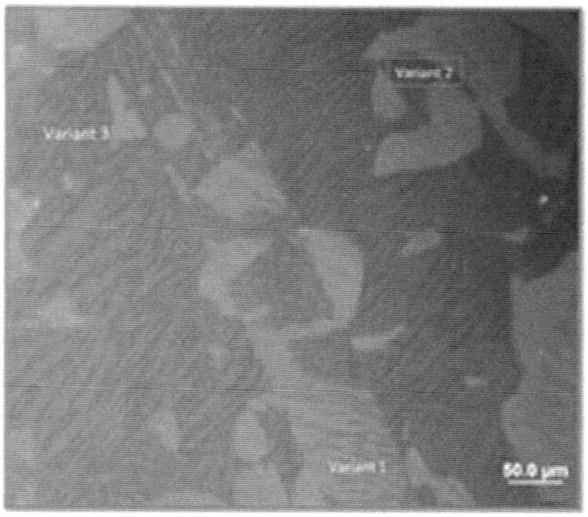

Figure 4: Polarized light micrograph of tetrataenite in the Appley Bridge LL6 chondrite. Three different crystallographic variants are indicated and are distinguished by different colors. Within each variant, elongated magnetic domains, corresponding to magnetically-polarized regions oriented 180° to one another may be discerned.

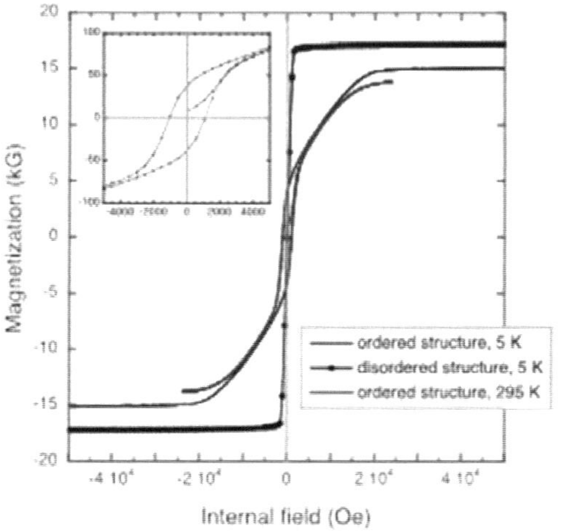

Figure 5: Hysteresis curves measured at 5 K and 295 K of a sample from meteorite NWA 6259. The hysteresis curve at 5 K after disordering at high temperature is shown for comparison. Inset: enlargement of low-field region of hysteresis data measured a 5 K, highlighting the approach to saturation.

defects (atomic vacancies) in the structure. However, these point defects must have a sufficiently long lifetime to allow ordering to take place. Insight into the origin of the very low Fe-Ni interdiffusion rate may be found in the work of Yang and Goldstein [3], who calculate that the magnetism present in FeNi alloys tips the Gibbs free energy of vacancy formation and migration in this system to positive values, resulting in a very highly reduced number of atomic vacancies present at a given temperature relative to non-magnetic alloys.

Within the $L1_0$ structure, chemical ordering can occur along any one of the three original cube axes (the <001> directions); thus three variants of the $L1_0$ phase may form from the parent A1 phase, each variant possessing a *c*-axis that is parallel to one of the three original cube axes, as shown in Figure 3. These variants determine the easy axis of the structure and thus control magnetic remanence of the specimen, impacting the energy product. It is necessary to align the $L1_0$ variants during synthesis and processing to provide the best magnetic performance. Figure 4 shows the well-developed crystallographic variant structure of tetrataenite in the Appley Bridge LL6 chondrite meteorite, imaged using polarized light optical microscopy (unpublished work). The magnetic domains, which are uniformly magnetized regions residing within the variants, may be clearly discerned as regions that are colored green, orange and brown.

4. Structure-Property Correlations in Natural Tetrataenite

Clearly, the main challenge that must be overcome to realize a tetrataenite-based permanent magnet is to develop a kinetic pathway to form the high-coercivity, high-magnetization FeNi $L1_0$ structure in an industrially-viable process on terrestrial timescales. Nonetheless, much can be learned from the study of natural tetrataenite, to ascertain aspects of its formation, its chemical order-disorder character and its potential performance as a future permanent magnet. To this end, selected intrinsic and extrinsic (technical) magnetic properties of tetrataenite ($L1_0$-FeNi) have been quantified, confirming the excellent potential of $L1_0$-type FeNi for permanent magnet applications [4, 5, 6].

Correlations between crystal structure, microstructure and magnetic properties of naturally-occurring tetrataenite have been achieved on material extracted from the meteorite NWA 6259. NWA 6259 (named for its location of discovery, Northwest Africa) was discovered in 2010 and has been verified to consist of largely single-phase tetrataenite. In previous work [5,6] the chemical composition of the microstructure of the meteorite NWA 6259 was determined with electron microprobe analysis (EPMA), confirming a slightly Fe-rich composition of $Fe_{55}Ni_{45}$ with 5 – 6% antisite defects. Optical microscopy and electron backscatter diffraction were employed to understand the texture and mosaic structure of the bulk meteorite sample, while transmission electron microscopy was utilized to verify the presence of the $L1_0$ FeNi structure throughout the sample. Magnetometry carried out in the temperature range from 5 K to 900 K allowed quantification of the technical performance of tetrataenite in its chemically-ordered, high-anisotropy state and its chemically-disordered, low-anisotropy state.

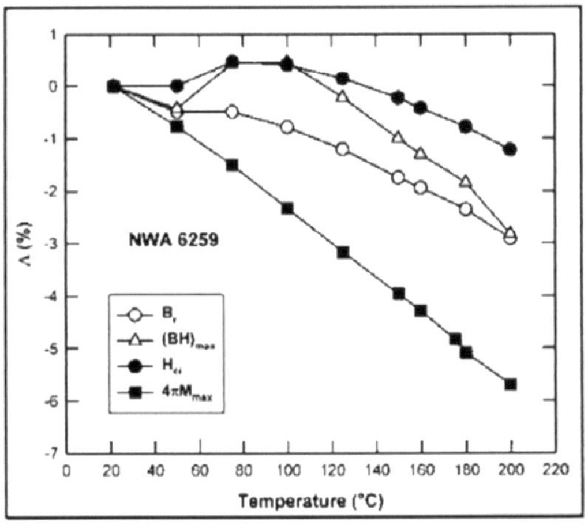

Figure 6: Relative change of NWA 6259 tetrataenite technical magnetic properties with temperature.

Figure 5 illustrates magnetic hysteresis loops of tetrataenite obtained from a portion of NWA 6259 measured at 5 K and at 295 K in its chemically-ordered and chemically-disordered states. Even in its highly nonoptimized state, the tetrataenite in NWA 6259 provides a room-temperature coercivity of 95.5 kA/m (1200 Oe) at room temperature.

After undergoing the phase transformation to the chemically-disordered A1 cubic structure above 800 K, the sample exhibits a significant decrease in coercivity to effectively zero while simultaneously demonstrating an increase in the saturation magnetization by 15% to 1.72 T (17.2 kG) at 5 K; the reason underlying the increase in magnetization upon chemical disordering is not clear. The magnetocrystaliine anisotropy energy K_u of tetrataenite in NWA 6259 is confirmed to be in the range 1.0 – 1.3 MJ/m^3; this measured value yields an estimated uniaxial anisotropy field of $H_A = 1.6 \pm 0.24$ MA/m (20 ± 3 kOe) at room temperature.

5. Potential of Tetrataenite as a High-Temperature Permanent Magnet

Elevated temperature measurements of the technical magnetic properties of tetrataenite indicate that the intrinsic coercivity H_{ci} is remarkably stable, exhibiting a total reversible loss of coercivity of only -1.2 % between room temperature and 200 °C (Figure 6). While the measured room-temperature coercivity and associated microstructure of tetrataenite in the meteorite NWA 6259 is far from optimized, this finding points to a major advantage for incorporation of this compound in motor design and operation at high temperature, with typical reference operating temperatures of 180 °C. In sharp contrast, the magnetic properties, especially the coercivity, of today's best rare-earth magnets based on the composition (Nd,Dy)-(Fe,Co)-B, decline drastically with increasing temperature. The best temperature coefficient of coercivity of Nd-Fe-B between room temperature and 180 °C is β = -0.64 to -0.80 %/K, even in materials engineered for high temperature by using a high Dy content. The corresponding value for L1$_0$ tetrataenite is β = -0.005 %/K, providing an approximate 100-fold improvement over that of Dy-modified NdfeB.

6. Conclusion

The combination of considerable magneto-crystalline anisotropy, high magnetization, high apparent Curie temperature and a very low temperature coefficient of coercivity highlight the enormous potential now evident in L1$_0$ FeNi, tetrataenite, as a candidate permanent magnet material. While synthesis and processing challenges for this material are very significant, it is now understood that optimized microstructures in tetrataenie will allow full manifestation of intrinsic magnetic properties for maximum coercivity and remanence to realize a high energy product. If fully realized, the coercivity-limited theoretical energy product present at room temperature is at least $(BH)_{max}$ ~ 335 kJ/m^3 (42 MGOe), competitive with that found in today's best magnets (64 MGOe). The totality of these results indicate that the composition and microstructure of L1$_0$–type FeNi may be tailored for high potential as a superior rare-earth-free permanent magnet.

Acknowledgement
Special acknowledge-ments to: K. Barmak (Columbia University), N. Bordeaux (Northeastern University), J.I. Goldstein and A. Mubarok (U. Massachusetts-Amherst), F. E. Pinkerton and E. Poirier (G. M. Global R&D Center).

References

[1] C.-Y. Yang, D.B. Williams, J.I. Goldstein, *J. Phase Equilib.* **17**, 1996, 522.
[2] R. B. Scorzelli, *Hyperfine Interact.* **110**, 1997, 143.
[3] J. Yang, J.I. Goldstein, *Metall. Mater. Trans. A* **35**, 2004, 1681.
[4] L. H. Lewis, K. Barmak, J. G. Goldstein, F. Pinkerton, R. Skomski, in: *Proc. 22nd Int. Workshop on Rare-Earth Permanent Magnets and Their Applications*, Nagasaki City, Japan, 2012.
[5] Laura H. Lewis, Frederick E. Pinkerton, Nina Bordeaux, Arif Mubarok, Eric Poirier, Joseph I. Goldstein, Ralph Skomski, Katayun Barmak, *IEEE Magn. Lett.* **5**, 2014, 5500104.
[6] L. H. Lewis, A. Mubarok, E. Poirier, N. Bordeaux, P. Manchanda , A. Kashyap, R. Skomski, J. Goldstein, F. E. Pinkerton, R. K. Mishra, R. C. Kubic Jr., K. Barmak, *J. Phys.: Condens. Matter.* **26**, 2014, 064213.

Role of the Applied Magnetic Field on the Microstructural Evolution in Alnico 8 Alloys

LIN ZHOU, WEI TANG, H. DILLON, R.W. MCCALLUM, I.E. ANDERSON, M.J. KRAMER
Ames Lab, Ames, IA 50011

Abstract: *Improving performance of permanent magnet alloys is a complex optimization of microstructure through control of chemistry and processing. Alnico alloys represent a class of chemically complex alloys whose functionality as a permanent magnet is dependent on the nano-structuring which develops during thermal heat treatments in an external applied magnetic field (H). This study showed that the microstructure of a specific alnico 8 alloy composition is very sensitive to magnetic field annealing temperature. A well-faceted mosaic structure will be formed at optimum magnetic field annealing temperature* (840°C)*, which results in optimum magnetic quality with a coercivity of 1845 Oe and a* $(BH)_{max}$ *of 5.9 MGOe. We demonstrate that the magnetic field annealing away from the optimum temperature can destroy the well-defined nanostructure crucial to the magnetic properties.*

Keywords: *Alnico magnets;, spinodal decomposition; transmission electron microscopy*

Address: Lin Zhou, Ames Lab of DOE, Ames, IA50011, USA, Tel: (515)294-7590,
E-mail: linzhou@ameslab.gov

1. Introduction

Permanent magnet-based motors and generators are crucial for hybrid electric vehicles and wind turbines. Recent concern for supply and price of the rare alloys, such as dysprosium and neodymium, the key elements in permanent magnets, has stimulated the searching of alternative magnetic materials [1,2]. Alnico, a family of magnetic alloys composed primarily of Al, Ni, Co and Fe, with excellent magnetic stability at high temperature, is an attractive near-term non-rare earth permanent magnet (PM) alloy. Key to the optimization of the magnetic properties is control of the spinodal decomposition (SD) into an Fe-Co ("α_1 phase") hard magnetic phase and a non-magnetic NiAl-based phase ("α_2 phase"). The properties of current commercial alnico alloys were optimized before 1970 mostly by empirical studies without the help of today's advanced characterization and simulation tools. The highest energy product $(BH)_{max}$ alnico alloys are type 9, which are both grain aligned and spinodally decomposed with an applied magnetic field.[1] To further improve properties of alnico alloys, a better understanding of the nanostructure of the SD phases, such as their chemistry, morphology and effect on domain structure, is very important.

Our recent extensive study on commercial alnico 5-7, 8 and 9 alloys showed the spinodal phase assembly is very sensitive to alloy chemistry and processing conditions employed. The spinodal phase assembly has a "brick-and-mortar" structure in alnico 5-7 and a "mosaic structure" in alnico 8 and 9. The α_1 phase is faceted on {100} planes in alnico 5-7, but on {110} and {100} planes in alnico 8 and 9. Additions of Ti transferred the α_2 phase from a B2-ordered structure in alnico 5-7 into an $L2_1$-ordered structure in alnico 8 and 9. Copper was pushed out of the α_2 phase and resides at corners of two <110> facets of the α_1 phase in alnico 8 and 9. The saturation magnetization is directly dependent on the α_1 phase volume ratio, but prediction of coercivity is more complex, which is attributed to the large α_1 rod diameter and interaction domains [3].

For alnico 8 alloy, initial phase separation during rapid quenching of a solid solution from 1250°C results in a network structure consisting of interpenetrating continuous α_1 and α_2 phases. Annealing polycrystalline alnico with a fixed **H** at 800°C causes isolation, coarsening and faceting of the α_1 phase with increasing time. Also, the volume fraction and the Al, Ni, Ti and Cu contents of the α_1 phase decreased, while the Fe, and Co contents increased with increasing field annealing time. The phase distribution and micro-magnetic domain structure is closely related to the relative orientation between **H** and the principal axes of each grain. The α_1 rods are elongated in each grain along the <100> direction with projected **H**, where the preferentially extended length of the α_1 rods along the selected <100> is proportional to the magnitude of projected **H** [4].

In this study, microstructure and magnetic properties of hot isostatically pressed (HIPed) alnico 8 samples that were magnetic field annealed at different temperatures were analyzed. Results indicate that the SD phase morphology is very sensitive to the magnetic field annealing temperature, which in turn affects the magnetic properties of alloys.

2. Experimental Methods

A simplified Alnico 8H alloy powder of 7.3Al-13.0Ni-38.0Co-32.3Fe-3.0Cu-6.4Ti (wt.%) composition was close-coupled gas-atomized (GA) using Ames Laboratory facilities. The resulting powders were spherical and averaged 30 μm in diameter. GA alnico 8H powders < 20 μm in size were loaded into a stainless steel HIP can. Before sealing, the powders were outgassed at 425°C for 2 hours under high vacuum (10^{-5} torr). The can was sealed under vacuum by electron beam welding. The HIP process was done under pressure of 300 MPa for 4 hours, at 1250°C. Center sections of the HIP consolidated alnico were cut into 3 mm diameter by 8 mm cylinders using electrical discharge machining (EDM).

The alloy was polycrystalline with random grain orientation. All cylinder samples were solutionized at 1250°C for 30 min. in vacuum (1.3×10^{-4} Pa) and quenched into an oil bath. The samples were then magnetically annealed in the temperature range of 800 to 860° C for 10 min., with an external applied field of 1T, followed by tempering at 650°C for 5 hrs and 580°C for 15 hrs. The samples that were only magnetically annealed were designated as MA only, while the samples that completed all of thermal processing were designated as full heat treatment (FHT). The FHT samples that were magnetically annealed at 800, 840 and 860°C were labeled as Sample A, B and C, respectively.

The magnetic properties were measured using a *Laboratorio Elettrofisico* Engineering Walker LDJ Scientific AMH-5 Hysteresisgraph with a 5 mm coil and a maximum applied field of 5.0 kOe at room temperature in a closed-loop setup.TEM analysis was performed on transverse sections (with electron beam parallel to magnetization direction) for all MA-only samples. TEM samples were prepared by mechanical wedge-polishing followed by a short time, low voltage Ar ion-milling with liquid nitrogen cold stage. A FEI Tecnai F20 (200kV, FEG) with Lorentz lens was used for microstructural characterization.

3. Results and Discussion

The effect of magnetic annealing temperature on the intrinsic coercivity (H_{cj}) is shown in Fig. 1. It is obvious that H_{cj} is very sensitive to the magnetic field annealing temperature. With increasing temperature from 800 to 860°C, the H_{cj} of the samples first increased from 760 Oe at 800°C, reach a peak value of 1360 Oe at 840°C and then decreased to 773 Oe at 860°C. After full heat treatment, the H_{cj} of all samples increased but followed the same trend as the MA only samples. The FHT sample magnetically annealed at

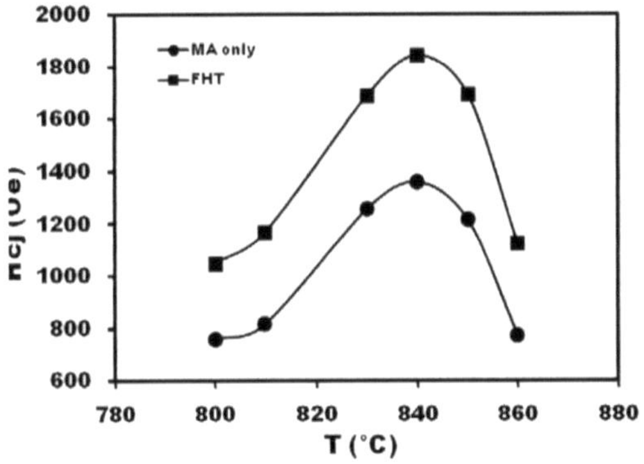

Fig. 1 Effect of magnetic annealing temperature and subsequent thermal annealing on H_{cj}.

840°C for 10 min. achieved a H_{cj} of 1845 Oe and a $(BH)_{max}$ of 5.9 MGOe.

High-angle-annular-dark-field (HAADF) scanning transmission electron microscopy (STEM) imaging, which emphasizes regions of high atomic number with brighter contrast because of greater electron scattering to large detector collection angles, clearly differentiates phase morphology in Samples A, B and C. HAADF STEM images of Samples A to C along the transverse directions are shown in Fig. 2. The α_1 phase is slightly brighter due to its higher average atomic number, while the darker region is the α_2 phase. For sample A, both diamond shape (~25nm) and rod shape (width ~25nm, length ~60-300nm) α_1 phase coexist. Most of Cu-rich particles are located at the corner of two {110} facets of the diamond shape α_1 phase. The longer axis of the rod shape α_1 phase is aligned along the <100> direction. The microstructure of sample B is similar to commercial alnico 8 alloy which shows a mosaic pattern with Cu-rich phase sitting at the corner of two α_1 phase facets. The α_1 phase has a diameter between ~30-40nm, indicating increasing of α_1 phase size with increasing annealing temperature. Further increase of magnetic annealing temperature to 860°C will destroyed the well-defined mosaic pattern as shown in Fig. 2(c). The morphology of α_1 phase is irregular. Both large α_1 phase patches with size up to 100nm and small α_1 phase particles with size of ~10nm were observed. Cu-rich particles were sometimes observed between two α_1 phase particles.

These results are consistent with the magnetic property difference shown in Fig. 1. Cahn [5] suggested that for SD with **H**, the shape of the particles is established during the first stage of decomposition, which was determined by the anisotropy of magnetic and elastic energy. For the alnico system, the elastic energy is much greater than the magnetic energy except near the Curie temperature.[5] As a result, when the magnetic field heat-treatment is close enough to (but below) the Curie temperature, it appeared to bias the growth of

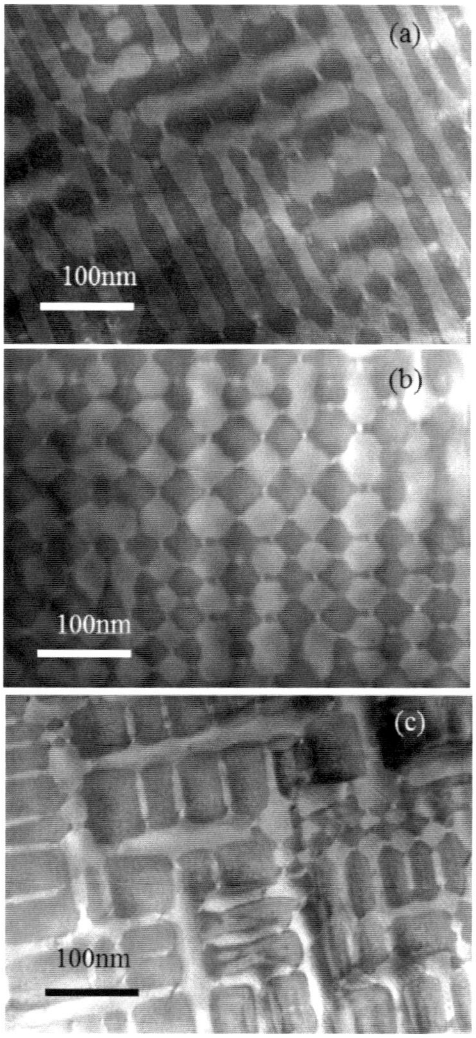

Fig. 2. HAADF STEM images of samples A(a), B(b) and C(c) taken close to [100] zone axis.

α_1 phase greatest and to create a uniform mosaic structure, resulting in an optimized H_{cj}.

4. Conclusion

In summary, this study showed that the magnetic field annealing temperature is very critical for the formation of a well-defined "mosaic" SD phase morphology in an alnico 8 HIPped alloy. The mosaic pattern "perfection" is directly related to good magnetic properties. The sample that was magnetically annealed at 840°C for 10 min. achieved a well-refined mosaic SD phase morphology and obtained the best magnetic properties. Magnetic field annealing below or above the optimum temperature destroyed the well-defined nanostructure and, in turn, worsened its magnetic properties.

Acknowledgement
This work was supported by DOE-EERE-VT-PEEM and Propulsion Materials Programs at the Ames Laboratory. Ames Laboratory is operated for the U.S. DOE by Iowa State University under contract no. DE-AC02-07CH11358.

References

[1] M. J. Kramer, R. W. McCallum, I. A. Anderson, and S. Constantinides, JOM, 64 (7), 2012,752.

[2] R. A. McCurrie, Ferromagnetic materials 3, North-Lolland Publishing Company, UK, 1982.

[3] Lin Zhou , M. K. Miller, Ping Lu, Liqin Ke, R. Skomski, M. McCartney, D. Smith, H. Dillon, Q. Xing, A. Palasyuk, S. Constantinides, R.W. McCallum, I. E. Anderson, V. Antropov, and M. J. Kramer, Architecture and Magnetism of Alnico, Acta Materilia, 74, 2014, 224.

[4] L. Zhou, M. K. Miller, H. Dillon, A. Palasyuk, S. Constantinides, R.W. McCallum, I. E. Anderson, and M. J. Kramer, Met. Trans. E., 2014, 1, 27.

[5] J. W. Cahn, J. Appl. Phys., 1963, 34 (12), 3581.

Templated Growth of Magnetic FeCo Nanostructures

M. GONG, S. REN
Department of Chemistry, University of Kansas, Lawrence, Kansas, 66045, USA

Abstract: *A synthetic route is reported to achieve a precise control of FeCo shell growth on AuCu core (AuCu/FeCo core/shell) nanoparticles, which could open up the metastable tetragonal FeCo growth. Due to nonmagnetic AuCu core, the FeCo shell exhibits a magnetic transition, which is determined by the particle radius and the thickness of the spheroidal shell. The magnetic state is further confirmed by deriving total magnetic energies of hollow magnetic nanospheres. In addition, the FeCo shell exhibits the excellent passivation against oxidation due to the annealing induced thin graphite shell. This work shows the uniqueness and versatility of the colloidal core/shell nanotechnology to manipulate nanostructures with desirable functionality.*

Keywords: *core-shell nanoparticle; nanomagnetism; FeCo and AuCu*

Address: Department of Chemistry, University of Kansas, Lawrence, Kansas, 66045, USA,
Email: Shenqiang@ku.edu

1. Introduction

The development of rare-earth-free, low cost and high energy product nanomagnets has become increasingly critical, especially for clean energy nanotechnologies.[1,2] The maximum energy density of permanent magnets is given by its saturation magnetization and magnetocrystalline anisotropy energy (MCA, K_u).[3] The FeCo alloys display the highest saturation magnetization of 1.95 MAm^{-1}.[4,5] However, these alloys are magnetically 'soft' meaning that their coercive field is small and its MCA energy is low, $K_u \approx 0.1 J/m^3$. To increase MCA, and therefore the maximum energy product of the material, the coercive field must be increased. To achieve this increase in MCA energy, controlling the metal alloy crystal growth via a templating approach has become a highly promising avenue to reach desired crystalline phases. This method allows thin film growth of the desired crystals using physical vapor deposition. Such studies have been conducted for alloys (e.g. FePt) that are vapor deposited onto a templating crystal structure (e.g. $L1_0$ ordered AuCu), which allows the decrease of the order-disorder transition temperature.[6,7] It will be critical to develop a solution processing technique that is low-cost and high-throughput for bulk nanomagnets, on which the energy product can be further improved by exchange-coupling.

Colloidal monodispersed magnetic nanoparticles (NPs) have been attracting significant interest due to their simple processing and high tunability of magnetic properties.[8-13] In addition, as the size becomes comparable to the size of magnetic domain, single domain NPs can exhibit interesting magnetic behavior. During the past decade, increased attention has been paid to ferromagnetic NPs, especially single domain NPs that are stable with respect to thermal demagnetization.[14] In contrast, creating a ferromagnetic shell coating onto a nonmagnetic core template has received limited attention due to the lattice mismatch between core and shell materials, as well as a lack of experimental progress in epitaxial core/shell growth.[15] However, theoretical analysis has indicated that different ratios of inner/outer radius of core/shell heterostructures can result in unique magnetic properties.[16] It will be necessary to overcome these synthetic barriers to open the door to these interesting magnetic properties.

Here, we report the nonmagnetic AuCu core to direct magnetic FeCo shell growth for the formation of AuCu/FeCo (core/shell) NPs, on which the magnetic vortex state is controlled by tuning the shell thickness and overall radius. The total energy of zero-field magnetization states within AuCu/FeCo NPs is examined, and we find that single domain configuration is formed under a thin FeCo shell, and the magnetic vortex state is realized when the overall particle radius exceeds a critical value R_e^{crit} of 9.6 nm at inner/outer radius ratio of a=0.51 ($a=R_i/R_e$). Our calculation confirms that the total energy of magnetic vortex is mainly determined by the exchange, which is 8.3 times larger than that of the sum of magnetocrystalline anisotropy energy and vortex energy. The AuCu/FeCo NPs exhibit excellent air stability due to a thermal annealing induced graphite shell.

2. Experimental Techniques

The starting AuCu core material is created following the previously reported synthetic method.[1] For a typical synthesis of AuCu/FeCo core/shell nanoparticles (NPs), a simple one-pot reaction was first employed to synthesis AuCu core NPs, which were subsequently used as template for the formation of AuCu/FeCo core/shell magnetic NPs. Briefly, stoichiometrically equivalent of $HAuCl_4{\cdot}3H_2O$ (0.25mM) and $Cu(acac)_2$

(0.25mM) were dissolved in 10mL oleylamine and 2mM 1,2-hexadecanedio mixture solution and heated to 160°C for 2 hr under argon atmosphere with rapid magnetic stirring. To prepare AuCu@FeCo core/shell NPs, the above AuCu colloidal solution was cooling down to 120°C, and then $Fe(CO)_5$ (1mM) and $Co_2(CO)_8$ (1mM) were injected simultaneously. The $Fe(CO)_5$ and $Co_2(CO)_8$ were dissolved in 1,2-dichlorobenzene under Argon atmosphere and kept at 80 °C. The mixture of AuCu-FeCo reaction solution was kept at 230°C for 30 min under Argon atmosphere with magnetic stirring. The as-prepared colloidal solution was then cooled to room temperature and crashed out for the magnetic testing.

3. Results and Discussion

The AuCu material is known to have two different crystal structures. Its disordered structure is face center cubic (fcc) where the Au and Cu elements are randomly placed in the lattice. In addition, the AuCu has an ordered face centered tetragonal structure (fct, $L1_0$), which is stable at low temperatures making it a prime candidate to use as an epitaxial growth template for potential tetragonal magnetic heterostructures.[17-19] Figure 1a exhibits transmission electron microscopy (TEM) image of the as-obtained (10.2 ± 0.5 nm) AuCu core NPs. The AuCu crystalline phase and ordering transition are confirmed using the x-ray diffraction and differential scanning calorimetry, respectively, which has reported in our previous paper.[20] The schematic Figure 1b demonstrates the AuCu/FeCo core/shell NPs. It was found that both reaction time and temperature played a considerable role on the FeCo shell thickness and crystallinity.

Figure 2 presents time dependent studies on the shell thickness of FeCo on AuCu cores reacted at 230 °C. Figure 2a shows TEM image of AuCu/FeCo NPs after cobalt carbonyl and iron carbonyl injected into the AuCu colloidal solution and keep temperature at 230 °C for 10min. It demonstrates that the FeCo shell coating is minimal on the surface of the AuCu cores. As the reaction is allowed to continue longer, the shells become more apparent as the precursors are

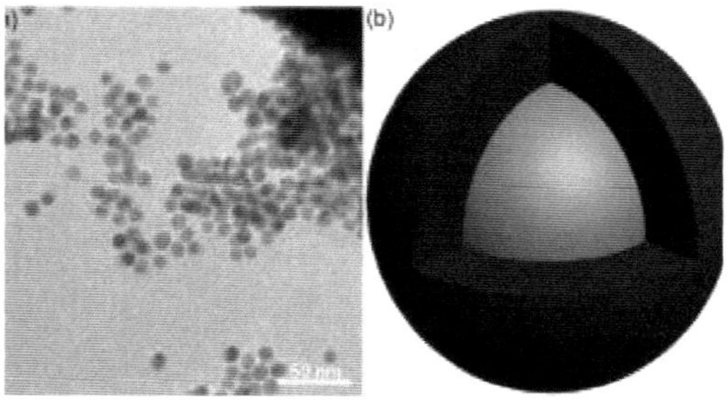

Fig. 1. (a)TEM images of AuCu Core nanoparticles. (b) Schematic of AuCu/FeCo core/shell magnetic nanoparticle.

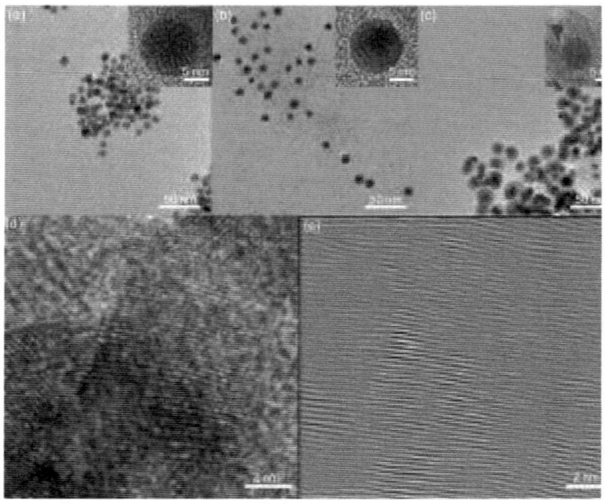

Fig. 2. TEM images of the AuCu/FeCo nanoparticles for different reaction times at 230 °C: (a) 10 min, (b) 20 min, and (c) 30 min. The insets are high-magnification images of the particles. (d) The high resolution TEM and (e) corresponding FFT images of AuCu/FeCo magnetic core/shell nanocrystals.

allowed longer to decompose. By 20 min reaction, a shell becomes discernable, which is evident by images shown in Figure 2b. After the 30 min into the reaction, the shell is complete, displaying the final thickness of 6.3±0.8 nm. This proves that the FeCo shell thickness can be controlled by the reaction time of the synthesis, which allows tuning of the final size of the particles. Knowing the size of the shell can be readily controlled by reaction time and temperature, the magnetic properties of these novel core/shell materials can be examined. The high resolution TEM and corresponding FFT images demonstrate the epitaxy relationship between AuCu core and FeCo shell (Fig. 2d-e). With desired phase of the shell material reached, it is imperative that the FeCo shell thickness is controlled so that the magnetic domain size can be optimized and compared to theoretical values.

Unique magnetic properties are observed for these AuCu/FeCo core/shell magnetic spherical NPs. The high resolution TEM image exhibits multiply-twinned boundaries for the polyhedral AuCu core NPs (Fig. 3a). Figure 3b displays magnetic hysteresis loop for the AuCu/FeCo magnetic core/shell NPs and FeCo-only NPs synthesized using the same method but no AuCu core. The AuCu/FeCo (core/shell) magnetic particles exhibit magnetic vortex characteristics with a high saturation magnetization. We attribute this vortex state to its unique core/shell structure templated on the multiply-twinned AuCu core. The FeCo shell can be treated as magnetic hollow spheres, considering the nonmagnetic AuCu core. Goll et al. show that magnetic domain structures of spherical hollow particles are mainly determined by the particle radius and the thickness of the shell, which can exhibit a single domain or vortex domain.[16] By comparing total energy

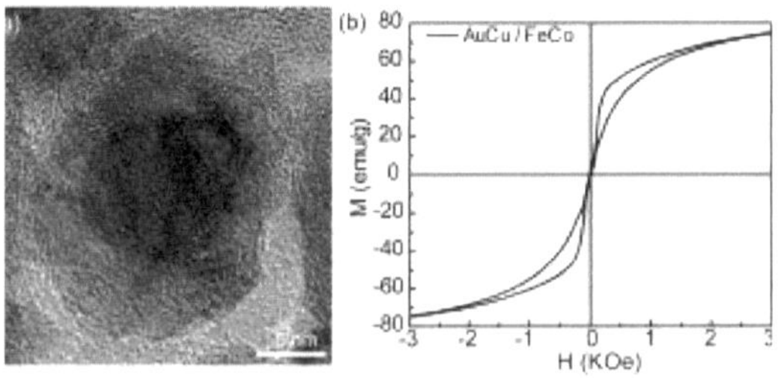

Fig. 3. (a) High resolution TEM image, with core and shell radii of 5.8 and 11.3 nm. (b) Magnetic hysteresis loops for AuCu/FeCo core/shell.

of single domain and vortex states of FeCo magnetic shells, we can calculate the lowest-energy configurations to model our experimental results.

The total energy of the zero-field magnetization states of FeCo shell particles was calculated in single domain state and curling-vortex state. In the case of single domain states, the entire energy consists of the stray field or magnetostatic energy.[16]

$$E_{tot}^{single} = -\frac{1}{2}\int H_z^{shell} J dV = \frac{2}{9}\pi\frac{1}{\mu_0}J_S^2 R_e^2(1-a^3) \quad (1)$$

Where E_{tot}^{single}, H_z^{shell}, μ_0, J_s, R_e, R_i and $a=R_i/R_e$ are the total energy for single-domain state, Lorentz field (due to uniform magnetic charges on the inner and outer surface), vacuum permeability, spontaneous polarization, particle radius, nonmagnetic core radius, ratio of particle radius and core radius. With single domain energy completed, we now calculate the curling-vortex state energy for the hollow sphere particle. To achieve this, we break up the hollow spherical particle to three different regions shown in Figure 4. It should be noted that two vortices are created to avoid a singularity due to exchange energy. The curling is assumed in the (x,y) plane in a three dimensional sphere. Region I represents the curling within $-R_i<z<R_i$. Region II represents the curling that takes place in the sphere caps, except for in the vortex region III. Region III (vortex region) is cylindrical disks with radius R_v and height R_e-R_i. The vortex region can be further broken into two parts. The core region with the radius b has a nonzero magnetization segment perpendicular to the (x, y) plane and the outer region between radius b and R_v has the magnetization vector within the plane. It should be noted that the magnetization configuration is independent of the z axis. Since the orientation of two vortices is oriented antiparallel to each other (Fig. 4), the energy of the curling vortex state is small. Due to long-range stray field interactions decreasing as $1/r^4$, interplay between the separate vortices can be neglected. Therefore the total energy of vortex energies is the sum of exchange, magnetocrystalline anisotropy energy and the vortex energies,

$$E_{tot}^{curling} = E_A^I + E_K^I + 2E_A^{II} + 2E_K^{II} + 2E_A^v + 2E_K^v + 2E_S^v \quad (2)$$

Where the E_A, E_K and E_S are exchange energy, magnetocrystalline anisotropy energy and vortex stray field energy. The combined energy expressions produce the following equation (more details of the starting expressions are shown in supporting information):

$$E_{tot}^{curling} = 2\pi A(2R_e ln\frac{2R_e}{R_v} + R_i ln\frac{R_v^2}{4R_i^2}) + \frac{1}{8}K[\frac{4\pi}{3}R_e^3(1-a^3) - 2\pi R_v^2 R_e(1-a)] + \{\frac{1}{2\mu_0}J_S^2 L_S^2 R_e(1-a)\left(2 - ln\frac{b}{R_v}\right) + 2\pi K R_v^2 R_e(1-a)[\frac{1}{8} - (\frac{65}{24} - 4ln2)(\frac{b}{R_v})^2] + \frac{4\pi J_S^2}{\mu_0}b^3[0.083 - (ln2 - \frac{1}{2})^2\frac{b}{R_e(1-a)}\} \quad (3)$$

Where A, K and J_s are exchange constant, anisotropy constant and spontaneous polarization, respectively. $L_s = \sqrt{2\mu_0 A}/J_s$ is the exchange length of the material,

and $b = \sqrt[3]{-\frac{F_2}{2} + \sqrt{C}} - \frac{1}{3}\frac{F_1}{\sqrt[3]{-\frac{F_2}{2}+\sqrt{D}}} + \frac{1}{3}\frac{N_2}{N_1}$; $F_1 = -\frac{1}{3}\frac{N_2^2}{N_1^2}$, $F_2 = -\frac{2}{27}\frac{N_2^3}{N_1^3} - \frac{L_S^2}{N_1}$, $C = \frac{1}{27}\frac{N_2^3 L_S^2}{N_1^4} + \frac{1}{4}\frac{L_S^4}{N_1^2}$, $N_1 = 12\pi \times 0.083\frac{1}{R_e(1-a)}$, $N_2 = \frac{8\pi\mu_0 K}{J_S^2}(\frac{65}{24} - 4ln2)$.

The total energies of single domain and vortex state are compared. A critical particle size R_e^{crit} appears when the total energies of single domain and curling-

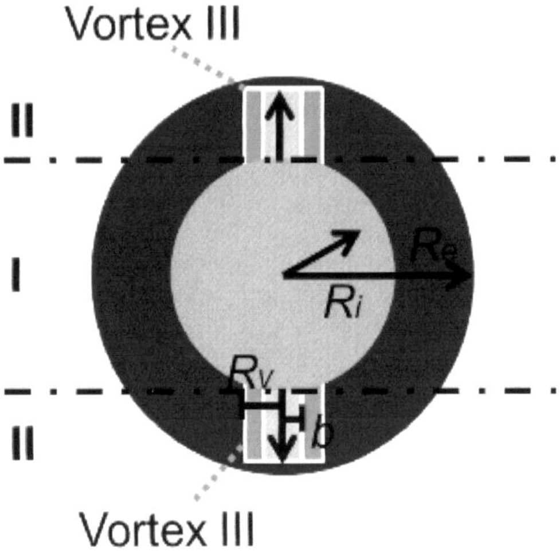

Fig. 4. Vortex-state model of Au/FeCo. The shell is divided into three regions: main (I), spherical caps (II), and vortex III-vortex region (III). In III, b is the radius of the vortex core and Rv is the radius of the vortex region.

vortex states are equal and one will transform into another. For a small particle size, single domain state is the energetically favorable configuration. Once the entire particle radius is above 9.6 nm (R_e^{crit}), it transforms from single domain to magnetic vortex state, where the critical radius of the vortex core (b) is 3.9 nm. In FeCo magnetic materials, the magnetocrystalline energy remains always small and the vortex state reduces the magnetostatic energy drastically. It is also seen that the exchange energy is ~8.3 times larger than that of other energy, meaning that the total energy of the vortex state (at R_e^{crit}) is strongly dependent on the exchange energy. Theoretical calculations confirmed the magnetic vortex formation within the AuCu/FeCo core/shell NPs due to their radius of 11.28 nm larger than the R_e^{crit}. Furthermore, our calculations will guide the formation of desired magnetic states (vortex or single domain) in the future controlled and precise synthesis.

4. Summary

We report a versatile and precise growth of magnetic FeCo shell onto the nonmagnetic AuCu core to form AuCu/FeCo core/shell heterostructures which demonstrate unique magnetic properties by controlling the shell thickness and particle radius. The magnetization states from single domain to magnetic vortex state of hollow FeCo nanospheres are reliant on the materials parameters J_s, A, K and the ratio of internal and external radius of the FeCo shell. The total energy of magnetic vortex state is mainly determined by the exchange energy. This allows us to control magnetic states of hollow sphere FeCo nanoparticles by tuning the shell thickness. In addition, the FeCo shell exhibits excellent air stability through the annealing induced thin graphite shell coating. Further work will include growth non-twinned, $L1_0$ AuCu crystalline cores to allow for improved epitaxial growth of FeCo to achieve the goal of creating a non-rare-earth magnetic material with high energy product for use in energy critical applications.

Acknowledgement

The work was supported by the National Science Foundation under Award No. NSF-CMMI-1332658 for material synthesis and assembly. The authors thank Dr. J. Cui from Pacific Northwest National Laboratory, and Prof. R.Skomski at the University of Nebraska, Lincoln for the result discussion.

References

[1] Gutfleisch, O.; Willard, M. A.; Brück, E.; Chen, C. H.; Sankar, S. G.; Liu, J. P. *Advanced Materials* **2011**, *23*, 821.
[2] Burkert, T.; Nordström, L.; Eriksson, O.; Heinonen, O. *Physical Review Letters* **2004**, *93*, 027203.
[3] Sort, J.; Suriñach, S.; Muñoz, J. S.; Baró, M. D.; Nogués, J.; Chouteau, G.; Skumryev, V.; Hadjipanayis, G. C. *Physical Review B* **2002**, *65*, 174420.
[4] Bai, J.; Wang, J.-P. *Applied Physics Letters* **2005**, *87*, 152502.
[5] Wang, C.; Peng, S.; Lacroix, L.-M.; Sun, S. *Nano Res.* **2009**, *2*, 380.
[6] Zhu, Y.; Cai, J. W. *Applied Physics Letters* **2005**, *87*, 32504.
[7] Shen, J.; Gai, Z.; Kirschner, J. *Surface Science Reports* **2004**, *52*, 163.
[8] Yang, C.; Wu, J.; Hou, Y. *Chemical Communications* **2011**, *47*, 5130.
[9] Hou, Y.; Kondoh, H.; Kogure, T.; Ohta, T. *Chemistry of Materials* **2004**, *16*, 5149.
[10] Sakuma, N.; Ohshima, T.; Shoji, T.; Suzuki, Y.; Sato, R.; Wachi, A.; Kato, A.; Kawai, Y.; Manabe, A.; Teranishi, T. *ACS Nano* **2011**, *5*, 2806.
[11] Kang, S.; Jia, Z.; Nikles, D. E.; Harrell, J. W. *Magnetics, IEEE Transactions on* **2003**, *39*, 2753.
[12] Puntes, V. F.; Krishnan, K. M.; Alivisatos, A. P. *Science* **2001**, *291*, 2115.
[13] Kang, S.; Jia, Z.; Nikles, D. E.; Harrell, J. W. *Journal of Applied Physics* **2004**, *95*, 6744.
[14] Ogi, T.; Dani Nandiyanto, A. B.; Kisakibaru, Y.; Iwaki, T.; Nakamura, K.; Okuyama, K. *Journal of Applied Physics* **2013**, *113*, 164301.
[15] Teng, X.; Black, D.; Watkins, N. J.; Gao, Y.; Yang, H. *Nano Letters* **2003**, *3*, 261.
[16] Goll, D.; Berkowitz, A. E.; Bertram, H. N. *Physical Review B* **2004**, *70*, 184432.
[17] Anraku, T.; Sakaihara, I.; Hoshikawa, T.; Taniwaki, M. *Journal of the Japan Institute of Metals and Materials* **2008**, *72*, 311.
[18] Sra, A. K.; Schaak, R. E. *Journal of the American Chemical Society* **2004**, *126*, 6667.
[19] Yang, J.; Chng, L. L.; Yang, X.; Chen, X.; Ying, J. Y. *Chemical Communications* **2014**, *50*, 1141.
[20] Maogang Gong; Alec Kirkeminde; Ralph Skomski; Jun Cui; Ren, S. *Small* **2014**, *DOI: 10.1002*.

Crystal Structure and Hard Magnetic Properties of Mn-Ga Compounds

T. MIX[1,2], L. SCHULTZ[1,2], T.G. WOODCOCK[1]
[1]IFW Dresden, Institute for Metallic Materials, PO Box 270116, 01171 Dresden, Germany
[2]Department of Physics, TU Dresden, Dresden, Germany

Abtract: *Mn-Ga binary alloys with composition in the range 50-75 at.% Mn were produced by arc melting. Annealing was carried out to produce single phase* $L1_0$ *and* $D0_{22}$ *structures. The magnetic properties of the materials were investigated up to a maximum applied field of 5T. A dramatic improvement in coercivity* (H_c) *was obtained by producing powder from bulk* Mn_3Ga $D0_{22}$ *and* $Mn_{60}Ga_{40}$ $L1_0$ *materials by mechanical milling. The* Mn_3Ga *powder showed a similar magnetisation at 5 T* (M_{5T}) *but an almost threefold increase in* H_c *compared to the bulk sample (cf. powder:* H_c = 1.409 T, *bulk:* H_c = 0.537 T*). The* $Mn_{60}Ga_{40}$ *powder had a similar* M_{5T} *but a fivefold higher* H_c *compared to the bulk sample (cf. powder:* H_c = 0.376 T, *bulk:* H_c = 0.073 T*). Furthermore, dense, isotropic compacts of powders with both structures were produced, in which the improved magnetic properties of the powders were retained.*

Keywords: *rare earth free magnets; coercivity; hot pressing; L10*

Address: Torsten Mix, Institute for Metallic Materials, IFW Dresden, PO Box 270116, 01171 Dresden, Germany, Phone +49 (0)351 4659 337, Email: t.mix@ifw-dresden.de

1. Introduction

The rapid growth in clean energy technologies, such as wind turbines and hybrid vehicles, has led to a large increase in demand for high performance permanent magnets based on Nd-Fe-B [1–3]. The recent fluctuations in the price and supply of rare earth elements are therefore a significant problem for industry [1–3]. In response, researchers are attempting to reduce the rare earth content in Nd-Fe-B magnets [1]. In addition, there is significant interest in the development of novel rare earth free magnets with intermediate performance between the ferrites and Nd-Fe-B magnets, but with much lower materials costs than Nd-Fe-B [2].

Interesting candidate phases for rare earth free magnets can be found in the Mn-Ga binary system. Depending on the composition, ferromagnetic $L1_0$ (*cP*4; *P4/mmm*) or ferrimagnetic $D0_{22}$ (*tI*8; *I4/mmm*) phases can be produced [4]. The $L1_0$ phase has been found to exist in a range of composition and the intrinsic magnetic properties vary greatly within this range [4]. The highest reported value of magnetisation measured at an applied field of 7 T (M_{7T}) for the $L1_0$ structure was M_{7T} = 0.78 T, for the composition $Mn_{54.5}Ga_{45.5}$ but the coercivity (H_c) was only 0.1 T [4]. The $D0_{22}$ structure has lower magnetisation (M_{7T} < 0.38 T) but higher coercivity (H_c = 0.25 T) than the $L1_0$ structures [4]. Although some of these properties are promising, the high raw materials costs of Ga are likely to prevent the commercial application of Mn-Ga magnets. At least partial substitution of Ga is therefore a critical aspect. Before substitution can be considered however, the upper limits of the magnetic properties of binary alloys should be thoroughly explored. The focus of this work is therefore the optimisation of both intrinsic and extrinsic magnetic properties in Mn-Ga binary alloys, with a view to producing a rare earth free magnet.

2. Experimental

Mn-Ga binary alloys with composition in the range 50-75 at.% Mn were produced by arc melting. Annealing was carried out between 500°C and 700°C for 7 days to produce the single phase $L1_0$ structure and at 400°C for 1 hour for the single phase $D0_{22}$ structure. The crystal structure was determined using x-ray diffraction. Rietveld refinement of the data was carried out using FullProf. The magnetic properties were measured at room temperature by SQUID magnetometry. Thermomagnetic measurements were gathered using a high temperature VSM with an applied field of 0.1 T. Powder samples with a particle size of less than 100 μm were produced with a vibration mill and a milling time of 1 hour. The hot compaction was carried out at 450°C for the $D0_{22}$ structure and 700°C for the $L1_0$ structure with a pressure of 300 MPa under vacuum conditions.

3. Results and Discussion

The crystal structures and lattice parameters of all materials were determined from XRD (data not shown here). The arc melted ingots all crystallised in a cubic A1 (*cF*4; *Fm*-3*m*) structure. In bulk Mn_3Ga, an annealing time of only 60 min at 400°C was needed to produce pure $D0_{22}$ from the initial A1 structure. The lattice parameters of the $D0_{22}$ phase were a = 3.910 Å and c = 7.113 Å. Pure $L1_0$ structure was produced by annealing the samples in the composition range 55-65 at.% Mn at 500°C to 700°C for 7 days. For the $L1_0$ structure the *c/a* ratio increased from 0.924 to 0.948 (*i.e.* the tetragonal distortion became smaller) with decreasing Mn content from 65 at.% to 55 at.% Mn.

SQUID data showed the magnetisation at an applied field of 5 T (M_{5T}) of 0.176 T for the bulk sample with the Mn_3Ga $D0_{22}$ structure (fig. 1). The small magnetisation is caused by the partial compensation of the magnetic moments in the two Mn sublattices in the ferrimagnetic $D0_{22}$ structure [5]. The coercivity (H_c) of the $D0_{22}$ bulk alloy was 0.537 T. (fig. 1).

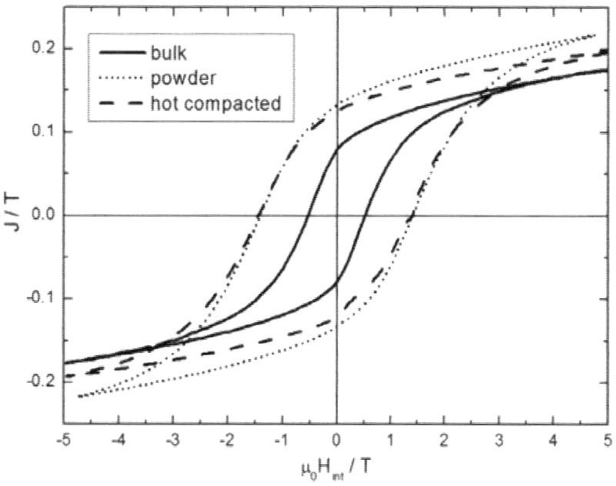

Fig. 1. Room temperature SQUID measurements of the Mn_3Ga bulk, powder and hot compacted samples, with a maximum applied field of 5 T.

It has recently been shown that further improvement in the properties of Mn-Ga alloys can be obtained by producing powder from a bulk material [4]. Mn_3Ga $D0_{22}$ powder was produced here by mechanical milling. The Mn_3Ga powder showed a similar M_{5T} but an almost threefold increase in H_c compared to the bulk sample (*cf.* powder: H_c = 1.409 T, bulk: H_c = 0.537 T) (Fig. 1).

To obtain a bulk magnet with this improved magnetic properties hot compaction of the milled powder was carried out. The compaction temperature was set to 450°C to avoid the phase transition of the $D0_{22}$ structure in to the antiferromagnetic hexagonal $D0_{19}$ structure. With this method hot compacted magnets with a density of 88.5% of the ideal value were produced. The increased coercivity of the powder sample (H_c = 1.409 T) was retained in the hot pressed compact (fig. 1). Although this improved H_c is high, considering that no rare earth elements are present, the low magnetisation of Mn_3Ga is likely to prevent the application of the material as a hard magnet. Alternative applications, *e.g.* spintronics have already been identified for Mn_3Ga [6].

The magnetisation in the bulk $L1_0$ alloys is in the range of M_{5T} = 0.465 T for the $Mn_{65}Ga_{35}$ to M_{5T} = 0.783 T for the $Mn_{55}Ga_{45}$ composition. Even the lowest magnetisation in this range is more than double that of bulk Mn_3Ga $D0_{22}$ (M_{5T} = 0.176 T). The H_c values for the bulk $L1_0$ alloys decreased with decreasing Mn content, from 0.118 T at 65 at.% Mn to 0.021 T at 55 at.% Mn and were significantly lower than that of the bulk Mn_3Ga $D0_{22}$ alloy (H_c = 0.537 T). The Curie temperature (T_C) of the $L1_0$ alloys also decreases with decreasing Mn content, from 431°C at 65 at.% Mn to 337°C at 55 at.% Mn (Fig. 2).

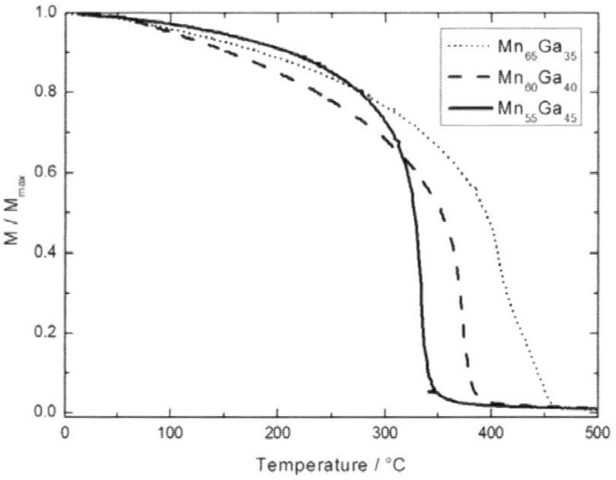

Fig. 2. Thermomagnetic measurements of Mn-Ga alloys in the Mn content range from 55 at.% to 65 at.% Mn.

Production of $Mn_{60}Ga_{40}$ powder showed a similar M_{5T} but a fivefold higher H_c compared to the bulk sample (*cf.* powder: H_c = 0.376 T, bulk: H_c = 0.073 T). The production of a hot compacted sample was carried out at 700°C as there was no risk of a phase transformation at this temperature. Therefore a better compaction of the pellet with a density of about 99% of the ideal value was achieved. As shown in figure 3 M_{5T} stayed constant and H_c is with 0.274 T slightly reduced compared to the powder sample.

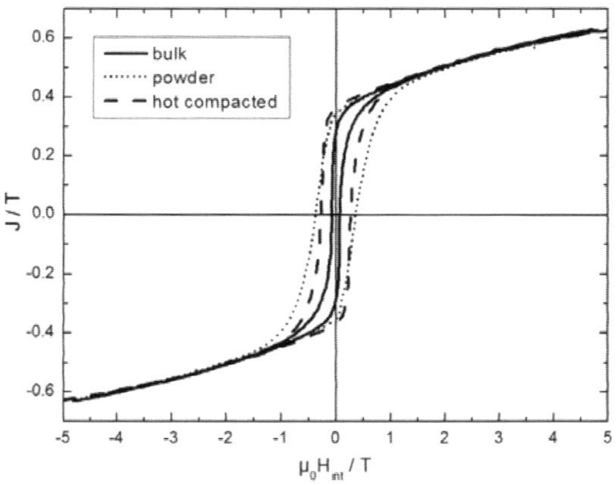

Fig. 3. Room temperature SQUID measurements of the $Mn_{60}Ga_{40}$ bulk, powder and hot compacted samples, with a maximum applied field of 5 T.

An upper limit for the maximum energy density can be estimated using $(BH)_{max} \leq \mu_0 M_r^2/4$ [7]. Assuming that a strong unixial texture could be induced in the sample so that say, $M_r \approx 0.9$ M_{5T}, $(BH)_{max} \leq 64$ kJm

^{3} could be obtained (based on M_r = 0.569 T), provided that $H_c \geq M_r/2$. The enhanced H_c of the powder presented here (0.376 T) fulfils this criterion but the H_c of the hot pressed compact (0.274 T) is slightly too low. This shows that $Mn_{60}Ga_{40}$ has some potentially attractive magnetic properties assuming a strong texture could be introduced. In order to achieve this, further work is required.

4. Conclusion

In summary, both $D0_{22}$ and $L1_0$ crystal structures have been produced in Mn-Ga binary alloys. The $L1_0$ structure was obtained in the composition range 55-65 at.% Mn. The T_C and H_c values decreased with decreasing Mn content within this range. The T_C was > 300°C for all alloys. The highest M_{5T} (0.783 T) was found at 55 at.% Mn. The $D0_{22}$ structure possessed a high H_c of 0.537 T but a low magnetisation (M_{5T} = 0.176 T). A dramatic improvement in H_c in all the alloys was obtained by producing powders (e.g. from bulk: H_c = 0.537 T to powder: H_c = 1.409 T for Mn_3Ga and from bulk: H_c = 0.073 T to powder: H_c = 0.376 T for $Mn_{60}Ga_{40}$). This confirmed and extended first results published in the literature [4]. The enhanced magnetic properties were retained in the production of fully dense, iostropic hot pressed magnets.

The results show some potential to develop a rare earth free hard magnet with intermediate performance in the Mn-Ga binary system. Further work is required both to optimise the magnetic properties and to reduce the materials costs through targeted substitution of Ga.

Acknowledgement

The authors would like to thank B. Gebel, M. Herrich and K. Pittruff for excellent technical support and K.-H. Müller for the fruitful discussions.

References

[1] O. Gutfleisch, M.A. Willard, E. Brück, C.H. Chen, S.G. Sankar, J.P. Liu, Adv. Mater. 23 (2011) 821–42.
[2] J.M.D. Coey, Scr. Mater. 67 (2012) 524–529.
[3] M.J. Kramer, R.W. McCallum, I.A. Anderson, S. Constantinides, JOM. 64 (2012) 752–763.
[4] Y. Huh, P. Kharel, V.R. Shah, X.Z. Li, R. Skomski, D.J. Sellmyer, J. Appl. Phys. 114 (2013) 013906.
[5] E. Krén, G. Kádár, Solid State Commun. 8 (1970) 1653–1655.
[6] J. Winterlik, B. Balke, G. Fecher, C. Felser, M. Alves, F. Bernardi, et al., Phys. Rev. B. 77 (2008) 1–12.
[7] J.M.D. Coey, Magnetism and magnetic materials, 1. publ., Cambridge Univ. Press, Cambridge, 2010.

Magnetic Anisotropy and Coercivity Mechanism of LTP MnBi Thin Films

T. HOZUMI[1,2], P. LECLAIR[1], G. MANKEY[1], T. SUZUKI[1]
[1] Center for Materials for Information Technology (MINT), The University of Alabama, Tuscaloosa, AL, U.S.A.
[2] Advanced Technology Development Center, TDK Corporation, Narita, Japan

Abstract: *The magnetic anisotropy as a function of temperature for low temperature phase (LTP) MnBi thin films is studied. Multilayers of Mn/Bi were fabricated onto silica-glass substrates by sputter deposition, followed by annealing. Two sets of thin films were prepared with i) the c-axis orientation along the film normal and ii) non-c-axis orientation. It is found that the coercivity for both the films starts to increase rapidly with temperature at about 200K, which is much different from that of bulk MnBi. The relation between the magnetic anisotropy constant, K and saturation magnetization $M_s(0)$ is found to be $K \sim M_s(0)^{-10.5}$ for the c-axis oriented sample.*

Key words: *MnBi magnet, thin film, crystal orientation, magnetic anisotropy*

Address: Toshiya Hozumi, Center for Materials for Information Technology (MINT), The University of Alabama, Tuscaloosa, AL 35487, U.S.A., Tel: 205-348-8574, E-mail: thozumi@jp.tdk.com

1. Introduction

The low temperature phase (LTP) of MnBi exhibits a large magnetic anisotropy constant (K) of the order of 10^7 erg/cc at room temperature, which increases with temperature. Therefore, LTP MnBi is very attractive for high temperature applications. However, while much work has been performed on the LTP MnBi thin films, very few systematic experimental studies on the temperature dependence of the magnetic anisotropy of the LTP MnBi can be found in literature [1-3]. The present paper describes the temperature dependence of magnetic anisotropy in LTP MnBi thin films.

2. Experiments

Multilayered MnBi thin films of [Bi(x nm)/Mn(y nm)]×N were fabricated by sputter deposition onto silica-glass substrates at an ambient temperature during deposition, where x = 1.1 ~ 7.9, y = 2.0 and N = 1 ~ 10. The deposition rates for Bi and Mn were 0.07 nm/s and 0.02 nm/s, respectively. After optimizing the fabrication conditions, the thicknesses of each Bi and Mn layer were chosen to be 3.2 nm and 2.0 nm, respectively. The samples were deposited at room temperature and subsequently annealed at various temperatures T_a from around 300 ºC to 550 ºC without breaking vacuum in the deposition system. After annealing, a capping layer of Ru was deposited at room temperature to prevent oxidation of the films.

The crystal structure of the films was characterized by X-ray diffraction (XRD) with Co Kα radiation. Measurements of temperature dependence of magnetic properties were carried out using a vibrating sample magnetometer (VSM) in fields up to 90 kOe. Torque measurements were carried out using a torque magnetometer in fields up to 90 kOe. All of the torque measurements were performed for the out-of-plane mode. The magnetic anisotropy constant, K was estimated by extrapolating the torque amplitude with two fold symmetry to H→∞.

3. Results and Discussion

Figure 1 shows the XRD patterns for the sample with x = 3.2, y = 2 and N = 10, annealed at T_a = 550 ºC for t_a = 30 minutes (film 1), and T_a = 350 ºC for t_a = 15 hours (film 2). The XRD patterns indicate that these samples are of the NiAs structure (LTP). The relatively strong peaks of (002) and (004) for film 1 indicate a preferential epitaxial growth of the c-axis normal to the film plane (Fig. 1 (a)). However, the presence of the weak intensity of (102) and (103)

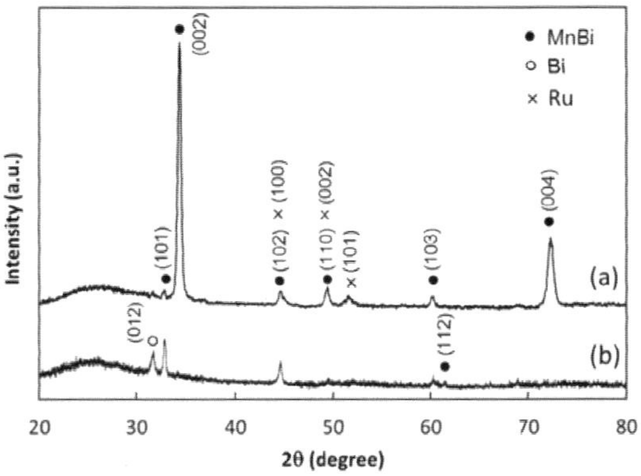

Fig. 1. X-ray diffraction patterns of MnBi films annealed at 550 ºC for 30 minutes (a) and 350 ºC for 15 hours (b).

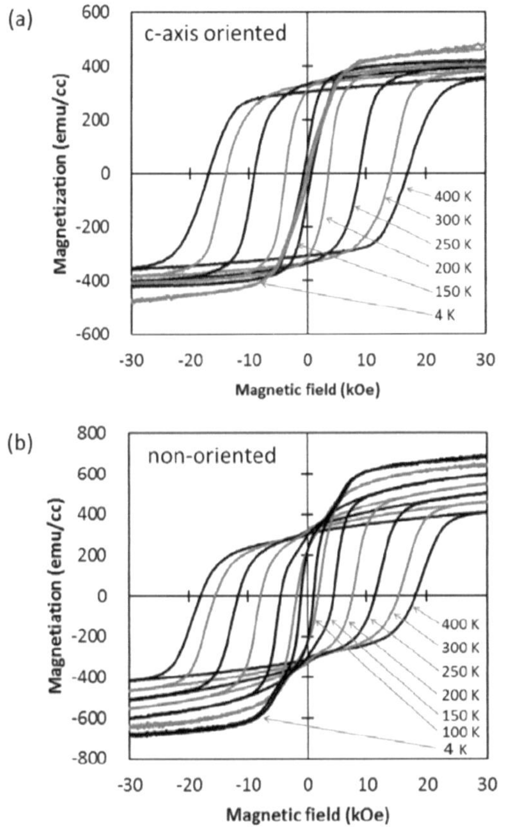

Fig. 2. Magnetic hysteresis loops in the temperature range of 4 – 400 K for the c-axis oriented film (film 1) (a) and the non-oriented film (film 2) (b).

peaks indicates that grains of the LTP MnBi with other orientations are also present in that film. On the other hand, the highest peak assigned to (101) for film 2 corresponds to the main peak for isotropic grains of LTP MnBi, indicating this film has non-oriented polycrystalline structure (Fig. 1(b)). The lattice constants of *a* and *c* were estimated to be 4.29 Å and 6.07 Å for film 1, and 4.28 Å and 6.11 Å for film 2. It is of interest to note that the orientation of the LTP MnBi can be controlled by the annealing condition.

Figure 2 shows the temperature dependence of out-of-plane magnetic hysteresis loops measured from 4 to 400 K for film 1 and film 2. Both the films show large coercivity at above 200 K and it increases monotonically with increasing temperature up to the maximum measurement temperature of 400 K. Figure 3(a) shows the temperature dependence of coercivity (H_c) for both the films. Interestingly, the coercivity for both the films has similar temperature dependence. The H_c increases with temperature, drastically for temperature beyond 200 K and the coercive fields at 400 K are 16.9 kOe and 18.0 kOe for film 1 and film 2, respectively. It is noted that the temperature dependence of H_c for the films is much different from bulk, where the larger slope in the temperature

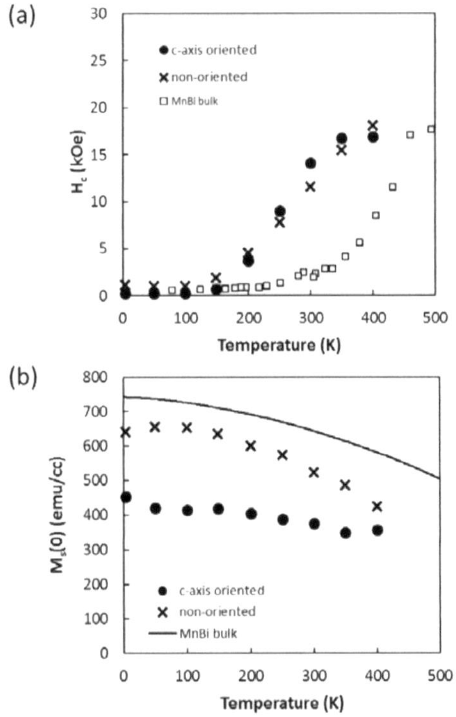

Fig. 3. (a) Temperature dependence of coercivity (H_c) for the c-axis oriented film (film 1) and the non-oriented film (film 2). (b) Temperature dependence of saturation magnetization ($M_s(0)$) for the c-axis oriented film (film 1) and the non-oriented film (film 2). The data for bulk MnBi [3] are also plotted.

dependence of coercivity occurs beyond 300 K. The measured coercivity values for the films of about 15 kOe at 300 K are about 30~40% of the magnetic anisotropy field, H_K (≈5 T). This high coercivity results from the unique microstructure of the LTP MnBi films, where LTP MnBi grains are isolated, being surrounded by Bi, leading to coherent rotation of the magnetization within the grains because the average grain size for the LTP MnBi film annealed at 550 °C is 30 – 50 nm. Further these grains are surrounded by an exchange-breaking layer of Bi [4]. In order to estimate experimentally the saturation magnetization, since the magnetization increases with H for even high fields above 4T due to a paramagnetic component, the extrapolation of the magnetization values at high fields to H = 0 was made for the M-H curves. The saturation magnetization thus estimated is defined as $M_s(0)$, which is shown in Fig. 3(b). The magnetization decreases gradually with temperature. The magnitude of $M_s(0)$ for film 1 is about a half of the bulk value. The detailed analyses by TEM, together with the EDS, indicate that about a half of the total sample volume is the LTP grains, the rest being Bi. Thus if one takes into account this result, the actual $M_s(0)$ would be nearly the same as the bulk value. Figure 4 shows the temperature dependence of H_K for the c-axis oriented film (film 1) which is

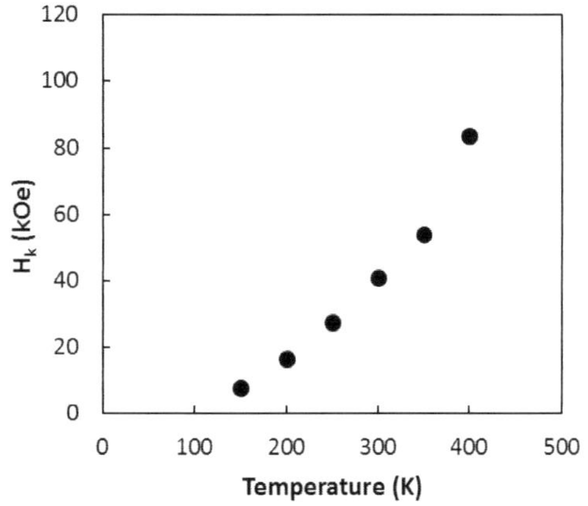

Fig. 4. The temperature dependence of magnetic anisotropy field (H_k) for the c-axis oriented film (film 1). The magnetic anisotropy field H_k is estimated as $H_k = 2K/M_s(0)$, where the K is the magnetic anisotropy constant estimated from the torque method.

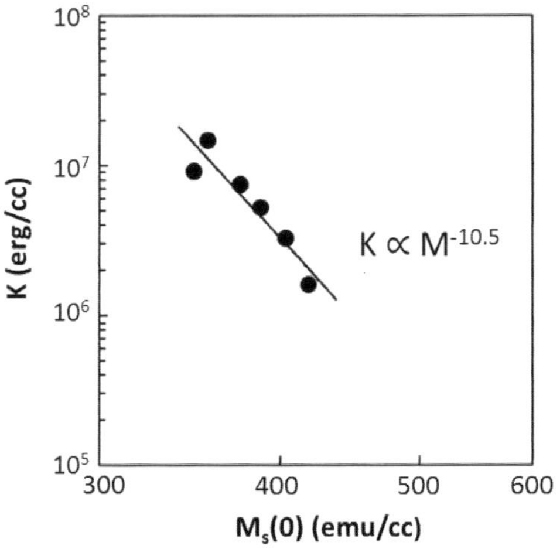

Fig. 5. The correlation between the magnetic anisotropy constant (K) estimated by torque method and the saturation magnetization ($M_s(0)$) for the c-axis oriented film (film 1).

estimated based on the torque curves. The H_k increases with temperature in a very similar way to the case for H_c. The magnetic anisotropy constant (K) was also estimated from torque measurements. The correlation between K and $M_s(0)$ for film 1 was investigated, which is shown in Fig. 5. It is found that K is proportional to $M_s(0)^n$, $n = -10.5$ for the c-axis oriented film. According to theoretical works, the magnetic anisotropy constant K changes with M_s^n, where n = 3 and 2 for a single-ion and two-ions models, respectively [5]. The presently observed temperature dependence is not well understood and a further study is necessary to reveal the correlation between K and M_s for the LTP MnBi.

In summary, the LTP MnBi thin films were fabricated by sputter deposition of Bi/Mn multilayer and subsequent annealing. Their crystal orientation can be controlled by the annealing condition. The film annealed at 550 °C for 30 minutes shows preferential growth of the c-axis along the film normal. On the other hand, the film annealed at 350 °C for 15 hours shows non-oriented structure. The H_c and K for the c-axis oriented film increase with increasing temperature and K is found to be inversely proportional to $M_s(0)^n$. To the best of the authors' knowledge, this is the first report on the correlation between K and $M_s(0)$ for the LTP MnBi.

Acknowledgement
This work was supported in part by National Science Foundation for the G8 program (CMMI-1229049) and TDK Corporation. The authors express their gratitude to Dr. Sepehri A. Hossein and Dr. Kazuhiro Hono at NIMS for their detailed analyses by high resolution TEM and for fruitful discussions.

References

[1] P. A. Albert, W. J. Carr, *J. Appl. Phys.*, 1961, 32, S201.
[2] T. Chen, W. E. Stutius, *IEEE Trans. Magn.*, 1974, 10, 581.
[3] X. Guo, X.Chen, Z.Altounian, J.O.Ström-Olsen, *Phys. Rev. B*, 1992, 46, 14578.
[4] T. Hozumi, P. LeClair, G. Mankey, C. Mewes, H. Sepehri-Amin, K. Hono, T. Suzuki, *J. Appl. Phys.*, 2014, 115, 17A737.
[5] O. N. Mryasov, U. Nowak, K. Y. Guslienko, R. W. Chantrell, *Europhys. Lett.*, 2005, 69, 805.

Enhancing the Magnetic Properties of High Aspect Ratio Co_xC Particles through Post Synthetic Processing

ZACHARY J. HUBA[1], KYLER J. CARROLL[1], VINCENT G. HARRIS[2], EVERETT E. CARPENTER[1]
[1]Virginia Commonwealth University, Richmond, Va 23284, USA
[2]Northeastern University, Boston, MA 02115

Abstract: *The solution processing of magnetic nanoparticles can allow for control of particle shape and size, resulting in enhanced magnetic properties. In this study we synthesize high aspect ratio Co_xC particles possessing high coercivities of 3.5 kOe. Development of an acid cleaning process resulted in an increase of coercivities to 3.9 kOe. Coercivity distribution measurements revealed significant switching events above 6 kOe, and helps to demonstrate the potential of the Co_xC system as an alternative hard ferromagnetic material to current technologies.*

Keywords: *cobalt carbide; hard ferromagnet; acid etching; polyol process*

Address: Everett E. Carpenter, Department of Chemistry, Virginia Commonwealth University, Richmond, Va 23284, U.S.A., E-mail: ecarpenter2@vcu.edu

1. Introduction

Rare Earth (RE) based permanent magnets (e.g. $Nd_2Fe_{14}B$ and Sm_xCo_y) are the mostly commonly used permanent magnetic materials in commercial and industrial applications, owing to their high intrinsic energy products [1]. However, many applications do not require the high energy products of RE magnets, nor their high cost. Current RE free magnets (e.g. doped hexaferrites and Alnico) possess decreased magnetic properties when compared to their RE counterparts, making them useful in only limited applications [2]. Hence, the search for new, alternative RE free magnets is a research area of increasing interest. This work reports the solution synthesis of high aspect ratio cobalt carbide (Co_xC) nanoparticles possessing enhanced magnetic properties over previous reports [3,4]. Also, a post synthetic processing technique is applied to further enhance magnetic properties. With further optimization, Co_xC based magnets could compete with current RE free magnets and be implemented into many of today's current technologies.

2. Expermimental Techniques

In a typical reaction, 10 mL of tetraethylene glycol and 3 μL of concentrated trace metal HCl were added to a round bottom flask. The solution was then degassed with N_2 and stirred mechanically for 5 minutes. After five minutes, the solution was rapidly heated to 327 °C under distillation conditions. Heating from room temperature to 327 °C took about 10 min, on average. Once at 327 °C, 100 mg of cobalt fumarate anhydrous was added as a dry powder to the glycol/HCl mixture. The synthesis of cobalt fumarate anhydrous can be found elsewhere [5]. After addition of the cobalt fumarate, the reaction was kept under distillation for 1 h. At this point, the heat source was removed and the reaction mixture was allowed to cool to room temperature naturally, still under an N_2 atmosphere and mechanically stirring. The resulting magnetic product was magnetically separated from the supernatant and washed with methanol numerous times. The collected powder was then dried in a vacuum oven at room temperature.

In attempts to better clean synthesized Co_xC particles, particles were subjected to a dilute acid etching process. In short, particles were sonicated in a mixture of 300 μL of HNO_3 in 4 mL of 190-proof ethanol. Sonication times were on the order of 15 min. The particles were then washed with methanol and magnetically separated after the sonication process.

Crystal structure analysis was carried out using a PANalytical X'Pert Pro MPD diffractometer under Cu Kα (λ = 1.5418 Å). Crystal grain size was determined using the Scherrer equation. Transmission electron imaging and analysis was conducted on a Zeiss Libra120 with an accelerating voltage of 120 kV. Elemental mapping of cobalt was conducted using Electron Energy Loss Spectroscopy at the L-edge. Magnetic characterization was collected using Vibrating Sample Magnetometry on a Quantum Design Versalab physical property measurement system. Measurements were collected in fields from 3 T to -3 T. Coercivity distributions were calculated from the first derivative of collected Direct Current Demagnetization Curves (DCD). For the DCD curves, a saturation field of 3 T and reversal field steps of 100 Oe were used.

3. Results and Discussion

Cobalt fumarate was chosen as the cobalt precursor because the fumarate ligand can act as a carbon source and shows high efficiency towards forming the carbide phases [5-7]. A representative XRD pattern for as prepared Co_xC powders is shown in Figure 1. Cobalt carbides can form two metastable orthorhombic crystal structures with stoichiometries of Co_3C and Co_2C. The use of cobalt fumarate commonly induces the formation of Co_3C, with only small amounts of Co_2C. The crystal phase composition for the sample shown in Figure 1 is 82.4% Co_3C and 17.6% Co_2C. Based on peak widths, a crystal grain size of 36 nm was calculated for the Co_3C phase.

From a magnetics standpoint, Co_3C is the preferred carbide crystal structure when compared to Co_2C. Theoretical calculations show Co_3C to exhibit a significantly higher magnetization than Co_2C [3]. Also, Co_3C was experimentally determined to possess an effective magnetic anisotropy value of 0.75 MJ/m^3[7]. The high magnetic anisotropy of the Co_3C phase caused the as prepared Co_xC particles to have a coercivity value of 3.5 kOe, as shown in Figure 2(a). A magnetization of 41 emu/g was recorded for the as prepared Co_xC particles.

In order to better clean the as prepared particles, an acid etching process was employed as described in the Synthesis section. The application of a single acid etch process resulted in an increase in coercivity to 3.9 kOe. Also only a minimal drop in magnetization was observed [Figure 2(a)]. However, acid etching a second time caused a dramatic decrease in magnetization and regression of the coercivity back to 3.5 kOe.

Inspecting the coercivity distribution revealed dramatic differences between the as prepared and acid etched samples [Figure 2(b)]. The as prepared sample showed multiple maximums, implying multiple magnetic phases. A low coercivity and moderate coercivity phase with coercivity modes of 1.8 kOe and 3.5 kOe, respectively, were observed. Also, significant switching events above 6 kOe were present. After subjecting the Co_xC particles to an acid etch process, the low coercivity phase is diminished and the coercivity distribution resembles a single magnetic phase, still with significant switching above 6 kOe. The second acid etch process causes the removal of high reversal field switching; a Gaussian like peak with a coercivity mode of 3.5 kOe resulted.

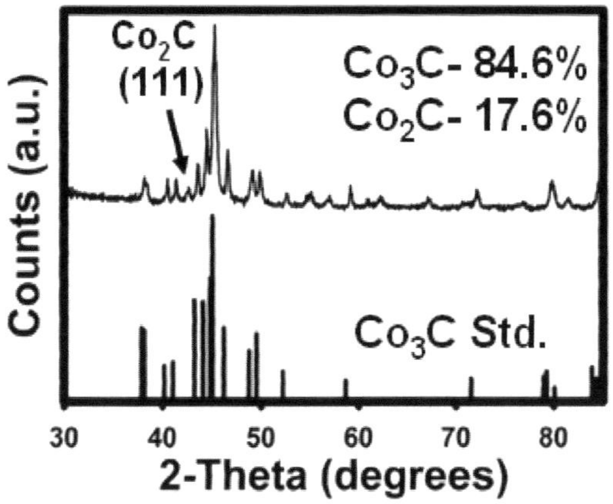

Fig. 1. XRD scan of as prepared Co_xC particles. Stick plot of a Co_3C standard is shown underneath for reference.

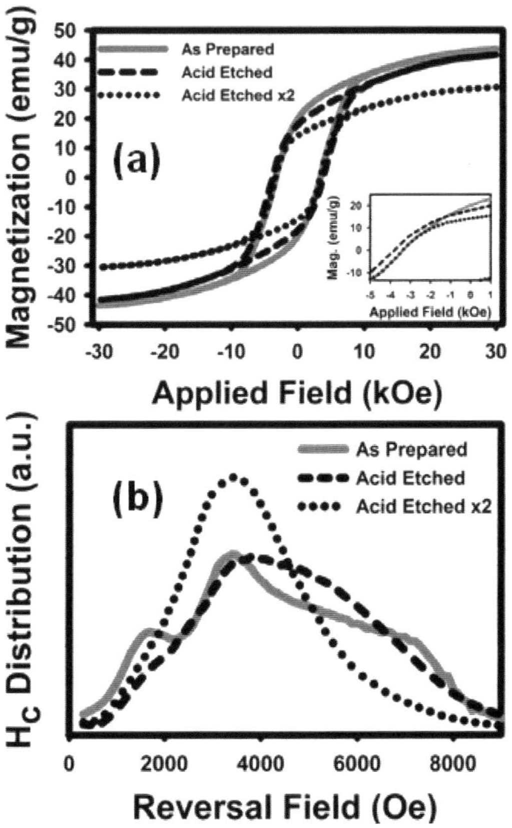

Fig. 2. (a) M(H) curves and (b) coercivity distributions of as prepared and acid etched Co_xC particles, collected at 300 K.

The high coercivity and changes in magnetics upon application of acid etching processed can be explained through visualization of the Co_xC particles (Figure 3). As prepared particles showed high aspect ratios; diameters were commonly less than 100 nm, with lengths well above 1 μm. A single acid etching process resulted in no observable change in particle morphology. However, a second acid etching process resulted in particles becoming porous, with many areas decreased density. The decreased density was confirmed to be a loss of cobalt through elemental mapping (not shown).

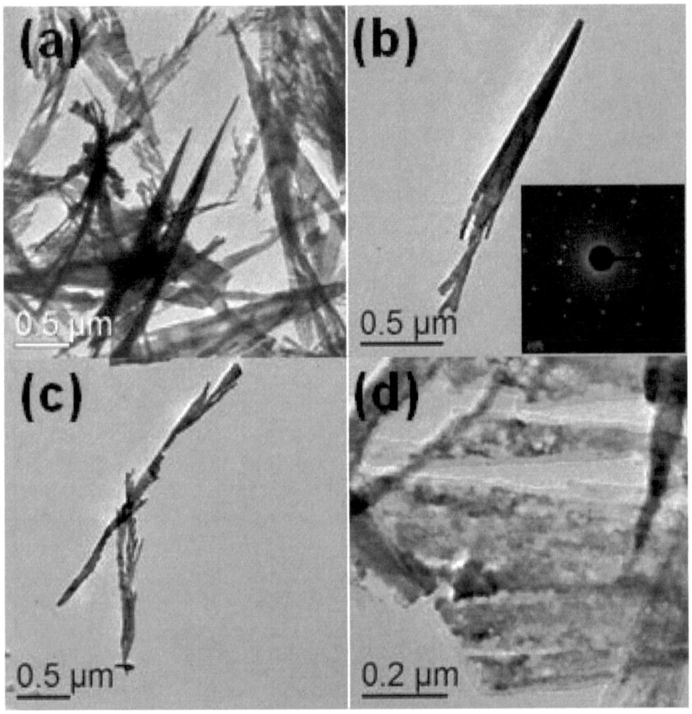

Fig. 3. TEM images (a-c) of as prepared Co_xC particles and (d) particles subjected to two acid etching processes. Inset in (b) shows SAED pattern of single high aspect ratio particle.

Taking all of the collected data into account, a mechanism for the effect of acid etching on magnetic properties can be proposed. The high coercivity (3.5 kOe) of the as prepared Co_xC particles can be attributed to the high magnetic anisotropy of the Co_3C crystal phase and the high aspect ratios of the formed particles. Application of a single acid etching process acts to eliminate contaminants on the particles' surface, without significantly affecting the morphology of the high aspect ratio particles. This results in an increase in coercivity to 3.9 kOe, and loss of low coercivity phases as observed in Figure 2(b). However, a second acid etching process begins to remove cobalt from the individual particles and causes a dramatic decrease in magnetization and coercivity values.

Conclusion

In this report, high aspect ratio Co_xC particles were synthesized using a wet chemical approach. The particles contained a high composition of the Co_3C crystal phase. Through etching of surface contaminants, coercivities as high as 3.9 kOe could be observed. With further optimization, the magnetic properties could lead to implementation of Co_xC magnets into many current technologies.

Acknowledgement

Financial support from the ARPA-e REACT program 1574-1674 is greatly acknowledged. The help of the staff of the VCU Nanomaterials Core Characterization Facility is also greatly appreciated. This work was also partially funded through a graduate research fellowship through Altria Group Inc.

References

[1] O. Gutfleisch, M. A. Willard, E. Bruck, C. H. Chen, S. G. Sankar and J. P. Liu, *Adv. Mater.* **23**, 2011, 821.

[2] J. M. D. Coey, *IEEE Trans. Magn.* **47**, 2011, 4671.

[3] K. J. Carroll, Z. J. Huba, S. R. Spurgeon, M. Qian, S. N. Khanna, D. M. Hudgins, M. L. Taheri and E. E. Carpenter, *Appl. Phys. Lett.* **101**, 2012, 012409.

[4] V. G. Harris, Y. Chen, A. Yang, S. Yoon, Z. Chen, A. L. Geiler, J. Gao, C. N. Chinnasamy, L. H. Lewis, C. Vittoria, E. E. Carpenter, K. J. Carroll, R. Goswami, M. A. Willard, L. Kurihara, M. Gjoka and O. Kalogirou, *J. Phys. D – Appl. Phys.* **43**, 2010, 7.

[5] Z. J. Huba and E. E. Carpenter, *Dalton Trans.* 2014.

[6] A. A. El-Gendy, T. Almugaiteeb and E. E. Carpenter, *J. Magn. Magn. Mater.* 348, 2013, 136.

[7] A. A. El-Gendy, M. Qian, Z. J. Huba, S. N. Khanna and E. E. Carpenter, *Appl. Phys. Lett.* **104**, 2014, *104*, -

Review of Synthesis and Characterizatin of $Fe_{16}N_2$ Powder

B. ZANDE[1], S. SIMIZU[1], R.T. OBERMYER[1], A. MARGOLIN[1], S.G. SANKAR[1], S. BENNETT[2], M. FEYGENSON[2], V. LAUTER[2]
[1] Advanced Materials Corporation, Pittsburgh, PA 15220 USA
[2] Oak Ridge National Laboratory, Oak Ridge, TN 37831 USA

Abstract: *Powdered samples of $Fe_{16}N_2$ and $(Fe_{16-x},Mn_x)N_2$ were synthesized in a fluidized bed reactor at temperatures between 120 ^0C and 160 ^oC. using mainly oxy-hydroxides as precursors. Powder x-ray and neutron diffraction patterns confirm that the samples, prepared under optimal conditions explored thus far, consist of nearly 98.5% of the 16:2 phase, balance being α-Fe. The neutron diffraction analyses indicate the average magnetic moment of the Fe atom in the $Fe_{16}N_2$ phase to be nearly 2.8 μ_B at room temperature. Extensive studies on the stability of the samples by thermo-gravimetric analysis and by high precision gas desorption measurements show that the samples begin to destabilize at temperatures around 200 ^oC, resulting in the formation of Fe_4N and α-Fe above about 240 ^oC. This meta-stability of the 16:2 phase is a serious impediment towards fabricating dense magnets via commercially viable conventional metallurgical techniques. Further, recent modeling studies published in the literature indicate that partial substitutions into the iron sites with other magnetic elements such as nickel, cobalt and manganese has a limited prospect of enhancing the thermal stability of the $Fe_{16}N_2$ phase or in significantly improving its magnetic properties. In addition, the magneto-crystalline anisotropy of the $Fe_{16}N_2$ phase is at least an order of magnitude lower than that of $Nd_2Fe_{14}B$, thus offering limited opportunity to fabricate permanent magnets with a high coercivity. However, reasonably high magnetic induction exceeding ~22 kG and modest coercivities exhibited by the $Fe_{16}N_2$ powder may find a few niche applications such as in proximity sensors, bonded magnets and fractional horse power motors. Further advances in stabilizing the 16:2 phase and related structures and in enhancing the magnetic properties, including magnetic anisotropy, are needed to make permanent magnets with very high energy product based on this structure.*

Key Words: *$Fe_{16}N_2$, powder synthesis, fluidized bed reactor, bonded magnets, stability*

Address: S.G. Sankar, Advanced Material Corporation, 850, Poplar Street, Pittsburgh, PA 15220 USA
Tel: (412) 921 9600; E-mail: Sankar@advanced-material.com

1. Introduction

For well over eighty years, several researchers around the world have investigated the Fe-N system. Lehrer [1] first reported the phase diagram of Fe-N and the low-field magnetic properties on Fe-N compositions. α"-$Fe_{16}N_2$ phase was first identified by Jack [2] in 1950 as precipitates in a matrix of nitrogen martensite (α') that was obtained by quenching nitrogen austenite (γ). He has published several papers on its crystal structure and pointed out its meta-stability. The $Fe_{16}N_2$ structure was found to form as a thin film on an appropriate substrate by Kim and Takahashi [3] and by Sugita and his co-workers [4]. The former authors first reported the most exciting observation that this phase exhibited giant magnetism. However, because of the difficulty in quantifying the amount of the material in thin film form, the exact magnitude of the moment of $Fe_{16}N_2$ has remained a controversial issue. Despite subsequent attempts to refine Jack's method by several groups, for example, by Wallace and co-workers [5] and by Coey [6], $Fe_{16}N_2$ phase could not be formed in bulk form without significant amounts of α- and γ-phases as secondary phases. The presence of these latter phases, whose relative amounts were difficult to assess in an unambiguous manner, has led to significant uncertainties in the evaluation of magnetic moment of the 16:2 phase and thus, the occurrence of giant magnetism in $Fe_{16}N_2$ remained uncertain.

2. Experimental

In the early nineteen nineties, Advanced Materials Corporation has undertaken an effort to fabricate $Fe_{16}N_2$ powder employing its proprietary technique using a fluidized bed reactor. The starting iron oxy-hydroxide was converted into α-iron with a relatively high surface area at temperatures below 440 ^oC and then reacted in-situ with either ammonia or mixtures of ammonia and nitrogen (or argon or helium) at temperatures between 120 and 180 ^oC. These reactions were carried out under computer control. The resultant powder, which is pyrophoric, was handled in protective inert atmosphere. Development of this work has resulted in obtaining the pure $Fe_{16}N_2$ powder in large quantities with attractive

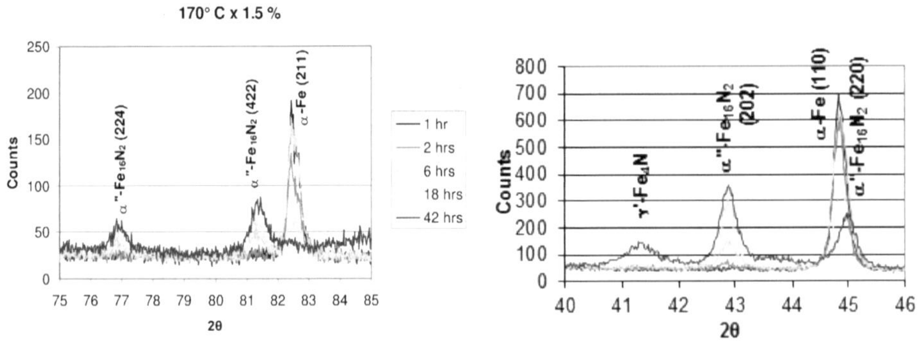

Fig. 1. Summary diagram showing the X-ray powder diffraction patterns of samples prepared at 170 °C for varying periods. 2-Theta regions relevant to the main peaks are shown. In the figure on the left hand side, reduction in the intensity of α-Fe (211) line and a corresponding increase in the intensities of α''-$Fe_{16}N_2$ lines (224 and 422) can be clearly seen as the reaction period increases from 1 to 42 hours. In the figure on the right hand side, we note the reduction in the intensity of α-Fe line (110) and the increase in the intensity of α''-$Fe_{16}N_2$ line (220). In addition, an increase in intensity of γ'-Fe_4N line (111) may be noted when the reaction is carried out for 42 hours.

compositional, morphological and magnetic properties.

In parallel, several other researchers have independently initiated detailed investigations on the 16:2 materials [7-9]. Fortunately, a few of them will be describing their work in this session and therefore, we are refraining from making any comments on their work in this paper.

2.1. The Process

Based on the processing variables, such as the chemistry of the starting material, reaction (reduction of the oxide and subsequent nitrogenation of α-Fe) temperature and its duration, flow rates of the gases etc., the relative fractions of the resulting nitrides vary. We have investigated nearly four hundred reactions. In this paper, we provide a summary of the important results.

For instance, the relative amounts of the three main phases obtained at a nitrogenation temperature between 150 and 180 °C for 18 hours result in the formation of varying amounts of $Fe_{16}N_2$, Fe_4N and α-Fe depending on the temperature, duration and relative concentrations of the reactive gases. It is pertinent to note that the formation of the γ-FeN was

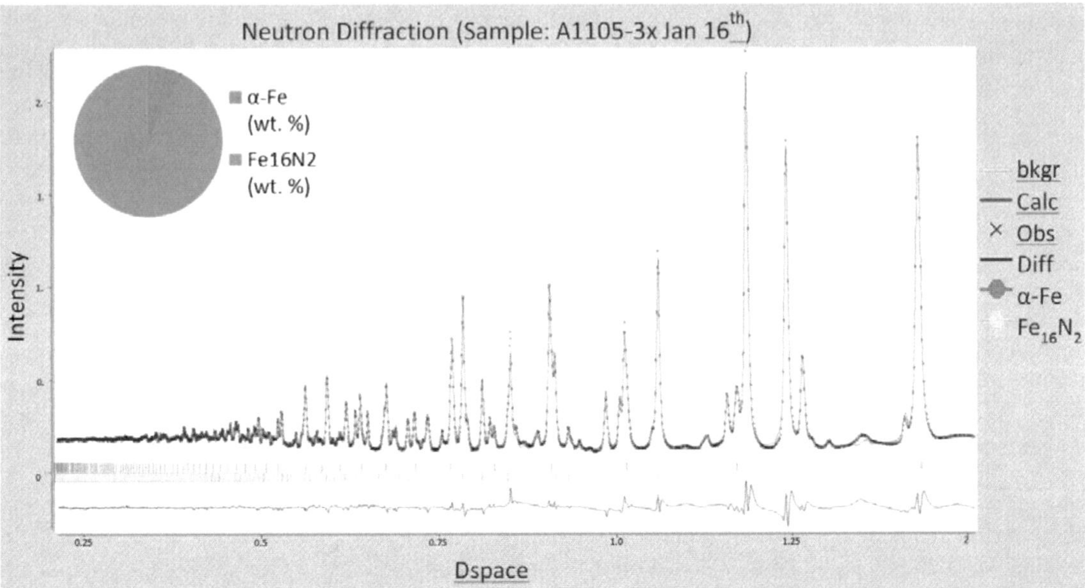

Fig. 2. Neutron diffraction pattern of a Fe16N2 powder sample. Rietveld refinement using the Fe16N2 and α-Fe phases resulted in a good statistical fit (Chi^2 = 63.10 for 73 variables). The weight percent of the two phases is 94:6.

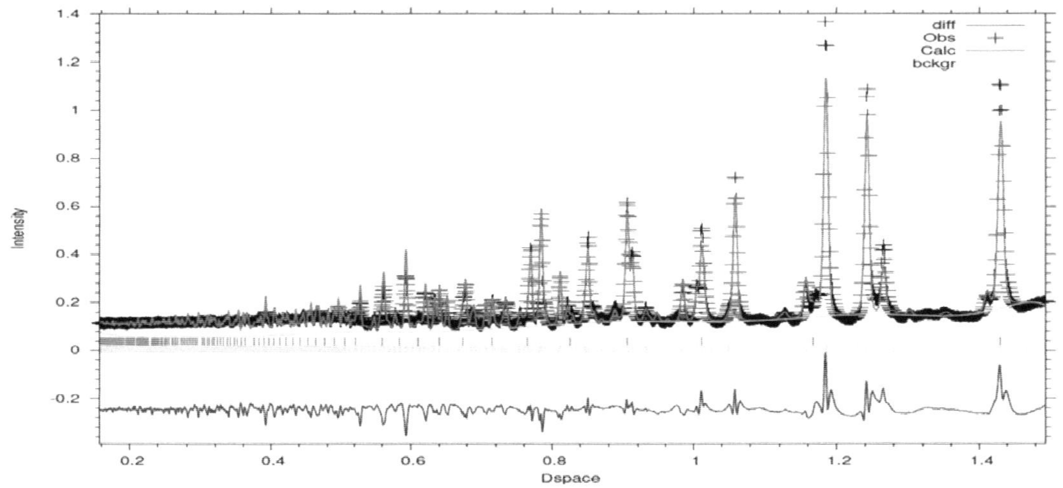

Fig. 3. Neutron diffraction pattern of a $(Fe,Mn)_{16}N_2$ powder sample. Rietveld refinement using the 16:2 and α-Fe phases resulted in a good statistical fit. The weight percent of the two phases is 98.5:1.5.

completely avoided in this approach. Further, by optimizing the process variables, we have now been successful in obtaining powder samples with nearly 98.5% $Fe_{16}N_2$, balance being α-Fe.

2.2. X-ray and neutron diffraction

The two main segments of the powder x-ray pattern of a typical reaction product is shown in Figure 2a-b. It shows the evolution of the 16:2 phase as the nitrogenation reaction proceeds from 0 to 42 hours. We note that, under these experimental conditions, nitrogenation for about 18 hours appears to produce an optimal amount of the 16:2 powder. It is also interesting to note that when the reaction is extended to nearly 42 hours, the undesirable γ'-phase (with a lower magnetization than that of the 16-2 phase) begins to form.

Neutron diffraction studies were performed on $(Fe, Mn)_{16}N_2$ samples at the Spallation Neutron Source at Oak Ridge National Laboratory. The powder sample was loaded into a 3 mm diameter quartz capillary for measurement on the Nanoscale-Ordered Materials Diffractometer (NOMAD). The data was analyzed by Rietveld refinement. The diffraction data was used to classify the phases present, and estimate their relative concentrations in the powder specimen. In the case of $Fe_{16}N_2$, initial fitting was performed using the 8 most probable phases based on elemental composition, (α-Fe, $Fe_{16}N_2$, Fe_3O_4, Fe_2O_3, Fe_8N, Fe_4N, Fe_3N, Fe_3C). Of these phases, α-Fe and $Fe_{16}N_2$ showed measureable phase fractions. Further refinement using these two phases resulted in a good statistical fit (Chi^2 = 63.10 for 73 variables). The weight percent of the two phases is 94:6 as shown in the figure.

Neutron diffraction studies were also performed at Oak Ridge on a second sample in which a part of the iron was replaced with manganese. This sample was prepared by preparing a mixed solution of iron nitrate and manganese nitrate (Nominal composition being ~7 atomic percent of manganese). Ammonia was added to the above solution at a temperature of about 80 °C to obtain a co-precipitate of the mixed metal hydroxide. This was filtered and washed thoroughly

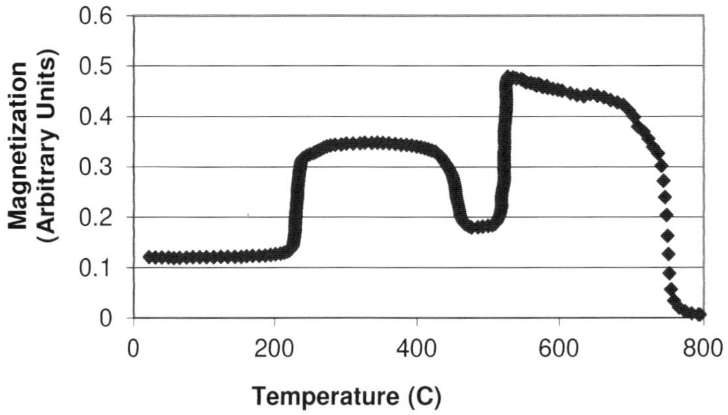

Fig. 4. Magnetization versus temperature behavior of $Fe_{16}N_2$ sample, showing the formation of Fe_4N at about 240 °C.

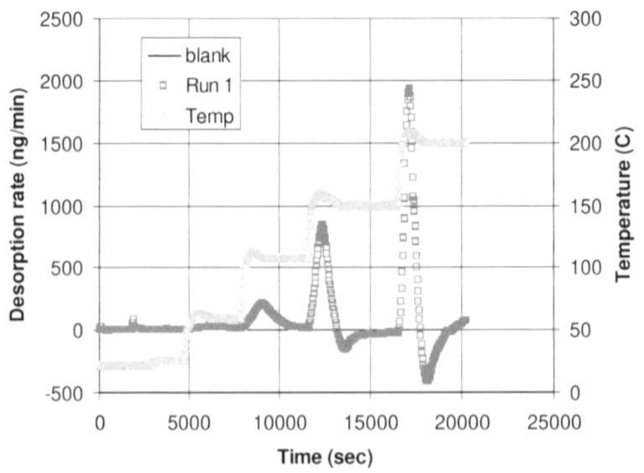

Fig. 5. Desorption rate of nitrogen from $Fe_{16}N_2$ sample, showing measurable desorption of nitrogen when the sample is heated up from 100 °C to 200 °C.

with deionized water. A few grams of the dried powder was loaded into the reactor and subjected to reduction followed by nitrogenation under reaction conditions similar to the those employed to obtain other 16:2 powders.

Results of the neutron diffraction analysis are given in Figure 3. It may be noted that this material contains 98.5% of the 16:2 phase, the balance being $_{a}$-Fe.

2.3. Thermal stability

As pointed out earlier, the meta-stability of $Fe_{16}N_2$ is of considerable concern, especially when we consider its potential for applications. Towards this goal, we have carried out two different types of experiments. Several samples prepared in our laboratory were first subjected to thermo-magnetic analysis at low applied fields in a vibrating sample magnetometer. A representative plot of magnetization (in arbitrary units) versus temperature is displayed in Figure 4. This curve shows that the 16:2 phase destabilizes at about 240 °C to form Fe_4N and α-Fe, which upon further heating exhibits the Curie temperature typical of Fe_4N and subsequently converts into pure Fe. From the relative intensity of the sharp increase in magnetization at ~240 °C, we have been able to estimate the phase purity of the powder.

We have also performed nitrogen desorption analysis of the $Fe_{16}N_2$ powders using a sensitive transducer in an automated gas desorption analysis unit. Results obtained on a typical sample are shown in Figure 5. In this experiment, the rate of nitrogen desorption from the sample is determined. These results show that some measurable quantities of nitrogen begins to desorb when the sample is heated from 100 to 150 °C; this becomes much more at higher temperatures.

Acknowledgement
The authors thank Dr. Mike Brady at ORNL for useful discussions. This work was supported by U.S. Navy, Army and DOE (ARPA-E) under a number of grants.

References

[1] E. Lehrer, *Z. Elektrochem.*, 1930, 36, 460.
[2] K.H. Jack, *Proc. Roy. Soc.*, 1951, A208, 200.
[3] T.K. Kim, M. Takehashi, *Appl. Phys. Lett.*, 1972, 20, 492.
[4] Y. Sugita, K. Mitsuoka, M. Komuro, H. Hochia, Y. Kozono, M. Hanazono, *J. Appl. Phys.*, 1991, 70, 5977.
[5] W. E. Wallace, M.Q. Huang, *J. Appl. Phys.*, 1994, 76, 6648.
[6] J. M. D. Coey, *J. Appl. Phys.*, 1994, 76, 6632.
[7] M. Takahashi, H. Takahashi, H. Nashi, H. Shoji, T. Wakiyama, M. Kuwabara, *J. Appl. Phys.*, 1996, 79, 5564.
[8] N. Ji, L. F. Allard, E. Lara-Curzio, and J. P. Wang, *Appl. Phys. Lett.*, 2011, 98, 092506.
[9] L.Q. Ke, K.D. Belashchenko, M. van Schilfgaarde, T. Kotani, V.P. Antropov, *Phys. Rev.*, 2013, B. 88, 024404.

Microstructure Evolution and Magnetic Properties of As-Cast Fe_2NiAl Alloy during Cooling After Homogenization at a Critical Rate

V.P. MENUSHENKOV, M.V. GORSHENKOV, I.V. SHETININ, E.S. SAVCHENKO
National University of Science and Technology "MISIS"

Abstract: *Microstructure and magnetic properties of as-cast Alni alloy were studied by transmission electron microscopy, X-ray diffraction and atomic force microscopy and using a vibrating sample magnetometer. Cooled Fe-Ni-Al samples have been characterized by modulated structure formed during the solid-solution decomposition into β- and β_2-phases within the miscibility gap. The rate of decomposition in the Alni alloy is so high that the decomposition cannot be suppressed by water-quenching. Therefore, subsequent annealing leads to the development of the zone structure instead of the decomposition of single-phase solid solution. The quenched zone structure and optimum modulated structure formed during cooling at a critical rate changes during additional aging at 780 °C.*

Keywords: *permanent magnet; Fe-Ni-Al alloy; heat treatment; zone structure; modulated structure*

Address: Vladimir Menushenkov, Leninskii pr. 4, Moscow 119049, Russia, E-mail: menushenkov@gmail.com

1. Introduction

In the last decades, due to the monopoly position of China on the market of rare-earth metals (RE) and the extensive soaring prices of Nd and Dy, interest of researchers once again shifts to RE-free magnets, including Fe-Ni-Al-(Co) alloys. Alni alloys with the coercive force $H_c \approx 700$ Oe still find application in simple devices due to its low cost and simplicity of manufacturing. Interest to these alloys could grow provided that hysteresis properties are increased [1]. Also, the Fe-Ni-Al alloys remain a convenient model system for studying the spinodal decomposition and formation of modulated microstructures. The magnetic hardness of as-cast Alni magnets results from the shape anisotropy of magnetic precipitates that are formed when the Alni alloys are subjected to a special heat treatment. The modulated microstructure is formed upon cooling of solid solution at a critical rate (heat treatment HT1), or during annealing of quenched solid solution (HT2) [2,3]. The H_c value reached after HT1 is higher than that reached after HT2 by a factor of 1.5 [4]. It was pointed out [2,3,5,6] that the cooling rate of the Fe-Ni-Al alloys during water quenching from 1200 – 1240 °C was not sufficient to stabilize the homogeneous solid solution. However, no detailed studies of the effect of zone structure on the subsequent solid solution decomposition during heat treatment have been carried out yet.

In connection with the foregoing, the aim of the present work is to investigate peculiarities of the structure of the Alni alloy (1) after the water quenching, (2) after cooling at a critical rate from the single-phase region, and (3) after aging of the as-quenched and cooled samples.

2. Materials and methods

The $Fe_{51.1}Ni_{23.5}Al_{23.7}Si_{1.7}$ Alni alloy was studied. The as-cast alloy was prepared by melting in an induction furnace using pure metals. The melt was cast into a copper finger-mold. The cast samples were additionally treated in accordance with the following regimes: water quenching from 1240 °C (after holding for 20 min); cooling of as-cast alloy from 1240 °C (after holding for 20 min) at a critical cooling rate (V ~ 2 K/min) up to an intermediate temperature T_q = 900 – 20 °C with subsequent water quenching; aging of the quenched and cooled alloy at 780 °C for 10 min.

The structures of the samples were examined by X-ray diffraction (XRD), transmission electron microscopy (TEM) and scanning electron microscopy (SEM). X-ray diffraction analysis was performed using a Rigaku diffractometer, Co $K\alpha$ radiation, and a graphite monochromator. The thin foils were examined using a JEM-1400 microscope and an accelerating voltage of 120 kV. The microstructure of samples was analyzed using a JEOL JSM-6610LV scanning electron microscope. Magnetic properties of powders were measured at room temperature in a maximum magnetizing field of 50 kOe using a PPMS EverCool-II (Quantum Design) magnetometer. Magnetic properties of cast samples were measured in magnetizing fields of up to 25 kOe using a hysteresisgraph AMT-4.

3. Results and Discussion

Fig. 1 shows (*a*) bright-field and (*b*) dark-field images of the structure of cast Alni alloy, which was water quenched from 1240 °C, and (1*a*, inset) associated

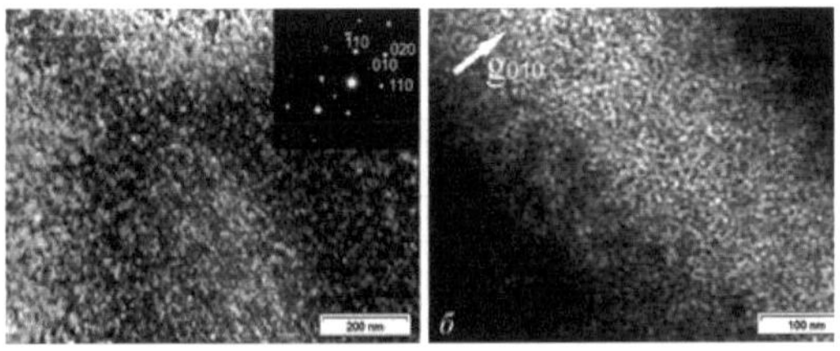

Fig. 1. Micrographs of the Alni alloy water-quenched from 1240 °C: (a) bright-field image, (b) dark-field image take in the (010) superlattice reflection of the B2 phase and (1a, inset) electron diffraction pattern, zone axis [001].

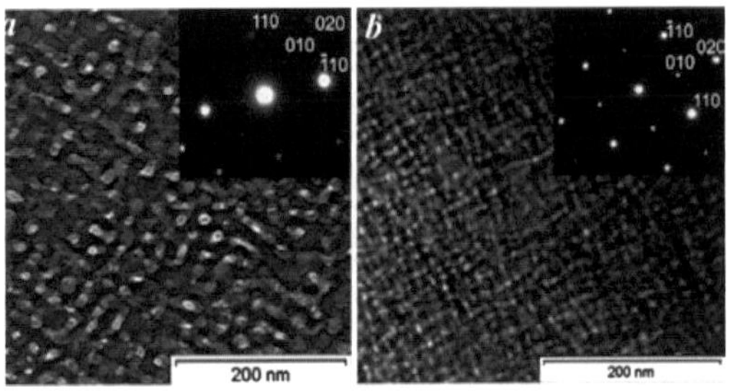

Fig. 2. Micrographs of the structure of cast Alni alloy cooled at a critical rate from 1240 °C up to (a) T_q = 860 °C and (b) 850 °C; and electron diffraction pattern (inset), zone axis [001].

electron diffraction pattern taken for an area with zone axis [001]. The microstructure of quenched sample does not correspond to the solid-solution state (zone structure). The presence of concentration inhomogenities ~10 nm in size, allows us to assume that, during water quenching from 1240 °C, the occurrence of partial decomposition of the solid solution into β and β_2 phases within the miscibility gap. Note that the coercive force of water-quenched sample is only ~ 4 Oe.

The electron diffraction pattern (Fig. 1*a* inset) is a superposition of two structures, such as the disordered A2 (β phase) and ordered B2 (β_2 phase) structures; the (010) superlattice reflections correspond to the β_2 phase. The detailed morphology of decomposition products is observed in the dark-field image of the quenched alloy (Fig. 1*b*), which was taken using the superlattice (010) reflection of the B2 phase in the electron diffraction pattern (Fig. 1*a* inset). Precipitates of the β_2 phase, which are ordered with the formation of B2 structure, are observed to be bright, whereas β-phase precipitates are dark. It is seen that alternating β and β_2 phase precipitates arranged in a random way form a labyrinth structure. The X-ray diffraction analysis showed that, similarly to electron diffraction pattern, the experimental X-ray diffraction pattern is the superposition of patterns of two A2 (β-phase) and B2 (β_2-phase) structures with close lattice parameters that are a = 0.28776 and a = 0.28782 nm, respectively.

The coercive force was found to exhibit a nonmonotonic dependence on the temperature T_q, which shows the minimum $H_c \leq 40$ Oe at T_q = 850 °C. Fig. 2 shows micrographs of the cast Alni alloy cooled from 1240 °C to 860 °C and 850 °C at a critical rate. The cooling to T_q = 860 °C has caused the formation of modulated microstructure and increases H_c to 370 Oe. However, cooling to T_q = 850 °C led to the destruction of modulated microstructure by splitting of β- and β_2-precipitates and forming the speckled microstructure that is similar to that formed at $T_q \geq 870$ °C.

The restoration of modulated structure and increase in the coercivity was observed already after quenching at $T_q \leq 840$ °C. Fig. 3 shows micrographs of the cast Alni alloy cooled at a critical rate from 1240 °C to T_q = 840 °C.

Fig. 3*a* (inset) shows the electron-diffraction pattern, zone axis [101]. The H_c of the alloy after such a treatment is 430 Oe.

Finally, the high-quality modulated microstructure giving the maximum H_c = 690 Oe was obtained for the sample cooled up to RT at the critical rate (Fig. 4). The comparison of bright- and dark-field images of the structure shows that this sample is characterized by formed modulated structure consisting of elongated β-phase particles that are oriented mainly along <100> directions and separated by matrix β_2-phase areas. As it can be seen in the dark-field image, which was taken in image-forming (010) reflection of the B2 phase, bright β_2-phase precipitates form an almost continuous net that separates dark β-phase particles. The size of β-phase particles varies from 20 to 80 nm; their aspect ratio l/d is 1 to 4. It is likely that the combination of factors, such as the small size, shape anisotropy and magnetic isolation of β-phase particles ensures the high H_c = 690 Oe of samples cooled at a critical rate.

The micrographs of the optimum cooled Alni alloy (Fig.4) after aging at 780 °C for 10 min followed by water quenching are shown in Fig. 5. The H_c of the

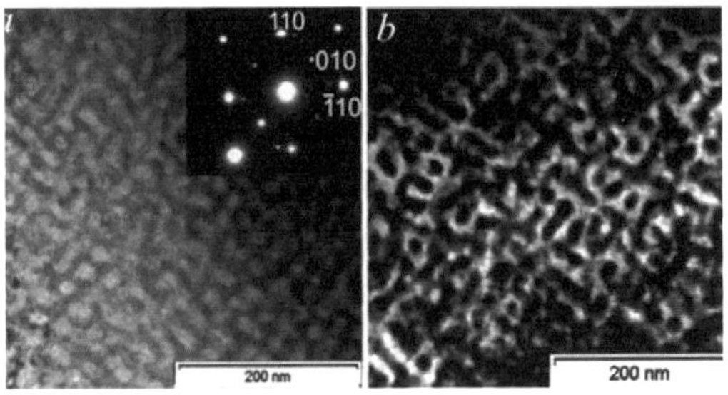

Fig. 3. Micrographs of the structure of cast Alni alloy cooled from 1240 °C to T_q = 840 °C at a critical rate: (a) bright-field image; (b) dark-field image taken in the superlattice (010) reflection of the B2 phase; (3a, inset) electron diffraction pattern, zone axis [001].

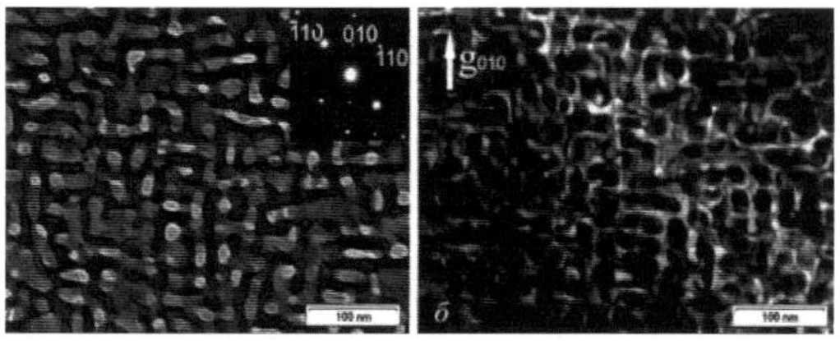

Fig. 4. Micrographs of the structure of cast Alni alloy cooled at a critical rate from 1240°C up to T_q = 20 °C: (a) bright-field image; (b) dark-field image taken in the superlattice (010) reflection of the B2 phase; and (4a, inset) electron diffraction pattern, zone axis [101].

aged alloy decreases to 320 Oe. Aging leads to the partial degradation of the modulated structure, which is accompanied by a noticeable (2 - 3 times) increase in the size of precipitates of β-phase and their partial disintegration into smaller fragments.

For comparison, Fig. 6 shows micrographs of the Alni alloy after water quenching from 1240 °C and aging at 780 °C (with subsequent quenching). The H_c increases from 4 Oe for the as-quenched sample to 350 Oe for the aged alloy.

The aging of quenched sample at 780 °C leads to the formation of the modulated structure, which, however, is markedly different from the microstructure of the sample in the optimal state.

The average size of the β precipitates (100 - 150 nm) increases almost twice in comparison with the size of precipitates in the optimally treated sample (Fig. 4). Furthermore, as is seen in the dark-field image (Fig. 6b) the bright β_2 precipitates will not form the continuous net that separates the dark β particles. This worsens insulation of the strongly magnetic particles and decreases the coercive force.

It is known that if the size of particles exceeds a critical single-domain size, the coercive force should be reduced. It can be assumed that the low H_c magnitude of sample after aging at 780 °C, like in the case of quenched sample (Fig. 6), and of optimally treated sample (Fig. 4) may be, primarily, due to the

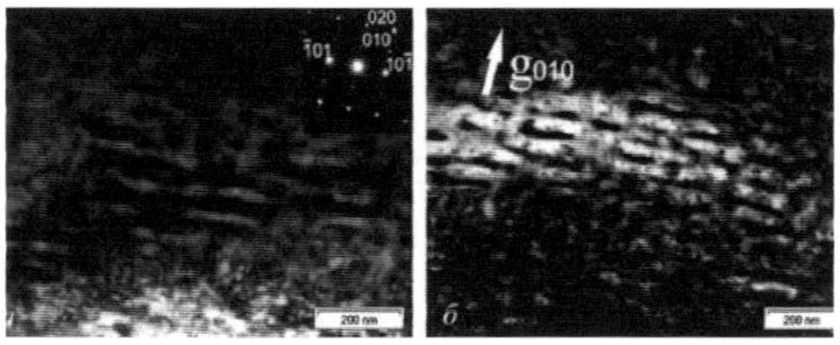

Fig. 5. Micrographs of the structure of cast Alni alloy after critical cooling from 1240 °C to T_q = 20 °C and aging at 780 °C for 10 min: (a) bright-field image; (b) dark-field image taken in the superlattice (010) reflection of the B2 phase; and (5a, inset) electron diffraction pattern, zone axis [101].

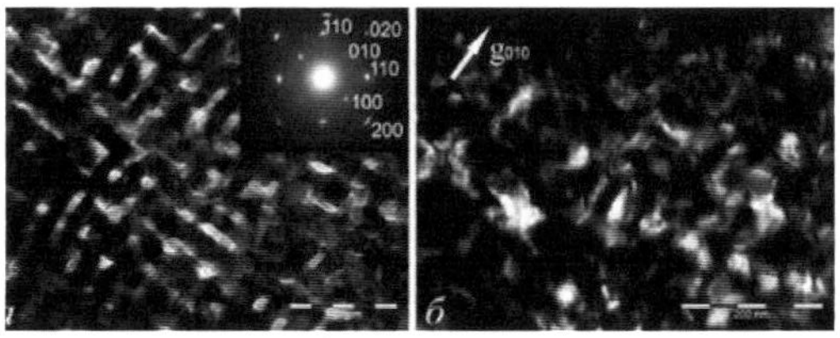

Fig. 6. Micrographs of the structure of Alni alloy after water quenching from 1240 °C and aging at 780 °C for 10 min: (a) bright-field image; (b) dark-field image taken in the superlattice (010) reflection of the B2 phase; and (5a, inset) electron diffraction pattern, zone axis [001]

enlargement of modulated structure components and the violation of single-domain state criterion for the β-phase particles. Another reason for the decrease in the H_c may be the change of β-phase and β_2-matrix compositions in accordance with the phase diagram. When heating the alloy to an aging temperature 780 °C, the β + β_2 region narrows and consequently, β_2 phase must be enriched with iron, which may transform it from the paramagnetic to ferromagnetic state. This will lead to the deterioration of magnetic insulation of strongly magnetic β-phase precipitates and as a consequence, to the decrease in the coercive force of the alloy.

4. Conclusion

The rate of decomposition of the solid solution in the Alni alloy within the miscibility gap is so high that the decomposition cannot be suppressed by water quenching from the single-phase region. The quenched samples are characterized by zone structure. During heating and aging of quenched Alni samples the development of the zone structure rather than the decomposition of single-phase solid solution, takes place. That is why the parameters of the microstructure formed during the isothermal aging are determined by kinetics of growth of already existing β and β_2-phase precipitates.

The optimum periodic modulated structure which is formed in the Alni alloy during cooling at a critical rate from the single-phase region (1240 °C) to 780 – 20 °C ensures the high H_c of 580 - 690 Oe. The periodic modulated structure, which is formed in the quenched sample during annealing at 780 °C, is characterized by large sizes of β-phase precipitates, which are likely to exceed the critical single-domain size. This facilitates the magnetization reversal and decreases the coercive force. The optimum modulated structure is formed during cooling to RT at a critical rate changes during additional aging (780 °C, 10 min); the changes are accompanied by substantial (2-3-fold) increase in strong magnetic β-phase precipitates and their partial decomposition into small fragments. This leads to the decrease in the coercive force.

Acknowledgement
This study was supported by the Ministry of Educations and Science of the Russian Federation and is performed in accordance with the basic part of State Assignment no. 2014/113 for 2014.

References

[1] M.J. Kramer, R.W. McCallum, I.A. Anderson, S. Constantinides, *JOM* **64**, 2012, 752.
[2] N.N. Buinov, R.M. Lerinman. *Dokl. Akad. Nauk USSR* **79**, 1951, 69.
[3] K.J. de Vos, *Z. Angew. Phys.* **21**, 1966, 381.
[4] B.G. Livshits. *Zh. Teor. Fiz.* **10**, 1940, 1981.
[5] E.G. Povolozkii, *FMM* **33**, 1972, 167.
[6] V.P. Menushenkov, T.A. Sviridova, V.V. Shelehov, in: *Proc. 19th Int. Metallurgical and Materials Conference*, May 18-20, 2010, Roznov pod Radhostem, Czech Republic, EU, 284.

First-Principles Study on Magnetization Easy-Axis and Crystal Field Parameters in $R_2Fe_{14}B$ Systems

TAKUYA YOSHIOKA[1], HIROKI TSUCHIURA[1], PAVEL NOVÁK[2]

[1] Department of Applied Physics, Tohoku University, Sendai, Japan

[2] Institute of Physics of ASCR, Prague, Czech Republic

Abstract: *Magnetic properties of intermetallic compounds $R_2Fe_{14}B$ (R = Pr, Nd, Tb, Dy, Ho) are studied based on first principles calculations and crystal field theory. We present magnetic moments and crystal field parameters $A_l^m\langle r^l\rangle$ (l = 2, 4, 6) by using the full-potential linearized augmented plane wave plus local orbitals method. The Fe magnetic moments for $R_2Fe_{14}B$ show good agreement with previous theoretical study. Except for R=Nd, the tilting angles of the magnetization are comparable to previous experimental studies.*

Keywords: *rare earth iron boron permanent magnet; crystal field parameter; spin reorientation phenomena; magnetocrystalline anisotropy energy*

Address: Hiroki Tsuchiura, Department of Applied Physics, Tohoku University, Aoba 6-6-05, Aoba-ku Sendai, Japan, Tel.: +81-22-795-5881, E-mail: tsuchi@solid.apph.tohoku.ac.jp

Because of the recent developments in renewable and sustainable technology, there has been emerging interest in improving the coercivity of Nd-Fe-B permanent magnets, and in revealing its mechanism. Theoretically, one of authors and coworkers have estimated the main contributions of the crystal field parameters (CFPs) of Nd ions around the surface of the crystalline $Nd_2Fe_{14}B$ based on first-principles calculations, and found that the Nd ions exposed on the (001) surface exhibit c-plane magnetic anisotropy [1,2], resulting in a reduction of coercivity of a single $Nd_2Fe_{14}B$ grain by half of the anisotropy field [3].

As in the examples given above, the coercivity mechanisms in the permanent magnets are very much complicated and affected by many factors. It has been widely accepted, however, that the large magnetic anisotropic energy due to the Nd ions is the dominant factor of the coercivity of Nd-Fe-B magnets. For deeper understanding of the coercivity mechanism, it is necessary to study the crystal field (CF) around the Nd ions which is the origin of the magnetic anisotropy of Nd. The experimental determination of CFPs requires a multi-parameter fit to experimental data, which involves inevitable ambiguity [4,5]. Although first-principles calculations can be applied to estimate CFPs without such ambiguity, the validity of the results is not evident. Thus in this study, we thoroughly investigate the CFPs in $R_2Fe_{14}B$ (R=rare earth) systems by using first-principles calculations, and construct crystal field Hamiltonians for the rare-earth ions using the obtained CFPs. We can determine the most stable direction of the magnetization by using the crystal field Hamiltonians, and can see whether they exhibit the so-called spin-reorientation phenomena or not. It has been known experimentally that $R_2Fe_{14}B$ systems undergo the spin-reorientation transition when R=Nd [6], Ho

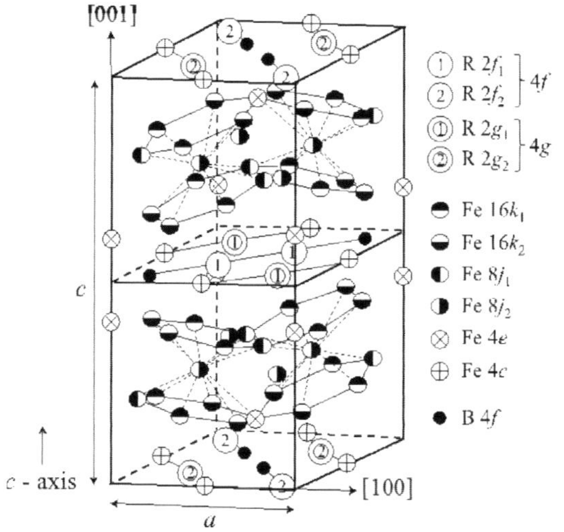

Fig. 1. Crystal structure of an $R_2Fe_{14}B$ compound. R-ion sites 4f and 4g are subdivided magnetically into $2f_1$, $2f_2$, $2g_1$, and $2g_2$.

[7], Er [7,8], Tm [7], Yb [9]. Therefore, to check the R-dependence of the spin-reorientation can be a reasonable criterion for the validity of the first-principles CFP estimation.

The magnetocrystalline anisotropy energy (MAE) of R ions is described by the Hamiltonian consisting of spin-orbit interaction, magnetic exchange, and CF interactions. The CF interaction energy depends on the orientation of 4f magnetic moment. At low temperatures, the 4f MAE depends mainly on the CF energy described by the standard model Hamiltonian of i-th R ion (i = 1 - 4 are correspond to $2f_1$, $2f_2$, $2g_1$, $2g_2$ sites),

$$H_{CF}(i) = \sum_{l,m} \Theta_l A_l^m(i)\langle r^l\rangle \hat{O}_l^m , \quad (1)$$

Table I. The local spin magnetic moments in μ_B for the crystalline $R_2Fe_{14}B$. For a comparison purpose, the results calculated by using the FP-LMTO [17] and the LMTO-ASA [18] method, are also shown.

	Pr	Nd		Tb		Dy		Ho	
	Present	Present	Ref[14]	Present	Ref[13]	Present	Ref[13]	Present	Ref[13]
$16k_1$	2.41	2.40	2.28	2.39	2.39	2.37	2.38	2.36	2.37
$16k_2$	2.32	2.31	2.22	2.30	2.19	2.28	2.17	2.28	2.17
$8j_1$	2.35	2.35	2.16	2.35	2.32	2.33	2.30	2.31	2.29
$8j_2$	2.78	2.77	2.67	2.77	2.60	2.76	2.59	2.76	2.59
$4e$	2.19	2.18	1.96	2.18	2.03	2.17	2.02	2.17	2.02
$4c$	2.52	2.50	2.43	2.48	2.47	2.45	2.44	2.44	2.44
Mean	2.42	2.41	2.29	2.40	2.33	2.39	2.32	2.37	2.31

where $\hat{O}_l^m$ are the Stevens operator equivalents and Θ_l are the Stevens factors [10,11]. The CFPs $A_l^m\langle r^l\rangle$ originating from the aspherical part of the total single particle discrete Fourier transform potential in the crystal [12,13]. To obtain the potential, we use the full-potential linearized APW+lo method implemented in the WIEN2k code [14]. The Kohn-Sham equations are solved within the generalized-gradient approximation (GGA). To simulate localized 4f states in the $R_2Fe_{14}B$ systems, we apply the open core treatment [15] was found to provide a 4f charge density being very close to that obtained from more rigorous SIC-DFT band calculations [16]. The lattice constants of the crystalline $R_2Fe_{14}B$ are set to the experimental values in Ref. [7].

We study the magnetic structures of intermetallic compounds $R_2Fe_{14}B$ (R = Pr, Nd, Tb, Dy, Ho). As the first step, we show the calculated local spin magnetic moments for the non-equivalent Fe sites and their mean values in Table I, in comparison with previous studies using the FL-LMTO [17] for R = Nd and LMTO-ASA [18] for R=Tb, Dy, and Ho. We can confirm that our series of local magnetic moments of Fe ions denote same tendency of previous theoretical calculations [18], however, the mean values are consistently larger than the previous ones with sufficiently large R_{MT} of Fe ions. Indeed, we have checked that the magnetic moments are monotonically converged as a function of R_{MT} for Fe ions.

Here we present the CFPs, $A_l^m\langle r^l\rangle$ in Table II for the crystalline $R_2Fe_{14}B$. Since the R ion has an orthorhombic symmetry, those values are complete set to construct the CF Hamiltonian in Eq. (1). We note that $A_l^{-2}\langle r^l\rangle$ (l = 2, 4, 6) and $A_6^{-6}\langle r^6\rangle$ of $2f_2$ and $2g_2$ sites have opposite sign to those of $2f_1$ and $2g_1$ sites, respectively. We found that each $R_2Fe_{14}B$ crystal has almost the same tendency, as shown in Table II.

Table II. The crystal field parameters $A_l^m\langle r^l\rangle$ in Kelvin for $2f_1$ and $2g_1$ sites in the crystalline $R_2Fe_{14}B$.

	Pr		Nd		Tb		Dy		Ho	
	$2f_1$	$2g_1$	$2f_1$	$2g_1$	$2f_1$	$2g_1$	$2f_1$	$2g_1$	$2f_1$	$2g_1$
$A_2^0\langle r^2\rangle$	486	358	463	358	381	356	375	355	362	349
$A_2^{-2}\langle r^2\rangle$	-316	869	-269	872	-86	839	-67	831	-46	817
$A_4^0\langle r^4\rangle$	-60	-53	-56	-51	-41	-41	-40	-40	-38	-38
$A_4^{-2}\langle r^4\rangle$	79	-94	70	-85	46	-62	42	-59	40	-57
$A_4^4\langle r^4\rangle$	116	-154	100	-146	59	-121	54	-117	49	-113
$A_6^0\langle r^6\rangle$	-2	-3	-2	-3	-1	-2	-1	-2	-1	-1
$A_6^{-2}\langle r^6\rangle$	-3	4	-3	4	-2	3	-2	4	-2	-3
$A_6^4\langle r^6\rangle$	-21	-31	-19	-27	-10	-15	-10	-14	-9	-12
$A_6^{-6}\langle r^6\rangle$	7	-4	5	-5	0	-5	0	-5	0	-4

Finally, to investigate the possibilities of spin-reorientation, we phenomenologically consider the MAE per R (R = Pr, Nd, Tb, Dy, Ho) ions at absolute zero, which is derived from the microscopic Hamiltonian in Eq. (1). Here, we take the quantization axis along the molecular field direction of R-4f and Fe-3d exchange interaction, assuming the field is the much larger than the CF potential. So the direction of the magnetization is expressed by the polar and azimuthal angles in the spherical coordinate [4]. From the MAE, we found that the spin reorientation phenomena only in case of R = Ho with tilting angle 15° of the magnetization from the [001] to the [110]. Except for R = Nd, these results for R = Pr, Tb, Dy, and Ho are well comparable to the experiments, where the tilting angle of R=Nd and Ho are 32° [6] and 23° [7], respectively.

It should be noted that the radial density of 4f electron decreases fast in heavy R ions as compared with light R ones, so in case of light R ions CFP calculations are hard to convergence as a function of muffin-tin sphere radius. To overcome this problem, we will apply the recently developed theoretical approach using Wannier basis [19], which is expected to be independent of atomic sphere radius..

Acknowledgment
We wish to acknowledge the support of the elements strategy initiative center for magnetic materials (ECICMM).

References

[1] H. Moriya, H. Tsuchiura, and A. Sakuma, *J. Appl. Phys.* **105**, 2009, 07A740.
[2] S. Tanaka, H. Moriya, H. Tsuchiura, A. Sakuma, M. Diviš, and P. Noák, *J. Appl. Phys.* **109**, 2011, 07A702.
[3] C. Mitsumata, H. Tsuchiura, and A. Sakuma, *Appl. Phys. Express* **4**, 2011, 113002.
[4] M. Yamada, H. Kato, H. Yamamoto, and Y. Nakagawa, *Phys. Rev. B* **38**, 1988, 620.
[5] T. S. Zhao and J. Lee, *J. Appl. Phys.* **75**, 1994, 3008.
[6] D. Givord, H. S. Li, and R. Perrier de la Bathie, *Solid State Commun.* **51**, 1984, 857.
[7] S. Hirosawa, Y. Matsuura, H. Yamamoto, S. Fujita, and M. Sagawa, *J. Appl. Phys.* **59**, 1986, 873.
[8] W. B. Yelon and J. F. Herbst, *J. Appl. Phys.* **59**, 1986, 93.
[9] P. Burlet, J. M. D. Coey, J. P. Gavigan, D. Givord, and C. Meyer, *Solid State Commun.* **60**, 1986, 723.
[10] K. W. Stevens, *Proc. Phys. Soc. A* **65**, 1952, 209.
[11] M. T. Hutchings, *Solid State Phys.* **16**, 1964, 227.
[12] M. Diviš, K. Schwarz, P. Blaha, G. Hilsher, H. Michor, and S. Khmelevskyi, *Phys. Rev. B* **62**, 2000, 6774.
[13] M. Diviš, J. Rusz, H. Michor, G. Hilsher, P. Blaha, and K. Schwarz, *J. Alloys Compd.* **403**, 2005, 29.
[14] P. Blaha, K.Schwarz, G. Madsen, D. Kvasnicka, and J. Luitz, *WIEN2k, and Augmented Plane Wave + Local Orbitals Program for Calculating Crystal Properties Karlheinz Schwarz*, TU Wien, Austria, 2001, ISBN 3-9501031-1-2.
[15] P. Novák, *Phys. Status Solidi B* **198**, 1996, 729.
[16] M. Richter, *J. Phys. D: Appl. Phys.* **31**, 1998, 1017.
[17] K. Hummler and M. Fähnle, *Phys. Rev. B* **53**, 1996, 3290.
[18] K. Hummler, T. Beuerle, and M. Fähnle, *J. Magn. Magn. Mater.* **115**, 1992, 207.
[19] P. Novák, K. Knížek, J. Kuneš, *Phys. Rev. B* **87**, 2013, 205139.

Impact of Different Nd-Rich and Cu Doped Crystal-Phases on the Coercivity of Nd-Fe-B Grain Ensembles

G. HRKAC[1], K. BUTLER[3], T.G. WOODCOCK[2], T. SCHREFL[4], O. GUTFLEISCH[5,2]
[1]College of Engineering, Mathematics and Physical Sciences, Univ. of Exeter, UK
[2]IFW Dresden, Institute for Metallic Materials, 01171 Dresden, Germany
[3]Centre for Sustainable Chemical Technologies, University of Bath, Bath, UK
[4]St. Pölten University of Applied Sciences, Matthias Corvinus Str. 15, Austria
[5]TU Darmstadt, Institute for Materials Science, Petersenstr. 23, Darmstadt, Germany

Abstract: *In this paper we show with atomistic simulations that Cu doped Nd-rich grain boundaries at interfaces to Nd-Fe-B grains can decrease the strain at the interfaces. We calculate the energy per atom for a* $NdCu_2$ *grain boundary and a Nd-rich grain boundary with a mono-layer* $NdCu_2$. *We find that by including this mono-layer of Cu the distortion width at the interface can be decreased and a recovery of the crystal phase is achieved, therefore increasing the coercivity of the Nd-Fe-B magnets.*

Keywords: *hard magnets; coercivity; atomistic model; micromagnetic modeling*

Address: Gino Hrkac, University of Exeter, CEMPS, North Park Road, EX44QF, UK, +447913801087,
E-mail: g.hrkac@exeter.ac.uk

1. Introduction

High performance Nd-Fe-B magnets are in great demand for applications in hybrid electric vehicles and wind turbines for electricity generation [1,2]. To increase the coercivity and stability at higher temperatures it is vital to understand the coercivity mechanism in Nd-Fe-B sintered magnets in greater detail [2]. Aberration-corrected transmission electron microscopy, combined with atomistic simulations is used to study anisotropy profiles of interfaces between metallic Nd (fcc and dhcp), Nd_2O_3 (hP5 and cI80), NdO and the $Nd_2Fe_{14}B$ phase. Atomistic interface models, based on TEM predicted the presence of distorted layers of the crystal structure at the interface. Distortions in the crystal phase are used to derive a magneto-elastic anisotropy energy from a first order perturbation of the magneto-elastic Hamiltonian and used in a numerical analysis to evaluate its effect on coercivity. These distorted layers have correspondingly lower magnetocrystalline anisotropy, depending on crystal structure, orientation, crystal-phase and type of Nd-rich phase and act as nucleation sites for magnetic reversal domains. In our previous work the resulting magnetic reversal curves show that different coercive fields are predicted for cubic (metallic fcc Nd, Nd_2O_3-cI80 and NdO), Nd_2O_3-hP5 and metallic dhcp Nd structures at this grain junction [3]. The largest contribution to the difference in coercivity originates from the thickness of the distorted layers. These are thinner for fcc Nd, Nd_2O_3-cI80 and NdO structures compared to the Nd_2O_3-hP5 and metallic dhcp Nd structures (*cf.* cubic: 0.7 - 1.2 nm, Nd_2O_3-hP5: 0.9-1.4 nm, metallic dhpc Nd: 1.2 to 2.0 nm). The cubic structures (metallic fcc Nd, Nd_2O_3-cI80 and NdO) appear to have a higher H_c (3.6 T) compared to Nd_2O_3-hP5 (3.2 T), which has a higher H_c than metallic dhcp Nd phase (2.8 T) [3].

In this paper, we investigated the impact of Cu doping in these intergranular phases and find that by including a thin Cu layer the distortion width can be decreased and a recovery of the crystal phase is achieved, therefore increasing the coercivity of the Nd-Fe-B magnets.

2. Theory

The system was modelled using Morse type potentials [3,4]. All molecular dynamics simulations presented in these calculations were run using the Lammps [5].

The first step in our procedure is to generate samples of $NdCu_2$ and surface cuts of Nd-Fe-B. The cell volumes were set and minimized by lattice minimization techniques.

Then this system was imported into the molecular dynamics code. In order to generate a system at elevated temperature, we started from the lattice minimized configuration and heated the system up to 250 K. The heating is done, by bringing the system into contact with a large heat bath. Under those conditions the probability to find the system in a given energy state is given by the Boltzmann distribution (Maxwell-Boltzmann velocity distribution).

In particular we obtain the simple relation between the imposed temperature T and the translational kinetic energy per particle. By using the kinetic energy per particle as a measure of the instantaneous temperature, this will result in local fluctuations of the temperature. To keep the average kinetic energy per particle constant one can use the so-called iso-kinetic MD scheme or velocity-scaling scheme. In our simulations of constant temperature we use the Nose scheme in the formulation of Hoover, the so-called Nose-Hoover thermostat.

Once we have exposed the super-lattice structure to the heat bath, we performed a velocity-scaling scheme for the first 150,000 runs and then let the system relax. This was done for 100/110 $NdCu_2$ and the tri-layer Nd/$NdCu_2$/Nd-Fe-B structures in a temperature range between 250 and 1100 K in 50 K steps.

3. Results and Discussion

The first system is the (100) $NdCu_2$ to (100) Nd-Fe-B phase. Here we are interested in the intermixture and diffusion of Cu into the Nd-Fe-B phase. Figure 1 shows the results of the temperature simulations for the (100) $NdCu_2$ to Nd-Fe-B phase. It can be seen that the Cu diffuses towards the interface and is concentrated there. We see a few lattice distortions but these are confined in the first few angstrom of the Nd-Fe-B crystal phase.

Another important parameter with temperature is the surface orientation of the Nd-Fe-B phase as function of temperature. From the lattice minimization calculations we have seen that the (110) surface is the most disruptive one, concerning the distortion regions and the depth. To understand the temperature effect on such a highly unstable system we performed temperature simulations in the range from 250 to 400 K. In Fig. 2, we see the super-cell structure simulation at 300 K.

The molecular dynamic simulation shows a diffusion of the Cu towards the interface and we can also observe that the distortions are reduced and confined in the first few angstroms and we can still see a strain

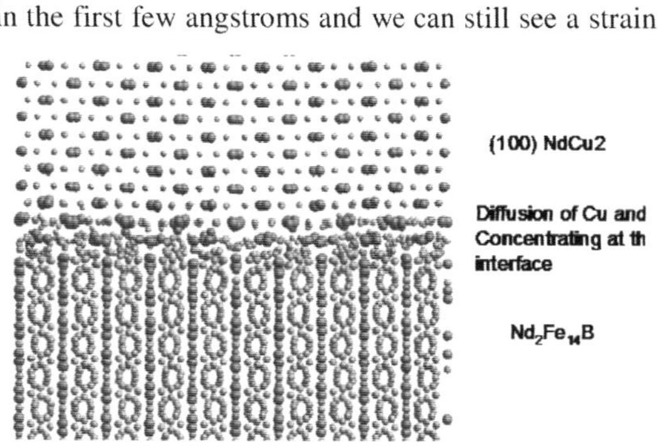

Fig. 1. Molecular dynamics simulations of (100) $NdCu_2$ to Nd-Fe-B at 300 K.

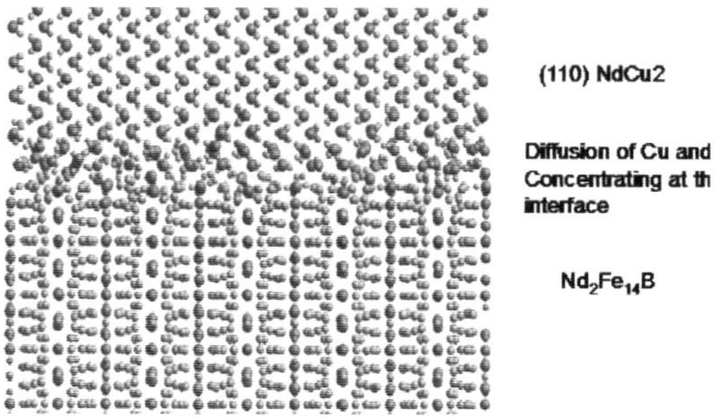

Fig. 2. Molecular dynamics simulations of (110) $NdCu_2$ to Nd-Fe-B at 300 K.

acting on the bulk Nd-Fe-B phase, shown by the periodic small distortions in the Nd-B layers.
But also as indicated by the lattice minimization calculations, the Cu is reducing the distortions and the penetration depth, meaning an improved surface phase of the Nd-Fe-B.

In the last simulations we have constructed a tri-layer system to mimic a small atom percentage of Cu in the inter-granular phase. The setup of this system is as follow, metallic Nd/$NdCu_2$/Nd-Fe-B. The thickness of the $NdCu_2$ phase is just one atomic layer, sandwiches between the Nd rich phase and the Nd-Fe-B phase.

The question we want to answer with this kind of simulation is how much Cu would you need to improve the surface morphology of the Nd-Fe-B phase.

In Fig. 3, we see the molecular dynamic results of the tri-layer system at 300 K. the interesting fact from the simulations is that the distortions are now more confined in the metallic Nd rich phase and only a small amount of distortions penetrate into the Nd-Fe-B bulk phase. Even the strain effects from the $NdCu_2$ crystalline phase, which we have observed before are highly suppressed.

As mentioned above, we have performed temperature simulations for all these systems in the range of 250 to 400 K. The energy equilibrium state is reached once the particles have reached an average kinetic energy, according to the velocity-rescaling scheme. This has been done for $NdCu_2$ to Nd-Fe-B interfaces (100 and 110) and the trilayer system, Nd-Fe-B with a metallic Nd phase with a $NdCu_2$ capping layer on the Nd-Fe-B surface. Energy wise it can be said that the tri layer phase is more stable compared to the $NdCu_2$ one.

In the (110) $NdCu_2$ surface, the energy per atom is -4.4 eV at 250 K and remains stable till 400 K reaching -4.45 eV. In the (100) phase the energy is -4.36 eV at 250 K and reaches -4.4 eV at 400 K. The trilayer system, on the other hand has an energy per atom of -4.6 eV and remains stable with temperature. This

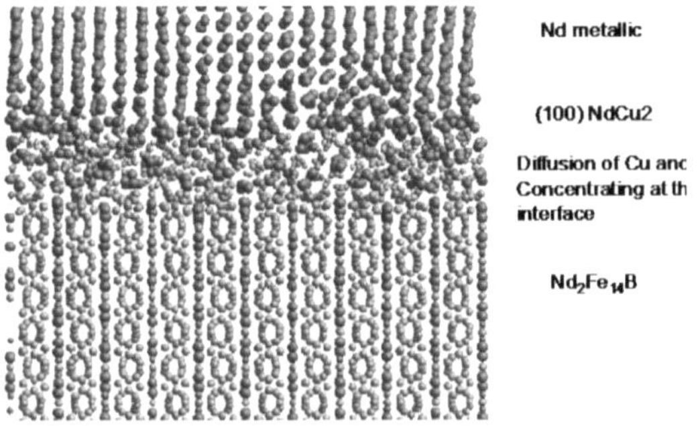

Fig. 3. Molecular dynamics simulations of Nd/$NdCu_2$ to Nd-Fe-B at 300 K.

indicates that a small amount of $NdCu_2$ can increase the stability and improve the surface energy.

We propose that the origin of the reduced coercivity in sintered magnets is the defect region at multi-junction sites, which locally reduce anisotropy, producing the primary nucleation sites during reversal.

References

[1] O. Gutfleisch, M.A. Willard, E. Brück, C.H. Chen, S.G. Shankar and J.P. Liu, *Adv. Mater.* **23**, 2011, 821.

[2] T.G. Woodcock, Y. Zhang, G. Hrkac, G. Ciuta, N.M. Dempsey, T. Schrefl, O. Gutfleisch and D. Givord, *Scr. Mater.* **67**, 2012, 536.

[3] G. Hrkac, T.G. Woodcock, K.T. Butler, L. Saharan, M.T. Bryan, T. Schrefl and O. Gutfleisch, *Scr. Mater.* **70**, 2014, 35.

[4] G. Hrkac, T. Woodcock, C. Freeman, A. Gontacharov, J. Dean, T. Schrefl, O. Gutfleisch, *Appl. Phys. Lett.* 97, 2010, 232511.

[5] S. Plimpton, *J. Comp. Phys.* **117**, 1995, 1.

Phase Boundaries in Hot Deformed Nd-Fe-Co-B-Ga Magnets Infiltrated with a Nd-Cu Eutectic Liquid

T.G. WOODCOCK[1], Q.M. RAMASSE[2], T. SHOJI[3], M. YANO[3], A. KATO[3], O. GUTFLEISCH[4]
[1]IFW Dresden, PO Box 270116, 01171 Dresden, Germany
[2]SuperSTEM Laboratory, STFC Daresbury Campus, Daresbury, WA4 4AD, UK
[3]Advanced Material Engineering Div., Toyota Motor Corporation, Susono 410-1193 Japan
[4]Materialwissenschaft, TU Darmstadt, Alarich-Weiss-Str. 16, 64287 Darmstadt, Germany

Abstract: *Phase boundaries in hot deformed Nd-Fe-Co-B-Ga magnets infiltrated with a Nd-Cu eutectic liquid were examined using Electron Energy Loss Spectroscopy elemental profiles and High Angle Annular Dark Field 'Z-contrast' images. The results showed that the Nd-Cu eutectic liquid penetrated the ≈ 1 nm thick intergranular regions, thus explaining the coercivity increase following infiltration. Co enrichment at an {001} surface of a* $Nd_2(Fe,Co)_{14}B$ *grain was observed, as was segregation of Cu to the interface between the* $Nd_2(Fe,Co)_{14}B$ *grains and the Nd-rich phase.*

Keywords: *STEM; coercivity; hot deformation; phase boundaries; EELS; Nd-Fe-B*

Address: Thomas G. Woodcock, Institute for Metallic Materials, IFW Dresden, PO Box 270116, 01171 Dresden, Germany, Phone +49 (0)351 4659 221, Email: t.woodcock@ifw-dresden.de

1. Introduction

In order to develop Nd-Fe-B magnets with high coercivity (H_c) at elevated temperature without using Dy substitution to increase the magnetocrystalline anisotropy of the 2:14:1 phase, precise engineering of the microstructure is needed. Hot deformed (die upset) Nd-Fe-B magnets are composed of platelet 2:14:1 grains (typically ≈ 100 nm thick and 300-400 nm wide) [1,2]. These platelets grains are significantly smaller than the grains in typical sintered Nd-Fe-B magnets and therefore higher H_c would be expected in hot deformed magnets [3,4]. Ultrafine grained materials contain a far higher number of grain boundaries per unit volume than coarse grained materials. A larger volume fraction of Nd-rich intergranular phases is therefore needed for complete coverage of the 2:14:1 grains in order to achieve high H_c. A 71% increase in H_c to 2.4 T (without Dy) has recently been achieved by infiltrating the grain boundaries of a Nd-Fe-Co-B-Ga hot deformed magnet with a Nd-Cu eutectic liquid [5]. The increase in H_c was attributed to the increased volume fraction and improved distribution of the Nd-rich phases [5,6]. Although the H_c of the infiltrated magnet was high, it reached only a small fraction of the anisotropy field of $Nd_2Fe_{14}B$ ($H_a \approx 8$ T at 300 K [1]). In order to investigate the causes of this discrepancy, the chemical composition of phase boundaries in the hot deformed and infiltrated materials has been investigated using 3D atom probe tomography [6] and aberration-corrected scanning transmission electron microscopy (STEM) plus electron energy loss spectroscopy (EELS) [5]. In the latter study, the chemical data, which resolved the composition of individual lattice planes, were additionally correlated with "Z-contrast" High Angle Annular Dark Field (HAADF) images of the crystal structure with atomic resolution [5]. Although novel features were resolved [5,6], the disadvantage of such high resolution studies is that only a small number of phase boundaries can be examined in practice. The aim of the current work is therefore to confirm and add support to the results in the previous study [5] by presenting further aberration-corrected STEM and EELS analyses of phase boundaries in hot deformed magnets infiltrated by a Nd-Cu eutectic.

2. Experimental

Hot deformed magnets of nominal composition $Nd_{14}Fe_{76}Co_{3.4}B_6Ga_{0.6}$ at.% were produced by hot pressing melt-spun ribbons, then deforming the resulting compact body to a height reduction of 80%. The hot deformed magnets were placed into contact with melt spun Nd-Cu ribbons of eutectic composition. The mixture was heated to 600 °C and was held at that temperature for 120 min in order to allow the Nd-Cu eutectic liquid to infiltrate the grain boundaries of the magnet. TEM lamellae were prepared from the magnets using the focussed ion beam lift out technique. Aberration-corrected STEM experiments were carried out at the SuperSTEM Laboratory using a Nion Ultrastem™ 100 (cold field emission gun operating at 100 kV) equipped with a C_5 Nion QO corrector, giving full correction up to six-fold astigmatism ($C_{5,6}$) and thus allowing the formation of an electron probe approx. 0.9 Å in diameter (full-width at half-maximum). EELS was carried out using a UHV Enfina EELS spectrometer, with a collection semi-angle of 32 mrad. Further details are given in [5].

3. Results and Discussion

Fig. 1 gives an overview of the analysis area. Three $Nd_2(Fe,Co)_{14}B$ grains (labelled "Grain 1" *etc.*) and two larger regions of a Nd-rich phase can be seen. Grain 1 shows the typical platelet grain shape for hot deformed magnets, where the crystallographic <001> axis is parallel to the short dimension. The top and bottom surfaces of Grain 1 are parallel to (001) and appear to be planar whereas the edge of the platelet is rounded except where it is flattened by contact to Grain 3. A thin intergranular phase separates Grains 1 and 3 (data not shown).

An EELS linescan was carried out from Grain1 into the Nd-rich phase (right-hand arrow in Fig. 1) and the resulting elemental profiles are shown in Fig. 2. The Fe and Nd profiles show some intensity variation across the 2:14:1 lattice planes. The interface from 2:14:1 to the Nd-rich phase occurs at a distance of approximately 5.8 nm. The Co profile has a constant intensity in the bulk of the 2:14:1 grain and then shows a clear peak at a distance of 5.3 nm, close to the edge of the grain, before falling to a low intensity in the Nd-rich phase. The peak Co intensity is approximately 3 times that in the bulk of the 2:14:1 grain. This Co enrichment at the edge of the 2:14:1 grain is similar to that observed previously [5]. The Cu distribution reaches its maximum at the interface between the two phases, and then decreases. The Nd profile only begins to increase at the interface (5.8 nm).

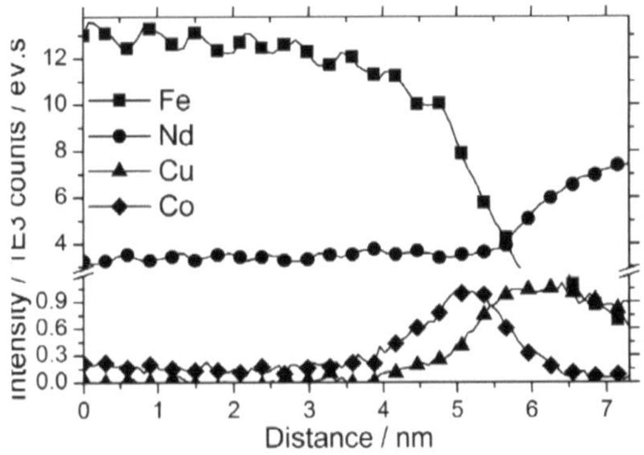

Fig. 2. EELS elemental profiles from the linescan going from a $Nd_2(Fe,Co)_{14}B$ grain into a large region of the Nd-rich phase (right-hand arrow in Fig. 1). One data point in four is plotted.

Fig. 3 shows the approx. 1.6 nm thick, amorphous, intergranular phase separating Grains 1 and 2. The crystallographic orientations of the grains were extracted from the FFT of the image. The *c*-axis of Grain 1 is in the plane of the image, perpendicular to the interface, whereas the *c*-axis in Grain 2 is misoriented by 29°. The total misorientation of the two grains can be described by a rotation of 50° about an axis close to [0-4-1]. The resolution of the lattice structure of Grain 1 with 'Z-contrast' in fig. 3 allows the planes of atoms in the 2:14:1 phase containing the Nd atoms to be identified. The terminating plane of Grain 1, forming the interface to the intergranular phase, is clearly between the planes containing the Nd atoms *i.e.* the terminating plane contains only Fe and Co atoms in this case.

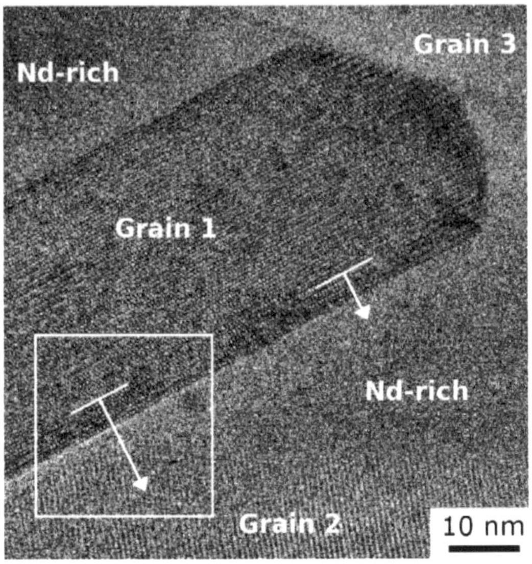

Fig. 1. Aberration-corrected STEM bright field image giving an overview. The right-hand arrow gives the position of the EELS linescan in Fig.2. The white box and the arrow inside it give the positions of the image in Fig. 3 and the linescan in Fig. 4, respectively.

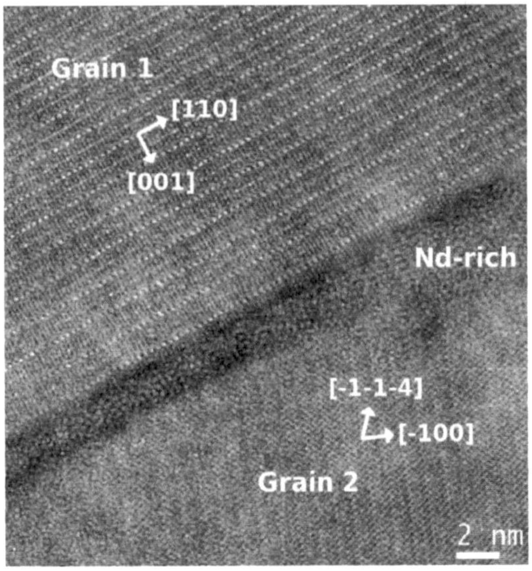

Fig. 3. Aberration-corrected HAADF image of the region shown by the white box in Fig. 1. The orientations of the two $Nd_2(Fe,Co)_{14}B$ grains are shown. The grains are separated by a thin intergranular phase, which broadens into the Nd-rich triple point.

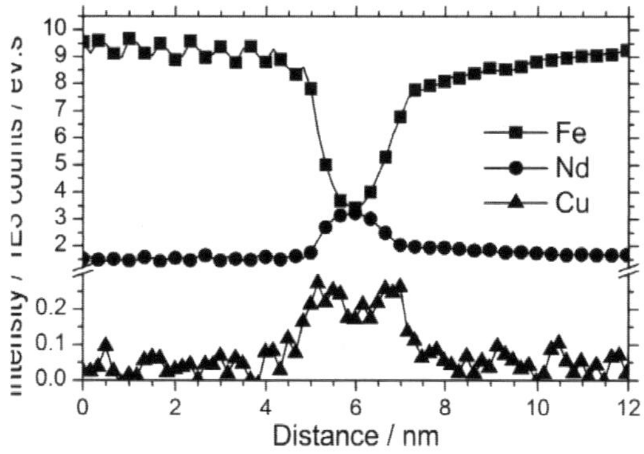

Fig. 4. EELS elemental profiles from the linescan across a thin, amorphous, intergranular phase (see Figs. 1 and 3). One data point in two is plotted for Fe and Nd.

The EELS linescan from Grain 1 into Grain 2 is shown in Fig. 4. In the centre of the intergranular phase (at a distance of 6 nm), the Fe trace falls to less than 1/2 its intensity in the 2:14:1 phase and the Nd trace reaches a maximum. It was not possible to extract a reliable Co profile from this data set. The Cu trace has two maxima, at the interfaces between the 2:14:1 grains and the intergranular phase, and shows a small minimum at the centre of the intergranular phase. The results in Figs. 2 and 4 show the tendency of Cu to segregate to the interfaces between the 2:14:1 and Nd-rich phases. Interfacial Cu segregation has been observed previously in these materials [5]. The presence of Cu in the nm-scale intergranular regions is evidence that the eutectic liquid penetrated those regions during the infiltration.

4. Conclusions

Co enrichment at the edge of $Nd_2(Fe,Co)_{14}B$ platelet grains has been observed by aberration-corrected STEM and EELS in a hot deformed magnet which was infiltrated by a Nd-Cu eutectic liquid. The peak Co intensity is ≈ 3 times that in the bulk of the 2:14:1 grain. Segregation of Cu to interfaces between the 2:14:1 and Nd-rich phases has also been observed. This showed that the Nd-Cu eutectic liquid penetrated the nm-scale intergranular regions during the infiltration process. The results shown confirm previous high resolution measurements [5], thus adding increased significance of the observations.

Acknowledgements

The authors thank Dr. T. Gemming, T. Sturm, D. Lohse and Dr. K.-H. Müller (all IFW Dresden) for technical support and fruitful discussions. SuperSTEM, the UK National Facility for Aberration-Corrected STEM, is supported by the EPSRC.

References

[1] J.F. Herbst, *Rev. Mod. Phys.* **63**, 1991, 819.
[2] R.K. Mishra, R.W. Lee, *Appl. Phys. Lett.* **48**, 1986, 733.
[3] S. Hirosawa, Y. Tsubokawa, *J. Magn. Magn. Mater.* **84**, 1990, 309.
[4] K. Uestuener, M. Katter, W. Rodewald, *IEEE Trans. Magn.* **42**, 2006, 2897.
[5] T.G. Woodcock, Q.M. Ramasse, G. Hrkac, T. Shoji, M. Yano, A. Kato and O. Gutfleisch, *Acta Mater.* 77, 2014, 111.
[6] H. Sepehri-Amin, T. Ohkubo, S. Nagashima, M. Yano, T. Shoji, A. Kato, T. Schrefl and K. Hono, *Acta Mater.* **61**, 2013, 6622.

Supercell Calculations of Magnetization, Exchange, and Anisotropy

P. MANCHANDA[1], R. SKOMSKI[1], A. KASHYAP[2]
[1]Department of Physics and Astronomy and NCMN, University of Nebraska, Lincoln, NE, 68588.
[2]School of Basic Sciences, Indian Institute of Technology Mandi, Himachal Pradesh, India 175001.

Abstract: *It is outlined how first-principle supercell calculations help to understand and develop permanent-magnet materials. After introducing supercell calculations based on density-functional theory using LSDA codes, we outline the capabilities and limitations of the approach to predict magnetization, Curie temperature, and anisotropy. We discusses various systems and phenomena of interest in permanent magnetism, namely Honda steels (tetragonally distorted Fe-Co permanent magnets), the Bethe-Slater curve predicting the sign of the exchange interaction, and disordered MnAl magnets.*

Keywords: *density functional theory; magnetic anisotropy energy;, MnAl; steel*

Address: Priyanka Manchanda, Department of Physics and Astronomy and NCMN, University of Nebraska, Lincoln, NE 68588, USA. Tel: (1-402)-560-3794, E-mail: pmanchanda2@unl.edu

1. Introduction

The ongoing search for novel permanent-magnet materials [1-4] has a strong first-principle computational component, dealing with intrinsic materials parameters, especially spontaneous magnetization M_s, Curie temperature T_c, and anisotropy constant K_1. The main aims of the research is the systematic understanding of known materials [5], the prediction of intrinsic properties of hypothetical materials [6, 7], and providing guidance to experimentalists in their quest for new materials [8, 9].

First-principle or *ab-initio* calculations are able to predict intrinsic magnetic properties of itinerant permanent magnets with impressive accuracy. Density-functional theory (DFT) has become the preferred method for electronic structure theory for metals, especially 3d, 4d, and 5d-transition metals. Our focus is on supercell calculations based on the generalized gradient approximation (GGA-PBE) [10]. Most of the examples below use the *Vienna Ab Initio Simulation Package* (VASP) [11], treating the electron-ion interactions with the PAW method [12].

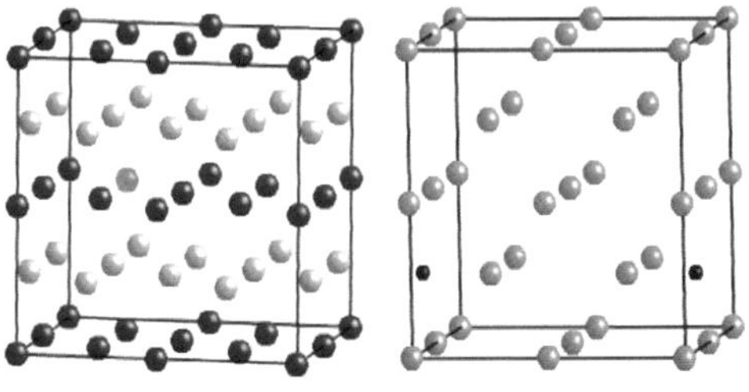

(a) (b)

Fig. 1. Typical supercell. (a) Fe doped MnAl and (b) $Fe_{16}C$ structure.

Fig. 1 illustrates the supercell approach. The magnetic solid is constructed as a periodic array of arbitrarily complicated supercells, which make it possible to treat real-structure effects such as atomic disorder so long as they are confined to the dimensions of the supercell. Computationally, the supercells replace the small unit cells simple elements and compounds without losing the benefits provided by Bloch's theorem.

The maximum size of the supercell depends on computer power and desired accuracy but is generally of the order of a few hundred atoms.

2. Capabilities and Limitations

Due to the breathtaking growth in computing power, first-principle calculations have become an effective tool to determine magnetic and other properties of condensed matter. The capabilities and limitations of supercell calculations largely reflect those of the underlying LSDA *ab-initio* approaches but also exhibit some supercell specific features.

2.1. Capabilities

Intrinsic magnetic properties of itinerant magnets, such as 3*d*, 4*d*, and 5*d* elements and alloys, can be calculated with high accuracies. The spontaneous magnetization is determined by local magnetic moments calculated from the difference between the majority and minority spin bands, integrating over the ↑ and ↓ densities of states (DOS). In the case of permanent magnets, the accuracy of the calculation is highest for the net magnetization and slightly lower for the atomic moments, both not much bigger than 1 - 2%.

The Curie temperature is calculated by exchange interactions which can be extracted from first-principle calculations. The simplest approach to estimate exchange interaction by taking total-energy differences of various spin configurations [13]. The other two approaches are real-space method [14] and frozen-magnon approach [15].

Magnetocrystalline anisotropy means that the magnetic energy depends on the magnetization directions relative to the crystal axes. It arises from the interaction of the spin magnetic moment with the crystal lattice due to spin-orbit interaction. Anisotropy calculations are more time-consuming than moment calculations and rather inaccurate for some cubic structures (Ni) and nearly cubic structures (*hcp* Co), but the anisotropy of most itinerant permanent magnets, such as $L1_0$-ordered magnets, is a chemical effect and reasonably well described by DFT, even if the error normally exceeds 10% often exceeds 20% [16, 17].

A practically important challenge is the treatment of atomic-scale disorder. For example, small C additions are important in the permanent magnetism of Fe [18] and MnAl [19], and off-stoichiometry is important in $L1_0$ magnets such as FeNi [20] and FePt [21]. Supercell calculations are well-suited for the treatment of interstitial, antisite, and other types of disorder, even if the calculations can be quite time-consuming due to required configurational or self-averaging in big unit cells.

The simplest approach to atomic-scale disorder is the virtual-crystal approximation (VCA), where the on-site potential of an *AB* alloy is averaged over all *A* and *B* atoms. This approach is trivial, because it treat the alloy as a homogeneous monatomic metal, without alloy-specific features in the electronic structure. A major improvement is provided by the coherent-potential approximation (CPA), where the alloy behavior is deduced by properly distinguishing between *A* and *B* atoms on any given site but treating the neighboring atoms as an effective medium [22-24]. As illustrated in Fig. 2(a-b), this amounts to a weighted average between *A* and *B* atoms. The CPA tends to predict magnetic properties fairly accurately, in striking contrast to the VCA, but it neglects cluster-localization effects [24, 25]. The dark region in the top-left part of Fig. 2(c) shows such a cluster, which can easily be treated by supercell calculations but may yield incorrect DOS in the "single-site" CPA.

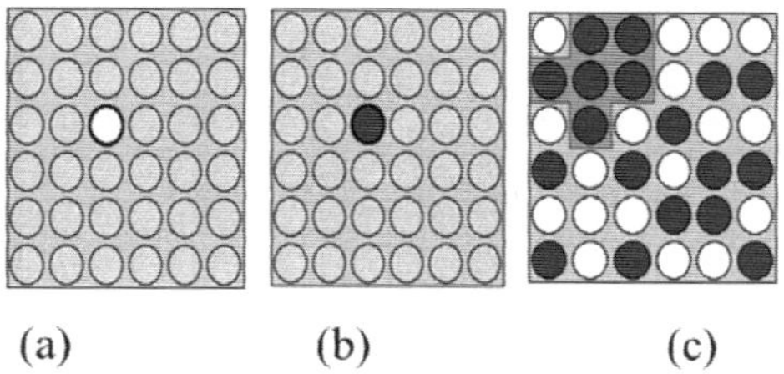

Fig. 2. Theoretical approaches to metallic disorder in an AB alloy: (a-b) coherent potential approximation (CPA) and (c) supercell approach.

2.2. Limitations

DFT is a quantum mechanical approach that describes interacting electrons in terms of the electron's particle density. In principle, DFT provides an exact description of ground-state properties, but practical applications of DFT are largely based on the independent electron approximation, mapping the electrostatic interactions between individual electrons onto a mean field. In particular, the local density approximation (LDA) replaces the exchange correlation energy by that of a homogeneous electron gas. This approach but fails when the density changes rapidly, for example at surfaces or in the 4*f* shells of rare-earth atoms, but it can be perturbatively improved by adding gradient corrections, as in the generalized-gradient approximation (GGA). The most widely used GGA functionals are the Perdew-Wang (PW91) [26] and Perdew-Burke-Ernzerhof (PBE) [10] functionals.

However, due to unphysical charge delocalization, LDA and GGA incorrectly predict some materials to be metals rather than insulators [27]. These errors especially occurs in strongly correlated systems, such as magnetic oxides and rare-earth magnets. In rare earths, there are not only strong correlations among 4f electrons, but also Kondo-like interactions between 4f and conduction electrons. (For the modelling of such interactions, see e.g. Refs. 28 and 29). Examples of first-principle approaches to approximately treat correlation effects are self-interaction corrections (SIC) [30] and the widely used LDA+*U* method [31].

3. Case Studies

The following subsections outline how supercell calculations and related approaches can be exploited in the understanding and development of permanent magnets.

3.1. Cobalt-steel magnets

Steel magnets, defined as carbon-containing iron alloys, have played an important role in the history of permanent magnetism [5] and recently received renewed attention in the light of rare-earth supply bottlenecks. Small additions of C are necessary to create pinning-type coercivity in steel magnets, and this mechanism involves both crystal-field interaction and martensitic strain. Both are caused by the interstitial carbon and yield anisotropy contributions of comparable magnitude [32].

Cobalt addition is known to greatly enhance the anisotropy. These 'Honda steels' were the energy-product record holders about 100 years ago [5, 33] and have recently attracted renewed attention as 'tetragonally distorted iron-cobalt' [34,35]. Supercell calculations are well-suited to treat small carbon concentrations. For instance, the anisotropy energy of $Fe_{16}C$ is -0.35 meV per supercell (-2.4 MJ/m^3), whereas for Fe_{16} with same the supercell (a = 5.642 Å, c = 6.076 Å) it is -0.8 meV per supercell (-5.4 MJ/m^3).

3.2. Bethe-Slater curve

As the next example, we investigate the magnetic order in metallic Mn magnets [36,37]. It is well-known that Mn compounds exhibit a trend towards antiferromagnetism (AFM), which negatively affects the utilization of the large Mn moment of up to 5 μ_B per atom. This trend is usually explained in terms of the Bethe-Slater-Néel curve [38], Fig. 3, which shows the dependence of the nearest neighbor exchange parameter on the interatomic distances. According to this curve, large and small interatomic distances lead to ferromagnetism and antiferromagnetism (or Pauli paramagnetism), respectively.

The Bethe-Slater curve predicts that Mn becomes ferromagnetic for sufficiently large interatomic distances $\langle d \rangle = 2r_a$. Unfortunately, large interatomic distances strongly reduce the energy product $(BH)_{max}$, because $(BH)_{max}$ is quadratic in the magnetization M and M scales as $1/\langle d \rangle^3$, leading to a strong $1/\langle d \rangle^6$ dependence. Reality seems to support this view: magnets such as MnBi and MnAl have rather low Mn contents and low magnetizations.

However, this conclusion is misleading. Elements in the middle of the 3d series, such as Cr and Mn, tend to exhibit AFM exchange due to nearly equally occupied bonding and antibonding electron levels in the ferromagnetic state, and $\langle d \rangle$ is merely a secondary consideration in this mechanism. A good example is (metastable) bcc Mn [39], which behaves very unusually from the viewpoint of Bethe-Slater curve. In Fig. 4, we show the corresponding phase diagram: bcc Mn is paramagnetic for lattice constants below 2.72 Å, exhibits a ferromagnetic low-spin state between 2.72 and 2.92 Å, and assumes an antiferromagnetic high-spin state above 2.92 Å. This is exactly the opposite of what is expected from Fig. 3, and in the next subsection we will see that similarly surprising trends also exist in alloys, specifically MnAl.

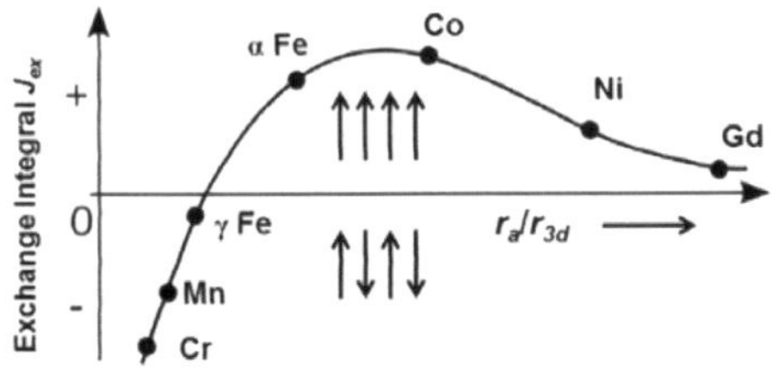

Fig.3. Bethe-Slater curve.

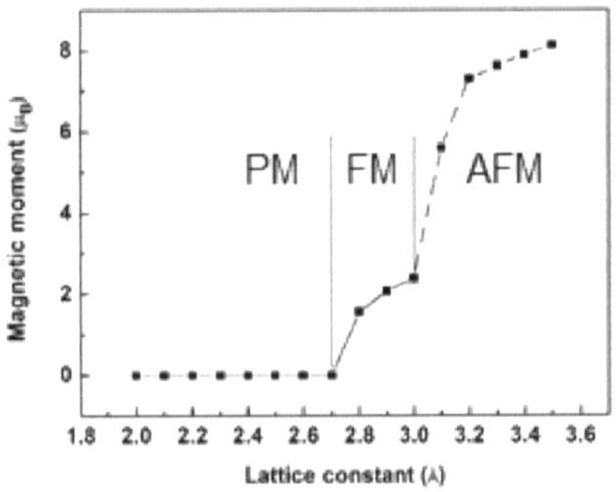

Fig. 4. Magnetic phase diagram for bcc Mn.

3.3. Exchange interactions in MnAl

As an $L1_0$-ordered alloy, MnAl consists of alternating planes of Mn, and the nearest-neighbor Mn-Mn distance in the planes is small. According to Fig. 3, this would mean AFM order, but our calculations shows that strong ferromagnetic (FM) exchange can exist even for very short Mn-Mn distances. In $L1_0$-ordered MnAl, the dense-packed Mn sheets exhibit an FM intralayer exchange J, whereas the interlayer exchange J^*, with enhanced Mn-Mn distances due to separating Al, is only very weakly ferromagnetic [2,36].

Figure 5 shows the dependence of the interplanar Mn-Mn exchange (in meV/unitcell) as a function of interlayer distance, parameterized by the c/a ratio at fixed a = 3.93 Å. The predicted exchange energy is calculated by taking the energy difference between ferromagnetic and layered antiferromagnetic spin configuration. The calculated exchange energy is maximum for c/a = 0.96.

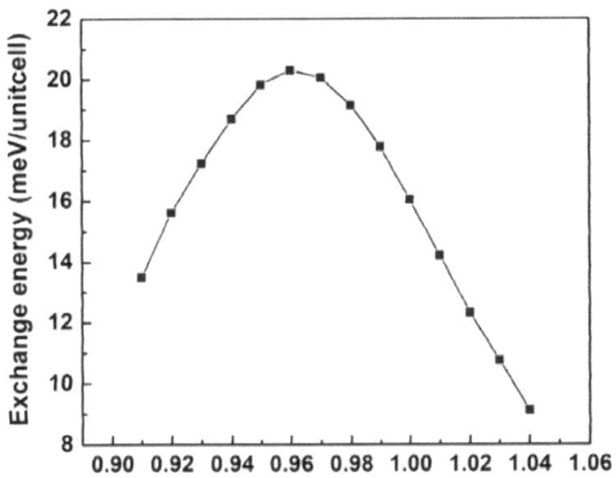

Fig. 5. Exchange energy (in meV/unitcell) as a function of c/a ratio.

Disorder strongly affects the coupling between neighboring Mn planes in MnAl. We have investigated various defects as sources of magnetization-reducing antiferromagnetic interlayer exchange interactions ($J^* < 0$). Starting from a supercell with 32 atoms ($Mn_{16}Al_{16}$ with J^* = 13 meV/unit cell), we have found the following main features: (i) $Mn_{16}Al_{16}$ with one antisite defect exhibits AFM exchange (J^* = - 10 meV/unit cell), (ii) putting one Fe atom in the Mn ($FeMn_{15}Al_{16}$) and Al ($FeMn_{16}Al_{15}$) planes yields J^* values of 13.25 and 40.25 meV/unit cell, respectively, and (iii) replacing one Al atom by one Mn atom ($Mn_{17}Al_{15}$) leads to J^* = 1.75 meV/unit cell. However, Fe tends to reduce the net magnetic moment [7].

4. Conclusions

In summary, supercell calculation have become a valuable tool in investigation of permanent magnets, supported by ever-advancing computational capabilities. We have treated three exemplary examples to elucidate interesting phenomenon in permanent magnets. A particularly interesting element is manganese, with counterintuitive dense-packed ferromagnetism in both its elemental form and in MnAl.

Acknowledgement
The authors are thankful to the J. Hafner and G. Kresse for providing the VASP code. This research is supported by PNNL, ARPA-E, ARO and NSF-MRSEC.

References

[1] J. M. D. Coey, *IEEE Trans. Magn.* 47, 2011, 4671; *Scripta Mater.* 67, 2012, 524.
[2] R. Skomski, P. Manchanda, P. Kumar, B. Balamurugan, A. Kashyap, D. J. Sellmyer, *IEEE Trans. Magn.* 49, 2013, 3215.
[3] M. J. Kramers, R. W. McCallum, I. A. Anderson, S. Constantinides, *JOM* 64, 2012, 752.
[4] M. D. Kuz'min, K. P. Skokov, H. Jian, I. Radulov, O. Gutfleisch, *J. Phys.: condens. Matter.* 26, 2014, 064205.
[5] R. Skomski, J. M. D. Coey, *Permanent magnetism*, Bristol: Institute of Physics,1999.
[6] P. Kumar, A. Kashyap, B. Balamurugan, J. E. Shield, D. J. Sellmyer, R. Skomski, *J. Phys.: Condens. Matter* 2, 2014, 064209.
[7] P. Manchanda, A. Kashyap, J. E. Shield, L. H. Lewis, R. Skomski, *J. Magn. Magn. Mater.* 365, 2014, 88.
[8] X. Zhao *et al. Phys. Rev. Lett.* 112, 2014, 045502.
[9] V. Sharma, P. Manchanda, R. Skomski, D. J. Sellmyer, A. Kashyap J. Appl. Phys. 109, 07A727 (2011).
[10] J. P. Perdew, K. Burke, M. Ennzerhof, *Phys. Rev. Lett.* 77, 1996, 3865.
[11] G. Kresse, J. Hafner, *Phys. Rev. B* 48, 1993, 13115; *Phys. Rev. B* 47, 1993, 558.
[12] P. E. Blöchl, *Phys. Rev. B* 50, 1994, 17953.
[13] P. Kurz, G. Bihlmayer, S. Blügel, *J. Phys.: Condens. Matter* 14, 2002, 6353.
[14] A. I. Liechtenstein, M. I. Katsnelson, V. P. Antropov, V. A. Gubanov, *J. Magn. Magn. Mater.* 67, 1987, 65.
[15] A. Hannemann, R. Hundt, J. C. Schön, M. Jansen, *J. Appl. Cryst.* 31, 1998, 922.
[16] G. H. O. Daalderoop, P. J. Kelly, M. F. H. Schuurmans, *Phys. Rev. B* 41, 1990, 11919.
[17] I. Galanakis, M. Alouani, H. Dreyssé, *Phys. Rev. B* 62, 2000, 6475.
[18] E. K- Koszó, G. Konczo, K. Lázár, G. Neuprandt, *IEEE Trans. Magn.* 10, 1974, 175.
[19] L. Pareti, F. Boizoni, F. Leccabue, A. E. Ermakov, *J. Appl. Phys.* 59, 1986, 3824.
[20] L. H. Lewis *et al. J. Phys.: Condens. Matter.* 26, 2014, 064213.
[21] K. Barmak, J. Kim, L. H. Lewis, K. R. Coffey, M. F. Toney, A. J. Kellock, J. –U. Thiele, *J. Appl. Phys.* 95, 2004, 7501.
[22] A. Gonis, Theoretical Materials Science, Material Research Society, Warrendale, PA, 2000.
[23] P. Soven, *Phys. Rev.* 156, 1967, 809.
[24] E. N. Economou, *Green's functions in quantum physics*, Springer, Berlin 1979.
[25] R. Skomski, *J. Appl. Phys.* 101, 2007, 09N517.
[26] J. P. Perdew, Y. Wang, *Phys. Rev. B* 45, 1992, 13244.
[27] G. Pacchioni, F. Frigoli, D. Ricci, J. A. Weil, *Phys. Rev.* B 63, 2000, 054102.
[28] P. Fulde, *Electron Correlations in Molecules and Solids*, Springer, Berlin 1991.
[29] R. Skomski, D. J. Sellmyer, *J. Appl. Phys.* 101, 2007, 09G524.
[30] A. Svane, O. Gunnarsson, *Phys. Rev. Lett.* 65, 1990, 1148.
[31] V. I. Anisimov, F. Aryasetiawan, A. I. Lichtenstein, *J. Phys. Condens.* Matter 9, 1997, 767.
[32] R. Skomski, V. Sharma, B. Balamurugan, J. E. Shield, A. Kashyap, D. J. Sellmyer, Anisotropy of doped transition-metal magnets, Proc. REPM'10 (Nagasaki), pp. 4-9.
[33] R. M. Bozorth, *Ferromagnetism*, Princeton, NJ: van Nostrand-Reinhold, 1951.
[34] T. Burkert, L. Nordström, O. Eriksson, O. Heinonen, *Phys. Rev. Lett.* 93, 2004, 027203.
[35] E. K. Delczeg-Czirjak *et al. Phys. Rev. B* 89, 2014, 144403.
[36] P. Manchanda *et al. IEEE Trans. Magn.* 49, 2013, 5194.
[37] J. M. D. Coey, *J. Phys.: Conden. Matter* 26, 2014, 064211.
[38] B. D. Cullity, *Introduction to Magnetic Materials,* Addison-Wesley, Reading, MA, 1972.
[39] G. Fuster, N. E. Brener, J. Callaway, J. L. Fry, Y. Z. Zhao, D. A. Papaconstantopoulos, *Phys. Rev. B* 38, 1988, 423.

Atomic Magnetic Properties of Pt-Lean FePt and CoPt Derivatives

RENU CHOUDHARY,[1,2] PANKAJ KUMAR,[1] PRIYANKA MANCHANDA,[2] YI LIU,[2] ARTI KASHYAP,[1] D.J. SELLMYER[2], RALPH SKOMSKI[2]
[1]School of Basic Sciences, Indian Institute of Technology, Mandi, Himachal Prasdesh, India
[2]Department of Physics and Astronomy, Nebraska Center for Material and Nanoscience , University of Nebraska, Lincoln, NE, USA

Abstract: *Transition-metal substitutions in $L1_0$-ordered FePt are investigated by first-principle calculations and compared with highly coercive high-magnetization $Fe_{50}Pt_{50-x}Ni_x$ thin films. VASP supercell calculations are used to determine atomic-moment and anisotropy changes due to Ni and Co subsitution for Pt. The magnetization increases with Ni content, but the theoretical increase is less pronounced than the experimental one, which we ascribe to the trend towards antiferromagnetism in perfectly $L1_0$-ordered FePt. In all cases, the magnetocrystalline anisotropy decreases with Pt content.*

Keywords: *Fe_2NiPt; Fe_2CoPt; supercell; local magnetic moment; magnetocrystalline anisotropy*

Address: Renu Choudhary, School of Basic Sciences, Indian Institute of Technology Mandi (H.P), 175001, India, Tel: +919459206370, E-mail: renu.khera12@gmail.com

1. Introduction

The replacement of expensive or critical raw materials by cheaper iron-series transition-metal elements is a major effort in present-day permanent-magnet research. The LI_0-ordered alloys FePt [1] and CoPt [2] have good permanent-magnet properties. As Pt is an expensive material, therefore, it is of interest to replace as much of the Pt as possible by cheaper iron-series transition metal (3d) elements without destroying the tetragonal $L1_0$ structure. Another important point is that the spin structure of perfectly $L1_0$ ordered FePt is antiferromagnetic, or very close to antiferromagnetism [3-5]. Small additions of transition-metal elements are therefore likely to improve the exchange coupling between neighboring Fe layers in the $L1_0$ structure, and this may also contribute to the record nominal energy products achieved in $Fe_{1+x}Pt_{1-x}$ [6,7]. In this paper, we investigate substitutions of Ni for Pt in FePt, both by first principle calculation and experimentally.

2. Methods

Our $Fe_{50}Pt_{50-x}Ni_x$ thin-film samples ($0 \leq x \leq 0.25$) were deposited on MgO, as described in Ref. 6, and characterized by x-ray diffraction, transmission electron microscopy and SQUID magnetometry. A comprehensive description of this work will be published elsewhere [8].

The first-principle calculations are performed by density functional theory based *Vienna Ab-initio Simulation Package* (VASP) [9], which uses a basis set of plane waves for valence electrons and the projected augmented wave (PAW) method. A generalized-gradient approximation (GGA) is used as the exchange-correlation functional. The plane-wave basis set is chosen by taking the energy cutoff as 350 eV. The lattice parameters are taken as $a = b = 3.85$ Å and $c = 3.71$ Å [10]. Using the Monkhorst-Pack scheme, sufficiently dense k-point meshes are selected to ensure convergence.

3. Results

Figure 1 shows a typical hysteresis loop for $Fe_{50}Pt_{50-x}Ni_x$ ($x = 6\%$), with nearly rectangular shape and a coercivity close to 2 T [20 kOe]. As the Ni concentration increases from 0 to 25%, the magnetic polarization increases from 1.33 T [1060 emu/cm^3] to 1.66 T [1320 emu/cm^3], whereas the coercivity decreases from 27 kOe to 0.5 kOe. A nominal maximum energy product of 52.9 MGOe was obtained for the film with 6% Ni ($Fe_{50}Pt_{44}Ni_6$). Figure 2 shows the saturation magnetization as a function of the Ni content and observe the slopes of the theoretical and experimental curves.

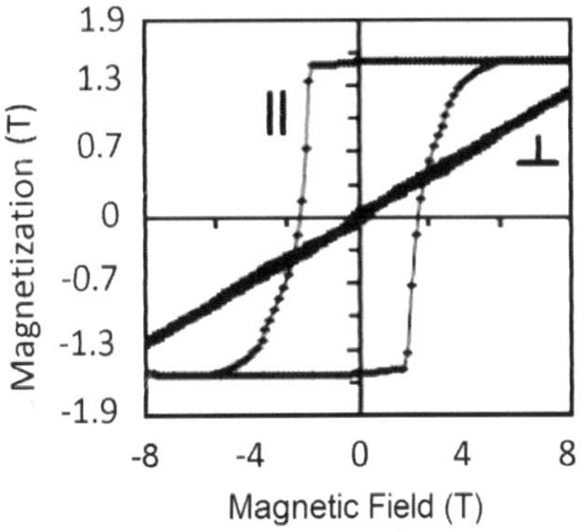

Fig. 1. Hysteresis loop of the $Fe_{50}Pt_{44}Ni_6$ film on MgO.

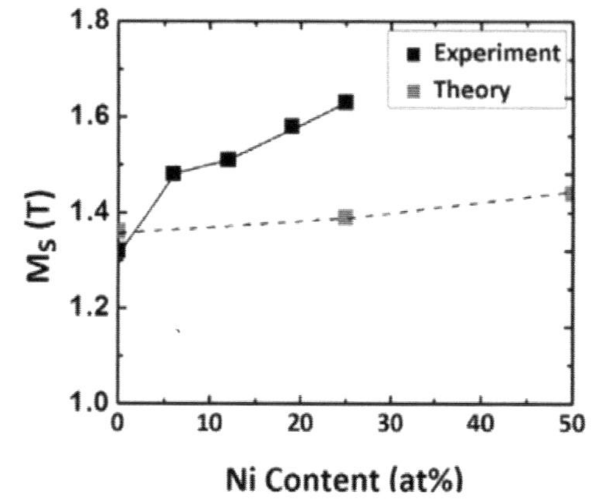

Fig. 2. Saturation magnetization of $FePt_{1-x}Ni_x$.

Figure 3 compares the total densities of states (DOS) of Fe_2NiPt and Fe_2CoPt, whereas Fig. 4 shows the element-specific partial DOS in bulk $Fe_{16}NiPt_{15}$. In both the total and partial DOS, the moment is the difference between the integrated ↑ and ↓ states.

To discuss magnetization trends caused by the Ni, we have performed first-principle moment and magnetic anisotropy calculations for $Fe_{50}Ni_xPt_{50-x}$ and for $Fe_{50}Co_xPt_{50-x}$. The original four-atom unit cell [11] can be used to treat Fe_2NiPt and Fe_2CoPt, whereas smaller Ni (and Co) concentrations require bigger supercells, such as 32 atoms for $Fe_{16}NiPt_{15}$ and $Fe_{16}CoPt_{15}$.

Table 1 summarizes the zero-temperature atomic magnetic moments extracted from the DFT calculations. The total magnetization is 1.08 MA/m (1.36 T) for FePt, 1.12 MA/m (1.39 T) for $Fe_{16}NiPt_{15}$, and 1.32 MA/m (1.42 T) for Fe_2CoPt. The addition of Ni and Co slightly redistributes the magnetic moment per Fe atom.

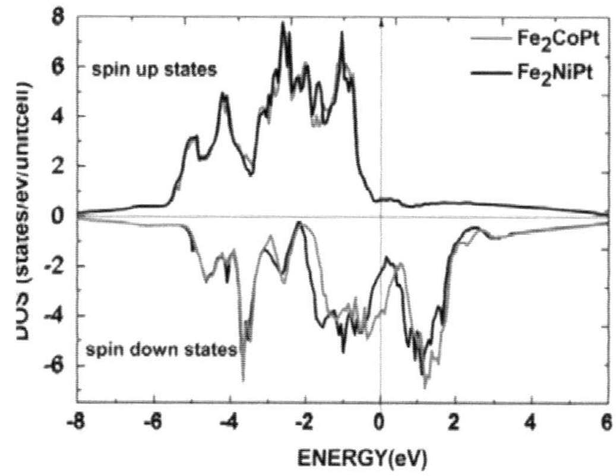

Fig. 3. Comparison of the total DOSs of Fe_2NiPt and Fe_2CoPt.

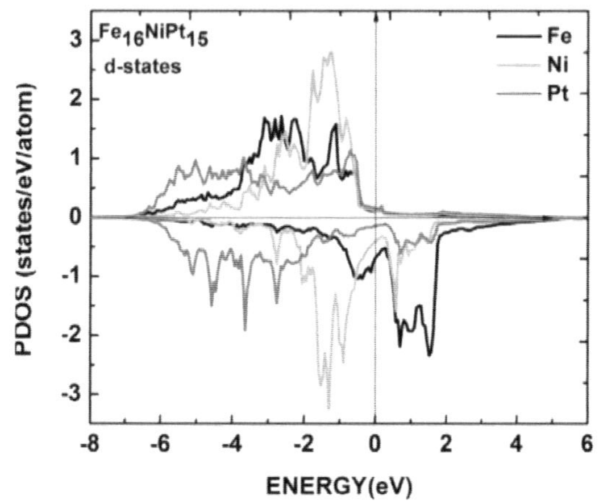

Fig. 4. Element-specific partial densities of states (DOS) for bulk $Fe_{16}NiPt_{15}$.

Table 1. Atomic magnetic moments and magnetizations of ferromagnetic $FePt_{1-x}Ni_x$ alloys.

Alloy	Magnetic Moment μ (μ_B per atom)				$\mu_0 M$ (T)
	Fe	Ni	Co	Pt	
FePt	2.89			0.32	1.36
CoPt			1.83	0.38	0.93
Fe_2NiPt	2.92	0.67		0.33	1.44
Fe_2CoPt	2.86		1.76	0.33	1.65
$Fe_{16}NiPt_{15}$	2.75	0.74		0.36	1.39
$Fe_{16}CoPt_{15}$	2.86		1.72	0.35	1.42

In $L1_0$ magnets, the cubic symmetry is broken by alternating planes of 3d and 5d atoms, in spite of the fact that $a = b \approx c$. The main contribution to the anisotropy comes from the 5d (Pt) atoms, which have large spin-orbit coupling, while the 3d atoms provide the necessary exchange splitting of the 5d sublattice (Fig. 4).

Table 2 summarizes our anisotropy results, obtained by using the total energy difference method [12]. The calculated anisotropy constants K_1 decrease from 7.04 MJ/m^3 in FePt to 3.42 MJ/m^3 in Fe_2NiPt, in agreement with experiment, and to 1.01 MJ/m^3 in Fe_2CoPt. Note that the calculated FePt and CoPt anisotropies agree well with experiment [10,13] but are somewhat at the lower end among first-principle calculations [14]. A pictorial explanation of the

Table 2. Magnetocrystalline anisotropy.

Alloy	K_1 (meV per unit cell)	K_1 (MJ/m^3)
FePt	2.421	7.04
CoPt	1.572	4.57
Fe_2NiPt	1.175	3.42
Fe_2CoPt	0.345	1.01

anisotropy trend is that Ni and Co make the environment of the Pt atoms more cubic, similar to the series $Fe_{2+x}Pt_{2-x}$, where the tetragonal $L1_0$ structure degenerates into cubic $L1_2$-ordered Fe_3Pt.

4. Conclusions

In summary, our focus has been on substitutions of 3d elements for 4d/5d elements, as contrasted to series such as $Fe_{1-x}Co_xPt$ [15], $Fe_{1-x}Mn_xPt$ [16], and $FePt_xPd_{1-x}$ [17]. The decrease of the $Fe_{50}Ni_xPt_{50-x}$ anisotropy with increasing Ni and Co contents is not surprising. By contrast, the calculated magnetization of $Fe_{50}Ni_xPt_{50-x}$ only qualitatively agrees with experiment: the experimental increase of M_s with Ni content is much larger than the one predicted theoretically (Fig. 2). Since DFT calculations are fairly accurate (with a magnetization error of less than about 2%), we ascribe this discrepancy to the assumption of ferromagnetic order for all Ni contents x. More generally, for $x = 0$, both spin structure and magnetic properties need further experimental and theoretical research.

Acknowledgement
This research is supported by DOE BES (DE-FG02-04ER46152), ARO (W911NF-10-2-0099) and NCMN.

References

[1] L. Graf, A. Kussmann, *Z. Phys.* **36**, 1935, 544.
[2] W. Jellinghaus, *Z. Tech. Phys.* **17**, 1936, 33.
[3] G. Brown, B. Kraczek, A. Janotti, T. C. Schulthess, G. M. Stocks and D. D. Johnson, *Phys. Rev. B* **68**, 2003, 052405.
[4] R. Skomski, A. Kashyap and J. Zhou, *Scripta Mater.* **53**, ***2005***, 389.
[5] R. Skomski, P. Manchanda, P. Kumar, B. Balamurugan, A. Kashyap, and D. Sellmyer, *IEEE Trans. Magn.* **49**, 2013, 3215.
[6] Y. Liu, T. A. George, R. Skomski and D. J. Sellmyer, *Appl. Phys. Lett.* **99**, 2011, 172504.
[7] P. K. Sahota, Y. Liu, R. Skomski, P. Manchanda, R. Zhang, H. Fangohr, M. Franchin, G. C. Hadjipanayis, A. Kashyap and D. J. Sellmyer, *J. Appl. Phys.* **111**, 2012, 07E345.
[8] Y. Liu *et al.*, in preparation, 2014.
[9] J. Hafner, *J. Comput. Chem.* **29**, 2008, 2044.
[10] M. Yua, H. Ohguchi, A. Zambano, I. Takeuchi, J.-P. Liu, D. Josell, L. A. Bendersky, *J. Mater. Sci. Eng. B*, **142**, 2007, 139.
[11] P. Manchanda, P. Kumar, A. Kashyap, M. J. Lucis, J. E. Shield, A. Mubarok, J. I. Goldstein, S. Constantinides, K. Barmak, L. H. Lewis, D. J. Sellmyer, and R. Skomski, *IEEE Trans. Magn.* **49**, 2013, 10.
[12] I. Galanakis, M. Alouani, and H. Dreysse, *Phys. Rev. B* **62**, 2000, 10.
[13] T. Klemmer, D. Hoydick, H. Okumura, B. Zhang, and W. A. Soffa, *Scripta Metall. Mater.* **33**, 1995, 1793.
[14] A. B. Shick and O. N. Mryasov, *Phys. Rev. B* **67**, 2003, 172407.
[15] J. A. Christodoulides, Y. Zhang, G. C. Hadjipanayis, and C. Fountzoulas, *IEEE Trans. Magn.* **36**, 2000, 4.
[16] Y.-Ch. Lai, Y.-H. Chang, G.-J. Chen, K.-F. Chiu and Y.-Ch. Chen, *Mater. Trans.* **47**, 2006, 2086.
[17] S. D. Willoughby, J. M. MacLaren, T. Ohkubo, S. Jeong, M. McHenry, D.E. Laughlin, S.-J. Choi, S.-J. Kwon, *J. Appl. Phys.* **91**, 2002, 8822.

Recent Advances in High-Performance Permanent-Magnet Motors

T. KONDO[1], Y. ASANO[1], A. YAMAGIWA[1], K. OHYAMA[2]
[1]Technology Research Association of Magnetic Materials for High-Efficiency Motors, Sakai, Japan
[2]Daikin Industries, Ltd. Environmental technology laboratory, Kusatsu, Japan

Abstract: *Recently, the requirements for high-performance motors have increased to contribute to environmental protection. It is expected that interior permanent-magnet synchronous motors (IPMSMs) perform with the highest efficiency among the various motor types. Further, it is important to reduce the amount of heavy rare-earth elements (HREEs) used from the viewpoint of resource issues. In this paper, we first review the improvements in energy-saving* technology *for the IPMSMs of air-conditioner compressor motors. Second, we show the trend in the amount of HREEs used in IPMSMs. Finally, we introduce the research of the Technology Research Association of Magnetic Materials for High-Efficiency Motors (MagHEM) on the design and measurement technology of high-efficiency motors for Hybrid Electric Vehicles (HEVs).*

Keywords: *demagnetization; iron loss; IPMSM; variable-magnetic-flux motor*

Address: Yoshinari Asano, Technology Research Association of Magnetic Materials for High-Efficiency Motors, Gakuen-cho 1-1, Sakai, Osaka 599-8531, Japan, E-mail: yasano@maghem.jp

1. Introduction

Recently, the requirements for high-performance motors have increased to contribute to environmental protection. It is expected that interior permanent-magnet synchronous motors (IPMSMs) perform with the highest efficiency among the various motor types. High-efficiency IPMSMs for compressors were achieved to improve the performance of air conditioners in Japan [1]. Thereafter, IPMSMs were employed for the traction motor of Hybrid Electric Vehicles (HEVs), in which a high coercive force is required from the magnet owing to the high environmental temperature.

In addition, the amount of rare-earth elements (REEs) used in the magnet continues to increase to improve the motor efficiency. In particular, it is important to reduce the amount of heavy REEs (HREEs) used, such as Dy and Tb, from the viewpoint of resource issues. For air conditioners, we developed a motor using grain-boundary diffusion processed Nd–Fe–B magnets that enable a dramatic reduction in the amount of Dy while retaining the high coercive force. For HEVs, motor applications using magnets with a lower amount of HREEs have been started, though a high coercive force is required owing to the higher temperature.

In this paper, we first review the improvements in energy-saving technology for the IPMSMs of air-conditioner compressor motors. Second, we show the trend in the amount of HREEs used in IPMSMs. Finally, we introduce the research of the Technology Research Association of Magnetic Materials for High-Efficiency Motors (MagHEM) regarding the design and measurement technology of high-efficiency motors for HEVs.

2. Energy-Saving Technologies for Compressor Motors

Table 1 summarizes the structures and features of induction motors (IMs), surface permanent-magnet synchronous motors (SPMSMs), IPMSMs, and switched reluctance motors (SRMs) for compressor drive applications. Fig. 1 shows the efficiency characteristics of compressor motors for residential air conditioners.

IPMSMs, in which magnets are embedded in the rotor, have advantages such as
1) high efficiency and high torque due to utilization of the reluctance torque in addition to magnetic torque and
2) a wide constant power range as a result of flux-weakening control.

Therefore, IPMSMs, which were produced in 1996 for the first time in the air-conditioning industry, play an important role in improving the intermediate load efficiency because they have a considerably higher efficiency at low speed in comparison with IMs and SPMSMs, which were produced by Daikin Industries in 1994 and 1995, respectively.

Furthermore, flux-weakening control of an IPMSM

Table 1 Comparison of the structures and features of compressor motors.

Motor type	IM	SPMSM	IPMSM	SRM
Structure	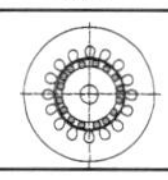	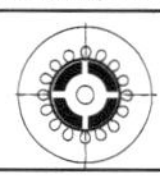	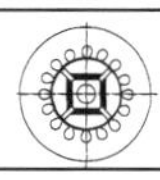	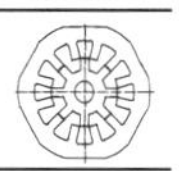
Efficiency at low speed	poor	good	excellent	fair
Rated Efficiency	fair	good	excellent	fair
Flux-weakening control	good	poor	good	good

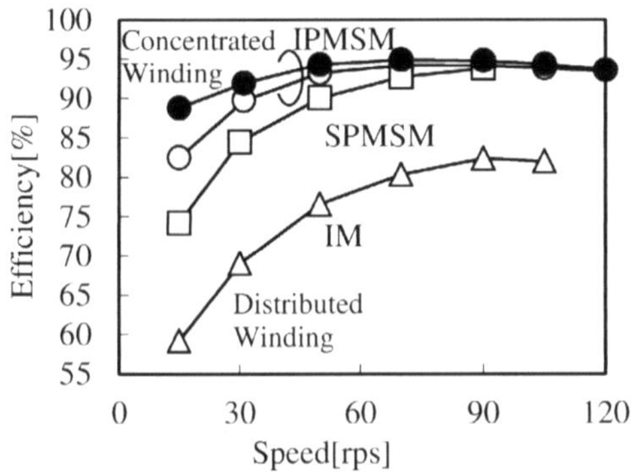

Fig. 1. Comparison of efficiency of compressor motors.

can increase the refrigeration capacity because it enables compressors to be driven at a higher speed, whereas this control is not easily applicable to an SPMSM.

The torque T and terminal voltage V_a are given by (1) and (2) using the variables and parameters in the rotating d–q coordinate system [2].

$$T = P_n\{\psi_a i_q + (L_q - L_d)(-i_d)i_q\} \quad (1)$$

$$V_a = \sqrt{(R_a i_d - \omega L_q i_q)^2 + (R_a i_q + \omega\psi_a - \omega L_d(-i_d))^2} \quad (2)$$

where, i_d and i_q are the d- and q-axis stator currents, respectively; ω is the electrical angular velocity; R_a is the stator winding resistance; ψ_a is the magnet flux linkage; L_d and L_q are the d- and q-axis inductances, respectively; and P_n is the number of pole pairs.

As summarized in Table 2, from the start of commercial production in 1996, Daikin Industries adopted a rotor structure with sintered rare-earth Nd–Fe–B permanent magnets embedded inside the outer surface of the rotor. Thus, the proportion of the reluctance torque increases because magnetic saturation can be avoided, and the saliency ratio can be increased [L_q–L_d becomes greater than zero in equation (1)]. A magnetic flux can be produced in the opposite direction to ψa by applying a relatively small current $-id$ (flux-weakening control) because the magnets are thin owing to the high coercive force of the Nd–Fe–B magnets. Thus, L_d is large in equation (2). As a result, it is possible to widen the constant-power operation range. These advantages were realized by both the development of the rotor structure and the increase in the remanent flux density and coercive force of the permanent magnets, as shown in Fig. 2.

In addition, the use of a concentrated winding, in which coils are wound directly around the stator teeth, has become the main technique for the stator winding since 2000. This technique shortens the length of the end windings; thus, the copper loss is reduced.

In addition to the improvements in the electromagnetic structure of the motor, progress in both permanent magnets (Fig. 2) and silicon steel sheets (Fig. 3) has been an important factor for

Table 2 Comparison of the structures and features of compressor motors.

Motor type	1996	2001	2007
Structure			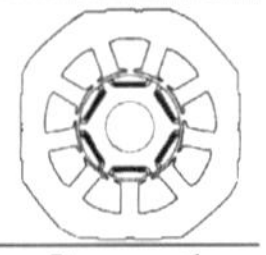
Rotor magnet	Rare-earth magnet	Rare-earth magnet	Rare-earth magnet
Stator winding	Distributed	Distributed	Concentrated
Driving waveform	Rectangular	Sinusoidal	Sinusoidal

improving motor efficiency. PM motors can reduce the copper loss in comparison with IMs because the excitation loss is eliminated. Because the iron loss is the dominant loss component in IPMSMs, which utilize the reluctance torque, a further decrease in the iron loss of the silicon steel sheets is desirable. At the early stages in the development of IPMSMs, the level of the saturation flux density of the silicon steel sheets tended to be sacrificed in order to reduce the iron loss. However, an increase in the saturation flux density has recently been demanded because new motor designs have a stator with a concentrated winding and a rotor in which the flux density is high as a result of magnetic flux focusing. Consequently, practical use of silicon steel sheets that exhibit both low iron loss and high saturation flux density has been extensively developed.

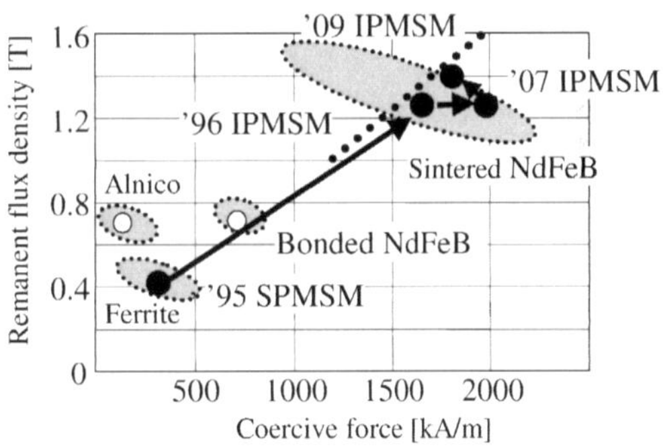

Fig. 2. Development trend for permanent magnets.

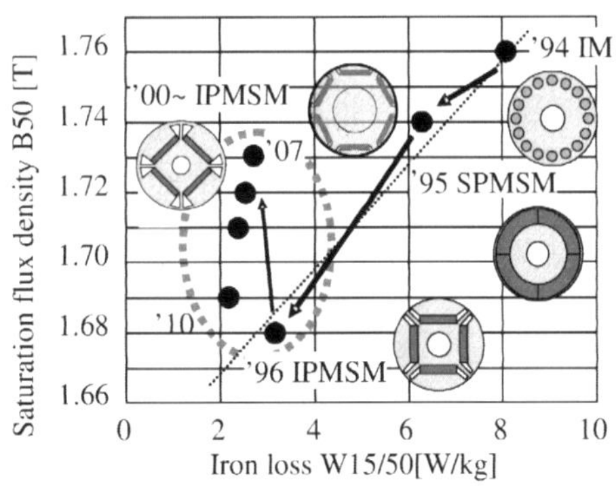

Fig. 3. Development trend for silicon steel sheets.

3. Trends in the Performance of Rare-Earth-Less Oriented IPMSMs

3.1. Trends in the amount of REEs used in IPMSMs for air conditioners

Table 3 summarizes the weights of Nd–Fe–B magnets and the amount of HREEs (Dy, Tb) contained in the magnets in an IPMSM for residential air conditioners. The values in the table are based on reference year 1996, when commercial production started earlier than other applications [3][4].

In the late 1990s, the expansion of IPMSM-installed products had become urgent to increase the efficiency of air conditioners. It was necessary to lower the cost by reducing the weight of rare-earth magnets, which were relatively expensive, in order to increase the number of IPMSM-installed products. However, the magnitude of the main magnetic flux in a motor cannot be reduced to increase the efficiency. Therefore, it is effective to reduce the magnet thickness and volume in order to lower the motor cost by reducing the magnet weight. At that time, the production of Nd–Fe–B magnets for motors expanded, and the cost of HREEs decreased. Therefore, thin Nd–Fe–B magnets having a high coercivity by increasing the amount of additives such as Dy were adopted, and the weight percentage and weight of HREEs used increased, as indicated in Table 3.

After that, in the mid-2000s, it was decided that the index for evaluating air-conditioner efficiency changed from the coefficient of performance (COP) to the annual performance factor (APF). To improve the APF, it is important to increase the energy consumption efficiency under the intermediate condition of cooling and heating. This can be achieved by improving the intermediate load efficiency of the motor. For the motor design, a stator with concentrated windings was adopted, and the surface area of the magnets in the rotor was increased to reduce the copper loss. At the same time, the amount of HREEs used increased to improve the demagnetization durability of the motors because the stack length was reduced to lower the cost. As a result, both the weight of the magnets and HREEs increased, as shown in Table 3, and the amount of HREEs used, such as Dy, in 2007 was 1.6 times higher than that in 1996.

For higher efficiency, grain-boundary diffusion processed Nd–Fe–B magnets, which reduced the amount of HREEs used by 60%, were adopted. This technique ensures that magnets have a coercivity equivalent to that of conventional ones while reducing the additional amount of HREEs used, causing a reduction in the remanent flux density. The remanent flux density of these magnets was increased by 11%, and the APF was increased by 1.5% in our development case. Thus, the increase in the amount of HREEs used halted, which had continued from the start of the installation of IPMSMs in air conditioners.

Table 3 Trend in amount of HREEs used in compressor motors.

Year	1996	2001	2007	2013
Rotor structure				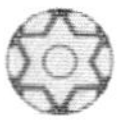
Weight of magnet	1.0	0.9	1.1	1.3
Weight percentage of HREEs [wt%]	6%	Over 6%	Over 6%	2%
Weight of HREEs	1.0	1.2	1.6	0.5

Furthermore, both high efficiency and a reduction in Dy were achieved earlier than other applications. A motor using grain-boundary diffusion processed magnets is a good example of a development to solve resource issues, and it is expected that the applicable range for mass production will be expanded for various applications.

3.2. Developed motors using magnets with less Dy

Fig. 4 shows an overview of a motor using magnets with less Dy installed in air conditioners in 2009. Grain-boundary diffusion processed magnets, of which the remanent flux density is increased by 11%, were adoped, and the surface area of the magnets was increased by using a V-shaped magnet arrangement to improve the motor efficiency. Fig. 5 shows the distribution of the magnetic flux density in the rotor calculated by using FEA. Demagnetization easily occurs in the parts of the two magnets where the magnet is adjacent to the others in this arrangement. For grain-boundary diffusion processed magnets, the problem of demagnetization in these parts can be prevented because the coercivity of the end parts of the magnets can be increased, even if the total amount of Dy is reduced. Therefore, these magnets are suitable for the V-shaped arrangement.

However, the iron loss due to harmonics increases when the magnetic flux is increased to improve efficiency. Therefore, we confirmed that the harmonic components in the rotor with the V-shaped arrangement were reduced by relieving the magnetic saturation due to the increase in the volume of the core of the magnetic poles in the rotor, as shown in Fig. 5. As a result, the motor efficiency improved by 1.4–1.7%, and the APF improved by 1.5% under cooling/heating intermediate and rated conditions, while the weight of HREEs used was reduced by 60% in comparison with that of conventional motors.

4. Development of Motors in MagHEM

MagHEM was founded in 2012 and consists of nine companies, an incorporated administrative agency, and an organization [5]. As shown in Fig. 6, the objective of MagHEM is the development of innovative magnetic materials by 2017 and 2022 and high-efficiency motors using the materials. In this paper, we

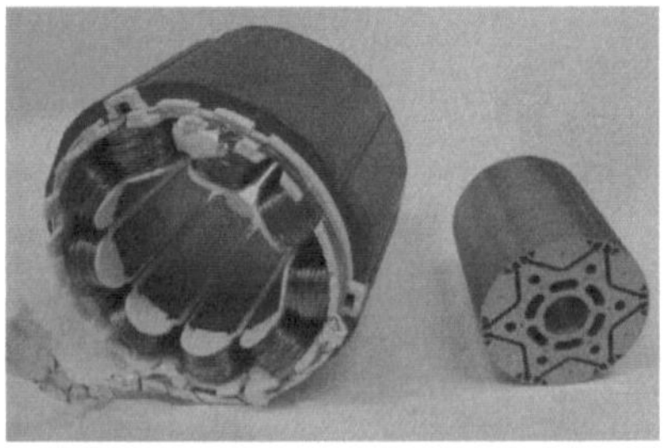

Fig. 4. IPMSM using magnets with less Dy.

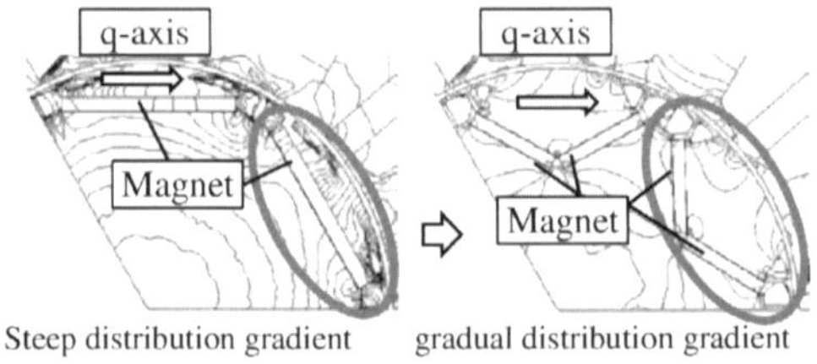

(a) Conventional rotor (b) V-shaped arrangement

Fig. 5. Distribution of the magnetic flux density in the rotor core.

introduce the activities for developing high-efficiency motors in MagHEM.

First, we show the development of motor material evaluation techniques for the development of high-efficiency motors using new magnetic materials developed by MagHEM. It is important to evaluate the demagnetization characteristics of magnets in a high-temperature environment because HEV/EV motors are used in this environment. However, the demagnetization state is not uniform in the magnet owing to the nonuniformity of the magnetic properties and the strength of the magnetic field applied by the armature coils. Furthermore, the flux density is only measured on the surface of the magnet to evaluate the demagnetization state, and the state inside the magnet is estimated by using FEA. Therefore, we develop a method to evaluate the three-dimensional demagnetization state including the inside the magnet by cutting the magnet into the cubes, as shown in Fig. 7, and measuring the *B–H* characteristics of each magnet cube.

Further, it is necessary to establish a high-precision motor-loss measurement technology, especially the iron loss, for accurate evaluation of the motor efficiency. The mechanical loss generated in the bearings makes it difficult to precisely evaluate the iron loss in a conventional measurement system. Therefore, we are developing a high-precision motor-loss measurement system that dramatically reduces the mechanical loss in the system, as shown in Fig. 8.

For the development of high-efficiency motors, we study IPMSMs and variable-flux magnetic-flux motors using the materials developed by MagHEM. The effects of the new magnetic materials on motor characteristics such as the efficiency and operating range were evaluated by FEA. Motors were analyzed by FEA by using the assumed characteristics of magnets without Dy that will be developed in 2017. One of the motors is shown in Fig. 9. It is expected that a reduction in the motor loss will be achieved as planned. Furthermore, future motor designs will be carried out by applying the assumed magnet characteristics with a maximum energy product of 50 MGOe at 180 °C, developed by MagHEM in 2022.

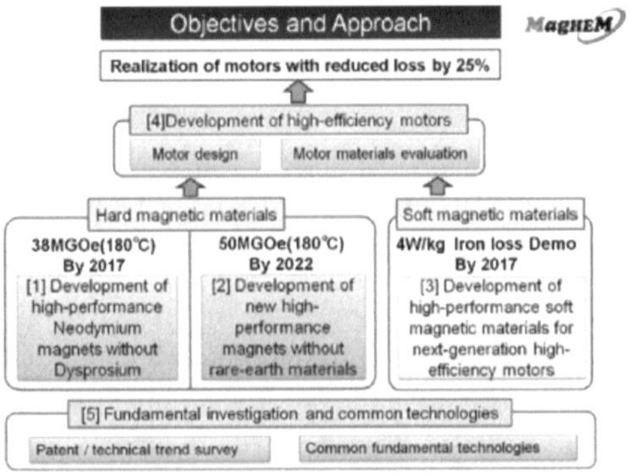

Fig. 6. Objectives of MagHEM.

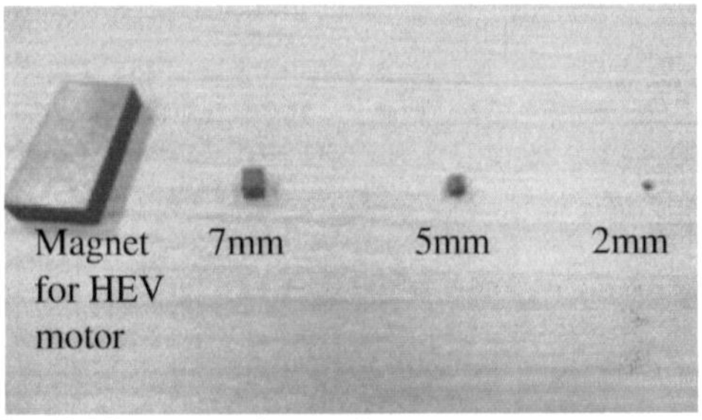

Fig. 7. Magnet cut into cubes.

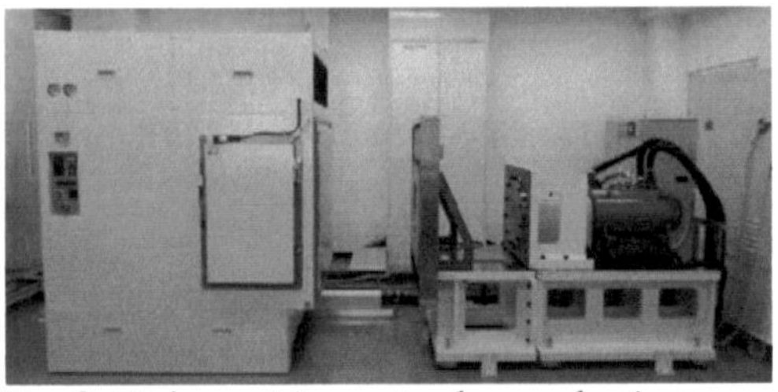

Fig. 8. High-precision motor-loss evaluation system.

Fig. 9. Developed motor.

5. Conclusions

In this paper, we described the improvements in energy-saving technology for the IPMSMs of air-conditioner compressor motors, the trend in the amount of HREEs used in IPMSMs, and the research activities for high-efficiency motor development by MagHEM.

Magnets with a high maximum energy product and soft magnetic materials with low iron-loss characteristics will be developed by MagHEM, and these materials will change the design of motors. We will develop high-efficiency motors that enable the extraction of the maximum performance of magnetic materials developed by MagHEM through these efforts.

Acknowledgments
The work was supported by the Future Pioneering Projects, Development of Magnetic Material Technology for High-Efficiency Motors.

References

[1] K. Ohyama, T. Kondo, *IEEJ Trans. Electr. Electron. Eng.*, 2008, Vol.3, No.2, pp.183-189
[2] S. Morimoto, T. Ueno, M. Sanada, Y. Takeda, T. Hirasa, A. Yamagiwa, *Rec. of IEEE Ind. Appl. Society Ann. Conf.*, 1993, pp.59-64
[3] K. Ohyama, *18th Magnetic Appl. Tech. Symp.*, 2010, p.A1-4
[4] K. Ohyama, *31st Motor Tech. Symp.*, 2011, p.B3-3
[5] Technology Research Association of Magnetic Materials for High-Efficiency Motors, http://www.maghem.jp/english/about.html

Optimizing Magnetic Effects through Shaped Field Magnets

G. MARTINEK[1], U. WYSS[2], D. MAYBURY[2], S. CONSTANTINIDES[3]
[1]Arnold Magnetic Technologies, Donaustrasse 7, 63452 Hanau, Germany
[2]Arnold Magnetic Technologies, Lupfig, Switzerland
[3]Arnold Magnetic Technologies, Rochester, NY, USA

Abstract: *Shaped field magnets exhibit a continuously varying magnetization direction over the volume of the magnet, resulting in significantly better performance in numerous applications. The optimized magnetization patterns in this new class of sintered magnets are achieved by implementing corresponding patterns for the magnetic anisotropy during particle alignment in the near-net-shape production process. These factors can be accurately modeled prior to manufacturing. Empirical examples from products in current serial production show more than 20% higher torque in permanent magnet couplings, or 30% weight reduction for sensor magnets.*

Keywords: *SmCo; sintered magnets; field shaping; flux concentration; torque coupling*

Address: Steve Constantinides, Arnold Magnetic Technologies, Rochester, NY, 14625, U.S.A., Tel: (1-585) 385-9010, E-mail: sconstantinides@arnoldmagnetics.com

1. Introduction

The overwhelming majority of modern sintered magnets are used with quasi-uniform magnetization. This is ideal for situations where the magnetic flux from the magnet can be conducted by soft-magnetic "iron" parts which direct the flux into the region of interest (e. g. the gap of a loudspeaker system). In cases where the magnet is used in an "open circuit" large portions of the flux will be in regions where it is not needed. This undesirable flux can be minimized by introducing a spatially varying magnetization direction. The most striking example for this principle is found in "Halbach" configurations [1,2], which maximize magnetic flux on one side of a planar magnet array (or inside a ring), nearly eliminating flux on the other side. Even before the theoretical treatments were published, similar principles had been applied in some applications, for instance, in Alnico braking magnets in Ferraris-type electricity meters.

In sintered magnets, examples of non-uniform anisotropy have been rare, limited essentially to segments or rings with radial magnetization. More often, they have been noted as undesirable side effects of the pressing process. However, developing the control of parameters to eliminate these side effects has opened other doors, as well. We now have successfully developed anisotropic "shaped field" sintered magnets with complex, optimized magnetization patterns.

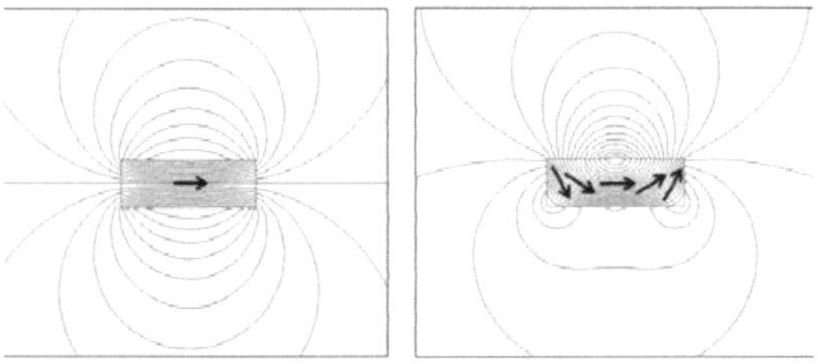

Fig. 1. Uniform magnetization vs "shaped-field" configuration.

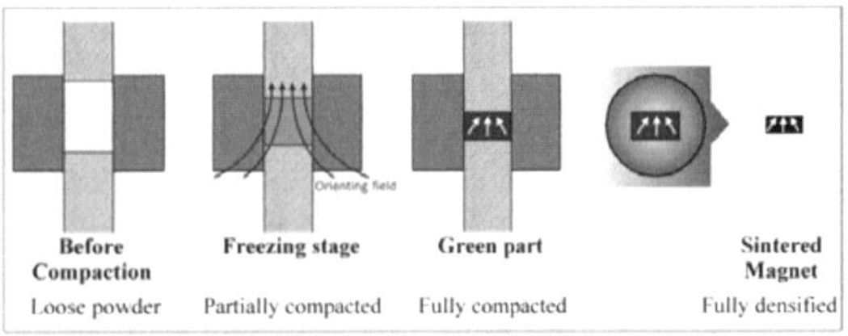

Fig. 2. Manufacturing process.

2. Manufacturing

The anisotropy in the common sintered magnet materials (hard ferrite, SmCo or NdFeB) is introduced by aligning the powder particles before and during compaction. The deliberate, controlled formation of strongly non-uniform anisotropy patterns therefore requires the application of a corresponding non-uniform field. This is achieved by a careful layout of magnetizing coils and permeable components in and around the tool. As the punches and powder move during compaction, the field will change. Special care must be taken to create the desired field configurations at the right stages.

3. Shaped Field Magnets for Angular Position Sensing

Manufacturers of angle sensors typically suggest cylindrical magnets with diametric orientation. A

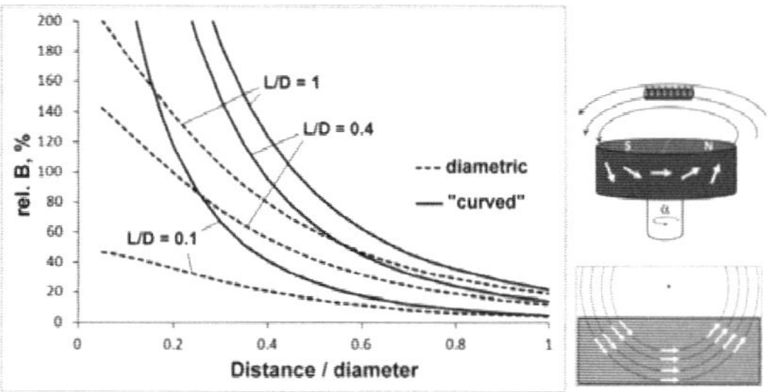

Fig. 3. Flux density on the axis of a cylindrical disc magnet of unit polarization and unit diameter. B = flux density in mT for a material with polarization 1T. L/D = ratio length/diameter.

more effective magnet, however, could show a curve pattern as indicated in Fig. 3 (upper right).

3.1. Modeling

The actual modeling of the magnet performance is done in 2 steps:

- Simulation of the magnetic fields on the press, giving the orientation pattern of the powder.
- Implementing this orientation pattern in a magnet of the appropriate size and shape for the finished sintered part.

For a simple approximation, the potential of shaped field magnets can be roughly assessed by assuming an idealized magnetization pattern which can easily be simulated. A suitable model for the magnets in question assumes a magnetization pattern following a circular path (Fig. 3, lower right). The position of the center of the circles was adapted to give the maximum field for each magnet shape and distance. The modeling indicates potential for significant improvements in the performance of the sensor magnet, as shown in Fig. 3 at left.

3.2. Experimental result

Cylindrical shaped field magnets of diameter 6.5 mm and thickness 2.5 mm were produced. The fields were then probed and compared with what was estimated by the rigorous modeling procedure outlined in the previous section.

The shaped field magnets are seen to give about 20% larger fields than a diametric magnet of the same dimensions and material (Fig. 4). In practical applications, this translates to a useful range extended by about 10%. It should be noted that rather than using the extended range, the magnet dimensions could be reduced, keeping the same distance from the sensor but reducing the cost of the magnet. This would result in a 30% smaller magnet volume for the same performance.

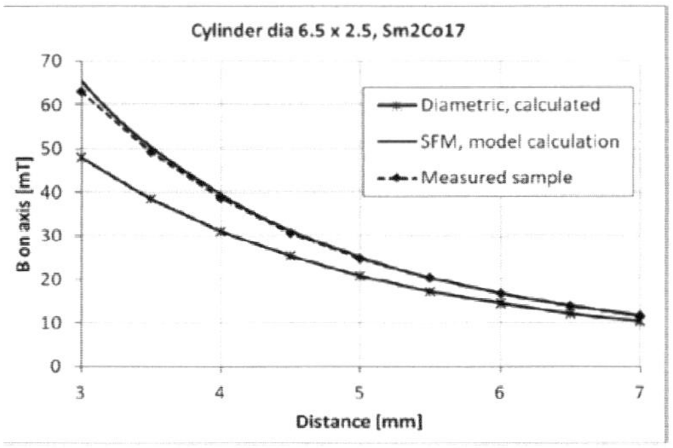

Fig. 4. Actual shaped field magnet example.

4. Shaped Field Magnets for Permanent Magnet Couplings

This type of magnet is optimized for performance in alternating-pole periodic arrays. Fig. 5 shows the traditional setup and 2 alternative configurations. The second configuration is commonly named "Halbach", although it is really just a rough approximation to a real Halbach array with continuously rotating magnetization direction.

4.1. Modeling

Figure 6 describes an easily implementable model for simulations. This model was used to demonstrate the potential for shape-field magnets in a very basic model: A planar coupling that extends infinitely, both in the periodic direction and perpendicular to the plane of projection (Fig. 7).

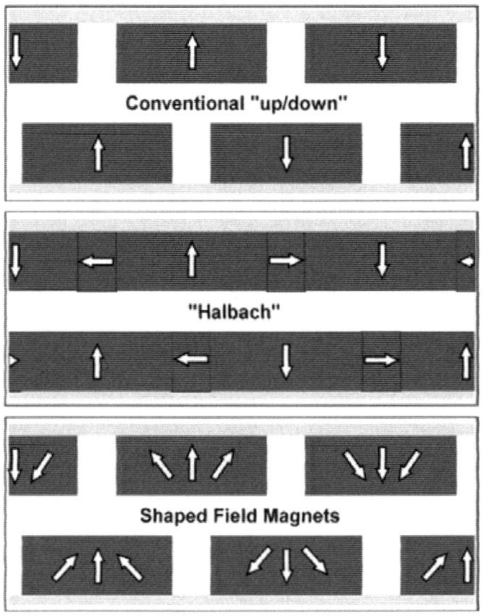

Fig. 5. Possible configurations for permanent magnet couplings.

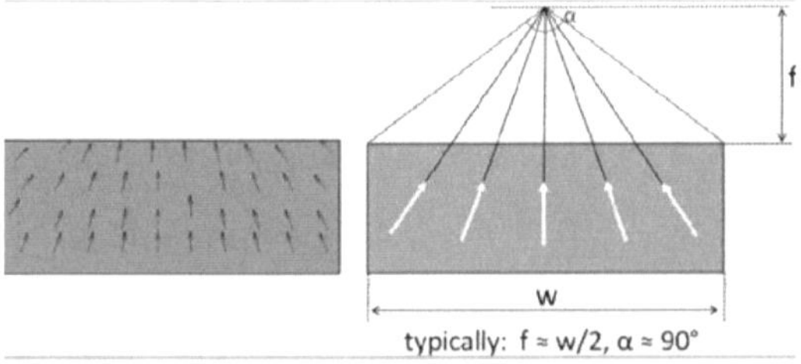

Fig. 6. Actual magnetization configuration and the approximation for modeling

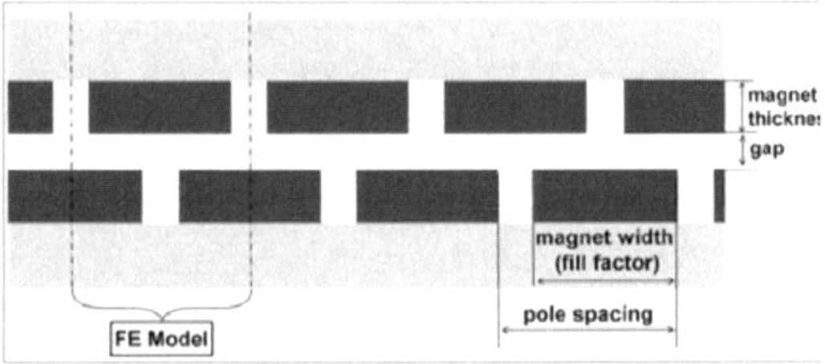

Fig. 7. Infinite planar coupling model.

The planar model contains only 4 parameters. It can be further simplified by scaling some of the dimensions against the gap, giving 3 independent parameters:

- magnet thickness / gap
- pole spacing / gap
- fill factor (= magnet width / pole/spacing)

In addition, for the shaped field magnets, the focusing parameter (α or f in fig. 6) was introduced.

Fig. 8 shows the shear force for a magnet material with polarization J = 1 T as a function of magnet thickness. Each point in the diagram represents a different configuration, where the remaining parameters (pole spacing, fill factor etc) were chosen to maximize the "efficiency" F per magnet volume.

4.2. Case study

The first implementation of this type of magnet was for a manufacturer of chemical pumps. Initially, the magnets in an existing coupling were simply exchanged for shaped field magnets of the same dimensions. This led to an increase of the transmittable torque by about 20%, both theoretically and empirically.

In second step, the coupling was extensively redesigned for more strength: The magnet thickness was increased and the number of poles was optimized, leveraging the advantages of the focused field. These changes yielded a torque gain of 54%.

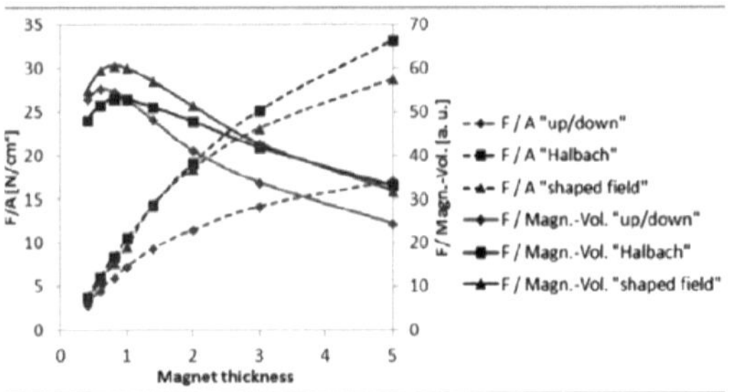

Fig. 8. Infinite planar coupling forces.

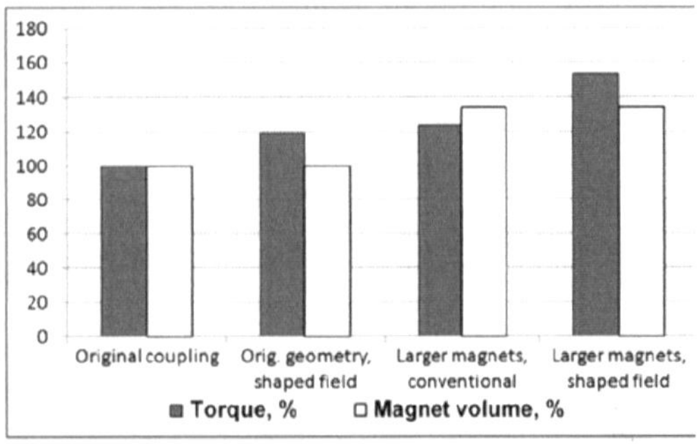

Fig. 9. Enhancements in torque in an actual coupling for chemical pumps.

References

[1] J. C. Mallinson, *IEEE Trans. Magn.* **9**, No. 4, Dec. 1973.

[2] K. Halbach, *Nuclear Instruments and Methods* **169,** 1980, 1.

Numerical and Experimental Root Cause Analysis of High Speed Motor/Generators

HEEJU CHOI, JINFANG LIU
Electron Energy Corporation, 924 Links Avenue, Landisville, PA 17538, USA

Abstract: *This paper discusses the design and failure mode analysis of an existing 125 kW 2-pole PM turbine machine rated at 75 krpm. The rotor speed is controlled by the waveforms, but the speed control is lost when these waveforms appear noisy. A root cause analysis of lower magnetic field, nonuniform field profile, and lower back-EMF was performed. The numerical finite element analysis of the magnetic circuit was carried out to compare the magnetic field and the back EMF with test data. In addition, the permanent magnet rotor assembly was investigated to verify the magnetic properties and uniformity. The results of root cause analyses helps to establish design guidelines and manufacturing procedures.*

Key words: *high speed motor; generator; back- electromotive force (EMF); finite element analysis (FEA)*

Address: Heeju Choi, Electron Energy Corporation, 924 Links Avenue, Landisville, PA 17538, USA, Tel: 1-717-898-2294, Fax 1-717-898-0660, E-mail: hchoi@electronenergy.com

1. Introduction

Permanent magnets (PMs) have become increasingly popular and are used in many applications including hybrid electric vehicles, motors, generators, and most consumer electronic devices [1]. The design of the magnetic circuit and the actual magnetic properties of the PMs have a significant impact on the performance of the magnetic systems. This is especially true for high speed turbomachines [2]. The design of rotating machinery requires a series of iterative computations based on the selection of different motor topologies, materials, geometrical dimensions, winding schematics, etc…[3]. The magnetic field density in the air gap provides valuable information in evaluating motor performance, torque, back electromotive force (EMF), and control [4].

In this paper, an existing 125 kW, 2-pole PM, 75 krpm rated turbine machine with a noisy waveform is taken as an example to discuss the design and failure mode analysis. The purpose of this study is to characterize the current rotor magnet and compare the tested magnetic performance with FEA data. This paper outlines the test data of rotor magnets in terms of magnetic alignment, magnetic field distribution, and Helmholtz testing. And FEA simulation will calculate the magnetic flux density in the interested air gap without the stator and also predict the back EMF with the stator winding.

2. Magnetic Characterization

There are many causes for turbomachinery failure. It was suspected that the magnetic circuit was under performing because design point conditions were not achieved. Hence the following works are performed to confirm the hypothesis.

A. Magnetic Alignment

The rotor assembly consists of 4 stacks of PMs on the rotor shaft and the magnetization direction is across the diameter. The purpose of this test is to determine if there is any misalignment between the stacks of PMs. Figure 1 shows the magnetic field viewing film on the rotor surface before and after remagnetization. Even after the remagnetization, the rotor magnet stacks are not aligned well and show the different division lines compared to the reference line. This misalignment may cause a signal noise in the controller due to the non-uniform field distribution.

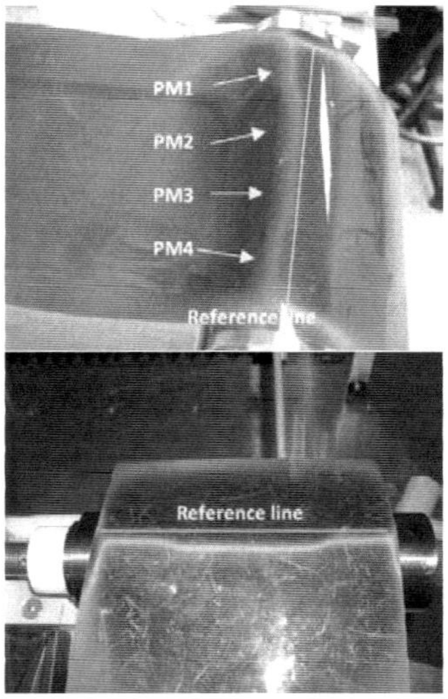

Fig. 1. Magnetic field alignment test: before re-magnetization (top) and after remagnetization (bottom).

B. Magnetic Field 3D Mapping

The purpose of this test is to determine the field variation by measuring the magnetic flux density around the rotor. This field mapping along the rotor axis is needed because the magnetic alignment is not enough to explain the field distribution near the peak field area. Figure 2 describes the test setup and defines the scanning area of 0.300" by 9.000" and the scanning angle of ±5° at 0° and 180° for the 3D magnetic field characterization. The magnetic field data is collected with the help of a data acquisition system incorporated into Labview. For the magnetic field uniformity study, Figure 3-a and 3-b show the magnetic field profile before and after remagnetization, respectively. The magnetic field in one end of the rotor is weaker than the other because some magnets are not fully saturated, as evidenced by the amount of difference shown in Figure 3-c. This magnetic non-uniform distribution may cause the signal noise problem of the controller. The average field is calculated and compared in Table 1.

Table 1. Magnetic Field Test Data Comparison Before and After Remagnetization

	Average Field at 0° (G)	Average Field at 180° (G)	Helmholtz Coil Test (mWb·cm)
Before	1,182	-1,181	3.507
After	1,382	-1,377	4.081
Change [%]	16.9↑	16.5↑	16.3↑

C. Helmholtz Coil Test

Using the Helmholtz coil test rig in Figure 4, the magnetic flux of the rotor magnets is measured. The total magnetic flux reading of the current rotor before

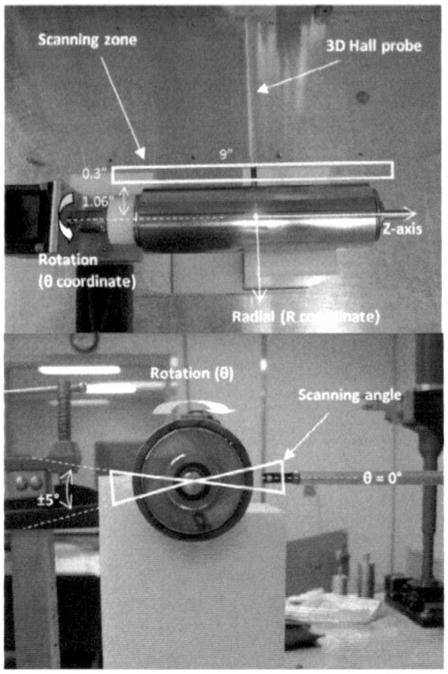

Fig. 2. Test setup and scanning zone definition

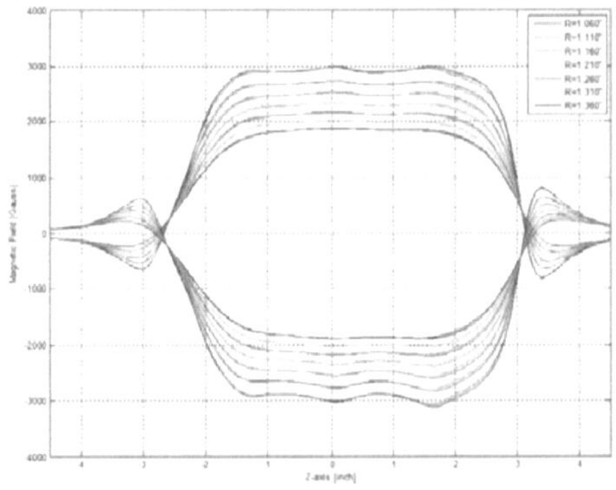

(a) Before remagnetization

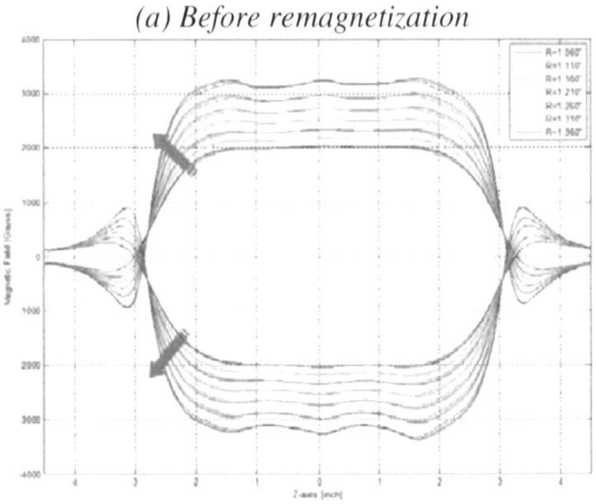

(b) After remagnetization

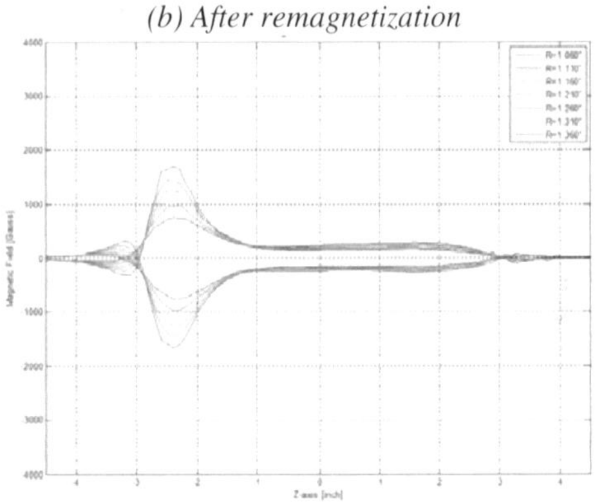

(c) Difference

Fig. 3. Magnetic field test data plot.

remagnetization is 3.507 mWb·cm while after remagnetization the total flux is 4.081 mWb·cm, which indicates a total flux increase of 16.3 % and corresponds to the percentage of the average field

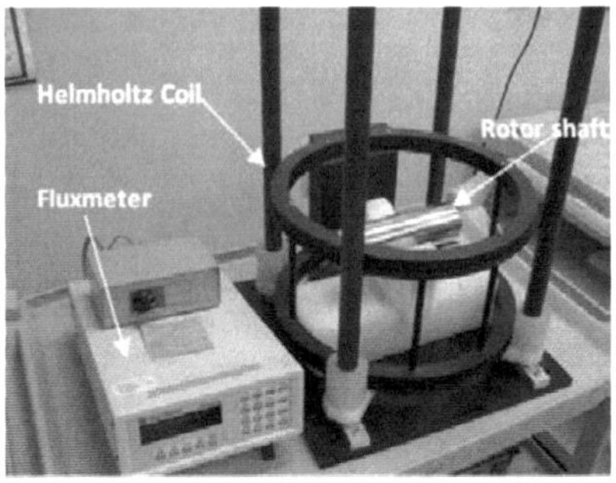

Fig. 4. Helmholtz coil test setup

increase in Table I. This shortage in the magnetic field strength may cause the low output of back EMF, which will be discussed in details in the following sections.

3. Magnetostatic Finite Element Analysis

Figure 5 shows the FEA rotor model without the stator: this is necessary for the magnetostatic analysis to calculate the magnetic flux density in the interested area. After calculating the FEA results, the FEA field plot in Figure 6 is comparable to the test data of magnetic field profile between before and after remagnetization. The peak field of FEA data is 3,410 G while that of the original rotor before remagnetization is 2,997 G, which is a 14% difference. This shortage in the magnetic field strength may cause the low output of back EMF.

4. Back-EMF Calculation

The back EMF is the voltage induced in the stator windings by the variable magnetic field in the air gap and important in motor control algorithms. The unexpected noisy and lower back EMF due to the PM is critical for the performance and stability. The purpose of this study is to calculate the back EMF and compare with test data. Figure 7 shows the FEA motor model with stator windings for the transient analysis. The motor has a 3-phases 'Y' connection. Figure 8 plots the back EMF calculation and its peak to peak voltage is 468 volts compared to the test data of 400 volts at the speed of 75,000 rpm. The difference is 17% which is close to the difference of Helmholtz and average field test data in Table I. This discrepancy may be due to the weak magnets because the rotor magnet is not fully saturated.

5. Conclusion

The root cause analysis of high speed turbomachinery failure is conducted to investigate the magnetic properties before and after remagnetization. Based on the magnetic field test and FEA data, it is found the PM stack is not well aligned in the assembly and not fully saturated.

References

[1] J. F. Liu, M. Jasinski, H. Choi, P. Dent, M. H. Walmer, in: *Proc. 21st Workshop on Rare Earth Permanent Magnets and their Applications,* 2010, 31-35

[2] H. Choi, G. Buckner, and N. Gibson, *American Control Conf.*, 2006, Minneapolis, MN, USA

[3] J. Liu, H. Choi, and M. Walmer, in: *Proc. 19th Int. Workshop on Rare Earth Permanent Magnets and Their Applications*, 2006, 383-387.

[4] H. Choi, J. Liu, R. Tucker, A. Kenny, A. Palazzolo, Z. Zhang, and A. Provenza, in: *Proc. 21st Workshop on Rare Earth Permanent Magnets and Their Applications*, 2010, 285-288.

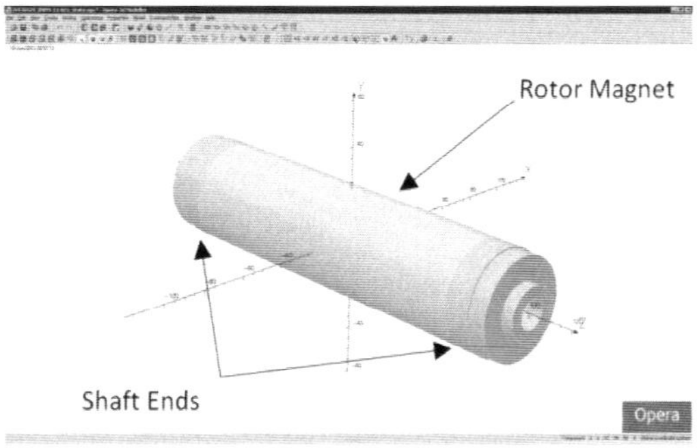

Fig. 5. FEA 3D model without stator

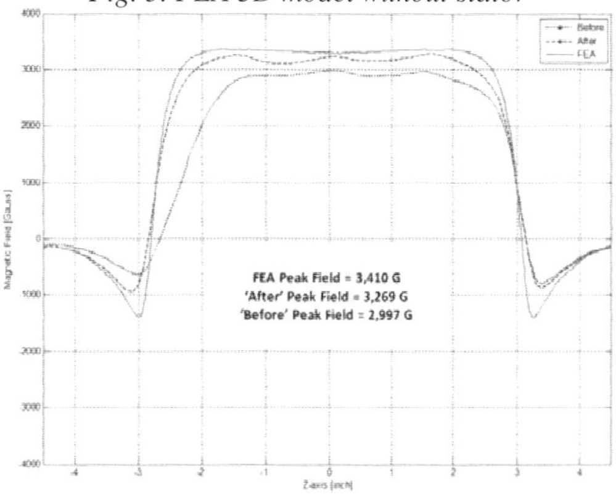

Fig. 6. Magnetic field comparison

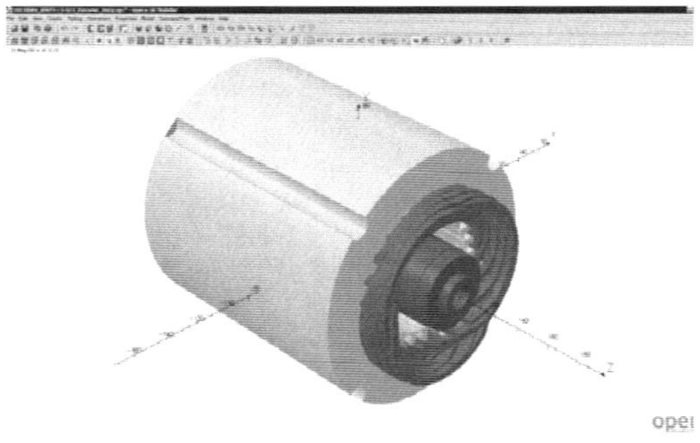

Fig. 7. FEA 3D model with stator winding

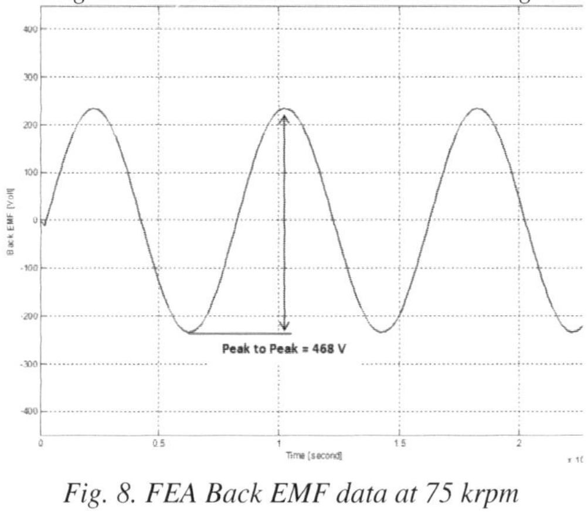

Fig. 8. FEA Back EMF data at 75 krpm

High Energy Magnets to Harness Energy from Sea Waves

EOBIN ALEX GEORGE[1], GAURAV TIWARI[2], S. PRAKASH NARAYAN[2]
[1]Yoyo Aerospace and Automation, Kochi (India)
[2]Mansarovar Institute of Science & Technology (MIST), Bhopal-462042 (India)

Abstract: *This paper describes an efficient and sustainable method of harnessing energy from sea waves using high energy magnets and directly converting it into electricity without multiple mechanical conversion stages. It is estimated that the global potential for electricity from sea waves is about 2,000 TWh/year which account for about 12% of the global electricity demand. Not only is this sources of energy clean and green, unlike solar energy it is available during day and night and throughout the year. This single stage Sea Wave Electricity Generator (SWEG) converts linear motion of waves directly into electricity using a revolutionary ramp generator due to its high magnetic flux density available from high energy permanent magnets in small sizes.*

1. Introduction

Sea waves are a continuous source of clean energy and available 24 hours a day& 365 days in a year. The energy harnessed from the sea waves is available throughout the smooth & even coasts except in certain areas that are inaccessible areas like rocks or are notified (biodiversity, industrial etc.). This potentially opens a huge avenue for harvesting energy and the advancement of high energy magnets allows efficient harvest of energy from sea waves. There are primarily 2 modes that can be used to produce energy from the waves, the horizontal stroke and the vertical height of the wave. We are currently limiting our studies to the electricity generation from horizontal motion of the waves in this phase of the project. Conventional systems convert the energy through multiple mechanical conversion cycles; the proposed Single stage Sea Wave Electricity Generator (SWEG)converts it directly.

1. Analyzing Sea Waves

Sea waves seem to consist of a wave washing at the coast at a certain frequencies. A close analysis of this indicates that the nature of waves is much more complex than just a simple linear amplitude and frequency variation. It also changes with location and the time of the day. The system consists of a sinusoidal variation of amplitudes of the waves washing at the shore which is superposed on another wave*. From data collected from the waves it is found that the waves have the following nature.

$$x = Q * \sin(\theta) \qquad (1)$$

Where $Q = Q_1$ for $\theta = 0$ to 180°
and $Q = Q_2$ for $\theta = 180$ to 360°

Where Q1 and Q2 are the stroke lengths of the upward and downward strokes of the swell waves respectively. We noticed this during field tests where the net velocity of a floating object in the swell is towards the coast. This could change depending on location and time which could affect the efficiency of our system due to the paddle system being pushed to one end for too long. To create a same stroke, we will be using a spring loaded slider along with a tilted slider platform. This is called a normalizer. This ensures that the spring is loaded by the wave during the swell wave opposite to the direction of net velocity allowing us to have almost equal transit times and stroke length. The value of Q is normalized assuming that we will be using a normalizer.

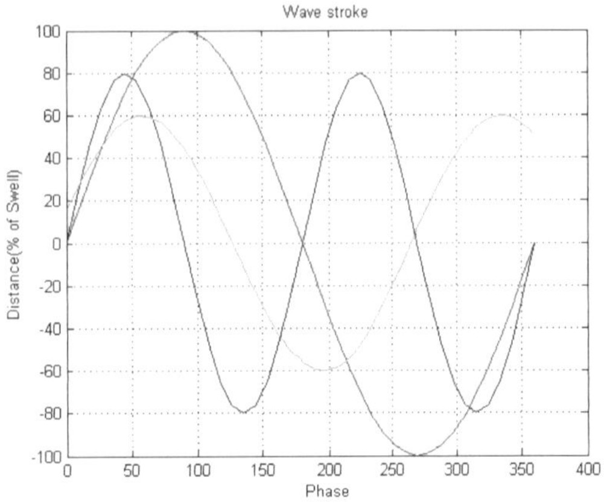

Fig. 1. Swell Stroke

3. Parameters of Interest

Though the parameters vary significantly with location, the general idea of this exercise is to understand the pattern and parameters involved in the design and calculation of the system and its output.

3.1. Effective Stroke

The effective stroke length of the waves washing at the shore line depends on parameters like the gradient of the shore area, the energy with which the wave is approaching, the height of the wave, frequency of the wave, wind nature and nature of shoreline. Typical swell stroke lengths range from 8.5 m to 80 m.

3.2. Speed and Time Period

Though it is difficult to model the actual nature of the waves, due to its complex nature due to the presence of multiple harmonics along with additional non harmonic components, we can approximate the stroke and amplitude variation approximately. This allows us to calculate the maximum speed of the wave and the reversal cycles to design the electric filters. The wave progresses at a particular speed dissipates its energy, decelerates and then returns back from maximum stroke accelerating on its way till it meets the next swell.

The wave velocities vary depending on the time of the day, the nature of coast and the weather and typically vary from 2 m/s to 8.9 m/s with a time period variation from 3.0 to 8.6 s.

3.3. Height

The height of the wave varies at different locations and duration of the day. The maximum height gives an idea of the second mode i.e. the vertical height head of the wave from which energy can be harvested. The height of the wave is also important from a safety point of view because of the stress which can be caused to the system by high waves. From the Douglas Sea Scale, we are limiting the operation of the system in coasts with calm to moderate waves i.e. wave heights from 0 – 4 m.

4. SWEG System and Operation

A single stage Sea Wave Electricity Generator (SWEG) system consists of a fixed coil system embedded in a rigid cylindrical device called a linear slider system. The length of the system and the material is decided depending on the maximum operational Douglas sea scale value of that particular area. The linear slider system is ideally made of poly-vinyl-chloride hollow pipe, due to its good chemical resistivity to sea water. The slider has 2 water proof end caps with wound copper coil stators encased in the. The sliders have a float system to hold it above water with a secure anchor system to hold it in place. A round high energy magnet is attached around the linear slider as shown in Fig. 2 along with a floating paddle system and a PVC slider casing friction reducer to avoid wear and friction on the linear slider. The latter is the movable device which moves to and fro along with the wave over the slider.

5. System Specifications

Conventional generators work on the techniques like using Wave height variation using fly-wheel system, using wave amplitude variation to pump a liquid and build pressure, rotating turbine from wave motion etc. But the SWEG system consists of just a slider and

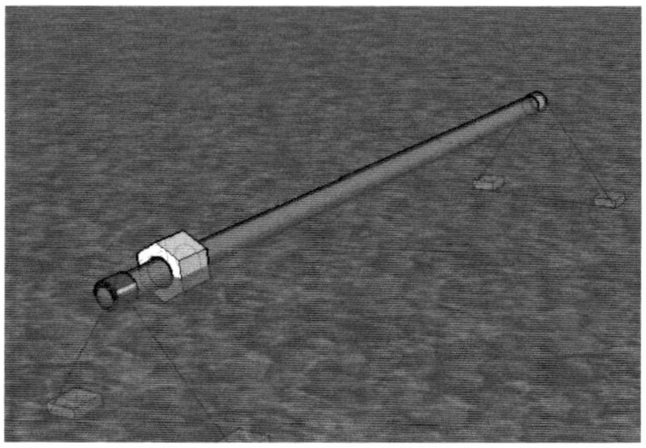

Fig. 2. SWEG System

float mechanism which causes a magnet to move to and fro due to sea waves which in turn causes the magnetic flux lines to be cut by the coil and generate electric charge directly which is accumulated in a capacitor, without any mechanical conversion stages unlike conventional systems.

5.1. Linear Slider Design

The stroke length, turns per coil type, coil type determined by the nature of the shoreline and waves. The coils are arranged with their cross sectional areas perpendicular to the axis of the slider as shown in Fig. 3. The flux lines of the magnets pass perpendicular to the slider and are parallel to the area vector of the coils, in such a manner as to cut the flux lines and change the area exposed to the coils as it moves to and fro due to sea waves. The coils are securely placed in the hollow cylinder using adhesives, which also ensures that the coils maintain their orientation as shown in Fig. 4.

The slider and stroke length is dependent on the maximum swell length and operational swell stroke length occurring at that location. Depending on the amount of cross flow (nature of flow perpendicular to the wave motion) and the sea state, the slider length can be reduced to minimize stress on the slider.

5.2. Paddle Magnet System Design

The movable section of the SWEG is a poly-urethane

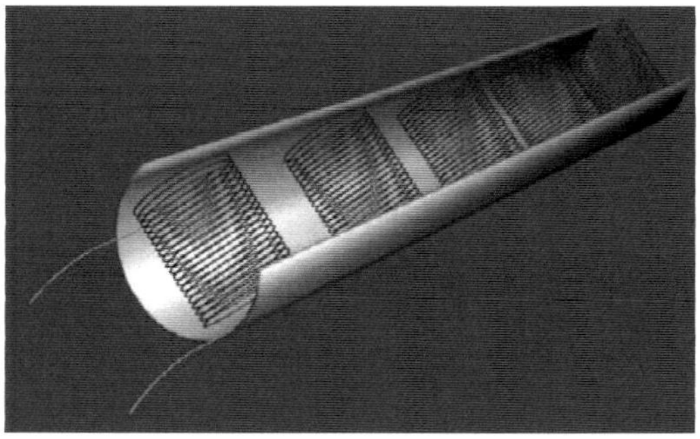

Fig. 2. The SWEG Coils in the Slider.

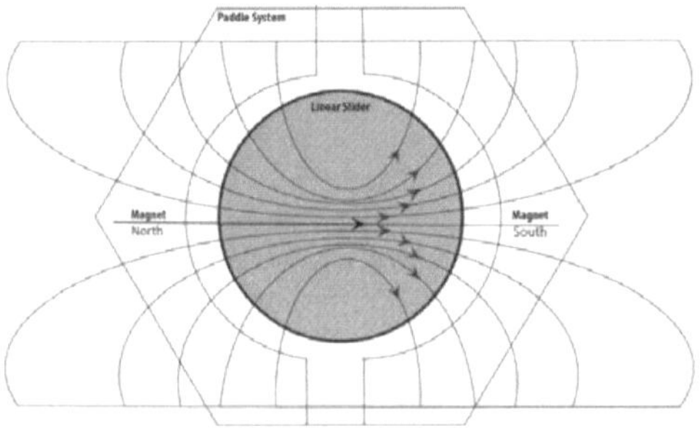

Fig. 3. Magnetic Flux lines.

cast paddle and float system which to move the magnet across the coils to generate EMF in the coils as they pass over them. The size of the float/paddle, the magnet size and strength and the nature of protective coating will depend on the nature of sea waves/swell in the area in which this system is deployed.

The overall performance of the system depends on the magnetic flex density (B) of the magnets used and its inertness to the environment especially sea water. Some of the magnets which can be used of our applications are Neodymium-Iron-Boron and Samarium Cobalt magnets. The polyurethane foam structure along with the coatings like nickel, enamel or rubberized coatings allows the magnets to withstand the corrosion and mechanical damages from the elements.

6. Principle of Electricity Generation

Any variation in the nature of magnetic field in the immediate vicinity of a coil causes an electric voltage (EMF) to be induced in the coil. Parameters which influence the direction and magnitude of the EMF are the magnitudeof magnetic field, orientation and the area of the coil exposed to the flux lines.

$$V = N * \frac{d(B*A)}{dt} \qquad (2)$$

Where: B - Magnetic Flux Density
A - Area; N - Number of turns in a coil

Voltage is generated in the coils as they cut magnetic flux lines produced by the magnets as they move to and fro through the sliders along with the waves. The value of B and N are constant which simplifies the above equation to

$$V = N * B * \frac{d(A)}{dt} \qquad (3)$$

The coils are arranged in series and they are connected in such a way that when the magnets is pulling away from the previous coil and entering into the region of the next coil, the direction of current flow is the same. i.e. when the magnet retreats form the first coil $\frac{d(A)}{dt}$ is negative since the area in the influence of the magnet is reducing. So to ensure that the EMF generated in the next phase does not cancel that of the previous coil, we reverse the connection as shown.

$$X_1.Y_1 - Y_2.X_2 - X_3.Y_3 - Y_4.X_4$$

where the X and Y are the coil endings.

The EMF generated by the coils can be calculated by using Equation 1 but the voltage patterns generated by odd and even coils will have a phase difference of 180°. The shape of the coils are aproximated to be a square of sides r for ease of computation.

Taking a small section of the coil, of width *dx*, we can calculate the change in area to be

$$d(A) = r * d(x); \qquad \frac{dA}{dt} = r * \frac{dx}{dt} \qquad (4)$$

By replacing d(x) with the differentiated equation of Equation 1 and using it in Equation 3 we get

$$V = N * B * r * Q * \cos(\theta) \qquad (5)$$
$$V = N * B * r * Q * \cos(\theta)\text{: Odd Coils} \qquad (6)$$
$$V = N * B * r * Q * \cos(\theta + 180)\text{: Even Coils} \qquad (7)$$
$$V = N * B * r * Q * (\cos(\theta) + \cos(\theta + 180))$$
$$\text{Total Voltage} \qquad (8)$$

Assuming an efficiency factor of just 50%, we have plotted the electricity generation pattern for a coastal area with sea state of less than 4 (Douglas Sea State). The swell wavelength is 35 meters, time period of 4.6 seconds, a 50-turn coil setup, coil dimension of 5cm X 5cm a10 coil slider segment and efficiency factor of 50% of electricity generation.

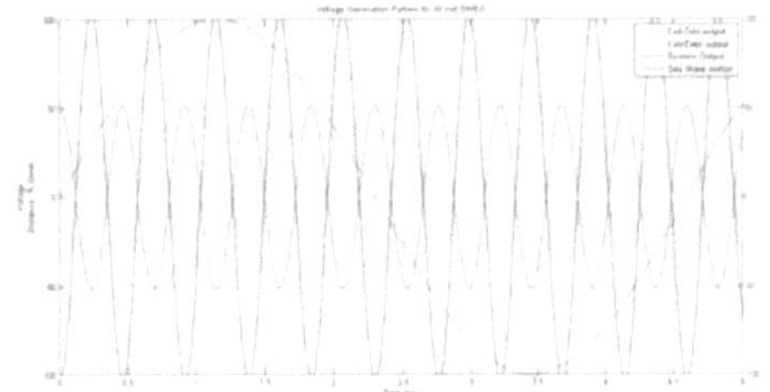

Fig. 4.

7. Final Design and Configuration

The SWEG system is designed for deployment as an array over large areas. The sliders will be secured to the shore at one end using rigid structures and will have a heavy weight and a float system on the seaward facing side. As soon as the system is taken into the water and the paddle starts moving to and fro, the SWEG will start producing electricity. The output which is a sinusoidal varying signal will be processed and stored in storage elements and discharged for transmission or used at the location for running other systems.

We are initially designing and testing a single slider SWEG system as a proof-of-concept before going into the array concept. From the output characteristics of an M segment SWEG system will just be a multiplication of the current single slider SWEG system output by a factor of M. From calculation and preliminary testing of the system, it is understood that a single SWEG system is capable of producing a 100 volts of electricity from about 1 meter of shoreline. Even if the system generates 400 milliamps of current, i.e 40 watts per meter of shore line, this translates to over 300 Mega-watts of uninterrupted power from the just the coastal belt of India.

8. Conclusion

The system was a proof-of-concept system and has been tested in a few locations in South India. Our system has shown that the energy in sea waves can be converted to electricity without multiple mechanical conversion steps in between. The SWEG system canbe designed to be deployed either as a single system or as an array for large scale deployment. The unique nature of the system like ease of operation, maintenance, ease of setup and very few components along with the renewable, non-polluting and continuous nature of sea waves makes this an ideal source of electricity.

Acknowledgment
The research and development team behind the SWEG system would like to thank the Mansarovar Institute of Science and Technology for its support in developing this system and to Yoyo Industries for providing resources for development of the system and requirement studies. I would also like to thank Dr. R N Yadava (CSIR) and Dr. S P Narayan (MIST) for their moral support.

References

[1] *www.maritime.nsw.gov.au/rec_boating/windwave.html*
[2] *http://en.wikipedia.org/wiki/Swell_(ocean)*
[3] *http://en.wikipedia.org/wiki/File:Deep_water_wave.gif*
[4] *http://www.omega.com/pdf/tubing/technical_section/chemical_chart_5.asp*
[5] *http://www.polyurethanes.basf.de/pu/Coastal-Defense/Wetterbestaendigkeit*
[6] *http://hyperphysics.phy-astr.gsu.edu/hbase/electric/farlaw.html*
[7] *http://www.rare-earth-magnets.com/Permanent-Magnet-Seletion-and-Design-Handbook.pdf*

Anisotropic Rare-Earth-Lean Pr-Fe-B Nanocomposite Magnets

RAJASEKHAR MADUGUNDO, GEORGE C. HADJIPANAYIS
Department of Physics and Astronomy, University of Delaware, Newark, DE 19716, USA

Abstract: *Magnetic and microstructure properties of hot-deformed Pr-Fe-B magnets with 13.5 and 12.5 at.% Pr were studied. The magnetic properties are correlated to the Pr-content and its effect on microstructure and texture. Texture shows a strong dependence on Pr-content with a texture parameter of 0.69 and 0.36 for the 13.5 at.% and 12.5 at.% sample, respectively. The magnet with 13.5 at.% Pr shows a microstructure consisting of oriented platelet-shaped grains of $Pr_2Fe_{14}B$ phase. Microstructure of the magnet with 12.5 at.% Pr show weak crystallographic orientation. A coercivity of 12.7 kOe and 40 MGOe of energy-product was obtained in the sample with 13.5 at.% Pr. Coercivity varied from 12.7 kOe to 8.5 kOe with the decrease in Pr from 13.5 to 12.5 at.%.*

Keywords: *R-Fe-B magnets; $Pr_2Fe_{14}B$; hot-deformed magnets; texture*

Address: Rajasekhar Madugundo, Department of Physics and Astronomy, University of Delaware, 217 Sharp Lab, Newark, DE 19716, USA, Tel: (302) 831-1498, E-mail: mraja@udel.edu

1. Introduction

The recent rare earth crisis led to worldwide efforts to develop rare-earth lean/free permanent magnets. Hot-deformation is known to be an effective technique to produce anisotropic R-Fe-B (R = rare-earth) from rapidly solidified isotropic nanograin ribbon powders (thickness of the flakes ~25-50 μm). Texture formation in the anisotropic magnet is critical for high energy product $(BH)_{max}$. It has been reported by many investigators that the R-rich phase is important to texture formation [1,2]. In the case of rare earth-lean magnets weak or no texture has been reported [3]. Grain boundary diffusion of low melting metals/eutectic alloys has proven to be a successful technique to induce texture in rare-earth-lean hot-deformed magnets [4]. However, so far most of the research was mainly focused on Nd-Fe-B system, and not much attention has been paid to the Pr-Fe-B system [5,6]. The coercivity (${}_iH_c$) in hot-deformed magnets is very sensitive to the R-content [2]. It is necessary to optimize ${}_iH_c$ for low Pr-content alloys before trying the grain boundary diffusion process by elements such as Zn, or eutectic Pr-Cu alloys. In the present work, we studied the hot-deformed magnets with decreasing Pr-content from 13.5 to 12.5 at.%.

2. Experimental

Alloys with nominal compositions $Pr_{13.5}Fe_{78.5}Ga_1B_6$ and $Pr_{13.5}Fe_{78.5}Ga_1B_6$ were prepared by argon arc-melting from pure Pr, Fe, B, and Ga elements. Ribbons of these alloys were produced by melt-spinning at a wheel speed of 20 m/s. The ribbons were then crushed to small flakes of < 300 μm size. The powders were hot-compacted at 650 °C for 30 min under a uniaxial pressure of 275 MPa. The compacts were then hot-deformed at 750 °C to a height reduction of ~75%. The magnetic properties of the samples were measured by a Quantum Design VersaLab vibrating sample magnetometer at room temperature. Prior to the measurements the magnets were saturated in an applied field of 6 T using a pulsed magnetizer. The hot-deformed magnets were characterized both parallel and perpendicularly to the press direction. The measurements were corrected for the self-demagnetization effect. The texture in the hot-deformed magnets was characterized by the remnant magnetization measurements (M_r) using the parameter $(M_r^{II} - M_r^{\perp})/M_r^{II}$ which varies from 0 for isotropic materials to 1 for a perfectly aligned ones. Micro-structure studies were performed using a JEOL (JSM-6335F) scanning electron microscope (SEM).

3. Results and Discussion

Demagnetization curves for the hot-compacted and hot-deformed magnets with 13.5 at 12.5 at.% Pr-content are shown in Fig. 1(a) and 1(b), respectively. The values of ${}_iH_c$ for the hot-compacted magnets with 13.5 and 12.5 at.% Pr are found to be 18.6 and 10.9 kOe, respectively. In hot-deformation samples ${}_iH_c$ reaches the values of 12.7 and 8.5 kOe respectively, at a loss of 31% in the hot-compacted magnets for both samples. Magnetic properties of the hot-compacted and hot-deformed samples are listed in Table 1. Demagnetization curves for the hot-deformed magnets are shown in Fig. 2(a) and 2(b). The value of ${}_iH_c$ decreases from 12.7 to 8.5 kOe on decrease in Pr from 13.5 to 12.5 at.%. The hot-deformed magnet with 13.5 at.% Pr exhibit a better squareness in the demagnetization loop with M_r and $(BH)_{max}$ values 13.1 kG and 40 MGOe, respectively. With decrease in Pr-content the value of M_r decreased to 10 kG and $(BH)_{max}$ to 20 MGOe.

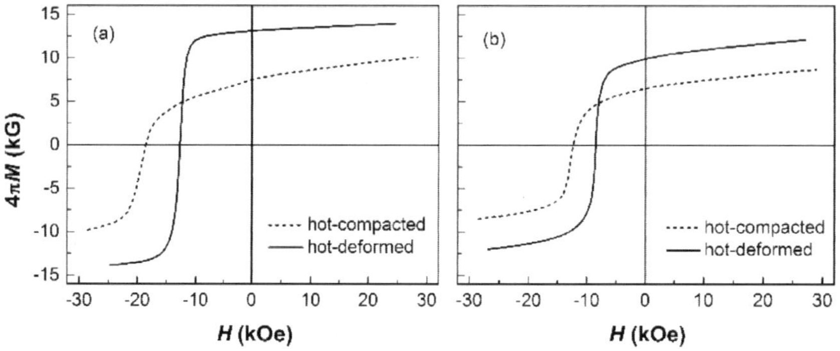

Fig. 1. Demagnetization curves for hot-compacted and hot-deformed magnets with (a) 13.5 at.% Pr and (b) 12.5 at.% Pr. Measurements were performed parallel to the compaction/deformation directions.

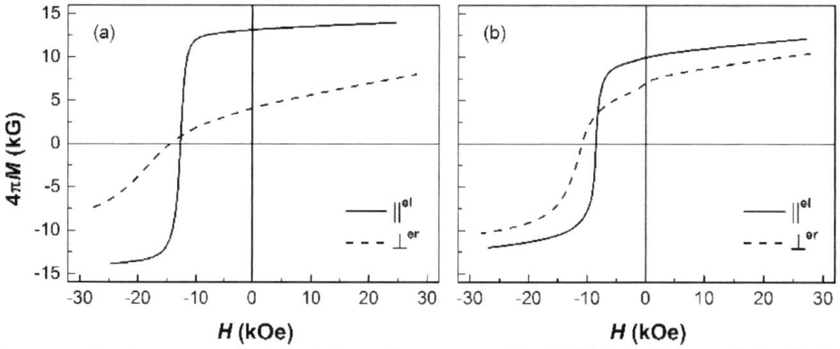

Fig. 2. Demagnetization curves for hot-deformed magnets with (a) 13.5 at.% Pr and (b) 12.5 at.% Pr. Measurements were performed parallel (∥^{el}) and perpendicular (⊥^{er}) to the deformation direction.

The effect of Pr-content on texture in the hot-deformed magnets was estimated by calculating the texture parameter from M_r values obtained by measurements in parallel ($M_r^{\parallel}$) and perpendicular ($M_r^{\perp}$) to the deformation direction. The texture parameter is found to vary from 0.69 to 0.36 in the samples with Pr-content of 13.5 to 12.5 at.%, respectively. The high M_r and $(BH)_{max}$ values in the magnet with 13.5 at.% Pr compared to 12.5 at.% magnet is attributed to the high degree of texture.

Microstructure analyses of the fractured surfaces for die-upset magnets with different Pr-content are consistent with the texture measurements. Figs. 3(a) and 3(b) show the SEM micrographs of the samples with 13.5 and 12.5 at.% Pr, respectively (the c-axis is in-plane). As seen from Fig. 3(a) the microstructure of 13.5 at.% Pr magnet shows the typical elongated platelet like grain structure observed in hot-deformed magnets. In this sample the presence of the R-rich phase facilitates a mass transport necessary for the growth of favorably oriented grains [1-3]. The microstructure of In the 12.5 at.% Pr magnet shown Fig. 3(b) only a small percentage of the area is oriented justifying the low texture parameter 0.36. The decreased orientation of the grains is attributed to insufficient Pr-rich phase. A similar decrease in the degree of texture has been reported in Nd-Fe-B hot deformed magnets with low Nd-content by Tang et al. [3] Coercivity and texture improvement can be achieved in these lean-rare-earth magnets by grain boundary diffusion process by low melting point alloys [3,4].

4. Conclusion

In summary, we made an attempt to understand the effect of Pr-content on microstructure and texture to

Table 1. Magnetic properties of hot-compacted (HC) and hot-deformed magnets (∥^{el})

Pr content (at.%)	M_r (kG)		$_iH_c$ (kOe)		$(BH)_{max}$ (MGOe)	
	HC	HD	HC	HD	HC	HD
13.5	7.5	13.1	18.6	12.7	11	40
12.5	6.5	10.0	12.3	8.5	9	20

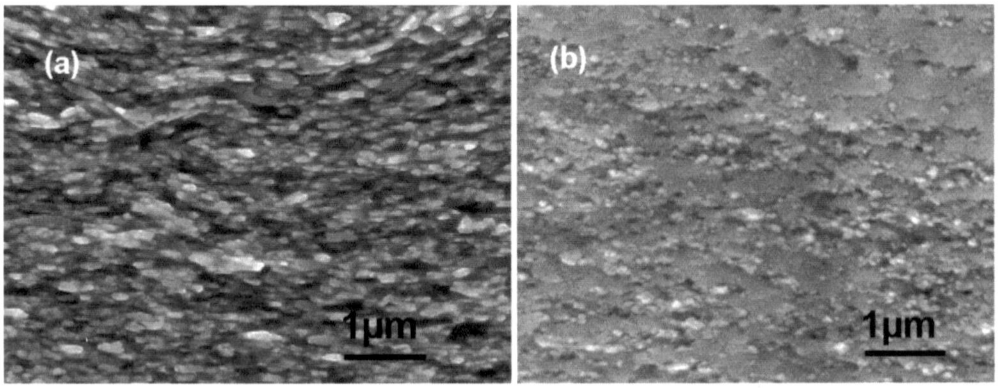

Fig. 3. SEM micrographs of hot-deformed magnets with (a) 13.5 at.% Pr and (b) 12.5 at.% Pr.

optimize the coercivity in lean Pr-content magnets. Coercivity and texture show a strong dependence on Pr-content. Coercivity varied from 12.7 kOe to 8.5 kOe with decrease in Pr from 13.5 to 12.5 at.%.

Acknowledgement
The work was supported by Siemens.

References

[1] C.D. Fuerst, E.G. Brewer, R.K. Mishra, Y. Zhu, D.O. Welch, *J. Appl. Phys.* **75**, 1994, 4208.

[2] J. Liu, H. Sepehri-Amin, T. Ohkubo, K. Hioki, A. Hattori, T. Schrefl, K. Hono, *Acta Mater.* **61**, 2013, 5387.

[3] X. Tang, R. Chen, W. Yin, J. Wang, X. Tang, D. Lee, A. Yan, *Appl. Phys. Lett.* **102**, 2013, 072409.

[4] H. Sepehri-Amin, T. Ohkubo, S. Nagashima, M. Yano, T. Shoji, A. Kato, T. Schrefl, K. Hono, *Acta Mater.* **61**, 2013, 6622.

[5] A.M. Gabay, Y. Zhang, G.C. Hadjipanayis, *J. Magn. Magn. Mater.* **302**, 2006, 244.

[6] A.M. Gabay, Y. Zhang, G.C. Hadjipanayis, *Appl. Phys. Lett.* **85**, 2004, 446.

Magnetic Properties of Pr-Ce-Fe-Co-B System Melt-Spun Ribbons

G. OBARA, K. KUSAKA
School of Science and Technology, Meiji University, 1-1-1 Higashimita, Tama-ku, Kawasaki 214-8571, Japan

Abstract: *Effects of Ce substitution for Pr on the magnetic properties of the Pr-Ce-Fe-Co-B system melt-spun ribbons were investigated. The results indicated that magnetization and coercivities decreased with an increase of Ce substitution, and the absolute value of the temperature coefficient of coercivities decreased with an increase of Ce substitution. In addition, the Curie temperature was decreased from 420 to 280 °C with an increase of Ce substitution.*

Keywords: *magnetic properties; melt-spun ribbons; bonded magnets; coercivity, magnetization*

1. Introduction

Melt-spun ribbons of (Nd,Pr)-Fe-B system alloys have been used on materials for high performance bonded magnets [1-3]. Recently, rare-earth metals as Nd, Pr and Dy etc. have increased in value owing to the effect of a rise in demand and resource strategies. The costs of rare-earth metals are rather stable at this time. There is however, a potential for increases in the costs of these metals. Generally, rare-earth metals are produced at the same time as many other rare-earth elements and compositions such as these differ according to area. For example not only Nd, Pr and Dy metals but also Y, La and Ce metals. The Y, La and Ce however, metals are being scrapped in spite of their large quantities. This is because the demand for Y, La and Ce metals is very low. It is thought that this is one of the causes for the rising costs of producing Nd, Pr and Dy metals. So, an increase in demand for these less-needed metals such Y, La and Ce is important [4].

In this research, we have investigated the effect of Ce substitution for Pr on the magnetic properties of Pr-Fe-Co-B system melt-spun ribbons.

2. Experimental Procedure

Alloy ingots with compositions of $(Pr_{1-x}Ce_x)_{12}Fe_{72}$-$Co_{10}B_6$ (x = 0 - 1) were prepared by arc melting. Melt-spun ribbons were prepared by single roller liquid rapid-quenching method. The wheel velocity was 20 m/s. Melt-spun ribbons were annealed with infrared gold image furnace at a temperature range of 600-800 °C for 10 min in an argon atmosphere. After 4.8 MA/m pulse magnetizing, the magnetic properties and temperature dependence of H_{cJ} and B_r for ribbons were measured by a vibrating sample magnetometer (VSM). The crystallization temperature of melt-spun ribbons was measured by a differential scanning calorimeter (DSC). The crystal structure was examined by X-ray diffraction method on the powder samples with Cu K_α radiation.

3. Results and Discussion

Fig. 1 shows the X-ray diffraction patterns of $(Pr_{1-x}Ce_x)_{12}Fe_{72}Co_{10}B_6$ (x = 0, 1) melt-spun ribbons with heat-treatment at 650 °C. The numbers in Fig. 1 are Miller indices of $RE_2Fe_{14}B$ crystal phase. It was found that the $RE_2Fe_{14}B$ single phase was approximately obtained as far as the XRD measurement. It was possible to define indexes in all the diffraction peaks. The same results were obtained in other samples (x = 0.2, 0.4, 0.6 and 0.8). The effect of Ce substitution on the lattice parameters of $(Pr_{1-x}Ce_x)_{12}Fe_{72}Co_{10}B_6$ melt-spun ribbons with heat-treatment at 650 °C are shown in Fig. 2. The value of lattice parameters a and c decreased with an increase in the x value. From this result, it was thought that the lattice constant decreased with an increase in the x value of $(Pr_{1-x}Ce_x)_{12}Fe_{72}Co_{10}B_6$ because atomic radius of Ce is smaller than Pr.

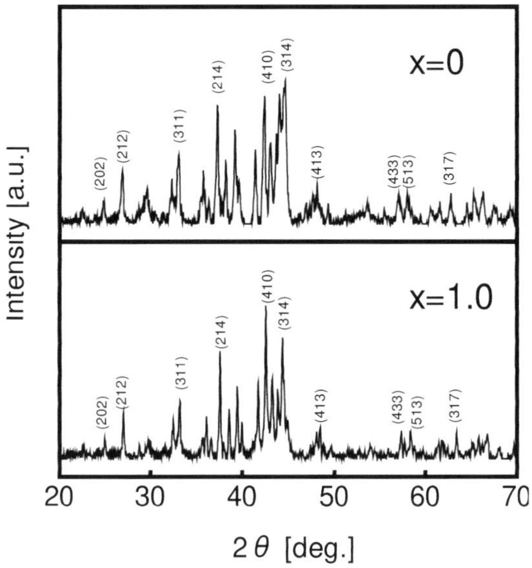

Fig. 1. X-ray diffraction patterns of $(Pr_{1-x}Ce_x)_{12}Fe_{72}Co_{10}B_6$ melt-spun ribbons with heat-treatment at 650 °C.

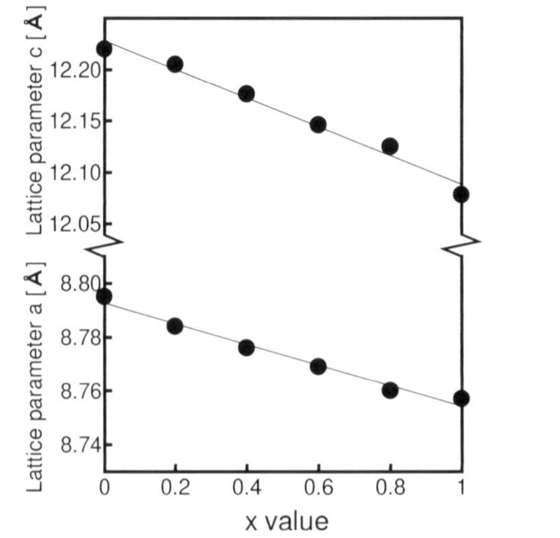

Fig.2. Effect of Ce substitution on the lattice parameters of $(Pr_{1-x}Ce_x)_{12}Fe_{72}Co_{10}B_6$ melt-spun ribbons with heat-treatment at 650 °C.

Additionally, since this result is subject to Vegard's law, it was considered that substitution of Ce for Nd went ahead smoothly.

Fig. 3 shows the effect of heat-treatment temperature on the magnetic properties of $(Pr_{0.6}Ce_{0.4})_{12}Fe_{72}Co_{10}B_6$ melt-spun ribbons. It was found that the values of B_r and H_{cJ} increased with an increase in heat-treatment temperature from 600 to 650 °C, and then decreased. Results of other samples with the different value of Ce substitution show the same tendency. It was decided from the results of this experiment that the optimum heat-treatment temperature was 650 °C.

Fig. 4 shows the effect of Ce substitution on the magnetic properties of $(Pr_{1-x}Ce_x)_{12}Fe_{72}Co_{10}B_6$

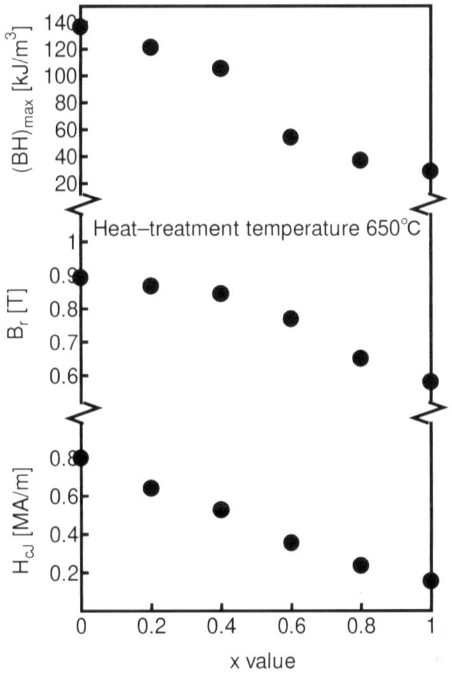

Fig.4. Effect of Ce substitution on the magnetic properties of $(Pr_{1-x}Ce_x)_{12}Fe_{72}Co_{10}B_6$ melt-spun ribbons with heat-treatment at 650 °C.

melt-spun ribbons with heat-treatment at 650°C. The coercivity H_{cJ} decreases linearly with an increase in the x value of $(Pr_{1-x}Ce_x)_{12}Fe_{72}Co_{10}B_6$ melt-spun ribbons. The remanence B_r and maximum energy product $(BH)_{max}$ gradually decrease with an increase the x value from 0 to 0.4, and then rapidly decrease. From this result, it was reasoned that the Ce substitution for Nd in this formula should be limited to under 0.4 of x value.

Fig. 5 shows the effect of x value on the temperature

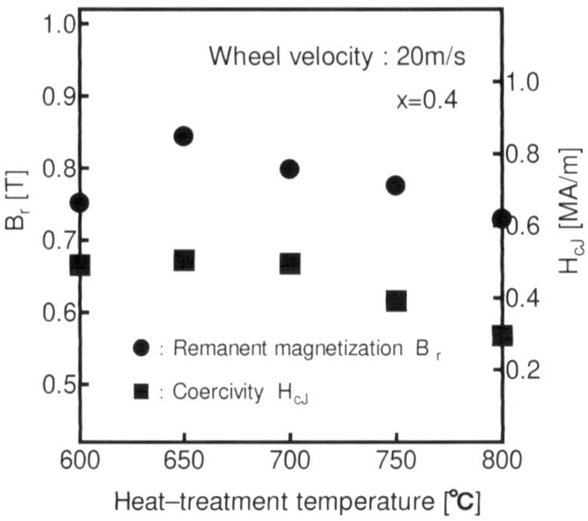

Fig.3. Effect of heat-treatment temperature on the magnetic properties of $(Pr_{1-x}Ce_x)_{12}Fe_{72}Co_{10}B_6$ melt-spun ribbons.

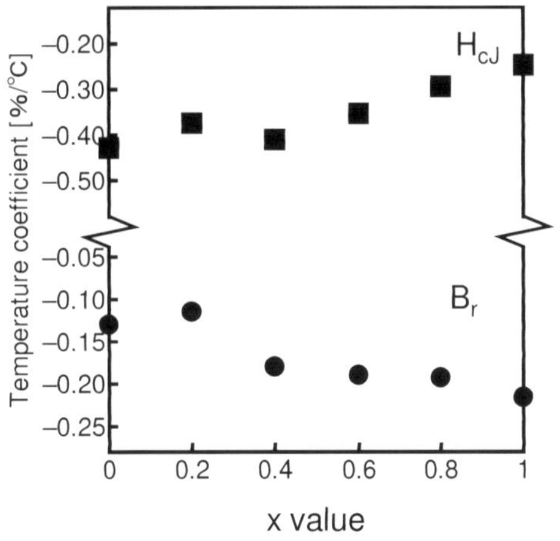

Fig.5. Effect of Ce substitution on the temperature coefficient of $(Pr_{1-x}Ce_x)_{12}Fe_{72}Co_{10}B_6$ melt-spun ribbons with heat-treatment at 650 °C.

coefficients of coercivity and remanent magnetization of $(Pr_{1-x}Ce_x)_{12}Fe_{72}Co_{10}B_6$ melt-spun ribbons with heat-treatment at 650 °C. The temperature coefficient was calculated from a straight-line approximation between 30 to 120 °C. The absolute value of the temperature coefficient of B_r gradually increased with an increase of Ce substitution. On the other hand, the absolute value of the temperature coefficient of coercivities decreased with an increase of Ce substitution.

The effects of Ce substitution on the Curie temperature of $(Pr_{1-x}Ce_x)_{12}Fe_{72}Co_{10}B_6$ melt-spun ribbons with heat-treatment at 650 °C are shown in Fig. 6. It was found that the Curie temperature was decreased linearly from 420 to 280 °C with an increase of Ce substitution.

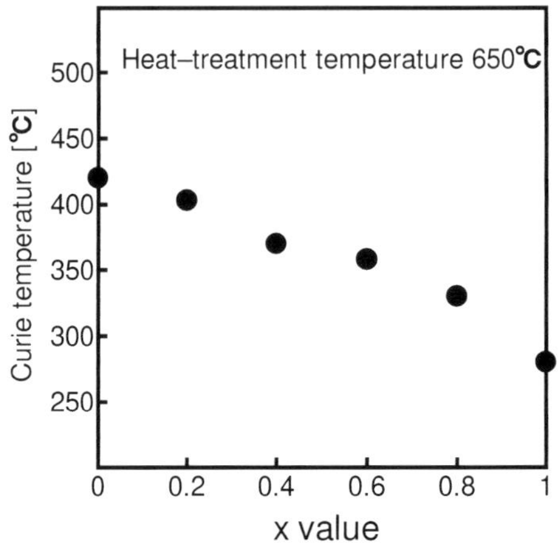

Fig.6. Effect of Ce substitution on the Curie temperature of $(Pr_{1-x}Ce_x)_{12}Fe_{72}Co_{10}B_6$ melt-spun ribbons with heat-treatment at 650 °C.

4. Conclusion

It was found that magnetization and coercivities decreased with an increase of Ce substitution. The remanence B_r and maximum energy product $(BH)_{max}$ gradually decrease with an increase the x value from 0 to 0.4, and then rapidly decreased. It is understood that the Ce substitution for Nd in this formula should be limited to under 0.4 of x value. The absolute value of the temperature coefficient of coercivities decreased with an increase of Ce substitution. On the other hand, the absolute value of the temperature coefficient of magnetization increased with an increase of Ce substitution.

References

[1] M. Daniil, H. Okumura, G.C. Hadjipanayis, D.J. Sellmyer, *J. Magn. Magn. Mater.* **267**, 2003, 316.
[2] K. Furusawa, H. Yamamoto, *IEEE Trans. Magn.* **41**, 2005, 10.
[3] J. F. Herbst, M. S. Meyer and F. E. Pinkerton, *J. Appl. Phys.* **111**, 2012, 07A718.
[4] D. Li and Y. Bogatin, *J. Appl. Phys.* **69**, 1991, 8.

Effect of Dy/Y/Gd/Ho Substitution on Magnetic Properties and Micrstructure of Nanocrystalline Monophase Nd-Fe-B Magnets

ZHI-AN CHEN, XIAO-LEI RAO, E NIU, BO-PING HU
Beijing Zhong Ke San Huan Research, No. 10 Chuangxin Road, Changping District, Beijing 102200, China.

Abstract: *Nanocrystalline* $Nd_{11.8-x}(Dy/Y/Gd/Ho)_xFe_{81.2}Nb_{0.5}Cu_{0.5}B_{6.0}$ *(x=0, 0.5, 1.0, 1.5, 2.0, 2.5) ribbons were prepared by melt-spinning and subsequent annealing. The effects of Dy, Y, Gd and Ho contents on the microstructure and magnetic properties especially the remanence, the Curie temperature and the squareness of the demagnetization curve were investigated, respectively. It was found that small amount of Dy/Y/Gd enhances glass forming ability of the over-quenched ribbons and stabilizes the amorphous phase during post annealing treatment. The microstructure is refined and uniformed with appropriate amount of Dy/Y/Gd/Ho substitution, which results in the enhancement of remanence and the improvement of the squareness of the demagnetization curve. What is more, different kind of element shows different optimum content and different effect on remanence. Excessive substitution, however, is harmful to the remanence and the microstructure.*

Keywords: *Dy/Y/Gd/Ho; nanocrystalline; Nd-Fe-B; squareness; remanence*

Address: Zhi-An Chen, No.10 Chuangxin Road, Changping District, Beijing 102200, China. Tel: 86-18901232481, E-mail: alvincza@gmail.com

1. Introduction

Melt-spun ribbons of Nd-Fe-B alloys comprised of exchange coupled nanocrystalline grains have received considerable attention due to the remanence enhancement phenomenon. Even through the grains of the ribbon are randomly oriented, the remanence can be much higher than the value expected for non-interactive grains. The first target for high performance Nd-Fe-B ribbon is the high remanence. In addition, in order to realize the high maximum energy product $(BH)_m$, the squareness of the demagnetization curve is as important as the remanence. Hence, how to optimize the squareness becomes the second key problem to be solved.

The shape of the hysteresis loop of nanophase magnets is highly sensitive to their microstructure. Several researches have demonstrated the effect of Dy addition on the microstructure of Nd-Fe-C/B nanograin alloy [1, 2]. It was found that small amount of Dy addition can effectively refine the microstructure of the alloy. This work focused on the influence of the Dy/Y/Gd/Ho substitution on the magnetic properties especially on remanence, the Curie temperature and the squareness of the demagnetization curve.

2. Experimental

Alloy ingots with nominal atomic compositions of $Nd_{11.8-x}(Dy/Y/Gd/Ho)_xFe_{81.2}Nb_{0.5}Cu_{0.5}B_{6.0}$ (x=0, 0.5, 1.0, 1.5, 2.0, 2.5) were prepared using commercial grade raw materials by arc-melting method in an Ar atmosphere for four times to obtain homogeneous composition. The over-quenched ribbons were produced by squeezing the melted ingot through an orifice of 0.6 - 0.8 mm in diameter onto the surface of a rotating copper wheel at the surface velocity of 25 m/s in high purity Ar atmosphere. The distance between the orifice and the wheel was maintained at approximate 0.5 mm. The ribbons were annealed at 550 °C-800 °C for 10 minutes to optimize crystallization and improve the permanent magnetic properties. The phase structure of the ribbons was preliminarily determined by X-ray diffraction with Cu K_α radiation and thermomagnetic analysis (TMA) in an applied field of 500 Oe. The crystallization behavior was examined by differential scanning calorimetry (DSC). The magnetic properties of the ribbons were measured with a vibrating sample magnetometer up to 2.5 T. The microstructures were observed by high resolution transmission electron microscopy with thin foils prepared by ion-beam thinning.

3. Results and Discussion

3.1. Phases analysis and crystallization behavior of the as-spun ribbons

XRD patterns for as-spun $Nd_{11.3}$ (Nd/Y/Gd/Ho)$_{0.5}Fe_{81.2}Nb_{0.5}Cu_{0.5}B_{6.0}$ (V_s=25m/s) are shown in Fig.1. It can be seen that the XRD patterns of Y-substituted (Fig.1a) and Gd-substituted (Fig. 1b) samples present primarily amorphous phase. Combined with our previous research [2], it indicates an increase in glass-forming ability (GFA) with slight amount of Dy or Y or Gd substitution. In contrast, some sharp peaks of 2:14:1 main phase appear in the diffractogram of Ho-substituted sample (Fig.1c) and sample without substitution (Fig. 1d), suggesting that the amount of 2:14:1 phase relatively increases compared to the Y or Gd-substituted samples due to the weaker GFA.

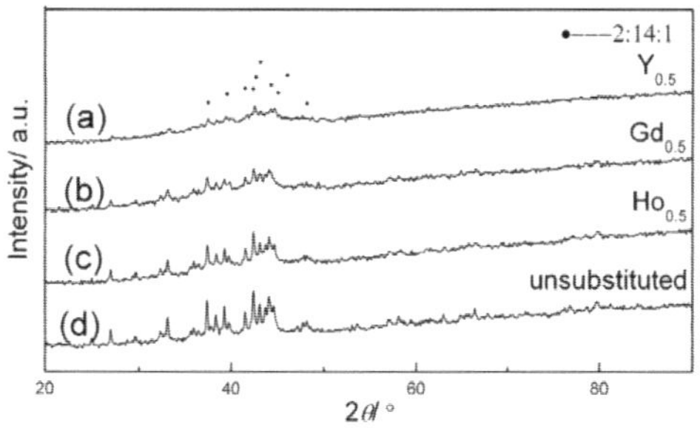

Fig.1. XRD patterns of the as-spun $Nd_{11.3}(Nd/Y/Gd/Ho)_{0.5}Fe_{81.2}Nb_{0.5}Cu_{0.5}B_{6.0}$ *(25 m/s)*

Shown in Fig. 2 are DSC curves of as-spun ribbons with 1.5 at% Ho, Gd, Y substitution and unsubstituted sample. Comparing with the curve of the unsubstituted sample (Fig. 2d), the curves of 1.5 at% Y, Ho and Gd substituted samples are observed to retard the crystallization by 10 °C, 20 °C and 26 °C, respectively, implying Y, Ho, Dy [2] and Gd addition can stabilize the amorphous phase during post annealing treatment.

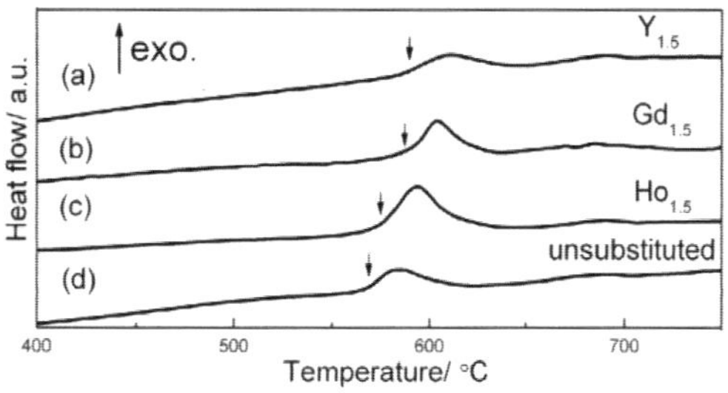

Fig.2. DSC curves of as-spun ribbons with different substitution

3.2. Influence of substitution on magnetic properties and microstructure

According to the peak temperatures shown in Fig. 2, a series of annealing treatment were applied individually to all the selected as-spun ribbons. Fig.3 summarizes the effect of substitution content and annealing temperature on the remanent magnetic polarization J_r of the ribbons.

The maximum remanent polarization of Dy and Gd substituted ribbons appear at 0.5 at% substitution at different annealing temperatures, which can be ascribed to the optimized microstructure showed in Fig. 6. What is more, with excessive substitution, the remanence decreases obviously led by the decrease in saturation magnetization of 2:14:1 main phase, although the average grain-size continuously decrease to enhance the exchange interaction between grains. As regard to Ho and Y substituted ribbons, the variation of remanence is complicated and hard to be summarized as a trend, which is still under research.

Thermomagnetic analysis results shown in Fig. 4 indicate that different kinds of substitution have different effects on Curie temperature T_c. For example, the optimally annealed Ho-substituted specimen presents an increase in T_c. On the contrary, the Y-substituted one shows an obvious decrease in T_c compared with the value of the unsubstituted specimen.

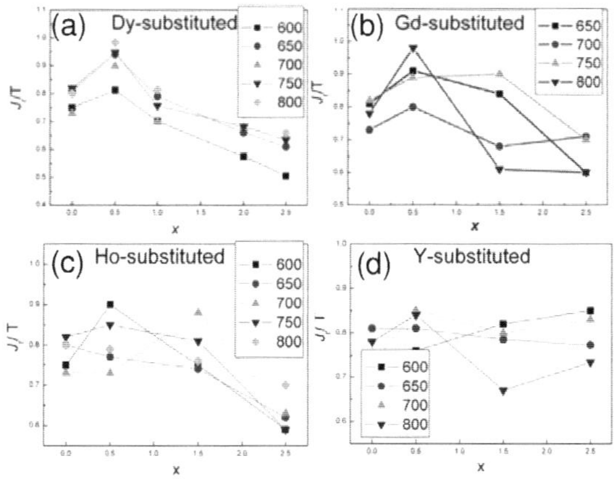

Fig.3. Distribution of J_r *of* $Nd_{11.8-x}(Dy/Y/Gd/Ho)_xFe_{81.2}Nb_{0.5}Cu_{0.5}B_{6.0}$ *ribbons annealed at different temperature as a function of substitution content*

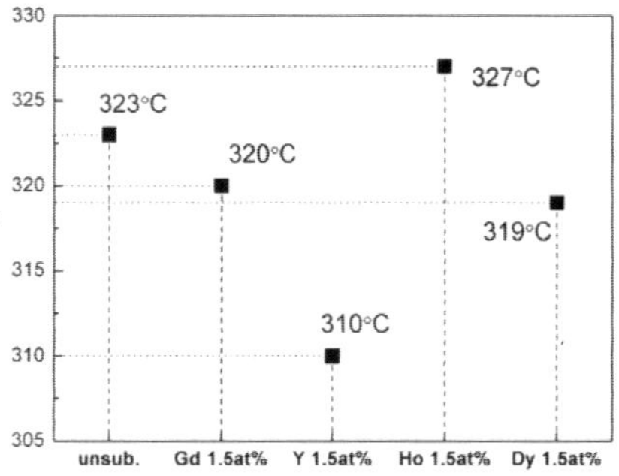

Fig.4. Distribution of Curie temperatures of optimally annealed ribbons with different kinds of substitution

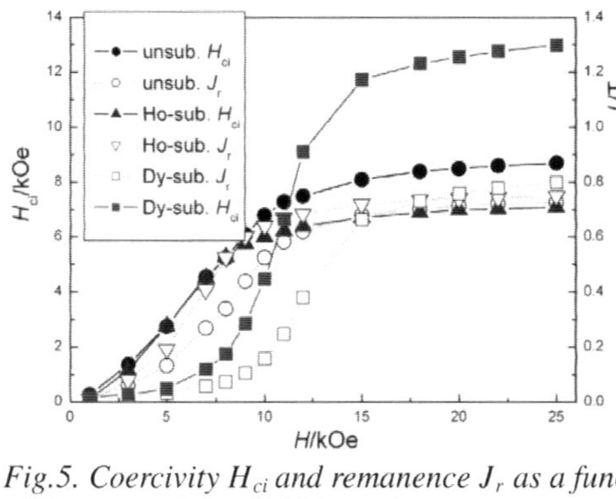

Fig.5. Coercivity H_{ci} *and remanence* J_r *as a function of the magnetizing field intensity*

The intrinsic coercivity H_{ci} and remanence J_r as a function of the magnetizing field intensity are shown in Fig. 5. The data were obtained from the minor loops of the optimally annealed ribbons with different kinds of substitution. As shown in Fig. 5, the coercivity and remanence initially rise very slowly followed by a drastic increase when the field exceeds a critical value corresponding to the value near coercivity H_{ci}. This behavior implies that the magnetization and reversal magnetization process is dominated by domain wall pinning mechanism [3]. Among all the ribbons, the Dy-substituted ribbon shows highest critical fields and coercive fields. For sure it is related to the large magnetocrystalline anisotropy field H_A of $Dy_2Fe_{14}B$ compound. But it is also attributed to the stronge intergranular exchange coupling interaction resulted from the uniform microstructure (Fig. 6). Perhaps the grain boundaries act as the domain-wall pinning centers.

Fig. 6 shows the microstructure of the annealed ribbons with different kinds of substitution. With increasing the Dy, Y and Ho contents from 0 to 0.5 at%, the average grain-size is decreased and the distribution of the grain-size becomes narrow.

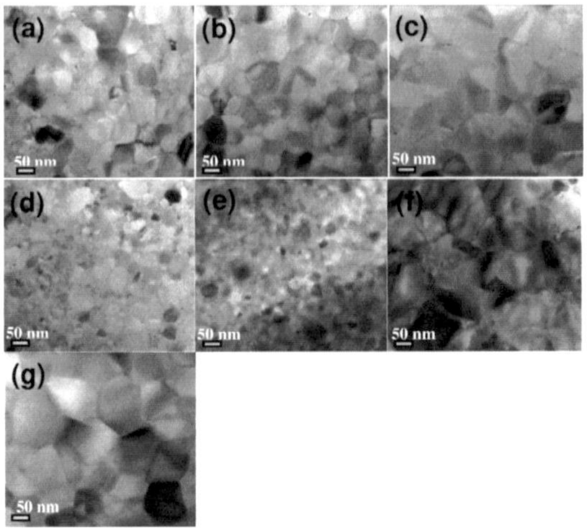

Fig.6. TEM images of optimally annealed samples with different substitution content: (a) 0.5 at% Y-substituted; (b) 0.5 at% Dy-substituted; (c) 0.5 at% Ho-substituted; (d) 2.5 at% Y-substituted; (e) 2.5 at% Dy-substituted; (f) 2.5 at% Ho-substituted (g) unsub.

With further increase in the substitution content to 2.5 at%, the microstructure of different rare earth substitution shows different change trend. For 2.5 at % Y-substituted ribbon (Fig. 6d), the grain size becomes finer but not uniform any more. Surprisingly, the grain-size of 2.5 at% Ho-substituted sample increases. And the precipitated phase appears in grain boundaries. Based on the theory from Kneller et al.'s works [4], in order to realize the crystallographic coherence as a necessary condition for mutual exchange coupling, the microstructure of nanocrystalline magnet should be a homogeneous distribution of the magnetic phases. There should not be any intergranular phase in this case. This may be the reason why the remanence of annealed 2.5 at% Ho-substituted ribbons is not so desirable.

To some extent, one may assume that the variation of $(BH)_{max}$ follows the same trend as the squareness of demagnetization curves. The demagnetization curves of the ribbons with different kinds of substitution after optimally annealing treatment are shown in Fig. 7. The squareness of the demagnetization curves seems to be insensitive to substitutional elements. As shown in Fig. 7, appropriate amount of substitutional elements such as Ho, Gd and Y are found to improve the squareness. As demagnetization fields reaching the two-thirds of their intrinsic coercivities, the magnetic polarization of unsubstituted ribbon, Y-substituted ribbon, Gd-substituted ribbon and Ho-substituted ribbon count as 57.2%, 79.8%, 82.6% and 81.7% of their remanent magnetic polarizations, respectively.

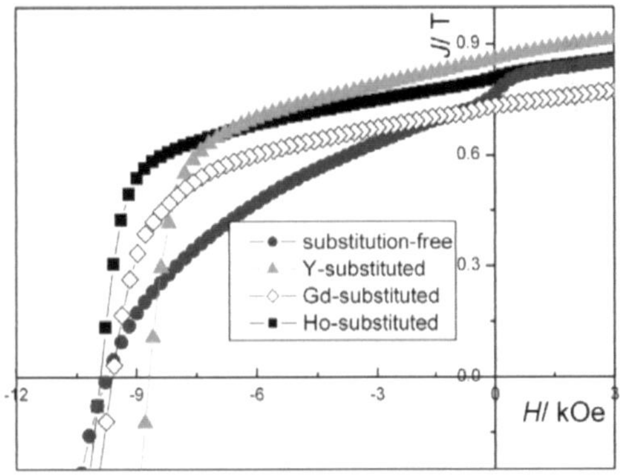

Fig.7. Room-temperature demagnetization curves of the ribbons with different kinds of substitution after optimum treatment

Two aspects in the refined microstructure may explain this phenomenon. At first, the intergranular exchange coupling interaction may be enhanced due to the increased specific surface area. In addition, the narrower distribution of the grain-size provides an opportunity for producing more pinning sites and uniformizing the domain-wall pinning strength which is extremely important for governing the reversal magnetization behavior in nanograin magnets.

4. Conclusion

The effects of Dy, Y, Gd and Ho content on the microstructure and magnetic properties of Nd-Fe-B nanocrystalline ribbons were investigated in this research. It was found that small amount of Dy/Y/Gd substitution enhances glass forming ability of the over-quenched ribbon. And all of Dy, Y, Gd and Ho substitution can stabilize the amorphous phase during post annealing treatment. Different kinds of elements show different optimum additional content and different effect on remanence and Curie temperature.

Furthermore, the microstructure is refined and uniformed with appropriate amount of Dy/Y/Gd/Ho substitution, which results in the enhancement of remanence and the improvement of the squareness of demagnetization curves compared with those of the unsubstituted counterpart. Surprisingly, the grains of 2.5 at.% Ho-substituted sample become coarse, and the precipitated phase appears in grain boundaries.

References

[1] T. Jang, Y. S. Kim. *IEEE Trans. Magn.* 36, 1999, 3310.
[2] Z. A. Chen, J. Luo, Z. M. Guo, *Int. J. Minerals, Metall. Mater.* **17**, 2010, 335.
[3] G. C. Hadjipanayis, A. Kim. *J. Appl. Phys.* **63**, 1988, 3310.
[4] E. F. Kneller, R. Hawig, *IEEE Trans. Magn.* **27**, 1991, 3588.

Fabrication and Magnetic Properties of Electrospun $Fe_{65}Co_{35}$ Nanowires and Nanotubes for Exchange-Coupled Permanent Magnets

MUHAMMAD ASIF WARSI, JOHN Q. XIAO
Department of Physics and Astronomy, University of Delaware, Newark, Delaware 19716, USA.

Abstract: *Exchange coupled permanent magnets are a promising candidate for future permanent magnets due to their potential for higher $(BH)_{max}$ and higher thermal stability. Recent studies have shown that soft core/hard shell exchange coupled cylinders can have maximum energy product higher than other practical geometries for mass production. We have fabricated $Fe_{65}Co_{35}$ uniform nanowires of small diameter of about 60 nm. The saturation magnetization (M_s) of fabricated nanowires is 222 emu/g that is very close to that of bulk $Fe_{65}Co_{35}$ alloys. $Fe_{65}Co_{35}$ nanotubes have also been fabricated with average diameter of 90 nm. Both of these nanowires and nanotubes can potentially be used as magnetically soft core in exchange coupled soft core/hard shell cylinders.*

Keywords: *electrospinning; nanowire; nanotube; exchange-coupled magnets*

Address: Muhammad Asif Warsi, Department of Physics and Astronomy, University of Delaware, Newark, Delaware 19716, USA, Fax: +1-302-831-1637, E-mail address: masif@udel.edu

1. Introduction

Permanent magnets (PMs) are used in motors, generators, turbine and many applications where PMs with high maximum energy products $(BH)_{max}$ and good thermal stability are highly desirable. Exchange spring nanocomposites consisting of magnetically soft phase with high magnetization and hard phase with high coercivity are potential candidate due to their ability to have high $(BH)_{max}$ and good thermal stability [1]. Soft and hard phase magnetic materials could be exchange coupled in multilayer, core/shell spherical or core/shell cylindrical geometries. Among these geometric multilayers is not an economical viable approach for mass production of PM. A recent theore-tical study compares the $(BH)_{max}$ for exchange coupled PM in different geometries (core / shell soft / hard cylinders and spheres) and results show that soft core / hard shell cylinders have the highest $(BH)_{max}$ [2]. $Fe_{65}Co_{35}$ alloy has the highest known magnetic moment per atom (~2.5 μ_B/atom) with a high Curie temperature (~ 900 °C) [3]. Due to its high saturation magnetization and high Curie temperature $Fe_{65}Co_{35}$ is a well-known choice as a soft phase in exchange coupled PMs. People have reported electrospun FeCo nanofibers in the past [4-6]. Barakat *et al.* reported carbon encapsulated FeCo nanofibers [5]. Due to carbon encapsulation of FeCo, it cannot be used in soft core/hard shell cylindrical exchange coupled PM. Xiang *et al.* reported $CoFe_2$ nanofibers with slightly larger diameter [6].

In this study, we synthesize $Fe_{65}Co_{35}$ nanofibers with controlled morphology (nanowire and nanotube) with small diameter of nanowire and high saturation magnetization M_s.

2. Experimental Section

2.1. Synthesis

All reagents were purchased from Alfa Aesar, USA. A viscous liquid solution was prepared for electro-spinning containing Fe and Co salts with atomic ratio 65 and 35, respectively. The solution consists of 10 wt.% of salts [$Fe(NO_3)_3 \cdot 9H_2O$ and $Co(NO_3)_2 \cdot 6H_2O$] and 5 wt. % of polymer polyvinyl-pyrrolidone (M.W. 1,300,000). N,N-Dimethylform-amide and 2-Propanol were used as solvent with volume ratio of (1:1). The solution was stirred for 12 h to uniformly mix the salts and polymer.

Electrospinning was done in a closed box with constantly purging dry air to keep the humidity below 20%. The solution was loaded into a plastic syringe which is attached to a pump. The solution was pushed with a constant flow rate of 0.2 ml/h. Plastic syringe is connected with a 22 gauge needle. A high electric potential of 13 kV was applied to the needle. A grounded rotating drum located 10 cm below the needle and served as a collector of electrospun fibers.

Electrospun fibers were first dried at 200 °C for 1 h. $Fe_{65}Co_{35}$ nanofiber formation involves two steps of heating. In the first heating step fiber was calcined in air to remove polymer and to convert Fe and Co salts into their oxides. In the second heating step, oxide fiber was reduced to pure $Fe_{65}Co_{35}$ by heating under reducing environment of 5% H_2 and 95% Ar.

2.2. Characterization

Nanofiber dried at 200 °C was subjected to thermo-gravimetric analysis using Pyris Diamond TG/DTA (PerkinElmer Instruments, USA). Morphology and

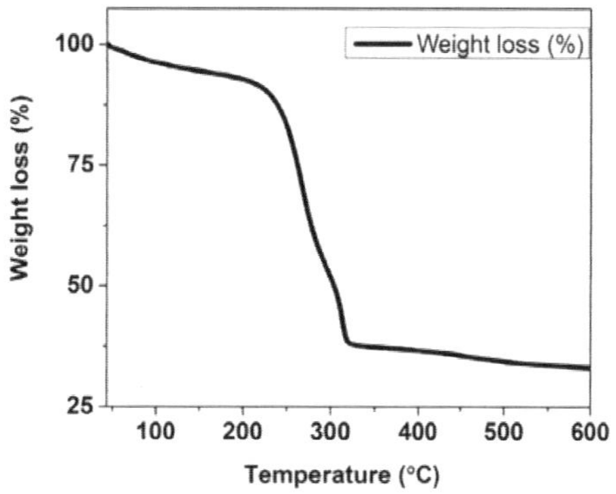

Fig. 1. TGA curve of nanofiber (dried at 200 °C).

diameter of nanofibers were determined by field emission scanning electron microscope (SEM, JEOL JSM 6330F). Chemical composition was determined by energy-dispersive spectrometer (EDS) attached to the SEM. The crystal structure was investigated with X-ray diffractometer (Rigaku Ultima IV). Magnetic properties were measured by vibrating sample magnetometer (Lakeshore 736, USA).

3. Results and Discussion

The nanofiber dried at 200 °C was subjected to thermogravimetric analysis (TGA) with a heating rate of 3 °C/min in air. Weight loss curve (Fig. 1) shows that there is no major weight loss below 200 °C. This is due to the fact that the spun fiber was first dried at 200 °C for 1 h. Weight loss (Fig. 1) due to the combustion of organic polymer (PVP) completes at temperature below 400 °C.

SEM images (Fig. 2) reveal the morphology of the nanofibers. Two different morphologies (nanowire & nanotubes) have been achieved due to different heat treatments. Although the heating steps are same, i.e. the first thermal treatment is to convert dry nanofibers into cobalt iron oxide and the second thermal treatment is to reduce fibers to $Fe_{65}Co_{35}$. Different heating temperatures result in different morphologies. To achieve nanowire morphology, dry nanofibers were calcined in air at 425 °C for one hour (heating rate = 3 °C/min) and then were calcined in a reducing environment (5% H_2 & 95% Ar) at 380 °C for one hour (heating rate = 3 °C/min). Average diameter of nanowire calculated from SEM is 60 nm. To achieve nanotube morphology dry nanofibers were calcined in air at 550 °C for one hour (heating rate = 3 °C/min) than were calcined in a reducing environment (5% H_2 & 95% Ar) at 300 °C for one hour (heating rate = 3 °C/min). Average diameter of nanowire calculated from SEM is 90 nm.

XRD pattern for calcined nanofibers at 425 °C in air [Fig. 3(a)] shows diffraction peaks that correspond to the standard peaks of cobalt iron oxide (ICDD # 00-022-1086), i.e. calcined nanofibers in air at 425 °C turns polymer fibers containing Co and Fe salts into cobalt iron oxide. The XRD pattern of nanofibers after the second heating step (reduction) is shown in Fig. 3(b). Strong diffraction peaks at the 2θ values of 44.78° and 65.14° correspond to the (110) and (200) crystal planes of $Fe_{65}Co_{35}$ (ICDD # 00-048-1817), indicating the formation of $Fe_{65}Co_{35}$ alloy. Average grain size of $Fe_{65}Co_{35}$ calculated by the Scherrer formula is 41 nm.

Hysteresis loops of $Fe_{65}Co_{35}$ nanowires reduced at 360 °C, 380 °C and 400 °C are shown in Fig. 4. Their saturation magnetizations are, respectively, 222 emu/g, 218 emu/g and 220 emu/g. This high M_s is close to that of bulk $Fe_{65}Co_{35}$ alloy. The coercivities of these are 490 Oe, 500 Oe, and 560 Oe, respectively, which is much higher than its bulk counterpart. The high coercivity is most likely due to the pining of the domain wall motion at nanofiber surface. This high coercivity is advantageous for forming a final exchange coupled PMs of high energy product.

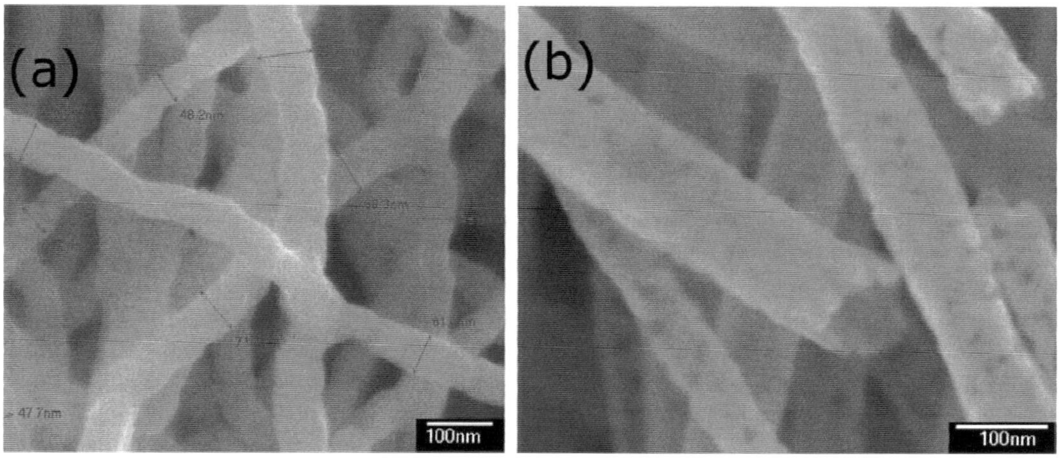

Fig. 2. SEM images of $Fe_{65}Co_{35}$ (a) nanowire and (b) nanotubes.

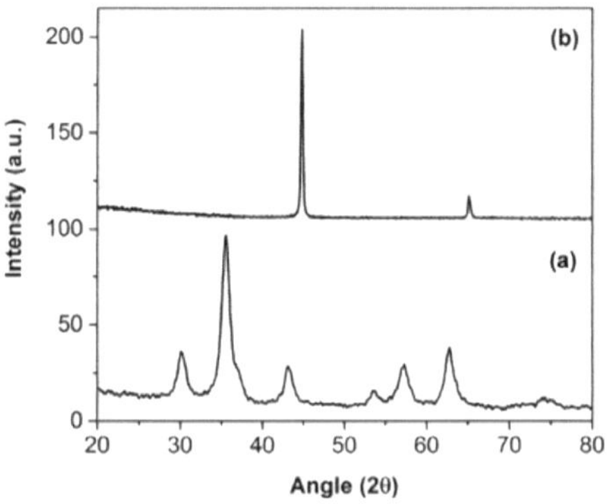

Fig. 3. XRD pattern for (a) cobalt iron oxide and (b) $Fe_{65}Co_{35}$.

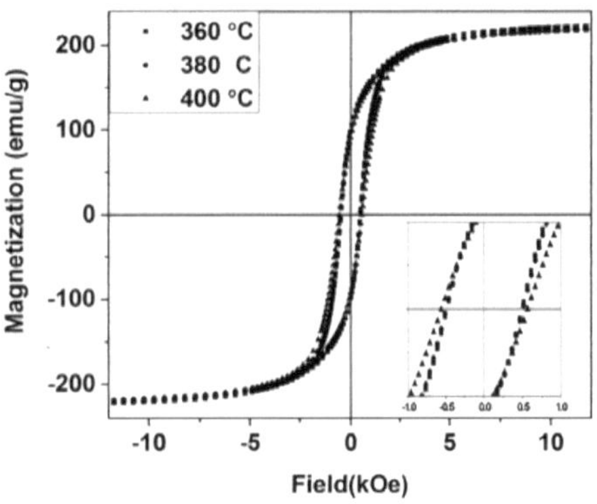

Fig. 4. Hysteresis loop for $Fe_{65}Co_{35}$ nanowires.

4. Conclusion

Electrospun $Fe_{65}Co_{35}$ nanowires and nanotubes have been successfully fabricated. These nanowires and nanotubes are uniform, small in diameter, and have very high aspect ratios. The average diameters of the nanowires and nanotubes are about 60 nm and 90 nm, respectively. The saturation magnetization of nanowire and nanotubes is about 222 emu/g. Due to their morphology and magnetic properties, these nanowires and nanotubes are ideal candidates as the soft magnetic core in exchanged coupled soft core/hard shell hybrid PMs.

Acknowledgments
This work is supported by the US Army Communications-Electronics Research, Development and Engineering Center (CERDEC), Command Power and Integration Directorate (CP&ID) via subcontract through General Technical Services under Grant # GTS-S-13-263.

References
[1] E.F. Kneller, R. Hawig, *IEEE Trans. Magn.* **27**, 1991, 3588.
[2] J.S. Jiang, S.D. Bader, *J. Phys.: Condens. Matter* **26**, 2014, 9.
[3] C.W. Chen, *Magnetism and Metallurgy of Soft Magnetic Materials*, Dover Publications, New York, NY, 1986.
[4] B. Paterson, P. Gyawali, D. McKeown, A. Buechele, I.L. Pegg, J. Philip, *Europ. Phys. J. - Appl. Phys.* **63**, 2013, 6.
[5] N.A.M. Barakat, M.F. Abadir, K.T. Nam, A.M. Hamza, S.S. Al-Deyab, W.I. Baek, H.Y. Kim, *J. Mater. Chem.* **21**, 2011, 10957.
[6] J. Xiang, X.H. Zhang, J.L. Li, Y.Q. Chu, X.Q. Shen, *Chem. Phys. Lett.* **576**, 2013, 39.

Microstructure and Crystallographic Texture Evolution in Hot Deformed $SmCo_5$ Permanent Magnet

M. YUE[1], C.G. WANG[1], C. ZHOU[1], D.T. ZHANG[1], W.Q. LIU[1], Q.M. LU[1], Z.H. GUO[2], W. LI[2]
[1] College of Materials Science and Engineering, Beijing University of Technology, Beijing 100124, China
[2] Division of Functional Materials, Central Iron and Steel Research Institute, Beijing, 100081, China

Abstract: *In present study, the electron backscattered diffraction (EBSD) and transmission electronic microscopy (TEM) have been applied to study the microstructure and crystallographic texture evolution in hot deformed $SmCo_5$ permanent magnet. Increase of height reduction of deformed $SmCo_5$ magnet leads to gradually enhanced c-axis crystallographic texture. Moreover, grain boundary planes are also textured. Further TEM analysis indicates that some $SmCo_5$ grains decompose into Sm_2Co_{17} grains and unidentified Sm-rich particles. The decomposition may undermine the crystallographic texture of $SmCo_5$ grains and the magnetic hardening of the magnets.*

Key words: *microstructure, crystallographic texture, $SmCo_5$ magnet, grain boundary, decomposition*

Address: Ming Yue, College of Materials Science and Engineering, Beijing University of Technology, Beijing, 100124, China, Tel: (8610) 67391760, E-mail: yueming@bjut.edu.cn

1. Introduction

Bulk nanocrystalline $SmCo_5$ permanent magnet with high coercivity and T_C is a promising candidate for practical application at elevated temperature [1,2]. More recently, strong c-axis crystallographic texture and magnetic anisotropy have been successfully developed in such kind of magnet by severe hot deformation method [3,4]. Up to now, however, mechanism of crystallographic texture development in nanocrystalline $SmCo_5$ permanent magnet during hot deformation process is still unknown. It is therefore of theoretical and practical value to clarify their structure evolution during deformation process. In present study, the electron backscattered diffraction (EBSD) and transmission electronic microscopy (TEM) have been applied to study the microstructure and crystallographic texture evolution in hot deformed $SmCo_5$ permanent magnet.

2. Experimental

Hot deformed $SmCo_5$ permanent magnets with height reduction of 80-90% were prepared by using the spark plasma sintering (SPS) method. The preparation details were reported elsewhere [3]. The crystal structure and microstructure of the magnets were studied by electron back scattered diffraction (EBSD) and Transmission electron microscopy (TEM).

3. Result and Discussion

3.1. EBSD analysis of the $SmCo_5$ magnets

Fig. 1 (a)-(c) shows the OIM-EBSD scans of the hot deformed bulk nanocrystalline $SmCo_5$ magnets with 80%, 85%, and 90% height reduction for the surface perpendicular to pressure direction, respectively.

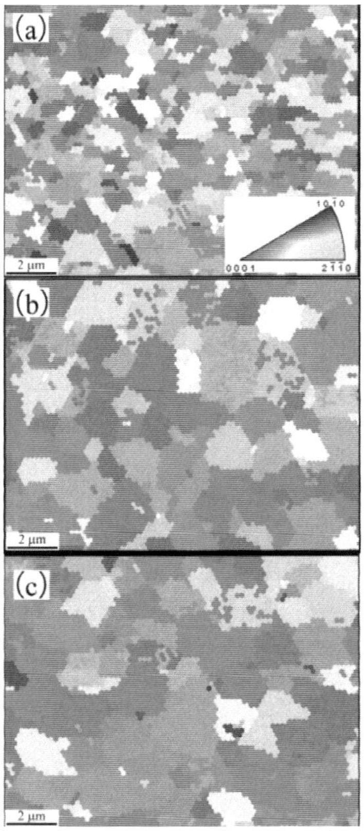

Fig. 1. OIM-EBSD scans of the hot deformed $SmCo_5$ magnets with (a) 80%, (b) 85%, (c) 90% height reduction for the surface perpendicular to pressure direction, inset of (a): color code for the interpretation of the OIM maps.

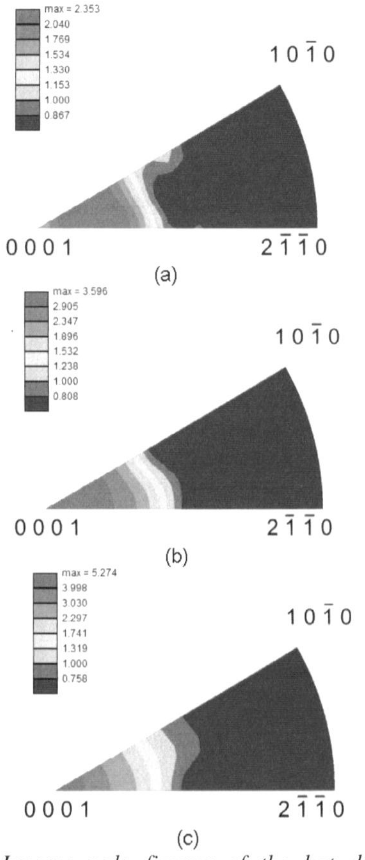

Fig. 2. Inverse pole figures of the hot deformed $SmCo_5$ magnets with (a) 80%, (b) 85%, (c) 90% height reduction.

According to the color code shown in the inset of Fig. 1 (a), it is observed that quite a lot grains are orientated close to (00*l*) direction for all three samples, and the bigger the height reduction of the magnets, the higher content of orientated grains in the samples. In addition, the average $SmCo_5$ crystal grain size in the sample enlarges remarkably with the increase of the height reduction associated with high deformation temperature, which leads to excessive grain growth.

In order to characterize the crystallographic alignment quantitatively, the inverse pole figures of the hot deformed bulk nanocrystalline $SmCo_5$ magnets with 80%, 85%, and 90% height reduction were examined and shown in Figure 2(a)-(c), respectively. By the height reduction of 80%, the texture intensity reaches to 2.353, suggesting the crystallographic alignment is already developed to some extent in the magnet. After that, the intensity rapidly increases with the height reduction increasing further to 85-90%, and intensity as high as 5.274, which indicates a strong c-axis texture in bulk nanocrystalline $SmCo_5$ magnet, was obtained in the magnet with 90% height reduction.

The orientation texture of $SmCo_5$/$SmCo_5$ grain

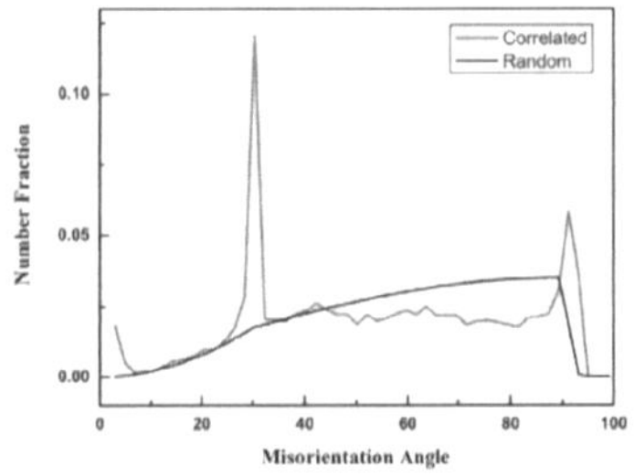

Fig. 3. Orientation texture of $SmCo_5$/$SmCo_5$ grain boundaries.

boundary planes is another major concern. The misorientation angle distribution is calculated, and the outcome is illustrated in Fig. 3. In the chart, the black and red lines represent the situations for an ideally random microstructure and the observed grain boundaries, separately. It can be seen that three symmetry equivalents of Σ13a boundaries, namely the 27.796°/[0001] boundary, the 32.204°/[0001] boundary and the 92.204°/[0001] boundary, are favored, and the occurring frequency of Σ13a boundaries is 5 times higher than that of the random boundaries.

3.2. TEM analysis of the $SmCo_5$ magnets

Fig. 4 shows the microstructure and corresponding SEAD patterns of $SmCo_5$ magnet. Area A and C are $SmCo_5$ and Sm_2Co_{17} phase, respectively, while B exhibits a transition from 1:5 to 2:17 phase. Further observation indicates that there are some unidentified Sm-rich particles (EDX result) near the transition area. The decomposition may undermine the crystallographic texture of $SmCo_5$ grains and the magnetic hardening of the magnets.

4. Summary

In summary, the microstructure and crystallographic texture evolution had been studied for hot deformed $SmCo_5$ magnet by EBSD and TEM. Increase of height reduction of deformed $SmCo_5$ magnet leads to gradually enhanced c-axis crystallographic texture. TEM analysis indicates that some $SmCo_5$ grains

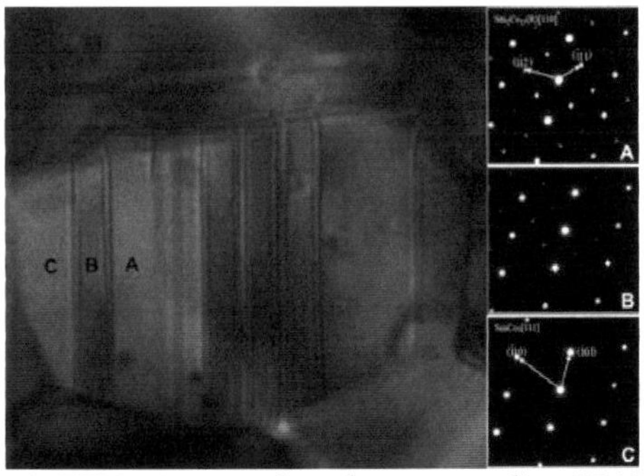

Fig. 4. TEM micrograph and corresponding SEAD of hot deformed $SmCo_5$ magnet.

decompose into Sm_2Co_{17} grains and unidentified Sm-rich particles. The decomposition may undermine the crystallographic texture of $SmCo_5$ grains and the magnetic hardening of the magnets.

Acknowledgement

This work was supported in part by the National Natural Science Funding (51331003) and the National Major Fundamental Research Program of China, Ministry of Science and Technology China (2010CB934600).

Reference

[1] J. Ding, *et al.*, *JAC.*, 1993, 191, 197.
[2] M. Q. Huang, *et al.*, *JAP.*, 2008, 103, 07E134.
[3] M. Yue, *et al.*, *JAP.*, 2011, 109, 07A711.
[4] A. M. Gabay, *et al.*, *JMMM.*, 2011, 323, 2470.

Fabrication of Size-Tunable Monodisperse $Nd_2Fe_{14}B@CoFe_2$ Nanocomplexes

BIN QI, DAVID P. ARNOLD
University of Florida, Gainesville FL, 32611, USA

Abstract: *Monodisperse, spherical core-shell $Nd_2Fe_{14}B@CoFe_2$ nanocomplexes are synthesized via a thermodecomposition procedure followed by calcium-assisted reduction annealing in a hydrogen environment. The core diameters are tuned from 4 nm to 34 nm by controlling the ligand/precursor ratio and refluxing temperature, and a fixed shell thickness of 2.5 nm is used. After reducing in hydrogen, the core-shell nanocomplexes range from 10 nm (4 nm core) up to 39 nm (34 nm core), exhibiting coercivity ranging from 3 kA/m to 40 kA/m and saturation magnetization ranging from 70 emu/g to 244 emu/g.*

Keywords: *$Nd_2Fe_{14}B$; core-shell; rare-earth magnets; thermodecomposition; nanoparticle*

Address: David P. Arnold, Dept. Electrical and Computer Engineering, University of Florida, Gainesville FL, 32611, USA, Tel: (1-352)-392-4931, E-mail: darnold@ufl.edu

1. Introduction

Hard-soft magnetic nanoparticle complexes have attracted considerable attention for their potential to leverage exchange interactions to increase the energy product of permanent magnets [1]. $Nd_2Fe_{14}B$ has a high coercivity, and $CoFe_2$ ($\sim Co_{35}Fe_{65}$) possesses a high saturation magnetization. However, there are few reports on $Nd_2Fe_{14}B$-metal core/shell structures. An important consideration is that achieving desirable exchange spring effects demands precise dimensional control [2], and hence necessitates uniform morphological control of the particles. The objective of this work is to precisely tune the dimensions of a hard, rare-earth magnetic core and a soft, transition metal-alloy magnetic shell in an effort to optimize the exchange coupling effect.

The general procedure is to first form monodisperse $Nd_2Fe_{14}B$ oxide nanoparticle cores by a thermodecomposition procedure modified from Park [3]. Core sizes are tuned by varying the ligand/precursor ratio and refluxing temperature. Next, a shell of $CoFe_2$ oxide is then grown on the cores, also via thermodecomposition. The core-shell nanocomplexes are then reduced to metal states via annealing in hydrogen.

2. Experimental

The materials used were: 99.9% neodymium chloride hexahydrate (Strem Chemicals), 99% iron(III) chloride (Alfa Aesar), 99.9% boron tribromide (Acros Organics), 98% cobalt(II) nitrate (Alfa Aesar), 97% sodium oleate (TCI America), 97% oleic acid (Fisher Chemical), 90% 1-octadecene (Acros Organics), 97% trioctylamine (Acros Organics), 99.5% calcium granules (Alfa Aesar), denatured anhydrous ethanol (Fisher Scientific Education), and certified ACS hexanes (Fisher Chemical).

Four different oleate precursors were first synthesized. To obtain neodymium oleate, 5 mmol neodymium chloride hexahydrate and 15 mmol sodium oleate were dissolved in a mixed solution of 20 mL ethanol, 35 mL hexanes, and 15 mL DI water in a three-neck flask and stirred vigorously via a magnet stir bar. The solution was heated to 60 °C for 4 hr. Then the upper organic layer containing the neodymium oleate was washed with 20 mL DI water three times. The aqueous phase at the bottom was discarded, and the upper organic layer was collected for further use. Iron oleate, boron oleate, and cobalt oleate were synthesized using the same procedure but with iron(III) chloride, boron tribromide, and cobalt(II) nitrate, respectively. In the boron oleate synthesis, an additional 15 mmol boron tribromide was added to compensate for material loss by volatilization. In the cobalt oleate synthesis, the sodium oleate was reduced to 10 mmol.

For thermodecomposition, organometallic precursors in stoichiometric ratio were decomposed at high temperature in the presence of the stabilizing ligands (oleic acid) in a high boiling point solvent (1-octadecene or trioctylmine). In a typical reaction of synthesizing 4 nm $Nd_2Fe_{14}B$ oxide nanoparticles, 0.06 mmol neodymium oleate, 0.42 mmol iron oleate, 0.03 mmol boron oleate, and 1.5 mmol oleic acid were dissolved in 10 mL 1-octadecene. The solution was heated 5 °C min^{-1} in a three-neck flask to 120 °C and kept at that temperature for 20 min with nitrogen bubbling. Then the solution was further heated to 318 °C with the same heating rate, and refluxed for 1 hr. After cooling to room temperature, the nanoparticles were precipitated by adding 50 mL ethanol and then isolated by centrifugation at 8000 RPM for 10 min. The obtained particles were washed by a mixture of ethanol and hexanes (volume ratio 2:1) three times. After washing, the product was redispersed in hexanes.

To form shells on the previously synthesized cores, hexanes containing 20 mg of $Nd_2Fe_{14}B$ oxide nanoparticles were mixed with 0.17 mmol cobalt oleate, 0.33 mmol iron oleate, and 1.5 mmol oleic acid and dissolved in 10 mL 1-octadecene. The same heating and purification procedures were used as in the $Nd_2Fe_{14}B$ oxide synthesis step. After washing, the $Nd_2Fe_{14}B@CoFe_2$ oxide nanocomplexes were redispersed in hexanes.

To reduce the core-shell nanocomplexes, 20 mg of the $Nd_2Fe_{14}B@CoFe_2$ oxide particles were dispensed on a silicon wafer and covered by 200 mg of calcium granules after evaporating the hexanes. The sample was then annealed at 450 °C for 3 h in a tube furnace purging with 5% hydrogen-95% argon gas. After cooling to room temperature, the calcium oxide and unreacted calcium was rinsed by de-oxygenated DI water, leaving the reduced $Nd_2Fe_{14}B@CoFe_2$ nanocomplexes on the substrate.

Samples for transmission electron microscopy (TEM) were obtained by dropping diluted particle solution onto a copper grid with carbon film. TEM images were acquired by a JEOL 200CX TEM system at a working voltage of 200 kV, and the mean average size of the nanocomplexes were extracted using ImageJ image analysis software. X-ray powder diffraction (XRD) was performed at 45 kV and 40 mA using a PANalytical X'Pert Powder X-ray diffractometer with CuKα radiation (λ =0.154056 nm) at a scanning rate of 5°/min. Hysteresis loops were measured using an ADE Technologies Model EV9 vibrating sample magnetometer (VSM) with applied magnetic fields up to ±2 T at 300 K. The measured moments were normalized by the sample under the assumption the nanocomplexes had the M_3O_4 oxidation state (magnetite) and were completely reduced in the annealing process. Elemental analysis was carried out by inductively coupled plasma atomic emission spectroscopy (ICP-AES) by Perkin-Elmer Plasma 3200RL.

3. Results and Discussion

Fig. 1 summarizes the core-shell oxide synthesis results (before annealing). The core size is increased from 4 nm to 17 nm by increasing the oleic acid/oleate molar ratio from 3:1 to 9:1. Moreover, the particle size is further elevated to 34 nm by raising the refluxing temperature from 318 °C to 365 °C, with a corresponding change in the solvent from 1-octadecene to trioctylamine. Fig. 1 shows the particle

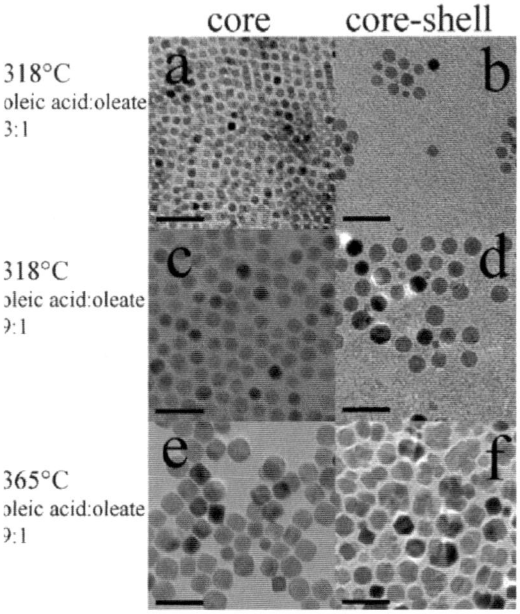

Fig 1. TEM images of (a) 4nm (c) 17 nm (e) 34 nm $Nd_2Fe_{14}B$ oxide nanoparticles and (b) 10 nm, (d) 22 nm, (f) 39 nm $Nd_2Fe_{14}B@CoFe_2$ oxide nanocomplex before annealing. Scale bars represent 50 nm.

size increase after adding the cobalt ferrite shell with an estimated shell thickness of ~2.5 nm.

Fig. 2 shows XRD patterns of the nanocomplexes before and after hydrogen annealing. The data confirms the phase changes of the core and shell from an oxidation to metal state. Crystal sizes of the annealed particles calculated by the Scherrer equation are 16 nm, 23 nm, and 40 nm respectively. The larger two values correspond well to the particle size from TEM images (Fig. 1), but the smallest 10 nm sample shows a grain size of 16 nm, which may be attributed to an increase in particle crystallinity and/or inter-particle sintering.

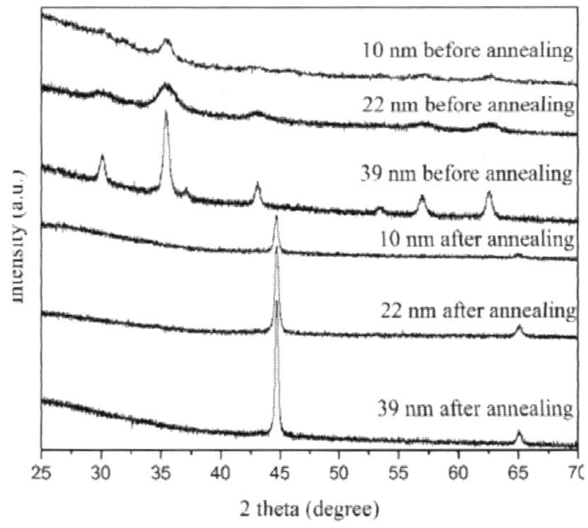

Fig 2. XRD patterns of nanocomplexes before and after annealing.

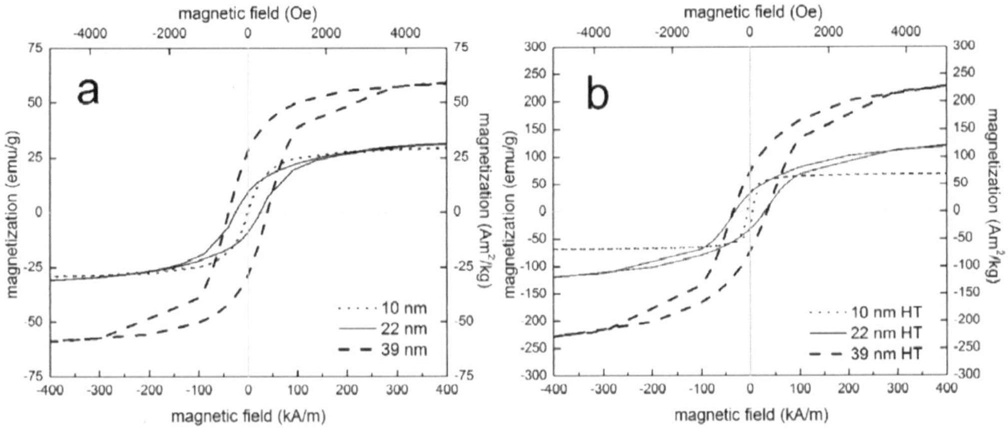

Fig 3. Hysteresis loops (300 K) of the core-shell nanocomplexes (a) before and (b) after heat treatment.

Fig. 3 shows the hysteresis loops of the three different core-shell nanocomplexes before and after annealing. While the coercivity values increase only modestly, the substantial increase in saturation magnetization after annealing gives further evidence of the reduction of the nanocomplexes from the oxide to metal state. Clear size dependencies are also observed. The reduced nanocomplex saturation magnetization grows from 70 emu/g for the 10 nm structures to 244 emu/g for the 39 nm structures. The coercivities correspondingly range from 3 kA/m to 40 kA/m. These value are much lower than bulk, mostly like because the hard $Nd_2Fe_{14}B$ cores of the nano-complexes are much smaller than their single domain size of ~350 nm [4].

4. Conclusions

This work demonstrates the ability to synthesize size-controlled monodisperse hard/soft core-shell nanocomplexes ($Nd_2Fe_{14}B$@$CoFe_2$). Higher coercivity and saturation magnetization were achieved with larger-sized nanocomplexes. Comparing to conventional procedures such as sol-gel or ball milling, nanocomplexes synthesized by this thermodecomposition procedure can create particles with uniform morphology and magnetic properties. This control can be conducive to maximize the exchange spring effect, since the distance between hard magnetic cores could be determined by the shell thickness after sintering. $Nd_2Fe_{14}B$@$CoFe_2$ complexes also have cost-effect advantages comparing to the well-studied CoPt/ FePt alloys, which contain noble metals.

Acknowledgements

This work was supported in part by the US Army Research Office (W911NF-90-1-0511). The thank Dr. J. Andrew from the UF Dept. Materials Science and Engineering as well as the UF MAIC facility for material analysis.

References

[1] S. B. Darling, S. D. Bader, *J. Mater. Chem.* **2005**, 15, 4189-4195.

[2] J. M. D. Coey, *Scripta Mater.* **2012**, 6, 524-529.

[3] J. Park, K. An, Y. Hwang, J. G. Park, H. J. Noh, J. Y. Kim, J. Park, N.M. Hwang, T. Hyeon, *Nat. Mater.* **2004**, 3, 891-895.

[4] F. Matsumoto, H. Sakamoto, M. Komiya, M. Fujikura, *J. Appl. Phys.* **1988**, 63, 3507-3509.

Synthesis of Well-Dispersed α"-$Fe_{16}N_2$ Particles

Y. KINEMUCHI[1,2], D. NAGAI[1], K. SUZUKI[1,2], A. TOWATA[1,2], M. YASUOKA[1,2], S. OKADA[1,2], K. TAKAGI[1,2], K. OZAKI[1,2]
[1]National Institute of Advanced Industrial Science and Technology (AIST), Nagoya 463-8560, Japan
[2]Research Association of Magnetic Materials for High-Efficiency Motors (MagHEM), ibid.

Abstract: *Isolated particles, without agglomeration and necking, is critical for magnetic applications. Up to now, such particles have been realized by means of an oxide coating for α"-$Fe_{16}N_2$ nanoparticles (NPs), at the expense of the saturation magnetization. Here, we report that hydroxyapatite, a well-known biomaterial, similarly avoids sintering during synthesis, and decomposes by chelating Ca ion from the structure. The resultant α"-$Fe_{16}N_2$ NPs were well dispersed without much deterioration of their magnetic properties, suggesting that the NPs are suitable for spin orientation.*

Key words: *α"-$Fe_{16}N_2$; nanoparticle; sintering; surface coating; hydroxyapatite*

Address: Yoshiaki Kinemuchi, National Institute of Advanced Industrial Science and Technology (AIST), Nagoya 463-8560, Japan, Tel: +81-52-736-7464, Fax: +81-52-736-7215
E-mail: y.kinemuchi@aist.go.jp

1. Introduction

Recently, the properties of pure α"-$Fe_{16}N_2$ nanoparticles (NP) with saturation magnetization (M_s) of 234 emu/g, i.e., 2.4 μ_B, and magnetocrystalline anisotropy of 0.96 MJ/m^3 have been reported [1]. Such magnetic properties present opportunities for practical applications in recording media [2]. On the other hand, its environmentally benign and abundant composition as a potential candidate for a rare-earth free magnet attracts attention as well. Successive low-temperature densification below 200°C has resulted in a sintered magnet with promising properties [3]. The required powder of α"-$Fe_{16}N_2$ for such applications is synthesized via the nitriding of Fe powders [4]. Because of its relatively low nitriding temperature, Fe powder less than 100 nm in diameter is usually applied in the synthesis procedure. It is known that mixing of large Fe particles causes deterioration of the purity of the product [5]. Reduction of iron-oxide NPs is a practical method for preparation of Fe NPs. Typically, heat treatment at 300 – 600 °C in H_2 atmosphere is carried out. One of the issues during the reduction is the sintering of Fe NPs, which can be solved by coating the iron oxides with Si, Al, and/or Y [2]. The resultant oxide layer on the NPs prevents sintering, and serves as a protective layer against air exposure. This is at the expense of the Ms, however. The sintering also occurs during the nitriding process even at a temperature lower than 150 °C.

In this study, we propose a way to impede the sintering of NPs via a removable coating on the iron oxides. We show that the coating material is robust in both H_2 and NH_3 atmosphere, can be removed by a chemical treatment after the nitriding process, and is effective in creating NPs without necking, indicating that the newly synthesized α"-$Fe_{16}N_2$ NPs can be employed for spin orientation.

2. Material Processing

Spherical hematite, α-Fe_2O_3, with an average size of 50 nm, was prepared as the starting raw material. In order to achieve homogeneous dispersion in water, ionic liquid assisted hydrothermal synthesis was implemented. Synthetic conditions were similar to that reported [6]. The hematite NPs were dispersed in distilled water, and subsequently mixed with water solution of calcium nitrate tetrahydrate, $Ca(NO_3)_2 \cdot 4H_2O$. After the pH of the mixture was adjusted to be 9 by aqueous NH_3, water solution of ammonium phosphate dibasic, $(NH_4)_2HPO_4$, was dropped into the mixture, resulting in the formation of hydroxyapatite (HAp), $Ca_{10}(PO_4)_6(OH)_2$. During this procedure, pH was kept at 9. The nominal molar ratio of Ca/P was 1.67, and the weight ratio of hematite/HAp was 0.5. In order to ensure the reaction, the above solution was mixed overnight. The HAp precipitated between hematite particles, so that a composite powder was formed. Because the morphology of HAp is needle-like, reaction gases can permeate the composite particles, and furthermore HAp maintains the distance between hematite particles, which is expected to prevent the sintering of the reactant particles. Besides the composite particles, commercially available γ-Fe_2O_3 NPs (C.I. Kasei Co. Ltd., NanoTek) were also used in the control experiment.

α"-$Fe_{16}N_2$ particles were synthesized via reduction and nitriding of the composite particles. The reduction was carried out in pure H_2 gas flow (99.99999%, 200 ml/min) for 4-8 h at 300-500°C. After the reduction, the remaining gas in the furnace was purged with pure Ar, and nitriding proceeded under NH_3 gas flow (99.9%, 200 ml/min) for 12-72 h at 130-150°C.

The surface of α"-$Fe_{16}N_2$ was passivated by keeping the products in N_2 and 100 ppm O_2 for one day, or by soaking the products in hexadecanethiol (HDT), $CH_3(CH_2)_{15}SH$, dissolved in absolute ethanol. The former method results in an oxidized layer of iron, while the latter contributes to the formation of a self-assembled monolayer of HDT [7].

Finally, the HAp were decomposed by chelating Ca by ethylenediaminetetraacetato (EDTA) in water with pH of 9 via ultrasonication, and the α"-$Fe_{16}N_2$ particles were collected using a centrifuge.

3. Results and Discussion

HAp, used as a coating material to prevent particle necking during H_2-reduction, is known as a stable biomaterial, yet its stability under a H_2 flow followed by a subsequent NH_3 flow is not certain. Especially, release of OH from the structure is a main concern, as the water vapor is considered to reduce the reaction yield of α"-$Fe_{16}N_2$ [5]. Figure 1 shows the X-ray diffraction (XRD) profiles of HAp after synthesis and also after exposure to the reducing and nitriding atmospheres. The profile of the as-synthesized powder shows rather broad peaks originating from its small crystalline size, and all peaks can be attributed to HAp. The profiles after exposure to H_2 flow as well as NH_3 flow were identical to the profile after synthesis, indicating the robust crystal structure of HAp. Furthermore, the negligible change in peak broadening indicates that the crystal size of HAp is maintained at the processing temperature, suggesting suitability as coating material. The IR spectra indicate libration mode of OH at 632 cm^{-1} maintained via the reducing and nitriding. Although the bending mode of CO_3 around 870 cm^{-1}, originating in contamination from the air, shifted to higher wave numbers, other modes were identical to the profile after synthesis, again confirming its rigid crystal structure. In addition, carbonated HAp, in which CO_3 ion substitutes the PO_4 ion, is reported to be a less thermally stable phase than pure HAp [8].

Such rigid HAp is an ionic crystal, i.e., Ca^{2+} binds the PO_4^{3-} tetrahedra and OH^- by ionic bonding, as shown in the inset of Fig. 1. Thus, HAp can be decomposed by extracting a Ca ion from its framework. Chelating Ca ion by EDTA was performed for this purpose. Figure 2 shows the IR spectra of the powders. Clear stretching modes of PO_4 were observed for the composite raw powder of hematite/HAp, as well as for the resultant product after reduction and nitriding. Chelating Ca completely extinguished the stretching modes, indicating decomposition of HAp.

The SEM images in Fig. 3 clearly reveal the effect of HAp. The starting hematite particles of 50 nm in diameter (Fig. 3a), disperse homogeneously in a cloud (Fig. 3b) which actually consists of HAp nanocrystals with needle-like morphology. Here, the chain network in the HAp nanocrystal can apparently be viewed as a cloud. White spots in the image are hematite particles that have become separated in the cloud. In this HAp cloud, gas reactions, i.e., reduction and nitriding, proceeds, resulting in α"-$Fe_{16}N_2$ formation. Because of the HAp, the sintering of particles is prevented, resulting in isolated particles after the decomposition of HAp (Fig. 3c). Without HAp, the particles would evidently sinter and grow, as shown in Fig. 3d. As reported earlier, such large particles remain in the

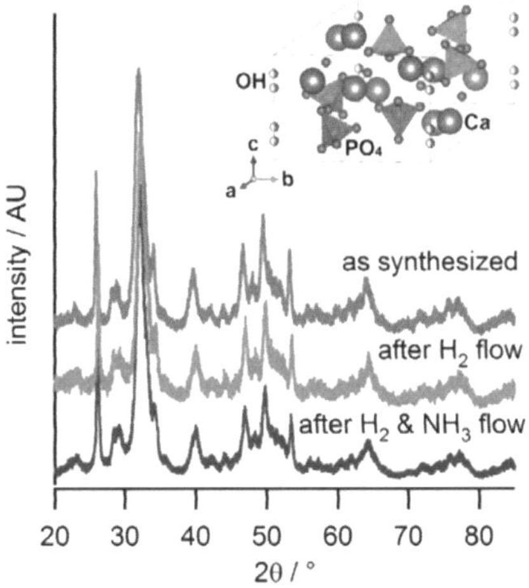

Fig.1. XRD profiles of HAp, as synthesized, after the exposure in H_2 flow at 450°C, and after the H_2 flow and subsequent NH_3 flow at 140°C.

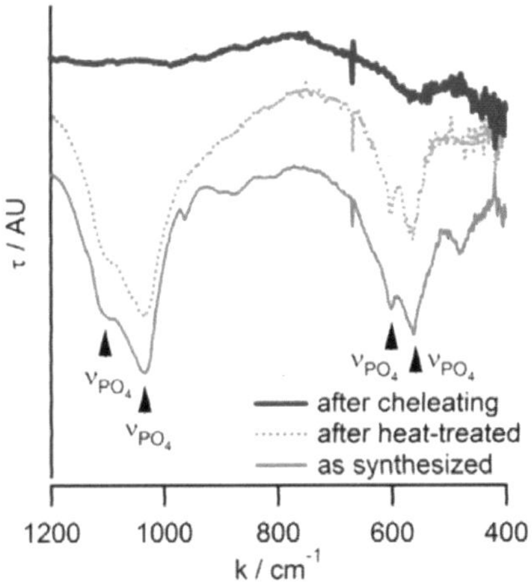

Fig.2. IR spectra of powders. As synthesized HAp/hematite composite, after the exposure in H_2 and subsequent NH_3 flow, and after chelating Ca from HAp.

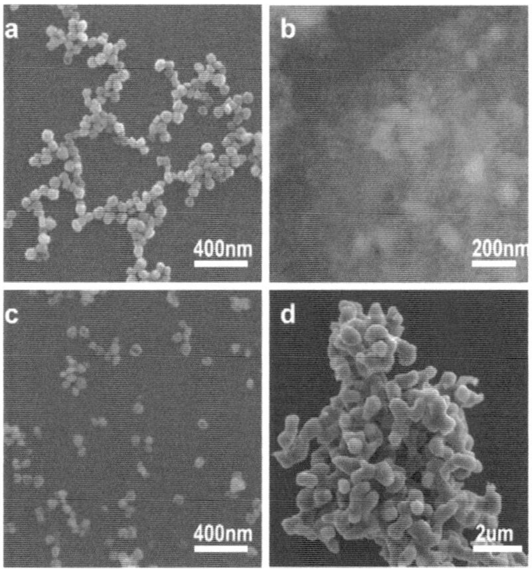

Fig.3 SEM images of (a) hematite NPs, (b) HAp/ hematite composite (raw material), (c) α"-$Fe_{16}N_2$ NPs (after chelating) and (d) sintered Fe powder (control).

α-Fe phase after the nitriding process [4].

The sintering occurs during the reduction as a result of the high process temperature. As well as the reduction, we also noticed that nitriding contributes to the sintering. $Fe_{16}N_2$ was synthesized without HAp following a reported procedure [9]. Nitriding at 130°C was assumed to be at enough of a low temperature to prevent sintering, but prolonged nitriding of 72 h caused obvious necking and coarsening of the particles.

From the XRD profile, the crystal structure of the synthesized powder was assigned to α"-$Fe_{16}N_2$. A minor iron phase was found, while no oxide phase was visible. Rietveld analysis revealed α-Fe of 6 mass% included in the powder. The saturation magnetization of 170 emu/g and coercive force of 2450 Oe at room temperature suggested further modification of the process is possible.

4. Summary

Well-dispersed α"-$Fe_{16}N_2$ NPs were synthesized. This was achieved by using a composite powder, i.e., a hematite NP surrounded by HAp nanocrystals, as the raw material. Thanks to the rigid structure of HAp, the NPs were separated via a gas reaction, leading to less sintering of the NPs. Subsequent chelating of Ca ion from HAp resulted in their decomposition, and an isolated α"-$Fe_{16}N_2$ NP was extracted as the final product.

References

[1] T. Ogawa et al., *Appl. Phys. Exp.* **6**, 2013, 073007.
[2] Y. Sakai et al., *IEEE Trans. Magn.* **41**, 2005, 3241-3243.
[3] K. Takagi et al., *J. Appl. Phys.* **115**, 2014, 103905.
[4] A. Nagatomi et al., *J. Jpn. Soc. Pow. Pow. Met.* **49**, 1999, 151-155. (in Japanese).
[5]K. Yamanaka et al., *J. Solid State Chem.* **183**, 2010, 2236-2241.
[6] J. Lian et al., *ACS Nano* **3**, 2009, 3749-3761.
[7] D. W. Lee et al., *J. Mater. Sci. Technol.* **26**, 2010, 367-370.
[8] A. Slosarczyk et al., *J. Mol. Struct.* **744-747**, 2005, 657-661.
[9] T. Hattori et al., *J. Magn. Soc. Jpn.* **25**, 2001, 927-930 (in Japanese).

Coercivity Enhancement in Nanocomposite Nd-Fe-B Alloys by Pr-diffusion

DANIEL SALAZAR[1], J. MANUEL BARANDIARÁN[1,2], RAJASEKHAR MADUGUNDO[3], GEORGE C. HADJIPANAYIS[3]
[1]BCMaterials, Camino de Ibaizabal, Edificio 500, Planta 1. Parque Científico y Tecnológico de Zamudio, 48160 Derio, Spain
[2]University of the Basque Country, Faculty of Science and Technology, P.O. Box 644, 48080 Bilbao, Spain
[3]Department of Physics and Astronomy, University of Delaware, USA

Abstract: *This study reports the magnetic and structural properties of optimally annealed melt-spun* $Nd_{12}Fe_{81}B_6Nb_1$ *and* $Nd_{10}Fe_{84}B_6$ *alloys which they were further subjected to a diffusion experiment with the low melting point* $Pr_{68}Cu_{32}$ *alloy. The maximum coercivity obtained in* $Nd_{12}Fe_{81}B_6Nb$ *was 8.76 kOe which increased further to 11.33 kOe after the Pr-diffusion. In the rare earth-lean* $Nd_{10}Fe_{84}B_6$ *alloy, the coercivity was found to decrease slightly after the diffusion experiment with a shoulder appearing on the demagnetization curve indicating decoupling of the soft Fe grains with the hard* $Nd_2Fe_{14}B$ *grains.*

Keywords: *Nd-Fe-B; nanocrystalline magnets; nanocomposite magnets; grain-boundary diffusion*

1. Introduction

In the last few decades the interest to study the hard magnetic materials for applications in engineering has increased, mainly due to their use in electric motors for vehicles and for the robotic industry as well as in medium sized generators. Ways to improve the performance of these materials is through the figure of merit known as *maximum energy product* $(BH)_{max}$. In the high energy product Nd-Fe-B magnets, however, the coercivity is low and makes them not suitable for high temperature applications. The most common technique to enhance the coercive field of these magnets is to replace some Nd by another element of heavy rare earths (Dy, Tb) [1]. However, this substitution results in a decrease of saturation magnetization due to antiferromagnetic coupling between Dy and Fe and therefore to a lower energy product.

Recently, several studies have reported, by means of structural and magnetic characterisation, an increase in the coercivity of Nd-Fe-B magnets [3-5] induced by a diffusion process of the heavy rare earth material (Dy) between the grain boundaries of the $Nd_2Fe_{14}B$ phase. This makes the Nd-rich core grains coated by a Dy-rich shell that leads to an increase in coercivity. Furthermore, the amount of Dy used for the increase in coercivity is much lower than the one used in sintered magnets (4 at.%). Likewise, diffusion process on Nd-Fe-B-type permanent magnet has been carried out using $Pr_{68}Cu_{32}$ alloy [6], where an increase in coercivity as well as an improvement in the thermal stability of their magnetic properties has been reported.

In this paper, we present preliminary results on the magnetic properties of nanocrystalline $Nd_{12}Fe_{81}B_6Nb_1$ and rare earth lean $Nd_{10}Fe_{84}B_6$ ribbons after diffusion of $Pr_{68}Cu_{32}$ through the grain boundaries.

2. Experimental

Cast samples with composition $Nd_{12}Fe_{81}B_6Nb_1$ and $Nd_{10}Fe_{84}B_6$ were prepared by arc-melting the pure constituents of Nd, Fe, Nb and B. Pieces of the cast samples were melt-spun into amorphous ribbons using a high wheel speed (v > 25 m/s). The amorphous samples were then crystallized by annealing under vacuum at different temperatures in the range of 650 - 700 °C and for different times to obtain the optimum magnetic properties. Small pieces of the optimally annealed samples were then mixed with polished tiny pieces of the low melting point (T_m = 480 °C) $Pr_{68}Cu_{32}$ ribbons and then heat treated under vacuum at 550 °C to diffuse Pr into the grain boundaries. The processed samples were then characterized by X-ray diffraction and magnetometry using an X'pert Philips diffractometer with Cu-K_α radiation source, a homemade vibrating sample magnetometer (VSM) and a SQUID magnetometer, respectively.

3. Results and Discussion

3.1. $Nd_{12}Fe_{81}B_6Nb_1$

The best hard magnetic properties for this alloy were obtained on a sample heat-treated at 650 °C for 60 min (Fig. 1) which showed a coercivity of 8.76 kOe. XRD data reveal the presence of 2:14:1 phase together with a small amount of α-iron phase (peak at 45°) (line 1 – Fig. 2). From the width of the peaks the grain size of this sample is estimated to be 76.6 nm using the corrected Scherrer's formula. The small

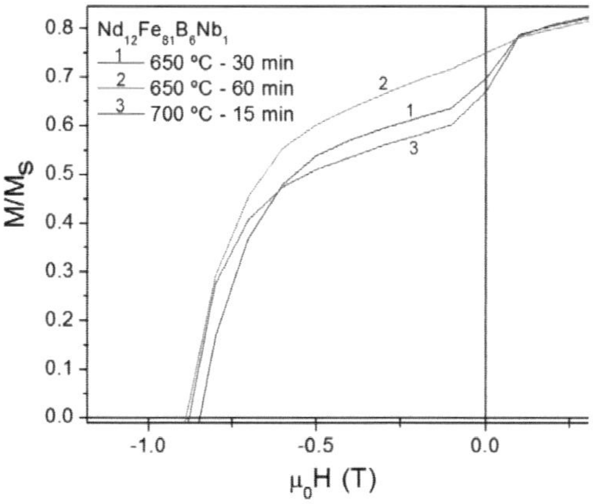

Fig. 1. Hysteretic loops of $Nd_{12}Fe_{81}B_6Nb_1$ heat treated at 650 °C and 700 °C for different times.

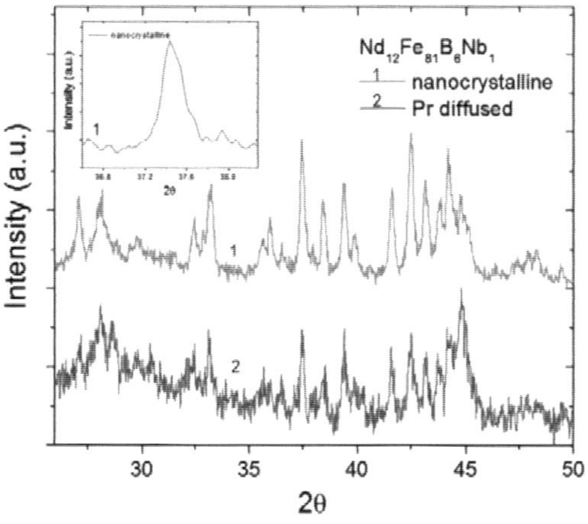

Fig. 2. XRD of $Nd_{12}Fe_{81}B_6Nb_1$ heat treated for 60 min at 650 °C, before (1) and after Pr diffusion (2). Inset: Peak of nanocrystalline sample used to estimate grain size by means of Scherrer's formula.

grain size and the high crystallinity of this sample explain its high coercivity field.

This optimally annealed sample was chosen for the preliminary diffusion experiments at 550 °C for different times with $Pr_{68}Cu_{32}$ ribbons previously polished to remove the oxidized surface layer. The last procedure resulted in an increase of coercivity to 11.33 kOe after a heat-treatment of 30 and 60 min (Fig. 3). The enhancement in coercivity increases with heat treatment time. The hysteresis loops measured with an 18 kOe field are minor loops. A more saturated hysteresis loop with a higher coercivity is obtained when the sample was measured with a SQUID magnetometer at 50 kOe. The XRD patterns of the Pr-Cu diffused samples have not changed (Fig. 2) showing the same small content of α-iron phase and the same broadness of XRD peaks indicating that the increase in the coercivity is due to the diffusion of Pr into the grain boundaries rather than an increase of nanocrystalline grains.

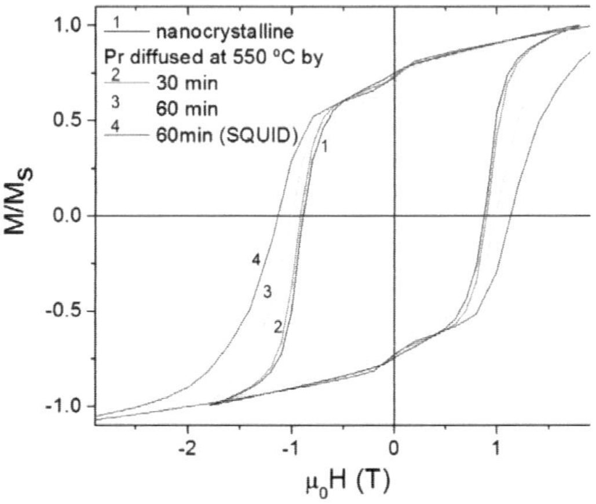

Fig. 3. Hysteretic loops of $Nd_{12}Fe_{81}B_6Nb_1$ with Pr diffused at 550 °C during 30 (2) and 60 min measured in VSM (3) and SQUID (4).

3.2. $Nd_{10}Fe_{84}B_6$

The optimization data for the rare-earth lean sample are shown in Fig. 4. The coercivity of this sample is smaller ($H_c \approx 4.4$ kOe) because of the presence of a larger amount of α-iron as shown by the XRD data (Fig. 5). From the XRD data a grain size of 80.3 nm was estimated for this sample. The lower coercivity obtained in this sample is expected based on previous studies with this composition [7]. From these results (Fig. 4) we have chosen the sample heat treated at 650 °C for 60 min (line 2) for the diffusion experiments.

We performed the same diffusion experiments on this sample but so far we have not observed an increase in coercivity (Fig. 6). We have also tried to diffuse Pr in both ribbon and powder samples at 550 °C, using a glove box to ensure a controlled atmosphere of Ar during mixing and grinding of the materials and

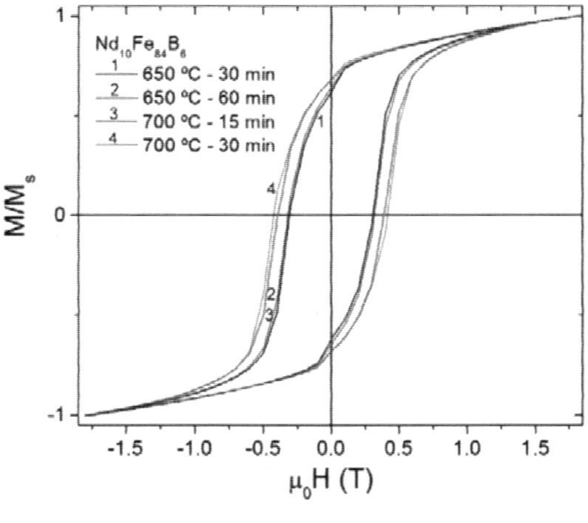

Fig. 4. Hysteretic loops for $Nd_{10}Fe_{84}B_6$ heat treated at different temperatures and times.

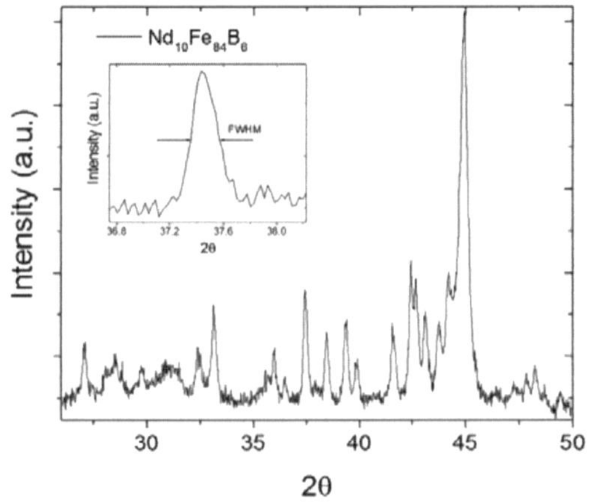

Fig. 5. X-ray diffraction of $Nd_{10}Fe_{84}B_6$ heat treated at 650 during 60 min. Inset: single peak used to estimate grain size.

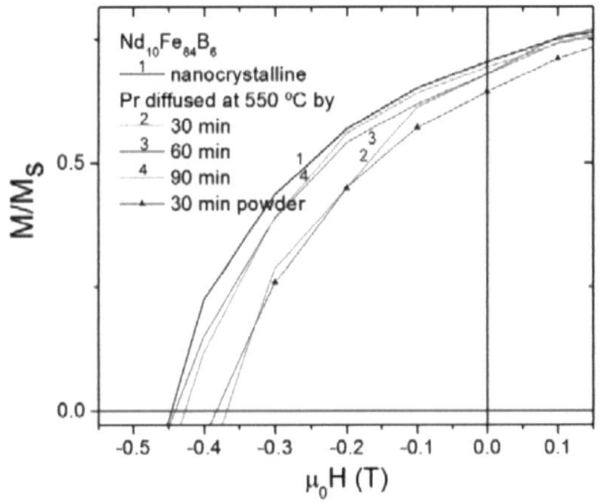

Fig. 6. Hysteretic loops of $Nd_{10}Fe_{84}B_6$ with Pr diffused at 550 °C during different times.

avoiding a possible surface oxidation by exposure to the environment, but the diffusion didn't result in a coercivity increase. However, the small shoulder observed in the loop after the diffusion experiment suggests that Pr is diffused into the grain boundaries leading to a decoupling of the soft and hard grains and therefore a lower coercivity.

We will continue our diffusion experiments on these samples at different temperatures and use TEM to obtain the microstructure of the optimally annealed samples before and after the diffusion experiments to obtain a better picture of the diffusion process in nanocrystalline Nd-Fe-B alloys.

Acknowledgments

This work was supported by the Department of Economic Development and Competitiveness of the Basque Government through ETORTEK 2013-2014. ACTIMAT project and Siemens.

References

[1] S. Hirosawa, Y. Matsuura, H. Yamamoto, S. Fujimura, and M. Sagawa, *J. Appl. Phys.* **59**, 1986, 873.

[2] Z. Lin, J. Han, J. Yang, X. Kong, X. Zhong, S. Liu, X. Zhang, C. Wang, H. Du, and Y. Yang, *Scr. Mater.* **65**, 2011, 206.

[3] Y. Ding, R. J. Chen, Z. Liu and A. R. Yan, *J. Appl. Phys.* **107**, 2010, 09A726.

[4] H. Sepehri-Amin, T. Ohkubo and K. Hono, *Acta Mater.* **61**, 2013, 1982.

[5] N. Watanabe, M. Itakura and M. Nishida, *J. Alloys Compd.* **557**, 2013, 1.

[6] Z. Lin, J. Han, M. Xing, S. Liu, R. Wu, C. Wang, Y. Zhang, Y. Yang and J. Yang, *Appl. Phys. Lett.* **100**, 2012, 052409.

[7] L. Withanawasam, Y. Zhang, A. S. Murthy, G. C. Hadjipanayis, and R. F. Krause, *Scr. Metall.* **33**, 1995, 1765.

Coercivity of Thermally or Mechanically Treated Nd-Fe-B-type HDDR Material

K.M. KIM[1], M.A. MATIN[1], H.W. KWON[1], J.G. LEE[2], J.H. YU[2]
[1] Pukyong National University, Busan, South Korea
[2] Korea Institute of Materials Science, Changwon, South Korea

Abstract: *The coercivity variation of thermally or mechanically processed HDDR-treated $Nd_{12.5}Fe_{80.6}B_{6.4}Ga_{0.3}Nb_{0.2}$ particles was investigated. The HDDR-treated powder contained significant amounts of residual hydrogen (approx. 1500 ppm) and significantly lost its coercivity when heated above around 600 °C. This significant coercivity reduction was attributed to disproportionation of the $Nd_2Fe_{14}BH_x$ hydride formed due to the residual hydrogen. Coercivity of the HDDR-treated Nd-Fe-B-type material was also radically reduced by ball milling, and this was attributed largely to the surface oxidation and the increased relative surface-grains-volume. The reduced coercivity in the milled fine particles was recovered remarkably by chemical etching of the oxidized surface.*

Key words: *Nd-Fe-B; HDDR; coercivity; residual hydrogen; chemical etching*

Address: Hae-Woong Kwon, Department of Materials Science and Engineering, Pukyong National University, Busan, 608-739, South Korea, Tel:(82-51) 629-6362, Fax: (82-51) 629-6353, E-mail: hwkwon@pknu.ac.kr

1. Introduction

The hydrogenation, disproportionation, desorption and recombination (HDDR) processed Nd-Fe-B-type materials feature important practical characteristics: high coercivity due to the very fine grain size, comparable to the single domain size (~300 nm for $Nd_2Fe_{14}B$). The HDDR-treated material has been widely used for bonded magnets and increasingly found in new applications, such as consolidated magnets [1-5]. For those applications, a thermal or mechanical processing of the HDDR-treated material is needed almost inevitably. In this article, the coercivity variation of the thermally or mechanically treated Nd-Fe-B-type HDDR-treated particles was investigated. The origin of radical coercivity reduction in the HDDR-treated Nd-Fe-B-type fine particles due to the thermal or mechanical processing is discussed. Feasibility of chemical etching for coercivity recovery in the ball milled particles was examined.

2. Experimental Work

The starting material used in the present study was HDDR-treated powder of $Nd_{12.5}Fe_{80.6}B_{6.4}Ga_{0.3}Nb_{0.2}$ alloy (iHc =13.5 kOe). The HDDR-treated material was heated in vacuum and Ar gas, and milled by ball milling (in cyclohexane) to control the size of the particles. Some of the milled particles were chemically etched using 1% Nital solution to remove the damaged surface. Hydrogen and oxygen content in the particles were determined by hydrogen determinator (LECO, RH-600) and oxygen analyser (LECO, TC-400), respectively. Microstructural characterization of the heated material was performed by TEM using hot-pressed compact. Coercivity of the prepared particles was measured by VSM. Prior to the VSM measurement, the particles were fixed with wax, and then magnetized by applying a pulsing field (4.5 T).

3. Results and Discussion

The influence of thermal processing on the coercivity of the HDDR-treated powder was examined by heating it in vacuum and Ar atmosphere. The coercivity variation of the heated powder is shown in Fig. 1, and it appears that the coercivity was reduced significantly above around 600 °C. Interestingly, the coercivity reduction was much more profound for the material heated in Ar atmosphere than in vacuum.

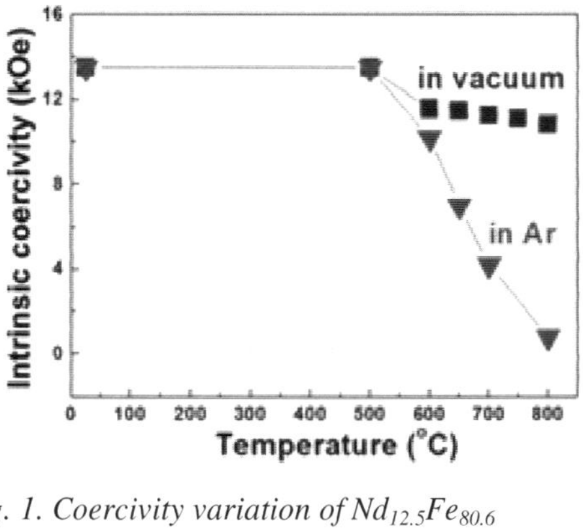

Fig. 1. Coercivity variation of $Nd_{12.5}Fe_{80.6}B_{6.4}Ga_{0.3}Nb_{0.2}$ HDDR-treated powder heated under vacuum or Ar atmosphere.

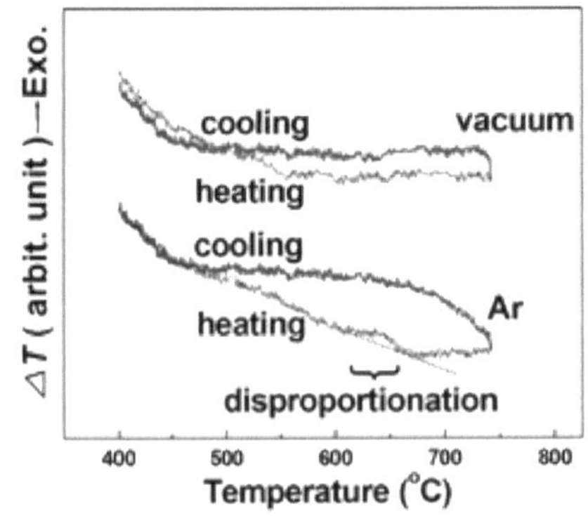

Fig. 2. DTA results for the $Nd_{12.5}Fe_{80.6}B_{6.4}Ga_{0.3}Nb_{0.2}$ HDDR-treated powder in different atmospheres.

Microstructure observation showed no significant grain growth after the heating in both the Ar and vacuum. The radical coercivity reduction in the sample heated in Ar may be closely related to the residual hydrogen in the HDDR-treated powder. The HDDR-treated initial powder contained significant amount of hydrogen (around 1500 ppm) [6,7]. The residual hydrogen was considered to exist in the form of $Nd_2Fe_{14}BH_x$ hydride, and it was disproportionated into α-Fe, Fe_2B and NdH_2 phases at an elevated temperature. The formed, magnetically soft α-Fe and Fe_2B may be responsible for the radical coercivity reduction above 600 °C in Ar atmosphere. The residual hydrogen may be desorbed more effectively in the course of heating in vacuum than in Ar gas atmosphere. This may explain the fact that coercivity reduction is less profound for the sample heated in vacuum. The disproportionation of the $Nd_2Fe_{14}BH_x$ hydride in the HDDR-treated powder was verified by DTA during heating in Ar and vacuum. As shown in Fig. 2, while no thermal event occurred during heating in vacuum, a noticeable exothermic event occurred at the temperature range of 620 °C - 655 °C during heating in Ar atmosphere. This exothermic event is

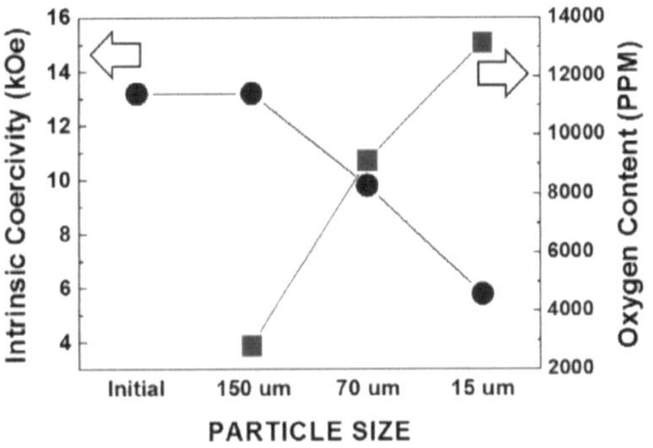

Fig. 4. Variation of coercivity and oxygen content of the particles prepared from ball milling of HDDR-treated $Nd_{12.5}Fe_{80.6}B_{6.4}Ga_{0.3}Nb_{0.2}$ alloy.

believed to correspond to the disproportionation of the $Nd_2Fe_{14}BH_x$ hydride in the HDDR-treated powder. The disproportionation due to the residual hydrogen was also evidenced by microstructural observation using the powder compact hot-pressed at a higher temperature (800 °C). In some local area in the hot-pressed compact, the α-Fe and Fe_2B phases were found as shown in Fig. 3. It is believed that these α-Fe and Fe_2B phases may have been formed by the disproportionation of the $Nd_2Fe_{14}BH_x$.

Coercivity variation of the HDDR-treated material due to mechanical processing was investigated using ball milled particles. Fig. 4 shows the coercivity variation of the HDDR-treated material as a function of particle size. Coercivity of the particles declined as the particle size decreased. The radical coercivity reduction in the milled fine particles may be attributed largely to the surface damage due to oxidation. Oxygen content in the milled particles increased radically with decreasing particle size as shown also in Fig. 4, indicating that surface of the milled particles was heavily oxidized during milling and handling afterwards. It is known that oxidation of the $Nd_2Fe_{14}B$-type compound occurs through

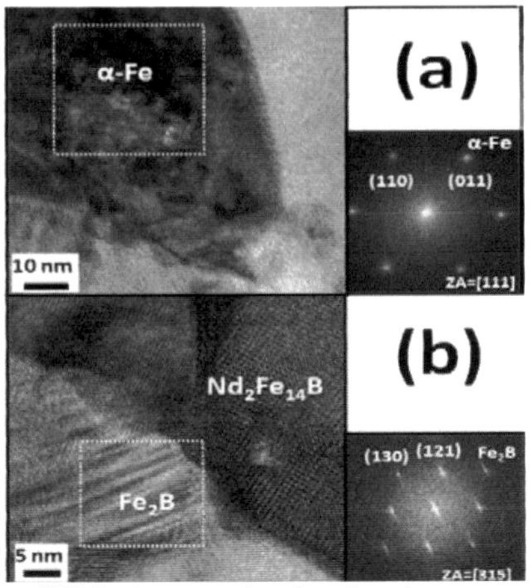

Fig. 3. TEM micrographs showing the presence of (a) α-Fe and (b) Fe_2B phases in the $Nd_{12.5}Fe_{80.6}B_{6.4}Ga_{0.3}Nb_{0.2}$ HDDR powder compacted at 800 °C.

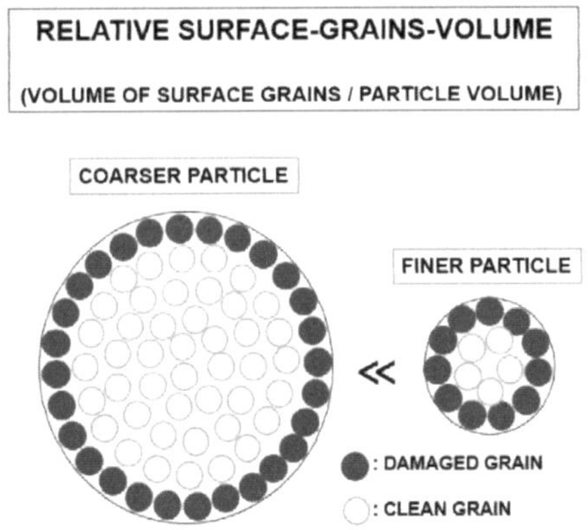

Fig. 5. Schematic showing the comparison of relative surface-grain-volume for the particles with different sizes [10].

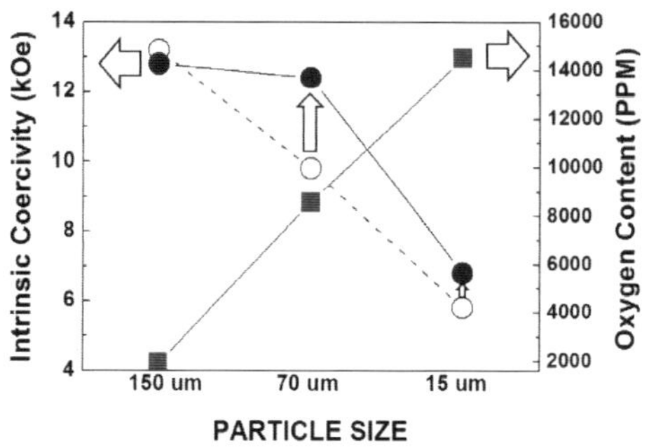

Fig. 6. Recovery of intrinsic coercivity by chemical etching and oxygen content of the fine particles prepared from ball milling of HDDR-treated $Nd_{12.5}Fe_{80.6}B_{6.4}Ga_{0.3}Nb_{0.2}$ *material.*

dissociation of the phase and leads to formation of the mixture of Nd-oxide, α-Fe and Fe-B phases [8,9]. The magnetically soft phases α-Fe, Fe-B at the surface of the fine Nd-Fe-B-type particle may facilitate the nucleation of reverse domain in a demagnetising field, hence reducing coercivity radically. Dependence of the coercivity reduction of the milled particles on the particle size can be explained by the relative surface-grains-volume. For the finer particles, the relative surface-grains-volume may be far greater with respect to the coarser particles (Fig. 5). Therefore, the impact of such a heavily oxidized surface on the coercivity deterioration may be far more profound for the finer particles. Removing the surface-oxidized layer, then, should result in the recovery of coercivity in the milled particles. The oxidized surface was removed with chemical etching using 1% Nital solution, and the coercivity recovery was presented in Fig. 6. It appeared that coercivity of the milled fine particles (in particular, 70 um particles) was recovered significantly by the chemical etching.

4. Conclusion

The HDDR-treated Nd-Fe-B-type material lost significantly its coercivity upon heating above around 600 °C, and this was attributed to the disproportionation of the $Nd_2Fe_{14}BH_x$ hydride formed by the residual hydrogen. Coercivity of the HDDR-treated material was also radically reduced by ball milling, and this was attributed largely to the surface oxidation and increased relative surface-grains-volume. The reduced coercivity in the milled fine particles was recovered remarkably by chemical etching of the oxidized surface.

Acknowledgement

The author H. W. Kwon would like to acknowledge that the present work was supported by Pukyong National University Research Promotion Program (2011).

References

[1] S. Yamashita, J. Yamasaki, M. Ikeda, N. Iwabuchi, *J. Appl. Phys.*, 1991, 70, 6627–6629.
[2] M. Nakano, R. Katoh, H. Fukunaga, S. Tutumi, F. Yamashita, *IEEE Trans. Magn.*, 2003, 39, 2863–2865.
[3] H. Nakamura, K. Hirota, M. Shimao, T. Minowa, M. Honshima, *IEEE Trans. Magn.*, 2005, 41, 3844-3846.
[4] O. M. Ragg, I. R. Harris, H. Nagel, P. Bohm, *IEEE Trans. Magn.,* 1996, 32, 4395-4397.
[5] N. Nozawa, H. S. A., T. Ohkubo, K. Hono, T. Nishiuchi, S. Hirosawa, *J. Magn. Magn. Mater.*, 2011, 323, 115-121.
[6] M. A. Matin, H. W. Kwon, J. G. Lee, J. H.Yu, T. H. Kim , C. W. Yang, *IEEE Trans. Magn.* 2013, 49, 3398-3401.
[7] T. Nishiuchi, S. Hirosawa, et al., *IEEE IEEJ Trans.,* 2008, 3, 390–393.
[8] Y. Li, H. E. Evans, I. R. Harris, I. P. Jones, 2003, 59, 167-182.
[9] H. W. Kwon, J. H. Yu, *J. Korean Magn. Soc.*, 2012, 22, 85-90.
[10] H. W. Kwon, J. G. Lee, J. H. Yu, *J. Appl. Phys.*, 2014, 115, 17A727-1 - 17A727-3.

Effect of DyCu Doping of Hot-Compacted and Die-Upset Nd-Fe-B Magnets

S. SAWATZKI[1], S. ENER[1], CHR. KÜBEL[2], O. GUTFLEISCH[1,3]
[1]Technische Universität Darmstadt, Materialwissenschaft, Alarich-Weiß-Str. 16, 64287 Darmstadt, Germany
[2]KIT, Institute of Nanotechnology & Karlsruhe Nano Micro Facility, P.O. Box 3640, 76021 Karlsruhe, Germany
[3]IWKS Hanau, Fraunhofer-Projektgruppe für Wertstoffkreisläufe und Ressourcenstrategie, 63457 Hanau, Germany

Abstract: *Nd-Fe-B melt-spun ribbons have been hot-compacted together with a $Dy_{70}Cu_{30}$ low melting eutectic in order to enhance coercivity. In the first part of this study, hot-compacted magnets have been annealed at 600°C which increases coercivity. Scanning transmission electron microscopy images as well as energy dispersive X-ray spectroscopy maps reveal a Dy and Cu enrichment within the grain boundaries well away from the initial flake boundary, which suggests a Dy and Cu diffusion during annealing. Following this, hot-compacted magnets have been directly die-upset in the second part without additional annealing in order to prepare textured magnets. High resolution transmission electron microscopy images show large $Nd_2Fe_{14}B$ grains which form at the Dy-Nd-Cu-O rich flake boundaries during die-upsetting. These large grains explain the low effective increase in coercivity of 0.11 T / wt.% Dy compared to 0.26 T / wt.% Dy for the hot-compacted sample after annealing.*

Keywords: *permanent magnet; Nd-Fe-B; grain boundary diffusion process; DyCu*

Address: Simon Sawatzki, Technische Universität Darmstadt, Alarich-Weiß-Str. 16, 64287 Darmstadt, Germany, Tel: +49(0)6151-16-75781, E-Mail: sawatzki@fm.tu-darmstadt.de

1. Introduction

The high price volatility of the heavy rare earth element Dy and the ongoing strong demand for high performance Nd-Fe-B magnets for electric hybrid vehicles (HEVs) and wind turbines enforces the development of new concepts to increase the thermal stability of Nd-Fe-B magnets without losing remanent magnetization [1]. One concept to use Dy more efficiently is the grain boundary diffusion process (GBDP), which has been widely studied for sintered magnets [2-4]. For nanocrystalline hot-pressed magnets, only a low temperature annealing can be applied for the diffusion process [5], therefore the use of heavy rare earth containing low-melting alloys have been investigated [6,7]. In our previous work the doping, especially of DyCu, was shown to be a promising alternative approach to the conventional coating process used for GBDP [8]. The present study provides a more detailed understanding of this process, by characterizing the microstructure with high resolution. Furthermore, first steps have been undertaken to prepare application relevant textured magnets be means of die-upsetting.

2. Experimental Procedure

The $Dy_{70}Cu_{30}$ low melting eutectic has been prepared by arc-melting and subsequent melt-spinning with a wheel speed of 30 m/s. The ribbons were ground and sieved with a mesh size of 250 μm and finally hot-compacted together with commercially available MQU-F melt spun ribbons (Molycorp Magnequench) at 725 °C at 150 MPa for 2 min. in vacuum. For a detailed analysis of the low melting eutectic, the reader is referred to [8]. First, hot-compacted magnets have been annealed at 600 °C in argon and subsequently rapidly quenched. Then, a second series of hot-compacted magnets have been die-upset in argon without having been annealed at 600°C before. The strain rate $\dot{\varphi}$ was 0.002 s^{-1} and the deformation temperature 750 °C. The degree of deformation $\varphi = \ln (h_{start}/h_{end})$ was 0.77 (with h_{start} and h_{end} representing the sample height before and after die-upsetting, respectively). This results in a height reduction of 54%.

Magnetic properties have been characterized in a pulse magnetometer (Metis Instruments) using fields up to 7 T or in a Permagraph C300 (Magnet Physik) using fields up to 2.3 T having magnetized the samples with a 5 T pulse field along the pressing direction beforehand. To study the phase distribution backscattered electron (BSE) images have been taken with a high-resolution scanning electron microscope (HR-SEM) JEOL 7600F operating at 20 kV.

Bright field (BF) and high angle annular dark field (HAADF) scanning transmission electron microscopy (STEM), energy dispersive X-ray spectroscopy (EDS)

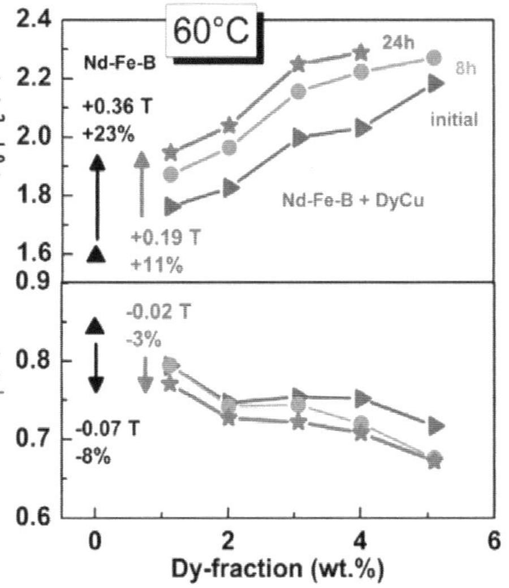

Fig. 1. Coercivity and remanence of hot-compacted samples measured at 60°C as a function of Dy-fraction for different annealing duration at 600°C.

and high resolution transmission electron microscopy (HR-TEM) were conducted using a FEI Tecnai F20-ST. TEM lamellas have been prepared by focused ion beam (FIB) in a FEI Strata 400S microscope using 30 keV Ga-ions.

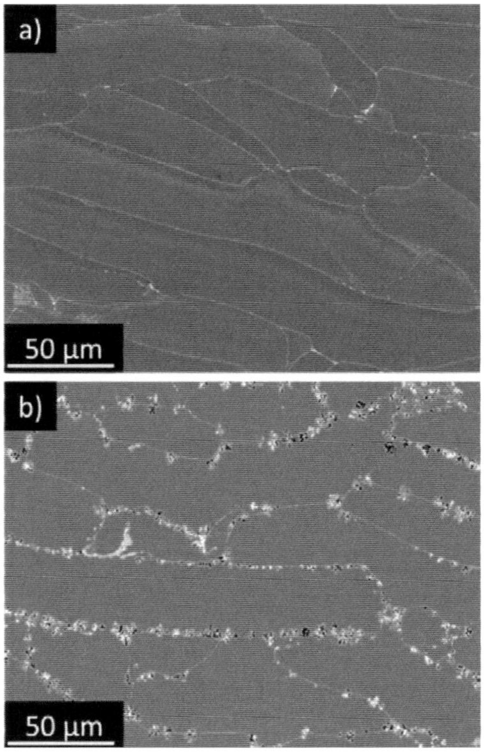

Fig. 2 BSE cross sections of hot-compacted samples with 2 wt.% Dy a) before and b) after annealing at 600 °C for 24 h.

3. Results and Discussion

The as-compacted magnets show a linear increase in coercivity and a linear decrease in remanence with increasing DyCu or Dy fraction, respectively (see Figure 1). The first can be explained by the formation of a $(Dy,Nd)_2Fe_{14}B$ phase with enhanced magnetocrystalline anisotropy compared to $Nd_2Fe_{14}B$. The latter is due to the addition of paramagnetic DyCu and the lower saturation magnetization of $Dy_2Fe_{14}B$. With longer annealing time at 600 °C, the coercivity increases by approximately 11%, whereas remanence decreases only by 3%. Both can be explained by Dy-diffusion along the grain boundaries and the formation of $(Dy,Nd)_2Fe_{14}B$ shells. The highest effective increase in coercivity compared to a Dy-free magnet is about 0.32 T / wt.% Dy (measured at 60 °C) and 0.26 T / wt.% Dy (measured at 23 °C) using 1.12 wt.% Dy. Both values are above 0.2 T / wt.% Dy which is a common value for a homogenous Dy distribution.

Figure 2 clearly shows that the microstructure changes drastically during annealing at 600 °C. In [8], it has already been reported that large Nd-rich precipitates form at the flake boundaries and that energy dispersive X-ray analysis in SEM does not reveal significant Dy-diffusion. From the STEM and EDS images in Figure 3 one can clearly see a Dy enrichment at the grain boundaries well away from the flake boundary after annealing, which supports the model of the GBDP and explains the increase in coercivity during annealing.

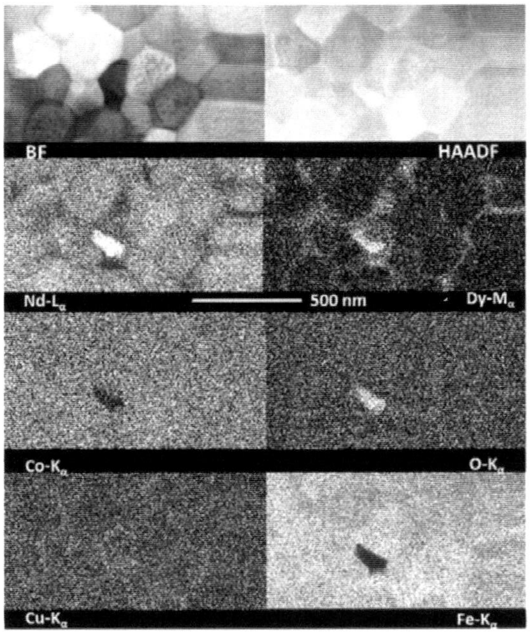

Fig. 3. STEM images and EDS elemental maps within the flake of a hot-compacted sample after annealing at 600 °C for 24 h.

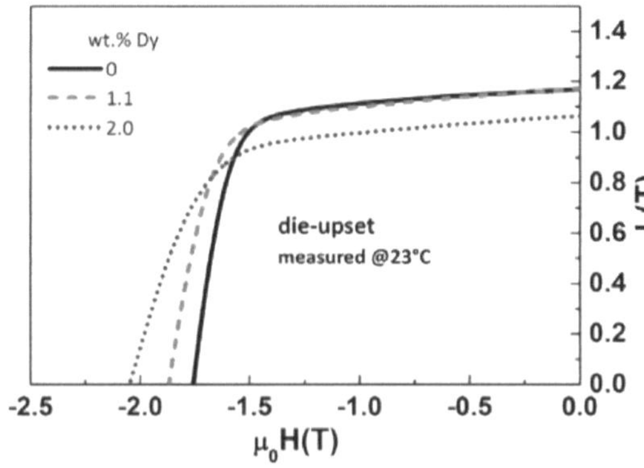

Fig. 4 Demagnetizing curves of die-upset magnets with different Dy fractions.

A second finding is a low Cu enrichment at the grain boundaries after annealing, which is also known to increase coercivity in die-upset magnets [9].

Die-upset magnets show an increase in coercivity with increasing Dy-fraction, in combination with an unreduced remanence for 1 wt.% Dy. Both features demonstrate that such a magnet can be used at higher temperature providing the same performance. The effective increase in coercivity amounts 0.11 T / wt.% Dy, which is below the average value of 0.2 T /wt.% Dy for a homogenous Dy distribution. From Figure 5 this reduced effective increase in coercivity can be explained by the formation of large $Nd_2Fe_{14}B$ grains during die-upsetting, which reduce the coercivity and diminish the positive effect of Dy. These large grains are delineated as a dark contrast in (d) at Nd-Dy-Cu-O-rich flake boundaries (a+b), which have been identified as large $Nd_2Fe_{14}B$ grains from Fourier transformed HR-TEM images (c).

4. Conclusion

It has been shown for hot-compacted DyCu doped magnets that after a low temperature annealing of 600 °C Dy and Cu is enriched in the grain boundaries. This feature explains the enhanced effective increase in coercivity of 0.26 T / wt.% Dy and 0.32 T / wt.% Dy measured at 23 °C and 60 °C, respectively. Die-upsetting of the as-compacted magnets, led to the formation of large $Nd_2Fe_{14}B$ grains at the Dy-, Nd-, Cu- and O-rich flake boundaries, which diminish the

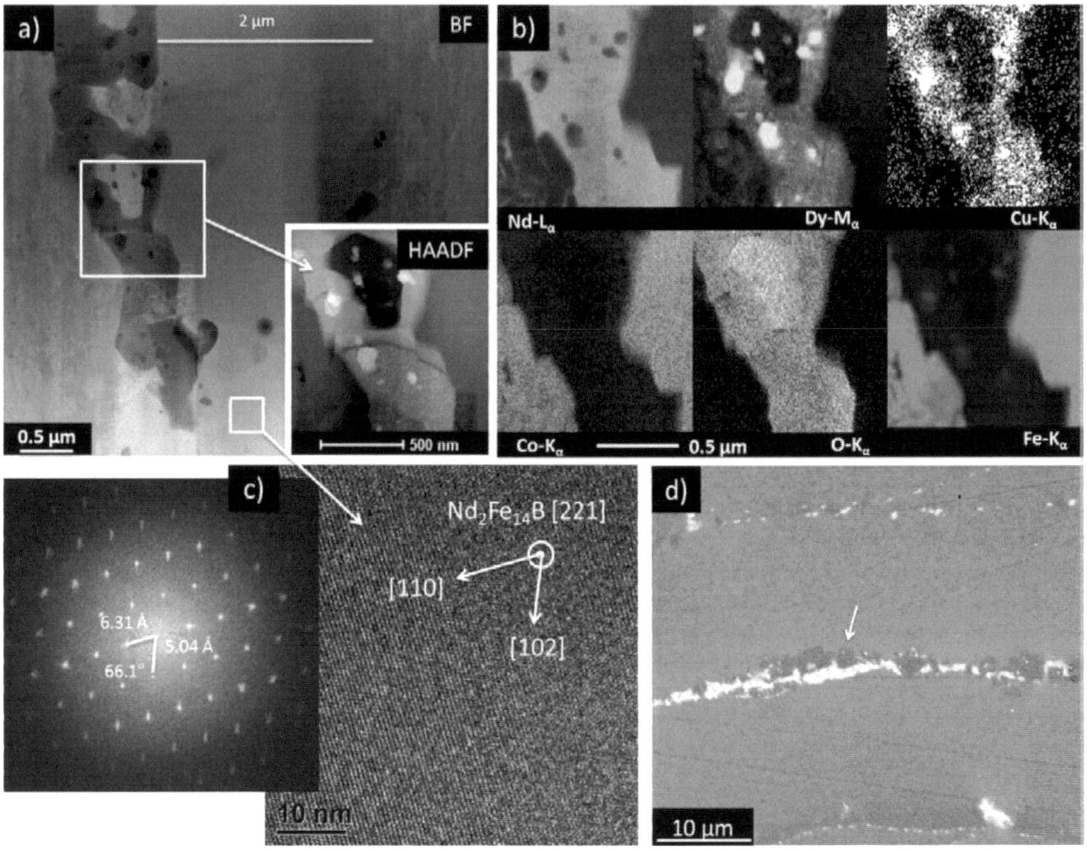

Fig. 5. a) STEM overview image with b) detailed EDS elemental maps. In d) SEM BSE cross section images of a flake boundary is shown for a die-upset magnet with 2 wt.% Dy. The arrow in d) marks the position of the TEM lamella and the 2 µm thick region in a.) The HR-TEM image in c) and the corresponding Fourier transformed identifies that this regions consists of $Nd_2Fe_{14}B$ grains.

effective increase in coercivity to 0.11 T / wt.% Dy. Nevertheless, the addition of 1 wt.% Dy enhances coercivity from 1.77 T to 1.88 T keeping remanence constant at 1.14 T. This demonstrates the potential of doping die-upset magnets with low melting eutectics.

Acknowledgements

We thank Almut Dirks and Bianca Frincu for scanning electron microscopy and the BMWi (Bundesministerium f. Wirtschaft und Technologie) via IGF (Industrielle Gemeinschaftsforschung), AiF (Allianz Industrie Forschung), FVA (Forschungsvereinigung Antriebstechnik e.V.) and the HMWK (Hessisches Ministerium f. Wiss. und Kunst.) via LOEWE RESPONSE for financial support.

References

[1] O. Gutfleisch, M. A. Willard, E. Bruck, C. H. Chen, S. G. Sankar, and J. P. Liu, *Adv. Mater.* **23**, 2011, 821.

[2] K. Park, K. Hiraga, and M. Sagawa, in: H. Kaneko, M. Homma, M. Okada (Eds.), *REPM Proceedings of 16th International Workshop on RE Magnets and their Applications*, The Japan Institute of Metals, Sendai, Japan, 2000, pp. 257–264.

[3] N. Oono, M. Sagawa, R. Kasada, H. Matsui, and A. Kimura, *J. Magn. Magn. Mater.* **323**, 2011, 297.

[4] H. Sepehri-Amin, T. Ohkubo, and K. Hono, *J. Appl. Phys.* **107**, 2010, 09A745.

[5] S. Sawatzki, I. Dirba, H. Wendrock, L. Schultz, and O. Gutfleisch. *J. Magn. Magn. Mater.* **358-359**, 2014, 163-169

[6] H. Sepehri-Amin, D. Prabhu, M. Hayashi, T. Ohkubo, K. Hioki, A. Hattori, and K. Hono, *Scripta Mater.* **68**, 2013, 167.

[7] B. Z. Cui, L. Y. Zheng, M. Marinescu, J. F. Liu, and G. C. Hadjipanayis, *J. Appl. Phys.* **111**, 2012, 07A735.

[8] S. Sawatzki, A. Dirks, B. Frincu, K. Löwe, and O. Gutfleisch. *J. Appl. Phys.* **115**, 2014, 17A705.

[9] C. Fuerst, E. Brewer, *Appl. Phys. Lett.* **56**, 1990, 2252.

Grain-Boundary Diffusion of Pr-Fe-B Magnets for Cryogenic Applications

C. BROMBACHER, K. UESTUENER, F.-J. BOERGERMANN, M. KATTER
Vacuumschmelze GmbH & Co. KG, Hanau, Germany

Abstract: *Conventional Pr-Fe-B magnets for low temperature applications frequently suffer the risk of partial demagnetization when handled at room temperature (RT). To increase the coercivity of Pr-Fe-B magnets at RT without sacrificing the remanent magnetic polarization, a grain-boundary-diffusion (GBD) process using Tb can be applied which allows the manufacturing of Pr-Fe-B magnets with H_{cJ} = 1800 kA/m and B_r = 1.41 T at 293 K and H_{cJ} = 6300 kA/m and B_r = 1.62 T at 77 K. The temperature dependence of the coercivity increase induced by the GBD correlates well with the different anisotropy fields of $Pr_2Fe_{14}B$ and $Tb_2Fe_{14}B$ supporting the model of higher nucleation fields due to Tb-rich high anisotropy $(Pr,Tb)_2Fe_{14}B$ layers along the grain-boundaries. The coercivtiy gradients induced by the GBD process have been determined and an increase in H_{cJ} has been observed up to a depth of ~4 mm.*

Keywords: *Pr-Fe-B, grain-boundary diffusion; spin-reorientation transition (SRT); coercivity; anisotropy*

Address: C. Brombacher, Vacuumschmelze GmbH & Co. KG, Grüner Weg 37, 63450 Hanau, Germany, Tel: +49 6181 382833, Fax: +49 6181 3882833, E-Mail: christoph.brombacher@vacuumschmelze.com

1. Introduction

It is well known that the usage of Nd-Fe-B magnets at cryogenic temperatures is limited to temperatures $T > \sim 140$ K due to the spin-reorientation transition (SRT) [1,2]. It was recently demonstrated that this transition temperature can be decreased by replacing Nd with Pr which allows the fabrication of magnets with a maximum energy density of $(BH)_{max}$ = 520 kJ/m³ at T = 85 K [3]. These Pr-Fe-B based magnet qualities have excellent properties for low temperature applications like cryogenic permanent magnet undulators [4–6]. However, due to the limited coercivity at room temperature (RT) and the corresponding risk of partial demagnetization when no cooling is applied, only a few prototypes using this class of material have been built. This issue can be solved by applying a grain-boundary-diffusion (GBD) process, a technology first established by Park et al. [7]. We will provide actual data on the performance of commercially available Pr-Fe-B based magnet grades after implementation of GBD. The temperature dependence of the magnetic properties as well as the thickness limitations associated with the application of the GBD process will be discussed.

2. Magnetic Properties

Typical demagnetization curves of Pr-Fe-B magnets fabricated by conventional pressing and sintering technology (VACODYM® 131 TP) as well as by state-of-the-art GBD technology using Tb as the diffusing heavy rare earth (HRE) element (VACODYM 131 DTP) are shown in Fig. 1. A minimum increase in coercivity by GBD of ΔH_{cJ} = 400 kA/m without a significant loss in remanent magnetic polarization can be observed.

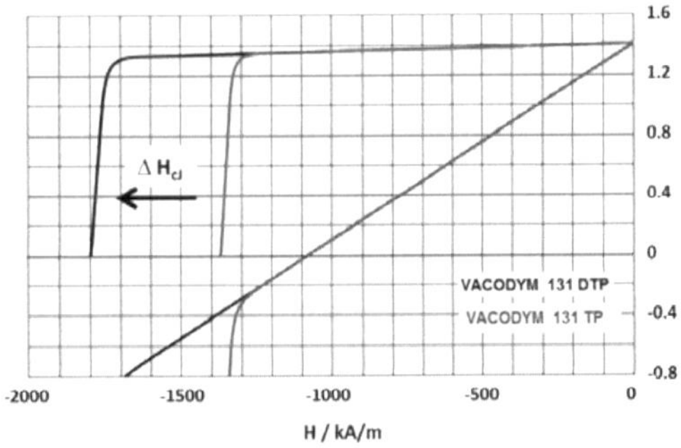

Fig. 1. Typical demagnetization curves of VACODYM 131 TP and VACODYM 131 DTP magnets at RT. The field was applied parallel to the direction of orientation.

Table I. Specifications of VACODYM 131 TP and VACODYM 131 DTP

Characteristic	VD 131 TP	VD 131 DTP
Remanence B_r at 293 K (T)	≥ 1.38	≥ 1.38
Coercivity H_{cJ} at 293 K (kA/m)	≥ 1230	≥ 1640
Remanence B_r at 77 K (T)	≥ 1.58	≥ 1.58
Coercivity H_{cJ} at 77 K (kA/m)	> 3185	> 3185

A summary of the minimum remanence and coercivity values of these new material grades are given in Table I. Please note that the magnetic specification of the GBD processed magnet quality is restricted regarding the dimensions of the magnet.

While the reversible permeability $\mu_{rev\parallel}$ along the direction of orientation is around 1.03 at RT and corresponds to typical values of Nd-Fe-B based magnet grades, the reversible permeability $\mu_{rev\perp}$ perpendicular to the direction of orientation is 1.2 ± 0.05 (Fig. 2). To minimize the occurance of domain wall motion the sample was saturated along the direction of orientation followed by a reverse field pulse with $H \sim H_{cJ}$ prior to the measurement of $\mu_{rev\perp}$. By extrapolating the *J-H* loops to higher fields the anisotropy field was estimated to $H_a \sim 6000$ kA/m which corresponds well with literature data [2]. As most of the magnet volume is not effected by the diffusion process, no difference in $\mu_{rev\perp}$ can be observed for conventional and GBD processed Pr-Fe-B magnet grades.

3. Temperature Dependence

The temperature dependence of the remanent magnetic polarization shows no indication of SRT down to temperatures of ~4 K and no significant differences between the two magnet grades can be detected [Fig. 3(a)].

Additionally, B_r shows only a small increase for temperatures below T = 77 K and consequently cooling with liquid helium does not lead to a superior magnetic performance.

Both magnet qualities show a pronounced increase in coercivity upon cooling to cryogenic temperatures and values of up to ~7000 kA/m can be achieved [Fig. 3 (b)]. The difference in coercivity ΔH_{cJ} between the conventional Pr-Fe-B magnet and the GBD processed quality is around 470 kA/m – 540 kA/m for temperatures below RT.

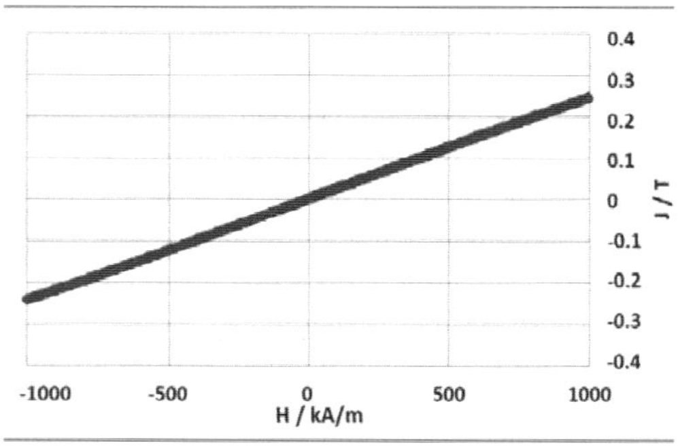

Fig. 2. J-H loop of VACODYM 131 DTP at RT with the field applied perpendicular to the direction of orientation.

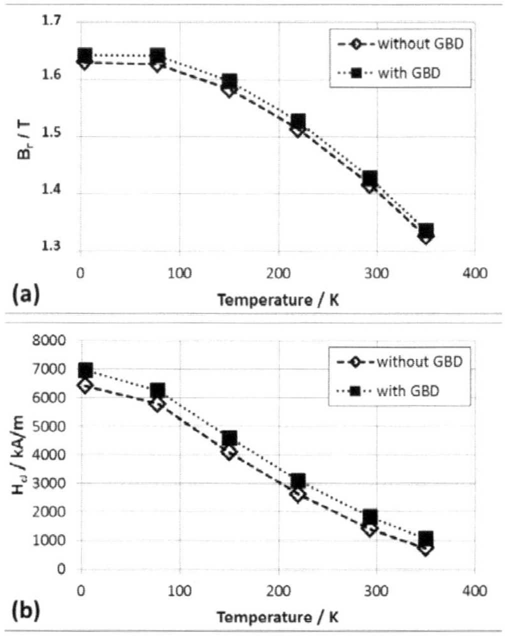

Fig. 3. Temperature dependence of (a) B_r and (b) H_{cJ} of Pr-Fe-B magnets after conventional fabrication without GBD and after fabrication involving a GBD process.

No scaling of the absolute value of ΔH_{cJ} can be observed in this temperature regime. The relative increase of ΔH_{cJ} with respect to the conventional magnet quality is, however, systematically decreasing towards lower temperatures (Fig. 4).

This trend correlates with the relative increase of $\Delta H_a = (H_{a,Tb2Fe14B} - H_{a,Pr2Fe14B}) / H_{a,Pr2Fe14B}$ indicating that the anisotropy differences of $Pr_2Fe_{14}B$ and $Tb_2Fe_{14}B$ have the major impact on ΔH_{cJ} . Thus, for sintered magnets with magnetically decoupled 2-14-1 grains, the origin for the coercivity increase is most likely related to the formation of Tb-enriched high anisotropy $(Pr,Tb)_2Fe_{14}B$ layers along the grain boundaries. No indication that the GBD process is

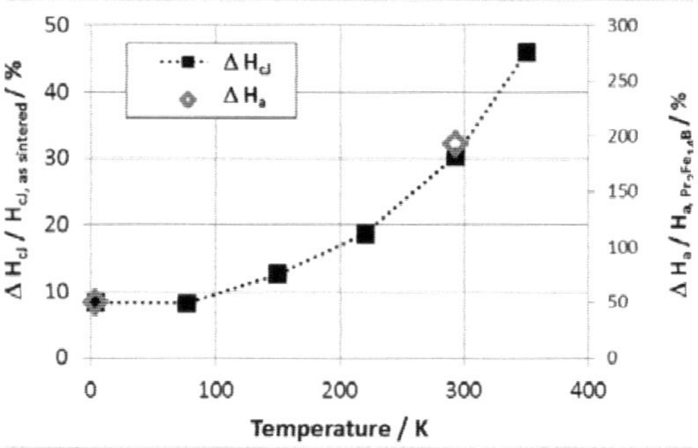

Fig. 4. Temperature dependence of the relative coercivity difference between conventional Pr-Fe-B magnets and Pr-Fe-B magnets after application of a GBD process, as well as the relative difference in H_a of $Pr_2Fe_{14}B$ and $Tb_2Fe_{14}B$ at 4 K and 295 K [2].

leading to a better decoupling of the grains, as for example reported for fine grained HDDR magnets [8], was observed.

4. Coercivity Gradient

The GBD process does not lead to homogenious local coercivities when it is applied to magnets with thicknesses t exceeding 5 mm. Figure 5 shows the distribution of the typical local coercivities at RT and 100°C of magnets with thicknesses >> 5 mm which have been processed with the GBD technology. It can be clearly seen that in the proximity of the Tb – coated surface, the local coercivity of the material can easily exceed 1800 kA/m at RT. With increasing distance d to the surface, the local coercivity drops and for $d > 4$ mm no increase in coercivity can be observed which is typically limiting the application of the GBD process to magnets with $t < 5$ mm. The application of the GBD process on thicker magnets is only beneficial if the strongest demagnetization fields occur close to the surface of the magnet.

5. Summary

With the development of two new magnet qualities based on Pr-Fe-B, magnetic material for the construction of cryogenic permanent magnet assemblies is commercially available. The implementation of the GBD process leads to an increased coercivity and sufficient resistivity against thermal demagnetization even at slightly elevated temperatures. The analysis of the temperature dependence of H_{cJ} reveals a good correlation with the anisotropy fields.

For thick magnets, the penetration depth of the diffusing element is limited to ~4 mm leading to a systematic drop of the local coercivity with increasing distance d to the coated surface.

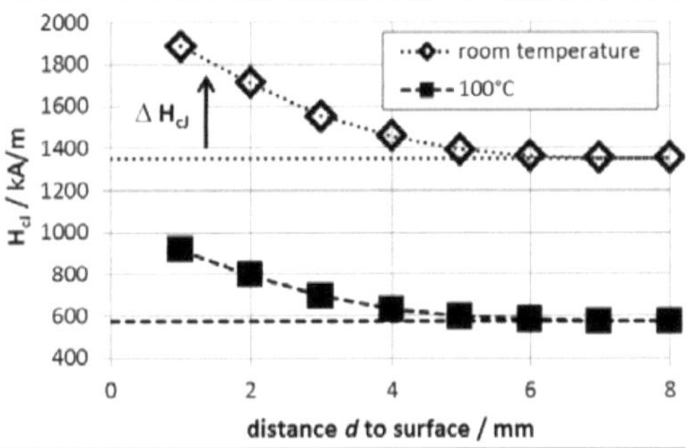

Fig. 5. Coercivity distribution of Pr-Fe-B magnets after GBD at RT and 100°C in dependence of the distance to the Tb - coated surface. The homogenious coercivity of Pr-Fe-B without GBD is indicated for comparison.

Acknowledgement
The implementation of low temperature magnetic measurements by Fraunhofer IWKS / TU Darmstadt is gratefully acknowledged.

References

[1] S. Hirosawa et al., *J. Appl. Phys.* **59**, 1986, 873.
[2] J. F. Herbst, *Rev. Mod. Phys.* **63**, 1991, 819.
[3] K. Uestuener et al., in: *Proc. 20th Int. Workshop on Rare Earth Magnets and their Applications*, Crete, 2008 , p. 397.
[4] C. Benabderrahmane et al., *NIM in Phy. Res. Sec. A* **669**, 2012, 1.
[5] T. Tanabe et al., SRI'09, Melbourne, *AIP Conf. Proc.* **1234**, 2009, 29.
[6] J Bahrdt et al., SRI'09, Melbourne, *AIP Conf. Proc.* **1234**, 2009, 499.
[7] K. T. Park et al., in: *Proc. 16th Int. Workshop on Rare Earth Magnets and their Applications*, JIM, 2000, p. 257.
[8] Z. Lin et al., *Appl. Phys. Lett.* **100**, 2012, 052409.

Grain Boundary Diffusion in Nd-Fe-B Permanent Magnets using an Electrochemical HRE Deposition Process

G. SUPPAN[1,2], M. RUEHRIG[2], C. BROMBACHER[3], M. KATTER[3]
[1] Institute of Physical and Theoretical Chemistry, University of Regensburg, Germany
[2] Siemens AG, Erlangen, Germany
[3] Vacuumschmelze GmbH & Co. KG, Hanau, Germany

Abstract: *To enhance the coercivity of sintered Nd-Fe-B magnets, the newly developed electrochemical deposition of dysprosium was investigated as the first step of the grain boundary diffusion process. For this purpose, an electrolyte consisting of the hydrophobic, air- and water-stable ionic liquid 1-butyl-1-methylpyrrolidinium bis(trifluoromethanesulfon)imide and tailor-made dysprosium bis(trifluoro-methanesulfon)imide salt were applied. A coating thickness of 2.6 µm was achieved and the coercivity increased by 20.4%.*

Key words: *grain boundary diffusion; electrochemical deposition; dysprosium; ionic liquids*

Address: Manfred Rührig, Siemens AG, Erlangen, Germany, Tel:+ 49 9131 31785 Fax: +49 9131 7-32469, E-Mail: manfred.ruehrig@siemens.com

1. Introduction

Due to their excellent magnetic properties, Neodymium-Iron-Boron magnets are widely used in high performance electric machines. In many of those applications, high coercivity grades are essential to avoid demagnetization, e.g., in high reverse fields and/or at high temperatures. It is well known that the anisotropy of the $Nd_2Fe_{14}B$ phase can be increased by substituting Nd with heavy rare earth (HRE) elements like Dy or Tb. However the substitution of Nd by the relatively scarce HRE elements is not only very costly but also results in a lower magnetization of the magnet. An increasing demand in Nd-Fe-B-based magnets for high performance applications like e-cars and wind turbines has made HRE-saving an earnest goal. A very efficient method to increase the coercivity H_{cJ} whilst substantially reducing the required amount of Dy is referred to as grain boundary diffusion process (GBDP) [1]. The GBDP is based on an interdiffusion of HRE at elevated temperatures along the grain boundaries of a sintered magnet, leading to a high anisotropy shell infolding the NdFeB grains. The high anisotropy shells lead to the suppression of reverse domain nucleation processes and thus to an enhanced coercivity. So far, various types of diffusion sources for the HRE have been reported, ranging from HRE vapor phase [2] to fluoride based coatings [3], and metallic layers deposited by PVD (sputtering) from HRE metallic targets [4].

In this work we describe for the first time a route to coat Nd-Fe-B sintered magnet blocks with HRE elements (Dy) using a novel electrochemical deposition process. The electrolytes are based on hydrophobic, air- and water-stable ionic liquids. The electrochemical deposition process leads to metallic coatings and avoids impurities such as halides or oxides which are introduced with the use of HRE-containing suspensions and powders.

2. Experimental Procedure

Commercially available sintered magnets (VACODYM 722 HR, Vacuumschmelze GmbH & Co KG) with an initial Dy-content of 0.5 wt% were used as staring material. 1-butyl-1-methylpyrrolidinium bis(trifluoromethylsuflonyl)imide, 1-butyl-3-methylimidazolium trifluoromethanesulfonate and copper trifluoromethanesulfonate were purchased from Sigma Aldrich and dried in vacuum at 100 °C overnight. Tailor-made Dy-salt was prepared after [6]. Pure Cu and Dy sheets were purchased from Sigma Aldrich and were used as counter electrodes for copper and dysprosium plating, respectively.

A 20ml Teflon cell was used for the plating process with a three-electrode-configuration and a Ag/Ag^+ reference electrode [6]. The coated samples were rinsed with dry acetone to remove any ionic liquid residue. All electrochemical measurements were performed in an argon filled glove box on an Autolab PGStat 30 (Metrohm Filderstadt, Germany) controlled by Nova 1.6 software. Subsequent to the coating procedure, the samples were annealed at 900 °C for 6h and aged at 500 °C for 2h. Magnetic characterization was done in a Capacitive Discharge Magnetizer (HyMPulse from METIS, Leuven, Belgium)

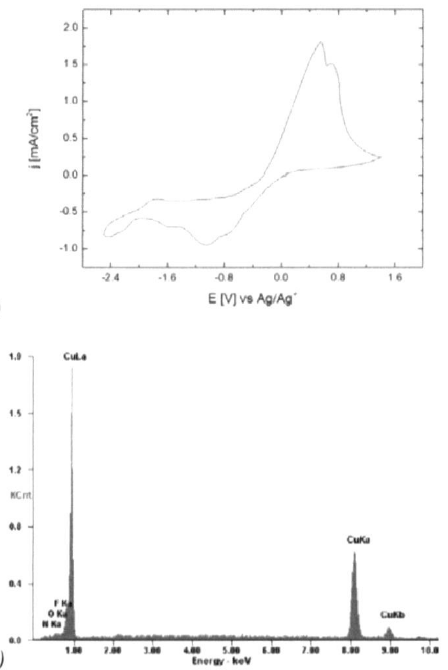

(a)

(b)

Fig. 1. (a) Cyclic voltammogram of the Cu electrolyte recorded with a scan rate of 5mV/s. (b) EDX pattern.

3. Results and Discussion

3.1. Electroplating of copper as adhesion layer

The reason for plating Cu before Dy was twofold:

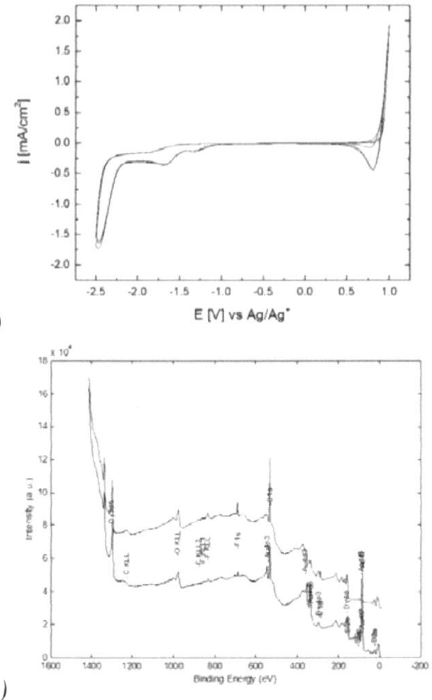

(a)

(b)

Fig. 2. (a) Cyclic voltammogram of the Dy electrolyte recorded with a scan rate of 5mV/s. (b) EDX pattern before and after sputtering

preliminary experiments showed the deposition of Dy to be feasible as a dense, adhesive layer on Cu substrates and small Cu additions showed not to be detrimental to the magnetic properties [7]; furthermore, the Cu-coating protects the sample from any hydrogen produced by residual amounts of water in the electrolyte during the Dy deposition. 10x10x3 mm³ sized Nd-Fe-B-sintered magnet samples were plated with copper from a deposition bath consisting of 1-butyl-3-methylimidazolium trifluoromethanesulfonate and 0.2 mol/kg copper trifluoromethanesulfonate in a potentiostatic procedure at -1.0V vs Ag/Ag^+ for 15 min at 100 °C to obtain coatings of about 100nm thickness. A cyclic voltammogram of the copper electrolyte on an Au substrate is shown in Fig. 1(a). EDX patterns of the as-deposited Cu are shown in Fig 1(b).

3.2. Electroplating of dysprosium

Dy was deposited on the Cu-coated samples from 0.2 mol/kg tailor-made dysprosium bis(trifluoromethylsulfonyl)imide in 1-butyl-1-methylpyrrolidinium bis(trifluoromethylsulfonyl)imide at 150°C for deposition times between 1 and 9 h in galvanostatic mode with a fixed current density of 0.5 mA/cm^2. The corresponding voltammogram is shown in Fig. 2(a). The XPS pattern of the as-deposited and cleaned (Ar-sputtered) surface of the Dy layer is shown in Fig. 2 (b).

3.3. Magnetic measurements and comparison after GBDP

Magnetic measurements after subsequent grain boundary diffusion process showed an increase in coercivity. Fig. 3 shows a comparison of electrochemically coated samples to reference samples based on conventional PVD-coatings

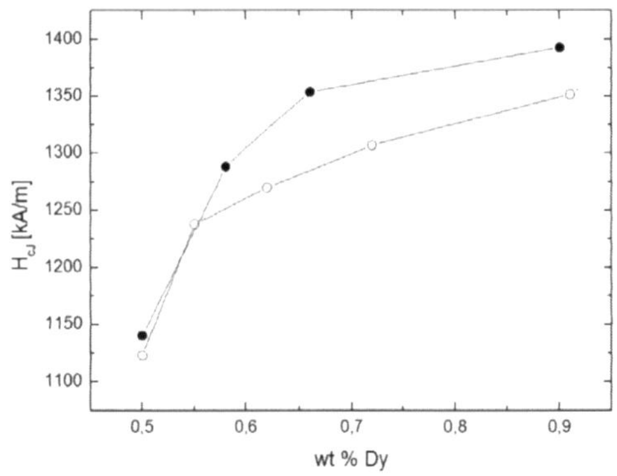

Fig. 3. Effects of Dy content on the coercivity of VACODYM 722 HR magnets having a base Dy concentration of 0.5 wt%. The additional Dy > 0.5 wt % is added by a GBDP. Full circles: Dy deposited by PVD (reference), empty circles: electrochemical deposition.

Table 1. Deposition times, mass of deposited Dy, coating thickness and relative changes in H_{cJ}.

Sample	Deposition Time [s]	Deposited Dy [mg]	Total Dy [wt%]	ΔH_{cJ} [%]
1	4500	1.01	0.55	10.3
2	12600	2.47	0.62	13.1
3	21600	4.55	0.72	16.4
4	39600	8.7	0.91	20.4

reported elsewhere [4].

Table 1 summarizes the deposition parameters together with the respective coercivity gain with respect to the untreated Nd-Fe-B samples.

4. Summary

In this study we present an alternative approach to deposit Dy layers on sintered RE magnets to be subsequently used as a diffusion source in a grain boundary diffusion process. The Dy layers were deposited by a novel electrochemical process, which, in principle, has the potential to be highly efficient and economical. With this process, we were able to deposit Dy coatings of up to 2.6 μm thickness on commercial sintered magnets and to enhance their coercitivity H_{cJ} by 20.4 % in a subsequent grain boundary diffusion process.

Acknowledgment

The authors would like to thank the German Federal Ministry of Education and Research for their support in the framework of the project "PerEMot"(FKZ 03X4621A)

References

[1] H. Sepehri-Amin, T. Ohkubo, K. Hono, *Acta Materialia*, 2013, 61, 1982-1990.

[2] K. Yoshimura, H. Morimoto, T. Odaka, *US Patent* 2008 / 0286595 A1

[3] M. Soderznik, K. Z. Rozman, S. Kobe, P. McGuiness, *Intermetallics*, 2012, 23, 158-162.

[4] C. Brombacher, K. Löwe, O. Gutfleisch, M. Rührig, M. Katter, *Proc 22nd REPM Workshop Nagasaki,* 2012, P2-034.

[5] D. B. Baudry, A. Dormond, F. Duris, J. M. Bernard, J. R. Desmurs, *J. Flour. Chem.*, 121, 233-238.

[6] K. Tsunashima, Y. Ono, M. Sugiya, *Electrochimica Acta*, 2011, 56, 4351–4355.

[7] B. E. Davies, R. S. Mottram, I.R. Harris, *Mat. Chem. Phys.*, 2001, 67, 272-281.

The Development, Process and Prospect of Rare Earth Permanent Magnetic Materials and Nanocrystalline Microstructure and Coercivity Mechanism Model of NdFeB Alloys with Nb and Ga

PAN SHUMING[1], LI SHOUYI[2], DAVID WONG[2], LIU JINFANG[1], LI ZHENGWEN[3], MA RUZHANG[3], PAN FENG[1], WANG HANCHUN[1]
[1]General Research Institute for Non-ferrous Metals, Bejing, China
[2]Feller Magnets Corporation
[3]Beijing University of Science and Technology,Beijing, China

Based on the model theory of metal phase transition, the publication systematically expounded the achievements and new results of rare-earth permanent alloys studied by the author during more than twenty years. The publication revealed the process of high-temperature phase transition and the correlation between the formation of nanocrystal and coercivity, which enhance the theories of high-temperature phase transition and magnetic properties for the rare-earth permanent-magnet alloys, The publication also discussed the principle and technology of sintered and adhesive rare-earth permanent-magnets, and the effect of composition and new technology on the magnetic properties and microstructure.

1. The Mössbauer analysis of the $Nd_2Fe_{12-x}Co_2Nb_xB$ ($x = 0.05, 0.10, 0.15, 0.20$) alloys indicates that H_A (anisotropic field) increases while M_s (saturation magnetization) and T_C (Curie temperature) decrease with Nb content increasing. The nano-microstructure of $(Nb_{0.9}Dy_{0.1})_{15}Fe_{76}B_7$ alloys shows that there are Fe_2Nb phases in the structure. The lattice constants are: $a = 0.482$ nm, $c = 0.787$ nm. The addition of Nb can decrease the grain size and mainly rich in grain boundary, which increases greatly the intrinsic coercivity (${}_jH_c$). Nb has little effect on the anisotropic field H_A because the elements mainly exist in the grain boundary and form Laves phases rather than enter into the crystal lattice. The microstructure of the alloys is dynamic tested by TEM with 1000kV from room temperature to 400 °C. It shows that there is not precipitates and change in the microstructure. But some precipitates emerge from $Nd_2Fe_{14}B$ phases of the Nd-Fe-B alloys without Nb at 280 °C. Therefore, Nb and Ga can improve the thermal stability of the alloys. The nucleation-hardening model and pinning model cannot comprehensively explain the coercivity mechanism of Nd-Fe-B alloys with Nb and Ga. Authors give out a new "grain finery local pinning" model. This model can explain the phenomena of any addition element increases the coercivity and improves thermal stability of Nd-Fe-B ternary alloy, which was the result of grain refinement and increment of the boundary local pinning.

2. The Mössbauer analysis of the $Nd_{15}(Fe_{1-x}Nb_x)_{78}B_7$ ($x \leq 0.04$) indicates that Nb primarily occupy *e* and *c* grain positions. But there are few neighbor atoms in *e* and *c* grain positions. Therefore, there are few Nb atoms in *e* and *c* grain positions, which cannot result in the hyperfine field change. Nb atoms mainly occupy 8*j*2 grain position.

3. The microstructure of Nd-Fe-B ternary alloys and Nd-Fe-B alloys with Nb are dynamically analyzed by TEM with 1000kV.

Sintered Magnets of HDDR Nd-Fe-B Powders with Artificial R-Cu Grain Boundary Phases

B.Z. CUI, M. MARINESCU, J.F. LIU
Electron Energy Corporation, Landisville, PA 17538, USA

Abstract: *This paper reports the structure and magnetic properties of sintered $Nd_2Fe_{14}B$-based magnets with enhanced cocerivities using precursors of jet milled HDDR $Nd_{13}Fe_{79.4}B_7Nb_{0.3}Ga_{0.3}$ powders and low melting-point eutectic alloy additives, such as $Nd_{70}Cu_{30}$, $Pr_{68}Cu_{32}$, $Tb_{70}Cu_{30}$, $Dy_{70}Cu_{30}$, and $Dy_{49}Er_{21}Cu_{30}$ (at.%). The intrinsic coercivity H_{ci} of the Nd-Fe-B sintered magnets was significantly increased due to the additives via a compounded effect of (1) the formation $(Nd,R)_2Fe_{14}B$ (R = Tb, Dy, Pr) phases with higher anisotropy fields, and (2) insertion of an 'artificial' R-rich intergranular phase to provide a magnetic 'insulation' of the grains. H_{ci} was increased by more than 200% for the Pr-Cu added magnets.*

Key words: *sintered Nd-Fe-B magnets; low melting-point eutectic alloy additives; intrinsic coercivity; R-rich intergranular phase*

Address: Bao Zhi Cui, Phone: 850-274-1245, E-mail: cuibz@yahoo.com

1. Introduction

Modification of the grain boundary microchemistry of poly-nanocrystalline $Nd_2Fe_{14}B$ magnets by thickening the Nd-rich grain boundary phase, which would weaken the exchange coupling between the $Nd_2Fe_{14}B$ grains, is a promising way to increase the coercivity. Coercivity enhancement of both hydrogenation – disproportionation – desorption – recombination (HDDR) processed Nd-Fe-B powders and Nd-Fe-B surfactant-assisted ball-milled flakes were reported due to the formation and/or thickening of a distinct Nd-rich phase at the grain boundaries via the diffusion of low-melting-point Nd–Cu eutectic alloys [1-3]. In this work, we report the structure and magnetic properties of sintered $Nd_2Fe_{14}B$-based magnets with enhanced coercivities using the precursors of jet milled HDDR $Nd_{13}Fe_{79.4}B_7Nb_{0.3}Ga_{0.3}$ powders and low melting-point eutectic alloy additives, such as $Nd_{70}Cu_{30}$, $Pr_{68}Cu_{32}$, $Tb_{70}Cu_{30}$, $Dy_{70}Cu_{30}$, and $Dy_{49}Er_{21}Cu_{30}$ (at.%) with melting points T_{melt} = 520°C, 472°C, 730°C, 790°C and about 820°C, respectively.

2. Experimental Procedure

The commercially available anisotropic HDDR Nd-Fe-B powders (particle size ~20-100 μm; grain size ~ 300 nm) with a composition of $Nd_{13}Fe_{79.4}B_7Nb_{0.3}Ga_{0.3}$ (at.%) were jet milled with 40 psi Ar for 1 pass. The low melting-point eutectic alloy ingots, $Nd_{70}Cu_{30}$, $Pr_{68}Cu_{32}$, $Tb_{70}Cu_{30}$, $Dy_{70}Cu_{30}$, and $Dy_{49}Er_{21}Cu_{30}$ (at.%), were prepared by arc-melting. Due to the ductility of these additive alloys, it was difficult to get fine microparticle powders by crushing and subsequently low or even high energy ball milling the ingots. Thus, ribbons of the these additive alloys were first prepared by melt-spinning at a copper wheel speed of about 25m/s, and then the ribbons were subjected to high energy ball milling for 20 min in Ar using a Spex mill/mixer (ball to powder ratio of 10:1). From this, fine additive ribbon powders with average particle sizes less than 10 μm were obtained. The mixtures with controlled ratios of jet milled Nd-Fe-B powders and ball milled additive ribbon powders were blended for 5 min in Ar using a Spex mill/mixer without any milling balls. The mixed powders were finally sintered and subsequently annealed at 1090°C, 900°C, and 580°C for 1 hr each, to produce the sintered magnets.

The structure and morphologies of the samples were examined by X-ray diffraction (XRD) with a Rigaku Ultima IV X-ray diffractometer using Cu Kα radiation and a scanning electron microscopy (SEM) with a JEOL JSM-6335F microscope equipped for energy-dispersive X-ray spectroscopy (EDS). The magnetic properties at temperatures in the range of 25°C to 250°C were measured with a hysteresigraph system (KJS Associates Model HG-700) after the specimens were pulse-magnetized at 70 kOe. Densities of the magnets were determined by a water immersion technique.

Fig. 1. SEM images of the jet milled HDDR $Nd_{13}Fe_{79.4}B_7Nb_{0.3}Ga_{0.3}$ powders. (b) is the enlarged image of an selected particle shown in (a).

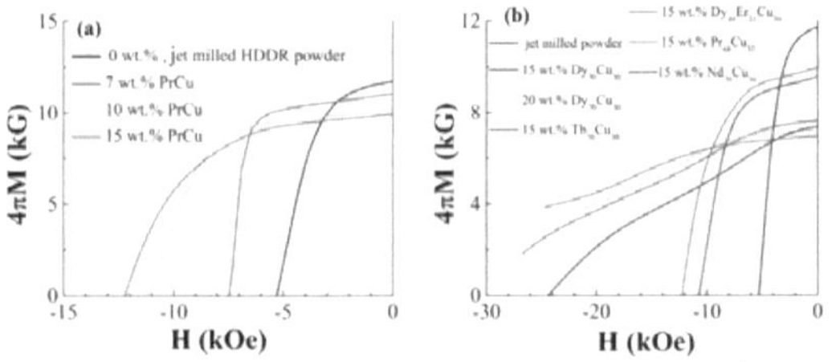

Fig. 2. Demagnetization curves measured at 25°C of the sintered magnets of (100-x) wt.% $Nd_{13}Fe_{79.4}B_7Nb_{0.3}Ga_{0.3}$ + x wt.% R-Cu additives.

3. Results and Discussion

The jet milled HDDR $Nd_{13}Fe_{79.4}B_7Nb_{0.3}Ga_{0.3}$ powders had a particle size of ~ 0.5-3 μm and a grain size of ~ 300 nm (see Fig.1). The demagnetization curves and magnetic properties of the sintered magnet with different additive alloys measured at different temperatures in the range of 25°C to 250°C are shown in Figs. 2-3 and Tables 1-2. Also shown in Table 2 are the temperature coefficients of the sintered magnets with different additive alloys between 100°C and 150°C of remanence, $\alpha_{100\text{-}150}$, and of coercivity, $\beta_{100\text{-}150}$, calculated with the formulas [4]:

$$\alpha = \frac{1}{B(T_0)} \cdot \frac{B(T) - B(T_0)}{T - T_0};$$

$$\beta = \frac{1}{H_c(T_0)} \cdot \frac{H_c(T) - H_c(T_0)}{T - T_0}$$

As a comparison, the jet milled anisotropic HDDR $Nd_{13}Fe_{79.4}B_7Nb_{0.3}Ga_{0.3}$ powder has an intrinsic coercivity H_{ci} of 5.2 kOe, a maximum energy product $(BH)_{max}$ of 21 MGOe and a remanence B_r (or $4\pi M_r$) of 11.7 kG. Whereas, the sintered counterpart without any additive alloys showed poor hard magnetic properties (B_r = 5.5 kG, H_{ci} = 0.16 kOe, $(BH)_{max}$ = 0.17 MGOe) due to the lack of the R-rich grain boundary phase to isolate the hard $Nd_2Fe_{14}B$ grains. As the amount of $Pr_{68}Cu_{32}$ additives x increased from

Table 1. Magnetic properties and densities at room temperature (25°C) of sintered magnets made from (100-x) wt.% $Nd_{13}Fe_{79.4}B_7Nb_{0.3}Ga_{0.3}$ + x wt.% additives at 1090°C, 900°C, and 580°C for 1 hr each.

x/additives	B_r kG	H_{ci} kOe	$(BH)_{max}$ MGOe	Density g/cc
0 (powder)	11.7	5.2	21	7.6
7/$Pr_{68}Cu_{32}$	11.1	7.5	26	7.4
10/$Pr_{68}Cu_{32}$	10.2	11.2	23	7.3
15/$Pr_{68}Cu_{32}$	9.9	12.2	22	7.3
15/$Dy_{70}Cu_{30}$	7.9	>30	15	7.4
20/$Dy_{70}Cu_{30}$	7.4	>30	14	7.4
15/$Dy_{49}Er_{21}Cu_{30}$	7.8	24.4	15	7.4
15/$Tb_{70}Cu_{30}$	7.2	>30	13	7.4
15/$Nd_{70}Cu_{30}$	9.5	10.0	19	7.3

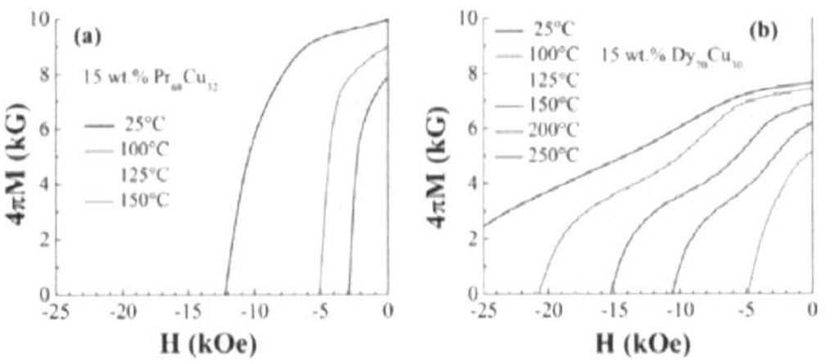

Fig. 3. Temperature dependent demagnetization curves measured at temperatures in the range of 25 °C - 250°C for the sintered magnets of 85 wt.% $Nd_{13}Fe_{79.4}B_7Nb_{0.3}Ga_{0.3}$ + 15 wt.% (a) $Pr_{68}Cu_{32}$ or (b) $Dy_{70}Cu_{30}$ additives.

7 to 15 wt.%, the H_{ci} increased and reached a maximum value of 12.2 kOe at x = 15 with B_r of 9.9 kG and $(BH)_{max}$ of 22 MGOe (see Table 1 and Fig.2). The oxidation level of the sintered magnets was below 0.7 wt.%. This method demonstrates an increase of the H_{ci} by more than 200% with x = 15 wt.% $Pr_{68}Cu_{32}$ additive compared to the powders without the artificial grain boundary additive.

Fig. 4 shows the SEM image and EDS elemental mapping of 85 wt.% $Nd_{13}Fe_{79.4}B_7Nb_{0.3}Ga_{0.3}$ + 15 wt.% $Pr_{68}Cu_{32}$ sintered and heat treated at 1090°C, 900°C, and 580°C for 1 hr each. The grain sizes of the sintered magnets are mainly in the range of 5-15 μm. The presence of a well-distributed artificial Pr-Cu grain boundary phase in the sintered magnets was observed by both the EDS elemental mapping and line scan (see Fig. 4). Both Pr and Cu were mainly distributed at the grain boundaries, while a small amount of Pr and Cu diffused into the hard matrix phases and formed $(Nd,Pr)_2(Fe,Cu)_{14}B$ phase (see Fig. 4).

For the same amount of additives (x = 15 wt.%), the

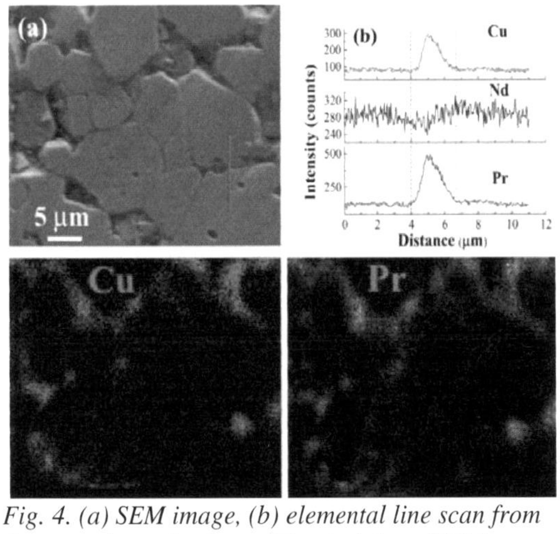

Fig. 4. (a) SEM image, (b) elemental line scan from the area shown by the red line in (a), and EDS elemental mapping of Cu and Pr (bottom left and right) of the sintered magnets of 85 wt.% $Nd_{13}Fe_{79.4}B_7Nb_{0.3}Ga_{0.3}$ + 15 wt.% $Pr_{68}Cu_{32}$ additives.

Table 2. Temperature dependent magnetic properties of sintered magnets made from (100-x) wt.% $Nd_{13}Fe_{79.4}B_7Nb_{0.3}Ga_{0.3}$ + x wt.% additives at 1090°C, 900°C, 580°C for 1 h each.

x / additives	Temp °C	B_r kG	H_{ci} kOe	BH_{max} MGOe	$\alpha_{100\text{-}150}$ %/°C	$\beta_{100\text{-}150}$ %/°C
15 / $Pr_{68}Cu_{32}$	100	9.0	5.1	14	-0.244	-0.863
	125	8.5	3.8	11		
	150	7.9	2.9	8		
15 / $D_{70}Cu_{30}$	100	7.5	20.7	13	-0.160	-0.522
	125	7.1	18.0	12		
	150	6.9	15.3	10		
	200	6.2	10.6	7		
	250	5.1	4.9	5		
15 / $Dy_{49}Er_{21}Cu_{30}$	100	7.3	15.7	11	-0.164	-0.573
	150	6.7	11.2	9		
	200	5.9	7.0	6		
	250	4.7	2.6	3		
15 / $Tb_{70}Cu_{30}$	100	6.7	> 25	11	-0.149	–
	150	6.2	> 25	9		
	200	5.6	16.8	7		
	250	4.8	9.6	5		

H_{ci} values of the sintered magnets are with $Tb_{70}Cu_{30}$ > $Dy_{70}Cu_{30}$ > $Dy_{49}Er_{21}Cu_{30}$ > $Pr_{68}Cu_{32}$ > $Nd_{70}Cu_{30}$ (see Table 1 and Fig.2). Whereas, the temperature coefficient values of $\alpha_{100\text{-}150}$, $\beta_{100\text{-}150}$ are with $Tb_{70}Cu_{30}$ < $Dy_{70}Cu_{30}$ < $Dy_{49}Er_{21}Cu_{30}$ < $Pr_{68}Cu_{32}$ (see Table 1). These results are consistent with the magnitude order of magnetocrystalline anisotropy fields of $R_2Fe_{14}B$ (R = Tb, Dy, Er, Pr, Nd) [4]. Especially, the H_{ci} of the magnets with $Tb_{70}Cu_{30}$ and $Dy_{70}Cu_{30}$ are as high as over 30 kOe. This implies that some of Pr, Tb, Dy, and Er diffused into the hard formed $(Nd, R)_2Fe_{14}B$ hard phase. On the other hand, the matrix phases during the sintering process and the well-distributed artificial R-rich phases at the grain boundaries were formed in the sintered Nd-Fe-B magnets, which was similar to that shown in the Pr-Cu added magnets (see Fig.4).

It is known that, besides the $R_2Fe_{14}B$ (R = Nd, Pr, Dy, Tb) phases with high anisotropy fields and refined grain sizes, another morphological component with a critical role in the value of coercivity for sintered Nd-Fe-B based magnets is the amount and distribution of the R-rich intergranular phases. For R-rich phases, the degree of their continuity and their smoothness are recognized as being important factors for the resulting coercivity of the magnets [5]. More specifically, the effect of the R-rich phases on H_{ci} is usually associated with the magnetic separation between the $R_2Fe_{14}B$ grains [6], thus weakening the exchange coupling between the $R_2Fe_{14}B$ grains, and with the ability of this phase to dissolve interface irregularities of the $Nd_2Fe_{14}B$ grains [7].Therefore, the H_{ci} increase for the magnets with the R-containing eutectic alloy additives in this work results from both the formation of the $(Nd,R)_2Fe_{14}B$ hard phase with larger anisotropy fields, and the non-magnetic R-rich grain boundary phases that offer more pinning sites in the domain walls.

However, the formation of $(Nd,R)_2Fe_{14}B$ (R = Dy, Tb, and Er) phases, the presence of non-magnetic R-rich phases and the resultant weaker intergrain exchange coupling results in a decline of the B_r, and thereby the $(BH)_{max}$ (see Table 1).

The H_{ci}, B_r, $(BH)_{max}$ and thermal stability of the magnets with the eutectic alloy additives can be further improved by optimizing the diffusion of R (R = Pr, Dy, Tb) into the Nd-Fe-B matrix and the concentration of the $(Nd,R)_2Fe_{14}B$ hard phases, and by improving the distribution of the R-rich phases.

Acknowledgement
This work was supported by US DoE, DE-SC0009199.

References

[1] H. Sepehri-Amin, T. Ohkubo, T. Nishiuchi, S. Hirosawac, K. Hono, *Scripta Mater.*, 2010, 63, 1124.
[2] B. Z. Cui, L. Y. Zheng, W. F. Li, J. F. Liu, G. C. Hadjipanayis, *Acta Mater.*, 2012, 60, 1721.
[3] B. Z. Cui, L. Y. Zheng, M. Marinescu, J. F. Liu, G. C. Hadjipanayis, *J. Appl. Phys.*, 2012, 111, 07A735
[4] J. F. Herbst, *Rev. Modern Phys.*, 1991, 63, 819.
[5] Y. Shinba, *et al.*, *J. Appl. Phys.*, 2005, 97, 053504.
[6] M. Sagawa, *et al.*, *J. Appl. Phys.*, 1984, 55, 2083.
[7] F. Vial, *et al.*, *J. Magn. Magn. Mater.*, 2002, 242–245, 1329.

The Mechanism of Coercivity in Sintered R-Fe-B Magnets Based on Misch-Metal

E NIU[1,2], Z.A. CHEN[1], G.A. CHEN[1,3], Y.G. ZHAO[1,3], J. ZHANG[1,3], X.L. RAO[1], B.P. HU[1], Z.X. WANG[1,2]
[1] Beijing Zhong Ke San Huan Research, Beijing 102200, China
[2] Institute of Physics, Chinese Academy of Sciences, Beijing 100190, China
[3] Sanvac (Beijing) Magnetics Co., Ltd., Beijing 102200, China

Abstract: *The R-Fe-B (R, rare earth) sintered magnets prepared with different ratio of alloys of MM-Fe-B (MM, misch-metal) and Nd-Fe-B by dual alloy method have been investigated. As expected, the high ratio of MM-Fe-B alloy degrades the intrinsic coerecivity (H_{cj}) heavily. The H_{cj} of the sintered magnets made from MM-Fe-B alloy only is even lower than 0.5 kOe. However the melt-spun ribbons of MM-Fe-B alloy have the H_{cj} as high as 7.5 kOe. It has been revealed that apart from the decrement of magnetocrystalline anisotropy fields (H_a) of $R_2Fe_{14}B$ matrix phase, the change of minor phase component and the deterioration in microstructure play fundamental roles in low H_{cj} in sintered MM-Fe-B magnets. The influence of minor phase component and microstructure on H_{cj} is different in melt-spun ribbon.*

Key words: *misch-metal, sintered Nd-Fe-B, melt-spun ribbon, coercivity, phase component, microstructure*

Address: E Niu, State Key Laboratory for Magnetism, Institute of Physics, Chinese Academy of Sciences, P. O. Box 603, Beijing 100190, China, E-mail: niue@aphy.iphy.ac.cn

1. Introduction

Recently, the issue on substitution of Pr-Nd by Ce or misch-metal alloys (MM) attracted renewed attention [1], because of the cost pressure of Nd and Dy metals. Although MM is much more inexpensive than pure Nd, the intrinsic magnetic properties of $La_2Fe_{14}B$ and $Ce_2Fe_{14}B$ are far inferior to those of $Nd_2Fe_{14}B$. Thus excessive substitution of Nd by Ce or MM will degrade the intrinsic magnetic properties and imply the deterioration of the extrinsic magnetic properties of sintered R-Fe-B magnet drastically [2].

In this work, sintered magnets [3] and melt-spun ribbons made from MM alloy were investigated to unveil mechanism of the intrinsic coercivity reduction for R-Fe-B with excess ratio of MM in sintered magnets.

2. Experimental

In our experiment MM is one of the typical misch-metals. It consists of La 27.06 wt.%, Ce 51.46 wt.%, Pr 5.22 wt.%, Nd 16.16 wt.% and other inevitable impurities. Dual alloy method was used to prepare sintered magnets with different ratio of Alloys A and B. Flakes of Alloy A in thickness of 0.3 ~ 0.5 mm were prepared from misch-metal in a nominal composition of $MM_{15.30}Co_{0.56}Cu_{0.08}B_{6.11}Fe_{bal}$ in atomic percentage by strip-casting. Flakes of Alloy B were prepared in the same way with a typical composition of Nd-Fe-B magnet as $(Pr,Nd)_{13.14}Dy_{0.73}Co_{1.0}Cu_{0.10}Al_{0.24}Nb_{0.21}B_{6.05}Fe_{bal}$. Alloys A and B were pulverized by hydrogen decrepitation, jet milled and blended according to different ratios listed in Table I. The blended powder was aligned in a constant magnetic field and pressed into green parts, then sintered in vacuum at 1000°C for 11 hours and annealed at 480 °C for 3 hours. Besides, ingot of the same nominal composition as Alloy A was prepared by arc-melting under argon. After that, the molten alloy was ejected onto the copper disk with a surface velocity of 25 m/s. The melt-spun ribbon with thickness about 30 μm was obtained and referred as b_{100}. Then a heat treatment in the temperature range of 550-700 °C for 10 minutes at high vacuum was applied to b_{100} for optimum magnetic hardening.

Table 1. Compositions of the sintered magnets a_0 to a_{100} and the melt-spun ribbon b_{100}. (R represents the total rare earth in the sample.)

Sample No.	a_0	a_{10}	a_{20}	a_{40}	a_{60}	a_{80}	a_{100}	b_{100}
A/(A+B) wt.%	0	10	20	40	60	80	100	100
MM/R at.%	0	10.8	21.5	42.2	62.1	81.4	100	100

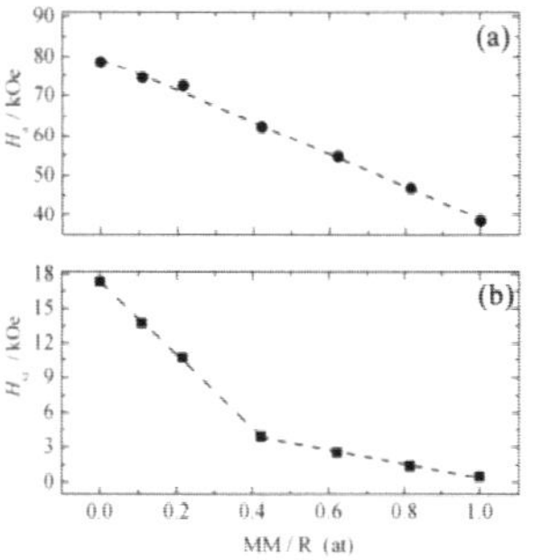

Fig. 1. MM/R dependence of (a) H_a and (b) H_{cj} at room temperature.

The extrinsic magnetic properties of all the sintered magnets were measured by a *B-H* tracer (NIM-200C) directly on cylinders of Φ8.0 × 6.5 mm^3 with its axis parallel to easy axis. The magnetization curves for sintered magnet cubes with side length of 1.5 mm were measured along and perpendicular to the easy axis by a superconducting quantum interference device (SQUID) VSM with the maximum field of 70 kOe. The magnetocrystalline anisotropy fields H_a of sintered magnets were estimated from the cross point of extension lines of the magnetization curves along and perpendicular to the easy axis. SQUID was also used to measure the magnetic properties of the melt-spun ribbons.

Phase component was characterized by X-ray diffraction (XRD) on powder samples. The microstructure was analyzed by scanning electron microscope (SEM).

3. Magnetic Properties

Fig. 1 shows the MM/R dependent H_a and H_{cj} of sintered magnets at room temperature. Different from the linearly decreasing H_a, H_{cj} decreases in two stages with the turning point near MM/R = 42.2%. In the first stage the H_{cj} drops rapidly with MM/R. When

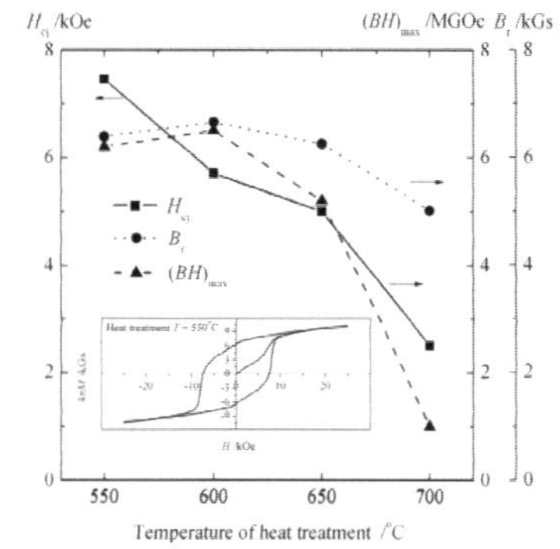

Fig. 2. The room temperature magnetic properties of melt-spun ribbons with heat treatment at different temperature. The inset is the magnetization curve of melt-spun ribbon with heat treatment at 550 °C.

MM/R ≥ 42.2% the H_{cj} declines slowly down to the value of 0.46 kOe with MM/R = 100%. It indicates that apart from the decrease of the H_a with substitution by MM, the extrinsic factors such as microstructure and phase component must play important roles in the declination of H_{cj}.

The magnetic properties of melt-spun ribbons with MM/R = 100% are shown in Fig. 2. The H_{cj} achieves highest value of 7.5 kOe when the heat treatment temperature is 550 °C. Then it decreases continuously as the heat treatment temperature elevating. However, the B_r and $(BH)_{max}$ increases first to reach a peak at 600 °C and then descends with the increasing temperature. The big gap of H_{cj} between the melt-spun MM-Fe-B and the sintered magnet of the same composition is mainly due to the difference in their microstructure and mechanism of coercivity.

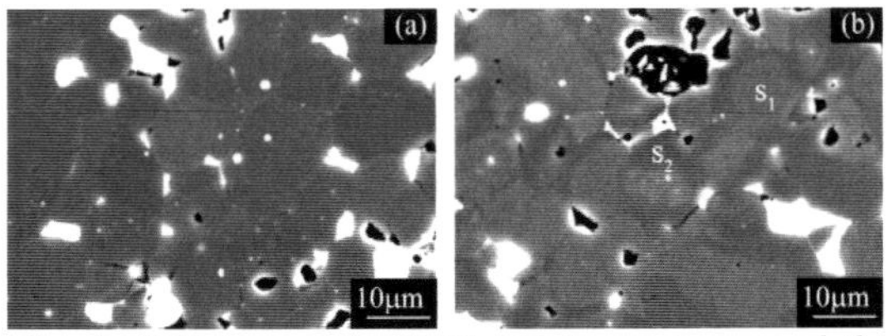

Fig. 3. BSE images by SEM of (a) sample a_0 and (b) sample a_{60}. (S_1 and S_2 are located in core region and shell region, respectively.)

4. Microstructure and Phase Analysis

Fig. 3(a) and Fig. 3(b) show the BSE images of samples a_0 (without MM) and a_{60} (MM/R = 62.1%). Different from sample a_0 in Fig. 3(a), there is no obvious intergranular rare-earth rich phase between neighbor grains in sample a_{60} shown in Fig. 3(b). Therefore main phase grains merge each other and are

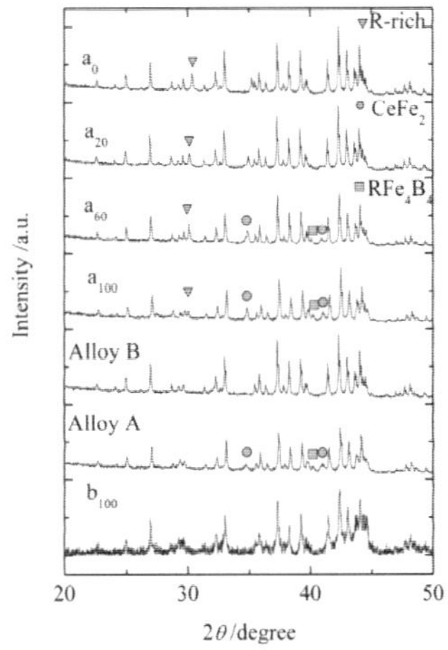

Fig. 4. X-ray diffraction diagrams (Cu K_α) for sintered magnets a_0, a_{20}, a_{60}, a_{100} after annealing, as-cast Alloys A and B, and melt-spun ribbon b_{100}. The unlabeled peaks are main phase $R_2Fe_{14}B$.

equivalent to large grains. In addition, in Fig. 3(b), it can be noticed that most of the grains in sample a_{60} show darker shell region, implying smaller average atomic numbers in shell than those in core. EDS data (not shown) indicate that the main phase grains in sintered magnets with high MM/R bear soft shell region which means lower H_a and the reversal domains tend to nucleate in this region.

Powder XRD patterns of sintered samples a_0, a_{20}, a_{60}, a_{100}, as-cast Alloys A and B, and melt-spun ribbon b_{100} are shown in Fig. 4. In Alloy A, sintered samples a_{60} and a_{100} of high MM ratio, a trace amount of $CeFe_2$ is observed ($2\theta \approx 35^o$ and 41°). $CeFe_2$ has a melting point of 925°C. It is much higher than that for Nd-rich phase or pure Ce metal. Therefore $CeFe_2$ exists as independent grains. The poor wetting ability of $CeFe_2$ phase implies low coercivity in high Ce-containing sintered R-Fe-B magnet.

4. Conclusion

Aside from the decrease in the intrinsic magnetic properties and strong oxidation tendency of MM-Fe-B, the degradation of H_{cj} in high MM/R ratio sintered R-Fe-B magnets is attributed to a) the growth of grain size, b) 'soft shell' region in main phase grains, and c) the existence of $CeFe_2$ grains.

References

[1] J. F. Herbst, M. S. Meyer, F. E. Pinkerton, *J. Appl. Phys.*, 2012, 111, 07A718.
[2] W. Gong, G. C. Hadjipanayis, *J. Appl. Phys.*, 1988, 63, 3513.
[3] E Niu, Z. A. Chen, G. A. Chen, Y. G. Zhao, J. Zhang, X. L. Rao, B. P. Hu, Z. X. Wang, *J. Appl. Phys.*, 2014, 115, 113912.

The Effect of Ni Impurities on HDDR Processing of Scrap Sintered NdFeB Magnets

M. FARR, A. CAMPBELL, I.R. HARRIS, A. BRADSHAW, R.S. SHERIDAN, V.S. MANN, A. WALTON[A]
School of Metallurgy and Materials, University of Birmingham, Edgbaston, Birmingham, UK, B15 2TT.

Abstract: *The Magnetic Materials Group (MMG) at the University of Birmingham have demonstrated previously that it is possible to use hydrogen to extract sintered NdFeB magnets from electronic waste* [1] *and to re-use the extracted alloy powders to form both sintered and resin bonded magnets* [2,3,4]. *One of the challenges in using scrap NdFeB magnets is that this material is likely to contain a number of impurities, for example, nickel from the protective coating. In this paper the effects of Ni contamination on the magnetic properties of HDDR NdFeB powders has been investigated. Nickel powder was blended with hydrogenated NdFeB powder in varying fractions from 1wt%-5wt% prior to processing using a modified version of the HDDR processing route developed by Sheridan et al (2012)*[2] *to produce anisotropic material. It has been shown that powders can be produced from voice coil magnets (VCM), which exhibit significant anisotropy and the anisotropy of the HDDR powder was shown to diminish with increasing Ni content. The Ni additions have been shown to lower the pressure at which the disproportionation reaction starts and ends, which, under the current conditions, could lead to over processing of the material.*

1. Introduction

The growing demand for NdFeB-based magnets, the potential for shortfalls in material supply, coupled with the increasing requirements to comply with the emerging WEEE Directives (Waste Electrical and Electronic Equipment)[4] on the recycling of electronic goods, are key drivers for the recycling of NdFeB-based magnets. Previous work has shown that uncoated sintered NdFeB-based magnets can be broken down into a powder using the hydrogen decrepitation process (HD)[5]. This powder can then be reprocessed into sintered magnets with comparable properties to those of the starting material [3]. The powder can also be processed further, using the Hydrogenation-Disproportionation-Desorption-Recombination (HDDR) process, for use in bonded or hot-pressed magnets. It has been shown previously that highly coercive, anisotropic powders can be produced using this method [2,6]. One of the main issues in trying to recycle the rare earth materials used in scrap electronics is the impurities, such as O, Ni, C and Si, that can be entrained in the HD powder after separation from the rest of the scrap. Ni will be one of the main contaminants as it is used to coat the surface of the magnets to protect against corrosion. These impurities could have an effect on the reprocessing routes and on the magnetic properties of the recycled magnets. VCMs from hard disk drives were used for this study, as they have been identified as one of the most abundant forms of magnetic scrap.

2. Experimental

Scrap sintered VCMs, supplied by Philips were used throughout this study. Ion coupled plasma (ICP) analysis was used to determine the composition of the magnets, which was shown to be: $Nd_{11.6}Dy_{0.6}Pr_{1.6}Fe_{77.9}Co_{1.4}Al_{0.7}Cu_{0.1}B_{6.1}$ (atomic%) A Leco oxygen analyser showed the oxygen content to be 5080 ppm. The sintered magnets were stripped of their Ni coatings and placed in a HD vessel where they were hydrogen decrepitated initially at room temperature, under 4 bar of hydrogen pressure. The resultant HD powder was then stored under argon in a glove box (Average O_2 level: ~4 ppm). 20 g samples of the HD powder were sieved to <90 μm and then blended with 1, 2 and 5 wt% Ni powder additions (99.9% purity, <90 μm particle size). The samples were then inertly transferred to an Inconel tube furnace for HDDR treatment. The powder was heated under vacuum (rotary pump, ~10^{-2} mbar) at a rate of 15°C/min up to 880°C, causing the hydrogen from the HD process to be desorbed. Once at temperature, the hydrogen pressure in the furnace tube was increased by 16 mbar/min up to 1200 mbar using a mass flow controller. The disproportionation reaction was considered complete when the hydrogen pressure stabilises at 1200 mbar. The pressure was then reduced at a rate of 100 mbar/min down to vacuum. Once the vacuum was achieved (~10^{-2} mbar), the material was quenched by rolling the furnace away and sliding a water-cooled copper coil over the Inconel tube. Temperature, hydrogen pressure and hydrogen flow rate were recorded during the measurement. The processing conditions are shown schematically in Fig. 1. HDDR powder samples of ~50 mg were mixed with molten wax and then aligned in a 1.5 T field while the wax solidified. The samples were then pulse magnetised in a 4 T field before measurement of the magnetic properties in the direction of alignment using a Lakeshore 7300 VSM. The samples were then re-magnetised in the 4 T field at 90° to the alignment direction, before being measured in that direction. The magnetisation values obtained by the VSM were converted to polarisation using a theoretical density of 7.5 g/cm^3. EDX analysis of the samples was carried out using a Hitachi TM-3000 SEM, with an accelerating voltage of 15000V, and a working distance of ~10mm.

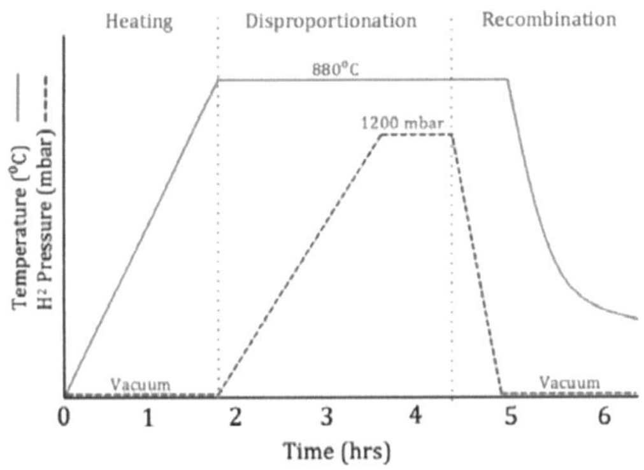

Fig 1. Schematic showing the HDDR processing conditions employed in this study.

3. Results & Discussion

In order to monitor the disproportionation reaction, the hydrogen pressure and flow rate into the reaction vessel were recorded. When the flow rate is plotted against pressure, a disproportionation peak is produced (Fig. 2). As the pressure is programmed to increase at a constant rate, any increases in flow rate would indicate that the sample is absorbing hydrogen. The first peak, at ~20 mbar, which can be a single, double or triple peak, represents the absorption of hydrogen by the Nd-rich phase. The second, larger peak (initiating at ~600 mbar) is associated with the $Nd_2Fe_{14}B$ matrix phase absorbing hydrogen and disproportionating into $NdH_{2\pm x}$, Fe_2B and αFe as shown in previous work[6]. When the flow rate levelled out, the disproportionation reaction is considered to be complete.

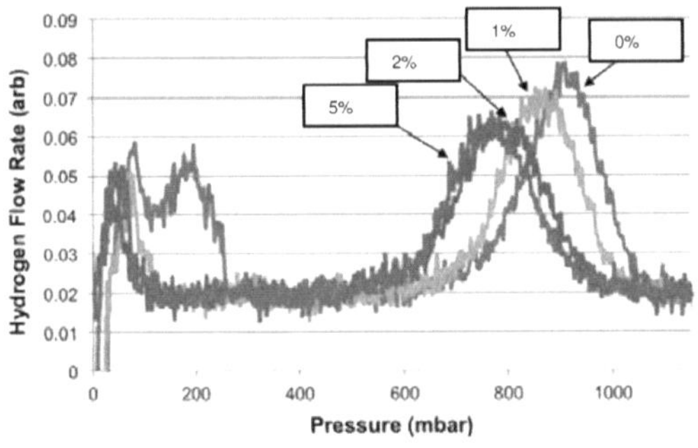

Fig 2. Hydrogen flow rate vs pressure at 880 °C. Graph shows the disproportionation peaks for samples with varying Ni impurities.

From Fig. 2 it can be seen that with increasing Ni content, the disproportionation pressure decreases. The disproportionation peak decreased in pressure from ~900 mbar to ~850 mbar when the Ni content was increased from 0-1 wt%. At 5 wt% Ni, the disproportionation pressure is reduced to ~760 mbar, a ~140 mbar decrease when compared to the sample with 0 wt% Ni. In the samples where a greater quantity of Ni is present, the disproportionation reaction is completed well below the processing pressure of 1200 mbar, which is likely to result in overprocessing. It has been shown previously that, with increasing time after disproportionation has been completed, the microstructure of NdFeB-type materials transformed from a lamella structure, to a more spherical morphology[7], thus reducing the anisotropy of the material and causing the magnetic properties to deteriorate. The magnetic properties of the samples with varying Ni impurities are shown in Table 1. In samples with 1 wt% Ni content, there is a 20.96% reduction in BH_{max} compared to those with 0 wt%. At 5 wt% Ni, the BH_{max} is reduced by 77.42% when compared to that of the 0 wt% Ni material.

Table 1. Magnetic properties of samples with varying Ni contents.

Sample	Remanence T (±0.02)	Coercivity, kA/m (±16)	$(BH)_{max}$, kJ/m^{-3} (±2.5)
0wt% Ni	0.84	720	90.67
1wt% Ni	0.77	766	71.67
2wt% Ni	0.44	873	34.33
5wt% Ni	0.38	550	20

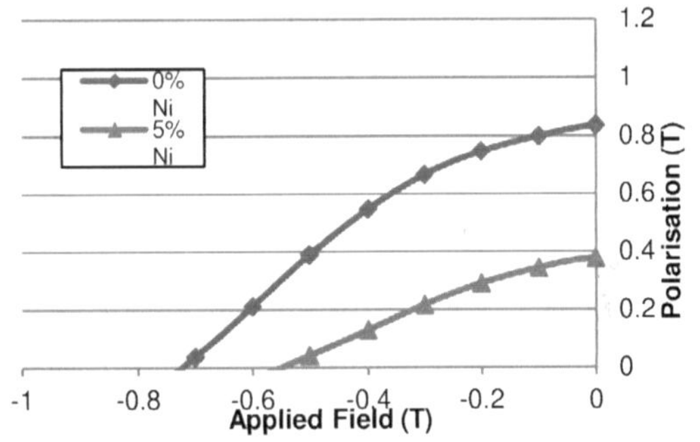

Fig 3. Graph shows the demagnetisation curves of samples with 0 wt% Ni and 5 wt% Ni additions.

Fig. 3 shows demagnetisation curves for samples with 0 wt% and 5 wt% Ni additions. It is very apparent that increasing the fraction of Ni dramatically reduced the remanence and coercivity. The effect of increasing Ni additions on the disproportionation pressure can be interpreted in terms of the progressive destabilisation of the $Nd_2Fe_{14}B$ matrix phase.

The extent of anisotropy in the HDDR processed material can be calculated by comparing the remanence in the easy and hard directions of magnetisation.

The figure of merit that describes the anisotropy can be calculated using:

$$Figure\ of\ merit = \frac{B_{r\,easy} - B_{r\,hard}}{B_{r\,easy}} \qquad \textbf{Equation 1[8]}$$

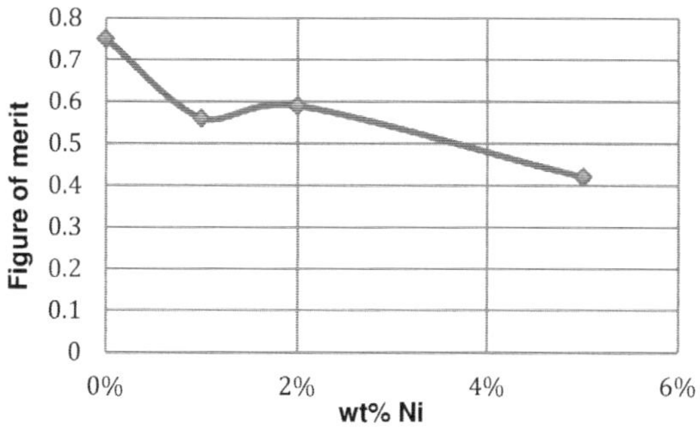

Fig 4. Change in figure of merit for anisotropy for samples with varying Ni impurities

From Fig. 4 it can be seen that the HDDR processed scrap sintered magnet with 0 wt% Ni exhibited significant anisotropy (0.75). This is relatively close to the highest anisotropy value found in previous work for this composition of magnet (0.84), which used a process optimised for producing anisotropic material [9]. As the Ni content increased to 5 wt%, the anisotropy was reduced, falling to 0.42 at 5wt% Ni. This could be due to over-processing of the material as a result of the lower disproportionation pressure in the higher Ni containing materials (Fig. 2).

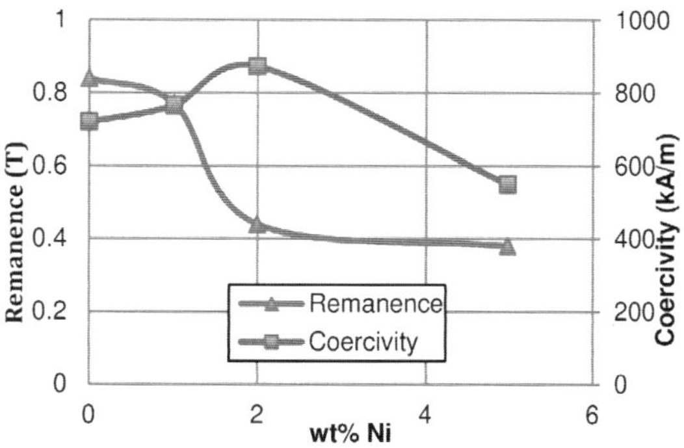

Fig 5. Change in remanence and coercivity in samples with varying Ni contents.

Fig. 5 shows both remanence and coercivity plotted against Ni impurity level (wt%). The remanence of the samples decreases as the Ni content increases. The BH_{max} values for these samples follow a similar trend to that of the remanence. The coercivity increases steadily up to 2 wt% Ni, however at 5 wt% it decreases significantly. It is possible that the Ni is substituting for one of the alloy constituents; however, the location of the Ni in the alloy is not known. EDX mapping software was used to locate Ni within the sample, to try to show any interaction with the starting material. Fig. 6 shows an EDX map for Ni in a sample with 5 wt% Ni. The Ni appears to be finely dispersed across the whole sample, however further high resolution studies are required to identify whether the Ni is located either in the grain boundary phase or in the $Nd_2Fe_{14}B$ matrix grains.

Fig 6. EDX map for Ni in 5wt% Ni sample

4. Conclusion

- Material with significant anisotropy can be produced by HDDR processing of scrap sintered NdFeB voice coil magnets from hard disk drives.
- A reduction in anisotropy is associated with increasing Ni content in hard disk drive VCMs that have been HDDR processed. This is possibly caused by over-processing of the material, causing the formation of a disproportionated microstructure with a more spherical, less orientated morphology.
- 1wt% Ni material showed a 20.96% decrease in BH_{max} when compared to that of HDDR powder with 0% Ni content. A BH_{max} reduction of 77.42% was observed in the 5 wt% Ni samples compared to those with 0 wt% Ni.

Acknowledgements

Less Common Metals for ICP analysis and Project Remanence: http://www.project-remanence.eu/

References

1. A.Walton, Han.Yi, V.S.J.Mann, A.I.Bevan, J.D.Speight, I.R.Harris, A.J.Williams, Proc. 22nd Int. Workshop on Rare Earth Magnets and Their Applications, p10 (2012)
2. R.S. Sheridan, A.J. Williams, I.R. Harris, A. Walton, Proc. 22nd Int. Workshop on Rare Earth Magnets and Their Applications, p394 (2012)
3. M. Zakotnik, I.R.Harris, A.J.Wiliams, J. Alloys Compd. 469, p314–321 (2009)
4. UK Environment agency, WEEE category 3: IT and telecommunications equipment
5. M. Zakotnik, I.R.Harris, A.J.Williams, J. Alloys Compd. 450, p525-531 (2008)
6. R. Harris and P. J. McGuiness, Journal of the Less-Common Metals, 172-174 (1991) 1273-1284
7. Han J, Tong C, Sun A, Xiao Y, Wang R, Journal of Magnetism and Magnetic Materials 270 136–141 (2004)
8. P. Guegan, PhD Thesis, University of Birmingham, UK (1999)
9. R. Sheridan, PhD Thesis, University of Birmingham, UK (2014)

The Development of Microstructure during HDDR Treatment of Sintered NdFeB-type Magnets

R.S. SHERIDAN, V.S.J. MANN, A. BRADSHAW, I.R. HARRIS, A. WALTON
School of Metallurgy and Materials, University of Birmingham, Edgbaston, Birmingham, B15 2TT, United Kingdom

Abstract: *The hydrogen absorption and desorption characteristics of the hydrogenation disproportionation desorption and recombination (HDDR) process on scrap sintered neodymium-iron-boron (NdFeB) type magnets has been investigated. The microstructural changes at each stage of the process have been studied using high resolution scanning electron microscopy (HR-SEM). These studies indicate that the hydrogenation of the grain boundaries and triple junctions during disproportionation may have been affected by the high oxygen content of the sintered NdFeB magnets in particular, some oxidised triple junctions appear to remain unreacted throughout the entire HDDR reaction and hence remain in the fine recombined microstructure.*

Address: R.S. Sheridan, School of Metallurgy and Materials, University of Birmingham, Edgbaston, Birmingham, B15 2TT, United Kingdom, E-mail: r.s.sheridan.1@bham.ac.uk

1. Introduction

The hydrogen decrepitation (HD) process has been shown to be an effective method for breaking down scrap sintered NdFeB magnets [1] into a powder and also for separation of NdFeB from end-of-life hard disk drive assemblies [2]. This HD-treated powder can be reprocessed back into new forms of magnet in a number of different ways, including chemical extraction of the rare earth elements, or by direct re-processing from the alloy by melting or re-sintering.

Another approach is to use the hydrogenation disproportionation desorption and recombination (HDDR) processing route which has been shown to be an effective method to produce anisotropic powders from scrap sintered NdFeB magnets [3,4,5]. The HDDR process is performed at high temperatures in hydrogen and it reduces the grain size of cast or sintered NdFeB to approximately 0.3 μm [6].
The HDDR reaction equation is described as:

$$\begin{array}{c} \textit{Disproportionation} \rightarrow \\ Nd_2Fe_{14}B + 2xH_2 \leftrightarrow 2NdH_{2x} + 12Fe + Fe_2B \\ \leftarrow \textit{Recombination} \end{array}$$

In previous work [3] the HDDR process has been optimised for direct re-processing of hydrogen decrepitated powder from scrap sintered magnets of specific compositions. However, the microstructural development of the HDDR process for sintered NdFeB material has not yet been covered in significant detail, which is the aim of this paper.

2. Experimental

Uncoated scrap sintered magnets with the composition of $Nd_{13.4}Dy_{0.7}Fe_{78.6}Al_{0.7}Nb_{0.4}B_{6.2}$ (at%) (minor constituents not included) and an oxygen content of 2665ppm were used throughout this work. The blocks of NdFeB were hydrogen decrepitated using a pressure of 2 bar to produce a hydrogenated powder.

The HD-treated sample was heated under vacuum to 885 °C, during which time the hydrogen is desorbed from the sample. In order to initiate disproportionation, hydrogen was then introduced at the same temperature at 16 mbar/min up to 1500 mbar and held under these conditions for 30 minutes to ensure completion of the reaction, which was monitored using mass flow controllers. The recombination reaction was then initiated by reducing the hydrogen pressure by 100 mbar/min to vacuum and held until full vacuum (~10^{-2} mbar) was recovered at which point the furnace was rolled off the furnace tube and a water-cooled copper coil applied to quickly cool the sample in order to prevent excessive grain growth. The schematic of this reaction is shown in figure 1.

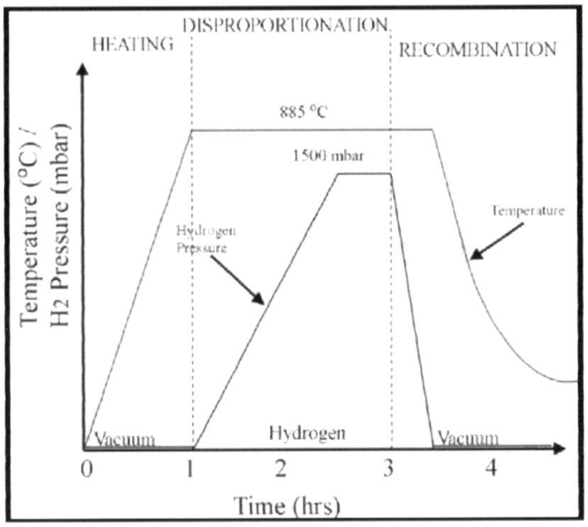

Fig. 1. Schematic showing the HDDR process.

The HDDR process was halted at carefully selected points in the reaction to examine the microstructural changes. A Jeol 6060 scanning electron microscope

(SEM) and a Jeol 7000 high-resolution scanning electron microscope (HR-SEM) were employed in backscattered imaging mode to reveal compositional aspects of the sample.

3. Results and Discussion

The sintered starting material consists of two main phases which can be identified using backscattered SEM imaging and these are shown in figure 2. The (grey) hard magnetic matrix phase, $Nd_2Fe_{14}B$, is surrounded by (white) Nd-rich grain boundary phases which accumulates at triple junctions and grain boundaries. The matrix grain size was calculated as 6.2 μm (with an estimated standard deviation of 2.3) using the Feret diameter method and minimal porosity is observed.

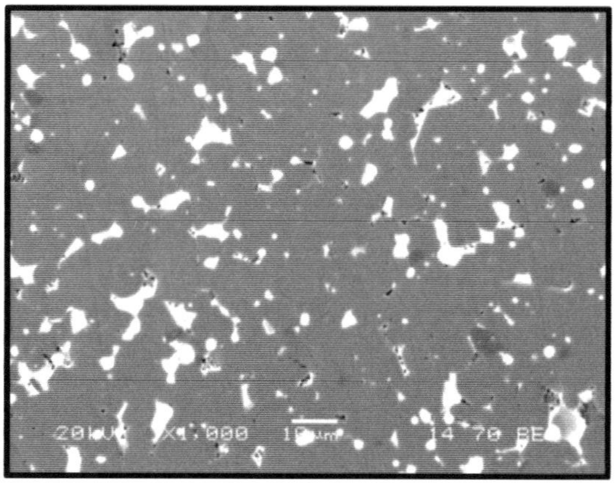

Fig. 2. Backscattered SEM micrograph of the sintered starting material.

The disproportionation reaction was halted part-way by quenching under hydrogen at the 2 hour mark on figure 1 and subsequently evacuated. Figure 3 shows a backscattered electron micrograph using HR-SEM of the partially disproportionated structure.

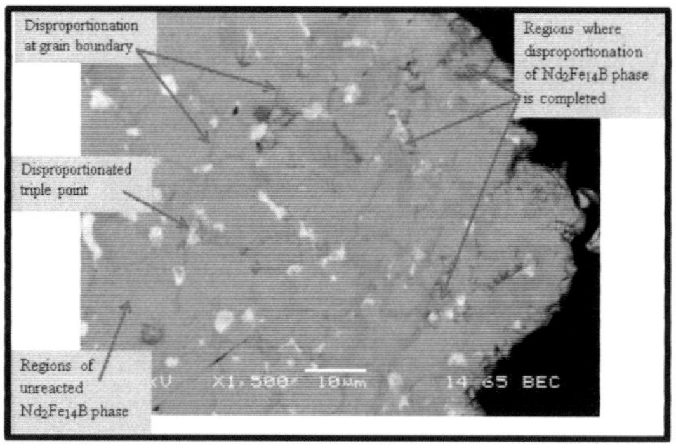

Fig. 3. Partially disproportionated structure at the edge of a particle.

It can be observed that hydrogen has begun to react at grain boundaries and triple junctions with a typical disproportionated microstructure being observed with light and dark regions representing the finely divided mixture of NdH_2 + α-Fe +Fe_2B.

It appears that the disproportionated structure is spreading in towards the centre of the $Nd_2Fe_{14}B$ matrix grains from the grain boundary regions, which has previously been observed when the HDDR process has been applied to cast material. It is also evident that the reaction has progressed further at the surface of the particles than in the centre.

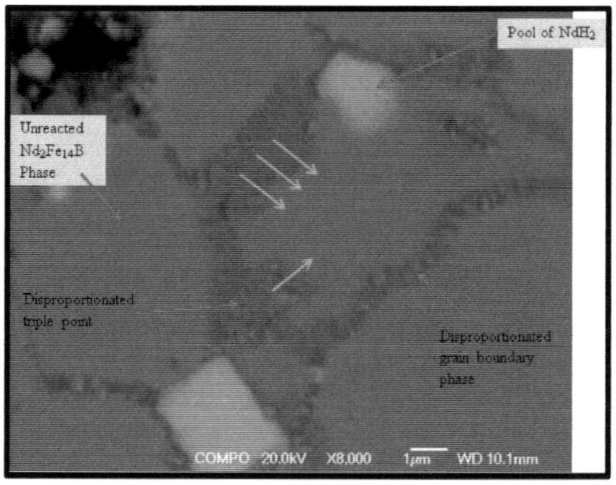

Fig. 4. HR-SEM micrograph of disproportionation occurring at grain boundaries and triple junctions.

Figure 4 shows clearly a region where the disproportionation reaction has initiated along the Nd-rich grain boundaries and triple junctions. The direction that the reaction takes from the grain boundaries into the matrix phase is demonstrated by the arrows on the micrograph. It should also be noted that there are two large pools of Nd-rich material which appear not to have reacted during this stage of the disproportionation reaction. It has been shown previously that in sintered NdFeB magnets, triple junctions contain large amounts of oxygen [7]. It is likely therefore, that the triple junctions are oxidised and that this process prevents the absorption of hydrogen, and hence the initiation of disproportionation.

The grain size of sintered NdFeB (<10 μm) is significantly smaller than that of cast NdFeB alloys (~300 μm), however the oxygen content of sintered NdFeB is an order of magnitude higher than that in cast alloys.

Figure 5 shows the completely disproportionated microstructure, consisting of rods of NdH_2 in an Fe matrix with finely dispersed Fe_2B. It is also evident that there are large regions of unreacted Nd-rich material from the triple junctions from the original sintered magnet.

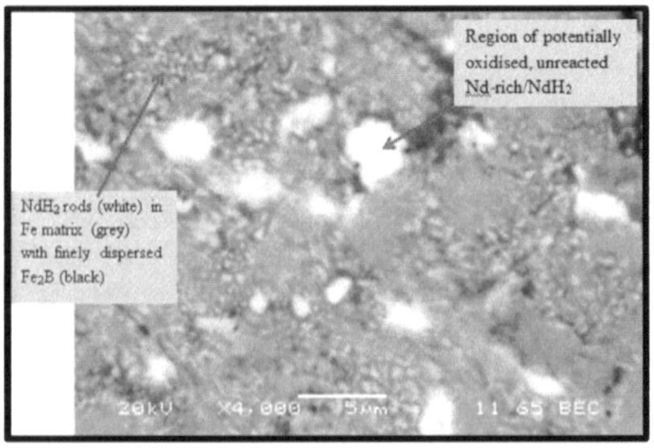

Fig. 5. Fully disproportionated structure.

To prevent the completion of the reaction, during the recombination reaction the sample was cooled quickly whilst still under a partial pressure of hydrogen (100mbar). The resultant microstructure is shown in figure 6. Uniformly across the sample, regions of $Nd_2Fe_{14}B$ have nucleated amongst the disproportionated mixture, however there is still evidence of unreacted Nd-rich material from the sintered microstructure and the formation of voids either from pull-out during polishing or due to cavitation resulting from redistribution of the Nd-rich phase during the HDDR reaction, as described by Williams et al (1996) [8].

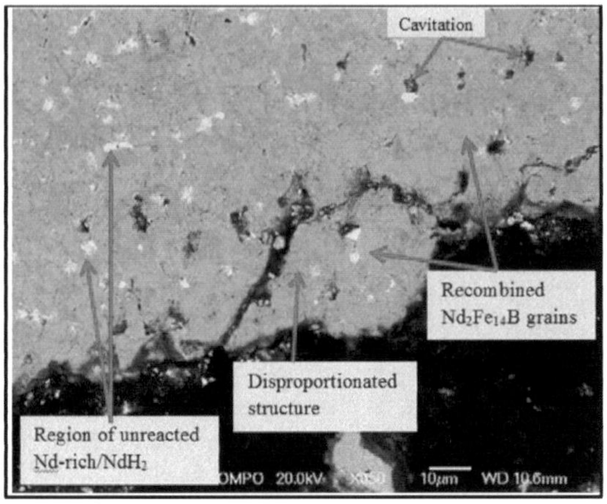

Fig. 6. Partially recombined microstructure.

The fully recombined structure is shown in figure 7. It can be observed that there are two different sizes of Nd-rich phase present within the structure. The characteristic redistribution of Nd-rich phase around a fine $Nd_2Fe_{14}B$ microstructure is accompanied by large pools of unreacted Nd-rich phase from the initial microstructure. There is also the presence of HDDR induced cavitation, however the amount of cavitation is likely to be reduced significantly due, to the presence of the unreacted triple junctions carried over from the previous sintered microstructure.

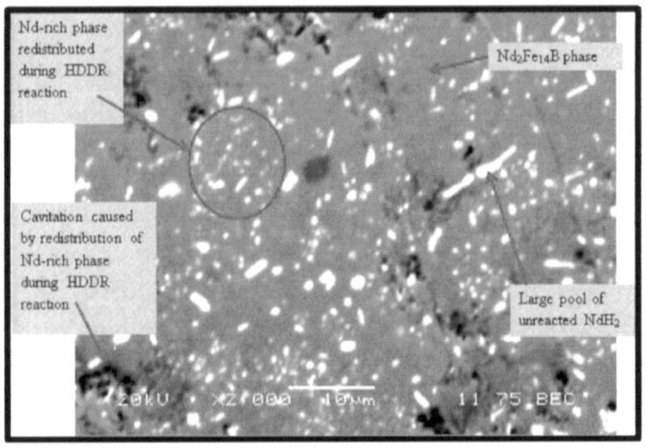

Fig. 7. Fully HDDR-treated microstructure

4. Conclusions

The disproportionation reaction initiates along Nd-rich grain boundaries and triple junctions, however some triple junctions do not react with hydrogen and these are assumed to be extremely oxidised. These pools of Nd-rich phase remain unchanged and in-tact throughout the entire HDDR reaction and are present in the final microstructure. It is not clear at this stage what the impact of these Nd-rich regions will be on the physical and magnetic properties of the final material and further work is required to determine this using samples with a known range of oxygen concentrations.

Acknowledgements

The work in this paper is dedicated to the memory of Dr. Andrew Williams, a colleague who sadly passed away in October 2011.

References

[1] S.Rivoirard, J.G.Noudem, P.de Rango, D.Fruchart, S.Liesert, J.L.Sobeyroux, Proc. 16th Intl REPM (2000) p355.

[2] A.Walton, H.Yi, V.S.J.Mann, A.I.Bevan, J.D. Speight, I.R.Harris, A.J.Williams, Proc. 22nd Intl REPM (2012) p10-13

[3] R.S.Sheridan, R.Sillitoe, M.Zakotnik, I.R. Harris, A.J.Williams, J. Magnetism and Magnetic Materials 324 (2012) p63-67

[4] J.J.Luo, P.deRango, D.Fruchart, J.N.Mei, L. Zhou, J. Alloys and Compounds 509 (2011) p4252-4259

[5] O.Gutfleisch, K.Guth, T.G.Woodcock, L. Schultz, J. Advanced Energy Materials 3 (2013) p151-155

[6] T. Takeshita & R. Nakayama. *Proc. 10th Intl. REPM* (1989) 551-557.

[7] S.C.Wang, Y.Li, J. Magnetism and Magnetic Materials 285 (2005) p177-182

[8] A.J.Williams, O.Gutfleisch, I.R.Harris, J. Alloys & Compounds 232 (1996) L22-26

From Neodymium Oxide to NdFeB Alloy: An Overview on the Reduction Methods

JOSÉ ADILSON DE CASTRO[1], DANIEL RODRIGUES[1,2], MARCOS FLÁVIO DE CAMPOS[1]
[1]PUVR– Federal Fluminense University, Volta Redonda, Rio de Janeiro, Brazil
[2]BRATS - Sintered Filters and Metallic Powders, Cajamar, São Paulo, Brazil

Abstract: *The main methods for producing metallic neodymium are briefly reviewed. These three methods are i) electrolysis using fluoride salts, ii) electrolysis using chloride salts, iii) calciothermic reduction. Fused salt electrolysis using fluoride remain are the most widely used commercial method for neodymium. An interesting possibility is the reduction of didymium oxide for production of magnets, avoiding the separation between Nd and Pr oxides. A mathematical model able to simulate the reduction is in development. The model takes into account parameters as cell size and geometry, distance between the electrodes and rate of carbon anode consumption.*

Keywords: *rare earth; reduction, oxides; neodymium; praseodymium*

Address: Jose´A de Castro, Universidade Federal Fluminense, Volta Redonda RJ, 27255-125, Brazil joseadilsoncastro@id.uff.br , marcosflavio@id.uff.br

1. Introduction

In the rare-earth business, two details are relevant, one of them is the rare-earth oxide separation in large scale, and the other is the production of rare-earth metal, or rare-earth magnetic alloy, from the oxide. This article is mainly devoted to the later: obtaining the metallic neodymium from oxide. Some of the main methods for producing metallic neodymium are discussed and reviewed, among them: i) neodymium electrolysis from fused fluoride salts; (ii) neodymium electrolysis from fused chloride salts; (iii) calciothermic reduction of neodymium oxide for production of the Nd-Fe-B alloy.

According Richardson [1], there was no commercial producer of metallic rare-earth in United Sates, at the beginning of 2013. The situation is different in Europe, where LCM [2] announced in mid 2013 the production of metallic rare-earth using molten salts. Brazil was a producer of metallic mischmetal in early 1990s, at the CIF company. However, after 1996, CIF focused on tantalum production [3], and stopped metallic rare-earth production. The process employed by CIF used fluoride molten salts.

The manufacture of metallic rare-earth is of special relevance for magnet production. In this article, details of the process for obtaining metallic rare-earth are reviewed. Calciothermic reduction of are-earth was very successful for $SmCo_5$ alloy production, but presents some difficulties for NdFeB alloy. The process of reduction using fused salts is discussed in analogy with the Hall-Heroult process for aluminum reduction. Present day technology usually makes use of fluoride salts for reduction of neodymium oxides.

2. Rare Earth Oxide Separation

The problem of the commercial rare-earth oxide separation starts in the 1880s when Carl Auer von Welsbach obtained ship ballasts consisting in monazitic black sand from Brazilian shore (coasts of South of Bahia, Espírito Santo and North of Rio de Janeiro States). An essential step in the rare-earth business is the rare-earth oxide separation, because the price of the oxide concentrate without any separation is very low. The separation method depends on the chosen ore [4]. In other words, the flow chart for rare-earth separation has to be optimized for each specific ore [5]. Rare earths with even atomic number (Z=60 for Nd) are much more abundant that their odd next neighbor (Z=59 for Pr). This is the so-called Oddo-Harkins rule. As consequence, in many ores, Neodymium and Praseodymium appear following the approximate proportion 3 Nd : 1 Pr [6]. This couple of elements is known as Didymium (from the Greek name for twins), after Mosander studies in the 1840s [7]. Only in 1885 Carl Auer von Welsbach demonstrated that Didymium was in fact Praseodymium and Neodymium. For magnet preparation, it may be better to keep the twins together. As the anisotropy field of praseodymium is higher than that of neodymium, a present day trend is the production of the didymium oxide as a commercial product, avoiding the separation of the didymium twins in the flow-chart. Due to recent renewed interest in rare-earth elements for many different technological applications, there are a number of recent reviews on the rare-earth oxide separation subject [8-11]. All of them emphasize that the separation process has to adapted or developed for each specific ore.

3. Obtaining the Neodymium Alloy

The focus of this brief review, however, is the production of the magnetic alloys. According David Kennedy [12], fused salt electrolysis employing fluorides remains the main method for metallic Neodymium as well as Dysprosium or Iron-Dysprosium production. This is essentially the same method used for mischmetal production in Brazil more than 20 years ago [3]. Many studies, however, have mentioned chlorides [13,14] instead of fluorides. A disadvantage of chlorides is that they are hygroscopic. Besides, the chlorides are less stable thermodynamically than the fluorides, generating Cl_2 and decreasing the current efficiency. Higher solubility of rare earth oxides and better conductivity also count in favor for choosing fluorides. Another interesting possibility is the calciothermic reduction of the Iron-Neodymium alloy. This was a subject of several academic studies in Brazil [15,16] and other countries [17,18]. Whereas a NdFe alloy oxidizes easily, a SmCo alloy not. Thus, a commercial $SmCo_5$ powder alloy was produced by co-reduction process [19] by Goldschmidt in the 1970s, and later by LCM (Less Common Metals) in North West England [20]. Many difficulties, however, have been found for production of NdFe alloys using calcium oxide for reduction. As consequence, reduction by electrolysis using fluoride fused salts remains dominant as commercial process up to present day. The electrowinning of neodymium and other rare-earth metals was investigated by Morrice and coworkers in the 1960s [21,22], and these studies remain a relevant reference up to the present day. The process employed by Morrice et al [21,22] has much in common with the process for metallic aluminum production [12], known as Hall-Heroult process. Continuing the research of Morrice et al [21], Dysinger and Murphy [23] discussed the possibility of increasing the size of the cells used for metallic neodymium production, and the effect of several processing variables. There is concern about fumes produced in the processing of metallic rare-earths [4, 24] and, thus, this detail has to be considered when designing the manufacturing plant. Several details may affect the reduction process, as for example cell size and geometry, current density and current efficiency, which depends on the distance between the electrodes. Another important detail is the carbon anode consumption during the reduction. All these details are being considered in a mathematical model [25] able to simulate the neodymium reduction process. The model uses the Navier-Stokes equations coupled with magnetohydrodynamics [25]. It is expected that the model may contribute for optimization of the processing parameters, for example the electrical energy consumption, which is usually high in the Hall-Heroult process of aluminum production.

4. Conclusions

The mines starting rare-earth concentrate or oxide production need to take into account that the price of rare-earth concentrate is very small, and that producing the separate oxides is necessary to increase the value.

Didymium oxide obtained directly from ore is very interesting for magnet production, presenting around ¼ Pr and ¾ Nd. Thus, the Didymium twins Praseodymium and Neodymium do not need be separated for producing the metallic alloy for magnet production.

The most used commercial process for metallic Neodymium production is the electrolysis using fluoride salts, and this process have similarities with the old Hall-Heroult process for aluminum production.

Acknowledgments

The authors would like to thank the National Council for Scientific and Technological Development (CNPq).

References

[1] http://www.magneticsmagazine.com/main/blogs/the-rare-earth-industry-where-do-you-fit/

[2] http://www.proactiveinvestors.com.au/companies/news/45536/great-western-minerals-successfully-produces-neodymium-metal-from-uk-manufacturing-unit-45536.html

[3] www.cif.ind.br/historia.html

[4] http://nepis.epa.gov/Adobe/PDF/P100EUBC.pdf

[5] http://qhxb.lib.tsinghua.edu.cn/myweb/english/2

006/2006e2/241-247.pdf

[6] Z. Chen: Journal of Rare Earths Vol. 29 (2011), p. 1–6

[7] F. Szabadvary "The History of the Discovery and Separation of the Rare Earths". In: Handbook on the Physics and Chemistry of rare-earths, Volume 11. Edited by: Karl A. Gschneidner, Jr. and LeRoy Eyring, Elsevier, 1988, p. 33

[8] A. Jordens, Ying Ping Cheng, K. E. Waters. Minerals Engineering Vol. 41 (2013), pp. 97–114.

[9] A. Golev, M. Scott, P. D. Erskine, S. H. Ali, G. R. Ballantyne. Resources Policy, Vol. 41 (2014), pp. 52-59.

[10] http://www.springer.com/earth+sciences+and+geography/geology/book/978-3-642-35457-1

[11] Feng Xie, Ting An Zhang, David Dreisinger, Fiona Doyle. Minerals Engineering, Vol. 56, (2014) pp. 10-28.

[12] D. Kennedy. In: Strategische Rohstoffe-Risikovorsorge. Springer Spektrum, Berlin, 2014, pp 201-217.

[13] N. Krishnamurthy, C. K. Gupta: Extractive Metallurgy of Rare Earths. CRC Press, Boca Raton Florida, 1st edition (2004)

[14] S. Singh, J. M. Juneja, D. K. Bose. Journal of Applied Electrochemistry Vol. 25 (1995), pp 1139-1142

[15] http://pelicano.ipen.br/PosG30/TextoCompleto/Eneida%20da%20Graca%20Guilherme_D.pdf

[16] P.F. Nogueira, F.B. Neto: Materials Science Forum Vols. 299-300 (1999), p. 200.

[17] Chiranjib Kumar Gupta .Chemical Metallurgy: Principles and Practice, Wiley, 2006

[18] http://www.jim.or.jp/journal/e/31/06/463.html

[19] http://hal.archives-ouvertes.fr/docs/00/21/88/83/PDF/ajp-jphyscol197940C5100.pdf

[20] http://www.tremcenter.org/index.php?option=com_attachments&task=download&id=31

[21] E. Morrice, T A. Henrie. Electrowinning high-purity neodymium, praseodymium, and didymium metals from their oxides [Washington, D.C.] U.S. Dept. of the Interior, Bureau of Mines, 1967.

[22] E. Morrice, E.S. Shedd, and T.A. Henrie: Direct electrolysis of rare-earth oxides to metals and alloys in fluoride melts [Washington, D.C.] U.S. Dept. of the Interior, Bureau of Mines, 1968.

[23] D. K. Dysinger and J. E. Murphy Electrowinning of Neodymium From a Molten Oxide-Fluoride Electrolyte, U.S., Bureau of Mines 1994. *stacks.cdc.gov/view/cdc/10116/cdc_10116_DS1.pdf*

[24] http://epa.tas.gov.au/documents/lynas%20services%20pty%20ltd,%20didymium%20pilot%20plant,%20ear.pdf

[25] J. A. de Castro, M. F de Campos. Modeling the neodymium metallic reduction from molten salts. Unpublished.

Development of Particle-Based Simulation for Magnetic-Aligned Compaction Process

R. SODA[1], M. AKADA[2], K. TAKAGI[1], K. OZAKI[1]
[1] National Institute of Advanced Industrial Science and Technology (AIST)
[2] Technology Research Association of Magnetic Materials for High-Efficiency Motors (MagHEM)

Abstract: *To understand the behavior of magnetic particles during the magnetic-aligned compaction process, we developed discrete element simulation models for permanent magnet particles with consideration of the crystal magnetic anisotropy and magnetic hysteresis. A numerical simulation was carried out to analyze the orientation behavior of particles in the pulsed-magnetic field. It was found that during applying the pulsed-magnetic field, the particles were completely oriented in the direction of the magnetic field. However, the orientation was somewhat disordered as soon as the pulsed magnetic field was finished. This orientation disturbance was revealed to be caused by the reverse rotation of small particles which were loaded with weak contact force.*

Keywords: *discrete element method; simulation; magnetic-aligned compaction; anisotropic permanent magnet*

Address: Rikio Soda; Powder synthesis and sintering Team, Green-Innovative Magnetic Material Research Center, AIST, 2266-98 Anagahora, Shimo-Shidami, Moriyama-ku, Nagoya, Aichi 463-8560 Japan, Tel:+81-52-736-7460 Email : r-soda@aist.go.jp

1. Introduction

Anisotropic permanent magnets are produced through a magnetic-aligned compaction process, which governs magnetization of the resultant magnets. Therefore, understanding the particle behavior in a magnetic field is essential for increased degree of orientation. Kotera *et al.* [1] and Tamura *et al.* [2] developed a numerical simulation model of particle motion in a static magnetic field based on particle-based simulation. This work aims to develop a three dimensional simulation model based on the discrete element method (DEM) [3] for tracking motion of the particles that were compacted under a strong pulsed magnetic field. DEM is capable of analyzing interparticle contact forces and rotation / translation movements of the individual particles. This paper reports the development of advanced simulation models for permanent magnet particles with consideration of the crystal magnetic anisotropy and magnetic hysteresis. Furthermore, the orientation behavior of particles in the pulsed-magnetic field was analyzed by the developed model.

2. Simulation Model

Particle motion and contact force were calculated by DEM. DEM is one of calculation method for tracking movements of particles while considering the viscoelastic force and frictional force. In this study, all particles were modeled as spheres, and the rotation of particles by a magnetic field was also considered. The translational motion and rotational motion were calculated by following equations:

$$m_i \frac{dv_i}{dt} = \sum_{j=1}^{k_i} \left(F_{ij}^n + F_{ij}^s\right) + mg + F_{i,\mathrm{mag}} \quad (1)$$

$$I_i \frac{d\omega_i}{dt} = \sum_{j=1}^{k_i} \left(r_i F_{ij}^s\right) + M_{i,\mathrm{mag}} \quad (2)$$

Where, m, v, t, g, I, ω, and r represent the mass of particle, transitional velocity, time, gravitational acceleration, moment of inertia, angular velocity and radius of particle, respectively. Suffixes i and j refer to particles i and j, respectively.

Normal and tangential components of contact force F_{ij}^n, F_{ij}^s were calculated by a spring-dashpot parallel system. To consider the frictional force, a slider element was added in the tangential direction as follows:

$$F_{ij}^n = K_n u_n + \eta_n \frac{du_n}{dt} \quad (3)$$

$$F_{ij}^s = \min\left\{\mu F_n, K_t(u_t + r\varphi) + \eta_t\left(\frac{du_t}{dt} + r\frac{d\varphi}{dt}\right)\right\} \quad (4)$$

Where, K, η, u, φ, and μ represent the spring coefficient, damping coefficient, relative

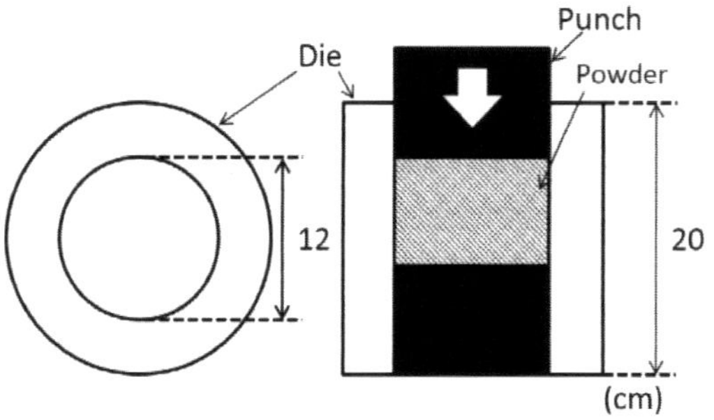

Fig.1. Schematic diagram of magnetic aligned compaction process.

displacement, relative angular displacement and frictional coefficient, respectively.

The magnetic force and magnetic moment acting on the particles were calculated by the following equations [4,5]:

$$F_{\mathrm{i,mag}} = (p_i \cdot \nabla)B_i \quad (5)$$

$$M_{\mathrm{i,mag}} = p_i \times B_i \quad (6)$$

where P is the magnetic moment of a particle, and B is the magnetic flux density. In addition, this study took into account crystal magnetic anisotropy and magnetic hysteresis.

3. Simulation Conditions

Figure 1 shows the schematic diagram of the magnetic aligned compaction model.

In this model, the particle size distribution was given by the Gaussian distribution. The mean particle diameter was defined as 6 mm and the diameter deviation was 2 mm. Note that the macro-scale DEM simulation conforms to the scaling law. Material properties were set based on Nd-Fe-B permanent magnets. An external pulsed-magnetic field was applied in parallel with the compressive load of 500N.

4. Results and Discussion

Figure 2 shows snapshots of the simulation result of the magnetic-aligned compaction process with a pulsed magnetic field of 4.0T.

Every particle was initially generated at random positions within a die (Fig.2 (a)). The circles and arrows represent the particles and their easy axis of magnetization. It was observed that during the application of the pulsed-magnetic field, the particles

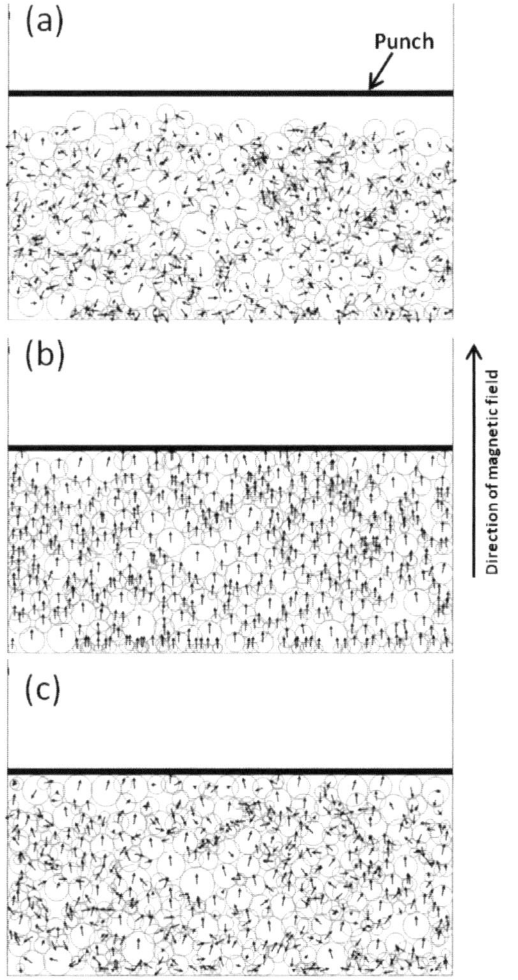

Fig.2 Snapshots of particle motion when applying a pulse magnetic field. (a) Initial state; (b) shortly after the applying a pulsed-magnetic field; (c) after the pulsed-magnetic field is removed.

were completely oriented in the direction of the magnetic field (Fig.2 (b)). However, the orientation was somewhat disordered as soon as the pulsed magnetic field was finished, (Fig.2 (c)). This orientation disturbance was revealed to be caused by the reverse rotation of small particles which were loaded with weak contact force.

5. Conclusion

A three-dimensional simulation model for a magnetic-aligned compaction process was developed based on the discrete element method. This simulation was successful in visualizing the decrease in the degree of orientation of the magnetization easy axis as the compaction proceeded.

Acknowledgment

This work has been supported by Future Pioneering Projects / Development of magnetic material technology for high-efficiency motors from Japanese Ministry of Economy, Trade and Industry.

Reference

[1] H. Kotera *et al.*, *J. Jpn. Soc. Powder Powder Metallurgy*, 1995, 42 1019-1026 .

[2] S. Tamura *et al.*, *J. Mater. Process. Technol.* 1994, 45, 353-358.

[3] P.A. Cundall *et al.*, *Geotechnique*, 1979, 29, 47–65.

[4] R. S. Paranjpe *et al.*, *J. Appl. Phys.*, 1986, 60, 418 – 422.

[5] N. Nakayama *et al.*, *Transactions of the Japan Society of Mechanical Engineers, Series (C)*, 2004, 70, 804-810.

Simulation of the Magnetic Alignment of Uniaxial Magnetic Powders in PLP Technology

O.A. GOLOVNIA[1], A.G. POPOV[1], A.N. SOBOLEV[2], G.C. HADJIPANAYIS[3]
[1]Institute of Metal Physics, 620990, Ekaterinburg, Russia
[2]South Ural State University (National Research), 454080, Chelyabinsk, Russia
[3]University of Delaware, Newark, DE 19716, U.S.A.

Abstract: *The numerical investigations of the process of alignment of magnetically uniaxial Nd-Fe-B powders in an applied magnetic field were carried out using the discrete element method (DEM). The influence of the particle shape anisotropy and friction coefficient on the alignment degree was studied. The increase in the friction coefficient leads to a decrease in the alignment degree; the simulation results qualitatively agree with experimental dependences.*

Keywords: *magnetic alignment; Nd-Fe-B; pressless process (PLP); discrete element method (DEM); LAMMPS*

Address: Oksana A. Golovnia, Institute of Metal Physics, 620990, Ekaterinburg, 18 S. Kovalevskoy Str., Russia, Tel. +73433783782, E-mail: golovnya@imp.uran.ru

1. Introduction

The PLP technology includes following stages: placing the powder with high filling density ρ_f into container for sintering, the magnetic alignment, and the sintering. In view of extensive applications of this technology, it is important to account for and understand in detail the effects of friction of the powder particles on their magnetic alignment. In the present work we continue to numerically simulate, using the discrete element method (DEM) [1], the process of magnetic alignment of uniaxial magnetic powders [2].

In the model, a powder is an ensemble of ferro-magnetic uniaxial particles with an average particle size d, mass m_i, and moment of inertia I_i. Each particle i experiences, along with the gravitational force $\mathbf{F}_i^g$, the contact force $\mathbf{F}_{ij}^c$ acting due to the interaction with a neighboring particle j and walls of the container and the non-contact force $\mathbf{F}_{ik}^{nc}$ caused by magnetostatic interaction. In addition, a torque $\mathbf{M}_{ij}$ acts on each particle. The governing equations for translational and rotational motion of particles are written as

$$m_i \frac{d\mathbf{v}_i}{dt} = \sum_j \mathbf{F}_{ij}^c + \sum_k \mathbf{F}_{ik}^{nc} + \mathbf{F}_i^g,\ I_i \frac{d\omega_i}{dt} = \sum_j \mathbf{M}_{ij}$$

and described in detail in [2,3].

DEM is implemented in the program software LAMMPS [3,4], i.e. Large-scale Atomic/Molecular Massively Parallel Simulator. In simulation, a packing of particles with the required filling density of the powder ρ_f is aligned in a magnetic field, which achieves the set value of its strength instantaneously after the application. Particles are anisotropic and formed from N_{sph} (ranged from 4 to 14) overlapping spheres of diameter d = 1 μm arranged in two rows in one plane, so that the minimum size of all designed anisotropic particles is d. The minimum distance between the centers of two overlapping spheres was chosen to be $d/2$, thus a ratio of maximum-to-minimum size of the particle $\alpha_A = L_{\max}/d$, where L_{max} is a maximum size of the particle; for spherical particles α_A = 1, for two-row particles $\alpha_A = (N_{sph}+2)/4$. The magnetic dipole moment **p** was perpendicular to the plane formed by rows of spherical particles.

In the model, we assume that the magnetic dipole moment of a real thermally demagnetized particle is changed at first because of the displacement of domain walls and does not achieve its saturation value in low fields. Therefore, the magnetic dipole moment is a linear function of its orientation and the applied field: $p = (p_0/H_d)\ H \cos\theta$, where p is magnitude of current magnetic dipole moment of the particle, p_0 is saturated magnetic dipole moment magnitude, H_d is the demagnetizing field of the particle, and θ is an angle between easy-axis and applied magnetic field H. Thus, orientation of the magnetic dipole moment of the constituent spheres was chosen to make the projection of the magnetic dipole moment on the field direction vary in the range from 0 to $|\mathbf{p}|$.

The number of anisotropic particles was near 5000, and the number of constituent spheres was 64512. For the estimation of the degree of alignment, the projection of magnetic dipole moment of the particles along the magnetic field direction, averaged over the ensemble, was employed. In the experiment, the degree of alignment is usually defined as $\alpha_T = B_r/4\pi M_s V\alpha_p = B_r/B_s$, where $4\pi M_s$ is the saturation magnetization of the ferromagnetic phase of the alloy at room temperature; V is the volume fraction of the ferromagnetic phase in the magnet; α_p is the relative (with respect to the density of cast alloy) density of the sintered magnet; B_r is the remanence. The present work is devoted to the simulation of powders of the Nd-Fe-B alloy; calculation parameters relate to Nd-Fe-B and are the following: Young's modulus, $E = 1.5\cdot 10^2$ GPa, elastic constants for normal and tangential contact, $k_n = 0.733E$, and $k_t = 2/3k_n$, viscoelastic damping constants for normal and tangential contact, $\gamma_n = 5\cdot 10^7\ s^{-1}m^{-1}$, and $\gamma_t = 2/7\gamma_n$, density, $\rho = 7.6\ g/cm^3$, specific magnetization, $\sigma = 148.6\ A\cdot m^2/kg$ [2].

2. Results and Discussion

Figure 1 represents the dependence of the calculated alignment degree α_T of the particles on α_A (represents the shape anisotropy) and ρ_f. The strength of the applied magnetic field $\mu_0 H = 3$ T, and friction coefficient was $\mu = 0.8$. If ρ_f is low, α_T is 100% for particles of any shape. At higher filling densities of the ensemble, the increase in α_A leads to a decrease in α_T. This result is in qualitative agreement with experiment. The magnetic dipole moments of the particles with low shape anisotropy ($\alpha_A \leq 2$) also align in the field direction. However, a higher α_A leads to a sharp decrease in α_T.

Figure 2 represents the dependence of the calculated α_T on μ in the magnetic field of 3 T. The dependences are obtained for particles with α_A equal to 3.5 and 4. Higher values of μ and ρ_f provide a decrease in α_T in all cases. In addition, an increase in the shape anisotropy of particles leads to a stronger dependence of α_T on μ. These results are in qualitative agreement with the experimental data [5,6].

Simulation of ensembles of particles of different diameters of constituent spheres showed that larger particles having greater moment of inertia take more time to approach steady state of the degree of

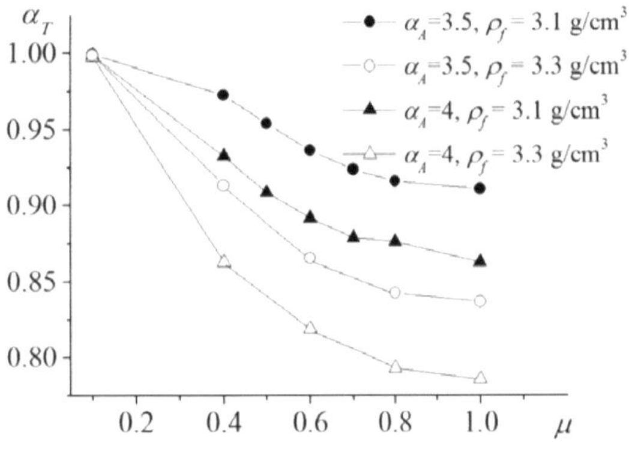

Fig. 2. Dependence of the alignment degree α_T on friction coefficient μ.

alignment. However, the value of α_T remains the same. The reason is in the identical spatial configuration of the system, i.e. space coordinates of the particles, while the greater masses and moments of inertia lead to more slow dynamics of the system.

In Fig. 3, dependences of the alignment degree on the strength of the applied magnetic field are shown for the ensembles with $\rho_f = 3.1\ g/cm^3$, which are simulated by the particles with $\alpha_A = 3.5$. The experimental and calculated dependences are in qualitative agreement. Accounting for demagnetizing factor of the particle is noticeable only in the fields less then demagnetizing field, which in our case was around 0.7 T. Thus, the magnetic dipole moment of particles does not achieve saturation value at 0.5 T, and $\alpha_T < 0.65$. In the fields higher than demagnetization field, the value of α_T does not change whether we take into an account the demagnetizing factor or not. In medium fields (1.4 – 3.0 T), the calculated dependences demonstrate higher values of α_T than the experimental ones. At $\mu_0 H \geq 5$ T, the experimental curve 1 corresponding to the powder prepared without an addition of internal lubricant [6] and the calculated curve with $\mu = 0.9$ (curve 4) coincide satisfactorily. The powder milled with an

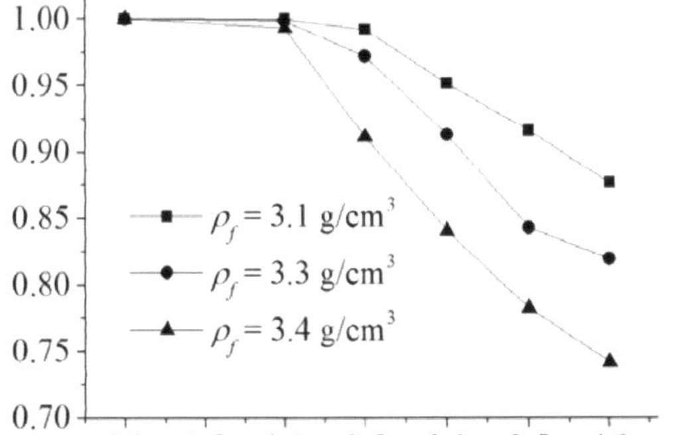

Fig. 1. Dependence of the alignment degree α_T on the shape anisotropy α_A and filling density of powder ρ_f.

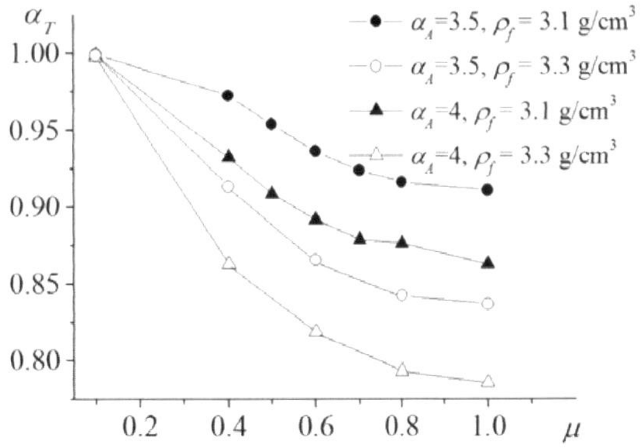

Fig. 3. Calculated (3, 4) and experimental (1, 2) dependences of the alignment degree on the strength of the applied magnetic field.

addition of 0.15 wt. % zinc stearate (curve 2) has a higher value of α_T; its field dependency can be approximated by the calculation dependence with μ = 0.6 (curve 3). Thus, in applied fields higher than 5 T, the calculated field dependences render the experimental data.

The discrepancy between the experimental and calculated results in low fields is likely to be caused by imperfection of the model presented. The experimental data are obtained for the case of alignment of powders in a pulsed magnetic field, whereas in the simulation, the magnetic field is constant and achieves its value instantaneously. In addition, the model magnetic dipole moment was oversimplified in comparison with the real one. In the process of alignment the projection of magnetic dipole moment on the field direction could change due to the rotation in the applied magnetic field and the magnetization in the effective field, $H \cos\theta$. The rotation of the real particle in the magnetic field occurs along with the displacement of domain walls; and this process hardly can be exactly taken into account by linear growth in the effective field. All these questions need further investigation.

3. Conclusion

In the work presented, the numerical investigations of the process of alignment of magnetically uniaxial powders in an applied magnetic field were carried out. The model of formation of anisotropic particles as a combination of spherical particles [2] was developed. The influence of the shape anisotropy and friction coefficient on the alignment degree was analyzed. It is shown that in magnetic fields higher than 5 T, the calculated field dependences of the alignment degree render the experimental data.

Acknowledgements
The calculations were performed using the "Uran" supercomputer of Institute of Mathematics and Mechanics UB RAS. The work is supported by UB RAS – CRDF GLOBAL (project RUP2-7104-EK-13) and UB RAS (project No. 12-M-23-2066).

References

[1] H.P. Zhu, Z.Y. Zhou, R.Y. Yang, and A.B. Yu, *Chem. Eng. Sci.* **62**, 2007, 3378.
[2] O.A. Golovnia, A.G Popov, A.N. Sobolev, and G.C. Hadjipanayis, *J. Magn.Magn. Mater.* **365**, 2014, 64.
[3] *LAMMPS Users Manual*, Sandia National Laboratories, 2013 (http://lammps.sandia.gov)
[4] S.J. Plimpton, *J. Comput. Phys.* **117**, 1995, 1.
[5] A.G. Popov, A.V. Shitov, E.G. Gerasimov, D.Yu. Vasilenko, M.Yu. Govorkov, D.Yu. Bratushev, V.P. Vyatkin, K.Yu. Shunyaev, T.L. Mikhailova, *Phys. Met. Metallogr.* **113**, 2012, 331.
[6] A.G. Popov, E.G. Gerasimov, P.B. Terent'ev, V.S. Gaviko, K.Yu. Shunyaev, T.L. Mikhailova, V.O. Vaskovskii, and N.A. Kulesh, *Phys. Met. Metallogr.* **114**, 2013, 285.

Effect of Low-Temperature Annealing on the Structure and Hysteretic Properties of Nd-Fe-B Magnets Prepared with Hydride-Containing Powder Mixtures

G.S. BURKHANOV[1], A.A. LUKIN[2], N.B. KOLCHUGINA[1], Yu.S. KOSHKID'KO[3], A.G. DORMIDONTOV[2], K. SKOTNICOVÁ[3], O. ŽIVOTSKY[3], T. ČEGAN[3], V.V. SITNOV[2]

[1]Baikov Institute of Metallurgy and Materials Science, Russian Academy of Sciences, Leninskii pr., 49, Moscow, 119991 Russia

[2]"JSC SPETSMAGNIT", Dmitrovskoe sh. 58, Moscow, 127238 Russia

[3]Vysoka Skola banska - Technical University of Ostrava, 17 Listopadu, 15/2172, Ostrava-Poruba, 70833, Czech Republic

Abstract: *The effect of low-temperature treatment on the structure and hysteretic properties of Nd-Fe-B magnets, which were prepared using strip-casting alloy (wt.%) Nd -24%, Pr – 6.5%, Dy – 0.5%, B – 1 %, Al – 0.2%, Fe – balance and 2 wt.% DyH_2 addition, has been studied. Hysteretic properties of the magnets subjected to the optimum heat treatment are B_r = 1.29 T, $_jH_c$ = 1309 kA/m, H_k = 1220 kA/m, $(BH)_{max}$ = 322 kJ/m^3. The subsequent combined heat treatment at 250 to 500 °C (for 20 h) does not change the hysteretic properties. The degradation of magnetic properties (decrease in $_jH_c$ and H_k to 1105 and 960 kA/m, respectively) is observed only after the repeated annealing at 550 °C. The hysteretic properties of the magnets can be restored completely by heat treatment 1050 °C (1 h) + 500 °C (2 h). The data obtained demonstrate the higher thermal stability of hysteretic properties of magnets prepared from hydride-containing powder mixtures. The observed effect is attributed to the formation of a non-uniform Dy distribution in $(Nd, Pr, Dy)_2Fe_{14}B$ principal magnetic phase grains.*

Keywords: *Nd-Fe-B-based magnets; coercivity; dysprosium hydride; low-temperature annealing*

Address: Kolchugina Natalia, Baikov Institute of Metallurgy and Materials Science, Russian Academy of Sciences, Leninskii pr. 49, Moscow, 119991 Russia, Tel. (7-499) 135-96-15, Fax (7-499) 135-94-18, E-mail: natalik@imet.ac.ru

1. Introduction

The coercivity of Nd–Fe–B magnets is structure-sensitive and dependent on the continuity and composition of RE-rich phases, grain-boundary defects, average grain size, exchange interaction between $Nd_2Fe_{14}B$ hard magnetic grains, etc. The coercivity of sintered magnets is reached by post-sintering annealing at the optimum temperature (around 500 °C) determined by the composition of Nd-Fe-B-based alloys. The role of the low-temperature heat treatment (LTHT) consists in the formation of continuous non-magnetic RE-rich layers between $(Nd,R)_2(Fe,M)_{14}B$ grains [1].

An obvious decrease in the coercive force of Nd-Fe-B magnets after annealing at temperatures slightly below the optimum temperature was reported, in particular in [2], and discussed recently in [3].

In a number of studies, the decrease in H_c has been attributed to the appearance of a minor B-rich phase ($Nd_{1+\delta}Fe_4B_4$) [4]. The presence of Nd-oxide-containing phases at grain boundaries and triple junctions was also considered, in particular in [5], as a possible cause for the coercivity decrease. The authors of [2] have related the decrease in H_c with the local stray field at cracks formed during the LTHT. Thus, the coercivity behavior at the LTHT stage is not completely understood; this makes it substantially more difficult to predict degradation of magnetic characteristics of permanent magnets during operation, in particular, at high temperatures (150 - 220 °C), under mechanical loading and radiation.

It was found in a number of studies [6] that, depending on the chemical composition and manufacturing procedure, the character of processes occurring at low temperatures (200 - 450 °C) can differ substantially. This fact manifest itself during repeated optimum heat treatment, which is performed to recover the properties [partial or complete recovery via single- or multistage heat treatment (HT)].

Some data on the important role of structural state of 2-14-1-phase grains in the formation of high-coercivity state are available in [7]. It is known that the formation of the non-uniform core-shell Dy distribution determines the increase in the coercive force of magnets [8]. The formation of such a structure in Nd-Fe-B magnets is reached by various Dy additions (DyH_x, DyH_x+DyF_3, Dy nanoparticles, etc.).

The aim of the present study is to investigate the formation and retention of the high-coercivity state of permanent magnets during LTHT, the manufacturing procedure of which includes mechanical alloying of Nd-Pr-Dy-Fe-Al-B composition and dysprosium hydride powders.

2. Experimental Techniques

Sintered magnets were prepared using strip-cast alloy (wt.%) Nd - 24%, Pr - 6.5%, Dy - 0.5%, B - 1 %, Al - 0.2%, Fe - balance and 2 wt. % DyH_2 added before the final milling stage. The preparation technique is available in [7].

The microstructure of prepared magnets and chemical composition of formed phases were studied using an electron microscope and JEOL JUMP 9500F Auger spectrometer, respectively. X-ray diffraction analysis of the strip-cast alloy and sintered magnets were performed using a Difrei 401 diffractometer and CrK_α radiation. X-ray diffraction patterns were processed using PowerCell software.

Magnetic characteristics of samples were measured after grinding and saturation magnetization. The measurements were performed at room temperature in magnetic fields up to 3 T using a close circuit of hysteresimeter.

3. Results and Discussion

Hysteretic properties of the magnets are B_r = 1.29 T, ${}_jH_c$ = 1309 kA/m, H_k = 1220 kA/m, $(BH)_{max}$ = 322 kJ/m^3. The temperature of the optimum HT equal to 500 °C (sample 1) is likely to be determined by the maximum wettability of grain-boundary R_{rich} [4] ensuring continuous 2-14-1-phase grain boundaries. The subsequent combined heat treatment in vacuum or inert atmosphere, which includes the stepped or progressive heating from 250 to 500 °C (the total heating time is to 20 h), does not change the hysteretic properties of magnets. Note that magnets of the same composition, but manufactured by traditional technology, demonstrate the abrupt decrease in hysteretic properties (${}_jH_c$ and H_k) upon heating in a temperature range of 350 – 400 °C. The degradation of magnetic properties (decrease in ${}_jH_c$ and H_k to 1105 and 960 kA/m, respectively) of magnets prepared from hydride-containing powder mixtures is observed only after the repeated annealing at 550 °C (sample 2). The annealing at 970 °C for 1 h does not restore the hysteretic properties. The hysteretic properties of the magnets can be restored completely by heat treatment 1050 °C (1 h) + 500 °C (2 h) (sample 3).

The degradation and recovery of hysteretic properties are discussed from the point of view of (1) formation and dissolution of impurity $Nd_{1.1}Fe_4B_4$ phase at triple junctions of 2-14-1 magnetic phase, (2) changes of grain boundaries; (3) presence of oxide phases; and (4) existence of compositional nonuniformity of 2-14-1 magnetic phase grains.

Figure 1 shows portions of X-ray diffraction patterns of samples subjected to optimum, degrading, and restoring HTs (samples 1, 2, and 3, respectively), which demonstrate the evolution of the NdO, Nd_2O_3 and $Nd_{1.1}Fe_4B_4$ phases in the magnets in the course of HTs. Along the main reflections of the $Nd_2Fe_{14}B$ phase, some additional reflections (belonging to other phases) are observed at 2Θ angles of 46.01°, 46.42°,

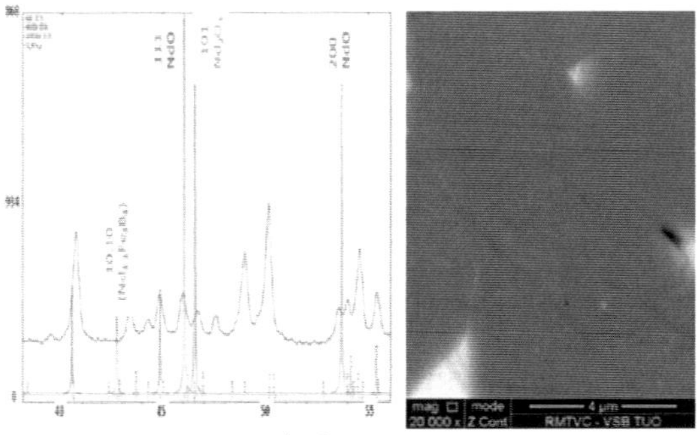

Sample 1

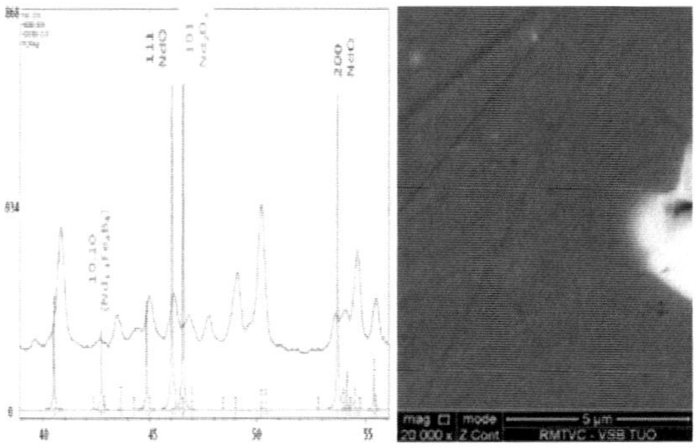

Sample 2

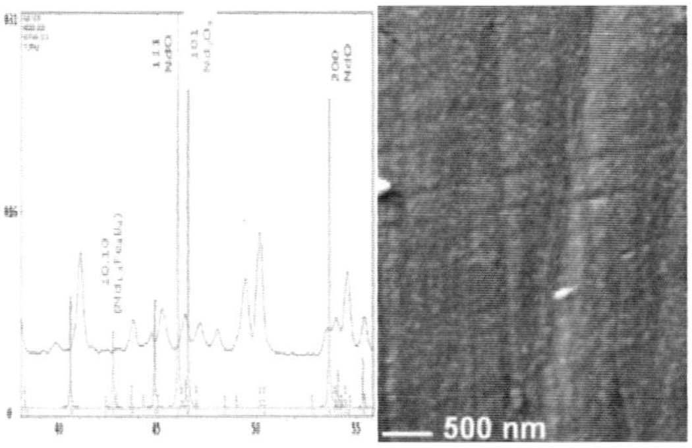

Sample 3

Fig. 1. Portions of X-ray diffraction patterns and SEM micrographs for samples after optimum (sample 1), degrading (sample 2), and restoring (sample 3) HTs. Simulated patterns corresponding to NdO (reflections (111),(200)), Nd_2O_3 (reflection (101)) and $Nd_{1.1}Fe_4B_4$,(reflection (10.10)) compounds are given with expanded scale for visualization. SE image for sample 3 was taken after 60-nm surface etching with argon ion beam.

53.58° and 79.13° which, according to the simulated NdO и Nd_2O_3 patterns, can be related to these oxides. Slight differences can be explained by the simulation performed for the NdO и Nd_2O_3 compounds (free from Dy and Pr, which are present in the composition).

The X-ray diffraction pattern for sample 2 exhibits a small peak at $2\Theta = 42.7°$ along with the other aforementioned reflections. We assumed that this reflection corresponds to the $Nd_{1.1}Fe_4B_4$ phase. The evolution of the peak after restored annealing allows us to state the decomposition of the phase.

The decrease in $_jH_c$, H_k and B_r after HT at 550 °C can be related to the appearance of the $Nd_{1.1}Fe_4B_4$ phase near 2-14-1-phase grain boundaries at the expense of near-surface decomposition of 2-14-1 phase; the 1-4-4 phase disappears after restoring annealing 1050 °C (1 h) + 500 °C (2 h).

SEM micrographs in Fig. 1 demonstrate transformations of grain boundaries during degrading and restoring HTs, which cause the formation of discontinuous and continuous boundaries, respectively.

The absence of any changes in $_jH_c$ and H_k after HTs at 250 - 500 °C is likely can be related to the substantial decrease in the invar effect (anomalous temperature dependence of the lattice parameters), which is due to magnetic ordering [9,10] at the expense of 2-14-1 phase structuring (Fig. 1, SEM for sample 3) [7].

The data obtained demonstrate the higher thermal stability of hysteretic properties of magnets prepared from hydride-containing powder mixtures. The observed effect is attributed to the formation of a non-uniform Dy distribution in $(Nd,Pr,Dy)_2Fe_{14}B$ principal magnetic phase grains [7], which is formed during the preparation of material from hydride-containing powder mixtures and determines the specificity of diffusion processes occurred during LTHT. These data are of importance for deciding the optimum heat treatment of Nd-Fe-B-based magnets and the prediction of their service stability.

4. Summary

The studies performed have demonstrated the high thermal stability of $_jH_c$ and H_k characteristics of sintered Nd-Fe-B-based magnets prepared from DyH_2-containing powder mixture during. The hysteretic parameters are unchanged in the course of HTs at 250-500 °C; the decrease in $_jH_c$ and H_k takes place only after 1 h annealing at 550 °C. The complete recovery of the high-coercivity state is reached by HT at 1050 °C (1 h) + 500 °C (2 h). The used binary mixtures technology also has allowed us to obtain the higher coercive force magnitude as compared to that of similar magnets prepared by traditional technology.

Acknowledgment
This study was supported by the Russian Academy of Science, program 5 and performed in terms of Opportunity for young researchers, no. CZ.1.07/2.3.00/30.0016).

References

[1] H. Seperhri-Amin, T. Ohkubo, K. Hono, *Acta Mater.* **61**, 2013, 1982.
[2] T. Akiya, T.T. Sasaki, T. Ohkubo, Y. Une, M. Sagawa, H. Kato, K. Hono, *J. Magn. Magn. Mater.* **342**, 2013, 4.
[3] T. G. Woodcock, F. Bittner, T. Mix, K.-H. Müller, S. Sawatzki, O. Gutfleisch, *J. Magn. Magn. Mater.* **360**, 2014, 157.
[4] T. G. Woodcock, O. Gutfleisch, *Acta Mater.* **59**, 2011, 1026.
[5] M. Matsuura, R. Goto, N. Tezuka, S. Sugimoto, *Mater. Trans.* **51**, 2010, 1901.
[6] A. A. Lukin, S. Szymura, *Arch. Mater. Sci.* **21**, 2000, 21.
[7] A. A. Lukin, N. B. Kol'chugina, G.S. Burkhanov, N. E. Klueva, K. Skotnicova, *Inorg. Mater.: Appl. Res.* **4**, 2013, 256.
[8] G. Yan, P. J. McGuiness, J. P. G. Farr, I. R. Harris, *J. Alloys Compd.* **491**, 2010, L20.
[9] A. V. Andreev, A. V. Deryagin, S. M. Zadvorkin, S. M. Terent'ev, *Fiz. Tverd. Tela* **27**, 1985, 1641.
[10] K. H. J. Buschow, *J. Less-Common Met.* **118**, 1986, 349.

Cold Hydrostatic Extrusion of Nd-Fe-B Powder

W. KASZUWARA[1], T. GIŻYŃSKI[1], M. LEONOWICZ[1], M. KULCZYK[2], P. PAWLIK[3]
[1]Warsaw University of Technology, Faculty of Materials Science and Engineering, Woloska 141, 02-507 Warsaw, Poland
[2]Institute of High Pressure Physics, Polish Academy of Sciences, Sokolowska 29/37, 01-142 Warsaw, Poland
[3]Czestochowa University of Technology, Institute of Physics, Al. Armii Krajowej 19, 42-200 Czestochowa, Poland

Abstract: *The melt-spun Nd-Fe-B ribbon powder was hydrostatically extruded (HE) at room temperature. It was found that HE leads to various processes such as refinement of the powder particles and deformation of the crystalline lattice, which cause slight deterioration of the magnetic properties. It was also found that, as a result of high deformation, a new phase is formed, which is probably a strongly disordered form of the* $Nd_2Fe_{14}B$ *phase, presence of which negatively affects the magnetic properties.*

Key words: *hydrostatic extrusion, Nd-Fe-B magnets, magnetic properties, melt-spun Nd-Fe-B powder*

Address: Marcin Leonowicz, Warsaw University of Technology, Faculty of Materials Science and Engineering, Woloska 141, 02-507 Warsaw, Poland, tel: +48 22 234 8450, E-mail: mkl@inmat.pw.edu.pl

1. Introduction

Hydrostatic extrusion (HE) can be applied for any standard extrusion, dedicated for either reduction of the billet diameter or densification of powder [1]. This is a very effective method because the force is exerted homogenously, through the liquid, at the extruded element. There is no danger that the extruded billet will undergo upsetting in the front of the die. High degree of strain is possible. Because of the high hydrostatic pressure, nucleation, growth and coalescence of material imperfections is suppressed, brittle solids and powder materials can be processed with achievable extrusion ratio substantially higher than in the conventional direct extrusion process. The characteristic feature of the HE is also high rate of the process (10 mm/s).

Application of HE for densification of Nd-Fe-B powders was reported only in [2], where it was demonstrated that the final density of the specimen depends on the applied strain and temperature of the process. At room temperature (RT) the true strain was 3.17 and it enabled for achieving of 90% of theoretical density. Higher density was achieved for extrusions at elevated temperatures, 700 and 800°C. The HD process resulted, however in a substantial reduction of the coercivity. The coercivity loss was higher for high strain, combined with high temperature. Especially interesting was achieving of reasonably good density and magnetic properties for the HE at RT. Densification of Nd-Fe-B powders at RT was also studied for MPQ-A powder [3] using a compression shearing method described in [4]. It was found that densification at RT leads to slight deterioration of the coercivity, however, application of higher temperatures results in substantial drop of this parameter due to the grain growth.

In this work the dependence of the magnetic properties on the deformation ratio was studied for initially densified Nd-Fe-B powders and subsequently hydrostatically extruded at room temperature. An attempt of correlation of the properties with microstructural changes was undertaken.

2. Experimental

MQU-F42 powder, having composition 30.5Nd-62Fe-6Co-0.9B-0.6Ga (wt. %), was provided by Magnequench. The powder was initially cold densified inside the copper capsules to green density of about 65% of the theoretical value. The capsules were sealed under vacuum and welded. The three-stage HE was applied. In the three consecutive stages the capsule diameter was reduced from 49.9 mm

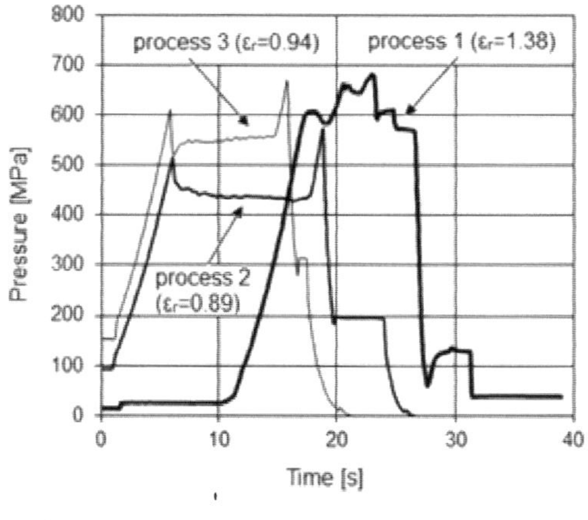

Fig. 1. Scheme of the HE processes.

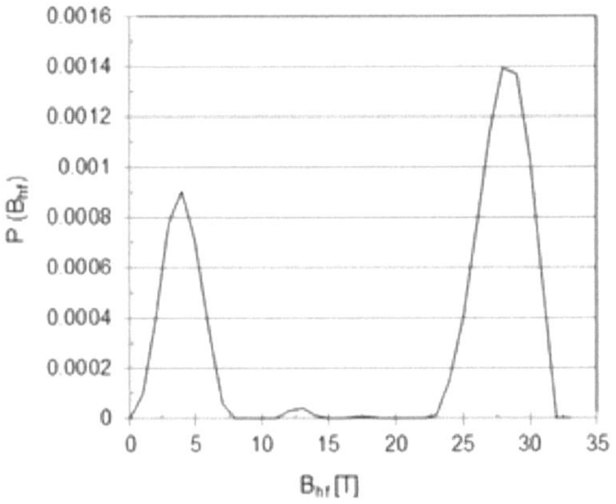

Fig. 2. Distribution of hyperfine fields for the disordered phase.

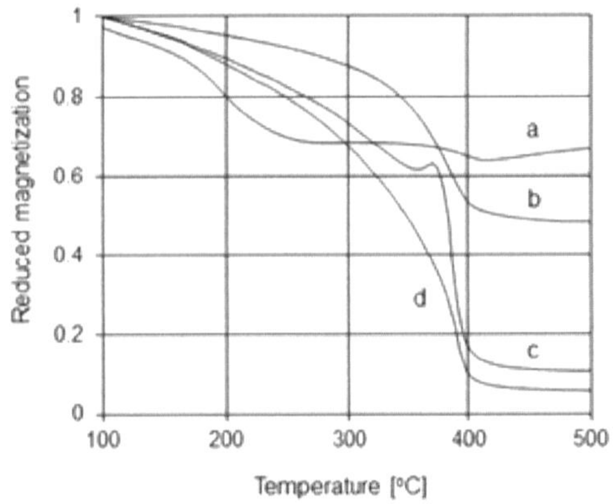

Fig. 3. Dependence of the magnetization on temperature for: a) extruded specimen – true strain εr=3.21, b) second heating of the same specimen, c) starting powder, d) second run of the starting powder.

down to 25 mm (true strain ε_r=1.38), from 25 mm down to 16 mm (ε_r=0.89), and from 16 mm do 10 mm (ε_r=0.94), respectively. Thus the specimens, after the consecutive stages of HE, experienced the summary strain of 1.38, 2.27 and 3.21, respectively. The magnetic properties of the samples were examined using a Lake Shore vibrating sample magnetometer. Samples were characterized by XRD with CuKα radiation. The crystalline lattice deformation of the $Nd_2Fe_{14}B$ crystallites was determined using the Williamson-Hall method. The Mössbauer were recorded using a POLON spectrometer, working in a transmission configuration with the constant acceleration of the Mössbauer source ^{57}Co in an Rh matrix, having the source activity of 50mCi. The quantitative analysis was done using the WinNormos for Igor package.

3. Results

In the initial stage of densification (process 1) large increase of the density is observed. For greater deformations (processes 2 and 3) the remanence decreases, in spite of the increasing density (Table 1). This dependence is especially pronounced when the effect of the reduced density ρ/7.54 is taken into account. The coercivity decreases with increasing deformation, however, still maintaining the useful level of values. The HE materials exhibit high crystalline lattice deformation.

It was noticed that the initial powder particles undergo refinement, in the course of extrusion [2]. Due to this process the particles have the ability of relocation among the neighbouring particles. Thus, the HE results in increasing the overall surface and surface of the grain boundaries, not isolated by the Nd-rich phase. This may lead to deterioration of the coercivity, however, the quantitative assessment of this phenomenon is difficult.

On the basis x-ray phase analysis changes in neither the phase constitution nor peaks intensity of the HE material, was found. The latter excludes texture formation [2].

The Mössbauer studies showed that the starting powder contained only the $Nd_2(Fe,Co)_{14}B$ phase. When fitting the experimental spectrum, besides the component related to the hard magnetic $Nd_2Fe_{14}B$ phase, a continuous component, which may be related to either amorphous or strongly disordered phase, formed in the course of extrusion, was detected. This phase is represented by the distribution of hyperfine fields $P(B_{hf})$, shown in Fig. 2. One can distinguish, in the disordered phase, two components: low- and high-field, respectively, which evidence two, various surroundings of the iron nuclei. On the basis of the analyses of areas of the sextet's components we found that the fractions of the hard magnetic and disordered phases in the material amount to 84% and 16%,

Table 1. Density and RT magnetic properties of the HE specimens.

Process	Density ρ [g/cm^3]	Coercivity H_c [kA/m]	Remanence B_r [T]	Remanence calculated for theoretical density ρB_r/7.54[T]	Lattice deformation [%]
Powder	7.54	1690	0.750	0.750	-
Process 1	5.48	1476	0.544	0.748	0.0485
Process 2	6.84	1477	0.583	0.643	0.0974
Process 3	6.89	1366	0.577	0.631	0.0989

respectively.

The existence of the new phase was confirmed by the dependence of the magnetisation on the temperature (Fig. 3). On the curve, demonstrating the dependence, for the three-stage extruded specimen (line a), one can distinguish, two characteristic temperatures, at which the magnetisation drops. The higher one, around 400°C, represents the Curie temperature of the $Nd_2(Fe,Co)_{14}B$ phase. This is confirmed by comparison of the Curie temperature, recorded for the starting powder (line c). The drop of the temperature around 200°C is probably related to the existence of the disordered phase. An interesting feature of the extruded material is demonstrated by the high magnetisation at elevated temperature; at 500°C it is still equal to 0.6 of the RT magnetisation, whereas for the starting powder, the respective value is 0.1 only. The both specimens were cooled down and reheated again (lines b and d). For the second run, for the HE specimen, the temperature drop at 200°C was not recorded, moreover, at 500°C this specimen still exhibited high magnetisation (line b). One can assume that, in the effect of transformation of the disordered phase, at a temperature of 200°C, a new ferromagnetic phase, having high Curie temperature, is formed. Thus, the formed during hydrostatic extrusion phase is not a typical amorphous phase.

4. Summary

Hydrostatic extrusion of the Nd-Fe-B melt-spun powder leads to various processes such as refinement of the powder particles and deformation of the crystalline lattice, which may cause the observed deterioration of the magnetic properties. It was also found that, as a result of high deformation, a new phase is formed. It is probably a strongly disordered form of the $Nd_2Fe_{14}B$ phase, presence of which negatively affects the magnetic properties.

Acknowledgement
The study was supported by the project co-funded by the European Union in Operational Programme Innovative Economy POIG 01.01.102.00/10 (ZAMAT). The powder was kindly provided by Magnequench.

References

[1] W. Pachla, M. Kulczyk, A. Świderska-Środa, M. Lewandowska, H. Garbacz, A. Mazur, K.J. Kurzydłowski, *Proc. of 9th Int. Conf. on Mat. Forming ESAFORM-2006, Glasgow, UK*, Nanostructuring of Metals by Hydrostatic Extrusion, 2006, April, 26-28, 535-538.

[2] W. Kaszuwara, M. Kulczyk, M. Leonowicz, T. Gizynski, B. Michalski, *IEEE Transaction on Magnetics,* Densification of Nd-Fe-B Powders by Hydrostatic Extrusion, - in press.

[3] T. Saito, H. Takeishi, *J. Appl. Phys.*, Consolidation of Nd-Fe-B melt-spun ribbon by compression shearing method, 2007, 101, 09K503.

[4] T. Saito, M. Fukui, H. Takeishi, *Scripta Mater.*, Sm–Fe–N bulk magnets produced by compression shearing method, 2005, 53, 1117–1121.

Coercivity Enhancement of the Sintered Magnets with Blending Magnetic Grains

HAIBO FENG, ANHUA LI, SHULIN HUANG, YANFENG LI, MINGGANG ZHU, WEIXING XIA, WEI LI
Division of Functional Materials, Central Iron & Steel Research Institute, China Iron and Steel Research Institute Group, Beijing 100081, P. R. China

Abstract: *The blending-magnetic-grain (BMG) method we developed and the grains with different Ce content were obtained in the magnets. The demagnetization curve of BMG magnet is smooth which is similar with the single-grain magnets. Microstructure and domain-structure of the BMG magnets were investigated. A hard-hard coercivity reinforcement mechanism was proposed and discussed. This coercivity enhancement effect is applicable in magnets with ternary and multi-magnetic grains system magnets.*

Keywords: *rare-earth; sintered magnet;* $Nd_2Fe_{14}B$*; microstructure; magnetic properties*

Address: Haibo Feng, Division of Functional Materials, Central Iron & Steel Research Institute, China Iron and Steel Research Institute Group, Beijing 100081, P. R. China

1. Introduction

With the growing demand for sintered $Nd_2Fe_{14}B$-type rare-earth magnets in new energy economic areas, reducing consumption of magnetic rare-earths and their substitution in the magnets were investigated [1-3]. Substitutes for Nd, such as La and Ce, were used in sintered RE-Fe-B magnets. Since the $Ce_2Fe_{14}B$ has lower saturation magnetization and weaker anisotropy than $Nd_2Fe_{14}B$, the magnetic properties decrease when Ce added to the magnets. Recently, we developed a blending-magnetic-grain (BMG) method: two powders with nominal composition of $Nd_{30}Fe_{bal}B_1$ and $RE_xNd_{30-x}Fe_{bal}B_1$ were prepared and mixed, then, aligned and sintered. The resulting magnet consists of Ce-free/lean grains and Ce-rich grains. A higher coercivity was obtained in the magnets with the BMG grains. The coercivity enhancement mechanism of the BMG magnets was proposed and discussed.

2. Experimental

The strip cast flakes with nominal compositions $Nd_{30}Fe_{bal}B_1$ (wt. %) and $(Nd_{0.5}Ce_{0.5})_{30}Fe_{bal}B_1$ were prepared. The two alloys were hydrogen-decrepitated (HD) and jet milled. Mixed powders with nominal composition of $(Nd_{0.7}Ce_{0.3})_{30}Fe_{bal}B_1$ were obtained by blending the two powders. Then, the powders were aligned and isostatically cold pressed. The compacts were vacuum sintered at 1000 - 1030 °C for 2 h. Then the magnets were annealed at 900 °C for 2 h and at 520 °C for 2 h and water-quenched to room temperature. Magnetic properties of the magnets were measured by the NIM-2000 hysteresis loop instrument. Microstructure was investigated by scanning electron microscopy (SEM, JSM-7001F) and transmission electron microscopy (JEM-2000).

3. Results and Discussion

The $(Ce_{0.3}Nd_{0.7})_{30}Fe_{bal}B_1$ magnet has a high performance when sintered at 1030 °C for 2 h: B_r = 13.5 kG, H_{ci} =9.5 kOe and $(BH)_{max}$ =42.8 MGOe. Fig. 1 presents the BSE image of the sintered magnet. The magnet has a grain size of ~5 μm, and the boundary phase is distributed between the $Re_2Fe_{14}B$ grains homogenously. As it can be seen in Fig. 1, the boundary phase is continuous and envelops the magnetic $Re_2Fe_{14}B$ grains thus contributing to the coercivity improvement. Because, the melting point of boundary phase decreases with the Ce content, the magnet can be sintered at lower temperature. A density of 7.61 g/cm^3 can be obtained for the $(Ce_{0.3}Nd_{0.7})_{30}Fe_{bal}B_1$ magnet sintered at low temperature. The EDS analysis results are presented given in Table1. Two kinds of grains with different Ce content were observed in the magnets. In the Ce-lean grains, the Ce content is below 2.5 at.%; Ce-free grains were observed. At the same time, the Ce content is above 6.5 at.% in the other grains. This indicates that the microstructure with BMG was obtained in the magnets.

Magnetic properties of the magnets with BMG were compared with the magnet prepared by the conventional method. The results are presented in Table 2. The remanence and maximum energy product of the BMG magnets were similar to the conventional magnets, but the coercivity of BMG magnets is 30% higher than that of common magnets. Moreover, the demagnetization curve of BMG magnet is smooth which is similar to that of the single-grain magnets, as given in Fig. 2. Demagnetization curve is not a linear combination of couplings between the $Nd_2Fe_{14}B$, $(Ce,Nd)_2Fe_{14}B$ grains and Ce-Nd-Fe grains. This indicates that an enhanced effect exists in

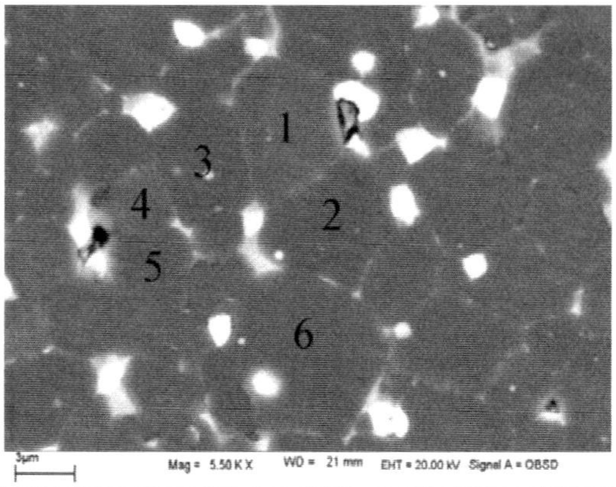

Fig.1. BSE image of the sintered magnet.

Table 1. EDS results of the grains (at.%).

Grain	Ce	Nd	Fe
1	0.42	14.51	85.07
2	6.55	7.81	85.64
3	6.95	7.57	85.48
4	2.29	12.76	84.95
5	7.08	7.53	85.39
6	1.71	13.72	84.57

the magnets with BMG microstructure. Typical magnetic domain structure of the BMG magnets is given in Fig. 2. Most magnetic domains stretch over several grains. So, the coercivity of (Ce,Nd)-Fe-B grains can be enhanced by the adjacent Nd-Fe-B grains with higher coercivity by a hard-hard reinforcement mechanism. This coercivity enhancement effect is applicable in magnets with ternary and multi-magnetic grains system magnets. So, higher coercivity can be obtained in the magnets with BMG microstructure. This coercivity enhancement effect is applicable in all the magnets with ternary and multi-magnetic grains.

Table 2. Magnetic properties of $Ce_9Nd_{21}Fe_{bal}B_1$ magnets.

Fabrication method	B_r (kG)	H_{cj} (kOe)	$(BH)_{max}$ (MGOe)
Conventional	13.43	7.22	42.5
BMG	13.53	9.53	42.8

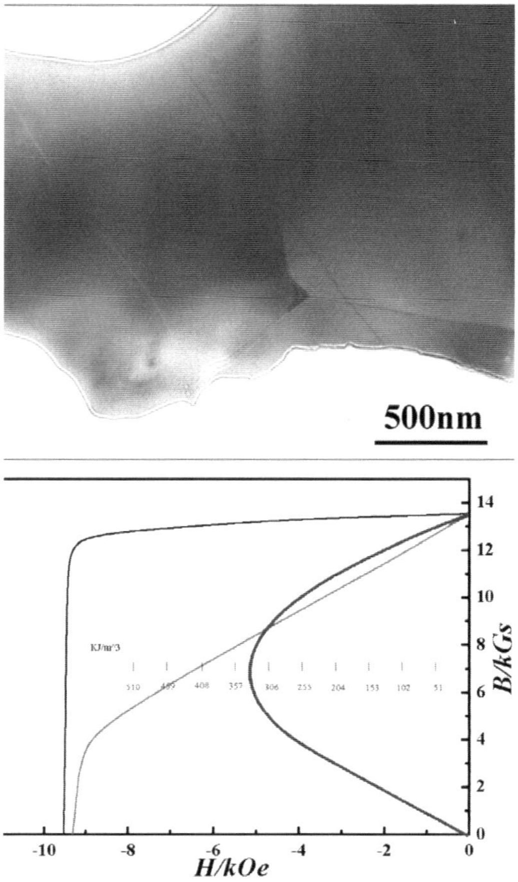

Fig. 2. Domain structure and demagnetization curve of the BMG magnet.

4. Conclusions

High performance Ce-Nd-Fe-B system magnets were obtained by BMG method. Two kinds of grains with different Ce content present in the magnets. The $Nd_2Fe_{14}B$ and $(RE,Nd)_2Fe_{14}B$ magnetic grains are distributed randomly in the magnets and they are surrounded by the RE-Nd-Fe boundary phase. The coercivity of (Ce,Nd)-Fe-B grains is enhanced by the higher-coercivity adjacent Nd-Fe-B grains by a hard-hard reinforcement mechanism. Higher coercivity of H_{ci} = 9.53 kOe was obtained; this is 30% higher than the magnets prepared by the conventional method.

Acknowledgements
This work was supported by National Natural Science Foundation of China (Grant NO. 50931001 and 51171048) and National Key Technology R&D Program.

References

[1] J.F. Herbst, *Rev. Mod. Phys.* **63**, 1991, 819.
[2] M. Velicescu, P. Schrey, W. Rodewald, *IEEE Trans. Magn.* **31**, 1995, 3623.
[3] S.X. Zhou, Y.G. Wang, R. Høier, *J. Appl. Phys.* **75**, 1994, 6268.

Elements Strategy toward High-Performance Permanent Magnets free from Critical Elements

S. HIROSAWA
Elements Strategy Initiative Center for Magnetic Materials, National Institute for Materials Science
1-2-1 Sengen, Tsukuba, Ibaraki 301-0047, Japan

Abstract: *Development of permanent magnet materials free from critical elements is strategically important for permanent magnet industries and all other industries on the downstream of the supply chains. Understandings of the coercivity mechanism and the thermodynamic landscape of the relevant systems are of key importance. Additionally, the search for a novel material with promising magnetic properties should be included in the package. Elements Strategy Initiative Center for Magnetic Materials (ESICMM) is the research center established in 2012 to conduct strategic and basic research activities on the theoretical search and mining of new permanent magnet materials and simultaneously pursuing processing technologies to improve the existing high-performance permanent magnet materials through collaboration among three research groups of computational physics, structural and property characterization, and material processing.*

Key words: elements criticality, coercivity, multi-aspects characterization, micromagnetic simulations, first-principles calculations, thermodynamic data base

Address: Satoshi Hirosawa, Tel: 81-29-851-2000, E-mail: HIROSAWA.Satoshi@nims.go.jp

1. Introduction

Development of permanent magnet materials free from critical elements is strategically important for the entire industries in the downstream along the value chains that use high-performance permanent magnets for energy conversion applications. The main issue in eliminating the critical element Dy from Nd-Dy-Fe-B magnets is to achieve a high coercivity at elevated temperatures on materials based on ternary $Nd_2Fe_{14}B$ that have only marginal magnetic hardness by means of microstructural manipulations [1,2]. Therefore, understanding the underlining physics and material science is of the key importance. Especially, deeper understandings of the coercivity mechanism and thermodynamic landscape of the relevant systems are required. The search for a novel material with promising magnetic properties is another key issue. The entire package of research programs to deal with the elements criticality is called "elements strategy initiative" in Japan. The second stage of this initiative has been carried out since 2012 as a project to form research centers, of which the Elements Strategy Initiative Center for Magnetic Materials (ESICMM) [3] was established in Aug., 2012. This article describes the basic concepts and recent research activities of the ESICMM.

2. Benchmarking

In civilian consumer applications, the operating temperature of permanent magnets may range from about –40 °C to about 200 °C in automobile applications. In most of the cases, the remanence and coercivity of permanent magnet materials have negative temperature coefficients, $\alpha(B_r)$ and $\alpha(H_{cJ})$, respectively. The temperature dependence of coercivity is mainly determined by that of anisotropy field, H_A, of the hard magnetic compound that composes the matrix phase. Two mutually independent fundamental magnetic parameters for hard magnetic materials are the uniaxial anisotropy constant K_{u1} and spontaneous magnetization J_S, with which H_A is expressed as $H_A = 2K_{u1}/J_S$. Fig. 1 shows K_{u1} and J_S of typical magnetic materials at room temperature and at 200 °C.

It is obvious that materials with a small K_{u1} will not have useful coercivity. As it was pointed out by Coey [4], the matrix compound of modern permanent magnets, which can be used in any block shape, must have K_{u1} large enough to hold magnetization along easy axis of magnetization by overcoming magneto static energy, and the criterion is expressed by magnetic hardness parameter, κ, which is defined as $[K_{u1}/(\mu_0 M_S^2)]^{1/2}$.

This parameter must be larger than unity for hard magnets if they are to be free from constraints concerning outer shapes for prevention of self-demagnetization. This sets a rigorous condition. The curved lines in Fig. 1 represent contours of constant κ values. All compounds that are used as the main phase in modern permanent magnets (i. e., Nd-Fe-B, Sm_2Co_{17}, $SmCo_5$, $Sm_2Fe_{17}N_3$, and magnetoplumbite compounds used for hard ferrites) have magnetic hardness factors slightly larger than 1.4, which is approximately equivalent to a statement that achievable coercivity values are only marginally greater than one quarter of H_A. The upper limit of

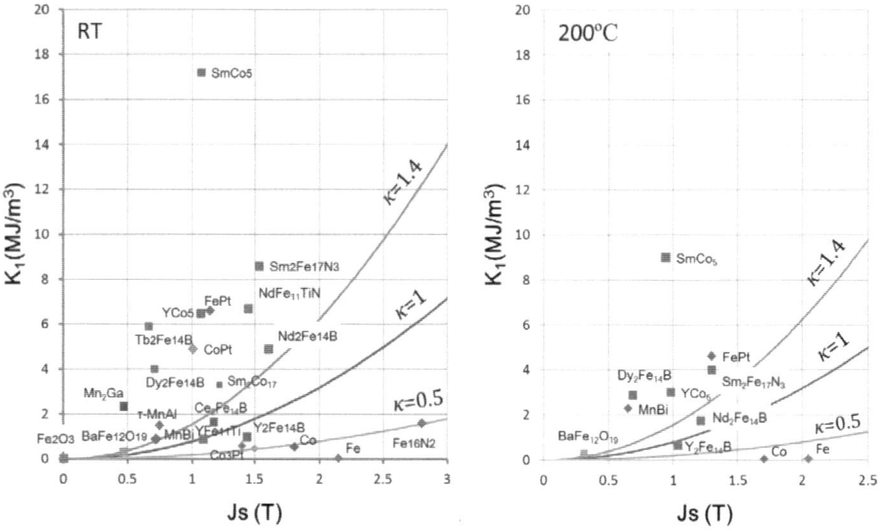

Fig. 1. K_{u1} and J_S of typical magnetic materials at room temperature and at 200 °C.

uniaxial shape anisotropy, which is the main resource of magnetic hardness in alnico and Fe-Cr-Co-type permanent magnets, corresponds to κ = 0.5, which is insufficient.

Non-rare-earth permanent magnets may be fabricated with hard magnetic compounds based on Mn-based intermetallic compounds such as $L1_0$-MnAl (τ) and $B8_1$-MnBi. These compounds have a small magnetization of about 0.7 T at room temperature, which leads to a relatively large magnetic hardness. The low-temperature phase (LTP) of MnBi which crystallizes in the $B8_1$ (NiAs-type hexiagonal) structure is of a particular interest because of its positive temperature coefficient of coercivity [5]. The relatively small magnetization of MnBi (at 200 °C, the spontaneous magnetization is 0.65 T) and low crustal abundance of Bi in an order of 0.1 ppm make MnBi less attractive as a candidate for a permanent magnet to replace commercial rare earth magnets or hard ferrites. $L1_0$-MnAl has once been utilized as a commercial permanent magnet with the addition of carbon (C) as a stabilizer of the $L1_0$ structure [6]. However, the Mn-Al-C magnet eventually disappeared from the main market after being largely replaced by hard ferrites and bonded (isotropic) Nd-Fe-B.

3. Elements Strategic Approach toward Dy-free Permanent Magnets

The most abundant elements in the 3d- and 4f-series carrying magnetic-moment are Fe and Nd, respectively, both of which have plural resources worldwide. The elements-strategically promising candidate remains $Nd_2Fe_{14}B$ (free from both Tb and Dy). In currently used magnets, HRE elements are used primarily to increase magnetic hardness in the main phase compound $(Nd_{1-x}HRE_x)_2Fe_{14}B$ by decreasing magnetization. To eliminate HRE, the most important issue is to achieve a high coercivity on $Nd_2Fe_{14}B$-based materials having only marginal magnetic hardness by means of microstructural manipulations. The basic strategy for this goal remains to be further reduction of grain sizes of the hard magnetic phase, which is rationalized by micromagnetic analyses showing that smaller grain size results in the reduction of local stray fields created by grains with reversed magnetization, which exist readily in defected surface regions of permanent magnets [7, 8]. Another important issue is to find whether there exist unknown compounds or materials with sizable magnetization and magnetic hardness.

The Elements Strategy Initiative Center for Magnetic Materials (hereinafter referred to as "ESICMM") was established in NIMS in August 2012, as a ten-year national project under the Element Strategy Initiative sponsored by the Ministry of Education, Culture, Sports, Science and Technology (MEXT), as a center to conduct multi-discipline team-work-oriented research activities on permanent magnets. About 150 researchers belonging to eight institutes are involved in this project. The current members can be seen on the URL of ESICMM [3]. ESICMM has three research groups: (1) the Computer Physics Group, (2) the Structural and Property Characterization Group, and (3) the Materials Processing Group. ESICMM researchers have formed a network beyond the boundaries of the respective research fields, making use of large-scale research facilities, such as SPring-8, J-PARC and the K-computer of RIKEN, and are thereby performing joint research from new perspectives. Research activities are performed using

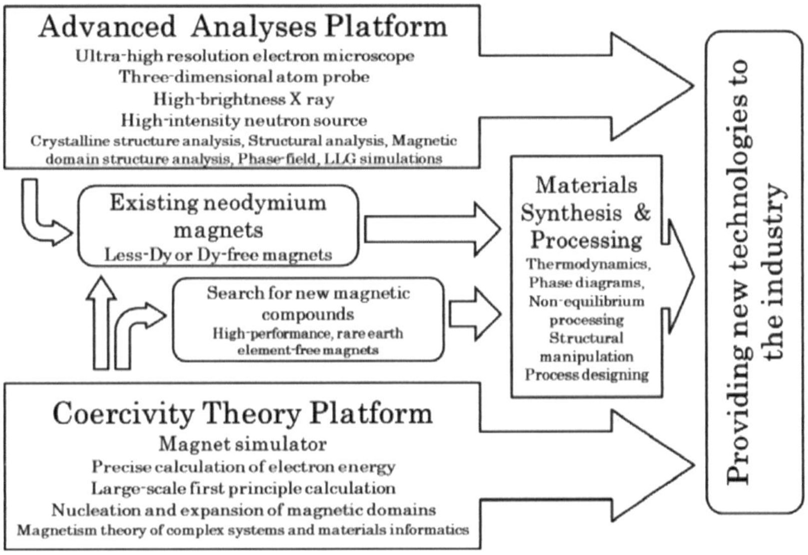

Fig. 2. Flow of research outputs in platforms and technology portfolio in ESICMM.

variety of advanced analytical and theoretical tools from the portfolio of the Advanced Analyses Platform and the Coercivity Theory Platform, construction of which is also an important subject of the project. Basic information of thermodynamics and phase diagrams will be also accumulated for materials synthesis and processing. The search for new materials currently include experimental investigations on Fe-based ordered alloys such as $L1_0$-FeNi, Fe-rich light-rare earth compounds in the $R_{m-n}Fe_{5m+2n}$ series, and feasibility studies on computational materials informatics. An image of the flow of information and research outputs in platforms and technology portfolio in ESICMM are shown in Fig. 2.

Output results of the research activities from different layers of investigations are circulated within ESICMM platforms and eventually flow into industry. A designed-in pathway is the parallel consortium project of METI called MagHEM [9]. As a whole, the deepened understandings of physics and materials science of permanent magnet materials acquired by ESICMM will be absorbed by engineers in the industry through academic communications and/or collaborated research programs.

4. Dy-free Nd-Fe-B Anisotropic Magnets

Using soft X-ray magnetic circular dichroism (XMCD), the intergranular phase which separates $Nd_2Fe_{14}B$ grains in sintered Nd-Fe-B magnets have been shown to be ferromagnetic [10] in agreement with recently performed investigations using holography [11] and spin-resolved SEM [12]. The soft XMCD investigation further evaluated the temperature dependence of magnetization and showed that the grain boundary phase has a low Curie temperature of about 250 °C, suggesting that the grain boundary phase might act as a domain-wall-pinning planar inhomogeneity [13]. A sub-micrometer branch-beam line for soft XMCD analysis has been recently constructed at BL25U in SPring-8 for acquisition of local magnetic properties and will be used for analysis of grain boundary phases in various hard magnetic materials.

Modification of structure and composition of the intergranular phase in fine grained HDDR-processed powders and hot-deformed bulk magnets, both of which have average grains sizes about one order smaller than those in sintered magnets, have been proved to result in significant increase in H_{cJ} by means of infiltration of Nd-rich alloys with low eutectic reaction temperatures [14-16], see Fig. 3.

Deeper knowledge of phase equilibria involving Cu, O, C, and other minor elements such as Al and Ga is expected to play a major role in further improvements of grain boundary chemistry and magnetic properties.

Nucleation of inversed magnetic domains at internal surfaces or interfaces with other Nd-rich phases existing at the relatively large multi-grain junctions is another possible event that may be a determinant in coercivity mechanism in these magnets. Previous investigations have suggested the importance of formation of the fcc-NdO_x phase (with a_0 = 0.55 nm) in conjunction with lattice defects in the $Nd_2Fe_{14}B$ interfacing with this phase [17]. The formation energy of this phase has been recently computed using a cluster expansion approximation combined with first-principles calculations and the fcc-NdO_x may exist as a stable phase derived from the ZnS-type

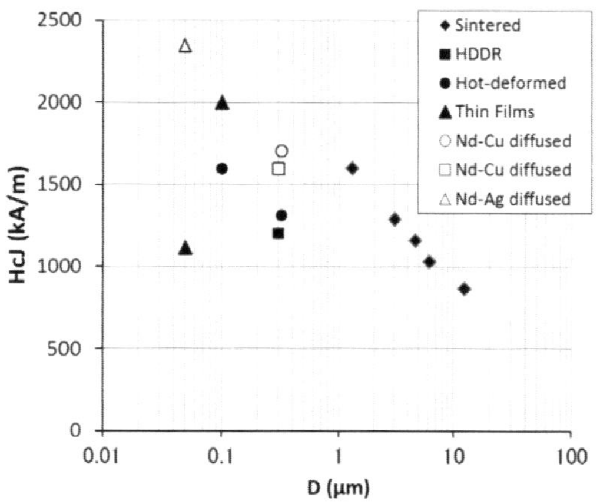

Fig. 3. Grain size dependences of Dy-free Nd-Fe-B anisotropic permanent magnets prepared with variety of processing routs. See text for original references.

NdO in a wide range of oxygen compositions from about 0.1 to about 0.5 and with a relatively large variation of the lattice constant [18]. In other words, the fcc-NdOx phase may be formed as an interfacial phase on surfaces of $Nd_2Fe_{14}B$-type phase without creating significant defects and large strain energy, which is consistent with the atomistic simulation of interfacial structures by Hrkac et al. [7]. First-principles calculation of interface atomic structure between $Nd_2Fe_{14}B(001)/NdO_{0.25}(100)$ is currently being undertaken.

The large difference of atomic arrangements in the interfacial region causes significant changes in electric fields acting on the 4f orbitals in Nd ions. First-principles calculation of electric field gradients on the Nd 4f and 4g sites due to asymmetry of the valence electrons of Nd are currently being performed, which suggests that even the sign of the principal crystal field parameter A_2^0 may be changed at the interface depending on directions of the strongest hybridization of 5d orbitals with p or d orbitals of surrounding atoms [19]. Such a change of sign of the magnetocrystalline energy can lead to a significant reduction of the nucleation field of reversed magnetic domains as previously shown by simplified micromagnetic calculation [20]. These results suggest possibilities for further improvements in coercivity of Dy-free Nd-Fe-B magnets.

5. Other Materials

Recent activities on other permanent magnet materials include a revisit on the $NdFe_{12}$-based materials from a theoretical point of view as the first try in the $R_{m-n}Fe_{5m+2n}$ series. Using first-principles calculations, Miyake et al. have clarified the mechanism of large changes of magnetic properties of the Fe atoms caused by incorporating Ti and N [21]. The fictitious compound $NdFe_{12}N$ has a large moment of 26 Bohr magnetons per formula unit. Thus, further searches for Fe-rich compounds appear to be worth trying. Characterizations of recently reported $L1_0$-Fe-Ni [22] and high coercivity Mn-Co-Sn-N alloys [23] will also be subjects of future investigations in ESICMM.

6. Summary

ESICMM focusses on the realization of Dy-free Nd-Fe-B through multi-discipline, multi-scale basic research including thermodynamic data acquisition and on the search for new hard magnetic materials with experimental and computational mining in its short term and long term programs, respectively. Progress toward the Dy-free Nd-Fe-B include clarification of grain boundary magnetism and some thermodynamic aspects concerning formation of grain boundary phases, which provide an optimistic outlook toward the realization of the Dy-free Nd-Fe-B anisotropic magnets.

Acknowledgement
The author is indebted to all ESICMM members for their hard work and to the Elements Strategy Initiative of the Ministry of Education, Culture, Sports, Science and Technology, Japan, for financial support.

References

[1] K. Hono, H. Sepehri-Amin, *Scripta Mater.*, 2012, 67, 530-535.
[2] K. Hono, S. Hirosawa, *Magnetics Japan*, 2012, 7, 290-299 (in Japanese) .
[3] NIMS, Elements Strategy Initiative Center for Magnetic Materials (ESICMM), http://www.nims.go.jp/research/ESICMM/index_e.html
[4] J. M. D. Coey, *Scripta Mater.*, 2012, 67, 514-529.
[5] M. Itoh, S. Yoshii, *Japan. J. Appl. Phys.*, 1974, 13, 809.
[6] T. Ohtani, N. Kato, S. Kojima, K. Kojima, Y. Sakamoto, I. Konno, M. Tsukahara, T. Kubo, *IEEE Trans. Magn.*, 1977, MAG-13, 1328-1330.
[7] G. Hrkac, T. G. Woodcock, C. Freeman, A. Goncharov, J. Dean, T. Schrefl, O. Gutfleisch, *Appl. Phys. Lett.*, 2010, 97, 232511 (3 pages).
[8] T. Schrefl, S. Bance, H. Oezelt, L. Exl, G. Zimanyi, M. Winklhofer, G. Hrkac, T. Shoji, M. Yano, A. Kato, *Digest of International Magnetics Conference, CD-4*, May 6th, 2014, Dresden, Germany.
[9] Technology Research Association of Magnetic Materials for High-Efficiency Motors, http://www.maghem.jp/english/index.html
[10] T. Nakamura, S. Hirosawa, T. Fukagawa, T. Nishiuchi, K. Saito, Y. Narumi, T. Hirono, T. Kinoshita, H. Nojiri, *P2-007, Proceedings of REPM* , 2012, Sep. 2-5, Nagasaki, 230.
[11] Y. Murakami, T. Tanigaki, T. T. Sasaki, Y. Takeno, H. S. Park, T. Tatsuda, T. Ohkubo, K.

Hono, D. Shindo, *Acta Mater.,* 2014, 71, 370-379.

[12] T. Kohashi, K. Motai, T. Nishiuchi, S. Hirosawa, to be published in *J. Appl. Phys.*

[13] T. Nakamura, A. Yasui, Y. Kotani, T. Fukagawa, T. Nishiuchi, H. Iwai, T. Akiya, T. Ohkubo, K. Hono, S. Hirosawa, Y. Gohda, to be submitted.

[14] H. Sepehri-Amin, T. Ohkubo, T. Nishiuchi, S. Hirosawa, K. Hono, *Scr. Mater.* 2010, 63, 1124-1127.

[15] H. Sepehri-Amin, T. Ohkubo, S. Nagashima, M. Yano, T. Shoji, A. Kato, T. Schrefl, K. Hono, *Acta Mater.*, 2013, 61, 6622-6634.

[16] T. Akiya, J. Liu, H. Sepehri-Amin, T. Ohkubo, K. Hioki, A. Hattori, K. Hono, *Scripta Mater.,* 2014, 81, 48-51.

[17] T. Fukagawa, T. Ohkubo, S. Hirosawa, K. Hono, *J. Magn. Magn. Mater.*, 2010, 322, 3346-3350.

[18] Y. Chen, A. Saengdeejing, M. Matsuura, S. Sugimoto, to be published in *JOM*, 2014, 66, (July Issue).

[19] Hiroki Tsuchiura, Takuya Yoshioka, Pavel Novak, to be published in *IEEE Trans. Magn.* conference proceedings paper of BE-7 presented at International Conference on Magnetics 2014, May 5 – 8, Dresden, Germany.

[20] C. Mitsumata, H. Tsuchiura, A. Sakuma, *Appl. Phys. Express*, 2011, 4, 113002 (3 pages).

[21] T. Miyake, K. Terakura, Y. Harashima, H. Kino, S. Ishibashi, *J. Phys. Soc. Japan*, 2014, 83, 043702 (4 pages).

[22] T. Kojima, M. Ogiwara, M. Mizoguchi, M. Kotsugi, T. Koganezawa, T. Ohtsuki, T-Y. Takahashi, K. Takanashi, *J. Phys.: Condens. Matter*, 2014, 26, 064207 (10pp).

[23] K. Isogaki, K. Shinaji, T. Mase, M. Matsuura, N. Tezuka, S. Sugimoto, *Mater. Trans.*, 2013, 54, 12361239.

Development of MnBi Based Permanent Magnet: Powder Synthesis and Bulk Fabrication

J. CUI[1], J.P. CHOI[1], G. LI[1], E. POLIKARPOV[1], M. BOWDEN[2], M.J. KRAMER[3], M. MARINESCU[4], S. REN[5], J.P. LIU[6]

[1] Pacific Northwest National Laboratory, Richland, WA 99354, USA
[2] Environmental Molecular Sciences Laboratory, Richland, WA 99354, USA
[3] Ames Laboratory/U.S. Department of Energy, Ames, IA 50011, USA
[4] Electron Energy Corporation, Landisville, PA 17538, USA
[5] University of Kansas, Lawrence, KS 66045, USA
[6] University of Texas at Arlington, TX 76019, USA

Abstract: *The metallic compound MnBi is a promising rare-earth-free permanent magnet material because of its high intrinsic coercivity (Hci) and its large positive temperature coefficient. However, the desired MnBi low temperature phase (LTP) is difficult to obtain. The reaction between Mn and Bi is peritectic, so Mn tends to precipitate out of the MnBi liquid during the solidification process. In addition, MnBi LTP decomposes at ~535 K, making the conventional sintering or warm compaction methods of fabricating bulk magnets difficult. Here we report our efforts toward developing MnBi permanent magnets. We found that the alloy with 55 at.% Mn exhibits the highest LTP MnBi content (~93 wt.%), and its magnetization is 74 emu/g with 9 T applied field at 300 K. After alignment, the energy product of the powder reached 11.9 MGOe, and that of the sintered bulk magnet reached 7.8 MGOe at room temperature. In addition to synthesizing single phase material, MnBi-Co core-shell particles were synthesized using a colloidal synthesis method. The Co layer can be controlled to ~20 nm and the overall magnetization exceeded 80 emu/g.*

Keywords: *MnBi, rare-earth free, permanent magnet*

Address: Jun Cui, E-mail: jun.cui@pnnl.gov, TEL.: +1-509-375-2028.

1. Introduction

MnBi compound is a promising permanent magnetic material because of its high coercivity and large positive temperature coefficient. MnBi exhibits a first-order structural transition between temperatures of 613 K and 628 K [1]. The phase that exhibits the desired magnetic properties is the low temperature phase (LTP). It has high magnetocrystalline anisotropy of (1.6×10^6 J/m^3), and relatively low saturation magnetization (81 emu/g, ~9 kG assuming 8.9 g/cm^3 density) at 300 K [2]. Its theoretical maximum energy product is estimated to be 20 MGOe using the formula $(BH)_{max} = M_s^2/4$, where M_s is the saturation magnetization. High purity MnBi LTP is difficult to obtain. This is because the peritectic reaction between Mn and Bi causes Mn to solidify and segregate from the Mn-Bi liquid during the solidification process. The kinetics of the segregated Mn reacting with the excessive Bi to form LTP MnBi is slow [3]. Many researchers have attempted to make MnBi alloys with high LTP content using various metallurgical methods, but none have exceeded 90 wt.% [3-5]. In the 90's, melt-spinning method was adopted for MnBi synthesis, and over 95 wt.% LTP MnBi was achieved [6-8]. However, a conventional metallurgical method, such as arc or induction melting casting followed by thermal-mechanical treatment, is preferred for its cost effectiveness. Some of the researchers have been working on developing such a method for the past two years, and have reported the properties of high purity powder with a composition near 56 at.% Mn [9].

This paper briefly describes a synthesis method for obtaining high purity MnBi with results given for an optimized composition. Obtaining high purity MnBi LTP is the first milestone to develop MnBi based permanent magnets. The next two milestones are consolidation of the LTP powder into a bulk magnet and improvement of magnetization through exchange coupling of the MnBi phase with soft phases such as Co or FeCo. This paper summarizes the current status of the fabrication of bulk magnets using warm compaction method and synthesis of MnBi-Co core-shell particles using a colloidal method.

2. Experimental Method

2.1. MnBi ingots, powder, and bulk magnet preparation

High purity Mn chips (Alfa Aesar: 99.98 wt.%) and Bi shot (Aldrich: 99.999 wt.%) were weighed according to the designed atomic ratio, and then mixed and pressed to a pellet. The pellet was arc melted three times before being cast into a button. In total 14 buttons were prepared. Their compositions varied from 45 to 80 at.% Mn. The buttons were heat-treated using a tube furnace under a pure hydrogen gas atmosphere. The heat-treatment schedule had two steps: 1) 528 K for 8 hours; 2) 625 K for 5 hours, then furnace cool to room temperature. Following the heat treatment, the buttons were crushed, ground and sieved to powders with three sizes (>44 μm, 37-44 μm, and <37 μm). The 37-44 μm powder was further heat treated under vacuum (~100 mTorr) at 563 K for 24 hours.

The heat-treated powder was then low-energy ball milled to reduce the particle size. About 5 grams of powder was sealed in a stainless steel jar filled with 100 gram stainless steel balls (1/4" in diameter) and 500 ml hexane. The jar was placed on a roller with the rotation speed set at 135 RPM. The size of the powder was reduced to ~3-5 μm after 3 hours of ball milling. The fine powders were aligned using a DC magnetic field and then packed under various loads and at various temperatures to optimize remanent magnetization and coercivity.

2.2. MnBi-Co core shell particle synthesis

A solution was prepared by mixing 5 mL N-Methyl-2-pyrrolidone (NMPO) and 35 μL Oleylamine (OLA) at 393 K. In a separate vial, another solution was prepared by dissolving 50 mg of $Co_2(CO)_8$ and 8 mg MnBi powder in 2 mL NMPO, then was quickly added into the NMPO/OLA solution. The mixture was then heated up to 453 K and held for 30 min. After cooling to 300 K, the solution was transferred into a nitrogen atmosphere glovebox where it was precipitated by adding ethanol followed by centrifugation. The product was then dispersed in hexane and stored in an intert argon atmosphere. The MnBi powder used in this process was synthesized using the metallurgical method described in the previous section.

2.3. Characterization

Samples compositions were analyzed using inductively coupled plasma atomic emission spectroscopy (ICP-AES). X-ray diffraction patterns of the powders were collected with a Panalytical X-Pert Bragg-Brentano diffractometer. Phase proportions were determined by whole-pattern Rietveld fitting using the fundamental-parameters approach implemented in Topas (v4.2, Bruker AXS) and crystal structures from the Inorganic Crystal Structure Database. Magnetic properties of the powders and bulk were characterized using vibrating sample magnetometer (VSM) and physical properties measurement system (PPMS). Microstructures of the ingots and morphology of the powders were analyzed using scanning electron microscopy (SEM) and transmission electron microscopy (TEM).

3. Experimental Results and Discussion

3.1. Effect of composition and heat treatment on LTP content

There are 4 steps to process a MnBi ingot into powder containing a high content of MnBi LTP. They are: arc melting, two-step hydrogen heat treatment, grind-&-seive, and vacuum heat treatment. Fig. 1 shows the XRD patterns of the powders after each processing step for the alloy with 55 at.% Mn. It shows that the intensity of the Bi peaks gradually decrease and eventually disappear as processing progresses.

The phase fractions of each composition, before and after heat treatment, are summarized in Fig. 2. The plot in Fig. 2(a) shows, after the grind-and-sieve process, that Bi decreases nearly linearly with increasing Mn content; however, small fluctuation in Bi are seen for Mn < 55 at.%; Mn increases more linearly with increasing Mn content. The amount of MnBi phase fluctuates around 65 mol.% when the Mn content is < 55 at.%, then linearly decreases with increasing Mn content. The overall trend of MnBi content is decreasing. Fig. 2(b) shows the phase fractions after the vacuum heat treatment. Clearly, the monotonic trends are broken and an optimum composition point (55%) emerges. Most of the Mn phase was converted to MnO and the percentage of MnO is relatively constant and independent of Mn content. This indicates that the kinetics of the Mn oxidization process is related to the heat treatment process. Bi quickly decreases to less than 2 mol.% at 55 at.% Mn, then remains constant. The amount of MnBi quickly increases to ~80 mol.% at ~55 at.% Mn, then decreases linearly with increasing Mn content.

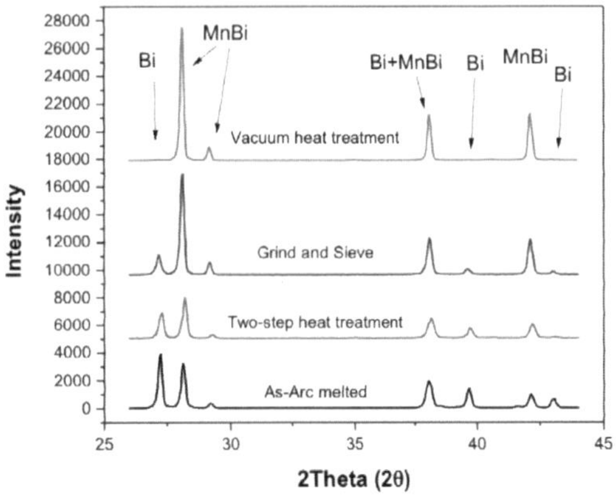

Fig. 1. The normalized XRD patterns after each thermal-mechanical processing step. The starting composition of the samples is 55 at.% Mn.

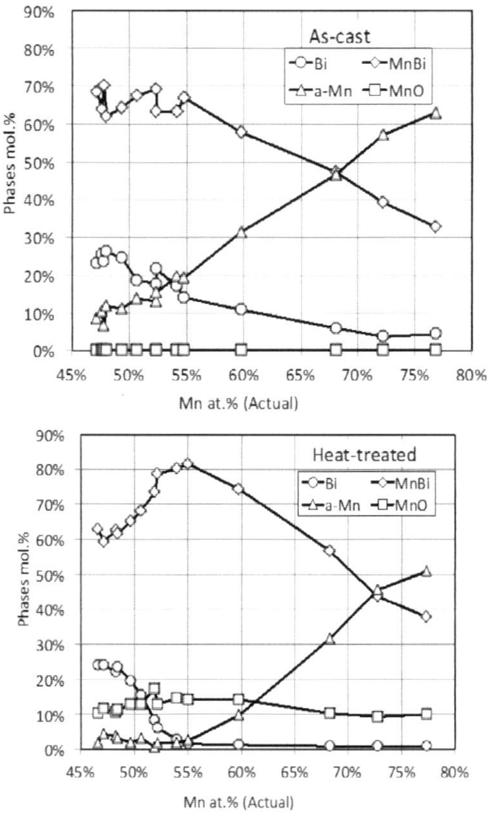

Fig. 2. Phase fractions analysis by XRD (a) before and (b) after vacuum heat treatment.

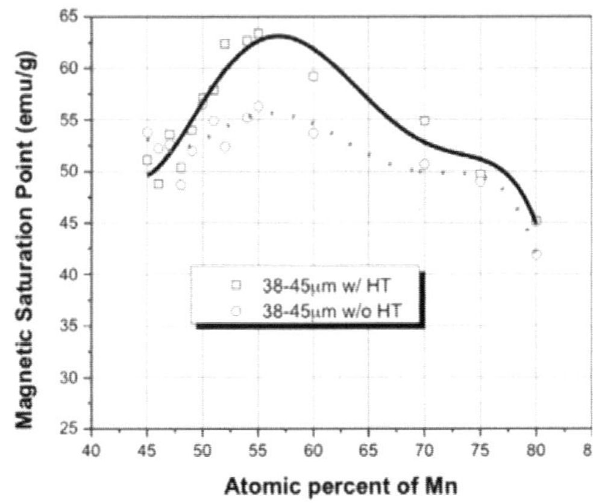

Fig. 3. Dependence of magnetization on compositions. The magnetizations were measured with 2.3 T field at 300 K.

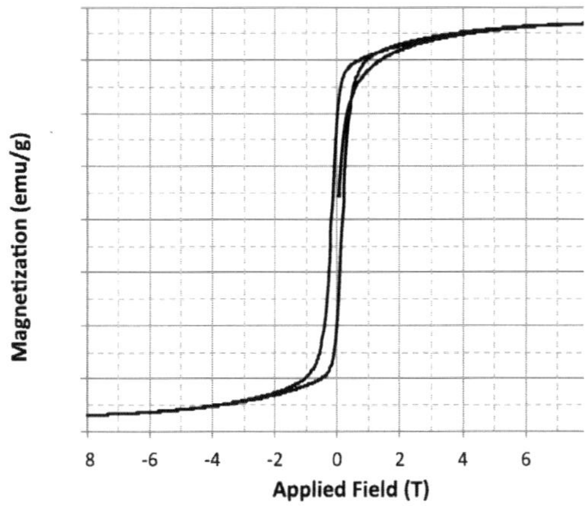

Fig. 4. MH loop of the MnBi powders at 300 K (55 at.% Mn).

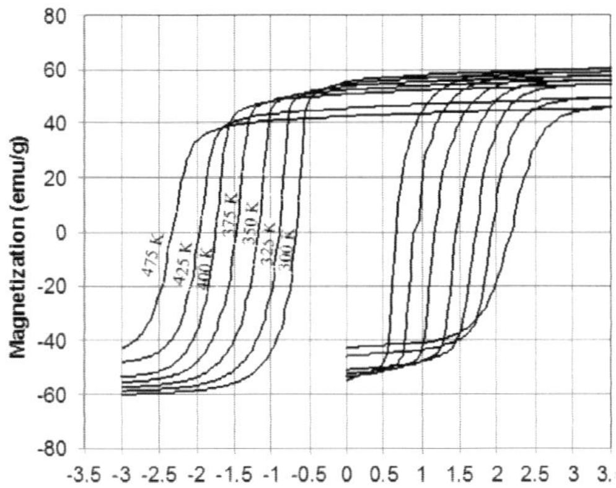

Fig. 5. MH loop of the MnBi bulk magnet fabricated using warm compaction method.

3.2. Magnetic properties of the MnBi powders and bulk magnet

The magnetizations of the MnBi powders versus compositions at 300 K are plotted in Fig. 3. The applied field was 2.3 T, which far exceeded the typical coercivity of these powders before alignment (< 3 kOe). Not surprisingly, the composition with 55 at.% Mn shows the highest magnetic moment because this is the composition possessing the highest LTP MnBi content. Compositions away from 55 at.% Mn show reduced magnetic moments. Fig. 4 shows the MH loop of the MnBi powder with 55 at.% Mn composition with an applied field of 9 T. It shows that the saturation magnetization of the 55 at.% Mn powder is about 74 emu/g at 300 K. Recall that the LTP MnBi content in this powder is about 93 wt.%. A powder with 100% LTP MnBi would show a saturation magnetization of 80 emu/g.

The magnetic properties of the bulk magnet were measured along the alignment direction. Fig. 5 shows part of the MH curves at different temperatures. The corresponding energy products are 7.8, 7.8, 7.0, and 5.3 MGOe at 300, 350, 400, and 450 K, respectively. Note that at 300 K, the bulk magnet has about 55 emu/g remanent magnetization, which is about 9% less than the 60 emu/g of the powder that was as synthesized. The loss of remanent magnetization is attributed to the oxidization of Mn, which was created by the thermal decomposition of MnBi particles at the

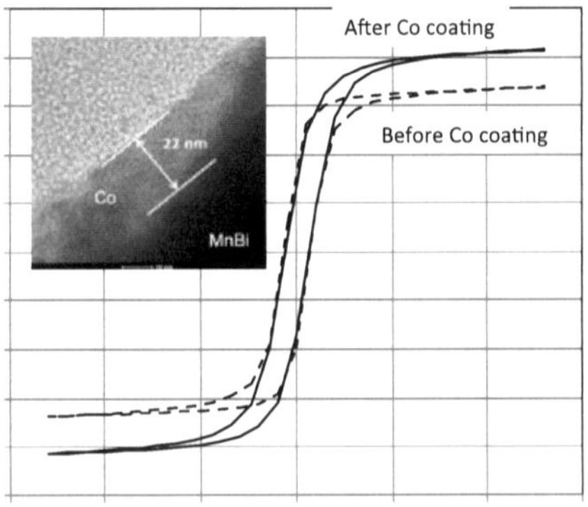

Fig. 6. TEM micrograph of a MnBi-Co core-shell particle and MH loops of the MnBi particles before and after Co coating.

fabrication temperature (563 K). This loss of M_r contributes to the 20% loss of $(BH)_{max}$.

3.3. Magnetic properties of the MnBi-Co core shell particles

The MnBi-Co core-shell particles were fabricated by coating MnBi particles with a thin layer of Co metal. Figure 6 shows a representative TEM micrograph of a MnBi-Co core-shell particle and the MH loop of the particles from the same batch. The thickness of the Co layer is sensitive to the solution annealing temperature and duration. By extending the reaction time to 4 hours, the thickness of the Co layer was increased from 22 nm to 44 nm. By lowering the reaction temperature from 453 K to 373 K, the thickness of the Co layer was reduced to 18 nm. MH loops of the MnBi particles before and after Co coating show the expected behavior, i.e., about 20% increase in magnetization and a slight reduction in coercivity.

4. Conclusion

High purity MnBi LTP is difficult to obtain because of the peritectic reaction between Mn and Bi, where the Mn phase starts to separate during the solidification process. Roughly 5 at.% excessive Mn is required to compensate for these Mn precipitations due to the preferential formation of the HTP, which later transforms to LTP and Mn phases. Through a series of thermal-mechanical treatments, high purity MnBi LTP (>93 wt.%) has been obtained.

To fabricate MnBi bulk magnets using a warm compaction method, load and temperature must be optimized. MnBi powder is mechanically softer at higher temperatures; therefore, fabricating the bulk magnet at higher temperatures could lead to full density. However, when temperature is close to the 533 K eutectic point, the MnBi LTP phase decomposes, leading to lower remanent magnetization. Conversely, if the fabrication temperature is below 473 K, the MnBi becomes hard and brittle. Large loads will break the particles, destroy alignment, and result in partial density. The optimum process temperature window is between 493 to 533 K, and the load between 30~40 kpsi.

MnBi-Co core shell particles can be synthesized using a colloidal synthesis approach. The purity can be high, and exchange coupling behaviors were observed for separate core-shell particles at 300 K. However, their performance after being fabricated into a bulk magnet is yet to be demonstrated.

Acknowledgement
This research was supported by the U.S. Department of Energy's Advanced Research Projects Agency-Energy (ARPA-E) under Contract No. 11/CJ000/09/03.

References

[1] T. Chen, W.E. Stutius. *IEEE T. Magn.*, 1974, Ma10, 581.
[2] C. Guillaud, *J Phys-Paris,* 1951, 12, 143.
[3] A.F. Andresen, *Acta Chemica Scandinavica*, 1967, 21, 1543.
[4] R.G. Pirich, *IEEE T Magn*, 1980, 16, 1065.
[5] N.V.R. Rao, A.M. Gabay, W.F. Li, G.C. Hadjipanayis, *Journal of Physics D-Applied Physics*, 2013, 46.
[6] X. Guo, A. Zaluska, Z. Altounian, J.O. Stromolsen, *J Mater Res*, 1990, 5, 2646.
[7] X. Guo, X. Chen, Z. Altounian, J.O. Stromolsen, *Phys Rev B*, 1992, 46, 14578.
[8] J.B. Yang, W.B. Yelon, W.J. James, Q. Cai, S. Roy, N. Ali. *J Appl Phys*, 2002, 91, 7866.
[9] J. Cui, J.P. Choi, G. Li, E. Polikarpov, J. Darsell, M.J. Kramer, N.A. Zarkevich, L.L. Wang, D.D. Johnson, M. Marinescu, Q.Z. Huang, H. Wu, N.V. Vuong, J.P. Liu, *Journal of Applied Physics,* 2014, 115, 17A743.

Exchange-Coupled Nanocomposite Permanent Magnets Using a Bottom-up Approach

FRANCIS JOHNSON, MIN ZOU, WANMING ZHANG, MOHAMMED HAOUAOUI
GE Global Research, One Research Circle Niskayuna, NY 12309, U.S.A.

Abstract: *The recent price volatility of critical rare earth elements used in permanent magnets has driven the search for substitutes to mitigate this supply risk. Nanocomposite magnets that contain a rare-earth permanent magnet phase and a rare-earth-free soft phase can potentially exceed the performance of* $Nd_2Fe_{14}B$, $SmCo_5$, *and* Sm_2Co_{17} *permanent magnets while requiring significantly less rare earth content. For this reason, exchange-coupled nanocomposite magnets would find use in high power density, high efficiency electric machines such as vehicle motors and wind generators. Realizing their potential requires nanometer-scale control of microstructural features such as grain size and intergranular spacing, as well as control of the crystallographic texture of the permanent magnet phase. One method for manufacturing nanocomposite magnets is a bottom-up approach in which discrete nanoparticles of the constituent phases are synthesized and consolidated into a nanocomposite permanent magnet. To achieve the highest performance, advanced manufacturing methods that can produce aligned, fully dense composites while avoiding grain growth must be employed. Recent work has focused on the development of scalable, shear-assisted thermomechanical consolidation methods that use shear strain to lower processing temperatures, in some cases to room temperature. Furthermore, a shear stress state may couple with anisotropically-shaped nanoparticles to provide an alignment mechanism. These methods face substantial challenges including residual impurities from nanoparticle synthesis, the sensitivity of rare earth containing nanoparticles to oxygen contamination, and a still limited understanding of the relationship of composite properties such as coercivity to microstructural features in bulk permanent magnets.*

Key words: *permanent magnets; rare earths; critical materials; electric machines; wind generators*

Address: Francis Johnson, Ph.D. GE Global Research, One Research Circle, MB-241, Niskayuna, NY 12309, Tel: 1-518-387-5087, Fax: 518-387-6232, E-mail: johnsonf@ge.com

1. Introduction

Electric machines utilizing rare earth-based permanent magnets have permeated the economy. These include electric vehicles and wind generators. In 2010, 274,600 hybrid electric vehicles were sold in the United States [1]. Each hybrid vehicle utilizes a permanent magnet electric motor that requires approximately 2 kg of high performance neodymium-iron-boron (Nd-Fe-B) permanent magnets [2] per motor. In 2012, 13,131 MW of wind power installations were completed in the United States [3]. Both on-shore and off-shore wind turbines can utilize permanent magnet based generators. Direct-drive off-shore wind turbines can require over 500 kg of Nd-Fe-B permanent magnets per MW of rated capacity. These clean energy technologies have driven substantial increases in the demand for the rare earth elements used to manufacture Nd-Fe-B and other permanent magnet compositions such as $SmCo_5$ and Sm_2Co_{17}.

Figure 1 illustrates the recent volatility in the price of critical elements. Nd and Dy have been identified as critical elements and are subject to supply constraint in the short and medium term [4]. Volatility of the price of rare earth elements highlights the importance of a coordinated strategy to mitigate their supply risk. The situation is complicated by the disparate functionality of the rare earth elements used in magnets coupled with the need for other critical

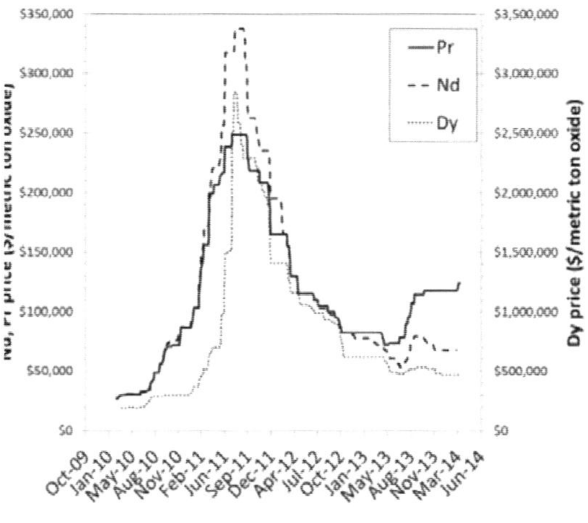

Fig. 1. Price series of oxides of praseodymium (Pr), neodymium (Nd), and dysprosium (Dy) as of May, 2014 [5].

elements like cobalt.

2. Materials Selection for Electric Machines

Permanent magnet machines operate by combining torque produced by permanent magnets with reluctance torque from the electrical steel laminations of the rotor. The magnetic flux produced by the magnets reacts across the airgap with an AC field generated by the windings on the teeth of the stator. The power density of permanent magnet machines is proportional to the remnant magnetization of the magnet. High-performance nanocomposite permanent magnets offer the potential to have flux densities similar to electrical steel. This would enable a potential step change in power density through the elimination of rotor iron mass.

3. Nanocomposite Permanent Magnets

Several technology development paths are being pursued to develop alternatives to rare earth permanent magnets such as Nd-Fe-B [6,7]. Material developments include advanced rare-earth permanent magnets that minimize the need of critical heavy rare earths such as Dy, nanocomposite permanent magnets that partly substitute non-critical elements, as well the search for new permanent magnets based compounds with no rare earths.

Nanocomposite permanent magnets have the potential to exceed the energy product of bulk Nd-Fe-B while simultaneously achieving reduced rare earth content [8,9]. In these materials a high magnetization, soft magnetic phase such as iron-cobalt is substituted for some fraction of a high-coercivity permanent magnet phase. The remanence is increased due to the increase in average magnetization of the two phases. An increase in energy product requires both exchange coupling between the constituent phases as well as crystallographic alignment of the hard phase grains. Satisfying these conditions requires achieving nanoscale control of the composite microstructure. This necessitates the development of novel processing methods to manufacture kilogram-scale magnets needed for electric machine applications. Figure 2 shows a schematic of a nanocomposite structure that could show an enhancement in energy product.

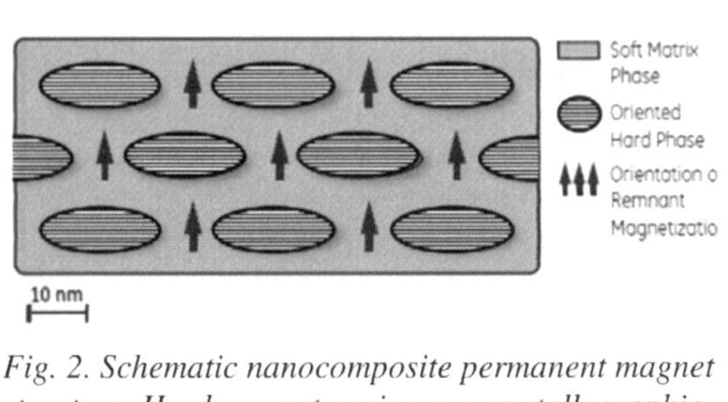

Fig. 2. Schematic nanocomposite permanent magnet structure. Hard magnet grains are crystallographically aligned and dispersed in soft magnet matrix. Length scales are on the order of 10 nm in order to promote exchange coupling of the two phases.

4. Bottom-up Synthesis via Extreme Shear Deformation

Nanocomposite magnets have been produced by consolidation and alignment of discrete hard and soft magnetic phases via extreme shear deformation methods. The hard magnetic phases are comprised of $SmCo_5$ nanoflakes produced via surfactant assisted milling of bulk $SmCo_5$ powder. The resulting nanoflakes (Fig. 3) have thicknesses in the range 30-50 nm with high aspect ratios. The microstructure of the nanoflakes indicates substantial disorder due to likely recrystallization of nanocrystalline grains, resulting in a remanant magnetization less than that of bulk, sintered $SmCo_5$. The intrinsic coercivity of the nanoflakes was consistently greater than 20 kOe.

The soft magnetic phase consisted of Fe nanoparticles produced by chemical precipitation of metal halide salts at elevated temperature using a superhydride reductant. The resulting nanoparticles (Fig. 4) were less than 10 nm in diameter with a saturation

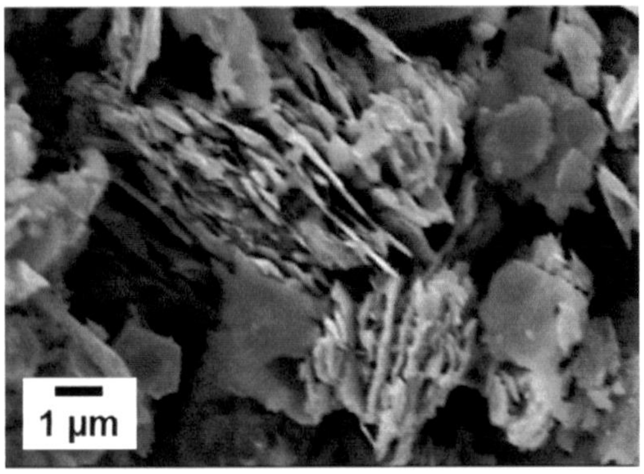

Fig. 3. $SmCo_5$ nanoflakes produced by high energy milling of $SmCo_5$ in heptane and oleylamine.

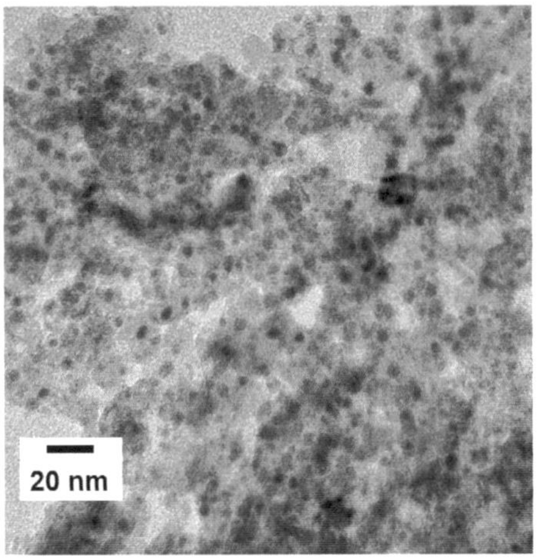

Fig. 4. Fe nanoparticles produced by reduction of Fe halide salts with a superhydride at high temperature.

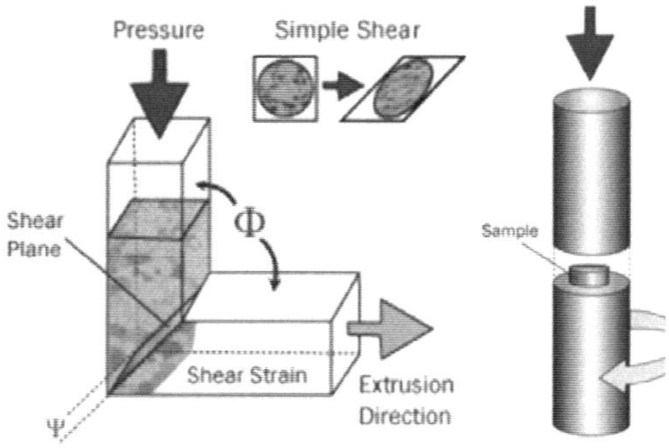

Fig. 5. (Left) *Schematic of Equal Channel Angular Extrusion (ECAE) process. The workpiece is extruded through die with angle Φ and extrusion ratio of 1:1. Simple shear strain accumulates parallel to extrusion direction with number of extrusion passes. (Right) Schematic of High Pressure Torsion (HPT) method. The workpiece is positioned between dies under uniaxial pressure. Circumferential shear strain is imparted by the rotation of one die.*

magnetization at room temperature greater than 200 emu/g.

Two extreme shear deformation methods were employed to both consolidate and align the soft and hard phase nanoparticles into nanocomposite magnets. The first method was Equal Channel Angular Extrusion (ECAE) and the second is High Pressure Torsion (HPT) [10]. Both methods apply anisotropic shear strains of greater than 100% onto blends of hard and soft phase nanoparticles. The shear stress mechanically rotates the high-aspect ratio $SmCo_5$ nanoflakes in order to achieve geometric alignment. The presence of the soft magnetic phase facilitates the rigid-body rotation of the $SmCo_5$. The deformation processing is conducted at temperatures near room temperature to avoid deterioration of magnetic properties through thermally activated grain growth.

In the ECAE process (Fig. 5, left), a blend of hard and soft phase powder is encapsulated within a copper can. The can is extruded through a die with a 90° bend but with no change in cross-sectional area. Each pass imparts a strain of approximately 100% and multiple passes may be used to achieve greater degrees of consolidation and alignment. In the HPT process (Fig. 5, right), a large (> 1 GPa) uniaxial pressure is applied to a thin envelope containing the blended hard and soft phase powders). Shear strain is imparted through angular rotation of the plunger at a low angular velocity (≈ 1 rpm). Total shear strain is a function of the radius of the die and the total number of turns.

5. Demonstration of Nancomposite Magnet Synthesis

A blend of 80 wt. % of $SmCo_5$ nanoflakes and 20 wt. % of Fe nanoparticles were prepared by mechanical milling in a solvent (heptane) and surfactant (oleylamine). The blended powder was washed with solvent and then degassed under vacuum. Approximately 0.5 g of the blend was sealed within tantalum envelopes. The envelopes were places within the HPT die set. Consolidation and alignment was conducted at room temperature under a uniaxial pressure of 5 GPa with an angular velocity of 1 rpm. Specimens were produced with total strain of 2, 5 and 10 turns. Figure 6 is an image of a nanocomposite magnet produced by HPT.

The samples were radially sectioned for characterization. Figure 7 shows the microstructure of a cross-section of an HPT processed nanocomposite magnet. The image was collected from backscattered electrons which reveal the contrast between the $SmCo_5$ (gray) and Fe (black) phases. Some degree of alignment is visually apparent, as well as evidence of deformation of the $SmCo_5$ nanoflakes during consolidation. In this image, the pressing axis is vertical.

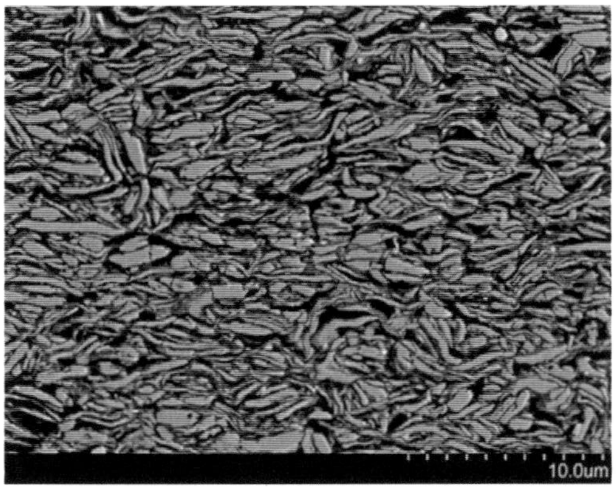

Fig. 7. Cross-sectional image of microstructure of 80% $SmCo_5$ / 20% Fe nanocomposite magnet consolidated and aligned by HPT. Gray regions are $SmCo_5$ and black regions are iron.

Table I. Magnetic properties of nanocomposite magnets produced by High Pressure Torsion. Total shear strain is proportional to number of turns. Increasing remanence B_r and energy product $(BH)_{max}$ correlates with number of turns.

Turns	H_{ci} (kOe)	B_r (kG)	$(BH)_{max}$ (MGOe)
2	11.0	6.0	4.2
5	11.0	6.2	4.5
10	11.5	6.7	5.3

Table I presents magnetic measurements of HPT processed nanocomposite magnets with 20% soft phase mass fraction. The nanocomposite retained approximately half of the intrinsic coercivity (H_{ci}) of the $SmCo_5$ precursor nanoflakes. An increasing amount of strain (turns) appears to correlate with increasing remanence B_r and energy product $(BH)_{max}$. The energy product is substantially lower than bulk $SmCo_5$ due to the lack of exchange coupling between the soft and hard magnetic phases. The microstructure shown in Fig. 7 shows a random distribution of soft Fe phase thickness between the $SmCo_5$ nanoflakes. Higher resolution microscopy reveals that the soft phase regions can be several hundred nanometers thick. This is two orders of magnitude higher than the magnetic domain wall width of $SmCo_5$, indicating that the magnetization of the thick soft phase regions is not able to be retained by the hard magnetic phases. Further progress in the magnetic nanocomposites depends on the development of processing methods capable of achieving uniform distribution of soft phase thickness.

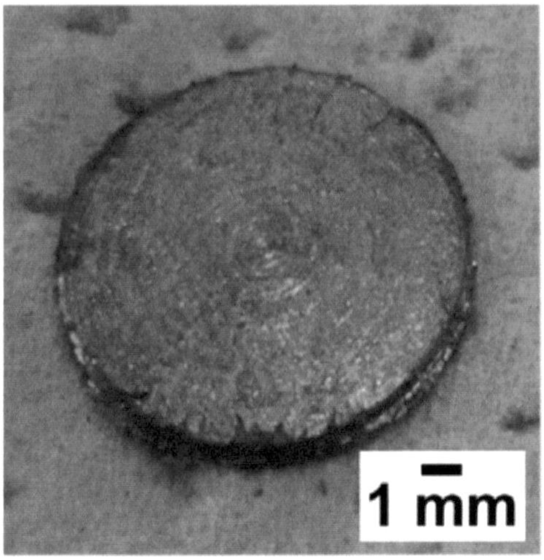

Fig. 6. Image of nanocomposite magnet produced by High Pressure Torsion consolidated at room temperature. Nanocomposite is comprised of 80 wt.% $SmCo_5$ nanoflakes and 20 wt. % Fe nanoparticles.

6. Conclusions

Extreme shear deformation methods have been used to consolidate and align blended $SmCo_5$ nanoflakes and Fe nanoparticles into nanocomposite permanent magnets. The nanocomposite permanent magnets retain over half of the intrinsic coercivity of the precursor $SmCo_5$ nanocomposite phase. The nanocomposite microstructure achieves geometric alignment of the high aspect ratio nanoflakes in a matrix of Fe. The remanent magnetization and energy product of the nanocomposite magnets correlates with the amount of shear strain imparted to the nanocomposite. An exchange-coupled magnet is not achieved due to a random distribution of Fe phase thickness between the $SmCo_5$ nanoflakes. Further process development will enable uniform distribution of soft phase thickness. A fully exchange-coupled permanent magnet based on $SmCo_5$ nanoflakes will enable improved system performance with less critical material content.

Acknowledgement
This information data, or work presented herein was funded in part by the Advanced Research Projects Agency - Energy (ARPA-E) U.S. Department of Energy under Award Number DE-AR0000158. The information, data, or work presented herein was funded in part by an agency of the United States Government. Neither the United States Government nor any agency thereof, nor any of their employees, makes any warranty, express or implied, or assumes any legal liability or responsibility for the accuracy, completeness, or usefulness of any information, apparatus, product, or process disclosed, or represents that its use would not infringe privately owned rights. Reference herein to any specific commercial product, process, or service by trade name, trademark, manufacturer, or otherwise does not necessarily constitute or imply its endorsement, recommendation, or favoring by the United States Government or any agency thereof. The views and opinions of authors expressed herein do not necessarily state or reflect those of the United States Government or any agency thereof.

References
[1] *Transportation Energy Data Book*, U.S. Department of Energy, 31st edition, 2012.
[2] *FreedomCar Advanced Traction Motor Development Phase I report*, ORNL/TM-2006/UQM, 08-04-2006.
[3] *2012 U.S. Wind Industry Market Update*, American Wind Energy Association.
[4] *Critical Materials Strategy*, U.S. Department of Energy, December 2011.
[5] Pricing data from *www.metal-pages.com* and *www.lme.com*.
[6] L.H. Lewis, F. Jimenez-Villacorta, *Metall. Mater. Trans. A* **44**, 2013, S2.

[7] N. Poudyal, J.P. Liu, *J. Phys. D: Appl. Phys.* **46**, 2013, 043001.
[8] E.F. Kneller and R. Hawig, *IEEE Trans. Magn.* **27**, 1991, 3588.
[9] R. Skomski and J.M.D. Coey, *Phys. Rev. B* **48**, 1993, 15812.
[10] F. Johnson, R.E. Colborn, J.S. Marte, P.J. Bonitatibus, B.I.I. Kandapallil, M. Haouaoui, C. Chen, *U.S. Patent Application US 2014/0002220*, filed June 29, 2012.

This page intentionally left blank.

Rare Earth Free Permanent Magnets

G. GIANNOPOULOS[1], C. SARAFIDIS[1], M. GJOKA[1], L. REICHEL[2,3], A. MARKOU[1], W. WALLISCH[4], V. PSYCHARIS[1], J. FIDLER[4], D. NIARCHOS[1]
[1]INN, NCSR Demokritos, Athens 15310, Greece
[2]IFW Dresden, PO Box 270116, 01171 Dresden, Germany
[3]TU Dresden, Institute for Materials Science, 01062 Dresden, Germany
[4]Vienna University of Technology, Institute Solid State Physics, Vienna, 1040 Austria

Abstract: *REFREEPERMAG is an EU-funded project to develop a new generation of novel materials without rare earths or platinum for high performance permanent magnets as a replacement of the existing ones mainly based on rare-earths. To achieve this objective our research is based on: a) exploitation of shape anisotropy of high magnetic moment materials produced in the form of nanoparticles (nanowires, nanorods) with high aspect ratio (>5) via chemical environmentally friendly polyol process, which will be then consolidated with novel processes for a new generation of permanent magnets with a maximum energy product* $(BH)_{max}$ *between 10 and 20 MGOe, and b) using a novel high-throughput thin film synthesis and characterization approach to search for very promising candidate materials of the type (Fe-Co-Mn)-X (X = other 3d or 4d metals and B, C) and/or Heusler alloys with high magnetization, that can be formed in a tetragonal or hexagonal structure by epitaxial growth on selected substrates, under various conditions of pressure, stoichiometry and temperature.*

Within the first two years we a) modeled libraries of candidate tetragonal FeCo-X (X = C, B, N, P) phases with large anisotropy, b) produced FeCo-X nanowires with coercivity values in excess of 0.5 T using a polyol process, c) deposited tetragonally distorted FeCo-C films on Au-Cu substrates using sputtering and laser ablation, and d) prepared tetragonally distorted Mn-Fe-Co-Ga phases with attractive magnetic properties. Up scaling and the combinatorial sputtering approach will be heavily employed in the last year of the project towards the final goal, following an integrated approach "Materials by design-fabrication-characterization" for low cost permanent magnets, leading to more efficient energy and power dense devices with positive environmental and socioeconomic impacts.

Keywords: *rare earth free; combinatorial; Heusler alloys; anisotropy*

Address: Dimitrios Niarchos, NCSR Demokritos, Greece, Tel. +302106503385,
E-mail: dniarchos@ims.demokritos.gr

1. Introduction

This work aims at developing a new generation of novel non Rare-Earth containing materials for high performance permanent magnets. To achieve this objective two approaches are used, high-throughput (HT) thin film and bulk materials synthesis and characterization techniques to identify new PM candidate phases.HT methods allow for screening of hundreds of possible compositions and synthesis conditions. Investigations focused on promising candidate materials of the type {Fe-Co}-Y (Y= B,C,P or N) and Heusler alloys of the type X_2YZ (where X is usually Fe, Co, Ni, Cu; Y other transition metals, most often Mn; and Z a group-B element (Al, Ga, Ge, Sn...). The goal of the research are materials with both high magnetic saturation (M_s) and magnetic anisotropies in excess of 10^7 erg/cm³. The latter is expected to be present in tetragonal or hexagonal structures grown epitaxially on selected substrates. The named range of anisotropies covers a wide field of possible applications. Soft Fe-Co is proposed already for exchange-coupled hard/soft type magnets [1,2]. The technique used was high-throughput synthesis using a multi-combinatorial sputtering system on highly textured substrates aiming to stabilize the fct-type tetragonal structure by exploiting the Bain path and the phase instability in the Fe-Co system.

For our work, we use the newest highly efficient high-throughput methods in order to develop PMs based on

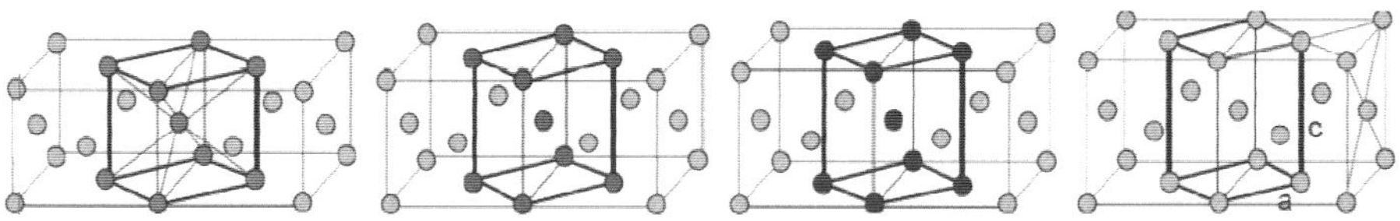

Fig. 1. Bain transformation.

FeCo. In calculations, this alloy is considered as a promising new class of PMs [3,4], which are both of great scientific interest but also have potential industrial impact. We have chosen well-developed combinatorial sputtering techniques for deposition of thin as well as thick films to produce materials libraries suitable for high-throughput characterization. HT techniques aim at fabricating materials libraries, where a well-defined set of materials is deposited in one experiment. Thus all the prepared samples of different chemical composition are very well-comparable. Rapid characterization techniques which automatically measure the whole material library with regard to the specific properties of interest are termed HT measurements. Structural measurements and analysis were performed using infrastructure Rigaku X-ray diffractometer.

2. Our Approach - Results

The challenge is to replace the rare-earth by other elements that ensure a high anisotropy without reducing M_s. The latter is crucial, because $(4\pi M_s)^2/4$ is the upper limit for the energy product of highly coer-cive materials. Thus, we extensively investigated:

(a) *Fe-Co-based alloys* close to the instability limit doped with B, C or with 3d or 4d transition metals.

(b) *Heusler alloys* - the family of ordered intermetallic compounds with the $L2_1$ structure having a composition of the general formula X_2YZ, where X is usually Fe, Co, Ni, Cu; Y is another transition metal, most often Mn; and Z is a group-B element (Al, Ga, Ge, Sn, ...). In their present structure, these materials have a low anisotropy and are not magnetically hard. We attempt to develop a high coercivity in these materials by going off-stoichiometry to obtain a microstructure with the fine Heusler phase in a nonmagnetic matrix like in the Cu_2MnAl using the HT approach. This approach may give rise to a high coercivity due to shape anisotropy, as in Alnico magnets.

We adjusted the deposition, following the theoretical calculations and reducing the former cubic symmetry along the "Bain path" of the Fe-Co alloy and at the selected Heusler alloys.

2.1. Thin films

A materials library of epitaxial buffer layers with tailored lattice parameters is needed to develop a "Bain library" of distorted Fe-Co-X. For this, we developed a layer system where the lattice constants are varying laterally - from one side of the substrate to the other. We could show that epitaxial growth of Cu-Au at various different composition is possible on Cr buffered MgO (100) substrates, which allows to vary the buffer fcc lattice constant from 0.361 nm to 0.407

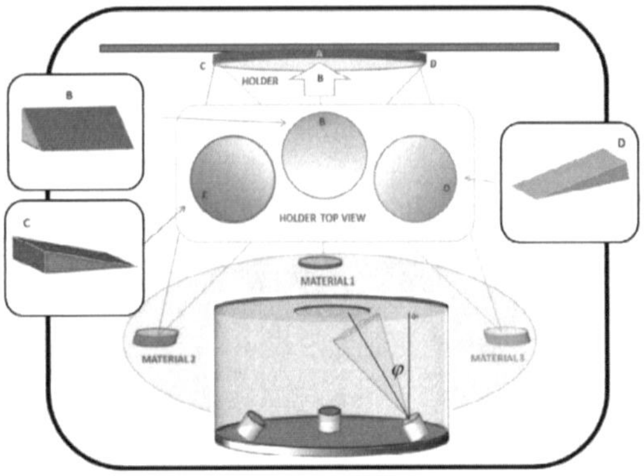

Fig. 2. Wedge type layer depositions using combinatorial sputtering technique.

nm [5]. On these buffers, Fe-Co-X films were deposited exhibiting a composition gradient perpendicular to the buffer lattice constant gradient.

Sputtering FeCo-C

By the incorporation of small C elements into the lattice of Fe-Co-C we tried to induce a tetragonal distortion using HT deposition method The main idea is that that when small atoms like C occupy interstitial positions inducing a stain into FeCo unit cell[6]

Several sputtering approaches have been employed in order to achieve a variable Fe-Co composition on two buffer layers of the different symmetry, either tetragonal ($Au_{50}Cu_{50}$) or cubic ($Au_{30}Cu_{70}$) Au-Cu. Deposition of three elements, Co, Fe and C via co-sputtering, was performed producing variable thickness, stoichiometry and carbon percentage in the magnetic layer. The samples were in situ annealed at 300 °C and carbon percentage varied up to 20%. Epitaxial growth of high quality $Fe_{45}Co_{55}$ layer was observed while magnetocrystalline anisotropy value K_u was estimated in the excess of $0.5 \cdot 10^6$ J/m^3, indicating tetragonal distortion of the FeCo unit cell.

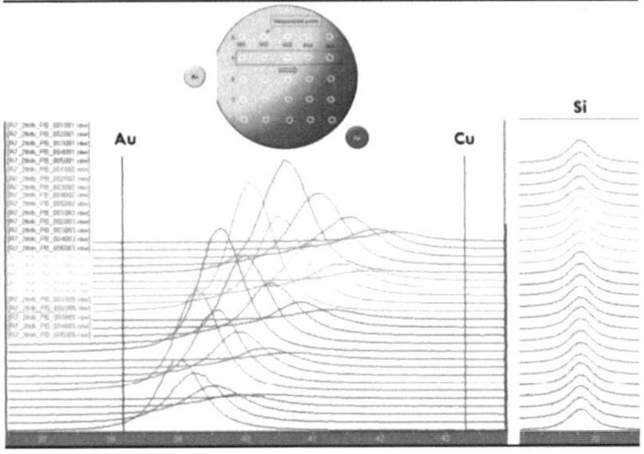

Fig. 3. Au-Cu buffer layer fabricated following combinatorial approach on a 4" Si wafer, showing variable lattice constant with alloy composition change.

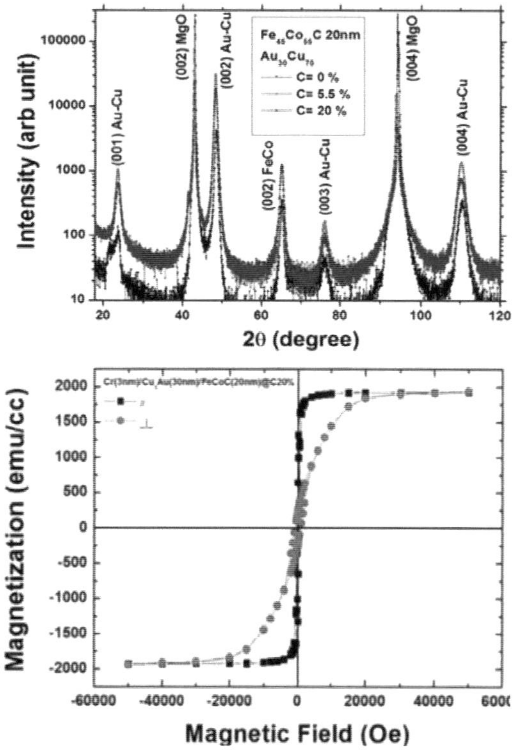

Fig. 4. X-ray diffraction of $Fe_{45}Co_{55}$ C thin films with variable C content (top) and representative in-plane / out-of-plane hysteresis loops for 3nm thick film (bottom).

Fig. 5. TEM characterization revealing high uniformity, continuous layer structure.

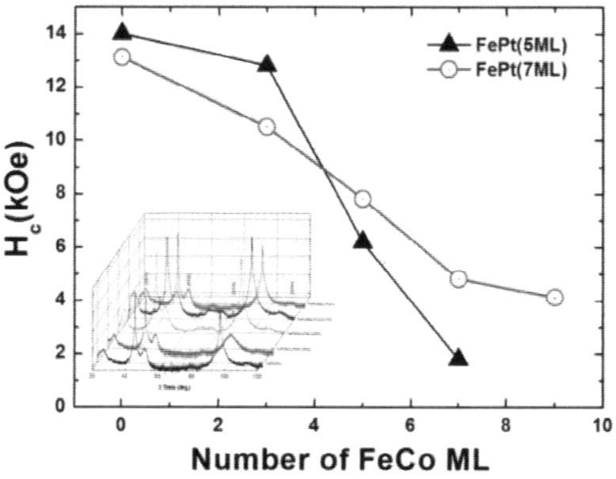

Fig. 6. Manipulation of the bilayers coercive field through exchange coupling of FeCo and FePt magnetic layers. FePt fct transformation and FeCo epitaxial growth is verified from x-rays measurements (inset).

To avoid strain relaxation a similar multilayer approach was followed, where the system consists of alternate magnetic (Fe-Co-C) and non-magnetic layers (Au-Cu) and is considered as a possible candidate for upscaling to higher thicknesses.

Moreover, a similar multilayer system fabricated by sputtering alternates magnetic layers, either Fe-C/Co or Fe/Co-C. The K_u value is even higher than the co-sputtering approach, while the easy axis is in plane, according to magnetic measurements analysis, as it was in all previous cases. Some representative results concerning Fe-Co-C are presented in Fig. 4.

FePt/FeCo multilayers

FePt $L1_0$ phase was used as an underlayer in order to strain the Fe-Co unit cell to obtain high coercivity and high energy product via an exchange spring system [7,8]. The thickness of the FePt layers varied between 5 and 7 monolayers (ML) while the FeCo thickness was up to 9 ML. Deposition temperature was fixed at 500 °C for FePt and 300 °C for the Fe-Co layer, respectively. Epitaxial FeCo growth observed on full fct transformed FePt, while the estimation of the energy product was in the order of 200 kJ/m^3.

2.2. Heusler alloys

Heusler alloys are a broad family of intermetallic compounds and include mostly ternary materials with XYZ (Half-Heusler) or X_2YZ stoichiometry (Full-Heusler) where X, Y are transition metal elements and Z main group element. In the last years, many new stoichiometries have been studied, experimentally and by theoretical calculations. Recently, combinatorial studies of Heusler alloys by first-principles computational methods, predict that Fe_2YZ alloys with tetragonal structure show magnetic moments close to 800 emu/cm^3, making them candidate materials for rare earth free permanent magnets [9]. Up to now, there is no Heusler alloy perfectly suitable for permanent magnetic applications. However, some present large magnetization combined with high Curie temperature (e.g. Co_2MnSi, M_s = 138.5 Am^2/kg, T_C = 983 K). Theoretical calculations, although not always confirmed by experiments, predict even better properties [10].

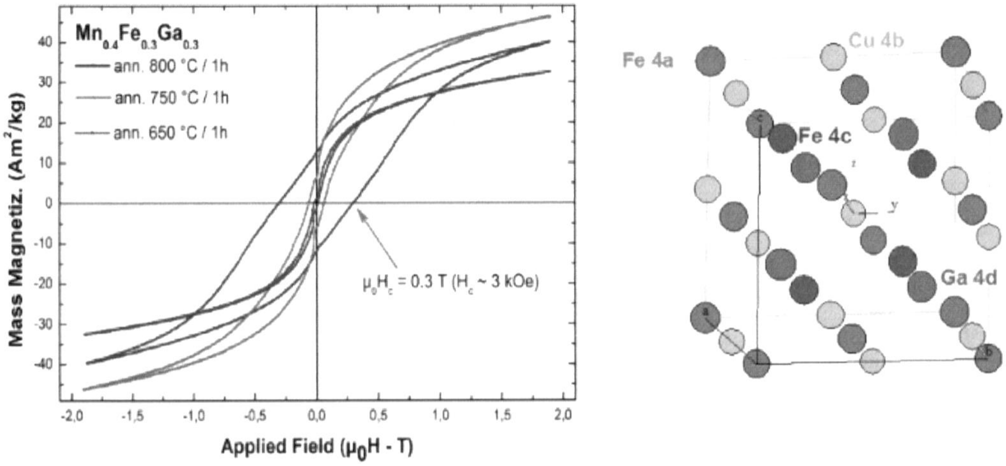

Fig. 7. RT magnetic loops of $Mn_{0.4}Fe_{0.3}Ga_{0.3}$ compounds annealed at various temperatures, larger coercivity corresponds to the sample annealed at 800 °C (left) and Hg_2CuTi-type "inverse Heusler" structure (S.G. F-43m, No 216) (right).

Our approach follows two paths. One is the exploitation of new alloys by introducing magnetic atoms (Fe, Ni, Co) in existing Heusler alloys. The second is the fine tuning of the structural and microstructural properties of the materials aiming at the improvement of their usually low anisotropy. We have focused mainly on stoichiometries which may be stabilized in a lower symmetry than the typical cubic.

Mn_2NiSn Heusler crystallizes in the inverse Heusler structure (Hg_2CuTi-type) with the two Mn atoms in an antiferromagnetic arrangement. It has been shown that changes in stoichiometry may turn the magnetic moments in a ferromagnetic arrangement. We have prepared $Fe_{2-x}Mn_xNiSn$ (x = 0.2 to 0.8) alloys in the form of ribbons after producing the initial alloys with Ar arc-melting. Heat treatment of ribbons was conducted in a temperature range 550 to 850 °C and for different time span, from 10 minutes to 1 hour under high vacuum followed by quenching. In large Mn concentration the cubic structure was found, while with increasing Fe content the hexagonal FeNiSn-type dominated. In all cases, magnetization was above 70 Am^2/kg which corresponds to a net magnetic moment about 4 μ_B per formula unit. Curie temperature of the materials is relatively high and increases with Fe content, from 578 K in the case of $x = 0.6$ up to 1008 K for the case of $x = 0.2$ alloy.

Mn_3Ga is practically a ferrimagnetic material with strong half-metallic character. The sum of the down spins exactly cancels the sum of the up spins, and thus the term compensated half metal (CHM) was introduced [11]. It is crystallizing in a tetragonal unit cell (I4/mmm) which is a disordered derivative of the cubic $L2_1$ structure but also in hexagonal and cubic variants while presenting frustrated and structure/stoichiometry sensitive magnetic properties [12]. We have successfully introduced Fe into the Mn-Ga Heusler system by synthesizing $Mn_{0.7-x}Fe_xGa_{0.3}$ series of compounds in the form of ribbons. Fe-rich compounds were found to crystallize in cubic $L1_2$ structure (Cu_3Au - SG 221), not previously detected in the Mn-Ga system. Heat treatment in various temperatures did not result in the appearance of the $D0_{22}$ tetragonal structure, however a tendency for the hexagonal $D0_{19}$ was observed instead. The magnetic properties of the materials are affected and annealing at higher temperatures improves the coercivity of the materials [13].

We have successfully synthesized $Fe_{2+x}Cu_{1-x}Ga$, $Fe_{2+x}Cu_{1-x}Al$ and $Fe_{2+x}Co_{1-x}Ga$ (x = 0 – 0.4) with the addition of excess B up to 12%, since B improves magnetic properties of intermetallics and helpful in synthesizing metastable phases. Although the materials did not adopt the tetragonal structure and the coercivity was low, small improvements with thermal treatment were observed. Small amounts of B

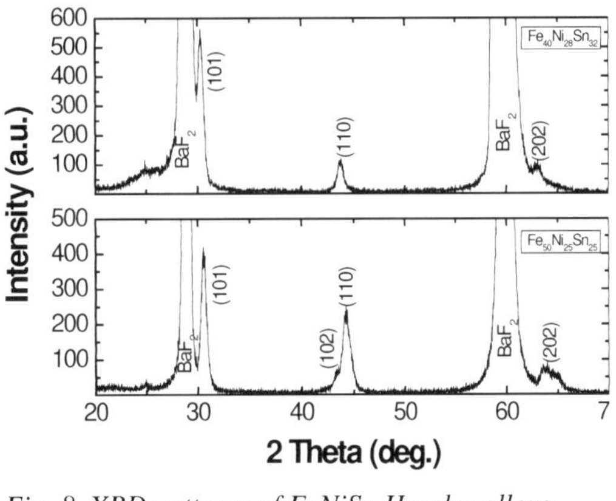

Fig. 8. XRD patterns of FeNiSn Heusler alloys deposited on epitaxial BaF_2 substrate.

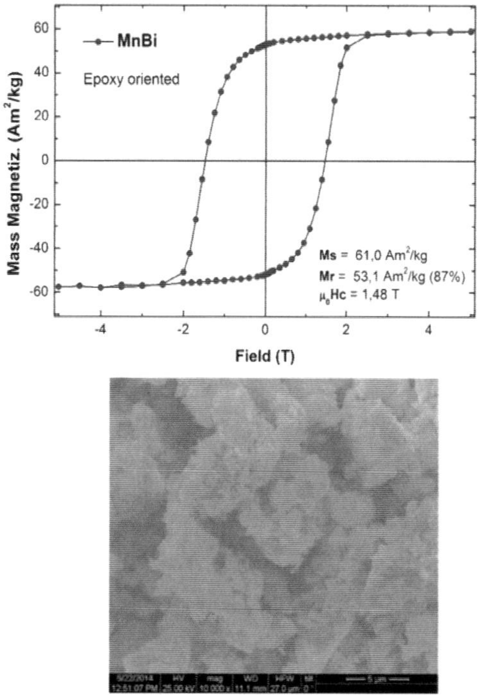

Fig. 9. Room-temperature hysteresis loop of epoxy-oriented MnBi sample and SEM image of MnBi powder showing well-distributed grains.

improve the saturation magnetization; 130 Am^2/kg (5.5 μ_B / formula unit) has been achieved in the case of $Fe_{2.4}Co_{0.6}Ga$ [14].

Apart from the bulk form, Fe-based Heusler films have been studied. FeNiSn films grown on BaF_2 (001), independently of film thickness and composition (from semi- to full Heusler) are crystallized in the hexagonal structure $P6_3/mmc$ (194) showing high magnetic moment 450 emu/cc.

2.3. Bulk materials – MnBi

MnBi has recently attracted large attention due to its potential for permanent magnetic applications. Although it presents little magnetization, it has a large coercivity, above 1 T, which results in a theoretical $(BH)_{max}$ value above 17 MGOe. It is also very interesting that the coercivity increases with temperature, up to 2.6 T at 523 K, for higher temperatures the structure is unstable [15,16].

The magnetic properties depend heavily on the quality of the basic material, which is difficult to synthesize. Microstructure plays also a dominant role, the best properties seem to be obtained for grain sizes from 0.7 to 4 μm. We have managed to achieve coercivity near 1.5 T at RT in epoxy oriented powder samples while saturation magnetization was 61 Am^2/kg. The production of high density bulk pieces from MnBi and exchange spring improved magnets could be an alternative for some technological applications.

Acknowledgements

Work is supported by the EU Programme REFREEPERMAG. We would like to thank our colleagues in REFREEPERMAG project (http://refreepermag-fp7.eu/project/).

References

[1] K. Sumiyama, S. Sawa, D. Liang Peng, Y. Kurokawa, T. Yamabuchi and T. Hihara, *Mater. Trans.* **53**, 2012, 1563.
[2] E.E. Fullerton, J.S. Jiang, M. Grimsditch, C.H. Sowers, S. D. Bader, *Phys. Rev. B* **58**, 1998, 18.
[3] T. Burkert, L. Nordström, O. Eriksson, O. Heinonen, *Phys. Rev. Lett.* **93**, 2004, 027203.
[4] C. Neise, S. Schönecker, M. Richter, K. Koepernik, H. Eschrig, *Phys. Status Solidi B* **248**, 2011, 2398.
[5] S. Kauffmann-Weiss, S. Hamann, L. Reichel, A. Siegel,V. Alexandrakis, R. Heller, L. Schultz, A. Ludwig, S. Fahler, *APL Mater.* **2**, 2014, 046107.
[6] E.K. Delczeg-Czirjak, A. Edstrom, M. Werwinski, J. Rusz, N.V. Skorodumova, L. Vitos, O. Eriksson, *Phys. Rev. B* **89**, 2014, 144403.
[7] D. Kim, J. Hong, *Surf. Sci.* **606**, 2012, 1960.
[8] D. Kim, Ar. Hashmi and J. Hong, *J. Korean Phys. Soc.* **62**, 2013, 918.
[9] M. Gillessen, R. Dronskowski, *J. Comput. Chem.* **31**, 2010, 612.
[10] T. Graf, C. Felser, S.S.P. Parkin, *Prog. Sol. State Chem.* **39**, 2011, 1.
[11] H. Luo *et al.*, *J. Magn. Magn. Mater.* **321**, 2009, 4063.
[12] S. Wurmehl, H. Kandpal, G. Fecher, C. Felser, *J. Phys.: Condens. Matter* **18**, 2006, 6171.
[13] C. Sarafidis, M. Gjoka, O. Kalogirou, N. Lupu, G. Ababei, D. Niarchos, *JEMS* 2013 (accepted for publication).
[14] C. Sarafidis, M. Gjoka, C. Wang, G. Hadjipanayis, O. Kalogirou, D. Niarchos, *Intermag* 2014 (accepted for publication).
[15] N.V. RamaRao, A.M. Gabay, G.C. Hadjipanayis, *J. Phys. D: Appl. Phys.* **46**, 2013, 062001.
[16] J. Cui et al., *J. Phys.: Condens. Matter* **26**, 2014, 064212.

Rare-Earth Free High Magnetic Anisotropy Materials: Temperature Dependence of Magnetic Anisotropy

T. SUZUKI[1], T. HOZUMI[1,2], S. ZHAO[1], P. LECLAIR[1], G. MANKEY[1]
[1] Center for Materials for Information Technology (MINT), The University of Alabama, Tuscaloosa, AL 35487-2507, U.S.A.
[2] Advanced Technology Development Center, TDK Corporation, Narita, Japan

Abstract: *The G8 research project is briefly described first. Then, the magnetic anisotropy constant for the τ-phase MnAl and the low temperature phase (LTP) MnBi thin films are discussed in conjunction with saturation magnetization. It is found that the correlation between magnetic anisotropy constant K and saturation magnetization M_s is found to be $K \sim M_s^{1.3}$ and $K \sim M_s^{-10}$ for MnAl and MnBi, respectively. The coercivity mechanism for LTP MnBi thin films is predominantly governed by a single domain type magnetization reversal mechanism.*

Key words: *MnBi thin films, MnAl thin films, magnetic anisotropy, coercivity mechanism*

Address: Takao Suzuki, MINT Center, University of Alabama, P.O.Box 870209, Tuscaloosa, AL 35487-2507, U.S.A. Tel. (205) 348-2508, Fax. (205) 348-2346, E-mail: takaosuzuki@mint.ua.edu

1. Introduction

1.1. G8 Research Councils Initiative

The G8 Research Councils launched in 2008 the multilateral initiative that was aimed at supporting research on topics of global relevance best tackled through a multinational approach, recognizing that global challenges need global solutions. Along this idea, the call "Interdisciplinary Program on Materials Efficiency – A first step towards sustainable manufacturing" was made in 2010, for which the present research topics on "High Performance Permanent Magnets sustainable for Next Generation" was selected in 2011. The project team members are PI: Takao Suzuki (University of Alabama), PPI: George Hadjipanayis (University of Delaware), Helmut Kronmüller (Max Planck Institute for Intelligent Systems), Oliver Gutfleisch (Technical University of Darmstadt), Kazuhiro Hono (National Institute for Materials Science) and Shin-ichiro Itoh (TDK).

1.2. Brief Description of the Project

To date, the best overall permanent magnets (PM) involve the ternary compound $Nd_2Fe_{14}B$ [1,2,3]. Such PM are of increased use in electric motor and generator applications of the energy sector as the coupling means between torque and electricity. The annual increase in NdFeB production has been more than 10% in the past decade and is expected to increase. However, there has been a growing concern that the export of those rare-earth (RE) from China, which has about 96% of the world production, would be further restricted, leading to a shortage in supply in other countries. Also, RE extraction processes lead to serious environmental problems [4]. Therefore, the development of high performance RE-free PM is an urgent necessity and of strategic importance for many high-tech applications.

Among various RE-free alloys and compounds, there are several potential candidates for future PM. Ferrite PM (including Ba- and Sr- ferrites) have been very extensively used for many applications, and represent more than 50% of the PM market. However, the $(BH)_{max}$ values are about 4 MGOe, much lower than that for NdFeB [5]. Recently, nano-crystalline particles of ε-phase Fe_2O_3 were reported to exhibit H_c of 20kOe and magnetic anisotropy constant (K) of $2x10^6$ erg/cc, but no report of $(BH)_{max}$ has been found in the literature [6]. Other types of PM including Alnico 5 have also been used, but their $(BH)_{max}$ values are about 5 MGOe.

There have been recently some developments for high magnetic anisotropy materials. A work on $L1_0$ FeNi thin films reported high K of $7x10^6$ erg/cc [7]. The stabilization of this phase requires a very rapid cooling process from the high temperature $L1_0$ phase. Also α"-$Fe_{16}N_2$, which has been reported to have high saturation magnetization (M_s) for many years, was recently reported to exhibit a very high K of the same order of magnitude as that for NdFeB. Certainly this is one of the potential candidates for future PM materials, although further work is needed [8].

The three Mn-based binary alloys (MnAl, MnBi and MnGa) are attractive materials for their magnetic properties and their economic advantages. In particular, the τ -phase MnAl [9,10], LTP MnBi

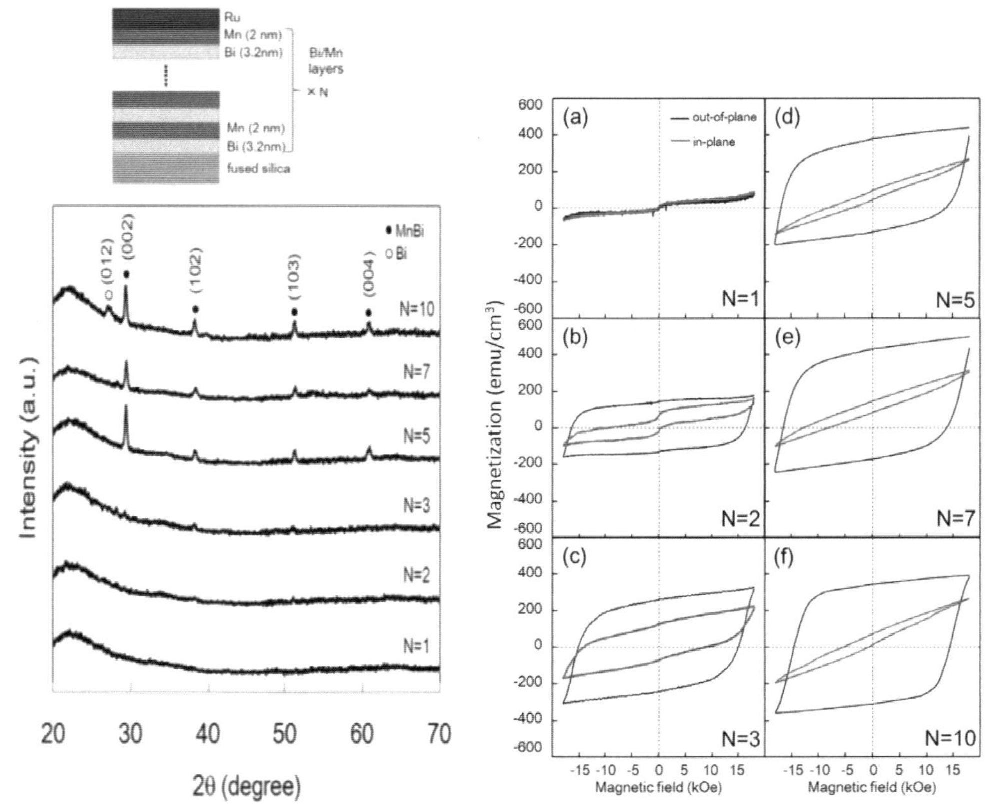

Fig. 1. The XRD patterns and the M-H loops for the MnBi samples with x=2 and y=3.2 for various N. The samples were annealed in vacuum at T_a=550 °C for t_a=0.5hr.

[11,12] and the δ-phase MnGa [13,14] exhibit high magnetic anisotropy of the order of 10^7 erg/cc at room temperature and also high H_c (more than 10 kOe). All three alloys, however, are challenging to stabilize with the desired high K, H_c, M_s and crystallographic structures. By investigating systematically the magnetic properties of the Mn-based systems with Al, Bi and Ga, and by controlling the atomistic structures to stabilize the new phases, the potential of Mn-based alloy systems with Al, Bi and Ga for future PM can be

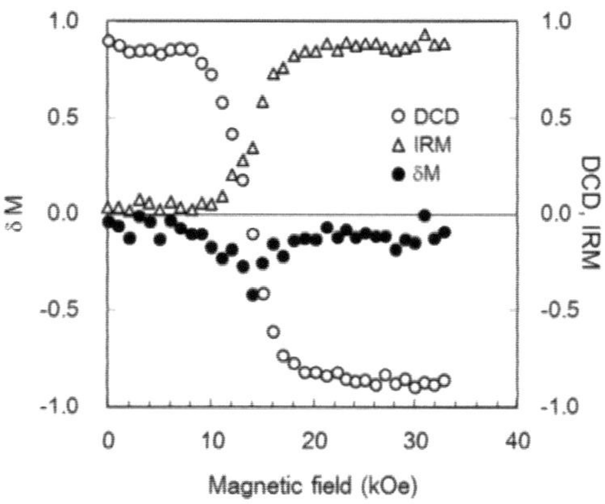

Fig. 2. The δM curve for the MnBi sample with x=2, y=3.2, N=10 and annealed at Ta = 550 °C for 0.5hr.

realized. The primary aim of this G8 project is to understand the interplay between structural, morphological and magnetic properties for those binary alloys. Control of the hard-magnetic properties by grain size and lattice structure will form the basis for the second step of combining the basic building blocks into novel multilayered structures engineered at the atomic level. Those materials in the forms of i) Thin films, ii) Multilayers, and iii) Particles will be fabricated by the sputter-deposition, pulsed laser deposition, chemical synthesis and ball milling techniques.

1.3. Objective

One of the fundamental properties governing $(BH)_{max}$ is the magnetic anisotropy constant, K. It is of interest to point out that all the binary alloys of MnAl, MnBi and MnGa exhibit K of the order of 10^7erg/cc at ambient temperatures, although Mn, Al and Ga do not possess high spin-orbit coupling by itself, which plays an important role in the magnetic anisotropy mechanism. Despite the importance of fundamental understanding of the anisotropy mechanism which is essential for developing new materials into PM with high $(BH)_{max}$, very little work on those binary alloy systems has been carried out. The present paper discusses first the coercivity mechanism of LTP

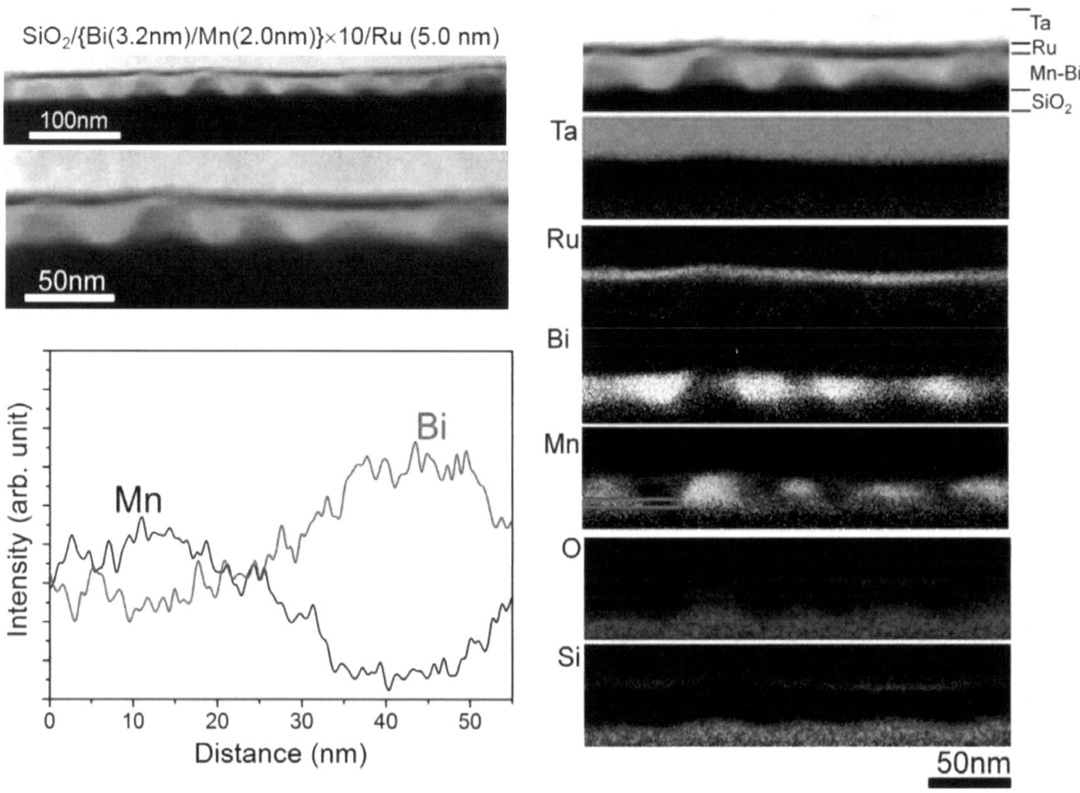

Fig. 3. The high resolution cross-sectional view and STEM-EDS analyses for the MnBi sample with x=2, y=3.2, N=10 and annealed at 550 °C for 0.5hr [15].

MnBi, and then the correlation between the magnetic anisotropy and the saturation magnetization of thin films of LTP MnBi and τ-phase MnAl.

2. Experimental Methods, Results and Discussion on MnBi and MnAl Thin Films

2.1. Thin-film fabrications

Multilayers of Mn-X (X=Al, and Bi) were fabricated by using a DC magnetron sputtering system. The multilayer structure was [Mn (x nm) / X (y nm)] x N / (silica glass). The substrate temperature during deposition was ambient, and the base pressure prior to deposition was better than $1x10^{-9}$ Torr. No bias voltage was applied. All the multilayers were subjected to a post annealing in vacuum at temperatures T_a for annealing times t_a.

2.2. Structural characterization

Measurements of magnetic properties were conducted by using a VSM and a torque-magnetometer over a temperature range from 5 to 400K in fields up to 9T. Structural characterization was carried out using XRD and high resolution TEM.

2.3. Low temperature phase (LTP) MnBi thin films

Figure 1 shows the results of the XRD patterns and the M-H curves for the samples annealed at T_a=550C for t_a=0.5hr with different N from 1 to 10 for x=2 and y=3.2. It is noted that the preferential growth of the c-axis orientation along the film normal for the LTP phase of MnBi thin films is observed for the samples with N ≥5. The M-H (minor) loops for those samples measured for both the perpendicular and parallel directions to film plane exhibit the easy axis for magnetization along the film normal, even for the samples with N=2 and 3, even though the XRD patterns of them hardly show any sign of the preferred c-axis orientation. The temperature dependences of saturation magnetization, magnetic anisotropy constant, as well as coercivity were measured in fields up to 9T.

It is pointed out that those thin films exhibit high coercivity of about 20~30kOe, which close to one half of a magnetic anisotropy field H_k (about 6T). In order to understand the coercivity mechanism, measurements of a so called δM curve were conducted, where δM is defined as { $2M_r(H)$ -1 + $M_d(H)$ }, where $M_r(H)$ and $M_d(H)$ are the isothermal remanence (IRM) and dc-demagnetization remanence (DCD) curves (normalized to saturation magnetization), respectively. Fig.2 shows the result

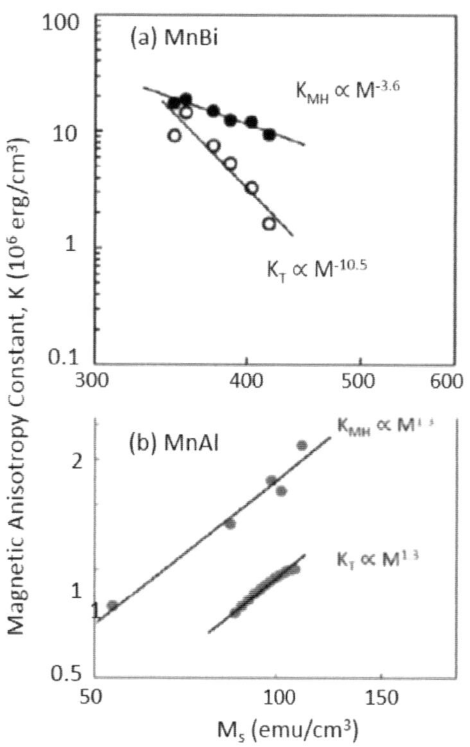

Fig. 4. The correlation between magnetic anisotropy constant K and saturation magnetization Ms for (a) the c-axis oriented LTP MnBi sample with x=2,y=3.2, N=10, annealed at 550 °C for 0.5hr, and (b) the τ-phase MnAl sample with x = 1, y = 1.25, N = 30 and annealed at = 580 °C for 190 min..

of δM curve for a sample with x=2, y=3.2, N=10 and annealed at Ta = 550C for 0.5hr. It is noted that the δM curve is negative, indicating that that a magneto-static coupling between grains is predominant for magnetization reversal.

Fig. 3 shows a high resolution TEM for a cross-sectional view together with STEM-EDS analyses for the sample fabricated under the same condition for that in Fig.3. It is found that the LTP phase grains are surrounded by Bi grains, the size of which is about 30~40nm. As a critical size for a single domain for LTP MnBi is about 500nm, which is much larger than the grain size of LTP MnBi, it is expected that the magnetization reversal may be governed by a coherent rotation, leading to a high coercivity, nearly a half of H_k [15].

Figure 4(a) shows the magnetic anisotropy constant K estimated based on the field dependence of torque curves at different temperatures, as $K_T = L_{2\theta}$ ($H \rightarrow \infty$), where the $L_{2\theta}$ is the amplitude of the two fold symmetry of a torque curve, and θ is the angle between the applied field and the easy axis direction. For comparison, the magnetic anisotropy constant K was also estimated based on the M-H curves at different temperatures, which is defined as $K_{MH} = \frac{1}{2} M_s H_s$ (H_s is the field where the magnetization becomes saturated). The result is shown in Fig. 4(a) for the c-axis oriented sample. The relation between magnetic anisotropy and saturation magnetization is found to expressed in terms of the power of (-10.5) and (-3.6) for K_T and K_{MH}, respectively.

2.4. The τ-phase MnAl thin films

Multilayers of Mn/Al were fabricated in a very similar way to that of MnBi thin films, as described in 2(a). The layered structure of the samples thus fabricated and subsequently annealed was found to be transformed to the continuous structure of the τ-phase in addition to the ε-phase. Measurements of magnetic anisotropy constant were carried out using the torque method, which is shown in Fig. 4(b) for the sample with x = 1, y = 1.25, N = 30 and annealed at T_a = 580 °C for t_a = 190 min. It is found that the correlation between K and M_s is found to be expressed in terms of $K \sim M_s^{1.3}$.

2.5. The correlation between K and M_s

Regarding the temperature dependence of magnetic anisotropy of LTP MnBi, the magnetic anisotropy constant K is expressed in terms of $K \sim M_s^{-10}$, as mentioned above. To the authors' knowledge, there has been very few papers found in literature concerning such a correlation. It is worthwhile mentioning that a recent experimental work by XMCD suggests that both the magnetic moments of Mn and Bi strongly depend on temperature, which could be strongly depending on atomic distances among Mn and Bi atoms (or c/a) [16].

For the τ-phase MnAl case, the correlation is found to be expressed as $K \sim M_s^{1.3}$. If Mn atoms contribute dominantly to the magnetic anisotropy, then one would expect the single ion model may apply to the case of MnAl, for which a theory [17] predicts the correlation of $K \sim M_s^3$. Therefore, the present dependence is not accounted for based on the single ion model. It is noted that a work on m-DO_{19} Fe_3Pt thin films [18], for which the two ion model is expected to be applied since both Fe and Pt atoms contribute to the magnetic anisotropy, reported a similar correlation ($K \sim M_s^{1.5\sim2}$). It is interesting to note that some recent theoretical works [19,20] showed that the effective spin-orbit coupling of the τ-phase MnAl is much larger, an order of magnitude than each of Mn and Al atom, thus leading to the high K value, comparable to that for CoPt and FePd.

3. Summary

The coercivity mechanism of LTP MnBi thin films is discussed. The coercivity is predominantly governed by a single domain magnetization reversal mechanism. The correlation between the magnetic anisotropy and saturation magnetization for MnBi and MnAl is presented. In order to explain the results, a further theoretical work is necessary.

Acknowledgement

The present work has been supported in part by NSF (CMMI-1229049), and also TDK Corporation. The authors are grateful to Dr. Sepehri A.Hossein and Dr. Kazuhiro Hono at NIMS for their fruitful discussions and TEM analyses.

References

[1] M. Sagawa, *et al.*, *J. Appl. Phys.*, 1984**,** 55, 208.
[2] K.H.J. Buscho, *J. Alloy and Compounds*, 1993, 193, 223.
[3] O. Gutfleisch, *et al.*, *Adv. Mat.*, 2011**,** 23*,* 821.
[4] Report by U.S. Department of Energy "Critical Materials Strategy", 2010, December.
[5] J.M.D. Coey, *Magnetism and Magnetic Materials*, 2010, Cambridge University Press, UK, 471-473.
[6] S. Ohkoshi, *et al.*, *J.Appl. Phys.*, 2005, 97, 10K312-1.
[7] M. Kotsugi, *et al.*, *J. Magn. Mag. Materials*, 2013, 326, 235.
[8] M. Takahashi, *et al.*, US Patent: US20120244356, 2010, Oct. 19.
[9] H. Kon, *J. Phys. Soc. Japan*, 1958, 13, 1444.
[10] A.J.J. Koch, *et al.*, *J. Appl. Phys.*, 1960, 31, 75S.
[11] T. Chen, W. Stutius, *IEEE Trans.*, 1974, MAG-10, 581.
[12] P.A. Albert, W.J.Carr, Jr., *J. Appl. Phys.*, 1961, 32, 201S.
[13] K.K. Wang, *et al.*, *Mate. Res. Symp. Proc.*, 2009, 1118, 118-K06-06.
[14] E.D. Lu, *et al.*, *Phy. Rev. Letter*, 2001, 97, 146101.
[15] T. Hozumi, *et al. J. Appl. Phys.*, 2014, 115, 17A737-1.
[16] E. Goering, Y-C. Chen, *G8 Second Workshop* 2014, May 9, Darmstadt, Germany.
[17] O.N. Mryasov, *et al.*, *Europhys. Lett.*, 2005, 69(5), 805.
[18] M.A.I. Nahid, T. Suzuki, *J. Appl. Phys.*, 2005, 97, 2005, 10K 307-1.
[19] Y. Kota, A. Sakuma, *J. Phys. Soc. Japan*, 2012, 81, 2012, 084705-1.
[20] Y. Kota, A. Sakuma, *J. Phys. Soc. Japan*, 2014, 83, 034715-1.

NANOPYME Project: In the Search of Improved Rare Earth-Free Permanent Magnets

A. BOLLERO, Project Coordinator
IMDEA Nanoscience, Madrid, Spain

Abstract: *NANOPYME ("Nanocrystalline Permanent Magnets based on Hybrid Metal-Ferrites") is a European project that addresses the design and development of high quality permanent magnets without rare-earths (RE). The goal of the project is to create novel magnets with no RE content, with a larger energy product,* $(BH)_{max}$, *by comparison with currently used ferrites and, with practical applications requiring* $(BH)_{max}$ *values between 35 and 100* kJm^{-3}. *NANOPYME groups 4 research centers, 4 academia and 3 industrial partners from 6 different countries to create a multidisciplinary frame combining the acquired knowledge in nanoscience and advanced production technologies [www.nanopyme-project.eu].*

Keywords: *ferrites; composites; nanocrystalline magnets; exchange-coupling*

Address: Alberto Bollero, IMDEA Nanoscience, C/Faraday 9, 28049 Madrid, Spain. Tel: (34) 91299 8758. E-mail: alberto.bollero@imdea.org

1. Introduction

There is a rapidly increasing demand of permanent magnets in nowadays technological applications strongly driven by large industrial machinery, wind turbines and electric vehicles markets [1-3]. Many nowadays applications traditionally use RE-based permanent magnets as no relevant problems raised when they were implemented in terms of availability or high and unstable pricing. The situation has dramatically changed in recent years due to the increased monopoly (mainly by China and, in particular, on heavy rare-earths) which has made mandatory searching for an alternative to RE-based permanent magnets.

The increased need of permanent magnets in combination with the strategically geographical situation of REs (especially heavy REs) make mandatory, first, an efficient and well-focused use of these elements for specific purposes (high performing applications or micro-scalable devices) and, additionally, a reinforcement in the search of permanent magnets alternatives in applications areas where the use of REs may be reduced or totally avoided. Successful achievement of these alternatives would also result in an added important benefit by reducing significantly the environmental impact of the permanent magnets sector development.

Tradition usually does not equal to unmatched efficiency and the latter should combine performance, low cost and environmentally friendly production. Since few years ago this is not the case for the REs market and some of their related applications, with a clear and alarming unbalance between these three points. Ferrites exhibit at present energy product values well below those achieved by RE-based permanent magnets. They count however with important advantages by comparison with other magnets in view of practical applications:

(i) Abundance of the constituent elements.
(ii) They are electrical insulators, therefore avoiding eddy currents (important for dynamic operating conditions such as those integrated in electrical motors).
(iii) They are chemically inert and they have practically no corrosion problems making possible air processing (key advantage over rare earth-based magnets), i.e., largely reducing fabrication costs.

They exhibit some limitations which must be considered in view of potential applications:

(i) Magnetization drops with increasing operation temperature more rapidly than for other permanent magnets due to the reduced Curie temperature.
(ii) Demagnetization resistance is reduced on cooling due to the positive temperature coefficient of the intrinsic coercivity.

An increase in the $(BH)_{max}$ for ferrites would result in a strong economic impact. Novel ferrites-based magnets, taking as starting point all the knowledge developed on classical ones, may be designed and fabricated to cover application areas that have been fully covered in the past by RE-based magnets. This together with the continuous advances in power electronics and control algorithms can lead to efficiently improved devices with an enhanced workability and reduced costs.

An effective permanent magnet requires as starting point adequate intrinsic magnetic properties, but this is not enough to guarantee a high-quality magnet. The interplay between the intrinsic properties and the microstructure will determine the magnetic behaviour of permanent magnets. A high remanence, together with preserving a high coercivity, is a requirement to achieve maximized energy densities. *NANOPYME* makes use of two complementary approaches in the search of novel ferrites-based magnets. The first one is based on the possibility of achieving improved microstructural and magnetic properties for ferrites when going to the nanometer scale because of surface/interface effects (grain sizes, adjacent phases…) different from those of bulk or microcrystalline materials by going to the nanometer scale. The achievements done will be translated in a second stage to the synthesis of novel hybrid nanocomposites based on exchange-coupled metals and ferrites in order to combine the complementary magnetic properties (high saturation magnetization and anisotropy, respectively) of both materials types.

2. *NANOPYME* - Project Objectives

NANOPYME aims to develop nanocrystalline ferrites-based magnets to compete with RE magnets in a large portion of nowadays technological applications where the latter are simply used because standard ferrites do not fulfill the magnetic energy product required [with a $(BH)_{max}$ target of 35-100 kJm^{-3}]. *NANOPYME* does not aim to achieve the record $(BH)_{max}$ values of RE based magnets [2,3] but to design novel magnetic materials with an enhanced magnetic performance

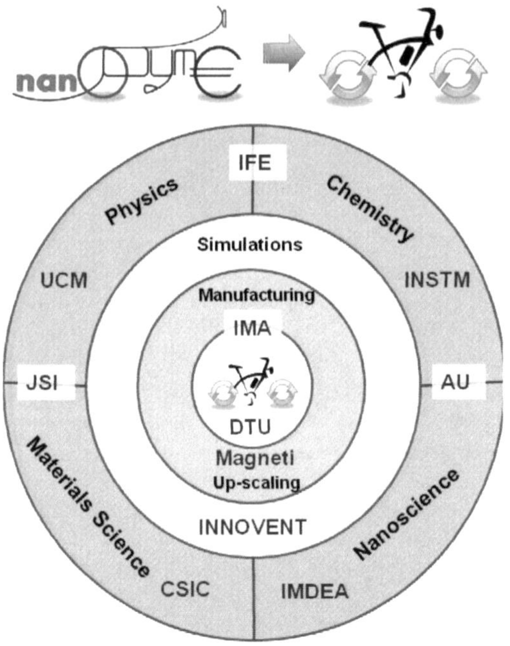

Fig. 1. Multidisciplinary structure of consortium established in NANOPYME project.

allowing significantly broader application fields than current ferrites and therefore substituting RE-based magnets in those applications.

The exchange-spring behavior between magnetically "soft" and "hard" magnetic phases that will be exploited in the project has been extensively studied in metallic systems [4-6]. This is not however the case for oxide nanocomposite permanent magnets where these studies are very scarce mainly due to the difficulty in optimizing the magnetic properties because of microstructural complexities. The variety of experimental techniques considered in the project will allow for different approaches to obtain optimized microstructures. It is important to take into consideration that, by comparison with conducting magnets, ferrites are insulators and the intergranular exchange-coupling will be related to a mechanism different from that of the formers. This makes of the proposed project a very interesting research topic from a fundamental as well as from a practical point of view where the complementary expertise areas of the different groups will match to achieve the proposed objectives.

2.1. The consortium

Successful achievement of the project objectives requires a multidisciplinary consortium configuration in order to achieve a full understanding and control of different correlated parameters (compositional, morphological, microstructural and magnetic) involved from the initial stages related to the synthesis of starting materials to the final products. This goes necessarily through an identification of the best processing routes (in terms of achieving an optimized performance of the produced materials matched by environmental friendly considerations and recyclability of the intermediate and final materials) and fabrication parameters. The diagram shown in Fig. 1 illustrates the multidisciplinary expertise fields of the partners involved in the project.

Public research institutions (Spain, Norway and Slovenia):

- IMDEA Nanoscience – Project Coordinator;
- Spanish National Research Council, CSIC;
- Institute for Energy Technology, IFE;
- Jozef Stefan Institute, JSI.

Academia centers (Denmark, Italy and Spain):

- Centre for Electric Technology - Technical University of Denmark, DTU
- Department of Chemistry - Aarhus University, AU
- Laboratory of Molecular Magnetism - Consortium for Material Science and Technology, INSTM
- Institute of Applied Magnetism - Complutense University, UCM

Small and medium-sized enterprises, SMEs (Germany, Spain and Slovenia):

- INNOVENT and GNRL;
- Applied Magnetic Engineering, IMA;
- Magneti Ljubljana.

2.2. Single-phase and nanocomposite materials

NANOPYME intends to exploit the properties of the interfaces in nanocomposite magnets to achieve enhanced energy products in ferrite-based low production cost permanent magnets. The materials exhibiting large saturation magnetization (mainly transition metals Fe, Co and Ni and their alloys) show low magnetic anisotropy values while contrary happens for ferrites. Therefore, the development of high performance permanent magnets represents a challenge for materials science and fabrication of well-designed composites becomes mandatory. One must keep in mind that in such magnetic systems, several competing effects are always present, and only through a careful control of the microstructure one is able to enhance or inhibit the desired mechanisms. We intend to exploit the exchange-coupling phenomenon [3] to produce nanocomposite magnets with high magnetic anisotropy and remanence values, i.e. enhanced magnetic performance. The effectiveness of the exchange-coupling, i.e. degree of remanence enhancement, depends on the intergrain exchange interactions between neighbouring grains which causes the spontaneous magnetic magnetization of each individual grain to deviate from its particular easy axis towards the direction of the magnetization of the nearest ones. Therefore our approach may be summarized in the production and processing of high performance nanomaterials considering two guidelines:

(a) Preparation of *nanometric sized ferrite-based materials* with improved microstructure and enhanced anisotropy. A key element is to match the design and production of novel materials with those for which the production to an industrial scale is solved. Strontium–type hexaferrites, cobalt-doped ferrites and the epsilon ferrite phase (exploratory material approach) are among the main materials used in the project.

(b) Preparation of *hybrid metal-ferrite nano-composites* with optimized nanostructures to obtain the adequate exchange-coupling between the two materials in such a way to obtain maximum magnetization with the smallest possible reduction of the anisotropy. The mechanism will follow the idea of the so-called “spring magnets” in the synergy between hard and soft phases giving rise to materials with enhanced energy product.

Besides this main goal, two additional significant improvements are investigated in the project through the fabrication of nanocomposites:

- Increase in the Curie temperature of ferrites to open the door to higher temperature applications.
- Improvement of the fragility of ferrites, allowing easier machining that would further decrease production costs.

The first part of the project has focused in the synthesis and processing of single-phase materials with adequate microstructure and magnetic properties to be used in a second stage as starting point for the production of hybrid metal-ferrite nanocomposites. A $(BH)_{max}$ = 9 kJm^{-3} was considered in the project as a quality threshold for isotropic powders in order to take them into consideration for further processing.

Figure 2a displays hysteresis loop for commercial Sr-ferrite powders used as starting material in the project. Despite of adequate magnetic properties, these powders show an inhomogeneous microstructure (Fig. 4a) constituted by a mixture of very large particles (several micrometers) and smaller ones (hundreds of nanometers) not suitable for the fabrication of

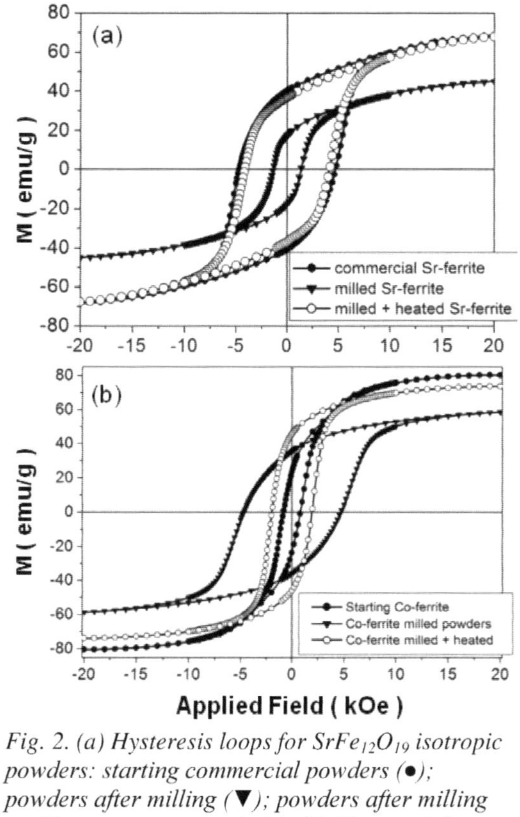

Fig. 2. (a) Hysteresis loops for $SrFe_{12}O_{19}$ isotropic powders: starting commercial powders (●); powders after milling (▼); powders after milling and heat treatment in air (○). (b) Hysteresis loops for $CoFe_2O_4$ isotropic powders: starting powders prepared by co-precipitation (●); powders after milling (▼); powders after milling and heat treatment in air (○).

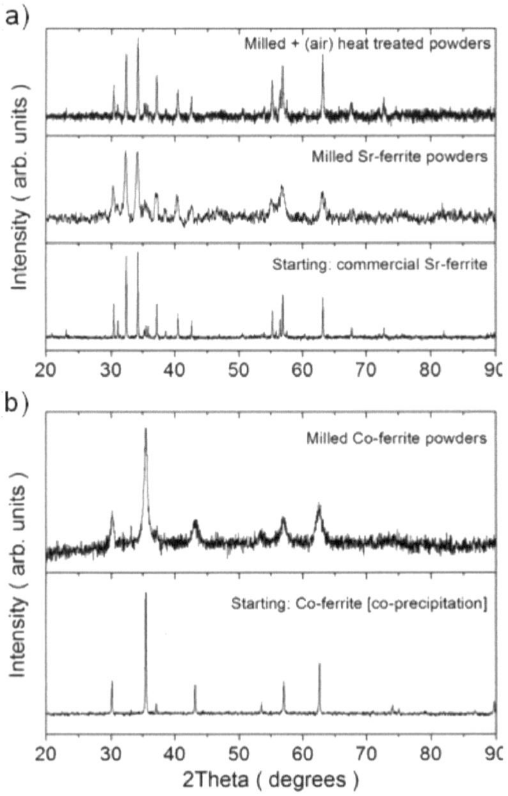

Fig. 3. XRD patterns for (a) $SrFe_{12}O_{19}$ powders (commercial; milled; milled and heat treated); (b) $CoFe_2O_4$ powders (synthesized by co-precipitation; and milled).

ferrite/metal nanocomposites. High energy ball milling followed by optimized heat treatment in air allows obtaining fine and homogeneous Sr-ferrite powders (see XRD in Fig. 3a) with a mean particle size well below the single domain size of 0.9-1.0 μm reported in the literature for Sr-ferrite (Fig. 4b) while maintaining practically unchanged the magnetic properties of the starting material (Fig. 2a). Thus the resulting milled and heat treated in air Sr-ferrite powders are good candidates to be used in the second part of the project to produce novel composite ferrites-based magnets.

Cobalt ferrite isotropic powders have been synthesized by co-precipitation (Fig. 4c) in the frame of the project following heat treatment to form stoichiometric $CoFe_2O_4$ powders with a uniform microstructure (200 nm particle size) [Fig. 4d]. High energy ball milling has been shown to be a very effective method to obtain isotropic Co-ferrite powders with outstanding magnetic properties (Fig. 2b). In good agreement with reported results [7], strains induced in the milled powders result in enlarge coercivities. XRD of milled Co-ferrite powders showed refection peaks corresponding to the $CoFe_2O_4$ phase (Fig. 3b).

Thus high quality $CoFe_2O_4$ isotropic powders have been obtained in the shape of three different products with hysteresis loops shown in Fig. 2b:

- Product 1: homogeneous Co-ferrite powders synthesized by co-precipitation.
- Product 2: Co-ferrite milled powders [high coercivity above 4.5 kOe].
- Product 3: Co-ferrite milled and heated powders [enlarged remanence and $(BH)_{max}$ > 17 kJ/m^3].

2.3. Up-scaling considerations

The project does not stop at the synthesis but it covers, as one of the main points, the development of production methods for nanomaterials -positively assessed in terms of magnetic, mechanical and corrosion tests- that allows fabricating them at industrial levels with economically viable costs. Alternative synthesis and processing routes, more eco-efficient than those conventional ones used in

Fig. 4. SEM images for $SrFe_{12}O_{19}$ (a) starting commercial and (b) milled powders. $CoFe_2O_4$ (c) starting powders synthesized by co-precipitation and (d) co-precipitated and heat treated powders.

industry are evaluated at the participant research institutions. Among them: microwaves synthesis, flow synthesis methods and rapid-quenching for production of hundreds meters long microwires. Ball milling, as an additional route, is a technique that has been successfully scaled from laboratory to industrial production for grinding multitude of materials (magnetic materials among them) but only at the macro- and micro-scale (while nanoscale has remained confined to an insignificant laboratory scale of typically a few milligrams to grams production).

Successful scaling from the laboratory to the mass production is considered in the project under the following premises: competitiveness, safety, recyclability and an eco-efficient production.

Processing of the materials is carried out under realistic considerations of scaling up the magnets production. Achievement of state of the art hybrid magnets goes through successful:

(i) controlled size distribution of particles;

(ii) increased intrinsic magnetization and/or anisotropy constant;

(iii) improved degree of crystallographic orientation;

(iv) increased density of sintered body after compaction of the magnetic powders.

Figure 5 illustrates the scenario for participant institutions and scaling up steps considered in the project. The goal is to achieve the industrial processing of magnets with restraints relating to price and manufacturing conditions. Each single step starting from the synthesis of the materials and ending in the compacted/sintered magnets will be carefully and systematically studied in order to optimize the magnetic properties of the final products as well as their stability (mechanical and against corrosion) in combination with an optimized and efficient energy use during the processing.

2.4. Demonstration

A prototype electric motor employing *NANOPYME*

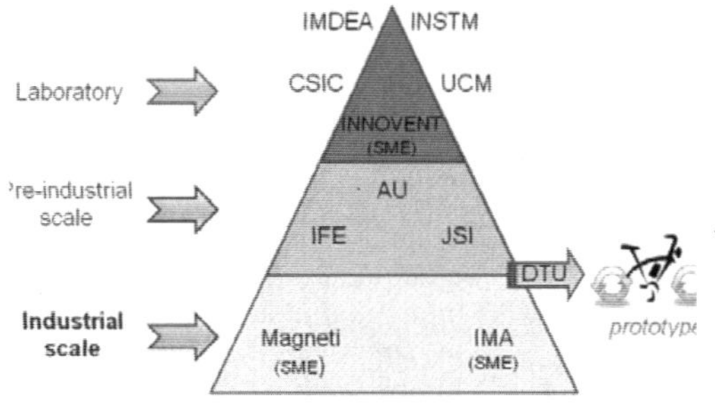

Fig. 5. Up-scaling through the different project stages and involved partners.

permanent magnets will be designed, constructed and tested in a last stage of the project. The *NANOPYME* magnets employed in the prototype will be fabricated in the consortium. The magnets will be manufactured by different methods according to the desired specifications and will include anisotropic as well as isotropic magnets. The prototype will be constructed in-house, with recyclability of the critical materials in mind. Tests will focus on the performance of the magnets under normal and extreme operating conditions, where possible deterioration or de-magnetization might occur.

3. Summary

The novelty of *NANOPYME* approach consists on preparing and processing hybrid metal-ferrite nanocomposites in such a way that different chemical-physical effects cooperate together to obtain materials with higher anisotropy and magnetization achieving enhanced $(BH)_{max}$ products by comparison with conventional ferrites.

NANOPYME focuses in the development of magnetic materials going through an eco-efficient production. The use of advanced techniques, in combination with the evaluation of a recycling program, are intended to allow for important cost reductions in the production process of these novel permanent magnets.

The development of the new ferrites-based magnets in *NANOPYME* will contribute to revert the situation of the permanent markets from the nowadays situation which is determined by the geographical distribution of the raw materials to a new market where the know-how and technological development will determine the market leader.

Acknowledgement
This research was supported by the EU-FP7 *NANOPYME* Project (No. 310516).

References

[1] NANOPYME website: www.nanopyme-project.eu

[2] O. Gutfleisch, M.A. Willard, E. Brück, C.H. Chen, S.G. Sankar and J.P. Liu, *Adv. Mater.* **23**, 2011, 821.

[3] L. H. Lewis and F. Jiménez-Villacorta, *Metall. Mater. Trans. A* **44**, 2013, 2.

[4] E.F. Kneller and R. Hawig, *IEEE Trans. Magn.* **27**, 1991, 3588.

[5] K.-H. Müller, D. Eckert, A. Handstein and P. Nothnagel, *J. Magn. Magn. Mater.* **104-107**, 1992, 1173.

[6] A. Bollero, A. Yan, O. Gutfleisch, K.-H. Müller and L. Schultz, *IEEE Trans. Magn.* **39**, 2003, 2944.

[7] B.H. Liu and J. Ding, *Appl. Phys. Lett.* **88**, 2006, 042506.

Dy-free, Reduced Nd, High Performance $Nd_2Fe_{14}B$-based Permanent Magnets

K.A. GSCHNEIDNER, JR.,[a] R.W. McCALLUM,[a] M. KHAN,[b] A.K. PATHAK, V.K. PECHARSKY,[a] L. ZHOU, K. SUN, K.W. DENNIS, M.J. KRAMER,
The Ames Laboratory, Iowa State University, Ames, IA 50011, U.S.A.
[a]Also Department of Materials Science and Engineering
[b]Present address: Department of Physics, Miami University, Oxford, OH 45056, USA
D. BROWN,
Molycorp Magnequench, Magnequench Technology Center, Singapore
C. ZHOU
MEDA Engineering and Technical Services, Southfield, MI 48075, U.S.A.

Abstract: *Mixed valent Ce when substituted for ~20% of the Nd increases the coercivity by about 20%. When Co is substituted for Fe in the $Nd_{0.8}Ce_{0.2}$ alloys a synergistic interaction between mixed valent Ce and Co leads to significantly improved properties, which exceeds those of Dy-sintered magnets at high temperatures >475 K.*

Keywords: *$(Nd_{1-x}Ce_x)_2Fe_{14}B$; $(Nd_{1-x}Ce_x)_2(Fe_{1-y}Co_y)_{14}B$; ribbons; die-upset*

Address: Karl A. Gschneidner, Jr., The Ames Laboratory, 255 Spedding Hall, Iowa State University, Ames, IA 50011-3020, U.S.A., Tel: (1-515) 294-7931, Fax: (1-515) 294-9579, E-mail: cagey@ameslab.gov

This research began as a project in response to the Department of Energy Advanced Research Project Agency-Energy's call for Rare Earth Alternatives in Critical Technologies Energy (REACT) proposals. The initial aim of our investigation was to substitute *mixed-valent* Ce for Nd in $Nd_2Fe_{14}B$ alloy, since semi-empirical alloy theory rules indicate that a two phase region may exist in the $(Nd_{1-x}Ce_x)_2Fe_{14}B$ system. If one phase were a soft magnet and the other phase a hard magnet the two phase alloy might form an exchange spring magnet which exhibited promising permanent magnetic properties. Initial X-ray and metallographic results indicate that $Nd_2Fe_{14}B$ and $Ce_2Fe_{14}B$ form a continuous solid solution but with a minor anomaly in the c lattice parameter at x = 0.15, see Fig. 1. This anomaly is also consistent with the anomalies observed in the magnetic property values around this composition – see the next few sentences and Fig. 2. Magnetization measurements of $(Nd_{1-x}Ce_x)_2Fe_{14}B$ rapidly solidified ribbons of drop-cast alloys showed that all of the basic properties $[(BH)_{max}, B_r, H_c, H_A$ and $M_S]$ initially drop gradually with increasing Ce content until $0.2 \le x < 0.4$, when they anomalously change, before falling-off predictably from the rule of mixtures once more for $x \sim > 0.4$, see Fig. 2. It is seen that the coercivity of the $(Nd_{0.8}Ce_{0.2})Fe_{14}B$ alloy is 19% larger than the undoped $Nd_2Fe_{14}B$ alloy (10.0 vs. 8.4 kOe). This is quite surprising and unexpected. A scanning electron microscopy (SEM) study of the drop-cast alloys around x = 0.2, revealed that the alloys from $x \ge 0.15$ to $x \le 0.5$ consist of two phases both having the 2:14:1 structure, but slightly different Ce concentrations, see Fig. 3. However, the rapid quenched ribbons are metastable single phase alloys.

This intriguing fact – an improved coercivity by adding mixed-valent Ce to the Nd-Fe-B magnets – prompted additional exploration. Since the x = 0.2 alloy has a low Curie temperature (548 K, i.e. 32 K lower than that of the undoped material) Co was substituted for Fe to increase T_C to permit the use of the Ce-doped alloy above room temperature. This led to another and even bigger surprise – a 50% increase in the maximum energy product from 10.6 to 16.0 MGOe for two Co atoms per formula unit substituted

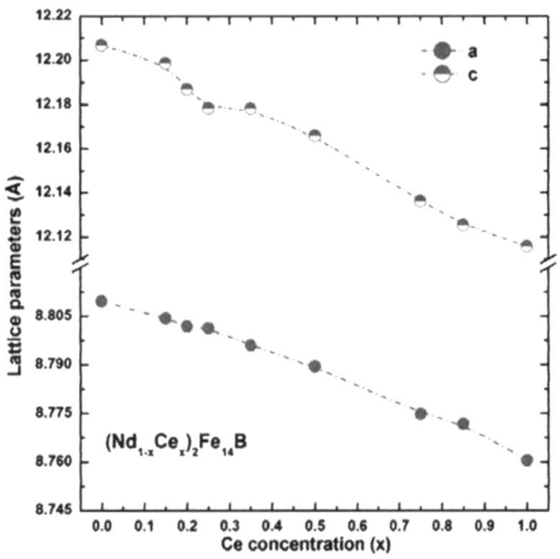

Fig. 1. Lattice parameters of $(Nd_{1-x}Ce_x)_2Fe_{14}B$ drop cast alloys as a function of Ce concentration.

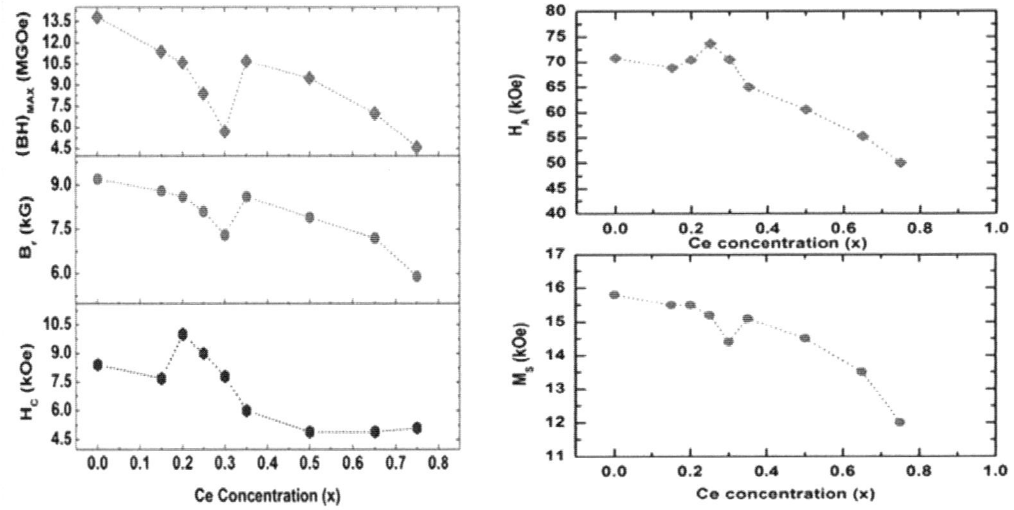

Fig. 2. $(BH)_{max}$, B_r, H_c, H_A and M_s of $(Nd_{1-x}Ce_x)_2Fe_{14}B$ ribbons as a function of Ce concentration.

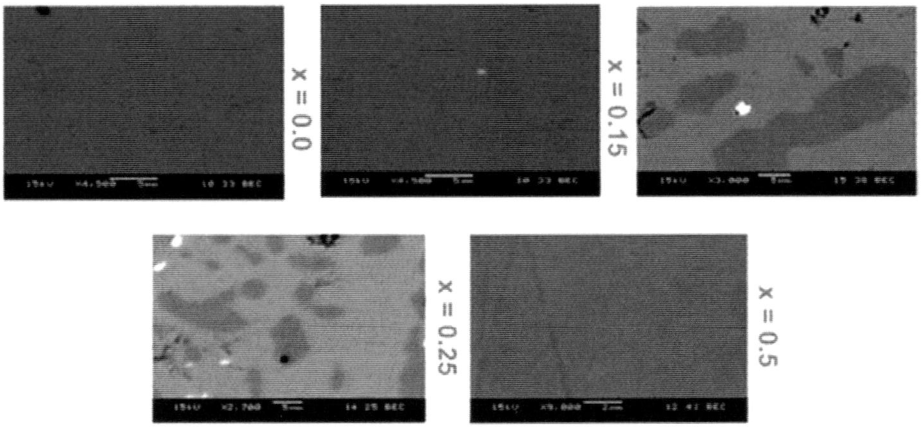

Fig. 3. SEM images of $(Nd_{1-x}Ce_x)_2Fe_{14}B$ drop cast alloys as a function of Ce concentration.

for Fe, in addition to increasing T_C by ~150 K to 695 K. Other than the coercivity, which dropped ~20% to 7.8 kOe, the other properties remained about the same. The enhanced $(BH)_{max}$ is due to a synergistic effect between the mixed valent Ce and Co, which results in a nearly perfect isotropic hysteresis loop, see Fig. 4. A further increase of the Co concentration resulted in a lower $(BH)_{max}$ and H_c, an increased T_C, and essentially no changes in B_r, H_A and M_S. Theoretical calculations have shown that the first two Co atoms substituted for Fe in the Fe(4c) position in the $Nd_2Fe_{14}B$ structure [1]. Any further Co additions require the Co atoms to occupy other Fe sites, which leads to a deterioration in the magnetic properties. The Ce atoms have a tendency to occupy the Nd(4f) positions [2]. It is noted that the Fe(4c) sites occupied by Co atoms are nearest neighbors to the mixed valent Ce atoms in the Nd(4f) site which probably accounts for the synergism between Co and Ce. Based on previous research on $Nd_2Fe_{14}B$ magnets TiC and ZrC were added as grain refiners of the rapidly solidified ribbons which increased the energy product but lowered the coercivity. When excess Nd and/or Ce were added, the corecivity could be enhanced significantly while maintaining the large BH_{MAX} value. This is shown in Fig. 5 for the Co-free alloy where the 2.5% TiC addition and 10% excess $(Nd_{0.8}Co_{0.2})$ results in a nearly ideal isotropic

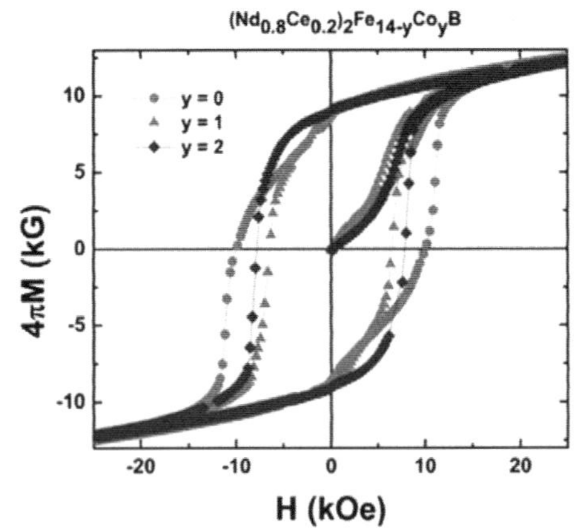

Fig. 4. Magnetization vs. field data for $(Nd_{0.8}Ce_{0.2})_2\,Fe_{14-y}Co_yB$ alloys.

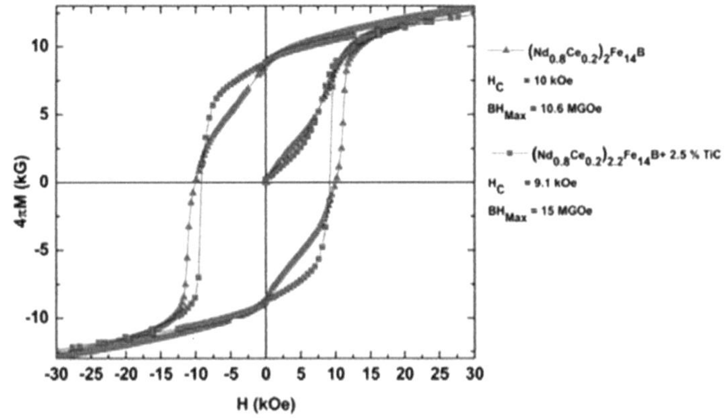

Fig. 5. Magnetization vs. field data for $(Nd_{0.8}Ce_{0.2})_2Fe_{14}B$ melt-spun ribbons with and without added TiC.

hysteresis loop. A similar improvement was realized in the Co-doped alloys, i.e. $(Nd_{0.8}Ce_{0.2})_2Fe_{12}Co_2B$ with TiC and excess Nd + Ce.

Further improvements were realized when TiC was replaced by ZrC, see Fig. 6. It is thought that Ti because of its similar size compound to Co (~17% larger than Co) partially substitutes for Co, while Zr which is 28% larger than Co does not displace a Co atom. More interesting is the temperature dependence of the coercivity for the Co-doped (Ce,Co)-$Nd_2Fe_{14}B$ alloy plus TiC or ZrC additions – it does not drop off as fast as that of the sintered Dy-doped $Nd_2Fe_{14}B$ material, see Fig. 6. The third surprise is that the coercivity of the ZrC additive alloy *exceeds* that of the Dy-doped alloy at 475 K (200 °C) and higher temperatures. This is very important for high temperature applications of the $Nd_2Fe_{14}B$-based permanent magnets, e.g. the motor compartment of gasoline or diesel powdered automobiles.

The $(Nd_{0.8}Ce_{0.2})_{2.4}Fe_{12}Co_2B$ alloys were

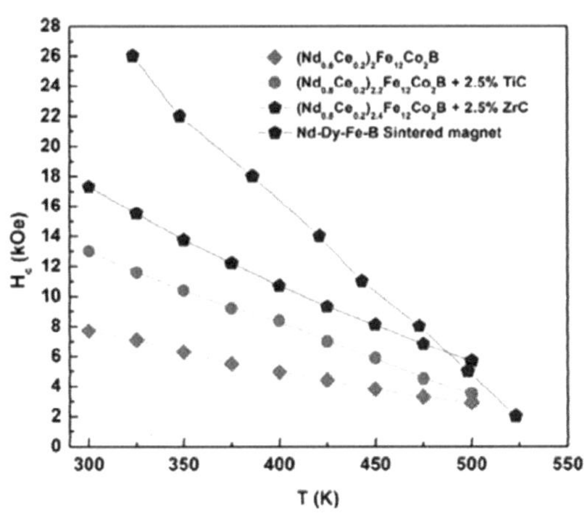

Fig. 6. Coercivity as a function of temperature for $(Nd_{0.8}Ce_{0.2})_{2+z}Fe_{12}Co_2B$ ribbons with excess rare earth and/or TiC, ZrC as a function of temperature. The coercivity of a Nd-Dy-Fe-B sintered magnet also presented for comparison.

mechanically deformed by hot pressing and by die-upsetting processes to further improve the magnetic properties. The first process yielded an isotropic microstructure and the latter an anisotropic microstructure. At 300 K the corresponding values for $(BH)_{max}$ are: 12.8 MGOe for the ribbons and hot pressed samples and 31.2 MGOe for the die-upset material.

To date our study basically developed five grades of high performance $Nd_2Fe_{14}B$ permanent magnet alloys:

$(Nd_{0.8}Ce_{0.2})_2Fe_{14}B$ (Co-free) ribbons,
$(Nd_{0.8}Ce_{0.2})_2Fe_{12}Co_2B$ ribbons,
$(Nd_{0.8}Ce_{0.2})_{2.4}Fe_{12}Co_2B$ + 2.5% ZrC ribbons,
$(Nd_{0.8}Ce_{0.2})_{2.4}Fe_{12}Co_2B$ hot pressed ribbons, and
$(Nd_{0.8}Ce_{0.2})_{2.4}Fe_{12}Co_2B$ die-upset alloys.

Our study has shown that alloys in which Ce substitutes for Nd plus Co substitutes for Fe have excellent coercivities and energy products which compare favorably to some of the Dy-sintered material, especially for high temperature applications (T > 475 K). Since there is a large excess of Ce the availability of these competitive Ce containing $Nd_2Fe_{14}B$-base alloys will help alleviate the critical shortage of Dy and Nd.

Acknowledgements
The author thanks Fred E. Pinkerton (General Motors R&D Center) for his useful comments and suggestions. This work was supported by the U.S. Department of Energy, Advanced Research Projects Agency - Energy, Rare Earth Alternatives in Critical Technologies for Energy. The research was performed at the Ames Laboratory which is operated for the U.S. DOE by Iowa State University under contract #DE-AC02-07CH11358.

References
[1] L. Ke, D. Kukusta, V. Antropov, unpublished personal communication, March, 2014.

[2] A. Alam, M. Khan, R.W. McCallum, D.D. Johnson, *Appl. Phys. Lett.* **102**, 2013, 042402.

This page intentionally left blank.

Anisotropy Inducement Mechanism in Hydrogen Disproportionation Desorption Recombination (HDDR) Processed Nd-Fe-B Powders

H. SEPEHRI-AMIN[1], T. OHKUBO[1], K. HONO[1], K. GÜTH[2], O. GUTFLEISCH[2,3]
[1]Elements Strategy Initiative Center for Magnetic Materials, NIMS, Tsukuba, Japan
[2]Fraunhofer ISC Projektgruppe IWKS, Germany
[3]Materialwissenschaft, Technische Universität Darmstadt, Germany

Abstract: *Microstructure evolution of dynamic-hydrogen-disproportionation-desorption-recombination (d-HDDR) processed $Nd_{12.8}Fe_{80.1}B_{6.6}Ga_{0.3}Nb_{0.2}$ alloy powders with different applied hydrogen pressure during HD process (P_{H2}^{HD}) have been studied to understand the origin of the texture development in the powders during the d-HDDR process. A high remanent magnetization was obtained in the powders when P_{H2}^{HD} = 30 kPa was used. Transmission electron microscopy analysis showed that Fe_2B grains memorize the crystallographic orientation of the initial $Nd_2Fe_{14}B$ phase and transfer it to the recombined $Nd_2Fe_{14}B$ grains in the highly textured sample. Boron segregation was found at the NdH_2/α-Fe interfaces which act as a boron source for the growth of the recombined $Nd_2Fe_{14}B$ grains during the DR process. The mechanism of the texture development will be discussed based on the microstructure observations.*

Keywords: *Nd-Fe-B permanent magnets; d-HDDR process; microstructure; texture*

1. Introduction

The hydrogenation-disproportionation-desorption-recombination (HDDR) process is an attractive and unique method for producing anisotropic nanocrystalline Nd-Fe-B powders [1,2]. In order to develop highly textured Nd-Fe-B powders, HDDR process parameters need to be carefully chosen and controlled [2]. Although lots of investigations have been carried out to understand the mechanism of the anisotropy development in HDDR powders [2-4], some questions still remain including how boron can be provided for the further recombination of $Nd_2Fe_{14}B$ phase after its nucleation at the interface of Fe_2B and NdH_2 phase. In this work, the microstructures of the Nd-Fe-B powders that were HD processed at different hydrogen pressure (P_{H2}^{HD}) were investigated to fully clarify the mechanism of the anisotropic microstructu- re evolution. Also, this work clarifies the existing sources of boron for the nucleation and growth of recombined $Nd_2Fe_{14}B$ grains during the DR process.

2. Experimental

Dynamic hydrogenation disproportionation (HD) desorption recombination (DR) process was carried out on $Nd_{12.8}Fe_{80.1}B_{6.6}Ga_{0.3}Nb_{0.2}$ alloy powders at different HD hydrogen pressure, P_{H2}^{HD} = 30 kPa and 100 kPa. The microstructures of the samples in early stages of the HD process, a full HD process, and an early DR process were investigated using SEM/FIB (Carl Zeiss 1540EsB) and TEM (Titan G2 80-200) to characterize the memory sites responsible for the texture development.

3. Results and Discussion

Figure 1(a) and (b) show magnetization curves measured parallel and perpendicular to c-axis of the fully d-HDDR processed Nd-Fe-B powders with different hydrogen pressure during HD process (P_{H2}^{HD}) of 30 kPa and 100 kPa, respectively. The

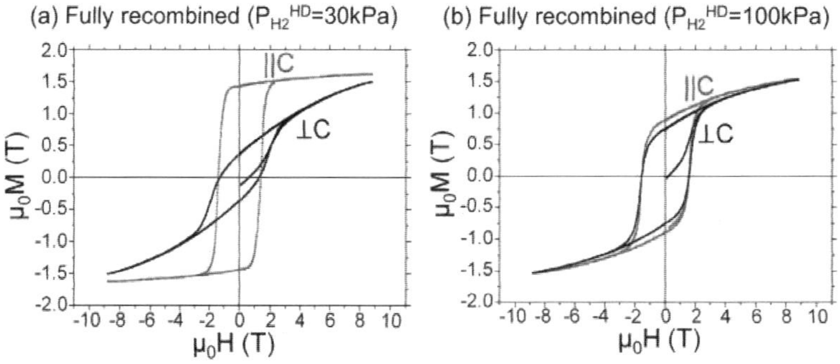

Fig. 1. Magnetization curves measured parallel and perpendicular to the c-axis of fully d-HDDR processed Nd-Fe-B powders with different hydrogen pressure during HD process (P_{H2}^{HD}) of (a) 30kPa and (b) 100kPa.

Fig. 2. (a) BF-TEM image and (b) superimposed energy filtered Fe (blue), Nd (red), and boron (green) maps of early HD processed sample with P_{H2}^{HD}: 30kPa. (c) Selected area diffraction pattern obtained from Fe_2B, $Nd_2Fe_{14}B$, and interface of α-$Fe/Nd_2Fe_{14}B$ and $NdH_2/Nd_2Fe_{14}B$ phases.

d-HDDR processed powders were aligned in a dc-magnetic field prior to the magnetic measurements. A high remanent magnetization of 1.43 T was obtained for the fully d-HDDR processed powder with P_{H2}^{HD} = 30 kPa, indicating a strong [001] crystallographic texture. However, P_{H2}^{HD} = 100 kPa led to the development of a weakly textured Nd-Fe-B powder with a remanent magnetization of 0.89 T.

Figure 2(a) shows bright field (BF) TEM image taken from the early HD processed P_{H2}^{HD} = 30kPa sample. Energy filtered elemental maps of different constituent elements were taken from the same area as BF-TEM image to get a hint about location of different phases. Fig. 2(b) shows superimposed energy filtered elemental maps of Fe (blue), Nd (red), and boron (green) obtained from the same region as BF-TEM image shown in Fig. 2(a). Based on the distribution of Fe, Nd, and B, location of initial $Nd_2Fe_{14}B$ phase, NdH_2, α-Fe, iron boride grains can be recognized as it is indicated in Fig. 2(a) and (b). Selected area diffraction patterns (SADP) obtained from different regions of Fig. 2(a), which are marked with circles with different colors, are shown in Fig. 2(c). Each SADP has a border color matched with the color of the marked circles in Fig. 2(a) indicating the region that the diffraction patterns are taken from. The indexed diffraction pattern from the boride region indicates that the iron boride phase is Fe_2B and no Fe_3B was found in the microstructure. A direct crystallographic orientation relationship was found between Fe_2B phase and initial $Nd_2Fe_{14}B$ grains, *i.e.* $[420]_{Fe2B}//[211]_{Nd2Fe14B}$ and $(00\bar{2})_{Fe2B}//(\bar{1}11)_{Nd2Fe14B}$. The diffraction patterns obtained from the interface of α-$Fe/Nd_2Fe_{14}B$ and $NdH_2/Nd_2Fe_{14}B$ grains showed that there is no crystallographic orientation relationship between the initial $Nd_2Fe_{14}B$ grains and NdH_2 and α-Fe phases as shown in Fig. 2(c).

Figure 3 shows BF-TEM image and superimposed energy filtered elemental maps of Fe (blue), Nd (red), and B (green) of fully HD processed samples processed with P_{H2}^{HD} = 30 kPa and 100 kPa. In these images, enrichment of boron not only at Fe_2B areas but also at the interface of NdH_2 and α-Fe can be seen. In addition, comparison of superimposed energy filtered elemental maps and BF-TEM images indicate that each iron boride region is comprised of several small Fe_2B grains.

Fig. 4(a) and (b) show BF-TEM and dark field (DF) TEM images from fully HD processed samples at P_{H2}^{HD} = 30 kPa and 100 kPa, respectively. Comparison of BF-TEM and DF-TEM images show that Fe_2B

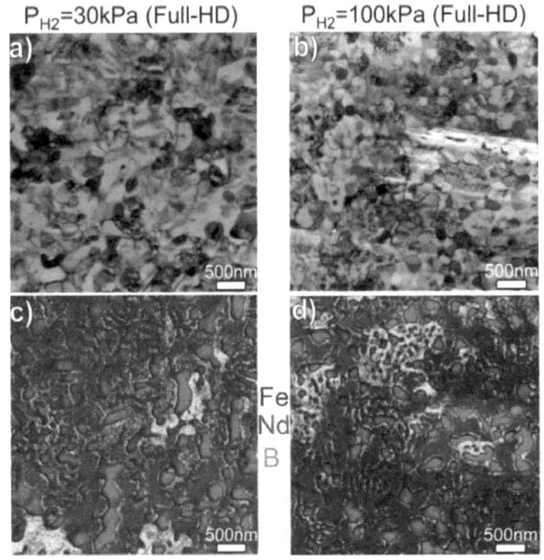

Fig. 3. BF-TEM image and superimposed energy filtered Fe (blue), Nd (red), and B (green) maps of fully HD processed (a) P_{H2}^{HD} = 30 kPa and (b) P_{H2}^{HD} = 100 kPa samples.

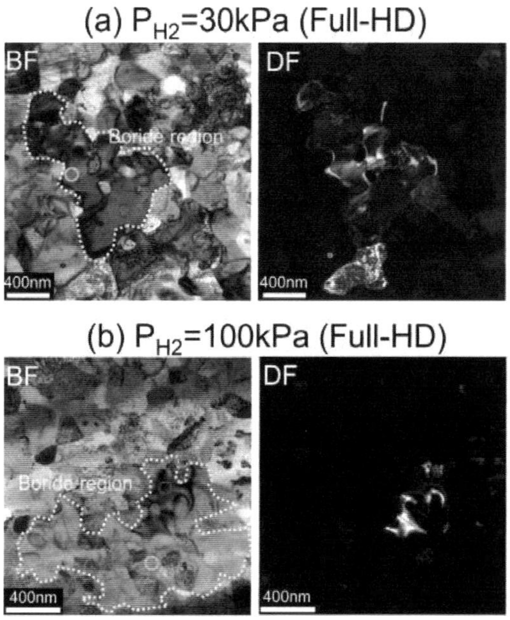

Fig. 4. Bright field (BF) and dark field (DF) TEM images of fully HD processed sample at (a) P_{H2}= 30 kPa and (b) P_{H2}=100kPa. Iron boride region are pointed out in BF-TEM images.

grains in the fully HD processed P_{H2}^{HD} = 30 kPa sample is very well textured while Fe_2B grains in the fully HD processed P_{H2}^{HD} = 100 kPa sample are isotropic.

TEM analysis of P_{H2}^{HD} = 30 kPa sample at early DR processed stage (data not shown) showed a crystallographic orientation relationship between Fe_2B grains and recombined $Nd_2Fe_{14}B$ grains, *i.e.* $[042]_{Fe2B}//[223]_{Nd2Fe14B}$ and $(\bar{1}12)_{Fe2B}//(\bar{2}20)_{Nd2Fe14B}$. These microstructure investigations indicate that the highly aligned Fe_2B grains act as memory sites for the development of the texture in the sample HD processed at P_{H2}^{HD} = 30 kPa, as shown schematically in Fig. 5. Importantly, it can now be shown that the boron segregated at the NdH_2/α-Fe interface acts as a boron source for the growth of the recombined $Nd_2Fe_{14}B$ grains during DR process.

4. Conclusion

d-HDDR process was carried out on $Nd_{12.8}Fe_{80.1}B_{6.6}Ga_{0.3}Nb_{0.2}$ alloy powders at different hydrogen pressure during HD process of P_{H2}^{HD} = 30 kPa and 100 kPa. A highly textured powders was found in the d-HDDR processed sample with P_{H2}^{HD} = 30 kPa. The microstructure evolution studies showed that highly aligned Fe_2B grains memorize the crystallographic orientation of the initial $Nd_2Fe_{14}B$ phase and transfer it to the recombined $Nd_2Fe_{14}B$ grains in the highly textured sample. These investigation confirm that highly aligned Fe_2B grains act as memory sites for the development of the texture in the sample HD processed at P_{H2}^{HD}=30 kPa, consistent with the previously proposed texture memory effect (TME) model [2]. Energy filtered elemental maps showed that B segregates at the NdH_2/α-Fe interface for both highly and poorly textured samples acting as a boron source for the growth of the recombined $Nd_2Fe_{14}B$ grains during DR process.

References

[1] T. Takeshita, R. Nakayama, in: *Proc. 11th Workshop on Rare Earth Magnets and their Applications*, Pittsburg, USA, 1990, 49-71.
[2] O. Gutfleisch et al., *IEEE Trans. Magn.* **39**, 2003, 2926.
[3] T. Tomida et al., *Acta Mater.* **47**, 1999, 875.
[4] Y. Honkura et al., *J. Magn. Magn. Mater.* **290-291**, 2005, 1282.

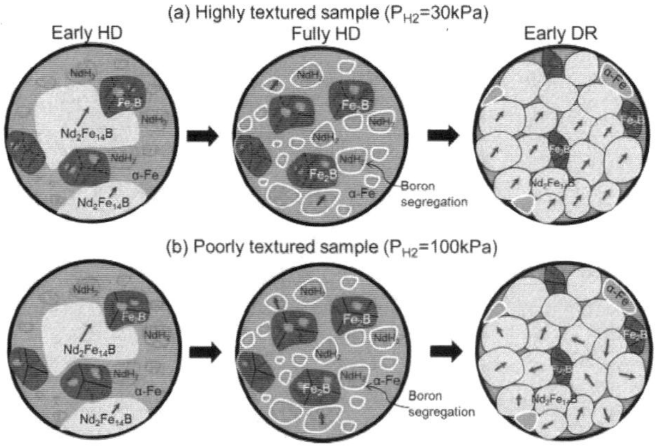

Fig. 5. Schematic illustration of microstructure evolution of HDDR processed sample with (a) P_{H2}^{HD} = 30 kPa (b) P_{H2}^{HD} = 100 kPa. This figure shows that in the highly textured powder, highly aligned Fe_2B grains act as memory sites and remembering the crystallographic orientation of initial $Nd_2Fe_{14}B$ grains and transferring the same orientation to the recombined $Nd_2Fe_{14}B$ grains.

SmCo-based Dual-Phase Nanocomposite Bulk Permanent Magnets

MIN ZOU, WANMING ZHANG, CHRISTINA H. CHEN*, JAE-HYUK HER, FRANCIS JOHNSON
GE Global Research Center, 1 Research Circle, Niskayuna, NY 12309, USA
*Current address: Magnet Energy Corp., San Jose, CA 95125, USA

Abstract: *This work explores a new approach for the microstructural control to ensure exchange coupling between the magnetically hard and soft phases. Dual-phase alloys are cast based on hard phase compositions with excess amount of soft phase metals, thus containing both hard and soft phases before milling down to the nanometer size. Crystallographic phase identification and magnetization measurement were conducted on bulk magnets made from dual-phase alloys $SmCo_6$ and $Sm_2(Co_{0.93}Fe_{0.07})_{21.7}$. The results show that after high energy ball milling and consolidation, the magnets made from $SmCo_6$ contain $SmCo_5$ and Sm_2Co_{17} phases and achieve B_r = 5.3 kG, H_{ci} = 10.9 kOe, $(BH)_{max}$ = 6.3 MGOe; the magnets made from $SmCo_6$ blended with 8.75 wt.% Fe and 8.75 wt.% Co contain Sm_2Co_{17} and FeCo phases and achieve B_r = 10.0 kG, H_{ci} = 7.4 kOe, $(BH)_{max}$ = 15.3 MGOe; and the magnets made from $Sm_2(Co_{0.93}Fe_{0.07})_{21.7}$ contain Sm_2Co_{17} and Co phases and achieve B_r = 11.1 kG, H_{ci} = 4.4 kOe, $(BH)_{max}$ = 7.9 MGOe. Henkel plots of the bulk magnets made from dual-phase alloys show positive δm peaks, and that made from $SmCo_5$ shows a negative δm peak.*

Keywords: *SmCo/FeCo nanocomposite; dual phase magnet; hot pressed magnet; spark plasma sintered magnet; high energy ball milling; Henkel plot*

1. Introduction

A key challenge facing nanocomposite exchange-spring bulk permanent magnets is ensuring exchange coupling between the magnetically hard and soft phases by controlling the microstructural features to the nanometer length scale [1-3]. Conventional methods consolidate blended nanosized hard and soft phases to produce bulk magnets. This work explores a new approach for achieving this microstructural control. SmCo alloys are cast based on hard phase compositions with excess amount of soft phase metals, such as Fe, Co, and their alloys. The as-cast alloys are therefore dual phase alloys containing both magnetically hard and soft phases. High-energy or surfactant assisted ball milling is then used to break the bulk dual-phase alloys down to nanoscale powders that comprise both hard and soft phases. The dual-phase powders can then be consolidated to form nanocomposite bulk permanent magnets either by themselves or when blended with additional soft phase nanopowders.

2. Experimental Details

Starting materials of two alloy compositions, $SmCo_6$ (equivalent to $SmCo_5$ + 12 wt.% Co) and $Sm_2(Co_{0.93}Fe_{0.07})_{21.7}$ (equivalent to $Sm_2(Co_{0.93}Fe_{0.07})_{17}$ + 18 wt.% $Co_{0.93}Fe_{0.07}$) were prepared by using vacuum arc melting. The alloy compositions were determined by using direct current plasma emission spectroscopy. The starting materials were crushed to < 300 μm and dry milled using a high energy SPEX mill, then consolidated using high vacuum uniaxial hot pressing (HP) and spark plasma sintering (SPS) at various temperatures between 550 and 700 °C and various pressures between 90 and 240 ksi for HP; between 14 and 22 ksi for SPS. The densities of the bulk magnets were > 95% of the theoretical density. The powders were not magnetically aligned prior to consolidation. All powder handling was conducted in an argon glove box with an oxygen level < 2ppm. The X-ray diffraction (XRD) data were collected using an Inel machine equipped with Rigaku rotating anode X-ray generator (50 kV × 80 mA, Mo K rad.) and a Bruker D8 machine equipped with sealed tube X-ray generator (40 kV × 40 mA, Cu K rad.). The program JADE [4] was used for phase identification. The magnetic measurements were carried out by using a Quantum Design PPMS. Demagnetization factor was applied to the magnetization data.

3. XRD Results

The XRD patterns of the $SmCo_6$ starting powder (Fig. 1a) and the bulk magnet made from it (Fig. 1b) can be indexed into hexagonal $CaCu_5$-type $SmCo_5$ and rhombohedral $Zn_{17}Th_2$-type Sm_2Co_{17} structures; and no soft phase is detected. To increase the volume fraction of soft phase, magnets were made from milled $SmCo_6$ powder blended with additional Fe and Co nanopowders to yield a composition of $SmCo_6$ + 8.75 wt.% Fe+ 8.75 wt.% Co. Fig. 2 shows that the bulk magnets made from these blended powders comprise a $Sm_2(FeCo)_{17}$ major phase and a FeCo B2 minor phase according to the XRD profiles. The intensity of the FeCo (011) peak decreases for the magnet made from the blended powders milled from 3, to 5 and 8 hours. Therefore, the starting $SmCo_5$ crystal lattice incorporated the Fe and Co atoms and transformed to the $Sm_2(FeCo)_{17}$ phase during high

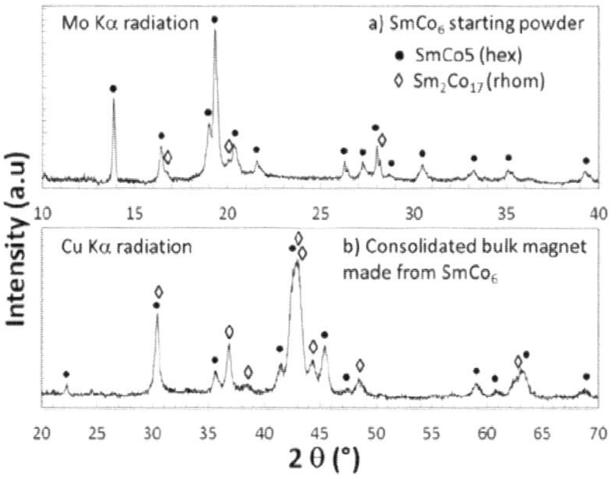

Fig. 1. XRD patterns of $SmCo_6$: (a) starting powder and (b) consolidated bulk magnet.

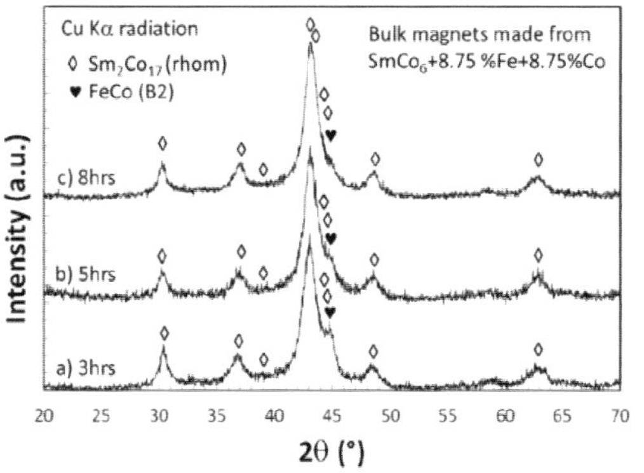

Fig. 2. XRD patterns of bulk magnets made from $SmCo_6$ blended with 8.75 wt.% Fe and 8.75 wt.% Co which were co-milled for (a) 3 hours; (b) 5 hours; and (c) 8 hours.

energy ball milling and consolidation. In fact, $SmCo_6$ + 8.75 wt.% Fe + 8.75 wt.% Co is equivalent to $Sm_2(Co_{0.88}Fe_{0.12})_{17}$ + 5 wt.% Sm. By further increase the soft phase volume fraction to a composition of $Sm_2(Co_{0.93}Fe_{0.07})_{21.7}$, while the starting powder is single phase with a rhombohedral Sm_2Co_{17} structure (Fig. 3a), the bulk magnet made from the milled powder comprises magnetically hard $Sm_2(FeCo)_{17}$ and soft Co fcc phases (Fig. 3b). No $SmCo_5$ phase was observed in $Sm_2(Co_{0.93}Fe_{0.07})_{21.7}$ bulk magnets.

4. Magnetic Properties

The magnetic properties of dual phase magnets are in good agreement with their crystallographic phase compositions. The demagnetization curves (not shown here) of the bulk magnets made from $SmCo_6$ and $Sm_2(Co_{0.93}Fe_{0.07})_{21.7}$ exhibit a step-like behavior, suggesting that the two magnetic phases, i.e. $SmCo_5$ and Sm_2Co_{17} for $SmCo_6$, and $Sm_2(FeCo)_{17}$ and FeCo for $Sm_2(Co_{0.93}Fe_{0.07})_{21.7}$, may not be fully coupled. The magnets made from $SmCo_6$ blended with 8.75 wt.% Fe and 8.75 wt.% Co does not show any step-

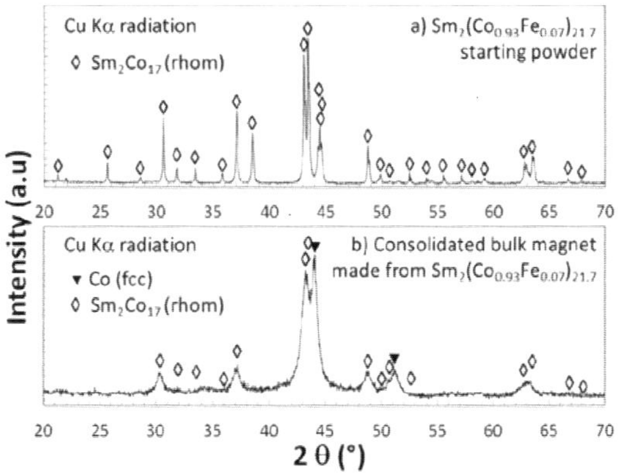

Fig. 3. XRD patterns of $Sm_2(Co_{0.93}Fe_{0.07})_{21.7}$ (a) starting powder; and (b) consolidated bulk magnet.

like behavior, which is in line with the very low FeCo peak intensities in their XRD patterns.

The highest magnetic properties of the isotropic bulk magnets made from the dual phase alloys are B_r = 5.3 kG, H_{ci} = 10.9 kOe, $(BH)_{max}$ = 6.3 MGOe for $SmCo_6$; B_r = 10.0 kG, H_{ci} = 7.4 kOe, $(BH)_{max}$ = 15.3 MGOe for $SmCo_6$ + 8.75 wt.% Fe+ 8.75 wt.% Co; and B_r = 11.1 kG, H_{ci} = 4.4 kOe, $(BH)_{max}$ = 7.9 MGOe for $Sm_2(Co_{0.93}Fe_{0.07})_{21.7}$. The variation of the H_{ci} and B_r in general agrees with the crystallographic phase composition of these magnets, because the $SmCo_5$ has a higher H_{ci} and a lower B_r than the Sm_2Co_{17} phase. The magnetic properties of the dual phase magnets are close to those of the bulk nanocrystalline $Sm(Co_{0.834}Fe_{0.166})_z$ with z = 6, 8.5, and 11, reported by Chen *et. al* [5]. It is not clear whether the $Sm(Co_{0.834}Fe_{0.166})_z$ magnets were made from dual or single phase alloys because the base alloys compositions were not disclosed.

To understand the magnetization reversal mechanism, Henkel plots were constructed for five bulk magnets made from $SmCo_5$, $SmCo_6$, $SmCo_6$ + 8.75 wt.% Fe + 8.75 wt.% Co, and $Sm_2(Co_{0.93}Fe_{0.07})_{21.7}$. These magnets were consolidated by using different techniques, such as hot isostatic pressing (HIP), HP, and SPS. While the $SmCo_5$ magnet shows a negative $\delta m = m_d - (1 - 2m_r)$ peak, where m_d and m_r are reduced magnetization from the DCD and IRM measurements, respectively, all dual phase magnets exhibit positive δm peaks. This suggests that the reversal of the $SmCo_5$ magnet is dominated by exchange coupling, and that of dual phase magnets is dominated by the dipolar interaction, which is opposite to what is commonly accepted [6] but reported by some other researchers [7]. It has been indicated by Wohlfarth [8] and discussed by Skomski and Sellmyer [9] that non-zero δm originates from not only particle interactions but also other factors, such as superparamagnetic, multidomain or incoherent

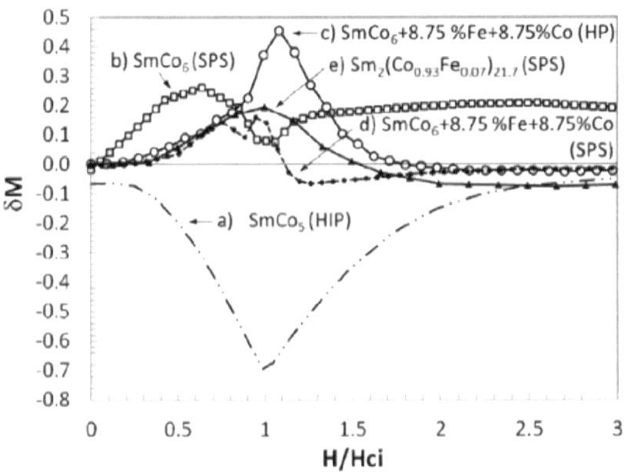

Fig. 4. Henkel plots of bulk magnets made from (a) $SmCo_5$; (b) $SmCo_6$; (c)&(d) $SmCo_6$ blended with 8.75 wt.% Fe and 8.75 wt.%; and (e) $Sm_2(Co_{0.93}Fe_{0.07})_{21.7}$. HIP: hot isostatic pressing; HP: hot pressing; SPS: spark plasma sintering.

rotation effects and non-uniaxial anisotropy. Given the existence of multiple magnetic phases with different anisotropy and unknown domain structure, our results suggest that besides the Henkel plots, further information is needed to determine the reversal mechanism of the dual phase magnets.

5. Summary

Dual phase nanocomposite bulk permanent magnets have been studied with alloy compositions $SmCo_6$ and $Sm_2(Co_{0.93}Fe_{0.07})_{21.7}$. The magnets made from $SmCo_6$ comprise of two magnetically hard phases, $SmCo_5$ and Sm_2Co_{17}. The magnets made from $Sm_2(Co_{0.93}Fe_{0.07})_{21.7}$ comprises $Sm_2(FeCo)_{17}$ hard phase and FeCo soft phase. Magnetization data show that the two magnetic phases may not be fully coupled and the dual phase magnets exhibit positive δm peaks in the Henkel plots.

Acknowledgement

This information data, or work presented herein was funded in part by the Advanced Research Projects Agency-Energy (ARPA-E) U.S. Department of Energy under Award Number DE-AR0000158.

References

[1] E. F. Kneller & R. Hawig, *IEEE Trans. Magn.* **27**, 1991, 3588.
[2] R. Skomski & J. M. D. Coey, *Phys. Rev. B* **48**, 1993, 15812.
[3] B. Balamurugan, D.J. Sellmyer, G.C. Hadjipanayis and R. Skomski, *Scr. Mater.* **67**, 2012, 542.
[4] Product of MDI, http://www.materialsdata.com.
[5] C.H. Chen, A.K. Higgins, M.Q. Huang, J.C. Horwath, Y. Shen, and S. Liu, *J. Appl. Phys.* **105**, 2009, 07A718.
[6] V. Patel, M. El-Hilo, K. O'Grady, and R. W. Chantrell, *J. Phys.D: Appl. Phys.* **26**, 1993, 1453.
[7] A. Bollero, O. Gutfleisch, K.-H. Müller, L. Schultz, and G. Drazic, *J. Appl. Phys.* **91**, 2002, 8159.
[8] E. P. Wohlfarth, *J. Appl. Phys.* **29**, 1958, 595.
[9] R. Skomski and D. J. Sellmyer, *J. Appl. Phys.* **89**, 2001, 7263.

Low Temperatures Magnetization Reversal Process in Nd-Fe-B Nanostructured Alloys

D.S. NEZNAKHIN[1], A.S. VOLEGOV[1], P.E. MARKIN[1,2], S.V. ANDREEV[1], A.S. BOLYACHKIN[1], N.V. KUDREVATYKH[1]
[1]Ural Federal University named after First President of Russia B.N. Yeltsin, Ekaterinburg, Russia
[2]Institute of Metal Physics UB RAS, Ekaterinburg, Russia

Abstract: *Isotropic samples of nanostructured rapidly quenched Nd-Fe-B-type alloy were investigated using SQUID base magnetic property measuring system and X-ray diffraction analysis method. Magnetization jumps were discovered at temperatures below 4 K on demagnetizing curves in magnetic fields around their coercivity value. It is shown that magnetization jumps have a stochastic nature and their number strongly depends on the temperature value and the mass of measured sample. This phenomenon is similar to the previous one for the anisotropic microstructural sintered magnets, but it cannot be described as the magnetic domain wall motions via micrograins. It requires the creation of proper models for magnetization jumps explanation in such nanostructured alloys.*

Keywords: *Nd-Fe-B nanostructured alloy; magnetization jumps; low temperatures*

Address: D.S. Neznakhin, Ural Federal University, Institute of Natural Sciences, 620083, pr. Lenin 51, Ekaterinburg, Russia, Tel:8(343)261-68-23, E-mail: D.S.Neznakhin@urfu.ru

1. Introduction

Low temperature magnetic hysteresis studies of rare-earth permanent magnets with a high $(BH)_{max}$ product revealed the existence of magnetization jumps on the demagnetizing curve of the hysteresis loop at the second and third quadrants [1-5]. These jumps were discovered firstly for the sintered Nd-Fe-B type anisotropic magnets at temperatures below 10 K and at the external magnetic fields near to its coercivity value. The coercivity mechanism in these samples originates from the reversed magnetic phase nucleations delay. Similar features of the demagnetization process were found in sintered magnets of Sm_2Co_{17}-type [1], where its hysteresis is caused by domain walls pinning.

Y.Otani *et al.* in their earlier work [2] have described the magnetization jumps in terms of domain wall "passage" from one $Nd_2Fe_{14}B$ phase grain to another through the layers of the $Nd_{1,1}Fe_4B_4$ phase. The Curie temperature of $Nd_{1,1}Fe_4B_4$ phase was relatively low (about 18 K); this was a reason to explain the "smooth" demagnetization curves at higher temperatures, by its paramagnetic state. After further investigations [3,4] Y. Otani has corrected the description of the anomalous demagnetization process at low temperatures and proposed a two-stage trigger/propagation process. The first stage is characterized by magnetization reversal in some micrograin volumes, whereas the second stage reflects the thermally activated domain-wall motions caused by the small lattice specific heat at temperatures below 10 K.

Paper [5] showed that magnetization jumps in Nd-Fe-B sintered magnets during the demagnetization process at low temperatures appear in both cases regardless of the $Nd_{1,1}Fe_4B_4$ phase. Thus, another model of giant magnetization jumps was proposed which describes them as domain wall tunneling through paramagnetic interfaces between neighboring $Nd_2Fe_{14}B$ phase grains. In further work, the authors [1] investigating magnets with another type of coercivity have come to an assumption about the importance of the local sample heating during magnetization jumps.

Aiming at verification of the possibility of applying the previous models to nanostructured exchange-coupled Nd-Fe-B hard alloys, as well as to check the presence of magnetization jumps, the magnetization reversal processes in such types of alloy at low temperatures were investigated in the present work. The demagnetization process occurs due to the irreversible magnetization rotations inside any $Nd_2Fe_{14}B$ phase nanograins without domain wall formation. The existence of magnetization jumps in these systems could not be expected from the perspective of view of the previous models.

2. Experimental Details

Commercially available, rapidly quenched isotropic MQP-B+ alloy has been taken as the object of this study. It is produced in the form of powder flakes, which are composed mainly of non-textured $Nd_2Fe_{14}B$ phase nanograins and some amounts of α-Fe inclusions. For magnetization reversal study, several samples of different masses have been prepared. Some of them were fixed in a copper capsule using wax; others were prepared as a minor assembly of isolated flakes glued to a nonmagnetic silicon wafer. The magnetic properties of a single flake (m = 0.05 mg) were also studied.

The phase composition of prepared isotropic samples was determined using X-ray diffraction analysis. The Sherrer-Selyakov formula was used to calculate an average grain size. Magnetic properties were measured in magnetic fields up to ±70 kOe using a MPMS-XL-7 EC magnetometer at temperature from 2 to 300 K. Before measurement, each sample was cooled from T = 300 K to the targeted temperature in the external magnetic field of +70 kOe, which exceeds anisotropy field (H_a) of $Nd_2Fe_{14}B$ phase at room temperature (H_a = 63 kOe [6]). Hence, all the presented hysteresis loops were ultimate.

3. Results and Discussion

From XRD analysis the $Nd_2Fe_{14}B$ phase was determined as the main phase for the investigated samples. The average grain size was also estimated as 30 nm, which in order of magnitude, is less than a critical single-domain $Nd_2Fe_{14}B$ phase size of d_c = 210 nm [7]. It means that the magnetization reversal process of the studied samples was realized by reversible and irreversible nanograins magnetization rotations.

Ultimate hysteresis loops measurements at low temperatures showed the magnetization jumps on demagnetizing curves below 4 K (Fig. 1).

The concave shape of the hysteresis loop branch in the second quadrant originates from the cone magnetocrystalline anisotropy type of $Nd_2Fe_{14}B$ phase caused by spontaneous spin-reorientation transition at T = 135 K [8]. Magnetization jumps appear on this branch in the magnetic fields close to coercivity value (-20.5 kOe) firstly in the second quadrant and spread mainly in to third one up to fields of about -25 kOe. At higher negative fields, as on the loop branches for the first and partially second quadrants, such jumps are not observed. Taking into consideration the easy cone anisotropy type in $Nd_2Fe_{14}B$ phase nanograins, and their random c-axis distribution inside the flake, this can be interpreted as irreversible magnetization rotations across the tetragonal lattice basal plane at an angle of about 116°. The magnetization jumps correspond to simultaneous magnetization rotations in the very large number of $Nd_2Fe_{14}B$ phase nanograins, since such jumps has a macroscopic scale value.

An increase of sample temperature from 1.8 K to 4 K has led to the jumps number decreasing with increasing separate jump magnitude (Fig. 2). Above 4 K magnetization jumps are not observed. The sample mass decrease has caused a similar effect (Fig. 3).

The statistical investigation of the ultimate magnetic hysteresis loops has demonstrated some stochastic behavior of magnetization jumps parameters (Fig. 4), which is impossible to connect with the uncertainties both for the external magnetic field and for the magnitude of magnetization jumps experimental determinations.

Using the $Nd_2Fe_{14}B$ phase nanograins sizes and the absolute magnetization jump magnitude, it was possible to estimate the sample volume and the grains number involved in the magnetization jump. It was thus inferred that such jumps "captured" about 10^{10} nanograins in the sample of 0.05 mg and about 10^{13} nanograins in the sample of 74.73 mg masses. As far as the average flake consisted of 10^{11} nanograins, it means that either the whole of the flake volume, or several flakes isolated from each other, are simultaneously involved in magnetization jumps.

The hypotheses of domain wall "passage" from one

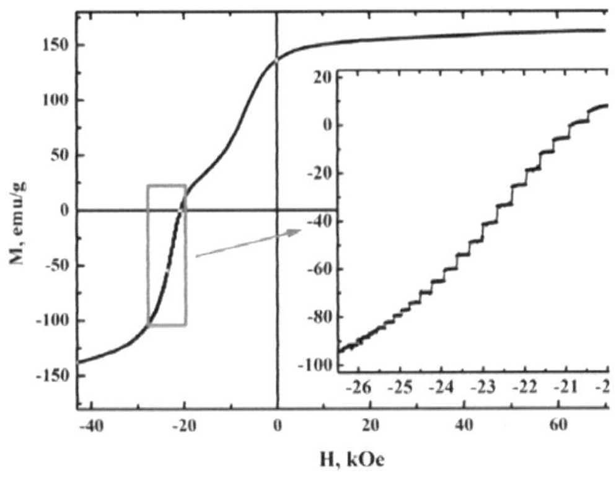

Fig. 1. Desending branch of ultimate hysteresis loop at T=2 K, for Nd-Fe-B alloy sample of 74.73 mg mass.

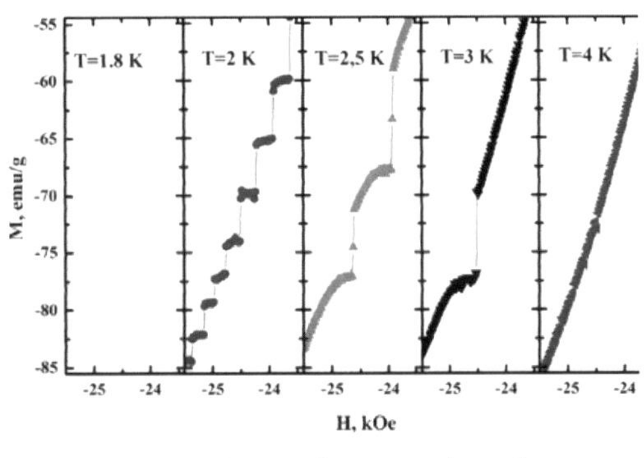

Fig. 2. Parts of ultimate hysteresis loop demagnetization curves at different temperatures for Nd-Fe-B alloy sample of 74.73 mg mass.

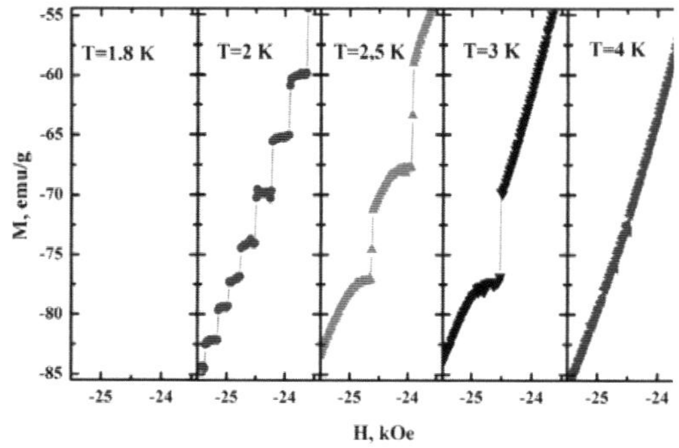

Fig. 3. Parts of ultimate hysteresis loop demagnetization curves at T= 2 K for Nd-Fe-B alloy samples of different masses.

$Nd_2Fe_{14}B$ phase nanograin to another through the layer of $Nd_{1,1}Fe_4B_4$ phase, or quantum tunneling between them, could not be used for interpretation of the observed magnetization jumps in the studied alloys, because of their single-domain grains state. For the same reason a model of two-stage trigger/propagation process could not describe this phenomenon adequately. Nevertheless, thermo-activating processes could play a significant role in magnetization jumps formation in nanostructured samples with the proviso that they cause a local irreversible magnetization rotation through the potential barrier between easy axes orientations laying on easy cone surface. Besides this mechanism in a nanostructured magnetic system because of size effect, an intergrains exchange interaction becomes strong enough in comparison to the one for microstructural samples and can intensify an avalanche demagnetization process observed as the large magnetization jump.

4. Conclusions

Magnetization jumps on the ultimate hysteresis loop demagnetizing branch of isotropic nanostructured rapidly quenched Nd-Fe-B-type alloy samples were discovered at temperatures below 4 K. The increasing of the sample temperature from 1.8 K to 4 K (or decreasing of the sample mass) has caused the decrease of the magnetization jumps numbers, and the increase in their magnitude. It is shown that the phenomena have a stochastic nature. For single-domain systems, this could be interpreted as thermo-activated "avalanche" irreversible magnetization rotation through the potential barrier between easy axes orientations via the crystallographic basal plane of the $Nd_2Fe_{14}B$ phase lattice. This process could be intensified by the intergranular exchange interaction, which is significant for nanostructured samples.

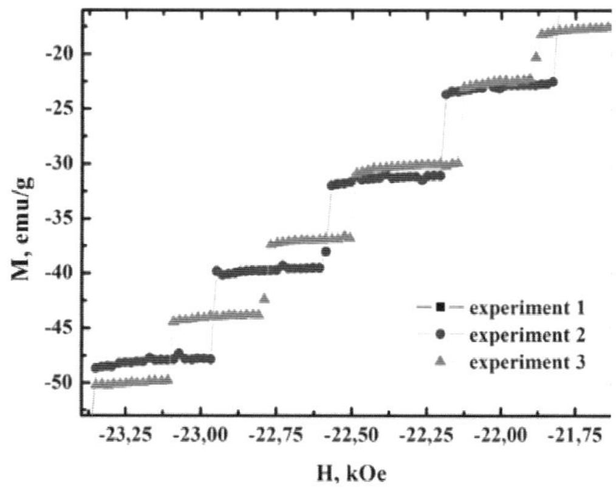

Fig. 4. Parts of ultimate hysteresis loop demagnetization curves at 2 K for Nd-Fe-B alloy sample of 74.73 mg mass measured three times after the same magnetizing field value of +70 kOe.

Acknowledgements

This research has been performed under the aegis of the state order project 2582 with the partial support of UrFU Young Scientists Competition grant. The authors acknowledge and appreciate the contribution of Tatiana Rasskazova (UrFU, Institute of Natural Sciences) and Mr. Ian Miller (UrFU, Institute of Social and Political Sciences) in the preparation of this article.

References

[1] A. Handstein, D. Eckert, K.-H. Müller, *IEEE Tran. Magn.* **30**, 1994, 598.
[2] Y. Otani, H. Miyajima, S. Chikazumi, S. Hirosawa, M. Sagawa, *J. Appl. Phys* **63**, 1988, 3316.
[3] Y. Otani, J.M.D. Coey, B. Barbara, H. Miyajima, S. Chikazumi et al., *J. Appl. Phys.* **67**, 1990, 4619.
[4] Y. Otani, R. Miyajima, S. Chikazumi, *IEEE Trans. Magn.* **25**, 1989, 3421.
[5] N.V. Baranov, E.V. Sinitsyn, E.A. Ignatyev, S.V. Andreev, *J. Magn. Magn. Mater.* **130**, 1994, 133.
[6] G.C. Hadjipanayis, *J. Magn. Magn. Mater.* **200** 1999, 373.
[7] H. Kronmüller, General Micromagnetic Theory, in: *Handbook of Magnetism and Advanced Magnetic Materials*, 2007, p. 19.
[8] J. Kamarad, Z. Arnold, *J. Magn. Magn. Mater.* **67**, 1987, 29.

Effect of Milling and Annealing Conditions on the Interphase Exchange Coupling of $Nd_2Fe_{14}B/\alpha$-Fe Magnetic Nanocomposites

S. MICAN[1], R. HIRIAN[1], O. ISNARD[2,3], I. CHICINAŞ[4], V. POP[1]
[1] Faculty of Physics, Babeş-Bolyai University, Cluj-Napoca, RO 400084, Romania
[2] Université Grenoble Alpes, Institut Néel, Grenoble, F 38042, France
[3] CNRS, Institut Néel, Grenoble, F 38042, France
[4] Materials Science and Engineering Department, Technical University of Cluj-Napoca, Cluj-Napoca, RO 400641, Romania

Abstract: *The effects of milling and annealing conditions on the microstructure and interphase exchange coupling of $Nd_2Fe_{14}B$+10 wt% α-Fe nanocomposites were investigated. We also address the problem of damaging the hard phase crystal structure during milling by using different milling energies. X-ray diffraction (XRD) investigations point to the destruction of the $Nd_2Fe_{14}B$ crystal structure during milling which is partially restored after annealing with a limited growth of the α-Fe crystallites. The $Nd_2Fe_{14}B/\alpha$-Fe exchange coupling was analyzed as a function of milling and annealing conditions. The best exchange coupling was obtained for the 6 h milled samples annealed at 700 °C for 2 min, with a maximum coercive field value of 0.48 T. It was found that lower milling energies increase the coercive field due to the reduced damaging of the hard phase crystal structure.*

Keywords: *$Nd_2Fe_{14}B/\alpha$-Fe nanocomposites;ball milling; short time annealing; interphase exchange coupling*

Address: Viorel Pop, Faculty of Physics, Babeş-Bolyai University, Cluj-Napoca, RO 400084 Romania, Tel: +40 (264) 405300, Fax: +40 (264) 591906, E-mail: viorel.pop@phys.ubbcluj.ro

1. Introduction

In the last decade permanent magnets have become crucial components in many devices and advanced technologies and, with the development of environmental technologies such as wind turbines and electric vehicles, their demand has steadily increased. Among the potential nanocomposite permanent magnets, the $Nd_2Fe_{14}B/\alpha$-Fe nanocomposites display interesting properties for both fundamental research and applications [1-4]. In addition to an increase in magnetization, the presence of Fe in exchange coupled nanocomposites could lead to an increased thermal stability [5] and higher corrosion resistance [6]. One way of preparing $Nd_2Fe_{14}B/\alpha$-Fe nanocomposites is mechanical milling [7, 8]. It was previously shown that the crystallite size of the soft magnetic phase is a critical parameter which affects the strength of the hard/soft exchange coupling [1, 9]. The structural and magnetic properties of mechanically milled (MM) $Nd_2Fe_{14}B$+10 wt% α-Fe nanocomposites were previously studied [7, 10]. It was shown that the restoration of the hard phase crystal structure without an excessive growth of the soft phase crystallites could be achieved through properly selected annealing parameters. It was suggested that a better interphase exchange coupling could be expected for 6 h MM samples followed by short time annealing [7]. We expect that the pre-milling of the soft phase powder could lead to smaller Fe crystallites after annealing the nanocomposites. In this paper, we aim to investigate the effect of milling conditions and short time annealing on the evolution of the microstructure and exchange coupling of milled $Nd_2Fe_{14}B$+10 wt% α-Fe nanocomposites. The problem of damaging the hard phase crystal structure during milling is addressed by using different milling energies.

2. Experimental Details

The $Nd_2Fe_{14}B$ ingot was prepared by induction melting in Ar, followed by annealing in vacuum at 950 °C for 68 h. The ingot was crushed and sieved through a 500 μm sieve. The soft phase starting powder consisted of Fe powder pre-milled for 4 h with benzene. The $Nd_2Fe_{14}B$ powder was mixed with the pre-milled Fe powder in a weight ratio of 90% $Nd_2Fe_{14}B$/10% Fe and dry-milled with Ø 10 mm and Ø 15 mm steel balls under Ar for 2, 4 and 6 h respectively. The ball-to-powder weight ratio was 10:1. The milled samples were annealed in an inert Ar atmosphere using a preheated furnace at 700, 750 and 800 °C for times ranging from 0.5 to 2.5 minutes followed by quenching in water. The structure and microstructure of the samples were investigated by XRD using a Brüker D8 Advance diffractometer using Cu Kα radiation. The average crystallite sizes were determined from the full width at half maximum of the diffraction peaks using Scherrer's formula. For magnetic measurements, the powder samples were blocked in Araldite resin. The hysteresis curves were recorded at room temperature using the extraction technique in applied fields up to ±10 T. Considering isolated magnetic particles we used a demagnetization factor of 1/3.

3. Results and Discussions

The XRD patterns for the samples milled for 2, 4 and 6 h with Ø 10 mm and Ø 15 mm balls along with those for the annealed samples are shown in Fig. 1. The peaks of the hard phase disappear even after 2 h MM for the samples milled with Ø 10 mm balls, whereas for the samples milled with Ø 15 mm balls, they are still somewhat visible after 6 h MM showing that Ø 15 mm ball milling has a lower energy, the damaging of the hard phase crystal structure being reduced. After annealing, the XRD peaks corresponding to $Nd_2Fe_{14}B$ become visible, pointing to the restoration of its crystal structure while the mean sizes of the Fe crystallites remain in the 10-25 nm range - Table 1. This shows that the excessive growth of the Fe crystallites was hampered during the short time annealing.

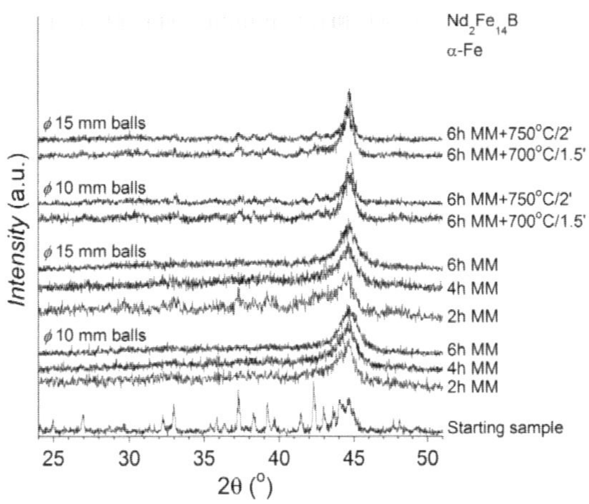

Fig. 1. XRD patterns for the as-milled and annealed $Nd_2Fe_{14}B$+10 wt% α-Fe samples.

The demagnetization curves and d*M*/d*H* vs. *H* plots of the annealed samples are shown in Fig. 2. The shape of the demagnetization curves for the annealed 2 and 4 h MM samples points mainly to the presence of decoupled magnetic phases, whereas the 6 h MM samples annealed at 700 and 750°C show a single magnetic phase behaviour. The d*M*/d*H* vs. *H* plots show two peaks, one at low field values of 0.1-0.2 T and the other centered around 0.5-0.6 T. The peak at low fields could correspond to badly coupled or uncoupled Fe or $Nd_2Fe_{14}B$ crystallites, while the peak at higher fields could be attributed to the exchange coupled nanocomposite. For the annealed samples milled at higher energies the exchange coupling occurs even after 2 h MM, whereas for the samples milled at lower energies, this only occurs after 4 h MM, due to a weaker soft/hard interphase coupling.

However, the intense peak at low magnetic fields proves that a significant percentage of crystallites are not yet coupled even after 4 h MM. The 6 h milled samples annealed at 700 and 750 °C show a much more efficient exchange coupling, the d*M*/d*H* vs. *H* curves showing a sharp peak at ~0.5 T and small peak around 0.2 T. The stronger exchange coupling in the 6

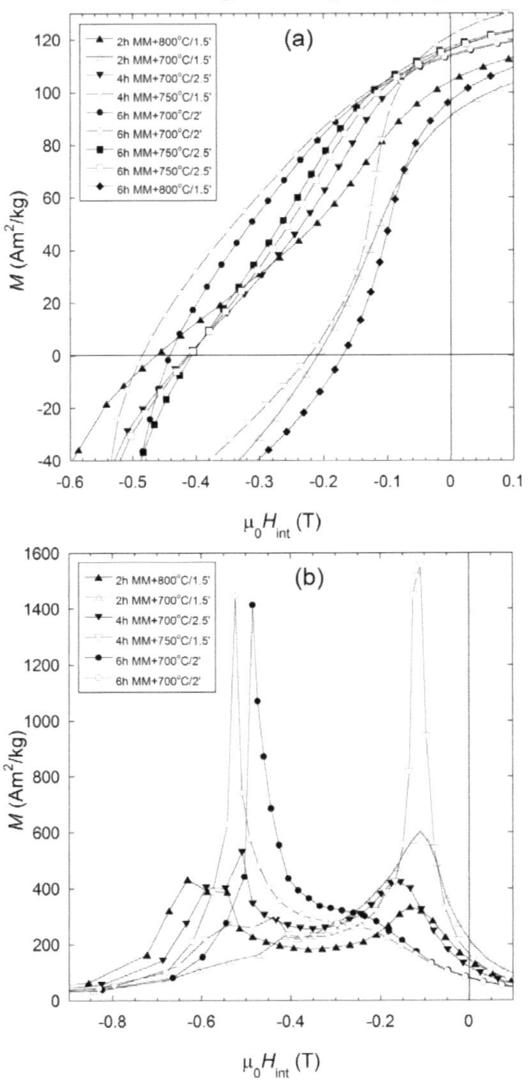

Fig. 2. Demagnetization curves after magneti-zation at 10 T (a) and dM/dH vs. H curves (b) of the annealed nanocomposites. The filled and empty symbols correspond to the samples milled with Ø 10 mm and Ø 15 mm balls respectively.

h MM samples could be attributed to lower Fe crystallite sizes and a better homogeneity of the composite mixture. The best interphase exchange coupling was obtained for the 6 h MM sample and annealed at 700 °C for 2 min. The coercive field and remanent magnetization values for the annealed samples are summarized in Table 1. The coercive field values increase with annealing time due to the progressive restoration of the hard phase crystalstructure. The slight decrease of these values with increasing annealing temperature could be attributed to a weaker interphase exchange strength determined by the growth of the Fe crystallites. The 6 h MM samples milled at lower energies exhibit higher coercivities due to the reduced damaging of the hard phase crystal structure. The large coercivity decrease of 6 h MM+800°C sample could be attributed to an increased interphase diffusion which could lead new phases. Our samples have slightly lower coercivities than previously reported values [7, 10], however, they show a higher remanence. This behavior could be attributed to the pre-milling of the soft phase evidenced by the lower Fe crystallite sizes. The lower coercive field values of our samples could be attributed to the pre-milling of Fe with benzene, however, further investigations are required.

Table 1. Mean crystallite sizes of Fe, coercive field and remanent magnetization values for the annealed nanocomposites.

Milling time (h)	Annealing temperature (°C)	Annealing time (min)	d (nm)	$\mu_0 H_c$ (T)	M_r (Am^2/kg)
6 (Ø 10 mm)	700	1.5	10	0.42	114
		2	15	0.44	114
	750	2	20	0.38	124
		2.5	21	0.41	117
	800	1.5	25	0.17	97
6 (Ø 15 mm)	700	2	17	0.48	114
	750	2.5	20	0.41	117
6	550 [10]	90	34	0.55	115
8 [7]	700	1.5	16	0.51	103
	800	1.5	26	0.54	96

4. Summary

The effect of milling conditions and short time annealing on the evolution of the microstructure and exchange coupling of milled $Nd_2Fe_{14}B$+ 10 wt% α-Fe nanocomposites was investigated. It was shown that lower milling energies lead to a reduced damaging of the $Nd_2Fe_{14}B$ crystal structure. After annealing, the hard phase crystal structure was restored with a limited growth of the Fe crystallites. Magnetic data showed a progressive strengthening of the interphase exchange coupling with milling time. It was shown that lower milling energies increase the coercive field due to a reduced damaging of the hard phase crystal structure. Our samples showed lower coercivities than previously reported values, possibly due to the pre-milling of Fe with benzene, however they showed a higher remanence.

Acknowledgment

The authors acknowledge support from the Romanian UEFISCDI Projects PN-II-ID-PCE-2012-4-0470 and PN-II-RU-TE-2011-3-0048.

References

[1] R. Skomski, J. M. Coey, *Phy. Rev.* B, *48*, **1993**, 15812.

[2] R. Skomski, P. Manchanda, P. Kumar, B. Balamurugan, A. Kashyap , D. J. Sellmyer, *IEEE Trans. Magn*, *49*, **2013**, 3215.

[3] G. C. Hadjipanayis, *J. Magn. Magn. Mater.*, *200*, **1999**, 373.

[4] E. F. Kneller, R. Hawig, *IEEE Trans. Magn.*, *27*, **1991**, 3588.

[5] D. Goll, M. Seeger, H. Kronmüller, *J. Magn. Magn. Mater.*, *185*, **1998**, 49.

[6] M. Jurczyk, J. Jakubowicz, *J. Alloys Compd.*, *311*, **2000**, 292.

[7] V. Pop, S. Gutoiu, E. Dorolti, O. Isnard, I. Chicinaş, *J. Alloys Compd.*, *509*, **2011**, 9964.

[8] W. Gong, G. C. Hadjipanayis, R. F. Krause, *J. Appl. Phys.*, *75*, **1994**, 6649.

[9] T. Schrefl, H. Kronmüller, J. Fidler, *J. Magn. Magn. Mater.*, *127*, **1993**, L273.

[10] S. Gutoiu, E. Dorolti, O. Isnard, I. Chicinaş, V. Pop, *J. Optoelectron. Adv. Mater.*, *12*, **2010**, 2126.

From High Aspect Ratio Nanoparticles Synthesis to Nano-Structured Permanent Magnets

E. ANAGNOSTOPOLOU[1], B. GRINDI[1], L.M. LACROIX[1], F. OTT[2], G. VIAU[1]
[1] Université de Toulouse, LPCNO, UMR 5215 INSA-CNRS-UPS, Toulouse, France
[2] Lab. Léon Brillouin, UMR 12 CEA/CNRS, Centre d'Etudes de Saclay 91191 Gif sur Yvette Cedex France

Abstract: *Dense and highly textured magnetic materials were obtained by controlled alignment in an electromagnet of cobalt nanorods (Co NRs) prepared by the polyol process. Square magnetization curves with M_R/M_S higher than 97% and H_C of 4.7 kOe were measured in the parallel configuration. The volume fraction of the three components of the material, cobalt, cobalt oxide and organics, were calculated through the combination of magnetometry and thermal analysis. The magnetic cobalt volume fraction was found in the range 45-54%, depending on the cobalt nanorods used, giving a remanence B_R in the range 0.80-0.96 T. BH_{max} as high as 165 kJ.m^{-3} could be reached. The shape homogeneity of the starting Co NRs is the key point to obtain the best performance of the dense material.*

Keywords: cobalt, nanorods, shape anisotropy, nanocrystalline magnets

Address: Guillaume Viau, Université de Toulouse, LPCNO, UMR 5215 INSA-CNRS-UPS, 135 av. de Rangueil 31077 Toulouse Cedex 4, France, gviau@insa-toulouse.fr

1. Introduction

The bottom-up approach for nanostructured permanent magnets is an interesting alternative route to the classical rare-earth metallurgy [1]. This approach is developed thanks to the recent progress in the magnetic nanoparticle synthesis by liquid phase methods, which now allow a good control of particle size, shape and chemical composition. Our motivation is to develop a new generation of permanent magnets relying on the shape anisotropy of high aspect ratio magnetic nanoparticles. A few years ago, it was proposed that ferromagnetic elongated nanoparticles prepared by wet chemistry process, either polyol process or organometallic chemistry, could be interesting building blocks for consolidation of nano-textured materials, combining high magnetization and high coercivity [2,3]. Single crystal cobalt nanorods (NRs) and nanowires (NWs) with a mean diameter in the range 10-20 nm and the long axis parallel to the crystallographic c axis were found particularly interesting due to their coercivity in the range 5-7 kOe. Actually, the challenge to obtain a permanent magnet based on cobalt nanowires is to reach a high volume fraction (>50%) with a nearly perfect alignment of the magnetic easy axes. This work reports on the formation of dense assemblies of cobalt nanorods prepared by the polyol process and the assessment of their BH_{max}.

2. Experimental Techniques

Cobalt nanorods (Co NRs) were synthesized following a published procedure [4]. Cobalt laurate (0.08M) was dispersed in a NaOH solution (0.075M) in 1,2 butanediol. Ruthenium chloride (molar ratio Ru/Co=2.5%) was added in the medium. The suspension was heated to 175°C with a slope of 8°C/min under mechanical stirring. After 30 min at 175°C the solution was cooled down to room temperature. The black particles were washed twice with ethanol and redispersed in chloroform. Synthesis in 1L of butanediol allowed preparing c.a. 5g of powder. The cobalt nanorods were characterized by transmission electron microscopy (TEM) using a Jeol JEM 1400. Mean diameter (D_m) and mean length (L_m) were measured with the image analysis on c.a. 200 rods using ImageJ software. Dense macroscopic assemblies of nanorods were prepared by drying at room temperature concentrated suspensions in an electromagnet under an applied field of 1T. These samples were characterized by vibrating sample magnetometer (QD, PPMS-6000) with a magnetic field parallel and perpendicular to the textured material. Thermo-gravimetric analysis (TGA) was performed on a Mettler Toledo balance in air and under H_2/Ar atmosphere. Scanning electron microscopy images were recorded with a SEM FEG JEOL JSM 6700F.

3. Material Characterization

The electron microscope showed that typical Co NRs prepared by the polyol process exhibited a mean diameter in the range 15-25 nm and a mean length in the range 150-250 nm. The drying of the concentrated suspensions of these rods made macroscopic needles (Fig. 1a) that consisted of dense and parallel alignments of Co NRs (Fig. 1b,c).

Fig. 1. (a) Picture of the macroscopic needles made up of a dense and parallel alignment of cobalt nanorods; SEM images of a needle with (b) low and (c) high magnification. Inset: TEM image of the Co NRs.

The magnetic volume fraction value was determined by the combination of magnetization measurement and thermal analysis. The saturation magnetization of these needles was found in the range 120 and 125 emu.g^{-1}. Taking into account a bulk value of 160 emu.g^{-1} for bulk Co, the mass fraction of ferromagnetic cobalt within our sample was calculated in the range 74-77%. This value is explained by a thin cobalt oxide shell and by organic molecules remaining at the surface of the cobalt rods. In order to measure the volume fraction of each component (metal Co, Co oxide and ligands) of the needles, thermal analyses were performed. A mass *m* of needles was first heated in air up to 700°C in order to remove all the organics and to fully oxidize the cobalt core. This treatment was followed by a reduction of the cobalt oxide in metal cobalt at 700°C under a mixture of H_2/Ar. The total mass variation of the two steps Δm gives the total mass fraction of cobalt, i.e. cobalt involved in the metal core and the cobalt oxide shell. This oxide shell was already characterized as a CoO shell [5]. Assuming that the density of Co, CoO and ligands are similar to the bulk values, namely 8.9, 6.4 and 0.9 g.cm^{-3}, respectively, it was possible to deduce the volume fraction of the three components. The cobalt volume fraction was

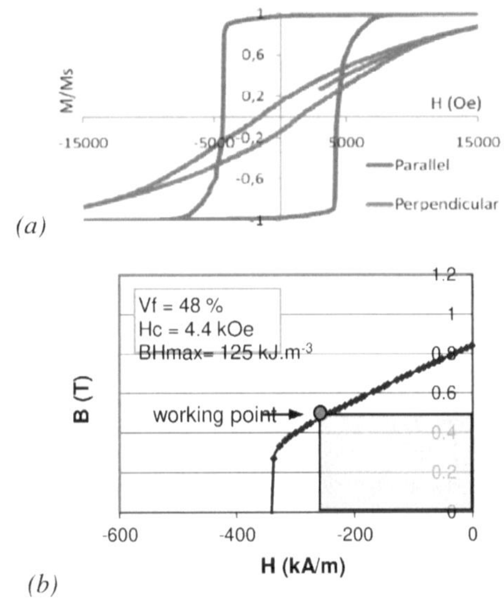

Fig. 2. (a) M(H) curve of a magnetic needle made up of dense alignment of cobalt nanorods, with the applied field H parallel and perpendicular to the needle; (b) Second quadrant of the B(H) curve calculated with the ferromagnetic cobalt volume fraction of 48%.

always found in the range 45-54%, depending on the sample and the washing procedure.

4. Magnetic properties

Magnetic needles were prepared with different batches of cobalt nanorods. The magnetic properties of single needles were measured with the applied field parallel and perpendicular to their long axis. Very square loops were obtained in the parallel configuration with a remanence to saturation ratio, M_R/M_S, higher than 97% and coercivity, H_C, in the range 3.9-4.7 kOe (Fig. 2a). In the perpendicular configuration, the loops collapsed with M_R/M_S lower than 20% and H_C lower than 2 kOe. These features show clearly that the easy axis is along the long axis of the needles. Moreover, the M_R/M_S value indicates a very narrow orientation distribution of the rod easy axis inside the needle. To our knowledge, this is the first time that such highly square hysteresis loops were reported for nanoparticles based materials.

The magnetic volume fraction value was used to calculate the B(H) curve (Fig. 2b) and to deduce the maximum of the energy product which is the BH_{max} value. This product was found in the range 60-165 kJ.m^{-3} depending on the sample. Actually, the BH_{max} is very dependent on the magnetization loop and on the magnetic volume fraction. The highest values were obtained with very square loops such as that given in Fig. 2a. For that, the rod alignment has to be nearly perfect. We observed that the presence of spheres or stars in the powder leads to a smoothing of the hysteresis loop and thus, to a drastic decrease of

Table 1. Properties of dense Co nanorods parallel assemblies.

BH_{max} (kJ.m^{-3})	H_C (kA/m)	B_R (T)
60 - 165	290 - 365	0,80 - 0,96

the BH_{max} value. The energy product is also very dependent on the magnetic volume fraction. For the same Co NR batch, only washed in a different way, the volume fraction in the needle increased from 48 to 54% and consequently the BH_{max} value increased from 125 to 165 kJ.m^{-3}, while the coercivity was found to be nearly the same. The ranges of BH_{max}, H_C and B_R obtained with different needles made up with different Co NRs are summarized in Table 1. These values showed that the Co NRs based materials can fill a gap between the ferrites or AlNiCo and the rare-earth based permanent magnets [6].

In order to assess the effect of the volume fraction and coercivity on the BH_{max} and on the working point, characterized in the second quadrant of the B(H) curves, we simulated a progressive increase of both parameters in the experimental B(H) loop presented on Fig. 2. Increasing the volume fraction to 60%, by removing the organics or by reducing the cobalt oxide shell, would increase Br, leading to a BH_{max} of 180 kJ.m^{-3} (Fig. 3a). Nevertheless, such increase would also shift the working point closer to the demagnetizing field, weakening the potential application of such materials. On Fig. 3b is plotted the B(H) extrapolated for an hypothetical H_C of 7.5 kOe, keeping constant the volume fraction at 48%. It appears that the BH_{max} value increases only very slightly but the curve is now almost linear (the knee has disappeared) which is more favourable for dynamic applications of permanent magnets.

Thus, an improvement of permanent magnets based on Co NRs would require to increase concomitantly the volume fraction and Hc. The coercivity of an assembly of nanorods depends on the intrinsic property of the rods and on dipolar interactions. The comparison between isolated rods and their assembly in dense needles showed that the coercivity decreased from 5.5 to 4.7 Oe due to dipolar interactions. If lowering the dipolar interaction, by increasing the interrods spacing, is contradictory with the high volume fraction needed, there is still room to optimize the intrinsic properties of the rods. The results presented here were obtained with NRs of diameter around 20 nm. Reducing the NR mean diameter could be a way to increase the H_C.

5. Summary

This work shows for the first time that Co NRs are interesting building blocks for dense permanent magnets based on the shape anisotropy. BH_{max} value as high as 165 kJ.m^{-3} were obtained. The shape homogeneity of the starting cobalt nanorods is the key point to obtain both high volume fraction and high remanence. The consolidation of these needles could be a way to make a new kind of magnet, filling a gap between ferrites and rare-earth based PM. Further investigations must now focus on the increase of coercivity. One possibility is to reduce the mean diameter on the rods.

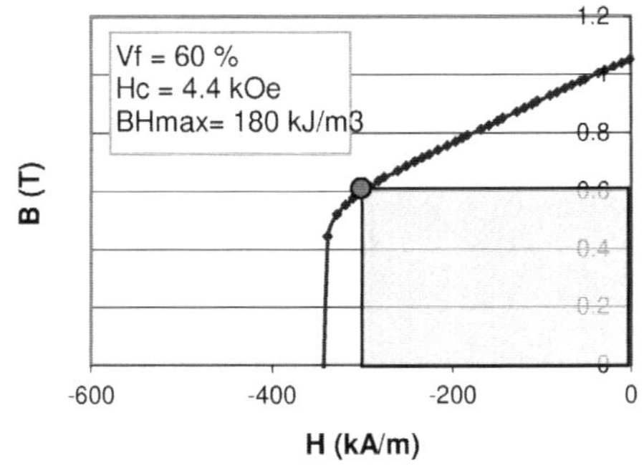

(a)

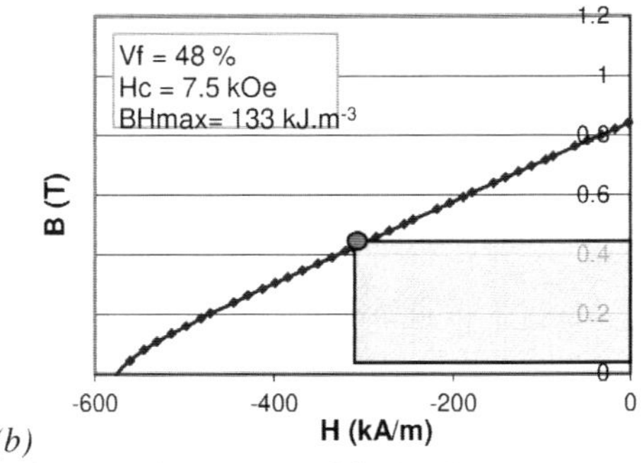

(b)

Fig. 3. Second quadrant of the B(H) curve extrapolated from the curve of fig. 2b by increasing the volume fraction from 48 to 60 % keeping Hc constant (a) and increasing Hc from 4.4 to 7.5 kOe keeping the volume fraction constant.

Acknowledgement

This work was partially supported from the European Commission FP7 for the REFREEPERMAG (No. EU NMP3-SL-2012-280670) Project.

References

[1] N. Poudyal, J. P. Liu, *J. Phys. D : Appl. Phys.*, 2013, 46, 043001.

[2] T. Maurer, F. Ott, G. Chaboussant, Y. Soumare, J.-Y. Piquemal, G. Viau, *Appl. Phys. Lett.*, 2007, 91, 172501.

[3] K. Soulantica, F. Wetz, J. Maynadié, A. Falqui, R. Tan, T. Blon, B. Chaudret, M. Respaud, *Appl. Phys. Lett.*, 2009, 95, 152504.

[4] Y.Soumare, C. Garcia, T. Maurer, G. Chaboussant, F. Ott, F. Fiévet, J.-Y. Piquemal, G. Viau, *Adv. Func. Mater.*, 2009, 19, 1971.

[5] T. Maurer, F. Zighem, F. Ott, G. Chaboussant, G. André, Y. Soumare, J.- Y. Piquemal, G. Viau, C. Gatel, *Phys. Rev. B*, 2009, 80, 064427.

[6] O. Gutfleisch , M.A. Willard, E. Brück , C.H. Chen , S.G. Sankar, J. Ping Liu, *Adv. Mater.*, 2011, 23, 821.

Texture Development in Nanocomposite Nd-Fe-B/α-Fe Rare Earth Magnets

S. PRAKASH NARAYAN[1], TAKASHI YANAI[2], HIROTOSHI FUKUNAGA[2]
[1]Mansarovar Institute of Science & Technology (MIST), Bhopal-462042 (India)
[2]School of Engineering, Nagasaki University, Nagasaki 852-8521, Japan

Abstract: *The nano-composite Nd-Fe-B/α-Fe Rare Earth Magnets have great potential to compete the permanent magnet demand with lower cost and less complicated processing. The isotropic magnets are much acceptable for commercial values, whereas the anisotropic magnets fall far behind due to limited degree of texture. Our investigations on hot deformation of these magnets have shown reasonable degree of texture of 64%, which may be still improved.*

Keywords: *nanocomposite Nd-Fe-B magnet; melt spun magnet; hot deformation; magnetic anisotropic in Nd-Fe-B magnet; plastic deformation induced magnetic anisotropy*

Address: S. Prakash Narayan, Director, Mansarovar Institute of Science & Technology (MIST) Bhopal-462042 (INDIA) Cell: +91 9425302319, E-mail:spnarayanbpl@gmail.com

1. Introduction

The nano-crystalline Nd-Fe-B magnets have generated a great commercial demand globally. However the growing price of the expensive metal neodymium is escalating up the cost of the magnets, day by day. The newly emerged nano-composite Nd-Fe-B/α-Fe Rare Earth Magnet shows great potential in complementing the demand with lower cost and less complicated processing. The ferromagnetic exchange coupling is the key factor in enhancing the magnetization value with moderate to stronger coercive force.

The magnetic properties; the energy product, coercivity and remanance of nano-composite Nd-Fe-B/α-Fe rare earth magnets depend on the alloy composition, microstructure and manufacturing techniques employed.

The addition of Mn can promote crystallization and enhance both coercivity and remanence ratio of exchange coupled $Nd_2Fe_{14}B$/α-Fe nanocomposites magnets. The manganese (Mn) addition reduces the Curie temperature (Tc) of the $Nd_2Fe_{14}B$ phase and raises that of α-Fe phase due to an exchange bias between the Fe–Mn alloy and the magnetic phases [1, 2]. Ti substitution enhances the glass forming ability and therefore consists of a significant fraction of amorphous phase, and show typical two-step magnetic behavior. It also helps to suppress the grain growth of 2:17 phase during the annealing process, and simultaneously promotes the growth of magnetically hard 2:14:1 phase and significantly improves the magnetic properties on annealing [3]. The Pr, Co and Dy additions can be used to achieve the highest values of $(BH)_{max}$ but it has the practical limit of $(BH)_{max}$ in the range ~160–180 kJ/m^3 and coercivity in the range ~ 400–800 kA/m (4).

The study of heat treatments and magnetic hardening of NdFeB-based melt-spun nano-composite ribbons has revealed that the magnetic hardening can be realized in by rapid thermal annealing for 1s with a typical coercivity of 10.2 kOe whereas the prolonged annealing did not give any increase in coercivity. Structural characterization has revealed that there is a close correlation between magnetic hardening and nanostructured morphology [5]. The magnetic annealing of melt-spun $Nd_{2.4}Pr_{5.6}Dy_1Fe_{84}Mo_1B_6$ nano composites in field of 1.2 T results in an enhancement of an out-of-plane (110) crystal texture of α-Fe and an in-plane uniaxial magnetic anisotropy of the 2:14:1 phase. It also introduces finer, less angular and more homogeneously distributed soft and hard nano-grains. The enhanced crystallographic texture, nanostructure refinement, and in-plane uniaxial magnetic anisotropy enhancement are responsible for a complex magnetization reversal mechanism in these nano-composites [6]. The combined addition of Cu and Ti is very effective in improving the magnetic properties and reducing the grain size and, in particular, the size of α-Fe grains as the crystallization temperature is increased by about 30K with a metastable hexagonal phase. The metastable 1:7 phase is decomposed into the α-Fe and $Nd_2Fe_{14}B$ phase which suppresses the growth of α-Fe grains and the microstructure becomes more uniform [7].

The small addition of lead (Pb) increases the coercivity after annealing of $Nd_{10}Fe_{84-x}Pb_xB_6$ (x=0–3) magnets at 923K. The maximum coercivity slightly exceeds whereas the remanence, attains a maximum for 1.5 at% [8].

In a study, α-Fe/ $Nd_2Fe_{14}B$ nanocomposite magnets with strong crystallographic texture were prepared by controlled melt spinning. For a relatively low wheel speed of 10 m/s, the *c*-axis texture of the $Nd_2Fe_{14}B$ crystals is predominantly perpendicular to the plane of the ribbon, but it switches to parallel to the ribbon plane direction at a higher wheel speed of 20 m/s. The magnets show strong magnetic anisotropy between in and out of the ribbon planes. High remanence of $0.74M_s$ and a large energy product of 24.3 MGOe were observed parallel to the ribbon plane direction in the magnets prepared at a wheel speed of 20 m/s [9]. The nominal boron:RE compositional ratio of the alloy may produce significant changes in the nature and stability of the metastable phases present in the nanocomposite system. In general, a high compositional ratio (B:RE ≈ 1–4) promotes the initial formation of Fe_3B and complex boron-rich intermetallic phases such as the cubic $Nd_2Fe_{23}B_3$, the hexagonal $NdFe_{12}B_6$ and the cubic $Y_3Fe_{62}B_{14}$-type phases in the quenched material, while a low compositional ratio (B:RE < 0.5) favors the formation of α-Fe and a 2-17-type phase [10].

The α-Fe/$R_2Fe_{14}B$-type exchange-coupled NdFeB nanocomposites magnets with a coercivity ($_iH_c$) of more than 11 kOe and energy product, $(BH)_{max}$, of more than 16 MGOe have been successfully obtained on melt spun $(Nd_{0.95}La_{0.05})_{7.5+x}Fe_{bal}Cr_2B_{10}$ alloy powders, where x ranged from 3 to 3.5. It was found that a slight substitution of Cr for Fe suppresses the formation of the $R_2Fe_{23}B_3$ and Fe_3B phases during crystallization and results in the formation of an α-Fe/ $R_2Fe_{14}B$ mixture. Increasing the total rare earth content has enhanced the remanence [11].

Magnetic anisotropy is one of the prime features of this class of magnet that generates good capacity of domain alignment to improve the intensity of magnetization to a very high level. Energy products of such anisotropic magnets are very useful for different fields of applications particularly to the electrical & electronics industries. The plastic deformation induced magnetic anisotropy in the nano-composite magnet has demonstrated the possibility of generating high value of magnetic anisotropy in such system under critically controlled processing parameters [12].

Our initial investigations have been focused on study the effect of addition of Niobium (Nb) and Gallium (Ga) and their hot deformation under controlled processing parameters to evaluate the generation of maximum induced magnetic anisotropy [i.e. the degree of texture (D_T)] as the poor anisotropy in this class of magnets, drastically limits their applications.

2. Experimental

A systematic study has been carried by us with the two different compositions ($Nd_{1.6}Fe_{14}B$ +0.5Ga) and ($Nd_{1.8}Fe_{14}B$+0.5Ga). The alloy was firstly melted between the temperature ranges of 1673-1700K in an induction furnace. The induction melted alloys were melt-spun at the rate of 10^5-10^6 s^{-1} to produce the amorphous or nano-crystalline ribbons of 5 - 25 mm length, 1 - 2 mm width and 25 - 50 μm thickness.

The melt spun ribbons were crushed to fine powder (<150 micron) and cold compacted in a cylindrical die of 10 mm bore. The solid cylindrical samples were hot compacted at 1073K in the argon (inert) atmosphere at 100-120 MPa pressure for 10-20 seconds. Thus produced performs were deformed at 1023K and 1073K at different true strain rates. In order to prevent the oxidation of pellets, a jet of argon gas was maintained during and after the hot compaction till the temperature dropped to nearly 773K.

The magnetic properties of all the samples were measured with VSM of the samples of cube shape (4mm) cut from deformed magnets after pulse magnetization in the 5 Tesla (6400 kA/m) field. The measurement was carried out in the parallel and perpendicular direction of the compression. The M-H plots were generated along the three axes. The degrees of the texture (D_T) for all the deformed magnets were calculated from the following relation:

$$D_T(\%) = [Br_{(//)}]^2 / [\{Br_{(//)}\}^2 + \{Br_{(\perp)}\}^2] \times 100 \qquad (1)$$

Where $Br_{(//)}$–remanence parallel to the compression axis and $Br_{(\perp)}$ remanence perpendicular to the compression axis (13). The degree of the texture (D_T) is 50% for isotropic and 100% for fully textured (anisotropic) magnet.

The Microstructure evaluation of hot compacted samples of $Nd_{1.8}Fe_{14}B$+0.5Ga and $Nd_{1.6}Fe_{14}B$ +0.5Ga were carried out by Optical microscope and by the SEM. The hot compacted samples showed flakes of melt-spun ribbons with the estimated porosity of 10-25%. This has also resulted in the drop of magnetization value.

3. Results and Discussion

EDAX and XRD examination of the solid samples were made to analyze the presence of different phases and the degree of magnetic orientation induced due to deformation. The XRD pattern of two different samples of $Nd_{1.8}Fe_{14}B$+0.5Ga show high intensity planes of (006) and (105), confirming the higher level of magnetic anisotropy. Analysis of the XRD pattern of $Nd_{1.6}Fe_{14}B$ +0.5Ga, shows that (I_{max}) is from (331) and (314) planes. The expected plane of reflection (006) and (105) were observed with low intensity,

Table 1

Sample No.	Sample details	Treatment	Br(//) (T)	Br(⊥) (T)	DT (%)
1	$Nd_{1.6}Fe_{14}B$+0.5Ga	1073 K, 10^{-2} s^{-1}	0.650	0.530	60.1
2	$Nd_{1.6}Fe_{14}B$+0.5Ga	1073 K, 10^{-1} s^{-1}	0.570	0.480	58.5
3	$Nd_{1.8}Fe_{14}B$+0.5Ga	1073 K, 10^{-2} s^{-1}	0.560	0.475	58.2
4	$Nd_{1.8}Fe_{14}B$+0.5Ga	1023 K, 10^{-2} s^{-1}	0.558	0.549	50.8
5	$Nd_{1.8}Fe_{14}B$+0.5Ga	1073 K, 10^{-1} s^{-1}	0.663	0.534	58.1
6	$Nd_{1.8}Fe_{14}B$+0.5Ga	1023 K, 10^{-1} s^{-1}	0.448	0.347	62.5
7	$Nd_{1.8}Fe_{14}B$+0.5Ga	1073 K, 10^{0} s^{-1}	0.480	0.360	64.0
8	$Nd_{1.8}Fe_{14}B$+0.5Ga	1023 K, 10^{0} s^{-1}	0.520	0.408	62.5

indicating the degree of texture induced was of low value.

It is observed in $Nd_{1.6}Fe_{14}B$+0.5Ga and $Nd_{1.8}Fe_{14}B$+0.5Ga nano-composite samples that with the lowering of Nd content where α-Fe phase is higher, the tendency for magnetic anisotropy is reduced. It shows very unique feature of isotropy of value within 5% in $Nd_{1.6}Fe_{14}B$+0.5Ga, whereas the value in $Nd_{1.8}Fe_{14}B$+0.5Ga system is not so. The degrees of the texture (D_T) have been calculated for all the deformed samples. The result shows 51 to 64% as shown in Table-1. It was surprising to note that the lowest texture was found in the sample deformed at 1073K at $1x10^{-2}$/sec, which is reported to be highest for nano-crystalline Nd-Fe-B magnets (14). The reason for the drop in texture was confirmed by the presence of (410) and (331) planes which are not the easy axis of magnetization. The optimum degree of texture (D_T) was obtained in the sample deformed at 1073K at the strain rate of $1x10^{0}$/sec. In this case it has the (006) and (105) planes along the axis of magnetization. The change in the deformation kinetics is due to the presence of second phase (α-Fe) either in (110) or (100) planes along the axis of magnetization, controlling the degree of texture. The observations show that there is great potential to improve the degree of texture under controlled process parameters of temperature and strain rate.

5. Conclusions

The following observations have been made:
The coercivity does not change with change in α-Fe phase or Nd content, as the grain size is not affected with the change in Nd content. Lower Nd content leads to high saturation magnetization because of increased α-Fe phase. The anisotropy induced in the system is limited because of the tendency to develop texture along (410) and (331) planes whereas the orientation should be along the (006) and (105) planes, which are in the easy direction of magnetization. In nanocrystalline Nd-Fe-B magnet, orientation is observed along the compression axis from (006) and (105) planes, which was found to be completely different in this system.

Acknowledgement

The research work has been supported under DST-JSPS exchange program.

References

[1] X. Guozhi, W. Yuping, L. Xiaoyan, W. Zehua, L. Pinghua, G. Benxi, D. Youwei, *Journal of Non-Crystalline Solids* 352 (21), 2006, 2137
[2] G. Xie, S. Yin, F. Zhang, P. Lin, B. Gu, M. Lu, Y. Du, Z. Yuan: *Materials Letters* 58 (5), 2004 636
[3] A.H. Li, C.H. Chiu, H.W. Chang, W.C. Chang, W. Li, *Journal of Alloys & Compounds* 437(1), 2007, 197
[4] Z.W. Liu, H.A. Davies, *Journal of Magnetism and Magnetic Materials* 313(2), 2007, 337
[5] Kung-Te Chu, Z Q Jin, Vamsi M Chakka, J P. Liu, *Journal of Physics D: Applied Physics* 38(22), 2005, 4009
[6] B. Z. Cui, C. T. Yu, K. Han, J. P. Liu, H. Garmestan, M. J. Pechan, H. J. Schneider-Muntau :*Journal of Applied Physics* 2005, doi:10.1063/1.1853693
[7] S. Yang, X. P. Song, X. S. Liu, S. D. Li, W. Qin, B. X. Gu, Y. W. Du: *Journal of Applied Physics* 2002 doi:10.1063/1.1530368
[8] W. Kaszuwara, M. Leonowicz: *Journal of Magnetism and Magnetic Materials* 242, 2002, 1366
[9] X. Y. Zhang, Y. Guan, L. Yang, J. W. Zhang: *Applied Physics Letters* 2001
[10] L. H. Lewis, V. Panchanathan: *Journal of Applied Physics* 1999 doi:10.1063/1.369130
[11] W. C. Chang, D. Y. Chiou, S. H. Wu, B. M. Ma, C. O. Bounds: *Applied Physics Letters* 1998 doi:10.1063/1.121446
[12] S. P. Narayan, B. K. Prasad, D. D. Mishra, H. S. Jain- Procd. of 20th International Workshop on Rare Earth Permanent Magnets and their Applications [REPM 2008]- (Greece)
[13] Y. Liu, L. Xu, Q. Wang, W. Li, X. Zhang:*Applied Physics Letters*, 94 (17), 2009 doi: 10.1063/1.3126444
[14] V. M. Chakka, B. Altuncevahir, Z. Q. Jin, J. P. Liu, *J.Appl. Phys.* 99, 2006, 08E912.

Magnetic Properties of Sm_5Fe_{17} Melt-Spun Ribbons and Their Nitrides

TETSUJI SAITO[1], SEIICHI SAITO[1], DAISUKE NISHIO-HAMANE[2]
[1]Chiba Institute of Technology, Narashino, Chiba 275-0016, Japan
[2]The University of Tokyo, Kashiwa, Chiba 277-8581, Japan

Abstract: *Sm_5Fe_{17} melt-spun ribbons were obtained that exhibited low coercivity and mostly or partly consisted of the amorphous phase. Annealing of Sm_5Fe_{17} melt-spun ribbons resulted in the formation of the Sm_5Fe_{17} phase. The annealed Sm_5Fe_{17} melt-spun ribbons exhibited a high coercivity of more than 25 kOe. Nitrogenation of the annealed Sm_5Fe_{17} melt-spun ribbons was carried out. Although the nitrogenated specimen had slightly lower coercivity than the non-nitrogenated Sm_5Fe_{17} melt-spun ribbons, their remanence was higher than that of the non-nitrogenated ribbons.*

Keywords: *Sm-Fe alloys; melt-spinning; nitrogenation; coercivity; microstructures*

Address: Tetsuji Saito, Department of Mechanical Science and Engineering, Chiba Institute of Technology, Narashino, Chiba 275-0016, Japan, Tel: 81-47-478-0315, E-mail: tetsuji.saito@it-chiba.ac.jp

1. Introduction

The Sm_5Fe_{17} phase is a new ferromagnetic phase in the binary Sm-Fe system [1,2]. It is a metastable phase and its formation has been reported only in sputtered films [3,4]. Recent studies have revealed that the Sm_5Fe_{17} phase can be obtained by the annealing of amorphous Sm-Fe melt-spun ribbons [5]. Sm_5Fe_{17} melt-spun ribbons show a high coercivity exceeding 25 kOe. However, their remanence is around 40 emu/g, which is significantly lower than that of Nd-Fe-B magnets. Nitrogenation of the Sm_2Fe_{17} phase has been reported to result in the formation of the $Sm_2Fe_{17}N_3$ phase and the resultant nitrides showed excellent magnetic properties [6]. In the present study, nitrogenation of Sm_5Fe_{17} melt-spun ribbons was carried out with the objective of improving the magnetic properties. The structures and magnetic properties of the Sm_5Fe_{17} nitridies were then examined.

2. Experimental Techniques

Sm_5Fe_{17} alloy ingots were placed in a quartz crucible with an orifice of 0.6 mm at the bottom. The alloy ingots were induction melted in an argon atmosphere and then ejected through the orifice with argon onto a copper wheel rotating at a surface velocity of 40 ms^{-1}. The resultant melt-spun ribbons were annealed for 1 h under an argon atmosphere at temperatures between 773 K and 1073 K. The melt-spun ribbon annealed at 973 K was subsequently nitrogenated under a nitrogen atmosphere at temperatures between 633 K and 713 K for 20 h. The phases in the specimens were examined by X-ray diffraction (XRD) using Cu Kα radiation. The microstructures of the specimens were observed using a transmission electron microscope (TEM) after ion beam thinning. The thermomagnetic properties of the specimens were investigated using a vibrating sample magnetometer (VSM) with an applied field of 500 Oe. The magnetic properties of the specimens were measured at room temperature by the VSM with a maximum applied field of 25 kOe after the specimens had been magnetized in a pulsed field of 50 kOe.

3. Results and Discussion

3.1. Sm-Fe melt-spun ribbons

The Sm_5Fe_{17} melt-spun ribbons were amorphous and exhibited a low coercivity value. It is known that crystalline phases can be produced by rapid solidification processing and subsequent heat treatment [6]. Thus, the Sm_5Fe_{17} melt-spun ribbons were annealed at temperatures between 773 K and 1173 K for 1 h. Figure 1 shows the XRD patterns of the annealed Sm-Fe melt-spun ribbons. It was found that annealing of the Sm_5Fe_{17} melt-spun ribbon at 873 K or higher resulted in the formation of the Sm_5Fe_{17} phase. However, the ribbon annealed at 1073 K consisted of the $SmFe_3$ phase together with the Sm_5Fe_{17} phase.

Figure 2 shows the dependence of the coercivity of the Sm_5Fe_{17} melt-spun ribbons on the annealing temperature. The specimens annealed at 873 K and 973 K showed high coercivity values. In particular, the specimen annealed at 973 K exhibited a high coercivity of more than 25 kOe. The hysteresis loops of the Sm_5Fe_{17} melt-spun ribbon and the specimen annealed at 973 K are shown in Figure 3. Since the specimens were measured by VSM under a maximum applied field of 25 kOe, the hysteresis loop of the annealed specimen is not symmetric. The actual coercivity of the annealed specimen was measured as 40 kOe using a superconducting magnet with a maximum applied field of 100 kOe.

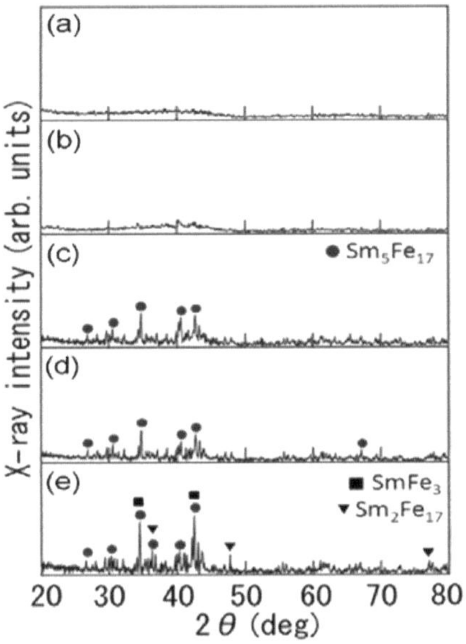

Fig. 1. XRD patterns of (a) the Sm-Fe melt-spun ribbon and the specimens annealed at (b) 773 K, (c) 873 K, (d) 973 K, and (e) 1073 K.

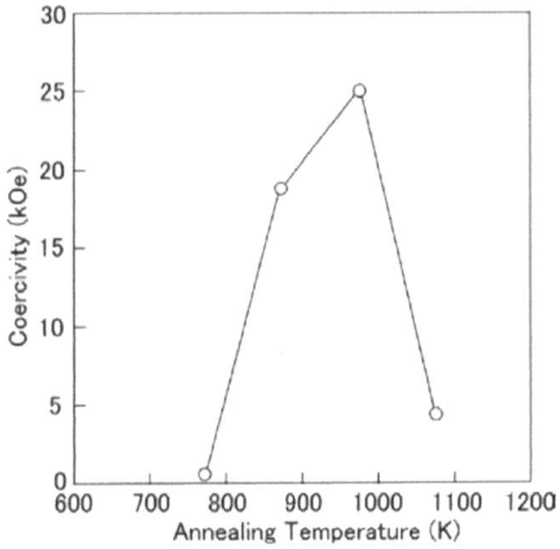

Fig. 2. Dependence of the coercivity of the Sm-Fe melt-spun ribbons on the annealing temperature.

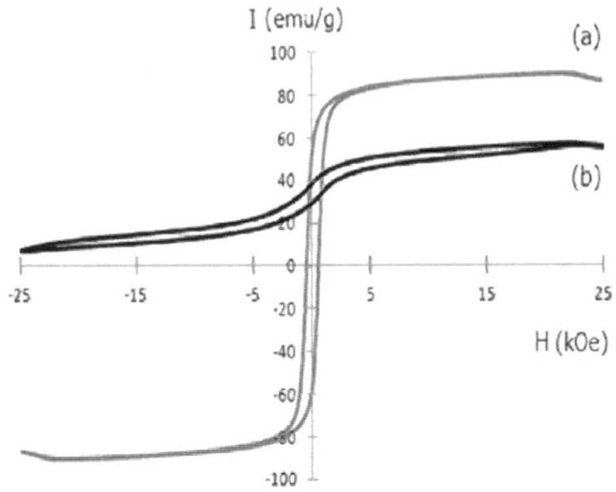

Fig. 3. Hysteresis loops of (a) the Sm-Fe melt-spun ribbon and (b) the specimen annealed at 973 K.

3.2. Sm-Fe nitrides

Although the Sm_5Fe_{17} melt-spun ribbon annealed at 973 K exhibits an attractively high coercivity, the remanence of 40 emu/g is significantly lower than that of Nd-Fe-B magnets. Thus, an attempt was made to improve the remanence of the Sm_5Fe_{17} melt-spun ribbon by nitrogenation at temperatures between 633 K and 713 K for 20 h. Fig. 4 shows the XRD patterns of the nitrogenated Sm-Fe melt-spun ribbons. The nitrogenation of the specimens resulted in a drastic change in the XRD patterns. The specimens annealed at 673 K or higher did not contain the Sm_5Fe_{17} phase, but consisted of a mixture of the α-Fe and unknown phases. This indicates that the specimens nitrogenated at 653 K or lower retained the Sm_5Fe_{17} phase, whereas decomposition of the Sm_5Fe_{17} phase occurred in the specimens nitrogenated at 673 K or higher.

Figure 5 shows the dependence of the coercivity of the Sm-Fe melt-spun ribbons on the nitrogenation temperature. The coercivity of the specimens decreases as the nitrogenation temperature increases. Before the nitrogenation experiments, the specimens were annealed in an argon atmosphere under the same conditions, at temperatures between 633 K and 713 K for 20 h. It was found that the annealing did not degrade the coercivity of the Sm_5Fe_{17} melt-spun ribbons. Therefore, the decrease in the coercivity value is considered to be due to the nitrogenation of the specimen.

Figure 6 shows the hysteresis loop of the annealed

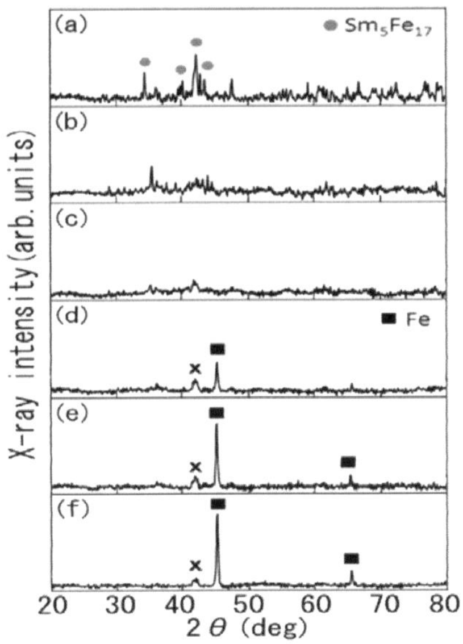

Fig. 4. XRD patterns of (a) the annealed Sm-Fe melt-spun ribbon and specimens nitrogenated at (b) 633 K, (c) 653 K, (d) 673 K, (e) 693 K, and (f) 1013K.

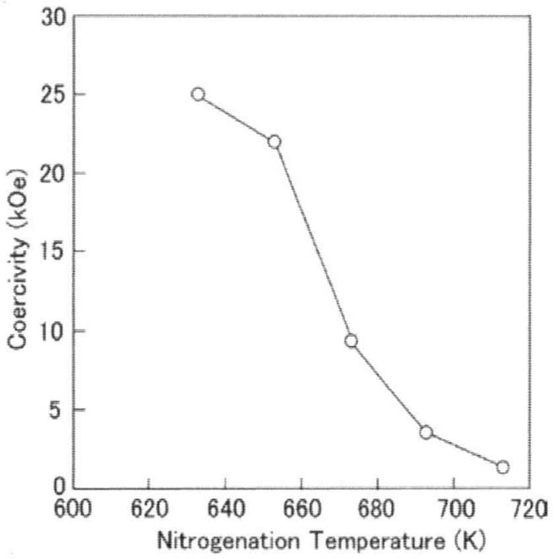

Fig. 5. Dependence of the coercivity of the Sm-Fe melt-spun ribbons on the nitrogenation temperature.

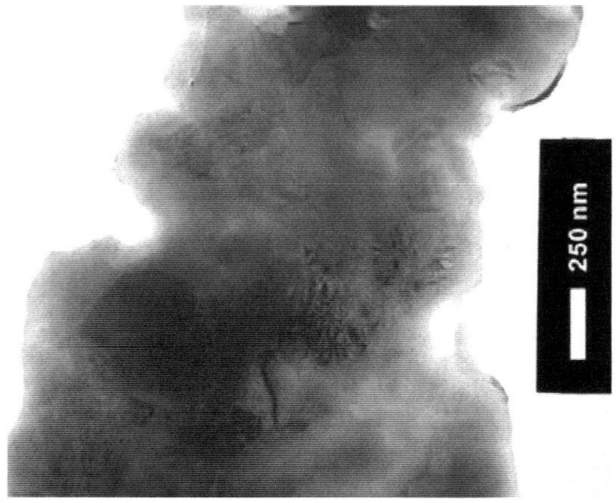

Fig. 7. TEM microstructure of the annealed Sm-Fe melt-spun ribbon nitrogenated at 653 K.

Sm-Fe melt-spun ribbon nitrogenated at 653 K. For comparison, the hysteresis loop of the annealed Sm-Fe melt-spun ribbon without nitrogenation is also shown. It was found that the remanence of the nitrogenated specimen was higher than that of the non-nitrogenated ribbon. Although the coercivity of the nitrogenated specimen is slightly lower than that of the non-nitrogenated ribbon, the nitrogenated specimen still exhibits an attractively high coercivity of 22.5 kOe. The TEM studies revealed that the nitrogenated Sm-Fe melt-spun ribbon consisted of fine grains of the Sm_5Fe_{17} phase. No significant growth of the grains was observed in the nitrogenated specimen.

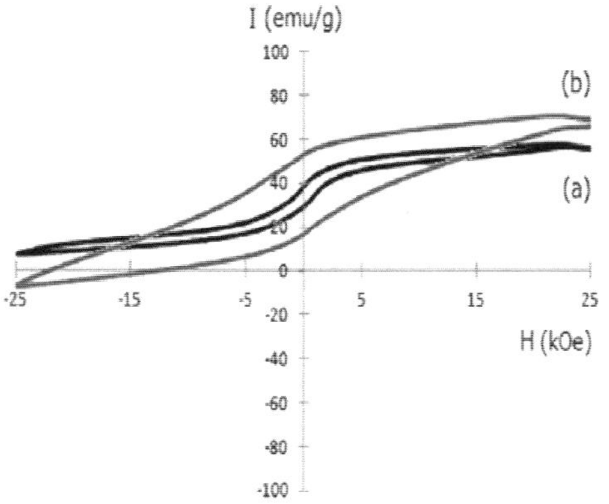

Fig. 6. Hysteresis loops of (a) the annealed Sm-Fe melt-spun ribbon and (b) the specimen nitrogenated at 653 K.

4. Summary

Sm_5Fe_{17} melt-spun ribbons produced that were amorphous and exhibited a low coercivity value. Annealing of the ribbon resulted in the formation of the Sm_5Fe_{17} phase. The Sm_5Fe_{17} melt-spun ribbon annealed at 973 K exhibited a high coercivity of more than 25 kOe with a remanence of 40 emu/g. Nitrogenation of the annealed Sm_5Fe_{17} melt-spun ribbons was carried out. Although the nitrogenated specimens had slightly lower coercivity, their remanence was higher than that of the non-nitrogenated ribbons.

References

[1] G. C. Hadjipanayis, A. Tsoukatos, J. Strzeszewski, G. J. Long, and O. A. Pringle, *J. Magn. Magn. Mater.* **78**, 1989, L1.
[2] C. Neiva and F. P. Missell, in: *Proc. 8th Int. Symposium on Magnetic Anisotropy and Coercivity*, 1984, 315-324.
[3] M. Katter, J. Wecker, L. Schultz, and R. Grössinger, *Appl. Phys. Lett.* **56**, 1990, 1377.
[4] F. J. Cadieu, H. Hegde, R. Rani, A. Navarathna, and K. Chen, *Mater. Lett.* **11**, 1991, 284.
[5] T. Saito, *J. Alloys Compd.* **440**, 2007, 315.
[6] J. M. D. Coey and H. Sun, *J. Magn. Magn. Mater.* **87**, 1990, L251.

Exploring New Ce-Fe-Based Permanent Magnet Materials

FREDERICK E. PINKERTON,[1] JAN F. HERBST,[1] MARTIN S. MEYER,[1] DAAD HADDAD,[1] CHEN ZHOU[2]
[1]Chemical and Materials Systems Laboratory, General Motors Research and Development Center, Warren, MI, 48090-9055
[2]MEDA Engineering and Technical Services, LLC

Abstract: *General Motors is pursuing several initiatives to explore new permanent magnet materials based on iron-rich cerium-iron materials. Among these are magnets based on $Ce_2Fe_{14}B$, for which energy products as large as 35 kJ/m^3 (4.4 MGOe) have been achieved, exceeding the properties of ferrites. Another approach is investigating $CeFe_{12-x}M_x$ compounds having the $ThMn_{12}$ structure, and their nitrides. Promising intrinsic magnetic properties have been demonstrated in Ce-based 1-12 systems; several nitrided systems have Curie temperatures T_c exceeding that of $Nd_2Fe_{14}B$, with reasonable magnetization ($4\pi M_s$ > 1 T) and technologically significant anisotropy fields H_a ~ 1.6 MA/m.*

1. Introduction

Global instability in samarium and cobalt price and availability in the early 1980's kindled world-wide research efforts to identify replacements for Sm-Co permanent magnets. These efforts came to fruition with the discovery of $Nd_2Fe_{14}B$ by GM [1] (rapidly solidified magnets) and Sumitomo [2] (sintered magnets). Nd-Fe-B magnets are now the world's premier permanent magnets, with ubiquitous applications in high performance devices. Recently a similar scenario played out for Nd-Fe-B: anticipated growth in demand for large quantities of low cost, high performance magnets for electric and hybrid vehicle traction motors and for wind generators has stimulated a renewed search for alternative permanent magnet materials with favorable performance/cost ratio. At GM R&D, we exploit nanocrystalline alloys made by rapid quenching as an expedient methodology for exploring a variety of potential permanent magnet materials. For example, Ce is much more abundant than Nd in rare earth ores and hence less expensive; we are exploring magnets based on (a) $Ce_2Fe_{14}B$ and (b) iron-rich $CeFe_{12-x}M_x$ compounds having the $ThMn_{12}$ crystal structure and their nitrides.

2. Experimental Procedures

We prepared samples by rapid solidification using melt-spinning, which for research purposes provides a versatile and robust preparation technique for magnetic hardening. The elemental constituents were combined by weight to the target stoichiometry, then alloyed by induction melting under Ar inert gas. Pieces of the ingot were placed in a quartz crucible having a 0.6 mm orifice, inductively remelted under Ar, then ejected via a 2.2 - 3.5 psi overpressure onto the surface of the Cr-plated copper quench wheel rotating with a surface velocity v_s between 5 and 60 m/s. Elemental compositions were confirmed using inductively coupled plasma atomic emission spectrometry (ICP-AES). Crystal structures, lattice parameters, and phase compositions were obtained via quantitative x-ray diffraction (XRD). Curie temperatures T_C were extracted from thermo-gravimetric curves during heating and cooling in a Perkin-Elmer TGA7 system while applying a small magnetic force. Demagnetization data on premagnetized powders were taken in a vibrating sample magnetometer (VSM) under an applied field of up to ±24 kOe.

3. $Ce_2Fe_{14}B$

We have successfully magnetically hardened $Ce_2Fe_{14}B$ by melt spinning [3]. Figure 1 shows the demagnetization curve for a sample of melt-spun $Ce_{17}Fe_{78}B_6$ ribbons with energy product $(BH)_{max}$ = 33 kJ/m^3 (4.1 MGOe).[3] Co substitution for Fe increases the Curie temperature T_c from 433 K for $Ce_2Fe_{14}B$ to 539 K for $Ce_2Fe_{12}Co_2B$ while maintaining technical magnetic properties exceeding those of ferrite [e.g., $(BH)_{max}$ = 35 kJ/m^3] [4]. The Curie temperature remains too low for high temperature applications, but $Ce_2Fe_{14}B$-based magnets could offer a viable inexpensive alternative to $Nd_2Fe_{14}B$ at ambient temperature.

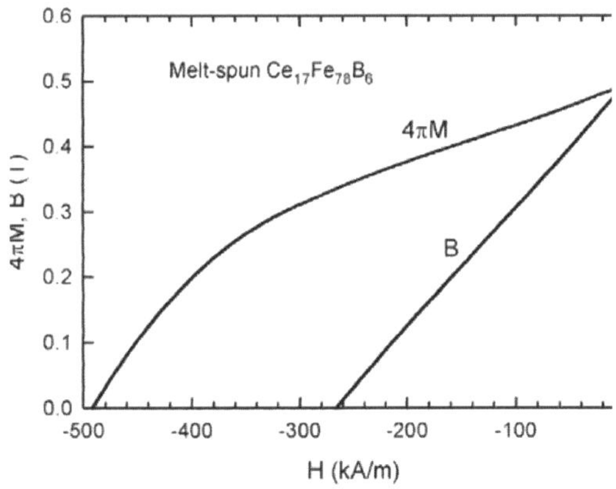

Fig. 1. Room temperature demagnetization curve for isotropic melt-spun $Ce_{17}Fe_{78}B_6$ ribbons.

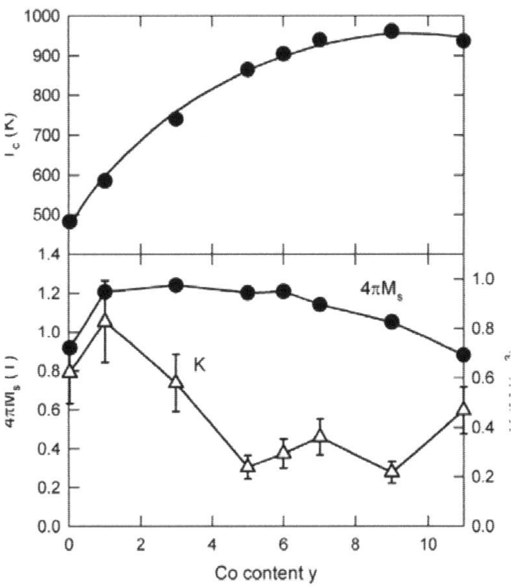

Fig. 2. $CeFe_{11-y}Co_yTi$ Curie temperature T_C, saturation magnetization $4\pi M_s$, and anisotropy K.

4. $CeFe_{12-x}M_x$ and Their Nitrides

GM is seeking magnets based on $CeFe_{12-x}M_x$ having the $ThMn_{12}$ crystal structure as part of an Ames Lab-led project funded by the ARPA-E Rare Earth Alternatives for Critical Technologies (REACT) program. Pure RFe_{12} does not form, but it is stabilized by adding $x = 1 - 2$ atoms of a suitable element M. The "1-12" compounds offer an intrinsic cost advantage because they contain one-third less rare earth than $R_2Fe_{14}B$, e.g., $CeFe_{11}Ti$ is 17.5 wt.% Ce compared to 26 wt.% for $Ce_2Fe_{14}B$. The 1-12s have promising intrinsic permanent magnet properties, especially when nitrogen is infused interstitially into the lattice. Nitrogen insertion expands the crystal lattice by 3 - 8 volume % and enhances the Fe-Fe exchange, greatly increasing T_c. For instance, the T_C of $CeFe_{11}MoN_x$ is ~60 K higher than in $Nd_2Fe_{14}B$ [5], implying substantially better performance at elevated temperatures. Co substitution for Fe also improves T_C; replacing one Fe by Co in $CeFe_{11}Ti$ increases T_C by 100 K [6]. Figure 2 shows T_C, the saturation magnetization $4\pi M_s$, and the anisotropy energy K for $CeFe_{11-y}Co_yTi$. At $y = 1$, T_C, $4\pi M_s$, and K all increase; the anisotropy field $H_a = 2K/M_s$ remains nearly constant. At present, achieving high coercivity remains challenging; although H_{ci} values of ~ ¼ H_a are expected when magnetically hardened by melt-spinning, results to date have been limited to values of $H_{ci} < 0.1H_a$. Efforts to optimize the microstructure continue in order to reach practical coercivities.

Acknowledgement

This research is funded in part by the Advanced Research Projects Agency – Energy under grant number 0472-1526.

References

[1] J. J. Croat, J. F. Herbst, R. W. Lee, F. E. Pinkerton, *Appl. Phys. Lett.* **44**, 1984, 148.
[2] M. Sagawa, S. Fujimura, N. Togawa, H. Yamamoto, Y. Matsuura, *J. Appl. Phys.* **55**, 1984, 2083.
[3] J. F. Herbst, M. S. Meyer, F. E. Pinkerton, *J. Appl. Phys.* **111**, 2012, 07A718.
[4] E. J. Skoug, M. S. Meyer, F. E. Pinkerton, M. M. Tessema, D. Haddad, J. F. Herbst, *J. Alloys Compds.* **574**, 2013, 552.
[5] C. Zhou, F. E. Pinkerton, *J. Alloys Compds.* 583, 2013, 345.
[6] C. Zhou, F. E. Pinkerton, J. F. Herbst, *J. Appl. Phys.* **115**, 2014, 17C716.

Development of Nanoparticle-Based Permanent-Magnet Materials: Challenges and Advances

B. BALAMURUGAN, B. DAS, P. MUKHERJEE, D.J. SELLMYER
University of Nebraska, Lincoln, NE-68588, U.S.A.

Abstract: *Next-generation permanent magnets require rare-earth-free or rare-earth-lean materials with suitable magnetic properties. An intriguing approach is the creation of nanostructured Co- or Fe-rich composite materials using nanoparticles having high magnetocrystalline anisotropies ($K_1 \geq 10$ Mergs/cm^3) as building blocks. There have been several formidable challenges, which include the control of particle size, crystal purity, easy-axis alignment, and compaction, limiting the prospects for nanoparticle-based permanent magnets. Here we review the structural and magnetic properties of high-anisotropy Co-rich nanoparticles (Co-X, X = Y, Sm, Hf, Zr) produced using a gas-aggregation-type cluster-deposition method. The development of novel nanostructured rare-earth-free magnetic materials, with energy products as high as 19.5 MGOe, is also discussed.*

Key words: *magnetic nanoclusters; high anisotropy; alignment, nanostructuring, composite magnets*

Address: Balamurugan Balasubramanian, Nebraska Center for Materials and Nanoscience & Physics and Astronomy, University of Nebraska, Lincoln, NE-68588, U.S.A., E-mail:bbalasubramanian2@unl.edu

1. Introduction

Magnetic nanoparticles can be used to build complex materials with improved magnetic properties because of their real-space and spin structures [1-5]. For example, an assembly of high-anisotropy magnetic nanoparticles with a high-magnetization soft phase has the potential to provide exchange-coupled magnetic materials with high energy products [1-3]. The theoretically achievable maximum energy product in a magnet is $J_s^2/4$ ($J_s = 4\pi M_s$ is the saturation magnetic polarization), when a magnet exhibits a square loop with remanent magnetization M_r equaling to the saturation magnetization M_s [6,7]. To achieve this, the magnetic nanoparticles ideally are aligned and compacted to form dense-pack magnetic materials. In this article, we discuss the recent research progress towards the development of permanent-magnet materials using high-anisotropy Co-rich nanoclusters.

2. High-Anisotropy Nanoparticles

Nanomagnetic assemblies produced using wet-chemical and gas-aggregation-type cluster-deposition methods have shown uniform distribution of particle sizes with well-controlled compositions and interfaces [1-3, 8-14]. Generally the wet-chemical methods require high growth or annealing temperatures (≥ 300 °C) to achieve desired high-anisotropy crystal structures in nanoparticles [1-3].

In comparison, the cluster-deposition method performed under high-vacuum conditions has been shown to produce Co-rich and Fe-rich nanoparticles having ordered structures without the requirement of a subsequent thermal annealing [8-14].This method has produced traditional RCo_5 (R = Y, Sm, La) alloys crystallizing in $CaCu_5$-type hexagonal structure (as shown in Fig. 1a), $L1_0$- ordered FePt, and new or metastable phases such as orthorhombic $HfCo_7$ (as shown in Fig. 1b) and rhombohederal Zr_2Co_{11} [8-14]. For example, transmission electron microscope images of YCo_5 and $HfCo_7$ nanoclusters are shown in Fig. 2a and Fig. 2b, respectively. The nanoclusters are single crystalline with a high degree of atomic ordering and the average diameter can be tuned between 2 and 20 nm with an rms standard deviation σ/d ≤ 20.

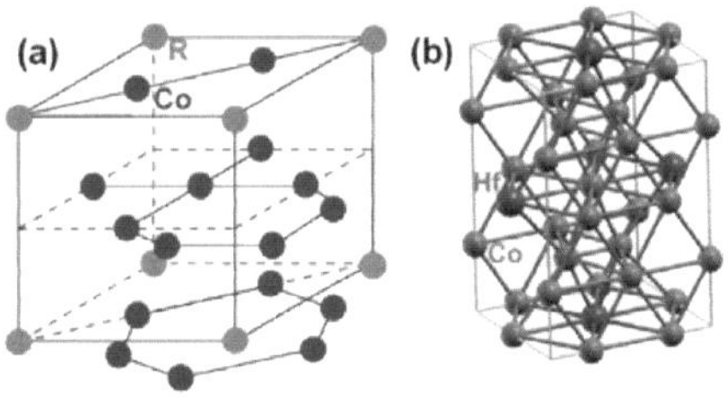

Fig.1. (a) Hexagonal $CaCu_5$-structure of RCo_5 alloys (R = Y, Sm, La) [5,15] and (b) orthorhombic $HfCo_7$ structure [14].

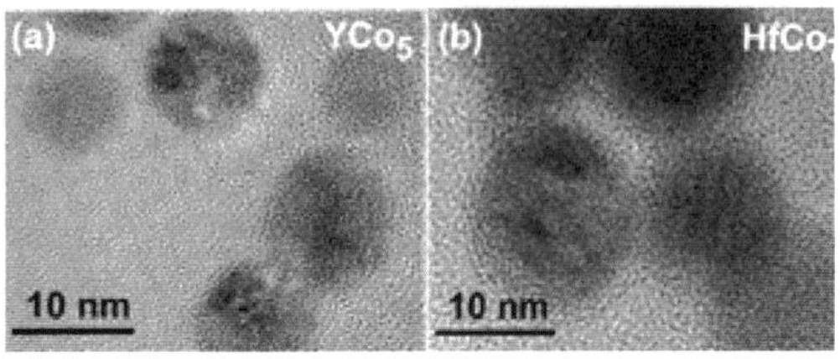

Fig.2 Transmission electron microscope images of the nanoclusters: (a) YCo_5 and (b) $HfCo_7$

3. Magnetic Properties

Generally the Co-rich nanoclusters having average diameters of around 10 nm have been used to fabricate permanent-magnet materials. An isotropic Zr_2Co_{11} nanocluster film exhibits a coercivity H_c = 2.3 kOe, J_s = 10.1 kG, and M_r/M_s = 0.60 at 300 K as shown in Fig. 3. The room-temperature magnetic properties of various Co-rich nanoparticles are summarized in *Table 1*.

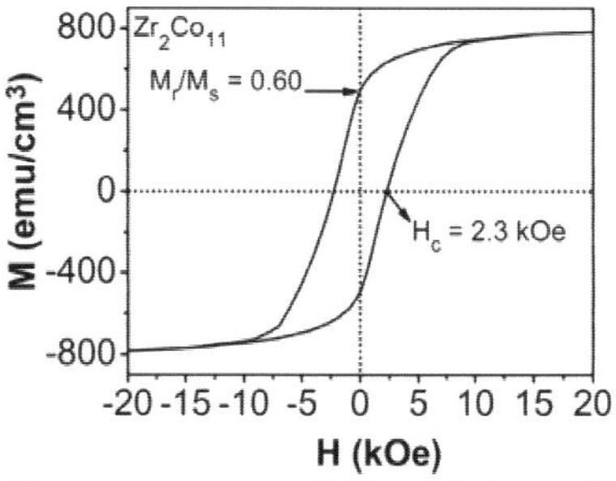

Fig.3. Room-temperature hysteresis loop of isotropic Zr_2Co_{11} nanoclusters.

Table 1. The measured H_c, J_s, M_r/M_s at 300 K for isotropic Co-rich nanoclusters [9-14].

Nanoparticles	H_c (kOe)	J_s (kOe)	M_r/M_s
$HfCo_7$	7.2	10.8	0.56
YCo_5	6.0	9.5	0.62
$SmCo_5$	4.4	11.1	0.57
Zr_2Co_{11}	2.3	10.1	0.60

4. Easy-Axis Alignment

The Co-rich nanoclusters show high J_s and appreciable H_c at 300 K as shown in *Table 1*, but they only exhibit remanence ratios of about 0.56 – 0.62 due to isotropic nature (random orientation of the easy axes). Thus, it is essential to align the easy axes of nanoclusters to improve M_r. In the case of wet-chemical methods, the annealing temperature required to obtain high-anisotropy crystal structure is often higher than Curie temperature T_c, and thus the alignment of nanoparticles during the growth/ deposition process by applying a magnetic field is challenging [16]. Since the nanoclusters are directly ordered during the gas-aggregation process, they can be aligned using a magnetic field before deposition on substrates [10,11]. A schematic of the alignment process used in our cluster-deposition system is shown in Fig. 4. In this process, the nanoclusters are extracted as a collimated beam towards the deposition chamber and subsequently aligned using a magnetic field H_{al} of about 5 kOe, prior to deposition on substrates as shown in Fig. 4.

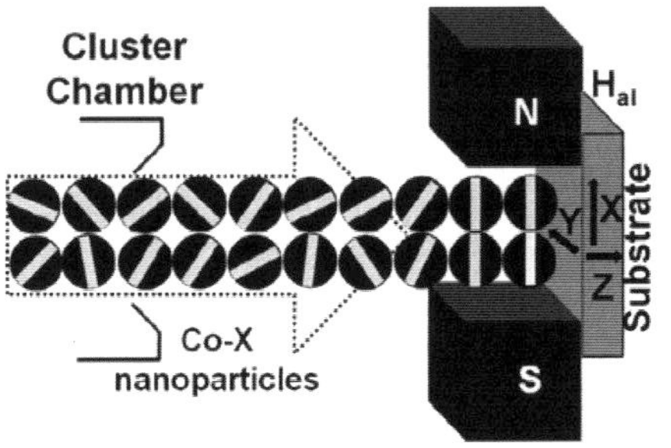

Fig.4. A schematic showing the alignment process of nanoclusters using a magnetic field H_{al} [10,11,14].

The degree of alignment in nanoparticles can be evaluated from the remanence ratios. The normalized average remanence of non-interacting nanoparticles is expressed as [11, 17-23]

$$M_N = \frac{M_r}{M_s} = \frac{\int m(\theta)P(\theta)\sin\theta d\theta}{\int P(\theta)\sin\theta d\theta} \quad (1)$$

where θ denotes the angle between the easy-axis and the direction of the measurement filed. M_N is the normalized magnetic moment of the individual nanoparticles. The normalized easy-axis distribution or texture function is expressed as [11,19,23]

$$p(\theta) = \frac{P(\theta)}{P(0)} = \exp\left(\frac{\cos\theta}{\delta}\right) \quad (2)$$

In eqn. 2, δ is a parameter defining the degree of easy-axis distribution or texture function. The remanence ratios along the easy- and hard-axis directions are plotted as a function of δ in Fig. 5 [19].

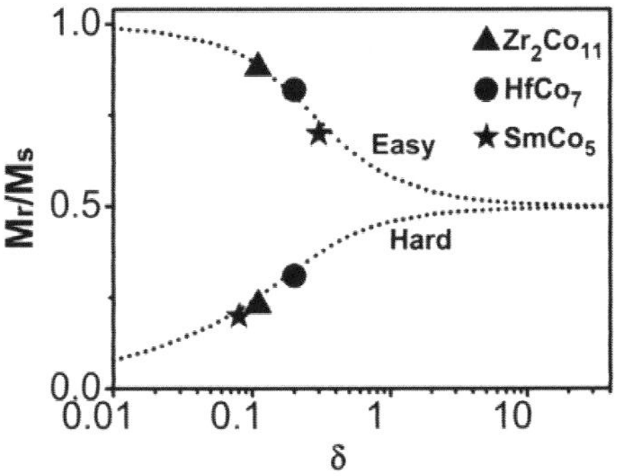

Fig.5. Remanence ratios of nanoparticles as a function of texture function δ [19]. The experimental M_r/M_s values for the aligned nanoclusters are also marked for comparison.

Aligned nanoparticles ideally exhibit $M_r/M_s \approx 1$ (easy-axis) and $M_r/M_s \approx 0$ (hard-axis), yielding $\delta \ll 1$. Experimentally, the Co-rich nanocluster films such as Zr_2Co_{11} (M_r/M_s = 0.88) and $HfCo_7$ (M_r/M_s = 0.82) along the easy-axis direction exhibit high remanence ratios, yielding low δ of about 0.11 and 0.20, respectively [11,12]. The effective alignment also leads to high coercivities in aligned Zr_2Co_{11} (4.4 kOe) and $HfCo_7$ (8.7 kOe) nanoparticle films [11,12], as compared to those values for the corresponding unaligned samples shown in Table 1.

5. Energy Products

The easy-axis alignment is a key processing step to achieve high coercivity and remanent magnetization. Zr_2Co_{11} nanocluster film show an appreciable coercivity of 4.4 kOe and a high remanent magnetic polarization of about 9.4 kG at 300 K, and thus exhibit a high nominal energy product of about 16.6 MGOe [11]. The energy products of $HfCo_7$ and Zr_2Co_{11} nanocluster films are compared with some of the rare-earth-free bulk alloys as shown in Fig. 6, and are higher among the magnetic materials that are free of critical rare-earth elements or expensive Pt.

The cluster-deposited films normally have packing fraction of nanoclusters below full compaction, and thus the energy products of $HfCo_7$ and Zr_2Co_{11} nanocluster films shown in Fig. 6 are nominal values. However, the packing fraction of the films was subsequently improved towards ideal value by dispersing the nanoclusters in a magnetically soft $Fe_{65}Co_{35}$ matrix [11]. Additionally, the soft phase also improved the magnetic properties of the composite films *via* strong exchange-coupling with the nanoclusters. For example, the aligned Zr_2Co_{11}:Fe-Co nanocomposite film with 15 vol. % of the soft Fe-Co phase has shown an improvement in J_s (11.7 kG) and M_r/M_s (0.90) with an appreciable H_c = 3.5 kOe as compared to the bare Zr_2Co_{11} nanocluster film (H_c = 4.4 kOe, J_s = 10.2, M_r/M_s = 0.88) at 300 K. This result subsequently leads to an energy product to 19.5 MGOe [11].

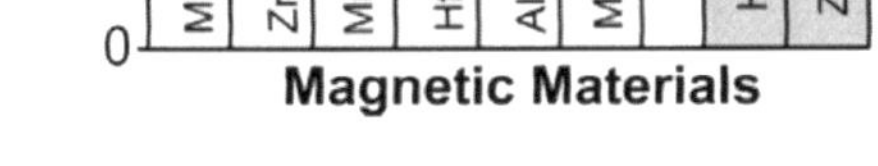

Fig.6. A comparison of energy products of the nanocluster films (dark colored bars) with those of rare-earth-free bulk magnetic materials reported in literature [6,7,11,12,24-28].

6. Summary

The Co-rich nanoclusters have shown appreciable coercivities (2.3 – 7.2 kOe) and high saturation magnetic polarizations (9.5 – 11.1 kG) at 300 K. Novel nanostructured rare-earth-free magnetic materials was fabricated by aligning the nanoclusters and subsequently assembling with a high-magnetization $Fe_{65}Co_{35}$ phase. The model nanostructured magnets show a high energy product of 19.5 MGOe, but it is also important to develop scale-up methods for producing bulk magnets.

Acknowledgement
This research is supported by the U.S. Department of Energy, BES Grant (DE-FG02-04ER46152, synthesis and magnetic characterization), U.S. Department of Energy, EERE, AMES Grant (DE-AC02-07CH11358, structural characterization and theory). The research also benefited from U.S. NSF, MRI Grant (DMR-0960110, electron microscopy). This work was performed in part in Facilities of the Nebraska Center for Materials and Nanoscience, which is supported by the Nebraska Research Initiative. We would like to acknowledge Ralph Skomski, G.C. Hadjipanayis, and J.E. Shield for helpful discussions.

References

[1] D.J. Sellmyer, *Nature*, 420, **2002**, 374-375.
[2] H. Zeng, J. Li, J.P. Liu, Z.L. Wang, *Nature*, 420, **2002**, 395-398.
[3] N. Poudyal, J.P. Liu, *J. Phys. D: Appl. Phys.* 46, **2013**, 043001.
[4] B. Balamurugan, D.J. Sellmyer, G.C. Hadjipanayis, R. Skomski, *Scripta Materialia*, 67, **2012**, 542-547.
[5] D.J. Sellmyer, B. Balamurugan, "Permanent-magnet materials: An assembly of nano-objects" *Magnetics Technology International, UKIP Media & Event Ltd.* **2011** pp. 26-29.
[6] B. Balasubramanian, B. Das, W.Y. Zhang, R. Skomski, D.J. Sellmyer, *J. Phys.: Condens. Matter* 26, **2014**, 064204.
[7] J.M.D. Coey, *Scripta Materialia*, **2012**, 67, 524-529.
[8] J.M. Qiu, J. Bai, J.P. Wang, *Appl. Phys. Lett.* 89, **2006**, 222506.
[9] B. Balasubramanian, R. Skomski, X.Z. Li, S.R. Valloppilly, J.E. Shield, G.C. Hadjipanayis, D.J. Sellmyer, *Nano Lett.* 11, **2011**, 1747.
[10] B. Balamurugan, B. Das, V.R. Shah, R. Skomski, *Appl. Phys. Lett.* 101, **2012**, 122407.
[11] B. Balasubramanian, B. Das, R. Skomski, W.Y. Zhang, D.J. Sellmyer, *Adv. Mater.*25,. **2013**, 6090-6093.
[12] B. Balasubramanian, P. Mukherjee, R. Skomski, P. Manchanda, B. Das, D.J. Sellmyer, Magnetic nanostructuring and overcoming Brown's paradox to realize extraordinary high-temperature energy products (submitted).
[13] a)B. Balamurugan, R. Skomski, D. LeRoy, G.C. Hadjipanayis, J.E. Shield, and D.J. Sellmyer,

Energy Technology 2012: Carbon Dioxide Management and Other Technologies, Eds. M.D. Salazar-Villalpando et al., TMS (The Minerals, Metals & Materials Society), 2012, pp 383-398.b) B. Balamurugan, R. Skomski, X.Z. Li, G.C. Hadjipanayis, D.J. Sellmyer, *J. Appl. Phys.* 111, **2012**, 07B527.

[14] B. Das, B. Balamurugan, P. Kumar, R. Skomski, V.R. Shah, J.E. Shield, A. Kashyap, D.J. Sellmyer, *IEEE Trans. Magn.* 49, **2013**, 3330-3333.

[15] O. Moze, L. Pareti, A. Paoluzi, K. H. J. Buschow, *Phys. Rev. B*, 53, **1996**, 11150 - 11156.

[16] S. Kang, Z. Jia, S. Shi, D.E. Nikles, J.W. Harrell, *Appl. Phys. Lett.* 86, 2005,062503.

[17] E.P. Wohlfarth, *J. Appl. Phys.* 29, **1958**, 595-596.

[18] C. Tannous, J. Gieraltowski, *European J. Appl. Phys.* 29, **2008**, 475-487.

[19] D. Le Roy, R. Morel, A. Brenac, L. Notin, *J. Mag. Mat. Mat.* 323, **2011**, 127-129.

[20] L. Néel, R. Pauthenet, G. Rimet, V.S. Giron, *J. Appl. Phys.* 31, **1960**,27S-30S.

[21] H. Rubio, S. Suárez, *J. Appl.Phys.* 87, **2000**, 7415-7424.

[22] K.H. Müller, D. Eckert, P.A.P. Wendhausen, A. Handstein, S. Wirth, M. Wolf, *IEEE Trans. Mag.* 30, **1993**, 586-588.

[23] D. Givord, A. Lignard, R. Perrier de la Bathie, P. Tenaud, T. Viadieu, *J. De Physique.* C6, **1985**, 313-317.

[24] J.H. Park, Y.K. Hong, S. Bae, J.J. Lee, J. Jalli, G.S. Abo, N. Neveu, S.G. Kim, C.J. Choi, J.G. Lee, *J. Appl. Phys.* 107, **2010**, 09A731.

[25] B. Balke, G.H. Fecher, J. Winterlik, C. Felser, *Appl. Phys.Lett.* 90, **2007**, 152504.

[26] M.A. McGuire, O. Rios, N.J. Ghimire, M. Koehler, *Appl. Phys. Lett.* 101, **2012**, 202401.

[27] J.B. Yang, K. Kamaraju, W.B. Yelon, W.J. James, Q. Cai, A. Bollero, *Appl. Phys.Lett.* 79, **2001**, 1846.

[28] N. Jones, *Nature*, 472, **2011**, 22-23.

Synthesis and Processing of Hard Magnetic Nanoparticles

NARAYAN POUDYAL, KEVIN E. ELKINS, KINJAL H. GANDHA, J. PING LIU
Department of Physics, University of Texas at Arlington, Arlington, TX 76019

Abstract: *Recent progress in nanotechnology has made it possible to prepare the nanoparticles with high magnetocrystalline anisotropy. By applying newly developed "salt-matrix annealing" and "surfactant-assisted milling" techniques, we have successfully synthesized monodisperse ferromagnetic FePt, NdFeB and SmCo nanoparticles. We also confirm there is a significant influence of shape anisotropy on the magnetic hardening of Co nanowires.*

Keywords: *magnetic nanoparticles; nanowires; salt-martix annealing; surfactant-assisted ball milling*

Address: J. Ping Liu, Department of Physics, University of Texas at Arlington, 502 Yates St. SH 108, Arlington, TX 76019, Phone: +1-(817)272 2815, Email: pliu@uta.edu

1. Introduction

Ferromagnetism is a size-dependent physical phenomenon. Ferromagnetic nanoparticles with controlled size and geometry have drawn great attention in the last decade for fundamental scientific studies and for their potential applications in advanced materials and devices such as exchange coupled nanocomposite magnets, ultra-high-density magnetic recording media and biomedicines [1-3]. However, synthesis of the highly sought ferromagnetic nanoparticles, especially hard magnetic nanoparticles with small size and controlled dimension turns out to be a non-trivial task. In this paper, we report our experimental results related to control in size, shape and composition of hard magnetic nanoparticles (FePt, NdFeB, and SmCo nanoparticles) prepared by various methods including chemical synthesis, salt-matrix annealing and the surfactant assisted ball milling technique. Significant influence of shape anisotropy on the magnetic hardening of Co nanowires is also discussed briefly.

2. Salt-Matrix Annealing

Recently, we successfully produced hard magnetic $L1_0$ FePt nanoparticles ranging from 3 to 15 nm by developing a novel annealing method known as salt-matrix annealing [4-8]. Interest in FePt nanoparticles is due to the very high uniaxial magnetocrystalline anisotropy of the $L1_0$-FePt phase, which is based on crystalline ordering of the face-centered tetragonal (fct) structure [2,3]. Generally, as-synthesized FePt nanoparticles take the disordered face-centred-cubic (fcc) structure without coercivity in nanoscale dimensions. High-temperature heat treatment (>600 °C) is required to completely transform the fcc structure to the fct structure resulting in $L1_0$ ordering [2,9]. However, conventional annealing at high temperature causes serious sintering of nanoparticles resulting in unwanted grain growth by destroying nanoscale morphology of the nanoparticles. By embedding nanoparticles in salt-matrix while annealing, particle aggregation and growth during the phase transformation can be completely avoided. Fig.1(a-i))shows the TEM images of $L1_0$ FePt nanoparticles obtained by using the salt-matrix annealing method. A very high coercivity over 35 kOe was achieved for 8 nm $L1_0$ FePt nanoparticles. It is found that magnetic properties including, magnetization, coercivity and Curie temperature (T_c) are strongly dependent on both the particle size and the chemical ordering (Fig.2(a-c)) [4,5,8]. It is also found that the relationship between the size effect and the chemical-ordering effect defines the magnetic behavior. The shift in T_c can be ascribed to the finite-size-scaling theory after considering the chemical-ordering effect on T_c [5].

3. Surfactant-Assisted Ball Milling

Although many attempts have been made with chemical synthesis, preparation of rare-earth containing nanoparticles with controlled particle size and phase purity is still very challenging due to their high chemical instability [10]. We developed a novel method to prepare rare-earth hard and soft magnetic nanoparticles by adopting an alternative approach, called surfactant-assisted ball milling including Fe, Co, FeCo, NdFeB and Sm-Co [11-16]. In conventional dry or wet ball milling of metallic systems, usually a submicrometer minimum average particle size is obtained even for an extended milling time because the crushed fine particles can be cold welded again during ball milling. Addition of surfactants during wet milling process prevents the cold welding and re-welding of crushed particles. Surfactants also play a key role for enhancing the dispersion of nanoparticles, and reducing the contamination during milling. Generally, as-milled products consist of particles with a wide size distribution. We developed a size selection process

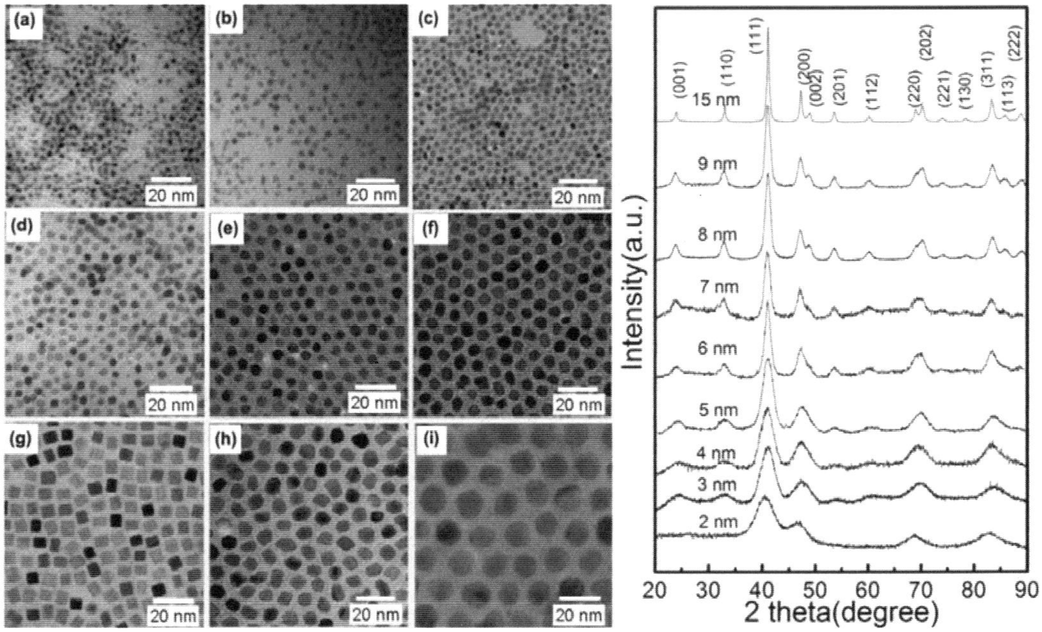

Fig. 1. (left) TEM images of salt-matrix annealed FePt nanoparticles of (a) 2, (b) 3, (c) 4, (d) 5, (e) 6, (f) 7, (g) 8, (h) 9 and (i) 15 nm and (right) XRD patters of different size nanoparticles. The annealing conditions for a 2 nm particle are 700 ℃ for 8 h, while those for other particles are 700 ° C for 4 h [8].

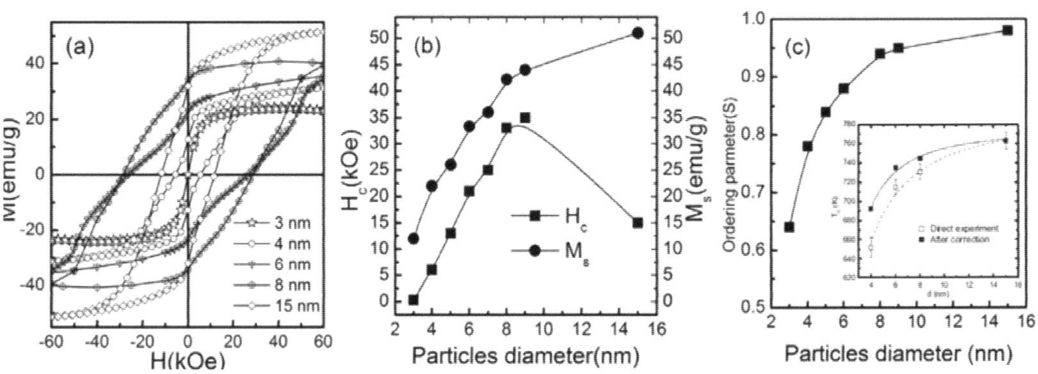

Fig.2. Salt-matrix annealed FePt nanoparticles at 700 ℃ for 4 h: (a) hysteresis loops, (b) size dependent coercivity and saturation magnetization and (c) dependence of the long-range ordering parameter on particle size (The inset shows dependence of Curie temperature on the particle size)[5,8].

based on a sophisticated control of the sedimentation time of the nanoparticle solutions and a proper use of centrifugal separation, that produce nanoparticles with narrow size distributions (see Fig.3(a-d) and Fig.4(a-c)) [12,14,15]. Anisotropic nanochips-like SmCo and NdFeB particles can be obtained by modifying the milling parameters, which are useful for fabrication of anisotropic nanostructured magnets [16]. It can be seen from the XRD patterns and demagnetization curves a substantial difference in two directions confirming the strong anisotropy resulting from the grain alignment along the *c*-axis in the $SmCo_5$ and $Nd_2Fe_{14}B$ nanochips aligned in 2T magnetic field (Fig. 5(a-d)). The aligned $SmCo_5$ nanochips particles measured parallel to aligned field direction had coercivity values about 20 kOe.

4. Magnetic Nanowires

Shape and magnetocrystalline anisotropy provides the basis of the coercivity for nanowires with the orientation and uniformity of the single-domain nanocrystals being essential for achieving high magnetic hardening [17,18]. Recently, we developed very high room-temperature coercivity in single crystalline Co nanowires with high aspect ratio, synthesized through a chemical solvothermal process. Our experiments revealed that Co nanowires with diameter of 15 nm and average length of 200 nm aligned in 2 T field have magnetic properties of saturation magnetization up to 150 emu/g and coercivity up to 10.2 kOe. The Co nanowires are ideal building blocks for fabrication of bonded,

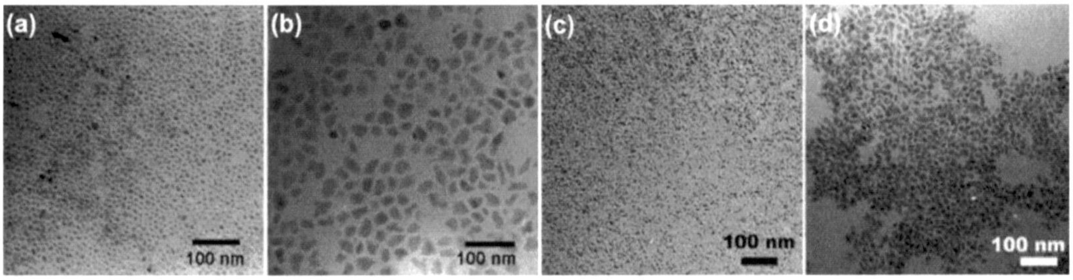

Fig. 3 TEM images of (a) ~ 6 nm and (b) ~ 20 nm Sm_2Co_{17} nanoparticles and (c) ~ 7 nm and (d) ~20 nm $Nd_2Fe_{14}B$ nanoparticles obtained by surfactant-assisted ball milling followed by the size selection process[14,15].

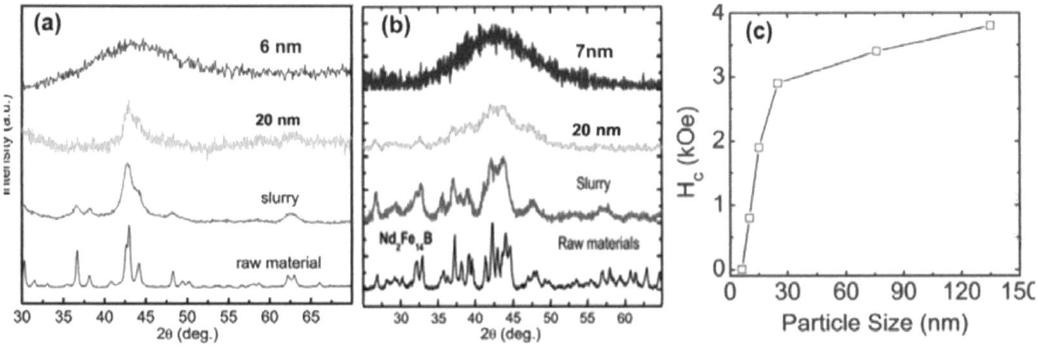

Fig. 4. XRD patterns of Sm_2Co_{17} ~6 nm, ~20 nm nanoparticles, submicron particles (slurry) and raw materials (b) XRD patterns of $Nd_2Fe_{14}B$ ~ 7 nm, ~ 20 nm nanoparticles, submicron particles (slurry) and raw materials and (c) size-dependent coercivity of Sm_2Co_{17} nanoparticles. Different size nanoparticles were obtained by surfactant-assisted ball milling followed by the size selection process [14,15].

consolidated and thin film magnets with high energy density and high thermal stability (Fig.6). It is found that the Co nanowires display typical Stoner-Wohlfarth behavior in magnetic hysteresis. The magnetocrystalline configuration, coupled with the shape and high aspect ratio, favors a coherent rotation of the magnetization process and thus gives a large coercivity of the nanowire assemblies when aligned magnetic field [18].

4. Concluding Remarks

In summary, interesting experimental findings on magnetic properties of hard magnetic nanoparticles have been reported from controlling the particle size, shape and orientation. Hard magnetic nanoparticles based on $L1_0$ structured FePt, SmCo, and $Nd_2Fe_{14}B$ with high magnetocrystalline anisotropy were produced by using the novel "salt-matrix annealing" and "surfactant-assisted ball milling" techniques. Size-dependent magnetic properties and Curie temperature have been observed in the ferromagnetic $L1_0$ FePt nanoparticles. Very high coercivity values have been measured in the Co nanowires at room temperature prepared via a solvothermal process as a result of shape anisotropy and orientation of the uniform length Co nanowire assemblies. The produced hard magnetic nanoparticles, nanochips and nanowires have a great deal of potential for advanced applications as well as for fundamental scientific studies.

Acknowledgement

The work reviewed in this paper has been supported by the DoD/DARPA/MURI/ARO under several grants, as well as by the Center for Nanostructured Materials and Characterization Center for Materials and Biology at the University of Texas at Arlington.

References

[1] H. Zeng, J. Li, J. P. Liu, Z. L. Wang, S. Sun, Nature, **420**, 2002, 395.
[2] S. Sun, *Adv. Mater.*, **18**, 2006, 393.
[3] D. Weller, A. Moser, L. Folks, M. E. Best, W. Lee, M.F. Toney, M. Schwckert, J. U. Thiele, M. F. Doerner, *IEEE Trans. Magn.*, **36**, 2000, 10.
[4] K. E. Elkins , D. Li , N. Poudyal, V. Nandwana, Z. Q. Jin , K. Chen and J. P. Liu, *J. Phys. D: Appl. Phys.*, **38**, 2005, 2306.

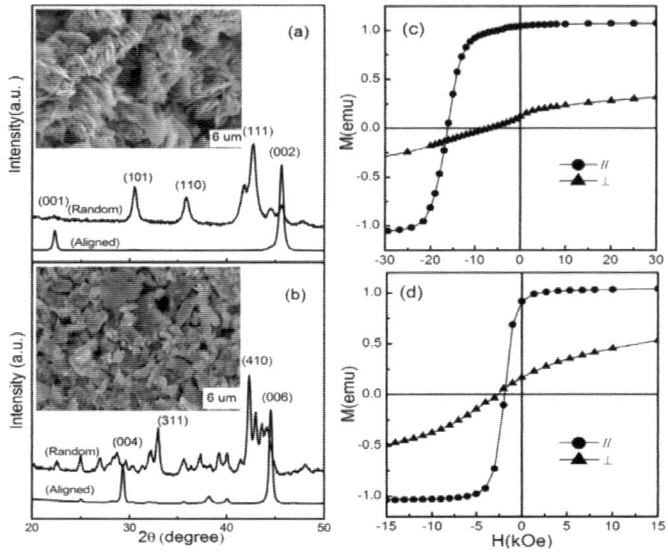

Fig. 5. XRD patterns of (a) $SmCo_5$ and (b) $Nd_2Fe_{14}B$ flakes randomly oriented and aligned in the magnetic field (insets show SEM images of the fakes-like particles).(c)and(d) demagnetization curves of the aligned samples measured in the directions parallel and perpendicular to the easy direction (alignment direction) for the $SmCo_5$ and $Nd_2Fe_{14}B$ samples, respectively.

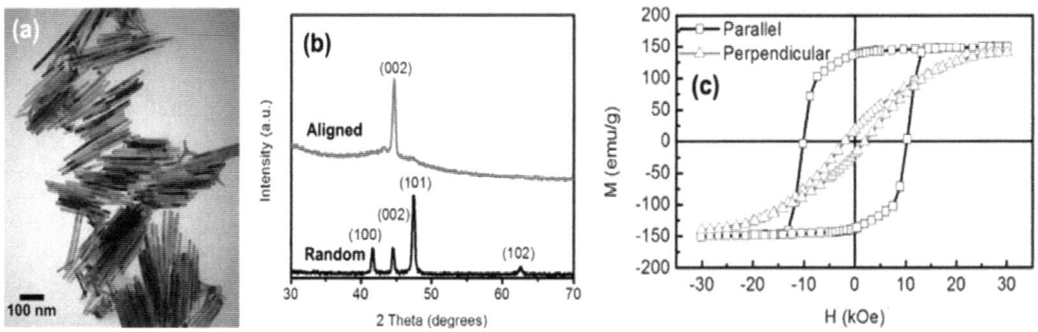

Fig.6. (a) TEM image of Co nanowires, (b) XRD patterns of randomly oriented and aligned Co nanowires assemblies in magnetic field and (c) hysteresis loops of Co nanowires measured hardening in epoxy parallel and perpendicular to applied magnetic field direction during alignment.

[5] C. B. Rong , D. Li , V. Nandwana , N. Poudyal, Y. Ding, Z. L. Wang , H. Zeng and J. P. Liu, *Adv. Mater.*, **18**, 2006, 2984.

[6] D. Li, N. Poudyal, V. Nandwana, Z. Jin, K. Elkins, J.P. Liu, *J. Appl. Phys.*, **99**, 2006, 08E911.

[7] J. P. Liu, K. Elkins, D. Li, V. Nandwana and N. Poudyal, *IEEE Trans. Magn.*, **42**, *2006,* 3036.

[8] N. Poudyal, The University of Texas at Arlington, ProQuest, UMI Dissertations Publishing, 2008. 3339158. (Available: http://ezproxy.uta.edu/docview/276043627?accountid=7117).

[9] V. Nandwana, E. K. Elkins, N. Poudyal, G.S. Chaubey, K. Yano and J. P. Liu, *J. Phys. Chem.* C, **111**, 2007, 4185.

[10] N. Poudyal and J. P. Liu, *J. Phys. D: Appl. Phys.*, **46**, 2013, 043001.

[11] V. M. Chakka, B. Altuncevahir, Z. Q. Jin, Y. Li, and J. P. Liu, *J. Appl. Phys.*, **99**, 2006, 08E912.

[12] Y. P. Wang, Y. Li, C. B. Rong, and J. P. Liu, Nanotechnology, **18**, 2007, 465701.

[13] M. Yue, Y. P. Wang, N. Poudyal, C. B. Rong and J. P. Liu, *J. Appl. Phys.*, **105,** 2009, 07A708.

[14] C. B. Rong, N. Poudyal and J. P. Liu, *Phys. Lett.* A, **374**, 2010, 3967.

[15] N. Poudyal, C. B. Rong, J. Ping Liu, J Appl. Phys., **107**, 2010, 09A703.

[16] N. Poudyal, C. B. Rong, V. N. Vuong and J. Ping Liu, *J. Phys.D: Appl. Phys.*, **44**, 2011, 335002.

[17] K. Gandha, N. Poudyal, Q. Zhang, and J. P. Liu, *IEEE Trans. Magn.* **49**, 2013, 3273.

[18] K. Gandha, K. Elkins, N. Poudyal, X. B. Liu, and J. P. Liu, *Sci. Rep.* **4**, 2014,5345.

Submicron Rare Earth - Cobalt Particles with Improved Hard Magnetic Properties

A.M. GABAY, G.C. HADJIPANAYIS
Department of Physics and Astronomy, University of Delaware, Newark, DE, USA

Abstract: *Polydispersed $R_2(Co,Fe)_{17}$ and RCo_5 powders consisting mostly of single crystal particles with average sizes ranging from tens to few hundreds of nanometers have been prepared through mechanical activation of a mixture of R_xO_y, Fe_2O_3, Co, Ca and CaO followed by short annealing and subsequent separation of the ferromagnetic particles. The room-temperature coercivities of the oriented powders of Sm_2Co_{17} (19.0 kOe) YCo_5 (20.6 kOe), $LaCo_5$ (9.6 kOe), $PrCo_5$ (19.1 kOe) and $SmCo_5$ (41.5 kOe) were significantly higher than those of traditionally ground powders. In the case of the Sm_2Co_{17} and $SmCo_5$ compounds which have been used in permanent magnets applications since 1970s, this improvement is primarily of a scientific interest. On the other hand, the preparation of the high-coercivity anisotropic YCo_5, $PrCo_5$ and especially $LaCo_5$ powders may have immediate technological implications.*

Keywords: *rare earth – cobalt magnets; coercivity; mechanochemical synthesis; anisotropic powders*

Address: Alexander Gabay, University of Delaware, 217 Sharp Lab, Newark, DE 19716, USA, Phone +1 302 831 6345, E-mail: gabay@udel.edu

1. Introduction

Magnetic hardness is usually induced in high-anisotropy magnetic materials through refinement of their crystals. Smaller crystals tend to be more resistant to magnetization reversal because they contain fewer anisotropy defects which serve as nucleation sites for the reversed magnetization. The intrinsic coercivity H_c emerging in prefabricated RCo_5 (R = rare earth) and Sm_2Co_{17} alloys subjected to mechanical milling reaches only 0.03 - 0.05 of the anisotropy field H_a of the respective compound [1-8]. The obvious reason for the limited efficiency of inducing H_c via milling is that simultaneously with decreasing the particle size, milling introduces new anisotropy defects [2,6]. Indeed, even large annealed Sm_2Co_{17} crystals with electropolished surfaces reportedly exhibit H_c of 6.9 kOe [9], almost three times the value achievable via milling [8]. It is true that significantly higher H_c values can be obtained through refinement of crystallites in milled *polycrystalline* alloys; however, this increase comes at the expense of the possibility to align the crystallites, i.e., at the expense of remanent magnetization M_r of the magnet. One technique which yields very fine, *separable* R-Co crystals without the defects associated with the milling and exhibiting a high H_c is mechanochemical synthesis. In this process, a reduction diffusion of oxide precursors is initiated by a high-energy ball milling and is completed during a subsequent annealing. The pioneering works by McCormick *et al.* demonstrated that it was possible to achieve $H_c \approx 0.15H_a$ for unseparated $SmCo_5$ nano-crystals (65 kOe) [10] and for separated Sm_2Co_{17} nanocrystals (14 kOe) [11]. In this paper, we review our recent studies [12-15] on mechanochemical synthesis of magnetically hard $R_2(Co,Fe)_{17}$ and RCo_5 single crystal particles for R = Y, La, Pr and Sm.

2. Overview of Synthesis Process

The mechanochemical synthesis employed for preparation of ultrafine R-Co(Fe) particles consisted of three principal steps. A mixture of precursor powders (typically, R_xO_y, Fe_2O_3 and Co; although, Co_3O_4 and Fe were also tried) with Ca granules (a reducing agent) and CaO dispersant powder (300 – 400 wt.% of the precursors) was subjected to several hours of high-energy ball milling in an argon-filled steel vial. Although the obtained black pyrophoric powder did contain particles of newly formed R-rich R-Co phases [13], the reduction at this stage was far from complete; the main purpose of the milling was to mix the reactants on a nanometer scale.

A subsequent annealing was done in argon at around 900 °C, i.e., above the melting temperature of Ca. The annealing completes the reduction of the oxide precursors and assures both sufficient homogenization of the R-Co(Fe) compounds and limited growth of their crystals. Figure 1 shows bright $LaCo_5$ crystals with an average size of 540 nm formed after 5 min at 900 °C. The particles are embedded in a darker matrix consisting of CaO (by-product of the reduction as well as the added dispersant) and excess Ca. The H_c of such as-grown single crystals is very high (the $LaCo_5$ particle of Fig. 1 exhibit the H_c of 24.9 kOe), but their easy magnetization directions cannot be aligned and they are greatly diluted by the non-magnetic phases.

Pure R-Co(Fe) hard magnetic particles were collected after repeated washing and electromagnetic

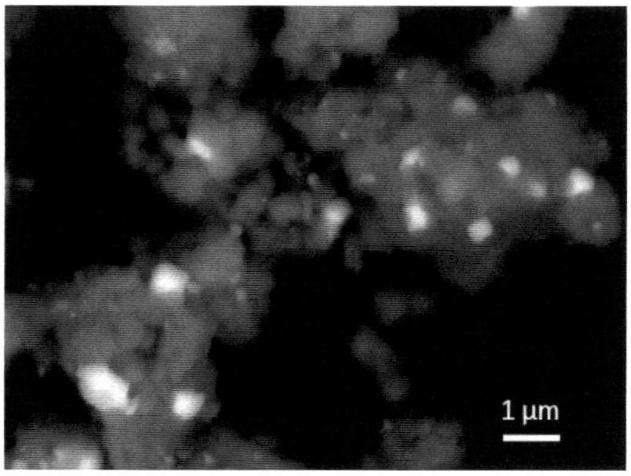

Fig. 1. Backscattered-electrons image of $LaCo_5$ particles embedded in CaO/Ca matrix.

separation; depending on the alloy, up to ten 1 - 8 min cycles were required. Typically, the washing - accompanied by a high-intensity ultrasound irradiation - was done with deionized water, 1 vol.% solution of acetic acid and ethanol. Only the $LaCo_5$ particles required a more gentle processing, the 1% acetic acid being replaced by consecutive application of 25 vol.% solution of glycerol and 0.1% acetic acid (these were also the only particles washed in an ice-water bath). After the last washing cycle (in ethanol) all particles were dried in a magnetic field.

The dry R-Co(Fe) particles collected after the washing were *not* pyrophoric (presumably, passivated) and they could be safely handled in air. The $R_2(Co,Fe)_{17}$ and especially $LaCo_5$ particles were found to be affected by hydrogen released during the washing. The absorbed hydrogen could be removed by annealing the particles in a dynamic vacuum, the exact annealing conditions being dependent on the weight of the charge. It must be noted that the vacuum-annealed particles became pyrophoric; capsules with them were opened under ethanol for a new passivation.

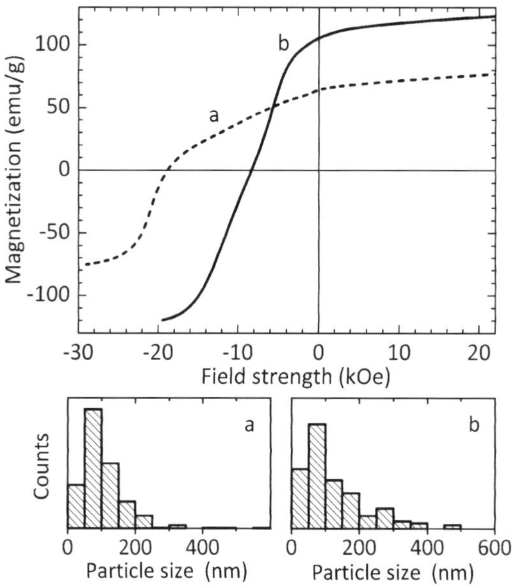

Fig. 2. Demagnetization curves and size distributions of (a) Sm_2Co_{17} and (b) $(Sm_{0.85}Pr_{0.15})_2(Co_{0.6}Fe_{0.4})_{17}$ particles synthesized at 925 °C. The magnetization data are for magnetically oriented particles.

3. Particles of Sm_2Co_{17} and Its Derivatives

3.1. Effect of Pr and Fe substitutions

The $(Sm_{1-x}Pr_x)_2(Co_{1-y}Fe_y)_{17}$ particles were prepared for $x = 0 - 0.15$ and $y = 0 - 0.5$. As one might expect based on the known behaviour of the fundamental magnetic properties (the saturation magnetization and magnetocrystalline anisotropy), the Pr and Fe substitutions resulted in higher M_r and lower H_c values. Figure 2 demonstrates the range of the hard magnetic properties obtained for the particles with average sizes $\langle D \rangle \approx 100$ nm: the binary Sm_2Co_{17} particles with $\langle D \rangle = 104$ nm exhibited an H_c as high as 19 kOe, whereas the M_r of the $(Sm,Pr)_2(Co,Fe)_{17}$ ($\langle D \rangle = 121$ nm) reached 106 emu/g and H_c of 8.3 kOe. Substituting more than 40% Fe for Co led to a rapid decline in the H_c. The highest H_c value obtained for $y = 0.5$ (at $x = 0.15$) was only 3 kOe.

3.2. Effect of excess calcium

The particles synthesized via the mechanochemical process are significantly polydispersed (see the bottom of Fig. 2), and narrowing their size distributions remains a priority of our ongoing studies. However, several factors controlling the *average* particle sizes have been already identified. The two obvious ones are the temperature and duration of the synthesis annealing. The third – and arguably the most powerful – tool for such control turned out to be the excess of metallic Ca over the amount nominally required for the complete reduction of the precursor oxides. In Fig. 3, this factor is presented as the ratio of the Ca and O atoms (not counting the added CaO dispersant). For given annealing conditions, the Ca/O ratio has a dramatic effect on the $\langle D \rangle$ and M_r. The X-ray diffraction (XRD) characterization [12] also revealed a strong effect of the Ca/O ratio on the chemical and

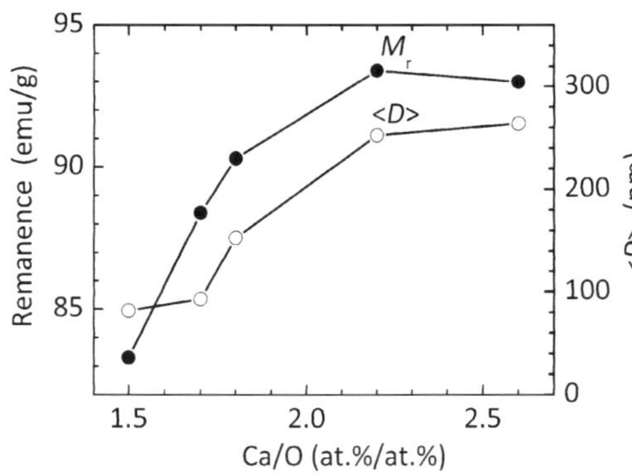

Fig. 3. Remanent magnetization and average size of $(Sm_{0.85}Pr_{0.15})_2(Co_{0.7}Fe_{0.3})_{17}$ particles as a function of Ca/O ratio in samples annealed at 925 °C for 5 min. The magnetization data are for magnetically oriented particles.

structural homogeneity of the particles. In [12,14], we attempted to link the observed effects with the assumed solution-precipitation mechanism of the particle growth. The liquid Ca phase is believed to facilitate diffusion necessary for this growth. We will return to this subject in section 4.1.

3.3. Effect of interstitial hydrogen

Unintended hydrogen modification of $Nd_2Fe_{14}B$ powders prepared through Ca reduction and occurring during washing the particles with water has been well documented [15,16]. The Sm_2Co_{17} compound is known to absorb the hydrogen atoms only at extreme conditions, yet the washed ultrafine particles prepared in our experiments consistently exhibited the characteristic lattice expansion. Unit cell volume increases by 0.65% in the case of the binary alloy and by up to ≈ 1.0% in the samples with the largest studied Pr and Fe substitutions. The results shown in Fig. 4 illustrate the removal of the interstitial hydrogen from the particles (the particles were similar to those featured in Fig. 2b). The contraction of the lattice was observed after annealing in vacuum at a temperature higher than 200 °C; this contraction is accompanied by a moderate increase in the M_r and similarly small decline of the H_c. One has to be careful, however, when linking these changes to the removal of the interstitial hydrogen. The annealing of the ultrafine particles may also be accompanied by their partial oxidation (even though the XRD characterization did not detect it, such oxidation still might have occurred in thin surface regions of the particles), which would also lead to a decline of the H_c. Although not fully conclusive, the available experimental results on the effects of the interstitial hydrogen suggest that, in the case of the Sm_2Co_{17} compound and its derivatives, the associated changes in the magnetic properties are rather small.

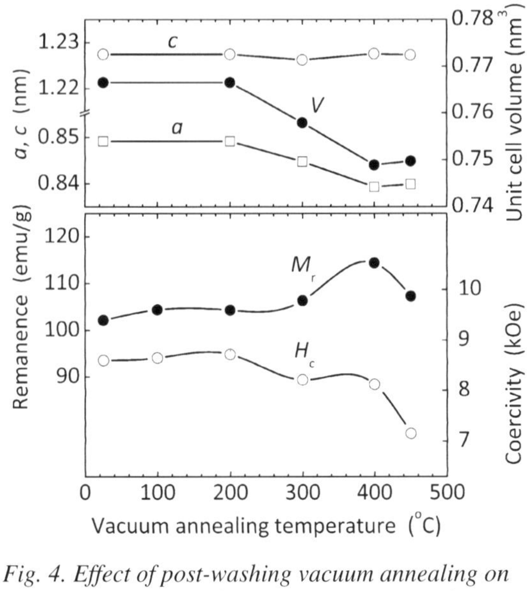

Fig. 4. Effect of post-washing vacuum annealing on lattice parameters and magnetic properties of $(Sm_{0.85}Pr_{0.15})_2(Co_{0.6}Fe_{0.4})_{17}$ particles. The magnetization data are for magnetically oriented particles.

4. Particles of RCo_5 for R = Y, La, Pr, Sm

4.1. Effect of synthesis temperature for R = Y, Pr, Sm

The highest room-temperature values of H_c obtained for oriented YCo_5, $PrCo_5$ and $SmCo_5$ particles were, respectively, 20.6, 19.1 and 41.5 kOe (see Fig. 5; the corresponding <*D*> values were 280, 260 and 400 nm). While obtaining RCo_5 *nanoparticles* (i.e., particles smaller than 100 nm) through adjustment of the Ca/O ratio is a subject of ongoing research, the effect of the annealing temperature on *larger* particles (150 nm ≤ <*D*> ≤ 400 nm) has been already studied in considerable detail. The data for $Sm_{0.25}Pr_{0.75}Co_5$ particles shown in Fig. 6 (annealing for 5 min) reflect the general trend, although the effects of the same absolute annealing temperatures may be quite different for the different RCo_5 (they become more universal if the annealing temperatures are normalized with the melting temperature for R = Y and with the temperature of the peritectic reactions for R = Pr and Sm [14]). Somewhat exceptional were (i) a significantly slower increase of the YCo_5 particle sizes with the annealing temperature and (ii) a virtually constant H_c of the $SmCo_5$ particles - it varied

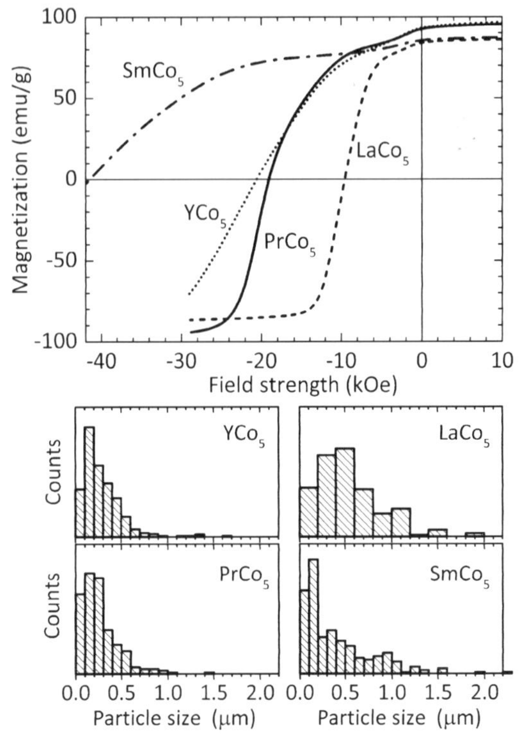

Fig. 5. Demagnetization curves and size distributions of RCo_5 particles for R = Y, La, Pr and Sm; the particles were synthesized at 1025 °C, 900 °C, 900 °C and 1000 °C, respectively. The magnetization data are for magnetically oriented particles.

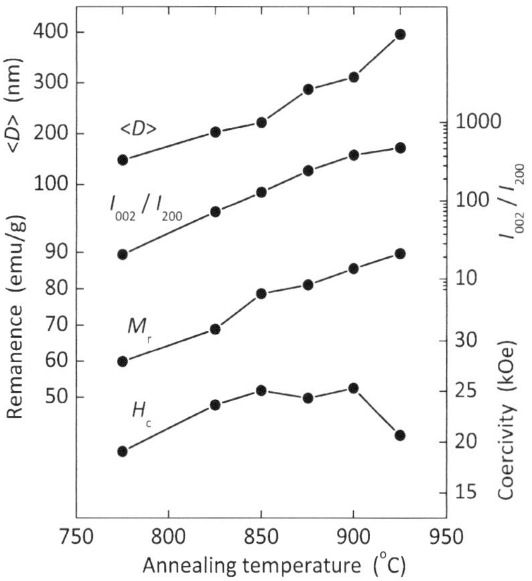

Fig. 6. Effect of the synthesis temperature on the average size, crystal anisotropy and magnetic properties of $Pr_{0.75}Sm_{0.25}Co_5$ particles. Crystal anisotropy of the particles was analysed by comparing intensities of the (002) and (200) XRD reflections for magnetically oriented samples.

by less than 1 kOe for six annealing temperature between 875 and 1000 °C despite the large differences in the particle sizes (see Fig. 7).

The variation of the M_r - the characteristic of a great practical importance - clearly reflects the difference in the degree of alignment of the magnetically oriented particles (expressed in Fig. 6 via the I_{002}/I_{200} ratio). Both are, apparently, determined by the fraction of *single crystal* particles. We theoretically explain the increase of this fraction with the annealing temperature assuming that many of the R-Co particles are initially formed as polycrystalline; the largest crystallite in such particle grows at the expense of the smaller ones until it consumes all of them. This model may explain why obtaining smaller particles requires – unfortunately – certain sacrifice of their M_r.

4.2. Effect of hydrogen on $LaCo_5$ particles

Whereas the H_c of the $R_2(Co,Fe)_{17}$ and $SmCo_5$ particles did not change after the washing (despite the evident absorption of hydrogen by the former) and that of the YCo_5 and $PrCo_5$ particles declined by about one third (since no lattice expansion could be detected, this decrease must have been be caused by an increased density of the anisotropy defects at the surfaces of the particles), the H_c of washed $LaCo_5$ particles collapses dramatically, from nearly 25 kOe to 7 kOe (when measured in randomly oriented samples).

The XRD data shown in Fig. 8 reveal changes caused by the washing; they are consistent with the absorption of hydrogen. As many as three derivatives of the original $LaCo_5$ structure emerge, two hexagonal

Fig. 7. Secondary-electrons images of washed $SmCo_5$ particles synthesized (a) at 875 °C and (b) at 1000 °C.

$LaCo_5H_x$ structures with different lattice parameters and an orthorhombic $LaCo_5H_3$ structure. Annealing in a dynamic vacuum drives the absorbed hydrogen away restoring the original $LaCo_5$ structure (spectra 3 and 4 in Fig. 8). Although the H_c of the (oriented) $LaCo_5$ particles increases only to 9.6 kOe (see Fig. 9), it is 2.5 times larger than the one reported for anisotropic $LaCo_5$ particles obtained via milling [2].

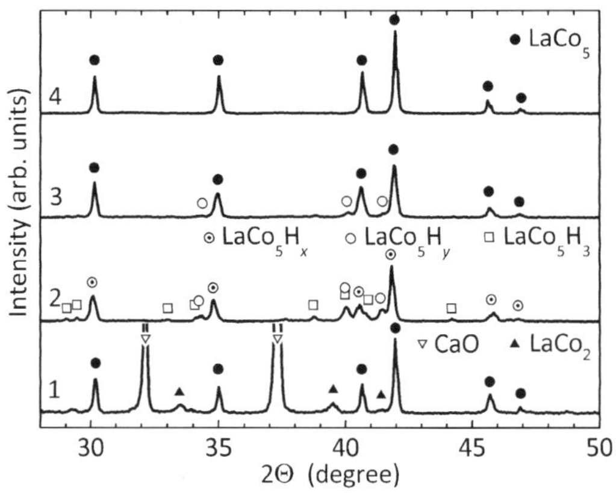

Fig. 8. XRD spectra of $LaCo_5$-based samples after synthesis at 900 °C (1), after the subsequent washing (2) and after additional vacuum annealing at 200 °C (3) and at 250 °C (4).

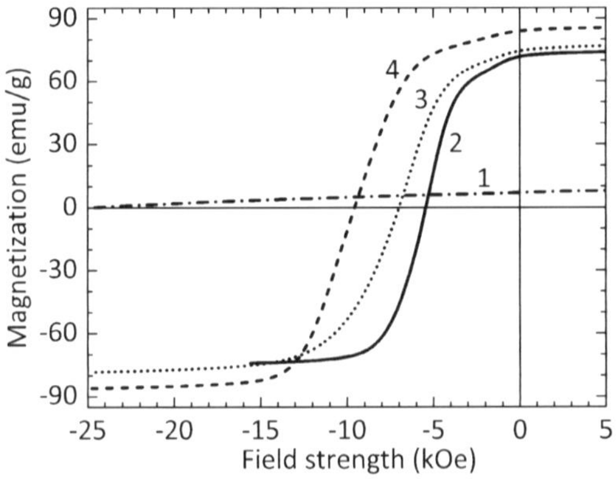

Fig. 9. Demagnetization curves of $LaCo_5$-based samples of Fig. 8. Sample 1 was not magnetically oriented, and measurements for it were not corrected for self-demagnetization.

5. Conclusions

Thus, mechanochemistry can produce single crystal R-(Co,Fe) powders with coercivity values several times larger than those of optimally milled alloys - most probably due to a lower density of anisotropy defects in *grown* crystals as compared to *ground* ones. Estimates for the maximum energy product values (made assuming a full density) are also impressive for the particles of these small sizes: up to 21 MGOe for $(Sm,Pr)_2(Co,Fe)_{17}$, 16.3 MGOe for YCo_5, 15.8 MGOe for $LaCo_5$, 19.6 MGOe for $PrCo_5$ and 19.3 MGOe for $SmCo_5$. In the mass-specific units, the remanence of the YCo_5 particles is actually higher than that for $PrCo_5$ and $SmCo_5$ (see Fig. 5), but the low density of YCo_5 compound reverses the order for the remanence values expressed in gausses.

At the present, the high room-temperature coercivity exhibited by the ultrafine Sm_2Co_{17} and $SmCo_5$ particles is primarily of a scientific interest as a further extension of the practical limits associated with hard magnetic materials (with their 41.5 kOe, the $SmCo_5$ particles are, probably, the "hardest" single crystals reported to the date), although use of these particles in novel nanocomposite magnets is being considered. On the other hand, synthesis of the anisotropic high-coercivity YCo_5, $LaCo_5$ and $PrCo_5$ powders from oxide precursors may have more immediate technological implications allowing the commercial utilization of more abundant and/or less expensive raw materials for permanent magnets.

Acknowledgments

This work was supported by DOE APRA-E grant DE-AR0000046 and DOE BES grant DE-FG02-04ER4612. The authors thank Dr. Wanfeng Li and Ms. Xiaocao Hu for contributing TEM characterization data.

References

[1] K. Strnat, G. Hoffer, J. Olson, W. Ostertag, J.J. Becker, *J. Appl. Phys.* **38**, 1967, 1001.
[2] W.A.J.J. Velge, K.H.J. Buschow, *J. Appl. Phys.* **39**, 1968 1717.
[3] K.H.J. Buschow, P.A. Naastepad, F.F. Westendorp, *J. Appl. Phys.* **40**, 1969, 4029.
[4] K. Strnat, J. Tsui, in: *Proc. 8th Rare Earth Research Conf.*, Reno, 1970, vol. 1, pp. 3-10.
[5] J.J. Becker, *J. Appl. Phys.* **42**, 1971, 1537.
[6] K. Inomata, S. Shikanai, H. Horie, K. Fukui, *Japan. J. Appl. Phys.* **12**, 1973, 565.
[7] C.H. Chen, S.J. Knutson, Y. Shen, R.A. Wheeler, J.C. Horwath, P.N. Barnes, *Appl. Phys. Lett.* **99**, 2011, 012504.
[8] C.H. Chen, S. Kodat, M.H. Walmer, S.F. Cheng, M. A. Willard, V. G. Harris, *J. Appl. Phys.* **93**, 2003, 7966.
[9] A.V. Deryagin, E.A. Barabanova, N.V. Kudrevatyhk, V.N. Moskalev, *Sov. Phys. J.* **22**, 1979, 664.
[10] Y. Liu, M.P. Dallimore, P.G. McCormick, T. Alonso, *J. Magn. Magn. Mater.* **116**, 1992, L320.
[11] W. Liu and P. G. McCormick, *J. Magn. Magn. Mater.* **195**, 1999, L279.
[12] A.M. Gabay, W.F. Li, G.C. Hadjipanayis, *IEEE Trans. Magn.* **49**, 2013, 3225.
[13] W.F. Li, A. Gabay, X.C. Hu, C. Ni, G.C. Hadjipanayis, *J. Phys. Chem. C* **117**, 2013, 10291.
[15] A.M. Gabay, G.C. Hadjipanayis, *J. Phys. D: Appl. Phys.* **47**, 2014 182001.
[14] A.M. Gabay, X.C. Hu, G.C. Hadjipanayis, *J. Magn. Magn. Mater.* **368**, 2014 75.
[15] E. Claude, S. Ram, I. Gimenez. P. Chaudoüet, D. Boursier, J.C. Joubert, *IEEE Trans. Magn.* **29**, 1993, 2767.
[16] A.M. Gabay, X.C. Hu, G. Hadjipanayis, *J. Alloys Compd.* **574**, 2013, 472.

Submicron Sm-Fe-N Magnet Powders with High Coercivity

YINGCHANG YANG
Peking University, Beijing 100871, China

Abstract: *The continuing trend of miniaturization of a wide range of electronic devices has provided robust demand for higher performance and more varieties of anisotropic bonded magnets. We have recently successfully mass produced Sm-Fe-N anisotropic magnet powders using strip casting, a significant development since Sumitomo Metal Mining Co started manufacturing Sm-Fe-N anisotropic magnet powders with the method of reaction and diffusion a decade ago. Our product achieves a maximum energy product* $(BH)_{max}$ *of up to 40 MGOe. The coercivity of the submicron Sm-Fe-N powders is characterized by a nucleation mechanism. In this talk, we will discuss the key issues involved in the production process.*

Keywords: $Sm_2Fe_{17}N_3$ *anisotropic powders; single particles; Nucleation and unpinning of domain boundaries*

Address: Yingchang Yang, School of Physics, Peking University, Beijing100871, China. Tel: 86-10-62757090 Fax: 86-10-62751615, E-mail: fuyang@pku.edu.cn

1. Introduction

It has been almost a quarter of a century since the discovery of Sm-Fe-N in 1990. Tireless efforts have been made since then to enable mass production of new Sm-Fe-N-based magnetic materials. We believe the opportunity of bringing this into reality is getting mature.

(1) Extensive experimental and theoretical research on spontaneous magnetization reveals the physical origin of the nitrogen interstitial effect on rare earth - iron intermetallics, providing a key for producing Sm-Fe-N nitrides with outstanding intrinsic magnetic properties [1-4].

(2) Thanks to research and development on magnetization process, magnetic domain structure and its demagnetization mechanism of the rare earth-iron nitrides have been studied, and many options have become available for the manufacture of Sm-Fe-N powders. A variety of processes are explored, including mechanical alloying, rapid quenching, HDDR, reduction and diffusion, melt-casting, strip casting and so on [5-10].

(3) Magnetic powder is used to manufacture bonded magnets. Different kinds of bonded magnets have been made with Sm-Fe-N powders using a variety of adhesive and molding techniques, including processes such as compression, calendering, injection, and extrusion. Injection magnets and flexible extrusion magnets based on Sm-Fe-N materials, in particular, seem to have a significant advantage over conventional bonded magnets [11-12].

(4) Cost of raw material is an important factor. In the past, the price of Sm was much higher than that of Nd. Now the situation is reversed with Sm becoming much cheaper than Nd.

In order to bring a new kind of material to market, the performance/cost ratio of the new material needs to be competitive. To achieve high performance, we have persistently pursued technologies for manufacturing anisotropic magnet powders. This is because, theoretically, the remanence of an anisotropic magnet is twice as high as that of an isotropic magnet based on of the same material, making the maximum energy product four times as high. In addition, we strive to reduce production cost by manufacturing the Sm-Fe alloys using the strip-casting method followed by nitrogenation and milling processes.

It is a challenging task to manufacture anisotropic magnetic powder with rare earth - iron compounds, whether using Nd-Fe-B or Sm-Fe-N. There are two ways to make anisotropic magnet powder. One is to prepare poly-crystal particles with aligned crystalline grains, e.g., the Nd-Fe-B HDDR anisotropic powders. Another is to prepare monocrystalline particles. We use the latter. Monocrystalline particles can be manufactured with a milling process. This is rather straightforward to manufacture Sm-Fe-N anisotropy powders. However, how to achieve a desirable coercivity with single crystals? It is well known that the coercive force of the Nd-Fe-B magnet powders results from domain wall pinning at the grain boundaries whereas no grain boundaries exist in the monocrystalline powders. The coercivity of Sm-Fe-N anisotropic powders is characterized by a nucleation mechanism. How to enhance the strength of the nucleation field and achieve a high coercivity with an ideal squarness for monocrystalline particles is the main topic of this paper.

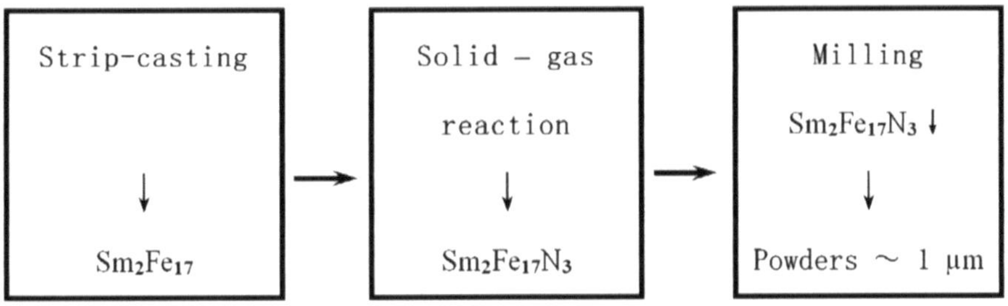

Fig.1. Process scheme of manufacture $Sm_2Fe_{17}N_3$ anisotropic powders.

2. Experimental Techniques

The Sm_2Fe_{17} alloys were fabricated by strip-casting method of 99.9% pure primary materials in a purified argon atmosphere. Nitrides were prepared by passing purified nitrogen gas at atmospheric pressure around 450 °C for several hours. X-ray diffraction (XRD) analysis was employed to detect the phase structure. Scanning electronic microscopy (SEM) was used to study the microstructures.

To investigate the intrinsic magnetic properties , the powder samples of cylindrical shape were aligned in the 15-kOe field and fixed in epoxy resin. Magnetization curves along and perpendicular to the orientation direction were respectively measured on aligned samples by SQUID magnetometer with a field of up to 90 kOe in a temperature range from 2 K to 400 K. The Curie temperatures were determined from *M-T* curves using a vibrating sample magnetometer (VSM) in a temperature range from 300 to 1000 K. For testing the permanent magnetic characteristics the hysteresis loop was measured by a VSM with an aligned sample without demagnetization field correction.

3. Results and Discussion

We develop a manufacture process for mass production of $Sm_2Fe_{17}N_3$ anisotropic powers by using powder metallurgy technique. As a starting point, Sm_2Fe_{17} alloys are prepared by strip-casting method. It is followed by a gas–solid phase reaction to form the $Sm_2Fe_{17}N_3$ nitrides. Finally, the $Sm_2Fe_{17}N_3$ nitrides are further pulverized by ball milling into fine monocrystalline particles. The production process consists of three steps as illustrated in Fig 1.

It is worth noting that each particle is a single crystal, but not a single domain. During the demagnetization process, domain nucleation and domain wall motion both should be considered. However, many experiments demonstrate that the Sm-Fe-N fine powders present a strong dependence of ${}_iH_c$ on magnetizing field H_m, as well as on the particle size. These facts suggest that the demagnetization process is associated with nucleation and unpinning of domain boundaries. In general, the nucleation of reverse domain can occur at lower field because of the defects associated with the materials, such as inclusion of other soft or non-magnetic phase, lattice defect, surface irregularities and surface oxides, etc. In the present work, it is required to minimize the product defects as much as possible during each step of the production process in order to enhance the nucleation field strength.

3.1. The master alloy Sm_2Fe_{17} is required to be a single phase

It is well known that in the melt-casting process, as Sm_2Fe_{17} alloy melts peritectically at 1280 °C and the conventional induction melt-casting method cannot attain rapid cooling, precipitation of both α-Fe and rich Sm phases is not avoidable, as demonstrated in Fig. 2(a). For this reason the strip-casting technique is used. The single phase of Sm_2Fe_{17} strips is identified in Fig. 2(b).

3.2. Complete gas-solid reaction in the nitrogen atmosphere is indispensable

The $Sm_2Fe_{17}N_3$-type material attracts strong attention as a useful material due to its outstanding intrinsic

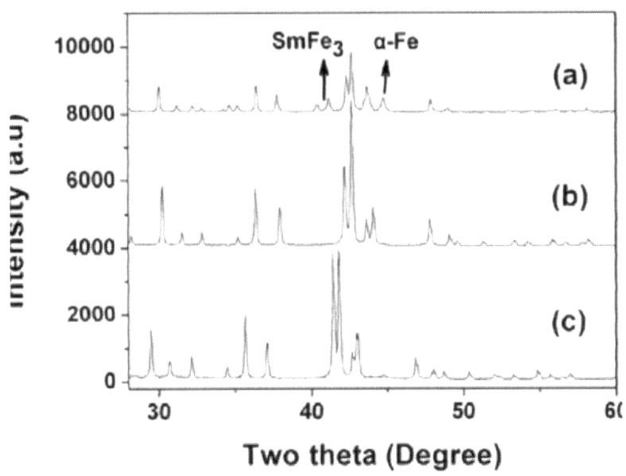

Fig. 2. X-ray diffraction patterns of (a) Sm_2Fe_{17} alloy made by induction melt–casting method, (b) Sm_2Fe_{17} alloy made by strip-casting method, (c) $Sm_2Fe_{17}N_3$.

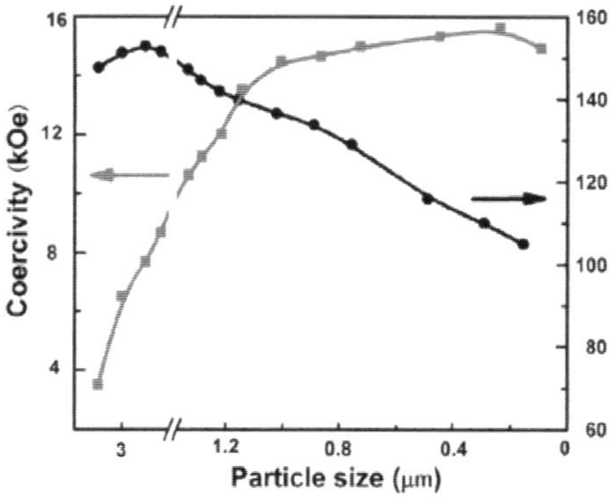

Fig. 3. Dependence of coercivity and remanence on the particle size of $Sm_2Fe_{17}N_3$ anisotropic powders.

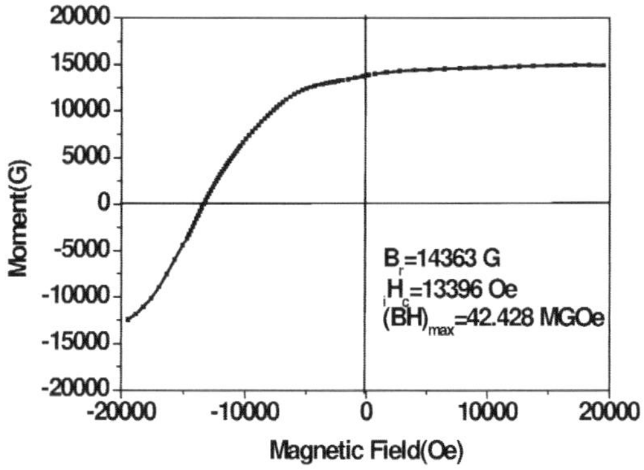

Fig. 5. Demagnetization curve of $Sm_2Fe_{17}N_3$ powder.

magnetic property, which is resulted from the interstitial nitrogen atom effect on the Sm_2Fe_{17} alloys. High intrinsic magnetic properties - including large anisotropy field H_a, spontaneous magnetization M_s and Curie temperature T_C - are a prerequisite for creating large coercive force $_iH_c$, remanence B_r, and maximum energy product $(BH)_{max}$. Thus, a complete gas–solid reaction in the nitrogen atmosphere is absolutely necessary. From the X-ray diffraction patterns of $Sm_2Fe_{17}N_3$, as illustrated by Fig. 2(c), α-Fe is negligible. Compared to the XRD pattern of the R_2Fe_{17} strips [Fig. 2(b)], all the diffraction lines shift to lower angle due to the volume expansion after nitrogenation, implying that nitrogen atoms have entered the interstitial sites of the Sm_2Fe_{17} structure, which guarantees the formation of high-quality nitrides. Fig. 3 presents the intrinsic magnetic properties of Sm_2Fe_{17} alloys before and after nitrgenation.

3.3. Each particle of Sm-Fe-N is a single crystal. Good particle size distribution is required

The nitrides are further pulverized to fine monocrystalline powders. Permanent magnetic properties of the powders are sensitive to their microstructure, especially their particle size. Fig. 3 shows the dependence of coercive force and

Fig. 4. SEM image of powders with the mean particle size of 0.2 μm.

Fig. 6. SEM image of powders with the mean particle size of 1.3 μm.

remanence of $Sm_2Fe_{17}N_3$ powders on their particle size. The coercivity first increases as the particle size decreases, and reaches a maximum value at the mean size close to 0.2 μm, see Fig. 4. The remanent magnetization also varies with the particle size, and reaches the maximum value around the mean size of about 2.5 μm. The maximum energy product of 42.2 MGOe, shown in Fig. 5, is obtained at the mean size of about 1.3 μm, demonstrated in Fig. 6.

Based on the experimental data of saturation magnetization shown in Table 1, the theoretical estimated value of $(BH)_{max}$ for $Sm_2Fe_{17}N_3$ is 60.0 MGOe at room temperature, and 69.4 MGOe at 2 K.

Table 1. Intrinsic magnetic properties of Sm_2Fe_{17} and $Sm_2Fe_{17}N_3$ compounds.

Material	T_C (K)	M_s (emu/g)		H_a (kOe)	
		1.5 K	300 K	1.5 K	300 K
Sm_2Fe_{17}	395	152.0	105.0	-	-
$Sm_2Fe_{17}N_3$	755	170.0	158.2	200	150

Accordingly, there still exists a lot of room for further improvement. At present, the submicron Sm-Fe-N magnet powder's performance is limited by milling facilities, because the conventional jet milling cannot crush strip-cast Sm-Fe-N alloys into submicron powders, whereas prolonging the milling by using other existing milling equipment affects the submicron particles through lattice deformation, oxidation and aggregation.

4. Summary

A manufacture process for mass production of $Sm_2Fe_{17}N_3$ anisotropic powers has been developed by using powder metallurgic technique. As to the product performance, a maximum energy product $(BH)_{max}$ of up to 40 MGOe has been achieved. The performance of the products is expected to improve with improvement of the milling process.

References

[1] J.M.D. Coey and H. Sun, *J. Magn. Magn. Mater.* **87**, 1990, L251.

[2] Y.C. Yang, X.D Zhang, L.S. Kong, Q. Pan, J.L. Yang, Y.F. Ding, B.S. Zhang, C.T. Ye, and L. Jin, *J. Appl. Phys.* **70**, 1991, 6018.

[3] S.S. Jaswl, W.B. Yelon, G.C. Hadjipanayis, Y.Z. Wang and D.J. Sellmyer, *Phys. Rev. Lett.* **67**, 1991, 644.

[4] J.P. Liu, K. Bakker, F.R. de Boer, T.H. Jacobs, D.B. de Mooij, K.H.J. Buschow, *J. Less-Common Met.* **170**, 1991, 109.

[5] J.F. Hu, T. Dragon, M.L. Sartoreli, and H. Kronmüller, *Phys. Status Solidi A* **136**, 1993, 207.

[6] Jinbo Yang, Weihua Mao, Benpei Cheng, Yingchang Yang, Hai Xu and Han Baoshang, *Appl. Phys. Lett.* **71**, 1997, 3290.

[7] W.B. Yelon and G.C. Hadjipanayis, *IEEE Trans. Magn.* **28**, 1992, 2316.

[8] Shin Tajima, Takeshi Hattori and Yoshio Kato, *IEEE Trans. Magn.* **31**, 1995, 3701.

[9] A. Kawamoto, T. Ishikawa, S. Yasuda, K. Takeya, K. Ishizaka, T. Iseki, K. Ohmori, *IEEE Trans. Magn.* **35**, 1999, 3322.

[10] I. Sasaki, H. Fujii, H. Okada, and S. Suzuki, *IEEE Trans. Magn.* **35**, 1999, 3319.

[11] S. Yoshizawa, T. Ishikawa, I. Kaneko, S. Hayashi, A. Kawamoto, K. Ohamori, *IEEE Trans. Magn.* **35**, 1999, 3340.

[12] T. Ihikawa and K. Ohmori, in: G.C. Hadjipanayis (ed.), *Bonded Magnets*, Kluwer Academic Publishers, 2003, p. 73.

Predicting the Crystal Structures of Magnet Materials Using Adaptive Genetic Algorithm

C.Z. WANG[1,2], X. ZHAO[1,2], M.C. NGUYEN[1,2], L.Q. KE[1], W.Y. ZHANG[3], M.J. KRAMER[1,4], D.J. SELLMYER[3], X.Z. LI[3], V.P. ANTROPOV[1], F. ZHANG[1], K.M. HO[1,2]
[1] Ames Laboratory – US Department of Energy, Ames, Iowa, 50011, USA
[2] Department of Physics and Astronomy, Iowa State University, Ames, Iowa, 50011, USA
[3] Nebraska Center for Materials and Nanoscience and Department of Physics and Astronomy, University of Nebraska, Lincoln, NE 68588
[4] Department of Materials Science and Engineering, Iowa State University, Ames, Iowa, 50011, USA

Abstract: *Fe and Co-based intermetallic compound have attracted a lot of interests as possible non-rare earth permanent magnet materials due to their strong magnetic moments and high Curie temperatures. However, the crystal structures of many of these compounds remain elusive. The uncertainty in the crystal structures greatly hinders further investigating and optimizing the materials for practical applications. We demonstrate that advanced computational algorithms and methods for crystal structure prediction can help unravel long-standing structural mysteries in complex intermetallic compounds. We show that the complex atomic structures of the orthorhombic, rhombohedral, and hexagonal polymorphs of Zr_2Co_{11} intermetallic compound can be resolved using a novel adaptive genetic algorithm in combination with first-principles calculations. The knowledge of the crystal structures at the atomic level allows us to identify the origin of the hard magnetic phase in Zr_2Co_{11} and provide useful insight for developing high performance permanent magnet without rare earth elements.*

Keywords: *non-rare earth permanent magnets; Zr_2Co_{11}; adaptive genetic algorithm; crystal structure prediction; first-principles calculations*

Address: C.Z. Wang, Ames Laboratory and Department of Physics and Astronomy, Iowa State University, Ames, Iowa, 50011, USA , Tel: (1-515) 294-6934, Fax: (1-515) 294-0689, e-mail: wangcz@ameslab.gov

1. Introduction

Permanent magnetic materials are an essential component in electrical generators and motors. Permanent magnets are also essential in computer hard drives and other electro-mechanical devices, including levitators. Because of the role of such devices in new energy economies there is a greatly increased demand for strong permanent magnet materials. Currently, the most widely used permanent magnetic materials are $Nd_2Fe_{14}B$ and $SmCo_5$, both containing rare earth (RE) metals. Owing to limited RE mineral resources and further limited RE metal supplies, the price of Nd and Sm and all other rare earth metals increased dramatically in the past several years. Thus, there is a strategic need to discover replacement magnet materials for rare earth permanent magnets (PM) to meet performance and cost goals for advanced electric drive motors and generators.

Since the middle of the last century, Edisonian's "trial and error" approach to magnetic materials discovery and design has led to many important technologies. At present there is an urgent need to develop new approaches to enable future advances in the field. Accurate and fast computational structure/property determinations can complement traditional experimental "trial and error" efforts in material design, and accelerate the pace of technological advances. With the rapid increase in computer power, it is now feasible to develop robust computational approaches that can theoretically explore the crystal structures of materials as a function of changing chemical compositions to help the discovery and design of new materials, especially when coupled with a strong synthesis effort to work in partnership to supply immediate feedback.

Recently, we have developed a robust and efficient computational algorithm, i.e., adaptive genetic algorithm (AGA), for computational phase diagram exploration and materials structure prediction [1-4]. We have applied the AGA to crystal structure perdition of magnetic materials [3,5-6], aiming at discovery of better non-rare earth magnetic materials with properties as good as, or exceeding, present rare earth magnets. In this paper, we demonstrate the power of the AGA approach for predicting the crystal structure of magnetic materials by solving a long-standing puzzle in the complex crystal structures of the orthorhombic, rhombohedral, and hexagonal polymorphs close to the Zr_2Co_{11} intermetallic compound. From our calculations, we identified the hard magnetic phase and the origin of high coercivity in this compound, thus guiding further development of these materials for use as high performance permanent magnets without rare-earth elements.

2. Adaptive Genetic Algorithm

To predict complex crystal structures from their chemical composition is one of the long-standing challenges in theoretical solid state physics and materials science. Development of the methodology for such an exploration requires not only computational algorithms for efficiently exploring configuration space, but also accurate and fast energy evaluations because the configuration space to be investigated is generally very large. The classical potential calculation is fast and applicable to big systems but it lacks accuracy. While density-functional theory (DFT) calculations give very accurate results, the calculation is too expensive to do a broad search in which the stochiometry and crystal structure can vary.

In order to perform a broad and accurate low-energy crystal-structures search, we have recently developed an adaptive genetic algorithm (AGA) method [1-4] which combines these two calculations in an efficient way to inherit both the speed of structure searches using classical potentials and the high accuracy of DFT calculations. In this new scheme, auxiliary classical potentials, which are adaptively adjusted based on the first-principles calculations during the GA search, are used to give a fast exploration of the configuration space, while the structures obtained from the GA search are evaluated by DFT and the results are used to guide the adjustments of the auxiliary potentials which will be used for further structure explorations.

In our AGA, the classical potentials are required to accurately describe only certain local configuration space regions so that it can capture the lowest-energy structures in the local basin under investigation. The AGA then investigates other local basins using different auxiliary potentials through the adaptive process. *Transferable* classical potentials are not required in the AGA search. Accurate classical potentials for different local configuration space can be fitted adaptively to the first-principles DFT results during the course of structure optimization. By iteratively adjusting the potentials parameters, the AGA search can explore various local basins in the configuration space effectively to locate the globally lowest-energy structures. In other words, the AGA can obtain a set of best candidate structures from each local basin (through the adaptive auxiliary potentials). Then, all the candidate structures from different basins are collected and evaluated by first-principles calculations to locate the globally best structures. Therefore the AGA is ready to apply to any systems of interested.

To validate of the power and accuracy of the AGA method for predicting the structures of Zr-Co systems, we performed the AGA search for Zr-Co alloys at selected compositions where the crystal structures are known. The adaptive GA searches were performed using only the information of chemical composition without any other assumptions on the Bravais lattice type, its basis or its dimensions. We successfully reproduced the structures of all the known phases in the Zr-Co system.

3. Unraveling the Structural Mystery of Zr_2Co_{11} Polymorphs

It has been shown by experiments that Zr-Co alloy could be promising materials for high performance permanent magnet without rare-earth due to their high magnetic anisotropy. The magneto-crystalline anisotropy K of Zr_2Co_{11} is reported to be 1.1 MJ/m^3 and the Curie temperature is around 500 °C [7-9]. However, the crystal structure of Zr_2Co_{11} alloy remains elusive. Different experiments [10-15] suggested different crystal structures and the number of atoms in the unit cell proposed by experiments is also controversy, ranges from 16 to about 120 atoms. The uncertainty in the crystal structures greatly hinders further investigating and optimizing the structures and properties of the material for high quality permanent magnets.

Using the AGA method, we performed a systematic search to determine the low-energy atomistic structures for Zr_2Co_{11-x} alloys (with x=0.0, 0.5, 0.6, 0.8 respectively) with the number of atoms in the unit cell ranging from 16 to 150. The global structure optimizations were performed without any assumptions on the Bravais lattice type, its basis or its dimensions. From the AGA search, we predicted the lowest-energy structures for Zr_2Co_{11-x} up to 150 atoms per unit cell [3]. We note that the lowest-energy $ZrCo_{5.25}$ structure with 50 atoms/cell from our prediction is consistent with the low-temperature orthorhombic phase reported by Ivanova *et al.* [13, 14] and Zhang *et al.* [15]. Two of its three lattice parameters (a=4.68 Å, b=16.34Å) match well with the experimental values. The third lattice parameter along the c axis is 8.10 Å in our structure, which is about 1/3 of that in the experiment (24.2 Å). If we allow this monoclinic structure to repeat three times along the c-axis to define a new unit cell, we can obtain a structure as shown in Fig. 1 (a) with an almost orthorhombic cell containing 150 atoms with a=4.68Å, b=16.54Å, c=24.08Å, $\beta=\gamma=90°$ and $\alpha=90.09°$, after refinement using first-principles calculations. The simulated XRD pattern from this "orthorhombic" structure agrees well with the experimental data as can be seen from Fig. 1(b). From

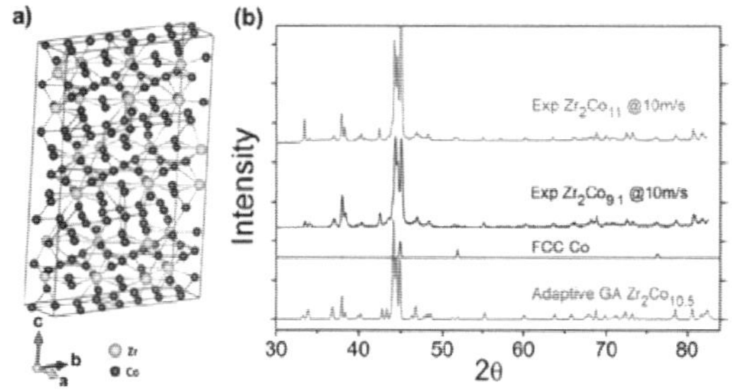

Fig. 1. ***(a)*** *Atomic structure of the 150 atom/cell "orthorhombic" phase predicted from our AGA search.* ***(b)*** *Comparison of simulated XRD spectrum from the predicted "orthorhombic" structure model (red) with experiments (black and green, 10m/s indicates the wheel speed). The blue line shows the XRD spectrum from fcc-Co structure.*

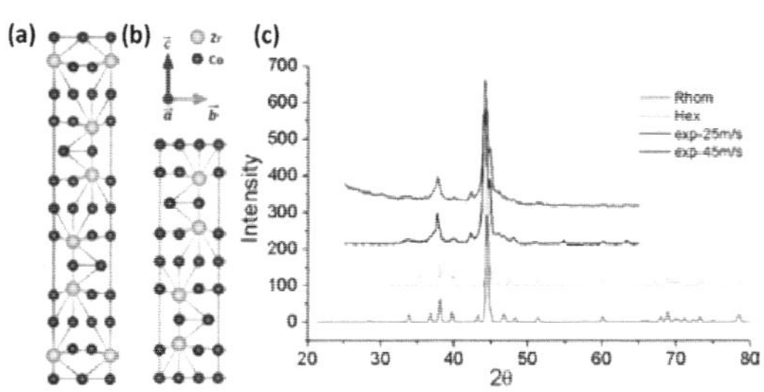

Fig. 2. *(a) The atomic structures of the (a) rhombohedral and (b) hexagonal polymorphs of Zr_2Co_{11} obtained from the AGA search. (c) shows the simulated XRD from the two structure in comparison with that from experimental rapid cooling samples.*

the AGA structure search, the complex atomic structures of the rhombohedral and hexagonal polymorphs of Zr_2Co_{11} intermetallic compound can also be obtained [3] as shown in Fig. 2. The simulated selected-area electron diffraction (SAED) patterns and high-resolution electron microscopy (HREM) images from the structure models predicted from our AGA are also in good agreement with experimental measurement.

4. Magnetic Properties of Zr_2Co_{11} Polymorphs

Using the atomic structures obtained from the AGA search, we carried out the all-electron full potential calculations to study the intrinsic magnetic properties of the Zr_2Co_{11} polymorphs. Results are listed in Table 1. The local density approximation (LDA) and generalized gradient approximations (GGA) were implemented with a generalization of the standard linear-muffin-tin-orbital (LMTO) basis set, where we used smoothed generalizations of Hankel functions for the envelope functions. For magnetic anisotropy energy (MAE) calculation, we also carried out the calculation with a "plane-wave+muffin-tin orbital" method [16] in which additional plane-waves are added into to the MTO basis to make the basis even more completed. The spin-orbit coupling is included in the calculations by traditional self-consistent solution of Pauli equation, which includes relativistic corrections of $1/c^2$ order. The MAE K is defined as $K=E_{100}-E_{001}$ (in a case of uniaxial MAE), where E_{001} and are the total energies with the spin quantization axis along [001] and [100] direction respectively. A positive K corresponds to a uniaxial, negative to a planar anisotropy. The integration over the Brillouin zone was done using the tetrahedron method with the Blöchl's correction. Very dense k meshes have been used to ensure a good convergence of MAE. For example, we used a 24x24x6 k-mesh for the hexagonal structure with 24 atoms in the unit cell. (It changed by less than 2% when the mesh was increased to 32x32x8 divisions).

The pairwise exchange coupling parameters J_{ij} have been obtained using a static linear response approach with Green's function (GF) method within the atomic spheres approximation (ASA) to LDA. Details can be found in Ref. [17]. In addition to making a spherical approximation to the potential, this method makes the long-wave approximation, so that the pair exchange parameters are proportional to the pair spin susceptibility. Once the magnetic part of the Hamiltonian is mapped to the Heisenberg model, the Curie temperature (T_C) is calculated using the mean-field approximation [18].

Our calculations revealed that both rhombohedral and hexagonal phases have rather high MAE, which compared satisfactorily with experimental data (see Table 1). To analyze the origin of MAE we used a

Table 1. *Calculated magnetic property of the structure models (M: magnetic moment; K: magnetic anisotropy energy; Tc: Curie temperature). GGA results are shown in the bracket.*

Structure	M (μ_B/atom)	K		T_c (K)
		(μeV/atom)	**(MJ/m^3)**	
Orthorhombic $ZrCo_{5.25}$	1.05 [1.07]	50 [42]	0.64 [0.54]	950
$ZrCo_5$ (Ni_5Zr type)	1.09[1.12]	~ 0	~ 0	1063
Rhombohedral (R32)	0.92[1.01]	81[111]	1.04 [1.42]	709
Hexagonal (P-62c)	0.94[1.01]	103 [104]	1.32 [1.33]	688

perturbative approach suggested in Ref. [19]. It is expected to be applicable in our case because the exchange splitting (1 eV) is much larger than the spin-orbit coupling energy (0.05eV) in Co-rich magnets. In this approach MAE is related to Δ, the sum of the atomic magnetic anisotropy energy (AMAE), which can be defined on each site as: $\Delta_i = \xi_i\, m_i(L_i^{001} - L_i^{100})/4$, where ξ_i is the spin-orbit coupling parameter, m_i and L_i are respectively the spin and orbital magnetic moments on site *i* . The orbital magnetic moment on Zr site is very small and variation with spin rotation can be neglected. For simplicity, here we used atomic parameter ξ =50 meV for Co atom to estimate Δ. In both the hexagonal and rhombohedral structures, there is a strong correlation between the variances of K and Δ during the spin rotation process. For all structures we investigated, the easy axis directions is always parallel to the spin quantization direction corresponding to the largest orbital moment. While this result is qualitative, calculation of AMAE using this model produces a rather good agreement with total MAE. This result advocate that the origin of large MAE in these materials is due to spin-orbit coupling and is related to enhancement of orbital moment on Co atoms along 001 direction. Thus these high magnetic anisotropy structures can be considered as hard magnetic phases due to their intrinsic magnetic properties.

5. Summary

In summary, we showed that the adaptive genetic algorithm method gives a convincing solution of the long-standing structural mystery in the Zr_2Co_{11} compounds which allows us to elucidate the physical origin of high coercivity observed in this system and provides useful insight guiding further development of these materials for use as high performance permanent magnets without rare earth elements. Resolving complicated atomistic structures with up to 150 atoms per cell by a first-principle computational approach in such a complex multiple-phase system demonstrated a new capability to aid the efficient materials discovery through the use of state-of-the-art supercomputers.

Acknowledgements

We are grateful to Dr. Iver E. Anderson and Dr. R. William McCallum for useful discussions. This work was supported by the US Department of Energy - Energy Efficiency and Renewable Energy, Vehicles Technology Office, PEEM program, and by the US Department of Energy, Basic Energy Sciences, and Division of Materials Science and Engineering, under Contract No. DE-AC02-07CH11358 for the operation of Ames Laboratory (USDOE). This research used resources of the National Energy Research Scientific Computing Center through the NISE program, which is supported by the Office of Science of the U.S. Department of Energy under Contract No.DE-AC02-05CH11231.

References

1. S. Q. Wu, M. Ji, C. Z. Wang, M. C. Nguyen, K. Umemoto, R. M. Wentzcovitch, K. M. Ho, *J. Phys. Condens. Matt.* **26**, 035402 (2014).
2. Min Ji, K. Umemoto, C. Z. Wang, K. M. Ho and R. M. Wentzcovitch,, Phys. Rev. B **84**, 220105(R) (2011).
3. X. Zhao, M. C. Nguyen, W. Y. Zhang, C. Z. Wang, M. J. Kramer, D. J. Sellmyer, X. Z. Li, F. Zhang, L. Q. Ke, V. P. Antropov and K. M. Ho, Phys. Rev. Lett. **112**, 045502 (2014).
4. Xin Zhao, Qiang Shu, Manh Cuong Nguyen, Yangang Wang, Min Ji, Hongjun Xiang, Kai-Ming Ho, Xingao Gong, and Cai-Zhuang Wang, J. Phys. Chem. C **118**, 9524-9530 (2014).
5. Manh Cuong Nguyen, Xin Zhao, Min Ji, Cai-Zhuang Wang, Bruce Harmon, and Kai-Ming Ho, J. *Appl. Phys.*, **111**, 07E338 (2012).
6. M. C. Nguyen, L. Q. Ke, X. Zhao, V. P. Antropov, C. Z. Wang, KM Ho, IEEE TRANSACTIONS ON MAGNETICS, **49**, 3281 (2013).
7. T. Ishikawa and K. Ohmori, IEEE Trans. Magn. **26** (5), 1370-1372 (1990).
8. E. Burzo, R. Grossinger, P. Hundegger, et al., J. Appl. Phys. **70** (10, Part I), 6550-6552 (1991).
9. A. M. Gabay, Y. Zhang, and G. C. Hadjipanayis, J. Magn. Magn. Mater. **236** (1-2), 37-41 (2001).
10. K. H. J. Buschow, J. H. Wernick and G. Y. Chin, J. Less-Common. Met. **59**, 61(1978).
11. K. H. J. Buschow, J. Appl. Phys. **53**, 7713 (1982).
12. B. G. Demczyk and S. F. Cheng, J. Appl. Cryst. **24**, 1023-1026 (1991).
13. G. V. Ivanova, N.N. Shchegoleva, A.M. Gabay, J. Alloys Compd. **432**, 135-141 (2007).
14. G. V. Ivanova and N. N. Shchegoleva, The Physics of Metals and Metallography, vol. **107**, No. 3, pp. 270-275, (2009).
15. W. Y. Zhang *et al.*, J. Phys. D: Appl. Phys. **46**, 135004 (2013).
16. T. Kotani, and M. van Schilfgaarde, Phys. Rev. B **81**, 125117 (2010).
17. M. van Schilfgaarde, and V. P. Antropov, J. Appl. Phys. **85**, 4827 (1999).
18. P. W. Anderson, Theory of Magnetic Exchange Interactions: Exchange in Insulators and Semiconductors, edited by F. Seitz, and D. Turnbull, (Academic Press, 1963), vol. 14 of Solid State Physics, pp. 99 – 214.
19. R. Streever, Phys. Rev. B **19**, 2704 (1979).

Better (Non)Rare-Earth Magnets – Using DFT Methods as a Computational Design Tool for Replacing Critical Materials

D.D. JOHNSON,[1,2] A. ALAM,[3] A. PATHAK,[1] V. PECHARSKY,[1,2] K. GSCHNEIDNER, JR.,[1,2] R.W. McCALLUM[1,2]
[1]Division of Materials Science & Engineering, Ames Laboratory, 311 TASF, Iowa State University, Ames, IA, 50011, USA
[2]Department of Materials Science & Engineering, Iowa State University, Ames, IA, 50011, USA
[3]Department of Physics, Indian Institute of Technology, Bombay, Powai, Mumbai 400 076, India

Abstract: *We provide an overview of improving magnet alloys and compounds and lowering their cost using materials theory and computational assessment of magnetic properties and materials stability for elemental reduction and/or substitution. Examples include key insights to desired properties and some experimental validation. Like all materials, defects and disorder often play an important role – and processing matters, such as adding small amounts of material to drive grain refinement!*

Keywords: *materials design; computational; DFT; experiment*

1. Introduction

Over the past few decades, $R_2Fe_{14}B$ permanent magnet compounds (with R a rare-earth element) achieved significant technological impact due to their high-energy products $(BH)_{max}$ at room temperature. Partly accomplished by resolving many materials issues, including grain refinement and magnetic domain boundaries effects, which relied on expensive ("rarer") rare-earth elements, such as Dy to protect against magnetization reversal at the surface of the grain which then engulfs the whole grain. However, at higher temperatures, those surpassing current operational temperatures of automotive traction motors, the coercivity declines dramatically. A well-known patent by Hitachi (its life now ended) was broad, encompassing additions of all transition-metal elements (TMs), for example, but never provided improved compounds, nor reduction in rare-earth content.

Revisiting $(R\text{-Ce})_2(\text{Fe-}M)_{14}B$ systems (R=Nd,La and M=3*d* metals), for example: Can density functional theory (DFT) methods *assessing carefully chosen design metrics (and trends)*, in combination with experimental synthesis and processing design, be used as a reliable guide to engineer new magnetic materials that have less or no (currently) critical elements but with equal engineering performance to current higher-cost magnets?

In short, yes. The oral presentation provided direct protocols and examples for a one-to-one connection to experiment, as a guide and "handshake" for validation. Specifically, computational design goals require reliably *reducing materials selection space by facilitating choice of alloy additions and composite structures/materials to enhance the performance needs*. The design metrics must make direct "handshake" between theory and experiment, and, more importantly, establish <u>accurate trends</u>, not necessarily quantitative values, for metrics.

2. Design Metrics

For better magnets, the design metrics are reflected in minimally four quantities that can be ascertained in experiment typically and must be provided by theory (not possible by all methods), namely:

(1) Saturation magnetization, M_s: [1 - 4 μ_B]

(2) Alloy formation energy (or enthalpy), ΔE_f: [1 - $100 \cdot 10^{-3}$ *m*eV]

(3) Curie temperature, T_C: [1 - $100 \cdot 10^{-3}$ *m*eV]

(4) Coercivity, H_c (really MAE, as $H_c \sim H_a \sim$ MAE): [1 - $1000 \cdot 10^{-6}$ *m*eV],

where H_a is the anisotropy field, and MAE is the *ideal* magneto-anisotropy energy, which can be calculated in DFT (albeit some oft-used approximations are invalid in some systems, such as MnBi). Clearly, M_s identifies trends in magnetization of a material (*the bigger, the better*); ΔE_f, provides information about thermodynamic stability, site preference for alloying elements, valency of rare-earths, etc. (*the more stable a favorable configuration, the better*); T_C reveals the stability of the preferred ferromagnetic state (the bigger, the better); and, finally, H_c dictates how stable the magnetic state is upon field reversal (*the bigger, the better)*. In the list above, the bracketed numbers provide a typical range for the quantities per atom.

3. Fast Estimations Required for Trends

Notably, H_c is a complex entity, dependent on domain boundaries (magnetic structure) and on intrinsic H_a or

MAE; in principle spin-dynamics simulations based upon DFT (magnet structures) could "predict" H_c. *But, this is not the fast "engineering" design estimate needed.* Better is a simple, empirical guide, as evidenced from experiment for decades: $H_c \approx 25\% H_a = 25\%$ (2 MAE / M_s). This rapid estimate provides rapid and reliable (almost quantitative) estimates – accurate trends, which is all that is required for design. Thus, using DFT to calculate MAE (already tricky in some cases) provides quick estimates of a very complex quantity. Hence, we can use DFT (DFT+U) to provide high-throughput assessment of design metrics (1) – (4) and assess accurate trends when changing material or alloying, for example, see [1-4] for details.

4. DFT Methodology

We employ two DFT methods to address alloying, spin-orbit ($L \cdot S$), and electron-correlation (Hubbard U) effects. The exchange-correlation is based upon local spin-density approximation (LSDA) or generalized gradient approximation (GGA), usually one developed by Perdew-Burke-Ernzerhof (PBE). We apply *Vienna ab initio simulation package* (VASP) with a pseudo-potential and projected-augmented wave (PAW) basis [5,6]. To address localized *f*-electrons in rare-earth systems, we use DFT+U with U introduced within a screened Hartree-Fock representation [7], as an on-site LSDA replacement. Spin-orbit coupling to the lattice of the hybridized R(4*f*)-Fe(3*d*) level is stronger than that for Fe(3*d*). VASP cannot address chemical disorder intrinsic to partially ordered alloys or solid solutions. Thus, we use an all-electron Korringa-Kohn-Rostoker (KKR) Green's function electronic-structure code [8] combined with the coherent potential approximation (CPA) to address the alloying, stability and site preference in homogeneously disordered, partially ordered, and perfectly ordered cases [9,10]. Details of the KKR-CPA calculation, especially T_C estimation can be found elsewhere [4]. The T_C is estimated using only the itinerant electron contributions, not those from the localized rare-earth moments, which would effectively contribute a constant shift to the estimate. The difference of the total energy per atom of the paramagnetic state (approximated by uncorrelated moments in a disordered local moment state) to that of the ferromagnetic state provides reliable T_C estimates for transition-metal alloys and excellent trends for rare-earth-based magnets.

5. Results: Reducing Rare-Earth Content

As a first pass, DFT methods were used to assess stability and properties for Ce-alloying in $Nd_2Fe_{14}B$ to create not a rare-earth-free magnet but use a readily available (almost "free") rare earth, i.e., cheaper Ce, to decrease Nd content. Note that $Nd_2Fe_{14}B$ has a 68-atom cell defining the structure [1,11]. Before experiments were completed, DFT results were used to provide validation of methods and "trust" factor for trends when providing future guidance.

First, DFT predictions for Ce site preference in $(La\text{-}Ce)_2Fe_{14}B$ was used as validation, as experiments have identified smaller R(4*f*) sites as preferred by Ce, easily justified by atomic size. Indeed, the La-Ce solid solution was weakly stable (as observed) with Ce preferring the smaller R(4*f*) sites [1]. Figure 1 shows that formation energy ΔE_f for $(Nd\text{-}Ce)_2Fe_{14}B$, based upon a rapid scan of favorability for Ce substitution and site preferences. Ce prefers the larger R(4*g*) sites, a trend also explained from atomic size effects. In the 2-14-1 structure, R(4*f*) sites are smaller in volume than R(4*g*); as such, a bigger (smaller) atom prefers the large (smaller) site, and Ce^{3+} ion is smaller than La^{3+} but larger than Nd^{3+}. Notably, when Co is doped on the Fe sublattices, atomic size effects and local chemistry then influence the Ce valence in the alloyed compound [3].

Clearly from Fig. 1, Nd-Ce 2-14-1 solid solutions are unfavorable, except at higher temperature processing (entropy). Before assessing ordered phases, how well is T_C predicted for the solid solutions developed via melting spinning and annealing? Figure 2 shows T_C versus x in $(Nd_{1-x}Ce_x)_2Fe_{14}B$, addressing only the itinerant electron moments via KKR-CPA results within a disordered local moment mean-field theory (MFT). Predictions are compared to in-house measurements, as well as the trend when KKR-CPA results are shifted by a constant (175 K), reflecting the neglect of 4*f* contributions. The trends are quantitative with experiment! Nonetheless, a 5% reduction in T_C

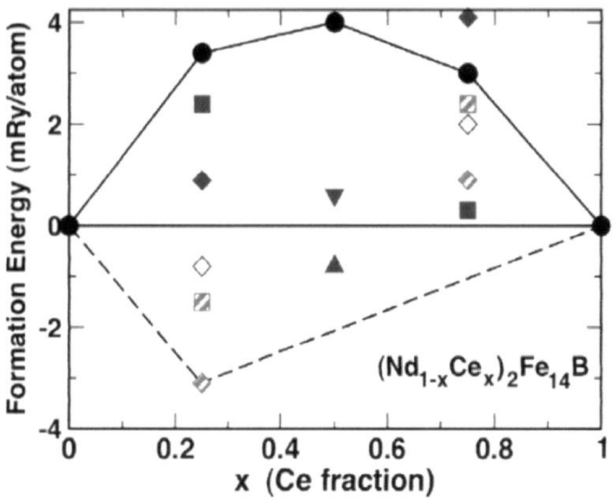

Fig. 1. ΔE_f vs. x for $(Nd,Ce)_2Fe_{14}B$. Negative (positive) values reflect favorable (unfavorable) stability for alloying. Circles are Nd-Ce solid solutions; solid symbols are partially ordered configurations; hatched symbols show an ordered configuration. Adapted from Ref. 1. Maxwell construction (dashed lines) shows only Nd-rich systems should be considered. Detailed calculations from 16 - 25% Ce show partially ordered states are favored at 20% Ce (Fig. 3).

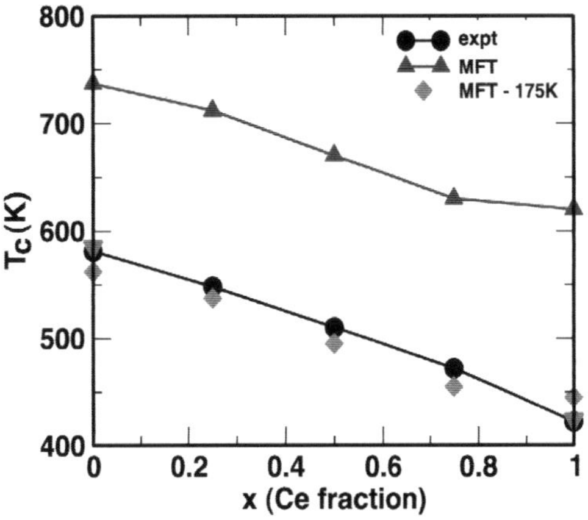

Fig. 2. T_C vs x for $(Nd,Ce)_2Fe_{14}B$ solid solution. Adapted from Ref. 1.

with 20% Ce is unavoidable, albeit still acceptable for operation conditions of most automotive traction motors.

In Fig. 1, by Maxwell construction, only Nd-rich systems should be considered as thermodynamically favored. Preliminary calculations (Fig. 3) show that specific partially ordered states from 15 - 30% Ce within a larger period supercell are more favored thermodynamically and entropically, with 20% Ce most favored. Details are presented elsewhere [12].

6. Mixed Valency and Co-doping

Interestingly, Ce exhibits a *mixed valence* with a valence of 3.53 determined from spectroscopy. We have predicted 3.5 by treating Ce 3+ and 4+ as "alloying" elements and performing direct configurational average over all possible arrangements on the R(4*f*) and R(4*g*) sites in the 68-atom cell [3]. In addition, doping Fe sublattice with Co does enhance magnetic properties, but Co occupies Fe sites, so-called Fe(k2), Fe(j1) and Fe(c) sites, see [**Error! Bookmark not defined.**], that surround the Ce favored R(4*g*) sites. However, Co atoms do not like to be adjacent to each other, reducing the possible fractional occupation. So, it is predicted that 20% Ce provides optimal reduction of Nd expected to be favorable, and about 10 - 20% Co on the Fe sublattice to maintain/enhance magnetic properties.

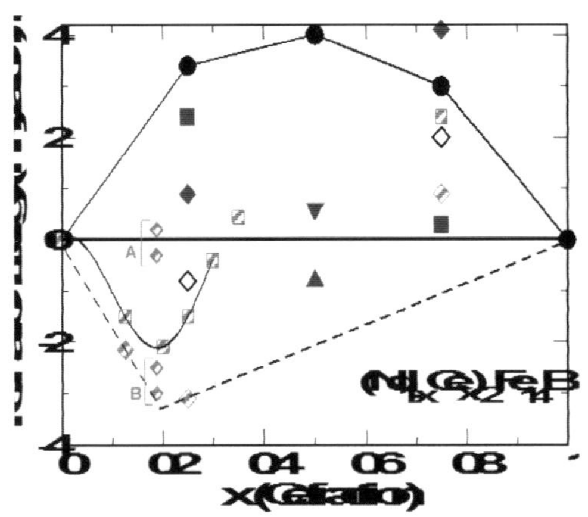

Fig. 3. Extension of ΔE_f vs. x in Fig. 1. Hatched symbols connected by solid line are partially ordered states with minimum at 20%Ce and favored by entropy.

How well does this agree with reality? Samples of $(Nd\text{-}Ce)_2Fe_{14}B$ and $(Nd\text{-}Ce)_2(Fe\text{-}Co)_{14}B$ were prepared as melt-spun ribbons and partially aligned in epoxy, and their magnetic hysteresis versus applied field ($4\pi M$ versus H) were measured. Importantly, no Dy was used to protect from domain reorientation, however, ZrC was used as a grain refiner during processing. As apparent from Fig. 4 comparison to pure $Nd_2Fe_{14}B$, Ce-only alloying has increased coercivity by 20%, with small decrease in remnant

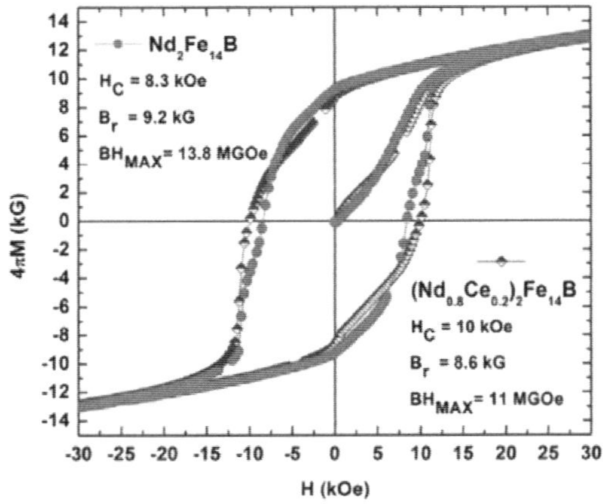

Fig. 4. Compared to pure $Nd_2Fe_{14}B$, $4\pi M$ versus H for $(Nd_{0.8}Ce_{0.2})_2Fe_{14}B$. H_c has increased 20%, B_r has decreased 7%, and $(BH)_{max}$ decreased by 10%.

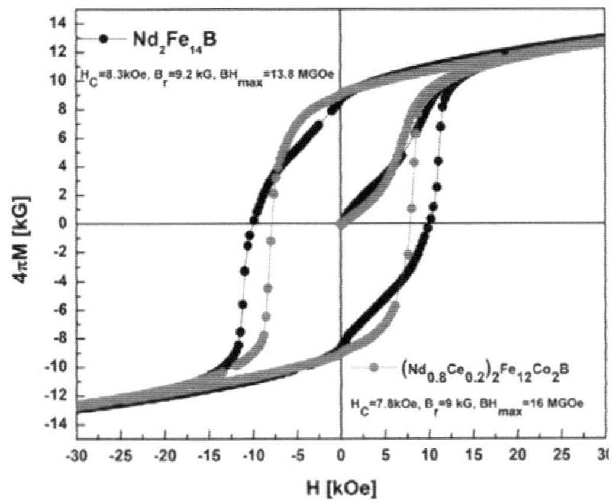

Fig. 5. Compare to pure $Nd_2Fe_{14}B$, $4\pi M$ versus H for $(Nd_{0.8}Ce_{0.2})_2Fe_{12}Co_2B$. H_c improved 20%, $(BH)_{max}$ improved 16%, and B_r is unchanged.

field and $(BH)_{max}$. However, from Fig. 5, increases are found in coercivity by 20% and $(BH)_{max}$ by 16%, with remnant field unchanged. Grain refinement was found to be a critical component of the treatment, and additional Co or Ce degrades the magnetic properties.

7. Conclusion

As should be now clear, computationally guided design using DFT-based methods with clearly defined metrics to predict trends has indeed help produce new magnets with a 20% reduction in expensive rare-earth with enhanced magnetic behavior found by further alloying on the 3*d*-metal sublattices, respecting that Co abhors Co neighbors while preferring Ce neighbors. Having DFT-based methods that can address disorder (not by ordered supercells, [13]) and thermodynamics (stability and Curie points) is key! Similar scans can be done in non-rare-earth systems, like MnBi [14,15].

Acknowledgements
This research was supported by the U.S. Department of Energy, Advanced Research Projects Agency - Energy (REACT Program) under contract 0472-1526 for Ce-based efforts, and contract 0472-1549 for MnBi efforts.

References

[1] A. Alam, M. Khan, R. W. McCallum, and D. D. Johnson, *Appl. Phys. Lett.* **102**, 2013, 042402.
[2] Supplementary material for "U" dependence of magnetic moments and further computational and experimental details is available at http://dx.doi.org/10.1063/1.4789527
[3] A. Alam and D. D. Johnson, *Phys. Rev. B* **89**, 2014, 235126.
[4] A. Alam, B. Kraczek, D. D. Johnson, *Phys. Rev. B* 82, 2010, 024435.
[5] G. Kresse, J. Furthmüller, *Phys. Rev. B* **54**, 1996, 11169; *Comput. Mater. Sci. B* **6**, 1996, 15.
[6] G. Kresse and D. Joubert, *Phys. Rev. B* **59**, 1999, 1758.
[7] A. I. Liechtenstein, V. I. Anisimov, and J. Zaanen, *Phys. Rev. B* **52**, 1995, R5467.
[8] D.D. Johnson, A. Alam, A.V. Smirnov, *MECCA: Multiple-Scattering Electronic-Structure Calculations for Complex Alloys*, KKR-CPA Program, Version 1.9, University of Illinois, 2008.
[9] D. D. Johnson, D. M. Nicholson, F. J. Pinski, B. L. Gyorffy, and G. M. Stocks, *Phys. Rev. Lett.* **56**, 1986, 2088; *Phys. Rev. B* **41**, 1990, 9701.
[10] Aftab Alam and D. D. Johnson, *Phys. Rev. B* **80**, 2009, 125123.
[11] J.F. Herbst, J.J. Croat, F.E. Pinkerton, and W.B. Yellon, *Phys. Rev. B* **29**, 1984, 4176.
[12] Aftab Alam and D.D. Johnson, in preparation.
[13] Aftab Alam and D. D. Johnson, *Phys. Rev. Lett.* 107, 2011, 206401.
[14] N.A. Zarkevich, L.-L. Wang, and D.D. Johnson, *APL Mater.* **2**, 2014, 032103.
[15] L.-L. Wang, N.A. Zarkevich, Y. Ye, M.J. Kramer and D.D. Johnson, in preparation.

New Rare Earth Lean Permanent Magnets by the Application of High-Throughput Methods

D. GOLL, J. HERBST, R. KARIMI, R. LOEFFLER, U. PFLANZ, R. STEIN, G. SCHNEIDER
Aalen University, Materials Research Institute, Beethovenstr. 1, 73430 Aalen, Germany

Abstract: *By high-throughput methods so far unexplored alloy systems can be searched for new permanent magnet phases with reasonable effort. The efficient synthesis methods utilize heterogeneous non-equilibrium states. The efficient analysis methods use the characteristic domain structures of the phases to estimate the magnetic properties of permanent magnets based on these phases. The high-throughput methods are shown to work properly to mine for novel permanent magnet phases with RE elements of better availability, smaller amount and free of RE metal.*

Keywords: *high-throughput approach; novel hard magnetic phases; RE lean permanent magnets*

Address: Dagmar Goll, Materials Research Institute, Aalen University, Beethovenstr. 1, 73430 Aalen, Germany, Tel: +49 7361 576-2187, E-mail: dagmar.goll@htw-aalen.de

1. Introduction

For efficient energy conversion in high-power motor and generator applications magnets as strong as Fe-Nd-B supermagnets, yet in combination with cost-effectiveness and longevity, are required. In consideration of the fact that the number of so far unexplored alloy systems is rather large (the total number of systems resulting from 4 transition metals (TM: Fe, Co, Ni, Mn), 7 rare earth metals (RE: La, Ce, Y, Pr, Nd, Sm, Dy) and 41 additives (X) by combinatorics is 1,000,000), there is big hope that such a material still can be discovered.

Previously, the authors have developed an elaborate concept to systematically mine for novel permanent magnet phases with success within a reasonable time frame [1,2]. The strategy of this multilevel bulk high-throughput approach is three-fold and composed of the following steps:

(1) Prioritization step: To handle one million systems a prioritization procedure has been developed. The procedure is based on the fact that the probability of a ternary or higher component system to form intermetallic compounds is larger when its boundary systems form already numerous intermediate phases. For ranking the systems this phase index can be additionally combined with the raw materials cost index and other physical principles. The prioritization step results in about 1000 hot candidates to mine for novel hard magnetic phases.

(2) Efficient synthesis step: To scan quickly through the systems of the prioritization list, an appropriate high-throughput synthesis method is needed. Using diffusion couples one sample is enough to cover the most relevant part of the corresponding phase diagram. Diffusion couples are based on the formation of concentration gradients between different elements due to thermodynamically guided diffusion processes.

(3) Efficient analysis step: To decide quickly whether so far unknown systems contain novel permanent magnet phases an appropriate high-throughput analysis method is comparably crucial. Using the typical stripe domain patterns of hard magnetic materials allows both direct visualization of the hard magnetic compounds and estimation of the corresponding intrinsic magnetic properties to evaluate the expected industrial relevance.

Once an interesting novel hard magnetic phase has been discovered it has to be synthesized in larger volumes. In the final step an optimal processing route is required to process the novel phase into a bulk permanent magnet. The focus of the paper is the application of the bulk high-throughput approach to search for novel high-performance permanent magnet materials with significantly reduced expensive RE content.

2. Development of Efficient Synthesis and Analysis for Ternary Fe-Nd-B

The efficiency of high-throughput synthesis and analysis which is described in detail in [2] is now demonstrated for known ternary Fe-Nd-B. For efficient synthesis a Fe reaction crucible is charged with a mixture of Nd and B granules. During isothermal aging (~1000 °C) and cooling intermetallic phases between melt composition and the crucible material and additionally by thermodynamic equilibria are formed.

Independent of the solidification path all ternary

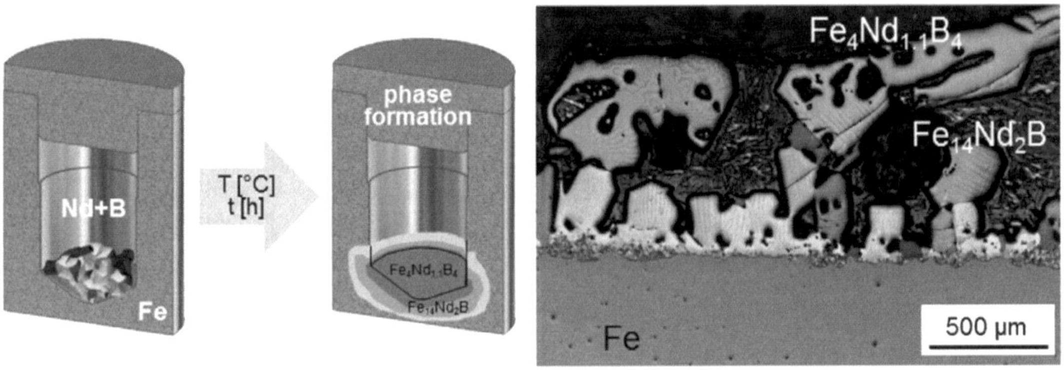

Fig. 1. Efficient synthesis for Fe-Nd-B.

intermetallic phases in the Fe-rich corner of the phase diagram, i.e. $Fe_{14}Nd_2B$ (ϕ) and $Fe_4Nd_{1.1}B_4$ (η) in the case of Fe-Nd-B occur (Fig. 1).

For efficient analysis various microscopy techniques are combined to identify all phases present (optical microscopy), to identify hard magnetic phases via their stripe and/or closure-type domain pattern (Kerr microscopy) and to determine their chemical composition (scanning electron microscopy / energy dispersive X-ray analysis). Additionally by quantitative image analysis the intrinsic magnetic material parameters can be obtained from the domain patterns (Fig. 2). The domain width is a measure for the anisotropy constant. The domain contrast is a measure for the saturation polarization. Using a hot stage in the microscopy from the temperature dependence of the domain pattern even the Curie temperature is achieved. The intrinsic material parameters estimated for Fe-Nd-B from the domain pattern are in good agreement to existing literature data.

3. Application to Find Novel Phases

The high-throughput approach has currently been applied successfully to novel systems with RE elements of greater availability and/or smaller contained RE amounts, but also to completely RE free systems. This is shown in the following for different systems.

A. Novel ternary Fe-Ce-X based magnets

For Fe-Ce-Zr one in literature so far unknown quasibinary ferromagnetic compound with uniaxial anisotropy could be found. The compound is judged to be $Fe_3(Zr,Ce)$ crystallizing in the hexagonal Ni_3Pu

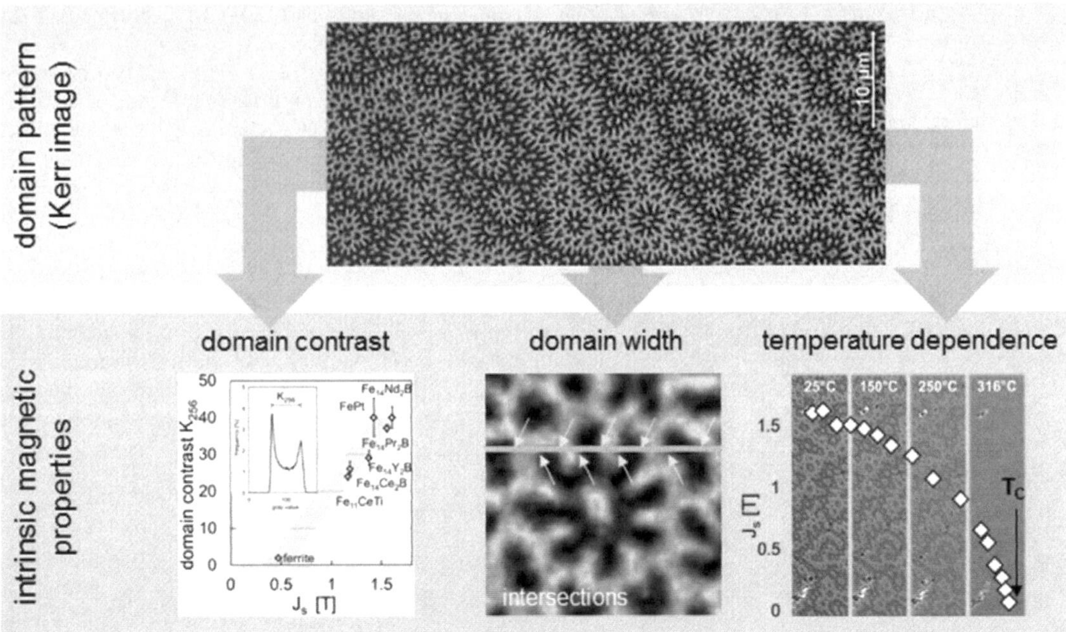

Fig. 2. Efficient analysis for Fe-Nd-B.

Fig. 3. Kerr microscopy image of novel compound with composition $Fe_{75.8}Zr_{13.9}Ce_{10.3}$ [$Fe_3(Zr,Ce)$] and uniaxial domain structure.

structure type (Fig. 3). This is supported by literature data where Fe_3RE and $Fe_3(Zr,RE)$ compounds are known to form. However, so far this compound was only reported with heavy RE elements [3,4]. The intrinsic magnetic properties of $Fe_3(Zr,Ce)$ as determined from domain structure analysis of the stripe domains are at least $J_s = 0.6$ T and $K_1 = 0.5$ MJ/m^3.

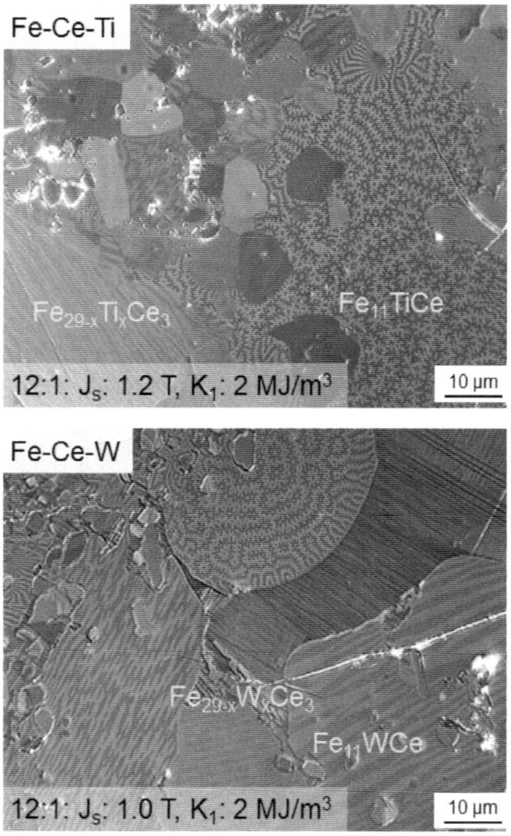

Fig. 4. Ternary Fe-Ti-Ce and Fe-Ti-W reaction crucibles showing 12:1 and 29:3 compounds.

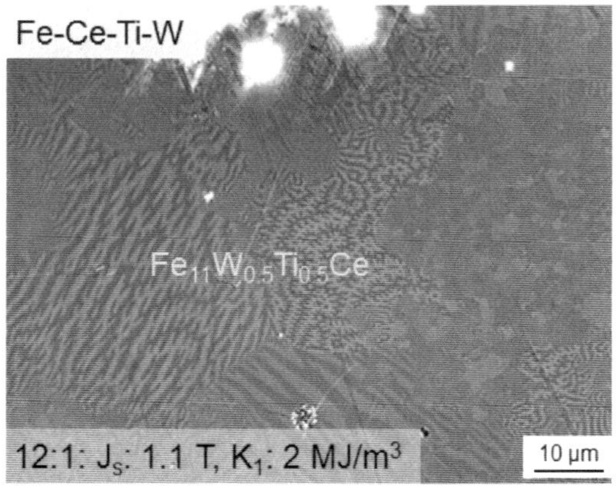

Fig. 5. Quaternary Fe-Ti-W-Ce reaction crucible.

For the system Fe-Ce-Ti the phases $Fe_{11}TiCe$ (12:1 structure) and $(Fe,Ti)_{29}Ce_3$ (29:3 structure) are known from literature [5-7]. However, for Fe-Ce-W the phases 12:1 and 29:3 so far have not been reported in literature. By high-throughput search it could be shown, that the two phases indeed form for Fe-Ce-W (Fig. 4). Compared to the intrinsic magnetic properties of $Fe_{11}TiCe$ ($J_s = 1.2$ T, $K_1 = 2$ MJ/m^3) the parameters of $Fe_{11}WCe$ amount to $J_s = 1$ T and $K_1 = 2$ MJ/m^3, respectively. For the 29:3 in both cases smaller values are found ($J_s \sim 0.5$ T, $K_1 \sim 0.5$ MJ/m^3). From Fig. 4 it becomes obvious that all phases occurring in the system coexist in one sample.

B. Novel quaternary Fe-Ce-X1-X2 based magnets

By mixing well-known Fe-Ce-Ti with Fe-Ce-W the quaternary system Fe-Ce-Ti-W is obtained. Using such a mixture crucible the intrinsic material parameters for all kind of Ti-W mixtures can be investigated in one sample at differrent locations. In Fig. 5 the $Fe_{11}Ti_{0.5}W_{0.5}Ce$ phase is shown. From the domain pattern shown values of the intrinsic magnetic properties of $J_s = 1.1$ T and $K_1 = 2$ MJ/m^3 have been estimated. For a reaction crucible Fe-(Co,Ti,Ce) the novel quarternary compounds $Fe_{11-x}Co_xTiCe$ and $Fe_{28-x}Co_xTiCe_3$ with a Co content of 2.5 at.% have been detected (Fig. 6). The 12:1 phase also here shows much larger values for domain contrast and domain width resulting in $J_s = 1.25$ T and $K_1 = 2$ MJ/m^3. For the 29:3 phase intrinsic magnetic parameters of $J_s = 0.5$ T and $K_1 = 0.4$ MJ/m^3 are received.

C. High-throughput approach on RE-free systems

The high-throughput approach also works for RE free systems as demonstrated in Fig. 7 for Mn-Bi and Fe-Pt. In the diffusion couples used, the hard magnetic $Mn_{50}Bi_{50}$ and $L1_0$-$Fe_{50}Pt_{50}$ are formed.

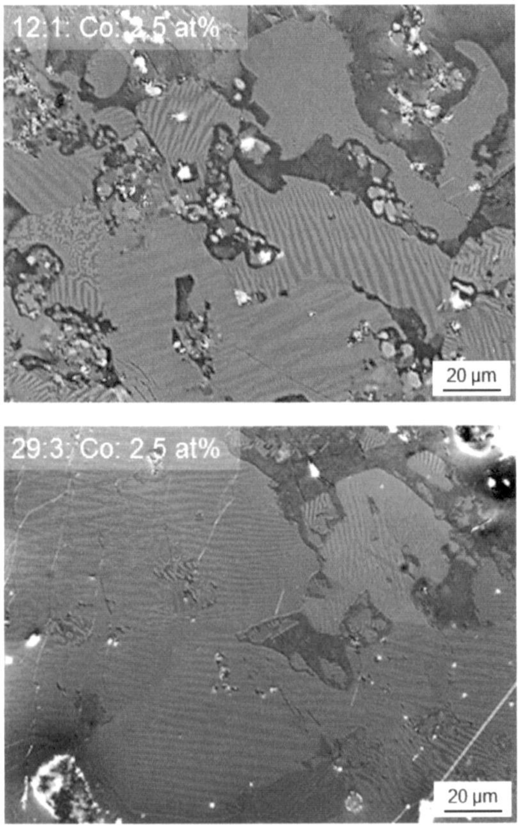

Fig. 6. Quaternary Fe-Ti-Co-Ce reaction crucible showing novel 12:1 and 29:3 hard magnetic phases.

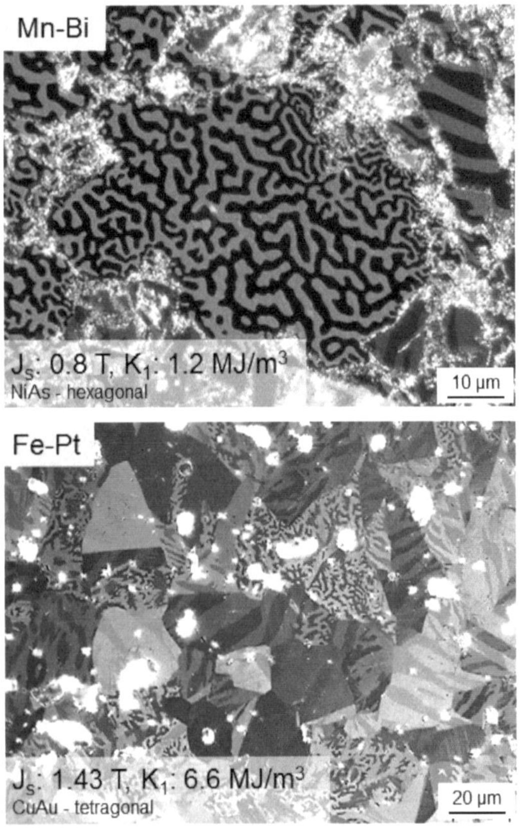

Fig. 7. Test of high-throughput approach on well-known RE-free systems Mn-Bi and Fe-Pt.

4. Conclusions

The high-throughput approaches for efficient synthesis and analysis of hard magnetic phases are established. By applying the high-throughput approaches search in about 450 different systems is completed and some interesting candidates of novel hard magnetic phases have been found (~ 50 RE-containing, ~ 10 RE-free systems).

Acknowledgement

The authors thank Carl Zeiss Microscopy, for providing special microscopy equipment. The authors acknowledge fruitful discussions with Fraunhofer IWM, MPI Intelligent Systems, Robert Bosch GmbH and Magnetfabrik Bonn. The work was funded by the German Federal Ministry of Education and Research.

References

[1] A. Luedtke, B. Stahl, I.R. Harris, G. Schneider, in: *Proc. 16th Int. Workshop on RE Magnets and their Applications*, The Japan Institute of Metals, 2000, p. 291.

[2] D. Goll, R. Loeffler, J. Herbst, R. Karimi, G. Schneider, *J. Phys.: Condens. Matter* **26**, 2014, 064208.

[3] K. Itoh, T. Okagaki, K. Kanematsu, *J. Phys. Soc. Jpn.* **58**, 1989, 1787.

[4] F. Stein, G. Sauthoff, and M. Palm, *J. Phase Equilibria* **23**, 2002, 480.

[5] M. Akayama, H. Fujii, K. Yamamoto, K. Tatami, *J. Magn. Magn. Mater.* **130**, 1994, 99.

[6] Q. Pan, Z.X. Liu, Y.C. Yang, *J. Appl. Phys.* **76**, 1994, 6728.

[7] W.A. Mendoza, S.A. Saheen, *J. Magn. Magn. Mater.* **195**, 1999, 136.

Magnetic Hardening Mechanism of Hard Magnetic Nanoparticles Prepared by Surfactant-assisted Ball Milling

M. Yue[1], Y. Q. Li [1], Q. Wu [1], W. Q. Liu [1], D. T. Zhang [1], M. L. Xu [1], Z. H. Guo [2], W. Li [2]
[1] College of Materials Science and Engineering, Beijing University of Technology, Beijing 100124, China
[2] Division of Functional Materials, Central Iron and Steel Research Institute, Beijing, 100081, China

Abstract: *In the present study, R-Fe-B (R=Nd, Dy, Tb), Sm-Co, Sm-Fe-N, and MnBi nanoparticles were prepared via Surfactant-assisted ball milling (SABM), and the effect of particle size on coercivity were discussed. For R-Fe-B and Sm-Co nanoparticles, the coercivity decreased with deceasing particle size; however, the coercivty of SmFeN and MnBi nanoparticle increases first and then decreased as the particle size decrease. The magnetization behavior indicates that the magnetic hardening process was governed by pinning mechanism for R-Fe-B nanoparticles. However, for the Sm-Fe-N nanoparticles, the magnetic hardening changes from a pinning mechanism to a nucleation mechanism with decreasing particle size, being responsible for their abnormal size-dependent coercivity.*

Key words: *nanoparticles, coercivity, particle size, pinning mechanism, nucleation mechanism.*

Address: Ming Yue, College of Materials Science and Engineering, Beijing University of Technology, Beijing, 100124, China, Tel: (8610) 67391760, e-mail: yueming@bjut.edu.cn

1. Introduction

Recently, hard magnetic nanoparticles have drawn considerable attention due to their potential application in magnetic recording, drug delivery, and nanocomposite magnet [1]. Surfactant-assisted ball milling (SABM) technique possessing mass production capacity has been developed to prepare hard magnetic nanoparticles via a top-down approach [2-4]. It is found that the coercivity depends on both particle size and magneto-crystalline anisotropy. It is therefore of theoretical and practical value to study their magnetic hardening mechanism. In the present study, R-Fe-B (R=Nd, Dy, Tb), Sm-Co, Sm-Fe-N, and MnBi nanoparticles were prepared via SABM, and the effect of particle size on coercivity was discussed.

2. Experimental

$R_2Fe_{14}B$ (R=Nd, Dy, Tb), $SmCo_5$, and MnBi alloy ingots, as well as commercial $Sm_2Fe_{17}N_3$ magnetic powders were used as starting materials in the present study. These materials were ball milled with heptane as solvent and oleic acid as a surfactant, and the ball to power ratio is 10:1. After ball milling, the resultant slurry was then dispersed into heptane by ultrasonic vibration and transferred to centrifugal tubes for size selection, which was controlled by the time of settling down process. Structural and morphological characterizations of the samples were studied by using X-ray diffraction (XRD), scanning electron microscopy (SEM), and transmission electron microscopy (TEM). Size distribution of the samples was examined by a laser particle size analyzer (LPSA). Magnetic properties were measured with a physical properties measurement system (PPMS) magnetometer with a maximum magnetic field of 9 T. No demagnetization correction was made for all the samples in the magnetic measurements.

3. Result and Discussion

3.1. Structure analysis of the nanoparticles

Based on the size selection process applied in the current research, three batches of nanoparticles were obtained from milled slurry of each type of alloy, namely the small particles(SP), the big particles(BP), and the flakes. As an example, here we show the structure analysis of the $Sm_2Fe_{17}N_3$ nanoparticles. Fig. 1 show the micrographs of Sm-Fe-N alloy

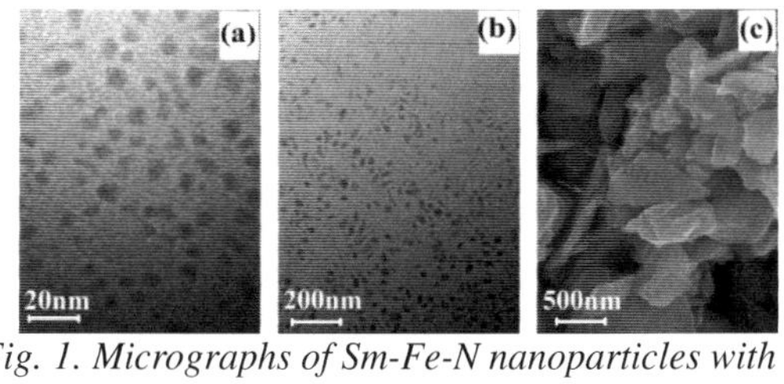

Fig. 1. Micrographs of Sm-Fe-N nanoparticles with (a) average particle size of 9.4 nm, (b) average particle size of 36.5 nm, and (c) flake-like ones with thickness of 60-80 nm and average length of 0.75 μm.

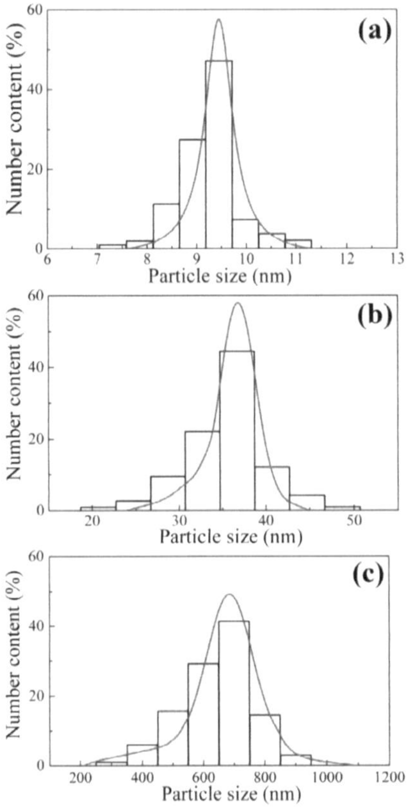

Fig. 2. Size distributions of $Sm_2Fe_{17}N_3$ nanoparticles of sample A: average particle size of 9.4 nm, sample B: average particle size of 36.5 nm, and sample C: flake-like ones with thickness of 60-80 nm and average length of 0.75 μm.

nanoparticles with different size and shape. It can be seen from Fig. 1(a) and (b) that these two types of Sm-Fe-N nanoparticles dispersed well and exhibit more or less equal-axis shapes. Further LPSA analyses confirm that average sizes of the particles shown in Fig. 1(a) and (b) are 9.4 and 36.5 nm, as shown in Fig. 2(a) and (b), respectively, and both of them possess narrow size distribution. On the other hand, Fig. 1(c) shows a typical flake-like Sm-Fe-N nanoparticles possessing noticeable shape anisotropy. Fig 2(c) shows that the mean diameter of the flakes is 750 nm, and the thickness is in the range of 60-80 nm, leading to a high aspect ratio of about 100.

Fig. 3 shows XRD patterns of the three types of Sm-Fe-N nanoparticles. For the flake-like particles (curve A), the rhombohedral Th_2Zn_{17}-type crystal structure is well preserved after the ball milling process, and a strong (0 0 *l*) crystal texture (see inset of Fig. 3) was obtained after magnetic alignment. As the particles size decreases, the diffraction peaks of the 36.5- and 9.4-nm Sm-Fe-N nanoparticles broaden remarkably. Besides the decrease in particle size, strain and amorphization induced by ball milling may also contribute to the broadening of the diffraction peaks.

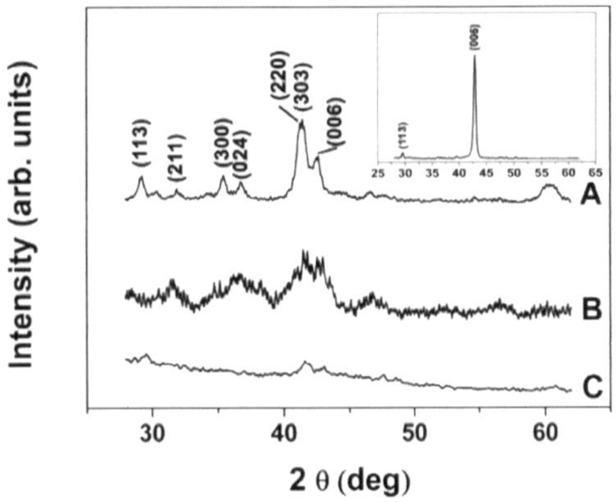

Fig. 3 XRD patterns of Sm-Fe-N nanoparticles of sample A: flake-like ones with thickness of 60-80 nm and average length of 0.75 μm, sample B: average particle size of 36.5 nm, and sample C: average particle size of 9.4 nm. Inset: XRD patterns of magnetically aligned sample A.

Note that most diffraction peaks of $Sm_2Fe_{17}N_3$ compound can be indexed in the XRD patterns of the 36.5 and 9.4 nm particles (curve B and C), indicating that the nanoparticles still keep the same crystal structure as the $Sm_2Fe_{17}N_3$ compound. In addition, it is worth noticing that no obvious diffraction peaks from rare earth oxides were detected in all XRD patterns of the Sm-Fe-N nanoparticles, indicating that the as-prepared nanoparticles were effectively protected from oxidation during the fabrication and examination process.

Table 1 shows the average particles size of the small particles, big particles, and nanoflakes of $R_2Fe_{14}B$, $SmCo_5$, MnBi, and $Sm_2Fe_{17}N_3$ alloys, respectively. It can be seen that the particle size of the small particles of all the alloys is in the range of 7.9-9.8 nm, indicating that similar ball milling and size selection process result in more or less same particle size for different alloys. Moreover, the big particles and flakes of different alloys exhibit similar results, which make our analysis on the coercivity and magnetic hardening mechanism reasonable.

Table 1. The average particles size of each batch of $R_2Fe_{14}B$, $SmCo_5$, MnBi, and $Sm_2Fe_{17}N_3$ nanoparticles. (Note: SP is small particle, BP is big particles, and the unit of size is nanometer)

	SP	BP	Flakes
$Nd_2Fe_{14}B$	9.1	30.7	840
$Dy_2Fe_{14}B$	7.9	35.8	1300
$Tb_2Fe_{14}B$	8.2	31.4	1100
$SmCo_5$	9.8	47.7	1400
MnBi	8.4	28.6	850
$Sm_2Fe_{17}N_3$	9.4	36.5	750

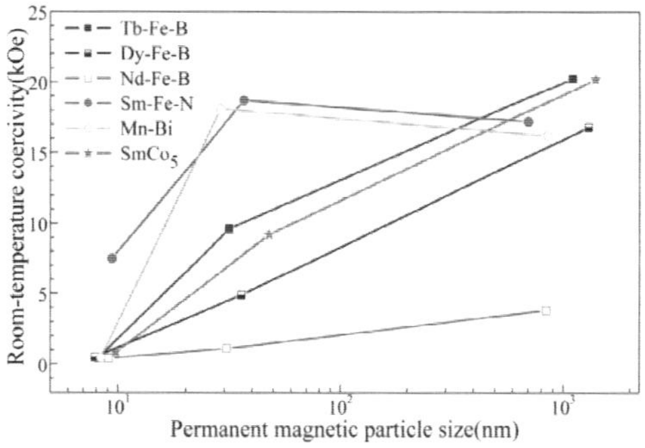

Fig. 4. Coercivity of the small particles, big particles, and nanoflakes of $R_2Fe_{14}B$, $SmCo_5$, MnBi, and $Sm_2Fe_{17}N_3$ alloys as a function of particle size.

3.2. Magnetic hardening of the nanoparticles

Fig. 4 shows the coercivity of the small particles, big particles, and nanoflakes of $R_2Fe_{14}B$, $SmCo_5$, MnBi, and $Sm_2Fe_{17}N_3$ alloys as a function of their particle size. It is interesting to found that the coercivity of $R_2Fe_{14}B$ and $SmCo_5$ nanoparticles reduces monotonically with deceasing particle size. On the other hand, the coercivty of SmFeN and MnBi nanoparticle increases first and then decreases as the particle size decrease. In addition, it was noted that for the $Sm_2Fe_{17}N_3$ alloy, the small nanoparticles with average particle size of 9.4 nm still keep coercivity as high as 7.5 kOe, which is amongst the highest reported coercivity at room temperature for rare earth containing magnetic nanoparticles smaller than 10 nm so far. The high coercivity of the $Sm_2Fe_{17}N_3$ nanoparticles demonstrates their practical application potential.

According to the coercivity behavior of the nanoparticles of different alloys, the $Sm_2Fe_{17}N_3$ and $Tb_2Fe_{14}B$ nanoparticles and nanoflakes were chosen to investigate the magnetic hardening mechanism. Fig. 5(a) - 5(c) show the initial magnetization curves and the corresponding differential susceptibility curves of the thermally demagnetized $Sm_2Fe_{17}N_3$ nanoparticles with particle size of 750, 36.5, and 9.4 nm, respectively. It can be seen from Fig. 5(a) that the magnetization curve rises slowly at low fields, and shows an inflection point at 12.9 kOe and rises more quickly at higher fields. Accordingly, the differential susceptibility curve shows a peak when the magnetization field reaches 12.9 kOe, and then decreases monotonically [inset of Fig. 5(a)]. It is therefore suggested that the magnetization reversal of the specimen is determined by the restriction of domain wall motion: i.e. the magnetic hardening mechanism of the magnetic powders should be pinning type. For the 36.5 nm $Sm_2Fe_{17}N_3$ nanoparticles, however, the magnetization curve rises steeply at the beginning of the magnetization field, and no obvious peak can be observed in the corresponding differential susceptibility curve, as

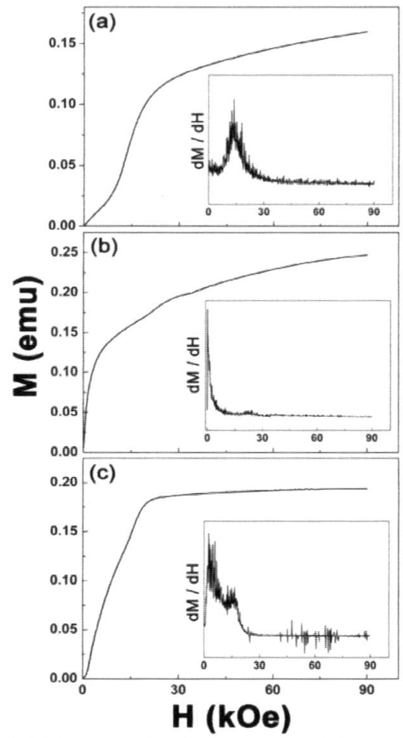

Fig. 5. Initial magnetization curves and the corresponding differential susceptibility curves (inset) of the thermally demagnetized $Sm_2Fe_{17}N_3$ nanoparticles with different particle size.

shown in Fig. 5(b), indicating that the pinning character weakens substantially, and instead, typical nucleation process is observed from the initial magnetization curve and the corresponding differential susceptibility curve. The magnetization behavior of the 9.4 nm $Sm_2Fe_{17}N_3$ nanoparticles is more or less similar to that of the 36.5 nm one, while a small peak at 15.9 kOe was observed in its differential susceptibility curve.

Fig. 6(a) and 6(b) show the initial magnetization curves and the corresponding differential susceptibility curves of the thermally demagnetized $Tb_2Fe_{14}B$ nanoparticles with particle size of 1100 and 31.4 nm, respectively. It can be seen from Fig. 6(a) that the magnetization curve rises slowly at low fields, and shows an inflection point around 20 kOe and rises more quickly at higher fields. Accordingly, the differential susceptibility curve shows two obvious peaks when the magnetization field reaches 20 kOe, and then decreases monotonically [inset of Fig. 6(a)]. Similar behavior was observed in Fig. 6(b), demonstrating that both the $Tb_2Fe_{14}B$ nanoflakes and big nanoparticles exhibit similar magnetization process. Both the initial magnetization curve and the corresponding differential susceptibility curve of the particles demonstrate that the magnetization reversal of the specimen is determined by the pinning of domain wall motion, and the pinning field is more or less equal to the coercivity of the nanoparticles.

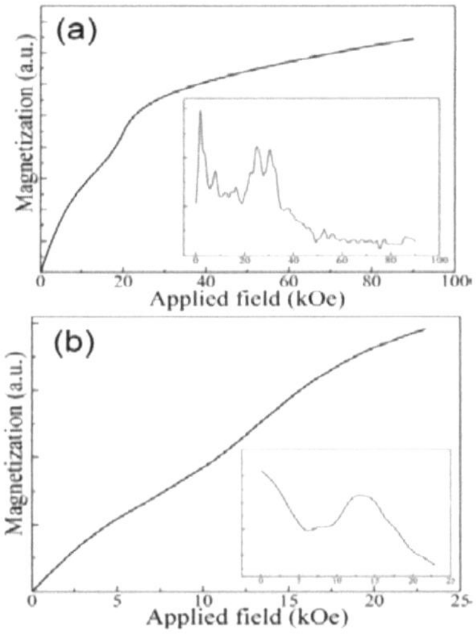

Fig. 6. Initial magnetization curves and the corresponding differential susceptibility curves (inset) of the thermally demagnetized $Tb_2Fe_{14}B$ nanoparticles with different particle size.

4. Summary

In summary, R-Fe-B (R=Nd, Dy, Tb), Sm-Co, Sm-Fe-N, and MnBi nanoparticles had been prepared via SABM. It is found that the coercivity of the nanoparticles exhibits varied in different way with their particle size. For R-Fe-B and Sm-Co nanoparticles, the coercivity reduces with deceasing particle size; however, the coercivty of SmFeN and MnBi nanoparticle increases firstly and then decreases as the particle size decrease. The magnetization behavior indicates that the magnetic hardening process was governed by pinning mechanism for R-Fe-B nanoparticles. On the other hand, for the Sm-Fe-N nanoparticles, the magnetic hardening process changes from a pinning mechanism to a nucleation mechanism with decreasing particle size, being responsible for their abnormal size-dependent coercivity.

Acknowledgement
This work was supported in part by the National Natural Science Funding (51371011), the National Major Fundamental Research Program of China, Ministry of Science and Technology China (2010CB934600), and the science and technology project of Beijing Municipal Education Commission (KM201010005025).

References
[1] S. Sun, *et al.*, *Science*, **2000**, *287*, 1989.
[2] V. M. Chakka, *et al.*, *J. Appl. Phys.*, **2006**, *99*, 08E912.
[3] Y. P. Wang, *et al.*, *Nanotechnology*, **2007**, *18*, 465701.
[4] M. Yue, *et al.*, *Appl. Phys. Lett.* **2011**, *99*, 162510.

SPONSORS

YSM Yantai Shougang Magnetic Materials Inc.

*One of top 3 NdFeB magnet manufacturers in China.
*ZL200910230609.7: the first Chinese Heavy Rare Earth Diffusion patent in China.
*JP5455056: the only Chinese Heavy Rare Earth Diffusion patent in Japan.
*45EN, 48VH and 50UH grade magnet can be available.
*More than 50,000 new energy vehicles with YSM magnet are running in the world.
*Baotou steel rare-earth Group, the biggest rare earth metal manufacturer in the world, is YSM's shareholder.

More information, please visit YSM website and contact us.
http://www.ysmagnet.com
Tel: 86-535-6302 681/2/3/6
E-mail: han@ysm.com.cn
Address: No. 888, Yongda Street, Fushan District, Yantai City, China

EXHIBITORS

OXY-GON INDUSTRIES, INC.

Hitachi Metals, Ltd.

Hitachi High-Tech Science Corporation

Hitachi High-Tech

DAIDO STEEL

Lake Shore CRYOTRONICS

SPONSORS

Department of Physics and Astronomy
UD Energy Institute
College of Arts and Sciences - Dean's Office
UD Research Office

ELECTRON ENERGY CORPORATION

Molycorp

GE Global Research, Materials Sustainability

147th Committee of JSPS

NIMS National Institute for Materials Science

SIEMENS

arpa-e U.S. DEPARTMENT OF ENERGY

REPM 2014
104 The Green, 217 Sharp Lab
University of Delaware
Newark, DE 19716
USA

ISBN 978-1-5108-4338-7

CURRAN ASSOCIATES INC.
proceedings.com

Scaling Decarbonisation Solutions: Reducing Emissions by 2030

Rotterdam, The Netherlands
29 November - 1 December 2022

The Royal Institution of
Naval Architects